# Britain in Revolution
## 1625–1660

# Britain in Revolution
# 1625–1660

## AUSTIN WOOLRYCH

OXFORD
UNIVERSITY PRESS

# OXFORD

UNIVERSITY PRESS

Great Clarendon Street, Oxford OX2 6DP

Oxford University Press is a department of the University of Oxford.
It furthers the University's objective of excellence in research, scholarship,
and education by publishing worldwide in

Oxford New York

Auckland Bangkok Buenos Aires Cape Town Chennai
Dar es Salaam Delhi Hong Kong Istanbul Karachi Kolkata
Kuala Lumpur Madrid Melbourne Mexico City Mumbai Nairobi
São Paulo Shanghai Taipei Tokyo Toronto

Oxford is a registered trade mark of Oxford University Press
in the UK and in certain other countries

Published in the United States
by Oxford University Press Inc., New York

© Austin Woolrych 2002

The moral rights of the author have been asserted
Database right Oxford University Press(maker)

First published 2002

All rights reserved. No part of this publication may be reproduced,
stored in a retrieval system, or transmitted, in any form or by any means,
without the prior permission in writing of Oxford University Press,
or as expressly permitted by law, or under terms agreed with the appropriate
reprographics rights organization. Enquiries concerning reproduction
outside the scope of the above should be sent to the Rights Department,
Oxford University Press, at the address above

You must not circulate this book in any other binding or cover
and you must impose this same condition on any acquirer

British Library Cataloguing in Publication Data

Data available

Library of Congress Cataloging in Publication Data

Data available

ISBN 0-19-820081-1

*CO 13484011*

1 3 5 7 9 10 8 6 4 2

Typeset in Sabon by
Jayvee, Trivandrum, India
Printed in Great Britain
on acid-free paper by
T. J. International Ltd.,
Padstow, Cornwall

# Acknowledgements

By far my greatest debt of gratitude is owed to two good friends, Professors John Morrill and Blair Worden, who read every word of my manuscript when it was still in longhand and sent me lengthy and immensely helpful lists of suggestions. They have saved me from very numerous infelicities and obscurities and not a few errors. Such of these as remain are of course all my own work. I am grateful to Dr Christopher Durston for enabling me to read his *Godly Governors: The Rule of Cromwell's Major-Generals* ahead of publication. My footnotes, deliberately limited in number, and my recommendations for further reading at the end of each of the book's six parts, convey only part of my indebtedness to the many fellow-scholars on whose researches I have drawn. And I warmly thank Ruth Parr and her colleagues Kay Rogers and Anne Gelling for their constant help and advice, and for making it such a pleasure (as always) to publish with the Oxford University Press. I also wish to express my gratitude to Katie Ryde, the Press' copyeditor, for her meticulous care and unfailing helpfulness.

# Contents

PART V: *Cromwell's Protectorate 1653–1658*

PART VI: *The Collapse of the Good Old Cause 1658–1660*

# List of Plates

# List of Maps

# Prologue

THE title of this book is a play upon two senses, old and new, of a word that has undergone a change of meaning since the times it describes. When a modern historian writes of revolution, he has in mind a violent upheaval affecting a whole state, profound enough to alter at least its system of government and probably the very structure of its society too. He means something more than just a *coup d'état*, and if he uses the term 'palace revolution', to describe a forced change of ruler which leaves the basic nature of the regime intact, he implies that it was something less than the real article. But in Cromwell's and Milton's time the only familiar sense of 'revolution' was its original one of circular motion, whether of a celestial body in its orbit or simply of a wheel turning full circle. Political writers sometimes applied the word by way of analogy to convulsions in the state—they had been doing so since Machiavelli's time in the early sixteenth century—but the metaphor still trailed its astronomical roots; it implied a return to a point of origin, however great the intervening upsets. It was related to the widely held notion, classical in origin, that the course of history moves in cycles, and only a little more distantly to that other favourite analogue of human destiny, the wheel of fortune. Thomas Hobbes, for instance, wrote after the Restoration: 'I have seen in this revolution a circular motion of the sovereign power, through two usurpers, from the late king to this his son'.[1] The very experience of the commotions of 1640–60, however, brought 'revolutions' (usually in the plural) into increasing use as a loose description of any major cataclysm in a country's history, and just occasionally a writer distantly prefigured the word's modern use, but its cyclical connotations remained dominant.[2]

Then as now, however, people employed metaphors without too close an attention to all that they implied, and there were many who did *not* believe that the course of history was following a circular path. Many, as we shall see, became convinced that the catastrophic events of the 1640s heralded the last times of this world, as prophesied by Daniel and the Book of Revelation: not the end of a cycle, but the end of history. And even if the modern concept of

---

[1] Thomas Hobbes, *Behemoth* (1679), quoted in Perez Zagorin, *The Court and the Country* (1969), p. 14.

[2] Christopher Hill dates the arrival of the modern sense earlier, in 'The word "revolution" in seventeenth-century England', in Richard Ollard and Pamela Tudor-Craig (eds.), *For Veronica Wedgwood These: Studies in Seventeenth Century History* (1986), pp. 134–51.

a revolution had not yet been formulated, that did not mean that such a thing could not happen. Whether it did or not is a question I would rather leave to the end of this book. I am rashly embarking on an attempt to make the events it describes intelligible to those who have not read much about them before, and I would hope that such readers will approach this crowded canvas without trying to fit it into the frame of some preconceived model of a revolution. I hope too that they will be struck, as I continue to be, by how little was inevitable in the way the course of events unfolded, and what different directions it might have taken at several crucial points if human beings with a genuine choice before them had taken other decisions than those they did.

There was a time, not so long ago, when you could make a fair guess at a historian's interpretative standpoint from whether he referred to the Civil Wars and Interregnum as the English Revolution or as the Great Rebellion. Marxists always wrote of the English Revolution, but many besides Marxists used the same label. Those who did so tended to assume that the upheavals of 1640–60 had a long germination, and constituted a breach in the continuity of our national history comparable, however remotely, with the French and Russian and other latter-day revolutions. This often went with a dogmatic assumption that all true revolutions are basically social revolutions, with their root causes in long-term economic change and in consequent conflict between social classes. Those who wrote of the Great Rebellion, on the other hand, generally assumed a more limited political causation, and saw more continuity between early Stuart and later Stuart England. Earlier, the favourite appellation had been the Puritan Revolution, to which the great Samuel Rawson Gardiner had given currency in the late nineteenth century, but it fell out of fashion during a long phase (now happily past) in which the religious factors in the mid-century conflicts tended to be played down or explained away in other than religious terms.

None of these labels is really satisfactory, though in the absence of a better one it would be pedantic to reject any of them out of hand. The Great Rebellion has a partisan ring; it was what royalists came to call the affair, and most parliamentarians would have hotly denied that they were engaged in rebellion at all. The Puritan Revolution suggests a monocausal explanation; it also obscures the facts that very many parliamentarians were not puritans, and that most of those who were disliked the word almost as much as they resented 'roundhead' or 'rebel'. As for the English Revolution, the objection is not only that it suggests questionable parallels with later revolutions but that it leaves out the Scots and the Irish. Present-day historians have rightly been emphasizing what Gardiner always knew: that the story of the period covered by this book can only be told intelligibly if it embraces all three nations.[3] They

---

[3] See particularly Conrad Russell, *The Causes of the English Civil War* (Oxford, 1990), esp. chs. 2 and 5.

have started a vogue for a new nomenclature, the Wars of Three Kingdoms, and for the period 1639–51 it serves very well; but after that the serious fighting was over, apart from some mopping-up in Ireland and Glencairn's rising in Scotland. We still lack a term for the whole hiatus in royal government, down to 1660. 'Interregnum', despite its royalist implications, is useful for 1649–60, but it really begins only with the abolition of monarchy.

I have tried to set forth the events of 1637–60 as a story of three kingdoms, though in calling this book *Britain in Revolution* I open myself to the charge of promising more than I deliver. There is much more about England in it than about Scotland and Ireland. This is not mere chauvinism, nor just a reflection of England's greater size and power. The fact is that England was where most of the crucial decisions were taken, and most of the crucial battles fought, which determined the fates of all three kingdoms. Sheer intelligibility commands a closer focus on England. To be sure, it was rebellion in Scotland which brought the personal rule of Charles I to an end and set all the troubles in motion, but that rebellion was a response to a decision taken in England, which England tried to impose by force. Three years later, it was rebellion in Ireland which more than any one factor tipped England over into civil war, but that rebellion was a reaction to a perceived threat from England. Later, it was convulsion in England that brought the king of all three kingdoms to the scaffold, and (later still) restored his son. Scotland's and Ireland's resistance to the king's enemies led to their conquest and subjection by England. The radical political and religious movements which give a unique interest to the years following the king's defeat—Levellers, Diggers, Fifth Monarchists, Quakers, and the rest—were English movements, and the thinkers who struggled most memorably to make sense of the collapse of the old political order—Harrington, Hobbes, Milton, to name only three—were English thinkers. For the prominence of England in what follows, therefore, I make no further apology, and I assure Scottish and Irish readers that it implies no lack of sympathy for what their ancestors suffered and strove for. I do apologize to purists, and still more to Irishmen, for using 'Britain' as though it included Ireland; it is just so useful to have one name to embrace the whole extent of the Stuarts' multiple kingdom and of Oliver Cromwell's rule. James I, who styled himself King of Great Britain, would have understood.

Historians still disagree quite widely about the causes of the Civil War (or the Wars of Three Kingdoms), and not least about where to begin looking for them. From the 1940s to the 1960s and beyond, the prevailing orthodoxy was that the roots of the conflict must be sought in certain socio-economic changes which took place in England during the century or so before 1640, and generated such tensions within the structure of society, and between government and the governed, that they finally reached breaking-point in civil war. The period 1640–60 was sometimes called Tawney's century, because of the great influence of an article on 'The rise of the gentry' which R. H. Tawney published in 1941. Even the most outspoken critic of the Tawney school, H. R. Trevor-Roper, looked for the origins of the war in changes and conflicts within England's governing class, though he interpreted them very differently. Lawrence Stone, writing in 1972, did look beyond socio-economic factors, but in *The Causes of the English Revolution* he took an equally long-term view, identifying the 'preconditions' for revolution in the century 1529–1629, the 'precipitants' which brought it inexorably on in the decade 1629–39, and the 'triggers' that set it off in 1640–2.[4] But before then the senior Tudor historian G. R. Elton, impatient with the distortions to which interpreters of the English Revolution were subjecting his own period and that of the early Stuarts, protested vigorously against their practice of reading a century of our history as a series of milestones along 'a high road to civil war'. He questioned indeed whether there was any grand inevitability about the war at all.[5] This was a timely call to order when historical thinking on the subject had been in danger of losing its way in a fog of determinism, and it was the more cogent because those sweeping and simplistic socio-economic interpretations were already being undermined by detailed and unprejudiced research. A series of close studies of particular social and political groups—the holders of office under Charles I, the members of the Long Parliament, the peerage, and the political communities in particular counties—were showing, and have continued to show, that the realities of the Caroline political nation were too diverse to be fitted into any Procrustean bed of 'rising' or 'declining' gentry, and that the Civil War required a much wider range of explanation than class conflict could supply.

It is an increase of knowledge, much more than a swing of fashion, that has turned historians away from those over-simple and anglocentric interpretations that held sway up to a generation ago. For the last twenty years and more most of us have been trying to write Stuart history without hindsight, and without ideological preconceptions. We are readier to admit the role of the personal and the contingent in bringing even catastrophic events to pass; a civil war, even the overthrow of an ancient monarchy, *may* be the climactic outcome of a gradual, inexorable increase of stresses in the fabric of society or the frame of government, but it may also come about through a failure of statesmanship. It may be something of the two. Some of our revisionists seem to me to go too far in reacting against earlier interpretations, whether of the old Whig school or the newer Marxist. Charles I's eleven-year rule without a

---

[4] Lawrence Stone, *The Causes of the English Revolution* (1972). Stone has also edited and introduced a useful anthology of the gentry controversy in *Social Change and Revolution in England 1540–1640* (1965).

[5] G. R. Elton, 'A high road to civil war?', first published in 1965, reprinted in *Studies in Tudor and Stuart Politics and Government* (3 vols., Cambridge, 1974–83), II, 137–54.

parliament, for instance, has been portrayed as neither intrinsically unviable in the long term nor widely unpopular, and discontent with the Laudian church as confined to a small but strident faction. Some writers have seemed to suggest that the storm-clouds of civil war loomed almost suddenly out of a clear sky. That strikes me as just as implausible as tracing their formation back to a non-existent 'opposition' in Elizabethan parliaments or to the redistribution of monastic land under Henry VIII.

It is possible to believe that the rebellions in Scotland and Ireland were until a late stage avoidable, and the English Civil War not only avoidable but unforeseeable, and yet to feel it necessary to look some way further back than their immediate causes for their preconditions. None of Charles I's three kingdoms was threatening to become ungovernable when he inherited them, but there were unresolved political problems in all three, as well as religious and social tensions of varying seriousness. These need never have led to civil war, but when a series of unanticipated crises did explode in war, and Scots, Irish and Englishmen (in that order) were forced to choose sides, they tended to split along existing lines of stress. All governments in early modern Europe were for varying reasons fragile and vulnerable, and the British monarchies were more lacking than most in the elementary means of enforcing unpopular governmental decisions. Yet when our period begins England had enjoyed a century and a half of almost unbroken internal peace, and Scotland more than sixty years. A glance at continental Europe will remind us how untypical they were.

France had suffered a succession of civil wars of religion from 1562 to 1598, and again (less severely) from 1622 to 1629; the Frondes of 1648–53 were shortly to come. The Spanish monarchy had been struggling vainly to suppress the revolt of the Netherlands since 1568, and was to be torn apart from 1640 by the rebellions of Catalonia and Portugal, followed by that of the kingdom of Naples in 1647. The German-speaking lands were locked in the Thirty Years War from 1618 to 1648, and for much of that time the Scandinavian kingdoms were involved in it too. The degree to which these conflicts were civil wars varied, but they put a heavy strain on the governments of all the countries concerned, few of which escaped the miseries of warfare on their own soil. Indeed so widespread were rebellion and civil strife in the 1640s that there was much debate a generation or so ago as to whether Britain's civil wars should be seen primarily as part of a general crisis of European monarchy. It came to be generally recognized, however, that the differences between the upheavals in these islands and those on the continent were so much more significant than any common features between them that the search for common causes was on to a false trail. No other mid-century rebellion generated so dedicated a fighting-force as the New Model Army, or cut the head off an anointed king, or altered ancient governments so drastically, or opened up so rich a vein of radical thought.

So where to begin? Any precise date must be to some degree arbitrary. But in November 1641, when the embryonic parliamentarian party prepared a comprehensive statement of all the ills that threatened the peace of the kingdom, it began its tally of the nation's grievances in 1625, the year of Charles I's accession. No historian regards this wildly partisan Grand Remonstrance as an objective analysis of the state of the nation, or lays such exclusive blame for the rifts within it upon royal misgovernment. But the perception that the new reign had wrought a great change in the prospects of all Charles's kingdoms was a true one, so his accession will be our starting-point too, as it was of Clarendon's classic *History of the Rebellion*—and he had lived through it. The next two chapters try to sketch with very broad strokes what England, Scotland, and Ireland were like when he inherited them, the first focusing on their social characteristics and political institutions, the second on the state of religion and on religious divisions within them. They pave the way for a chapter on the nature of Charles's rule before its peace was broken by rebellion in Scotland. Readers may understandably feel that they have an unconscionable way to go before the action starts, and those who already know their bearings in early Stuart history will need no prompting on how to skip through the first three chapters.

A word as to footnotes and reading lists, neither of which are as full as they would be in a work addressed to an academic readership. Footnotes are confined mainly to direct quotations, or controverted points on which I have preferred one interpretation to another, or places where I have plundered a fellow-historian's work specially heavily. Bibliography was a problem; a full one would have been very long, and inappropriate to the kind of book that this sets out to be. So at the end of each of its six chronological parts I have appended a page or two of advice on further reading, addressed to the interested general reader or student who feels the need for a broader background or wishes to pursue a particular topic further. The recommendations are highly selective, and they are mostly confined to books that might be found in a municipal public library or a smaller university or college library. For that reason, articles in learned journals are cited only where there are exceptional reasons for including them. Spelling has been modernized in the titles of seventeenth-century books and pamphlets, and in quotations from contemporary sources. The place of publication is London unless specified otherwise.

# PART I

## Background and Beginnings
## 1625–1640

# King Charles's Inheritance I:
# Three Kingdoms, Three Peoples

ENGLAND was not only the largest and richest of Charles's three kingdoms, but politically the most highly developed. Compared with the other major monarchies of early modern Europe, that of England possessed both strengths and weaknesses. In the later sixteenth century England had been arguably the most stable and best governed realm in Europe, and there was no sharp decline under James I.

Its greatest asset was its political unity. The authority of the king and his privy council extended on an almost equal footing into every corner of the land, and the system of local government was virtually uniform throughout. The regional jurisdictions of the Council of the North and the Council in the Marches of Wales, and the palatine privileges of Durham, Lancashire, and Cheshire, constituted only minor exceptions. A single system of common law operated throughout England and Wales; a single parliament represented the whole realm (except County Durham, though the Bishop of Durham sat in the Lords), and the taxes that it voted were levied equally (at least in theory) throughout it. The contrast with the regional diversity within the French and Spanish monarchies could not be stronger. In the former, only the central Île de France enjoyed anything approaching England's political and legal uniformity. The great outlying provinces from Brittany through Guyenne and Gascony, Provence and Dauphiné to Burgundy and Lorraine had to differing degrees retained their own institutions when they were absorbed into the French kingdom; some still kept their own representative assemblies, some their own *parlements* (or semi-sovereign courts of law), while most clung to their own legal codes and judicial systems and their own distinct forms and levels of taxation. In the Spanish monarchy, the imperfect assimilation of the kingdom of Aragon to that of Castile was shown not only in their separate institutions but in the former's revolt in 1591–2 and the major rebellion of Catalonia in 1640. Portugal remained even more a distinct kingdom, and the attempt to increase the Spanish king's authority over the Spanish Netherlands led to their revolt in 1566 and to their final loss eighty-two punishing years later.

In France too the provinces often showed separatist tendencies when the crown's position was weak, as it so often was during the long wars of religion. There were strong regional loyalties in various parts of England, but never such as to impair the overall sense of nationhood and (until 1642) loyalty to the crown. That was largely true even of Wales, despite its separate language and relatively recent assimilation, as its strong popular royalism was to show in the Civil Wars. Shakespeare's cameo of Captain Fluellen in *Henry V* is perhaps evidence of a certain affection on England's side, as well as of Welsh pride. It is a striking difference between England's civil wars and France's that loyalty to Charles I was firmest in the north, in Wales and the West Country, the regions furthest from his capital, whereas the French king was usually strongest in the nuclear Île de France and most under threat in the imperfectly assimilated provinces. The Fronde was to be only a partial exception, because after the short-lived Fronde of the Parlement was overcome the movement was hijacked by overmighty princes and nobles, playing their time-dishonoured game of raising rebellion in their provincial power-bases.

Such 'overmighty subjects' had long ceased to be a threat to the English monarchy, and that was one of its great strengths. In France and Spain the king's justice, while gradually asserting its supremacy, still coexisted with the jurisdiction of the great feudal lords, and even minor nobles commonly had some judicial powers over their tenants. But in England (though not Scotland) the battle had long been won; the king's courts had a monopoly of criminal jurisdiction, and all important civil cases came before them too. The ecclesiastical courts still wielded significant power over the laity in certain areas, but they too were ultimately under the power of the king as the church's Supreme Governor. Feudal jurisdiction survived in the manorial courts, at least in the more highly organized manors, but they dealt with little more than the rights and obligations of tenants within the manorial community. The military powers of the English nobility were as attenuated as their judicial rights. Whereas in the French wars of religion the greatest magnates had been able to build up large clienteles of dependent nobles, whose lords they literally were, and who brought their own retinues of armed vassals with them, the Tudor kings had finally established the principle that allegiance to the monarch took precedence over all other allegiances, and that to raise military forces by any other authority but that of the crown was treason. The long Tudor peace, and England's even longer immunity from invasion, had much diminished the ancient military role of the aristocracy; indeed by 1625 few English nobles had any military experience at all. England was fortunate too in having among her magnates no princes of the blood, whose closeness in lineage to the king could offer a dangerous alternative focus of loyalty. The last Englishman to try to play the overmighty subject had been Elizabeth's favourite the Earl of Essex, and the fiasco of his fling had shown what an anachronism it was.

The English nobility not only had fewer powers and privileges than their continental counterparts; they were relatively much fewer in number. In 1633 the English lay peerage, from barons up to dukes, numbered only 122, in a national population of about 4.75 million. Queen Elizabeth, parsimonious with titles as in everything else, had let the total fall to a mere fifty-five. James I had more than doubled it, mainly through openly selling peerages to raise revenue, but thereby he had only restored the proportion of titled nobles in the total population to roughly what it had been when the Tudors first came to power. Despite his blatant sale of honours, however, the deference in which the peerage was held was only slightly dented, and the political influence of the older and greater houses remained large, whether through the House of Lords, or the privy council (which they dominated), or senior officers in the royal household, or the patronage that they exercised in and around their territorial bases in the counties. The notion, once widely held, that a general rise of the gentry in the century 1540–1640 was balanced by a decline of the titled aristocracy has been very heavily modified by more recent research. At the latter date the peerage did indeed hold a smaller proportion of the land of England than at the earlier, but most of them had weathered the crisis that the long inflation of the sixteenth century had inflicted on them, and on the eve of the Civil War their mean landed incomes were in real terms slightly higher than they had been at Queen Elizabeth's accession, despite there being more than twice as many of them. They had mostly risen to the challenge of managing their estates better and maximizing their resources, and they had benefited as the chief recipients of the large profits that flowed from royal patronage.[1]

A corollary of the small number of the titled nobility was that very many substantial landowners who would have ranked as nobles in a social structure like that of France or Spain were classed in England among the gentry, so that in law they were commoners. The gentry played such a crucial part in the English Revolution that it is helpful to have an idea of their status, wealth, and numbers. They were of several degrees. At the top was a small elite, numbering just over 300 in 1633, which consisted mainly of baronets, a new title that James I had created simply in order to sell it, but which also included some eldest sons of senior peers who bore courtesy titles and some English holders of Scottish and Irish peerages, which James had also sold. The titles of these 300 or so were hereditary, but did not qualify them to sit in the English House of Lords. Next came upwards of 1,500 knights, whose title was conferred by the monarch but was not hereditary. Below them were between 7,000 and 9,000 esquires, still substantial men with a landed income averaging around

---

[1] Lawrence Stone, *The Crisis of the Aristocracy 1558–1641* (Oxford, 1965).

£500, as compared with a mean of over £5,000 enjoyed by the peerage and with the £10 that an agricultural labourer might earn in a year if he was regularly employed. Most members of parliament and justices of the peace were esquires and above, who constituted what were recognized as the county families in their home territory. The lowest and largest category among the gentry were those who styled themselves simply gentlemen, which was a far from meaningless social distinction, though impossible to define with precision, as contemporaries acknowledged. It was very much a matter of social acceptance: if you lived like a gentleman and were accorded the title by your fellow-gentry, that was sufficient. Most of the 10,000 to 14,000 'mere' gentlemen in Caroline England were landowners, but a growing minority were gaining recognition as such through office-holding, mercantile wealth, or practising as barristers or in other professions. Taken as a whole, however, the gentry formed essentially a landed class, and at the top of the scale their wealth overlapped with that of the nobility. Their collective landed income probably came to more than ten times that of the whole peerage.[2]

England's governing class was a more open society than that of France or Spain, in that entry into it required less formality. The ranks of the gentry were volatile during the century before the Civil War, and successful newcomers had no difficulty in obtaining a coat of arms from the College of Heralds if they had a sufficient estate and paid the fee. Many of the lesser gentry, however, were not armigerous. There was indeed a rise of the gentry in the sense that the numbers of knights, esquires, and gentlemen increased at a considerably greater rate than the population as a whole, but against their success stories must be set large numbers of small squireens who struggled unsuccessfully to keep up the life-style of a gentleman and fell out of the race. Failure of male heirs was the commonest cause of the disappearance of gentry families, though incautious borrowing or too many daughters to find dowries for could be fatal too. Oliver Cromwell was one whom hard times almost forced out of the ranks of the gentry. Yet the thesis that the sixfold price rise that began around 1510 and was levelling out by 1625 spelt ultimate disaster to gentlemen who lived by their landed income alone has not been found generally true. Some, especially the smaller, went under because of it, but landowners of whatever degree who managed their estates in a businesslike fashion, lived within their means and had reasonable demographic luck could generally keep their heads above water, and even prosper. Although gentry estates seem to have changed hands more rapidly from about 1540 to 1640 than before the Reformation or after the Restoration, it was not only their members that rose but the amount of the land of England

---

[2] This paragraph is heavily indebted to G. E. Aylmer, *The King's Servants: The Civil Service of Charles I* (rev. ed., 1974); see esp. Table 35, p. 331.

that they collectively owned. Most of the monastic lands sold off by Henry VIII came into their hands, if not immediately then in the course of the next generation or two. When Elizabeth and James I sold off large quantities of crown land to make ends meet, and when overspending peers had to part with real estate to meet their debts, the gentry were generally the purchasers. Some were investing the profits of office or courtiership or success in trade or the law, but many were of established landowning families, taking the opportunity to expand or round off their estates. Newcomers to landownership might take a generation or so to make their mark in county society, but generally it remained true, as Sir Thomas Smith had written in 1565, that 'as for gentlemen they be made good cheap in England'.[3] There was no nation-wide clash of interest between old and new gentry, or between rising and declining ones; no quasi-geological fault-line ran through the landed classes, such as would determine which way they split when it came to civil war.

Nobility and gentry formed a single economic class in England, and the social gap between the barons and the upper crust of commoners was not wide. Marxist attempts to identify the gentry, or at least a very substantial part of the gentry, with the bourgeoisie have fallen right out of favour, and with good reason. The gentry themselves were strongly aware of the social distinction between the landed and the landless, whatever the latter's wealth, even though they intermarried with wealthy merchant families more freely than on the continent, and often put their younger sons into trade or the law. Merchants and clothiers had their ups and downs under James I, but in the longer term they were flourishing. By 1625 they collectively possessed a considerably larger share of the nation's wealth than a century earlier, but they had not increased their political weight proportionately. This was partly because of the prestige that continued to attach to landownership, which led the most successful merchants to invest their gains in real estate and acquire gentry status. Two spectacular Jacobean examples were Sir Arthur Ingram, the company promoter and customs farmer who built Temple Newsam near Leeds, and Baptist Hicks, the silk merchant and moneylender who became a viscount. The City of London, with its prestigious corporation and its well armed, well trained militia, was to become a power in English politics in the 1640s, but until then its political influence rested largely on the crown's dependency on it for loans. The capital grew prodigiously in population and wealth, from about 60,000 in 1500 to 185,000 by 1600 and 355,000 in 1640.[4] At James I's accession there were only three other cities in England

---

[3] Sir Thomas Smith, *The Commonwealth of England* (1589 ed.): excerpt in G. W. Prothero (ed.), *Select Statutes and Other Constitutional Documents Illustrative of the Reigns of Elizabeth and James I* (Oxford, 4th ed., 1913), p. 177.

[4] R. Finlay and B. Shearer, 'Population growth and suburban expansion', in A. L. Beier and R. Finlay (eds.), *London 1500–1700: The Making of the Metropolis* (1986), pp. 37–59, esp. Table 3, p. 45.

with populations over 10,000: Norwich with about 15,000, Bristol with 12,000, and York with 11,000, and none were growing at anything like the rate of London.[5] The concentration of foreign commerce on the capital was excessive, and the living conditions for its thousands of poor were horrible. London was handling about four-fifths of England's entire foreign trade, and paying three-quarters of all the customs revenue received by the crown.

If the mercantile classes ranked rather modestly in the political nation (meaning that part of the population which had some say in the running of the country's affairs), there was a large and ill-defined 'middling sort', to use the favourite contemporary description, on the fringe of it. The term embraced yeomen and substantial tenant farmers in the countryside and lesser merchants, shopkeepers, and independent craftsmen in the towns. They were on the whole a more flourishing class than in most of continental Europe (the Netherlands excepted), and they carried real responsibility when they served as high or petty constables, overseers of the poor, or in other unpaid local offices. In parliamentary elections, they voted at the county hustings if they were freeholders, and they were being admitted to the franchise in an increasing number of boroughs. They were becoming steadily more literate and politically aware, and were capable of strongly independent religious opinions.

The century prior to Charles I's accession had not been kind to the poorer folk who made up the majority of the people of England. The greatest strains upon English society had been the relentless rise in prices, already almost sixfold, and a doubling of the population from about 2.3 million in 1524 to 4.6 million in 1625. Wage-earners were a minority in this pre-industrial society, but there was a surplus of labour, and the real value of wages fell by half. Small landholders, mostly customary tenants with a plot that they could regard as their own and hope to pass to their heirs, were more numerous than wage-labourers, and enjoyed varying fortunes. But landlords facing rising prices had strong motives for getting rid of small tenants whose rents they could not easily raise, and where such husbandmen did hang on their holdings became too small to subdivide, so younger sons had to leave home and seek employment. Some found it in neighbouring or more distant parishes; others swelled the ranks of London's poor, or took up the travelling trades of pedlars or minstrels or quacks. Many were driven to begging or crime, or both. Vagrancy became a serious social problem. The Elizabethan Poor Law made more humane provision than many a European country could boast, but it discriminated heavily against incomers to a parish, and poor rates were still levied reluctantly. During the century down to 1625 the poor had been getting poorer and the rich richer. The lot of the poor was brutally harsh by

[5] P. Clark and P. Slack, *English Towns in Transition 1500–1700* (Oxford, 1976), p. 83.

modern western standards, but England was not an uncharitable country, and few of them starved. The year 1623 was the last—it was one of acute dearth—in which English people died of hunger in considerable numbers, and they did so mainly in the more inaccessible parts of the north.

Civil war, however, was to come about not through the desperation of the poor or the resentment of oppressed tenants, but through a quarrel which until shortly before the fighting started involved few outside the governing class. The unique structure of that class in England vitally affected the composition of parliament; indeed it goes far to explain why the English parliament survived so vigorously when most of the corresponding representative assemblies in the rest of Europe were far gone in decay. Those had typically developed during the Middle Ages as meetings of the three estates of clergy, nobles, and commons, whose representatives usually debated separately. The noble estate generally spoke for the landowning class as a whole, and the third estate, typically composed of lawyers, officials, and merchants, was too inferior in status or too subject to royal pressure to wield much independent influence. Astute monarchs, unwilling to accept any check on their power to make laws or raise taxes, exploited the inherent antagonism between the nobility and the third estate, and played one off against the other. But there was no chance of that in England, where parliament was uniquely composed of two houses, both dominated by landlords. The clerical estate was represented solely by the twenty-six bishops, who sat in the Lords with the lay peers. The House of Commons represented the communes or communities of the counties and boroughs; formally it comprised 90 knights of the shire and a still growing number of burgesses—372 in 1601 and 417 by 1641. There was an old law that members should be residents of their constituencies, and if it had been observed there would have been over four times as many townsmen as country gentlemen in the House. By late Elizabethan and Jacobean times, however, the actual ratio was almost the reverse. Many parliamentary boroughs were already long decayed, and among the country gentry there was an insatiable appetite for the prestige of a seat in parliament—far more than the county constituencies could supply. So they had long been invading the borough seats, and the crown was under constant pressure to create new ones, both from aspirant local gentry and from magnates, courtiers, and ministers of the crown who had the monarch's ear and wanted parliamentary patronage to dispose of. Many of the boroughs enfranchised by Elizabeth and James were sleepy little backwaters from the start. The gentry who vied for these seats, however, were not all plain country landowners; they included holders of royal offices and successful lawyers, who regularly outnumbered the forty-odd wealthy merchants who typically got elected to early Stuart parliaments.

Disputes between Lords and Commons were by no means unknown, but there was a fundamental homogeneity about the English parliament that the

États-Généraux of France or the Cortes of Castile, for example, had never possessed. There was no gulf of economic interest or social class between the two Houses, for most MPs were landowners like the peers, and the richest overlapped with them in wealth. The Commons' chief strength lay in their consisting mainly of the 'natural rulers' of the counties, rather than of humble burgesses from small provincial towns, yet mercantile wealth was not felt to be inadequately represented, and clashes between landed and bourgeois interests were rare. Ministers of the crown sat in both Houses, and non-noble privy councillors had long been aware of the importance of finding themselves seats in the Commons, so that the policies and wishes of the king's government could be properly spoken to there. When they neglected that duty, as in the Addled Parliament of 1614, the king's interests suffered seriously. Parliament, especially the Commons, needed to be carefully managed, and the art whereby Elizabeth's great ministers had effected this was in decline.

But the trend towards worsening relationships was not irreversible. The picture that we used to be offered of a House of Commons seeking relentlessly to increase its initiative in face of a monarchy inspired by an ideal of absolutism is one that historians have rightly discarded. A strong parliament need not necessarily imply a weak crown, or vice versa. The great Tudors, in their more successful phases, had recognized that the king (or queen) in parliament was more powerful than an English monarch could possibly be acting on his or her own, and they had achieved more through parliamentary statutes than their cousins of France and Spain could ever do by more absolutist methods. The Reformation statutes, the transfer of monastic property to the crown, Henry VIII's and Elizabeth's Acts of Supremacy, the imposition of successive liturgies on the church, the several Treasons Acts, and the tampering with the succession to the throne are just the more obvious examples of what the crown could do in partnership with parliament. But parliaments were still special occasions for specific needs; no one imagined that they should be sitting for most of the time. James I took time to realize that his interests and parliament's were not necessarily opposed, but his relations with his last parliament were altogether more cordial than with his previous ones. It was still true when he died that parliaments met in the hope of reaching mutually beneficial agreement with the king rather than of opposing him; the expectation still was that they would vote the subsidies he needed, and he would assent to the statutes that they desired for the people they represented.

An inadequate revenue was the greatest weakness of the early Stuart monarchy, and the commonest source of friction between crown and parliament. The Tudors and James I had not had the pretext of foreign invasion and war on their own soil that had justified most continental monarchies in levying taxes without the consent of representative assemblies. The regular revenues of the English crown—rents from crown lands, fines imposed by the courts, and a clutch of ancient fiscal prerogatives—had not risen proportionately with the great inflation. The customs, which parliament had voted to the king for life at the start of every reign since Edward IV's, were levied on the nominal values of merchandise, which were fixed by royal authority, but fell far below their real values in the course of the long price rise. When James's Lord Treasurer issued a new Book of Rates in 1608, partly redressing over half a century of undervaluation, he raised a storm that blew in the parliament of 1610 and was still blowing in that of 1614. During Elizabeth's reign the crown became increasingly dependent on direct taxes that only parliament could impose. But the units in which parliament voted supplies, the 'subsidies' of early Tudor origin and the more ancient 'tenths and fifteenths', not only failed to adjust to inflation but fell steadily in even their nominal value. The whole fiscal system should have been overhauled many years before James inherited the crown. Elizabeth had been urged to take it in hand at a time when the war with Spain would have made parliament not unsympathetic, but to the despair of her ministers she had refused to consider it, out of sheer dislike of 'novelty'.

Parliament rarely resorted to withholding subsidies as a lever for exacting concessions or the redress of grievances; it happened only four times before the Civil War. But when the Commons did vote supplies, they were invariably less than the king asked for and needed. Even when they thought they were being generous and voted multiple subsidies and tenths and fifteenths, they had little idea of how far these units had shrunk in real value. And when these taxes were collected, local gentry commissioners were entrusted with assessing their fellow gentry's estates, and undervalued them to a degree that to modern eyes looks scandalous—until we remember that the gentry's equivalents abroad, the lesser nobility, were often exempt from direct taxation altogether. James I was driven to various unpopular expedients, the most lucrative being the levying of special import duties, known as impositions, which were additional to tonnage and poundage, the customs duties regularly granted by parliament at the start of each reign for its duration. But this caused a parliamentary outcry, as an abuse of the royal prerogative. Robert Cecil, Earl of Salisbury and Lord Treasurer, made a brave effort in 1610 to rationalize the crown's revenue and parliament's responsibility towards it. His scheme was called the Great Contract. The crown was to give up the impositions and some anachronistic fiscal rights, including the wardship of heirs to noble and gentry estates who inherited while under age, in return for a guaranteed annual parliamentary grant of £200,000. Added to the customs and other regular revenues of the crown, that would just have sufficed a frugal monarch in peacetime. But James was far from frugal, and the whole deal eventually fell through, basically because neither the king nor the Commons really trusted each other. Yet the Great Contract was not forgotten in

Charles I's early parliaments, and if the new king had had a happier touch in managing them, and had kept out of wars he could not afford, an overdue reform of the fiscal system need not have had to wait for another generation.

James was deeply reluctant to be drawn into the Thirty Years War, which broke out in 1618, but his only daughter Elizabeth was married to the Calvinist Frederick, Elector Palatine, who rashly accepted the crown of Bohemia. He soon lost it, and his own Palatinate was invaded by a Spanish army in 1620. Family honour and the protestant cause were at stake; Prince Charles and James's favourite the Duke of Buckingham were eager that England should come to Frederick's aid, and a strong current of public feeling supported them. But James realized, as they did not, that England had become unfitted to engage in any large-scale war, except at sea. For more than a century a military revolution had been taking place on the continent. Musketry and artillery necessitated a sophisticated battle drill, which along with developments in siegecraft made war a far more costly and professional business than when York had fought Lancaster. No power could engage in it on equal terms without at least the nucleus of a fully trained and equipped standing army, and in 1625 England was the only significant country in Europe without one. Apart from the tiny garrison of the Tower of London, the defence of the realm rested entirely with a county-based militia, consisting of select companies known as the trained bands. They were of course spare-time soldiers, and even the modest requirement that they should muster for training on one day in each summer month was not always met. In 1604, when the long war with Spain ended, parliament repealed the Tudor statutes which had regulated the militia, so from then on it rested on no other legal foundation than the royal prerogative. During the years of peace the trained bands tended to be trained less and less, because the responsible gentry magistrates were often unwilling to levy the necessary rates to buy them muskets and to pay a professional soldier as muster-master. There were to be patchy attempts to improve their effectiveness, but their most serious limitation lay in their extreme reluctance to march beyond the bounds of their own counties. They were never a match for professional soldiers, and the Scottish Covenanters were to expose their weaknesses cruelly in 1639–40. To engage in landed warfare overseas, the crown had to enlist or press men who were usually quite untrained, and the result in Charles's early years was one fiasco after another.

The same financial stringency that denied the early Stuarts a standing army deprived them of that other mainstay of absolute monarchy, a nationwide salaried bureaucracy. In France and Castile, for example, the men who really directed local government, especially in the towns, were the king's paid servants; so were the magistrates who locally administered his justice, and the collectors who brought in his taxes and customs duties. In England the government of the counties lay in the hands of the leading gentry families, and that of nearly all significant towns in the mercantile elite from which the mayor and corporation were drawn. The all-important magistrates in the counties were the justices of the peace, who in their quarter sessions not only adjudged all but the most serious crimes but carried out a wide range of administration. There were getting on for 2,000 of them in England and Wales by 1625. They derived their commission from the crown; they acted under the direction (not in normal times very close) of the privy council, and the law that they executed was the king's law, the common law of the land. They were unpaid, but the commission of the peace set a coveted seal on their standing in the county, so that their loyalty and co-operation could normally be depended upon. They varied greatly, however, in the seriousness with which they took their work; some did very little, but the active core who attended sessions regularly showed an impressive sense of social duty to the local community, and not least towards the poor.

The JPs were the most versatile and indispensable of the crown's unpaid local commissioners, but they were not the only ones. At the head of the county community stood the lord lieutenant, usually a senior nobleman, sometimes a great minister, but either way often absent at court. He had special charge of the militia, but the real responsibility for it fell on half a dozen or so deputy lieutenants, chosen from the senior JPs of the shire. Their commission was prestigious enough to find ready takers, but colonels of regiments and captains of companies in the trained bands were growing harder to come by, since their duties were both expensive and inconvenient. There was widespread reluctance, too, to take on the ancient office of sheriff, though his irksome and costly duties lasted only a year. When parliament voted subsidies, gentry commissioners supervised their collection, though the hardest work fell on the village constables, who were also unpaid.

The JPs and all the other commissioners in the counties depended heavily on the assistance of the high constables in the hundreds and the petty constables, churchwardens, and overseers of the poor in the parishes. So much reliance on unpaid local service might look like a weakness in the English state, though it had not seemed so when Tudor government was at its best. Arguably the crown was better served, and its subjects too, by the voluntary service of gentry magistrates than more absolute monarchs were by their salaried bureaucrats, for the latter's offices had in very many cases been made purchasable when the king was desperate for revenue, and their holders tended to be more intent on extracting a good return on their investment than on serving either the crown or the community. But the English system of local administration, coupled with the strong survival of parliament, did make Stuart government ultimately dependent on consent to a degree that was very rare in the seventeenth century. If the kind of direction that king and council

gave to their indispensable agents in the localities became seriously unacceptable, the waves of discontent could spread far down the social scale. But in
1625 the notion that large numbers of the 'natural rulers' of the counties
might withdraw their obedience, and take their orders from a parliament that
was defying the king's commands to the point of civil war, as was to happen
in 1642, would have seemed quite incredible.

James was a less popular monarch than Elizabeth had been in her prime,
and most of his ministers were inferior to hers. He lacked both the art and the
inclination for the kind of continuous public spectacle through which she had
wooed her people, and his court, in contrast with hers, was vulgar, venal, and
extravagant. Yet the older historians, put off by his unprepossessing manners, his homosexuality, and his love of pontificating about his royal powers,
overdrew the contrast between him and Elizabeth, whose regime had come
some way down from its high plateau of success and popularity in her later
years. He had been, and remained, a very shrewd and successful King of Scotland. In England he made his mistakes, of course, but he generally learnt from
them; his intelligence and experience usually restrained him from persisting in
unwise courses or engaging in dangerous confrontations. There was no
calamitous fall in the prestige and authority of the monarchy.

James used to be excessively blamed for courting constitutional trouble by
preaching a novel doctrine of the divine right of kings and rousing fears of
royal absolutism.[6] But there was nothing of substance in his ideas of divine
right that had not been common coin under the Tudors; all that was new was
the frequency, and sometimes the overblown rhetoric, with which he asserted them. None of his subjects doubted that the king held his authority from
God. Government, it was universally agreed, was ordained by God as necessary for the control and welfare of fallen mankind; England's government
was unquestionably a monarchy, therefore the king's power was divinely
sanctioned and resistance to it was a mortal sin. Only if he commanded something contrary to the laws of God might a subject refuse to obey him, but in
that case he or she must passively submit to the consequences of disobedience.
If more was heard now of divine right than in the high Tudor period, it was
not just because James had a good conceit of himself as a political philosopher
but because doctrines of resistance had lately been so much in the air—not in
England certainly, but in his native Scotland as well as on the continent.
During the French wars of religion and the revolt of the Netherlands, both
Calvinist and catholic (especially Jesuit) theorists had argued that their co-
religionaries had a right, indeed a duty, to resist rulers who persecuted them,
since all kings derive their title from the consent of their people, and their

---

[6] *The Oxford History of England* furnishes a good example: see Godfrey Davies, *The Early
Stuarts 1603–1660* (Oxford, 1937), pp. 30–2.

authority ceases to be legitimate if they abuse the power that the people confer on them. No one had advanced such resistance theories more eloquently than James's own former tutor, George Buchanan.

It was to counter such doctrines rather than to promote a systematic absolutism that James wrote his two major treatises on divine right, both published before he became King of England. Scotland's constitution was different from England's, and in Scotland James had had to deal both with armed resistance and with a strong clerical challenge to his royal authority. In his writings he was much more concerned with what legitimized kingly authority and whence it derived, namely God's ordinance, than with its precise extent in practice. Belief in its derivation from God did not necessarily imply that royal authority was absolute; indeed for James's English subjects the doctrine of divine right was quite compatible with their equally widely held belief that kings were obliged to rule according to the laws of the land. James did not dispute this; indeed in a famous message to parliament in 1610 he authorized Salisbury to say on his behalf that 'though he did derive his title from the loins of his ancestors, yet the law did set the crown upon his head, and he is a king by the common law of the land.' Though it was 'dangerous to submit the power of a king to definition', he further acknowledged 'that he had no power to make laws of himself, or to exact any subsidies *de jure* [as of right] without the consent of his three estates'.[7] On other occasions James's pronouncements were more questionable, but in his central claim he was consistent: what the king lawfully commanded had God's sanction, and must be obeyed as a religious as well as a civic duty; and whatever he commanded, even if it was against the laws of God, he must not be actively resisted, because ultimately he was accountable only to God. Few Englishmen would have quarrelled with that in 1625, or for quite a long time after.

This is not to suggest that James always saw eye to eye with parliament and the common lawyers in constitutional matters. The common law enjoyed an extraordinary prestige, even veneration, in England. Lawyers regularly outnumbered merchants in early Stuart parliaments, but the proportion of MPs who had had a smattering of a legal education was much higher—well over half the House in the Long Parliament. Very many of the wealthy gentry sent their sons to one of the Inns of Court for a year or two, not to become professional barristers but to acquire a bit of metropolitan polish, form useful friendships, and (optimistically) to acquire enough legal lore to be useful to them as landowners and JPs. They may not in fact have learnt much law, but they did absorb the notion, beloved by the profession, that the common law of England went back to time immemorial, that it had survived the Norman Conquest essentially intact, and that parliament as an institution antedated

---

[7] J. P. Kenyon, *The Stuart Constitution* (2nd ed., Cambridge, 1986), p. 11.

the Conquest by centuries. Histories were published under the early Stuarts which showed what a breach the Conquest had really made and when parliament had really originated, but they scarcely dented these cherished beliefs, which were upheld with all the authority of Sir Edward Coke, the most renowned, revered, and belligerent of common lawyers. James had several serious clashes with Coke as Lord Chief Justice, before he finally sacked him in 1616. Few held Coke's extreme view that the law and the constitution had survived unchanged in essence from the mists of Anglo-Saxon antiquity, but very many believed that they had evolved since then through scarcely perceptible adjustments in the nation's changing circumstances, so that at every stage they embodied its collective wisdom and fitted its needs like a glove.

Despite much common ground, there could be clashes between James's conception of the royal authority and that of the common lawyers, and clashes certainly occurred. Coke and his kind held that the law itself was the supreme source of authority, and that the royal prerogative was simply that area of it that the law committed to the king's personal exercise and discretion. James believed that the divine origin of his authority placed him intrinsically above the law, but that a good king obliged himself to rule in accordance with it in all matters that touched the lives, liberties, and property of his subjects. This difference of principle surfaced in disagreement as to the source of parliament's precious customary privileges, which first came in 1604 and returned more acutely in 1621: were they a grace, which the king granted anew to each parliament when the Speaker made his formal request, or were they (as the Commons asserted in 1621) 'the ancient and undoubted birthright and inheritance of the subjects of England'?[8] Such conflicts of principle might lead to serious trouble under a more stiff-necked and less astute monarch, but James forbore from pressing them too far. Most of his substantial disputes with parliament, including those over the impositions in 1610 and 1614 and over foreign policy in the early 1620s, were conducted without raising really disturbing questions of constitutional theory. By keeping the language of divine right to that generalized plane on which it could be used uncontroversially, in order to inculcate obedience, and by respecting the common law tradition in those legal and constitutional areas which involved the liberty of the subject, James learnt to play his part in maintaining a high degree of consensus, right to the end of his reign.[9]

Yet if neither clashes of ideology nor conflicts of class interest carried in them the seeds of civil war, there was a more disturbing symptom of malaise in the body politic in the emergence under James of the terms 'Court' and

[8]  J. P. Kenyon, *The Stuart Constitution*, p. 42; cf. pp. 31–2 for the Commons' statement of their position in 1604.

[9]  Glenn Burgess, *The Politics of the Ancient Constitution: An Introduction to English Political Thought, 1603–1642* (1992), esp. ch. 6.

'Country' to describe opposing interests. Henry Parker, in a famous pamphlet of 1642, took it as axiomatic that 'we have ever found enmity and antipathy betwixt the Court and the Country';[10] but 'ever' was quite mistaken, and 'enmity and antipathy' would have been an overstatement in 1625. Both terms need to be defined, though they were used loosely and not always in quite the same sense. 'The Court' with a capital C embraced the king, his royal household, and his whole entourage of councillors and courtiers; by extension it could include all who made their living by paid employment in the crown's service, and even those who were not so employed but looked to great ministers or favoured courtiers for patronage. Modern distinctions between the government, the civil service, and the royal household were far less clear-cut in Stuart times. The highest household offices were worth more to their holders than any strictly political ones except Lord Treasurer, Lord Chancellor, and Secretary of State,[11] and were regarded as legitimate remuneration for busy politicians. Buckingham, for instance, was Master of the Horse as well as Lord Admiral, to name only two of his places, and the Earl of Pembroke, an influential privy councillor (and incidentally the co-dedicatee of Shakespeare's first folio) was Lord Chamberlain as well as a Commissioner of the Great Seal. All the more successful of the king's ministers were pluralists of this kind. In terms of the number of its officers and its cost to the Exchequer, the king's household, especially if the queen's and the prince's are added, was a much larger establishment than the whole of the central administration, taking that to mean the privy council and its staff, the two Secretaries of State and theirs, the Exchequer, the Court of Wards, the Duchy of Lancaster, the Mint, the Navy Office, the Ordnance, and all the central courts of law.

The word 'country' carried a wider range of nuances. It could mean England as a whole, of course, or the political nation which had some share in running its affairs. But it was often used synonymously with county; anyone who spoke of his 'country' could well mean (say) Cornwall or Lancashire or Suffolk. Used in contradistinction from the Court, however, the Country signified all those of gentry status who held no paid office and had no other material ties with government or the royal entourage. It became an idealized and somewhat smug stereotype, contrasting the Country's independence with the Court's sycophancy, the health of rural life with the filth and disease of the capital, the honesty and neighbourliness of country living with the intrigue and treachery of courtiers, and the wholesomeness of country recreations with the court's debauched and costly pleasures. During the

[10] Henry Parker, *Observations upon Some of His Majesty's Late Answers and Expresses* (1642), reprinted in facsimile in W. Haller (ed.), *Tracts on Liberty in the Puritan Revolution, 1638–1647* (3 vols., New York, 1934), II, 177.

[11] Aylmer, *King's Servants*, ch. 4, esp. Tables 7 and 9.

pro-Spanish phases of James I's foreign policy 'the Country' also carried overtones of superior patriotism and firmer protestantism.

Yet Court and Country were by no means synonymous with government
and opposition, and they were not remotely comparable with political parties. Still less should they be thought of as royalists and parliamentarians in
embryo. That polarization was nowhere in sight in 1625, and when it came in
1641–2 it split both the Court and the Country interests more or less down the
middle. The Country around 1625 was not to be identified with any coherent
set of agreed national policies opposed to those of the government, and the
Court was quite normally an arena for contending factions, not only competing for influence and reward but promoting different policies in opposition to
each other. For all the rhetoric of Court and Country, there was no hard and
fast line between them; they interpenetrated. Even the most successful ministers and courtiers had need of a power-base of loyal and satisfied client-
gentry in the provinces, if they were not to be wholly dependent on the king's
capricious favour, and no dishonour attached to accepting their patronage.

What has to be explained is why 'the Court' came to be an object of suspicion during James's reign, and why 'the Country' felt alienated by it. The fact
is that the crown and the king's senior servants exercised so much patronage,
and redistributed so much of the country's wealth, that to manage the court
with reasonable probity and good judgement was a significant part of
kingcraft. It was the part in which James was most lacking. Too much of his
patronage was bestowed on unworthy recipients, and he was lavish with
gifts and pensions which he could not afford. He sold not only the highest
honours that the crown disposed of, but an increasing number of offices
(though not those carrying high political responsibility). His court was not
only disorderly, but at times the centre of serious scandal. It also overspent
quite grossly, and precious revenue drained away through its extravagance
and corruption. The efforts at reform and retrenchment by James's best Lord
Treasurer, Lionel Cranfield, Earl of Middlesex, were frustrated by his
favourite Buckingham, who in 1624 was largely responsible for engineering
Middlesex's impeachment. The shortcomings of his court were not irremedi-
able, however, and there seemed every hope that things would be better under
the new king, with his blameless morals, his passion for decorum, his young
wife and his dislike of sleaze. But though there was eventually some check to
waste and venality, Charles was as attached to Buckingham as James had
been, and after the favourite's death his court was to fall into disrepute for
new and graver reasons.

Charles's other two kingdoms were very different from England, and even
more different from each other. Scotland's population was rising fast when
James assumed the English crown, but it was barely a quarter of England's:

maybe a million, maybe slightly less. That gave a density of 28 people per square mile, compared with about 100 in England and 70 in Ireland. The gap in relative wealth was wider, and the inflation which both countries suffered was exacerbated by debasement of the Scottish currency; £1 sterling exchanged for £6 Scots in 1565 but for £12 in 1601.[12]

James had wanted to unite his two kingdoms as well as their crowns, and had been wounded and angry when his first English parliament rejected an Act of Union. Englishmen, he was hurt to discover, tended to look down on the Scots, and were selfishly unwilling to admit them to the benefits of full fellow-citizenship. It may be doubted, however, whether on balance a full union would have advantaged either nation at that stage. Extraordinary tact and skill would have been needed to incorporate within one realm two very different societies (or rather three, taking the Highlands as they then were), two quite distinct legal and judicial systems, two churches far apart in their ethos and government, and a whole set of institutions from parliament downward that differed more in fact than in name. Union proved hard enough to bring off just over a century later, when both countries had benefited by the experience of the intervening period. A premature attempt would have broken the homogeneity which was the English kingdom's greatest strength, and would probably have subjected Scotland to a greater degree of subordination than she actually experienced, without yielding enough economic advantage to compensate for it.

Scotland was a far less unified realm than England, for the Gaelic-speaking Highlands and Islands were almost a kingdom apart. There the clan chieftains held their territories as tenants-in-chief of the crown, but the clansmen took their law, as they took their land, from the chief, in accordance with ancient custom. Yet heavily mediated though the king's authority was in those wild parts, Charles I was to have no braver champions than the Highlanders who followed the Marquis of Montrose, whereas Lowland Scotland was to lead the way in raising rebellion against him. His most formidable Scottish enemy, however, was to be a Highlander, and Archibald Campbell, Earl of Argyll, typifies the kind of overmighty subject who could make the government of Scotland very difficult. As hereditary Justice-General over his vast territories Argyll was little less than a viceroy. His powers were exceptional, but other Scottish magnates, in the Lowlands as well as the Highlands, still wielded a feudal jurisdiction that the English nobility had long lost, some as hereditary sheriffs, others through 'grants of regality'. They also retained a powerful patriarchal hold over their kin and tenants, and could raise them in arms. They had violently interrupted James's reign more than once, but he had finished by mastering them. He had checked their feuds, restricted their

---

[12] Jenny Wormald, *Court, Kirk and Community: Scotland 1470–1625* (1981), pp. 166–7.

armed retinues, arbitrated their quarrels, and steadily taught them to bow to the rule of law. When necessary he made them enter into large bonds to keep the peace, and imposed heavy fines when they breached it, but on the whole he achieved his impressive success by his personal touch—by knowing them thoroughly and gaining their willing loyalty, rather than by confronting or coercing them. After four years as King of England he would fairly boast that he governed Scotland with his pen, and though he did not govern it as well at a distance as he had done from within, the country quietly prospered and remained at peace. Over forty years passed between the last serious riot in Edinburgh, in December 1596, and the one that was to launch the Scottish rebellion and thereby, quite shortly, to plunge all three kingdoms in crisis.

James kept a firm control over the Scottish privy council, which became more a channel for his commands than a fully responsible executive and advisory body. It included enough loyal Scottish magnates to reassure the nobility that they were not neglected, which made it look on paper too large for effective administrative action; but its working core was much smaller, and consisted mainly of lairds (who corresponded to the English gentry), lawyers, a few bishops, and others of good burgess stock—all men who saw their own advancement in devoted service to the king. James freely rewarded his most efficient councillors and officers with hereditary noble titles, which served both to satisfy their aspirations and to establish a sector of the peerage with strong ties of loyalty to the crown. There were already between fifty and sixty Scottish peers in 1603, as many as in England at that date, despite Scotland's much smaller population. By 1641 there were 105, not because titles were sold, which was the main reason for their even greater increase in England, but mostly through the ennoblement of deserving royal servants. The older aristocracy was still a power that needed to be managed, as Charles would learn the hard way, but James in his long reign put the Scottish crown in such a position that a competent king need have no fear of overmighty subjects. He might have more to fear from an overmighty Kirk, but James dealt shrewdly and firmly with that too in his time, as will be seen in the next chapter.

Scottish parliaments were very different from English ones, and thanks again largely to James's efforts they were much more easily managed by the crown. Scottish peers sat in them by right, of course, and so after 1597 did the bishops. Commissioners elected by the royal burghs were a long-established part of the membership, commissioners of the shires only a recent one, dating from an act of 1587. James insisted that his chief officers of state should sit in parliament ex officio, but in face of objections he agreed to restrict the number so entitled to eight. The shire commissioners were drawn from the lairds and lesser barons, but in contrast with England most burgh commissioners really were residents of the towns they represented, and engaged in commerce or other urban occupations. The bishops, the officers of state, and the first-generation nobles had all been chosen by the king, and since all the significant towns were royal burghs he could exercise a good deal of influence over their representation too.

The biggest difference between Scottish and English parliaments, however, was that the former sat not in two houses but in a single assembly. If the estates that composed it held any discussions apart, it was on an informal basis and by specific arrangement. But there was seldom much time for debate at all, for after the opening session the parliament regularly referred all the business before it to a committee of the estates called the Lords of the Articles. It met again in full session only to pass the measures that this committee laid before it. Even before 1621 the king's government could generally manage the choice of the Lords of the Articles in its favour, but in that year the procedure was made watertight: the bishops collectively chose eight nobles, who then chose eight bishops, who then joined with the eight nobles to choose eight shire and eight burgh commissioners. If even that did not suffice to deliver the Articles into the crown's hands, the presence *ex officio* of the senior officers of state could be counted on to do so. Such blatant manipulation did not go unresented, but since only one more parliament was to meet after 1621 before the revolutionary ones of 1639–41 there was not much opportunity for protest.

Rather less successful was James's attempt to establish commissioners of the crown in every shire to deal with petty crime and various administrative duties. It was launched in 1610 and widened by a comprehensive act of 1617, which clearly showed its inspiration in the English system of JPs. But it cut across the ancient rights of the burghs as well as the feudal jurisdiction of the magnates, and by 1625 well under half the shires had JPs in operation. There was never much prospect of introducing them except in the Lowlands, but James was not greatly interested in the Highlands, and the gulf between the two Scottish cultures unhappily widened during his reign.

Jacobean Ireland was a country of even more widely differing cultures. Its status was not like that of Scotland, which remained a distinct kingdom, theoretically on an equal plane with England, with whom it now shared a king. Ireland by contrast was regarded as a dependency of the English crown; members of the Long Parliament would liken its constitutional position to that of Jersey or Guernsey. That was going too far, of course; Ireland had its own council and parliament, but they were subordinate to those of England in a way that Scotland's institutions had never been. That was true even before the late Elizabethan conquest, which was undertaken after the two greatest lords of Ulster, the Earls of Tyrone and Tyrconnell, had in the name of the Irish nobility offered the crown of Ireland to Philip II of Spain, with whom England was at war. In 1601 a small Spanish army had landed at Kinsale, but Elizabeth's general, Lord Mountjoy, had forced both Tyrconnell and the

Spaniards to surrender, and followed up his success with the most complete conquest of Ireland that England had yet effected. Mountjoy was just completing it when James came to the throne, and for the rest of the reign Ireland, with her power of resistance seemingly broken, was storing problems for the future rather than manifesting them pressingly in the present.

Ireland had a higher population than Scotland—perhaps 1,400,000 in 1600, rising very fast to as much as 2,100,000 by 1641[13]—though most of it was even poorer and economically more backward. It was no less culturally divided, consisting as it did of three unequal and imperfectly assimilated elements. Much the largest was the ancient native stock, Celtic in race and Gaelic in language (closely related to that spoken in the Scottish Highlands), whom the English have often called the Old Irish, to distinguish them from the Old English. Theirs was a clan culture, though Irish clans were called septs; it dominated western Ireland, and until the Jacobean plantations it was supreme throughout Ulster. Its system of landholding was hardly compatible with English conceptions concerning individual ownership, and its customary brehon law clashed uncomfortably with the English common law. The Old Irish were passionately catholic, though their catholicism was largely untouched by the reforms associated with the Council of Trent and the Catholic Counter-Reformation. There was already tension between the native clergy who never left Ireland and the sons of the gentry who trained for the priesthood in the several Irish colleges in Rome and in the Spanish Netherlands, for the latter aspired to bring Irish catholicism into line with the Counter-Reformation. The Old Irish spanned a wide social spectrum, for poor as most of them were they boasted a native nobility whose greater members shared a life-style and often intermarried with the second element in the population, the Old English (or Anglo-Irish).

Before the Tudor and Stuart plantations the Old English were indisputably the ascendancy class. They were mostly the descendants of Anglo-Norman lords who had settled and carved out great estates for themselves in the Middle Ages, and they represented an older colonial dominance. They included such great houses as the Fitzgeralds, Butlers, and Burkes (originally de Burghs), but there were a few lords of Gaelic extraction who so fully shared their outlook and interests as to be inseparable from them; Donough Mac-Carthy, Lord Muskerry, is an example. Except in those regions where the great Old Irish families held sway—mainly Connaught and Ulster (before the plantation)—the Old English dominated local government, and regarded themselves as an essential part of the colonial regime. They had stayed loyal during the rebellion of 1593–1603, but their loyalty was already under strain,

---

[13] T. W. Moody, F. X. Martin, and F. J. Byrne (eds.), *A New History of Ireland*, III (Oxford, 1978), pp. 388–90 (by L. M. Cullen).

and the strain became increasingly severe under the early Stuarts. In the first place the great majority remained Roman Catholics, and whatever de facto toleration they enjoyed, their religion subjected them to various disabilities. They saw it as the ultimate aim of the English government to bring the whole Irish population within a protestant Church of Ireland. Secondly, the policy of plantation, which began on a small scale under Mary Tudor, threatened their possession of their own estates, for their title could seldom satisfy the strict criteria of English law. Thirdly, the increasing efforts by the English crown, from the 1530s onward, to rule Ireland through an English Lord Lieutenant or Lord Deputy and a council in Dublin threatened their status and encroached on their very large power in their own regions. They therefore found themselves more and more in conflict with the third element in the population, the New English who acquired Irish estates under the various plantation schemes.

These settlers were nearly all protestants, and though they developed interests that were not always at one with those of the English government they stood much closer to it than the Old English did. It was from the crown that they had acquired their grants of land and other privileges, and they looked to it for further opportunities, and for protection. But the only part of Ireland that was fully under English rule was the Pale, which extended from Dundalk to a little south of Dublin, and up to thirty miles inland. Even there the New English shared their dominance with the longer-seated Old English Lords of the Pale. It was only in the Pale and the plantations that the Church of Ireland held any real sway, for as the next chapter will make clearer it scarcely pretended to be more than the church of the protestant settler community. Its Calvinistic doctrine and its identification of the papacy with Antichrist put the rest of the Irish people literally beyond redemption, and although there was no attempt to force catholics to attend its services it was no friend to the Old English. It upheld the exclusion of catholics from public office, implied that their professions of loyalty were not to be trusted, and opposed any formal toleration of the exercise of their religion. Fortunately the realities of political and social life in Jacobean Ireland were not as intolerant as its established church's professions, but the fears among Irish catholics of protestant intentions had far more substance than the fear of popery among protestants in England.

Ulster, which had been the centre of rebellion in the 1590s, remained the least anglicized and most wholly Gaelic province of Ireland in James's early years. The dominant families were the Old Irish houses of O'Neill and O'Donnell, whose heads, the Earls of Tyrone and Tyrconnell, wielded great territorial and political power. They continued to give grounds for suspicion after the defeat of the rebellion, and in 1607 the English privy council summoned them both to London. Instead of obeying they fled to France. The

English government construed the 'Flight of the Earls' as proof of their treasonable intent, and they were adjudged to have forfeited all their estates to the crown. It was a golden opportunity to extend the policy of plantation to Ulster. The original plans were quite small-scale and made generous provision for those Irish who lived peaceably, but there was a minor rising in 1608, unnecessarily provoked by the governor of Derry, and James and the privy council panicked. The revised plan opened almost all the six counties of Armagh, Cavan, Coleraine (renamed Londonderry), Donegal, Fermanagh, and Tyrone to English and Scottish settlers, allocating at the most a quarter of the territory to the native Irish. Most of the latter received nothing, and few of those who did get grants were allowed to retain the land that they actually occupied. The rest of the territory was divided into estates, mostly of 2,000 acres, and allotted to 'undertakers', who accepted specific obligations to reside on them, settle a quota of colonists on them, and defend them. These obligations were seldom met. The aim was the complete segregation of the Irish and settler populations, but the new owners found it economically impossible to subsist without taking Irish tenants, though their terms forbade it. Consequently there were few parts of Ulster where settlers were not greatly outnumbered by natives, even by James's death. By 1622 about 3,700 families (roughly 13,000 adults), with English and Scots in about equal numbers, had been introduced into the six 'escheated' counties, while another 7,500 adults had settled in Down and Antrim, where plantations had been established in Elizabeth's reign. Large numbers of Scots had also settled in Munster.

Naturally enough, the Irish population of all ranks had been resentful of the plantations, and the early settlers had gone in fear of their lives. But by the end of the reign the threat of violence had receded, amid a surprising amount of mutual accommodation. The English common law had made solid progress, but in other ways, such as housing, the settlers had to some degree gone native. There was still a latent store of discontent, however, for most Irish tenants had no security of tenure and they had not forgotten their old loyalties. Living as they did in Church of Ireland territory, they also felt the subjugation of their religion more acutely than their compatriots elsewhere.

English political dominance over Ireland was greater after the Elizabethan conquest than before, but there were quite strong practical limitations to it. Constitutionally, the Lord Lieutenant (or Lord Deputy—the powers were the same whatever the title) was a colonial governor, and the Irish council in Dublin existed purely to advise and assist him. By Poynings's Law (1494) no bills might be introduced in the Irish parliament without prior approval, not only by the Lord Lieutenant and his council but by the king and the English council. The Irish parliament, like the English, had two houses, and hitherto the Old English had numerically dominated both. But before James summoned it for the only time in his reign, in 1613, he created new seats on a lavish scale, nearly all in Ulster and many representing newly incorporated tiny boroughs of protestant settlers, little more than villages in size. His blatant aim was to ensure a protestant majority in the Commons; of the sixty-four members who represented Ulster, only one was a catholic. Sixteen of the twenty lay peers who attended were catholics, but they were outvoted by twenty Church of Ireland bishops, all in effect royal nominees. Yet despite such gerrymandering the Dublin government could not have things all its own way, and no English monarch could rule Ireland by decree. With little of military force to dispose of, with even less of a bureaucracy, and with a chronic problem in pursuing financial self-sufficiency, government could not dispense with the co-operation of the Old English at least. If England's rulers could have accepted that the catholicism of the Old English and of the more anglicized Old Irish was not incompatible with their loyalty, if they could have conceded them their religious liberty and their right to full political participation (especially office-holding), and if they had limited the colonization of an admitted underpopulated country so as to preserve the property rights of the peaceably inclined Irish, the history of the country in the coming decades and for many generations after might have been less tragic. Seen with hindsight, Ireland was the kingdom in which James's rule was least successful.

The fact that Charles I inherited a multiple monarchy certainly made his task complex and demanding. Each of his three realms presented problems (what seventeenth-century state did not?), yet none was in a state of crisis, and there was no inherent reason why he should not have gone on governing them with the sort of imperfect success that his father had achieved. He needed to be sensitive to the state of feeling in all three, to keep himself accurately informed, and to judge competently what were the limits of the politically possible in each. On all three counts he was to fail. His throne was unlikely to be in danger unless all three became seriously destabilized at the same time, and that was not to be foreseen in 1625, because there was no need for it to happen. That it did happen was more due to errors of policy—not all of them of course his personal errors—in the twelve or fifteen years following his accession than because of anything intrinsically doom-laden in the situation which he inherited. One element in that inheritance, however, which called for a special degree of understanding and statesmanship was the state of religion in each of his kingdoms. Religious fears and aspirations were to be the prime cause of the Scottish rebellion in 1638 and a major factor in the Irish rebellion of 1641; and though religion was not foremost among the immediate issues over which the English Civil War broke out, religious convictions played an incalculable part in the way men and women chose sides when it came to the breach. The subject therefore calls for a chapter to itself.

# TWO

# King Charles's Inheritance II: The Matter of Religion

So large did religious differences and fears loom in the course of Charles's reign that it may come as a surprise to find how relatively stable the religious situation was when he came to the throne, at least in England and Scotland. James had inherited a Church of England which had won the loyalty of the great majority of the English people, and thanks to the firm measures of Elizabeth's later years it had little to fear from either catholics on the one side or Presbyterians or separatists on the other. That was still true when he died.

The fear of popery was something about which neither the English nor the Scottish peoples were wholly rational, but Gunpowder Plot apart there was little enough reason for it during James's reign. The vast majority of English Roman Catholics were loyal, law-abiding subjects, located mostly in a few rural areas where concentrations of catholic gentry families protected the priests who risked fearful penalties (though these were hardly ever enforced now) to minister the sacraments on which their religion depended for survival. Counting both the recusants, who submitted to regular fines and other disabilities rather than attend parish worship as the law required, and the more numerous 'church papists' who conformed just far enough to avoid such penalties, the catholic community under James I numbered around 40,000 men, women and children—a mere one per cent of the whole population, though about a tenth of the gentry and a fifth of the peerage were recusants. James himself was very firmly protestant, though his penchant for crypto-catholic councillors and courtiers aroused some suspicion. The catholic threat from overseas receded during most of the twenty years of peace with Spain that began in 1604, especially after Spain concluded the Twelve Years Truce with the Netherlands five years later. The international scene changed in 1619, however, when the rebellious protestant nobility of Bohemia elected Frederick, the Elector Palatine and James's son-in-law, as their king. As such, Frederick would have had a second voice in the electoral college which chose the Holy Roman Emperor, thus altering its balance from a catholic to a protestant majority of four to three. This was a nightmare prospect for the House of Habsburg, but an imperial army routed Frederick at the Battle of the White Mountain in 1620, and a Spanish one occupied his own principality on the Rhine. Frederick was to be an exile for the rest of his reign.

James had for years been rousing misgivings by his close working relationship with the Spanish ambassador, the Count of Gondomar, and by his keenness on marrying Prince Charles to a Spanish Infanta. He now thought that the best prospect of securing the return of the Palatinate to Frederick lay in concluding a diplomatic deal with Spain, whose king was kinsman to the Emperor, and sealing it with a Spanish match. Charles himself was so taken with the idea that in 1623 he set off for Spain incognito, in company with Buckingham, to woo the Infanta in person. It was a mad escapade, but the wild public rejoicing when the pair came home without the lady showed how unpopular James's policy was, and how easily the fear of popery could be revived. It rose again in 1625 when Charles married Henrietta Maria, the fifteen-year-old sister of Louis XIII of France, not least because of well-grounded suspicions that there was a secret clause in the marriage treaty, promising to suspend the penal laws against catholic recusants. But this time the fear was less acute, because France's commitment to the international catholic cause was heavily qualified by her enmity with Spain, her friendship with the Dutch, and her toleration of her own Huguenot population. Moreover Charles's relations with his young bride were for the first few years reassuringly cool.

If the fear of papists was later to swell until it significantly contributed to the genesis of civil war, conflict within the Church of England was to play an even greater part in dividing the nation. Such conflict was kept within quite narrow bounds during James's reign, and consensus prevailed; but to understand why the potential for division remained present, and why it widened so unhappily under Charles, it is necessary to go further back. The Church of England had always affirmed an identity distinct from that of the Roman, Lutheran, and Reformed (Zwinglian or Calvinist) churches, though that identity underwent quite rapid changes in its early years. The liturgy in use down to the Civil War, the Book of Common Prayer of 1559, was a compromise, like the rest of the Elizabethan settlement, in this case between the earlier Prayer Books of 1549 and 1552. The Thirty-Nine Articles, the church's confession of faith, were not formulated by convocation until 1563 (though they were based on the Forty-Two of ten years earlier), and Elizabeth did not allow parliament to give them statutory authority until 1571. She disliked religious controversy, especially if it challenged her own authority as the church's Supreme Governor. She did not want to stir the hostility of the large numbers of her subjects who were still at heart attached to the old catholic rites, and she distrusted the zeal of the opposed minority who hoped that the 1559 settlement would prove to be just a half-way house to the full reformation that some of them had embraced, as exiles, during Mary's reign, in Geneva or Zürich.

During the early part of her reign, opposition to her settlement focused mainly on clerical vestments and liturgical ceremonies, but as under Charles I seventy years later, this was symptomatic of deeper disagreement as to how a church should be constituted and what a Christian should believe. In the early 1570s a puritan movement emerged which in many ways prefigured the opposition to Charles, though its main objectives and preoccupations changed considerably over the years. For most of Elizabeth's reign it was mainly concerned with church government and discipline. Various developments were impelling strongly committed English protestants to seek a closer identification of interest with the Reformed churches abroad; they included the unique authority that Geneva developed under Theodore Béza after Calvin's death in 1564 as an exemplar of Reformed ideals, the onset of the French Wars of Religion and the revolt of the Netherlands, then England's own involvement in war with Spain and the succession of catholic plots against the queen's life. Militant puritans strove to give the national church a form of government and jurisdiction that would render it virtually independent of its lukewarm Supreme Governor—a Presbyterian form. In place of archbishops, bishops, archdeacons, and their various courts, they would have built the church's polity on the base of a consistory in every parish, consisting of a minister and a group of lay elders with powers of justice over the faith and morals of the congregation, which meant the whole local population. Within a defined area called a *classis* or classical presbytery, the constituent ministers and elders were to meet regularly, exercise powers of ordination and excommunication, and from time to time elect representatives to a provincial synod. A national synod was to crown the whole pyramidal structure, which could operate if need be quite independently of the secular state, though the ideal was a partnership.

To Elizabeth, who was very much her father's daughter, such a threat to her authority was anathema. She and her bishops nipped the first wave of the Presbyterian movement in the bud in the early 1570s. It revived in the mid-1580s, however, in the so-called classical movement, on a sufficient scale to threaten a serious rift in the church, and with some lay support in parliament. This time she had an Archbishop of Canterbury after her own heart in John Whitgift, and within a few years he and his fellow-bishops, with the help of the Court of High Commission, had scotched the attempt to presbyterianize the Church of England from within. By James's accession it was virtually dead. What survived of Elizabethan puritanism was a certain doctrinal bent, to which we will turn shortly, and a strong zeal to extend the preaching of the

Word, at a time when large numbers of parish clergy were still too ignorant and ill-educated to put together a simple sermon. In regions with a large infusion of puritan clergy and laity, the practice survived of holding 'exercises', which were meetings of neighbouring ministers in which the more proficient tutored the less in the expounding of the Scriptures, before a lay audience. This usage descended from what had more usually been called 'prophesyings' in Elizabeth's earlier years, and which she (who distrusted preaching) had disliked so much that she had suspended Whitgift's predecessor Archbishop Grindal from all his episcopal functions when he bravely refused to prohibit them. Another way of securing regular sermons where the incumbent could not or would not provide them was to fee a 'lecturer' (an ordained minister, but not beneficed in the parish concerned) to preach every Sunday and market-day. Sometimes this was done by the more well-to-do parishioners; sometimes neighbouring clergy took turns to fill a gap, or to preach in the nearest market town; and in some towns the corporation or other benefactors endowed weekly lectures (i.e. sermons), to be delivered on market-days. Endowed lectureships embodied in a relatively unobjectionable form the Reformed churches' principle that pastors and teachers should receive a calling from their congregations.

Until quite late in Elizabeth's reign, differences over church government bulked much larger than controversies over doctrine. Predestination, over which there was to be so much contention in the next two reigns, was hardly an issue yet among English protestants. They all believed that since the Fall the will of man was so corrupted by sin that nothing he did by his own mere volition could earn him merit in the sight of God; salvation could come only through faith, and that saving faith was attainable only through the free gift of divine grace. All agreed that humankind was divided into the elect and the reprobate, and that God had predestined the elect to salvation; the reprobate would of course go to hell. The unresolved question—and this is an area that became so filled with eggshell-fine distinctions that non-theologians tread in it at their peril—was whether God had absolutely predestined the reprobate to damnation, so that no effort of theirs to believe and repent could save them: whether, in other words, Christ had died for all mankind or only for the elect. The early English reformers, including Hooper and Latimer, taught clearly that Christ died for all, and so did Bishop John Jewel, whose works carried great authority in the early Elizabethan church; in their belief, saving faith was available to all who opened their hearts to it, and the reprobate excluded themselves from salvation by their deliberate sins. Béza, however, elaborating on Calvin's own teaching, enunciated the doctrine of double predestination in its harshest form: the reprobate were no less fore-ordained to damnation than the elect to salvation. The rigour and logic of his formulation, coupled with the prestige of Geneva among the converted, had a strong attraction for many of the more intellectual Elizabethan churchmen, and high Calvinism eventually took a powerful hold on the universities. It was the more attractive for standing at the furthest distance from the abhorred Roman Catholic doctrines concerning free will and the shocking assumption that men and women could acquire merit in God's eyes through good works. It requires an effort to understand its appeal today, but there are some who are still drawn by it.

In the Church of England there was always a spectrum of opinion on the troubled points of free will, free grace, and predestination, single or double. But late in the sixteenth century the theological centre of gravity shifted towards Calvinism within the establishment, and not only in the universities. When young Samuel Harsnett, whom Charles I was to make Archbishop of York forty-five years later, boldly went against the grain and attacked the harshness of the prevailing predestinarian doctrine in a famous sermon at Paul's Cross in 1584, Whitgift censured him for it and ordered him to preach no more on the subject. A more sustained attack on high Calvinism developed at Cambridge a decade later, led by the Lady Margaret Professor of Divinity, who was the Huguenot refugee Peter Baro, and a young fellow of Caius College called William Barrett. They drew down on themselves the wrath of the Vice-Chancellor and the senior heads of colleges, but the noise of the ensuing disputes spread far beyond Cambridge, until Whitgift felt obliged to intervene. In 1595 he approved a set of nine statements of the Church of England's position on the troubled points of doctrine which became known as the Lambeth Articles. The first stated that 'God from eternity predestined certain men to life and condemned others to death'; the fourth that 'Those who are not predestined to salvation shall of necessity be damned on account of their sins'; the seventh that 'Saving grace is . . . not given to all men by which they may be saved if they so will'.[1] The Lambeth Articles have often been taken as proof that Whitgift was a thorough-paced Calvinist in doctrine, but some modern scholars have argued that he dissociated himself from the belief that God gave his elect a certain knowledge of their salvation, and that his aim was to put a check on both sides in the current controversy. The main argument, now and for some time to come, was not between predestination and free will but about the precise manner in which predestination operated. Nevertheless the Lambeth Articles acquired such authority among puritans in the early seventeenth century that they repeatedly pressed to have them added to the Thirty-Nine in the Prayer Book.

---

[1] The Lambeth Articles, translated from the Latin, are printed in Claire Cross, *The Royal Supremacy in the Elizabethan Church* (1969), p. 205. For views on their interpretation, see H. C. Porter, *Reformation and Reaction in Tudor Cambridge* (Cambridge, 1958), pp. 344–90; Peter Lake, *Moderate Puritans and the Elizabethan Church* (Cambridge, 1982), pp. 209–26; and Peter White, *Predestination, Policy and Polemic* (Cambridge, 1992), pp. 101–11.

Elizabeth's reaction to the episode was characteristic. Having signified her high displeasure to Baro for raising the theological dust, she showed scarcely less of it to Whitgift for venturing to pronounce on the points at issue by virtue of his authority as primate. She forbade him to publish the Lambeth Articles and threatened him, only half in jest, with the penalties of praemunire for clerical encroachment on royal authority, through which her father had brought down Cardinal Wolsey. Elizabeth, it should be remembered, intervened in ecclesiastical affairs at times more autocratically than either James or Charles ever did, at least in England. It was not good to get on the wrong side of her. Baro left Cambridge in 1596, when his tenure of his chair was not renewed, and Barrett had to make two recantations to save himself from expulsion from the university. Yet though such anti-Calvinists were a small and disfavoured minority at that time, there was a direct continuity between them and the school of divines that Charles I was to promote.

James I shared Elizabeth's dislike of public disputation over the mysteries of the divine decrees, though unlike her he was keenly interested in theology and seriously knowledgeable about it. Soon after his accession he received a petition from a sizeable group of puritan ministers, calling for a number of modest reforms in the practices of the church. In response he summoned a group of bishops and moderate puritan clergy to confer under his presidency at Hampton Court. He hugely enjoyed himself, but initially he mistook the aims of the puritans, speaking as if the Elizabethan movement was still in its militant phase. His much reported words, 'no bishop, no king', were quite wide of the mark, because no one in the conference was opposed to bishops as such, or to the royal supremacy; episcopacy was not to become an issue again in England until 1641. Predestination was discussed, but it was not the central matter of debate, because nearly everyone present would have found common ground in the Lambeth Articles. James was opposed to any changes of substance in the church's government or worship, which he profoundly admired, but the discussions were generally harmonious, and out of the conference came the priceless jewel of the Authorized Version of the Bible.

Fifteen years later James sent delegates to a much more important meeting of divines, the Synod of Dort, whose repercussions were still affecting theological debate down to the Civil War. By the time that the synod met at Dordrecht in Holland in 1618–19, doctrinal dissension was not only tearing the continental Reformed churches apart but threatening actual civil war in the Dutch Republic. In the late sixteenth century a professor of theology at Leiden called Jacob Hermandzoon, or by his Latinized name Arminius, had led a challenge to the Bezan doctrine of predestination parallel to that which troubled Cambridge, though the two movements arose independently. He believed in the predestination of the elect, and he did not hold that it lay within the free will of every individual to embrace or reject salvation, but he did teach that those who truly believed and repented could be assured that Christ would exercise his power to save them. This shocking 'heresy' led to a bitter controversy which lasted far beyond his death in 1609 and ramified deeply into Dutch politics. The Arminians, or Remonstrants, were supported by Jan van Oldenbarnevelt, the virtual chief minister and leader of the Estates of Holland, by the great jurist Hugo Grotius, and by most of the regent class that governed the Dutch towns. The Contra-Remonstrants (i.e. the high Calvinists) were backed by the stadtholder Maurice of Nassau (William the Silent's son) and most of the nobility and clergy. The dispute became a power struggle between Maurice and Oldenbarnevelt, between those who opposed Holland's dominance of the Union and those who supported it, and between those who wanted to renew the war with Spain when the Twelve Years Truce ran out in 1621 and those who did not. People felt so passionately about Arminianism in the run-up to the English Civil War that one needs to know what they understood by it.

James's contribution to promoting the international synod was some-thing of a diplomatic coup. His delegation openly supported the Contra-Remonstrant side and applauded its victory, but his diplomatic approval of the hard-line decrees whereby the Arminian tenets were condemned should not be taken as a declaration of his personal beliefs. He had genuine objections to Arminius's doctrines, and in England he preferred the Calvinist theologians' position to that of their more liberal challengers; but the four divines whom he sent to Dort, though regarded as Calvinists, took a mediatory stance there and repudiated the Bezan doctrine of predestination to reprobation. It seems that he disliked the attempt by both sides to probe the working of God's decrees further than mortal minds can go, and there was an element of diplomacy in his public support for the synod's decrees. He still felt a need for Maurice's friendship, and judged that a Contra-Remonstrant victory would best restore unity of a kind in the Dutch Republic and keep it effective as a bastion of the protestant interest in Europe. The outcome of the synod was naturally very welcome to English puritans, who from then on smeared their fellow-countrymen who questioned their high Calvinism as Arminians, whether or not they subscribed to Arminius's own beliefs or had even read his works. The intense interest in the synod led to acrimonious controversy in the universities, and to a spate of anti-Arminian sermons at Paul's Cross. This was not to James's liking, and in 1622 he commanded his Archbishop of Canterbury to enforce a set of 'Directions concerning preachers', limiting their subject-matter, forbidding any below a bishop or dean 'to preach in any popular auditory the deep points of predestination, election, [or] reprobation', and prohibiting 'railing speeches against the persons of either papists or puritans'.[2]

---

[2] Kenyon, *Stuart Constitution*, pp. 128–30. Some points in this paragraph may need to be qual-ified in the light of R. B. Patterson, *James I and the Reunion of Christendom* (Cambridge, 1999).

Few of the English divines who reacted against the harsher formulations of predestinarianism owed much to Arminius, least of all the senior of them, the learned and saintly Lancelot Andrewes, who was seventy in 1625 and had only a year to live. Theirs was mainly a native tradition. James was not unfriendly to them, though in his personal beliefs he stood nearer to the Calvinist camp. When Canterbury fell vacant, he chose the strongly Calvinist George Abbot as archbishop rather than Andrewes, who had been widely expected to succeed. Buckingham patronized puritans, and through him their most prestigious divine, John Preston, was made a chaplain to Prince Charles. But James appointed Andrewes to both the English and Scottish privy councils, and made him dean of the Chapel Royal from 1618. Andrewes's liturgical practices there, including the placing of the altar, were the pattern for what Charles tried to impose on the whole church in the 1630s. James gave bishoprics to five so-called Arminians, including Andrewes and the future Archbishops of York and Canterbury, Harsnett, Richard Neile, and William Laud—though he appointed Laud reluctantly, and only to the remote see of St David's, under pressure from Buckingham, for he distrusted his 'restless spirit'.[3] Five was not a large proportion of a bench of bishops numbering twenty-six, but James grew more sympathetic to the group in his later years, not because he was converted to their theology but because he shared their dislike of puritans. This was strengthened by the puritans' bitter hostility to the Declaration of Sports that James issued in 1618, ordering the toleration of lawful recreations (including dancing!) after the time of divine service on Sundays, and by puritan preachings against his plans for a Spanish match for Prince Charles, which he regarded as an unwarranted intrusion into matters of state.

The international situation and the prince's marriage did bring some sharpening of religious differences towards the end of the reign, and so did the increasing confidence of the 'Arminian' faction. The latter were regularly congregating at Durham House, Bishop Neile's London residence, which became so notorious as an academy of anti-Calvinism that it was called Durham College. The circle included two future bishops who were to become particularly unpopular in the 1630s, Matthew Wren, chaplain successively to Andrewes and Prince Charles, and John Cosin, chaplain to Neile. Wren accompanied Charles to Madrid in 1623, and after his return he assured Andrewes, Neile, and Laud that the prince's judgement was 'very right', adding that 'for upholding the doctrine and discipline and the right estate of the church, I have more confidence of him than of his father'.[4] Another of the circle, one of the king's own chaplains called Richard Montagu, was at the

---

[3] H. R. Trevor-Roper, *Archbishop Laud* (2nd ed., 1962), pp. 56–7.

[4] Quoted in Kevin Sharpe, *The Personal Rule of Charles I* (New Haven and London, 1992), p. 279.

centre of a *cause célèbre* in 1624–5. He had already been under fire in the 1621 parliament for asserting the church's divine right to tithes in print, but he was in worse trouble with that of 1624 for publishing *A New Gag for an Old Goose*. This was a defence of the Church of England's doctrines against a Roman Catholic attack. It did not affirm the doctrines of Arminius, whom Montagu had never read, but it did not support the Calvinist position on pre-destination either; it maintained that the church left the finer points touching the divine decrees undefined, as 'secrets reserved to God alone'.[5] Where Montagu really gave offence was by branding those who took a rigorous line on predestination as puritans, for their position had always been accommodated within the spectrum of the Church of England's tolerated beliefs, and to stigmatize a *doctrine* as puritan—one moreover widely accepted by the Reformed churches—was novel and disturbing. Montagu raised the stakes by defending himself against the Commons' attack, which had allegedly been orchestrated by Archbishop Abbot, in a book which he entitled with the king's permission *Appello Caesarem* (I appeal to Caesar), and James saw to it that it was published, despite Abbot's refusal to license it. The row rumbled on into the next reign.

Despite such episodes, one should not exaggerate the extent of religious dissension in England when Charles succeeded to the throne. Most of the controversy between Calvinists and anti-Calvinists took place at a fairly rarefied academic level, and most English Calvinists had lately been retreating from the full rigour of Béza's double predestination. James maintained to the end a policy of holding a balance within the church, discouraging any polarization between theological extremes, and if necessary using his authority to dampen public disputation over mysteries that human reason had no power to resolve. Consequently the minority in the episcopate and the universities who held unpopular 'Arminian' views were mostly content to keep fairly quiet about them. Another reason why the Jacobean church accommodated such differences with a minimum of strife was that most of its active members cared more about preserving its broad evangelical front than about probing what was potentially divisive within it. For there really was a consensus in the Jacobean church—probably a more general one than at any time since the Reformation, or for a long time to come. The search for causes of the Civil War has led to too much concentration on disputations among the most highly educated clergy, few of whom held a cure of souls that involved ministering to the laity, and until recently too little on the life of the church as a whole, including not only the parish clergy but the broad religious public.

It had taken a long time—longer than historians used to realize—to wean the English people from the old faith and turn the great majority into a truly protestant nation. A great evangelistic drive was afoot in Jacobean England, for much still remained to be done, and the educated laity were partners with the more active clergy in the enterprise. A high proportion of parish livings were in the gift of lay patrons, generally local landowners. The hitherto lowly position of parish parsons in the social scale was improving and a growing proportion were university educated, but a great many were still incapable of preaching, and lay-endowed lectureships helped to supply what was seen as an urgent need. The godly among the gentry—and not only those who came to be called puritans—played their part as patrons by appointing zealous men to parish livings, by supporting lectureships, by hospitality to preachers, by conducting daily devotions and rehearsing the weekly sermon in their households, and by upholding Christian morality as squires and magistrates.

Much distortion has resulted from attempts to trace a fundamental breach between 'Anglicans' (an anachronistic term) and puritans back into James's reign or even earlier. The reality of the Jacobean church was more like a spectrum, dominated by a broad middle band of agreement. Yet puritans were recognized as existing and Ben Jonson satirized them on the London stage. Mr Zeal-of-the-Land Busy was of course a crude and hostile caricature, but laying such stereotypes aside, what can be said about puritans at this time, and what distinguished them from middle-of-the-road English protestants? There was certainly no sharp line of division, and some historians have questioned whether they still existed at all; but that leaves us wondering why contemporaries were so plainly conscious of them. Apart from a small and radical minority, they were no longer organized as a militant movement. They are best thought of as representing a distinctive strain of piety within the broad protestant establishment, a strain whose roots lay in an intense preoccupation with personal salvation. Puritans had no monopoly of predestinarian doctrine, but they generally held it in a rigorous form, as expounded by their favourite divine William Perkins, whose works (though he died early in 1602) held an almost canonical authority for them. The separation of humankind into the elect and the reprobate was central to their view of both this world and the next. They acknowledged that the elect are known only to God, but they took it as a sign of grace if they could keep God's commandments—'by their fruits ye shall know them' was a favourite text—and that was the main reason for the uncompromising austerity of their moral code. They were given to constant anxious self-searching; they read every personal adversity as a trial or judgement and every piece of good fortune as a blessing of providence. And since faith was the key to God's saving grace, they set enormous store by the preaching of the Word and the reading of the Scriptures. The puritan clergy constituted an informal preaching brotherhood, and the appetite of their flocks for sermons was insatiable. Preachers had two supreme tasks: first, to awaken sinners to repentance and guide them through the dark night of the soul to the assurance (if grace were granted) that salvation could be theirs, and second, to instruct the faithful in the full meaning of the sacred texts and keep them at a high pitch of dedication to their spiritual calling. They held the authority of the Scriptures to be absolutely paramount, and in matters of faith and worship they were suspicious of any other authority at all.

Puritans were of course not alone in being anxious about the state of their souls, as any reader of Donne's sermons or Holy Sonnets will appreciate. But they placed a massive weight on every individual's personal responsibility, whereas churchmen of an older tradition trusted more to the sacraments as the media through which saving grace was transmitted, and were content to accept the operation of the divine decrees as ultimately a mystery. Such men generally cultivated a serener faith, though not necessarily a less intense one. It is movingly exemplified in the life and poetry of George Herbert, who renounced the prospects of a career at court (he was a kinsman of Pembroke) to become a country parson, and died in 1633 before he was forty. To such as Herbert the church was a temple and the clergy a priesthood, whose highest function was the celebration of the sacraments; desirable though it was that priests should preach it was not essential, as the sacraments were. To puritans, however, priesthood was an uncomfortable concept, except in the protestant sense of the priesthood of all believers. In their attitude to the sacraments they were anxious to avoid any tincture of popish 'superstition', and their clergy disliked wearing the surplice and the liturgical vestments; a plain black gown seemed more appropriate to their calling as ministers of God's Word. The central tradition of the Church of England, as against its puritan and later 'Arminian' wings, had been immensely strengthened by Jewel's protégé Richard Hooker, who published the essential parts of his magisterial *Laws of Ecclesiastical Polity* between 1593 and 1597. In contrast with puritans who exalted scriptural authority at the expense of all others, Hooker venerated the example of the early church and the teaching of the early Fathers, and he stressed the English church's medieval inheritance. Unlike the puritan who identified the papacy with Antichrist, he did not deny that Rome was a true church, though he strongly affirmed the distinctness and superiority of that of England. Convinced that God's grace would be denied to none who truly sought it, he firmly believed that the visible Church of England must aim at embracing all the people of the realm. In justifying the Royal Supremacy, he granted the absolute authority of the Scriptures in matters of faith, but he argued that they did not and could not prescribe every detail of ecclesiastical organization and liturgical practice, which were likely to vary according to the needs and traditions of particular societies in different ages. There was, therefore, an area of 'things indifferent' which could legitimately be regulated by the civil magistrate, and that is why the Acts of Settlement and Uniformity and subsequent orders by the church's Supreme Governor should be obeyed. Puritans remained queasy about the concept of 'things indifferent', but Hooker's answers to both Roman and puritan questionings of the Church of England's authority and rites held great authority in early Stuart England.

Another contentious puritan characteristic was their hankering after a 'godly discipline', to keep the faithful in the paths of righteousness and to prevent the reprobate from giving scandal to them. Puritans were deeply dissatisfied with the existing ecclesiastical courts, mostly survivals from pre-Reformation times, which they felt to be too much concerned with enforcing clerical conformity and the church's financial dues, and far too little with raising the moral tone of the nation. In some parishes with a puritan patron, he and the parson of his choice and a core of like-minded parishioners operated something like a consistory, with the churchwardens and overseers of the poor taking the role of elders. There were towns, too, where a strongly puritan magistracy worked in similarly close concert with the minister or ministers in a holy war against drunkenness, fornication, swearing, and sabbath-breaking. And there were whole regions, some quite large, where two cultures were in conflict: the one traditional, attached to old festivals and customary merry-makings such as church ales, maypoles, dancing, and games of football (then a rough free-for-all), the other suspicious of carefree revelling and hostile to any occasions that encouraged boozing, brawling, and the begetting of bastards. Very broadly speaking, the older festive culture tended to survive best in regions given mainly to open-field arable farming and characterized by close-knit manorial communities, whereas puritanism and its discipline had a stronger hold in pastoral and woodland country, which commonly had a less cohesive and more shifting population, and in the clothing districts, which were also less manorialized. The older order tended to flourish where local society was aristocratically dominated, unless the nobleman or greater gentry concerned were themselves strong puritans, while the godly had their way more where the middling sort had a common interest with the gentry in imposing discipline on the unruly lower orders. There was to be some correlation between this sort of division, involving religion, economic occupation, and social structure, with the way in which regions aligned with one side or the other in the Civil War, but the differences within and between them were not remotely likely to lead to civil war on their own account; they just help to explain how people, when forced (often reluctantly) to make a choice, took the sides they did.

The prevalence of puritanism in many towns, in the clothing districts and in other regions where godly gentry made common cause with the middling sort has led some historians to account for it as primarily an instrument of social control, designed to teach the feckless poor to labour soberly and diligently in their callings. Such an interpretation distorts the other-worldly focus of the puritan faith and does less than justice to its preachers' efforts to evangelize the under-privileged and the illiterate. Their social teaching was compassionate towards the honest poor, and they kept reminding the well-to-do that they were merely stewards of their worldly wealth. Puritans had a notably good record for charity under Elizabeth and the early Stuarts. There were stronger reasons than economic interest why puritanism struck root among the middling sort in many towns and in the rural clothing areas. Weavers and skilled craftsmen were mostly literate, able to study the Scriptures for themselves and to ponder them at their looms or counters or workbenches. Towns brought people of similar callings and convictions into close proximity and provided an apt milieu for the mutual propagation of their beliefs. The larger ones offered a choice of places of worship, and hence a better chance of sitting regularly at the feet of a puritan preacher, especially if there was a lectureship within the walls. But it would be quite wrong to think of puritanism as the faith of a particular class, or as an urban rather than a rural phenomenon. It was widely disseminated through the social scale, and its propagation owed an incalculable amount to aristocrats such as the Earls of Bedford, Huntingdon, and Leicester in Elizabeth's reign—not to mention the Duchess of Suffolk—and Lord Brooke, Viscount Saye and Sele, and the Earl of Warwick in Charles I's. At least a fifth of the peerage were to some degree puritan in sympathy in 1641,[6] but even they wielded less influence collectively than the hundreds of puritan gentry with parish livings in their gift and a powerful role in the county magistracy.

The puritans' concentration on drawing out and cherishing those men and women who appeared to have the seeds of grace in them carried with it a tendency to conceive the visible church as a community of the elect, and to think of the unregenerate many as somehow outside it. Church-puritans, who constituted the great majority, were aware of the dangers of separation, but there were small splinter groups who rebelled against the whole conception of a national church embracing the godly and ungodly alike, and split off to form congregations purporting to consist only of 'visible saints'. In their eyes the only true church of Christ was a community of men and women who, under their chosen pastor, entered into a mutual covenant to 'walk together in the ways of the Lord' and to submit to a common discipline. These sectaries or separatists, sometimes called Brownists after one of their early leaders, incurred the heavy displeasure of church and state alike. They first attracted the attention of government in the 1580s. In 1593 three of their pastors were executed for sedition, and an Act against Seditious Sectaries was passed,

---

[6] Stone, *Crisis of the Aristocracy*, p. 742.

giving those who persisted in attending 'conventicles' the choice between death or banishment. There was some resurgence of separatism soon after the Hampton Court Conference, when Archbishop Bancroft (Whitgift's successor and former chaplain) carried out a drive for conformity which led to about ninety puritan ministers being ejected from their livings, at least temporarily. The English General Baptists had their beginning in 1608, when John Smyth, being convinced that no surviving church possessed the true ordinances, baptized first himself and then the rest of his congregation. But separatists remained few, and most of them went into exile, in Amsterdam or some other Dutch city, rather than face the harsh penalties that threatened them at home. The most famous of these congregations made an even harder choice in 1620 when it chartered a little ship called the *Mayflower*, and bound itself anew in a covenant, some time before it made landfall at Plymouth, Massachusetts. Theirs was quite a different migration from the much larger one that followed in the 1630s. Until Charles and Laud formed their fateful partnership, mainstream puritans felt no need to consider leaving England, for they felt tolerably at home in its established church.

James's problems with the puritans were as nothing compared with what he had suffered from the high Calvinists in his native Scotland. There the Reformation had followed a totally different course from that in England. Instead of being initiated and controlled by a dominant monarch, it had been carried to victory by an aristocratic rebellion against a catholic queen, and between her abdication in 1567 and her son James's twenty-first birthday two whole decades passed. The leading role of the laity and the long minority resulted in the establishment of a predominantly Presbyterian Kirk of Scotland, with no royal supremacy comparable to that in Tudor England. Consistories, called kirk sessions, took a powerful hold on the religious and social life of Lowland Scotland. Episcopacy was never formally abolished, but it fell into a long eclipse, and the main role in governing the Kirk was assumed by General Assemblies with a strong lay presence. Catholicism, however, survived more strongly than in England among the nobility and gentry; it was estimated to claim as many as a third of them, as late as 1600. But it was weaker than such a figure suggests, since it was mainly confined to scattered regional pockets, the chief being Aberdeenshire, parts of the Highlands, Ayrshire, and the borders.

The high tide of Scottish Calvinism really began to flow in 1574, when the famous scholar Andrew Melville returned from Geneva to assume the headship of the little University of Glasgow, which was sunk in deep decline. He inaugurated an impressive intellectual revival, not only in Glasgow but in St Andrews too, but he was power-hungry for the Kirk, which he fought through the 1580s and 1590s to make totally Presbyterian. He aimed to abolish not only episcopacy but all lay patronage over ecclesiastical appointments, and to make the Kirk virtually independent of the crown. He taught a doctrine of two kingdoms, the church being supreme and self-sufficient in all matters spiritual and the state having power only over the outward man. In modern Iran he would have made a good ayatollah. He lectured James to his face in 1596, calling him 'God's silly vassal'. By then, however, such overweening clerical pretensions were becoming too much for most of the laity and not a few of the clergy, and in the following year James got a statute passed which restored the bishops to the Scottish parliament. The tide was now running his way, but when he was called to England the struggle was still on for control of the General Assembly, with its powerful representation of nobles, lairds, and burgesses as well as clergy. James claimed the power to determine when and where it should meet; Melville affirmed its right of free assembly. Eventually, in 1606, Melville with seven other ministers was summoned to London, where his invective against the Church of England's forms of worship and Archbishop Bancroft's 'Romish Rags' so incensed the privy council that it committed him to the Tower. There he remained for nearly five years, and he was released only on the understanding that he would live the rest of his life in France. He died at Sédan in 1622, a figure of the past.

From then on, James gradually restored both the bishops and the crown to a considerable measure of authority in the Kirk, making use of deftly managed Scottish parliaments and carefully packed General Assemblies. The Kirk became once more a blend of episcopacy and Presbyterianism, with the kirk session continuing to exercise a godly discipline at parish level and with parishes grouped in presbyteries, but with bishops presiding over diocesan synods and sitting in both the General Assembly and parliament. James would have liked to go further, and bring both the government and the worship of the Kirk closely into line with those of the Church of England, but he knew where to stop. He did manage to press the Five Articles of Perth through a reluctant Scottish parliament in 1621, which forced the Kirk to accept the observance of the great Christian festivals, confirmation by bishops, kneeling to receive holy communion, and the validity of private communion and private baptism for the sick. The Articles of Perth were to remain a smouldering grievance until they were swept away in rebellion, and in face of the hostility they aroused James wisely shelved his tentative plans to introduce a Scottish prayer book, loosely based on the English Book of Common Prayer. The last General Assembly for twenty years met in 1618, and James left the Scottish ecclesiastical scene in a rather sullen state of peace. He had got his way by exploiting lay (especially aristocratic) suspicion of clerical ambition. To build on his success, it was essential to avoid alienating the clergy and the nobles and lairds at the same time, and giving them a common cause. That was just what Charles was to do.

Religious problems in Ireland were altogether more intractable, and the main reason why they did not become explosive under James was that for a long time after the Elizabethan conquest the Irish were incapable of organized resistance. The official attitude of the king's servants in Ireland was that the way to overcome the natives' resentment of colonial rule was to 'civilize' them, and since they held it axiomatic that English institutions were supremely civilized, that meant anglicizing them. But if there were difficulties in introducing English models of local government and jurisdiction, the English common law, and English practices in matters of land use and inheritance, they were as nothing to the problems of imposing an alien religion. It was not only that the Old Irish were devotedly catholic; so too were most of the Old English, who were used to being a powerful part of the colonial system and were most reluctant to accept that their faith should debar them from public office, as officially it now did.

James was personally averse to forcing catholics to abandon their faith or conform to protestantism. But early in his reign he was under some suspicion of being soft towards popery, and in 1605 he gave way to his Irish council's request for a tough policy. He issued a proclamation denying that he was prepared to tolerate catholic worship, ordering the catholic clergy to leave the country, and commanding the laity to attend divine service in the established Church of Ireland. That was never possible to enforce. Over much of Ireland the parish churches were in ruins, and no worship could be held in them. The church owned plenty of land, but in the course of time so much of its assets had been appropriated by laymen or the higher clergy that most of its livings were too poor to support an educated clergyman—even if a protestant pastor could have found a flock. The Church of Ireland showed little of the will or capacity for the impossible task of converting the Irish, whose language very few of its clergy could speak. It settled to the role of ministering to the masters of the Pale and to the protestant settlers in the areas of plantation. Trinity College Dublin had been founded in 1591, largely to furnish it with protestant parsons, but in James's reign clergy for Ireland still had to be sought in England or Scotland, and even towards its end only about one Irish parish in six had a preaching minister.

That did not of course mean that the Gaelic-speaking mass of the population went unprovided for. They had their own priests, living in and sustained by the local communities, and in sept territory especially these were often monks or friars. Seven Irish colleges (or seminaries) in the Spanish Netherlands and north-eastern France trained a steady flow of recruits to the priesthood, and though there were tensions between their Counter-Reformation ideas and the traditional practices of the old Gaelic church, Irish catholics were still capable of closing ranks if the threat from the protestant ascendancy became acute.

The Old English organized in protest against James's proclamation and the threat to their faith, and it soon became clear that the Irish and English governments disagreed about the treatment of Irish catholics. The former was all for severity; the latter favoured a policy of conversion rather than compulsion, though it supported the imposition of recusancy fines, which were however only patchily collected. The illegal Irish hierarchy presented a problem, and in 1612 the aged Bishop of Down and one of his priests were tried and executed for treason, *pour décourager les autres*. That left just one catholic prelate resident in Ireland and four others in exile. Thereafter the orders from England were that priests should not be hunted unless they were suspected of treason; and the papacy responded, on the advice of the exiled primate of Ireland, by appointing as resident bishops only men who were unquestionably loyal to the king. The Irish government made examples of some towns which obstinately elected recusants as officials, seldom with lasting results, and tried even less effectively to broaden the imposition of recusancy fines. The latter were suspended during Prince Charles's jaunt to Madrid in 1623, and the greater leniency continued into the new reign. But an intolerable policy made bearable by non-enforcement was hardly a permanent solution.

Meanwhile the Church of Ireland was taking a theological direction distinct from that of Canterbury. Trinity College Dublin, its intellectual centre, had been modelled on Cambridge's most puritan college, Emmanuel, and was largely staffed with Emmanuel graduates. Instead of embracing the Church of England's Thirty-Nine Articles, the first protestant convocation of the Church of Ireland approved and adopted its own articles of religion in 1615. They were formulated by the outstanding intellect of the early Stuart Church of Ireland, Dublin-born James Ussher, who was one of Trinity College's first scholars and was to become Archbishop of Armagh and primate in 1625. The articles, which embodied Whitgift's Lambeth set among many others, did not directly conflict with the Anglican Thirty-Nine, but they were far more positively Calvinist, and expressly affirmed the doctrine of double predestination. They also firmly identified the pope with the 'man of sin', or Antichrist. They were held in great esteem by the anti-Arminian party in England, many of whom, right down to the Civil War, would have liked to see them adopted by the established church at home. They made the Church of Ireland more than ever the communion of the New English, for they virtually condemned the rest of the population of Ireland to eternal torment. But even as the colonial class at prayer the Church of Ireland was under strain, having difficulty on the one hand in accommodating the increasing number of Scottish Presbyterian settlers in Ulster, and on the other containing a minority that would respond sympathetically to the efforts of Archbishop Laud. Its divisions were to widen under Charles I.

# THREE

# The New Reign

IT will (I hope) be clear by now that Charles's inheritance was by no means an impossible one, but that success in managing it would depend very much on his personal qualities. That was true of all monarchies in an age when the sovereign's power of decision was so great, but Charles's throne was particularly vulnerable because he ruled over three disparate kingdoms, and because in England successful government depended to a degree then unusual on consent. The task before him called for insight, judgement, tact, flair, and dedication. He possessed the last quality in abundance, but he was short of all the others.

He certainly had a lofty conception of his office and an earnest desire to exercise it worthily; if good intentions had been enough he would have been among the best of British kings. He worked harder at the business of governing than his father had done; he would never be found in the hunting field when he should have been attending to matters of state, or at Newmarket when he should have been at Westminster. He revered his father and in many ways took him as a model, accepting as dogma the doctrines of divine right that for James had had just a touch of the intellectual exercise. But in certain respects, some conscious some perhaps not, he reacted against him. His strict personal morality and his abstemious habits doubtless had deeper roots than a distaste for his father's looser ways, but the rapid transformation of the royal court represented a deliberate rejection of the coarseness and license of the last reign. In contrast with James's bonhomous familiarity towards those whose company he enjoyed, Charles imposed on his entourage his own almost obsessive predilection for order, hierarchy, and decorum. The court became infinitely more dignified, and in a deeper sense more civilized, for the connoisseurship that he showed in collecting the treasures of the past and in patronizing the finest artists and architects of the present adorned it with many things of rare beauty. But the severely formal ritual that he prescribed widened the gap between him and all but a very narrow circle of his subjects.

He was a much more deeply religious man than his father, and was the first monarch to grow up in the faith of the Church of England, as defined in the Elizabethan settlement. In contrast with James's preference for Calvinism, he was an enthusiastic patron of the Durham House or Arminian divines, though their appeal for him lay more in their exaltation of authority and hierarchy in ecclesiastical government, and their insistence on a seemly ritual in worship, than in their doctrines concerning the availability of divine grace. He lacked his father's intellectual interest in theology, and the ban he imposed on public disputation concerning predestination, either for or against, seems to have sprung from a personal aversion to the probing of such mysteries. This was one of many things that he shared with William Laud, whom he chose as Dean of the Chapel Royal when Andrewes died in 1626. At the first opportunity he translated Laud from St David's, the poor and remote Welsh see to which James had reluctantly appointed him, to Bath and Wells in 1626 and to London in 1628; only Abbot's longevity kept him from Canterbury until 1633. Charles and Laud met each other's needs, for Laud was as assiduous in exalting the royal authority in both church and state as the king was in commanding obedience to the church and its bishops. Yet the two men were not as personally close as used to be thought. Laud lived in constant uncertainty as to just where he stood with his royal master, and it was probably not until the late 1630s that he felt fully secure in his favour.[1] Even those in close and frequent contact with Charles found his mind and character hard to read, and later generations have found it no easier; it is significant that no fully satisfactory biography of him has yet been written.

Three of James's qualities were conspicuously lacking in his son: his shrewd intelligence, his wisdom in the ways of the world, and a certain natural authority. Charles was not stupid, but his mind was narrow and inflexible, and since his imagination was severely limited he too often failed to foresee the results of his decisions or to gauge their impact on other people. Indeed decisions did not come easily to him, and once he had painfully arrived at them he tended to affirm them so uncompromisingly that if a tactical withdrawal should prove necessary, as it often did, it was bound to be humiliating. James had not cut a very regal figure, but by the time he came to the English throne he was thoroughly at home in his royal office, and when he gave commands he had a healthy confidence that he would be obeyed. Charles was apt to insist obtrusively on his royal authority because for much of his reign he lacked assurance in the exercise of it; the habit of command did not come naturally to him.

One can only conjecture how much his diffidence and lack of easy contact with others stemmed from his upbringing: his parents' joyless marriage, his sickly childhood, in which he saw little of his unsatisfactory mother and seems to have formed no other warm attachments, and his having been overshadowed until he was nearly twelve by a more able and outgoing elder

---

[1] Sharpe, *Personal Rule of Charles I*, pp. 284–5.

brother. Prince Henry's immense popularity, and the outbreak of national grief at his early death, may have driven Charles further into his shell. His mind was well on the way to being formed before he became heir to the throne, so his self-preparation for kingship was a conscious rather than an instinctive process. The portrait of him in his late teens, probably by Abraham van Blyenberch and now at Montacute,[2] tells us almost as much about him as the later Van Dycks; the pose and expression strive for authority, but the hands (and not only the hands) hint at some lack of inner conviction. After he became king, at twenty-four, he often spoke like an autocrat, and at heart he leaned more strongly towards absolutism than James had done, even though his mind accepted that an English king's powers were not unlimited. He lacked, however, the sheer zest for the actual exercise of power, and the satisfaction in the demanding day-by-day deploying of it, that a successful autocrat really needs. The court masques in which he delighted projected an idealized image of benign kingship that encouraged him in his tendency to take his good intentions for deeds. He had no flair for managing people, because he did not easily understand them. With a very few individuals he formed deep and loving relationships, but in his contacts with most of his councillors and nobles and courtiers he lacked his father's common touch. He could express himself clearly and cogently, in spite of his famous stammer, but in his public pronouncements one too often senses an urge to justify himself to his own satisfaction rather than to make a convincing case to his auditors and his subjects at large. His dignified affability was carefully cultivated, but behind it a natural warmth was lacking. He seems to have been totally humourless.

His diffidence and his lack of instinctive political judgement made him unusually dependent on advice. He listened to it conscientiously, and not only from those counsellors who were naturally congenial to him, but he was not easily persuaded when it ran counter to his own opinions or inclinations, and in such cases he was apt to be suspicious of it, however honestly it was given. Buckingham exercised a greater sway over him than he ever had over James, but in contrast with James's infatuation with the Duke there was nothing homosexual in the relationship, at least at a conscious level. Buckingham was a consummate courtier, and he cultivated the heir for a considerable time before the old king died. The journey to Madrid together bound Charles to him in total devotion. His age advantage of eight years was just right for his purpose of building up an almost total ascendancy over the unsure and inexperienced prince, to whom he seems to have given the confidence in his actions that so far he naturally lacked. Charles never gave his love and trust

[2] Plate 8; for attribution see Malcolm Rogers, *Montacute House* (National Trust, 1991), pp. 77–8.

so freely to anyone else except his wife, and he only turned to her after Buckingham's death.

One of the puzzles is to explain why a man who so prided himself on his rectitude as Charles did, and who professed to set such store by honest dealing, acquired from early in his reign a reputation for deviousness and untrustworthiness. It was partly because a certain habit of distrust made him secretive, so that his intentions were often imperfectly understood. He was also prone to interpret opposition, even the principled dissent of good subjects, as disloyalty, and he regarded loyalty as so absolute a duty that he could consider himself released from his undertakings when he thought it wanting. Central to his political creed was his belief in the sanctity of an anointed king's authority and in his sacred duty to preserve it. If a conflict arose between keeping his word and acting as he believed a king should act for the safety of his crown and people, then his regality absolved him, and if a subject seemed to be posing a threat to the crown itself, no holds were barred in dealing with him. When it came to civil war, he did not believe that the king need keep faith with rebels. The casuistry which in those times permitted crowned heads to conceal or even deceive was widely understood in the sphere of international relations, but Charles exercised it rather freely towards those of his own subjects whom he regarded as his enemies. Yet deviousness was not his main failing as a king, for what princes in his time did not practise deception? More serious were his lack of insight into human motivation and his fatally weak sense of what was politically possible and what was not. He was tragically miscast: the things that gave him the deepest satisfaction in his mature years, his religious faith, his wife and family, and his art treasures, bespeak a sensitive and essentially private man. The unluckiest chance of his life was his brother's death, which exposed him to the most public and taxing of all callings.

The first fifteen years of his reign, down to the crisis that set in when he confronted the Short Parliament, fall into three phases. The first continued the run of frequent parliaments that had begun in 1621, with three within a span of under four years. It ended with Charles so violently at odds with the third of them that he resolved to dispense with parliament in England (though not in Scotland and Ireland) for an indefinite period. The so-called personal rule that followed lasted for eleven years, but its outward calm was broken when Scotland rebelled against his attempt in 1637 to impose a Prayer Book on the Kirk. That inaugurated the phase of Anglo-Scottish war which lasted almost until the Long Parliament was summoned. This chapter is concerned with the first two phases. The events of both were still so vividly in the minds of the members of that parliament, and raised so many issues that they felt they had to settle, that an outline of them forms a necessary background to our main story.

The reign opened with England on the brink of war with Spain, for James had felt impelled finally to help his son-in-law back to his principality. It was still undeclared, for James had refused to take the formal step until parliament voted him enough money to wage it, but an English expeditionary force of pressed men had already crossed the Channel under the mercenary leader Count Mansfeld. Unfortunately, instead of fighting its way into Germany to recover the Palatinate for Charles's brother-in-law the Elector Palatine, this force was rotting away through disease and desertion in Holland. The inadequate sum which James's last parliament had voted for the war was already being swallowed up fast when he died.

Charles felt no hostility towards parliament as an institution when he came to the throne. Encouraged by his father, he had attended the House of Lords in the last two parliaments, and he had enjoyed the experience. The last one had been the most amenable since Elizabeth's death, and he would have kept it in being if he could, but by law it terminated with the demise of the monarch, so he had to call another. When it met in June 1625 it was basically well disposed towards him, but it was suspicious of the French marriage treaty and concerned over Mansfeld's unhappy expedition. Instead of voting generous supplies, as Charles hoped, for the war to which the last parliament had committed him, the Commons made only a token grant and called for an investigation into how the previous subsidies had been spent. Furthermore, instead of following the precedent of every reign since Edward IV's and granting tonnage and poundage to the king for life, they voted them for one year only. This was not a deliberate attempt to deprive the crown of essential revenue. What they had in mind was to review the antiquated structure of the customs revenue and negotiate a deal that would rationalize it, eliminating the hated impositions in the process. But that would take time, and since London was currently stricken with the plague they did not want to spend the summer months there. The Lords, however, declined to pass the temporary bill, seeing it as an affront to the king, so he went on collecting tonnage and poundage without parliamentary consent. He really had no choice, for he could not govern without the customs, but it remained a source of grumbling until 1641. The Commons angered him further by complaining of an increase in recusancy and blaming it on his marriage treaty; they also reopened the attack on the doctrines of Richard Montagu, who had angered them with his *Appello Caesarem*, published earlier in the year. Provocatively, they had him arrested; Charles warned them to desist and reappointed Montagu as a royal chaplain. The quarrel rumbled on through the next two parliaments, especially after the king, equally provocatively, made him a bishop.

Desperate for revenue to carry on the war, Charles adjourned parliament to Oxford, and in Christ Church hall he appealed to the patriotism of both Houses. A great fleet, he told them, was getting ready to sail. He was doing his best to keep the lines of parliamentary government open, and he had reason to feel let down. But the Commons' support for the war was evaporating, for they believed that the crown's financial difficulties arose mainly from mismanagement and self-enrichment at the state's expense. As Sir Edward Coke put it in a major speech, 'the ship hath a great leak'.[3] The finger was pointed more and more plainly at Buckingham, and not without reason. That was more than Charles would stand for, and on 12 August he dissolved parliament.

The great fleet duly sailed in October with Cadiz as its objective, but the operation was so bungled that more than half its men were lost. The sight of the miserable survivors who landed at Plymouth in December, ragged, stinking, and sick, transformed one west country MP, Sir John Eliot, from a client of Buckingham into his bitterest opponent. Buckingham bore the blame because he was Lord Admiral, though the expedition was seriously underfunded (which was not his fault) as well as incompetently led. It was also held against him that English warships which had been loaned to the King of France under the marriage treaty had been used in action (through no wish of his) against a Huguenot fleet. Buckingham's relations with France, where Cardinal Richelieu had recently become Louis XIII's all-powerful minister, were steadily worsening.

Sheer financial necessity forced Charles to call a new parliament, the third in three years, in February 1626. In the false belief that opposition sprang from only a few factious men, he debarred the members who had most displeased him in 1625 (including, ironically, his future minister Sir Thomas Wentworth) by making them sheriffs. Sheriffs could not stand because by law they had to reside in their counties throughout their term. The result, however, was merely to give more influence over the House to the fiery Eliot and others who were less restrained and responsible than the men excluded. Nevertheless the Commons were ready to consider ways of giving the crown a sufficient revenue for its peacetime needs on a permanent basis, but at a price: Buckingham must be brought to account for wasting the king's estate. Since Charles would not hear of this, they gradually advanced to the point of impeaching the favourite. Impeachment was an ancient judicial process, disused since the fifteenth century until something like it was revived in 1621, in which the Commons preferred the charges and appointed prosecutors, and the whole House of Lords sat as judges. It was used only in the case of 'high crimes and misdemeanours', and of men who might be too great, or too strongly protected, to be subject to the process of the ordinary courts of law. It had recently been employed to bring down James I's Lord Chancellor, Francis Bacon, Viscount St Albans, and his Lord Treasurer, Lionel Cranfield,

---

[3] Conrad Russell, *Parliaments and English Politics 1621–1629* (Oxford, 1979), pp. 244–6.

Earl of Middlesex; Buckingham had had a heavy share in the latter's down-fall. The charges against Buckingham were many, but there were four main reasons why both houses were ready to proceed against him: he had grossly enriched himself at the kingdom's expense; he had perverted the exercise of the crown's patronage in favour of himself, his kin and his creatures; he had dominated the king's counsels to an extent that virtually eclipsed the proper authority of the privy council; and he had been seriously incompetent as Lord Admiral. Charles, in an effort to halt the impeachment, summoned both houses to Whitehall. He ordered the Commons to drop the proceedings, and told them that unless they voted supplies immediately and unconditionally, he would dissolve parliament that very week. 'Remember', he said in words ominous for the future, 'that parliaments are altogether in my power for their calling, sitting and dissolution; therefore as I find the fruits of them either good or evil, they are to continue or not to be.'[4] Despite his threat, he hung on for over two and a half months before he actually dissolved the parliament. By then there was no other way to stop the impeachment from proceeding, and he had not received a single subsidy.

Still believing that only a few malevolent politicians were standing between him and his subjects' loyalty, Charles had letters sent to all the deputy lieu-tenants and JPs in the country, requesting them to collect as a free gift the four subsidies and three fifteenths that the Commons had been prepared to vote if their grievances were remedied. The result was abject failure; county after county responded that it would give by way of parliamentary grant or not at all.

Charles and the privy council then sailed into even more troubled constitu-tional waters and demanded a Forced Loan. The Tudor monarchs had quite often demanded forced loans from corporations and wealthy individuals, but in 1626 commissioners were appointed to levy the equivalent of five subsidies from everyone who was rated in the subsidy books. To the public at large it was indistinguishable from a large parliamentary grant, except that parlia-ment had not granted it. Financially the Forced Loan was a success because very nearly five subsidies were collected, but seventy-six gentlemen went to prison rather than pay it. (At least fifteen peers also refused to pay, but signifi-cantly only one was imprisoned; peers were privileged, even in disobedi-ence.) Five of the imprisoned refugees launched a *cause célèbre* by taking out writs of habeas corpus, which required the crown to state the reason for their imprisonment; they hoped thereby to bring the legality of the Loan under the judgment of the common law. The judges had collectively declined the king's request to pronounce it legal in advance, and he had sacked the senior Lord Chief Justice in consequence. They were faced with a dilemma, however,

---

[4] Quoted in Roger Lockyer, *Buckingham* (1981), p. 316.

when the privy council's return to the habeas corpus stated simply that the prisoners had been confined *per speciale mandatum domini regis* (by special command of our lord the king). The crown was exercising its prerogative power, which the judges collectively had upheld in 1592, to detain individuals without declaring the cause. When used, as it normally was, in circumstances where reason of state enjoined secrecy, as in the case of suspected spies or conspirators, there was no objection to it; a trial would be expected to follow, if those arrested were not released. But it was another matter to deny both bail and trial to loyal subjects who were taking a principled stand against arbitrary taxation, and to prevent the Court of King's Bench from adjudging the legality of the Loan. In this famous Five Knights' Case the court simply ruled that the prisoners should not be bailed, probably expecting that in due course the council would inform it of what their offences were. The case left both sides dissatisfied. By keeping the five in prison, the court's ruling implied that the king was within his powers in demanding a loan and in punishing those who refused it. On the other hand Charles failed to get it to affirm the general right of the crown to imprison subjects without declaring the cause.

Meanwhile England embarked upon war with France in 1627, not long after that country had made peace with Spain. The causes were complex, involving the hiring of English warships by France and the threat to use them against a Huguenot revolt centred upon La Rochelle, as well as the seizure by each country of merchant ships belonging to the other. Rather than go to war with the two greatest European powers simultaneously, while lacking the financial and military resources to fight either, England would have been far wiser to settle the quarrel by diplomacy, as Richelieu wished to do. But Buckingham thought he saw a chance to gain some much-needed popularity by relieving the Huguenots in La Rochelle, which he tried to do in June 1627 by leading in person a large amphibious expedition against the offshore Ile de Rhé. He lost more than half of it and sailed home defeated in November—a third national humiliation to add to Mansfield's expedition and Cadiz, and the worst. The proceeds of the Forced Loan had been spent, and the government could only meet its debts to the City of London by a massive sale of crown lands. There was nothing for it, the privy council advised, but to call a new parliament.

It met in March 1628, united as never before in pursuing the redress of grievances, but for the most part anxious to avert another premature dissolution. The Commons therefore held back from attacking Buckingham or venting their religious grievances, strongly though they felt about both. They offered the king five subsidies, an unprecedented grant though far short of what he currently needed, if he would assent to a Bill of Rights that would make it statutorily unlawful to levy any tax or loan without parliament's consent, to imprison any subject without trial, or to billet soldiers on uncon-senting civilians (as had widely been done in the current war). All these prac-tices lay in the king's view within the royal prerogative, which he regarded as a power entrusted to him by God to employ as he thought fit for the good of the people, and hence outside the reach of the law. Sir Edward Coke, who introduced the bill, believed on the other hand that the law was the supreme authority in the land and conferred on the king all those prerogatives that he legitimately exercised. If he abused or exceeded them, parliament could define them by statute. But Charles would not hear of a statutory limitation upon his prerogative, and after much search for a compromise it looked as though another deadlock had been reached. Then Coke proposed an expedient: let them proceed not by a bill but by a petition of right. This was a procedure open to any subjects who believed themselves wronged by an action of the crown or its agents; the crown could not be sued, but they could formally peti-tion to enjoy their right according to the law of the land. What parliament now agreed to present to the king was a unique Petition of Right on behalf of all his English subjects, to secure them in perpetuity from the three abuses that the bill had treated, and in addition to ban the exercise of martial law within the realm—a matter that was to become important again in 1639–40.

The Lords gave their concurrence, and Charles seemed on his way to a bet-ter relationship with parliament than he had yet enjoyed. He almost threw it away, however, by his first answer, which merely granted 'that right be done according to the laws and customs of the realm, and that the statutes be put in due execution'. This was wholly unsatisfactory, for it implied that no change was to be made in the laws, whereas the whole point of the Petition of Right was to state the law unequivocally in those areas where its scope and the exercise of the royal prerogative had been in dispute. His evasive response set the Commons upon preparing a Remonstrance concerning the whole state of the kingdom which remarkably prefigured the Grand Remonstrance of thirteen years later, when the country was heading for civil war. During the debates on it the members displayed more sustained anger (though it was mixed with grief) than at any time before 1640, and the main object of their wrath was Buckingham, despite Charles's express command not to name him. But the essence of this Remonstrance, as in that of 1641, was its linking of two major general grievances, namely innovation in government and innov-ation in religion, and its attribution of both to the machinations of a 'popish and malignant party', with which the king's favoured Arminians were allegedly hand in glove. Equally prophetic was the fear of the Irish which John Pym, a rapidly rising figure, brought into the debate—fear of their open prac-tice of popery, of the catholics in high places and in commands in the Irish army, and of the Irish soldiers among the forces still afoot in England. A fur-ther parallel with 1641 was that detestation of Buckingham, as the great evil counsellor who poisoned the channels of royal authority, spilled over from parliament into the capital and the country at large, though not to the extent that it would do in the case of Strafford. And already anxiety was expressed about the possibility of an armed *coup d'état* which distantly prefigured the feverish response to the Army Plots of 1641.

Charles eventually gave his assent to the Petition of Right in a form that made it as binding as a statute, and received his five subsidies. He was conscious of defeat, and he resented it deeply. But his concession did not halt the progress of the Remonstrance, which culminated in a forthright request for Buckingham's removal, and after it was presented the Commons went ahead with a second remonstrance, declaring that the king's collection of tonnage and poundage and other impositions not granted by parliament was 'a breach of the fundamental liberties of this kingdom' and contrary to the Petition of Right. Before it could be presented Charles prorogued parliament, declaring as he did so 'that I owe an account of my actions to none but to God alone'.[5] By delaying his acceptance of the inevitable he had widened the constitutional quarrel to a degree hardly conceivable in his father's lifetime, and all in a mere three years.

Two months after the dissolution, a melancholic naval lieutenant who had been on the Rhé expedition stabbed Buckingham to death with a tenpenny knife that he had bought for the purpose. He was motivated partly by personal grievances, but also on his own admission by the Commons' Remonstrance. Charles was utterly grief-stricken, and the public jubilation over his friend's murder must have wounded him more than all the bonfires and bell-ringing that had celebrated his final assent to the Petition of Right. But Henrietta Maria hastened to his side, and quite soon she began to fill the void in his heart that Buckingham's death had left. She was still only eighteen, and so far her relationship with him had been neither easy nor close. Now it blossomed; soon she was pregnant, and the royal couple's delight in each other's company was the talk of the court. Charles for the first time began to discuss affairs of state with her, but she told him truthfully that she had no ambition to influence him in such matters. That would change with time, but it would be another nine years or so before she became a serious force in English politics. Nevertheless the king's devotion to her meant that more indulgence was shown to her catholic entourage, and to the English catholics who worshipped in her chapel. Her friends naturally tended to become his friends too, and the growing catholic presence at court was to be a constant source of rumour and disquiet.

---

[5] S. R. Gardiner (ed.), *The Constitutional Documents of the Puritan Revolution 1625–1660* (Oxford, 3rd ed. 1906), p. 73. See ibid. for the draft Bill of Rights, pp. 65–6, the Petition of Right and the king's two answers to it, pp. 66–70, and the remonstrance against tonnage and poundage, pp. 70–3.

Meanwhile Charles decided to recall parliament for a second session in January 1629 and give it one more chance (as he saw it) to enable him to continue governing 'in a parliamentary way'. The touchstone was to be the Commons' willingness to regularize his collection of tonnage and poundage with a formal grant. But he had seriously damaged his credit with them by perverting the record of the Petition of Right. His printer had produced 1,500 copies of it, as both Houses and he himself had agreed, with his second and binding answer following the text. As soon as the last session ended, however, he had had this edition suppressed and destroyed, and a new one printed with only his evasive first answer, followed by two further speeches which put his own gloss on the whole document.[6] Not surprisingly, the Commons launched an investigation into the deceit as soon as they met, and so far from voting tonnage and poundage they took up the case of the merchants who had refused to pay them and had had their goods seized in consequence. One such was a member of their own House, and when they summoned the customs officers concerned to appear before them, Charles forbade them to proceed. An angry confrontation developed, but though tonnage and poundage was superficially the primary issue, there was a deeper one between king and Commons over religion, as both sides soon recognized.

Charles had made some attempt to damp down religious controversy by republishing the Thirty-Nine Articles and requiring all clergymen to 'agree in the true usual literal meaning' of them, as expressing the doctrine of the Church of England. But he had insisted on licensing for publication a sermon which Roger Manwaring had preached before him, and which had justified the Forced Loan in such blatantly absolutist terms that its author was impeached for it; and in the recess he had not only saved Manwaring from the Lords' sentence by granting him a pardon but had given him a rich benefice and made him a royal chaplain. At the same time he issued special pardons to three other high churchmen who were in trouble for their words or deeds, John Cosin, Robert Sibthorpe, and Richard Montagu, and it was now that he made Montagu a bishop. More disturbing was his advancement of Laud to London and Neile to Winchester, and his appointment of both to the privy council. He also made Laud Chancellor of Oxford University and gave the influential deanery of Windsor to Matthew Wren. So far from holding a balance between ecclesiastical factions, as his father had done, he was showing a strong partiality for one of them, and the more unpopular.

The situation called for restraint and statesmanship in the Commons, but both were lacking. Old age had taken Coke into retirement, and Thomas

---

[6] The full story is told by Elizabeth Read Foster in 'Printing the Petition of Right', *Huntington Library Quarterly* XXXVIII (1974), and more briefly in Russell, *Parliaments and English Politics 1621–1629*, pp. 401–2, and L. J. Reeve, *Charles I and the Road to Personal Rule* (Cambridge, 1989), pp. 91–2.

Wentworth, another who had tempered opposition with discretion, had accepted a barony and the presidency of the Council in the North. The threat of Arminianism clouded the judgement of even such a politician as Pym, as the threat to parliamentary authority did that of the great lawyer John Selden. Eliot and his fellow-hawks gradually gained an ascendancy over the House, which lost the sense that it had had in the first session of what Charles could with patience be brought to accept. At its direction, a powerful sub-committee drafted a set of resolutions on religion for presentation to the king which plainly stated that he had been ill advised and that both church and kingdom were in imminent danger from papists and Arminians. They comprehensively attached the teachings and practices of his favourite churchmen, stated where the church's true doctrines were to be found, and proposed ten drastic means whereby its abuses should be remedied.[7] The implied claim was that parliament had the ultimate power to declare what the religion of the Church of England was. Queen Elizabeth must have been turning in her grave.

On the day fixed for the House to debate the resolutions, and in all probability to adopt them, the king ordered a five days' adjournment. When it met again on 2 March, the Speaker announced that the king had ordered a further adjournment to the 10th. On his putting the motion for it, there were shouts of 'No!' on all sides. The king had personally commanded the Speaker to leave the chair immediately if anyone tried to speak, but when he attempted to do so two members, Denzil Holles and Benjamin Valentine, thrust him back into it and held him down. After further impassioned scenes and a wild speech by Eliot, the House passed three resolutions by acclamation, while the Usher of the Black Rod was waiting outside its locked doors with a message from the king, and with a guard sent by him to force a way in if necessary. The first resolution was that whosoever should make innovation in religion or seek to introduce popery or Arminianism 'shall be reputed a capital enemy to this kingdom and commonwealth'. The second laid the same anathema on anyone who advised or participated in the collection of tonnage and poundage, and the third condemned anyone who *paid* those dues as 'a betrayer of the liberty of England, and an enemy to the same'.[8]

Such language was profoundly ominous. A capital enemy to the kingdom, one deserving death, must mean a traitor; but treason was by law a crime against the king, as the personification of the nation-state. It consisted in plotting the king's death, or levying war against him, or adhering to his enemies. Yet here was the House of Commons holding forth a kind of secondary treason against the whole community of the realm ('kingdom and commonwealth'), of which a subject might be guilty to the point of incurring the death penalty if he did what the king commanded, or if he propagated religious

---

[7] Text in Gardiner, *Constitutional Documents*, pp. 77–82.    [8] Ibid., pp. 82–3.

beliefs which the king, the church's Supreme Governor, showed every sign of holding. We should not try to squeeze too much out of words that were recited in heat, and by memory from a paper that Eliot had just burnt, and we should not suppose that he or anyone else involved in that angry scene was remotely contemplating the possibility of civil war; but the ideas implicit in the Three Resolutions were uncomfortably prophetic of those that the Long Parliament would be taking up in 1642. The inevitable dissolution followed, accompanied by a long declaration in which the king blamed the failure of the session on 'some few malevolent persons'. Ten of them—Eliot, Holles, Valentine, Selden, and five other members who had resisted the adjournment—had already been committed to prison by the council, and only one of them secured his early release by making the total submission that Charles required. Except for those prisoners, it was no bad thing that the country should be given a respite from parliamentary activity, since it had gone so sour. What remained to be seen, however, was whether or not the opportunity would be taken to begin mending the rifts in the political nation.

There was certainly a sense of crisis in the air during the first weeks and even months after the dissolution. The popular support for Eliot in his own west country was vociferous enough to threaten public order. Many prominent men, peers included, visited him and his fellow-prisoners to express their sympathy. The third of the Three Resolutions led many merchants to refuse to pay customs duties; indeed the Merchant Adventurers, who handled most of England's cloth exports, ceased all trading until the middle of May, and so did many Dutch merchants in London. Foreign commerce did not return to a normal level until late in the summer. But public reaction did not run all one way, for much of it was critical of the Commons' conduct during the last session, especially at the end of it. There was a real fear abroad that Charles was so outraged by their conduct that he had formed a resolution to rule without parliament indefinitely, perhaps even to suppress it permanently.

That does seem to have been his first reaction, but wiser counsels dissuaded him from publishing such an intention, notably those of his Secretary of State Dudley Carleton, Viscount Dorchester, who knew how essential the continuance of parliament was to the pursuit of an active foreign policy in support of the protestant cause. Dorchester drafted an important 'proclamation for the suppression of false rumours touching parliament', which the king worked over carefully and published on 27 March. In it Charles claimed to have demonstrated his 'love to the use of parliaments' by his frequent calling of them; 'yet [he went on] the late abuse having for the present driven us unwillingly out of that course, we shall account it presumption for any to prescribe any time unto us for parliaments, the calling, continuing and dissolving of which is always in our own power'. He would be more inclined to summon them again 'when our people shall see more clearly into our intents and actions', and when those who had been misled by the 'false and pernicious rumours' surrounding the recent dissolution 'shall come to a better understanding of us and themselves'. But first the men who had 'bred this interruption' must 'receive their condign punishments'.[9]

This proclamation probably expressed what Charles truly felt and intended at the start of the personal rule, once he had got over his first sense of outrage over the behaviour of Eliot and his colleagues. No one any longer describes the period now commencing as the Eleven Years' Tyranny, though assessments of its character and achievements vary very widely. Charles, sure as he was of his own good intentions, really believed that he had been traduced by men who wished him and his people no good, and that a substantial spell of benevolent government, uninterrupted by parliamentary broils, would in time win from his subjects the loyalty that he felt he deserved. But the men who had alienated them from him must be punished, and he would not have mere subjects telling him when to call another parliament. Within the circle of his government, however, there were always some ministers about him who desired an early return to parliamentary rule, and though several episodes indicate that his aversion to the prospect remained strong, he never closed his mind to it, or seriously contemplated a systematic royal absolutism. The weakness of parliament's position at the start of this eleven-year intermission was to a considerable extent its own fault, because by persistently living in the past in its reckoning of the government's financial needs, and by expecting heavy concessions in return for inadequate supplies, it had made the king and many of his ministers wonder whether the game was worth the candle.

Rather than attempt a comprehensive outline history of England in the 1630s, the rest of this chapter will focus on five topics that were to be of particular concern to parliament and people when the personal rule eventually collapsed. They are, in roughly ascending order of importance, the treatment of the members imprisoned for their part in the violent end of the last parliament, the winding up of the wars and the abandonment of the Elector Palatine, the financial expedients whereby the crown managed to get by without parliamentary grants, the general quality of provincial government in the absence of a parliamentary safety-valve, and the religious policies of the king and Archbishop Laud.

Charles was not totally unforgiving to those who had shown opposition in his early parliaments. Several besides Wentworth received preferment during the personal rule, including Sir Dudley Digges, who had launched the

---

[9]  Text in J. F. Larkin (ed.), *Stuart Royal Proclamations*, II (Oxford, 1983), pp. 226–8; quoted and illuminatingly discussed in Reeve, *Charles I and the Road to Personal Rule*, pp. 109–12.

impeachment of Buckingham with a speech that had landed him in the Fleet prison, William Noy, who had defended in the Five Knights' Case and became Attorney-General in 1631, and Edward Littleton, a promoter of the Petition of Right (like Digges) and counsel for Selden after his arrest, who rose through successive high legal offices in the 1630s to become Lord Keeper of the Great Seal in 1641. But towards Eliot and his associates whom he held responsible for the last parliament's violent end Charles was implacable. They were in the King's Bench prison pending trial, and for many months to come the eyes of the public were closely upon them. Their case is significant because it illustrates Charles's conviction that the law must bend before reason of state, or to put it bluntly his regal authority, and because it was remembered with still warm indignation by the members of the Long Parliament when they drew up the Grand Remonstrance.

Whatever was thought of their conduct, an important point of parliamentary privilege was at issue, for the prisoners were being arraigned for what they had said and done in the House of Commons. For that reason Eliot and his bolder fellows refused to reply to the privy council's interrogations and denied that either the common law courts or Star Chamber had jurisdiction over them; they were (they claimed) accountable only to a parliament. In Charles's view on the other hand they were guilty at the very least of sedition, wherein privilege should not protect them, so he was determined not to release them unless they admitted their guilt and threw themselves on his mercy. The judges, however, did not fully share his assumptions about their criminality, and it was clear that if they were brought to an open state trial in King's Bench they would take a stand for the rights of parliament that could do him grave political damage. His wiser councillors urged him to make a gesture of clemency and conciliation, but unless the prisoners submitted he would not forgive them. If he could not secure their conviction, he would punish them by long confinement. They naturally took out writs of habeas corpus, and Littleton bravely and brilliantly contended for their right to bail. The justices of King's Bench duly decided in favour of bail, but the king commanded them to deliver no judgment until all the judges had been consulted. He then put the prisoners out of the court's reach by transferring them from the King's Bench prison to the Tower, where they were held in close captivity all summer. Two did submit after this, one because his counsel was too frightened to appear for him. Before the Michaelmas law term began in October, the crown relented to the extent of granting bail on condition that they gave bonds for their good behaviour, but five refused, demanding their bail as of right. To cut a long and complex story short, the crown eventually communicated their alleged offences to the King's Bench, whose judges, under heavy royal pressure, sentenced Eliot, Holles, and Valentine in February 1630 to large fines and imprisonment at the king's pleasure, despite their refusal to plead. Holles, Selden, and Sir Miles Hobart were released during 1631 upon giving security for their good behaviour. Not so Eliot; Charles had him moved to a fireless room, because rumours of a new parliament were bringing him a stream of visitors. He developed consumption, but his petition for leave to go into the country for his health was refused, and he died in November 1632. Valentine and Strode were kept in captivity until 1640. Both were elected to the Long Parliament, which voted them compensation; Strode and Holles were among the five members whom Charles disastrously attempted to arrest in January 1642.[10]

One obvious price that he had to pay for ruling without parliament was to wind up the wars with France and Spain. The Peace of Susa with the former was swiftly concluded in April 1629, but the Treaty of Madrid with Spain was not signed until the following November. The reason for the longer and more difficult negotiation was that Charles felt real compunction about abandoning the cause of his sister Elizabeth and her husband the Elector Palatine, whose various territories were currently occupied by the forces of Spain, the Empire, and Maximilian of Bavaria. To make matters worse, the Emperor had transferred Frederick's electoral title to Maximilian. Eventually Charles got an empty promise from Philip IV of Spain that he would do all he could to get Frederick's lands restored to him, and arguably this was the least hopeless diplomatic course to pursue, though some of Charles's best servants were shocked by the peace. Dorchester wrote to Elizabeth in admiration of 'our godly people, who, weary of this wicked land, are gone (man, woman and child) in great numbers to seek new worlds'. Her friend Sir Thomas Roe, ambassador, explorer, and patriot, who under another monarch would surely have had a career worthier of his talents, had earlier written to her that 'if there be an America I can live'.[11] The Great Migration was indeed under way, for 1630 was the year in which John Winthrop and his little fleet sailed to Massachusetts and founded Boston. Dorchester and Roe, like Winthrop, felt a kinship with the international protestant interest that the Palatines personified for most Englishmen; Charles did not, though he remained committed to doing what he could for his sister, little though it was while he declined to meet another parliament.

Peace made the drain on the crown's finances less ruinous, but it came at a time when the king could no longer pay for the provision of his own household. When Richard Weston took over the treasurership in 1628 he inherited a debt of around £2 million, roughly the equivalent of three years' peacetime expenditure in the mid-1630s. Crown lands were being sold on a vast scale to make ends meet; £640,000 worth went in the first ten years of the reign, most

[10] For the full story of the proceedings against the imprisoned MPs, see Larkin (ed.), *Stuart Royal Proclamations*, II, ch. 5.

[11] Ibid., pp. 111 (Roe), 210 (Dorchester).

of them in the first five. But this of course was living on capital, and by 1635 there was not a lot left to sell. The customs, the largest source of revenue, were depressed by the stop of trade in 1629 and did not make a full recovery until 1631. Thereafter they throve on the increasing share of the carrying trade that English merchants took over while the Dutch and (from 1635) the French were at war; they yielded £358,000 in 1635, well over half the Exchequer's total receipts, and rose to £482,000 by 1640. But they stirred a steady under-current of resentment for three reasons: they had not been granted by parlia-ment, they included the disputed impositions as well as tonnage and poundage, and the greater part of them was farmed. The crown, instead of collecting customs through its own officials, negotiated a rent for them with syndicates of financiers (the farmers), who took the task over and made what profit they could. This suited the crown because the rent was paid in advance, and because in time of need the farmers could usually be called upon for large loans or anticipatory payments. But they were unpopular, partly because they were levying duties that parliament had not voted, partly because their profits were generally large, and partly because when the government did have enough funds to repay loans the farmers got paid first.

To the merchant community in general the crown was a bad creditor and often an unwelcome interloper in their business interests. A large loan that James had raised from the corporation of London in 1617, to take one ex-ample, was still being repaid in the 1630s. A gap was widening between the middle rank of merchants, whom Charles's personal rule did much to alien-ate, and a smallish elite of really rich concessionaires who profited from the crown's needs. They included, besides the customs farmers, the brokers of some lucrative patents and monopolies, from some of which they wrung more profit than the crown. The sale of monopolies had been a grievance under James I, but the 1624 parliament thought it had remedied it with its Statute of Monopolies. That act, however, had exempted companies and cor-porations for trade from its ban, intending thereby to safeguard the exclusive rights of such bodies as the Merchant Adventurers, the Levant Company, and the London livery companies. Charles I exploited this loophole by granting monopolies under charters of incorporation, and by the late 1630s a whole vexatious range of them was bringing him nearly £100,000 a year, of which over £30,000 came from a particularly oppressive monopoly for soap.

Very little of his revenue during the personal rule came from unobjection-able sources; most of them were to be declared illegal by the Long Parliament, or (in the case of the customs) brought firmly under parliamentary control. It is difficult to say how strongly the fiscal expedients of the 1630s were resented at the time, and historical opinion varies quite widely on the subject. They fell mainly on those who could afford to pay, and by European standards Eng-land remained a lightly taxed country—far less burdened than it was to be in the 1640s and 1650s. The chief objections to them were that they were often arbitrary in their incidence and that they were blatant devices to enable the king to dispense with parliament.

Some of them were ancient, and no longer bore any relation to political and social realities. Wardship was the most famous of these sources; parliament had sought to abolish it in 1604, and again in the Great Contract. It fell on landlords who held their estates as tenants-in-chief of the crown, as most of the gentry did. If such a landowner died leaving an heir under age or an unmarried heiress, the king had the right to all the rents and profits of the estate until the boy reached his majority or the girl married, and to a further payment when that event occurred. The historic justification was that a tenant-in-chief owed him service in war as a mounted knight, and that if he could not serve in person the crown needed his revenues to hire a substitute. But feudal military service had long passed into history, and the general practice of the Court of Wards was to sell the wardship to the family of the heir for a large lump sum. Sometimes, however, the king granted valuable wardships by way of reward to royal servants or favoured courtiers. Wardship was therefore a matter of demographic luck; most families survived, but two or three minorities in near-succession could ruin a house. In Charles's reign, mainly from 1635 onward, wardships were sold more dearly and their yield almost doubled, reaching about £84,000 a year by 1640. Purveyance was another archaic due whose abolition parliament had long been seeking. It entitled the crown to purchase provisions, cartage, and other services below the market rate; it dated from the days when the royal household was peripatetic, but it was levied on counties that never saw the court. Its burden too was increased, to the accompaniment of much vexation, until it brought in nearly £38,000 a year.

To these old examples of fiscal feudalism a newly reinvented one, distraint of knighthood, was added in the 1630s. By reason of that same obligation of mounted military service that lay behind wardship, landowners worth £40 a year had anciently been required to present themselves at the king's coronation to be knighted, or incur a fine in default. Knighthood, however, had long been an honour conferred by the crown, and thanks to the great inflation £40 was only about five per cent of the mean landed income of actual knights in the 1630s. Nevertheless in that decade 9,280 men, ranging from peers down to well-to-do farmers, were fined for failing to claim a title which most of them had no right to assume, and which they did not acquire by paying up. But pay up they had to do, and they brought the Exchequer more than £174,000.

Even more widely unpopular, because it affected many more people, was the revival of ancient crown rights over vast areas of what had once been royal forest, reserved for the king's hunting or for timber for his ships. Whole counties were mulcted; Essex is an example. All the inhabitants of such areas could be fined for encroaching on forest land, and most were; the sums were from the shillings demanded of poorer tenants to the £20,230 imposed on Sir John Winter (though he negotiated a reduction to £4,000, as most of the more heavily taxed did). Another lucrative dip into fiscal antiquarianism was the fining of many people who had built in London's spreading suburbs, under an ancient ban on building 'under the wall', because houses outside their perimeter would provide cover for the sappers and miners of a besieging army. The walls were already largely non-existent, and ironically the only enemy that London was ever likely to have to defend itself against (at least before Hitler) was Charles I. A revenue-raising scheme that aimed more genuinely at improvement was that for the drainage of the fens, but it aroused great local hostility because of its failure to provide adequately for the dispossessed poor, its disproportionate benefit to foreigners and courtiers, and general distrust of the government's motives. The fenlands, like the forests, witnessed serious rioting during the personal rule, and there were cases where local gentry and poor commoners joined in protest against the court concessionaires. The divisions wrought in both fens and forests would be reflected in their inhabitants' choice of allegiance when it came to civil war.

Ship Money was the most controversial of the financial devices of the personal rule, though for five years it was the most successful. It had ancient origins, for since Plantagenet times the crown had occasionally, in times of special need, required the ports and maritime counties to furnish ships for the navy or money in lieu. James I had levied £48,555 in Ship Money in 1619. What was new was its extension to the whole country. Charles's government first tried this in 1628, issuing demands for a total of £173,411, but it withdrew them in face of hostile reactions from many counties; the Forced Loan was still being collected then. Ship Money was next demanded in 1634, from the maritime counties in the traditional way, and it was collected without undue difficulty. There was more protest when fresh writs were sent out less than a year later, this time to all inland as well as seaboard counties, and for an unprecedented total of £218,500—nearly as much as parliament's five subsidies had realized in 1628-9. Yet nine-tenths of this sum was brought in within a year, and the arrears eventually came down to little more than a fiftieth. When further writs were issued in 1636 it was clear that Ship Money was to be an annual levy instead of an infrequent expedient, warranted by national emergency, and protest mounted. A remonstrance against it was prepared for presentation to the king, and the Earl of Warwick told him frankly that he doubted its legality. Viscount Saye and Sele refused to pay it, and sued a constable who distrained two of his oxen in consequence, but the government preferred to avoid a test case at this stage. The king put the question formally to the judges in February 1637. They replied that by law he could compel his subjects to furnish ships for the defence of the kingdom when it was in danger, and that he was the sole judge of that danger and the necessary means to avert it.

Each year, however, the collection of Ship Money became a little slower and less complete, though even in 1637 nine tenths of the £196,413 demanded was eventually paid. But at the time that that sum was being brought in, two new factors were making the public drag its feet. One was Scotland's progress towards rebellion and Charles's preparations for meeting it with force; the other was John Hampden's trial. Flat refusals to pay were still uncommon, but the government could no longer ignore them, and Hampden, a close associate of Eliot who had sat in all the parliaments of the 1620s and had already been imprisoned for refusing the Forced Loan, was chosen for a test case. It began in November 1637 amid intense public interest, and it was over three months before all the judges had delivered their judgments. Only seven of the twelve found for the crown, and though the grounds on which the other five upheld Hampden were narrow and technical, the minimal majority for the government spelt a moral defeat. Oliver St John's brilliant speech as Hampden's counsel was in effect an eloquent assertion of the necessity of parliaments, whereas Justice Berkeley's extravagant claims for the crown did Charles no favours. For pronouncements such as '*rex* is *lex*, *lex loquens*, a living, a speaking, an acting law' Berkeley was to be impeached by the Long Parliament.[12]

It can be said for Ship Money that it was paid into the Treasury of the Navy and used for nothing else but the king's ships and their crews. From 1635 the Ship Money fleet was the best that England had put to sea for many years; it raised her standing in Europe, and its protection of the growing volume of English shipping was undoubtedly in the national interest. But the navy had never before depended on regular extra-parliamentary taxation, and it was never to do so again. An even finer fleet was to be maintained under the Commonwealth out of parliamentary revenue, including of course the customs. Contemporaries were justified in seeing Ship Money, once it was levied annually, as a means of averting the calling of a parliament indefinitely and as a breach of the spirit of the Petition of Right; for the official arguments that it was a rate and not a tax, and that the king was not demanding money but commanding the provision of ships, cut little ice with men whose possessions were distrained if they did not pay a very specific sum in cash.

The shortfall in payment only became really worrying in 1638, when the Scots openly rebelled in a cause that commanded much English sympathy, and collection only collapsed in 1639, when the counties were facing the

---

[12] Gardiner, *Constitutional Documents* gives long extracts from Berkeley's speech on pp. 115–24, and from St John's on pp. 109–15.

simultaneous costs of fielding an army in the First Bishops' War. The striking success of Ship Money until then has been taken as evidence that it was not seriously unpopular until the government's policies aroused widespread opposition for other reasons. We should not suppose, however, that the fact that it was paid more or less obediently for five years is any indication that it was paid willingly. The habit of obedience was strong among gentry magistrates and subordinate officers in counties and towns and villages, because any breach in co-operation between them and the privy council, or among themselves, could pose a serious threat to peace and order in their localities. Outright refusal was a risk that few were willing to take until men of Hampden's standing set an example, because with no prospect of a parliament to liberate them they might languish in prison as long as Strode and Valentine. Moreover the amounts demanded of individuals were not large, because Ship Money was paid by several times as many people as were assessed for parliamentary subsidies. The poorest contributed as little as a penny, while the gentry were as usual grossly under-assessed; the sum which Hampden, one of the richest squires in Buckinghamshire, refused to pay was £1. The sheriff, to whom the Ship Money writs were addressed, had a strong motive for putting the pressure on the constables and other subordinate officers, since if he failed to deliver his county's quota he had either to pay the deficit himself or face the council's wrath and stay in harness until he had collected the arrears. Ship Money made the sheriff's office so nearly intolerable that fewer and fewer members of county families were willing to undertake it; thus forcing the government to fill it in some cases from lower in the social scale or from men who lived outside the county, and so straining the delicate system of co-operation upon which local administration depended.

Despite the rarity of open refusals before 1638, there were so many protests over the sums demanded of particular localities that they only half-conceal a resentment of the levy itself. As soon as Ship Money was extended to the inland counties, the privy council was so overwhelmed with complaints, appeals, and requests for direction that it was unable to continue the programme of reform that it had been genuinely trying to pursue in the earlier 1630s, and the efficiency of central government was impaired. And when the country finally went on a tax strike in 1639, under the double burden of Ship Money and 'coat and conduct' money (for the troops on the march towards Scotland), it was largely because unpaid constables would no longer go on wringing pennies out of neighbours poorer than themselves.

The traditional system of local government by unpaid magistrates survived the years of personal rule in fair working order, but this should not be taken as evidence (as it sometimes has been) that non-parliamentary rule was broadly acceptable to the gentry elite of the shires. They shared a common interest with central government in maintaining order and keeping the poorer sort tolerably content, and they were reluctant to forfeit the prestige which the commission of the peace conferred. The king had sharply warned them against agitating for a parliament, and if he chose not to call one there was nothing they could do about it. Non-cooperation was not an option. The lines were kept open between central and local government when the assize judges went on their circuits twice a year, and commenced their proceedings in each county by delivering a charge to the assembled JPs. It was a reminder that they were engaged in the common enterprise of enforcing the law of the land, and before they set out the judges were collectively briefed by the Lord Keeper of the Great Seal in Star Chamber. The lord lieutenant could be another channel of communication, especially if he resided in his county for at least part of the year.

Early in 1631, in a time of dearth and high unemployment, the privy council sent out to all counties a comprehensive set of directions known as the Book of Orders. It used to be seen as inaugurating a new and paternalistic social policy and as a major extension of royal control over local government. In fact it was essentially traditional in spirit, in line with occasional earlier drives to improve the quality of local administration, and it was almost entirely the work of the Earl of Manchester, the father of the parliamentarian general. The remedies that it prescribed—poor relief, provision of work, securing adequate local supplies of grain and so on—were mostly of Tudor origin and already widely applied in many counties. What was new in the Book of Orders was that it required the quarter sessions everywhere to return quarterly certificates to the council, reporting their execution of its directions. This, rather than the directions themselves, caused some resentment, because local magistrates felt that they could judge their communities' needs better than the men in Whitehall, and that they were already doing their best to meet them. For a year or two the Book had a noticeable effect, but the quarterly reports came in very irregularly. In 1633 more than half the counties failed to return any at all, and those that sent fewest included some of the best governed. The results might have been more positive if the council had had the time and the personnel to read and act on the reports that *were* sent in, but from the mid-1630s it all but sank under the labour of administering Ship Money. The Book of Orders merely created a short-term stir in a long-term momentum towards improvement which owed more to the initiative and concern of county magistrates than to central direction; the provision of poor relief, for instance, improved more under the Commonwealth than in Charles's reign down to 1640.[13] The Book was almost certainly less of a strain

---

[13] B. W. Quintrell, 'The making of Charles I's Book of Orders', *English Historical Review* XCV (1980); P. Slack, 'Books of Orders: the making of English social policy, 1577–1631', *Transactions of the Royal Historical Society*, 5th series, XXX (1981); Anthony Fletcher, *Reform*

The New Reign 71

on the gentry's tolerance of non-parliamentary rule than Ship Money and the other financial exactions that bore on them. But strain there certainly was.

Turning from the country to the court, the greater formality that Charles had introduced at his accession became even more marked during the personal rule. What he had seen of the King of Spain's court—its august ceremony, its hierarchy, its reverence for the throne, and its highly ritualistic religious worship—had left an enduring mark on him. In or about 1630 he personally signed a comprehensive set of regulations for the conduct of his household and entourage which demonstrate his preoccupation with the physical presentation of majesty. Entry into the precincts of the court was to be strictly checked, and access to the Presence Chamber, Privy Chamber, and above all the royal bedchamber was exactly regulated. Misconduct by officers of the household was to be severely punished, and immorality on the part of courtiers, even the highest, was not to be tolerated. It was an austere ethos that he aimed to inculcate, far from the pleasure-loving cavalierism of the popular image. The ceremony laid down for the Chapel Royal might have made a modern intruder wonder quite who was being worshipped, God or his lieutenant on earth, though Charles would have been shocked by the suggestion. The enormous importance that he attached to the Order of the Garter and its ceremonies again reflects his constant attention to the image of royalty. He longed for the brave new Whitehall Palace that Inigo Jones had designed, and of which only the Banqueting House was built; it would have given the royal presence a setting of appropriate splendour, and set him at a proper distance from all but his closest servants and greatest subjects.

In recent years there has been great interest in the masques, plays, and poems that entertained the court, and in the paintings and music that the king or his chief courtiers commissioned. It need hardly be said that the work of such men as Anthony Van Dyck, Inigo Jones, Ben Jonson, Thomas Carew, Richard Lovelace, Sir John Suckling, and the brother composers Henry and William Lawes is highly worthy of attention in itself. It has been argued, however, that the Caroline court masques should be studied as not merely the diversions of an elite but as the very deliberate expressions of a political ideology. They belong to an age in which images did not merely represent authority, but were held to have a power in themselves to inculcate virtue and disseminate it. Their purpose therefore (so the case runs) was not just to entertain but to communicate political values to men holding positions of responsibility from the king's ministers downward; they have been described as 'the high mass of Neoplatonic monarchy performed by the whole clerisy of court'.[14] They

*in the Provinces: The Government of Stuart England* (New Haven and London, 1986), pp. 56–9, 123–5, etc.

[14] By P. Thomas, quoted by Sharpe in *Personal Rule of Charles I*, p. 230, in the course of a

certainly embody the ideals whereby Charles and his ministers strove to steer the ship of state—ideals of peace, order, service, and the subjugation of rebellious passions—but the question is whether they had much impact outside the narrow circle of those who witnessed or participated in them. They are most unlikely to have done so. They did reach a wider audience through printed editions, but one suspects that they were read more for their aesthetic and entertainment value than for their rather insipid political messages. It would have been different if the Caroline court had been as open and popular as the Elizabethan, but since medieval times there can rarely have been a monarch who was known by sight to so few of his subjects as Charles. He not only restricted access to his presence, but he really tried to enforce the order (which was not novel) that noblemen and gentlemen should reside on their country estates, and should not come to London even on business, unless it was the king's, without permission.

In actual government, the great change that coincided with the personal rule was the privy council's return to full activity, after Buckingham's dominance had threatened to reduce its functions to routine, or to the execution of policies decided elsewhere. With around forty-two members it might appear too large to act with the corporate authority of a modern cabinet, but in contrast with Tudor practice many council appointments were honorific, and the typical attendance was around a dozen or less. Charles involved himself more in the daily business of government than James had done and attended far more council meetings. We do not know quite how many, because by a royal order of 1630—one of many that aimed to regulate conciliar procedures—no clerks were to be present when the king was, so an unknown number of his attendances probably went unrecorded. The council still bore traces of its past as part of the royal household; the Council Chamber faced the king's bedchamber in Whitehall Palace, though it also met at times in the Star Chamber in the Palace of Westminster, or in whichever royal residence the king was occupying when on progress. The full Council Board always met on Wednesdays and Fridays, to which Sundays were added from 1635, to cope with the burden of administering Ship Money. But business was constantly increasing under the government's efforts at administrative reform, and thirteen or fourteen meetings a month were quite common in the second half of the decade.

There were few matters on which Charles did not seek the council's advice, and the active members were never confined to a single political viewpoint. Contemporaries spoke of the Spanish, Dutch, and French factions, but they over-simplified. Nevertheless there was a rough correlation between those on the one hand who favoured friendship with Spain and were opposed to

discussion of the whole nature of court culture (pp. 222–35). See also the same author's *Politics and Ideas in Early Stuart England* (1989).

calling another parliament, and those on the other who supported a protestant foreign policy, sought to keep the way open for England to intervene
again in the continental wars, and desired an early return to traditional constitutional ways, including parliaments. The most prominent of the former
group were doubtful protestants, at best. Chief among them until his death in
1635 was Richard Weston, the Lord Treasurer who laid the financial foundations of the personal rule and was made Earl of Portland in 1633. He kept
up a personal correspondence with the Count-Duke of Olivares, the great
minister who virtually ruled Spain, and though he attended Anglican services
for much of his life he was married to a declared catholic and converted formally to Rome before he died. Weston was an old friend of the great magnate
Thomas Howard, Earl of Arundel and Earl Marshal of England, who had
been a privy councillor since 1616 and after 1629 rose high in Charles's esti-
mation, not least because he too was a great collector and connoisseur.
Brought up a catholic, he had converted to the Church of England in 1615.
Weston's protégé Francis Cottington, who was Chancellor of the Exchequer
throughout the personal rule, a baron from 1631, and Master of the Court of
Wards four years later, had been a diplomat at the Spanish court at intervals
since 1605 and had become 'almost a naturalized Spaniard'.[15] Amusing, flam-
boyant, and cosmopolitan, he was nevertheless a serious politician and a useful minister. At heart a catholic, he alternated between Anglican conformity
and professed Romanism, generally according to the state of his health; he
died in the old faith.

The committed protestants, whose sympathies lay with the Dutch and with
Sweden and Denmark in the continental wars and who would have gladly
returned to parliamentary government, were a dwindling force in the council.
The third Earl of Pembroke died in 1630, Dorchester in 1632, Archbishop
Abbot in 1633, and Sir Thomas Roe was passed over for the secretaryship on
Dorchester's death in favour of another suspected crypto-catholic, Sir Francis Windebank, a great protector of catholic priests, though he was probably
an Arminian in the 1630s, and only finally converted to Rome in 1646. The
other Secretary of State, Sir John Coke, was a firm enough protestant, but he
was more a man of business than a policy-maker, and age was creeping up on
him; he was 77 when he was finally persuaded to pass on the seals in 1640.
There was a phase in 1631–2 when the protestant constitutionalists seemed
to be in the saddle. Gustavus Adolphus of Sweden was striking triumphantly
southward after his sensational victory at Breitenfeld, and the reconquest of
the Rhine Palatinate lay in his grasp. He asked England for financial and
diplomatic support, and Elizabeth begged her brother to give it. This would
have meant calling a parliament, but Gustavus was such a hero in England

[15] Reeve, *Charles I and the Road to Personal Rule*, p. 185.

that it would almost certainly have been generous, and Charles would have got a more sympathetic consideration of his own financial needs than at a later time, for Ship Money still lay in the future. But there were reasons for doubting whether Gustavus would restore Frederick to his territory, since other allies of his had claims to it, and in the end Charles drew back from breaking with Spain and committing himself to another parliament. He also detested the Dutch, whose ally he would have become, and he sympathized with Spain's phobia about an international protestant conspiracy, of which he saw his own puritan subjects as a part. England soon resumed the orientation towards Spain which characterized most of the 1630s.

There was one more significant break in it, between 1635 and 1637, following upon France's declaration of war against Spain. Again the Palatinate lay at the root of it. Frederick having died, his elder son Charles Louis was now the titular Elector, and French forces were now in occupation of much of his territory. For various reasons, English hopes of getting it restored to him though Spanish influence were dashed by the Peace of Prague, which the Emperor Ferdinand signed with the Elector of Saxony in 1635. Charles had hitherto disliked the France of Richelieu almost as much as he did her Dutch allies, but he was much drawn to the alliance that the cardinal now offered him, on terms that included an undertaking not to make peace without securing the restoration to the Palatinate of Charles Louis, who arrived in England in November 1635 to add his own pleas for joint Anglo-French action. It all came to nothing in the end, but the episode is significant because it aroused the queen to a more active role as an ardent supporter of the proposed alliance, and it brought to prominence a 'French faction' which was to be a force in the coming years. Its leading numbers were Henry Rich, Earl of Holland, and James, Marquis of Hamilton. Holland was High Steward to the queen, Chancellor of Cambridge University, Groom of the Stool from 1636, brother of the puritan Earl of Warwick, and a favourite of both the king and the queen. Hamilton was Master of the Horse, Charles's principal Scottish adviser, and from 1633 a member of the English privy council as well as the Scottish. He was given the English title of Earl of Cambridge, which was to lay him open to trial as an English traitor in 1649. Cottington and Windebank also gravitated towards the queen and France, despite their Hispanophile reputations, and Arundel returned from a mission to the Emperor in 1636 so thoroughly ill-satisfied with the response he received that he too advised allying with France and breaking with Spain. Any such prospect ended, however, when revolt began to stir in Scotland in 1637, for Richelieu listened sympathetically to Scottish appeals for support, and England's need to keep clear of foreign entanglements soon became very plain.

It may seem surprising that so little has yet been said of Wentworth and Laud, the two most famous of the king's servants during the personal rule, and the two who incurred the most odium and paid most dearly for their participation in it. But Wentworth had few friends at court (other than Laud), and little direct influence on the government of England until 1639, for he was physically distanced from it, first in York as President of the North and then from 1633 in Ireland as Lord Deputy. Laud was always a power in religious matters, but Charles at first discouraged him from engaging too closely in temporal affairs. Laud scored a success when his protégé Windebank got the secretaryship in 1632, but it was only during Portland's last illness that he rose to really high political influence. With his strict principles and genuine zeal for reform he got on badly with Portland, who figures in his letters to Wentworth as 'the Lady Mora', signifying the spirit of dilatoriness, procrastination and venality that frustrated the policies that he and the Lord Deputy tried to pursue under the name of 'Thorough'. He called Cottington, less than fairly, 'Lady Mora's waiting maid'. It was a mark of his new standing that he got William Juxon, Bishop of London, appointed Treasurer after Portland's death, despite Cottington's more obvious claim to the succession. Juxon executed the office with probity, though hardly with distinction or originality, but to have the three highest prelates in England—Arminians all—in the inner ring of the privy council did not endear the government to public opinion. Elizabeth, whose reign was increasingly looked back on as a golden age, had had only one clerical privy councillor, Whitgift, in all her fifty-four years as queen.

Of all aspects of the personal rule, its religious policy is the hardest to assess, yet probably the most important to understand. With Scotland there is no great problem, and in the next chapter it will be shown how Charles's treatment of the Kirk generated the national rebellion which launched the Wars of Three Kingdoms. The case of Ireland is not so straightforward, but it will not be too difficult at a later stage to describe how fears for the religion of the catholic majority of the Irish people helped to drive them too into rebellion. As for England, most historians can now agree that though the immediate issues over which king and parliament came to blows were primarily political and constitutional, men and women were profoundly influenced by their religious standpoints when they formed a judgement about the claims of the two sides for their support. But just what the religious policies were that they were approving or condemning, and how far they departed from Elizabethan and Jacobean norms, and who was mainly responsible for formulating them, and what in them was most objectionable and to whom, and consequently where the main lines of religious division ran—these are all questions over which historians disagree widely. The differences are not just between revisionists and the older schools. One distinguished revisionist sees religious issues as so fundamental that 'The English civil war was not the first European revolution; it was the last of the Wars of Religion'.[16] Another, while acknowledging that Caroline ecclesiastical policies offended particular sectors of the community, suggests that at parish level they engendered 'a growing commitment to and affection for the church', and that most of the religious strife of 1640–2 was of very recent origin, stirred up by a puritan minority in the wake of the Bishops' Wars.[17] The version offered here, therefore, can only be one historian's reading of a complex web of evidence and argument, at one stage of a controversy that is obviously far from finished.

To this writer the least plausible of recent interpretations is one which contends that Charles and Laud were simply resuming the efforts of Whitgift and his successor Bancroft to secure conformity to an Anglican church order and ethos that went back to the Elizabethan settlement; in other words they introduced no essential change, other than to end the laxity of Abbot's archiepiscopate.[18] This flies in the face of abundant evidence that most educated contemporaries were aware of very considerable change, beginning before the personal rule and intensified in the course of it, with the result that when the Long Parliament at last had a chance to address the grievances of the realm, most members gave priority to religious ones. But this should not be attributed, as it often used to be, to a 'rise of puritanism', or interpreted as a straightforward conflict between puritans and Anglicans. 'Anglican' was a term virtually unknown to contemporaries, and mainstream puritanism was (as has been argued) a strain of piety within the established church, which accommodated it reasonably comfortably during most of James's reign. A much favoured recent interpretation has identified the Laudians rather than those they called puritans as the innovating party, thanks to a partnership between the king and the leading members of the hierarchy, and has substituted for the rise of puritanism 'the rise of Arminianism'.[19] This is much nearer the mark, but as a label it lays too much emphasis on doctrine. There certainly was controversy over doctrine, of course, but by no means all those stigmatized as Arminians shared the beliefs of Arminius, and doctrine was not the main concern of most of the people involved—least of all the king, whose initiative in the ecclesiastical policies of his reign has until recently been underestimated.

Perhaps the mainspring of the change in direction was a reaction against the prevailing evangelical, lay-oriented ethos of the Jacobean church. Some leading clergy, especially the Durham House group and the disciples of

[16] John Morrill, 'The religious context of the English Civil War', reprinted as ch. 3 of *The Nature of the English Revolution* (1993).

[17] Sharpe, *Personal Rule of Charles I*, p. 387 and ch. 6 *passim*.

[18] This is the broad argument of White in *Predestination, Policy and Polemic*, chs. 12–15.

[19] Nicholas Tyacke, *Anti-Calvinists: The Rise of English Arminianism c.1590–1640* (Oxford, 1987), and the same author's chapter 4 in Conrad Russell (ed.), *The Origins of the English Civil War* (1973).

Lancelot Andrewes, felt that the emphasis on preaching, at the expense of prayer and the sacraments, was distorting the character of the historic Church of England. They wanted to reaffirm its unique identity, and to check the tendency to align it with the Reformed churches in other countries. They felt a need to reassert the priestly nature of their calling, and to reinstate the sacraments, especially holy communion, as the main channel through which grace was conveyed to believers. Lay influences, they believed, had gone too far; they aimed to restore the authority and independence of the clergy, and especially of the episcopate. Their insistence that the bishop's office was *jure divino* proved particularly obnoxious, and not only to puritans; indeed the divine right of bishops was a much more contentious issue under Charles I than the divine right of kings. They sought to restore a sense of the inherent sanctity of consecrated churches, which were tending to be regarded just as preaching-houses. Laud presided over a much-needed drive to repair delapidated churches and to provide the many that lacked them with decent furnishings.

More controversial was the aim of Laud and his bishops to re-dignify the church's worship, and especially the celebration of the sacraments, with a reverent ritual and priest-like vestments. They insisted that services must be performed according to the letter of the Book of Common Prayer, and clamped down on those puritan clergy who abridged the liturgical part to make time for longer sermons, or substituted extempore prayers for the prescribed forms. Many, though not all, of the clergy who promoted these policies were Arminians in the loose sense that was current after the Synod of Dort, in that they deplored the harsh literalness of the Bezan doctrine of double predestination and believed that Christ had died for all. Lancelot Andrewes exemplifies the link between their more liberal theology and the outward forms that Charles sought to impose on all Anglican worship, for it was as Dean of the Chapel Royal that he introduced the prince (as he then was) to the raised and railed-off communion table, placed like an altar at the east end of the chancel, and to those rituals like bowing at the name of Jesus which were to become so contentious in the 1630s. Charles's continued promotion of Arminian divines to bishoprics, deaneries, and headships of colleges changed the whole balance in the episcopate, even before Abbot's long-awaited death enabled him to advance Laud to Canterbury in 1633.

All but one of the Caroline bishops stood quite firm on the differences of doctrine and ecclesiastical polity that separated England from Rome and on the superiority of Ecclesia Anglicana, but whereas most of the previous generation had emphasized its affinity with the Reformed churches abroad, they sought to present it as an alternative and purer embodiment of a catholic, apostolic church, a *via media* between the corruptions of Rome and the excesses of Geneva. Calvin had less authority for them than the early Fathers and the practice of the early church, whose traditions they sought to recover. Unlike the majority of Elizabethan and Jacobean protestants, who had identified the papacy with Antichrist, they regarded Rome as a true church that had become tainted through the ages by erroneous doctrine, superstition, and false political pretensions. They were therefore objectionable to the broadly Calvinist sector of English protestants on three grounds: they failed to recognize the utter falsity and iniquity of popery; they were suspect on those doctrines which had long been a touchstone of the differences between the Reformed churches and Rome; and their ritual practices smacked of popish superstition. In particular their placing of the communion table where the pre-Reformation altar had stood, their raising it above the level of the chancel and shutting it off with rails, and their insistence that communicants should kneel at the rail to receive the sacrament, all offended the puritan view of the Lord's Supper as essentially an act of commemoration by suggesting the catholic belief that the celebrant was re-enacting the sacrifice of Christ's body. Thus Arminianism came to be seen as a kind of creeping popery, and even as part of a design, in partnership with catholics and crypto-catholics in high places, to lead the national church back by degrees into the Roman fold. This was as unjustified as the attempt by some so-called Arminians to brand their opponents as puritans merely for upholding doctrines, especially predestinarian doctrines, which had not only been permissible in the established church but had until lately predominated in it.

With these changes came a sharp contraction of the de facto toleration that had characterized Abbot's long archiepiscopate. The new authoritarianism and the drive for uniformity owed at least as much to the king as to Laud and his fellow bishops. Charles's support for the Arminians was based less on a preference for their doctrine than on a growing hatred of puritans, who he thought were bent on subverting his own royal authority. Church and state, he believed, needed a parallel assertion of discipline and hierarchy. Convinced that kingship itself was sacramental in character, he sensed a strong affinity between the reverence, ceremony, and mystery with which the Arminians sought to endow religious worship, and the deference and ritual with which he surrounded his own presence. For laymen to challenge the one was as bad as for disrespectful subjects to profane the other. 'Popular reformation', in his words, was 'little better than rebellion', and as he said to Archbishop Neile in 1634, 'the neglect of punishing puritans breeds papists'. He forbade public preaching and discussion concerning the vexed points of predestination, not because he himself held strong views about them, but because they were 'too high for the people's understanding'.[20] There was no

---

[20] Quotation from Julian Davies, *The Caroline Captivity of the Church* (Oxford, 1992), pp. 10, 11, 17. I am greatly indebted to Dr Davies's profound study and if my brief account fails to reflect its depth and originality adequately it is for lack of space rather than any reservations.

total ban on the publication of theological and devotional works upholding Calvinist doctrine, but all books had to be licensed by the Bishop of London (or his officials) or by one of the two universities, and after the transformation wrought by Charles's wholesale promotion of Arminians it was undoubtedly easier to obtain licenses for writings of their school than for those of a strongly predestinarian standpoint.

Charles had a deep distrust of unregulated preaching, and especially of lecturers supported or endowed by laymen. The Instructions that he issued in 1629, based on a document prepared by Archbishop Harsnett of York, went much further than his father's 1622 ban on public controversy over predestination. The only lecturers that they sanctioned were clergymen holding livings in the town concerned or in the near neighbourhood, and all lecturers were required to read divine service, wearing surplice and hood, before they preached. Afternoon sermons, with which puritans had widely supplemented the morning one (if it was preached at all), were to be replaced by catechizing, according to the strict form prescribed by the Prayer Book. The Instructions also sought to put a stop to the practice of many of the gentry who kept unlicensed clergymen in their households as domestic chaplains or as tutors for their children, for they restricted the keeping of chaplains to those—mainly the peerage—who were specifically qualified by law to employ them. Not long after, Charles and Laud put an end to a venture that had been launched in 1625 by twelve Londoners, who had formed a trust to collect charitable donations in order to buy up tithes that had fallen into lay hands and church livings whose right of presentation had become lay property. In the next half-dozen years these Feoffees for Impropriations raised considerable funds and many bequests, and applied them to endowing lectureships, supplementing the stipends of inadequately paid preaching ministers, and acquiring the right of presentation to many livings. This was undoubtedly a puritan enterprise, though a moderate one, and Laud saw it as a cunning conspiracy to overthrow established church government. In 1632 the Attorney-General prosecuted the Feoffees in the Exchequer court as an illegal corporation; next year they were dissolved by its order, and their assets confiscated to the crown.

It was essentially Charles's decision to reissue his father's Book of Sports in 1633, and to require every beneficed clergyman to read it out in his church. He disliked the strict observance of the sabbath, which he regarded as a specifically puritan tenet—wrongly, because it had been enjoined by churchmen of all colours in James's reign. It was also almost certainly his personal decision in the following year, though Bishops Wren and Piers probably advised it, to order that communion tables must be kept at the east end during the communion service, and that communicants must kneel at the rails to receive the sacrament. Even Laud had reservations about this, and did not enforce the instruction rigidly; indeed only three bishops imposed it really strictly, including Wren and Piers. Significantly, enforcement was to be most rigorous in much of East Anglia, which was to be the most strongly parliamentarian region of rural England, whereas royalist support was to be firmest in dioceses where receiving at the rail was not insisted upon.

But if Laud had to carry the odium for some policies which were really more the king's, there were others for which he more than shared the responsibility. His was a complex character, which comes over much more sympathetically in his diary and his letters to his friends than in his public actions and pronouncements. He was utterly upright, dedicated to an ideal of a purified church, and punishingly hard-working in pursuit of it. He was as keen as any puritan to recover for the church the impropriated tithes and other assets that had fallen into lay hands and apply them to the maintenance of an educated and devoted parish clergy, but he could not abide lay initiative in the work, and the clergy he supported had to be conformist. Though deeply authoritarian, he was not at heart inhumane or tyrannical. But he had a brusque, forbidding manner and a fiery temper, which he frequently lost, not least at meetings of the privy council. On one famous occasion the Lord Chief Justice, Sir Thomas Richardson, acceded to a petition from some JPs in Somerset and issued an order for the suppression of church ales and wakes in the county. Unfortunately he went beyond his powers by requiring it to be published in the local churches. Furious at this encroachment on ecclesiastical authority, Laud had him summoned before a committee of the privy council and so savaged him there that this most senior judge complained that he had 'been almost choked with a pair of lawn sleeves'.[21] Laud was a somewhat lonely figure at court, not only on account of his hectoring manner and total lack of courtly graces, but because of the conspicuous gap between his social origins (his father had been a clothier in Reading) and the pomp that he assumed as archbishop. When he rode out from Lambeth Palace, forty or fifty mounted attendants accompanied him, and ushers roughly cleared the way for his cortège.

During the 1630s an unprecedented number of clergymen were prosecuted for nonconformity in the diocesan courts. Laud's drive for stricter regulation reached its peak between 1634 and 1637, when he revived a pre-Reformation procedure and instituted a 'metropolitical visitation' of the whole province of Canterbury. Armed with a voluminous questionnaire concerning the fabric and furniture of churches, the behaviour and garb of the clergy, the precise conduct of services, sermons, catechizing, and a great deal else, his Vicar-General Sir Nathaniel Brent traversed the whole of England south of Trent, interrogating parsons and churchwardens on every point. Needless to say he uncovered many disorders, many evasions of the strict letter of the Prayer

---

[21] Trevor-Roper, *Archbishop Laud*, pp. 156–8.

Book, and much equivocation over the controversial 'ceremonies'. Laud's own preference was to secure conformity by persuasion rather than coercion, and fewer clergymen were suspended or deprived than might have been if his and the king's instructions had been enforced with full rigour, but the pressure to conform was keenly felt. Some bishops, notably Wren of Norwich (later Ely) and Piers of Bath and Wells, applied it more high-handedly than Laud himself. And behind the diocesan judicial machinery stood the Court of High Commission, which acquired a quite new unpopularity in the 1630s— an unpopularity that rubbed off on the crown, since it ultimately derived its authority from the royal prerogative. It was used not only to discipline errant clergy but to prosecute noblemen and gentlemen for moral offences, and to harass them into making ever more of their impropriated tithes to the maintenance of the clergy.

Laud also bears much responsibility for making the other great prerogative court, Star Chamber, unpopular as it had never been before. The most notorious case tried there, in 1637, was that of William Prynne, John Bastwick, and Henry Burton, who had committed the unpardonable crime of attacking in print the whole order of bishops. They were sentenced to be branded, to have their ears cut off, to stand in the pillory, to pay fines of £5,000 each, and to suffer life imprisonment. Their prosecution proved to be one of Laud's and Charles's worst mistakes, for the oppressive proceedings and the savagery of the sentences recoiled against their accusers; branding, mutilation, and the pillory were not penalties to be imposed on gentlemen. The demonstrations of sympathy that greeted the victims' addresses from the pillory and accompanied them to their places of imprisonment gave them a moral victory. It was quite an achievement to make martyrs of men as unlovable as Prynne and Burton but Laud believed that people who attacked the principle of hierarchy in the church could be no loyal subjects of the king, and Charles agreed with him. Preaching at the opening of parliament in 1626, Laud said:

They, whoever they be, that would overthrow *sedes ecclesiae*, the seats of ecclesiastical government, will not spare (if ever they get power) to have a pluck at the throne of David. And there is not a man that is for parity, all fellows in the church, but he is not for monarchy in the state.[22]

This was of the same order of extravagance as the belief of Laud's opponents that he and his fellow-Arminians were hand in glove with papists in a design to bring the Church of England back to Rome.

Not everything that Laud attempted was unpopular, and endeavours that were disliked by some were probably well taken by others. The firm pressure that he put on patrons of livings to bear their share in repairing delapidated churches may have been resented by the gentry who felt it, but welcome

---

[22] Prothero, *Select Statutes and Constitutional Documents*, p. 435.

enough to their humbler fellow-parishioners. Squires doubtless complained at the enforced removal of their high-sided box pews, whose privileged position often cluttered the chancel, but ordinary worshippers must have been glad to get a proper view of the services for the first time. The reverent rituals, the fuller observance of the church's festivals, and the enhancement of worship with what Laud called 'the beauty of holiness' all offended puritans, but may well have been better liked by simple countryfolk, and not only by them. When the Long Parliament tried to outlaw the Prayer Book rites and services after the Civil War, it encountered a deep and widespread popular affection for them. Even the bitterly opposed altar rails cannot have been universally unpopular, for many parishes restored them spontaneously on the eve of the Restoration, before the Anglican order was formally reinstated. Laud's efforts to make well-to-do Londoners pay tithes may have done more to heighten anticlericalism than to raise the clergy's living standards, but it was an honest attempt to redress the unfair share of the tithes burden that small countrymen bore. Laud laboured hard to recover all sorts of ecclesiastical assets that had been quietly appropriated by the laity, and to apply them to improving the incomes of the clergy, but his achievement was very limited, because of all his major aims this was the one in which he had least support from the king.

Looking at the Caroline church from the perspective of 1640, few if any of the directives that Charles and his favoured prelates had imposed on it were totally without precedent, yet collectively they effected a qualitative change in its character. Where there had been a fairly wide and often longstanding variety of liturgical and ritual practice there was now a high degree of conformity, much of it unwillingly yielded. Whereas the main thrust of the Jacobean church had been evangelical and the involvement of the laity in the work had been generally welcome, the emphasis was now on sacerdotalism and sacramentalism; preaching was constrained and lay initiatives discouraged. There was a much stronger assertion of clerical authority, especially episcopal authority. The church courts, busier now but scarcely more efficient, acquired an unprecedented unpopularity. The swing from a predominantly Calvinist to a predominantly anti-Calvinist theology had begun before Charles's accession, but his weighting of the scales in the Arminians' favour and the relative difficulty with which strict predestinarians could preach, publish, or find preferment raised fears that the church's protestant faith was under threat. Absurd though the charges were that Charles and Laud were heading the country back to Rome, these changes did amount to what can fairly be called a catholicization of the Church of England, a kind of counter-reformation in a minor key. They shifted it away from sisterhood with the Reformed churches of Europe, and claimed it as a true daughter of the catholic apostolic church of the early Christian centuries.

To many modern Anglicans the ecclesiastical policies of the 1630s may look almost entirely admirable, but we have to consider how they struck contemporaries. Charles's subjects saw them against the background of the strongly protestant church in which they had grown up; against the background too of the long and bloody wars on the continent, which to many represented a struggle between the gospel and Antichrist. They linked them with the crucifix on the altar in the Chapel Royal, with the ritual observed there, with the king's practice and advocacy of frequent confession, with his uxoriousness towards his catholic wife, with his frank pleasure in the company of successive papal agents to her court, and with the increasingly fashionable conversions that they effected among her courtiers. It was not enough that he publicly deplored those conversions, and disapproved of the freedom with which English catholics worshipped in her chapel and in those of foreign ambassadors, or that he trebled the crown's income from recusancy fines. Since some of his own senior ministers were generally believed to be crypto-catholics, the association in the public mind of Arminianism with popery and of the court with both is not surprising, especially after the return to a strongly pro-Spanish orientation in foreign policy from 1637 onward. Fears of a pervasive popish plot were of course less rational, but Gunpowder Treason and the conspiracies against Queen Elizabeth's life were vivid in the folk memory.

The Great Migration to New England coincided almost exactly with the personal rule. Between 1629 and 1640 about 60,000 men, women, and children made the journey, and far more than in the case of Virginia and the other older colonies whole families wound up their affairs in England and sailed to Massachusetts together. By no means all of them emigrated for religious reasons, but the high proportion who did brave such a vast and perilous change of life for the sake of their faith, and the number of ordained ministers who sailed with them, are eloquent testimony that for a significant sector of the English people the only religion permitted to them by law had become offensive to their consciences to a degree unprecedented before Charles's reign. In contrast with the Mayflower pilgrims, who were avowed separatists, the great majority who sailed in the 1630s had always regarded themselves as members of the national church, and severed communion with it reluctantly. Many more were contemplating emigration as the only way of finding religious freedom, including one Oliver Cromwell, when the change in Charles's fortunes gave them fresh hope at home. The Massachusetts Bay Company was not the only colonizing venture with a religious complexion, for Viscount Saye and Sele and Lord Brooke, both strong puritans, founded the Saybrook Company for the settlement of Connecticut; while the Providence Island Company, which aimed to establish a puritan colony in the Caribbean, became politically important at home because it kept so many future leaders of the

Long Parliament in close touch during the years when the two houses at Westminster stood empty.

The effect of Caroline policies on Ireland and its religious communities will be traced in a later chapter. It was in Scotland, however, that they first provoked open rebellion, so to Scotland we must turn next.

# FOUR

# Storm over Scotland

WHEN James VI (as he was styled in his native land) died he left his Scottish subjects nursing a number of discontents, but none so serious as to threaten to make them ungovernable. Rule by an absentee king imposed an inevitable strain, but James knew his people and understood the problems. When he first departed for England he promised to revisit Scotland every three years, but he did so only once, in 1617. During his first decade or so as James I of England he surrounded himself with Scots to an extent that aroused serious resentment among English courtiers, and for much longer he kept in touch by summoning his chief advisers in Scotland, one after another, to come and report on the state of affairs there and counsel him on his Scottish policy. He also added a powerful group of Scottish peers to the English privy council, thus giving it, quite informally, a British dimension.

He was sensitive to Scottish fears of being reduced to a province, but he could not wholly allay them because they had some foundation. The absence of a royal court denied the old nobility the natural arena in which they had hitherto wielded political influence, and deprived the merchants and manufacturers around Edinburgh of a vital economic stimulus. Scottish administration became increasingly the preserve of a smallish group of leading civil servants and courtiers, among whom faction was rife and corruption not uncommon. James's practice of freely ennobling the more successful of them created a potential rift between the old aristocracy and the new *noblesse de robe*. In his later years his government became less sensitive to Scottish aspirations and susceptibilities. New taxes, and (as in England) the sale of monopolies to courtiers and speculators, raised doubts about the government's probity, and its failure to protect the Scottish currency against the circulation of dubious foreign dollars gave the mercantile community a serious problem and a well-founded grievance. On the political and religious front, the forcing through of the Five Articles of Perth made many think that even the emasculated Scottish parliament had been pushed too far, and revived what had been a waning Presbyterian faction among a new generation of ministers.

Charles showed no awareness that ruling Scotland as an absentee monarch presented any serious problem at all. Until he had reigned for nearly eight years the only Scotsmen whom he knew personally were those at his English court. He had been less than four years old when, as a sickly child who had only recently learnt to walk and talk, he had followed his parents south in 1604. He did not revisit Scotland until his coronation as King of Scots twenty-nine years later, and his next and last appearance there was in 1641. He had none of his father's old hankering for a union of the crowns and an integrated kingdom of Great Britain, and he was far less sensitive to Scottish fears of becoming a mere province. His aim was not, however, to subordinate Scotland to England but to subject it to his personal authority. It suited him that it was a separate kingdom, because with its weaker institutions he thought he could control it better.

Like James, he governed through a privy council in Edinburgh, but in various ways he changed its character as well as its personnel. He initially appointed forty-seven councillors, including twenty-seven noblemen who held no office of state. But since attendance gave the latter no direct contact with the king, few of them ever appeared, and the real decision-making devolved upon a small core of officials. These indeed protested when he raised the quorum to eight, for they did not always muster so many. The real innovations, however, lay in his rigid separation of the privy council from the Court of Session, Scotland's highest law court, and the exclusion from the latter not only of councillors but of noblemen. In principle it seemed a progressive move to separate the executive from the judicial function and to clear the Court of Session of nobles with no professional qualification in law. In practice it involved the removal from the court of some who had been appointed judges for life, which was doubtfully legal, and the disqualification from the council of some of its most expert and experienced members, the legally trained ones who were also judges. There had been a time in James's reign when *all* members of the Court of Session had been privy councillors. The real purpose of these 'reforms' was not to achieve constitutional propriety, however, but to forestall any questioning by either the council or the judiciary of a measure that Charles had prepared with an absolute minimum of consultation, and now expected his Scottish servants to implement without discussion. This was his act of revocation.

There had been so many royal minorities in Scotland—Charles was in fact the first monarch in over two centuries to inherit the crown at an age above fifteen—that it had become the accepted right of a new king, on arriving at an age between twenty-one and twenty-five, to revoke any grants of royal property that had been made in his name before he assumed the personal exercise of the royal authority. Since there had been no minority, he being twenty-four at his accession, Charles's right to an act of revocation was questionable, yet he intended not only to exercise it but to extend it beyond the practice of his predecessors. On the basis of earlier statutes which had made it illegal ever to alienate land annexed to the crown without parliament's consent, his act revoked grants not only of crown property but of that of the Kirk, and not only those made during minorities but *all* such grants since 1540—sixty years before he was born. The significance of the date is that it preceded the Scottish Reformation and the dissolution of the religious houses, so the title of all ecclesiastical property that had passed into lay hands during and since those events was now in question. Not only were vast quantities of land at stake, but a comparable slice of the country's wealth in the shapes of tithes, or teinds as they were called in Scotland. And unlike most earlier acts of revocation, Charles's had teeth.

Every substantial landowner in the country was threatened by Charles's act, the nobility most of all, but he never intended to exploit the powers that he had assumed to the full. He had several objects in mind, most of them justifiable in principle. He wanted to show the magnates who was master, and to curb the power that they wielded through hereditary offices and other feudal rights. He wanted to make the terms on which some of them held their land more favourable to the crown, and generally to improve its revenues. He wanted to settle the confusions and ambiguities that undoubtedly beset the payment of teinds, and by means of them to provide better for the many parish clergy with woefully inadequate livings. What he failed to appreciate sufficiently was that by threatening most of the landed classes with large-scale dispossession, and then graciously regranting to them most of what they had long regarded as their own, he would earn not gratitude but resentment and distrust. It looks very much as though, in assuming such powers and implementing them as secretively and selectively as he did, he was bent on asserting his authority in a manner that would set the tone for his reign. Equally without consultation, and to scarcely less consternation, he erected a council of war and a similarly novel commission of exchequer, and he re-established a commission for grievances (first set up in 1623) with powers so enlarged that it was plausibly seen as an attempt to introduce a Scottish Star Chamber.

Amazingly, he expected his chief ministers to authenticate the act of revocation unquestioningly with the great seal and privy seal of Scotland, and the privy council to enforce it without even having a sight of its text before it was a fait accompli. He must have been very ill-informed about previous revocations, for he was genuinely surprised that his own raised such a fuss. When the privy council protested against the whole packet of measures that it was ordered to implement in October and November 1625, he was seriously offended. A group of councillors took the wintry roads south to put their case to him, which they did at a series of meetings in the withdrawing chamber at Whitehall in January. It tells us something about his style of kingship that on these occasions he alone was seated; Buckingham stood on his left, the Lord Chancellor of Scotland on his right, and when the Scottish councillors spoke they knelt. They made rather more progress in less formal sessions with Buckingham, seated round a table.[1]

The detailed execution of the revocation and these other early measures need not concern us. Charles proved not entirely inflexible, and he scored a limited success in the regulation of teinds—though very little in improving his regular Scottish revenue. Achievement fell far short of expectation. His clumsy authoritarianism simultaneously alienated the older nobility and his Scottish administrators, and made bad blood between the latter and the Scottish people. These tensions were eased somewhat during a period of five years, beginning early in 1628, when William Graham, Earl of Menteith, established himself as Charles's chief agent in the government of Scotland. As president of the council he managed it adroitly when he was present, and by travelling on average twice a year between Edinburgh and the English court he kept the king in closer touch with Scottish affairs and Scottish feelings than at most other times during the reign. He knew better than to oppose Charles's policies directly, but his advice as to what was practicable often took the hard edges off them. In particular, his success in tempering the implementation of the act of revocation took much of the heat out of the nobility's animosity towards it. His disgrace in 1633 left the faction-ridden Scottish administration weakened, and deprived the king of a vital link with the Scottish aristocracy. The tortuous story, too long to tell in full here, is typical of Scottish politics and reflects no credit on any of the participants. Menteith had royal blood in his veins, being descended from David, Earl of Strathearn, who was reputedly King Robert II's son by his highly dubious first marriage. King James I of Scotland made David's grandson surrender the earldom of Strathearn for the greatly inferior one of Menteith. In a fit of antiquarian vanity Charles's minister, the seventh earl, persuaded him to reverse the exchange and restore him to the earldom of Strathearn. Thereby he made enemies, and some jealous magnates and privy councillors, chief among them his confidant the Earl of Traquair, Treasurer Depute, made out that Menteith had never renounced his rights as a blood descendant of Scottish kings. They speciously charged him with having actually said he should rightfully be King of Scotland. Charles made some effort, but not enough, to ward off his disgrace, and Menteith, financially ruined, languished under house arrest until December 1637.[2]

Traquair was now the rising power, and after a long and devious quest he secured the dominant post of Lord Treasurer in 1636. He was an adroit political fixer and a tolerably competent financial administrator, but in a serious

---

[1] Peter Donald, *An Uncounselled King: Charles I and the Scottish Troubles, 1637–1641* (Cambridge, 1990), pp. 16–17.

[2] Maurice Lee, Jr., *The Road to Revolution: Scotland under Charles I, 1625–37* (Urbana and Chicago, 1985), chs. 2 and 3.

crisis he could be counted upon only to put his own advancement or survival before his obedience to the King's commands. Charles, it must be said, was not making his Scottish council's task any easier. Having excluded most of its best talent by debarring the judges of the Court of Session, he further altered its balance by appointing bishops to it on a lavish scale. By the end of 1634 eight of the Scottish bishops were privy councillors, and John Spottiswoode, Archbishop of St Andrews, had just been appointed Lord Chancellor, the first churchman to hold that office since the Reformation. This injudicious involvement of the bishops in secular administrative and political functions went down even worse in Scotland than in England, for they were regarded as very much the king's creatures; they have been well described as 'the civil servants of absolutism'.[3] For advice on Scottish affairs, however, Charles looked not to his council in Edinburgh, whose job (as he saw it) was to carry out his commands, but on those Scottish nobles who had been his courtiers, and hence to a greater or lesser degree anglicized. Sixteen of them held offices in his household in 1638. Highest in rank was his kinsman James Stewart, Duke of Lennox, the hereditary Lord Chamberlain and Lord High Admiral of Scotland and the kingdom's premier peer. But Lennox had little Scottish blood in his veins; he was born and bred in England, and he did not even visit Scotland until he accompanied the king there for his coronation. His personal influence as Charles's close companion was not inconsiderable, but he was a political lightweight. More effective and ambitious politically was James Hamilton, Scotland's only marquis. He had come to England with his father, James I's trusted friend, when he was ten, and before he was fourteen he was married to a neice of Buckingham. He was still only nineteen when both James and his father died, but such was Charles's favour and affection towards him that in addition to lavish royal gifts, he received Buckingham's lucrative office of Master of the Horse on the favourite's death. By 1635 he was a member of both the English and Scottish privy councils, but at that time he had paid only one visit to Scotland since his early boyhood. In contrast with Lennox, however, he had his roots and the bulk of his landed wealth there; nevertheless after Menteith's fall Charles was woefully short of counsel from men who knew the Scottish political scene at first hand. English historians have not on the whole been kind to Hamilton, and it is true that he was not equal to the impossible tasks that Charles imposed on him from the outbreak of its Scottish rebellion onward; but a case can be made that he always strove to serve his master after his fashion, sometimes in despite of himself, and at the end he sealed his loyalty with his life.

Charles's sole visit to Scotland before the troubles began was for his coronation in 1633. It had been announced five years earlier and several times

---

[3] Julian Goodare, 'The nobility and the absolutist state in Scotland, 1584–1638', *History* LXXVIII (1993), 177, 180.

postponed, and if the long delay was not enough of a wound to Scottish pride the ceremony was made an aggressive display of alien rites. Whether it even occurred to Charles to be crowned at Scone, as most Scottish kings had been since early times, or Stirling, which had been more recently favoured, we do not know. His first choice of venue was St Giles's, Edinburgh's principal church and soon to be designated a cathedral, but he settled for the abbey kirk at Holyrood, where James II had been crowned. A splendid procession down the royal mile set forth his regal power with suitable pomp, but the four-hour coronation service aroused deep disquiet. Its framework was that of Holy Communion according to the English Book of Common Prayer, which struck the Scots, who were quite unfamiliar with it, as half way to the Mass. A stage 24-feet square had been constructed at the east end, from which further steps led up to a communion table placed altarwise. Two lighted candles stood on it, and behind it hung a tapestry depicting the crucifixion, before which the bishops genuflected as they passed. Five of them officiated with Archbishop Spottiswoode, all wearing white rochets and stoles of blue and gold, the likes of which had not been seen in Scottish worship since the Reformation. Laud, whom Charles had just made a privy councillor of Scotland, was prominent with them on the dais. Other bishops, who may have jibbed at such vestments, sat below it in their black gowns. To the coronation oath prescribed by Act of Parliament in 1567 Charles pointedly added a promise to preserve to the clergy all their canonical privileges, and specifically to defend the bishops.[4] He was not to foresee that before he next visited Scotland episcopacy there would be swept away lock, stock, and barrel.

The first Scottish parliament since 1621, and the last before the rebellion, began its business two days after the coronation and held its final plenary session eight days after that. Virtually all initiative was delegated as usual to the Lords of the Articles, whose selection was manipulated in the same way as in 1621, but to encourage them to dispatch swiftly the programme of legislation which he personally had helped to prepare, Charles himself attended most of their meetings. The Articles were docile enough, and he decreed that there should be no debate in the final full meeting of parliament. Nevertheless some of his most cherished measures had a quite unusually rough passage there, despite the fact that he ostentatiously took down the names of those who spoke against them. He got his revocation ratified, but there was real resistance to the confirmation of the Five Articles of Perth and of his power to regulate clerical dress, while some of his new taxes came close to being thrown out. The powerful Earl of Rothes was particularly bold in opposition, and two lords whom he was about to elevate to earldoms, Loudoun and

---

[4] John Morrill (ed.), *The Scottish National Covenant in the British Context* (Edinburgh, 1990), ch. 1 (by Morrill), pp. 2–3.

Lindsay, had their promotions stopped because of their outspokenness. All three were to be leading Covenanters five years later.

Charles had no desire to linger in Scotland. He made a brief progress, which took him no further north than Stirling, and then set off home. His whole stay in the country had lasted just over a month, the same time, almost exactly, as he had spent on his leisurely journey northward to the border. He left a fair number of individuals gratified by the favours he had dealt out, and a royal visit was such a rare event that it was naturally greeted with a good deal of popular acclamation. Charles himself reckoned it a great success, but he was never very clever at distinguishing between the spontaneous popular enthusiasm that royal appearances nearly always generated in those times and the considered responses of the political nation. He left the nobility chafing at their loss of power and influence under their chilly and alien monarch, who knew them little and seemed to value them less. He left the tax-paying classes, those of Edinburgh in particular, resentful of the heavy increase in their burdens that he had steamrollered through parliament. Above all, he left a deeply religious nation justifiably apprehensive that he intended to bring its faith and worship and church government into conformity with those of England.

That fear rested in more than the coronation service. Wherever Charles worshipped during his Scottish visit he insisted on the use of the Anglican rite and vestments. Soon after he got home he sent orders to Bishop Wedderburn, the Dean of the Chapel Royal at Holyrood, that all services there should be conducted according to the English prayer book, pending the preparation of a Scottish one, and that communion should be received kneeling. Next May he instructed all members of the Court of Session to take the sacrament there twice a year. In the same month he formally directed the Scottish bishops to prepare a Book of Common Prayer and a set of canons, the first to secure uniformity in worship, the second the same in discipline. Some months earlier he had decided to create a new bishopric of Edinburgh, with St Giles's as its cathedral. The building currently housed three kirks, divided by partition walls. He ordered that these should be demolished and that two new churches should be built in compensation; one, the beautiful Tron Kirk, was actually erected. There were good administrative grounds for a see of Edinburgh, and the opening up of St Giles's was a great architectural gain, but he had interfered autocratically with the way the people of the Scottish capital had chosen to worship, and since the heavy building costs fell on them they did not thank him. He could not foresee that in restoring St Giles's to its full glory he was creating a theatre for the most fateful riot of his reign.

In all the vast changes that he intended to make in the religious life of Scotland, he never had a thought of involving what nearly all protestant Scots still regarded as the highest ecclesiastical authority in the realm, the General

Assembly of the Kirk, even though it had not been allowed to meet since 1618. He approved the new book of canons in 1635 and had it published in January 1636, upon no other authority than that of his royal prerogative. Regarding church government, it took the power of bishops over their dioceses for granted, but made no mention of presbyteries or of the General Assembly. It forbade ministers to offer extempore prayers, as was their common practice, or to use any other than the forms prescribed. Most provocatively of all, it commanded the use of the Scottish Book of Common Prayer, which was not yet completed, on pain of excommunication. It reaffirmed the Five Articles of Perth, which *inter alia* required communicants to receive kneeling, and it ordered that communion tables should be placed at the east end of the church. In December 1636 a proclamation of the Scottish council ordered that the new prayer book should be used everywhere, and that every parish should purchase two copies by Easter; yet the first printed copies only reached Scotland in May 1637. The Scottish bishops had done their work on it with reasonable dispatch, but the king insisted on closely scrutinizing every draft, in consultation with Laud and Bishops Juxon and Wren; Laud himself records that Charles 'carefully looked over, and approved every word in this liturgy'.[5] Laud was his willing lieutenant, but it was essentially the king's decision to impose the book on Scotland, and the Scottish bishops found their freedom in drafting it heavily restricted by his requirement that it should be based as closely as possible on the English Book of Common Prayer of 1549 (not 1559). They did secure significant concessions, notably in the office of Holy Communion, and in the use throughout of the word 'presbyter' instead of 'priest', but they could not shake Charles's insistence on the retention of numerous saints' days in the church's calendar, and on the inclusion of a dozen chapters from the Apocrypha, which the Scots rated much further below the canonical scriptures than English churchmen did.

The differences between the Scottish and English books were greater than used to be supposed, but the new services were so much closer to the English rite than any form of worship that the Scots had known for generations that they can be forgiven for seeing them as much the same. The preface to the Scottish book was quite open about the king's desire for uniformity of worship throughout his three kingdoms on the basis of the English Common Prayer, and expressly condemned the practice of praying extempore. The ban on this, and the insistence that sermons should only be preached in the context of long sequences of set forms, seemed to the Scottish clergy a denial of their mission and an insult to their gifts. The book's emphasis on the sacraments ran counter to their conception of the Kirk's main function. As to the

---

[5] Quoted from Laud's *Works*, VI, 504–6 in Donald, *An Uncounselled King*, p. 48. The classic account, with all relevant texts, is by Gordon Donaldson, *The Making of the Scottish Prayer Book of 1637* (Edinburgh, 1954).

Communion itself they saw a world of difference between a congregation seated at the table while their minister, facing them, broke the bread as Christ had done among his disciples, and a surpliced celebrant performing an act of consecration at what looked all too like an altar, with his back to the communicants, while they awaited their turn to kneel at the rails and receive. The rubric was not specific about his stance, but this is what it suggested, and though kneeling had been prescribed by the Articles of Perth it had not been widely enforced. There was of course not a word in either the canons or the Prayer Book about lay elders and kirk sessions, which played such a vital part in Scotland's religious life.

The manner of imposing such great alterations upon the nation's worship and church order was almost as objectionable as their content. For the Articles of Perth James had obtained the reluctant assent of a General Assembly and a parliament, but Charles decreed the use of the Prayer Book, as he had the canons, simply as an act of prerogative. The only Scottish clergy whom he consulted were the bishops, who instantly became far more unpopular than they already were. The despotic and threatening tone of the royal proclamation which commanded the universal and exclusive use of the book, months before the public could have a sight of it, was typical of Charles's style. The Scots, besides loathing it for its own sake, saw it as one more move in the subordination of their country to England, even though that does not seem to have been his intention. But they had before them the recent *cause célèbre* of John Elphinstone, Lord Balmerino, who typified the link between religious opposition and national pride, and whose fate warned others who might be tempted to resist—or so Charles thought, not reckoning that it might prove more of a beacon to the Scots than a deterrent. Balmerino had been boldly critical of the king's ecclesiastical measures in the 1633 parliament, especially of his claim to determine what apparel ministers wore when conducting public worship. Subsequently he was found in possession of a remonstrance against such policies, which he had not himself drafted but had annotated in his own hand. It was never presented, and it is not clear that he showed it to anyone but Rothes and his own man of business, but the offending copy was leaked to Archbishop Spottiswoode, who took it to the king. Charles immediately had Balmerino arrested, and on his refusal to submit insisted that he be tried for treason. Traquair presided over the trial in March 1635, and when the packed jury was equally divided he gave his casting vote for a verdict of guilty, merely because Balmerino had not revealed the document and betrayed its author. But such was the public outcry that Traquair himself joined in persuading the king to grant a reprieve, which was followed a year later by a full pardon. The whole shabby business helped to ensure that when ministers of the Kirk held meetings during 1635–6 to concert their opposition to the king's ecclesiastical policies, they were not short of sympathizers among the nobles and lairds, though it was agreed that their lay champions should keep their heads low until public reaction to the Prayer Book could be gauged.[6]

The Scottish council fixed Sunday, 23 July, for the introduction of the new services, and its members walked in procession to St Giles's for morning worship—except for Traquair, who preferred to attend a kinsman's wedding far away, and Lord Lorne, the old Earl of Argyll's heir, who found himself suddenly indisposed. The rest soon found themselves at the heart of the riot of the century. They and the dean, who conducted the service, were pelted with folding-stools, clasped bibles, and other missiles, while a great crowd outside battered at the doors and hurled stones at the windows. The bishop was stoned as he fled from his cathedral; the dean shut himself up in the steeple. There were simultaneous demonstrations in other Edinburgh churches, and women took the same conspicuous parts in them as they did in St Giles's. They were of course by no means spontaneous; we have a glimpse of a planning meeting where some enterprising Edinburgh matrons agreed that women should lead the protests so that their men could take over when the disturbances really got going.[7]

The Scottish council had expected some trouble, but not the explosion of public outrage which actually confronted it. It soon showed how little stomach it had for the struggle that the distant king had wished on it, and how differently its lay and ecclesiastical members viewed the situation. Three days passed before it sent a report of the riots to the king, and then, nervous of his reaction, it misleadingly played them down, blaming them on the bishops' 'imprudent precipitation' in imposing the Prayer Book—though the bishops had of course merely obeyed the king's and the council's own orders. Spottiswoode and some fellow-bishops sent him their own account, blaming Traquair; but the bishops themselves were split between conservative men with Erastian leanings (the majority) and a few thorough-paced allies of Laud, the chief of these being Maxwell of Ross, Whitford of Brechin, and Wedderburn of Dunblane. On the advice of Spottiswoode and some of the former, the council ordered on 29 July that until the king's pleasure was known both the new and the old forms of service should be suspended, at least in Edinburgh, where for several weeks the only public worship consisted in listening to Sunday sermons. Faced with more and more petitions against the Prayer Book, it declared that its order to the parishes to purchase it did not extend to actually using it!

This was not only in flat contradiction to the Book of Canons and its own earlier directives, but an act of direct disobedience to the king's orders. The

    [6] Lee, *Road to Revolution*, pp. 157–62, 208–12; David Stevenson, *The Scottish Revolution 1637–44* (Newton Abbot, 1973), pp. 56–61.
    [7] Stevenson, *The Scottish Revolution 1637–44*, p. 58, citing H. Guthry, *Memoirs* (2nd ed., Glasgow, 1747), pp. 23–4.

council had already had his reply to its first report of the riots, which was angry and uncompromising: he directed it to support the bishops in enforcing the use of the new services, without any intermission. He wrote separately to the bishops, instructing them similarly. Largely because the council had not informed him fully and promptly of the full seriousness of the situation, he was not yet aware that it could not both obey his commands and maintain the public peace. A concerted campaign of petitions against the prayer book was under way; sixty-eight of them had come in by 20 September, from presbytaries, burghs, and parishes. Most had been drawn up by ministers and signed by their associated elders, but leaders of lay society were mustering in Edinburgh to lend them support. A group of nobles met there on 19 September to distil the gist of the local petitions into a national one, which was endorsed next day by a larger meeting of twenty nobles (including Rothes, Balmerino, Loudoun, and Lindsay), over eighty ministers, numerous lairds, and commissioners from many burghs and parishes. This national petition was presented that same day to the council, which had belatedly written to the king to tell him how grave a confrontation he faced in Scotland, and proposed that some of its members and some leading ministers should come and confer with him. It was now digesting his reply. He would have none of it; to concede a conference, he wrote, would make it appear that he had either 'a very slack council or very bad subjects'. The Prayer Book must be enforced at once, and the rioters against it must receive exemplary punishment.[8]

The council made some tokens of compliance, but Traquair connived with the authors of the national petition in producing a toned-down version of it, such as the king might be expected to read without exploding. This was committed to Lennox, who was in Scotland for his mother's funeral, along with samples of the more violent local petitions, in the hope that such evidence would convince Charles that some degree of compromise was imperative. A few days later the city of Edinburgh sided decisively with the petitioners. So far the burgh council had tried hard to avoid offering any open defiance of the king's commands, without necessarily going so far as to obey them; but the last straw was an order from him, most reluctantly complied with, to elect as the city's provost Sir John Hay, clerk register of the privy council and his most sycophantic supporter on it. On 26 September it presented its own strong petition against the prayer book to the council, and the effect on the other Scottish burghs was dramatic. Very shortly all but Aberdeen had joined the cause. The leaders of national resistance, still assembled in Edinburgh, decided to send out an 'advertisement' to all the presbyteries in the country; they entrusted the drafting of it to Archibald Johnston of Wariston, a fanatically Presbyterian lawyer with a gift of words that he was soon to apply to the

National Covenant itself. It brought in not only several hundred fresh petitions but a much larger gathering of supporters, especially laymen, than ever before. Nobles, lairds, burgesses, and ministers took to holding their separate meetings; opposition was beginning to take on the complexion of a movement of the estates of the realm, acting consciously as such.

Charles's reply to the council's letter and the petitions might have seemed calculated to pour fuel on the flames, but neither he nor anyone else in England yet appreciated how hot the situation in Scotland had become. If Lennox really tried to convey it, he failed. The king's letter, read on 17 October, removed the affairs of the Kirk from the council's authority altogether, so that it could neither receive petitions nor make concessions on matters of religion. He ordered the council and the Court of Session to leave Edinburgh, first for Linlithgow and then for Dundee, and commanded that all the petitioners assembled in the capital should depart within twenty-four hours. The council issued proclamations accordingly, but the petitioners stayed put and the people of Edinburgh broke into violent riots—more violent than those of July. In one episode the Bishop of Galloway, notorious as a Laudian and a persecutor of conventicles, was mobbed by several hundred angry citizens, and when Traquair, Hay, and other lay councillors came to protect him they too were roughly handled. Soon afterward the council, finding itself besieged in its own chamber, had to swallow its pride and seek the protection of the leading petitioners, who escorted it to the temporary safety of Holyroodhouse.

The nobles gathered in the city were not responsible for the riots, but they now took an important initiative. They instructed the lairds and ministers to stay there, regardless of the council's orders, while they considered a 'Supplication' which had been drafted for them by David Dickson, one of the leading dissident ministers. In contrast with the watered-down national petition that Lennox had taken to London, it roundly denounced the bishops as the authors of a pernicious book of canons and a liturgy riddled with errors, and charged them with sowing discord between the king and his subjects. Indeed its attack on them went further than some of the clergy had so far wanted to go, for not all who opposed the prayer book shared the aristocracy's animosity towards the episcopate in general. But the national Supplication was signed on 18 October by 30 nobles, 281 lairds, 48 burgesses, and 123 ministers, and then widely circulated through the country for further signatures. Within a month about half the Scottish nobility had put their names to it, including young James Graham, Earl of Montrose, the king's future champion. So had all the burghs that mattered except Aberdeen, St Andrews, and Inverness.

The Supplicants, as they were henceforth called, organized themselves ever more closely, and were not without sympathizers on the council itself. One such was Sir Thomas Hope of Craighall, the king's Lord Advocate. They returned to their homes after the Supplication had been signed and presented, but they reassembled in Edinburgh in mid-November, partly to elect a hold-ing committee to stay and consider the king's reply to it, but also for larger purposes than they cared to disclose. The folly was now revealed of removing the council to Linlithgow, when so many of its members were lukewarm or disaffected that at first it could not even find a quorum there, while abandon-ing the capital to the Supplicants. It deputed Traquair, Lorne, and the Earl of Lauderdale to go to Edinburgh and persuade them to go home; if necessary they were to charge them to do so in the king's name (though who was to enforce such a charge was an unanswerable question). The Supplicants refused, claiming their right to meet for peaceful petitioning under a recent concession by the council itself. In a tough negotiation the next day, a small committee of nobles, lairds, burgesses, and ministers pressed for permission to hold meetings in the shires to elect commissioners to come to Edinburgh in order to hear the king's answer. Most of the council were unhappy about granting it, but Sir Thomas Hope gave his authoritative legal opinion that the right to assemble was theirs by law.

In the election of commissioners that now began lay the origins of the so-called Tables, which developed early in the next year into something like a provisional government of Scotland, though their organization as such evolved by stages. What the Supplicants planned at this stage was a represen-tative body consisting of all the nobles active in the cause, together with two lairds from each shire, one or two burgesses from each burgh, and a minister from each presbytery; but no assembly ever sat in quite this form because far more lairds and ministers came up to Edinburgh than the scheme provided for. The four estates continued to hold separate meetings, and soon adopted the practice of choosing small committees to sit on in the capital during the lulls in the developing conflict, when the majority could safely go home. These committees came to be called Tables because in Scottish usage the word could be used, like board in English, to describe the men who did business round the piece of furniture in question; being less formal, 'table' carried less of an impli-cation than 'council' or even 'committee' that its members were usurping the functions of the established agencies of the king's government (as they increasingly were). Each estate had its Table, but the most formidable was the fifth or general Table, consisting of the active core of the first (that of the nobles) with a few representatives of each of the other three. It was consti-tuted effectively on 6 December 1637 and more formally on 23 February 1638, just before the National Covenant was launched; it was after that that the term Tables became publicly current. By then the general Table had become a revolutionary executive, with Johnston of Wariston as its highly influential clerk and chief publicist.[9] The organization of the Tables in general probably

[9] Allan I. Macinnes, *Charles I and the Making of the Covenanting Movement 1625–1641*

owed something to freemasonry, which had been attracting members of the nobility and others of the Edinburgh elite during the 1630s.

Meanwhile Charles had not even deigned to reply to the national Supplication, and his response to the October riots was typically provocative. His first hint of conciliation came in an instruction to the council, received on 7 December, to issue a proclamation declaring his abhorrence of all popish superstition and disclaiming any innovations against the laws of his native kingdom. That was not going to satisfy anyone. Placed in an impossible position, Traquair and Roxburgh for the council met on the 9th with five leading Supplicants at Holyroodhouse and tried to induce them to moderate their stance. But the Supplicants rejected their proposals, and proceeded to submit a 'declinator', which formally denied the right of the bishops on the council (i.e. most of them) to sit in judgement on their grievances because they were interested parties. They also presented an enlarged supplication which extended its condemnation to the Scottish Court of High Commission. The council, which was now sitting by the king's orders at Dalkeith, wriggled until 21 December before it gave way to heavy pressure and agreed to receive these unwelcome documents; but in the interim Wariston drew up a protestation for the Supplicants, affirming that their grievances must be redressed through accepted constitutional channels. This was an early intimation of the pressure for a General Assembly and a parliament that was soon to become irresistible. Upon the council's receiving the declinator and the new supplication the Tables dispersed from Edinburgh, but they left behind a strong holding committee, whose chief members were Rothes, Loudoun, and Balmerino.

At this stage Charles sent for Traquair, though not so much in order to consult him on how to save the situation in Scotland as to berate him for trafficking with the Supplicant leaders and failing to support the bishops. Traquair reportedly told him that to enforce the use of the Prayer Book he would need an army of 40,000 men; his advice was to withdraw it and concentrate on asserting his civil authority. Charles was not to be convinced, and he sent the Treasurer back with a proclamation that utterly dismayed him, though he warned his master of its consequences in vain. The council, now moved again on Charles's orders to Stirling, heard it read there on 19 February. It offered no concessions on the prayer book, for whose contents the king took full personal responsibility. Those who had gathered without his permission to frame petitions and declarations against it were liable to 'high censure, both in their persons and their fortunes', but he would overlook their offences if they returned home at once and engaged in no more meetings. Any who disobeyed, however, would be subject to the penalties of treason. As Gardiner

(Edinburgh, 1991), pp. 166–9; and see the same author in Morrill (ed.), *The Scottish National Covenant in the British Context*, pp. 107–8.

wrote, the proclamation 'was virtually a declaration of war'.[10] In the shorter term, it triggered the National Covenant.

News that the king's response was utterly negative sped back to Scotland much faster than Traquair travelled. By 6 February the holding committee knew enough to summon the Tables back to Edinburgh, and by the 16th Wariston was apprised (one would like to know by whom) of the main points of the king's proclamation. When it was first published at Stirling, the leading Supplicants were there to make a protestation, and they organized further formal protests when it was read out at Linlithgow on the 21st and Edinburgh on the 22nd. There were now about 2,000 of them and their sympathizers in the capital, and they sent further circular letters to their potential supporters far afield, summoning them to Edinburgh for 'the most important business that ever concerned this nation'.[11] This was the context in which, on the 23rd, they publicly constituted the fifth or general Table as potentially a provisional government. Its first act, unanimously approved by the other Tables that same day, was to commission 'a band of mutual association for offence and defence', which was published five days later as the National Covenant. Wariston was again the chief draftsman, assisted by Alexander Henderson, and the text was revised by a sub-committee of the first Table consisting of Rothes, Balmerino, and Loudoun, who carried the ultimate responsibility for it. Henderson was perhaps the most eloquent and influential of all Scottish ministers, and prominent in opposition to the prayer book from the beginning. He combined a convert's enthusiasm for Presbyterianism with considerable diplomatic skill. Wariston was still in his twenties, and one of the most complex characters to be caught up in these events. He kept a voluminous diary which presents him as a soul in torment, endlessly wrestling with his conscience, engaging in long dialogues with his God, and alternating between utter dejection in face of supposed divine judgements and exaltation over apparent blessings. Yet the Covenanting leaders appreciated his astuteness as a man of business, his precociously acute political sense, and his knowledge of Scottish history. He was also well versed in the story of the Dutch revolt, with its useful parallels, and in the political thought that it had generated, particularly in the work of Althusius (Johann Althaus). In the public declarations and manifestoes that he prepared he showed a flair for finding forms of words that would gloss over potential divisions, and in pursuit of unity he was adept at presenting a revolutionary cause as a conservative one. The contrast between his public and his private persona parallels that between the lucid English of the documents that he drafted for the Supplicants and Covenanters and the broad Scots in which he communed with his maker in his diary.

[10] S. R. Gardiner, *History of England from the Accession of James I to the Outbreak of the Civil War* (10 vols., 1883–4), VIII, 326–8.
[11] Stevenson, *Scottish Revolution*, p. 82.

'Banding' had a long history in Scotland, and it had first been turned to religious use when the protestant nobility formed the Band of the Lords of the Congregation in 1557. This married the magnates' age-old practice of joining together under mutual bonds for some political or social purpose to the Reformers' concept of a covenant, whereby the faithful entered into a solemn pledge to each other and to God to walk together in the ways of the Lord. The last such national band had been in 1596. The present National Covenant began by repeating in its entirety a confession of faith dating from 1581, variously known as the Negative Confession or the King's Confession. It had been sanctioned and signed by James VI and ordered to be subscribed throughout the kingdom, but James had been only fourteen at the time, and it must be seen historically as a move in the intense power-struggle that followed the overthrow of the regent Morton rather than an expression of the king's personal convictions. But in a phase of Presbyterian ascendancy it had been confirmed by a General Assembly in 1590 and reimposed by the king's council, and it was obviously helpful to invoke the stamp of royal authority for its condemnation of saints' days and auricular confession, its branding of the papacy as Antichrist, its rejection of the Roman religion as utterly corrupt and erroneous, and much else that implicitly repudiated the spirit if not the letter of the new Prayer Book. It affirmed convictions that were very far from those of Charles and Laud, but very close to what most Scots had grown up in.

Having rehearsed the confession of 1581, the Covenant recited a long list of Scottish statutes which condemned popery and idolatry and upheld the true protestant religion as professed by the Kirk. The Covenanters' fear that the Prayer Book and Canons were the thin end of a popish wedge was genuine, and not only because they shared the suspicion of English puritans that Laud and the Arminians were deliberately heading the Church of England back towards Rome. There was a strong catholic element among Charles's Scottish courtiers, including the Earls of Douglas, Nithsdale, Semple, and Abercorn. George Con, the papal agent at the court of Henrietta Maria from 1636 to 1639, was a Scot and an astute charmer; Charles notoriously loved his company, and enjoyed plenty of it. The catalogue of statutes that the Covenant reaffirmed was studiously selective, omitting the confirmation of the Articles of Perth and all those that had granted authority to the bishops, or confirmed them in it. There is indeed no mention of bishops in the Covenant, other than a passing disapproval of the 'civil places and power of kirkmen', though it expressly upheld the authority of national assemblies, presbyteries, and kirk sessions. This silence was obviously tactical, aimed at accommodating the many who hated the Caroline innovations and the threat to Scotland's political integrity in the manner of their imposition but had no quarrel with the Jacobean synthesis of episcopacy and Presbyterianism.

Constitutionally, the Covenant's careful listing of the statutes which its sub-scribers swore to uphold implied that there were other acts whose authority they disputed. Herein lay a challenge to the positive law of the land such as would not be heard in England until after the first Civil War.

In the final and positive part of the Covenant, it solemnly committed its subscribers to the same objectives as had inspired the earlier general bands, namely to defend true religion and uphold the king's authority. As regarded religion, they would neither implement the innovations in worship or church government, nor recognize the civil offices and authority conferred on churchmen, until these had been 'tried and allowed in free assemblies, and in parliaments'. In civil matters they would maintain to the uttermost 'the king's majesty, his person, and authority, in the defence and preservation of the foresaid true religion, liberties, and laws of the kingdom'. Thus their commit-ment to true religion (as they defined it) was absolute, while to the king's authority it was conditional, depending upon his employing it to uphold their religion, laws, and liberties. In defence of these ends they pledged their mu-tual support and assistance, 'so that whatsoever shall be done to the least of us for that cause, shall be taken as done to us all in general, and to every one of us in particular'.[12]

There has been much argument as to whether the Covenanting movement was really as centrally concerned with religion as the Covenant itself pro-fessed, or whether it was essentially a nationalist revolution in which religious issues acted as precipitants. But these are not mutually exclusive alternatives; it meant different things to different participants, and for most of them it was a matter of degree. Those who see its inspiration as primarily secular point to the ways in which Charles's rule as an absentee king had alienated all classes of society, and to the nobility's assumption of the leadership some months before protests escalated into rebellion. They note how politically sophisti-cated the organization of petitions, supplications, and protestations was, cul-minating in the Covenant itself, and how all the four estates were involved at each stage. They rightly point out that some leading nobles, Rothes in particu-lar, were neither strong in their religious convictions nor godly in their per-sonal lives. It can readily be granted that quite a number of magnates were drawn to the Covenant more by a hope of recovering their old ascendancy in central and local government than by devotion to the Kirk. The Scottish aris-tocracy was never homogeneous. It included a substantial court interest, for besides the sixteen peers already mentioned who held places in the king's household, a dozen more were linked to the court through kinship or direct contact. That accounts for a significant proportion of the eighty-nine adult

---

[12] Full text in *A Source Book of Scottish History, Vol. III, 1567 to 1707*, ed. W. C. Dickinson and G. Donaldson (1954), pp. 95–104.

peers living in 1638, and there were others, including the non-courtier catholics, who were thoroughly alienated by what was going on in Edinburgh. A list of the nobility, probably drawn up in the middle of 1638, named slightly more as for the king than for the Covenant.[13] Nevertheless a strong core of Covenanting nobles was as devoted to the religious cause as anyone engaged in it. We shall see how they and the *politiques* parted company in the second Civil War of 1648.

It has also been argued that the economic grievances of merchants, craftsmen, miners, and fisherfolk played a greater part in aligning the burghs behind the Covenant than has generally been allowed. Grievances there certainly were, not only because Charles's government failed to meet Scotland's urgent needs, especially in the provision of a sound currency, but because it constantly tended to subordinate her interests to England's. That was the case with the fishing, coalmining, and saltmaking industries, and the raising of the duties levied on Scottish exports to match the English rates was also much resented. But the burghs were never foremost in the protest movement against the religious changes, and the corporation of Edinburgh, where so much economic activity was concentrated, was notably hesitant about joining it. Discontent with policies that hurt people in their callings and their pockets doubtless made them readier to embrace the Covenant, but would never have led to rebellion by itself. For all their grievances the Scots were a very quiet people before 1637. The imposition of the prayer book transformed them.

For some time before then there had been a large and rapid increase in the number of devotional and theological works published in Scotland, especially in the 1630s. It suggests that the educated laity's interest in such matters had been growing, well before the crisis of 1637–8. Scottish divines had been preoccupied with the biblical concept of a covenant between a dedicated nation and God for years before that crisis gave it such dramatic immediacy. But when the day came round in March 1638 for mass subscriptions to the Covenant to be taken in the churches throughout the land—a day of national fasting appointed for the purpose—there were scenes of deep popular emotion that took even the ministers by surprise. A highly charged spirit of evangelism attended these solemn ceremonies; the rejection of the prayer book evoked a passionate response from great masses of the laity, who evidently found in the Covenant a release from spiritual bondage. Support for it was not universal, but it is significant that where pressure had to be applied to gain subscriptions it was in those areas where Presbyterianism had least taken root, such as Aberdeen and some other parts of the north. Elsewhere, from now on, the preachers held forth Scotland as a chosen and covenanted

---

[13] Bodleian Library MS Dep. 6.172, fo. 11, cited and discussed by Morrill in *The Scottish National Covenant in the British Context*, pp. 15, 27.

people, a second Israel, taking up the vanguard of the people of God in Europe and leading the nation towards a more perfect reformation—even a new heaven and a new earth. The Covenanters, especially their lay leaders, were fired by a variety of motives, but what gave the national movement its main force was an intense religious fervour.

Was the Covenant itself a revolutionary document? The continuing disagreement among historians over the question is really a tribute to the skill with which it was composed, so as to draw in both those who did and those who did not desire it to have revolutionary consequences. The actual outcome did not depend so much upon the text, which was left wide enough open to cater for a broad range of possible eventualities, as on what the Covenanters were able to hammer out with the king. With another man than Charles, whom as yet they knew little, it could have been quite different. It is fascinating to speculate on what political aims and expectations they had when they launched their movement, beyond forcing the withdrawal of the Prayer Book. All that the Covenant itself committed them to politically was to admit no changes in worship or church government that were not passed by free General Assemblies and parliaments, and to debar kirkmen, meaning mainly bishops, from civil office. They denied that they had any intention of diminishing the king's greatness and authority, but that was common form in seventeenth-century manifestoes, and rather hollow in view of the powers that the Tables had already usurped from the council. The constitutional safeguards that the Covenant invoked were time-honoured. Its promoters certainly meant to put a stop to Charles's style of autocratic rule from afar, and some leaders doubtless looked further into the future than others, but there is no sign that most of them, at the outset, desired any more than a return to the kind of government that Scotland had enjoyed before James set about subjugating General Assemblies and muzzling parliaments. Most may well have hoped that the banding of the nation would suffice to make the king give way.

They may not even have seriously contemplated the possibility that he would go to war against them with an English army in order to get his way. If they had, they would surely have made contact with potential allies in England before embarking on the Covenant. There were some later allegations that they did so, and Laud suspected it at the time, but the evidence for it is slight and unconvincing. They did, however, send copies of the Covenant to London as soon as it was signed, and a Scottish minister called Eleazar Borthwick who resided there, and had been employed in diplomatic work by Hamilton, sought to win friends for it in court circles. But there was no open propaganda to enlist English support until later, when they found themselves faced with war in good earnest.

The Covenant was formally launched when the nobles and lairds in Edinburgh signed it in Greyfriars kirk on 28 February, followed next day by nearly three hundred ministers and the commissioners of the burghs. While the ministers were subscribing, the privy council met in Stirling at the summons of Chancellor Spottiswoode and other bishops, but only one of their order attended it. Most bishops now were not so much keeping a low profile as staying out of sight altogether. Spottiswoode himself wrote to excuse his own absence, honestly registering his advice 'to lay aside the book and not to press the subject with it any more, rather than to bring it in with such trouble of the church and kingdom as we see'.[14] Traquair wrote to Hamilton that it would be as easy to establish the mass in Scotland as the new prayer book. The council virtually gave up trying to execute the king's instructions or to counter 'the general combustion'. It sent Sir John Hamilton of Orbiston, the justice clerk and a respected moderate, to explain to the king that the country was in crisis because of religious innovations which were generally seen as contrary to law, and to beg him to suspend the offending orders and listen to the Covenanters' grievances. Charles returned a cold reply, expressing surprise at the disorders in Scotland and at the council's advice. He asked that Traquair or Roxburgh should come and explain what it really intended. Both men came to London, and so did Lord Lorne, very likely at Charles's request; Traquair may have suggested that Charles should appoint him as his commissioner in Scotland. He and Lorne certainly travelled back in the same coach. Lorne, who was soon to succeed his father as Earl (later Marquis) of Argyll, was to become the leader of the Covenanters, but he had not formally joined them yet. He brought with him a paper from some of the chief of them, however, stating their minimum demands, which now included annual General Assemblies, abolition of the High Commission, a reduction in the power of bishops, and no further enforcement of the Articles of Perth. In a long private interview with the king, Lorne acknowledged his own general concurrence with these objectives and spoke very frankly about his country's grievances. Charles showed respect for his outspokenness, but appointed Hamilton as his commissioner to treat with the leaders of the Covenanters in Edinburgh.

Hamilton did not want the job, and he has often been judged unduly harshly for failing to execute it with credit. The fact is that he was given an almost impossible brief, and this goes much further to explain his ill-success than any shortcomings of his own. He lacked first-hand experience of Scottish affairs, for he had not resided in Scotland for the last ten years (he was twenty-two when he left it), and in some moods he frankly hated the country. He was a courtier rather than a statesman, and he had a somewhat inflated view of his own political skills, as he had of his military prowess. But those skills were not inconsiderable, and he did his best according to his lights to employ them

---

[14]  Quoted in Stevenson, *Scottish Revolution*, p. 87.

in his master's interests. He and Lorne were friends, but unlike Lorne he was not burdened with strong personal beliefs about the religious merits or demerits of the prayer book and canons. If he had been given more freedom to manoeuvre, his relative detachment from the confessional and personal strife that were keeping Scotland on the boil could have been an advantage. He has been accused of lacking firmness and boldness, but he was bold enough in telling the king the truth about Scottish feeling when he became aware of it, and in warning him what the consequences would be if he persisted in his policies. Charles got much better advice from Hamilton the *politique* than from Wentworth the despot, who counselled that Scotland should be reduced by force and brought 'under the government of an English Deputy, if not an English law'.[15]

Unfortunately Charles was already contemplating force when he sent Hamilton to Edinburgh. Among his courtiers were a number of other Scottish nobles, and he sent home as many of them as he could, ahead of Hamilton, to raise a royal interest north of the border. They merely increased the distrust with which Hamilton was received when he finally arrived in Edinburgh on 8 June 1638. He was hobbled by the king's instructions. Charles furnished him with two alternative proclamations and gave him discretion as to which to publish. Both promised that the prayer book and canons would not be pressed except in 'such a fair and legal way' as would satisfy his subjects that he intended 'no innovation in religion or laws'.[16] The first version promised pardon for past disorders on condition that all signed copies of the Covenant were surrendered, but warned that those who retained them or refused to renounce the document would be declared traitors. The second did not specifically demand surrender, but threatened that force would be used to restore order if the Covenanters did not pledge their total obedience to the king; and if the necessary force was not to be found in Scotland, he would lead an army from England in person to reduce them. He empowered Hamilton to dismiss disloyal councillors, to arrest anyone who engaged in public protestations, and in the last resort to proclaim rebellious lords as traitors. It was in vain that Hamilton warned Charles frankly that he could only get what he wanted by force, and that his English subjects would be unwilling and his Irish ones unable to supply it. He tried to persuade the king, now and later, that the Covenant need not necessarily be incompatible with royal rule over Scotland, but Charles would not hear of it. 'So long as this Covenant is in force,' he wrote, 'I have no more power in Scotland than as a Duke of Venice; which I

[15] Quoted in C. V. Wedgwood, *Thomas Wentworth, First Earl of Strafford 1593–1641: A Revaluation* (1961), p. 251. On Hamilton see John Scally, 'Counsel in crisis: James, third Marquis of Hamilton and the Bishops' Wars, 1638–1640', in John R. Young (ed.), *Celtic Dimensions of the British Civil Wars* (Edinburgh, 1997). Dr Scally is preparing a full-length study of Hamilton.

[16] Quoted in Gardiner, *History of England*, VIII, 339.

will rather die than suffer.'[17] One is left wondering how many more of his subjects in all three of his kingdoms might have died in their beds if he had died in his in 1638. The Covenanters were justified in distrusting him, for he had by now set his mind on war. The apparent concessions regarding the prayer book in his draft proclamations were so worded that he could put what construction he liked on them once Scotland was fully in his power.

In the end Hamilton published neither version, but he did agree to return to England and convey the Covenanters' point of view and minimum demands to the king. There was no question of their renouncing the Covenant itself, and they insisted on the calling of a General Assembly of the Kirk and a parliament. Just after he left Edinburgh he received from Charles a third proclamation, with a firm order to publish it. Over the prayer book and the canons it went no further than the previous two, but it did promise that the king would summon a free assembly and a parliament at his convenience. In order to promulgate it, Hamilton needed an act by the council to register it. Returning to Edinburgh, he persuaded all but two of the still active councillors, who now met at Holyroodhouse, to sign the act, but the leading Covenanters were so dissatisfied with the king's offer that they persuaded the majority to change their minds. So the king's commissioner was forced to tear up the act ratifying a proclamation expressly ordered by the king, because the king's Scottish councillors were threatening to sign the Covenant themselves if he did not.

Both sides were openly preparing for war by this time. The Covenanters were already buying arms in the Dutch Republic, and bracing themselves for a fight on more than one front. Invasion from England was not the only threat, for they faced possible resistance in the north and west. The northeast, especially Aberdeenshire, was the territorial base of the Gordons, whose head, the second Marquis of Huntly, had been brought up at the English court with Charles and his elder brother Prince Henry, and was a staunch episcopalian. The attachment to episcopacy in the region was not solely due to Huntly's influence; Kings College Aberdeen played its part, and a group of its theologians and associated ministers known as the Aberdeen Doctors helped to put up a determined resistance to the Covenant. Westward, in the Highlands and Islands, opposition to it came mainly from the catholic chieftains and their clansmen, whose loyalty the king had an obvious interest in cultivating. The main bulwark of the protestant interest in the west lay in the territory of the clan Campbell, whose chief, the Earl of Argyll, was the most powerful of all Scottish magnates. The old earl, who was to die in November, had converted to catholicism in 1617, but his heir Lorne was very firmly protestant, though not yet a committed opponent of episcopacy and not yet a

---

[17] Quoted in Conrad Russell, *The Fall of the British Monarchies 1637–1642* (Oxford, 1991), p. 56.

Covenanter. Given his friendly relations with Hamilton, it was not inevitable that he should become the king's most formidable enemy in Scotland. That he did so was a measure of Charles's outrage to Scottish patriotism and his disregard for Lorne's own legitimate interests.

A complicating factor, which linked Scotland with Ireland, was the old clan enmity between the Campbells and Macdonalds, over a wide extent of Highlands and Islands territory. The Macdonalds were very consciously of the same stock as the MacDonnells of Ulster, whose current chief, Randal MacDonnell, second Earl of Antrim, will crop up again in our story. Given the right circumstances and leadership, Macdonalds and MacDonnells could still act together as one clan. Antrim was by far the largest landowner in Ulster, indeed one of the greatest in all Ireland. He was a grandson and a great admirer of the Earl of Tyrone who had fled the country in 1607, and a patron of the present earl's Irish regiment in the Spanish Army of Flanders. But his father had cultivated James's favour by supporting the plantation of Ulster, surrendering around 2,000 acres near Coleraine, and adopting an English lifestyle and English landlord–tenant relationships. He leased a lot of land very profitably to Lowland Scottish settlers and built on a lavish scale, yet he kept a foot in both cultural camps, for he clung to the catholic faith and the old Gaelic language and values, and brought up his son in them. Young Randal, after completing his education in France, came to Charles's court in 1627 and spent over ten years there, visiting Ireland only on brief occasions, though he kept an astute eye on the improvement of his Ulster estates. In 1635 he married Buckingham's widow, who already had four children and was his senior by seven years. But she was hugely wealthy, both through her late husband and as the Earl of Rutland's daughter, so he put up with his deserved notoriety as a fortune-hunter to enjoy both the income and the privileged access to the king and queen that his marriage secured for him. After succeeding to his father's title in 1636, Antrim and his wife drew well over £20,000 a year from land, pensions, Irish customs, and other sources, which was getting on for five times the mean landed income of the English peerage. Yet Antrim was such a reckless spender and gambler that he was nearly always heavily in debt. His more serious contemporaries found him shallow, vain, untrustworthy, of mediocre intelligence, and prone to nasty tantrums, and despite a recent attempt to put him in a better light it is not easy to disagree with them. But as a young man he had good looks, including striking red hair, and he was clearly an accomplished courtier. Both the king and the queen enjoyed his company, and his wife, besides being one of the leading catholics at court, was an intimate of Con.

Good as the pickings were in England, however, Antrim had to return to Ireland in September 1638 to try and reduce his debts, which were running at over £40,000. His homecoming was most unwelcome to Wentworth, who thoroughly disliked and distrusted him. His debts were not the only reason for his return. He had a longstanding claim to the peninsula of Kintyre in western Scotland, which the Campbells had taken from his Macdonald cousins many years ago, and which James I had assigned to the seventh Earl of Argyll in 1607, along with the island of Jura. He saw in Charles's present needs a chance to reverse that grant, so in May and June 1638 he offered to raise his clansmen on both sides of the Irish Sea for the king's service. His friend Hamilton commended the scheme to Charles, who allegedly promised Antrim whatever of his former lands in Kintyre he could recover from the Campbells. Lorne got wind of the deal, which not unnaturally helped to drive him into the arms of the Covenanters. It brought the king nothing.[18]

Since early in June the central authority of the Covenanters had been further formalized. Representatives of the lairds, burgesses, and ministers served on the fifth Table according to a system of rotation, ostensibly to secure wide involvement and spread the workload. But in practice a small caucus wielded most of the initiative when it came to policy-making. Rothes was probably the most powerful figure, though Loudoun and Montrose were very prominent too, and the influence of Johnston of Wariston as clerk to the fifth Table is incalculable. Wariston had contacts in England and Ireland, and received good intelligence of the king's military preparations. He had a particularly fruitful meeting on 10 June with Sir John Clotworthy, a puritan Anglo-Irishman with a large estate in Ulster, who was en route for England and promised to keep him well posted. Wariston also busied himself with propaganda designed to enlist friends for the Covenant in England. He was the main author of *A Short Relation . . . for Information and Advertisement to our Brethren in the Kirk of England*, whose burden was that the Reformation was in danger in both kingdoms. The Scottish Prayer Book (it warned) portended further popish innovations in England, for the English prelates who lay behind it were acting in concert with the catholics.

Hamilton returned to Scotland in mid-August with fresh instructions which were designed merely to hold off a conflagration until the king was ready to invade. He was to summon a General Assembly, but to ensure if possible that the bishops should sit and vote in it, and that one of them should be its moderator. He was first, however, to present a list of demands that the Covenanters must meet before he sanctioned its election, the stiffest being that they should dissolve all their meetings (including presumably the Tables) and stop pressing for signatures to the Covenant. Charles was still hoping to delay the assembly until he could deploy enough armed force to avert it. But Hamilton found the Covenanters adamant in rejecting his demands, and

---

[18] The last two paragraphs are heavily indebted to Jane H. Ohlmeyer, *Civil War and Restoration in the Three Stuart Kingdoms: The Career of Randal MacDonnell, Marquis of Antrim, 1609–1683* (Cambridge, 1993), chs. 1–3.

interestingly the strongest resistance to them came from the lairds' Table. The most they would agree to, and that reluctantly, was to postpone elections until Hamilton had had time to consult the king again. They gave him until 20 September.

Before leaving Scotland he privately met Traquair, Roxburgh, and another councillor, the Earl of Southesk, and signed with them a set of articles of advice to the king. They urged him to abandon the Prayer Book and canons unequivocally, annul the High Commission, and suspend the Articles of Perth, pending a Scottish parliament. But their constructive proposal was for an alternative covenant, which became known as the King's Covenant, and was quite cleverly designed to take the wind out of the Covenanters' sails. Like the National Covenant, it reaffirmed the Negative Confession of 1581, but instead of the rebellious band devised by Wariston it repeated a relatively loyal one of 1590, whereby subscribers bound themselves to support the king in suppressing papists and promoting true religion and obedience to the crown. Charles hated the Negative Confession and was loath to give up the Prayer Book, but he realized by now that he could not go to war with the Covenanters before 1639. This was partly because in his determination to keep Scottish policy in his own hands he had not put the state of Scotland before the English privy council until 1 July. So eventually he agreed to all the Scotsmen's advice, empowering Hamilton not only to revoke the prayer book and canons and to summon an assembly and parliament, but even to promise his assent to the repeal of the Articles of Perth. It is most unlikely that he meant to honour these concessions permanently, but he saw it as his prime need to stave off open rebellion until he could confront it with sufficient military force.

The King's Covenant had sufficient success to disconcert the Covenanters, until the Glasgow Assembly consigned it to history. It collected about 28,000 signatures, 12,000 of them in the region of Aberdeen. But the Covenanters themselves were not idle while Hamilton was in England. As soon as he had departed, Wariston and two others drew up directions for the holding of elections to a General Assembly between 21 and 25 September, regardless of whether or not he formally summoned one. They also decided vital questions about its composition without giving Hamilton or the king any say in the matter, and after a twenty-year intermission there were large questions to be settled. Three main interests were in conflict. The strict Presbyterians, including the majority of ministers, wanted the assembly to be constituted as Andrew Melville had conceived it and to consist exclusively of representatives of church courts. The lay Covenanters, however, dependent though they were on the support of the ministers and the religious fervour that their preaching kept on the boil, had a particular need in the political situation of 1638 for the large presence of nobles and lairds that General Assemblies had always included in the past. Third and very much last was the interest of the king, which if he had to face an assembly at all was to maintain his father's methods of rendering it amenable. James had not only brought bishops into it in increasing numbers; he had appointed king's commissioners as full members on his sole authority, and added various nobles and lairds as their 'assisters' or assessors, all with voting rights.

The Covenanters had no intention of admitting any bishops at all, except as plaintiffs to submit to the assembly's judgement on their offences, and they claimed that the Jacobean assemblies of 1606–18 had been unlawful. They took as the basis for the forthcoming one an act of 1597 which had sought to eliminate royal intruders and to compose the General Assembly exclusively of members elected by the presbyteries, but they modified its manner of implementation so as to secure a strong presence of nobles, lairds, and burgesses in the guise of lay elders. This caused consternation among strict Presbyterian ministers, and threatened to cause serious dissension between lay and clerical Covenanters, for though it had been intended that presbyteries should include some elders when they were originally established they had come to consist only of clergy. The objection was overcome, because the need for strong lay representation in the context of 1638 was obvious, but the dispute portended a rift which was to open wide ten years later. Under covert prompting from the central leadership, powerful local Covenanters exerted a lot of crude pressure, often bullying reluctant ministers into returning useful nobles and lairds as ruling elders, even when their previous activity in church affairs had been slight indeed. Most burgh commissioners seem to have been elected by their town councils from the local oligarchy, and they included many present or future magistrates and past or future members of parliament; but the kirk session to which each belonged was asked for its consent to their election, so a semblance of ecclesiastical representation was preserved. In the event these nominal elders were only a part of the lay presence in the assembly, for in October the Tables ordered that all nobles who had signed the Covenant should attend, and that four to six gentlemen from each presbytery should accompany its elected representatives, to sit with them and advise them as assessors, though not to vote. Each burgh commissioner too was to have up to six assessors, and even gentlemen who were not chosen as assessors but wished to attend were permitted to do so. In these ways the assembly was flooded with supernumeraries, well after the formal elections had been completed. The laymen all came armed.

The Tables, in their covert directions to their trusted friends in the localities, not only told them whom they wanted elected but instructed them to collect all the damaging information against the bishops that they could rake up, whether personal or ecclesiastical. They meant to arraign them before the assembly, and then move to abolishing episcopacy outright. The fate of the bishops became more and more the central issue during the weeks between Hamilton's return to Edinburgh in mid-September and the opening of the assembly on 21 November. He appointed Glasgow as its venue, since it was the one major town besides Aberdeen where the Covenant had met considerable opposition, and lay within his own territorial power-base. The same proclamation announced that a parliament would follow in May 1639 in Edinburgh; it also set forth the king's new concessions and ordered his subjects to sign the King's Covenant. When it was read in Edinburgh, according to Wariston, the common people shouted 'God save the king! But away with bishops, these traitors to God and man, or any other covenant but our own'.[19] Wariston engaged in some ugly correspondence with friends who were planning so to terrorize the bishops that they would not dare to show themselves in public. The King's Covenant worried the Tables, but it rebounded upon Hamilton, whose idea it had been, when Sir Thomas Hope of Craighall, still the King's Advocate but no friend to the king now, declared that episcopacy was contrary to the Negative Confession and urged all Covenanters to sign, since by so doing they could proceed to abolish bishops in the king's name. Not many did so, but the effectiveness of the King's Covenant was seriously undermined.[20]

The formal membership of the assembly consisted of about 150 ministers and 100 ruling elders (including 15 nobles, 36 lairds, and 39 burgesses), but its appearance as it sat in Glasgow cathedral, with all the additional nobles and gentry who sat as assessors or supernumeraries, resembled that of a plenary meeting of the Tables. Hamilton was empowered to dissolve it if necessary as soon as it opened, but he struggled for six days to defend the king's interest, and though he failed on most points of substance he certainly did his best. He contested its composition and exposed serious irregularities in the elections, but he secured no changes. He tried to get candidates acceptable to the king elected to the key offices of moderator and clerk, but the Covenanting leaders had decided beforehand that Henderson and Wariston, the authors of the National Covenant, should be chosen, and so they were. Henderson asked, and was granted, that he might have assessors to assist and advise him, and the fifteen who were elected acted with him as a steering committee for the full assembly, almost as the Lords of the Articles had done for the emasculated parliament. James had used assessors similarly to manage the muzzled General Assemblies of his reign in England, but when Hamilton tried to secure similar powers for assessors of his own they were denied the power to vote. He failed to get a declination and protestation by the bishops heard

[19] *Diary of Sir Archibald Johnston of Wariston*, ed. G. M. Paul, D. H. Fleming, and J. D. Ogilvie (3 vols., Edinburgh, 1911–40), I, 392.
[20] Stevenson, *Scottish Revolution*, pp. 111–14.

until after the assembly's composition had been determined, and when it was finally read it was received with derision.

By the end of the session on 27 November he had run out of procedural devices to delay the broaching of business that he knew would be carried against him, and that he could not possibly countenance. The assembly was now formally constituted, and poised to proceed to judgement upon the bishops, against whom heavy charges had been prepared. He decided to dissolve it the next day, and in reporting this to the king he wrote as though he feared for his life. On the 28th, when Henderson called on the assembly to vote on its competence to judge the bishops, Hamilton broke in, maintaining that it could discuss only what the king had summoned it to discuss. Revealing his knowledge of the Tables' secret directions for the fixing of the elections, and complaining of the way the assembly had treated himself as the king's commissioner, he declared that he could not give his consent to anything that was done in it. Isolated as he was, and forced to quarrel publicly with powerful and popular men, some of whom had been his friends, his stand required courage, but it was unavailing. After a prolonged and bitter alteration with Rothes and Loudoun, and after denouncing the whole way in which the Covenanters had usurped the king's power, he finally pronounced the words of dissolution: 'I in his majesty's name discharge this court to sit any longer'.[21] He attempted to leave, intending that the assembly should terminate with his departure, but the cathedral door had been locked and the key hidden, so he had to wait until it was broken open. As soon as he was gone the assembly voted that it should remain in session, and that the bishops were subject to its judgement.

With great difficulty, Hamilton got the rump of the council to issue a proclamation confirming the dissolution and ordering all the assembly's members to leave Glasgow. It was of course ignored. He could rely on very few of the councillors now. The most serious defection was that of Lorne, who had just succeeded to the earldom of Argyll; he was one of Hamilton's assessors, but did not follow him when he walked out, as the others did. Argyll basked in the warmth of the assembly's response to his continuing presence, even though he was not formally a member and had not yet signed the Covenant. He was even more popular when he announced that like Craighall he had signed the King's Covenant on the assumption that the Negative Confession precluded episcopacy. Seven more privy councillors made declarations to the same effect during the next few days. Argyll had not yet given up all hope of serving the king, but his role in the Glasgow Assembly marked a vital stage in his progress to the leadership of the Covenanting movement.

The assembly sat on for a full three weeks after Hamilton pronounced it

<hr />

[21] Stevenson, *Scottish Revolution*, pp. 121–3.

dissolved, and the Covenanters had cause to feel vindicated in insisting on a strong representation of all four estates. A purely clerical body would probably not have proceeded so boldly, and even if it had it would not have carried so much of the nation with it as the Glagow Assembly did. It not only condemned the Prayer Book as unlawfully introduced and full of popish errors, and deposed all the bishops; it abolished episcopacy outright, annulled the canons and the Articles of Perth, and forbade kirkmen to hold any civil offices or powers. It declared the government of the Kirk to be by kirk sessions, presbyteries, synods, and general assemblies, condemned the six assemblies held between 1606 and 1618 under royal dominance as unlawful and null, and asserted the Kirk's right to annual assemblies in future; it appointed that the next one should meet in Edinburgh on 17 July 1639. It ordered that the Covenant should be signed and sworn anew, together with a supplementary 'Glasgow Declaration' which made it clear that its subscribers bound themselves to abjure episcopacy and the Articles of Perth. These momentous things done, it dissolved itself on 20 December.

With these acts the Covenanting movement took the final step from opposition to rebellion. The participation of so many nobles, lairds, and burgesses ensured that the forthcoming parliament would endorse the assembly's decisions. Yet however strongly secular aims were intermixed in the motivation of many lay Covenanters, the proceedings at Glasgow focused the call to arms on religious issues that drew on deep springs in the national consciousness. The response to that call was fired by the concept of a chosen people covenanted with God, which was preached with intense fervour throughout Lowland Scotland. Yet the Glasgow acts divided as well as united. They went further than many who had opposed the Caroline innovations desired; they supplanted the broad Kirk of King James's days, which had possibly satisfied a higher proportion of protestant Scots (Argyll among them) than any other ecclesiastical regime before or since, with something altogether narrower and less tolerant. Many ministers wondered whether they were exchanging subjection to the dictates of an absentee king for subordination to oppressively present nobles and lairds. Although the nationwide subscription to the Covenant in 1638–9 involved more Scotsmen in a political act than ever before in the country's history, the nation was by no means fully united by it. The autumn and winter's events suggest how easily the crisis might have been averted by more sensitive and flexible handling on the king's part, and raise the question whether war might yet have been averted.

Hamilton, just before his vain attempt to dissolve the assembly, wrote to warn Charles that Argyll must be watched, 'for it fears me that he will prove the dangerousest man in this state'.[22] Yet he kept in cordial touch with Argyll

[22] Quoted in Macinnes, *Charles I and the Making of the Covenanting Movement*, p. 190.

behind the scenes, despite the latter's now open support for the Covenanters. He has been accused of treachery for it, but his conduct will bear a kinder interpretation, even though his personal interests as a Scottish magnate were involved. Whereas Argyll's firm grip on the vast Campbell territories and their inhabitants made him easily the most powerful noble in Scotland, Hamilton's long absence had weakened his power to call on his own dependants and tenantry, large though his estates were. His strong-minded mother, who despite her lately deceased catholic husband was wholeheartedly on the Covenanting side, had successfully courted their loyalty, and when on his first arrival back in Scotland Hamilton had summoned them, few had attended. Since then he had been forced to play a deeply unpopular role, and to be seen as Argyll's friend could help him to regain his personal and territorial influence. Yet the two men shared a larger interest in keeping the conflict within bounds; after all, their failure to do so was to cost them both their heads in the end, and in different ways each man's death was a result of his convictions.

If Charles could have brought himself to listen to Hamilton rather than Laud, and if Argyll had gone on using his powerful influence to moderate the Covenanters' mood of defiance, something might yet have been saved. It was a slender chance, and it would have called for concessions such as Charles was not prepared to contemplate, but it was the only one. Argyll did not cease to attend the privy council until March 1639, or sign the National Covenant until April. Hamilton had two strong reasons other than personal ones for regarding an English attempt to conquer Scotland with deep apprehension, and he was to be justified in both of them. First, as he had told Rothes, if it came to war he expected never to see peace in his country again; and secondly he doubted whether the king would find sufficient support in England to carry it through successfully. In advising Charles, back in June 1638, that he could have his way in Scotland only by armed force, he had warned him that by resorting to it he might hazard all his three crowns. 'The conquering totally of this kingdom will be a difficult work', he wrote, and he feared that England would not be as forward in it as she ought; 'there are so many malicious spirits among them that no sooner will your back be turned, but they will be ready to do to you as we have done here, which I will never call by another name than rebellion. England wants not its own discontents, and I fear much help they cannot give'.[23] It was honest and prescient advice, but it went unheeded. Charles would not entertain the possibility that the English people, so superior in wealth and numbers, would not support him in his just quarrel. He was obsessed now with punishing the Scots; they had dared to pit their notion of authority against his, and his must prevail.

---

[23] Quoted in Russell, *Fall of the British Monarchies*, p. 56; see p. 60 for Hamilton's words to Rothes.

# FIVE

# The Bishops' Wars

As Charles prepared for war during the early months of 1639 he was confronted with three discouraging contrasts. One was between the grand sweep of his plan of campaign and his likely capacity to execute it. Another lay between the effectiveness with which the Scots mobilized their military resources and the dragging, bumbling efforts of the English. And behind both lay the third, which was between the passionate commitment of the Covenanters to their cause and the lukewarmness of most Englishmen—and the downright hostility of some—towards the king's.

He originally planned that the war should be won on Scottish soil with the support of his loyal Scottish subjects, whose number he heavily overestimated. The bulk of his English army was to stand defensively on the borders, while his fleet patrolled the Firth of Forth and strangled Scotland's trade. Hamilton was to land about 5,000 men in Aberdeenshire and join forces with Huntly, who by March had a similar number of men under arms there. The two marquises were to sweep southward together, enlisting as they marched the host of loyal Scotsmen whom Charles fondly imagined to be chafing under the Covenanters' yoke. In Ulster, Antrim had undertaken to raise 5,000 foot and 200 horse, though so far he had had no formal commission. Late in February, Charles abruptly ordered him to have this force ready to invade western Scotland by the beginning of April. Wentworth was thoroughly hostile to this enterprise, and nothing came of it. He had little but contempt for these 'naked and inexperienced Irishmen',[1] who lacked trained officers and looked to his government for arms and equipment which he was most reluctant to furnish, needing them as he did for his own army. He also sensed that Antrim was less interested in collaborating in a grand strategy against the Covenanters than in making himself formidable in Ulster and recovering his clan territory in Kintyre.

Antrim's contribution, however, was never intended to be more than peripheral to the main effort of Huntly and Hamilton in Scotland. There, unfortunately for Charles, the Covenanters struck first. During March the

---

[1] Quoted in Ohlmeyer, *Civil War and Restoration in the Three Stuart Kingdoms*, p. 83.

royal castles of Edinburgh and Dumbarton fell to them without a blow, and at Dalkeith Traquair was forced on the 24th to surrender not only a precious store of arms and powder but the crown, sceptre, and other regalia of the Scottish kingdom. The day after, before he can have heard of that humiliation, Huntly had intelligence that Montrose and David Leslie were marching towards him with a force slightly larger than his own. On the advice of his council of war he sent his troops home rather than risk a battle, and he was forced to accompany Montrose back to Edinburgh as a virtual prisoner. Aberdeen submitted to a Covenanting garrison, and most of the supposedly loyal magnates' castles fell like ninepins.

So even when Charles rode into York on 30 March to place himself at the head of his army, his intended strategy was already in tatters. Since there was now no question of Hamilton attempting an opposed landing in Aberdeenshire, Charles sent him to the Firth of Forth instead, with just three raw regiments. But Hamilton found Leith fortified against him and the whole of Fife and the Lothians up in arms; his own mother appeared in public, pistol in hand, and threatened to shoot him if he set foot ashore. Frustrated, he disembarked his men on two small islands in the Firth and set about shaping them into soldiers. Charles turned to Antrim again, ordering Wentworth to stop refusing him arms and ships, and then on 11 April to give him and his army a commission under the Great Seal of Ireland. This last was promptly countermanded from London by Windebank, who sensibly suggested that the expedition should be put off until the spring of the next year. Antrim welcomed the postponement (as well he might), and was directed, for the present, merely to make a show of threatening invasion.

By May, therefore, the only way of carrying the war to the Covenanters was for the English army to invade Scotland. For this it was quite unprepared, and Charles had not expected so to use it. So far there had been a strong element of theatre in his military preparations, which had been planned more to frighten the Scots into submission than to fight them in the field. For infantry he relied largely on the trained bands, supplemented by pressed men (i.e. conscripts). For cavalry, he summoned all the nobility of England to attend him at York on 1 April, with such horse and foot as they could personally raise. There was more of pageantry than of serious military purpose in this chivalric gathering under the royal banner, though over 800 horsemen attended it. He had planned to raise an army of 24,000, three-quarters of it consisting of trained militiamen and the levies of the nobility and gentry. He actually raised between 15,000 and 20,000, but at least a third and perhaps a half were pressed men. Impressment, in living memory, was something that had mainly befallen the dregs of society—vagrants, prisoners, petty criminals, and other masterless men. It carried a heavy taint, and serious danger too, for not too many pressed men had come home. It is no wonder then that parish constables were unwilling to conscript respectable fellow villagers or townsmen, and that very many who did have the king's shilling thrust upon them either bribed the captain or 'conductor' who had charge of them to let them off or deserted at the first opportunity.

The trained bands should have furnished better material. The deputy lieutenants, on whom the main responsibility rested, made a considerable effort to furnish their counties' quotas, but at heart they were generally inclined to put those counties' interests before the king's. It would doubtless have been different if there had been a deeply felt national cause at stake, as there had been when the Armada threatened England half a century ago, and as there was now for the Scots. As things were, there was a lot of resentment when the king took a county's stock of arms for use outside its bounds, or introduced professional officers with no local roots to help make good the general lack of military experience among the trained bands' own captains. The spirit of localism was at least as strong among the men themselves, who regarded themselves very much as defenders of their own shire, and wanted a very good reason before they would march beyond its borders. Being freemen, mostly of some small substance, very many of them took advantage of a right which the council in its weakness granted them to furnish a substitute to serve in their place. The substitutes were of course untrained, and probably unarmed too, since a militiaman's weapon was often his own property and he would not part with it. So what with substitutes and pressed men, the bulk of the king's infantry were raw levies with little heart in his cause.

Financial provision for his army was precarious, and the troops were kept more or less in pay mainly by the personal contributions of his councillors and courtiers. The payment of Ship Money was for the first time falling far below the quotas set, and the council had to spend an inordinate amount of its time in attempting to enforce it. It was being resisted on a new scale partly because Hampden's test case had been decided so narrowly in the crown's favour, and partly because it was being exacted at the same time as coat-and-conduct money, and two levies of questionable legality were more than many people were prepared to pay, or could afford to. Coat-and-conduct money was a rate imposed on the whole county to furnish each soldier with a good coat and maintain him on the march, at 8*d.* a day, until he crossed the county boundary or arrived at the royal standard. And while there was just enough money to keep the men paid, there was nothing like enough to arm them properly. Such of the trained bands' arms as reached the king's camp were in many cases rusted through or obsolete, and there were never enough pikes and muskets to go round the thousands of pressed men.

The senior commanders of this raw and reluctant army were hardly likely to stir it to great deeds. Charles chose as its general Thomas Howard, Earl of Arundel, partly because he had been Earl Marshal of England since 1621, partly because he had large estates and many tenants in northern England, but chiefly because he knew and trusted him so well. Arundel was (after the king) the greatest connoisseur and collector in the country, but he was also the head of its greatest catholic family, and though he had converted to the Church of England he was widely believed, however inaccurately, to be still a crypto-papist. In a time when most people aged earlier than they do today, he was fifty-four years old and he had no military experience whatsoever. His appointment typifies Charles's hierarchical, quasi-theatrical approach to his confrontation with the Scots. It meant that a great deal of responsibility rested on the shoulders of Arundel's second-in-command, the Earl of Essex, who was appointed Lieutenant-General and General of the Horse—the two commands commonly went together. Essex was one of the few English nobles who had had any serious military experience in the continental wars, and though he had won no glory as commander of the ill-fated expedition against Cadiz in 1625 he might at least be presumed to have learnt from its mistakes. No one had more respect from the serious soldiers in the royal army. But Charles, after appointing him, detached the command of the horse from the lieutenant-generalship and bestowed it, on the pleas of the queen, upon her favourite the Earl of Holland, whose experience of action was confined to a brief spell as a gentleman volunteer at the siege of Juliers in 1610. Arundel was outraged, and Wentworth regarded Holland with deserved contempt. There was bad blood too between Arundel and the Master of the Ordnance, the Earl of Newport, and that was not the end of the animosities among the courtiers who were masquerading as soldiers in the army of 1639.

Whether the Scottish army could have sustained a serious campaign in that year is an open question, but the contrast between the two forces began at the top. The Covenanters' general was Alexander Leslie, who was older than Arundel but had been toughened by thirty years' distinguished service under the great Gustavus Adolphus, who had honoured him highly and finally made him a field marshal. The irony is that when Leslie retired from the Swedish army in 1638 his first intention was to serve Charles I, who before the Scottish rebellion had been hoping to send a force into Germany to aid the Elector Palatine. Once home in his native Scotland, however, Leslie was won to the Covenanters' cause and soon became their invaluable military adviser. It was not only his professionalism in raising, organizing, training, and disciplining troops that gave them the advantage; this 'old, little, crooked soldier' commanded the willing obedience of the Covenanting nobles with as sure a knack as he fired the military spirit of his subordinates. His manner of giving directions to both was 'very homely and simple',[2] but (as Robert Baillie tells us) he knew the difference between commanding mercenaries and

---

[2]  Robert Baillie, quoted in Gardiner, *History of England*, IX, 32.

volunteers, and his combination of military expertise with natural authority was something that would not be found in English armies until the rise of Fairfax and Cromwell.

He had an uphill task, for Scotland had a quarter of England's manpower at the most, and had had even less direct experience of war in the last thirty years. Very few home-dwelling Scotsmen had had even the rudimentary military training of the English militia, except in the Highland clans, and outside Campbell territory very few clansmen were friends to the Covenant. Yet Scotland's very poverty gave her a reservoir of potential military strength in the thousands of young men who left home to serve in the armies of Sweden or Denmark. When recruitment was at its height between 1625 and 1632, around 25,000 went off to fight for pay and the protestant cause—roughly one in ten of all adult Scottish males—and many more were to follow. They included officers as well as men, and a fair number rose from the ranks. Late in 1638 the Tables issued a general summons to all Scottish protestant officers in foreign service to return home, and men of all ranks responded. So although most colonels of regiments and captains of companies were nobles or lairds, the Tables could stipulate that the lieutenant-colonel and major in every regiment and the ensign and two sergeants in every company should be veterans of the continental wars. This leavening of seasoned professionals gave Leslie's army an incalculable advantage, and was probably the chief factor in deterring Charles from launching his own forces against it in 1639.

Nevertheless the raising, equipping, and financing of such an army put an acute strain on Scotland, and its preparedness in that summer should not be exaggerated. Compared with the localism that bedevilled the English war effort, however, the Tables' strong central authority was a great benefit, and the rates that they levied were generally more cheerfully paid than Ship Money or coat-and-conduct money south of the border; if not, they had no hesitation in employing force. The organization that geared the country for war was an interesting mixture of the civil, the ecclesiastical, and the feudal, laced with a strong tincture of Swedish practice, thanks to the influence of Leslie and other veterans. Each county had its powerful committee for war, consisting of a commissioner and other representatives from every presbytery within its bounds, and each maintained two commissioners (or one in the case of the smaller shires) in Edinburgh. The county committees were responsible for raising the quotas of men specified by the central authority and for quartering the regiments stationed in their territory, but the actual selection of recruits lay with the ministers and elders in the rural parishes and with the burgh councils in the towns. Pressed men, however, bulked less large in the Scottish army than in the English, for the fervent preaching of the clergy brought in many volunteers, and the nobles and lairds who took the initiative in raising regiments and companies brought in many of their own kinsmen, tenants, and servants.

Late in May the king established his camp at Birks, three miles from Berwick, and the Covenanting army stood on the defensive some distance north of the border. Estimates of its strength vary, but it may have totalled only half the 20,000 that Gardiner once reckoned, and it was probably outnumbered very considerably by the English forces. But its morale was so far superior as to more than make up the difference in numbers, for its members believed they were fighting for their faith and for their country. Many ministers attended them in the camp and in the field, and the call from the pulpit that had enlisted many of them was refreshed by frequent sermons. On the English side, some priests ministered clandestinely to the fifty-odd catholic officers under Arundel's command, but otherwise chaplains were few, and they did not impress. We get a glimpse of them riding before the troops at their ease and puffing at their pipes of tobacco, but we hear nothing of their preaching. Even if they had tried, they would have had to preach very hard to persuade the average English soldier to put up gladly with the lack of shelter and the shortage of decent victuals and drinkable water (let alone beer) in the camp at Birks. He might share his countrymen's traditional dislike of Scotsmen, but he had no quarrel with their religion, and no particular sympathy with what the king was trying to do to it.

Here is where Charles was very vulnerable, for whereas those Scots who professed loyalty to him had been largely neutralized, there were already many influential Englishmen who felt a positive sympathy with the Scottish cause. The Countess of Westmorland warned Windebank in May that the Scots 'know our divisions, and the strength of their own combination, and that they have a party amongst us, and we have none amongst them'.[3] There was very little open disaffection towards the king in England, but when he had required the nobles assembled at York to swear an oath to fight for him to the utmost of their power and hazard of their lives, Viscount Saye and Sele and Lord Brooke had flatly refused, and were briefly imprisoned. They were probably the two peers who, according to intelligence from Sir John Clotworthy in the summer of 1638, had been seriously thinking even then of settling in Scotland. Clotworthy thought that forty or fifty leading gentry were inclined the same way. Brooke was discovered in treasonable correspondence with the Scots in 1639, but Charles thought it not politic to prosecute him. The Scots were now addressing printed propaganda to a wider English audience. An example is *An Information to all good Christians within the Kingdom of England*, written partly by Wariston and published in February 1639. It roundly blamed the English prelates for seeking to subvert true

---

[3] Quoted in Russell, *Fall of the British Monarchies*, 81.

religion in Scotland, and warned English readers that this was but a step in a design to bring both kingdoms back to Rome. It hoped that an English parliament would shortly vindicate the Scots and recognize that both peoples had a common cause. Its play on the fear of a popish plot touched a raw nerve, as will shortly be seen. It worried the privy council enough to set going a search of suspect houses, and copies were found in about forty of them.

In his uncertainty about the capacity of his forces to engage Leslie across the border, Charles asked Wentworth in May for a thousand men from his Irish army. The Lord Deputy replied that with all the Scots in Ulster taking sides with Covenanters, with all Connaught still to be settled and with the native Irish burning Englishmen's houses in Munster, he would be courting disaster if he split his forces. He offered to concentrate them at Carrickfergus, so as to make the Scots think he intended to invade, but his advice to Charles was to postpone his attack for a year and meanwhile to spin out time with negotiations.

An unhappy military manoeuvre on 4 June helped to convince the king that Wentworth was right. Intelligence had come in the evening before that Leslie had advanced a force to Kelso, only just within the border, contrary to a royal injunction not to come within ten miles of it. Holland was dispatched with about 1,000 horse and 3,000 foot to reconnoitre, and if possible drive them out. His cavalry left his infantry far behind, and came unsupported upon a force of Scottish foot that he reckoned at between 6,000 and 10,000, though Leslie had probably positioned it so that it looked much larger than it was. Holland sent a trumpeter to ask the Scots what they were doing so close to the border; Leslie retorted by asking what the English cavalry were up to on the wrong side of it, and suggested that they should withdraw immediately; which is what Holland did. His humiliating retreat was a blow to the morale of the English forces and gave the Covenanters a political advantage. They advanced their main army to Duns Law on the 5th, and from that position of strength, less than a dozen miles from the king's camp, they sent to him to propose a negotiation. They were uncertain whether their still raw and outnumbered army could sustain a serious campaign; they were still fighting Scottish royalists in the north-east, and they seized what they saw as an opportunity to secure the essentials of what they had taken up arms for without the hazard of a battle.

Charles was strongly urged to treat by the nobles in his camp, and he yielded. His reasons were probably as much political as military. Having learnt, or partly learnt, how limited was the support he could expect from Scottish royalists, he needed time to think and plan afresh. He was beginning to learn how many English, besides the overtly pro-Scottish minority, looked coldly on his quarrel. The Earl of Bristol told him publicly in the camp at Birks that most of the lords there, including the privy councillors present, were resolved to petition for a parliament. That was almost the last thing he wanted, but a military reverse would probably force it upon him, and make it unmanageable. So a treaty it would have to be—though not in his mind as a means to the definitive settlement that the Scots sought but as a stalling operation, to give him time to exploit such political opportunities as it might offer or, if that failed, to renew war with better prospects.

Commissioners from both sides met on 11 June, and signed the Pacification of Berwick a week later. Charles personally participated in the negotiation; indeed he and Hamilton did most of the talking on the English side, and he showed considerable debating skill. He certainly deceived the Scots as to his intentions, but how far this was deliberate is uncertain. It may be, as Conrad Russell has argued,[4] that he and the Covenanters came to the table with such totally different assumptions about the relation between royal and ecclesiastical authority that they found it difficult to speak a mutually intelligible political language. Moreover both sides wanted so badly to avoid fighting, at least for the present, that they were prepared to blur the central issues. The Scots agreed to disband their forces, free royalist prisoners, and restore the king's castles and property; Charles undertook to withdraw his army and convene a General Assembly in Edinburgh in August, closely followed by a Scottish parliament. But on the crucial question of episcopacy the Pacification said nothing directly. It laid down that in future all ecclesiastical matters would be settled by assemblies of the Kirk and all civil ones by parliament, but as to whether Charles was prepared to accept the assembly's inevitable verdict on episcopacy, and to assent to parliament's ratification of it, the two parties left Berwick with very different impressions. The Scots took it that he was so prepared. So did Hamilton; otherwise he was not willing to act as his commissioner in either the assembly or the parliament. But Charles is reported to have promised verbally that he would agree to whatever an assembly *lawfully constituted* should determine, and in his mind an assembly without bishops could not be so described, nor could a parliament. Yet he left the Scottish commissioners believing that in promising a free assembly he was conceding one that was free to determine both its own composition and the future (or non-future) of Scottish bishops. It seems unlikely that he was quite unaware of arousing expectations that he had no intention of fulfilling.

The commissioners had a poor reception when they returned to Edinburgh, and the Tables circulated a letter which openly expressed their disappointment that so little had been gained. They particularly regretted that the king had not been brought to accept the Glasgow Assembly's acts. They also felt that Edinburgh Castle had been surrendered too easily, especially as Hamilton was already provisioning and fortifying it. Their fears were confirmed on

[4] *Fall of the British Monarchies*, pp. 64–7.

1 July when the Scottish council issued a proclamation on the king's orders, summoning to Edinburgh all archbishops, bishops, commissioners, and others who had a right to sit in General Assemblies. They published a paper denying that the bishop had any such right, while the people of Edinburgh vented their indignation by stoning Traquair's coach and roughly handling him and other prominent royalists.

Charles originally intended to attend the assembly and the parliament in person, and it was ostensibly to discuss his journey that he summoned fourteen leading Covenanters to Berwick. Many suspected, however, that he meant to make them prisoners, and they may have been right. Why so many, they asked each other? Only six came, but one of them was Montrose. He had just secured the key objective of Aberdeen for the Covenanters. The city had changed hands three times in a matter of weeks, but on 19 June he routed its latest royalist occupiers at the Brig o'Dee and made sure of it. But he was having doubts now about the Covenanters' objectives, and he and Charles made a strong impression on each other. This was probably when he pledged his future service to the king. After a week's talks, Charles sent the six back to Edinburgh with instructions to return with the other eight. But only two came, the uncompromising Loudoun and the more pacific Lindsay. Charles gave up any idea of going to Edinburgh and sent Traquair as his commissioner. Hamilton was unwilling to act, feeling that Charles had not taken him completely into his confidence, and knowing that he had lost that of the Covenanters almost entirely. He knew he could not handle the assembly without making concessions that were odious to the king, and he told him so frankly. Charles did not trust Traquair, but that did not greatly matter, for he had decided by now that he would have to go to war again, and if he eventually had to renounce the proceedings of the assembly and the parliament, as now seemed certain, it would be easier to repudiate promises made by his commissioner than any that might have been wrung from him in person.

On 27 July he sent Wentworth a brief note in his own hand, calling him home to England. 'Come when you will', he wrote, 'ye shall be welcome to your assured friend, Charles R.'[5] Wentworth's policy towards Scotland was nothing if not robust: it should be reduced to obedience by conquest, and governed as a province.

A week later Charles was back in Whitehall, having left Traquair detailed instructions for his conduct in the general assembly. They show that he was now prepared if necessary to concede the abolition of bishops, though with reservations that neither the assembly nor parliament were likely to accept, and with an obvious intent to leave the way open for restoring them when circumstances improved. He instructed the bishops not to attend, but assured

---

[5] Quoted in Wedgwood, *Thomas Wentworth*, p. 259.

Archbishop Spottiswoode that he meant to remedy in time what he was forced at present to yield. The assembly duly met in St Giles's on 12 August, and after a few days passed a single act which confirmed the condemnation of episcopacy as unlawful 'in this Kirk', the abrogation of the Prayer Book, canons, High Commission and Articles of Perth, the exclusion of kirkmen from civil offices, and the Kirk's right to annual assemblies—everything in fact that the Glasgow Assembly had enacted, though Traquair did succeed, as instructed, in excluding any specific reference to that body. But by assenting on the king's behalf to the act as it stood he went beyond his brief, and he did so again when he and the council, at the assembly's request, passed an act requiring all subjects to subscribe the National Covenant and the Glasgow Declaration. It was no use his trying to qualify these derelictions by entering glosses in the council's register; the king was understandably furious with him.

The assembly was dissolved on 30 August, and parliament met the next day. Whether the king or his commissioner had any control over its proceedings depended on how the Lords of the Articles were chosen, for there had been no challenge yet to their dominant initiative. In the last two parliaments the bishops had played the crucial role in their selection,* but no bishops sat in this one. Nor could the crown rely on its other mainstay, the senior officers of state, who had hitherto sat ex officio with the articles and in parliament. Such was the Covenanters' control over elections that only three officers of state were returned, though one more sat as a noble in his own right. Faced with this difficult situation, Traquair handled it with some skill. He persuaded the nobles to retire with him from the full session to discuss the selection of the lords of the articles, and then argued that in the bishops' absence the eight noblemen should be chosen by the king. Four or five hours of intense debate ensued, in which some including Montrose supported Traquair, while Argyll and others argued that each estate should elect its own articles, which would have destroyed the crown's chief control over legislation at a stroke. As a compromise, the assembled nobles chose their own eight representatives, but allowed Traquair formally to appoint them on the king's behalf. Those eight then selected the eight shire commissioners and eight burgesses, to the vociferous indignation of both estates when parliament reassembled in full session.

All might not have been lost yet for Charles, for the eight elected nobles included not only Argyll and Rothes, his chief opponents, but Huntly, Montrose, and Southesk, his present or future supporters. But the lairds and burgesses whom they chose to sit with them were all Covenanters, and thanks largely to them the Lords of the Articles voted by a majority of two for an act

---

* See above, pp. 27, 90.

whereby in future each of the three estates, now redefined as nobles, shire commissioners, and burgesses, should elect its own representatives on this crucial committee. Traquair declined to commit the royal assent to this measure, but parliament's casting off of its fetters was merely deferred. These Lords of the Articles sat for an unprecedented seven weeks, and most of the momentous constitutional changes wrought by parliament in the following year originated from acts that they drafted. Parliament would have enacted them immediately if Traquair had let it, but he postponed its reassembly in full session no fewer than eight times. Finally he received orders from the king to prorogue it until 2 June 1640, by which time it was hoped in London that the Covenanters would have been subdued by force. The parliament denied the king's power to prorogue it without its own consent, in a protestation drafted by Wariston which broke new constitutional ground. It did not, however, sit on defiantly, as many expected, but appointed representatives of each estate to await the king's reply. The resultant committee was in effect a continuance of the Tables under another name, and was empowered to do whatever was necessary until the full parliament resumed. On 19 November, a few days after it took over, the king's birthday was saluted by a firing of the cannon in Edinburgh Castle, where 130 workmen had been toiling since July to make it defensible. The shock of the gunfire brought down part of the walls, an omen that cannot have been lost on the citizens of the capital.

Earlier in the autumn, Charles had been humiliated by an episode in the Channel which had a most damaging impact on English public opinion, inflamed as it already was by the aid that he was giving to the Spaniards against the Dutch, in the vain hope that it would persuade Spain to restore the Palatinate to Frederick. Five more shiploads of Spanish troops had recently disembarked at Plymouth, to march through southern England and take the shortest sea passage to the theatre of war in the Netherlands. Early in September a fleet of over seventy ships, both Spanish men-o'-war and hired English transports, sailed up the Channel with 10,000 soldiers on board. A much smaller Dutch fleet under Admiral Tromp attacked it in the Straits of Dover, and after a sharp fight the Spaniards took refuge in the Downs. There Tromp blockaded them for over a month, while the Ship Money fleet under Sir John Pennington watched from a distance. Charles sold powder to the Spaniards at an exorbitant rate and haggled with the Spanish ambassador over the price of his continued protection, but he also made contingency arrangements for billeting the troops on English soil if their ships should be driven ashore. Thereby he fanned an already widespread rumour that the Spanish soldiers' real mission was to fight for him against his own rebellious subjects. On 11 October Tromp, now heavily reinforced, attacked the Spanish vessels with gunfire and fireships, within sight of joyous crowds of English spectators. Over twenty ships were driven ashore, others were burnt or captured, and only a dozen or so got away. Pennington had orders to prevent any fighting, but his men might have mutinied if he had tried to protect the Spaniards, and he had the excuse of a fog and a contrary wind; only the catholic faction at court blamed him for keeping out of it. Tromp, before sailing off in triumph, fired a salute of nineteen guns in acknowledgement of English sovereignty over these territorial waters, but that did nothing to assuage the king's indignation or save his loss of face.

This unhappy affair heightened the suspicion that there was a popish plot afoot in England. This had been intensifying over the past two years or so, and was to colour the whole political debate when parliament eventually met.[6] Its factual basis was slender, but it was linked to the current fashion of alluding to the political rivalries at court and in the council in terms of a French faction ranged against a Spanish one. This too was over-simple, for the so-called French party were not so much pro-French as anti-Spanish. Since Richelieu represented the strongest force ranged against the Habsburgs of both Spain and Austria in the Thirty Years War, they looked to France as potentially England's best ally. They included most of the firmest protestants on the political scene, including the Earls of Bedford, Warwick, and Northumberland, Viscount Saye and Sele, Lord Brooke, and Secretary Sir John Coke, and they were in eclipse from 1637 onward. The so-called Spanish party were a mixed group, and those with the most political weight among them favoured a neutrality biased towards Spain rather than active commitment to the Spanish side. They included Laud, Wentworth, Cottington, Windebank, and Arundel. There was nothing 'popish' about Wentworth, but Laud's attitude to Rome was widely misunderstood, Cottington and Windebank were accounted crypto-papists, and most of Arundel's family, including his wife, were avowed catholics. More positively pro-Spanish, to the point of urging a full alliance, were a group of catholic courtiers, including Manchester's son Wat Montagu, Sir Toby Matthew, Endymion Porter (who refrained from professing his faith only so as to retain his court office), and George Gage. They were mostly close to the queen, whose sympathies were with the anti-Richelieu, pro-Spanish *dévots* in France. The virtuoso Sir Kenelm Digby was another catholic who enjoyed great favour at court.

It was not only the number of the court catholics but their open evasion of the laws that fed the fears of a popish plot. The queen and her entourage were privileged, of course. Her splendid new chapel at Somerset House, designed by Inigo Jones and over a hundred feet long, was opened late in 1636. It was thronged on Sundays and holy days, when one mass swiftly followed another, and between masses more than a hundred candles surrounded the reserved

---

[6] This and the next four paragraphs are heavily indebted to Caroline M. Hibbard, *Charles I and the Popish Plot* (Chapel Hill, NC, 1983).

sacrament on the high altar. Henrietta Maria's rash proselytizing, which her uxorious husband was too slow to check, received fresh encouragement after the pope's envoy to her, the Scotsman George Con, took up residence in 1636. Charles took to him, saw him almost daily, and freely discussed foreign affairs with him; there were intimate dinners between the royal couple, Con, and the queen's confessor Father Robert Philip. Con's aim was to convert the king, and though we know that he stood no chance it was not so obvious to contemporaries, especially since the papacy stood ready to ease Charles's financial straits if he went over. Con also attempted to convert Charles Louis, the Elector Palatine, and his younger brother Prince Rupert. Through his intercessions many an English and Irish catholic won relief from the penal laws, which around the court and the capital became almost a dead letter. On feast days up to nine masses were said in his chapel, largely for the benefit of English catholics, who also worshipped freely in the chapels of the ambassadors of the catholic powers, as well as in the queen's. Laud hated all this, and in December 1637 he persuaded the king to issue a proclamation against catholic proselytizing and the participation of English subjects in privileged catholic worship, but the queen got it toned down, and its effect was only temporary. Catholicism remained chic in court circles in the late 1630s, and what was becoming a stream of fashionable conversions continued.

Con did his best to weld the court catholics into something like a party. There were currently nearly forty Jesuits on mission in London; Charles had hitherto disliked their ultramontanism and wanted them withdrawn, but Con's warm relations with them brought them more into the court circle. In the spring of 1638 he secured the appointment of their close associate Sir John Winter, a nephew of the catholic Earl of Worcester, as the queen's secretary. He was on the friendliest terms with Arundel and his catholic countess, indeed Arundel sometimes drove to meetings with the king in Con's coach, emblazoned with the papal arms. Con's aim was not only to gain converts and protect his English, Irish, and Scottish co-religionaries, but to strengthen the Spanish interest in English government circles and weaken that of France. The court catholics were never as weighty or as homogeneous a group as he would have wished, but their political influence has until recently been underrated, just as that of Laud and Wentworth has been exaggerated, at least until Wentworth returned from Ireland. It strongly encouraged Charles to entertain a whole series of proposals, between the middle of 1638 and the outbreak of the Civil War, for bringing in seasoned troops from the Spanish Netherlands to fight for him, in return for English naval support in the Channel and recruiting rights in Ireland. In January 1639, for instance, Father George Gage, the queen's cupbearer and dean of the secular catholic priests in England, carried a commission to his brother Henry, who commanded a regiment in the service of Spain, to negotiate with the governor of the Spanish

Netherlands for 4,400 veterans to fight against the Scots. The privy council was not told of his mission. Nothing came of any of these proposals, but they add to the evidence that those who scented a popish plot were not just imagining things.

Imagination certainly inflated their suspicions, but catholic indiscretion gave them something to feed on. From early in the year a special contribution to the king's military expenses had been demanded from catholics throughout the country, and it was known as the queen's contribution because she pressed it so strongly. Protestants denounced it as a device to stave off the calling of a parliament, and most of the provincial catholic gentry paid up so reluctantly that it was hardly worth the hostility that it aroused. Far from bringing in the £50,000 expected, the first £10,000 was not collected until after the Pacification of Berwick, and its final yield was only about £14,000. The number of catholic officers in the king's army was not very large, but the presence of some well-known courtiers among them made them conspicuous. Taken together with Charles's readiness to employ Antrim's catholic Ulstermen in mainland Scotland, and his desire to bring over a contingent from Wentworth's largely catholic army, it is no wonder that zealous English protestants wondered whose side they should be supporting.

The catholic presence at court was swollen by aristocratic refugees from Richelieu's France. Their political influence was not great, but they fuelled the king's hostility towards the cardinal, whom he suspected of colluding with the Covenanters. The queen saw much of them, especially that arch-conspirator the Duchess of Chevreuse, who was later to make even more trouble for Cardinal Mazarin than she had for Richelieu. She moved to England from Spain in May 1638 and stayed for two years. An even more illustrious and troublesome guest was Marie de Medici, the queen-mother of France, who arrived in October 1638 with scores of her hard-up courtiers. The king did not desire her visit, which was politically very unpopular and horribly expensive, but he could not deny her the honours due to fellow-royalty and his own mother-in-law. He did finally stop her pension in January 1641, but not before she had cost him £800,000 (according to Henrietta Maria), which was not far short of the bill for the first Bishops' War. She finally left for Italy late in June, but died before she got there.

Wentworth's presence was soon felt after he arrived in London on 21 September. It was probably on his advice that Charles set up a committee for Scottish affairs consisting of eight privy councillors. Unfortunately Hamilton was the only Scot among them, but at least it brought Scottish policy formally within the purview of the English government. The committee gave Traquair a rough reception when it heard him report on the Scottish situation on 27 November, which was somewhat hard, since he had incurred the wrath of the Covenanters as a creature of the court. The occasion was historic, however, because Wentworth seized on it to urge that the only remedy now lay in calling an English parliament. Laud and Hamilton supported him; the committee concurred, and the king was soon persuaded. The full privy council unanimously endorsed their advice on 5 December. The Spanish party had hitherto resisted a parliament, fearing an onslaught upon popish counsels and upon catholics generally, but the affair in the Downs had lowered their stock. Laud must have accepted the necessity reluctantly, but Wentworth had a more positive attitude. He had first made his political reputation in the House of Commons, and in 1634–5 he had managed an Irish parliament with considerable skill. To prevent the forthcoming assembly from over-exploiting the crown's financial needs, this same council meeting pledged its members to a loan totalling £300,000. Wentworth headed the list with £20,000, and £200,000 was brought in by Christmas. In January, Charles marked his trust in his new chief minister by making him Earl of Strafford and promoting him from Lord Deputy to Lord Lieutenant.

Charles's sole object in conceding a parliament was to raise the money he needed to renew the war. When the Covenanters sent four commissioners to protest against the prorogation of the Scottish parliament and to request his assent to the acts prepared by the Lords of the Articles, he kept them waiting more than a month before granting them a few strained audiences in late February and March. He then forbade them to leave London, detaining them virtually as hostages. He had got hold of a letter that some leading Covenanters, including Rothes, Loudoun, Mar, Montrose, and Alexander Leslie, had just sent to Louis XIII, justifying their conduct and begging him to intercede for their people with his cousin of England. He confidently hoped that it would be a trump card when he faced the coming parliament. In his own frankly expressed view, he was making one last trial of the traditional way of raising supplies for his and the kingdom's necessities, and if the parliament failed in its duty he would be justified in using extraordinary means. He felt no need to *consult* it about his recourse to arms, though in the recent campaign he had been the first English monarch to go to war without calling a parliament since 1323. As he saw it, he had no obligation to seek the estates' advice, for what he faced was rebellion and they had an unquestionable duty to assist him in suppressing it. It was of course inconceivable that the Commons would vote the million or so pounds that he needed without first securing the redress of at least the major grievances that had been piling up for eleven years.

Historians disagree about the depth and motivation of the opposition that Charles faced when at last he had to listen to parliament. In extreme reaction against the traditional Whig interpretation, which depicted a House of Commons steadily increasing its initiative and striving for a stronger voice in government from Elizabeth I's reign onwards, one revisionist view is that during the personal rule Charles and his ministers built up a viable and not seriously unacceptable system of government, which was brought to an end only by the avoidable error of provoking rebellion in Scotland. England was merely conforming, a little late, to the declining trend of medieval representative institution in Europe as a whole. On this reading, the opposition that exploded in the Short Parliament, and in the first session of the Long, was largely opportunist, factional, and shallow-rooted, and with the emergence of a royalist party in 1641–2 a large part of the political nation rejected its policies.[7]

Those who find this version unconvincing do not have to revert to the old Whig mythology in order to furnish an alternative one. There *is* evidence of a groundswell of discontent in the 1630s, growing stronger as the interval between parliaments stretched out longer and the financial expedients through which they were avoided became more blatant. Dislike of the changes in the Caroline church was by no means universal, but neither was it narrowly based or shallow. The expression of such discontents was muted for several reasons: because the king had publicly warned that pressure for a parliament would be taken for disaffection, because the presses were controlled and private correspondence sometimes intercepted, but above all because government had to go on. Unpopular government was a lesser evil than lack of government, and if gentry magistrates had refused to accept the directions of the privy council they would have courted anarchy, not to mention the disgrace of dismissal. If the king declined to call a parliament there was not much they could do about it, but that does not mean that they suffered gladly the long denial of the traditional mechanism for the expression and redress of grievances. Their hankering for such a remedy did not imply any desire to change the fundamental constitution of the realm, indeed it was consistent with a profound conservatism. It is undeniable that the personal rule was shattered by the Scottish rebellion; the question is how long its flimsy structures could have survived if that misfortune had been avoided. Any war, surely, would have brought them tumbling down, and there is no evidence that Charles ever intended to renounce war permanently in order to preserve them. If some continental entanglement had not provided the trigger, Ireland could well have done so.

The elections to the Short Parliament are a very imperfect gauge of current public opinion, because the majority of elections were still uncontested. In the county constituencies the principal landowners traditionally pre-selected two candidates, and only two, on the basis of social standing rather than political stance. In many cities and boroughs the corporation, often in collusion with the local gentry, presented the electors with a similar fait accompli, and in

---

[7] This is an over-compressed summary of the interpretation advanced by Sharpe in *Personal Rule of Charles I*.

many more an individual patron had a virtual right of nomination. Contested elections, which gave the choice to the populace, were reckoned to mark the failure of the local elite to settle the representation in its own interest. But except in unshakably 'close' boroughs, responsiveness to the electorate was increasing, as was the total number of voters in the country. Only thirteen elections had been contested in James's first parliament, but the number ranged between twenty and forty in the 1620s, and with the Short Parliament it rose significantly to sixty-two. Since two-member constituencies were almost universal, that meant that a quarter of all MPs reached Westminster through a contest of some sort. Nor is that the full measure of this election's response to public feeling, since in many cases where the elite did get their nominees elected unopposed they had to take care, in selecting them, to avoid rousing popular antagonism, and hence rival contenders, by putting forward politically unpopular candidates. By 1640, too, the gentry's own choice often reflected their collective antagonism to the policies of the court, and there were certainly counties in which the godly interest ran a concerted campaign to secure the return of men of their own kind. One way and another, questions of national policy, rather than merely local interests, were of more concern than ever before to both the typical selectors of candidates and to the broader electorate. The sentiments that emerged most widely were hostility towards courtiers and disquiet over the advance of popery—two attitudes closely linked in the public mind. Their expression was to become still more marked in the second elections of the year, in the autumn.

After so long a gap there were far more new faces in the Commons than usual when parliament assembled on 13 April. Only John Pym and Sir Francis Seymour were there out of the score or so of really prominent parliament-men of the 1620s. Seymour typified the conservative gentry who had been antagonized by Charles I's policies but had no wish for constitutional change. He had been made a sheriff in order to keep him out of the 1626 parliament and he had refused to pay Ship Money in 1639, but he was to accept a peerage early in 1641 and ultimately to fight for the king, alongside his elder brother the Marquis of Hertford. Pym by contrast was not a typical member at all. He had no real territorial base and spoke for no county community; nor did he owe his influence to favour at court. Since 1607 he had been an official in the Exchequer as receiver of crown lands for Wiltshire, Hampshire, and Gloucestershire, and the Exchequer remained the chief focus of his loyalties until far into the 1620s. So far, his legendary prominence in the Short and Long Parliaments would have been unpredictable, though he had made his mark in the proceedings against Buckingham and (still more) in the struggle for the Petition of Right. By the 1630s he had leased out his small estate, and he lived in London until his friend Richard Knightley took him into his home at Fawsley in Northamptonshire. His emergence as a major politician is largely to be explained by two changes in his life, both dating roughly from the accession of Charles I. One was the patronage that he won from Francis, Lord Russell, who became Earl of Bedford in 1627, and also in time from the Earl of Warwick; the other was the new direction that ecclesiastical policy took under Charles, for this gave him a cause in which he believed passionately.

Bedford and Warwick were two of the most powerful puritan peers in England, and Pym was closely associated with the latter in the Providence Island Company, which was founded in December 1630 with the purpose of founding an ideal puritan settlement in a rather insalubrious Caribbean Island. As a colonizing venture it was largely unsuccessful, but it kept some of the most influential future leaders of the Long Parliament in close touch during the long years of non-parliamentary rule. Alongside Warwick, Viscount Saye and Sele and Lord Brooke were among its most active members, as were Knightley, John Hampden, Oliver St John, Saye's son Nathaniel Fiennes, and Sir Thomas Barrington. They met regularly at Saye's London house, or at his seat at Broughton. Pym was their treasurer and general factotum, and though he kept his Exchequer post the company absorbed most of his energies in the 1630s. Many of its members refused to pay Ship Money, whose legality the company was responsible for getting tested before the courts. Hampden's case made him a national figure, and St John won scarcely less fame as his counsel; he and Pym spent months in planning strategy with Hampden before the trial opened. Another puritan colonizing enterprise with a largely overlapping membership was the Saybrook Company, named after the two peers most actively involved, and with territory in what is now Connecticut. Pym, Hampden, and Knightley were active in this venture too. Both companies displayed a typical combination of colonizing and commercial initiative with a spirit of constitutionalism and a quest for a truly godly community.

Pym had always been deeply concerned for the purity of religion, though he had not felt it to be in serious danger under James. Never an extremist, he had been angered by those who sought to brand all godly protestants as puritans. But with the Caroline innovations and the rise of the divines whom Pym and his kind called Arminians, religion became a matter of profound concern to him. He had already emerged as a defender of the ancient constitution and an upholder of the supremacy of the law, not least because he believed the true protestant religion to be protected by both. When he found religion, law, and constitution simultaneously under threat, his zeal for all three redoubled. He became the leading champion of the powers and privileges of parliament, not just for their own sakes, but because they were impugned by the likes of Montagu, Neile, and Laud, and because parliament had to take responsibility for preserving the national church against popery when neither its hierarchy nor its Supreme Governor could be trusted to do so.

It was the Speaker of the last parliament, who had been held down weeping in his chair during its violent final scene eleven years ago, who made the opening speech to the Short Parliament, by virtue of his new office of Lord Keeper. Lord Finch, as he now was, had dealt brutally with several opponents of the prerogative in Star Chamber, and as Lord Chief Justice he had pronounced judgment for the crown in the Ship Money case. Speaking now in the king's presence and by his instructions, he conspicuously failed to make any mention of Ship Money, though he did ask for an act to confirm his master's right to tonnage and poundage from his accession onward. His main request, however, was for an immediate, unconditional, and generous grant of subsidies. If that was forthcoming, the king would call another session in the late autumn and would then grant redress of 'just' grievances, though he would expect a further supply then. Finch's rhetoric pitched the king's divine right to determine matters of state uncomfortably high, and there was no mistaking the implied warning against any questioning of his policy towards the Scots, who were guilty of 'foul and horrid treason'.[8] As soon as Finch sat down, Charles himself introduced the Covenanters' letter to Louis XIII, which he commanded the Lord Keeper to read. Through Finch, he made great play of the fact that it was endorsed '*Au Roy*', claiming that its authors had thereby acknowledged the King of France as their sovereign. That was absurd, and probably struck his hearers so; the two words were probably meant merely to direct the bearer and distinguish it from others addressed to other contacts in France—Richelieu, for instance.

On the first day of more than formal business, Windebank read the letter again to the Commons. Harbottle Grimston answered him that there were dangers at home as great as any that he had presented; the liberty of the subject had been widely infringed, contrary to the Petition of Right, and it was parliament's duty to expose 'the authors and causers of all our miseries and distractions in church and commonwealth'.[9] We shall meet Grimston again, as Speaker of the Convention Parliament twenty years later, welcoming King Charles II home with expressions as fulsome as any of Finch's, but now he was taking the lead in putting grievances before supply, and focusing on the king's evil counsellors. Sir Francis Seymour struck the same note: 'though the king be never so just, his bad ministers may corrupt his justice'.[10] That same opening day witnessed heated exchanges in the Lords, after Laud moved that according to custom they should not sit the next day because the bishops would be in convocation. Saye objected, maintaining that their presence was not essential for the House's proceedings to be valid, and Finch eventually

[8] *Proceedings of the Short Parliament of 1640*, ed. Esther S. Cope and Willson H. Coates (Camden Society, 4th series, XIX, 1977), pp. 115–18.
[9] Ibid., p. 137.    [10] Ibid., p. 141.

saved their faces from the chair by pleading his own indisposition, upon which the House voted to adjourn during his enforced absence.

There was a crucial debate in the Commons next day, and the key speeches were by Pym and his older half-brother Francis Rous, a moderate puritan of profound conviction and author of widely respected theological works. The two had spoken in concert before, in 1629, and this time Rous rose first. Contrary to the rules of the House, both men spoke from scripts, and their speeches were early examples of a genre that was addressed as much to the public as to the House itself. They were widely copied and circulated in manuscript, though it was not until the licensing laws began to break down in the following year that Pym's appeared in print. Rous declared that 'the root of all our grievances' was 'an intended union betwixt us and Rome',[11] and repeated the now familiar complaint that upholders of the true protestant religion were being stigmatized as puritans. Conscientious ministers were subjected to illegal burdens, suspended, and driven out. He touched more briefly on Ship Money and other secular discontents, but left these largely to Pym.

Pym spoke for two hours, which was a length to which parliaments were quite unaccustomed, but his masterly exposition of the nation's grievances was an immediate success with the House. Religion, he agreed with Rous, was 'the greatest grievance to be looked into', but he would turn first to the liberties and privileges of parliament, because verity in religion depended on parliament's freedom of debate. In words that Charles must have found deeply subversive, he declared that 'the parliament is as the soul of the commonwealth, that only is able to apprehend and understand the symptoms of all such diseases which threaten the body politic'. It was 'the intellectual part which governs all the rest'; so much for the king's claim to a unique capacity to comprehend and decide matters of state. The first breach of its liberties of which Pym complained was the silencing of debate when the last parliament had been dissolved before grievances had had redress, or even full expression. He spoke for the members who had been wrongfully imprisoned; the judges had had no right to question them over what had gone on in the House, for 'the court of parliament is a court of the highest jurisdiction and cannot be censured by any law or sentence but its own'. He dealt next with grievances concerning religion, starting with the official encouragement given to papists, their intrusion into places of power, their virtual immunity from the recusancy laws, and the presence of a papal nuncio at court. It amounted to a campaign to convert England to Rome, and the bishops' claim to authority *jure divino* and the popish ceremonies that they inculcated were part of it. Finally he expounded comprehensively the abuses of civil government and

[11] Cope, p. 146.

infringements to rights of property, stating them with precision and moderation. The true cause of all these evils, he said, was the long intermission of parliaments, which by law should be held every year. He desired that all these grievances should be set down, after debate, in a remonstrance, with a petition from both Houses for redress.[12]

Before the Commons rose that day, three members proffered petitions concerning grievance from their counties, and four more followed suit the next morning. Between them they covered much the same ground as Pym had done, and they bear the signs of a concerted operation, for the puritan interest was highly organized in all the constituencies involved (Middlesex, Hertfordshire, Essex, Suffolk, Norwich, Northamptonshire, and Northampton town). The counties of origin were contiguous, and all the members who presented the petitions were to be prominent parliamentarians. It was a technique to be more fully exploited in the Long Parliament, with the dual purpose of swaying the Houses and publicizing the issues in the shires and cities concerned. On this first manifestation, however, it struck some unsympathetic hearers as smacking of the practices of the Covenanters.

Pym's speech set the agenda for the Commons' next two working days, most of which they spent in grand committee. This was a procedural device of Jacobean origin, otherwise known as the committee of the whole House, which facilitated freer discussion by replacing the Speaker with an elected chairman, suspending the record in the Journal and relaxing the formal rules of debate. So ready were the members to follow Pym in taking up the unfinished business of the last parliament that they fastened for hours on end on the first of the grievances he had put to them, namely the violent manner of its ending and the proceedings against the eleven imprisoned members. It was the last straw for the king when they sent for the judicial records of the Ship Money case, and he peremptorily summoned both Houses to Whitehall on the afternoon of 21 April. Because of his stammer, he again entrusted the Lord Keeper with the delivery of his message. It was a disadvantage to him that his spokesman was just coming under the Commons' hostile scrutiny, both for his conduct as Speaker in 1629 and for his more recent pronouncements on Ship Money, but it was a self-inflicted one, since he had appointed Finch to the office which gave him this function after he had decided to call a parliament. In a long speech delivered at very short notice,[13] Finch set forth the crown's financial needs as cogently as he could, truthfully declaring that the army now afoot was costing £100,000 a month and that the Ship Money fleet was a far greater charge than tonnage and poundage or any other

[12] Ibid., pp. 148–57; lengthy extracts from the printed version are in Kenyon, *Stuart Constitution*, pp. 183–9.
[13] *Proceedings of the Short Parliament*, pp. 164–7, 303–5.

regular revenue could support. In defending Ship Money, however, he strained belief when he affirmed that the king 'never had so much as a thought to make it an annual revenue', nor was his citing of the Irish parliament's recent generosity as an example likely to impress the Commons. In urging the latter to vote large supplies without delay, he had no specific concessions to offer in return, and he—or rather Charles—was courting trouble when he told the Lords that their assistance would be expected if the Commons were backward in their duty. Charles had yielded to his council's advice so far as to call a parliament, but not so far as to pay the necessary price for a successful one. The very minimum that members could be expected to take back to their 'countries' as a justification for a record load of subsidies were the abolition of Ship Money and a guarantee of frequent parliaments in the future. In imagining otherwise he simply displayed a lack of political competence.

The Commons spent another day on their own business before going into grand committee to consider the king's demand. They debated at length whether they should put supply before redress, and finally decided to request a conference with the Lords on the nation's grievances. To their minds, 'Till the liberties of the House and kingdom were cleared, they knew not whether they had anything to give or no'.[14] On hearing of this, Charles angrily broke off his supper and summoned an emergency meeting of the council to consider an immediate dissolution. Strafford advised him instead to go to the Lords next morning before the Commons' message was read, and to appeal to them to support him in seeking an immediate supply and the postponement of redress of grievances to a winter session. Charles agreed, and before the smaller auditory and familiar faces of the Upper House he spoke in person. His necessities, he said, were 'so urgent that there can be no delay', and he expected a pledge of the Lords' concurrence and assistance before they rose that day. A tough debate ensued, in which all the noble councillors had evidently been briefed to support his plea. But Strafford's repeated appeals to their loyalty were repeatedly countered by Saye, who stubbornly stood up for the Commons' sole right to initiate votes of supply. Eventually the Lords did resolve that in the present situation supply ought to have precedence over grievances, but of the sixty-eight lay peers present (the bishops being of course solidly for the king) twenty-five voted against the motion.[15]

When the conference with the Lords that the Commons had requested was held on 25 April, a Saturday, it was devoted not as they had intended to grievances but to a report of the king's speech and the peers' resolution. The result, when the Commons sat again on the Monday, was entirely predictable. They took great offence at the Lords' invasion of their historic initiative in matters

[14] Quoted in Gardiner, *History of England*, IX, 108.
[15] *Proceedings of the Short Parliament*, pp. 69–79; Russell, *Fall of the British Monarchies*, pp. 111–12.

fiscal, and after much debate they voted it a breach of privilege. The Lords in turn took umbrage, and voted by a massive eighty to two that it was nothing of the kind. Strafford's tactics had succeeded in setting the two Houses against each other, but had split the Lords and brought the desperately needed subsidies no nearer. Very possibly, however, his main purpose by now was to put the Commons in the wrong and so place an early dissolution, if it came to that, in a better light.

Meanwhile trouble was brewing on the ecclesiastical front. On 24 April the Commons threatened a serious challenge to the king's authority as Supreme Governor of the church by questioning the commission that he had recently given to convocation, empowering it to make new canons. In a long debate of religious grievances on the 29th, two things were clear: a fair number of more conservative members were not prepared to go all the way with the godly party, but the great majority, including many future royalists, were profoundly alienated by what had been happening to the church under Charles and Laud. Another conference with the Lords on 1 May, however, and another message from the king through Secretary Vane the next day, brought them back to the matter of supply. 'A delay will be as destructive as denial', Vane told them, adding that the king wanted an answer that day. They knew now, if they did not already, that they were debating under imminent threat of dissolution, and they were so unhappy about it that they were seriously divided. They failed to reach a conclusion, and since it was a Saturday they appointed Monday for a definite answer to the king's demand. When Monday came, Vane brought them a final offer from him: he would give up Ship Money in return for twelve subsidies, spread over three years. They would have been worth £840,000 at the yield of 1621, though considerably less in 1640, and Charles actually needed about £1m for the current year's campaign. What he was offering to give up was worth on paper around £200,000 a year, but Ship Money was already collapsing, for payments had fallen off drastically as soon as elections were called, in the general expectation that parliament would condemn the levy. However, although twelve subsidies fell far short of his needs, no parliament had ever voted so many before, and some members said they could not face their constituents if they granted so much. Others tried to add other concessions to the price ticket, including the abolition of coat-and-conduct money. The debate dragged on till six in the evening, ten hours after the House met, without its coming to a vote.

That was enough for Charles, and he dissolved the parliament the next day. He probably had a further reason, besides its persistent failure in its duty, as he saw it. In the last two days of debate an occasional voice had been raised against the war itself, and that he would not stand. Sir Robert Cooke, for instance, had said how ill an opinion the country had of the war, adding that the king stood in greater need of hearts than of men or purses, but that this war only took heart from some great clergymen, who themselves called it *bellum episcopale*.[16] There is some evidence, though it is not conclusive, that some members had been conferring with the Scots commissioners with a view to bringing Scotland's grievances formally before the House, and that Pym was planning to speak in support of their printed vindication of their case on the very day of the dissolution. Immediately after it, Saye, Brooke, Pym, Hampden, and Erle had their studies searched, presumably for evidence of correspondence with the Scots. None was found, but three other members were brought before the council to answer questions about their speeches in the House, and were imprisoned when they declined to reply. Charles's attitude to parliamentary privilege had not changed much in the past eleven years.

The parliament had lasted a mere three weeks, and it had not passed a single bill. Was its failure inevitable? Success was certainly impossible on Charles's terms of an unprecedented and unconditional grant of supplies on the spot and a vague assurance of redress of grievances (but which grievances?) next winter. If Strafford thought any differently, it shows how far he had lost touch with the political nation. Yet this House of Commons was a more moderate body than its successor in the Long Parliament, and was genuinely divided over whether to go some way towards meeting the crown's needs without delay. Compared with its successor, most of it was less pro-Scottish, and less disposed to religious and constitutional change; a return to the Elizabethan and Jacobean status quo in church and state would have satisfied the majority. If Charles had offered to renounce Ship Money on the first day of this parliament instead of the penultimate one, he might even have got those subsidies.

So can it be argued, as some have done, that he missed a great chance by not coming to terms with the Short Parliament, since he would have had to part with less of his prerogative than he was forced to do later? Any such argument has to assume that Charles was other than the man he was. But even if he had suddenly become amenable to political reason, he could not wipe out the record of his reign so far, and given that he was wholly bent on continuing his war against the Covenanters, twelve subsidies were not going to change the outcome of the coming summer's campaign. In face of the accumulated discontents of eleven years, and after he had gone to war without calling a parliament and then failed to win it, no conceivable package of concessions was likely to swing the hearts and minds of his English subjects wholly behind him in his quarrel with the Scots, or fire his unwilling conscripts with the will to fight Leslie's army. *If* he had been ready to come to terms with the Scots as

---

[16] *Proceedings of the Short Parliament*, pp. 187–97; *The Short Parliament Diary of Sir Thomas Aston*, ed. Judith D. Maltby (Camden Society, 4th series, XXXV, 1988), pp. 120–44.

well as with the parliament, the latter might have helped him to a face-saving peace and paid off his troops; but such a change of course was never in his mind, and nor as yet were the guarantees against non-parliamentary rule in the future that would surely have been asked of him.

But if a resumption of personal rule was no longer a viable option for Charles, nor was any lasting solution to be found in merely reaffirming an idealized ancient constitution, as conservative parliament-men were content to do. They still had no realistic conception of the crown's financial needs. Sooner or later, the Commons were going to have to face a fundamental restructuring of the financial system, going even deeper than the Great Contract would have done—something on the lines of the future Restoration settlement, though with a better estimate of the actual yield of the main revenues than the Convention Parliament was to make. There is no sign that such an exercise was contemplated in the spring of 1640, though something like it was to be forced upon the Long Parliament.

As soon as Charles returned to Whitehall after the dissolution, he called a meeting of the committee for Scottish affairs. A great deal hung on its debate, and Vane took notes of it. The key question was whether, without parliamentary subsidies, it was still possible to carry on the war. The Earl of Northumberland, who had been designated commander-in-chief, more than hinted his doubts, and Vane advised a merely defensive war. But Charles had summoned them for advice, not on *whether* to take the offensive—his mind was made up on that—but on *how* to. Strafford made the crucial speech, and it was just what the king wanted to hear. A defensive war he utterly rejected; only 'loss of honour and reputation' could come of it. 'Go on with an offensive war as you first designed', he urged. Having appealed to parliament for supply and been denied it, the king was 'acquitted towards God and man'. Indeed 'being reduced to extreme necessity', he was 'loose and absolved from all rules of government' and justified in resorting to naked power. He need not fear disaffection at home, for 'the quiet of England will hold out long'. A forced loan of £100,000 from the City and a sharp drive to collect Ship Money would sustain a short campaign, and Strafford was 'confident as anything under heaven' that Scotland would succumb within five months. 'You have an army in Ireland', he said, that 'you may employ here to reduce this kingdom'.[17]

Those last words, more than anything else in his record, were to cost Strafford his life a year later. He was referring to the army of 8,000 that he was currently raising in Ireland, and in the context it is quite clear that by 'this

---

[17] Quoted in Gardiner, *History of England*, IX, 120–3, from Vane's notes; I have made one change in the order of sentences.

kingdom' he meant Scotland. But his words were somehow leaked, and within days the rumour was spreading that he had advised the bringing over of catholic Irish soldiers to crush opposition in England. That was never on the cards before the Civil War, but why was the Irish army not used against the Scots? Probably because it was not ready in time; it looked to England for arms and horses, which were in too short supply to be spared.

In assuring Charles that 'the quiet of England will hold out long', Strafford was right in that the country was nowhere near the brink of revolt, but quiet did not imply willing support, and in London it was not unbroken. Immediately after the dissolution the City apprentices began to threaten violence against Laud—'William the Fox', their placards called him—whom they unreasonably blamed for it, and on 11 May they attacked Lambeth Palace. In another riot three days later they broke open the White Lion prison, where two of their comrades were held, and released them. Charles was sufficiently alarmed to order an extra guard for his children, who were not in the least threatened. He also wrote with his own hand the warrant whereby John Archer, who beat the drum at the apprentices' march on Lambeth, was put to judicial torture before being executed—the last Englishman ever thus punished. The privy council, not trusting the City's own militia, mobilized 6,000 of the trained bands of Essex, Hertfordshire, and Kent, but there was no sequel to these brief disorders, and London remained generally calm until Strafford's fate stirred it to fever nearly a year later.

If organized resistance was not a threat to Charles's and Strafford's plans, wholesale non-cooperation was. The drive to collect Ship Money was being thwarted, not only because individuals were refusing to pay it but because local officials right down to parish constables were refusing to collect it. Some admitted that they were more afraid of their neighbours than of the government, and spontaneous violence was becoming a real threat. Coat-and-conduct money was by now even more resented than Ship Money and it too was widely refused, despite threats to conscript those who would not pay. On top of these there was billeting money for troops on the move or awaiting marching orders. The legality of these levies was more and more questioned.

During the spring and summer of 1640 the king aimed to raise an army of 30,000 men, drawn from the trained bands throughout the whole of England. Mustering and drilling were supposed to have begun before the parliament met, and all counties were ordered to hold a general muster and review on 20 May. The intention was to use impressment as little as possible, but the reluctance of militiamen to serve and their wholesale resort to substitution resulted in a serious shortfall and a high proportion of untrained and unarmed men among those were embodied. Deputy lieutenants often had the utmost difficulty in raising their county quotas, and were finding their once prestigious jobs so disheartening that the government had to forbid them to resign without special licence.

Before this ill-starred army was even assembled, however, a new religious grievance in England and political defiance in Scotland weakened the king's position still further. Normally, when a parliament was dissolved, convocation came to an end with it, but this time Charles decided to keep it in being and directed Laud to proceed with the new canons that it was framing. They were ready by the end of May and published by royal authority on 16 June. The canons themselves, and especially the royal preamble to them, unmistakeably bear Charles's stamp as well as Laud's. Their purpose was to justify the ecclesiastical policies of the reign, to 'prove' that these made no innovations but were in accord with the Elizabethan settlement, and by requiring stricter conformity to expose any unsound churchmen who might be inclined to take the Scots' side in the present quarrel. They began by affirming that 'The most high and sacred order of kings is of divine right, being the ordinance of God himself'; moreover the Scriptures accord kings 'a supreme power' and commit to them 'the care of God's Church'. 'Tribute, and custom, and aid, and subsidy' are due from subjects to kings for the public defence 'by the law of God, nature and nations', and this obligation does not conflict (so it was affirmed) with subjects' right to their property. The assertion of the doctrines of divine right and non-resistance were even more high-flown than brief quotations can convey, and they were none the more digestible for being followed by directions that in every church and chapel the communion table should stand sideways under the east window and be 'decently severed with rails'.

But the most controversial canon was the one intended to demonstrate that the church was committed to *oppose* all innovations and to *maintain* the order established by law. It imposed an oath on all the clergy never 'to alter the government of this church by archbishops, bishops, deans and archdeacons, etc. as it stands now established'. What, it was asked, might not the Arminian prelates and their church courts read into that deceitful 'etc.'? Was it to shut the door on further reformation of religion through the common consent of King, Lords, and Commons? No wonder that the 'Etcetera Oath' soon became the butt of vehement protest, and not only by radical puritans. Its unhappy form probably derived from clumsy drafting rather than sinister intent, but what had been designed to unite and reassure became in itself a fresh source of division.[18]

Meanwhile the date (2 June) had come to which the king had prorogued the Scottish parliament. He had decided in May to prorogue it again until 7 July,

[18] For generous excerpts from the canons see Kenyon, *Stuart Constitution*, pp. 149–53 and for the best commentary Julian Davies, *The Caroline Captivity of the Church* (Oxford, 1992), ch. 7.

but most of its members came to Edinburgh for the earlier date, and at a crucial meeting the leading Covenanters not only decided that it should open that day but planned what should be done in it. Among themselves, they discussed the theoretical right of subjects to depose a king who invaded or deserted his kingdom, and though they almost certainly stopped short of seriously contemplating the actual deposition of King Charles there was talk of a temporary dictatorship. Parliament duly assembled without the presence of either king or commissioner, publicly declaring its right to sit on the grounds that the Pacification of Berwick had committed to it the ratification of the Edinburgh General Assembly's acts and the settlement of all matters civil. It further declared that Scotland was threatened with destruction by war, and in just ten days it enacted a veritable constitutional revolution.

It permanently excluded bishops, indeed any churchmen, from its membership. It finally struck off the shackles of the Lords of the Articles, ruling that if parliament should decide to appoint them (which it did not), they were to be freely chosen by each estate and to consider only what the full parliament referred to them. All grievances and matters of substance were to be debated in full parliament. Over eight months ahead of England's Triennial Act, it enacted that in future parliaments must meet at least once every three years. It naturally ratified the acts of the previous year's General Assembly and the National Covenant. It appointed a new executive committee of estates, comprising twelve each of nobles, lairds, and burgesses, and invested it with full power over the army and civil government. It adjourned on 11 June, but declared its own continuance until 19 November. It said nothing of asking the king's consent to its acts; it just assumed that they were binding without it. So much for its repeated declaration that it had no intention of entrenching upon his civil authority!

During June and July the Covenanters consolidated their hold on what had been disputed territory in Scotland. A plundering expedition into Gordon country finally subdued the north-east; Huntly along with other royalists had already retired to England. By late July it was possible to hold a General Assembly at Aberdeen without any challenge by royalists or episcopalians, though few Covenanting nobles attended it; the measures that they most cared about had already been passed in Glasgow and Edinburgh, and they were busy preparing for war. From mid-June to early August Argyll marched a force of 4,000 men through a very broad sweep of Highland territory, which ended for the time being any threat to the Covenanters' dominance from that quarter. It did, however, widen the growing breach between Argyll and Montrose, which stemmed partly from territorial rivalry and partly from political differences.

Charles's original plan had been for a three-pronged assault on Edinburgh, but by July the question was less and less whether an English army would invade Scotland, and more and more whether the Scots would invade England. A desperate shortage of money and arms forced the king to put off the rendezvous of his forces twice, the second time to 1 July. His persistent hopes of getting veteran troops from the Spanish service were finally killed when disorder in Catalonia swelled into full rebellion during June, for from then on the King of Spain had troubles enough of his own. In desperation, the government early in July seized £130,000-worth of bullion, belonging to the Spanish crown, which was lodged in the Tower of London and waiting to be minted into Spanish coin for transport to the Netherlands. It promised repayment in six months' time, but the City merchants were aghast at the breach of faith and fearful of reprisals. This disreputable shift was said to have been Hamilton's idea, but Strafford was behind a still worse plan launched on 11 July, for a debasement of the coinage. There was to be a huge issue of copper shillings, worth only a quarter of their face value. Bowing to the outraged protests of the mercantile community, the government restored the bullion and abandoned the debasement, but not before the crown's credit had sunk to its nadir. Or almost, for in August Cottington, the Chancellor of the Exchequer, seized about £70,000-worth of pepper from an incoming ship of the East India Company and sold it at around 30 per cent of its market value. The amount that the crown finally raised in 1640 was quite considerable, but most of it came in too late to pay and arm the troops who faced the Scots.

Among those troops, desertion and indiscipline were even more rife than in 1639. Quite a number of them, on their march to the general rendezvous at Selby, broke open gaols and released the prisoners. Others threw down enclosures, but there was on the whole comparatively little violence against private property. In at least five counties they destroyed the altar rails in churches, though that is not necessarily evidence that they were puritans; in some cases we know that they were not. The targets on which the soldiers most often vented their anger and resentment suggest a generalized sense that authority had been abused, both in church and state. Mutinies were frequent throughout the summer, and since martial law had been so expressly condemned by the Petition of Right there was a real problem in dealing with them. Arms were desperately short, and there were cases where even though they were available the temper of the men was such that their officers dared not distribute them. Only two cases are certainly known of officers being murdered by their men (both were reputed catholics), but many more feared it. Somewhere between a third and a quarter of all the king's infantry were still unarmed when they faced battle in August. Well before then, Northumberland was put out of action by chronic illness, probably malaria, and Strafford took over the generalship. But he himself was suffering miseries from gout and the stone, so the main military responsibility fell upon Viscount Conway, the commander of the cavalry, and Sir Jacob Astley, a veteran of the continental wars since the 1590s, who did what could be done as commander of the foot.

The Covenanters had been thinking of striking first since June, but they wanted first some assurance of active support from highly placed sympathizers in England. They sought it through the channel of Lord Savile, the son of Strafford's bitter rival in Yorkshire; Johnston of Wariston wrote to him on 23 June. Savile tried to engage some of the greatest puritan nobles—Bedford, Essex, Warwick, Brooke, Mandeville, and Scrope—but in their joint reply to Wariston the seven peers stated that they could not invite the Scots into England or take up arms with them, since that would be treason. They would, however, stand with them in all such ways as honour and the law permitted. Understandably, that was not enough for the Covenanters, but Savile's fellow-correspondents would go no further. He then, at about the end of July, sent the Scots another letter, assuring them of the whole group's unqualified support if they invaded, and very skilfully forging the signatures of the other six. The shamelessness of his subsequent career supports an impression that he was motivated by hatred of Strafford rather than by anything that could be called principle. How much difference his action made it is impossible to say, for by this time the Scots may have found reason enough for taking the military initiative in the wretched state of the opposing army.

During July General Leslie had encamped his own army at Duns, less than ten miles from the border. Against him, Conway intended to defend the line of the River Tyne, but most of the king's forces remained in Yorkshire, to the misery of that unhappy county. Not unexpectedly, the Scots struck first. Their decision to invade was taken with apparent unanimity by a meeting of the committee of estates and the senior army commanders on 3 August, but it did not command the assent of all the Covenanting nobles, and least of all that of Montrose. He was the chief author of a pact called the Cumbernauld Band (or Bond), which was secretly drawn up early in August and signed, then or later, by eighteen or nineteen other noblemen. It was a studiously vague document, affirming its signatories' 'duty to religion, king and country' and their continued adherence to the Covenant in defence of all three, but objecting to 'the particular and indirect practicking of a few'.[19] They did not pledge themselves to any specific line of action, however, and while a few like Montrose were to go over to the king, others remained firm Covenanters. What bound them at this point in time was doubt about an offensive war and dislike for current talk about deposition or dictatorship. That course would have been bound to confer huge power on Argyll, and the Cumbernauld Band is chiefly significant for its evidence that Argyll's command of the Covenanting nobility was never total.

[19] *A Source Book of Scottish History*, ed. W. Croft Dickinson and Gordon Donaldson (1954), p. 121.

The Covenanters supported their invasion with fresh propaganda directed at their 'brethren of England'. It is not easy to gauge how much English support they could call upon in 1640. In denouncing Laud and Strafford as the twin enemies of both peoples, and in calling for a common front against a popish plot to subvert the true protestant religion in the churches of both countries, they could draw upon widespread sympathy. But far fewer concurred with the specific Presbyterian church polity enshrined in the Covenant, not only because the majority of English people remained attached to the liturgy and government of the pre-Caroline Church of England, but also because a considerable proportion of puritans preferred the congregational way, as adopted in New England, to Presbyterianism. Sympathy was also offset by the old chauvinistic dislike of Scotsmen, especially at popular level; by doubts about the legitimacy of a war waged by subjects against their king; and by the hurt that national pride suffered through armed invasion of English soil. The Scots were certainly dismayed by the lack of welcome that they found as they marched through north-east England, though they won some respect by their discipline and by their practice of paying for what they took on the way.

They crossed the border on the night of 20 August, bypassing the garrison at Berwick and striking boldly south towards the Tyne. Charles had set out from London only hours earlier to place himself at the head of his army in York. Strafford, who had just assumed command as Lieutenant-General from the stricken Northumberland, was forced by illness to break his own journey north, and did not reach York until the 27th. His forces were at this point divided, with about 12,000 foot and 500 horse based around York and 10,000 foot and 2,000 horse forward in the vicinity of Newcastle under Conway. The Scots had all but reached the Tyne, and were on the brink of a dramatic victory; but before they won it, Charles was already under heavy pressure to call a new parliament, and it was not only military defeat that made him give way. Three days before he arrived in York the gentry of Yorkshire petitioned him for a parliament for the second time in a month, in order to relieve the heavy burdens that their county suffered through the presence of his forces and to redress their more general grievances. A more powerful plea for a parliament, together with a blunt and comprehensive summary of the nation's grievances, starting with the war itself, was signed four days later by twelve peers, most of whom were to play a very prominent role when that parliament met. They were Bedford, Essex, Warwick, Saye, Brooke, Mandeville, Rutland, Bolingbroke, Exeter, Mulgrave, Howard of Escrick, and Hertford, who was the only future royalist among them. Their petition was drawn up at Bedford House in the Strand, allegedly by Pym and St John; Hampden was also present at the meeting, but only the peers signed it. They called for an early meeting of parliament so that the authors and counsellors of England's ills could be brought to trial and punishment, and the present war ended without bloodshed.[20]

The only blood to be shed in battle in the Bishops' Wars was spilt on the very day that the twelve peers met. Conway had rightly guessed that Leslie's objective was Newcastle, and that he would attack its almost defenceless southern side rather than its fortified northern approach. The Scots would therefore cross the Tyne before developing their assault, and Conway reckoned that they would do so by the bridge at Hexham, twenty miles upstream. He divided his forces accordingly; but Leslie chose to ford the river at Newburn, only six miles from Newcastle, and although a high tide delayed his attempted crossing for some hours—long enough for the English to throw up some hasty earthworks—he had at least three times as many men as Conway managed to range against him in the time. The fire of the English musketeers repelled the first attempt of the Scottish horse to ford the river, but Leslie had at least forty cannon in skilfully concealed placements, besides many snipers, and the sheer weight of his cannonade put the inexperienced infantry—mostly Somerset men—to flight. Some of the English cavalry, notably those led by Commissary-General Henry Wilmot and Captain George Vane, son of the Secretary, fought very bravely to stem the Scottish advances, but they were overwhelmed, and the defeat became a rout. It was the first Scottish victory on English soil in anything more than a raid since Chevy Chase in 1388. Newcastle being indefensible on the southern side, Conway pulled his forces out of the city, and the Scots occupied it on the 30th. They were relieved to find it well stocked with victuals, for their own had almost run out.

Newburn was a small-scale and one-sided action in comparison with what was to come in the 1640s, but it finally determined that the royal authority would never again be what Charles conceived it to be, in either kingdom. It ensured too that the Scots would be a major force in the politics of both for years to come, and that their Kirk would permanently preserve its identity, despite the eclipse between the Restoration and the Revolution of 1688. Leslie very soon resumed his advance, confident that there was no line that the English could hold north of the Vale of York. What the Scots wanted, however, was not more territory than they could hold but a settlement that would secure for them what they had fought for. They were in communication now with some at least of the twelve petitioning peers, and the chief intermediary seems to have been Saye's son Nathaniel Fiennes, who wrote to them with intelligence of the state of the king's forces and advice as to how they and the peers could best work to a common end. So after Leslie had occupied Durham on 4 September, the Scots sent the king a respectful supplication,

---

[20] Gardiner (ed.), *Constitutional Documents*, p. 134.

asking for a treaty through which peace terms might be agreed, with the advice of an English parliament.

Charles's reaction to the political and military situation was very different from that of most of his councillors. He still assumed that he could continue the war and rally the country behind him. He did not receive the twelve peers' petition until the day after the Scots's request for a treaty, for it had been presented to the privy council, the greater part of which remained in London; but he was not seriously shaken by it. Strafford wrote to him in cheerful terms, but in a letter to his friend Sir George Radcliffe he confessed to a deep despondency. The councillors in London reacted to the news of Newburn with something like panic, issuing orders for the defence of Whitehall and the Tower against full-scale military attack. They took the twelve peers' petition very seriously, especially when they became aware that it was intended as a signal for a national petitioning campaign for a parliament, and they opened contacts with its authors. Some of them felt that nothing but a parliament would meet the case, and said so, but they decided instead to advise the king to summon a Great Council. This was an assemblage of all the peers of England—a thoroughly archaic institution, revived only once before since the fifteenth century, and then on the inauspicious occasion when Mary Tudor had announced her impending marriage to Philip of Spain. But it was one way of getting formal negotiations with the Scots moving, and in advising Charles to bow to the inevitable, as it surely would, such an assembly would shift some of the odium from the privy council's shoulders.

Charles duly summoned a Great Council to meet at York on 24 September, and when he opened it he announced that writs would be issued for a parliament to meet on 3 November. He had been forced to realize that he could not carry on the war without more money, and that without a parliament he could not get it. He was discouraged by the news that Edinburgh Castle had surrendered on 15 September, after holding out against the Covenanters since the spring. He had doubtless already made up his mind when he received a petition for a parliament signed by 10,000 Londoners on the 22nd. He evidently still hoped that the peers would support his quarrel with the Scots, for he called on Traquair to restate his case against them. But the Earl of Bristol, whose record of political independence earned him the respect of most of his fellow peers, bravely assumed the task of bringing him to a sense of realities. Bristol moved to appoint a committee to negotiate with the Scots and consider their grievances, and defended the necessity for doing so against Strafford's protests at treating with rebels. The Great Council, in response, named sixteen lords as commissioners to negotiate a treaty, and of these ten proved sympathetic to the Scots' cause. In answer to the king's request for assistance in raising an urgently needed £200,000, Bristol again eased the way to a loan from the City, which had so long refused one, but it advanced the sum on the peers' security, now that a parliament was promised.

Charles tried to insist that the treaty with the Scots should concede nothing more than the Pacification of Berwick, but Bristol found a formula that would save the king's face and yet give himself and his fellow commissioners a chance of success. The latter met their Scottish counterparts at Ripon, and came to terms with them in mid-October. The Scottish army was to remain in occupation of the six northern English counties, and England was to pay £850 a day for its maintenance. The terms of the long-term settlement were to await the meeting of the English parliament. The Great Council broke up on 28 October 1640, having secured little more than a truce. The course of both England's and Scotland's political future was to depend on the parliament about to meet, and the expectations that the king and most of his subjects had of it were tragically at odds.

# PART I: FURTHER READING

There is a wealth of good books which place the period covered by this book in a longer setting, but Derek Hirst, *England in Conflict 1603–1660* (1999) is outstanding, not least for its bibliographical essay. Also recommendable are Roger Lockyer, *The Early Stuarts: A Political History of England 1603–1642* (1989), Barry Coward, *The Stuart Age* (2nd ed. 1994), and on a slighter scale Mark Kishlansky, *Monarchy Transformed: Britain 1603–1714* (1996). The European context is probingly and sometimes controversially discussed by Jonathan Scott in *England's Troubles* (Cambridge, 2000). Conrad Russell emphasizes the British dimension and the problems posed by a multiple kingdom in *The Causes of the English Civil War* (Oxford, 1990), themes taken up in his major work on *The Fall of the British Monarchies 1637–1642* (Oxford, 1991). Some of the most helpful writing on the background to the troubles in both England and Scotland is to be found in collections of essays, notably Alan G. R. Smith (ed.), *The Reign of James VI and I* (1973), Howard Tomlinson (ed.), *Before the English Civil War* (1983), Richard Cust and Ann Hughes (eds.), *Conflict in Early Stuart England*, and Conrad Russell (ed.), *The Origins of the English Civil War* (1973).

The key work on English government under Charles I is G. E. Aylmer, *The King's Servants* (1961), while on a much smaller scale the same author's *The Personal Rule of Charles I* (1989) and Brian Quintrell, *Charles I 1625–1640* (1993) both offer good brief introductions. L. J. Reeve, *Charles I and the Road to Personal Rule* (Cambridge, 1989) is admirable on the early years of the reign, while Esther S. Cope, *Politics without Parliaments 1629–1640* (1987), though less original, has some insights. Much fuller, and based on profound research, is Kevin Sharpe, *The Personal Rule of Charles I* (New Haven and London, 1992), and though most critics have found it over-favourable to the king and his government the thoughtfulness and independence of its arguments command respect. On the king's favourite, Roger Lockyer, *Buckingham* (1981) is excellent. On the later years of the personal rule, C. V. Wedgwood's beautifully written *The King's Peace 1637–1641* (1955) has won an enduring place as a work of art, but has sometimes been underrated as a work of scholarship. On seventeenth-century parliaments and electoral practices, Derek Hirst, *The Representative of the People?* (Cambridge, 1975) and Mark Kishlansky, *Parliamentary Selection: Social and Political Choice in Early Modern England* (Cambridge, 1986), offer somewhat conflicting accounts, but Hirst's work stands up to most of Kishlansky's criticisms. On English local government the best survey is Anthony Fletcher, *Reform in the Provinces* (New Haven and London, 1986).

On English society and its institutions, see Keith Wrighton, *English Society 1580–1680* (1982), and two books by David Underdown: *Revel, Riot and Rebellion* (Oxford, 1985), whose emphasis is on popular culture and politics, and the broader and briefer *A Freeborn People* (Oxford, 1996). Most helpful on its subject is Felicity Heal and Clive Holmes, *The Gentry in England and Wales 1500–1700* (Basingstoke,

1994), while on the nobility Lawrence Stone, *The Crisis of the Aristocracy 1558–1641* (Oxford, 1967) retains its authority.

The background to our period in Scottish history is very well established by Jenny Wormald, in *Court, Kirk and Community: Scotland 1470–1625* (1981), supplemented on the social side by Part I of T. C. Smout, *A History of the Scottish People 1560–1830* (1969; paperback 1972). Charles I's reign is well served by Maurice Lee, Jr., *The Road to Revolution: Scotland under Charles I, 1625–37* (Urbana and Chicago, 1985) and David Stevenson, *The Scottish Revolution 1637–44: The Triumph of the Covenanters* (Newton Abbot, 1973), while Peter Donald searchingly examines the king's role in *An Uncounselled King: Charles I and the Scottish Troubles, 1637–1641* (Cambridge, 1990). John Morrill (ed.), *The Scottish National Covenant in its British Context* (Edinburgh, 1991) is an excellent collection, in which Margaret Steele and Morrill himself argue that religious issues were primary in the Covenant and Allan I. Macinnes gives greater weight to its political and constitutional objectives. Macinnes argues his case more fully in his *Charles I and the Making of the Covenanting Movement* (Edinburgh, 1991). See also W. Makey, *The Church of the Covenant* (Edinburgh, 1979) and G. Donaldson, *The Making of the Scottish Prayer Book of 1637* (Edinburgh, 1954). Many relevant documents are printed by W. C. Dickinson and G. Donaldson (eds.) in *A Source Book of Scottish History, Vol. III: 1567 to 1707* (1954).

Events in Ireland will figure more prominently in later parts of this book, but developments from 1600 onward to the eve of the 1641 rising are splendidly covered in five long chapters by Aidan Clarke in volume III of *A New History of Ireland*, ed. T. W. Moody, F. X. Martin, and F. J. Byrne (Oxford, 1976).

There is a rich literature on the religious issues underlying the troubles in England. Patrick Collinson, *The Religion of Protestants: The Church in English Society 1559–1625* (Oxford, 1982) is outstanding on the longer background, and his pamphlet on *English Puritanism* (1983) is more than a mere introduction. Of great value too are the essays edited by Kenneth Fincham in *The Early Stuart Church, 1603–1642* (1993), while Nicholas Tyacke's rightly influential *Anti-Calvinists: The Rise of English Arminianism c.1590–1640* (Oxford, 1987) stands up in the main to the criticism of Peter White in *Predestination, Policy and Polemic* (Cambridge, 1992). Julian Davies, *The Caroline Captivity of the Church* (Oxford, 1992) powerfully reinforces the view that the Church of England underwent a very significant change under Charles I, and emphasizes the king's own part in the process. Despite all that has been written since, H. R. Trevor-Roper, *Archbishop Laud* (1940; 2nd ed. 1962) remains a classic biography. Though not on the same plane, and despite its questionable title, William Haller, *The Rise of Puritanism* (New York, 1938; paperback 1957) remains worth reading, and J. T. Cliffe, *The Puritan Gentry* (1984) is illuminating on lay puritanism. On Roman Catholicism see John Bossy, *The English Catholic Community 1570–1850* (1976), and on the activities of catholics and crypto-catholics at court, Caroline M. Hibbard, *Charles I and the Popish Plot* (Chapel Hill, NC, 1983).

On the crisis sparked off by the Scottish Prayer Book, Russell's *Fall of the British Monarchies* comes into its own with its counterpointing of developments in England and Scotland, as do the works on the Covenant already cited. C. V. Wedgwood, *Thomas Wentworth, First Earl of Strafford 1593–1641: A Revaluation* (1961) supersedes her earlier *Strafford*. Mark Charles Fissel, *The Bishops' Wars: Charles I's Campaigns against Scotland, 1638–1640* (Cambridge, 1994) gives the fullest and best account of its subject, though it is much stronger on the English than on the Scottish side. Jane H. Ohlmeyer very thoroughly covers Antrim's activities in *Civil War and Restoration in Three Stuart Kingdoms* (Cambridge, 1993).

Behind all the studies cited here lies the monumental pioneering work of Samuel Rawson Gardiner, *History of England from the Accession of James I to the Outbreak of the Civil War* (10 vols., 1883–4). Its first two volumes were originally published in 1863, and it still remains immensely worth reading. At the time of writing it is available in a recent paperback reprint.

# PART II

*War in Three Kingdoms*
*1640–1646*

# Climacteric I:
# 'a Posture of Defence'

IN the autumn of 1640 all three Stuart kingdoms were heading towards crisis. Ireland would come to the point of confrontation a little later than Scotland and England, but the waters of rebellion were already being stirred. All three countries, though they did not know it, were on course for a decade or more of intermittent war, which would bring varying degrees of subjection to Scotland and Ireland and a period of startling political convulsion to England. The coming twenty years indeed are apt to seem so anarchic in their complexity, so bewildering in their pace of change, that it may help to preface them with a rough chart of the shoals ahead.

During their course there were four fairly short crucial phases, in which political crisis was particularly intense and decisions particularly momentous. They varied in length between about nine and twenty months; the first, which occupies this chapter and the next, was the longest. The years in between them were far from uneventful, but what happened during those intervals can be seen as mainly the following through of the course set by the preceding crisis-period or the building up of the tensions that generated the next one. Educated people of the time, if they had perceived such patterns, might have been disposed to describe these bursts of crucial change metaphorically as climacterics, for the word was widely used to denote not only the menopause but other supposed turning-points in the cycle of human life. Climacterics were reckoned to occur at intervals of seven years, and the four key phases of the 1640s and 1650s were not dissimilarly spaced.

The first ran from the meeting of the Long Parliament to the outbreak of the first Civil War. The second was triggered by the New Model Army's defiance of the Long Parliament in 1647, embraced the Second Civil War, and culminated in the execution of the king and the establishment of the Commonwealth. The third and shortest extended from Cromwell's final quarrel with the Rump Parliament to the establishment of his Protectorate, all within the year 1653. The last began with the army's violent confrontation of his son Richard in 1659, and ended with the restoration of Charles II.

All our climacterics have one remarkable feature in common: the men who set them moving did not initially intend or foresee their actual outcomes. In each case the authors of political change enjoyed a brief illusion of success, but what they established failed to withstand the internal stresses or external buffetings to which it was subjected. When the Long Parliament first met, none of its members or supporters desired or seriously anticipated a prolonged civil war, yet that is what came to pass. The army that abducted the king in 1647, far from seeking his deposition or death, wanted to restore him on more favourable terms than his parliamentary captors were offering, yet eighteen months later it was mainly instrumental in bringing him to the scaffold. When Cromwell expelled the Rump it was not his aim to become head of state and he had a sincere aversion to military dictatorship, yet he became Lord Protector before the year was out. After his death, the last thing that those who overthrew his son wanted was to bring back the Stuart monarchy, yet back it came just a year later. To a striking degree, the story to be told in this book is a story of unforeseen consequences.

What then were the hopes and expectations of the main actors on the political stage, and of the broader political nations of England, Scotland, and Ireland, when the Long Parliament met on 3 November 1640? Least realistic was the king, for he seriously hoped that the parliament would furnish him with the means to renew the war against the Scots, unless they abandoned their opposition to the prayer book and episcopacy. He saw them only as rebels and invaders and he could scarcely believe that his English subjects would not rally and drive them out. He could not or would not grasp that one reason why his calling of a parliament was so popular was that nearly all Englishmen hoped and expected that it would seal a peace with the Scots. It seemed the obvious outcome, since none of the twelve peers appointed to negotiate with them favoured the war. Strafford, almost alone of Charles's councillors, encouraged him in carrying it on, though he was realist enough to doubt whether the English would fight. He offered again to bring over an army that he was raising in Ireland, if shipping could be found, but he was surely over-sanguine if he thought it could be a match for the Covenanters. Most of the privy council would have had the king extricate himself from the war with as little loss of face as possible, but they accepted that he would have to give up Ship Money and make such other concessions as were necessary to 'the uniting of your Majesty and your subjects together, the want whereof [they] conceive is the source of all the present troubles'.[1]

Such a reconciliation between king and people could not have been easy, in face of the accumulated grievances of the past eleven years, but there was a

---

[1] Quoted from *Clarendon State Papers* (Oxford, 1767), II, 97–8, by Conrad Russell in 'Why did Charles I call the Long Parliament?', *History* 69 (1984), 375. My whole paragraph is much indebted to this article.

very wide desire for it when the parliament first met. The picture that some textbooks used to convey of a House of Commons dominated by an organized opposition, and bent on countering the threat of absolutism with a programme of reform inspired by an ideal of parliamentary monarchy, was wide of the mark. This parliament was indeed more responsive than any previous one to the desires of the electorate, and feelings throughout the broad political nation that returned it ran high. The prevailing hope, however, was not for drastic change, and certainly not for prolonged confrontation, but for a return to an idealized norm: to the ancient constitution as it had functioned in Queen Elizabeth's golden days, and to the protestant Church of England of pre-Arminian times.

The autumn elections of 1640 aroused even wider excitement and competition than those of the spring, and there were contests in somewhere between a third and a half of the constituencies. In more of them than ever before, candidates appealed to the voters on national issues, and since the electorate as a whole was growing in numbers quite rapidly, political involvement reached further down the political scale. Voters were multiplying for several reasons. In the counties, the forty-shilling freeholders who held the franchise had been men of substance when the act of 1429 first gave them the vote, but more than a century of inflation had brought many quite poor men within its entitlement—so many indeed that sheriffs could not distinguish just who were freeholders and who were not when a large concourse assembled on polling day. The loudest shout generally carried it. In the boroughs, which returned over four times as many members as the shires, the long Tudor trend towards oligarchy was being decisively reversed. This was partly because more and more townsmen were literate and politically aware, and hence eager for a say in choosing their representatives, and partly because gentlemen from outside the constituency, on the look-out for parliamentary seats, were courting the popular vote and encouraging the mass of inhabitants to challenge the corporation's right to select their members for them. Hence there were more and more disputed elections, which went to the Commons' Committee for Privileges to be determined, and in 1624, 1628, and above all in 1640-1 the committee ruled in favour of a wide franchise in borough after borough. England was still a long way from democracy as we understand it, but by the time the Long Parliament had finished settling disputed elections, something like a third of all adult males in the country were entitled to vote.

In opening up the borough franchises since the 1620s, the Commons had been deliberately trying to make it harder for courtiers and royal officials to go carpet-bagging. There was a very widespread animus against court candidates in the elections to the Long Parliament, thanks not a little to the efforts of puritan preachers, and the number of elected members with court connections was an unprecedentedly low 15 per cent, compared with over a third in

1614. Within the gentry elite, those of the godly interest strove to advance men of their own kind. To take one famous example, it is most unlikely that Oliver Cromwell would have been elected for Cambridge twice in 1640, against opposition, if he had not been on the fringe of the Earl of Warwick's puritan circle, for in the 1630s he had been far below the social level of the county families and had had to work for his living.[2]

Even more widely than in the spring elections, petitions of grievances were drawn up in the name of the constituents and presented to their members-to-be, sometimes after being read out and acclaimed in the county court where the election was held. Such petitions were produced in at least eighteen counties and in a number of towns, including Newcastle, Boston, and Scarborough. On the first day of more than formal business in the Commons, member after member rose to voice what his electors had charged him to put before the House and to present their petitions, and more followed two days later. This was not just a one-sided campaign by an organized opposition, for of the sixteen members named as speaking to their constituents' petitions by John Rushworth, the House's Clerk Assistant and chronicler, ten were to take the king's side when it came to civil war. The most striking feature of these petitions is the priority that most of them gave to the threat to true religion, and the depth of feeling with which they spoke of it. The other main grievances that they expressed were the predictable ones: the long intermission of parliaments, the financial exactions and the various other breaches of the rule of law during the personal rule. But they voiced no desire for revolutionary change. The general assumption was that the king had been 'seduced by evil counsel', and that if parliament recovered its control over taxation, ensured its own regular meeting, and upheld the supremacy of fundamental law, all would be well. Inside parliament a particular party had a more specific programme, as will be seen shortly, but it too was far from revolutionary in its aims.

For the Scots as well as the English, the meeting of the Long Parliament was an important event, and they depended much on its goodwill. At the Treaty of Ripon they had already secured that the final peace terms should be ratified by the English parliament, rather than being subject to the mere will of the king, and that England should pay their occupying army until those terms were settled. That meant that parliament would have to find the money. The Scottish commissioners appointed at Ripon had been greeted by cheering citizens when they arrived in London at the end of October, and they had enough friends among their English opposite numbers to be confident of the outcome. There were eleven of them—Henderson, Wariston, and three representatives of each lay estate—and four leading ministers accompanied them.

[2] J. S. Morrill, 'The making of Oliver Cromwell', in *Oliver Cromwell and the English Revolution*, ed. J. S. Morrill (1990), pp. 43–5.

Parliament assigned a church to their use, and Londoners thronged to hear the Scottish preachers, who fuelled the already strong anti-episcopal feeling in the capital. The commissioners' first objective was to get the sweeping recent acts of their own parliament ratified, and their first public demand was that the king should publish them in his own name. Charles tried to baulk them by attending the negotiations in person, but they steadfastly refused to treat in the presence of anyone except the commissioners appointed at Ripon.

To look ahead for a moment, Charles (after some wriggling) surprisingly agreed on 3 December to publish the acts of the Scottish Parliament. Thereby he not only bowed to the rejection of the prayer book, the abolition of episcopacy, and the other religious changes enacted by the Glasgow and Edinburgh assemblies; he accepted regular triennial parliaments, shorn of bishops and officers of state, and uncontrolled by compliant Lords of the Articles. He held out longer against the demand that 'incendiaries'—men held responsible for inflaming the quarrel between him and his peoples—should be brought to justice by their respective parliaments. The commissioners were eventually satisfied with his assurance that he would not employ anyone whom the Scottish parliament judged incapable—and well they might be, for it gave that body a veto on his choice of Scottish councillors and officials. One cannot believe that he intended these concessions to be permanent, for they were quite inconsistent with his stance at the start of the treaty, when he had tried to insist that the peace terms should go no further than the Pacification of Berwick. They probably reflected his bitter education in the true temper of the Westminster parliament during the first month of its sitting. When he realized what a contest he had on his hands there, he wanted the Scots and their army out of the way at all costs, because their occupation of northern England was his English opponents' strongest suit.

But much though the Scots had gained by the end of the year, they hoped for much more. Their long-term aims were to persuade the English parliament to abolish episcopacy, agree with them in a common church polity, confession of faith, and directory of worship, and join in imposing them on all Charles's three kingdoms. They overestimated, however, the amount of positive support in England for their rigid Presbyterianism, both in the country generally and in parliament, where only about 15 peers and a core of around 130 MPs were prepared to go all the way with them. They were more realistic in looking to the English parliament to put it out of the king's power to make war on them ever again without its consent.

The political leaders at Westminster welcomed the Scots' support, in so far as they had a common interest in asserting parliamentary power. They knew how much they benefited from the Scottish military presence, since Charles was virtually denied his prerogative of dissolution while money had to be raised to pay Leslie's army and the English regiments facing it. But as time went on the occupying force was perceived to be wielding a two-edged sword, for its continuing cost could erode parliament's popularity, and Scottish pressure for some widely unpopular objectives, especially in the sphere of religion, could jeopardize the more moderate policies that the leading spirits in both houses favoured. Between them and the Scottish commissioners there was always a mutual wariness.

For Ireland too a great deal hung on the transactions of the Long Parliament, though the prospect of its spelling good news for the majority of the Irish nation was bleak. A brief retrospect of Irish affairs in the earlier part of Charles's reign is overdue. In its first three years, when he was at war with Spain and France, he was aware of the danger (as was said at the time) of having the pope as keeper of the keys of his back door, so he felt a strong need to expand his small Irish army. Since he could not finance it from England, he needed to draw upon the tax-paying classes in Ireland without jeopardizing their already strained loyalty. What strained it were the burdens and disabilities they bore as catholics and the threat posed to their landed property by the policy of plantation. Traditional Irish law gave them all too little security in their estates; what they craved was a firm title, recognized by English law. The prospect of a deal was opened by two large meetings of nobles in 1626–7, which were sweetened by an offer to suspend the collection of recusancy fines from propertied catholics. The nobles and gentry were asked for voluntary subsidies, to pay for an enlarged Irish army, and a representative delegation of eight Old English catholics and three protestant settlers was sent to England early in 1628 to treat. They negotiated a mixed bundle of concessions that came to be known as the Graces, some of which eased the strains that the law imposed on the consciences and purses of Irish catholics. The most practically important Grace, however, would have extended to Ireland the benefit of a recent English statute which laid down that sixty years' possession of an estate conferred a valid title. That would have given most Irish landowners the security of title that they wanted so badly. They were led to believe that this and the other concessions would be laid before an Irish parliament, which was scheduled to meet in November 1628.

But the Graces were strongly opposed by the Irish Privy Council, whose members (being mainly New English) had a vested interest in extending English colonization into new areas, and by the Church of Ireland. Archbishop Ussher and his fellow prelates published a statement accusing the king of putting the people's souls up for sale and making the state a party to the damnation of those who died in the idolatrous Church of Rome. By the latter part of 1628, with peace in the offing, the need for a larger Irish army ceased to be pressing. The promised parliament was deferred and then in effect cancelled; the recusancy laws, though little enforced, remained unrepealed, and the Graces, unconfirmed, fell into limbo.

When Sir Thomas Wentworth arrived as Lord Deputy in 1632, his immediate need was to get the subsidy negotiated with the Old English renewed, so he gave them to understand that he would use his influence with his master to get the Graces implemented. But this was just a short-term tactic. His ultimate aim was not only to make the government of Ireland financially self-supporting but to raise a surplus for the king's use in England. A large-scale plantation of Connaught, which the Graces would have precluded, was an essential part of his plans. By 1634 he felt confident enough to call an Irish parliament, the only one to meet between 1615 and 1640. Thanks to a combination of pressure, deceit, and gerrymandering, it was almost as blatantly managed as the Scottish parliament of a year earlier. Wentworth played off the Old and the New English against each other; the indigenous Irish were as always grossly under-represented. He promised two sessions: the first, limited by the king's commission to three weeks, was to be devoted to supplying the crown's needs, while the second, in the following spring, was to attend to the interests of its subjects. The Old English, being led to expect the confirmation of the Graces, gave their support to a handsome grant of subsidies in the first session, but were cheated in the second. The vital sixty-year title to their land was denied them, and a committee was set up to plan the plantation of Connaught.

After seeming to ally with the Old English in the first session, Wentworth made some show of siding with the New English in the second, but the appearance was almost equally deceptive. Not without reason, he regarded the established New English politicians as self-serving and dishonest, and he soon confronted them head-on: first the Earl of Cork and Lord Wilmot, and then (after a brief tactical alliance) Lord Mountmorris. He had a genuine aversion to corruption, factiousness, and procrastination in government, and he had made his name as a figure of opposition in the parliaments of the 1620s. But he was convinced by the conduct of the last one that parliament could not be trusted to provide the remedies, and thenceforward he pursued an ideal of strong, disinterested royal government, standing above faction and venality. He was set on establishing himself as the crown's all-powerful viceroy in Ireland, and he ruled with the help of able friends whom he brought with him and of a circle of like-minded associates from the settler community. He dealt with opposition ruthlessly through the Court of Castle Chamber in Dublin, a prerogative agency of similar status to Star Chamber in England, though much more deserving of Star Chamber's posthumous reputation for tyranny. It wore the trappings of a judicial tribunal, but it was composed of members of the executive, and it became the arbitrary instrument whereby anyone who thwarted the intentions of Wentworth's government could be fined, imprisoned, or corporally punished. It did, however, display a certain brutal impartiality, in that it was almost as ready to dispossess New English as Old English landowners.

Wentworth certainly transformed the administration of Ireland, improving its efficiency, increasing its revenue, making it more amenable to royal direction, and curbing corrupt self-interest. But he did so at the cost of alienating all the main interest-groups in the country, and he sacrificed any claim to the moral high ground by his own rapacious self-enrichment. The Old Irish saw him as an enemy because of his drive to extend plantation and subjugate them increasingly to English rule. Despite his recognition that it was not politic to enforce recusancy fines for the present, they rightly suspected that his ultimate goal was protestant uniformity throughout Ireland. The Old English shared many of their fears; they also felt robbed of their old ascendancy and cheated over the Graces, and they resented their exclusion as catholics from offices of profit in central and provincial government (though not from unpaid commissions such as JP and sheriff). Most of the New English saw Wentworth as governing through his own friends in the interests of a distant king, and thrusting them out of the power and the pickings that they regarded as their right, sometimes by methods as dubious as their own.

His relations with the Church of Ireland also became strained. He found it already a divided body when he took up office. One part of it, a minority, was represented by William Bedell, Bishop of Kilmore, who had come to Ireland at 56 to take up the Provostship of Trinity College Dublin, which he held from 1627 to 1629. Though English himself, Bedell appointed Irish-speaking parish clergy whenever he could, and minimized the differences between his church's faith and that of the catholic population. He was denounced for his maverick stance on a range of issues, and he fell out with Archbishop Ussher, who had the support of the majority of the bishops—men as Calvinistic as himself. The divergence between Ussher's Church of Ireland and Laud's Church of England widened with the growing influx of Scottish settlers, for the former connived at the ordination of Presbyterian Scots to minister to parishes where they predominated. This was anathema to Laud, and Laud was Wentworth's close friend and constant correspondent. John Bramhall came to Ireland as Wentworth's chaplain in 1633, and after being made Bishop of Derry next year he attained a power to rival Ussher's. It was Wentworth's and Bramhall's aim to model the Church of Ireland as closely as possible on the Laudian Church of England, and in 1634 the Lord Deputy compelled it to accept the latter's Thirty-Nine Articles in place of Ussher's distinctive Irish articles of 1615. Laud's influence became more direct after he was made Chancellor of Trinity College. Many Church of Ireland clergy sensed a sinister plan to 'draw us back again into popery',[3] and gave Wentworth most of the blame for it. In 1638–9 he seriously antagonized the

---

[3] Quoted by Aidan Clarke, 'The 1641 rebellion and anti-popery in Ireland', in *Ulster 1641: Aspects of the Rising*, ed. Brian Mac Cuarta (Belfast, 1993), p. 148.

Scottish settlers by forcing them to take an oath—the black oath, they called it—abjuring the Scottish National Covenant and swearing allegiance and obedience to King Charles. A fair number returned to Scotland rather than submit to it.

Wentworth, when the king called him home, left Ireland a better governed country than he found it, though all its disparate elements had one grievance in common: they felt they had been subjected to a despotism. His power was still intact, and he left an able Lord Deputy (he being now Lord Lieutenant) in his friend Christopher Wandesford, but it could not survive the collapse of that of his master. He counted on Ireland to make a substantial contribution, both financial and military, to defeating the Scottish rebellion. He was raising a new Irish army for the purpose, and he was confident enough to persuade the king to call a new Irish parliament for March 1640. He had paved the way by disfranchising some of the less reliable boroughs and tampering with the charters of others, so with the help of some heavy electoral pressure by his henchmen the spring session went tolerably well for him. Irish fears of the rabidly anti-popish pronouncements of the Scottish Covenanters and their English puritan sympathizers helped him to get the subsidies he needed to pay his new regiments. But there were already enough signs of opposition, especially from the Old English, to give pause to a man less sanguine than Strafford, and when parliament reassembled for a second session in June it was already out of control. Wandesford hurriedly prorogued it until October. The government party was disintegrating, because outside the ranks of Strafford's personal supporters most of the New English inclined more towards the parliamentary opposition in England, as manifested by the Short Parliament, than towards the king, and many aligned themselves with the Scots. The Irish council itself reflected these divisions, and could no longer be relied upon. The interests of the Old English chimed more with the king's, and if he had been in a position to grant them the Graces and at least a de facto toleration of their religion he could have drawn on a great deal of Irish support.

So when the Long Parliament met, the hopes and prospects of the several interests in Ireland differed considerably, but for the present they could nearly all join in attacking Strafford. In the Irish parliament's autumn session, Wandesford was powerless to prevent the Commons from adopting a remonstrance which amounted to a massive indictment of his master's oppressive rule. They sent it over to England, in defiance of his prohibition, in the charge of thirteen members who spanned the whole gamut from Irish and Old English catholics to New English puritans and Scottish Presbyterians. They included Sir Donagh McCarthy, who as Viscount Muskerry was to join the Irish rebels in the name of the king, and Sir Hardress Waller, who was to fight against them as Cromwell's major-general of foot, after signing the king's death warrant. The remonstrance was intended as much for the English parliament's ears as for the king's, and Pym conveyed the substance of it to the Commons on 19 November, three weeks before Charles agreed to receive it. There was not a hint in it of the Irish separatism that the coming rebellion would eventually unleash; it invoked Magna Carta, and claimed for Ireland an equal right to be governed according to the fundamental laws of England. Wandesford, Strafford's devotedly loyal lieutenant, died on 3 December, perhaps lucky in the hour of his going. To replace him, Charles appointed two lords justices of considerably lesser stature, Sir John Borlase, an elderly soldier, and Sir William Parsons, a veteran of the old Dublin administration and a member of the Court of Castle Chamber.

The removal of Strafford was high on the agenda of the parliamentary leadership at Westminster, and the evidence from Ireland was essential to the case against him. Pym launched his impeachment on 11 November, and the Lords promptly concurred in it. But more than four months were to pass before he was brought to trial, and for at least the first two of them the records of the Commons' proceedings leave one half wondering whether they had any clear agenda at all. The early sittings were dominated by matters that members had been commissioned to put before the House by their constituents, in petitions or otherwise. This led to a lot of repetition, for the same predictable grievances recurred again and again. In response, the House showed a far clearer sense of what it disliked than of what it positively desired; many of its votes, well into the new year, seem directed more to making its members feel better than to finding constructive remedies for the real ills of the body politic.

The speech that best caught its mood on its first day of free debate, judging by its wide dissemination in manuscript and later in print, was made by Sir Benjamin Rudyerd. Its content and its popularity stand as warnings against any supposition that there were clear political camps in the Commons at this stage. Rudyerd was a contemporary and friend of Ben Jonson, a poet in his own right, and an intimate of the Earl of Pembroke, the highest officer in the king's household (and incidentally the co-dedicatee of Shakespeare's first folio). He himself held the very lucrative office of Surveyor of the Court of Wards. The complete courtier, you might think; but Rudyerd was also a member of the Providence Company and a close friend of Pym, with whom he had sat in all the parliaments of the 1620s. His speech reads like a reaffirmation of the typical Jacobean values of his early manhood. Urging the House to give precedence to religion, he began by lamenting 'what disturbance hath been brought upon the church for vain petty trifles', such as the positioning of the altar and the Book of Sports' encouragement of dancing on Sundays. Those who troubled it over such matters were hostile to preaching per se, he said, 'for I never yet heard of any but diligent preachers that were vexed with these and the like devices . . . They would evaporate and dispirit the power and vigour of religion, by drawing it out into solemn, specious formalities, into obsolete, antiquated ceremonies new furbished up'. As for traditionalists in church and state like himself, 'They have brought it to pass that under the name of puritans, all our religion is branded', for 'whosoever squares his actions by any rules, he is a puritan; whosoever would be governed by the king's laws, he is a puritan; he that will not do whatsoever other men would have him do, he is a puritan'. Rudyerd was typical in seeing the country's religious and political ills as closely linked; for 'it is a known and practised principle, that they who would introduce another religion into the church, must first trouble and disorder the government of the state, that so they may work their ends into a confusion, which now lies at the door'. The first remedy, therefore, must be to remove the authors of such counsels, who 'have almost spoiled the best instituted government in the world, for sovereignty in a king, liberty to the subject; the proportionable temper of both which, makes the happiest state for power, for riches, for duration'. 'I am zealous for a through reformation', he concluded, 'which I humbly beseech this House, may be done with as much lenity, as much moderation, as the public safety of the king and kingdom can possibly admit.'[4]

That same day Pym also made a carefully prepared speech, two hours long. He too put religious grievances first, and he too maintained that the threats to the church and to the laws and the constitution came from the same source, though he diagnosed it more explicitly as a design to return the country to popery. As in his famous oration to the Short Parliament, he presented a comprehensive exposition of the evils from which the country was suffering. He was not specific, however, about the long-term remedies, apart from frequent parliaments and the upholding of the rule of law. Prominent though he was in the House's proceedings from the start, because of his flair for articulating its sentiments and his experience of all the parliaments of the 1620s, it should not be supposed that he yet had clear plans for the whole set of constitutional reforms enacted in 1641, let alone for the further demands that would lead to civil war. His reputation as 'King Pym', loved or loathed, lay almost a year ahead. His present standing owed much to his practised skill as a House-of-Commons man, but much also to the patronage of the Earl of Bedford, and to the confidence of other puritan peers and politicians that he had earned as a tireless and effective man of business in the Providence Company. He was the chief representative in the Commons of a small and mainly aristocratic group of men who had been working out a programme for political settlement since the famous twelve peers had publicly petitioned for a parliament last August, and perhaps for longer. Bedford, the leading signatory, was at the centre of the group; his associates in the Lords included Saye, Brooke,

---

[4] J. Rushworth, *Historical Collections* (8 vols., 1680–1701), III, pt. i, 24–6.

Essex, Warwick, and Mandeville, and in the Commons Pym, St John, Hampden, Denzil Holles (the Earl of Clare's son), Nathaniel Fiennes, and William Strode. These men had a possible channel of communication with the king through the two Sir Henry Vanes. The elder was from February 1640 Secretary of State, and his son a Treasurer of the Navy, a friend of Pym and an altogether more radical figure, in both religion and politics. The members of the group were not of one mind as regards religion, but they had close contacts with Archbishop Ussher and with John Williams, Bishop of Lincoln, who was shortly to succeed Neile at York. Most of them would probably have settled for a scheme of limited episcopacy that Ussher had recently worked out in an attempt to find common ground between Anglican and Scottish forms of church government. More will be said about it shortly.

Deeply though some of the group cared about religion, however, their primary concerns in the winter of 1641–2 were to detach the king from the 'evil counsels' that had landed the country in a fratricidal war (and in Pym's view threatened it with popery), to put the government in safe hands, and to make it financially viable. The essence of their plan was that the king should give the key offices of state to members and associates of the group, in return for which they would place his revenues on a sound and permanent footing. Central to the deal was that Bedford should become Lord Treasurer and Pym Chancellor of the Exchequer. Pym's plans for making the crown solvent included an excise, a greatly enhanced customs revenue (by bringing the rates at which duty was levied into line with current prices), and the sale of the lands of the deans and chapters of cathedrals, which were let at grossly undervalued rents. The terms on which the nobility and gentry held their lands as tenants-in-chief of the crown were to be changed, so that they would be freed of anachronistic burdens like wardship, but would have to pay both an annual rent and an entry fine on first inheriting.

In principle, the scheme carried echoes of the Great Contract and in some ways prefigured the Restoration settlement. But more basically it was of the kind that parliaments had always sought to impose on monarchs whose exercise of their regal powers had become intolerable, ever since parliament had existed. The substance of all such attempts was to oblige the king to take advice from, and entrust authority to, ministers who had the confidence of his parliament, and now as in the past it was assumed that a large role would fall to his 'natural' counsellors, the heads of great noble houses with very broad acres. Pym played an important role, of course, but his most frequent employment in these early months, before the trial of Strafford absorbed him, was not in drafting legislation, nor in steering Commons' committees (he sat on a number, but others sat on more); it was in acting as a messenger from the Commons to the Lords and as a spokesman for the former in conferences between the two houses. He was very little involved in the introduction and preparation of all but one of the major constitutional acts of 1641, which were to place unprecedented limitations on the royal prerogative and change the whole balance between crown and parliament. The one exception, and the only such measure to become law during the first six months of the parliament's existence, was the Triennial Act, which had its third reading on 20 January. It laid down procedures which ensured that parliament would meet in every third year at the least, whether the king summoned it or not, though it did not set any limit to the duration of a particular parliament or require elections at regular intervals. Regular sessions, however, were not only nationally desired, as many petitions attested, but were essential to the Bedford–Pym scheme, since its financial provisions would need to be subject to regular parliamentary renewal if its beneficiaries were to be sure of their tenure of the seats of power. It should come as no surprise that further limitations of royal authority were not seriously pursued until the scheme was facing failure. If the group succeeded in gaining the dominance that it sought in the king's counsels, curbing his prerogative in other spheres than the financial would only limit its own power.

There were obvious obstacles in the way of the scheme's success. Charles would need to be convinced that it would do more for him than any other strategy still available to him, and that was not going to be easy. He was loath to give up his inherited right to choose his own ministers, and still more reluctant to throw Strafford to the wolves. He would fight hard against conceding to parliament the ultimate authority over the church, and Ussher's plan for it was to be quite unacceptable to him. For their part, the Bedford–Pym connection had to maintain the support of both houses of parliament if it was to deliver the goods that it offered, and the Commons' response to some of Pym's earlier financial proposals were not encouraging. Furthermore it had to keep up its alliance with the Scots, lest the king should make his own terms with them behind its back and resort to another sudden dissolution. Admittedly, Charles was most unlikely to satisfy the Scots' religious demands, but those demands were something of a millstone round the group's own neck. Finally, the group was not monolithic; the strains imposed by its dealings with the king, the two houses and the Scots eventually opened breaches in its own unity.[5]

One almost instinctive reaction of the Commons in their early days was to take up the hue-and-cry against papists. Among various measures against them that they considered was a particularly unpleasant proposal by Pym himself (thankfully not adopted) that papists should be made to wear a

---

[5] On Bedford's group and its plans see Russell, *Fall of the British Monarchies*, especially ch. 6, 'The projected settlement of 1641'.

distinctive mark or badge. On a more positive note they instituted the first of the many public fasts, when all business was nationally set aside to seek God's guidance in prayer, that were to punctuate the parliament's proceedings throughout its long life. The sermons preached to the Commons in St Margaret's church were regularly published, and provided an important channel through which an idealized picture of the parliamentarian cause was disseminated to a wider public. On this first occasion two famous puritan divines, Stephen Marshall and Cornelius Burges, both sounded the call of the Reformation in danger and of a design to reimpose the Roman yoke. Burges dwelt on Israel's delivery from Babylon by an army from the north, a bold allusion when the Scottish forces were still on English soil.[6]

The Commons did not altogether neglect secular grievances. They pronounced Ship Money illegal in a resounding declaration on 7 December, affirming that no plea of public danger could justify the king in raising any tax without parliament's consent, but they showed little urgency about facing up to the crown's real financial predicament. It was easier to impeach Lord Keeper Finch, chiefly for his leading part in the Ship Money judgment, and six other judges (who were never brought to trial). But the Laudian church and the threat of popery remained the most popular targets. The canons of 1640 were condemned without a dissentient voice on 9 December, though the three-day debate preceding the vote did hint at some of the religious differences to come, especially as to where the power to legislate for the national church ultimately lay. Pym initiated the impeachment of Laud himself on 18 December, and the two bishops who had executed his policies most zealously, Wren and Piers, were impeached a few days later. More than three years were to pass before Laud was brought to trial, and the other two never were, though Wren was to spend nineteen years in the Tower of London. An earlier victim of impeachment was Secretary Windebank, for signing letters saving priests and other catholics from the rigour of the laws, though he had probably done no more than the king and queen instructed him to do. He fled abroad rather than face trial (as did Finch), and was received into the Roman Catholic church shortly before he died in Paris in 1646.

The Commons took special pleasure in rehabilitating Laud's victims. Within a week of their first meeting they took up the petitions of Prynne, Burton, and Bastwick, and proceeded not only to release them but to declare their Star Chamber convictions illegal and to vote them reparations (which were never paid). The triumphal reception that greeted Prynne and Burton in late November (Bastwick followed a fortnight later), both along the road to

---

[6] Anthony Fletcher, *The Outbreak of the English Civil War* (1981), pp. 92–4; Russell, *Fall of the British Monarchies*, pp. 174–5. On the fast sermons generally, see H. R. Trevor-Roper, 'The fast sermons in the Long Parliament', in his *Religion, the Reformation and Social Change* (1967), and J. R. Wilson, *Pulpit in Parliament* (Princeton, 1969).

London and still more on their arrival there, testified to a genuine popular hatred for the repressive side of the Caroline church and Caroline government. This surfaced again in an uglier manner when Laud was transferred to the Tower. A crowd gathered as soon as he was identified and reviled him all along the way, threatening to kill him in his coach; the Lieutenant of the Tower had to call out the yeomen of the guard to quell the riot.

Another prisoner to be swiftly freed was young John Lilburne, the future leader of the Levellers. He had fallen foul of Star Chamber in 1638 for smuggling Bastwick's most notorious anti-episcopal tract to Holland, to be printed there for redistribution in England. He had been fined £500, far beyond his capacity to pay, and flogged all the way from the Fleet prison to Westminster, tied to the back of a cart. Despite receiving (at his own guess) two hundred lashes, he had still found strength to harangue a sympathetic crowd until he was gagged. Back in the Fleet, he had been kept in irons ever since, even through weeks of serious illness. The member who pleaded his case to the House was then probably less well known in London than Lilburne was; Sir Philip Warwick, proud of being as well dressed as a Lord Treasurer's secretary ought to be, noted disdainfully this backbencher's plain ill-cut suit, his none too clean linen (with a spot or two of blood on it to suggest that his 'swollen and reddish countenance' had had a rough shave), his 'sharp and untunable' voice, and (to Warwick's mind) his exaggeratedly fervid eloquence.[7] The speaker was Oliver Cromwell, making his first speech in the Long Parliament and perhaps the second that he had ever made at Westminster, the only previous one on record having been in 1629. His championship of Lilburne might appear ironic in the light of the later antagonism between them, but there is no reason to suppose that he ever regretted it.

The Commons spent a great deal of time during November and December in considering petitions concerning particular acts of injustice by the courts and alleged oppressions by individual churchmen, so many indeed that there was a danger of their clogging national business. But not all petitions secured a favourable response, especially when they aroused suspicion of popular or factional pressure. The most famous case of this kind was the original petition for the abolition of episcopacy 'root and branch', which was brought to Westminster by about 1,500 London citizens, headed by two aldermen. Several hundred of them crowded into Westminster Hall, to the scandal of Secretary Vane, while Alderman Isaac Pennington, one of London's four MPs, presented it to the House. It was the work of a group of radical London ministers, and its sponsors had been gathering signatures to it for weeks. They were hand in glove with the Scots; Robert Baillie, the best known of the

[7] Sir Philip Warwick, *Memoirs of the Reign of King Charles I* (1701), quoted in W. C. Abbott, *The Writings and Speeches of Oliver Cromwell* (4 vols., Cambridge, Mass., 1937–47), I, 121.

chaplains who accompanied the Scottish commissioners, had been shown it almost as soon as they arrived in London. The language of the Root and Branch Petition was strong and its demands uncompromising. It blamed the government of the church by archbishops and bishops, and their claim to an immediate calling from Christ, for all the evils of the time, and not only for the religious ones such as the silencing of godly ministers, the ban on the preaching of predestination, the profusion of idle and ignorant parish clergy, the censorship of godly books and the free circulation of lewd and subversive ones, the unchecked increase of popery, priests, and Jesuits, the pushing of the Church of England's liturgy and ceremonies ever closer to those of Rome, the profanation of the sabbath, the rottenness of the church courts, and the abuse of excommunication; it even blamed the bishops for Ship Money, impositions, and monopolies. In a final paragraph that may have been added by Baillie it warned that

The present wars and commotions happened between his majesty and his subjects of Scotland . . . will not only go on, but also increase to an utter ruin of all, unless the prelates with their demandings be removed out of England who as we . . . do verily believe and conceive have occasioned the quarrel.[8]

The Root and Branch Petition was not welcome to Pym and his allies, for they knew how divisive it would be. The Scots were urged by their friends in parliament to help hold it back, at least until Strafford's trial was sure of a successful conclusion. But while bishops survived in England they did not believe that their own church order was safe, and they were bent on converting England to it; Root and Branch could clear the way. They mistook the religious temper of the English nation, however, and overestimated the support they enjoyed among it, for London was not England. Whereas most Scots were anxious to guard against the subjection of the spiritual authority to the civil, most Englishmen were temperamentally suspicious of clerical power as such. In a phrase that was to be much repeated, Bedford's son-in-law George Digby warned the Commons against exchanging a bishop in every diocese for a pope in every parish.

The Laudian church as it stood in 1640–1 found no defenders in the House, but between that extreme and the Scottish Presbyterian model, there were three main positions among the members. Many believed like Digby and Lord Falkland that episcopacy should not be destroyed but reconstituted, by bringing bishops back to what they had been under Queen Elizabeth and asserting parliament's ultimate authority over church matters. In the country at large, that position probably commanded the widest support, though not the most vociferous. Then there were the Erastian abolitionists who wanted

---

[8] Gardiner (ed.), *Constitutional Documents*, pp. 137–44.

to replace the bishops' authority, not with presbyteries and synods but with a mainly lay commission in each diocese, appointed by parliament. This was what the Root and Branch Bill was to propose, when it was eventually introduced in May 1641. Thirdly there was the scheme devised by Archbishop Ussher, whose profound erudition and personal goodness even Strafford had acknowledged. Drawing on the practice of the earliest churches, he aimed to build bridges between the Anglican and Scottish forms of church government. He proposed that parish ministers should be assisted by elders, who could be the long-familiar churchwardens and sidesmen, and whose duty it would be to present any who lived scandalously for admonition and reproof. In every rural deanery the ministers of the constituent parishes were to meet in a monthly synod under a suffragan, and exercise the power of excommunication. Twice a year, representatives of the monthly synods were to meet in a diocesan synod under a bishop or superintendent ('call him what you will', wrote Ussher), and in every third year the provincial synods of Canterbury and York should combine in a national council, sitting in time of parliament as convocation did. It was ingenious, for it offered close parallels with Scotland's consistories, presbyteries, provincial synods, and general assembly, while preserving an episcopal framework. But it provided for no lay participation above parish level, and anyway the Scots would have no truck with 'limited prelacy'; one of them published a tract against it in January. Charles for his part would never have submitted to an ecclesiastical polity that cut him out as Supreme Governor, or countenanced bishops in whose choice he had no say. 'A purely clerical compromise', Professor Trevor-Roper has called it; 'a combination, at the expense of the laity, of new Presbyter and old Priest'.[9] Nevertheless it was very seriously considered, and it would surface again more than once during the next twenty years.

The Commons were much divided as to whether to receive the Root and Branch Petition at all. They finally agreed to consider it on 17 December, but what with pressure of business, and perhaps a reluctance to grasp the nettle, they did not actually do so until 8 February. Before then, the London petition proved to be the harbinger of a campaign of similar petitions from the counties—thirteen of them by the end of January and six more later in the year. Most came from areas where 'Arminian' bishops had been particularly zealous. So unpopular were those prelates that some people signed the petitions who did not really want to see episcopacy totally abolished. Sir Edward Dering, for instance, the knight of the shire who presented Kent's petition, had already presented an earlier anti-episcopal petition in November and was to introduce the Root and Branch Bill in May; yet by

---

[9] Hugh Trevor-Roper, 'James Ussher, Archbishop of Armagh', in his *Catholics, Anglicans and Puritans* (1989 ed.), p. 152.

November 1641 he was singing the praises of 'good' bishops, especially the 'incomparable' Ussher.[10]

Hoping to check the anti-episcopal pressure, and at the same time to hasten parliament's overdue provision for the two armies and the navy, Charles addressed the two Houses at Whitehall on 25 January. He would concur with them, he said, in investigating all innovations in church and state, for his intention was 'to reduce all matters of religion and government to what they were in the purest time of Queen Elizabeth's days'.[11] But he deplored the wave of root-and-branch petitions, and he would never consent to depriving the bishops of their votes in the Lords, let alone to abolishing them; nor would he assent to the Triennial Bill while it prescribed means for assembling parliament in default of his summons. The trouble with Charles, now and later, was that his 'never' too often turned out to mean 'not until the temperature gets hotter'.

He had just aroused angry suspicion by reprieving a Jesuit priest named John Goodman, who had been sentenced to death under the harsh Elizabethan law that made it treason for members of his order simply to be on English soil; it was suspected that Charles was deliberately creating a precedent for future reprieves of Strafford and Laud. This not only provoked a clamour for Goodman's execution, but caused the City to suspend a vital £60,000 loan, and spurred the Commons into one of their periodic drives against catholics in the royal entourage. They demanded the banishment from court of Sir Kenelm Digby, Wat Montagu, Toby Matthew, the queen's secretary Sir John Winter, and the papal nuncio Count Rossetti, who had succeeded Con late in 1639. They sent for the first two and examined them on their part in raising the so-called queen's contribution to the Scottish war. Outside parliament Henrietta Maria herself was coming under attack from the godly party. Understandably upset by the nasty scriptural parallels with which they insulted her, she set afoot a tactical rumour that she would soon be leaving for France.

At this point Charles began to make concessions, partly to take the heat out of the situation, partly to sow divisions among his opponents. He agreed to leave Goodman to the justice of parliament, which declared itself satisfied and left him to lie in prison, where he died in 1645. On 29 January he appointed St John to the office of Solicitor-General, and during the next four interesting weeks it looked as though the Bedford connection's scheme for a settlement might be coming to fruition. Two or three days later Bedford, Saye, and Pym were reported to have been closeted with the queen, who bewildered the Commons on 4 February with a cordial message, assuring them that

---

[10] Rushworth, *Historical Collections*, III, pt. i, 426; D. Hirst, 'The defection of Sir Edward Dering 1640–1', *Historical Journal* XV (1972).

[11] Key passages of the speech are in Kenyon, *Stuart Constitution*, pp. 17–18.

Rossetti was about to return to Rome, excusing her part in persuading catholics to contribute to the Scottish war, and promising to do all she could to promote a good understanding between her husband and the parliament. Then on the 16th Charles unexpectedly gave his assent to the Triennial Bill, with its offensive clauses intact, and three days later he created seven new privy councillors. They included six of the twelve peers who had petitioned for a parliament, among them such leading promoters of the settlement scheme as Bedford, Saye, Essex, and Mandeville. Charles is said to have hated appointing them, but to have been persuaded to it by Hamilton. It was an astute move, calculated to drive a wedge between these powerful men and the Scots, split the ranks of the Root-and-Branch party, and maybe save Strafford from the scaffold. But despite persistent rumours that Bedford was to receive the crucial office of Lord Treasurer he never did, nor did Pym get the Exchequer. Promotion to the privy council brought little power, because from now on Charles rarely summoned it.

There were other signs that his tactic was to divide Bedford's group rather than suffer a loss of political initiative by submitting to it. He bowed to antipapist pressure by issuing a proclamation, which his new councillors signed, banishing all priests and Jesuits, but the Commons were clamouring for all recusants to be removed from the court, including the queen's servants, and specifically Winter. Bedford's allies in both Houses were disunited on the matter. They split again over the larger issue of Root and Branch. After the moderate episcopalians had tried and failed to get it rejected out of hand, the Commons at last took the London petition into consideration on 8 and 9 February. At the end of long and inconclusive debates they referred it to a committee, but reserved the central question of whether to preserve or abolish episcopacy to the House itself. Strafford was another source of division, some of Bedford's group supporting his pleas for more time to prepare his case, others pressing that he should be tried for his life forthwith. He was given a further week, and 24 February was appointed for him to present his answer to the charges against him in the House of Lords. Charles saw him privately for an hour before the hearing began; then he unexpectedly took his seat on the throne in the Upper House, and by his solicitous, even tender demeanour towards the accused man he made his sympathies abundantly clear. The Lords were incensed, and on his departure they declared their proceedings in his presence to be void and went through them all again. The king's demonstration, however, gave notice that it would be difficult for his new councillors, all of them peers, to vote for Strafford's death and keep their places.

On the same day that Strafford appeared before the Lords, the Scots, to whom the Commons had voted a 'Brotherly Assistance' of £300,000, played into the king's hands by clumsily intervening. A paper drafted by Henderson, demanding the execution of Strafford and the abolition of episcopacy in

England, was circulated to members of parliament, but it was leaked to a stationer and publicly sold as a pamphlet. The Scots were seen trying to apply rather gross pressure on their English allies, especially the new privy councillors, to choose between the king and themselves. Charles was understandably furious and said that the Scottish commissioners deserved to be hanged as traitors. Their paper won them no friends in the Commons either, for the debate on it revealed a new strength of anti-Scottish and anti-puritan feeling. Members like Edward Hyde, Sir John Culpepper, Sir Ralph Hopton, and George Digby, who had been eager for the redress of the grievances of the 1630s, were beginning to display the sentiments that would gradually turn them into constitutional royalists. For his part Charles, who had seemed so isolated during the parliament's first two months, began to see a better way out of his troubles than by bending to ministers not of his choosing and to policies not to his liking. He glimpsed the possibility of cultivating a party that would unite old loyalists with men who had been moderate opponents— a party with the common bonds of love for the historic Church of England, traditional loyalty to the throne, attachment to the ancient constitution, dislike of the Scots, and belief in social order. With the latter went a revulsion against riotous demonstrations, threatening petitions, fanatical iconoclasm, and other manifestations of popular pressure.

As for the bishops, the Commons voted on 10 March that they should be deprived of their legislative and judicial role and be barred from secular employment, which plainly implied that they were not to be abolished altogether. But the question remained deeply divisive, and it was not until 1 May that they sent a bill to exclude bishops from parliament up to the Lords. It met with predictable hostility there, and it sowed dissension between the two Houses just when the prosecutors of Strafford most needed to hold them on a common course.

But the case of Strafford in itself opened divisions between the Houses and within each; indeed it split the Bedford–Pym connection. Scarcely anyone disagreed that he had to be removed from the political stage, and permanently; for his Irish army posed a real threat while the king persisted in refusing to disband it, and if ever Charles saw a chance to cast off parliament's shackles through a sudden dissolution, Strafford could quickly become his all-powerful minister again. But had he committed treason, and did he deserve death? He was not the apostate from parliamentary constitutionalism or the renegade exponent of royal absolutism that the old Whig historians used to portray, but he had fallen considerably short of his own self-projection as the disinterested executant of firm, benevolent, incorruptible, faction-free royal government. His arrogance and self-righteousness had made him many enemies in his native Yorkshire before ever he went to Ireland; the same qualities, and the record of his ruthless treatment of his Irish opponents, made him many more after his return. The Lords had proposed on 18 February that he should be removed from all his public employments, but that was widely felt not to go far enough. Permanent disqualification from office might have been a solution, or even banishment. But the Bedford–Pym group was divided as to whether the possibility of sparing his life might be used as a lever to exact further concessions from the king, or whether his crimes were so heinous (or the danger he still posed so great) that death was the only appropriate penalty. If that was the case, the charge had to be treason, and a conviction for treason was what the Commons determined to press for.

The weakness of the prosecutors' case was that nothing Strafford had done constituted treason by any unforced interpretation of the law of England. Treason was a crime against the king, in whom the state was personified: making war upon him, or plotting his death, or siding with his enemies. But Strafford had had the king's total trust, and his offence was that he had sought not to diminish his master's authority but to raise it too high. It was just possible to argue, as had been done against Empson and Dudley when the young Henry VIII was courting popularity, that making a division between the king and his people amounted to treason, but that was a charge that could be retorted on Strafford's accusers. Pym's way round the problem was to contend that there was a higher treason than that, classically defined in the statute of 1352, against the monarch: a treason against the constitution itself, the 'fundamental laws' in which the king's powers were enshrined and demarcated. Strafford's policies and practices (Pym argued), by perverting those laws, made the king the fountain not of justice but of injustice, not of peace but of confusion, not of protection but of public misery and calamity. 'This treason would have dissolved the frame and being of the commonwealth', he maintained; 'it is a universal, a catholic treason.'[12] So although the crimes charged against Strafford might not singly constitute treason, they did so cumulatively when considered together, and amounted to a so-called 'constructive treason'. This was dangerous doctrine, and Strafford exposed its legal and intellectual flaws with searing eloquence. But the case against him was fuelled more by hatred and fear than by law or reason, and men as different as Arundel, Essex, Pembroke, and the elder Vane were scarcely less eager than Pym to see him dead.

His trial eventually opened on 22 March, and it was designed to be a great semi-public spectacle. Impeachment was a process in which the whole body of lay peers acted as judges (but not the bishops, when the charge carried the death penalty), and a committee of 'managers' prosecuted on behalf of the Commons. It was normally conducted in the House of Lords, but for this trial the much larger space of Westminster Hall had been prepared with elaborate

---

[12] Kenyon, *Stuart Constitution*, pp. 191–3.

carpentry. Steep banks of benches on either side accommodated the Commons, the Scots commissioners, some other privileged persons, and anyone else who could fight their way in. In the central enclosure the peers lined either side, in two ranks. There was a raised throne at one end, but the king did not occupy it because the peers were not prepared to proceed if he was formally present. He and the queen watched the proceedings from a box, just behind the throne and a little to one side; a lattice had been inserted to screen them from view, but Charles promptly removed it. At the opposite end, Strafford stood or sat in a dock on a raised platform, with four of his secretaries behind him and several lawyers, whom he was allowed to consult on points of law. The new Lord Keeper, Edward Littleton, should have presided, but he was unwell, and the Lords chose Arundel to take his place. His chair was immediately below the throne, with the judges seated in front of him to give him such legal advice as he might need.

The chairman of the Commons' managers was Bulstrode Whitelocke, a 35-year-old lawyer who was to hold high office under the Commonwealth, but it was Pym who opened their case with a scalding attack on Strafford's alleged tyranny and corruption in Ireland. Strafford, however, defended himself with extraordinary eloquence and skill, though he was far from well. As the days went by his unruffled courage, matched against the dubious rhetoric and the harassing tactics of his prosecutors, won him some sympathy. By 5 April, when they came to what they regarded as their deadliest charge, his alleged advice a year earlier that the king had an army in Ireland which he might 'employ here to reduce this kingdom', they had already lost some ground. Secretary Vane, their chief witness, stuck to his allegations that Strafford had indeed spoken the words (which was very likely true) and that by 'this kingdom' he had meant England, not Scotland (which was palpably false). But Vane proved to be their sole witness, for the other councillors present at the time remembered Strafford's words differently, and for proof of treason the law required two. Thereafter every day that passed seemed to make it more uncertain that the peers would find him guilty.

Then on 10 April the case was given an entirely new direction by Sir Arthur Haselrig, a newcomer to parliament in 1640 and still in his early thirties, but a brother-in-law of Lord Brooke and already displaying the political thrust that would carry him high in the next dozen years. That day, without consulting the managers of the impeachment, he introduced a bill of attainder against Strafford. Whereas impeachment was a judicial process, requiring proof, an act of attainder was a piece of legislation; it simply declared the accused to be guilty and enacted, by the authority of King, Lords, and Commons, that he should suffer the appropriate penalties. Haselrig's bill indicted Strafford for 'endeavouring to subvert the ancient and fundamental laws and government . . . of England and Ireland, and to introduce an arbitrary and tyrannical government against law.'[13] Specific offences, which his prosecutors had been hard put to substantiate, were stated as facts, though very summarily, for the whole bill fills less than two printed pages. The attainder was in effect a confession of the impeachment's failure, and Pym and Hampden were at first among those who opposed it, though Pym came round to it when he became convinced that there was no other sure way of bringing Strafford to the scaffold. The Lords were greatly angered by it, and carried on with the trial in Westminster Hall. There on the 13th Strafford made a noble final speech in his own defence, and once more rebutted his accusers' depiction of him as a ruthless promoter of unfettered royal absolutism. 'I ever did inculcate this [he said]: the happiness of a kingdom consists in [the] just poise of the king's prerogative and the subject's liberty, and that things should never be well till these went hand in hand together.'[14] Pym drew on his own best eloquence in reply, but there were moments when he and Strafford seemed in principle not so very far apart, as when he said: 'if the prerogative of the king overwhelm the liberty of the people it will be turned into tyranny; if liberty undermine the prerogative, it will grow into anarchy'.[15]

Strafford's fate, however, hung not so much on his principles as on the emotions aroused by his political role in the last two years. It was determined by the bill of attainder, which passed its third reading on 21 April by 204 votes to 59. It may seem surprising that on a matter of such intense public interest little more than half the House was present, whereas a few weeks earlier 379 members had voted on whether to send an obscure clergyman to the Tower for saying from the pulpit 'From lay puritans and lay parliaments good Lord deliver us'.[16] The explanation is that many members absented themselves, either because they felt (as we know Hampden did) that to kill Strafford without convicting him by due process of law was an abuse of parliamentary power, or because they were afraid of exposing themselves by voting against the bill. Their fear was not unreasonable, for the names of the 'Noes' were posted up around London and Westminster under the heading 'These are the Straffordians, the betrayers of their country'. A crowd of 10,000 brought a petition to the House for his execution. Pym himself took the bill up to the Lords.

Various moves were afoot behind the scenes to save Strafford's life. Bedford was quite ready to bargain over it, but his associates in the former settlement scheme, which finally perished now if it was not dead already, were utterly divided. Saye was being tempted with the very lucrative office of Master of the Wards, which Pym's financial plans would have abolished, and he was invested with it a few days after Strafford's death. Essex by contrast

---

[13] Gardiner (ed.), *Constitutional Documents*, pp. 156–8.
[14] Kenyon, *Stuart Constitution*, pp. 193–5.     [15] Ibid., p. 196.
[16] Quoted in Russell, *Fall of the British Monarchies*, p. 279.

would have no compromise; 'stone dead hath no fellow', he said.[17] Pym is reported to have been twice with the king during April, and when Cottington resigned the Chancellorship of the Exchequer on the 27th he was very hotly tipped to succeed him. He is said to have actually been offered the post but to have declined it. He could hardly do otherwise. He had deeply and publicly committed himself to securing Strafford's death, and reports of his contacts with the court were damaging his standing in the House. He also knew that until Strafford's head had fallen the City would never advance the loans that the next Chancellor would desperately need.

Charles was intensely anxious to save his minister, and wrote to him on 23 April, promising 'that, upon the word of a king, you shall not suffer in life, honour or fortune'.[18] Unfortunately he was dabbling in a conspiracy whose ultimate effect was to strengthen the clamour for Strafford's death, even though Strafford had no part in it. There had been growing discontent among the officers of the king's army in the north over the chronic shortage of pay, the unsympathetic attitude (as they saw it) of the House of Commons and the civil courts, and the very doubtful legality of martial law, without which they could hardly hold their forces together. They drew up a petition stating their grievances on 20 March, and sent it to their sick general Northumberland in London by one Captain Chudleigh. This officer was taken to see the queen, and was drawn into what at first were two distinct plots. Both were well known to the king by the end of March. One, which he fully supported, was managed by Northumberland's brother Henry Percy, and the gist of it was that the army should put pressure on the parliament by petitioning it for the Irish army to be kept up, for episcopacy to be preserved, and for the king's revenue to be made good. The other, a courtiers' conspiracy involving Henry Jermyn, the poet Sir John Suckling, William Davenant (the future pioneer of English opera), and Sir George Goring, was a wilder scheme to seize control of the Tower and procure Strafford's escape, while simultaneously bringing the army south. Charles was highly interested, but other courtiers were opposed to this plot, and when Chudleigh, back in Yorkshire, sounded a meeting of officers at Boroughbridge on 3 April the response was generally cool. Lieutenant-General Sir John Conyers, the senior officer in the north, got wind of it and responsibly reported what he knew to Northumberland. The Commons were soon informed, and voted on 6 April that anyone who moved the army without parliament's advice and consent would be accounted 'enemies to king and state'. At about this time Goring revealed 'the main of the business' to Saye, Bedford, and Mandeville, among others; Charles reportedly countermanded the wilder plot when he heard of the poor response to it at

[17] Edward Hyde, Earl of Clarendon, *History of the Rebellion*, ed. W. D. Macray (6 vols., Oxford, 1888), III, 318–21.
[18] Quoted in Gardiner, *History of England*, IX, 340.

Boroughbridge, but it has been plausibly suggested that he encouraged Goring (who lost none of his favour) to leak it to the parliamentary leaders, in order to warn them that if they pursued Strafford to death they ran the risk of a military coup.[19] If this was indeed Charles's tactic, he was playing with fire.

Although the design to bring the army south was in abeyance by the time Strafford was attainted, the plot to seize the Tower remained very much alive. Three days after the Commons passed the attainder, Suckling set about recruiting a hundred men under Captain Billingsley, an officer of Strafford's Irish army—not a large force, but sufficient to overcome the forty Yeomen Warders of the Tower. On 28 April a plot for Strafford's escape was discovered; a ship had been chartered and was waiting for him at Tilbury. Three days later the Commons were summoned to the Lords' chamber to hear the king address his parliament. They feared a sudden dissolution, but Charles was intent only on saving Strafford. He gave his minister's judges certain assurances, including a belated undertaking never to employ Strafford again in any capacity (which might have been helpful earlier in the year); then he declared that his conscience would never allow him to assent to the bill of attainder. Since the Lords had not yet passed the bill, he was in effect claiming that his royal conscience was a bar to the will of parliament. To Laud's sad thinking, this personal intervention brought his friend's death nearer.

Charles made an even worse misjudgement early on 3 May when he ordered Billingsley and his men into the Tower. The Lieutenant, Sir William Balfour, refused to admit them, and some watchful citizens who witnessed the incident promptly alerted the Lords, who immediately sent the Earl of Newport, Master of the Ordnance, to secure the Tower. Charles was forced to back down and discharge Billingsley, while the peers who assembled that day to consider the bill of attainder had to pass through a huge crowd of mainly respectable, well-to-do London citizens, shouting 'justice and execution!' The debate on Strafford's fate could hardly have opened under more inauspicious circumstances. When on the same day Alderman Pennington reported Billingsley's failed attempt to the Commons, Pym promptly made capital of it. It was part of a design by the papists to overthrow the kingdom, he said, and members must bind themselves to maintain the liberties of the subject against any such conspiracies. Others, notably Henry Marten, invoked the Elizabethan precedent of an oath and bond of association. A committee was set up to draft what became one of the key documents of the next year and more, the so-called Protestation. Reported, debated, amended, and passed that same day, it was intended to be subscribed not only by members of both Houses but by men of goodwill throughout the kingdom.

---

[19] Russell, *Fall of the British Monarchies*, pp. 291–3; C. Russell, 'The first Army Plot of 1641', *Transactions of the Royal Historical Society*, 5th series, XXXVIII (1988), esp. pp. 100–1.

Deploring the designs of priests and Jesuits to undermine the established protestant religion, the preamble alleged that there still were 'endeavours to subvert the fundamental laws of England and Ireland, and to introduce the exercise of an arbitrary and tyrannical government by most wicked counsels, practices, plots and conspiracies'. The core of the Protestation was a solemn vow to maintain and defend 'the true reformed protestant religion expressed in the doctrine of the Church of England', the king's person and estate, and the powers and privileges of parliaments. Those who took it pledged themselves to bring to condign punishment all who did anything contrary to these ends, and to promote union and peace between the three kingdoms.[20] Its promoters conceived it as almost an equivalent to the Scottish National Covenant, and soon afterwards passed a bill to impose it on all Englishmen. The Lords eventually rejected this, but all the protestant peers present took the Protestation on 4 May, and it was soon circulating widely for signatures, first in London, than further afield.

A rougher mob, armed with swords and staves, noisily beset the Upper House on the 4th and threatened those lords whom they took to be Straffordians. But the peers were very angry over the army plot, and let the Commons know that only their unwillingness to act under crude popular pressure was holding up their final decision on the attainder bill. That same day, Strafford wrote a brave and moving letter to the king, releasing him from his promise and beseeching him to pass the bill, rather than incur 'the many ills that may befall your sacred person and the whole kingdom should yourself and parliament part less satisfied one with the other than is necessary for the preservation both of king and people'.[21] There is no reason to doubt the sincerity of his gesture, but he probably hoped that Charles would divulge the letter to the parliament, and there is some evidence that he advised him to do so. Perhaps there was just a hope that the Lords might be moved by such magnanimity in a fellow peer, but the advice, if given, was not acted upon.

The tumults around the Palace of Westminster continued during the next few days. On the 5th Pym disclosed all he knew of the army plot to the Commons, and embellished it with unfounded statements that French troops were massing near the Channel coast, allegedly with Portsmouth as their objective. Since Goring had recently been fortifying Portsmouth, and the queen had packed all her plate with the intention of taking refuge there from the threatening Londoners, the House's reaction came close to panic. When a board in the gallery broke with a sharp crack, a member cried that he smelt gunpowder and set off an ignominious rush for the lobby; the spreading wave of rumour that ensued brought out the City trained bands. In sober fact, Car-

[20] Text in Gardiner (ed.), *Constitutional Documents*, pp. 155–6.
[21] Wedgwood, *Thomas Wentworth*, pp. 373–5, where almost all of Strafford's letter is printed.

dinal Richelieu was totally unsympathetic to Henrietta Maria's appeals for French assistance to her husband and had strongly advised her not to return to France. But the army plot fever was inflamed next day by the news that Percy, Jermyn, Suckling, and Davenant had fled; the first three got away to France, but Davenant was captured. In those febrile days of early May both Houses, but especially the Lords, began to take direct executive action in areas that traditionally lay firmly within the king's prerogative. They disposed of the trained bands and the command of the king's ships, and they secured Portsmouth, which Goring handed over to parliament's commissioners. They also requested changes in the Lords Lieutenant, to ensure that the militia should be in safe hands. For the first time they sensed a threat of civil war in the air, and their reactions anticipated much of what they were to do in 1642. Such was the fear that Charles would resort to a sudden dissolution, rather than assent to the attainder, that a bill providing that the present parliament (and only the present one) could not be dissolved or adjourned without its own consent was rushed through all its stages in both Houses in four days.

There was a considerable exodus from the Lords before they gave the attainder bill its third reading on Saturday 8 May. The catholic peers had ceased to attend after refusing the Protestation, and the bishops had withdrawn on a motion by Williams of Lincoln. Others who might have voted against the bill may have been deterred by the intimidatory mobs, others again by a more responsible fear of a general breakdown of order if parliament tore itself apart on the issue. London was still in a violent mood, gripped that day by a false report that a French fleet had seized Jersey and Guernsey. Only the French ambassador dissuaded the queen from fleeing immediately, by warning her that she was sure to be stopped on her way to Portsmouth (neither of them knew that it was already in parliamentary hands). The Lords passed the attainder bill, according to Secretary Vane's contemporary report, by 51 votes to 9; a later account gave the figures as 26 to 19.[22] Either way it was a thin house, for there were nearly 120 peers in England, including minors, and some recent attendances had been much higher.

The parliamentary delegation that took the bill to the king for his assent was followed by an armed multitude, and on and off during that weekend Whitehall Palace was beset with threatening mobs, shouting for Strafford's blood. Charles agonized for long before coming to a decision. On his moral dilemma he received conflicting advice from the five bishops whom he

[22] Russell in *Fall of the British Monarchies*, pp. 296–8, cautiously accepts 51: 9; Fletcher in *Outbreak of the English Civil War*, p. 14, opts for 26: 19, as do several other historians. The latter figure derives from *A briefe and perfect relation of the answers and replies of Thomas Earle of Strafford* (1647), p. 85. The evidence of the Lords' Journal is lacking because the record of the vote was expunged at the Restoration.

consulted, but most of the privy council, who found him in tears when they met at his summons on the Sunday, advised him to give way. On the Monday he did so, moved by fear for the safety of his terrified wife and his children. It lay on his conscience for the rest of his life.

Strafford received the news with apparent shock, which suggests that he had really hoped that his letter to the king might save him. He asked in vain for a last meeting with Laud, but sent him a message by Ussher, bidding him be at his window when he went by on his way to the scaffold. As the procession passed, he bowed low to his old friend, who managed to raise his hands in prayer and blessing before falling to the ground in a faint. Strafford met his death on Tower Hill, before a hostile crowd of 100,000, with that touch of the heroic that had characterized the best parts of his flawed career. What might his talents have achieved, one may wonder, if he had served a wiser master, within a sounder political framework.

At the same time as he passed the attainder, Charles assented to the bill whereby he gave up his prerogative right to terminate the present parliament. It could now be dissolved only be an act of parliament, and adjourned only by order of each House. The Lords had tried unsuccessfully to limit its operation to two years, but neither they nor anyone else can have foreseen that all but twenty years would pass before the Long Parliament enacted its own dissolution. These were not Charles's only concessions, for two days earlier he had ordered the disbandment of the army that Strafford had raised in Ireland. He could see no way of raising the money to pay it.

His dabbling in schemes for some kind of military coup had not only done Strafford more harm than good; it had seriously set back his own best hope for the future, that of building up a party of conservative constitutionalists on the basis of a common devotion to the established church and the principle of order. He dealt a further blow to such a prospect when he announced, within a week of Strafford's execution, that he intended to visit Scotland as soon as the peace treaty, now in its final stages, was concluded. The English parliament took its time in approving the terms of the Treaty of London, but got through it by the end of June. The Scottish parliament passed it on 24 July, and the king ratified it on 10 August, just before he set out for Scotland. The Scottish army pulled out of England later in the month, and all but three regiments were disbanded. The slow disbandment of the English army began at the same time. This should have led to détente, but relief over the reduction of these costly forces was offset by suspicion of Charles's motives in travelling north of the border. Four future royalist lords, including Montrose and Napier, were being held in Edinburgh Castle for what the Covenanters called a plot, but what they saw as the pursuit of an alternative policy for Scotland. Charles was interested in exploring what they had to offer, and hoped to build a party for himself in Scotland.

He would have been better engaged in an exercise of damage limitation in England, for the full investigation of the army plot by a parliamentary committee did him great harm, especially in the House of Lords. But far from learning his lesson, he proceeded to involve himself in a second army plot. Late in May or very early in June, he sent Daniel O'Neill, his agent in the first plot, back to the army in the north with the draft of a petition, initialled by himself, intending that it should be circulated for signatures. It deplored the turbulent spirits who were advancing new and unreasonable demands, backed by a tumultuous multitude who threatened a total subversion of government, and it purported to offer the army's services for the defence of the king, the parliament and the established laws. The design came to nothing because the army's responsible commanders would have nothing to do with it, and it was not made public until the autumn, but it almost certainly came to Pym's knowledge well before the end of June.

In the immediate aftermath of Strafford's execution the two Houses continued to be divided, both internally and in their relations with each other, over the question of episcopacy. The Lords did not throw out the Bishops' Exclusion Bill until 8 June, but they made their intentions clear on 25 May by voting that the bishops should continue to sit in their House. The Commons retorted on the 27th with a bill to abolish bishops root and branch, which passed its first reading by 139 votes to 108. The majority probably included others besides its introducer, Sir Edward Dering, who were moved more by detestation of 'Arminian' bishops and exasperation with the Lords than by a desire to abolish episcopacy totally. Until the approach of civil war removed the royalists from Westminster in the following year, there never was an outright majority in either house opposed to episcopacy in principle. The bill proved deeply divisive, and the long debates on it played a considerable part in turning devoted Anglicans like Hyde, Falkland, and Culpepper towards the king. It never reached the Lords, though it was much elaborated in committee during the summer months. It did not satisfy the Scots, for what it proposed in place of bishops were not presbyteries and synods but commissioners, some lay and some clerical, appointed by parliament. The result would have been as Erastian as the system it replaced, and the main purpose of most of its promoters was not so much to reform religion as to ensure that the king never controlled the church again. The hours that it consumed and the contentious feelings that it aroused helped to frustrate other bills with a more positively religious purpose, such as those for requiring ministers to preach regularly, checking pluralism, removing scandalous clergy, tightening sabbath observance, and abolishing idolatry and superstition. A bill to disarm Roman Catholics came back from the Lords too heavily amended for the Commons to accept it, though even they laughed down a proposal by Sir John Clotworthy for a bill to castrate priests and Jesuits.[23]

Although religious issues continued to divide the two Houses, the repercussions of the army plot and distrust of the king's intentions brought them closer together on constitutional issues. Between late June and early August the Long Parliament passed a series of acts which placed unprecedented limitations on the royal prerogative and proved to be its most enduring work. These measures, unlike the attacks on episcopacy and the prayer book, generally had the support of the future constitutional royalists in both Houses. The first tackled the sixteen-year-old conflict over tonnage and poundage by granting these essential dues, the largest single source of the crown's revenue, for an initial period of less than two months. It therefore strengthened parliament's security against a dissolution because it needed frequent renewal, but its enduring feature was its unequivocal denial that any duties whatsoever could be imposed on either imports or exports without parliament's consent, for this settled the much older controversy over impositions.

Two more acts, to which the king gave his reluctant assent on 5 July, abolished the Courts of Star Chamber and High Commission. Both derived their authority from the royal prerogative, and their abrogation at the instance of parliament diminished the monarch's powers significantly. Henceforth the courts of common law were to be the sole arbiters between his interests and the rights of his subjects, and the only ways in which he could interfere with their sometimes archaic and dilatory processes was through his power of pardon or by exercising direct pressure on the judges, whom he still had the power to appoint or dismiss. Star Chamber had played a useful part in mitigating the deficiencies of the common law and had been a generally popular institution until its authority had been abused in the notorious political cases of the 1630s. Had it not been for those it would not have come under attack. The High Commission, however, had few if any mourners outside the Laudian clergy, though they had themselves to thank for its peak of unpopularity in 1641.

These measures were followed early in August by acts declaring Ship Money to be illegal, setting firm limits to the royal forests (and hence to the fines inflicted under the forest laws), and prohibiting the exaction of fines for failing to assume knighthood. Taken with the Tonnage and Poundage Act, they closed all the significant loopholes through which taxes had been raised without parliamentary consent and made a recurrence of the personal rule legally impossible. It might look as though the king had suffered a serious political defeat by the time that he departed for Scotland on 10 August. Yet the parliament's position was less happy than it might appear, and there were

---

[23] Fletcher, *Outbreak of the English Civil War*, pp. 69–70. Pym, however, gave the proposal a serious reply: Russell, *Fall of the English Monarchies*, p. 340.

serious issues, in addition to the religious ones, on which it remained divided. The Bedford–Pym group's scheme for a settlement lay in ruins, not just because Bedford had died on 9 May but because such unity of purpose as it once possessed had disappeared. Charles had made enough 'bridge appointments' to split it apart, but not enough to make him part with the power of decision. Just before he left for Scotland he balanced the recent 'country' appointments to his privy council by adding three court-oriented peers to it, but since it had seldom met since February this made no significant difference.

The crucial problem of ensuring that royal policies were guided by ministers whom parliament trusted, and of securing the removal of ministers whom it did not, had not been solved. Pym, probably under the immediate stimulus of his personal knowledge of the second army plot, signalled a radical new approach to it in a speech to the Commons on 23 June. What he proposed was referred to a committee of seven to put into definitive shape and carried to the Lords next day in the form of Ten Propositions. The most vital one, somewhat toned down by the Commons, was that both Houses should petition the king 'to remove such evil counsellors against whom there shall be any just exceptions', and that he should commit the affairs of the kingdom 'to such counsellors and officers as the parliament may have cause to confide in'.[24] This was as far as the majority of members would go for the present in matching the Scottish parliament's new power to control the appointment of councillors and ministers, but for Pym and his allies the intention was the same. Pym also raised the other major issue that was to lead to civil war, the control of the armed forces, but the drafting committee moderated his first proposal that all the lord lieutenants and deputy lieutenants, who had charge of the trained bands, should be nominated in parliament and that the forces of every county should be 'put into a posture of defence'. What the two Houses finally requested was 'That there may be good lord lieutenants and deputy lieutenants', that the trained bands should be fully armed and made fit for service, and that all who commanded them should take a special oath, to be framed by parliament. Many in the Commons were prepared to bid higher; in July they gave two readings to a militia bill which would have put the trained bands under named commissioners for nine months, but it went no further after the king left for Scotland.

Others of the Ten Propositions were particularly offensive to the queen, who was to be allowed no Jesuits or British-born priests in her service and was to be attended by a guard to prevent the resort of papists to her. The education of the royal children was to be committed to protestants, the college of Capuchins at Somerset House was to be dissolved and its members banished,

---

[24] Gardiner, *Constitutional Documents*, pp. 163–6, prints the Ten Propositions as they emerged from the Commons' committee. On their passage through parliament and their repercussions see Fletcher, *Outbreak of the English Civil War*, ch. 2.

and it was to be made treason for a papal nuncio or agent to enter the kingdom. The Lords demurred only at the most gratuitous of these affronts to the queen; they agreed to all the rest of the Propositions with striking readiness.

Pym's personal standing was now nearing its peak, but he had difficulty in managing parliament because so many members of both Houses were slipping off home. It had already been an unprecedentedly long session, and with plague and smallpox spreading seriously from the City to Westminster it was dangerous as well as uncomfortable to stay in the capital through the hot summer months. From July onward there was often difficulty in assembling a quorum of forty members, especially early in the morning and after a break for dinner. But the leadership felt it essential to keep the parliament sitting through August and beyond, because they simply did not feel safe until the armies—especially the king's, of course—were disbanded. In one way their task was easier, since it was mainly the lukewarm who went home, and about sixty activists who enabled them to keep going. In consequence the religious temper of the House became less moderate and more aggressively anti-papist. Late in July the Commons sent up an oppressive bill to compel all Englishmen to sign the Protestation or face the penalties of recusancy; peers who refused it were to be debarred from parliament. When the Lords predictably rejected the bill, the Commons published a vote declaring that all who refused the Protestation were unfit for office in church or state. This they had printed and sent out to their constituencies, to the Lords' intense resentment. They also instituted impeachment proceedings against thirteen bishops for their alleged part in preparing the 1640 canons.

Despite such irritants, however, Pym usually found enough support among the dwindling number of peers still at Westminster to get essential business done. In the hazardous situation created by the king's departure, while two armies were still afoot, the two houses went further than before in taking executive action of a kind that had never belonged to the legislature. During the last three weeks of the session they issued the first five parliamentary ordinances. Most of these were relatively innocuous measures, justifiable by the king's absence. But the ordinance for disarming recusants, which the Lords were now willing to pass, went further than enforcing existing law, for it extended the definition of recusancy to include new categories of offenders and suspects, and added to the catholics' disabilities. That great lawyer John Selden warned the Commons that it 'made new laws which it could not'.[25] It was a significant step towards the assertion of parliamentary sovereignty that would become explicit in the following spring.

[25] Quoted in Fletcher, *Outbreak*, pp. 76–7. Fletcher explains the objections to the ordinance more fully than is possible here.

The ninth of September was the date appointed for a six weeks' adjournment, and as it drew close the attenuated House of Commons was overcome by a sense that it had not done enough to restore the purity of religion. On its own sole authority it published an order on the 8th, commanding the churchwardens in every parish to move the communion table away from the east end of the church, take down the rails, and remove any crucifixes, images of the Virgin Mary, and 'scandalous pictures of any one or more persons of the Trinity'. The order forbade bowing at the name of Jesus, as well as dancing or other sports on the Lord's Day.[26] It was not passed without exposing deep differences among the members; it angered the Lords and caused great division in the country generally. Much of what it banned was neither contrary to law nor universally disliked, and it led to much destruction of medieval carving and stained glass. The iconoclasm that was so often ascribed uncritically to 'Cromwell's soldiers' began nearly a year before the Civil War, and much of it was carried out by civil agencies on the orders of the people's representatives. The Lords responded by publishing an order of their own, first passed in January, commanding that divine service be performed as appointed by acts of parliament, and not otherwise. On these discordant notes the two houses adjourned themselves until 20 October.

Each named a committee to look after parliament's interests in the interim, and to correspond with a joint committee that they had appointed to attend the king in Scotland. The Commons nominated forty-seven MPs, but attendance sometimes sank as low as twelve; the plague was at its worst in October. Pym as their chairman, however, was never more powerful, and many of their executive orders bore his sole signature. It was at this time that he began to be called King Pym; but the sobriquet was not used affectionately, and he was quite widely unpopular. Many backbenchers disliked the tactics whereby his policies were driven through parliament, and he and his faction were attacked in printed libels, scattered and posted up in the streets of London. They were particularly accused, unjustly, of working hand in glove with sectaries, tub-preachers, and other radical puritans of the City. They themselves were totally convinced of the need to curb the king's powers further than they had yet done, and though they may have been unduly alarmist about his present capacity to cast off the restraints imposed by their recent measures, and unrealistically obsessed with popish plots, they were not mistaken about his long-term intentions or his trustworthiness. They had not succeeded, however, in conveying their sense of urgency to the provinces, where there was by now quite a widespread reaction in Charles's favour. This stemmed partly from a dislike of the activities and pretensions of the godly interest, but many

[26] Text in Gardiner (ed.), *Constitutional Documents*, pp. 197–8; the Lords' order of 9 September is on p. 199.

people also felt that the king had been driven too hard. If he had not been far away in Scotland, he might have exploited this reaction to considerable advantage. But while his opponents' suspicions were concentrated on his activities north of the border, they were quite unaware of the imminent danger of an explosion in Ireland. This unforeseen tragedy, more than any other factor, was to wreck the widespread hopes of a new constitutional deal in England and Scotland.

# SEVEN

# Three Kingdoms in Crisis

WHEN Charles arrived in Edinburgh on 14 August 1641 he was delighted by the warmth of his reception. He did not yet appreciate that most Scots believed they had already won the substance of what they had fought for in the Treaty of London, and expected to secure the rest in the course of his visit. After his ceremonial entry into parliament on the 17th he made a gracious speech which seemed to confirm their hopes. But when he offered to touch the acts passed by the parliament in 1640 with his sceptre, the traditional way of conferring the royal assent, a pretext was found for requesting him to delay the ceremony. Parliament, it transpired, was not prepared to acknowledge that his assent was necessary, and he allowed the acts to be published a few days later without it. After what he had conceded earlier in the year he could hardly do otherwise, but this was more than a symbolic defeat for him.

He genuinely desired to come to agreement with the Scottish parliament, but three unsettled questions still stood in the way of it. One was the treatment of those whom the Covenanters branded as 'incendiaries', the chief of whom were Traquair and Montrose. He eventually agreed not to grant them access to him or give them public employment without parliament's consent, and he conceded that parliament should bring them both to trial, on the understanding that it would refrain from passing final sentence. A more serious difference was over the appointment of officers of state; just what had he agreed to in the previous year? His assumption was that he would nominate them, subject to parliament's approval, which he expected it to give unless it advanced specific objections, but parliament's understanding was that it would name a list of candidates from whom he would choose. There was a direct clash over the two highest offices of all: the Covenanters wanted Argyll as Chancellor and his brother Loudoun as Treasurer. But Charles could not stomach Argyll in the powerful place of Chancellor, which eventually went to Loudoun, while the treasury, for which he had proposed the Earl of Morton, was put into commission. The third divisive issue, which was really not resolved at all, was whether the Scots had a right to be formally heard when decisions were taken at Westminster which deeply involved their country's interests.

In most of these points of difference, personalities were almost as much concerned as principles. Argyll remained the most powerful man in Scotland, with or without the Chancellor's office. Hamilton was much associated with him at this time, and he also kept in close touch with the English commissioners appointed by the Long Parliament to attend the king. Charles was displeased with Hamilton and frankly suspected that his main concern was with his own self-preservation, but he did not break with his old friend, who still attended upon him and regularly slept in his bedchamber. Nothing was ever simple in Hamilton's motives, but he may have been genuinely striving to keep the channels open between the king and the Covenanting nobles. Montrose was a personal enemy of his; that too played a part in his rapport with Argyll, which was bitterly criticized by the Scottish royalists, and led Roxburgh's son Lord Ker to challenge him to a duel.

An extraordinary plot came to a head in the second week of October, which came to be known simply as the Incident. The evidence is complex and shot through with uncertainties, but the plan seems to have been to assemble four hundred armed men and seize Argyll, Hamilton, and Lanark in the king's withdrawing room. The three were to be brought there by Will Murray, Charles's Groom of the Bedchamber; Lord Almond (who had signed the Cumbernauld Band) and the catholic Earl of Crawford (who commanded one of the three Scottish regiments still under arms) were to perform the arrest. Almond, it is reported, intended to bring the three to legal trial, Crawford to murder them. Murder, we can be sure, Charles would never have countenanced, and there is no certain proof that he was privy to the plot. But the fact that his intimate servant Murray had a central role in it makes it scarcely conceivable that he knew nothing of it, and so does the conduct of Montrose, who wrote to him three times from prison asking for an audience, and on 11 October was given one. What he wanted to offer, according to Crawford, was an accusation of high treason against Argyll and Hamilton. It was never levelled, because one of the several soldiers of fortune involved, Colonel John Urry or Hurry (who was to change sides three times before the wars were over) divulged the plot to General Leslie. Leslie, like the man of honour he was, made Urry repeat it to Hamilton and Argyll. They could scarcely believe it, but after some hesitation they fled to Hamilton's house at Kinneill, some miles outside Edinburgh. Soon the wildest rumours were running, and they were not kind to the king. Charles furiously denounced the whole affair as a fabrication of his enemies, designed to discredit him, and he had the gall to throw most of the blame for it on Hamilton, one of its intended victims. But he did not help his cause by coming to parliament next day with a guard of several hundred armed royalists. He demanded a public investigation, to clear his honour; parliament decided on a secret one, and named only one royalist to the committee entrusted with it. After it had produced a face-saving report, Hamilton returned to Edinburgh and to attendance upon the king.

Charles's credit was seriously damaged. He stayed in Scotland until the parliament dissolved itself on 17 November, but when he departed he had achieved none of the objectives for which he had come north. Any thoughts he may have had of mustering a following strong enough to help him recover his position in England must have withered under the chill realities of the Scottish political scene. Montrose was released just before he left, in a general amnesty following the Incident, but the Covenanters remained so dominant that the Scottish royalists were almost powerless to help him. The parliament had stood its ground to him; when a new Scottish privy council was named shortly before the dissolution, ostensibly by him with parliament's advice and consent, he was allowed four or five royalists on it, but eight more whom he had proposed were overruled, and Covenanters appointed in their place. The four commissions that parliament had set up to look after its various interests until its successor met ensured that its constitutional standing would be fully safeguarded. Charles sought to sweeten his departure by making Argyll a marquis, Hamilton a duke, Leslie an earl and Wariston a knight, but these and other honours that he conferred were to have no effect when it came to civil war and their recipients had to choose sides. A full military alliance between the Covenanting leadership and the English parliament would be only a matter of time. Edward Hyde's subsequent verdict, writing as Earl of Clarendon, was 'that he seemed to have made that progress in Scotland only that he might make a perfect deed of gift of that kingdom'.[1]

The lurid reports of the Incident came as a godsend to Pym, for he badly needed something to revive a sense of urgency in England, now that the armies were disbanded. On the first day of the new session the Commons had to wait idly after prayers for a quorum of forty members to assemble, and Pym waited longer for a fuller House before he broke the news from Scotland. Hyde and Falkland tried to cast doubt on it, but a majority in both Houses were ready to believe that they too might be threatened with violence and ordered a guard to be posted on the Palace of Westminster night and day. Next day (21 October), in a House so thin that it again had difficulty in maintaining a quorum, a new bill was introduced to exclude the bishops from parliament, and it passed its three readings so rapidly that it was sent to the Lords two days later.[2] The Commons followed it up with a resolution asking the Lords to suspend the bishops when the vote on the bill was taken. But Charles, from Edinburgh, had just let it be known to the peers through Secretary Nicholas

---

[1] Clarendon, *History of the Rebellion*, I, 415.
[2] On the thin attendances see *The Journal of Sir Simonds D'Ewes*, Oct. 1641–Jan. 1642, ed. W. H. Coates (New Haven, 1942), pp. 11–15, 29, 32–3, 49.

that he had no intention of altering the government of the Church of England, and he shortly underlined his message by appointing five new bishops and translating others. Episcopacy, however, was not the issue uppermost in Pym's mind. His main plan for the new session was to revive something that had been mooted at intervals since the parliament first met: a comprehensive remonstrance of the state of the kingdom, which would tabulate all that had gone amiss since Charles's accession, state what parliament had achieved so far by way of remedy, and set out what still remained for it to do. The first of November was set aside for the Commons to consider a draft of this Grand Remonstrance; meanwhile on 30 October Pym kept the temperature up by divulging to the House, with all the oratory he could command, its committee's full report on the second army plot.

On the appointed day for the great debate, however, the Grand Remonstrance was thrust aside by the appalling news that a major rebellion had broken out in Ireland. It was to bring terror and carnage to the settler population, and in the longer term it set in train a great tragedy for the Irish people as a whole. In between, it was to have a powerful bearing on the course of events that culminated in civil war in England.

There were two connected parts to the initial design: a plot to seize Dublin Castle and incapacitate the English administration, and a rising in Ulster to recover the estates of the dispossessed Irish nobles and gentry. There had been no Lord Lieutenant in Dublin since Strafford's recall, and Lord Deputy Wandesford was dead. Robert Sidney, Earl of Leicester, had been appointed Lord Lieutenant in June 1641, but Charles had charged him not to go to Ireland until he personally ordered him to do so. Responsibility in Dublin lay with two elderly Lords Justices, both closely associated with the settler interest: Sir William Parsons, who had sided with the Irish parliament's opposition to Strafford, and Sir John Borlase, an indolent ex-soldier. The design against Dublin Castle, like the Ulster rebellion, had been timed for 23 October, but the Lords Justices were informed of it the very night before. They were able to arrest the chief conspirators, Lord Maguire, Hugh MacMahon, and about thirty others, and they made Dublin safe, but they could not cope with the forest fire that was spreading in the north. Now that Strafford's levies were disbanded they had only the older regular army at their disposal. It numbered fewer than 2,300 foot and 950 horse; it was widely dispersed, and some of its units were already disarmed by the Ulster insurgents. The Lords Justices proclaimed a state of rebellion, describing it as 'a most disloyal and detestable conspiracy intended by some evil-affected Irish papists'.[3] Before long they

---

[3] Quoted in *A New History of Ireland*, III, 292. On the outbreak of the rebellion see also M. Perceval-Maxwell, *The Outbreak of the Irish Rebellion of 1641* (Dublin, 1994); Aidan Clarke, *The Old English in Ireland* (Ithaca, N.Y., and London, 1966), ch. 9; the chapters by M. Perceval-Maxwell, Raymond Gillaspie, Hilary Simms, and Aidan Clarke in *Ulster 1641*, ed. Mac

were depicting it as a general rising by the 'mere Irish' against English rule and a popish-inspired design to massacre all the protestants in Ireland.

Their reports were far from the truth. At first, their misrepresentations can be largely attributed to panic, prejudice, and imperfect knowledge, but they probably became more deliberate quite soon. It suited the books of the settler class to portray the rebellion as a general attempt by the catholic Irish to extirpate the English crown's authority and the protestant religion, because that would lead (they hoped) to a massive military response, a total subjugation of Ireland, and the release of untold quantities of land for easy purchase and colonization. Their attitude was tested on 24 and 25 October when eight of the chief Old English Lords of the Pale, all catholics, approached the Lords Justices, professing their loyalty to the king and asking to be furnished with arms for their own defence. The Lords Justices replied that they were not sure whether they had arms enough to defend the city, which was manifestly untrue, since the store in Dublin Castle included all those handed in by Strafford's disbanded army, and sufficed for nearly 10,000 men. But their reluctance to arm catholics of any kind was understandable, though soon afterwards they proclaimed their belief in the personal fidelity of the Lords of the Pale.

To understand what really lay behind the Irish rebellion, it is necessary to make some distinctions between the attitudes of the Old English and the Old Irish, though the line between them was anything but clear-cut. The Old English lordships were scattered over most parts of Ireland except the north; Ulster was Old Irish territory, where it had not been taken over by English or Scottish settlers, though there were Old Irish landowners in all the provinces. It will be remembered that in December 1640 Charles had received a delegation and a remonstrance from the Irish parliament.[4] The Old English members of that delegation entered into a negotiation with him, and he appointed a committee of the privy council to consider their grievances in general and the Graces in particular. During the time of Strafford's trial, when he was dabbling in the first army plot, he was hoping to save at least part of Strafford's army, and he needed a non-parliamentary source of revenue to keep it afoot. On 3 April, in return for the promise of a subsidy from the Old English, he agreed to cancel the future plantations that had been planned, authorize a statute conferring good title on landlords with sixty years' possession, and grant the enactment of others of the Graces. In return for two more voluntary subsidies he offered further far-reaching concessions in July, and ordered that the bills to implement them should be prepared. His raising of Old Irish hopes was of course a tactical move, and part of the same strategy as his planned

---

Cuarta; and William Kelly's essay on Ormond in *Celtic Dimensions of the British Civil Wars*, ed. J. R. Young (Edinburgh, 1997).

[4] See pp. 163–4.

visit to Scotland. If he could enlist a substantial party in both kingdoms and rally a large part of the English nobility, he might (he thought) be able to pull off what he most desired, a dissolution of the Long Parliament.

His concessions were highly unwelcome to the Irish council in Dublin, which had a strong interest in further plantation, especially in Connaught, and resented not being consulted. It took steps to frustrate the passage of the promised bills through the Irish parliament, but before that was necessary Charles was given a pretext to withdraw the Graces again (which he did willingly enough, once he had to give up hope of keeping up any part of Strafford's army). A row developed over a Scottish settler in Ulster who had been imprisoned for refusing the black oath. The leadership in Edinburgh took umbrage and pressed his case on the English House of Lords, which at one stage summoned the entire Irish council to appear before it as delinquents. Naturally there were protests from Ireland, to which the Lords responded by requesting the king not to grant the Graces, and to declare the Irish parliament to be subject to that of England. Charles complied.

Aggrieved though the Old English were by this treatment, few of them thought of resistance, let alone rebellion. Their loyalty to the king, though strained, survived, since a political triumph for the ultra-protestant elements in the English parliament, in partnership with the Scottish Covenanters, could harm them more than ever he could. Nor was it a matter merely of calculation, for they felt honour bound to maintain their old partnership with the crown, however ill it had been rewarded. But another party, mainly of Old Irish, were coming to feel that they would need to resort to force to secure what they considered to be their rights. A group of them began to make contingency plans to that end in February 1641, and it was not long before the second denial of the Graces and the English parliament's evident intent to treat Ireland as a subject province took the brakes off their enterprise and improved its prospects of finding wide support. In their own minds they were not plotting a rebellion against their king, for they too saw themselves as his loyal subjects—certainly more so than the Scottish Covenanters, in their estimate. Their plan was for a coup against the government in Dublin, which they regarded as disloyal to him, coupled with a seizure of strongholds and towns in Ulster. What they sought for Ireland were the liberties that the king's English subjects enjoyed: the rights of an independent kingdom under a common monarch, with a government answerable to him but not to that of England, a parliament with the same powers and privileges as that of Westminster, and a free judiciary. For themselves they sought the same security of title as English landlords had, and the right to practise the catholic religion—the national religion, in fact if not in law—without political or financial disabilities. They were anxious to demonstrate that, contrary to English prejudice, their catholicism was in no way incompatible with loyalty to the crown.

They planned to seize Dublin Castle on 23 October 1641, but their design was betrayed and foiled. According to Lord Dillon, who was in on their secrets, they intended to replace the Lords Justices with James Butler, Earl of Ormond, a rare protestant among the great Old English families and a staunch though not uncritical royalist. He was a close and trusted friend of Strafford, who in 1638 made him Lieutenant-General of the Irish army and commander-in-chief during his own absences in England, despite the fact that Ormond was not quite twenty-seven when so promoted and had seen no military action. He was also Lord President of Munster, where most of his vast estates lay, though they extended well into Leinster. For all his loyalty to the king and his attachment to Strafford, he had serious misgivings about their plans to use the Irish army against the Covenanters, and in the spring of 1640 he withdrew to his seat at Kilkenny, ostensibly because of his anxiety about his wife's pregnancy, though he stayed there for more than two months after she bore him a daughter. The interesting question, then and ever since, is whether he knew in advance of the intended strike against Dublin Castle, but the surviving sources leave us no certain answer.

The planned coup in Dublin was aimed mainly against the Long Parliament's plans, of which the Lords Justices were the agents, to subject Ireland to itself and make her an even more subordinate kingdom than she had become already. Its betrayal did not put a stop to the wider movement, centred on Ulster and aimed at redressing the grievances of the 1630s: the massive plantations, the failure to grant the Graces, the religious, political, and economic disabilities of Irish catholics, and so on. Sir Phelim O'Neill, the catholic leader in Ulster, punctually set off the rising there on 23 October by capturing the key fortress of Charlemont, but he immediately issued a proclamation, declaring that they were not in arms against the king but only in defence of their liberties. Lord Dillon, the head of a gaelicized Anglo-Norman house but nevertheless a protestant and an Irish privy councillor, had visited Charles in Scotland shortly before, probably to assure him that whatever he might hear of commotions in Ireland the participants' intentions were loyal and their aims just. Perhaps his mission was their last bid to secure those aims without having to resort to rebellion. Charles is reported to have told him that he would come to Ireland in person in the spring or summer of 1642, presumably hoping by then to have crushed the Covenanters. Dillon came to see him again in London late in November 1641, when the rebellion was in full swing, with a document signed by many Irish catholic nobles and gentry, offering to suppress it themselves if he would grant certain not unreasonable demands,[5] of which more will be said shortly.

So why did a rebellion in one province, with such limited objectives, lead to

---

[5] Russell, *Fall of the English Monarchies*, pp. 396–8.

so much brutal bloodshed and swell within months into almost a national movement, in which some elements aimed ultimately at national independence? One reason, as we shall see, was that political strife in England prevented the English government from giving the concessions and assurances that would have held the mass of the Old English nobility and gentry to their allegiance. Another was that the rebellion passed rapidly out of control and unleashed popular violence on a scale that its planners had never intended, and mostly deplored. This outbreak of terror took everyone by surprise, for in spite of all the dispossession caused by the plantation Ulster had not looked like a powder-barrel waiting for a spark to explode it. There had been much mutual rapprochement since the plantation began; landlords who had settled only a generation or two ago were living on easy social terms with their Irish gentry neighbours, and without fear of their Irish servants. The richer were building not fortified castles but typical undefendable Jacobean mansions with as much glass as masonry in their walls. Intermarriage was not uncommon, and many native Ulster gentry bore a part in local government. But the ruling elite, whether long or lately settled, did not appreciate the gulf that had grown between them and the smaller folk who had been the worst losers when their clan territory was parcelled out under English law. Such people would never have risen if their superiors had not raised the standard of rebellion, and not all did so; there were cases of planters being saved by their Irish servants. But such was the pent-up resentment of the majority that once let loose it became uncontrollable. The early successes of the rebellion were almost too rapid and sweeping for its own good. Some of the settlers' castles and some walled towns, including Derry, held out, but the rebels secured much of central Ulster within two days and controlled eight of its nine counties after two weeks. Very early they began to advance southward; they took Dundalk on 31 October, Ardee in the Pale two or three days later, and then they laid siege to the vital port of Drogheda. Wherever they went they spread shock and terror. Social order collapsed, for many Irish JPs joined the insurgents, and many less sympathetic magistrates were killed or driven to flight. Although O'Neill publicly ordered that no hurt should be done to anyone on pain of death, there was a spontaneous surge among the common people to settle old scores and help themselves to the planters' possessions. In the early stages there was more robbery than murder, though from the start many settlers were turned out of their property, some to be killed, many set adrift, others made prisoners in order to be ransomed. Most of them probably knew their attackers, and had hitherto seen no reason to fear them. More probably died of exposure than were actually murdered, for many who were forced to take to the roads were stripped of their clothes as they fled.

Certainly there were horrible incidents, later enshrined in the folk memory of protestant Ulster, like that of the hundred or so men, women, and children who were imprisoned in Loughgall church, then marched to Portadown and drowned in the River Bann, some after being tortured. In another well attested case about thirty were herded into a house at Shewic and burnt alive in it. Refugees were soon landing in England with harrowing tales of murder, mutilation, and rape, which seemed to bear out the wildly exaggerated reports in the public prints of a general massacre. Generally the rebel leaders did what they could to restrain the savagery, and some catholic priests ritually cursed those who perpetrated it, warning the people against bringing down the wrath of God on what for them was a holy cause and a fight for the faith. We who have seen in our own time how far humanity can be forgotten in the heat of racial hatred, ethnic cleansing, religious fundamentalism, and reaction against colonial exploitation should not find it difficult to comprehend what happened in Ulster, which had elements of all these phenomena.

Modern catastrophes of such kinds, however, at least stand some chance of accurate and objective reporting, whereas what England heard and read of Ireland in 1641–2 was not only grossly overstated from the start, but dwelt solely on one side's atrocities. It is still very hard to form an estimate of how many perished in the Ulster rebellion. A careful attempt has been made for Armagh, one of the province's nine counties, which probably had between 3,000 and 5,000 settlers in 1641.[6] Reports of the numbers killed, whether in 'massacres' like Portadown or in individual murders, yield a minimum of 527 and a maximum of 1,259. Allowing for a tendency to exaggerate, balanced by some incompleteness in the evidence, one might conclude that about a fifth of the settler population was actually killed; the estimates do not include deaths by exposure. These calculations, lacking in precision as they necessarily are, suggest that the most widely accepted older estimate (made by Ferdinando Warner, an Anglican parson, in 1767) of 4,028 murder victims and perhaps twice as many refugees who died of cold, sickness, or hunger[7] is of the right order of magnitude, though it does not refer exclusively to Ulster. Considering that there were about 34,000 English and Scottish settlers in the province in 1641, these figures are tragic enough. But they bear no relation to the 'statistics' of protestants killed in Ireland that circulated most widely in England: 154,000 in April 1642, rising to 250,000 in 1644 and 300,000 in what became the standard authority, Sir John Temple's *The Irish Rebellion* of 1646. If it had been known that in 1641 there were fewer than 100,000 protestants in all Ireland, the absurdity of these confident allegations should have been self-evident, but this was a pre-statistical age.

---

[6] Hilary Simms, 'Violence in County Armagh, 1641', in *Ulster 1641*, ed. Mac Cuarta, pp. 123–43.

[7] F. Warner, *The History of the Rebellion and Civil War in Ireland* (1767), p. 297. Among those who have accepted Warner's estimate as the best available are W. E. H. Lecky (in *History of Ireland in the Eighteenth Century*, I, 46–89), Gardiner, *History of England*, X, 69, and *A New History of Ireland*, III, 291–2.

England's response to the Irish rebellion was vitiated by three things: mis-information from Dublin, blind prejudice against papists, and total lack of sympathy for legitimate Irish aspirations. Parliament's first reaction—to order the raising of 8,000 men to reinforce the Lords Justices' inadequate army and to request Leicester to go to Dublin at once—was reasonable enough. But it created a dilemma for Leicester, a studious, indecisive man, because of the king's instruction to await his personal command. The command never came, and Leicester never went. The Commons' second reaction, on the day after news of the rebellion first broke, was to demand that all prominent English recusants should be not only disarmed but arrested, and they launched an impeachment of the queen's confessor, Father Philip, large-ly because he, when interrogated, refused to swear on a protestant bible.

Pym, however, brought them to the central issue on 5 November with a motion to instruct the commissioners attending upon the king to put to him an unequivocal demand for parliamentary control over the composition of his government. The suppression of the Irish rebellion clearly necessitated the raising of a sizeable army; parliament had already voted for it. But could the king, whose army it would be, be trusted with it? If he could not, parliament needed to ensure that political and military decisions which would normally have been his to take were subject to the control of men that it could trust. The time was not yet ripe, though it soon would be, for parliament to claim direct control over the armed forces, though the very next day Cromwell carried a motion that the Earl of Essex, as Captain-General south of Trent, should be empowered to assemble the trained bands in that great area at any time, until parliament took further order. That however was an emergency measure, prompted by an unreal fear that the catholics in England were about to rise in arms, and that an army from Ireland would cross the sea to join them. Pym's motion, and the draft that he put to the House, looked beyond immediate contingencies, and the great debate on it on 8 November separ-ated future parliamentarians from future royalists more clearly than any previous one. The resultant 'Additional Instruction' to the commissioners in Scotland, approved by 151 votes to 110, alleged that the king continued to take counsel from 'favourers of popery, superstition and innovation', and blamed them not only for 'contriving by violence to suppress the liberty of par-liament', in other words for devising the army plot—but also for the present 'conspiracies and commotions in Ireland'. The commissioners were to request him to get rid of such advisers and 'to employ such counsellors and ministers as shall be approved by his parliament';[8] if he did not, parliament would be forced to take its own measures for dealing with the Irish rebels. This demand that parliament should positively approve all ministerial

---

[8]  Gardiner (ed.), *Constitutional Documents*, pp. 199–201.

appointments went significantly further than the request in the Ten Propositions that he should employ only such as parliament had cause to confide in,
and it was a direct result of the rebellion. It was never formally put to him,
because the Lords kept on putting off their debate of the Additional Instruction until he was back in England, but he was soon informed of it.

It would be fascinating to know whether Pym believed that there was some
complicity between the king and the rebels. He never directly accused him,
but the speech that Pym made when he delivered the Additional Instruction
to the Lords on 8 November suggests that he did suspect Charles, not of
approving the massacres, but of countenancing the conspiracy that sparked
them off.[9] Considering what little evidence he had before him, and how long
it has taken historians (with much more to go on) to arrive at a consensus that
puts the king in the clear, Pym's suspicion is understandable. It could feed on
Charles's earlier willingness to employ a force to be raised in Ulster under the
catholic Earl of Antrim against the Covenanters in western Scotland, on his
readiness to employ Strafford's Irish army, and on his reluctance to disband
it. Pym may or may not have known that Antrim, by his own later account,
received orders from Charles in the late summer of 1641 to reassemble all he
could of Strafford's disbanded troops and hold them ready, if occasion
should offer, for use against the English parliament. Antrim, however, held
aloof from the plots to surprise Dublin and Ulster, and afterwards wrote of
the rebellion that the business was 'spoiled by bloodshed and robbery'.[10]
Much more damaging at the time was a proclamation that Sir Phelim O'Neill
and a fellow-commander in Ulster issued on 4 November, for it published a
commission purporting to come from the king himself, authorizing all Irish
catholics to rise in defence of his person and to seize the lands, goods, and
persons of all English protestants. It looked authentic, bearing as it did the
great seal of Scotland, but this had been purloined from another document.
The commission was beyond doubt a forgery, but that is clearer now than it
was then.

In the Commons the great business of mid-November was the Grand
Remonstrance, which was first read on the 8th and finally passed in the small
hours of the 23rd. The debates on it were punctuated by worsening news
from Ireland and alarms about a catholic rising in England. Members were
seriously perturbed when a tailor called Thomas Beale came rushing to the
House on the 18th to report that he had miraculously escaped injury when a
pair of popish plotters had caught him eavesdropping from behind a hedge in
Moorfields. They had attacked him with drawn swords, run him through his
cloak, and left him for dead, so he told the members, and they swallowed it.

[9] See the discussions in Fletcher, *Outbreak*, pp. 137–8, and Russell, *Fall of the English Monarchies*, pp. 418–20.
[10] Ohlmeyer, *Civil War and Restoration in the Three Stuart Kingdoms*, pp. 98, 102–3.

The plot that he overheard was allegedly hatched by some priests; it was for 108 picked men to assassinate an equal number of puritan peers and MPs on the 18th, in order to create a tumult in London while the catholics rose in six widely scattered counties. Needless to say the 18th passed without incident, but Pym and Hampden repeatedly interrupted the debates on the Remonstrance with hot new 'evidence' of the plot in the counties. One may well wonder whether they believed any of it themselves.

The text of the Remonstrance antedated the Irish rebellion, for its preparation had been entrusted to a committee of eight on 3 August. Pym himself wrote most of it. It spoke only for the Commons, for it was never presented to the Lords, and though it was addressed to the king it was essentially propaganda directed at the public, aiming to bring the political nation round to its authors' view of the political situation. It was a wildly tendentious document, falling into three main sections. The first and longest catalogued all the grievances, oppressions, illegalities, and blunders of the first fifteen years of the reign, which were were rooted in 'a malicious and pernicious design of subverting the fundamental laws and principles of government'. There were echoes here of the charge against Strafford, but now the design was attributed to an unholy alliance of 'the Jesuited papists', the bishops and other corrupt clergy, and councillors and courtiers engaged in promoting the interests of foreign catholic powers for their private ends. Together they had striven to sow division between the king and his people, to disaffect him towards parliaments, and by cherishing the catholicizing faction in the church to build up a party of papists, Arminians, and libertines, fit to advance their sinister purposes. The same malignant party was held responsible, in what was obviously a newly added passage, for the rebellion and massacres in Ireland.

After devoting nearly a hundred numbered clauses to the abuses of 1625–40, the Remonstrance gave the next sixty or so to boasting of the present parliament's achievements. But its most interesting part was the third, in which it set forth what the Commons intended to do in the matter of religion, and what they expected of the king. They meant to reduce the exorbitant power that the bishops had assumed and debar them from temporal office, but not (it was implied) to abolish them. They denied the malignant party's slander that they intended to dissolve all church government, but the king's power as Supreme Governor was to be exercised 'by such rules of order and discipline as are established by parliament'. Sensitive to current accusations that they were encouraging sectaries and fanatics, they declared

that it is far from our purpose and desire to let loose the golden reins of discipline and government in the church, to leave private persons or particular congregations to take up what form of divine service they please, for we hold it requisite that there should be throughout the whole realm a conformity to that order which the laws enjoin according to the word of God.

In other words they were as opposed to religious toleration as the Scottish Covenanters were. In order to effect the intended reformation and frame the prescribed order, there was to be 'a general synod of the most grave, pious, learned and judicious divines of this island; assisted with some from foreign parts, professing the same religion with us'.[11] The words 'of this island' implied that the synod should include Scottish divines, and the addition of foreign ones carried an assumption that the religion of (say) Dutch and French Calvinists was the same as the Church of England's. Whatever church order the synod prescribed, it would not be the Prayer Book order enshrined in the existing laws, and that was the main reason why the Grand Remonstrance played a powerful part in driving Anglicans into the royalist camp. But it was not likely to satisfy the Scots either, since besides envisaging the survival of episcopacy, it made the synod's recommendations subject to the approval and confirmation of parliament.

Following the committee stages, the final debate on the Remonstrance as a whole began at about noon on 22 November, when the king, on his way back from Scotland, was two days' ride from London. Strangely, Cromwell expected it to be short. In fact, it was the longest and probably the most impassioned debate that there had ever been in a single sitting. More sharply than in any previous one, future royalists were pitched against future parliamentarians. More speeches are recorded against the Remonstrance than for it, and its opponents had a powerful case. They deplored its raking over grievances long past, and in many cases already remedied. They scored strong points against the unprecedented manner of proceeding without even seeking the concurrence of the Lords. Above all they attacked as subversive the device of presenting as an address to the king what was plainly an appeal to the public against his manner of exercising his royal authority, for the fiction that everything amiss could be blamed on his evil counsellors was wearing very thin now. 'Wherefore is this descension from a parliament to a people?' asked Sir Edward Dering, who had shifted a long way since he had introduced the Root and Branch Bill; 'I did not dream that we should remonstrate downward, tell stories to the people, and talk of the king as of a third person.' To such objections, Pym retorted that all the plots and designs that had created the current critical position had been rooted in popery, and popery had been rampant at court. 'It's time to speak plain English', he said, 'lest posterity shall say that England was lost and no man durst speak truth.'[12]

It was well past midnight when the House finally divided and carried the Remonstrance by a bare eleven votes, with over 300 members still present. But that was not the end of the night's work, for two bitter disputes broke out

---

[11] Full text in Gardiner (ed.), *Constitutional Documents*, pp. 202–32; quotations on religion from p. 229.

[12] *Journal of Sir Simonds D'Ewes*, ed. Coates, pp. 184–5.

after many of the Remonstrance's supporters had gone home. One was over an attempt by its opponents, ultimately unsuccessful, to stop it from being printed or published. The other, even angrier, broke out when the royalist Geoffrey Palmer pressed a motion to allow those who opposed the Remonstrance to have their protestations entered in the Journal of the House. This was against precedent, for the registration of individual dissents was a privilege enjoyed by peers but not by MPs. But it expressed the extremely strong feelings that the Remonstrance aroused, especially in those who detested it. Members took their sheathed swords out of their belts, holding them menacingly before them, and for a while it looked as though fighting would break out on the floor of the House. Mercifully they were persuaded to adjourn without taking a decision on Palmer, and they finally went home as the clock struck two. Yet such was the division he provoked that the House spent more than eight hours during the next two days in debating first whether to question him, which they did, and then on how he should be punished. For much of this time the attendance was higher than during the final debate on the Remonstrance itself, despite the fact that a large number of members had failed to resume their seats after the summer recess. Palmer in the event spent twelve days in the Tower, but was not expelled.[13]

When the king entered London on 25 November, the City fathers had the fountains flowing with wine and entertained him to a splendid banquet in the Guildhall. This may seem surprising after the Londoners' demonstrations against Laud and Strafford and the tumults aroused by the army plot, especially considering that three of the City's four MPs were strong supporters of Pym and the fourth a moderate parliamentarian. But there was a division of interest and opinion between the majority of the citizens and the narrow oligarchy which dominated the City's government, and the past year's events had been widening it. Over the centuries, immense authority had accrued to the Lord Mayor, who was elected annually, and the Court of Aldermen, whose twenty-six members were elected for life, and from whom the Lord Mayor was traditionally chosen. The aldermen constituted an elite of wealth and power; typically, they belonged to more than one of the chartered trading companies which derived their exclusive privileges from the crown, whose needs they frequently met by raising loans, to their own considerable profit. Some profited even more as farmers of the customs, which forged another link between them and the court; some helped to manage the corporate monopolies whereby the crown had evaded the 1624 Monopolies Act. These interests did not make them creatures of the court, for until 1641 the grievances which they shared with the bulk of London merchants against the

---

[13] *Journal of Sir Simonds D'Ewes*, pp. 191–200. On 14 December a member complained (with exaggeration) that over 200 MPs were regularly absent, most of them since the summer recess (ibid., p. 287).

crown's fiscal exactions, its damaging interferences in their commercial operations, its appalling record in repaying loans, and its punishment of the City
for failing to carry out the Londonderry plantation outweighed, for most of
them, the personal profit that their links with the king's government brought
them. But they were mostly conservative men, and during 1641 they became
alarmed at the radical temper of the lesser citizenry and at the rising tide of
iconoclasm and sectarianism. They drew closer to the crown for much the
same reasons as the constitutional royalists like Hyde and Culpepper in the
Commons and the Earls of Hertford and Southampton in the Lords did,
because the crown stood for the defence of order and traditional values. The
annual election of the Lord Mayor on 28 September generated quite unusual
heat, but the successful candidate was a royalist, Sir Richard Gurney. The
corporation's welcome to Charles was quite sincere, but he was mistaken in
supposing that he could henceforth look to the City for support against the
parliament, because the oligarchy's hold on its government was shortly to be
thrown off.

London indeed was about to enter upon a phase of turbulence even greater
than that which had accompanied Strafford's attainder and the scares about
the army plot. The parliament buildings were the main target for popular
demonstrations until about the end of the year, when the focus shifted to
Whitehall. Since the start of the session parliament had continued to have a
guard of trained bands set at its own request by the Earl of Essex, but the king
had removed it as soon as he got back from Scotland, on the ground that his
presence was guard enough. Essex accepted that his commission as Captain-
General south of Trent had lapsed with the king's return, but parliament
requested the king to continue the guard. Charles did so, but appointed the
Earl of Dorset, a moderate royalist, to command it. On 29 November a
menacing crowd of citizens, armed with swords and staves, filled the parliamentary precincts, persistently chanting 'No bishops!' They pressed against
the door of the House of Lords and intimidated members of both chambers.
The Lords directed Dorset to call up the guard and disperse the mob, and
when the demonstrators defied his repeated requests to clear Palace Yard he
ordered his men to open fire. Fortunately they did not obey, but the shaken
citizens made off hastily, and the incident rankled. Next day the Commons
dismissed Dorset's guard on their own authority, and on a motion by Pym
two MPs who were also JPs of Westminster undertook to set another in its
place. The episode is interesting not only for the constitutional clash, but
because the Commons' debate on it showed that the majority regarded the
demonstrating citizens as their allies. They wanted a guard not against them
but against the king, for a fear was already being hinted that he was nursing
a design against some of themselves.

Early in December a mass petition was afoot in London, calling for the exclusion of the bishops from the Lords and for the reform of abuses that had crept into the City government. The chief organizer was John Fowke, a rich City merchant, and soon, as Alderman Fowke, to be a major power in City politics. The systematic gathering of signatures was accompanied by a good deal of pressure and led to some unruly scenes; the Lord Mayor and Recorder used even more pressure to stop it, but at least 15,000 were collected, and plans were laid for a procession of 10,000 supporters to accompany it to the Commons on the 10th. To prevent this, the JPs of Middlesex, under instructions from both the king (via the Lord Keeper) and the House of Lords, set a guard on the parliament-house of 200 men with halberds. The Commons took great offence; they voted that to set a guard without their consent was a breach of their privileges, discharged the guard, sent for the offending JPs, and committed one of them to the Tower. The big procession was abandoned, but the petition was brought to Westminster on the 11th by four representatives of each ward and a company of City notables riding in fifty coaches. Fowke presented it, and received the House's warm thanks.[14] The Commons gave a more mixed reception on the 23rd to a petition for the outright abolition of episcopacy, said to have been signed by 30,000 apprentices, but they did express appreciation of the orderly manner in which it was presented.

Meanwhile the news from Ireland was worsening, for the rebellion was threatening to become nationwide. The tragedy was that the escalating crisis in England was not only distracting the government in Westminster from taking the necessary steps to prevent that from happening, but was blinding most of the parliament to what those steps should be, and making them politically impossible for Charles to contemplate, at least in public. In a less inflamed situation, justice and common sense should have pointed to the sort of concessions that the king had seemed ready to grant earlier in his reign, especially public exercise of the catholic religion, a secure title for landowners who had possessed their estates for sixty years or more, recognition of the rights of the Irish parliament, and free access to public office for those who were prepared to take the oath of allegiance but not the oath of supremacy. If such legitimate aspirations could have been met, the rebellion could have been confined mainly to Ulster and defused. But the fiercely anti-papist temper at Westminster, heated by wickedly exaggerated tales of massacre, put concessions to catholics out of the question, and made it impossible for Charles to appear to consider them without gravely damaging his cause. In Dublin the Lord Justices and the council, like the English parliament, thought in terms of suppression rather than concession, but for the present they could do little more

---

[14] *Journal of Sir Simonds D'Ewes*, ed. Coates, pp. 271–3; Brian Manning, *English People and the English Revolution 1640–1649* (1976), pp. 61–7; Russell, *Fall of the British Monarchies*, pp. 431–4.

than defend the territory surrounding the capital. They called in what they could of the scattered Irish army, and about three quarters of it managed to comply. It was still of course the king's army, and he appointed Ormond as its lieutenant-general. Ormond recruited three new infantry regiments, mainly from refugees from Ulster, and he commissioned Sir Charles Coote and two other protestant colonels to raise more. He decided to take the offensive against the Ulster rebels, but the Lords Justices countermanded it. They were strongly identified with the planter interest, and he with that of the Old English aristocracy, but there were probably military motives as well as factional ones behind their decision. They may have thought it rash to commit all their military resources against the rebels before they could be reasonably sure of beating them, for they were expecting the English government to send them powerful reinforcements as a matter of urgency. At their distance from Westminster they could not know how swiftly England was sliding towards civil war, or how long it would be before any forces could be spared outside her own confines.

In mid-November the leaders of the rebellion drew up an oath of association to be sworn by all who joined them. It was clearly a bid to make their cause acceptable to the Old English nobles and gentry, who so far were mostly holding their fire. It carries strong echoes (which may have been conscious) of the English Protestation of six months earlier, though its commitment was of course to the catholic and not to the protestant faith. It pledged those who took it to defend the free and public exercise of the true catholic religion against all who should oppose it, to bear faith and allegiance to their sovereign lord King Charles, and to defend him against all who should attack his prerogative or commit any acts contrary to regal government, the power and privileges of parliament, or the lawful rights of subjects. It had its effect on the Irish parliament, which reassembled on 16 November, for the Commons (where the Old English had the ascendancy) refused to describe those in arms as rebels or traitors, though they did agree reluctantly to 'detest and abhor their abominable actions'.[15] The Old English members then sent Lord Dillon on the mission (his second) to the king already mentioned, with a petition urging that the rebellion could and should be suppressed without intervention from England or Scotland, that the implementation of the Graces would be more effective than military force, and that Ormond should be put in charge of the government of Ireland. It amounted to an offer to support the king against the rebels if he fully granted the concessions that he had earlier offered, if the Irish people were allowed the free exercise of their religion, and if the hostile and self-interested Lords Justices and their like-minded councillors were removed from the Dublin government.

[15] Clarke, *Old English in Ireland*, pp. 169–70, 173.

If it had been possible for the king and the English and Irish parliaments to agree in confronting the rebellion on some such terms as these, an incalculable number of Irish and English lives could have been saved and the whole subsequent history of Anglo–Irish relations could have run differently. But of course it was not possible. For Charles to have entertained a pact with the Old English ascendancy on the basis of toleration for papists would have been political death to him, while at Westminster the Commons thought only of forceful suppression. On 3 December they heard reports of settlers stripped naked, bound hand and foot, and left to die of cold. Ten days later they were informed that 30,000 had already been put to the sword, and next day Sir John Clotworthy communicated a letter telling of eyes plucked out, women's bellies ripped open, male genitals hacked off, children's brains dashed out, and other horrors. Vivid woodcuts, illustrating them in gory detail, were soon finding a brisk sale on the bookstalls. Meanwhile Pym divulged the proposals that Dillon had just brought from members of the Irish Commons to the king, and obtained a vote from the House 'that they will never give consent to any toleration of the popish religion in Ireland, or in any other of His Majesty's dominions'. Pym also welcomed the Scots' offer of military co-operation in reconquering Ulster, and got the king to agree to it.

England's utterly uncompromising response to the rebellion was one reason why it spread far beyond the bounds that its originators had intended. Another was that the spontaneous violent uprising of the Ulster peasantry, born of generations of repression, was proving infectious, and a threat to the landed elite in general as well as to English overlordship. Catholic landowners, whether of Irish or Old English stock, felt menaced from two sides. On the one was an English parliament in increasingly close accord with the Scottish Covenanters, utterly opposed to their religion, unsympathetic to their property rights and political aspirations, and bent on further plantation; on the other was a populist movement which posed a threat to landlords' rights, as well as to life and property generally, if it got further out of control. Louth and Meath were lost to the rebels by the end of November, as was county Wexford to the south. In between, many rose in Wicklow too, but Sir Charles Coote recovered that territory with a brutal efficiency that inaugurated, on a small scale, a protestant counter-terror. He was rewarded by being made governor of Dublin. Drogheda, however, remained under siege by the rebels, and a small force that was sent from Dublin to relieve it was ambushed on the way, and most of it killed or captured. The territory of the Pale was threatened on all sides, and since more than four-fifths of it was still in Old English ownership much depended on the attitude of the chief landowners there, the so-called Lords of the Pale. They had been prepared to defend it against the rebels, but the Dublin government had (as we have seen) unwisely antagonized them by refusing to allow them, as catholics, to arm themselves and their tenants. Like the catholic Old English elsewhere, they faced the prospect of a military reconquest of Ireland, directed by a puritan-dominated English parliament in partnership with Presbyterian Scottish Covenanters, both lured by the prospect of further confiscation and settlement of Irish land. No wonder they felt they had common ground with the insurgents who had framed the oath of association. The latter invited a large number of Old English nobles and gentry to a meeting early in December on the Hill of Crofty in Meath, where their representatives urged upon them that 'you are marked forth for destruction as well as we'.[16] On being assured that the rebels remained loyal to King Charles, all those present agreed to join them in arms, and the pact was cemented at a second meeting at Tara a few days later. But for the present it was an alliance, not a fusion of forces, for the Old English appointed their own commander in the person of Viscount Grandison; and by no means all the Old English or even Old Irish magnates in other parts of the country joined it. Others besides Ormond who stood out against the rebellion included the Earls of Clanricard, Thomond, and Inchiquin.

By Christmas the outlook from Dublin was bleak but not hopeless. The arrival of a regiment of 1,100 foot under Sir Simon Harcourt, the first troops to reach Ireland from England since the outbreak of the rebellion, relieved the immediate threat to the territory of the Pale. Drogheda was still surrounded by an estimated 20,000 men, but since they had no artillery and not much military skill it was not in imminent danger of falling. Munster and Galway were still quiet, though they would not remain so for long. Above all, there was no overt sign yet of the rebellion developing into a war for national independence. Two classes of Irishmen had some motivation to head it in that direction, the exiles in the service of Spain and the catholic clergy who had had their training on foreign, especially Spanish, soil. But though the Spanish Army of Flanders included a whole Irish tercio (a unit larger than a regiment), whose officers and men came in large part from Ulster, it was to be some time before they returned in significant numbers. As for the clergy, they did their best from the start to give the rebellion the character of a crusade, but it was not to their advantage to pursue objectives at odds with those of its leaders and their patrons, the indigenous catholic gentry. The great majority of the latter still hoped to attain theirs within the framework of the monarchy that had so nearly granted them the Graces. When, in the coming year, they found Charles powerless to meet their desires, and control passing to a parliament bent not only on denying them but on an almost limitless threat to their property, the whole situation would change.

That unhappy outcome stemmed mainly from England's own constitutional conflicts. The main problem was to raise a force for Ireland that the

<hr />

[16] Quoted in Clarke, *Old English in Ireland*, p. 181.

king could not use against opponents even nearer home. Early in December
the Commons, with the rebellion in mind, did pass an Impressment Bill,
which would have empowered parliament to conscript men for military service, but many peers shared the king's objection that it was his sole prerogative right to raise armed forces, and it stuck in the Lords. On the 7th
Sir Arthur Haselrig introduced a more sweeping Militia Bill which would
have appointed three generals, one north of Trent and two south, with power
to raise men and money and to exercise martial law. But this was a still grosser invasion of the prerogative, and it died in the Commons. It had little to do
with Ireland anyway, and the Dublin government's military needs were to
remain neglected at Westminster until the crucial question of who ultimately
controlled England's military resources had been settled. Charles chose a
most unfortunate way to emphasize his own claim. Since the disbandment of
his army in the north, many unemployed officers had collected in London,
some to press for their arrears of pay. Conspicuous among them was a brutal
and disreputable soldier of fortune called Thomas Lunsford, who had been
gaoled seven years earlier for attempted murder, though he had partly
redeemed himself by his courage in trying to stem the rout at Newburn.
Charles, partly to reassert his prerogative and partly to secure a more than
symbolic stronghold in his troubled capital, dismissed the Lieutenant of the
Tower and on 23 December appointed Lunsford in his place. Sober Londoners were horrified, and the concerted protests of the Lord Mayor, Common
Council, and House of Commons persuaded him to dismiss Lunsford three
days later—though with a knighthood and a pension to console him. It was
only a partial climb-down, and it helped Charles little, for the new Lieutenant
he appointed, Sir John Byron, continued to fill the Tower with soldiers and
ammunition. In the wake of the worse crisis that Charles was to precipitate
early in January, pressure for Byron's removal made his position so intolerable that he was pleading to be relieved.

Well before that Charles lost the considerable influence that the crown had
hitherto wielded over the government of the City of London. Normally the
Lord Mayor and Court of Aldermen ran it as they thought fit, but certain
decisions and functions such as the making of bye-laws required the consent
of the Common Council, a larger body (numbering 237 in 1641) elected
annually by the City's wards. It met only when the Lord Mayor summoned
it—typically five or six times a year, though less during Charles's personal
rule—and it normally considered only what had already been approved by
the Court of Aldermen. Most common councilmen were very wealthy, generally with an interest in more than one trade and livery company, and a fair
number benefited (like so many aldermen) from lucrative crown concessions,
so they were not inclined in normal times to rock the political boat. But a
significant proportion of them were strong puritans, receptive to the

campaigning zeal of London's puritan ministers and lecturers. Those clergy were a close-knit group, and they were extremely active in 1641–2, canvassing for anti-episcopal petitions, holding house-to-house collections, and (so it was alleged) using their pulpits to organize popular demonstrations. They brought a special influence to bear on the 1641 elections to the Common Council, which fell on 21 December. The result was an exceptional influx of new men, who for the first time tilted the balance decisively in favour of Pym and the parliamentary leadership. As soon as they took their seats the Common Council showed a new self-assertiveness; in particular it challenged the cosy oligarchies in the vestries which had traditionally managed its elections and claimed that all the freemen of the City had the right to vote. It also set up a committee of its own to adjudicate disputed elections. The large political results of this quiet revolution will be seen shortly.[17]

Meanwhile the Grand Remonstrance had been presented to the king on 1 December, prefaced by a petition asking him 'to concur with the humble desires of your people in a parliamentary way' by agreeing to exclude the bishops from parliament, abolish 'oppressive and unnecessary ceremonies' in church services, and remove his offending councillors in favour of such as could command parliament's confidence. He promised an answer at a later date, but when two weeks passed without one the Commons, after several hours' debate, ordered the Remonstrance to be printed. This angered him, and on the 23rd he published a reply which had been skilfully drafted for him by Hyde to appeal to fellow constitutional royalists and lovers of the Church of England. It was an answer to the petition only, since Charles considered the Remonstrance itself to be unparliamentary, proceeding as it did from one House only. Concerning religion, he said he would continue to concur with his people's *just* desires in a parliamentary way, but the bishops' membership of the Lords was grounded in the fundamental law of the kingdom and the constitution of parliament, and (since the bill to exclude them was still stuck in the Lords) he would give no further answer at present. As for alleged corruptions in religion and church government, he was convinced 'that no church can be found upon the earth that professeth the true religion with more purity of doctrine than the Church of England doth, nor where the government and discipline are jointly more beautified and free from superstition, than as they are here established by law'. He would maintain it in its purity and glory, 'not only against all invasions of popery, but also from the irreverence of those many schismatics and separatists, wherewith of late this kingdom and this city abounds'.[18] If he had held to this widely popular course and waited

---

[17] On London's role in 1640–2, see Valerie Pearl's masterly *London and the Outbreak of the Puritan Revolution* (Oxford, 1961); pp. 132–40 deal with the 1641 Common Council elections.

[18] Gardiner, *Constitutional Documents*, pp. 202–5 for the petition accompanying the Grand Remonstrance, pp. 233–6 for the king's answer.

for his opponents to make false moves, Pym and his party might have been thrown back on their heels, at least temporarily.

Parliament took only two days off for Christmas, and there were serious disorders when it reassembled on the 27th. A large mob filled Palace Yard and crowded into Westminster Hall, shouting 'No bishops!'. Lunsford and some fellow-swordsmen happened to be there, to press for their arrears and solicit employment in Ireland. Under some provocation they drew their swords and chased the citizens from the hall, shedding blood in the process; the demonstrators pelted them with stones and roof-tiles in reply. But the mob's main object was to prevent the bishops from getting to the House of Lords, whether by coach or by barge, and it certainly made their passage difficult. Archbishop Williams, who had recently been translated from Lincoln to York, grabbed at one insolent youth, and was roughly handled by the lad's comrades until a couple of peers came to his rescue. Worse things were to happen in the coming years than Williams's torn tippet, but on the 29th he and eleven other bishops presented a protest to the king, claiming that since they had been violently prevented from attending the Upper House, its proceedings in their absence were null and void. This angered the Lords, who only the day before had rejected a motion declaring that because of the mob's pressure parliament was not free. For Pym the bishops' protest was a windfall, and he immediately moved the impeachment of all its twelve signatories. The earlier impeachment of thirteen bishops for their part in the 1640 canons had been hanging fire in the Lords, despite frequent proddings from the Commons, probably because many peers saw it as a stratagem to deprive the bishops of their votes; but this time the Lords felt their own privileges offended and promptly accepted the charges against the twelve, who spent a cold winter's night in prison while church bells tolled and bonfires blazed in the City. Their folly had brought the two Houses closer after some weeks of strained relations, and it hastened the nineteen-year eclipse of their order. That same night Charles entertained Lunsford and about 120 other former officers to dinner at Whitehall.

By the turn of the year Charles and Pym each nursed a fear of a violent coup by the other. On 30 December Pym dramatically moved that the door of the House should be shut, and announced that there was a plot afoot to destroy it that very day. Next day, after long debate, the Commons sent a request to the king to provide them with a guard of City trained bands under the command of Essex. What they feared was the growing number of ex-officers gathered around the court at Whitehall—four or five hundred 'desperate and loose persons', they were told on 3 January.[19] Charles for his part felt that it was Whitehall that most needed a guard, and indeed on New Year's Eve

[19] *Journal of Sir Simonds D'Ewes*, ed. Coates, pp. 365–6, 372–3, 376.

about two hundred demonstrators with swords and staves did beset the palace, clashing with the swordsmen, who injured a few of them. It was around this time that the popular names that were to stick to the two sides in the Civil War first became current: Cavaliers, denoting the swashbuckling military types who associated with Lunsford and swaggered around White-hall, and Roundheads, referring to the sort of puritan City agitators whose tumults the Commons were accused of encouraging: men of the middling sort and lower orders who wore their hair cropped, instead of long like gentlemen.

Charles genuinely feared that the queen's life was in danger from these London mobs. A rumour was spreading that she was about to be impeached, and he believed it. He resolved to forestall such a move by himself impeach-ing those he thought likely to attempt it, but before doing so he strengthened his government by taking on board two leading constitutional royalists, in both of whom parliament should have had every 'cause to confide'. He had already, on returning from Scotland, dismissed the elder Vane from his Sec-retaryship of State, since his loyalty was becoming more and more suspect, and the younger Vane from his Treasurership of the Navy. What with Winde-bank's flight to France, Charles had both secretaryships to dispose of, and he had appointed the faithful Sir Edward Nicholas to one of them. Now, on 2 January 1642, he gave the other to Lord Falkland, and at the same time made Sir John Culpepper Chancellor of the Exchequer. Their friend Edward Hyde was already his close adviser, but preferred for the present to remain without office. Writing to his wife, Sir Edward Dering transmitted an extra-ordinary story that hours before giving the Exchequer to Culpepper, Charles sent for Pym and offered it again to him. This has to be mentioned, since some distinguished historians, including Gardiner, have been inclined to believe it; but it is scarcely credible that Charles could have contemplated giving a key place in his government to a man who he believed to be threatening his wife's life, or that he could have supposed that at this stage Pym might be tempted by such a poisoned chalice. The time when political rifts might have been mended by 'bridge' appointments had surely passed with Bedford's death, Strafford's execution, and the first army plot.

Pym in fact headed the list of those whom Charles now charged with trea-son. The others of the famous Five Members were Pym's close ally and friend Hampden; Holles and Strode, who had been imprisoned (Strode all through the personal rule) for their part in the stormy closing scene of the 1628–9 par-liament; and the much younger Haselrig, a prime mover in the Root and Branch Bill, Strafford's attainder, and the recent Militia Bill. By an after-thought Charles added a single peer, Manchester's son Lord Mandeville. The Attorney-General, Sir Edward Herbert, laid articles of impeachment against the six before the House of Lords on 3 January, but he had had no part in framing them. His own account, given admittedly when he was threatened with impeachment himself, was that he presented them only at the king's peremptory command, after he had twice tried earnestly to dissuade him from proceeding with them. Charles was acting under strong pressure from Henrietta Maria, and was himself probably responsible for their content. They sound like an attempt to retort the charges against Strafford upon his accusers' heads. The six were arraigned for 'traitorously endeavour[ing] to subvert the fundamental laws and government of the kingdom of England' by placing an arbitrary and tyrannical power in mere subjects, of alienating the affections of the people by their foul aspersions upon their sovereign, of inviting a foreign power (the Scots) to invade England, and of actually levying war against the king.[20] Not all the accusations (there were seven) were preposterous, and the Five Members could have had an uncomfortable time answering them if the majority of the Lords had been as staunch for the king as he imagined. It was all very well to invoke parliamentary privilege, as the Five loudly did, but privilege did not avail against treason. Nevertheless most of the peers, and not only the future parliamentarians, saw the king's move as an attack on the authority of parliament itself, and they doubted whether his manner of proceeding was lawful. Historically, in impeachments, the Commons preferred the charges and appointed prosecutors, and the Lords collectively sat as judges. For the crown to assume the prosecutor's role was not only unprecedented but contrary to the spirit of this great judicial process. So instead of ordering the immediate arrest of the accused, as Charles had expected, the Lords appointed a committee to consider whether the Attorney-General's procedure was according to law.

Charles, however, was so determined that the Five Members should not escape arrest that he decided to go to the House of Commons in person next day to apprehend them. Late at night he sent a messenger to the Lord Mayor, forbidding him to send any of the City trained bands to protect the parliament-house, but authorizing the militia to fire on the crowd if there should be any tumults. At Whitehall on the 4th, where Lunsford had charge of the guard, he assembled about four hundred armed men to accompany him. Pym, thanks to his friend Essex and to the French ambassador, was fully informed of Charles's intentions and movements. He and his fellow-accused took their seats, determined not to spare the king the irreparable harm that he was evidently about to do himself. When they got word at about three in the afternoon that he was on his way, they left the House and took a waiting barge to the City. Charles, on arriving, left most of his cavalcade outside, but about eighty men armed with pistols and swords entered the lobby behind him, and remained visible and threatening through the open door. He entered the Chamber with his nephew the Elector Palatine at his side and took over the

<hr />

[20] Gardiner (ed.), *Constitutional Documents*, pp. 236–7.

Speaker's chair. He announced his purpose, making many pauses while his eyes searched in vain for the five whose arrest he demanded. He called for Pym, then for Holles, by name; he was met by total silence. He asked the Speaker where they were. Lenthall was a timorous man by nature, but on this occasion he found words that have become immortal. 'May it please your Majesty,' he said, falling to one knee, 'I have neither eyes to see, nor tongue to speak in this place, but as this House is pleased to direct me, whose servant I am here.'[21] He begged the king's pardon that he could give no further answer. Charles groped for some face-saving words, but passionate anger showed on his face as he left the chamber, followed by shouts of 'privilege! privilege!' from the members.

That same day, all the shops in the City were shut, and the Common Council took the unprecedented step of electing a Committee of Safety, consisting almost entirely of the more prominent supporters of the parliamentary leadership. It later assumed control of London's trained bands. Pym's allies among the City fathers henceforth wielded unchallenged power in the capital, and Lord Mayor Gurney's authority was cut from under him. Charles cannot have been aware of this development when he rode to the Guildhall next day to make a personal demand that the City should hand over the fugitive Five. He was evidently shaken, however, by the hostility of the crowds through which he passed, and by their repeatedly shouted slogan: 'privileges of parliament!' The same cry was echoed in his presence by members of the Common Council, though others shouted 'God bless the king'. His fruitless visit was a second humiliation within two days.

On 6 January the Commons voted by two to one to seek the City's protection and adjourn until further order to the Guildhall. Legally they could not change their venue without the king's command, but they got round this by sitting as a committee open to all members to attend. That night, London rocked to an alarm that Charles was sending in horse and foot to arrest the Five Members by force. Their supporters went round the streets, knocking from door to door and shouting 'arm! arm!' It was reckoned (no doubt with some exaggeration) that 40,000 citizens turned out completely armed, while 100,000 more stood to in their houses with halberds, swords, or clubs. Yet when the alarm proved false, the streets were cleared within an hour. Next day in the Guildhall the Commons voted that power over the City's armed forces lay with the Lord Mayor, Aldermen, and Common Council, 'or the greater numbers of them', which meant that the now friendly majority of the Common Council could outvote their royalist or neutralist seniors. On the 10th, after consulting with their Common Council friends, the Commons voted that until the City ordered otherwise its forces should be commanded by

---

[21] Gardiner, *History of England*, X, 140.

Sergeant-Major-General Skippon, a seasoned professional who had risen from the ranks and had the common touch, as well as being a strong puritan and parliamentarian. By way of reinforcement, Hampden announced that some thousands of his Buckinghamshire constituents were marching towards London, and there were offers of support from the apprentices, the Southwark trained bands, and the seamen on the Thames.[22]

Charles now decided that his capital had become too hot to hold him. He left it for Hampton Court in the night of the 10th, never to see it again until he was brought back seven years later as a prisoner, to be tried for his life. Through his attempt to silence his parliamentary opponents by proceeding against them as traitors, he had strengthened their hold on the Commons, boosted their popularity in the country, alienated the Lords, and dealt a fatal blow to what was left of his support in the City. Next day the Commons returned to Westminster by barge, to the sound of martial music and volleys of shot from a whole regatta of festively decked boats, while Skippon's trained bands, 2,400 of them, marched to the same destination by way of the Strand and Whitehall. Many of them bore copies of the Protestation on their pikes and muskets, and many citizens hung the printed sheets like little banners on lines strung between their houses. It had become the very emblem of the parliamentary cause.

Charles was constantly being spurred by his queen to stand up to his enemies, and his first actions after leaving London suggest that he already wanted to go to war. He and she believed that away from the seditious politicians and subversive preachers of the capital he could draw on a great fund of loyalty in provincial England. They were planning that she should go to Holland with a substantial part of the crown jewels, to pawn or sell them and procure both men and arms. The Commons were alarmed to hear on 12 January that Lunsford had mustered a considerable body of cavaliers at Kingston-upon-Thames, where the county magazine of Surrey was stored. Lord Digby had come over from Hampton Court with instructions from the king, and it may have been part of a plan to secure Portsmouth, where Charles was probably hoping to embark his wife. Lunsford's party, however, was dispersed after a scuffle by the Surrey trained bands.

Charles also tried to secure control of Hull, which was important not only as a fortified port where Dutch or Danish troops might be landed, but because its magazine held most of the weapons and artillery that had been collected for the war with Scotland—enough to arm 16,000 men. On 11 January he secretly appointed the Earl of Newcastle as governor of Hull, and sent Captain Legge, his agent in the army plot, to secure its magazine and ensure the

---

[22] *Journal of Sir Simonds D'Ewes*, pp. 392, 398, 400–1; Pearl, *London and the Outbreak of the Puritan Revolution*, pp. 141–5; Russell, *Fall of the British Monarchies*, pp. 450–1; Manning, *English People and the English Revolution*, pp. 96–8.

citizens' obedience. But the Commons got wind of the design and ordered Sir John Hotham, member for nearby Beverley, to take Hull over with the Yorkshire trained bands, with instructions not to deliver it up without orders from parliament. His son Captain John Hotham, MP for Scarborough and a soldier like himself, got to Hull before Legge and held it safe until his father arrived and took command. It was a striking example of the Commons' readiness to give direct orders in a sphere that undoubtedly lay within the royal prerogative, but with the king threatening war it was an act of self-defence.

The issues over which the war would be fought were fast becoming defined. Cromwell, who was prominent by now among the 'fiery spirits' in the House, successfully moved on 14 January for a large committee to consider how to put the kingdom in a posture of defence. Four days later it recommended that the militia in every county should be put under the command of a lord lieutenant and deputy lieutenants appointed by an ordinance of parliament. No one quarrel led so inexorably to war as that over the resultant Militia Ordinance, which went to the Lords on 15 February and won their immediate assent. On 17 January the committee of the whole House resolved, on a motion by Pym, that the king should be requested to dismiss all his present privy councillors and to appoint in their place such men as the two Houses should advise. The Commons were ahead of the Lords on this issue, but it was the most sweeping bid so far for parliamentary control over the composition of the executive. To show who was the real master of the king's servants, they impeached the Attorney-General for preferring the articles of impeachment against the Five Members, even though he had done so reluctantly, under the king's written command, and though Charles had subsequently withdrawn them. Despite an order from the king not to proceed, the Lords eventually found him guilty, and after a brief imprisonment banned him from London and Westminster. They would not give their consent, however, to an order of the Commons on 20 January for a printed letter to be sent from the Speaker to the sheriff of each county, requiring all males over eighteen to swear to the Protestation, and directing that the names both of those who complied and of those who refused should be recorded. The letters were nevertheless sent, and during the ensuing weeks much of the country was sworn village by village, often after Sunday service. For those outside court circles, and not of the catholic faith, it was the first real whiff of parliamentary tyranny. It was not to be the last.

Charles had moved to Windsor on 13 January. His court there was small, and consisted too much of swordsmen and sycophants. Essex, his Lord Chamberlain, and Holland, his Groom of the Stool, had refused to obey his command to attend him, and few other lords came to Windsor. Sir John Holland MP, who went there on parliamentary business on the 28th, 'found a desolate court, saw not one nobleman and scarce three gentlemen'.[23] Charles seriously lacked good counsel and sound intelligence about the state of feeling in the country, but he nevertheless came to realize that war was not an option for the present, since far too few of his subjects would be prepared to take up arms for him. He would have to rally them personally in those regions that he believed still loyal, so he needed time. Sensing that his opponents were running ahead of public opinion, he now sought to take the wind out of their sails by offering a prospect of negotiated agreement. He wrote to both Houses on 20 January, asking them urgently to draw up a single document, stating what they intended to do to settle his revenue, what further safeguards they desired for the privileges of parliament and the property and liberty of the subject, and what they proposed for 'the security of the true religion now professed in the Church of England' and for settling its ceremonies. He promised that he would respond so graciously that if the kingdom's present distractions did not 'end in a happy and blessed accommodation', he would call on God and man to witness that it would be through no failure on his part.[24] It was a skilful appeal to all who longed for a peaceful settlement and loved the established church, and the Lords responded with warm thanks. But when their answer came before the Commons for their concurrence, Hampden moved and carried an addition to it, asking that the Tower, the other forts, and all the trained bands should be put in the charge of men whom parliament could trust. The Tower was still commanded by Sir John Byron, the royalist Lieutenant with whom Charles had replaced Lunsford, and though he was virtually blockaded by Skippon's trained bands, London's citadel had symbolic significance. Hampden's addition irritated the Lords and greatly offended the king, but it gauged not unfairly the sincerity of Charles's intentions. It effectively blocked the negotiation that he sought, as it was intended to do.

While Charles was courting the religious conservatives the Commons were alienating them. In response to a petition from puritan Colchester, they voted on 21 January that the present liturgy stood in need of reformation, and they resolved next day that no one should be penalized for omitting any of its ceremonies pending parliament's intended revision of it. The Book of Common Prayer had come under threat before, but this was the first time that its defenders had failed to stave off a specific condemnation of it. Hitherto the Lords could have been trusted to come to its rescue, but at the end of the month the king, feeling his isolation at Windsor, summoned fourteen faithful peers to join him there. Other royalist lords followed them, and the balance in the Upper House changed critically. It passed the Bishops' Exclusion Bill

---

[23] *The Private Journals of the Long Parliament, 3 January to 5 March 1642*, ed. W. H. Coates, A. S. Young, and V. F. Snow (New Haven, 1982; hereafter *Private Journals*, I), pp. 71–3, 218, 356–9, 363.

[24] *Lords' Journal*, IV, 523, also printed with one omission in *Private Journals*, I, 125.

on 5 February and the Impressment Bill soon after. It gave an immediate welcome to the Militia Ordinance, though for many peers, as Conrad Russell has well said, 'the object seems to have been, not to enable the Commons to start a war against the king, but to disable the king from starting a war against the Commons'.[25]

Charles, however, was still pursuing the path of conciliation, if only because he was so anxious to get the queen and her chests of treasure safely out of England. As he travelled with her towards Dover, he finally dropped the charges against the Five Members, and gave his assent first to the Bishops' Exclusion Bill and then to the Impressment Bill. He also yielded to Byron's plea to be released from his untenable position as Lieutenant of the Tower, and to his replacement by Sir John Conyers, who was parliament's choice. Unkind winds delayed Henrietta Maria's departure for a tense week, during which Charles was presented with the Militia Ordinance for his assent. This was too much for him, and he temporized. It was a matter of such high importance, he said, that he would defer an answer until he had seen the queen safely on her way to Holland. She sailed on 23 February, but without waiting for a fuller reply the Commons declared on the 21st that his response was 'as unsatisfactory and destructive as an absolute denial'.[26] The Lords finally passed the ordinance on 5 March, over the recorded protests of sixteen peers, and both Houses claimed for it the force of law, despite the withholding of the royal assent. It was not the first ordinance of parliament, though no previous one had attempted anything as momentous as the assumption of control over the kingdom's land forces.

It is probable that for some time now neither King Charles nor King Pym had had any serious hopes of a negotiated settlement, unless one side or the other could be forced to accept terms of virtual surrender. But Charles had to find a party to fight for him, and the parliamentary leaders had to persuade the gentry of provincial England that their differences with him could not be resolved through what everyone was calling an accommodation. Here we are given an unusually broad view of local feelings, because between December 1641 and May 1642 no fewer than thirty-seven of England's forty counties sent petitions to parliament, while others came in from Wales and from a number of English towns. Most were the fruit of close liaison between MPs and leading figures among their constituents, and they obviously convey the views of future parliamentarians rather than of royalists. But they are not to be discounted, as they used to be, as a mere propaganda campaign, orchestrated by the activists at Westminster. As Anthony Fletcher has demonstrated, most of the petitions were submitted for discussion and approval to

---

[25] Russell, *Fall of the British Monarchies*, p. 472; *Private Journals*, I, 384–5.
[26] *Private Journals*, I, 431.

large meetings of the county gentry, and they represent a genuine attempt to express a consensus of local opinion. Most bore large numbers of signatures, ranging between 3,000 and 30,000, with even little Rutland mustering 560, so they spoke for a fair number of the middling sort as well as for the gentry.[27]

The petitions testify that parliament's supporters in the provinces were seeing current issues and conflicts in much the same terms as the parliamentary leadership, for the view of these that they expressed was broadly that of the Grand Remonstrance. The gap that had opened during the previous summer, when it was widely felt in the shires that Pym's faction was driving too hard and pressing the king too far, had closed. The petitioners were full of praise and thanks for what parliament had achieved so far, but they believed that further reform was needed and that a malignant party was obstructing it. They shared Pym's conviction that papists were at the heart of that party, and that Arminians were no better than fellow-travellers. These petitions were generally more moderate as regards religion than those in the root and branch campaign of a year or so earlier, for they represented a broader range of opinion; only one called for the total abolition of episcopacy, but twenty-two demanded the removal of scandalous ministers. The one major difference between the temper of the provinces and that of the central actors was that whereas King Charles and King Pym were well aware that they were on a collision course, the petitioners still spoke the language of accommodation. They clung to their faith in the ancient constitution, and to their hope that present differences could be reconciled and desirable reforms achieved without any essential violation of it. Many counties called for the improvement of defences and the better arming and training of the militia, and many supported the Militia Bill (or Ordinance, in the later ones), but they were not contemplating, let alone desiring, an imminent civil war. Their temper was defensive. They were moved by lingering alarms about the army plots, and by more present ones arising from the newsbooks' stories of atrocities in Ireland, the tales told by protestant refugees, and the persistent fear of a general uprising by English catholics. Scares were endemic during the early months of 1642, and Lancashire and Cheshire in particular were acutely apprehensive of an invasion from across the Irish Sea.

It is easier now than it was then to see that such fears were foolish. The Irish rebellion did reach its greatest territorial extent during January and February. Its partisans secured Waterford, Tipperary, and Kilkenny during January; the Earl of Thomond tried in vain to prevent county Clare from joining them, and when Viscount Muskerry declared for them late in February most of county Cork was lost. But Lord Clanricard managed to keep most of Galway from open revolt, and at the end of January Ormond launched the first major

[27] Fletcher, *Outbreak*, ch. 6.

counter-offensive. The initiative was beginning to pass to the Dublin government. On 20 February a proclamation by the king, declaring all those in arms against it to be rebels and traitors, at last arrived in Dublin (it was dated 1 January). Henceforth the insurgents could no longer plausibly claim to be his loyal subjects, and by this time further reinforcements had arrived from England under George Monck and Sir Richard Grenville.

When the Lords finally passed the Militia Ordinance, the king had set off on a slow journey to York, where he was hoping that his presence would animate what he supposed to be the greater loyalty of the northern gentry. A delegation from both Houses met him at Newmarket on 9 March and presented a declaration, setting forth in offensive detail the grounds for fear and distrust that his prolonged absence from his parliament gave rise to, and requesting him (not for the first time) to return to his capital. Charles received it with unconcealed anger. Next day the Earl of Pembroke, whom Charles had dismissed from the office of Lord Chamberlain in the previous July for persistently siding with his opponents, asked him whether he might not concede that the Militia Ordinance should be operative for a limited time. Charles 'swore by God, not for an hour; you have asked that of me in this, [that] was never asked of any king, and with which I will not trust my wife and children.'[28] In his formal reply on the 15th he declared that his subjects could not be obliged to obey any act or order which lacked his consent, and he forbade them to put the Militia Ordinance into execution. That same day, independently, the two Houses voted that the country was in imminent danger and that the ordinance 'ought to be obeyed by the fundamental laws of this kingdom'. On receiving the king's reply, they declared that those who advised him to it were 'enemies to the peace of this kingdom, and justly suspected to be favourers of the rebellion in Ireland'. There were times when their political judgement was as dubious as their constitutional position.

Charles reached York on the 19th, but he received no such welcome as he expected, from either the city or the Yorkshire gentry, and he was deeply disappointed. At the end of March he had only thirty-nine gentlemen and seventeen personal guards attending on him. He thought of travelling on to Scotland, but Henrietta Maria, with whom he corresponded constantly in cipher, discouraged him. She did, however, urge him to seize Hull by force. He caused consternation at Westminster when he announced on 8 April that he intended to go to Ireland in person with a force armed from the Hull arsenal, for parliament's natural fear was that once he was at the head of an army he would find another use for it. The two Houses begged him not to risk his life in such an expedition, and refused their consent to his departure. He

---

[28] Rushworth, *Historical Collections*, III, pt. i, 533. Parliament's declaration, presented on 9 March, is on pp. 528–32; the king's reply, parliament's vote thereon, and the vote of 15 March on the Militia Ordinance are on pp. 533–5.

was doubtless angry that they supposed he needed it. The Commons were anxious about the precious magazine in Hull and had recently ordered that its whole contents should be shipped to the Tower, but the Lords had amended the order to a request to the king to authorize the transfer, which he indignantly refused. He had the support of about a score of Yorkshire gentry who petitioned him on 22 April not to let the arms leave the county but to seize them himself.

Next day he set out for Hull with about three hundred horsemen, after sending a letter ahead to Sir John Hotham, announcing his intention to inspect the magazine. He did not believe that Hotham would defy him face-to-face. Hotham's position was uncomfortable, for the Lord Mayor and most citizens would gladly have admitted the king, but he had strict orders from parliament, so he ordered the gates to be shut and the drawbridges raised. His small garrison was loyal to him, and from the city wall he refused his monarch's personal demand to be admitted. Charles had him proclaimed a traitor on the spot, and rode off furious and humiliated. It was the first direct military confrontation between an Englishman and his sovereign for more than a century and a half, and the prolonged pamphlet controversy that ensued testifies to the profound impression that it made.

The Hull affair was only one of the topics that fuelled the paper war that was waged all spring and summer. There was a constant exchange of declarations between the king and parliament, and all of them were promptly printed, for they were addressed at least as much to the public at large as to the formal recipients. Each side was trying to put the better case to the political nation, primarily to win its support, but partly (one senses) to stoke up the fires of their own self-righteousness to a heat that would nerve them for a war for which few were temperamentally ready in the spring. From May onward most of the king's declarations were drafted by Hyde, who was not only a master of language but understood equally the mentalities of his parliamentarian opponents and those of the conservative country gentry whose allegiance was in the balance. One of the most interesting questions for the historian is how Charles, who seemed so isolated in the early months of 1642, was able to fight the first battle of the Civil War on equal terms and to keep up a fair chance of outright victory for nearly three more years. Part of the answer lies in the skill with which his propaganda was conducted during the crucial months when the English people were having to choose sides. His declarations took all possible credit for what he had already conceded, especially in the legislation of 1641; they expressed his total condemnation of the Irish rebellion; they affirmed his devotion to the laws of the land, which they claimed were now being violated by parliament. They portrayed him as the defender of order against lawless tumults and seditious petitions. And above all they repeatedly affirmed his commitment to the true protestant religion, as embodied in the Church of England, which despite all attempts to smear the court with popery and Arminianism was his strongest suit. Radical, icono-clastic puritanism had made many enemies in the past year, and sectaries were almost as much a bogey as papists.

The parliament had a harder task in putting its case to the conservative majority of provincial England. It was committed to calling an Anglo-Scottish synod of divines, whose brief was to include the revision of the prayer book, and the Scots were pressing to have it assembled soon. To allay the jus-tified fears that Anglicans felt about it, the two Houses published a declar-ation on 8 April, saying that while its purpose was to reform the government and liturgy of the church, it was intended 'to take away nothing in the one or the other but what shall be evil and justly offensive, or at least unnecessary and burdensome'.[29] To all who loved the church as it was, or as it had been under James I, this was a hollow reassurance, and it proved to be a false one.

On the constitutional side, parliament's very real need to deny control over the country's military resources to the king forced it into an equally uncom-fortable position. When it publicly declared on 5 May that the Militia Ordin-ance was to be put into immediate execution, he responded, first in a printed answer and then in a formal proclamation on the 27th, by again charging his subjects on their allegiance not to obey it. The two Houses replied by declar-ing that parliament was constitutionally empowered to provide for the king-dom's peace and safety,

and what they do herein hath the stamp of the royal authority, although His Majesty, seduced by evil counsel, do in his own person oppose or interrupt the same; for the king's supreme and royal pleasure is exercised and declared in this high court of law and council, after a more eminent and obligatory manner than it can be by personal act or resolution of his own.[30]

They accordingly declared the king's proclamation to be void, and com-manded all constables and other officers to execute the ordinance under par-liament's protection. Their claim rested on a very forced application of the medieval doctrine of the king's two bodies, which distinguished his natural person from his embodiment of a public authority established by law. Every-one accepted that whenever a judgment was delivered in one of the king's courts it was the king's judgment, whether he personally agreed with it or not, and that no other court stood as high as the High Court of Parliament. But it was one thing to say that he could not interfere with the due process of law and quite another to deny him the monarch's ancient power to make binding decisions in matters of state. Since Charles was not a minor like Edward VI, the implication was that he was *non compos mentis* like Henry VI, and this

---

[29] Gardiner (ed.), *Constitutional Documents*, pp. 247–8.     [30] Ibid., pp. 256–7.

made a great many people uneasy. The parliamentarians were in fact making up a theory of constitutional monarchy as they went along, and by and large posterity has thanked them for it, but they can have convinced few but the converted when they claimed to have the fundamental laws on their side. As the law and custom of the constitution then stood, the king had the better case, but the idealized King Charles presented by Hyde and his other apologists was a different creature from the inconsistent opportunist with whom the parliamentarians actually had to deal.

At almost the same time as the contentious declaration just quoted, the two Houses issued a more comprehensive statement of their objectives. The Nineteen Propositions of 1 June were a response to another request from the king's camp for a full set of proposals, as a basis for a negotiated settlement, but they are significant not as a recipe for an accommodation, which they plainly were not, but as the fullest public statement of the aims for which the parliament first went to war. They went further than ever before in seeking to subject the executive and the judiciary to parliament. Not only were all privy councillors to be approved by both Houses, but all political decisions which were properly the council's business were to require the consent of the majority of councillors, attested by their signatures. The size of the council was prescribed: not more than twenty-five members or less than fifteen. The seventeen highest officers in the government, the judiciary, and the royal household were not only to be chosen with the approval of both Houses but were to 'hold their places *quam diu bene se gesserint*' (so long as they conducted themselves satisfactorily). They were no longer to be removable at the king's pleasure. His children were to be educated by governors and tutors approved by parliament, and to marry only with its consent. Among other anti-papist proposals, there was to be an act requiring the children of all catholics to be brought up by protestants in the protestant religion. The king was required to consent to whatever reforms parliament should advise in the government and liturgy of the church, after consulting with the forthcoming assembly of divines. Catholic peers were to lose their votes in the Lords, and henceforth newly made peers were not to be admitted to sit without the consent of both Houses. Invading yet another sphere of the prerogative, the king was requested to enter into a closer alliance with the United Provinces and other protestant powers.[31]

The severity of these terms suggest that their authors believed that Charles was incapable of making war and would have to capitulate. That was rapidly becoming less likely, for between mid-May and mid-June a stream of valuable supporters left Westminster and joined him in York. They included a bevy of moderate peers and Lord Keeper Littleton, but the most important of

---

[31] Gardiner (ed.), *Constitutional Documents*, pp. 249–5.

them were the leaders of the constitutional royalists in the Commons, Hyde, Falkland, and Culpepper. Hyde had hitherto sent Charles the drafts of his answers to the parliamentary declarations from Westminster, but now he could advise him personally. It was Falkland and Culpepper, however, who were entrusted with framing his answer to the Nineteen Propositions, in a document that came to assume as much significance as the Propositions themselves. The King's Answer was an eloquent vindication of the traditional constitution as most parliament-men had understood it before the current crisis. It upheld the authority of parliament as the king's 'Great and Supreme Council', but maintained that he was very much a part of it. Hyde subsequently objected to it because it presented the king alongside the Lords and Commons as one of the three estates of the realm, whereas he himself identified the estates as the Lords Spiritual, Lords Temporal and Commons, with the king as head and sovereign over them all. But the Answer's purpose, which was very apposite to the circumstances of the summer of 1642, was to reaffirm the time-honoured functions of the crown and the two Houses in a constitution which held the classical elements of monarchy, aristocracy, and democracy in an ideal balance. 'The power, legally placed in both Houses,' it argued, 'is more than sufficient to prevent and restrain the power of tyranny' which the monarch might threaten without such a balance, but the House of Commons was 'never intended for any share in government, or the choosing of them that govern'. Only ill comes from 'the encroaching of one of these estates upon the power of the other'. If the monarchy fell, the church would follow and in all probability the Lords too, and in the end

the common people [would] set up for themselves, call parity and independence liberty, devour that estate which had devoured the rest, destroy all rights and proprieties [properties], all distinctions of families and merit, and by this means this splendid and excellently distinguished form of government [would] end in a dark, equal chaos of confusion, and the long line of our many noble ancestors in a Jack Cade or a Wat Tyler.[32]

Such arguments were probably almost as effective in rallying conservative country gentlemen to the king as were their fears for the Church of England. The most effective counter to them came not from parliament itself but from the pamphleteer Henry Parker, whose *Observations upon some of His Majesty's Late Answers and Expresses* appeared at the beginning of July. It was the most influential and widely discussed statement of radical parliamentarian theory in all the proliferating pamphlet war of 1642. Parker was a barrister and the younger son of a Sussex knight, and he had already made his

[32] Kenyon, *Stuart Constitution*, p. 20. For the full text, which is considerably more interesting than Kenyon's brief excerpts convey, see J. Malcolm (ed.), *The Struggle for Sovereignty: Seventeenth-Century Political Tracts* (2 vols, 1999), I, 145–78.

name with a tract on the illegality of Ship Money. Addressing the problem that subjects faced when parliament was commanding one thing and the king commanding the contrary, he grasped that the issue had come to be one of sovereignty, which was a concept alien to the common-law mind. Where did *ultimate* authority in the state lie? On his very first page he confronted the king's claim to derive his from God and the law. God, he retorted, was no more the author of royal than of aristocratic power, but gave his sanction to all power, whether supreme or subordinate, that was rightly bestowed. 'Power is originally inherent in the people', Parker resoundingly asserted, and the law that governed its exercise was whatever particular human societies had agreed among themselves: 'When by such or such a law of common consent and agreement it is derived into such and such hands, God confirms that law: and so man is the free and voluntary author, the law is the instrument, and God is the establisher of both.'[33] The people, when consenting to the bestowal of power, may fix what bounds and ordain what conditions they please, so the power vested in the English crown is not absolute but fiduciary, a trust conveyed by the people for the people's good. In normal circumstances, Parker acknowledged, the power to make laws or ordinances in England lay with the king and parliament jointly, but in the present situation, when the king had *deserted* parliament (by withdrawing his presence and rejecting its repeated pleas to return), it lay with parliament to take order for the safety of the people. If king and parliament issued contrary commands, parliament must be obeyed, because it represented 'the whole community in its underived majesty'.[34] Monarchy, if unrestricted, tended of its nature towards tyranny, but the Lords and Commons so perfectly represented the whole nation that they could not conceivably ordain anything that was not advantageous to it. Considering the arbitrariness of the franchise and the large number of rotten boroughs, this to modern eyes is the weakest part of Parker's argument, for experience tells us that no amount of parliamentary reform will guarantee that elected legislators unfailingly serve the public interest or refrain from promoting their own. He maintained that parliament, in its composition, was 'so equally, and geometrically proportionable' that the interests of none of the estates of the realm could be overswayed. He was a democrat only to a limited degree; he happily accepted that the two Houses consisted essentially of the nobility and gentry, who, he said (borrowing the very words of the *Answer to the Nineteen Propositions*) 'serve for an excellent screen or bank . . . to assist both king and people against the encroachments of each other'.[35] For Parker, tyranny and 'ochlocracy' (government by

---

[33] H. Parker, *Observations upon some of His Majesty's Late Answers and Expresses* (1642; reprinted in facsimile in W. Haller (ed.), *Tracts on Liberty in the Puritan Revolution* (New York, 1933), II), p. 1.
[34] Ibid., p. 15.　　[35] Ibid., p. 23.

the populace) were two extremes to be avoided. His object in 1642 was to convince men of substance that their interest lay in supporting parliament, and when, five years later, the Levellers came forward with far more radical ideas than his, he was to deplore them.

Although the greatest controversy was over the control of the land forces (Parker's tract being one of many to which the militia question gave rise), king and parliament clashed just as directly over that of the navy. The Earl of Northumberland was Lord Admiral, but he was too ill in March to take command of the fleet in person. Parliament requested him to name the Earl of Warwick as Vice-Admiral and to delegate the active command to him, but the king had already appointed Sir John Pennington to the post. Charles refused to back down, warned parliament to keep out of the matter, and forbade Warwick's appointment. Parliament nevertheless directed Northumberland to instate him. Later, as Northumberland's parliamentarian leanings became plain, Charles dismissed him and made Pennington Lord Admiral, yet Warwick (on parliament's directions) was in the Downs before him, and it was Warwick whom the fleet wanted. All but five captains accepted him as Admiral on 2 July, and those five were overborne by their own crews. Thereby the navy was lost to the king for the whole of the first Civil War, though a considerable part of it was to rally to him in the second.

The navy, being a close-knit, professional organization, was in a position to make its own choice of allegiance; the county militias, being neither close-knit nor professional, were not. A contest for the control of the trained bands was waged desultorily through the summer and autumn. Following parliament's order to put the Militia Ordinance into execution, they were mustered in fourteen counties by mid-July, and in nine more between August and October. They were to be of limited use when it came to civil war, partly because their arms and training were so often defective, still more because they were so reluctant to march beyond their own county boundaries; but Charles could not afford to relinquish them to his opponents, and he wanted their weapons, such as they were. Since parliament had pre-empted the normal channels of command, through the lord and deputy lieutenants, he resorted to a procedure which dated from long before the lieutenancy. He began on 11 June to issue Commissions of Array, which directed named local magnates to raise and train men for his service. Their use went back to Edward I's time, and had been regulated by a statute of 1405 which had lapsed long ago. They were archaic in form, and in Latin. It was nearly a century since they had last been seriously employed, and when Charles had tried tentatively to revive them during the Bishops' Wars their legality had been strongly challenged. It was disputed again now; nevertheless his commissioners of array succeeded in holding musters in eleven counties between July and October, and they attempted to do so in a dozen more. In a number of shires they came into

sharp conflict with the deputy lieutenants or others who were trying to execute the Militia Ordinance. Musters were held by both sides in Lancashire,
Cheshire, Warwickshire, and Leicestershire, all deeply divided counties.

Success in mustering the trained bands, however, gives us only a very
limited clue to the strength of local feeling for or against king or parliament.
In some cases the motive for assembling them was to defend the county
against the military preparations that were afoot in neighbouring territory,
rather than to contribute to a warlike situation. There were quite large areas
where neither side held musters, but this did not necessarily betoken apathy.
It could mean that the local gentry were mostly like-minded, and confident
enough of their ascendancy to put off any military preparations until they
were forced to face the fact of a war that they had hoped to avert, and would
anyhow rather see fought elsewhere. That must help to explain why there
were no musters in the four northern counties or in the whole of Wales,
regions where gentry royalism was particularly strong, and why in the
parliamentarian heartland of East Anglia the Militia Ordinance was executed only in Essex before the Civil War began, and not at any time in
Cromwell's native Huntingdonshire.

Yet there were areas where the musters did give a clearer indication of genuinely popular support, and that is where volunteers for the parliament came
in spontaneously. In Warwickshire and Northamptonshire they outnumbered
the enrolled trained bands substantially, and at least thirty-four towns, not
counting London, raised volunteers for parliament between June and September. By contrast the only town known to have displayed popular royalism
at this stage was Hereford, where the common people shouted down a minister who tried to preach a 'Roundhead' sermon in the cathedral.[36] The king
indeed found great difficulty in raising foot soldiers. On 20 May he formed a
small personal guard of 200 gentlemen volunteers, all from Yorkshire and
many of them catholics, but though he caused his drums to be repeatedly
beaten in the county during the next three months very few volunteers
came in. He did little better when he made recruiting forays into Lincolnshire,
Leicestershire, and Nottinghamshire. Here and there, groups of loyal gentlemen were willing to raise troops and even regiments of horse, using their
influence among their substantial tenants and their yeomen neighbours, but
at the lower social level from which infantrymen were drawn the response
was miserable. He tried to broaden his territorial base by making William
Seymour, Marquis of Hertford, lieutenant-general of all the western parts
from Oxford to Land's End, including much of Wales. But when Hertford
came to Somerset at the end of July with a small armed force, hoping to raise
it into an army by means of the king's Commissions of Array, he met with

---

[36] Ronald Hutton, *The Royalist War Effort 1642–1646* (1982), p. 4.

massive popular resistance. A crowd of 12,000 or more countrymen turned out to oppose him, and after a week in Wells he beat a humiliating retreat to Sherborne, having raised only about 900 men. The king himself, when he set out from York for Nottingham in August to raise his standard, commanded only about 800 horse and even fewer foot.[37]

If public reaction in the provinces to the increasingly warlike confrontation between king and parliament seems muted, this should not necessarily be attributed to ignorance or indifference. There were many ways whereby all levels of the population were made aware that a great quarrel was afoot, and likely to culminate in war: public readings of royal and parliamentary declarations by magistrates and parsons, many sermons, musters of the trained bands, a spate of pamphlets, and any amount of talk in taverns and ale-houses. There was a very widespread reluctance to accept the war as inevitable, and something will be said in the next chapter about the many attempts to keep it at bay by local accommodations and pacts of neutrality. These were not evidence of apathy—rather the opposite. But if there was once a tendency (which I shared) to underestimate the degree to which people below the ruling class were aware of and involved in the issues of the day, it is possible to go too far in the other direction. It has been argued, for instance, that the increasing pressure and self-assertion of the middling sort, right down to artisans and apprentices, transformed the political confrontation of 1640-1 into a social revolution by 1642, and that in consequence of this, royalism came into being as essentially the party of order. This is to overstate the political initiative and consistency of purpose among the protesting classes, and to take evidence from the London area too far as typical; it also over-simplifies the motives of most royalists, though it points to a very significant factor in the process whereby the king, who had seemed so isolated after his attack on the Five Members, was able to fight on at least equal terms in the first battle of the Civil War.

One cannot fix a precise point in time at which the war became inevitable. The issues, as we have seen, were defined long before the fighting started, but only a minority of those who took up arms were striving for the same object-ives as the protagonists. Few royalists fought, as the king, did, to restore his personal powers to what they had been before the Scottish rebellion; the aims of most were to defend the ancient constitution (as reinforced by the acts of 1641) and the Church of England, both of which they rightly saw as threat-ened by parliament in 1642, and to safeguard the age-old social hierarchy from the threat of subversion. On the other side, only a minority of parlia-mentarians outside the capital really desired the more drastic political

[37] David Underdown, *Somerset in the Civil War and Interregnum* (Newton Abbot, 1973), pp. 32-8; Fletcher, *Outbreak*, pp. 363-4; J. L. Malcolm, *Caesar's Due: Loyalty and King Charles 1642-1646* (1983), p. 41.

changes demanded in the Nineteen Propositions. The majority were as attached to the ancient constitution, as reinforced in 1641, as the moderate royalists were, but rightly saw it as still under threat from a king whose political judgement was disastrous and whose word could not be trusted. If there had been some sure way of restraining Charles's power to do mischief without impairing the powers of his successors, most would probably have been content. Most parliamentarians were social conservatives, but over the future of the church they were deeply divided. The primarily defensive attitudes of both moderate parliamentarians and constitutional royalists is the main reason why the war was so long in coming about. They could not see why their differences could not be bridged by negotiation, and it was only the slow realization that the king and the parliamentary leadership were irreconcilable that made them accept, with dismay, the need for military preparations.

Such preparations went ahead slowly from June onwards, on both sides. Parliament passed an ordinance on the 9th, calling on the public to contribute money, plate, or horses for its service, and most members of both Houses who were still at Westminster pledged generous sums from their own purses. The queen was now making large purchases of arms in the Netherlands with the proceeds of the crown jewels. On the 17th the Earl of Newcastle secured the city of that name for the king, and went on to garrison Tynemouth Castle and fortify Shields at the mouth of the river—a good place for the queen to land her purchases. The activities of the commissioners of array gave parliament a pretext on 4 July to set up a Committee of Safety, consisting of leading activists from both houses, to advise on what was necessary to preserve the peace of the kingdom. It rapidly became an embryonic government, the distant ancestor of a modern war cabinet.

There followed a series of debates from the 9th onward on the raising of an army. Many members faced the prospect with deep dismay. Old Sir Benjamin Rudyard reminded the House of all that parliament had already secured, and urged it to 'beware we do not contend for such a hazardous unsafe security, as may endanger the loss of what we have already . . . Every man here is bound in conscience to employ his uttermost endeavours to prevent the effusion of blood: blood is a crying sin, it pollutes a land; let us save our liberties and our estates, as we may save our souls too'. Bulstrode Whitelocke, who unlike Rudyard was to play a prominent political role under the Commonwealth and Protectorates, said unhappily:

It is strange to note how we have insensibly slid into this beginning of a civil war, by one unexpected accident after another, as waves of the sea, which hath brought us thus far, and we scarce know how, but from paper combats . . . we are now come to the question of raising forces, and naming a General and officers of our army.[38]

---

[38] Rushworth, *Historical Collections*, III, pt. i, pp. 753–4.

He would have had a committee consider how the Nineteen Propositions might be modified, in order to reach an accommodation; but the House finally voted on the 12th that an army should be raised forthwith, and that Essex should be its General.

Charles had just appointed Robert Bertie, Earl of Lindsey, the 59-year-old former commander of the Ship Money fleet, as his commander-in-chief. But within days he made his nephew Prince Rupert, the present Elector Palatine's brother, general of the horse, and authorized him to act if he thought fit without orders from Lindsey, which made the latter's position impossible. He was still desperately short of money, and he was sustained through the summer largely by a series of enormously generous gifts from the catholic Earl of Worcester, whose son Lord Herbert of Raglan acted as their bearer.

With increasing numbers of men under arms, and mobs turning out with makeshift weapons, there were bound to be some violent episodes, as well as a certain amount of casual pillage. A confused affray occurred at Manchester on 15 July when Lord Strange, the Earl of Derby's heir, was being feasted by the chief townsmen. Three of parliament's deputy lieutenants called out some of the militia in protest, and a fight broke out between them and some of Strange's 120 attendant cavaliers. Blood was shed on both sides, and a militiaman who died of his wounds has sometimes been reckoned the first fatal casualty of the Civil War. He may have been preceded by a victim of one of several skirmishes near Hull, which was beset by royal troops from 4 July.[39] There might have been heavier losses at Marshall's Elm in Somerset on 4 August when John Pyne MP, at the head of about five hundred trained bands, was ambushed by Henry Lunsford and a hundred or so cavaliers, if Pyne and his men had not made off so quickly. But both sides were, on the whole, so reluctant to strike the first blow that such skirmishes as these were quite exceptional until after the king had given the formal signal for war.

There were, however, enough breaches of the peace and rumours of war to nourish the fear of a general breakdown of order, and this was reflected in widespread difficulty in collecting rents, reluctance to bring cattle to market, and other symptoms of economic dislocation. In the fenlands there was more destruction of enclosures and ditches than usual, but that was more because the commoners were expecting parliament to relieve them from exploitation than because they were kicking over the traces in expectation of civil war. A violent mob that gathered for the purpose in Lincolnshire early in April, however, was heard to say 'that if the parliament would not help them, they would help themselves by club law'.[40] Many landowners in other parts sensed

[39] Manning, *English People and the English Revolution*, p. 167; E. Broxap, *The Great Civil War in Lancashire* (Manchester, 2nd ed., 1973), pp. 16–20.

[40] *The Private Journals of the Long Parliament, 7 March to 1 June 1642*, ed. V. F. Suon and A. S. Young (New Haven, 1987), p. 132; Manning, *English People*, pp. 133–4; C. Holmes,

a greater than usual tension between their tenantry and themselves, and there were enough examples of open defiance by angry mobs to feed an apprehension that the law was breaking down. Perhaps the worst episode began on 20 August in puritan Colchester, when it was learnt that Sir John Lucas, who lived nearby, was about to set off to join the king with twelve horses and sundry arms. The trained bands assembled, along with 400 or more volunteers for the parliamentary army and a crowd of men, women, and children variously estimated at between 2,000 and 5,000. They besieged Lucas's house. Next day the mob broke into it, seized him and his family, and forced a terrified mayor and aldermen to shut them in the town gaol for their own safety. Then when they had done all the damage they could to Lucas's property they split up and attacked other royalist houses in the neighbourhood. Order was quickly restored, however, when the House of Commons sent down Sir Thomas Barrington and Harbottle Grimstone to make it clear that this was not how parliament wished to be served, despite the formal commencement of war on the 22nd.[41] Outbreaks like this were exceptional, and even now the fear that the rule of law was collapsing was exaggerated. The king's judges rode their circuits and held the assizes as usual in July and August, and the JPs held their quarter sessions almost everywhere, not only in July but in October too.

The gathering clouds of war were distracting public attention from Ireland, and diverting military resources that would surely have been employed there if England had not been obsessed with her own troubles. Although the military situation in Ireland did not change dramatically after the rebellion reached its maximum extent early in 1642, there were important political developments during the spring and summer. Most of the Old English had now joined the rising while retaining a distinct military organization, but an important minority of Old English and anglicized Irish nobles, led by Ormond and including Clanricard, Thomond, and Inchiquin, continued to hold out against them and aligned themselves with the English royalists. The enmity between the rebels and the English parliament was increased when the latter decided in February that the suppression of the rebellion should be financed by raising £1,000,000 from the sale of 2,500,000 acres of confiscated Irish land to any 'adventurers' who would put up the money. The king gave his assent to the resultant Adventurers' Act on 19 March. He could hardly have refused it without appearing soft towards the rebels,

---

*Seventeenth-Century Lincolnshire* (Lincoln, 1980), pp. 154–6. Keith Lindley, in *Fenland Riots and the English Revolution* (1982), p. 139, argues that most fenland commoners were indifferent to the national issues of the Civil War, except when the political situation enabled them to further their immediate social and economic interests.

[41] Manning, *English People*, pp. 171–4.

who were still declaring their loyalty to him, but he made it harder for them to do so with any sincerity. King and parliament were both committed now to a policy of total reconquest and large-scale confiscation, and the prospects for Irish landlords became bleaker when the Scots asked for, and got, the right to participate in the adventurers' scheme. Scotland also secured a substantial share in the military programme, and the first contingent of 2,500 Scottish troops under Colonel Robert Monro landed in Ulster early in April. The Dublin government's forces had already cleared the Pale, and on 15 April Ormond soundly beat a rebel army of 6,000 at Kilrush. He could not keep up the campaign because his unpaid and ill-shod men refused to march again, but the rebel cause was looking a little shaky by the late spring.

It was given new life in the summer, first by a striking initiative on the part of the Irish catholic clergy, and then by the return of Owen Roe O'Neill and other distinguished soldiers from the Spanish army in Flanders. The clergy, led by those of Armagh but soon on a nationwide basis, urged the need for a central decision-making organization for the whole of Ireland, embracing both churchmen and laymen. They held a series of crucial meetings at Kilkenny in May and early June, to the latter of which they invited leaders of the catholic laity. From their joint deliberations there emerged a scheme for a central supreme council, to be chosen by an elected national assembly and backed by four provincial councils. Together they declared that the current war was a just war, and that catholics who declined to take part in it should be automatically excommunicated. They pledged themselves to put an end to rivalry between provinces, and to make no difference whatever between Irish and Old English. They framed a new oath of association to bind together the 'confederated catholics of Ireland' in what came to be known as the Confederation of Kilkenny. The Confederates swore to bear true allegiance to Charles, 'King of Great Britain, France and Ireland', to maintain the power and privileges of the Irish parliament, the fundamental laws of Ireland, the free exercise of the Roman Catholic religion and the lives, liberties, estates, and rights of all their associates, and to obey the commands of the supreme council. They set up a provisional executive of twelve men and made arrangements for the election of a representative General Assembly to meet in October.

The Confederates expressly disclaimed the title and authority of a parliament for their General Assembly, in the same way as they constantly affirmed their allegiance to the king. But they were in fact creating an alternative government to that which he sought to maintain through his Lord Lieutenant Ormond, and they were of course defying the proclamation that he issued on 26 February 1642, ordering all those in arms in Ireland to surrender. They could maintain the assumption that in commanding them thus, and in the

Adventurers' Act, he was acting under duress; and in the English Civil War that was so clearly imminent when they set up the Confederation it was obviously more advantageous to them that the king should win, rather than the parliament in alliance with the Covenanting Scots. Moreover they had to take account of the deeply felt royalism of so many of the Old English nobles and gentry whose alliance they needed, and there was always the chance that Charles's military needs would give them the chance to strike an advantageous deal with him.

Yet although these considerations militated against the Confederation becoming a movement for national independence in its early years, the potential was there, and there were two elements within it whose interests might tend that way. There were the clergy, especially the higher clergy whose training had given them a cosmopolitan and ultramontane outlook. They had little of the ingrained loyalty to the heretical royal house that most of the Old English still felt, and their natural hope was ultimately to recover the alienated wealth of the church, which the crown was never likely to grant. Much of it had stuck to the fingers of lay landowners, who were consequently inclined to put a curb on clerical pretensions. The senior clergy's loyalty was not undivided, but in the last resort it went mostly to Rome. They were instrumental, by enlisting a bit of diplomatic pressure from the papacy, in persuading the governor of the Spanish Netherlands to release Owen Roe O'Neill, the nephew of the Earl of Tyrone who had fled Ireland in 1607, and the veteran of over thirty years' distinguished service in the forces of the King of Spain. Spain herself, with Catalonia and Portugal in rebellion and the long, grinding war with France on her hands, could neither spare further help nor afford to provoke England, but O'Neill brought some other officers (and some munitions) when he slipped home at the end of July 1642, and more were to follow. They formed the other significant group whose ties to the house of Stuart were weaker than those of most of the indigenous landed class. O'Neill was to go on professing his allegiance to King Charles until he himself died in 1649, but how long it would have survived the establishment of the Commonwealth is matter for doubt. At any rate the return of the exiles transformed the military direction of the rebellion. O'Neill was promptly accepted as general of the army of Ulster. Two other senior veterans followed him home to Ireland in September: Thomas Preston, an uncle of Lord Gormanston, who became general of the army of Leinster, and John Burke, a kinsman of Clanricard, who took over that of Connaught. Garret Barry, another veteran of the Spanish service, was a less successful appointment in Munster and did not last long, but on the whole the military competence of the commanders in the field improved dramatically. It would take time to turn the Irish irregulars into soldiers, and money and munitions would remain woefully short; but time would not be lacking while England became engrossed in civil war, and the Confederation's constitution provided a means of raising taxes. That and the disposal of armed forces were not the only sovereign powers that the Confederation assumed, for over the next six years it would also enact laws, issue coinage, and appoint and instruct ambassadors to foreign powers.

# EIGHT

# The Blast of War

THERE was no sharply defined beginning to the English Civil War. The king sought to give it one by ceremonially raising his standard at Nottingham on 22 August 1642 and summoning his subjects to aid him in suppressing the rebellion headed by the Earl of Essex, but even as a symbolic gesture this was to fall flat. There had already been clashes of arms in various parts of the country for some weeks past, and it would be many weeks more before Charles's military commanders felt capable of offering battle. Very many of his subjects clung to a hope that open war might yet be averted by a negotiated settlement, or expected that if it came to the worst the quarrel might be decided by a single battle. Many thought first about the interests of their own communities and set about negotiating local pacts of neutrality, hoping thereby to keep any war there might be outside the bounds of their particular counties or cities.

Charles, unlike most of his subjects, felt no reluctance about going to war; his problem was that he lacked the men and the means to wage it. When he ran up his standard, Essex already had a strong military advantage and enjoyed much broader support. He had the authority, indeed the command, of parliament to raise horse and foot, and that gave him the head start of launching his recruiting campaign in the capital. London's citizens not only furnished a unique concentration of truly popular support for the parliament's cause, but had for some time been showing a growing enthusiasm for amateur military exercises. This found an outlet in the Honourable Artillery Company and other voluntary societies, as well as in the best trained bands in the kingdom. The home counties too had a strong vein of puritanism and a greater than average awareness of national political issues, and they too provided Essex with many volunteers. At this stage, also, there was public financial support for those who were willing to raise men and lead them. To each captain who undertook to furnish a troop of horse parliament gave £1,000 as 'mounting money', and each colonel of foot received a sum of 'levy money' when he had raised a certain number of men. Essex was personally popular, both as the bearer of a great name and as an outspoken Country peer, and he threw himself into the task of raising an army with energy and panache. His military expertise was apt to be exaggerated, for his service in the German wars lay far in the past and was limited to defensive operations, while his role in the 1625 Cadiz expedition as Vice-Admiral and Colonel-General had been decidedly less than glorious. But with the help of some more experienced subordinates he made a fair professional job of organizing a sizeable army at short notice.[1] If he had shown a similar zest for leading it against the enemy, the war might have been shorter. There was great public enthusiasm when he held a general muster of volunteers in the Artillery Garden on 26 July, and before Charles had raised his standard Essex and his General of the Horse, the Earl of Bedford, had recruited fifty-nine troops of cavalry, each nominally of sixty men, and four of dragoons. On 9 September he set out to engage the king with an army estimated (probably with slight exaggeration) to number 15,000. With him in his life guard rode a bevy of men who were soon to make their own military and political reputations, including Henry Ireton, Charles Fleetwood, Thomas Harrison, Nathaniel Rich, Edmund Ludlow, Matthew Thomlinson, and Francis Russell.

The king was far from ready to meet him. He had been deeply disappointed by the response of the Yorkshire gentry to his presence among them. During July and August his drums had beaten for recruits in various parts of the county and in adjacent shires, but very few men indeed had come in. He had made a series of personal progresses to Doncaster, Lincolnshire, Nottinghamshire, and Leicestershire, but though many of the gentry and some town corporations gave him a loyal welcome he found very little response at the social levels from which the rank and file of armies were drawn. He fared no better with the trained bands. Those of Yorkshire had a total nominal strength of about 12,000, but when he commanded their 'strict appearance' at a rendezvous on 4 August it was reported that barely 200 turned up. As has been seen, Hertford's recruiting campaign in the west country was meeting with no more success. The Earl of Northampton was doing rather better in Warwickshire, partly because his intense rivalry with Lord Brooke of Warwick Castle was causing most of the local gentry and many commoners to take sides. During August he conducted a small-scale siege of the castle, which was threatening enough to induce parliament to send Brooke a relieving force. On the 18th, just outside Warwick, about 6,000 horse and foot under Brooke confronted about 5,000 under Northampton, who formally demanded Brooke's submission and the surrender of the castle. But this was before the royal signal for war had been given, so after Brooke had defied the royalist lords with similar flights of rhetoric the two forces backed off.

---

[1] This account of the king's recruiting campaign is based largely on Joyce Lee Malcolm, *Caesar's Due: Loyalty and King Charles 1642–1646* (1983), and Ronald Hutton, *The Royalist War Effort 1642–1646* (1982). That of Essex is described in Vernon F. Snow, *Essex the Rebel* (Lincoln, Nebr., 1970), ch. 12.

Charles had, however, published a proclamation on the 12th, announcing his intention to raise his standard at Nottingham ten days later. When he set out from York he had only about 800 horse and not so much as a regiment of infantry with him. Hoping apparently to capitalize on Northampton's efforts in Warwickshire, he swiftly moved far beyond Nottingham to Coventry, where the county's magazine was kept. He was making a practice now of securing the trained bands' arms even when he could not enlist the men themselves, but it was meeting with growing resistance. Coventry had a royalist mayor and a divided corporation, but there was a strong puritan element among the citizens. The city had as yet no garrison, but when Charles appeared before the walls some of the citizenry turned out in arms and fired on his troops, wounding several and killing some horses. The puritan party kept Coventry firmly on the parliament's side for the rest of the war.

The raising of the standard followed upon this rebuff. It was a cheerless and muted ceremony, at which Charles's looks betrayed his own melancholy. So few came to witness it that some in his small retinue suggested postponing it; but it went ahead, though he had not even enough foot soldiers to furnish his standard with a round-the-clock guard. Two or three nights later a strong wind blew it down. On the very day he raised it the parliamentarian relief force for Warwick Castle, which included John Hampden and the regiment that he had personally raised in Buckinghamshire, forced Northampton to abandon the siege. On the night of 22–3 August, and sporadically through the next morning, these parliamentarians, together with Brooke's men and other local levies, skirmished with Northampton's forces near Southam, east of Warwick. This clash has been claimed as the first battle of the Civil War, but though there was some cannon-fire and a few fatal casualties, mainly on the royalist side, it hardly amounted to that. The parliamentarians had the better of it, and were rapturously welcomed in Coventry next day.

Charles's commissions of array proved to be a quite ineffective way of raising a field army. He only began to assemble the makings of one when he settled at Shrewsbury for three weeks in late September and early October. He did so by a method which the crown continued to employ down to the Napoleonic wars, and was similar to what Essex and the parliament were currently employing; namely by granting commissions to individual noblemen and gentlemen to raise regiments in his name. On this basis the Earl of Derby raised three foot regiments in Lancashire, and other prominent landowners in Wales, Cheshire, and Staffordshire recruited eleven more, all largely at their own expense. In practice this left the choice of subordinate officers almost entirely to the colonels in charge, and since losses of men through casualties or desertion were seldom fully made good, the royal army faced a growing problem as the war went on of over-officered regiments with a mere fraction of their complement in troopers or foot soldiers.

Another problem was that in some of the most fertile recruiting areas a high proportion of the gentry were Roman Catholics. Two thirds of the royalist gentry in Lancashire were of that faith. Catholics outside court circles had little to thank the king for (though they might reckon that a parliamentarian triumph would make their condition even worse), and their support for him varied widely from region to region. Publicly they got no thanks for it, for Charles had ruled in his formal orders of war that 'No papist of what degree or quality soever shall be admitted to serve in our army',[2] and he solemnly repeated the ban in the royal declaration that accompanied the raising of his standard. One cannot believe that he intended to keep such pledges, and they did not deceive anyone for long. The Earl of Newcastle, his commander in the four northern counties, was raising a separate army for him in those parts, and making no discrimination against catholic officers. In the country as a whole, but especially in the north, the number of catholics who took up arms for the king was impressive. Of the 603 officers whom he commissioned as colonels in the course of the war, 117 were catholics, and so (by one estimate) were two in five of all the officers who died fighting for him.[3] Catholics were no less generous in their financial support. His war effort was still being sustained, apart from the sale of a few peerages, very largely by voluntary contributions, and by far the most munificent were those of the catholic Earl of Worcester. Ironically, he still relied on the recusancy fines which catholics had to pay for not attending parish worship, and which most of them settled by an annual composition. In September he appealed to the recusant gentry of Shropshire and Staffordshire to help him with a two or three years' advance, and they promptly came up with between £4,000 and £5,000.[4]

At Shrewsbury he did not feel immediately threatened by Essex's army, which was making very sluggish progress. Essex reviewed about 15,000 men when he held a general muster at Northampton on 14 September, but many of them lacked training, discipline, and equipment, and he stayed in the town a whole week. On the 19th he set out again for Worcester, believing that to be the king's objective. Sir John Byron, the poet's ancestor and a devoted cavalier, had indeed arrived in Worcester from Oxford with much of the plate of the university and its colleges, some chests of money, his own regiment of horse, and a band of student volunteers. The king sent Prince Rupert to secure the city and provide Byron and his treasure with an escort, but Rupert decided on arrival that Worcester's delapidated fortifications were indefensible

---

[2] Quoted in Malcolm, *Caesar's Due*, p. 49. On Lancashire catholic royalists see B. G. Blackwood, *The Lancashire Gentry and the Great Rebellion, 1640–1660* (Chetham Society, Manchester, 1978), esp. pp. 27, 64.

[3] P. R. Newman, *The Old Service: Royalist Regimental Colonels and the Civil War, 1642–46* (Manchester, 1993), ch. 4; Malcolm, *Caesar's Due*, p. 51.

[4] Clarendon, *History of the Rebellion*, II, 338–9.

and directed Byron to take his precious convoy to the king in Shrewsbury. To cover his withdrawal he positioned about 1,000 horse and dragoons in the vicinity of Powick Bridge, two miles south-west of the city. Essex meanwhile had sent Colonel John Brown ahead with a roughly equal number of dragoons to clear his advance, and on 23 September Brown unexpectedly ran into Rupert's skilfully posted rearguard. Brown was desperately keen to attack, and though his troop commanders, who included three MPs, advised caution he overrode them. He did not know that he was taking on not only Rupert in person but his brother Prince Maurice and such skilled commanders as Byron and Henry Wilmot. His men were caught in a defile, and when Rupert charged them the result was very soon a rout. He lost at least fifteen officers and many more soldiers, including fifty or more taken prisoners.

Few actions involving only 2,000 men have been so much written about as Powick Bridge, but its significance really was disproportionate to its scale. It came at a time when many still doubted the king's ability to field an army capable of engaging the parliament's, and its effect on the morale of both sides altered the terms on which they met in their first major battle a month later. It also launched Rupert's English reputation. The prince was only twenty-three, but he had commanded a cavalry regiment when he was sixteen, and in addition to his prowess in the field he was a serious student of fortification, siege warfare, and the use of artillery. Three years as a prisoner of war in the castle of Linz on the Danube had given him leisure for study, and may have sharpened the pricklier side of his nature. He was not an easy colleague in the king's council of war, and his attitude to the civilian population smacked too much of the German campaigns in which he had learnt his profession. His capacity to take overall charge of an army in a major battle was, and remains, an open question, but he was beyond doubt a formidable and charismatic leader of cavalry, and his devotion to his uncle's cause was complete.

Essex duly entered Worcester the day after the clash at Powick Bridge, and he stayed there for over three weeks. Despite his earnest injunctions to his officers to maintain discipline, his men plundered the houses of nearby catholic gentlemen and systematically vandalized the cathedral. They demonstrated their godly horror of superstition by urinating in the font, ripping down the organ, breaking every statue within sight, and relieving themselves as and when they felt inclined. When the royalists reoccupied the city later in the year they were naturally appalled by the sacrilege and the stench. This sort of behaviour is so commonly attributed to 'Cromwell's soldiers' that it is worth mentioning that none of his troops were with Essex in Worcester and Cromwell himself was far away. His men were not guiltless of iconoclasm, but it was, regrettably, a characteristic of parliament's forces generally and by no means peculiar to his command.

Worcester and Shrewsbury are only fifty miles apart, and it is a measure of both sides' limited eagerness for battle that their armies remained rooted so close to each other for nearly three weeks before either sought the other out. The king moved first, on 13 October, and he boldly set his march towards London. Essex left Worcester on the 19th, only when he knew where the royal army was heading. Charles had never lacked the will to fight, but it was only now that he felt that he had the means to do so. He set off with about 6,000 infantry, 2,000 cavalry, and 1,500 dragoons (mounted troops who normally fought on foot), and by the time the three Lancashire regiments joined him in the Midlands his army totalled about 14,000. Numerically it was almost a match for Essex's, but it was indifferently equipped, despite the recent arrival of a large convoy of weapons purchased on the continent; many of the Welsh foot were armed only with pitchforks and clubs.

For days the two armies groped their way towards each other, neither with much knowledge of the other's movements. Essex naturally intended to place his between the royalists and London, but he seems to have thought mistakenly that the king was aiming to attack Banbury and he marched to its relief. Charles had marginally better intelligence and the advantage of Rupert's sense of terrain, so on the prince's advice he formed up his army, early on Sunday the 23rd, on the ridge of Edgehill near Kineton, across the road from Warwick to Banbury and Oxford. When Essex learnt where the enemy really was, just as he was about to go to church at eight in the morning, he found that the king's forces were ranged in line of battle between him and London, instead of the other way round. He did not want to fight, since he was expecting to be joined next day by John Hampden with three foot regiments and eleven troops of horse, the force which had relieved Lord Brooke and Warwick Castle. But he had no choice, and even without Hampden's brigade he was not outnumbered, though the royalist cavalry was superior both in strength and quality. Seeing that the royal army had moved forward from the steep slopes of Edgehill to positions just forward of the village of Radway, he deployed his own half way between it and Kineton, facing south-east.

There had been an acrimonious dispute between Lindsey, the king's general, and Rupert as to the battle formation to be adopted. Lindsey favoured the Dutch order that he had learnt in the service of Maurice of Nassau, Rupert the more complex Swedish model which had been highly effective in Gustavus Adolphus's armies but required more training and expertise than their present forces could boast. Charles eventually ruled in Rupert's favour, whereupon Lindsey said that 'since His Majesty thought him not fit to perform the office of Commander-in-Chief, he would serve him as a colonel', and asked that his own regiment of foot be posted opposite Essex's. He fought at its head, and in the bitter infantry battle that followed he was mortally wounded.

The basic formation of both armies was the usual one of the period, with the infantry in the centre and most of the cavalry on either wing. After an hour or so of rather ineffective cannonading, Rupert on the king's right launched the battle proper with a cavalry charge which completely broke the parliamentarian horse opposite him. Almost simultaneously Henry Wilmot, the king's Commissary-General, led an equally successful charge on the left wing. Both commanders chased the fleeing parliamentarian cavalry to Kineton and beyond. It was always difficult to halt victorious horsemen in the full excitement of a pursuit, with the prospect of booty before them, and most of these were in their first fight; but it was deplorable that Byron, commanding Rupert's second line of cavalry, joined with it in the chase instead of turning it against the now almost unprotected parliamentarian infantry. He might have won the battle decisively for the king. What is most striking about Edgehill, however, is not that both sides lacked the professional skill and discipline to bring it to a decisive conclusion, for that was to be expected so early in the war, but that most of the infantry on both sides fought with extraordinary tenacity and bore heavy casualties. Essex had kept two cavalry regiments in reserve, and one of them under his Scottish Lieutenant-General, Sir William Balfour, inflicted such losses on the exposed royalist foot that they might have broken if Rupert and his troops had not returned in time to prevent a rout. The two armies broke off only when darkness was falling, having fought themselves to a standstill. Both spent the night in the field; Essex and the king both took what sleep they could close to their men, and both decided next morning not to renew the fight. More perhaps hinged on the outcome of this battle than of any other before Naseby, and there is a kind of natural justice, given the state of feeling in the country generally, in the fact that it was indecisive.

Militarily the honours were fairly even, but Charles had the potentially great advantage that the road to London lay open to him. He was in no hurry to take it, however; there were many dead to bury and even more wounded to be tended. He secured Banbury on the 27th, and shortly after occupied Oxford, which was to be his headquarters for the rest of the war. Essex had no thought of pursuing him, but drew back to Warwick to rest his battered army. Casualties and (still more) desertions had reduced it to about half its initial strength, despite its reinforcement by Hampden's brigade. At Westminster the will to fight was wavering; the Lords voted to reopen peace negotiations, and on 2 November the Commons concurred. Without yet knowing this, Charles set off next day on a march for Reading, with London as his obvious final objective. At Reading, he snubbed the parliament's peace initiative by refusing to admit one of its commissioners, Sir John Evelyn, on the ground that he had just proclaimed him a traitor. Without waiting for its response, he authorized Rupert to clear his way to London by attacking Brentford.

Essex meanwhile brought his army back to London by way of Watling Street, and received a hero's welcome on arriving there on the 7th. He posted the regiments of Denzil Holles (who had fought very bravely at Edgehill) and

Lord Brooke in Brentford, but Rupert's fierce onslaught on the 12th drove them out with heavy losses, hard though they resisted. When he had taken the town, Rupert gave it over to his soldiers to sack. This put a strange gloss on a gracious message that the king had sent to parliament the day before, promising to receive its peace proposals wherever he might be and suggesting Windsor as the place of negotiation. From now on his pragmatic attitude to peace overtures deceived only those whose wishes dimmed their judgement.

Brentford was little more than ten miles from London, and the closeness of the threat caused great consternation there; but it also aroused a strong spirit of resistance. Essex left at once to organize what was left of his army, and he ordered an immediate rendezvous of all the troops in the London area—his own, the City trained bands, and any other able-bodied citizens who could appear in arms—at Turnham Green, halfway between Brentford and Westminster. Thousands of apprentices responded enthusiastically to the call, as did many militiamen from Hertfordshire, Essex, and Surrey. About 24,000 men mustered in all, almost as many as the combined parliamentary and Scottish armies at Marston Moor, and far more than either side brought to any other Civil War battlefield. These were not all trained soldiers, of course, but Essex and Major-General Skippon, the commander of the City trained bands, posted them in effective defensive positions among small enclosures, with musketeers lining the hedges to deter a cavalry attack and with well emplaced guns covering every road and passage. Skippon rode round his companies, exhorting them in homely terms that spoke from the heart to the heart. Essex too made the round of the defenders, accompanied by members of both Houses, and the soldiers threw their caps in the air, shouting 'Hey for old Robin!' It was a Sunday, but they did not go hungry, for their wives and girls made picnics of their Sunday dinners, which were trundled out to Turnham Green in nearly a hundred carts, along with quantities of beer and sack. The king's army confronted this display of genuine and formidable popular resistance for some hours, and Essex's guns fired a few shots at it; then it drew off. The sheer numbers and the disadvantageous terrain would have made an assault extremely hazardous, and even if Rupert had carried it, his and the king's problems would barely have begun. The royal forces caused some further alarm by taking Kingston, but Charles returned to Oxford on the 23rd, and he did not leave it again for another six months. His army did not remain entirely inactive, for Wilmot stormed and sacked Marlborough on 5 December, and Rupert did the same to Cirencester on 2 February.

Essex for his part thought of nothing but defence during the winter months. His army very quickly wore out its welcome in the capital, for his men were so extremely disorderly that parliament promptly passed an ordinance subjecting them to martial law, which despite the Petition of Right gave him powers of life or death over them. He set up his headquarters at Windsor, and he established garrisons in such important cities as Bristol, Gloucester, Exeter, Plymouth, Southampton, and Dover, but as time wore on a growing war party at Westminster began to murmur at his evident unwillingness to carry the war to the king.

Against most people's expectations, the first brief campaign of the war had gone better for Charles than for the parliament. Indeed if full use had been made of the superiority of his cavalry at Edgehill, the battle could have been clearly won for him. But would even the clearest of victories in one battle have decided the outcome of the war, as so many of his subjects on both sides hoped? It is most improbable. The moral effect would have been great, but the forces under the direct command of the two commanders-in-chief were only a fraction of those under arms in the country as a whole, and if either army had gone down to total disaster at Edgehill—which was unlikely, given the limited military proficiency of both—the other side would still have had men enough in its regional forces to carry on the struggle. At the end of 1642 the king was perhaps marginally better placed, with the Earl of Newcastle in the northern counties, Sir Ralph Hopton in the south-west, and the still scarcely tapped fund of loyalty in Wales to draw upon, but if Essex had been the loser the Scots would not willingly have let the parliament suffer total defeat; and parliament too had its regional forces.

In Yorkshire they were raised and led by Ferdinando Lord Fairfax, with his son Sir Thomas in command of the horse, but hostilities in the county had been suspended in the early autumn while some of its leading gentry, mainly from the West Riding, negotiated a treaty of neutrality. This was intended to isolate Yorkshire from any war that might develop elsewhere, and it was an early example of a series of such treaties. Lord Fairfax and the king's local commander, the Earl of Cumberland, both approved it, though Fairfax stipulated that it must be subject to parliament's consent. Among those who signed it near Leeds on 29 September were members of parliament on both sides and the fathers of two outstanding statesmen of the next reign, the Earl of Danby and the Marquis of Halifax. But parliament could not tolerate such a challenge to its claimed right to determine national policy, and it was denounced nearer home by the Hothams, father and son, who had defied the king in Hull and were still holding the city against Newcastle's forces. The Hothams were old rivals of the Fairfaxes, and deeply resentful of the authority that had been given to them over the county's forces. Sir John attacked the treaty in a published declaration for presuming 'to call the conclusions of England before the bar of Yorkshire, and to indict a parliament (the greatest council) before the judgement of some few gentlemen, and half of them delinquents too'.[5] His son Captain Hotham reacted more physically by

---

[5] *Reasons Why Sir John Hotham Cannot Agree to the Treaty of Pacification . . .* (1642).

threatening the walls of royalist-held York and capturing Cawood Castle, the archbishop's seat. Archbishop Williams had been fortifying it at his own expense, but he fled to north Wales rather than stay and defend it. Yet one wonders whether the Hothams were moved more by zeal for the parliamentary cause or jealousy of the Fairfaxes. The son was in correspondence with Newcastle by early January and the father before the end of April, by which time he fully intended to betray Hull to the king.

Once parliament had condemned the neutrality treaty, a struggle for the control of Yorkshire ensued between the Fairfaxes and Newcastle; the ineffectual Cumberland soon retired from the scene. Puritanism was strong among the small clothiers of the West Riding towns, and they supported the Fairfaxes with both men and money, especially in Bradford and Halifax. In Leeds, however, they were held down for a time by a royalist ruling oligarchy, whose authority rested on a charter granted by Charles in 1626, and who now admitted a royalist garrison. Newcastle's wealth and territorial influence, coupled with his status as a privy councillor and (until recently) governor of the Prince of Wales, enabled him to raise a sizeable army, which numbered about 8,000, including 2,000 horse, when he moved into Yorkshire late in November. Captain Hotham, who had not yet changed sides, tried in vain to deny him the passage of the Tees at Piercebridge, and Lord Fairfax with about 1,500 men fought him at Tadcaster for most of the day on 7 December before having to fall back. By the end of the year the parliamentarians still clung to Hull, Scarborough, Selby, Cawood, and most of the clothing towns, and on 23 January Fairfax took Leeds by storm. But Newcastle was master of most of the county and its coast, where he stood ready to welcome the queen when she should land with a convoy of ships carrying the munitions that she had purchased in the Netherlands. She first set sail on 6 January, but was driven back by storms.

Far away in the West Country the king's lieutenant-general, the Marquis of Hertford, was recruiting with more success after Charles had raised his standard than he had had earlier, when he had met with the spontaneous popular resistance of the men of Somerset and adjacent parts. Operating from Sherborne, he engaged in rather desultory hostilities against the local parliamentarians, but late in September he embarked most of the men he had raised for Wales, whence he marched them to join the king's main army. He left behind, however, his Lieutenant-General of Horse, Sir Ralph Hopton, who was soon to prove himself one of the finest soldiers in all the king's forces. He had seen some professional service on the continent; he and Essex had been comrades in arms in the English volunteer force that fought for the Elector Palatine. Hopton was a moderate puritan, and as MP for Wells he had voted for Strafford's attainder, but he had subsequently rallied to the king with the other constitutional royalists and had been expelled from parliament. After

Hertford's departure he took his small body of cavalry into Cornwall, where the gentry on both sides had concluded a treaty of pacification similar to that in Yorkshire. They indicted him for breaking the peace, and he willingly submitted to trial, for he aimed to win the county by persuasion rather than coercion. He was acquitted; and when the Cornish royalist gentry indicted their opponents in turn, the latter fled the county to join their fellow-parliamentarians in Devon. With Cornwall now firmly in royalist hands he did a fine job of recruiting, though most of his volunteers needed to be trained from scratch.

Hopton found much less response, however, in Devon, a county with a thriving and growing clothing industry, though that was only one basis of its relatively strong parliamentarianism. In December his attempts to capture Plymouth and Exeter were foiled by the local parliamentarian commander Lord Ruthin, a Scottish professional—not to be confused with Patrick Ruthven, another such, whom Charles had recently appointed as his commander-in-chief in succession to Lindsey and made Earl of Forth. Ruthin was checked in turn when he first tried to carry the war into Cornwall. Hopton was short of arms and money, but was saved when three parliamentarian warships carrying both were driven by a storm into Falmouth on 17 January. The windfall was timely, for Ruthin was advancing westward again. Hopton joined battle with him at Braddock Down, between Lostwithiel and Liskeard, and his Cornish infantry put their opponents to ignominious flight; they captured at least 1,250 prisoners, many arms and five pieces of artillery. It was the first of a string of brilliant victories for Hopton, but for the present the urge for peace among the western gentry was still strong. They agreed a truce on 28 February, and soon afterwards a serious negotiation opened between the Cornish royalists and Devonian parliamentarians; it was even proposed to extend it to Dorset and Somerset. Hopton agreed to it because he hoped it would neutralize the south-west while he took his own army to join the king's, and though that was not to come about the cessation of arms did not finally end until 22 April.

Other local commanders who played a significant part in the war will come into our story later, but one who earned a national reputation in its early months was Sir William Waller. Now in his mid-forties, he had as a young man fought with the English volunteers in the Elector Palatine's service alongside Essex and Hopton, but he was no more a professional soldier than they were. A strong though moderate puritan, he was currently MP for Andover and a colonel of horse in Essex's army. Essex sent him with a small force to reduce Portsmouth, which Goring was holding for the king, and after a three-week siege Goring surrendered to him on 5 September. During the next four months Waller went on to capture Farnham Castle, Marlborough, Winchester (which he gave over to plunder, and did not hold for long), Arundel

Castle and Chichester. On his triumphant return the London citizens hailed him as 'William the Conqueror', and parliament made him Sergeant-Major-General of Gloucestershire, Bristol, Somerset, and Wiltshire, with five new regiments of horse and five of foot under his command. He received his commission from Essex, but during the next year and more he came to be seen by the war party as not so much a subordinate of the Lord General as an alternative commander. He was soon to be pitched against his old friend Hopton, with whom he could scarcely have imagined a quarrel two years earlier. They had been contemporaries at Oxford, as well as in the wars together; their estates were in neighbouring counties, and until well into 1641 they had both seemed typical Country MPs.

To explain how the Civil War came about it has been necessary to focus first on the breakdown of political relations at the centre and the activities of the armed forces that the king and the parliament raised. This has involved concentrating on the committed activists on both sides: on the politicians at Westminster who took the crucial decisions (though not all peers and MPs were activists); on the king and his close entourage, and others strongly linked to the crown by service or patronage; on passionate puritans on the one side and passionate anti-puritans, whether Anglican or Roman Catholic, on the other; and on soldiers old and new who found their *métier* when the quarrel escalated into war. But such activists were still not typical of England, let alone of Britain, as a whole.

Very many of the country gentry, and still more of the middling sort, could not understand why the king and parliament could not come to an 'accommodation', since their public declarations spoke so fair. There seemed to be so much common ground between them. The actual outbreak of hostilities heightened most people's sense that civil war was the worst of evils, for the year 1642 had seen a marked increase in riots against enclosures, many attacks on gentlemen's houses, frequent panics over popish plots, much iconoclasm by both puritan fanatics and soldiers, and a great deal of lawbreaking by ill-disciplined troops. There was a widespread fear of a general breakdown of order. This kind of reaction did not usually express indifference to the issues between the two sides, but rather a feeling that war was not the way to settle them. Those who shared it tended to put their local community's interests first and to try to exempt it from war's ravages, in the hope that the antagonists on the national stage could come to their senses and to some agreed terms. There were attempts to negotiate pacts of neutrality in twenty-two English counties—well over half, that is—and in many towns.[6] The commonest type was that we have seen in Yorkshire, where leading men of both

---

[6] John Morrill, *Revolt in the Provinces* (1999), ch. 1, esp. pp. 52–7.

sides suspended the execution of the Militia Ordinance and the commissions of array, and bound themselves to renounce all hostilities. But there were some more ambitious initiatives in counties, notably Cheshire, Staffordshire, and Lincolnshire, where moderate men dominated the commission of the peace and used their collective authority not only to demilitarize their territory but to raise a third force in order to resist any who attempted to invade it. And lest it be thought that neutralism was most to be found in the sleepier and less committed parts of rural England, it was widespread in the puritan and parliamentarian heartland of the east—in Essex, Hertfordshire, Cambridgeshire, Norfolk, and most of all in Suffolk.

The local pacifications were predictably doomed to failure. The parliament could not allow whole counties to opt out of its war effort, and though the king posed as the friend of peace and took tactical advantage of such overtures as were made to him, he had his mind too firmly set on victory to treat them seriously for long. Activists might be a minority in the political nation, but once they had the sword in their hand their will prevailed. There was never a chance that a locally organized militia could keep out increasingly professional armies, if they felt a need to enter 'pacified' territory. On the parliamentary side, the winter of 1642–3 saw the establishment of county committees with such varying responsibilities as overseeing the maintenance of troops in the area, the raising of various dues, and the impressment of recruits. Comparable though less systematic institutions emerged in royalist territory, with the result that the local gentry, including the magistracy, found themselves increasingly subject to direct commands from one side or the other, and in disputed territory from both. They might choose which to obey, but it was not practicable for JPs, who bore a responsibility to the whole local population, to defy both.

Sir William Waller gave a typical parliamentarian activist's view of local neutrality pacts in a letter to a knight of Devon who had been involved in negotiating the south-western one:

There can be nothing more destructive to the kingdom and their own counties than these treaties. The kingdom will lose by this neutrality the strength which might have been derived from your county, and in this way . . . His majesty will with the more ease subdue our party in the field . . . and then all the privileges these poor counties shall obtain that sate down first will be to be devoured last.[7]

Yet Waller himself had taken up arms with no light heart, and he was soon to give poignant expression to his sense of the tragic nature of the conflict which engulfed his country. There was to come a point in his campaign against Hopton, in June 1643, when he was in a tight corner and Hopton wrote to

---

[7] Quoted in Mary Coate, *Cornwall in the Great Civil War and Interregnum, 1642–1660* (Oxford, 1933), p. 56.

him to suggest a personal meeting, no doubt to urge him to consider suing for terms. Waller's letter of refusal has become justly famous, but it is worth repeating in part because it says so nobly what many who fought on both sides must have felt:

Certainly my affections to you are so unchangeable, that hostility itself cannot violate my friendship to your person, but I must be true to the cause wherein I serve. . . . I should most gladly wait on you according to your desire, but that I look upon you as you are engaged in that party, beyond a possibility of retreat. . . . And I know the conference could never be so close [i.e. secret] between us, but that it would take wind and receive a construction to my dishonour. That great God, which is the searcher of my heart, knows with what a sad sense I go upon this service, and with what a perfect hatred I detest this war without an enemy, but I look upon it as *opus domini* [the Lord's work], which is enough to silence all passion in me. The God of peace in his own time send us peace, and in the mean time fit us to receive it: we are both upon the stage and must act those parts that are assigned to us in this tragedy. Let us do it in a way of honour, and without personal animosities; whatsoever the issue be, I shall never willingly relinquish the dear title of

Your most affectionate friend and faithful servant.[8]

On the royalist side, an even greater hatred of the war, united to a sense that a man of honour could not opt out of it, was soon to drive Lord Falkland to seek and find death in battle.

From the first winter of the war onward, men of substance found themselves under increasing pressure to declare themselves for one side or the other, whether they wished to or not. Few can have been so lucky as the Midlands parson who wrote in his parish register: 'When an uncivil war was being waged most fiercely between king and parliament throughout the greater part of England, I lived well because I lay low'.[9] Those who did not meet the demands for money, horses, provisions, and services by the county committee or by the king's agents were liable to have their goods distrained, or were simply plundered. Landowners who regularly supported the royalists, even if they had little choice, were liable to have their estates seized by the parliament's Sequestration Committee, established in March 1643, and to have to redeem them after the war by paying a heavy 'composition'.

Yet neutralism did not die with the collapse of the early pacification treaties, and a surprising number even of the gentry managed to avoid outright commitment. Defiant neutrality, however, was less common than a preparedness to co-operate just far enough with whichever side had local military dominance to avoid actual plunder or worse. There were some communities

---

[8] Coate, *Cornwall in the Great Civil War and Interregnum*, p. 77.
[9] Quoted in D. R. Guttery, *The Great Civil War in Midlands Parishes* (1950), p. 11.

in disputed territories which tried to obey both sides. Magistrates and others in authority who thus bowed to the prevailing wind were not necessarily acting out of cynical opportunism, but rather out of a desire to preserve what they could of local autonomy and save the people under their charge from the worst depredations of war. In south Wales, where such gentry were in the majority, they were called 'ambidexters', and they thought it no shame to transfer their nominal allegiance if their counties changed hands. Such as they were common enough in most counties to make nonsense of those old maps which divided all England and Wales into red and blue areas, purporting to show which were for the parliament and which for the king. The most that maps can convey is which side had the military ascendancy and where *at a given date*, and they should always allow for disputed territory.

Yet however widespread such pragmatic attitudes were, the Civil War would not have been fought to a finish over nearly four wasting years if there had not been large numbers of more positively committed men on both sides. What moved people to give their allegiance to one or the other is a question of endless interest to historians, and the answers are neither simple nor free from controversy. We know most about the prominent activists because they were the most articulate, but even among them there was a wide spectrum of motive and aspiration on both sides. On the parliament's they ranged from conservative constitutionalists like Denzil Holles or Sir Robert Harley, who would have rested content with England's time-honoured frame of government as safeguarded by the statutes of 1641 if they could have trusted the king to honour the latter, to such a crypto-republican as Henry Marten, who was expelled by the House of Commons in August 1643 for saying: 'it were better one family [the king's] should be destroyed than many'. Republicans were very rare birds, however, before the late 1640s. On the king's side there was an equally wide range between out-and-out cavaliers such as the Gorings, father and son, and the courtiers Henry Jermyn and Jack Ashburnham, who regarded the 1641 reformers as little better than rebels and had no qualms about the likely political outcome of a total royalist victory, and on the other hand the constitutional royalists like Hyde and Falkland who had rallied to the king after the 1641 reforms (which they supported) were enacted, and remained as concerned for the rights of parliament as for the prerogatives of the crown. Ideologically, the constitutionalists of both sides were closer to each other than to the extremists in their own camp.

It is not very fruitful to debate (as many have) whether political or religious convictions had the greater influence on allegiance. It was a matter of degree, and it varied greatly between individuals; religion, one senses, played a negligible part in the motivation of Sir Thomas Lunsford or Henry Marten, and a very large one in that of Hyde and Falkland and Cromwell and Milton. But the idea of politics and religion as *alternative* grounds for their allegiance would have seemed strange to most seventeenth-century minds, which saw the two as intertwined. They would have seen no inconsistency between acknowledging that the immediate issues over which king and parliament had come to blows were secular ones, such as the powers and privileges of parliament, the extent of the royal prerogative, the control of the armed forces, and the appointment of councillors and ministers, and yet making their choice according to which side they thought would better uphold the religious ideals and ecclesiastical principles in which they believed. Nor was it just a matter of making a judgement as to which cause most deserved God's blessing, though most people must have tried to do so. It also came naturally to them to associate particular political principles with particular forms of religion— to believe on the one side that absolutist tendencies in the state were part and parcel of popery and Arminianism, or to hold with Laud on the other that puritans hankered after 'parity' in both church and state and were therefore no good subjects for a monarchy. To royalists, taking up arms against the Lord's anointed was simply wicked in itself; 'rebellion is as the sin of witchcraft' (2 Samuel 15: 22) was a favourite biblical text. The manner in which religious considerations swayed the allegiance of parliamentarians, especially those of the middling sort, is well conveyed in a much quoted passage from the reminiscences of Richard Baxter, a youngish clergyman (in 1642) whom the local royalists drove out of his living in Kidderminster, and who after ministering to the garrison in Gloucester became a chaplain in the New Model Army. He wrote:

But though it must be confessed that the public safety and liberty wrought very much with most, especially with the nobility and gentry who adhered to the parliament, yet it was principally the differences about religious matters that filled up the parliament's armies and put the resolution and valour into their soldiers, which carried them on in another manner than mercenary soldiers are carried on. Not that the matter of bishops or no bishops was the main thing (for thousands that wished for good bishops were on the parliament's side) . . . But the generality of the people through the land (I say not *all*, or *every one*) who were then called puritans, precisians, religious persons, that used to talk of God, and heaven, and Scripture, and holiness, and to follow sermons, and read books of devotion, and pray in their families . . . I say, the main body of this sort of men, both preachers and people, adhered to the parliament.[10]

Baxter conjures up well the strain of piety that inclined people to the parliament's side, and rightly acknowledges that they included many moderate episcopalians. Many royalists were motivated by equally sincere religious convictions, including a strong attachment to the Prayer Book services and sacraments, a liking for reverence and hierarchy, a devotion to the annual round of Christian festivals, and a sense that the church was a guarantor of the

---

[10]  *Reliquiae Baxterianae*, ed. M. Sylvester (1696), p. 31.

traditional order in the state and society. Many gentry felt a strong antipathy towards Presbyterianism, which became an imminent threat when the Scottish alliance was sealed. Lay elders, they feared, would introduce a popular element in parish discipline and subvert the traditional partnership in authority between squire and parson.

There has been controversy over the role of Roman Catholics in the Civil War. Given the parliament's extreme hostility to papists, their choice lay between supporting the king or staying as neutral as they could. Over the country as a whole the great majority chose the latter option, especially those below the ranks of the gentry. But the high proportion of catholic colonels in the king's service has already been noted, and there were wide regional differences in the response of the catholic gentry. Almost two thirds of the *actively* royalist families in Lancashire were catholics, as were a third of those in Yorkshire, and in Cheshire too the proportion of committed royalists among the catholic gentry was much higher than that among the protestant ones. These were counties with large recusant populations, but in others where catholics were thick on the ground, notably Monmouthshire, Cumberland, and Westmorland, the majority remained inactive. It seems generally true that among the catholics who did commit themselves to the king's cause an impressively high proportion actually fought for him. Their loyalty is striking, for outside court circles the catholic community as a whole had little to thank Charles for. The leadership of the great catholic magnates, especially Derby, Worcester, and Winchester, enlisted many in his cause. They may well have calculated that an outright parliamentarian victory would be likely to worsen their lot, but, most were probably more strongly moved by the same spirit of ingrained loyalty to the crown that fired their Anglican fellow-officers.[11]

So far, little has been said about social distinctions between the two sides. A generation or two ago that would have seemed very shocking, for in the post-war decades socio-economic explanations of the Civil War were de rigueur. But all attempts to depict it as some kind of class war have foundered, because closer research (especially into county and other local communities) has shown that every order of society was substantially represented on both sides. That is not to say that royalists and parliamentarians were socially indistinguishable, but rather that the pattern again varies from region to region, and that attempts to establish socio-economic factors as the *primary* determinants of allegiance, nationwide, have proved unfruitful. Some

---

[11]   K. J. Lindley, 'The part played by catholics', in B. S. Manning (ed.), *Politics, Religion and the English Civil War* (1973), is illuminating on regional differences, but underestimates the proportion of active royalists among the gentry of Lancashire, Yorkshire, and Cheshire. Lindley's and other recent research on the subject is evaluated by John Morrill in *The Nature of the English Revolution* (1993), ch. 9.

generalizations hold true, the simplest being that (as one would expect) the higher one looks in the social scale the higher the proportion of royalists one finds. Men of rank had the biggest interest in preserving the old hierarchical social order, and many felt it threatened by the violent mob demonstrations, the anti-enclosure riots and the arming of the plebs from 1642 onward. The peerage most of all felt their estate to be tied up with that of the monarchy, for the king knew nearly all of them personally, and they were the greatest beneficiaries of his patronage. Yet only about half of them actively supported him in the war, and the minority that sided with the parliament was a sizeable one, though it dwindled with the years. Even at this social level not a few stayed neutral, and some changed sides.

The gentry were much more evenly divided, though over most of the country a greater proportion of the knights, the wealthier esquires, and the older, more deeply rooted families were royalist than parliamentarian. It was not so everywhere; in Suffolk and Dorset, for example, the leading county families leaned more towards the parliament. In no county were the gentry solid for one side or the other. The many small squireens who were finding it a struggle to keep up their gentry status tended to be the least engaged either way, but in some regions they inclined towards the king, as the upholder of the social order to which they clung precariously; there were hundreds of such in the south-west, in Wales and the Marches, and in the far northern counties. In East Anglia on the other hand the vein of radical puritanism that gave parliament some of its staunchest support was strong among the lesser gentry.

One might have expected the Court interest, comprising the courtiers and paid office-holders who had made their living in the service of the crown, to form a central element in the royalist party. But their response varied widely, and it would be equally unsafe to assume any strong correlation between the Country peers and gentry of the 1630s and the active parliamentarians of the 1640s. The issues over which the Civil War was fought were not the same as those in contention during the personal rule, and many routine offices in the administration, like Pym's, did not commit their holders to a sense of personal loyalty to the monarch through thick and thin, especially if they had been obtained by purchase. Gerald Aylmer, in his magisterial study of the king's servants, reckons that of the 900 or so men of gentry or noble status who enjoyed paid employment in the king's household or in his central government, those who actively supported him in the Civil War were slightly outnumbered by those who either stayed out of it or sided with parliament.[12]

But though most people formed their own judgement of the merits of the opposed causes and the worth of the parties that upheld them, their choice

---

[12] G. E. Aylmer, *The King's Servants: The Civil Service of Charles I, 1625–1642* (rev. ed., 1974), ch. 6. The estimate is based on a large sample.

was often influenced by local interests and loyalties. The pattern of allegiance differed so greatly from county to county that to do justice to the wealth of recent studies, even in summary, would require a chapter to itself. Sampling must suffice, and it may convey the sheer variety if we compare two pairs of adjacent shires, in the north, the Midlands, and the south.

Lancashire was one of the more divided counties, the main contrast being between the rural areas, especially where the Earl of Derby wielded a semi-feudal authority over a gentry that included a high proportion of his fellow-catholics, and the clothing districts around Manchester and Bury, which were strongly puritan and parliamentarian, like the West Riding clothing towns just across the Pennines. There were about twice as many Lancashire royalist gentry as parliamentarians, but both combined were far outnumbered by those who have left no trace of any commitment to either side. Neighbouring Cheshire was more homogeneous. Most of the leading families were polarized in two groups, competing with each other for precedence in county affairs, but most were moderate in their political outlook and were drawn into the war reluctantly; they made one of the strongest attempts to keep it out through a neutrality treaty. When that failed, they split mainly along the lines of their local factions, resulting at the outset in slightly more royalists than parliamentarians. More than twenty changed sides, however, and many of the nominal royalists lapsed into submission when parliament gained military control over most of the county in 1643. But one of the knights of the shire, Sir William Brereton, headed a minority party of active parliamentarians, drawn mainly from the puritan lesser gentry, and as local parliamentarian commander he won a victory at Nantwich late in January 1643, taking the town a few days after Sir Thomas Fairfax recaptured Leeds. He could not dislodge the royalists from Chester, however, until the war was almost over.[13]

Northamptonshire and Leicestershire, Midlands neighbours, were at least as strongly contrasted. Most of the former was in the hands of wealthy landowners who had risen to gentry status within the last two or three generations, whether through office-holding or mercantile success or marrying heiresses. The majority of these were parliamentarian, but the chief local magnate, the Earl of Northampton, was as we have seen a strong royalist, and he carried most of his clientele among the county gentry with him. Northamptonshire thus looks like a perfect illustration of R. H. Tawney's class-war interpretation of the English Revolution, with rising 'bourgeois' gentry opposed to aristocratically orientated 'feudal' types. But next-door Leicestershire presents a quite different picture, of a county peopled mainly

---

[13] Blackwood, *Lancashire Gentry and the Great Rebellion, 1640–1660*; J. S. Morrill, *Cheshire 1630–1660: County Government and Society during the English Revolution* (Oxford, 1974).

by small gentry with long-set local roots and rather narrow horizons. By far the deepest division among them had little to do with politics or religion or economic interest, and most were dragged into the war reluctantly, if at all. They were split by the competing patronage of the two great noble houses in the county, the Greys, Earls of Stamford and the Hastings, Earls of Huntingdon, who had long been at feud. Both families had long been puritan, but when the Greys became strongly parliamentarian and the Hastings just as strongly royalist, their clienteles among the gentry went the same way. There was a slight tendency for the older families to adhere to the king and the newer to parliament, but patronage was the main key to allegiance. Consequently the north and west of the county were predominantly royalist and the south and east parliamentarian, but Leicestershire saw little of the war until 1645.[14]

Our southern examples, Sussex and Kent, present different kinds of contrast. Sussex was even more emphatically divided geographically than Leicestershire, here between a parliamentarian east and a royalist west, but for different reasons. There were no dominant magnates after Elizabeth's reign, and local influence lay mainly with about ninety county families, many with ancient roots in the county. Many, too, were puritan, especially in east Sussex, but Richard Montagu, who was Bishop of Chichester until 1638, had been planting fellow-Arminians among the parish clergy wherever he could. Caroline religious policies were the strongest single source of anti-royalism in the county. In 1642–3 the ninety leading families split fairly equally between royalists, parliamentarians, and neutrals, but the east Sussex gentry's prevailing allegiance to parliament was backed by enthusiastic popular support. The commitment of the parliamentarian activists was far stronger than that of their opponents and the rather lukewarm royalism of west Sussex cooled further after Waller captured Chichester. Kent was different again, except in being free of magnate dominance. It was home to an exceptionally large number of gentry, but activists on either side constituted quite a small minority, and most of them were relative newcomers to their estates. The majority, especially among the long-established Kentish families, were moderates, and inclined towards neutralism. They were not much given to puritanism, and they tended to put local interests before national issues. Most were lukewarm or merely nominal supporters of parliament at the outset, thanks in part to the proximity of its military forces, but they were rapidly alienated by the heavy hand of the county committee of Kent. They were still more antagonized by the radical turn that parliamentary politics took from 1645 onward, and

[14] A. M. Everitt, *The Local Community and the English Civil War* (Historical Association Pamphlet G. 70, 1969).

when they rose in large numbers in 1648 they were moved not so much by devotion to the king as by exasperation with parliamentary tyranny.[15]

Such wide regional differences, and such a tendency for allegiance to be swayed by local interests and attachments, may seem incompatible with the claim that most people, at any rate from the middling sort upward, judged the merits of the two sides for themselves, whether or not they actively support-ed either. But no one makes judgements in a vacuum, and in the thinly popu-lated, pre-industrial England of 1642 bonds of neighbourhood were strong. So were the vertical ties between patron and client, landlord and tenant, and master and man. Information about current events and issues came to most people through such channels, or from the pulpit, for the media as we know them did not of course exist. Even weekly newsbooks, the ancestors of our newspapers, were a novelty, and only a tiny proportion of the population can have seen them. The tendency to react politically in the same way as one's neighbours or immediate superiors was naturally strong, but the fact that so many communities and even families were divided in their allegiance shows that individual choice was by no means stifled.

Towns and cities were specially close communities, and the minority of the nation that lived in them showed the same tendency to division and attach-ment to local interests as we have seen in the counties. The tradition that most towns were 'nurseries of faction and rebellion', providing centres of active support for parliament even in regions predominantly royalist, goes right back to the time of the Civil War, but modern research is steadily revealing that the reality was much more complicated. Popular enthusiasm for the par-liamentary cause was mainly found in towns where puritanism was preva-lent, for example in the clothing regions already noted, in Coventry, Birmingham, and urban Norfolk, and above all in London. There were sever-al reasons why puritanism took strong root in urban communities. It was a religion of the book, and literacy was high in towns; many craftsmen could read the bible as they worked. Larger towns provided a choice of places of worship, and many supported puritan lectureships. Itinerant sectarian preachers commonly targeted the urban middling sort. The puritan code of values conferred dignity on the 'callings' of craftsmen and traders, and incul-cated the self-discipline needed for success in them. From the ranks of such men and their apprentices, and from townsmen lower in the scale such as porters and watermen, the parliamentary service drew many volunteers. Very few of this sort enlisted in the king's forces.

But the active parliamentarianism of many urban puritans does not imply that the towns in general showed the same commitment. A great deal usually

---

[15] A. J. Fletcher, *A County Community in Peace and War: Sussex 1600–1660* (1975); A. M. Everitt, *The Community of Kent and the Great Rebellion* (Leicester, 1973).

depended on the attitude of the governing corporation, which was generally drawn from the mercantile elite. Wealthy aldermen and common councilmen had every reason to fear the interruption of trade and damage to property that war was likely to bring. Moreover, many of them enjoyed commercial and political privileges under royal charters, and this could sway them in the king's favour even where there was a strong vein of parliamentary feeling among the citizenry; such was the case in Newcastle and Leeds, for example. The commonest reaction of city and borough corporations to the onset of war was one of dismay; they wanted no part in it, and their first care was to save their community from its impact if they could. Puritanism was strong in Gloucester, but the city fathers were so reluctant to admit a parliamentarian garrison that it had to force its way in. Bristol's corporation locked one out for two days in December 1642 before reluctantly opening the gates to it. Worcester, after refusing to admit the king's commissioners of array in August, let in a parliamentary garrison most unwillingly in December, but soon made its soldiers wish they had never come. The prime concerns of most corporations were to preserve their autonomy and to protect their inhabitants' livelihoods, and where they were persuaded to fortify and defend themselves, it was frequently with the object of keeping out both warring parties rather than actively supporting either. Their relations with both military governors and county committees were commonly poor.[16]

The middling and lower orders of rural England outnumbered the entire urban population several times over, but it is harder to generalize about their allegiance. There is less evidence about them, and the lower they stood in the social scale the less chance they usually had of making a free choice, unless they actually enlisted in one army or another. Nevertheless the once prevalent notion that the mass of the rural population was ignorant of the issues between king and parliament, or indifferent to them, will no longer hold water, and before the war was over the popular voice was to find striking expression in the Clubmen movement, of which more later. One clue to popular preference may lie in the geography and social organization of rural communities. Historians have for some time been distinguishing two broad types. One is found where arable farming had long been the main occupation, and since open-field systems required strict communal organization, such regions were characterized by close-knit village communities, often cemented by still operative manorial institutions. Such social units generally valued ancient customs, ceremonies and festivals, and hierarchy prevailed in them. The other type occurred mainly in regions less suited to tillage, such as heath or fens or

---

[16] The best survey is by Roger Howell, 'Neutralism, conservatism and political alignment in the English Revolution: the case of the towns, 1642-9', in John Morrill (ed.), *Reactions to the English Civil War* (1982).

woodland, where there were (or had been) large amounts of common land and where population had until recently been thin. Such areas, as well as the towns, had taken the overspill during the rapid demographic growth of the last few generations, so they contained many newcomers. They were suitable for pastoral farming or rural industry, including the overflow of clothmaking from the old urban centres. Their characteristic occupations called for no such close control as agrarian communities needed, so besides being less bound by tradition they were generally subject to considerably less social and political organization. Yet poverty and vagrancy tended to be constant problems in them, and in many such parishes (it has been argued) the gentry and the middling sort found a common interest in promoting a puritan code of godly reformation, not only to save souls but to impose a degree of discipline on the often unruly lower orders. Hence the greater individualism of the pastoral and woodland regions, coupled with their tendency towards puritanism, predisposed them towards the parliamentary side, whereas the traditionalist values and organization of agrarian communities inclined them to the king's.

It would be premature to claim that we have here an *explanation* of why some regions were predominantly royalist in sympathy and others parliamentarian, and more work needs to be done before we can say how widely a *propensity* towards one side or the other coincided with such contrasted types of rural community. Clearly there were exceptions: not all wood-pasture parishes developed a striving after godly discipline, and there were arable regions, notably in East Anglia, where an alliance of puritan squire and parson carried many a village with them. On the other hand one might have expected the lead miners of Derbyshire to be parliamentarian, but they were mainly royalist. Yet this line of approach seems to offer far less distortion than the crude old contrast between a royalist north and west and a parliamentarian east and south, or than the now happily less frequent attempts to portray the armed struggle of the 1640s as some kind of class war. It certainly deserves to be pursued further.[17]

Before the campaigns of 1643 got seriously under way, the winter and spring saw a prolonged attempt at national level to find a basis for a negotiated peace. The shock of the king's military threat to London, the revelation of his

---

[17]  The pioneer of this line of interpretation is David Underdown, in *Revel, Riot and Rebellion: Popular Politics and Culture in England, 1603–1660* (Oxford, 1985). Morrill offers a critique of it in *Nature of the English Revolution*, ch. 11: 'The ecology of allegiance in the English Civil Wars'. A stimulating local study with wider implications is Mark Stoyle, *Loyalty and Locality in Devon during the Civil Wars* (Exeter, 1994). For the Derby lead miners see Andy Wood, *The Politics of Social Conflict: The Peak Country, 1520–1770* (Cambridge, 1999).

evident capacity to fight an extended war, and the widespread revulsion against such a prospect which local neutrality pacts continued to demonstrate, all served to create a strong peace party at Westminster. It dominated the small body of peers who continued to sit there, and it was too well supported in the Commons for Pym to stifle it, even if he had wanted to. He was probably prepared to consider a compromise settlement, so long as it did not surrender what he regarded as essentials. Long preparation and debate were given to a set of propositions which was presented to the king on 1 February, and inaugurated the so-called Treaty of Oxford. The first of them proposed that the armies on both sides should be disbanded and that the king should return to his parliament. He was most unlikely to accede to this, but the terms as a whole did recede significantly from those in the Nineteen Propositions of eight months earlier. They tacitly dropped the demand that every appointment to the privy council and the major officers of state, including the governors of the king's children, should be permanently subject to parliamentary approval. They no longer required the consent of both Houses before new peers were admitted to parliament. But they still demanded much that Charles could not in conscience concede: the handing over of 'delinquents' for trial by parliament, his assent to the recently passed bill for the total abolition of episcopacy and to whatever parliament should enact in the near future concerning the government of the church, and his acceptance of whatever parliament should determine concerning the control of the armed forces by sea and land. This was not a realistic agenda for an agreed settlement.

Charles's response showed that he did not really want one. Instead of disbandment on both sides he proposed an armistice, but since he stipulated that his forts, his ships, and his revenues should be restored to him he might as well have openly demanded parliament's surrender. He also asked it to prepare a bill for the preservation of the Book of Common Prayer, though he offered in vague terms to consider a clause in it for the ease of tender consciences. Pym could see that without mutual disbandment there was no hope of a satisfactory peace, and he just managed to carry a very divided House of Commons with him; but when the Lords voted for a twenty-day negotiation under a mere cessation of hostilities, the Commons by a bare three votes concurred. No such cessation in fact occurred, nor could it while Charles expected it to be accompanied by the surrender to him of the navy and the forts, which included the Tower of London. But so unwilling was the peace party to give up hope, and so well did it suit him to appear willing to negotiate, that it was mid-April before parliament finally broke off the 'treaty'.

How little Charles was really interested in ending the war by compromise and negotiation can be gauged from the fact that in the middle of March, shortly before parliament's commissioners arrived in Oxford, he had a secret commission prepared, empowering seventeen prominent London citizens headed by the former Lord Mayor Gardiner to organize an armed rising in the city on his behalf. He did not activate the commission immediately, but at the beginning of May he sent it to London with instructions to his agents to enlist as many as possible of the peace party in both Houses. The chief conspirator was the MP and poet Edmund Waller, who had just been one of parliament's commissioners in the Oxford treaty. Waller's contacts included the Eart of Northumberland and other peers, and in the Commons John Selden, Bulstrode Whitelocke, and the diarist Sir Simonds D'Ewes, though the degree of their implication varied, and stopped short of treachery. At the end of May, however, the Commons discovered the commission and exposed the plot. Two prominent conspirators, one of them Waller's brother-in-law, were hanged in front of their own houses, but Waller himself, who was rich as well as treacherous, saved his life by a combination of bribery and informing on his contacts. He got off with a £10,000 fine and banishment.

The king in fact had a stronger will for victory at this stage than the parliament collectively was displaying. He also had more positive plans for achieving it, for the direction of parliament's war effort lay in the hands of an unwieldy Committee of Safety, and Essex was continuing to show himself a rather supine general, in imperfect control of various nominally subordinate forces and in no hurry to take the field with his main army, despite repeated pleas to do so from the parliamentary activists. His sympathies were with the peace party, and while he wintered at Windsor his army shrank to about a third of its original size, partly because parliament was not providing enough money to pay his men, and partly because many of them just melted away while their colonels and other commanders went home for a prolonged winter's leave. He did not march out of Windsor until 13 April, the day that parliament recalled its commissioners from Oxford.

The royalists meanwhile were far more active. Charles had three concentrations of forces large enough to be called armies: his own, based in Oxford, Newcastle's in the north, and Hopton's in the south-west. He has often been credited with a grand strategy involving them in a three-pronged attack on London, but there is no documentary evidence of such a co-ordinated plan. Judging from his military decisions month by month, his main concern was to extend the territory under his control, and that made sense in the circumstances, for the only way he could pay his men was by levying contributions wherever he held sway. The more territory, the more revenue; and the same went for recruits, for from May 1643 onward his commanders were raising men by impressment. Should he have gone for the jugular and banked everything on a swift concerted attack on London? This has been suggested, on the grounds that time was ultimately against him and that his enemies were almost bound to grow stronger, especially when the Scots came in on the parliament's side. But the risks would have been enormous, and in military terms the tide was not really to turn against him until 1645. Parliament had quite sizeable local forces in Yorkshire, the Midlands, East Anglia and Devon, and it is more than doubtful whether Newcastle and Hopton could have fought their way through to the capital, even if they had been able to hold their troops together so far from home. London had the will to defend itself when really threatened, as Turnham Green had shown, and if the king's army had met with a decisive defeat, he might have been left without the territorial resources to raise another before parliament established an overwhelming advantage. As it turned out, he and his commanders did so well in 1643 that it must be doubted whether a more grandiose strategy would have served him as well.

During the early part of the year Charles appointed three more regional commanders, in addition to Newcastle and Hopton: the Marquis of Hertford in Herefordshire, Monmouthshire, and south-east Wales, the Earl of Carbery in south-west Wales, and Lord Capel in Cheshire, Shropshire, Worcestershire and north Wales. During March and April he sent Prince Maurice, Rupert's younger brother, with a detachment of his main Oxford-based army to meet the threat that Sir William Waller's force was posing in the Severn valley, in company with Sir Edward Massey, the parliamentarian governor of Gloucester. Before Maurice arrived, however, Waller defeated Herbert's Welshmen at Highnam on 24 March, and then went on to take Monmouth and Chepstow, while Massey at his direction seized Tewkesbury. Maurice checked Waller's further advance towards Worcester with a clear victory at Ripple Field on 13 April, but he was then recalled to Oxford. Waller went on to capture Hereford on the 25th, together with a whole clutch of local royalist leaders, and he could reckon that for the present his battle for the Severn valley was won.

Meanwhile Hopton and his Cornishmen continued to wage a minor campaign against the parliamentarians of Devon under the Earl of Stamford. His second attempt to strike into Devon ended in a defeat at Modbury on 21 February, and it suited both sides to agree on a forty-day cessation of hostilities. When this ran out, Stamford had a slight superiority with about 3,500 foot and 8 troops of horse, but Hopton's nucleus of 3,000 infantry was reinforced by many volunteers. The parliamentarians made the first move, led by the 25-year-old Major-General James Chudleigh, Stamford being laid low by the gout. They struck at Launceston and gave Hopton a hard time holding it, but a day-long fight on Beacon Hill on 23 April turned in his favour when badly needed reinforcements reached him during the course of it. Chudleigh was eventually forced to withdraw to Okehampton, but when Hopton pursued him into Devon he set a skilful ambush at Sourton Down, where he got rather the better of a confused night action on the 25th. The royalists retreated into Cornwall in disorder, leaving 1,000 muskets, 100 horses, 5 precious barrels of powder, and all Hopton's own papers behind them. From the latter, Stamford learned that the king had ordered Hopton to lead his Cornishmen into Somerset and join Prince Maurice's forces, so he decided to foil this by a pre-emptive strike into Cornwall while Hopton's men were still shaken by their recent defeat. He had a two to one advantage when he posted his army for battle on Stamford Hill—a lucky name, did he think?—just north of Stratton on 15 May. But Hopton's little army was in good heart again, and he resolved to attack next morning. The battle of Stamford began at 5 a.m. with the Cornish foot charging uphill in four columns, and after many repeated assaults it was still undecided eight hours later, by which time their powder was almost spent. But these tired brave men made one final effort, holding their fire until they faced the enemy on the level top of the hill, where they put them to total rout. Stamford, who had committed his few cavalry elsewhere, lost about 300 dead, 1,700 prisoners, all his guns and powder, and all his baggage and treasure.

Hopton never won a finer victory, and thanks to it he duly joined up with Maurice's and Hertford's forces at Chard on 4 June, even though he had to leave Plymouth and Exeter in parliamentarian hands in his rear. This conjunction gave the king a sizeable army in the west, though not a harmonious one. There was rivalry among the commanders and friction in the ranks, with no love lost between Hopton's foot and Maurice's favoured cavalry, who jibbed in turn at the Cornishmen's lack of discipline when not in action. But the royalists' strength in Somerset drew Waller off from Worcester, which he had been besieging, and when they took Taunton and threatened Wells he followed after them. Waller had the better of a heavy cavalry skirmish at Chewton Mendip on 10 June, which gave him a much needed breathing-space in which to build up his depleted army. With about 2,500 horse he was strong enough in that arm but seriously short of infantry, for most of Stamford's Devonians had gone off home. He was now directly opposed to his old friend Hopton, who despite Hertford's superior rank was really the effective commander of their combined forces. The war in the West was entering a new phase, but before recounting its dramatic course in July we must catch up with what had been happening in central and northern England.

While Essex lay inactive all through the Treaty of Oxford, Charles's local commanders secured Ashby-de-la-Zouch, Tamworth, Lichfield, Stafford, and Stratford-on-Avon for him. The queen had landed at Bridlington on 22 February with several ships carrying munitions and money, and after surviving a frightening bombardment she had, under Newcastle's protecting forces, carried these welcome supplies to York. One object of the fighting in the Midlands during the spring was to clear her further passage to Oxford, for she brought not only arms but a considerable body of troops that she had recently raised herself. The main resistance came from Lord Brooke, who was commissioned under Essex to command the counties of Warwick, Stafford, Leicester, and Derby. He recaptured Stratford by storm, secured all Warwickshire for the parliament, and went on to attack Lichfield, but there a defender's bullet struck him in the eye and killed him instantly. His death was a serious political loss to the parliament, and a worse was soon to follow. Lichfield fell soon after to Sir John Gell, the parliamentary governor of Derby, whose troops were as notorious for plundering as he was for womanizing (it is well to be reminded that neither activity was confined to the side which became most notorious for it). Gell, however, was challenged by Northampton's forces, now near Stafford, having lately been strengthened by several cavalry regiments under Henry Hastings, the king's Colonel-General of Leicestershire. Gell planned to make a rendezvous with Brereton's Cheshire troops on 19 March on Hopton Heath, three miles from Stafford, prior to attacking that town. But Brereton arrived late, and before his and Gell's men had effected a proper junction they were furiously attacked by Northampton's cavalry. The result of this fierce little action was a decided royalist victory, in which the parliamentarians lost all their guns and about 500 men. The victors lost fewer than fifty, but one of them was Northampton, who was unhorsed in a rash charge and slain after refusing quarter.

Charles now sent Rupert to secure his corridor to the north. On the way, the prince was resisted for two hours by the citizens and tiny garrison of Birmingham, for which insolence he fired the town and give it over to plunder. This was a whiff of the continental wars in which he had learnt his trade, and it earned him a mild rebuke from the king. He went on to recapture Lichfield on 21 April, after a two-week siege, but at that point Charles recalled him and his brigade to Oxford, to counter a threat from the parliament's main army.

Essex was on the move at last, and heading towards Oxford. He took Reading on 26 April after a short siege, but with his army struck by an epidemic and further thinned by desertions he advanced no further for six more weeks. On 10 June he occupied Thame, only ten miles from Oxford, and he posted some of his units even closer, but he was not prepared either to assault or to besiege the city, and by dispersing his forces over a wide area he made them vulnerable. Colonel John Urry here made the first of his three changes of side and carried full information of Essex's dispositions to royal headquarters, along with intelligence that a convoy was on its way to him with £21,000 for his soldiers' pay. Rupert set out to intercept it with some 1,350 horse and dragoons and 500 picked infantrymen, but a countryman gave the parliamentarians warning of his approach, and their nearest units tried to cut off his retreat to Oxford. These included John Hampden's own foot regiment, and in a minor cavalry action on Chalgrove Field Hampden exposed himself far beyond the call of duty and was mortally wounded. He died six days later. Only Pym would be missed more among the parliamentary leaders, and his days too were numbered. Essex got no further in his sluggish moves against Oxford, for during July a series of disasters in the west forced parliament upon the defensive. But it was not only there that the war was going badly for it.

In the north, the Fairfaxes' hold on the West Riding had been secured by Sir Thomas's capture of Leeds in January, but their position in the rest of York-shire was precarious at best. The Hothams had not yet betrayed Hull, though they were wobbling, but Scarborough was lost when its governor Sir Hugh Cholmley MP, who had fought at the head of his own regiment at Edgehill, went over to the king soon after the queen had landed in the country. New-castle's forces dominated the north-east, and southward in Nottinghamshire there was a strong royalist garrison in Newark, which beat off a large-scale attack on 27 February with heavy losses to the assailants. Late in March the Fairfaxes decided to abandon their headquarters at Selby and fall back on Leeds; Sir Thomas occupied Tadcaster to cover their withdrawal. Newcastle sent George Goring with a strong body of horse and dragoons to retake the town, and on the 30th Goring struck at the retreating Yorkshiremen on Seacroft Moor near Leeds, killing 200 of them and taking 800 prisoners.

By late April the concentration of royalist forces around Newark was rais-ing serious fears in parliament that they intended to advance southward through its heartland in eastern England and threaten London itself. To defend it, an Eastern Association had been formed in December, embracing Norfolk, Suffolk, Cambridgeshire, Essex, and Hertfordshire (Lincolnshire was later added), and at parliament's direction Essex had commissioned Lord Grey of Warke as its Major-General. In February 1643, however, Grey and most of his forces were sent to reinforce Essex's shrunken army in the Thames valley, leaving Colonel Cromwell (as he now was) with his own regiment of horse and a small scratch body of foot to guard the territory on its threatened Lincolnshire frontier.

Cromwell was forty-four and had no military experience whatever when he first raised a troop of horse at the outbreak of war, but by the spring of 1643 the troop had grown to a full regiment—about half of the eventual double regiment of fourteen troops that was to become famous as the Iron-sides. It already had a special character, for he had sought from the start to enlist, not only as officers but as troopers too, 'such men as had the fear of God before them, and made some conscience of what they did'. Especially after witnessing the superior mettle of the royalist cavalry at Edgehill, he looked for 'men of a spirit that is like to go as far as a gentleman will go'.[18] When the Suffolk county committee cavilled at the modest birth of one of his troop commanders, he replied: 'I had rather have a plain russet-coated captain that

---

[18] Abbott, *Writings and Speeches of Oliver Cromwell*, I, 471.

knows what he fights for, and loves what he knows, than that which you call a gentleman and is nothing else. I honour a gentleman that is so indeed.'[19] His method of defending the Eastern Association was to attack those who threatened it. He occupied Peterborough, then bombarded Crowland into submission on 28 April. He joined up with Sir John Hotham and Lord Willoughby of Parham, with their forces from Hull and Lincolnshire respectively, intending a combined attack on Newark. That did not materialize, but on 13 May he and his own cavalry routed a body of royalist horse at Grantham. It was a minor action and his subsequent career has inflated its reputation, but it was the first to be fought under his command and it staked his Ironsides' claim to meet the cavaliers on more than equal terms. More might have been achieved if he and Hotham and Willoughby had all been of the same purpose, but between them they failed to prevent the queen from taking two successive convoys of munitions from Newark to Oxford. Cromwell and Hotham were 'ready to cut each others' throats',[20] and no wonder, since Hotham and his son were just waiting for their chance to betray Hull, and Lincoln too if they could, to the king. Their treachery was discovered in time, however, and both were captured, tried, and executed. How far it was due to a genuine revulsion against the parliament's proceedings, and how far to frustrated ambition and jealousy of the Fairfaxes, it is difficult to say.

Once the queen was safe in Oxford, Newcastle moved against the Fairfaxes with the intention of mastering the whole of Yorkshire. He had about 10,000 men, they about 4,000, plus an uncertain number of untrained countrymen with improvised weapons. They appealed to Hotham, Willoughby, and Cromwell to come to their aid with their combined forces, but Cromwell had his own territory to defend and Hotham's heart was on the other side. Unsupported, they gave battle to Newcastle on Adwalton Moor near Leeds on 30 June, and at the end of a hard-fought action, in which the cavalry on both sides distinguished themselves, the larger forces won. Bradford and Leeds defended themselves with Sir Thomas's help for as long as they could but had finally to yield, and the Fairfaxes retreated first to Selby and then to Hull. It was the nadir of parliament's fortunes in the north.

July was a month of royalist victories, and the most striking were in the west. When it began, Waller was defending Bath and Hopton was advancing against him. On the 4th Waller took up a strong position on Lansdowne Hill, north-west of the city, and Hopton attacked it next day. In the bitter battle that ensued the royalist cavalry were repelled and suffered heavy casualties, but the hill was eventually won by the heroic Cornish infantry. They were still

---

[19] Ibid., I, 256.
[20] Quoted in Clive Holmes, *The Eastern Association in the English Civil War* (Cambridge, 1974), p. 74.

unsure of their success when night fell, but the lighted matches and bristling pikes which Waller left on his last position proved to be feints to cover his withdrawal. It was an inconclusive victory, however, and a costly one, for Sir Bevil Grenville, Hopton's loyalest and most popular commander, was killed as he led the Cornish foot in their final triumphant assault. Next day Hopton himself was badly burnt and injured when a powder-wagon blew up very close to him. Temporarily blinded and paralysed, he insisted on being carried to councils of war, for he would not leave his post while the royalist forces remained threatened by Waller's still unbroken army.

Those forces took up a defensive position in Devizes. They were seriously short of ammunition, and the council of war decided to send Hertford and Maurice and their cavalry back to Oxford as fast as possible with an urgent plea for reinforcements. It was promptly met, and by the morning of 13 July Lord Wilmot (as he now was) was approaching Devizes with 1,500 horse from the king's main army. For two or three days Waller had been trying to bombard Devizes Castle into submission, and he had his army drawn up for battle on Roundway Down, just to the north of it. Wilmot attacked, expecting Hopton's infantry to come out of the town and support him. But they did not do so until the battle was in its last stages, and the total rout of Waller's army in which it ended must be credited to Wilmot's leadership and the tremendous courage of his cavalry, which included Byron's and Maurice's and the Earl of Crawford's regiments as well as his own. Most of Waller's forces that escaped death or capture quietly melted away, many to their homes, and he took the remnant first to Gloucester, then to Evesham, and finally back to London.

Wilmot returned to Oxford after his victory, but as he did so Rupert set out with a very substantial force to join the western army, which had already occupied Bath. His objective was Bristol, and on 24 July he summoned the city to surrender. Its governor, Saye's son Nathaniel Fiennes, refused, though his garrison of 1,500 foot and 300 horse was insufficient to man the three-mile circumference of its defences. Rupert's council of war was divided about storming it, but he carried a decision in favour. The action began at 3 a.m. on the 26th and was fought fiercely, with heavy losses, until Fiennes asked for terms in the early evening. He had defended the city for as long as he reasonably could against very determined assailants, skilfully directed and greatly superior in numbers. He did not deserve to be court-martialled and sentenced to death, as he was on his return to London, but Essex to his honour secured his reprieve. The loss of Bristol, however, was a very severe blow. After its fall the Earl of Caernarvon set about reducing Dorset, while Maurice did the same in Devon. Plymouth, Exeter, Lyme, and two or three smaller outposts remained in parliamentarian hands, but almost all the rest of England to the west and south of Gloucester lay under the king's control. Charles appeared in person to summon Gloucester itself on 10 August, but Massey defied him. As the summer wore on, Gloucester's precarious resistance to its besiegers seemed the one bright spot in a bleak picture.

On the political front, the run of reverses was already serious enough by mid-July to bring the Lords to agree to what the Commons had been urging since May, namely to seek the support of a Scottish army. A convention of estates, similar to a Scottish parliament in composition but with more limited powers, had assembled in Edinburgh on 22 June. The English parliament sent commissioners to negotiate with it for a military alliance, but serious doubts about its own will to continue the struggle began to arise before they even arrived in Edinburgh. On 4 August the Lords gave their assent to a set of propositions for peace which amounted to virtual surrender, and the Commons voted two days later to take them into consideration. Many of the less pusillanimous members were of course absent on active service, but the terms proposed were abject, and a crowd of 5,000 demonstrated angrily against them in Palace Yard. Essex refused to support them, and the Commons rejected them on the 7th, though by only seven votes. It was a close thing, and during the next two days crowds of women clamoured for peace outside the House, pelting its guards with stones, and some shouting 'Give us that dog Pym!' This was the context in which Henry Marten was expelled from parliament for suggesting that it should rid itself of the house of Stuart.

But the mood in the capital was not totally defeatist, and the City corporation remained staunch. Largely at its instigation, parliament was persuaded to raise a new army of 11,000 under Waller's command, with the remnants of his western brigade as its nucleus and the defence of London as its main role. Essex, whose dislike and resentment of Waller were strongly reciprocated, was unwilling to grant him a commission, but under pressure from the Commons and at the persuasion of Pym, to whose steady support he owed much, he did so on 7 August. Five days later, again in compliance with directions given by parliament on Pym's recommendation, Essex commissioned the Earl of Manchester as Sergeant-Major-General of the Eastern Association in place of Grey of Warke, who was ineffectual as a commander and suspect in his commitment to the parliamentarian cause. Manchester was empowered to recruit up to 20,000 men, but though his army never achieved anything like that strength it was to play a major part, with Cromwell as Lieutenant-General of the Horse, in the campaigns of 1644. As for Essex himself, however much his sympathies lay with the peace party his loyalty to parliament was never in doubt. With an army reinforced from the London trained bands to 15,000 he set off resolutely on 26 August to relieve Gloucester. He swept aside an attempt by Rupert and a cavalry force to check his progress near Stow-on-the-Wold on 4 September, and then, when the Gloucester garrison was down to three barrels of powder, he forced the royalists to raise the siege.

But even as he marched, Barnstaple and Bideford surrendered to the king's forces, and Maurice took the greater prize of Exeter on 4 September. Charles was determined to bring Essex to battle, and sought to bar his passage back to London. The two armies, both about 14,000 strong, shadowed each other for days, in long marches through almost continuous rain. On 19 September Essex found his way barred by the royalists at Newbury and was forced to give battle. Charles and Rupert had high hopes that it would be a decisive one, for they had the advantage in cavalry, and many of Essex's foot were London militiamen. But in the fierce fight that lasted all the next day these part-time soldiers acquitted themselves heroically under Skippon's leadership, and the outcome was still undecided when darkness fell. Casualties were heavy, and the saddest of all was Falkland, who felt such misery over the war that he rode deliberately into a gap raked by musket fire. As Secretary of State he had no call to be on the field at all, but he was riding in Byron's own troop as a volunteer. In the end the royal army, which was short of powder and shot, left the field in the dark and retired to Oxford, leaving Essex a clear road to Reading and London. The Lord General never fought a better campaign.

The remaining military actions of the autumn confirmed that the tide of royalist victory was ebbing for the present, though they left the ultimate outcome of the war still wide open. In the north Newcastle, whom the king had just made a marquis, laid siege to Hull early in September with an army of about 15,000, but he did not press it vigorously and he lost many men through desertion. Sir Thomas Fairfax was able to get his cavalry out of the city, and Manchester to reinforce its garrison with 500 Eastern Association foot. Manchester himself took Lynn, which had declared for the king in August, after a brief siege on 16 September. He and Cromwell and Sir Thomas Fairfax then joined forces at Boston and advanced further north to besiege Bolingbroke Castle. A strong force from the Newark garrison rode out to challenge them, but it was routed with heavy losses in a brief but fierce battle at Winceby on 11 October. It was mainly a cavalry action, and it is memorable as the first in which Cromwell and Fairfax fought together. Fairfax played the greater part in it, for Cromwell's horse was shot dead in the first charge and fell with him beneath it, and though he got back into the action on a trooper's mount it is not clear how far he affected its outcome.

On the same day as the Winceby fight, the elder Fairfax's garrison sallied out of Hull and fought all day against its besiegers with such effect that Newcastle broke up the siege that night. Nine days later Lincoln surrendered to Manchester, and all danger of a southward advance by the royalists through eastern England now seemed past. The king was doing better in the south, however, for units of his main army retook Reading on 3 October, and others briefly occupied Newport Pagnell and Towcester, though they were forced to abandon them before the month was out. Hopton was advancing eastward again, but he suffered two severe setbacks when Waller stormed Alton on 13 December and captured Arundel Castle on 6 January, taking large numbers of prisoners in both actions. Hundreds of them promptly enlisted in the parliamentarian forces, a sign that war was already becoming a way of life for many a common soldier.

By the turn of the year 1643 the prospect of an outright royalist victory, which had looked bright in July, had dimmed, but it was uncertain whether either side could win decisively with the forces at their disposal, and both were looking outside England for allies. In December parliament lost the man who more than any other had held it on course in adversity, piloted through the measures needed for it to sustain a protracted war, and set up the vital Scottish alliance. John Pym died of cancer, but being the consummate politician that he was, he probably sensed that he had done enough to ensure ultimate victory for the cause he believed in.

# NINE

# The Conflict Widens

Now that parliament realized that the path to victory would be long and hard, it was inevitable that it should pursue an alliance with the Scottish Covenanters. The king, however, had been first in seeking allies outside his English kingdom, and the diplomatic efforts of both sides in the course of 1643 turned what had begun as an English civil war into a true war of three kingdoms.

The situation in Ireland was complicated for both king and parliament. The Confederated catholics had established a form of provisional government, but they continued to profess their loyalty to the king, and they had strong reasons for wishing that he and not the parliament should win the war in England. The first General Assembly, which they summoned to Kilkenny in October 1642, had abjured the title of parliament because their oath of confederacy bound them to defend the king's rights, which included the sole authority to summon a parliament. It had accepted the English common law as the law of Ireland and recognized the binding force of existing English statutes that legislated for Ireland, so long as they were not against the Roman Catholic religion or the liberties of the Irish people. It had petitioned the king for the free exercise of their religion and security for their estates and liberties, 'which granted [it said], we will convert our forces upon any design your majesty may appoint'.[1]

Charles had no personal compunction about enlisting Irish catholics to fight for him, but he had publicly condemned all those in arms against the Dublin government as rebels and traitors. At this stage he was more interested in neutralizing the Confederates than in bringing them over to fight for him. Ormond, his most loyal servant in Ireland, was fighting against them, and Charles's primary aim was to release Ormond and his mainly English troops for service in England. But Ormond's was only one voice in the council in Dublin, which was divided in its loyalties, with the majority leaning towards the English parliament because of their fear and hatred of the rebels. Late in

---

[1] *New History of Ireland*, III, 302, quoting T. Carte, *Life of Ormonde* (6 vols., Oxford, 1851), V, 368–70.

October 1642 the parliament sent a committee to Dublin with the object of winning the council wholly to its side and detaching the army from its obedience to Ormond. But Ormond's officers remained loyal to him and the king, and when the Irish parliament reassembled for a brief session in November and December it too continued to be divided in its allegiance.

Early in the new year Charles ordered the Dublin council to expel the committee from Westminster, which it did, and then sent a commission to Ormond, Clanricard, and five others, authorizing them to meet representatives of the Irish catholics and to hear their grievances. Ormond and his colleagues set fairly stiff conditions before agreeing to a meeting with delegates of the confederates, who reciprocated his caution. This was understandable, for the council was planning a military campaign to capture New Ross and Wexford, and had appointed the parliamentarian Lord Lisle, son and heir to Lord Lieutenant Leicester, to command it. Ormond sensed in this another ploy to take the command of the army away from him, and insisted on leading the expedition himself. But it failed to take New Ross, and Ormond had to fight his way past the confederate army of Leinster on 18 March to bring it safely back to Dublin. The first meetings with the Confederates' delegates took place while the siege of New Ross was still in progress. They asked for the repeal of the penal laws, so as to allow catholics full admission to public office as well as freedom of worship, and for the redress of their grievances by an Irish parliament, free of the shackles of Poynings' law. These things were more than Charles could grant, but he did comply with their request for the removal of Sir William Parsons, the senior Lord Justice and the dominant parliamentarian in the Dublin council. This strengthened the hand of Ormond, to whom Charles sent a commission on 23 April, directing him to seek a one-year truce with his 'Roman Catholic subjects in arms'.

That was to bear fruit in September, but it was not the king's only iron in the diplomatic fire, either in Ireland or Scotland. Earlier in the year the Earl of Antrim was in correspondence with such Scottish royalists as Nithsdale, Aboyne (Huntly's son), and Airlie, and also with Newcastle in England, about a plan for raising the king's supporters in Scotland and making common cause with his own people in Ulster. Most of Antrim's Ulster estates were under the occupation of Colonel Robert Monro and the Covenanting forces that he brought from Scotland in April 1642, and he was prepared to do anything to get them back. He was not the only proponent of a rising in Scotland, for Charles's future champion Montrose visited the queen soon after her landing at Bridlington and urged her to persuade her husband to authorize one. Antrim came to see her in April, and she sent him back to Ireland to negotiate a cessation of arms and raise Confederate support for the king. But Antrim was captured at sea in mid-May, with a number of letters which revealed all too plainly what he and the queen had been planning. The

English parliament published them, and their disclosure helped to win public support for its own negotiation of a treaty with the Scots.

During the spring and early summer Charles was inclined to see his best hope of support outside England neither in Irish catholics nor in uncompromising Scottish royalists like Huntly, Aboyne, and Airlie but in an emerging party of 'royalist Covenanters'. They were mainly allies of Hamilton, who was raised to a dukedom in April, and whose advice Charles was probably following. Hamilton was hoping to ally this group with non-Covenanting royalists of a more moderate stamp than Huntly, and with their support to build bridges between the king and the central Covenanting leadership personified by Argyll. The latter asked Charles to call a new Scottish parliament in 1643, and it was because he refused that Argyll summoned a convention of estates instead. That in itself, however, was an invasion of the royal prerogative, and Charles's first reaction was to forbid it to meet; but Hamilton persuaded him to accept the concession as an act of grace and to give him a chance to try and manage the convention. His hopes of success, however, were all but wrecked by the revelations that followed the capture of Antrim, and by the interception of a letter from six Scottish earls to the queen, offering advice on how the war against the parliament in England should be conducted. Even so Hamilton had the support of most of the nobles present, though the lairds and burgesses were almost solidly for Argyll. Their party carried an 'act of constitution' which enlarged the convention's powers far beyond what the king had sanctioned, whereupon Hamilton and many of his allies withdrew, leaving the field to Argyll and the strict Covenanters.

The convention of estates was all the better disposed towards the English parliament's plea for military help by the fact that on 1 July, soon after it opened, the promised assembly of divines met at Westminster. It consisted of 121 ordained ministers, with ten peers and twenty MPs as lay assessors, and the Scots were invited to send commissioners. They sent eight, five clerics and three laymen. It is fascinating to speculate on what the Westminster Assembly would have prescribed for the Church of England if the Scots had not been involved. A moderate episcopalian solution, which would have had the broadest national support, was ruled out because parliament, shorn of its royalist members, had already abolished episcopacy. A Presbyterian settlement was a possibility, for a Presbyterian party was developing among the puritan clergy, but little or nothing was left of the old Elizabethan Presbyterian movement, and lay support for such a system must at this stage have been small indeed. When English puritan settlers in New England had had a free hand to establish a church polity after their own hearts, it was a congregational model that they followed, not a Presbyterian one, and congregationalism or Independency was a growing force in the England of the mid-1640s. The balance between Presbyterians, Independents, and Erastians would surely have been different if the English parliament's need for a Scottish army, and the consequent Solemn League and Covenant, had not skewed the Westminster Assembly's agenda; there might even have been a tincture of toleration.

The parliamentary commissioners arrived in Edinburgh on 7 August 1643 with the prime object of obtaining at least 10,000 Scottish foot and 1,000 horse to fight in England. But the Covenanters were more intent on bringing the two kingdoms into a closer and more equal union, and in particular on so reforming the Church of England as to bring it into line with the Scottish Kirk. A General Assembly had just met in Edinburgh, and it politely maintained the pressure for ecclesiastical conformity. The Scots would not discuss the terms of a military alliance until the English commissioners had agreed to a joint band or covenant that would commit them to the religious and political objectives which were an essential part of its price. The result was the Solemn League and Covenant, which was drafted mainly by Alexander Henderson and approved unanimously by both the General Assembly and the convention of estates on 17 August. Vane, the chief negotiator on the English side, strove hard to keep 'a door open in England to Independency', which is where his own convictions lay, but the Scots were adamant against it.[2]

The Covenant was adopted by the English parliament with small amendments, and all the members of the Commons and the Assembly of Divines solemnly swore to it in St Margaret's church on 25 September. Parliament then passed an ordinance requiring all male Englishmen over eighteen to subscribe it, and in Scotland a committee of estates joined with the commission of the Kirk to impose it on all Scottish subjects, on pain of having their goods and rents confiscated. In theory it imposed a common religion on every subject of both nations, with no concessions to any who might conscientiously dissent from it; and since it also rigidly defined England's and Scotland's war aims, and hugely affected their subsequent relations with the king and between each other, its terms were of unusual importance. In form it was an oath, to be sworn by the subjects of England, Scotland, and Ireland, 'living under one king, and being of one reformed religion', to *preserve* the religion of the Church of Scotland and *reform* that of England and Ireland, 'according to the word of God, and the example of the best reformed churches', and to bring the churches of all three kingdoms into uniformity of creed, liturgy, and government. Vane was later credited by Bishop Burnet with getting 'according to the word of God' inserted, so that the example of the Scottish Kirk should not be the sole pattern for the settlement of the Church of England, but it was the narrowest of loopholes since the rest of the clause so clearly implied uniformity on the Scottish model. Next came a pledge to extirpate

[2] Stevenson, *Scottish Revolution 1637–44*, pp. 283–6.

popery, episcopacy, superstition, heresy, and schism (another rejection of toleration), so 'that the Lord may be one, and his name one in the three kingdoms'. The Covenant further bound those who swore to it to preserve both the rights and privileges of the two parliaments and the king's person and authority, to bring all incendiaries and malignants to public trial and condign punishment, and when the war had been concluded to endeavour that the allied kingdoms 'may remain conjoined in a firm peace and union to all posterity'.[3]

When political union was eventually achieved on a lasting basis sixty-four years later, it recognized the enduring religious diversity between England and Scotland. The Covenant, by failing to do so, was to prove a grave obstacle to a peaceful settlement when the war ended, both because the king would never submit to what he regarded as the betrayal of the church of which he was Supreme Governor, and the English people would never let themselves be forced into an ecclesiastical strait-jacket in which only a fraction of them felt comfortable. Parliament anyway lacked the will to attempt it seriously; many in both Houses tried at the time to save it from committing itself to a Presbyterian Church of England, but the need for a Scottish army after the run of royalist victories in the summer of 1643 overruled them. From now on, however, religion was to be an even greater source of division in the parliamentarian ranks than it had been before.

The commissioners whom the General Assembly in Edinburgh sent to the Westminster Assembly included Henderson and Baillie among the ministers and Johnston of Wariston among the laymen. They were no more troubled about imposing an alien religious system on an unwilling nation than a group of Soviet commissaries would be when delivering the pure milk of Marxist-Leninist orthodoxy to a satellite country after the Second World War. They did not see themselves as engaged with the Westminster divines in a common quest for a confession of faith and a form of church polity that accorded most closely with the word of God, for they knew the answers already. What they brought was the truth, which their Kirk possessed in unique perfection, and they assumed that its blessings had only to be experienced to be eventually embraced. They were not content just to sit on the Assembly; they insisted on treating formally with a committee of representatives of both parliament and the divines on the specific point of uniformity, and they got their way. The Scottish army under negotiation in the simultaneous but separate military treaty was now raised to 21,000 men under the command of the veteran Earl of Leven, and it was an offer that the English parliament could not refuse.

Parliament's acceptance of the Covenant was encouraged by the king's conclusion of a truce with the confederate Irish, initially to release Ormond's

---

[3] Text in Gardiner (ed.), *Constitutional Documents*, pp. 267–71.

troops to return and fight for him in England, but with who knew what possibilities of further military aid from Irish catholics. Ormond's cautious negotiation with the Confederates was opposed by a papal envoy called Pier Francesco Scarampi who joined them in mid-July, but the Marquis's position had been strengthened, and theirs weakened, by a severe defeat that Owen Roe O'Neill had suffered at the battle of Clones on 13 June. In it O'Neill had lost many of the officers who had returned to Ireland with him, and he needed a breathing-space in which to recruit his army and give it some serious military training. Ormond's fellow protestant commanders such as Thomond and Inchiquin and Coote had misgivings about his treating with the Confederates, but in accordance with the king's instructions he concluded with them, on 15 September, a one year's armistice that became known as the Cessation. It exposed the king to much propaganda in England about the iniquity of enlisting murdering Irish papists against his English subjects, but in fact the 5,000 or so troops that Ormond sent home after its conclusion were all protestants and nearly all English. Their military value to the royalists was small compared with that of Leven's Scottish army to their opponents, and many of them, when captured in England, cheerfully changed sides. But Ormond deserved his reward of the office of Lord Lieutenant, and his stature grew steadily over the next five years. He was still only just thirty-three, and as an Old English magnate most of his kinsmen and former friends were with the Confederates, but he remained firm in his protestant faith and his loyalty to the king was unwavering.

He was not, however, the only channel of communication between Charles and the catholic Irish. Antrim was as usual pursuing grandiose projects which might have been of advantage to himself, and even to his king, if he had been able to deliver what he proposed. He was currently angling for the position of Lieutenant-General of all the Confederate forces in Ireland. He visited Charles in Oxford in December 1643 and won him over to a plan whereby 10,000 Confederate troops would be sent over to fight against the Scottish army that was about to enter England. Ormond was excluded from this negotiation, and justly resented the fact. The scheme eventually came to nothing because the Confederates' supreme council refused to sanction it, though (as will be seen) they would be willing to send a small force to fight alongside Montrose.

When the year 1643 began, there had still been a widespread hope that the war might soon be wound up and a common desire to preserve as far as possible the forms of government known to the law. Since then, however, both sides had had to devise the measures and institutions needed to recruit, pay, and supply field armies and garrisons on a long-term basis. The result by the end of the year was that England had what amounted to two rival governments, and a large part of that which operated in parliamentary territory was of necessity new.

The king was naturally better able to act through time-honoured channels, and he made a virtue of so doing. When he appointed officers of state, privy councillors, and military commanders he was exercising what had until very recently been his unquestioned prerogative, and he could denounce parliament's attempts to usurp it as a breach of the fundamental laws. In practice the privy council's function was now partly taken over by his new council of war, in which his generals sat side by side with selected civilian councillors and officials. This was the centre from which his war effort was directed, and it gave instructions to the commissioners of array who continued to impress soldiers for his armies in the territories that he controlled. For civil administration and justice, however, he went on working as far as possible through the JPs, sheriffs, constables, borough corporations, and other traditional authorities. The chief officers of state from the Lord Chancellor and Lord Treasurer downward had moved to Oxford with him, along with much of his central bureaucracy, and continued to perform most of their old functions, though the financial demands of his armies led to the increasing use of a special treasury of war. Late in the year he tried to take some of the constitutional wind out of his enemies' sails by summoning parliament to meet in Oxford. His objects were to lure peace party members away from Westminster, to broaden support for his war effort and to add some legitimacy to the financial exactions that he was being forced to make. The royalist peers and MPs whom he addressed in Christ Church Hall on 22 January 1642 were quite impressive in number, but the Oxford 'Parliament' disappointed his hopes. If the members who fought for him in the field are added to those who sat in Oxford they amounted to not far short of a third of the original House of Commons, and the peers at Oxford greatly outnumbered those at Westminster, though their ranks were swollen by his many new creations. But very few MPs seem actually to have left Westminster for Oxford, and most of the royalists who did answer his summons brought their constitutionalist notions with them. Often they seemed more interested in terms of peace than in prosecuting the war, and he became increasingly exasperated with them. In his council of war Rupert and Digby, who were usually at daggers drawn, were at one in detesting the Oxford parliament, with its pacific and legalistic tendencies.

The Westminster parliament, which in normal times had had no executive authority except in respect of its own members and privileges, almost had to invent a system of central and local government as it went along. During most of 1643 the bicameral Committee of Safety acted tolerably effectively as a national executive, though it depended far more constantly on the votes of the two Houses than a modern cabinet does. Pym's unique authority in both the

Committee and the Commons had helped to keep the wheels turning until his final illness laid him low. A new solution was then needed, not only because of the vacuum that he left but because the Solemn League and Covenant demanded a Scottish presence in whatever body directed the joint war effort. It was found in the Committee of Both Kingdoms, which was established in February 1644 and consisted of seven peers, fourteen MPs, and four Scottish commissioners. The man who did most to pilot its formation through a suspicious parliament was Oliver St John, the one-time counsellor to Hampden and prosecutor of Strafford, and his main ally in the Commons was the younger Vane. St John was emerging as the chief successor to Pym, who had greatly trusted him, and he carried on Pym's efforts to hold together a middle group of politicians who steered a path between the defeatism of the peace party on the one hand and the disruptively radical aspirations of some members of the war party on the other. Despite his strong commitment to winning the war he remained a friend of Essex, and strove to avoid a fatal breach between the Lord General's supporters and those who wanted him removed. He was a reserved, unsmiling man, very much of 'the godly interest' and leaning towards Independency—his correspondence with Cromwell is full of the language of the saints—but broad enough in his sympathies to enjoy the respect and trust of moderate Presbyterians.[4]

The Committee, which was given larger powers to direct the conduct of the war than the Committee of Safety had had, was a well balanced body. Its commoners included, besides St John and the elder and younger Vanes, such advocates of an aggressive war policy as Waller, Haselrig, and Cromwell, as well as supporters of Essex like Sir Philip Stapleton, John Glyn, Sir Gilbert Gerard, and William Pierrepoint. Essex and his brother-in-law Warwick were naturally among the peers on the Committee, as was Manchester, but so were three men who were to be closely associated with the New Model Army in 1647, Saye, Northumberland, and Wharton. The Scots who sat with them were Loudoun (the Lord Chancellor), Johnston of Wariston, Lord Maitland (the future Earl of Lauderdale), and Robert Barclay. This disparate body of men seems to have worked together better than might have been expected, but during 1644 it made the mistake of trying to direct the commanders in the field more closely than was wise, robbing them of initiative and causing them to miss opportunities because the information on which it acted was often stale long before its consequent orders got to their headquarters. The Committee had rather more success in directing the county committees, which were the parliament's main agencies at the local level, but its instructions to them were not always obeyed.

---

[4] Valerie Pearl, 'Oliver St John and the "middle group" in the Long Parliament: August 1643–May 1644', *English Historical Review* CCCXX (1966), 490–519.

The county committees, which became hugely unpopular during the war and after, were an almost haphazard growth, and they differed in structure and function from shire to shire. They had two origins. One was in the Deputy Lieutenants, whom the parliament had so greatly relied upon when first raising armed forces, and who continued to hold regular meetings of reliable fellow-magistrates in many counties. In others the committees grew out of the various financial measures whereby parliament financed the war, including the regular direct tax on every county and major town under its control, called the assessment (first weekly, later monthly), and the sequestration of the estates and rents of royalists. Each of these involved the appointment of county commissioners, answerable to central committees or commissions; so did the ordinances regulating the militia and governing the removal of refractory or unworthy parish clergy and their replacement by 'godly' ministers. In many counties, though by no means all, these functions all came to be performed by a single committee. However they took shape, the county committees generally consisted mainly of JPs, including the Deputy Lieutenants, but their powers went far beyond those exercised by the bench in peacetime and were not subject to the same legal restraints. Milton, in the proposals that he published on the very eve of the Restoration in an attempt to shore up the tottering commonwealth, hoped that the local democratic assemblies that he then advocated 'will henceforth quite annihilate the odious power and name of committees',[5] so enduring was their unpopularity a decade after they had lapsed.

Their role in bringing in the revenue was a major cause of their unpopularity, for the burden of taxation was extremely heavy. The monthly assessment alone was fixed at about double the total regular revenue that Charles had had at his accession, and it was levied upon a much higher proportion of the population than the old parliamentary subsidies. It all had to be found from those regions over which parliament had effective control, and it was none the better liked for being assessed on much the same basis as Ship Money. It was by no means the only new imposition. The excise, introduced in 1643 and destined to continue till the Restoration (and beyond), was especially hated. It was charged at first on beer, tobacco, and other non-essentials (if beer can be so called in the seventeenth century when water was so often lethal), but it was extended as the war went on to such basic commodities as meat and salt. By the end of the first Civil War it was yielding about £330,000 a year, which was more than half as much again as the highest annual demand for Ship Money. The excisemen, unlike the constables who collected the assessment, were not always local men, and their inquisitorial searches for excisable commodities were quite often met with violence. Royalists at first

---

[5] *Complete Prose Works of John Milton*, VII (New Haven, rev. ed., 1980), 443.

denounced the excise as another example of parliamentary tyranny, but the king soon introduced it in the regions under his control. He levied his own equivalent of the assessment too, though less systematically and effectively. The differences between living in a parliamentarian and a royalist-controlled country was a matter of swings and roundabouts. The parliament's tax burden was heavier because it was more efficient, but where the king's forces held sway the population was more subject to irregular demands and casual pillage, and had no hope of recovering the cost of what had been commandeered when the war was over. The unluckiest people were those who lived in disputed territory, for they had difficulty in not paying the demands of both sides.

Heavy taxation was a cross borne by the whole country; so to a varying extent was the disruption by war of normal commercial life, though some trades and manufactures flourished, especially those which supplied weapons, ammunition, armour, shoes, stockings, and other clothing to the armies. The other miseries of war fell more unequally on the civil population, according to whether or not they lived in areas much crossed by field armies or in the vicinity of hungry garrisons. The approach or proximity of troops in large numbers was always bad news, whichever side they were on. The damage that they did through pillage, theft, and wanton destruction, as well as the scars inflicted on civilians and their property by military action, will be considered further when the time comes to reckon the overall cost of the war in terms of human suffering. But two of its inevitable burdens, free quarter and the commandeering of goods and services, may be reckoned alongside that of taxation, of which they could be considered a form. For all the initial promises by both sides that their armies would pay their way, money was always short, soldiers were very irregularly paid, and discipline was never perfect. Soldiers needed food for themselves, utensils to cook it in, fodder for their horses, and whenever possible beds to sleep in. Looking at the last first, they had to be billeted on civilians, and they were rarely welcome guests. Strictly, the householders concerned should have been given 'tickets' for quarter, and the sums recorded should have been reclaimable or deductible from taxes due, at any rate on the parliamentary side. But it did not always work out like that, and there was no redress after the war for those who had been forced to billet royalist troops—indeed they might even be penalized for assisting the enemy.

As for the commandeering of goods and services, the line between requisitioning and robbery was a blurred one in active service conditions. Horses were very frequently taken, both as mounts and for transport, and to a small husbandman the consequent loss to his livelihood could be severe, whether he was later compensated or not. Soldiers helped themselves to untold quantities of livestock and chickens and corn and hay, and when poor housewives lost their pots and pans and beds and bedding they felt it sorely, for such things cost far more in relation to their income than in these days of mass-production. Soldiers also often brought sickness with them, especially typhus and dysentery; disease was certainly more rife in the war years than before and after. And when battles were fought, it was local householders who were left with the care of most of the wounded, and their chances of being paid for it were problematic: fair, if they were tending parliamentarian casualties after a parliamentarian victory, otherwise more doubtful.

The 1644 campaigning season began early, with actions involving the forces acquired by both king and parliament through their recent treaties. Released by the Cessation, five infantry regiments from Ormond's army in Ireland had landed at Chester in November and had been taken under the command of Lord Byron, the king's governor of the city. He was aiming to build up a second royal army in the north-west to match Newcastle's in the north-east. He soon took the field against Brereton's now greatly outnumbered Cheshire parliamentarians and drove them into Nantwich, to which he laid siege on 13 December. Sir Thomas Fairfax, who was wintering in Lincolnshire, set out to relieve Brereton with 2,300 horse and dragoons and such infantry as he could pick up on the way, including many who had fought with him at Adwalton Moor. As he approached, Byron tried to storm Nantwich on 18 January, but was repulsed with heavy losses. A week later Fairfax brought him to battle outside the city and totally defeated him, capturing all his guns and baggage. Two of the regiments from Ireland broke and ran; 1,500 men were taken prisoner, and when offered service under the parliament more than a third—one account says more than half—promptly accepted. They cannot fairly be accused of disloyalty, because as Englishmen who had enlisted under a protestant Dublin government and a protestant general to fight Irish catholic rebels they would not necessarily see the king as having the better cause in the Civil War in England. So many others of the men from Ireland simply made off home that most of the military gains from the Cessation were lost before January was out, though a few more troops were still expected at Chester and two regiments were on their way to join Hopton's army in the south.

Fairfax had no difficulty in mopping up most of the remaining royalist garrisons in Cheshire and Lancashire, while young John Lambert, his most brilliant colonel of horse, was fast recovering the clothing towns of the West Riding. By the spring the only significant royalist outpost in the north-west to the north of Chester was Lathom House, a great moated castle near Ormskirk belonging to the Earl of Derby, who was away fighting for the king—at least for the present, though after the battle of Marston Moor he withdrew to the Isle of Man. His remarkable French countess, however, a granddaughter of

William the Silent, cousin of the late Elector Palatine and mother of nine children, was defying Fairfax's besieging forces with a garrison of little more than 300 men. This was the first of two long sieges in which she commanded the defence in person.

Meanwhile across the Pennines parliament's alliance with the Scots was bearing better fruit. A Scottish army, close to its nominal strength of 21,000 men, crossed the Tweed on 19 January under Leven's command and advanced slowly towards Newcastle. The veteran general's sixty-odd years made him disinclined for unnecessary exertions, but he was immensely experienced in the practical craft of keeping large bodies of men in fighting trim. There was more dash in his much younger general of the horse David Leslie—no relation, but schooled like him in the Swedish service. Every regiment in this army was constituted as a kirk session, with its minister and lay elders, but for all the praying and preaching to which they were treated Leven's blue-bonnets soon gained a bad reputation for plundering and otherwise ill-treating the civil population. This was no doubt partly due to the anti-Scottish prejudice of English reporters, but the main explanation is that the Scottish army's pay, which England was bound by treaty to furnish, was always in arrears. Heavy snow and floods slowed Leven's advance through Northumberland, but he met with no other resistance until he launched an assault on Newcastle on 3 February. There the Scots found that the Marquis who took his title from that city had arrived in the nick of time to defend it, and they met with a sharp repulse. They settled around it for the next two months, Leven thinking it enough to prevent Newcastle and his forces from joining the king.

Two days before that clash of arms Montrose, who was visiting Charles in Oxford, at last obtained the commission that he had long sought to raise the Scottish royalists in arms. Formally he was made Lieutenant-General of all the king's forces in the northern kingdom, Prince Maurice being appointed Captain-General, but the command was really his, for Maurice never went to Scotland. As part of the plan Antrim, who was also in Oxford, was sent to Ulster with orders to muster 2,000 Irish troops and land them in Argyllshire by 1 April. Montrose's return to Scotland in April and May was something of a fiasco, for he was excommunicated by the Kirk and forced by the hostility of the Lowlanders to retreat into England again. But his day was to come.

By an intriguing coincidence another commission as Lieutenant-General was sealed on the same day as Montrose's. Its recipient was Oliver Cromwell, and it formalized his position as second-in-command and general of the horse in Manchester's Eastern Association army. Essex was incensed by the build-up of this army, backed as it was by his political opponents; he protested to the Lords two months later at the reduction of his own to 7,000 foot and 3,000 horse while parliament was financing Manchester's up to a total of 14,000. With Waller in command of another independent army, now almost as large as his own, the Lord General's position was far from comfortable, but the war party's dissatisfaction with him was not groundless, and its confidence in the Eastern Association army was to be well justified. But reluctant though he regrettably was to carry the war to the enemy, Essex could never be accused of overt disloyalty. Late in January he received a letter from the Oxford parliament, signed by 44 peers and 118 MPs, urging him to mediate with the two Houses at Westminster and help to bring about a negotiated peace. They sent with it a letter addressed by the Oxford to the Westminster parliament. He declined to present it, but he did return a declaration by the Lords and Commons at Westminster, promising a pardon to all who returned to their duty and took the Covenant, of which he enclosed a copy. Nothing on the face of it could have been more correct, but the almost vice-regal pomp that Essex was assuming aroused some concern.

The month of March brought mixed fortunes to both sides. For the parliamentarians, Sir John Meldrum laid siege to Newark with a mainly local force of about 5,000 foot and 2,000 horse, and with Newcastle bottled up by the Scots in his namesake city the king was in some danger of losing the whole of the north. But Rupert, who was in Chester to oversee the arrival of the remaining forces from Ireland, collected a scratch force, led it to Newark before Meldrum had any idea of his approach, caught him at a hopeless disadvantage and forced him to surrender. This was Rupert at his vigorous best; his booty included over 3,000 muskets, but he had to return most of his men to the garrisons from which he had taken them and go back to his task of building up the king's main army. He spent the rest of the spring in Shrewsbury, raising and training recruits for it.

In the south the duel between Hopton and Waller was continuing. Hopton had been shaken by his reverses at Alton and Arundel Castle, and he repeatedly asked for reinforcements from Oxford. They came early in March, 1,200 foot and 800 horse under the command of no less than the king's Captain-General, Patrick Ruthven, Earl of Forth, who had succeeded Lindsey in the post. Now in his seventies and somewhat slow, bibulous, and gouty, the old Scottish professional courteously insisted on treating Hopton as a partner rather than a subordinate, but the very fact that he had been put in charge of so modest a force showed that the king's council of war no longer had quite its old confidence in Hopton. Together they commanded about 3,200 foot and 3,800 horse, but Waller had 5,000 foot, including a brigade of London trained bands, and his 3,000 horse were reinforced on the Committee of Both Kingdoms' orders by a whole brigade of cavalry from Essex's army. On 4 March the Committee ordered him to march against Hopton, and the result was the battle of Cheriton, fought on the 29th seven miles east of Winchester. It went in Waller's favour, thanks mainly to his superior numbers and to the courage and resource shown in a long and fierce cavalry fight by Sir Arthur Haselrig and his regiment, known as the Lobsters because unlike nearly all other Civil War cavalry they wore full armour. But the battle did not reflect much credit on the generalship of either side, and its immediate results were less positive than they might have been. The royalists took much the heavier casualties, especially among their officers, but Hopton got his guns and most of his infantry away in the night to the safe shelter of Basing House, and Forth escaped westward with his surviving cavalry.

Cheriton did put an end to any further drive eastward by the royalists through southern England, and it checked a serious attempt by the peace party at Westminster to make overtures to the king once more. How might parliament have reacted, one wonders, if Waller had been beaten. As things were, Charles was thrown on the defensive; he ordered both Forth and Hopton to rejoin him with their forces in Oxford, where his army currently numbered only about 10,000. Waller did not pursue them, but moved west-ward to mop up the remaining garrisons in Hampshire and Wiltshire. He was deterred, however, from striking further into the West Country by intelli-gence that the king was massing forces around Marlborough to prevent such a move, and his infantry were depleted when the London trained-band regi-ments decided, as they always did sooner or later, that it was time to march back home.

In mid-April the Committee of Both Kingdoms decided to concentrate all its forces south of Trent, including Manchester's Eastern Association army, in the Aylesbury area, intending a direct attack on Oxford. But already a more immediate opportunity was beginning to open up in the north. Sir Thomas Fairfax, having already recovered most of the West Riding, rejoined his father before Selby, and on 11 April they stormed the town, taking over 3,000 prisoners. Leven was on the march again, having left a sufficient force to keep Newcastle surrounded. The Marquis of Newcastle, when he heard of Selby's fall, gave up disputing the Scots' advance and drew back his army of 6,000 foot and 5,000 horse to defend York. Leven joined up with the Fair-faxes near Wetherby on the 20th, and together they agreed to lay siege to York. Manchester and his army retook Lincoln by storm on 6 May, where-upon the Committee of Both Kingdoms wisely cancelled their instructions to him to join Essex and sent him to reinforce the besiegers of York. Essex and Waller had enough men between them to tackle the king's Oxford army, unless Rupert was able to strengthen it considerably, and the threat to York was more likely to draw him northward. There was not much love lost between Essex and Waller, but they agreed to co-operate in the operation against Oxford on the terms that each would direct his own army, with Essex of course in overall command.

Rupert did indeed respond to the threatening moves of the Scots and the Fairfaxes. He set off from Shrewsbury on 16 April, but having only 8,000 men, three quarters of them infantry, he needed to collect many more in Cheshire and Lancashire before he could confront them. He was much strengthened, especially in cavalry, when he added Byron's forces to his own on reaching Chester. He captured Stockport on 25 May and gave the town over to plunder. His near approach was enough to relieve Lathom House, at least for the time being. Its besiegers withdrew to Bolton, which he stormed on the 28th. For daring to resist him, he let his men slaughter 1,600 of its defenders and sack the town. Next day he introduced himself to the Countess of Derby at Lathom and presented her with twenty-two standards captured from her besiegers. The day after, he was joined by Sir Charles Lucas and George Goring with further reinforcements, including most of Newcastle's cavalry, which the marquis sent out of York when he came under siege. Many Lancashire royalists came in to him, but he met with stubborn resistance at Liverpool, which he took on 11 June, though only after five days' bombardment and more than one assault. The defenders paid the now usual price in butchery and pillage.

By now, however, it was a question whether Rupert's first priority was to relieve York or rescue the king. Charles had been forced to strengthen his main army by pulling in some of Oxford's outlying garrisons, including the 2,500 in Reading, whose fortifications were dismantled. Essex took the town over on 19 May, and occupied Abingdon a week later. On that same day Massey, who from his base in Gloucester had been capturing a whole series of royalist garrisons in Gloucestershire, Herefordshire, and Wiltshire, received the surrender of Malmesbury. Charles still had a western army of about 5,000 in Dorset under Prince Maurice, but it was occupied in besieging the little town of Lyme (its 'Regis' was very much in abeyance), whose heroic resistance was through no fault of its defenders to distort the whole parliamentarian strategy. By the end of May most of Essex's army was in and around Islip, with detachments to the south covering the east banks of the Thames and Cherwell, while to the west Waller had his headquarters at Newbridge and forward units in Eynsham and Woodstock. Oxford and the king's army were almost surrounded; the gap between Woodstock and Islip was little more than five miles wide.

The Committee of Both Kingdoms, however, had received false intelligence that Charles intended to come to London and negotiate a peace. In transmitting this to Essex on 30 May, it also informed him that Lyme was in desperate straits and instructed him to send immediately a force sufficient to relieve it, adding that such an operation would be 'a means . . . to recover the whole west'.[6] The Committee therefore must take its share of responsibility for the debacle that followed, for it acted on a report about Charles's

---

[6] Quoted in Snow, *Essex the Rebel*, p. 430.

intentions which was inherently most improbable, it put the relief of Lyme before the opportunity to engage his main army at an advantage, and it encouraged Essex in dreams of conquest in the west. Charles had no intention of either seeking peace or exposing himself to capture. With admirable audacity he mounted a feint attack toward Abingdon, causing Waller to move south and loosen the noose, then slipped through the gap and headed west with 3,000 horse and 2,500 foot. By evening on 4 June he and they had got beyond Burford. Essex and Waller were soon in pursuit, respectively two days' and one day's march behind him, and their chances of bringing him to battle were still very good. But they held a council of war on the 6th at Stow-on-the-Wold, with all their commissioned officers present, and there the disastrous decision was taken to separate the two armies. Essex would take the whole of his to relieve Lyme and reconquer the West Country, while Waller would go on pursuing the king, combine forces with Massey, and *then* seek battle. Waller opposed the plan strenuously but had to submit to Essex's express orders, though he protested hard to parliament about them. Essex had the pretext that he had the heavy guns and the more experience of sieges, but one cannot but believe that he was drawn by the prospect of a victorious campaign on his own in what had been Waller's territory, in co-operation with his cousin Warwick the Lord Admiral, who was operating off the Dorset and Devon coasts. He might even capture the queen, who was in Exeter and expecting very shortly the birth of her fourth child. What a game in high politics that might open up!

The Committee of Both Kingdoms was appalled by Essex's decision, and again directed him to send only a detachment to the help of Lyme, but in a reply which made his jealousy of Waller all too plain he insisted on sticking to his course. He duly relieved Lyme, then occupied Weymouth; parliament bowed to the fait accompli on 25 June and gave its sanction to his further advance westward. The ruinous consequences will be seen shortly, but if Essex and Waller had fought and beaten the Oxford army, and supposing that Rupert's northern campaign went the way it did, the Civil War could have been over in 1644.

Charles and his army made their way by 6 June to the relative safety of Worcester, a garrison city in friendly territory. He did not have too much to fear now that only Waller was challenging him, and he did not want Rupert to abandon York to its fate in order to come to his own assistance. But the orders that he sent to the prince on 14 June were far from unambiguous, and obviously reflect divisions and misgivings in his council of war. The letter must have worried the prince sick, and though he never produced it in order to refute his critics he carried it on him to his dying day. It reads as though it was deliberately intended to make it possible to blame Rupert if either the king's army or the relief of York met with disaster, and if Sir Philip Warwick is right that Digby drafted it the suspicion is probably justified. But for all its distracting references to alternative strategies its operative words are clear enough, and Charles of course signed them: 'Wherefore I command and conjure you . . . that all new enterprises laid aside, you immediately march, according to your first intention, with all your force to the relief of York'. Only if he found York already lost, or already freed from its besiegers, or if he had not enough powder to engage them, was Rupert to march with all his troops to Worcester, to assist the king and his army.[7] It is clear from the letter that Charles recognized that Rupert could not relieve York without offering battle, and he must have known that that would mean fighting against heavy numerical odds.

Charles and his forces were in fact already on the move and countering Waller's threat with a series of daring and successful manoeuvres. They marched first up the Thames valley to Bewdley, as if heading for Shrewsbury, but they then doubled back through Worcester, made a rendezvous with the Oxford garrison at Witney, and next advanced north-eastward as far as Buckingham. This caused a scare at Westminster that they were about to descend on Eastern Association territory while its army was far away at York, and Waller was urgently ordered to prevent it. After sundry manoeuvres, with the opposing forces marching in sight of each other for hours, Waller struck on 29 June from a strong position near Cropredy, three miles north of Banbury. He had as many cavalry as the king (about 5,000) and rather more infantry, though these again included a brigade of London trained bands. He caught the royal army on the march and might have given it a severe mauling, but the untidy and inconclusive battle that ensued went very much in the royalists' favour, thanks particularly to the dash and initiative shown by their cavalry under the Earl of Cleveland and Lord Wilmot. Waller took much the heavier casualties and lost most of his guns. In the aftermath his demoralized infantry virtually disintegrated; one City regiment deserted en masse, other companies mutinied or simply made off home. He had strong reason for telling parliament, as he afterwards did, that the war would never be won by makeshift armies or part-time soldiers.

Rupert did not know that the king and his army were no longer under threat when he set off from Preston on his 'York march' on 23 June. His harshness in Stockport and Bolton and Liverpool had not been without purpose, because it had caused the Committee of Both Kingdoms to urge the generals before York repeatedly to send a strong detachment to the defence of Lancashire. But they refused to split their forces, and they were right. Inside York, rations were down to one meal a day for soldiers and civilians alike. Three mines had been set under strategic points in the walls, in preparation

---

[7] Eliot Warburton, *Memoirs of Prince Rupert and the Cavaliers* (3 vols., 1849), II, 436.

for simultaneous assaults by all three armies, and if Manchester's major-general of foot, the Scotsman Lawrence Crawford, had not sprung his prematurely the city might have fallen before Rupert reached it.

Rupert rested his troops for three nights at Skipton, a royalist garrison. He had collected so many of them en route that he needed to make sure they were adequately armed and battle-ready. Setting off again on the 29th, they had two long days' marches by way of Otley to Knaresborough, only seventeen miles from the walls of York. Speed mattered, for Meldrum and the Earl of Denbigh were on their way with enough local forces from the Midlands to man the siege works and enable Leven, Fairfax, and Manchester to march out and give battle. But they were still four days' march away when Rupert's rapid approach caused the three generals to reluctantly abandon their lines, their siege guns, and 4,000 pairs of shoes and boots, and to form lines of battle seven miles west of the city on the broad expanse of open heath called Marston Moor. They thus covered Rupert's obvious line of approach, whether he marched north of the River Nidd or south via Wetherby.

But Rupert took neither route. He led his army north-west through Boroughbridge to the first crossing of the River Swale at Thornton Bridge, and thence joined the road from Thirsk to York. By the time he quartered it in the forest of Galtres, three miles north of the city, his infantry had marched twenty-two miles, making all but fifty in the past three days. His appearance there caused great consternation among the allied commanders, who met in a council of war that evening. If he chose to fight he could now add the York garrison to his forces, which they had counted on preventing. They still wanted to bring him to battle (at least most of the English officers present did—the Scots were less keen), but they feared he might slip away southward, perhaps to add the Newark forces to his own and attack the exposed eastern counties, perhaps to join up with the king's army somewhere in the Midlands. That could spell disaster, with Essex's army far away in the west and Waller's in a state of decomposition. As they saw it, he had good reasons for avoiding battle, since their combined forces outnumbered his, even when reinforced by Newcastle's men in York, by nearly three to two. Nor would he be leaving York to certain surrender, since by marching south he would draw off at least Manchester's army, and Newcastle was expecting reinforcements from Cumberland and Westmorland. They were of course unaware of the king's instructions to him, which he took as a command to fight, and they failed to appreciate his own eagerness for battle. Even less could they know that Rupert came to Newcastle that evening and insisted, against the marquis's misgivings and the stronger objections of his infantry commander, James King, Baron Eythin, that the York garrison should come out and fight alongside his own forces next day.

Consequently the allied generals decided to march their combined armies to Tadcaster, intending to block Rupert's southward passage at the crossings of the Wharfe and Ouse, and their infantry set off from Marston Moor early in the morning of 2 July. Their foot regiments were strung out for eight miles along the lanes towards Tadcaster when they became aware that Rupert's cavalry was massing in strength on the Moor, clearly intent on battle. The royalist horse almost equalled theirs in numbers, and included such formidable commanders as Goring, Byron, Sir Charles Lucas, and Sir Marmaduke Langdale; the allies' numerical advantage was nearly all in infantry, and in a battle of this scale, in mainly very open terrain, the infantry rarely decided the outcome. So although they may have commanded a total of 28,000 men against perhaps 18,000 (we do not know just how many of the York garrison came out to fight), their troops were of varying experience and quality, and Rupert was not wildly rash to engage them. If he could have fired Newcastle with his own enthusiasm and confidence, and if Eythin had not borne him a grudge going back to an incident in the German wars long ago and been uncooperative to the point of obstructiveness, the day might have gone differently. As it was, when Eythin's foot were mustered for action many had not returned from plundering the besiegers' abandoned lines, and those who did appear refused to march until they were given their overdue pay. So although Rupert's horse were in position by 9 a.m., the infantry were not fully deployed on the Moor until far into the afternoon.

There for hours the two armies faced each other, the cavalry on the two flanks no more than 400 yards apart and the foot not much further. From about two o'clock there was a desultory exchange of artillery fire, but after five little broke the silence except the chanting of metrical psalms in the Scottish and parliamentarian ranks. A shallow valley with a ditch running through it separated the two hosts, and neither seemed willing to abandon its high ground and charge uphill. Soon after seven Rupert decided that it was too late for a battle, saying to Newcastle: 'We will charge them tomorrow morning'. The marquis retired to his coach for a pipe of tobacco, doubtless glad of the chance to take shelter because a huge storm was threatening. As it broke, amid loud thunder and a downpour of hail, the allied armies advanced together to the charge and crossed the ditch right along its length. On their right, Cromwell's Eastern Association cavalry routed that of Byron opposite, and though Rupert led a counter-charge in person and checked it, David Leslie's Scottish horse were in support and came in gallantly to restore the advantage. Soon the royalist cavalry on the western flank were in flight. At the other end of the battle, however, Sir Thomas Fairfax's northern horse had to advance over very difficult ground, hotly defended, and were eventually put to flight by Goring, who went on to wreak havoc upon the Scottish infantry. Many Scots fled the field; indeed at one stage all three generals were

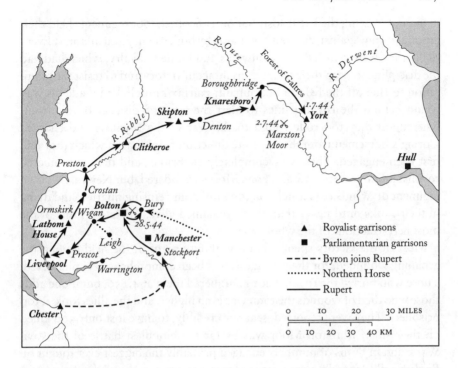

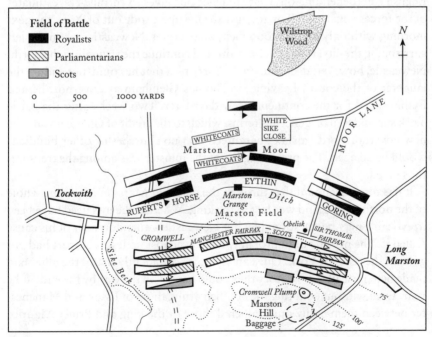

MAP 1. Marston Moor Campaign of 1644.

in flight, believing the battle lost. But other Scottish foot regiments held their ground grimly against charge after charge by both cavalry and infantry. Eventually they were relieved by Cromwell's and Leslie's cavalry, which had had the discipline to keep their formations intact in victory and to resist the temptation to ride off the field in hot pursuit. Fairfax himself had made his way round behind the royalist lines to alert them to the disaster on his front, whereupon they too rode round to the rear of the royalists and charged Goring's horsemen from the opposite direction from that in which they had first been engaged. They were completely victorious, and the outnumbered royalist infantry were now at mercy. Most surrendered, but Newcastle's own regiment of Whitecoats fought on for a full hour refusing quarter, and dying in their ranks until fewer than thirty remained alive. Theirs was one of the most heroic actions of the whole war.

Most of the victors spent a hungry, thirsty night in the field among the groaning wounded, for their waggons had been comprehensively plundered. Those who buried the royalist dead numbered them at 4,150, but if one adds those who died of wounds the total was even higher, and the allies took 1,500 prisoners. They were reported, scarcely credibly, to have lost only 300 killed on their side.[8] Marston Moor was by far the bloodiest battle of the Civil Wars, and in terms of numbers engaged probably the biggest ever fought on English soil (depending on what credence one gives to chroniclers' estimates of the forces engaged at Towton in 1461). Rupert rode out of York the next morning with only about 6,000 men, after urging Newcastle, whom he left garrisoning the city, to recruit his army and continue the struggle in the north. Newcastle, however, declined, on the sorry plea that he could 'not endure the laughter of the court'. Leaving Sir Thomas Glemham as governor, he and Eythin sailed for the continent a few days later. Two weeks after the battle York surrendered on generous terms, which to the credit of Glemham and the new governor Lord Fairfax guaranteed that no churches or other buildings would be defaced. The precious glass of the minster was among the treasures thus saved.

It has often been said that through the defeat at Marston Moor the whole of the north of England was lost to the king. Whether the loss need have been irrevocable may be questionable, but Newcastle's abandonment of his cause sealed it. The north would probably have been lost no less if Rupert had not gone to the relief of York. One can say more confidently that if the allies had made better use of their victory they could have won the war by the end of the year. Even without counting the Scottish army, those of Essex and Manchester between them easily outnumbered those of the king and Prince Maurice

---

[8] I have slightly modified the account that I gave of the numbers engaged in the battle in *Battles of the English Civil War*, ch. 3, in the light of Peter Newman's careful study, *The Battle of Marston Moor 1644* (1985).

combined, and the more local royalist forces did not approach the combined total disposed of by the Fairfaxes, Edward Massey (commander of a brigade based on Gloucester), Brereton, Meldrum, and Denbigh, not to mention the 4,000 or so that were left of Waller's troops. The failure to grasp the opportunity lay partly with the Committee of Both Kingdoms, which itself represented divided interests, but neither the Scots nor Manchester were exactly eager for total victory, and Leven in particular had an old professional's preference for keeping his army in being, rather than risking the casualties that aggressive tactics were bound to entail. But the really calamitous decision was that of Essex to pursue his attempted conquest of the west.

At first all went quite well with him. He was flattered by the welcome he received from the gentry of Devon and Dorset after he relieved Lyme, and having concerted tactics with Warwick, who carried his ammunition by sea, he reduced a whole series of towns. He threatened Exeter, where the queen had given birth on 16 June to Henrietta Anne, better known later as Charles II's beloved sister Minette. Her confinement left her in bad health and she asked Essex for a safe-conduct to Bath, so that she could get good medical care. He refused, and brutally offered instead to conduct her personally to London, knowing that parliament had voted her impeachment. She then made her way to Falmouth and took ship for France, leaving her baby behind. She and Charles never saw each other again.

The king and his council of war had meanwhile decided on 7 July that he would go to her rescue with his own army and Hopton's, with which he joined up in Bristol about a week later. When, after reaching Exeter, he added Maurice's forces to his swelling ranks he had a formidable numerical advantage over Essex, who was unaware how seriously threatened he was until almost too late. Essex appealed for reinforcement, but all that could be sent to him were 2,000 horse from Waller's ruined army, and they were intercepted and routed at Bridgwater. For all his initial welcome in Devon, very few recruits came in to him. He relieved Plymouth, but that released the besieging forces under Sir Richard Grenville to join those of the king. After leaving garrisons in the more important towns that he had taken he had about 10,000 men to pitch against at least 16,000 of the combined royal forces, which were now pursuing him purposefully. He made the almost inexplicable decision to press on westward into Cornwall, whose population was hostile almost to a man. He prepared to defend himself in Lostwithiel, sending a strong infantry detachment to secure the little port of Fowey, five miles to the south. He was short of provisions and counting on Warwick's ships to supply him, but they were constantly hampered by contrary winds. As August wore on he was more and more effectively cut off and surrounded, until on the 31st he sent out his cavalry by night. Most of them got through to the safety of Plymouth, but he strove in vain to extricate his exhausted and demoralized infantry by way of

Fowey. Charles himself was directing operations against him, and most effect- ively. Before the night was out Essex made off in a fishing-boat for Plymouth, leaving Skippon, his major-general of foot, to treat for the surrender of his men, almost 6,000 of them. They were allowed to march away with their colours, but all their arms and powder and no fewer than forty-two guns fell to the victorious royalists. It was Charles's most resounding victory, and from the start of the campaign to the finish it was essentially his own. Essex tried to lay the blame for his disaster on his enemies in parliament and on its conse- quent failure to support him, but he really had only his own obstinacy, vanity, and misjudgement to thank for it.

As has been said, however, he was by no means solely to blame for the missed opportunities of 1644. The three generals who had found themselves victorious at Marston Moor, after fleeing the field, shared a wholly mistaken opinion that Rupert's defeat would suffice to bring the king to terms, for they jointly urged parliament to pursue 'a settled peace' and rested on their laurels. Lord Fairfax arguably had enough to do in garrisoning York and reducing such royalist strongholds as remained in Yorkshire, but Leven's army relaxed for five weeks before resuming the siege of Newcastle. Manchester, after a brief stay in Doncaster, returned to Lincoln, where he was impervious alike to the Committee of Both Kingdoms' orders to go to the rescue of Essex and to his own officers' pleas to move against Newark. Under their pressure he did allow them to reduce two or three minor garrisons, but he seemed reluctant to engage in any further action whatsoever. Lieutenant-Colonel John Lil- burne, the future Leveller leader who commanded his dragoons, asked his leave to move against Tickhill Castle, which was waiting only for a pretext to surrender. 'Get thee gone!', he replied angrily, 'thou art a mad fellow'; and when Lilburne took Tickhill without a shot fired, Manchester dressed him down furiously in front of the prisoners he had taken. He did in the end respond to peremptory orders from the Committee of Both Kingdoms to go to the aid of Waller, who was retreating through Dorset and Wiltshire before the king's much stronger forces, but he moved so dilatorily that his infantry were still in Reading on 17 October.

Manchester was no coward, and he held no traffic with the royalists until the later 1650s, but he hoped and believed that 'this war would not be ended by the sword'.[9] His gentle, humane nature was probably shocked by the slaughter and suffering he had seen, and like most parliamentarian aristocrats he thought that a lasting peace needed to be achieved by negotiation, on terms that both sides could honourably accept. That would have been a tenable point of view if the king had shared it, but he did not. Essex's surrender had

[9] C. Holmes, *The Eastern Association in the English Civil War* (Cambridge, 1974), pp. 197–8.

revived Charles's hopes of winning the war outright, though he was not (as some feared at Westminster) contemplating an advance on London that year. He spent most of September trying vainly to take Plymouth, then moved eastward in mid-October with the object of relieving his beleaguered garrisons in Basing House, Donnington Castle, and Banbury. This is what spurred even Manchester into obeying orders, for the royal army was within fifty miles of London. The Eastern Association army effected a junction with Waller's remaining forces, Essex's now rearmed infantry and a brigade of London trained bands. Together they numbered about 18,000, very nearly twice as many as the king had after sending a detachment to raise the siege of Banbury. The royal army prepared to engage them from a strong position just north of Newbury, but well chosen though it was the parliamentarians had the opportunity to inflict a crippling blow on it, and in the battle fought on 27 October they bungled it. Divided command was part of the problem, for Essex was laid up sick in Reading. An over-ambitious plan of battle, involving a thirteen-mile march by night and a simultaneous attack on the royalists' front and rear, came unstuck largely because Manchester's arm of the pincer moved very late.[10] The outcome of the fight was still uncertain when darkness broke it off, but the king's council of war wisely decided not to renew it in the morning, and his army made good its retreat to Oxford. As it did so the parliamentarians held their own acrimonious council of war. Manchester predictably opposed any further action, and was persuaded only with difficulty to let Waller, Haselrig, and Cromwell take their cavalry off in pursuit—too late to do anything effective.

After some ineffective manoeuvres the parliamentarians tried to storm Donnington Castle, where the king's train of artillery had found a safe refuge, but they were repulsed with quite heavy casualties. They laid siege to it, but the appearance of the king and his army on 9 November forced them to draw off. The royalists took up battle positions just outside Newbury, challenging them to fight, but the third battle of Newbury did not take place, because the parliamentarian council of war declined it. Manchester urged the case against it. 'The king cares not how oft he fights,' he said, 'but it concerns us to be wary, for in fighting we venture all to nothing. If we beat the king ninety-nine times he would be king still, and his posterity, and we subjects still; but if he beat us but once we should be hanged, and our posterity be undone.' 'My lord,' Cromwell replied, 'if this be so, why did we take up arms at first? This is against fighting ever hereafter. If so, let us make peace, be it never so base.'[11]

---

[10] An attempt to shift the blame for the failure of co-ordination from Manchester to Cromwell is made by Dr T. J. Halsall in *Cromwelliana* (1996), pp. 37–8. I find it unconvincing.

[11] My version of Manchester's words is a conflation of Haselrig's and Cromwell's recollections of his words, which agree closely in substance. Both are printed in Abbott, *Writings and Speeches of Oliver Cromwell*, I, 299, 310.

But Manchester as senior officer had his way, and the royal army marched off the field in triumph. The relief force that Charles sent to Basing House found the siege already raised.

When his army went into winter quarters around Oxford it was 15,000 strong and in better fettle for the next year's campaigns than could ever have been expected in the early summer. The progress of the war so far is an object-lesson against the supposition, once common among non-military historians, that its outcome was inevitable because parliament commanded superior resources (above all through London's support) and exploited them more effectively, or because it had one social class or another mainly on its side. Parliament's superiority in resources is unquestionable, but wars are commonly won in the field, and the English Civil War was no exception. So long as the royal forces were (on balance) better led; so long as their officers could fire their men to fight as Hopton's Cornishmen or Newcastle's Whitecoats or most of the royalist cavalry troopers fought; above all so long as a greater will to win prevailed in the king's council of war than among the politicians who attempted to direct the allies' armies and among most of their senior commanders, the royalists could overcome their material disadvantages and spring up again after setbacks—even after such a defeat as Marston Moor. It is remarkable that they were in as strong a position as they were after two years of warfare, and it was not a foregone conclusion that their run of fortune was bound to come to an end. It depended on whether the parliament was prepared to shake up its ramshackle armies, concentrate its war effort, dedicate itself to total victory, and commit its forces in the field to commanders single-minded in pursuit of it. All these things would eventually be achieved, but not without a struggle.

That the royalists had succeeded against the odds so far was largely because of Charles's indomitable will, strengthened as it was by a steady faith that God would not let the cause of his anointed go under. His council of war was often divided in its advice, but the decision always rested ultimately with him, and he missed few opportunities and made few mistakes. He now decided to make Rupert his Captain-General, having the pretext that old Forth (now Earl of Brentford), who was far past his best, had been wounded at Newbury. It was a sign that he was looking forward to an aggressive strategy in 1645, but the appointment was to cause problems. Rupert outshone his rivals in military talent, but he was on bad terms with other powerful men on the council of war, especially Digby and Culpepper, and he was not liked by the royalist nobility. They were partly placated when George Goring, the Earl of Norwich's son, succeeded Rupert as general of the horse. Goring was a brave soldier and (when sober) a skilled leader of cavalry, but he was personally ambitious and not too good at obeying orders. He immediately began to intrigue for an independent command, and he soon wangled one. It was to contribute to the outcome of the decisive battle of the war in 1645.

Two days after Marston Moor, one of those meetings took place that make historians dream of a time machine and a chance to eavesdrop. It was at Richmond in Yorkshire, where Rupert, still in the first bitterness of defeat, was joined by Montrose, a marquis now but still lacking the means to execute the king's commission to raise royalist Scotland. There was no news of the 2,000 Ulstermen whom Antrim had undertaken to contribute to the enterprise. Montrose asked Rupert for 1,000 horse, but understandably none could be spared, so he set off for Scotland again with just two trusted companions, they dressed as troopers in Leven's army and he as their groom. He did not know that 1,600 exiled Macdonalds and Macleans, raised by Antrim in Ulster, had just landed at Ardnamurchan, the most westerly point of Argyllshire. They were commanded by Antrim's kinsman Alasdair MacColla, whom the Lowlanders were to call Colkitto, though Coll Keitach ('Coll who can fight with either hand') was actually his father's nickname. For six days MacColla had to live in hiding, for he soon had a Covenanting force on his tail and very few clansmen came in to him. But he managed to get a message to Montrose, and the two men met in the nick of time at Blair Atholl. Montrose, whose authority as the king's lieutenant in Scotland MacColla gladly accepted, raised the royal standard, and before the government in Edinburgh knew he was in the country he had the beginnings of an army. But it numbered at most 2,700, nearly all infantry, when Lord Elcho brought it to battle on 1 September at Tippermuir near Perth. Elcho had nearly 7,000 foot and 700 horse, properly armed, whereas Montrose's third line of infantry had only stones to fight with and MacColla's musketeers had only one round apiece. Yet a wild Highland charge routed Elcho's none too warlike levies, of whom hundreds were slain in the ensuing pursuit. Perth surrendered to Montrose without a shot fired. He allowed no violence or pillage, but he took a fair booty in cannon and hand weapons and cloth, to arm his ragged soldiers and warm them through the coming winter.

  This first of his brilliant run of victories struck consternation among the Covenanters in both Edinburgh and London, and caused troops to be recalled to Scotland from the forces besieging Newcastle, which did not surrender to them until 19 October. The drain was to continue as his successes multiplied during 1645, and the Committee of Estates quite failed to check them by putting a price of £1,500 on his head. He had not enough troops, however, to garrison Perth, which Argyll retook on 11 September, and he failed in an attempt on Dundee. It was a recurrent problem that as soon as his clansmen got their hands on some booty they made off home with it, so he had constantly to keep recruiting. It was the hope of raising men in Huntly territory that took him next to Aberdeen, but he found Lord Burleigh barring his way into the city with at least 2,000 foot and 500 horse, and Argyll was on the way with a larger army. On 13 September Montrose summoned the city magistrates to surrender, warning them that if they refused the inhabitants could expect no quarter. Refuse they did, and a drummer-boy who accompanied his envoy was treacherously shot dead as the two returned. Furious, Montrose promised MacColla the sack of the city, and with a mere 1,500 foot and 70 horse they fell on Burleigh's Covenanters. In a fight lasting several hours they routed them with heavy slaughter, giving no quarter to men under arms. The city was then looted for three whole days, during which about 150 unarmed citizens were killed, including old men, women, and children. It was an atrocity uncharacteristic of Montrose, and one wonders how far it was due to sudden rage and how far to the problem of holding together such a force as his, and particularly Macdonald's Irishmen, when regular pay was so hard to provide. It spoilt his chances of recruiting in Aberdeenshire, and it gave fuel to the Covenanting propaganda that depicted him as a cruel marauder, threatening civilized Scotland with a band of bloodthirsty popish barbarians.

He was on the defensive during October and November, for Colkitto and many of his men left Montrose temporarily in order to attack the Campbells and drum up recruits in Macdonald territory. He had only 800 foot and 50 horse when Argyll caught up with him near Fyvie Castle with a force five times as large, but he fought his way free. When MacColla rejoined him in Atholl late in November his army totalled about 3,000, for the fame of his exploits was making recruitment in the Highlands much easier. But Lieutenant-General William Baillie, a professional who had done distinguished service under Gustavus Adolphus, had been recalled from Leven's army to take command of the Covenanting forces in Scotland. Henceforth Montrose faced a sterner challenge. He also had to recognize that many of his and Mac-Colla's clansmen had enlisted to fight not so much for the king as against the Campbells, so in December he led them deep into Campbell country, which they torched and ravaged mercilessly, causing considerable loss of life. Argyll, who had hastened home to defend Inverary, fled at their approach, and for the rest of the year they lived high on the fat of their old foes' land. Whatever more they might accomplish, they had already depleted the Scottish army in England and lowered the stock of the Covenanters, not least in English eyes. 'This is the greatest hurt our poor land got these fourscore year', wrote commissioner Robert Baillie from London; 'it has much diminished our reputation in England already.'[12] Thanks to Montrose, it was going to be harder to force the less popular provisions of the Solemn League and Covenant down English throats.

[12] Quoted in D. Stevenson, *Revolution and Counter-Revolution in Scotland, 1644-1651* (1977), pp. 24-5.

Back in England one sorry piece of unfinished business, closely linked with the religious settlement, was wound up in the winter of 1644–5. Archbishop Laud had lain in the Tower for over three years before parliament, at the insistence of the Scots, proceeded with his impeachment in March 1644. His former victim William Prynne had the managing of the charges against him, which he did with a bigotry and malevolence that stooped to tampering with witnesses and 'editing' Laud's diary to make it more damning as evidence. Even so, as the proceedings dragged on into the autumn, it became doubtful whether the remnant of the Lords who still attended would convict him of treason (which of course he had not committed), so the Commons switched to an ordinance of attainder, as they had with Strafford, though now they did not have the king's assent to worry about. They sent it up to the Lords on 22 November, but despite pressure from the London mob the peers held out against passing it until 4 January. The 71-year-old prelate was beheaded on Tower Hill, as Strafford had been, and he died as bravely. The Hothams, father and son, had suffered the same fate there a few days earlier, for trying to betray Hull. Unlike them, Laud had never broken faith and had long ceased to pose a threat to the parliament. The malignity with which it pursued him to death is a stain on its cause.

# TEN

# Towards a Resolution

IT was clear by the end of the 1644 campaigning season that if the parliament was to win the war it must concentrate its resources and reorganize its armies. Yet if the need was obvious, the obstacles to fulfilling it were formidable. For a start there was the problem of military leadership. Essex would take some shifting; his standing in parliament was not as badly damaged by his recent defeat as might have been expected, he still had powerful friends and allies, and he remained popular with all who hoped as he did for a negotiated peace. Waller had once seemed a plausible alternative commander, for he had shown an altogether stronger fighting spirit. But Cropredy Bridge and the second battle of Newbury had exposed serious limitations in his generalship, and by his own later admission he had become 'so perfectly tired with the drudgery' of military command that he was ready to lay it down.[1] As for Manchester, whose Eastern Association army had once been the white hope of the war party, he had become so reluctant to engage it in action that a running quarrel had developed between him and Cromwell, his Lieutenant-General.

War-weariness in the country at large and divisions at Westminster were further impediments to the forging of the means of victory. Vane, St John, Saye, and other surviving stalwarts of Pym's old middle group were finding it hard to hold a solid parliamentarian centre together in support of the war effort, whilst fending off a defeatist peace party on the one hand and a disruptively radical tendency on the other. During 1644 parliament increasingly tended to polarize between two parties, which came to be commonly referred to as the Presbyterians and the Independents. As the nomenclature implied, religious differences had much to do with this division, but religion was never the sole reason for it and the labels were partly misleading. The old middle group and the original war party coalesced in the Independents, who covered a broad political spectrum and were not homogeneous. The Presbyterians included the old peace party, though some who were Presbyterian in religion were strongly committed to the war effort. The political differences

---

[1] J. Adair, *Roundhead General* (1969), p. 176, quoting Waller's *Vindication* (1793), p. 109.

between the parties at this stage have often been exaggerated, for neither was contemplating a post-war settlement that would exclude the king; Henry Marten was almost alone in having voiced such a possibility. Several historians have followed Gardiner in believing a report that Vane, when he was sent as an emissary from parliament to Leven, Manchester, and Fairfax during the siege of York, was briefed by his fellow-Independents to enlist the generals' support for deposing the king, as an agreed war aim. But the story rests only on the speculative tattle of foreign diplomats, and is profoundly improbable.[2] Vane, like Cromwell and Saye and other leading Independents, would still be seeking for means to reinstate the king on safe and honourable conditions more than three years later. The parties differed on the terms rather than the principle of a future settlement, and religion was a major point of difference.

It came to the fore because all through 1644 the Westminster Assembly was debating the form of government which it would recommend for the Church of England. The Scottish Commissioners were pressing for the pure Presbyterian model, with a church session exerting its coercive jurisdiction in every parish, with parishes grouped in classical presbyteries, provincial synods elected by and from the presbyteries, a national synod at the summit, and with lay participation by ruling elders at every tier of the pyramidal structure. Since episcopalians were unrepresented in the Assembly, most of the English divines were prepared to endorse such a system in its essentials, but they were persistently opposed by a small group of Independents who became known as the Dissenting Brethren. In January 1644 the five most prominent of them published *An Apologetical Narration*, in order to distinguish their position from those of the Presbyterians on the one hand and of the separatists or sectaries on the other. They were all men of learning, trained in the universities and ordained in the Church of England, who had gone into voluntary exile during the Laudian regime and ministered to congregations of their fellow-exiles in Holland. There they had followed 'the congregational way', like their brethren in New England. Unlike the separatists they fully accepted the authority of the civil power and valued a partnership with it, so long as it did not oppress the churches over essential matters of faith and conscience. Doctrine was not a point at issue, for in theology these moderate Independents professed a common Calvinist orthodoxy with the Presbyterians. What they rejected was the concept, common to Anglicans and Presbyterians, of a church co-terminous with the nation, embracing saints and sinners alike; they could never accept that church membership was conferred merely by being born and baptized in a parish. A true church for them could consist only of a congregation of committed believers, men and women who had given mature

---

[2] Compare Gardiner, *History of the Great Civil War*, I, 430–1 and Wedgwood, *King's War*, p. 349 with Woolrych, *Battles of the English Civil War*, p. 88, and L. Kaplan, *Politics and Religion during the English Revolution* (New York, 1976), pp. 55–6.

testimony of their faith and entered into a mutual covenant to live in accordance with it. Every such 'gathered church', they held, should have the right to choose its own pastor and the power to discipline its members, even in the last resort to cast them out; so the Presbyterians' entrustment of ordination and excommunication to presbyteries was unacceptable to them. But they did not claim the total autonomy for each congregation that most separatists demanded, for besides accepting (within limits) the civil magistrate's authority over their churches their ideal lay in a kind of federal association. They acknowledged the right of sister-churches to meet and censure a congregation that fell into error, and to renounce communion with it if it proved incorrigible, but they rejected the power claimed by presbyteries and synods to deliver whole churches over to Satan. They did not like being called Independents, because they believed 'the truth to lie and consist in a middle way betwixt that which is falsely charged on us, Brownism, and that which is the contention of these times, the authoritative Presbyterial government in all the subordinations and proceedings of it'. They asked only for 'a latitude to some lesser differences with peaceableness'.[3]

Few though they were in the Assembly, the Independents had powerful supporters in parliament, including Cromwell, Vane, and St John in the Commons and Saye and Wharton in the Lords. These and most other lay Independents were strongly committed to a vigorous prosecution of the war, so it is understandable that 'Independent' became a loose label for all who pursued total victory and 'Presbyterian' for those who would have preferred a negotiated peace. It was also generally true that most Independents advocated some degree of liberty of conscience in religion, whereas most Presbyterians favoured the continuance of a single national church, conformity to which would be enforced by the state. Yet the labels could be misleading, partly because many peace-party politicians were at best lukewarm Presbyterians in religion, and would have preferred a limited episcopacy and a modified Anglican liturgy if that option had been open, and partly because there were committed religious Presbyterians like Zouch Tate and Samuel Brown who were keen to fight the war to a finish. There were also a few radical Independents like Henry Marten and Thomas Chaloner who were virtual freethinkers, and anything but puritan in their morals. It would be perverse to eschew altogether the use of terms that were so widely employed at the time, but it is often necessary to distinguish between the political and religious senses of Presbyterian and Independent, since the correlation between them was so imperfect. It may help here if 'Presbyterian' and 'Independent' are henceforth spelt with capital initials when they denote religious denominations, and without capi-

---

[3] Tho. Goodwin and others, *An Apologetical Narration* (1644), pp. 24, 31; facsimile in W. Haller, *Tracts on Liberty in the Puritan Revolution* (3 vols., New York, 1934), II.

tals when they refer to the opposed political groupings—'parties' suggests a greater degree of identity, coherence, and organization than actually existed in the 1640s, though the term is hard to avoid.

There was a social dimension to the mutual opposition between Presbyterians and Independents. Politicians like Cromwell, Vane, and St John would have extended freedom of worship not only to their fellow-Independents but to the more peaceable sects—Baptists, Seekers, and others—which were proliferating in the unsettled climate of the 1640s. Conservative souls, however, distrusted the whole principle of electing ministers of religion, and were horrified by the prospect of giving free rein to sectarian tub-preachers with no academic credentials, elected by their fellow-plebeians. They might feel uncomfortable over the authority about to be given to lay elders, many of whom were bound to be of the middling sort, but the Westminster Assembly promised the continuance of a single, exclusive national church in which the majority of the parish clergy would go on being chosen by wealthy gentry patrons. Such a church was likely to cement the existing structures of society, whereas sectarian preachers were seen as potential social dynamite.

There was particular concern among the orthodox and conservative over the high proportion of religious radicals in Cromwell's cavalry. Cromwell, in his efforts to enlist men who knew what they were fighting for and loved what they knew, had found them mainly among those who saw their cause as that of the people of God, and many of them were puritan enthusiasts. He was accused unjustly of favouring sectaries at the expense of moderate, orthodox men, for he did not probe into their beliefs if he sensed that they had what he called 'the root of the matter' in them. He had a famous row in March 1644 with the commander of the infantry in Manchester's army, Major-General Crawford, a narrow Presbyterian Scot who arrested the lieutenant-colonel of his own regiment and sent him up to headquarters, apparently because he was unwilling, as a Baptist, to sign the Covenant. It was hardly the place of the lieutenant-general of horse to rebuke the major-general of foot for disciplining his own subordinate for not complying with the law as laid down by parliament, but rebuke him Cromwell did:

Sir [he wrote], the state, in choosing men to serve them, takes no notice of their opinions; if they be willing faithfully to serve them, that satisfies . . . Take heed of being sharp . . . against those to whom you can object little but that they square not with you in every opinion concerning matters of religion.[4]

For a while after this episode he did promote Independents and sectaries in preference to rigid Presbyterians, not because of the latter's religious convictions but because of their intolerance towards comrades-in-arms who did not

---

[4] Abbott, *Writings and Speeches of Oliver Cromwell*, I, 278.

share them. But the phase did not last long, and his true spirit spoke in his dispatch to the Speaker after the New Model Army's heroic storming of Bristol in 1645: 'Presbyterians, Independents, all had here the same spirit of faith and prayer, the same presence and answer; they agree here, know no names of difference: pity it is it should be otherwise anywhere.'[5]

Such sentiments were anathema to the Scots, and they helped to bring about an interesting reversal of alliances in the course of 1644. When the Scots first came into the war, they saw Pym's middle group and the war party as their natural allies, and the abortive treaty of Oxford deepened their suspicions of the peace party. Several things changed this alignment, and turned them particularly against Cromwell: his quarrel with Crawford, followed by his demand for the man's dismissal; the excessive credit that they thought he received for the victory of Marston Moor; and above all the so-called Accommodation Order which Cromwell and St John piloted through the Commons in September. This was a directive to the parliamentary committee that was then in liaison with the Scottish commissioners and a committee of the Assembly divines, and it requested them 'to endeavour the finding out some way how far tender consciences, who cannot in all things submit to the common rule which shall be established, may be borne with according to the Word'.[6] This was moderate enough, and its immediate effects were slight, but the Scots saw it as a betrayal of the Covenant's commitment to a common religious uniformity based on the faith and practice of their Kirk. They drew steadily closer to the presbyterians, partly because the latter were friendlier towards their religious aspirations and partly out of a shared hostility towards Cromwell and the independents.

Furthermore the Scots lost their appetite for outright victory when they began to fear that it would carry the independents to ascendancy, a prospect so disturbing that they came to share the presbyterians' predilection for a negotiated peace. The Scottish commissioners, indeed, were the main initiators of a new set of peace proposals which parliament approved and sent to the king in November 1644, and on which the so-called treaty of Uxbridge was conducted early in the new year. There is no need to consider them in detail, for they made demands that would have been excessive even if the parliamentarians and the Scots had found the means to beat the king in the field, which so far they had not. No wonder Charles told the commissioners who brought him these preposterous proposals that there were three things he would not part with, his church, his crown, and his friends—'and you will have much ado to get them from me', he added.[7] Nevertheless it suited him to

---

[5] Abbott, *Writings and Speeches of Oliver Cromwell*, I, p. 377.    [6] Ibid., p. 294.
[7] Quoted in Gardiner, *Great Civil War*, II, 25; text of the propositions of Uxbridge in Gardiner (ed.), *Constitutional Documents*, pp. 275–86.

appear amenable to overtures for peace, and the peace party did not give up on the Uxbridge treaty until late in February 1645.

Long before then the parliament was riven by an altogether more serious debate. This opened on 25 November when, at the Commons' request, Waller and Cromwell gave their accounts of what had gone wrong in the recent campaign. Widely though they differed in their politics and religion, both men were heavily critical of Manchester, and both pressed the point that the war could not be won while three armies in varying degrees of delapidation were competing for parliament's resources. Cromwell's accusations against Manchester were detailed and devastating, indicting his 'continued backwardness to all action' with a frankness remarkable enough in a commoner criticizing an earl but sensational, and to many shocking, in a second-in-command publicly censuring his own general. He did acknowledge, however, that Manchester was motivated by a sincere conviction that the issues between king and parliament should not be resolved by war. Manchester, replying in the Lords, made counter-accusations of a more personal kind. One was that Cromwell had said 'he hoped to live to see never a nobleman in England', which sounds improbable, since Cromwell remained a believer in social hierarchy all his life. Others were that he had called the Assembly divines persecutors, and said that he would as soon draw his sword against the Scots as against any in the king's army, and that he wanted none but Independents in his own.[8] These were not Cromwell's considered sentiments, but his temper had a short fuse, and words he had spoken in heat may have been heightened in the telling.

While the Commons' Committee for the Army was considering the evidence against Manchester, Essex summoned the Scottish commissioners and five MPs including the Presbyterian leaders Denzil Holles and Sir Philip Stapleton, to a secret conference at Essex House, late at night on 3 December. They met to consider a proposal by the Scots that Cromwell should be impeached before parliament as an incendiary between the English and Scottish nations, in breach of the Solemn League and Covenant. Holles and Stapleton were all for proceeding, but the lawyer-MPs Bulstrode Whitelocke and John Maynard persuaded the Scots that Cromwell had too much support in parliament for the charges to stick.

Cromwell was not pursuing a personal vendetta against Manchester, nor did he relish the antagonisms within and between the two Houses that their quarrel was generating. He was waiting only for the Committee of the Army to endorse the evidence of Manchester's persistent unwillingness to fight since

---

[8] Quoted in Ian Gentles, *The New Model Army in England, Ireland and Scotland, 1645–1653* (Oxford, 1992), pp. 4–5. The sources for the whole episode are printed in D. Masson (ed.), *The Quarrel Between the Earl of Manchester and Oliver Cromwell* (Camden Society, 1875).

the fall of York. It did so when it reported to the House on 9 December, and towards the end of a long debate he rose to make the most important speech of his career so far. The long continuance of the war, he said, had brought the nation into such a state of misery that unless they conducted it more urgently and effectively they would make the people hate the name of a parliament.

> For what do the enemy say? Nay, what do many say that were friends at the beginning of the parliament? Even this, that the members of both Houses have got great places and commands, and . . . will perpetually continue themselves in grandeur, and not permit the war speedily to end, lest their own power should determine with it . . . If I may speak my conscience without reflection upon any, I do conceive if the army be not put into another method, and the war more vigorously prosecuted, the people can bear the war no longer, and will enforce you to a dishonourable peace.[9]

So let them cease pursuing particular complaints against any one commander, since none was infallible, but apply themselves rather to the necessary remedy; and he hoped no member of either House would take offence at it, or hesitate to sacrifice private interests for the public good.

He did not directly specify the remedy, but he was plainly colluding with the chairman of the Committee for the Army, Zouch Tate, a Presbyterian but a firm believer in fighting to a finish. Tate immediately moved, as from his committee, that for the duration of the war no member of either House should hold any military command or civil office conferred by parliament. Vane seconded him, offering to give up his own post as Treasurer of the Navy. Such a Self-Denying Ordinance was one half of the remedy; the other would be a thorough recasting of the parliament's military forces, but that would be fruitless unless they were put under commanders with a whole-hearted will to win. Removing Essex and Manchester was the first problem to be faced, though there were other peace party peers and MPs holding less exalted commands. To have sought their individual dismissal would have caused huge offence to honourable men and deepened already serious divisions, but to call for a sacrifice by *all* legislators who held places of profit was practical politics, though it was much resisted. It was an imperfect solution, for it proposed to end the military careers not only of seven peers, who were mostly of the peace party, but of seventeen MPs, including Cromwell himself, Waller, Lord Fairfax (MP for Yorkshire—his Scottish peerage gave him no seat in the Lords), Haselrig, Brereton, and half-a-dozen others who were equally committed to total victory. Waller was not sorry to go, and Fairfax was over sixty, but for Cromwell to have hung up his sword would have been a serious military loss. Yet the indications are that he accepted the necessity and thought it worthwhile. He told the Commons that the recall of their fellow-members to Westminster 'will not break, or scatter our armies. I can speak this for my own

⁹ Abbott, *Writings and Speeches of Oliver Cromwell*, I, 314.

soldiers, that they look not upon me, but upon you; and for you they will fight, and live and die in your cause.'[10] From an early date it was suspected that he was counting on being personally exempted from the ordinance, as eventually he was; but there was just such an attempt to exempt Essex, which his allies narrowly defeated, and Cromwell could hardly have expected them to treat him differently. The loophole that would permit his continuance in the army lay in the future.[11]

The twin measures which were to transform the conduct of the war, the Self-Denying Ordinance and its follow-up the New Model Ordinance, were not the product solely of the war party leaders in the Commons. They were devised in concert with a small group of like-minded peers, chief among them Viscount Saye and Sele, who had been St John's patron in the 1630s, and also including Lord Wharton and a convert from the peace party, the Earl of Northumberland. These formed a coherent group with their allies in the Commons, a group that some historians have called the royal independents, and which was to assume even more importance between the first and second Civil Wars. Saye proposed the principle of self-denial in the Lords on the same day that it was first moved in the Commons, but the peers took great offence, seeing it as aimed primarily against their own members, and promptly rejected it. When the Self-Denying Ordinance formally came up to them from the Commons, who passed it on 19 December, they laid it aside and resisted all pressure to take it into consideration until 13 January, when they threw it out; only four peers then recorded their dissents.

What finally prodded them into action was the reading of the New Model Ordinance, which the Commons had passed without a division. This measure had three main objects. One was to forge a genuinely national army out of the remnants of the earlier ones, an army free of the regional ties which had made Waller's London trained bands and Manchester's East Anglian foot look over their shoulders when they had been away from home ground for any length of time. A second aim was to create a fully professional army whose officers were wholly dedicated to prosecuting the war, with no political by-ends. Thirdly, this army was to have an undisputed first call on parliament's financial resources. The creation of so powerful a force aroused the deepest misgivings in the Lords, especially since peers were to be precluded from holding command in it. Its promoters sought to forestall opposition, however, by writing the names of its generals and colonels into the ordinance itself, and by letting it be known that the peace negotiations at Uxbridge would not proceed unless parliament first committed itself to remodelling its forces.

[10]  Ibid., p. 316.
[11]  For slightly different readings of Cromwell's motives and expectations compare J. S. A. Adamson, 'Oliver Cromwell and the Long Parliament' in J. Morrill (ed.), *Oliver Cromwell and the English Revolution*, pp. 61–5, with my own chapter in the same volume at p. 102.

The choice of a commander-in-chief was far from simple, because the Self-Denying Ordinance ruled out almost everyone who had commanded any-thing larger than a regiment. Massey and Skippon were exceptions, but Massey was a strong presbyterian who had sided with the king in 1642 and would do so again in 1647. Skippon was nominated to the post to which his experience best suited him, that of major-general of the infantry. For that of General of the New Model Army the choice fell boldly on Sir Thomas Fair-fax. He was only thirty-two, he had no pre-war military experience, his high-est command had been that of the horse in his father's small army, and he had not been lucky at Adwalton Moor or Marston Moor. But wherever he had fought he had shown the dash and flair of a born leader of cavalry; his nor-mally mild nature was fired in the furnace of battle to a white heat, which he communicated instinctively to his officers and men. A further virtue was that he had no known political leanings beyond a steady devotion to the parlia-ment's cause, and in religion he was a devout but undogmatic puritan. Cromwell had seen him in action more than once, and it may further have helped him that his father had corresponded with Wharton and Northum-berland. The vote to appoint him, taken in the Commons on 21 January, was a trial of party strength, with Cromwell and Vane as tellers for the 101 ayes and Holles and Stapleton for the 69 noes.

The Lords delayed passing the New Model Ordinance until 15 February, despite constant pressure from the Commons, and they disputed the lists of officers submitted by Fairfax for more than a month after that. Although Fairfax proposed no one for the service who did not already hold a commis-sion, they tried to make no fewer than 57 changes in his recommendations, and most of them were politically motivated; 35 of the 52 officers whom they tried to demote or remove were independents or men of radical views. They tried to make every officer take the Covenant and undertake to conform to the church government to be settled by parliament, and to cashier or disqual-ify any who refused. Under extreme pressure from the Commons and the City, and under the threat of both to withhold essential financial provisions until they gave way, an evenly divided House of Lords finally approved Fair-fax's nominees on 18 March with the help of the proxy vote of his own grand-father, the Earl of Mulgrave. Even then the new army was not in the clear, for at the end of the month Essex, Manchester, and Denbigh had still not resigned their commissions, and the presbyterian peers were holding up Fairfax's because it did not bind him, as previous commanders had been bound, to pre-serve the safety of the king's person. Without his parliamentary commission, Fairfax had no legal authority to discipline what was left of Essex's infantry, who were in a state of mutiny. Earlier, some of Essex's cavalry had refused to serve under Waller when the latter had been ordered to take them to the relief of Weymouth, which was under severe threat by royalist forces. By their obstructiveness the Lords were jeopardizing the whole parliamentarian war effort, and they still had not passed the Self-Denying Ordinance. The Commons, to break the deadlock, passed a modified ordinance which discharged all members of both Houses from their military commands or civil offices, but gave them forty days' grace and did not debar them from being reappointed. The Lords then approved Fairfax's commission by one vote; Essex, Manchester, and Denbigh resigned their commands on 2 April, and the second Self-Denying Ordinance passed the Upper House next day. Ironically, it paved the way for Cromwell's later appointment to the command of the cavalry in the New Model Army, which so far was left vacant.

Mere pique and injured pride seem inadequate explanations of the tenacity with which the Lords obstructed the measures essential for the continuance of the war. It has been persuasively argued that Essex and his allies had, since at least 1642, been nursing a dream of a resurgent aristocracy, in which the power-vacuum left by the king's incapacity to rule would be filled by the magnates as his 'natural' counsellors. There is some evidence that Essex's aim was to have the medieval office of Lord High Constable, which had carried supreme military authority, revived for him, as a possible step towards even more vice-regal powers. His repeated failures to obey the Committee of Both Kingdoms' directions may be attributable to an ambition to be the master of the war and the architect of the peace—an ambition to which the New Model Army and its political sponsors were fatal obstacles. Not all the peers supported him, of course. At the same time as parliament finally passed the New Model Ordinance it appointed Northumberland, Saye's ally and the senior peer still attending the Lords, as Governor of the king's children, and it was reported that if Charles refused reasonable terms of settlement, his youngest son, the eight-year-old Duke of Gloucester, would be made king and Northumberland Lord Protector. The new elevation of Northumberland looks very like an aristocratic move to scupper Essex's pretensions once and for all.[12]

Sheer military necessity forced the Committee of Both Kingdoms, with the Commons' backing, to go ahead with forming the New Model Army before it received parliament's legislative blessing. It was to consist of 6,600 cavalry, 1,000 dragoons, and 14,400 infantry, and the general aim was to embody in it intact such units in the existing armies as had proved their military worth. Fairfax was entrusted with the nomination of all officers below colonel, and he faithfully observed the principle of keeping together officers and men who had already forged a bond in war. Despite acute Scottish suspicions to the

---

[12] J. S. A. Adamson, 'The baronial context of the English Civil War', *Transactions of the Royal Historical Society*, 5th series 40, pp. 93–120 (esp. 105–19). I do not attribute quite as much motive force to aristocratic faction as Dr Adamson does, and I believe Fairfax to have been chosen more on his military merits than as the candidate of the Saye–Northumberland group, but it is a most interesting argument.

contrary, there was no deliberate design to create an army of a specific political or religious complexion; the overriding criterion was military effectiveness. The senior officers named in the ordinance covered a wide ideological
spectrum, though the greater commitment of Independents both religious
and political to outright victory gave them a certain preponderance. Proven
fighting quality ensured the embodiment of most of Cromwell's Eastern
Association cavalry, which furnished five of the New Model's original regiments of horse.

There was no difficulty in filling the ranks of the cavalry, indeed quite a
number of redundant officers enlisted as troopers. The service carried much
more prestige and better pay and conditions than the infantry enjoyed. A
trooper's two shillings a day was about twice what he basically needed to feed
man and horse, whereas a foot soldier's eightpence was the wage of a common labourer, and his rations in the field usually consisted only of cheese with
bread or biscuit. The infantry of the older armies were so depleted that just
over half of the New Model foot had to be raised by conscription, and they
were not raised easily. An impressment ordinance was hurriedly passed at the
end of February, and most of the burden fell on London, which had to find
2,500 men, and on Norfolk, Suffolk, Essex, and Kent, whose quota was 1,000
apiece. None of these targets was easily met, and the pressed men were so
prone to mutiny or desert that they had to be guarded all the way to their regiments. They were drawn from the lowest levels of society, for anyone worth
£3 in land or £5 in goods was exempt, and so were a whole range of occupations from students to seamen. Death was the penalty prescribed for desert-
ers, but many were homeless men who had little trouble in disappearing
without trace. During the New Model's first year nearly twice as many men
were impressed as actually served in it for any length of time, for desertion
rendered it chronically short of infantry, who were down to only 8,000 late in
September 1645. As Ian Gentles has written, 'conscripting infantry in 1645–6
was like ladling water into a leaky bucket'.[13] Fairfax reportedly said at the end
of the war that his best private soldiers were the many former royalists who
had promptly enlisted in his army after being captured.[14] By that time many
of them knew no other occupation. The problem of recruitment did ease,
however, as the New Model's reputation rose on its tide of victories, whereas
for the royalists it became ever more acute.

The New Model was certainly better armed and equipped than its predecessors, and it was the first English army to wear uniform: red coats faced

---

[13] Gentles, *New Model Army*, p. 33. In all that concerns the formation of the army I am greatly indebted to Dr Gentles's work. Mark A. Kishlansky also throws much light on the subject in
*The Rise of the New Model Army* (Cambridge, 1979), though on some points of interpretation
he is questionable.

[14] C. H. Firth, *Cromwell's Army* (3rd ed., 1921), p. 37, citing Sir Philip Warwick's *Memoirs*.

with blue (Fairfax's colour) and grey breeches. It was even paid fairly regularly while the war lasted, but that did not stop its men from taking free quarter and 'liberating' large quantities of livestock, bacon, beer, grain, firewood, and household goods wherever they marched. Its discipline and its reputation for paying its way improved markedly after its run of victories began at Naseby, but in its early months many of its infantry behaved as one would expect of unwilling conscripts. 'An ungodly crew', Sir Samuel Luke, the Presbyterian governor of Newport Pagnell, found them as they advanced towards their first battle; 'I think these New Modellers knead all their dough with ale, for I never see so many drunk in my life in so short a time.'[15]

Hostile commentators, both royalist and presbyterian, misrepresented the general character of the new army from the start. They sneered at the base birth of its officers, but of the thirty-seven who fought at Naseby with the rank of colonel or above nine came from noble families and only seven were not gentlemen born, while a high proportion of the more junior officers were also of gentry stock. Over the years, casualties and resignations led to more and more promotions from the ranks, but the resultant social change was gradual. The New Model was widely feared as the supposed military wing of the independent party, but in fact it refrained from engaging in any kind of collective political activity until a presbyterian-dominated parliament threatened it with virtual extinction in 1647; and when that happened the number of conservative officers who left it rather than resist the civil power was, as we shall see, substantial. This is not to suggest that before then it was apolitical in the sense of being indifferent to political issues, for most of its officers and very many of its men, especially in the cavalry, cared passionately about what they were fighting for. But under Fairfax's leadership and example it scrupulously fulfilled, for more than two years, its creators' intention that it should be wholly dedicated to beating the enemy in the field.

The religious tone of the army also changed over the years. At the outset, those units which already contained a high proportion of Independents and sectaries, such as the cavalry drawn from the Eastern Association, retained their old character, but in choosing officers for regiments that had to be reorganized or newly raised the criteria were military fitness and previous service. In practice a broad toleration prevailed in most of the army during its fighting years. Something can be gleaned from the names of its chaplains, whose appointment, outside army headquarters, lay with the regimental commanders. But chaplains proved hard to find, and though over thirty have been traced who served with various regiments between 1645 and 1651 few stayed with the colours for more than a few months. Of the nine in post during 1645 five were Independents and four either certainly or probably Presbyterian,

---

[15] British Library, Egerton MSS 786, fos. 30, 33.

but of the sixteen traceable during 1646 the Independents numbered at least eight and possibly ten.[16]

Even at full strength the New Model accounted for less than half the men under arms in England. Although it absorbed what was left of Essex's, Manchester's, and Waller's armies, Massey's Western Association army and Brereton's Cheshire brigade were kept up, and the Northern Association forces were placed in 1645 under Major-General Sydenham Poyntz, a professional soldier recently returned from service overseas. There were also numerous local garrisons, as well as the London trained bands. None of these forces was to play a significant part in what remained of the first Civil War, though they were to assume considerable political importance after its end.

The delay in getting the New Model ready for action allowed the initiative to pass to the royalists in the early months of 1645. They took Weymouth in February, though it was quite soon recovered. Colonel Mytton scored a rare success for parliament by capturing Shrewsbury on 22 February, but some of its defenders had come from Ireland, and in accordance of a barbarous ordinance passed in the previous October Mytton hanged thirteen of them. Rupert promptly retaliated by hanging thirteen parliamentarian prisoners; the war was getting rougher. Plymouth and Abingdon managed to survive determined royalist assaults, but Goring's cavalry captured Farnham, only thirty-eight miles from London. He was, however, soon forced to draw them back. More threateningly, the king sent the Prince of Wales with a group of privy councillors to Bristol, to reanimate the war in the West Country and create a new field army there. He ordered Goring and his forces to join it, with the specific aim of besieging the much-contested town of Taunton. Its governor was Robert Blake, earlier the heroic defender of Lyme, who had taken it in 1644 and had already withstood a three-month siege with only a tiny garrison. Now he faced a more formidable threat, but he was partly saved by the quarrels among his opponents. Goring wangled a commission for himself as commander-in-chief of all the western forces, and thereby gave great offence not only to Rupert but to Sir Richard Grenville, who commanded the troops besieging Plymouth, and to Sir John Berkeley, the governor of Exeter. Neither Grenville nor Berkeley was willing to take orders from Goring, and they were on bad terms with each other. Charles's indulgence to Goring shows that his growing skill in military strategy was not matched by any improvement in his judgement of men. Goring at his best was a brave and resourceful commander of cavalry, but drink and debauch were taking their toll of his talents, and he was all too prone to put his own advancement and reputation

---

[16] Anne Laurence, *Parliamentary Army Chaplains 1642–1651* (Woodbridge, 1990), ch. 4, esp. p. 54. This work supersedes all previous studies of the subject.

first. His unwillingness to obey orders which did not promote them was to hasten the king's defeat.

Rivals though they were, Goring and Grenville had one thing in common: their discipline was lax and they let their troops oppress the civilian population to a degree that was already causing a backlash. They were not unique in this, but they were especially notorious. A movement of popular protest was arising that could at times significantly affect the conduct of the war. Rupert was one of the first to encounter it. In March 1645 he was sent to relieve Chester, which was being seriously threatened by Brereton. Leven then dispatched 5,000 Scots under David Leslie to reinforce Brereton, and it looked as though a major battle was impending. Rupert, however, was forced to fall back by a popular uprising in Herefordshire which threatened his rear. It was neither for parliament nor for the king, but a spontaneous act of resistance by exasperated countrymen, who had formed an association to defend themselves against lawless, plundering soldiers, whichever side they fought for. They were called Clubmen because most of them were armed only with cudgels and farm implements, though some had firearms. Clubmen had first appeared in Shropshire in the previous December, and in March they rose in Worcestershire as well as Herefordshire. At this stage they were mostly yeomen and husbandmen and other small landholders, though quite early some of the lesser gentry joined their associations. The Herefordshire men were particularly aggressive; an estimated 15,000 of them virtually laid siege to Hereford, fired on its royalist defenders and demanded the withdrawal of all but local troops from the county. Massey marched out of Gloucester to offer them support and enlist them on the parliamentary side, but to his disgust they would have nothing to do with him. To have closed with him would have compromised their objectives, which were peace for their community and freedom from the military presence of either side's forces. They were crushed by Rupert's and Maurice's combined forces, and their county was punished when Rupert quartered his troops there and let them loose on it. But though force of arms stamped out the movement in the Marches for the time being, further Clubmen risings were to follow: in Wiltshire, Dorset, and Somerset in the late spring and summer, in south Wales and the border from August onward, and in Berkshire, Hampshire, and Sussex in the autumn.

The Clubmen associations varied as to whether they were more aggrieved with the armies in their midst or with the county committees, whose powers were much increased by the New Model Ordinance, but they all expressed resentment at the ways in which the demands of war were infringing local autonomy and rights of property, especially the property of those who had none to spare. Yet although most were neutralist in origin, they were not wholly indifferent to the issues between king and parliament, and they became less so as the rural middling sort who formed their original core were joined by increasing numbers of gentry, lawyers, and clergy. Their sympathies differed from region to region, but rather more inclined towards the royalist cause; indeed they stand as a warning against any facile assumption that in the countryside the middling sort were as a class basically parliamentarian. They were moved by an attachment to old ways and to the rule of law, and many of their declarations called for the retention of the Prayer Book services, which became formally illegal in March 1645 when parliament prescribed the exclusive use of the Assembly's Directory for Worship. They breathed some of the same grass-roots conservatism, at a more popular level, as the abortive neutrality pacts of 1642–3, though no one still believed that with a bit of collective goodwill his county could be spared the ravages of war. Self-help was needed now, and what nerved untrained countrymen to confront battle-hardened soldiers was not just exasperation but sheer mass. In most counties where they appeared they easily outnumbered the locally stationed troops, claiming as they did (perhaps with some exaggeration) 20,000 adherents in Wiltshire, for example, and 16,000 in Berkshire.[17]

Fairfax was to have much experience of the Clubmen, but they were not among his problems when he took the field at the end of April, with his army still at barely half strength. His main impediment was the Committee of Both Kingdoms, which insisted on directing his operations from Westminster, and showed the characteristic tendency of chairborne strategists to think defensively and react to the enemy's last move but one. It ordered him, against his own judgement, to march to the relief of Taunton, but when he had got all the way to Blandford it recalled him, directing him to detach six regiments for Taunton. It was alarmed by the movements of the king's forces and lured by a false report that the faithful governor of Oxford, Colonel Will Legge, was ready to betray the city. Fairfax must have thought that there were better ways of raising the morale of raw and reluctant infantry recruits than taking them on long marches with no evident purpose. The chimera of besieging Oxford before engaging the king's main army in the field continued to seduce the committee for weeks, but there was indecision and misjudgement on the royalist side too. Rupert wanted to march north, first to relieve Chester from Brereton's besieging forces and then to attack Leven's now much reduced Scottish army, which was besieging Pontefract Castle. But Cromwell was still in the field with a brigade of horse, making the most of the forty days that the Self-Denying Ordinance allowed him, and on 25 April he captured Bletchington House, an important garrison only seven miles from Oxford. He went on

---

[17]  Morrill gives the best brief survey of the Clubmen movement in *Revolt in the Provinces*, pp. 132–51, 200–4. The earlier version of this book, *The Revolt of the Provinces* (1976), prints a number of Clubmen manifestoes (pp. 196–200). See also R. Hutton, *The Royalist War Effort* (1982), and D. Underdown, 'The chalk and the cheese: contrasts among the English Clubmen', *Past & Present* no. 85 (1979), 25–48.

to harry the outer defences of the city itself, and frustrated the northward movement of the king's artillery by driving off most of the draught horses. This caused Charles to change his plans; he recalled Goring from the west and summoned all his army, including Maurice's forces in the border counties from Worcestershire southward, to a general rendezvous at Stow-on-the-Wold on 8 May. There he mustered at least 5,000 foot and 6,000 horse, as much as Fairfax had when he first set out, and the arrival of Sir Marmaduke Langdale with his northern horse gave him an appreciable advantage in cavalry. With 5,000 men detached for the relief of Taunton, Fairfax was temporarily very vulnerable, yet the Committee of Both Kingdoms ordered him to advance against Oxford.

At Stow, however, the king's council of war was as usual divided, and it proceeded to throw away its advantage. Rupert and Langdale wanted to stick to their plan for a northern campaign, but most of the rest, including the civilians, pressed for the whole army to move westward and engage Fairfax while the New Model was still raw and under strength. That surely was what the parliament and its general had most to fear, but Rupert opposed it strenuously, and he broke what was becoming an impasse by proposing a division of forces: Goring and his men should be sent westward to check Fairfax, while the rest of the royal army proceeded northward. It was not a good solution, but it pleased Goring, whose authority it enhanced, and it was adopted. It did at least force Brereton to lift the siege of Chester. The Committee of Both Kingdoms had tried to keep it going by requesting Leven to hasten to Brereton's assistance and by ordering all available local forces, including Lord Fairfax's Yorkshiremen, to do likewise. But Leven, though he did not refuse, was deflected by the news of the most brilliant of all Montrose's victories at Auldearn. Montrose had owed most of his successes to the unwillingness of reluctant Lowland levies to stand up to the fierce mettle of his plunder-hungry Highlanders and of Macdonald's Irishmen, but at Auldearn he was up against four regular regiments of foot who fought hard, and he left at least 2,000 of them dead. Leven seriously feared that Montrose might advance through the Lowlands and eventually join forces with the northward-moving royal army. He had already had to send home nine regiments, while five were garrisoning Newcastle and five more were besieging Carlisle. So his way of answering the call of Lancashire and Cheshire was to make a long northward detour through Westmorland, in case he had to answer an urgent summons from Scotland. Needless to say Brereton did not receive the help he needed in time, and Chester's defenders under Lord Byron were freed to join the king's main army, which had reached Market Drayton.

Leven would have been prepared to commit his army against the king's if England had sent the New Model north to join him, and that is what the Scottish commissioners urged the Committee of Both Kingdoms to do. They hoped for a kind of rerun of Marston Moor. But the committee was still lured by the mirage of an easy siege of Oxford, and the independent politicians were looking now for an ultimate victory which would owe as little as possible to the Scots, who had become more and more of a political liability as their military value had shrunk. After six days of wrangling, the proposal to send the New Model north was referred to a special committee of both houses and rejected by one vote. As a compromise, Fairfax was ordered to send 2,500 of his cavalry and dragoons to assist Leven and to move what he had left against Oxford. His political masters thus succeeded in splitting his army into three parts before it was even up to strength, with nearly half his cavalry posting northward, 4,000 or more men in Taunton (which was duly relieved, though Goring soon had the relieving force bottled up in the town), and maybe 10,000 preparing to lay siege to Oxford. By the end of May he had received at least 4,000 infantry recruits since he first took the field, but he probably lost 3,000 men through desertion or otherwise in the course of his gruelling march into Dorset and back.[18]

Rupert too had to contend with politically motivated civilian tacticians in the king's council of war, but at Market Drayton he guided it towards wiser decisions than those he had urged at Stow. Byron wanted the royal army to continue northward, but Rupert, who had been so keen on a northern campaign, was aware that the major part of the divided New Model had returned as far as Newbury and he was eager to engage it while he could still catch it at a disadvantage. He had already sent urgent orders to Goring, who was obsessed with retaking Taunton, to return with his whole force and rendezvous with the main army at Market Harborough. He now successfully urged that by striking eastward towards the parliamentarian heartland he would be sure to draw Fairfax off from Oxford, and he hoped on the way to collect 3,000 Welshmen that Charles Gerrard had been raising and the bulk of the cavalry from the Newark garrison. Since the royal army already numbered at least 11,000 he had a good prospect of giving Fairfax battle on equal or better terms. If Goring had obeyed, there is no knowing what the outcome might have been. But Goring was in Bath, indulging in drinking bouts that incapacitated him for days on end, and he responded to Rupert's pressing orders by merely promising that he would come as soon as he had taken Taunton, which he undertook to do within a few days. That was unlikely, with his men deserting fast and his siege lines so slack that the defenders were bringing in provisions almost unhindered. When Charles and Rupert learnt that Fairfax had actually begun besieging Oxford they commanded Goring even more urgently to return and relieve it, but in vain.

To draw Fairfax off, they marched against Leicester. It was a wealthy

---

[18] Gentles, *New Model Army*, pp. 35–7.

town, but inadequately garrisoned, and its hastily built fortifications were compromised by suburban buildings which gave cover to an attacking force. Its plunder would fill the hungry soldiers' pockets and still leave plenty over for the king's own coffers. Rupert invested it methodically and summoned it to surrender on 30 May. Not getting an immediate response, he opened fire with his siege guns in mid-afternoon, and by six they had breached its best defended quarter, the Newark. At midnight he launched a general assault, which was resisted with extraordinary tenacity by the defenders, a mere 480 foot and 400 horse, assisted by 900 townsmen in arms. They had to be driven back street by street until they were finally cornered in the market-place and forced to surrender. They did not all receive quarter, and women perished in the night's slaughter as well as men, for Rupert had lost thirty officers in storming the town and he was exasperated by its resistance. The ensuing plunder went on for days, and at the end of it 140 cartloads of booty were carried off to Newark. It was reported that no royalist prisoner taken between Leicester and Naseby had less than forty shillings on him—two months' pay for a foot soldier. Others who may have taken more made off home with their spoils and were not seen again.

Leicester's agony had the expected effect of making the Committee of Safety abandon the folly of besieging Oxford. Parliament promptly accepted its recommendation that Fairfax should take the field against the king forthwith, and it soon freed him from the shackles of constant direction from Westminster. It simply instructed him to follow the royal army's movements and left the rest to his judgement. Not knowing this, the king's council of war decided that the relief of Oxford must have first priority; Rupert was overborne by Digby and the courtiers, whose ladies in the unprotected city were badly frightened. But there were better reasons for not being in too great a hurry to take on the New Model. What with the casualties at Leicester, the garrison that had to be left there, the desertions of loot-laden soldiers, the return to Newark of many of the cavalry borrowed from its garrison, and a mutiny by Langdale's horse, who rode off when they learnt that the army was not going to march northward, Charles reckoned that he had barely 4,000 foot and 3,500 horse left. Langdale's northerners were brought back with difficulty before his army reached Market Harborough on 5 June, but there was still no sign of Goring and his men or of Gerrard's Welsh levies.

That same day Fairfax set off from Oxford. Three long marches took his army to a rendezvous near Newport Pagnell with the 2,500 men whom he had sent to support Leven, and on the 8th he held a crucial council of war. He put two questions to it: how best to bring the king's army to battle, and how to fill the vacant post of lieutenant-general of the horse. For that place he proposed Cromwell, and the assent was unanimous. He sent the 24-year-old Colonel Robert Hammond posting to Westminster to request the appointment, to which the Commons immediately agreed. The Lords, whose concurrence was legally required to exempt Cromwell from the Self-Denying Ordinance, declined to give it, but the Commons' assent was enough for Fairfax. Cromwell was in Ely, recruiting both horse and foot, and Fairfax at once sent for him. He was the obvious choice, and a very popular one in the army, and when he rode into the lines with about 700 horse, early on the day before the crucial battle of the war, he was greeted 'with a mighty shout'.[19]

Fairfax had equally strong support for seeking battle at the first opportunity, and on the 11th he advanced his headquarters to Stony Stratford, only twenty-five miles from where the royal army was entrenched in an almost impregnable position on Borough Hill near Daventry. There it remained immobile for nearly six days from 7 June onward, mainly because 1,200 cavalry had been detached to escort vast quantities of cattle and sheep to Oxford, and did not rejoin the army until the night of the 11th. Rupert cannot have approved this, for he knew by the 7th at the latest that the siege of Oxford had been raised, but he was never sure of his position in the king's counsels. He wrote on the 8th to his old friend Will Legge that there had been a plot among the civilian councillors, Digby and Ashburnham in particular, to persuade Charles to return to Oxford, so that they could reassert their influence over him and counter that of 'the soldiers', meaning chiefly himself. Charles sharply rejected the proposal, but Rupert felt insecure.[20] His own judgement was fallible, however, for he shared the royalists' facile contempt for 'the New Noddle' (the word could mean booby), and he was poorly informed of its current strength. He was also quite unaware of its present proximity, whereas Fairfax had excellent intelligence of royalist movements from Sir Samuel Luke.

Fairfax and Skippon had much to do during the week before the impending battle, for many infantry recruits were recent arrivals and were not even armed when the army left the Oxford lines. A large consignment of muskets overtook them on the march, but there were still basic skills to be mastered. Fairfax began his final advance against the royal forces, still in position on Borough Hill, in foul weather on the 11th. His men slogged all day along muddy country lanes, avoiding the more frequented roads, and when they quartered at Wootton that night their approach was still unsuspected. The rain may have made Rupert's scouts slack in patrolling, for he was still oblivious of the New Model's proximity until late in the next afternoon, when its 'forlorn hope' of forward cavalry surprised two of his outposts only two miles out of Daventry. His army was dispersed and resting, its horses at grass, while the king was enjoying a hunt in Fawsley Park, several miles away from its nearest positions.

[19]  Abbott, *Writings and Speeches of Oliver Cromwell*, I, 355–6.
[20]  Warburton, *Memoirs of Prince Rupert*, III, 100.

Great as his advantage was, Fairfax could not attack immediately, because the day was too far gone and his infantry were too far behind. He quartered his army around Kislingbury that night, and most of it must have slept in the wet fields. He himself stayed in the saddle till 4 a.m., riding round his regiments to check their preparedness against a night attack, and then advancing beyond Flore until he could make out the dim bulk of Borough Hill. There the king's army stood to its arms in its prepared positions all night; Fairfax could see many little fires twinkling, and he rightly deduced that the soldiers were burning their huts prior to moving off. At about five his invaluable scoutmaster-general, Leonard Watson, brought him confirmation that it was indeed retreating, and also a splendid windfall: an intercepted letter from Goring to Rupert, begging him not to give battle until he could join him, but explaining that he could not leave the west just yet. It must have rejoiced Fairfax to know that he could tackle the king's army and Goring's forces consecutively rather than in combination, and that Rupert was deprived of this vital intelligence. He held a council of war at 6 a.m., and it was actually sitting when the cheer went up that greeted Cromwell's arrival. It agreed most readily to pursue the retreating royalists and make them fight.

By nightfall on the 12th Rupert was at last aware that he had seriously underestimated the enemy's numerical strength. He and the king decided to retreat northward by way of Melton Mowbray to Belvoir Castle, where they could reinforce themselves from Newark and other Midlands garrisons. To throw off a possible pursuit they marched westward for some miles, as if for Warwick, before wheeling north-east for their chosen quarters for the night around Market Harborough. But all through the 13th a strong detachment of what was now Cromwell's cavalry, under his old comrades Henry Ireton and Thomas Harrison, shadowed the royal army's movements, and the New Model advanced on a parallel line with it at a much closer distance than Rupert knew. He had posted an outer guard of about twenty horse at Naseby, seven miles from Harborough. They were not very alert, for Ireton fell on them while they were at supper or playing quoits and captured most of them. But a few escaped and carried the alarm to headquarters. The king was roused from his bed, and he and Rupert held a council of war at two in the morning. The great question, of course, was whether to offer battle, and the answer was not easy. The alternative proposal was to make speedily for Leicester, where the addition of its small garrison and the shelter of its defences, such as they were, would give about 10,000 men a better chance to hold off at least 15,000. There were great risks either way. A retreat with Cromwell's cavalry in close pursuit could have led to a savage mauling, not least for the 200-odd wagons in the royalist train. But it is very significant that Rupert, who was usually so eager for action, advised against giving battle. It was Digby and Ashburnham who pressed for it, arguing that retreat would

demoralize the king's men, whereas they supposed Fairfax's to be already discouraged by their failure to take Oxford and by a bloody repulse that they
had lately suffered in an attempt to storm Boarstall House. Even less realistically, they urged that Fairfax should be engaged before he could join forces
with the Scots. The decision rested of course with the king, and he opted for
battle.

It has been said that 'the Royalist cause committed suicide at Naseby',[21] but
in fairness one has to consider what might have happened if battle had been
declined. Even if the king had got his army through to Leicester unscathed he
could not shelter there indefinitely, because Fairfax was intent on fighting and
could in the long run muster more reinforcements than he. Now that parliament had learnt how to deploy its superior resources and found commanders
with the will to win, the terms of war had turned in its favour. And yet if Goring had obeyed orders and added his troops to the king's, Naseby would have
been fought on more equal terms, with better if fewer infantry and with a
numerical advantage in cavalry. If the untried New Model's first battle had
ended in defeat, who can be sure that it would have developed the collective
spirit that took it within a year to total victory? Because of that intercepted
letter, Rupert did not know that Goring was still stuck in Somerset, and may
have advised against an immediate engagement in the assumption that his
forces were well on their way. In deciding to fight, Charles was going against
the odds, but the outcome was not a foregone conclusion.

Both armies were on the move in the early hours of 14 June. Fairfax, as he
ranged his on the ridge north of Naseby, did not know yet whether the royalists would accept his challenge, but the appearance of their cavalry in force on
another ridge four miles away reassured him. After much manoeuvring the
two armies drew up about 1,000 yards apart (less at the eastern flank, more
at the western), both near the crests of gentle rises, with the open expanse of
Broad Moor between them. The king had probably slightly more than 9,000
men, the parliamentarians something over 15,000, including Cromwell's 700
cavalry and Colonel Rossiter's Lincolnshire regiment, which arrived just after
battle was joined. The royalists were outnumbered mainly in infantry, though
those they had were seasoned soldiers, a high proportion being hard-fighting
Welshman; in cavalry they had about 5,000 against 6,600.[22] As usual, the
foot were ranged mainly in the centre and most of the horse on either flank.
Cromwell commanded on the right, facing Langdale and his northerners and
as much of the Newark horse as had not returned to that garrison. Ireton,

[21] Hutton, *Royalist War Effort*, p. 178.

[22] I have slightly revised the figures I gave in *Battles of the English Civil War* in the light of
Glenn Foard's *Naseby: The Decisive Campaign* (Guildford, 1995), which is now much the fullest
and best account of the battle, and makes fruitful use of archaeological evidence. The figures
exclude officers. For a briefer narrative see Gentles, *New Model Army*, pp. 55–60.

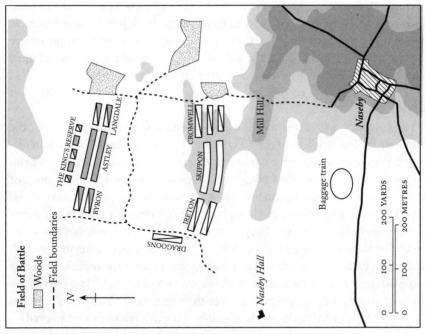

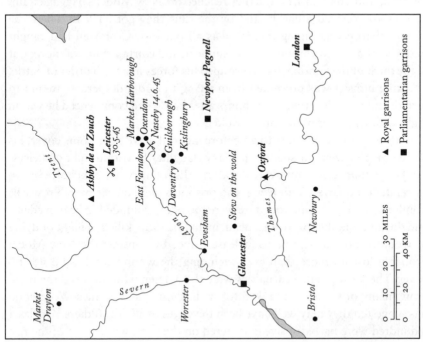

MAP 2. Naseby Campaign of 1645.

who was promoted that very morning to commissary-general (second-in-command of the cavalry), was ranged against both Rupert and Maurice, riding at the heads of their own regiments. Opposite Skippon in the centre was the 66-year-old Lord Astley, who had commanded the royalist infantry since the war began. His men were outnumbered by seven to four and had slept little since their 20-mile march the day before, but they fought most bravely.

The royalists began the battle in mid-morning with an assault along the whole front. The first line of the New Model foot buckled and fell back in disorder; Skippon was severely wounded, though he refused to leave the field. To his left the charge of the two princes carried all before it, putting much of Ireton's cavalry to rout. Ireton too was wounded, and temporarily taken prisoner. Everything now hung on the right, where Cromwell's veteran regiments had a numerical advantage. They were completely victorious, but it was his control of them that saved the day for the parliament. Detaching just enough of them to pursue Langdale's fleeing horsemen, he kept the remainder intact and used them to turn the tide of battle on the rest of the field. It is not easy to check triumphant cavalry when they see their opponents break and flee, and Rupert signally failed to do so. He joined his men in a pursuit that careered on for a mile and a half until he and they reached the New Model's baggage train. There they received a check, and by the time they got back to where the infantry battle was raging the day was all but lost. Cromwell had caught Astley's gallant men without cavalry support, and Fairfax, who was never out of the thick of the fighting, had regrouped his forces in a fresh order of battle. The king himself was prevented from trying to lead a desperate attempt to turn the tide, and less than three hours after battle had commenced he was in flight with whatever of his forces could get away.

With eight or more hours to go before nightfall gave them some cover, his fleeing cavalry were pursued with heavy slaughter to within sight of Leicester. Fewer than 4,000 got away to safety. His infantry had no choice but to surrender on quarter, and over 4,500 prisoners were on the march towards London next day. About 500 more were too badly wounded to be moved far, and the total number of royalist dead, including those killed in flight or dying of wounds, probably came to at least 1,000. By contrast the New Model probably lost no more than 200, including the wounded who did not recover. The most pitiable casualties were the women who followed the royal army, many of whom were taken for Irish, though as Veronica Wedgwood has suggested they may well have been the wives of Welsh soldiers.[23] At least a hundred were barbarously slaughtered on the spot, while most of the rest had their faces slashed or their noses slit to mark them as whores.

---

[23] Wedgwood, *King's War 1641–1647*, p. 455.

The king's army also lost all its guns and wagons, in which was found a rich haul of his secret papers, including his correspondence with the queen. This laid bare his hopes of bringing an army of native Irish into England and of obtaining money and mercenaries from foreign princes, as well as his readiness to consider granting toleration to English papists. These letters, published as *The King's Cabinet Opened*, created a sensation and did him immense harm. To add to his misfortunes, his garrison in Leicester was forced to surrender three days after the battle.

Naseby naturally gave a great boost to the New Model's morale. Fairfax lost far more men through desertion than in battle, for many of his foot soldiers slipped off home with the booty that they took from the royalist dead, wounded, and prisoners. In the pursuit Cromwell had forbidden his horsemen to dismount for plunder on pain of death—an unpopular order, but it seems to have been obeyed. In a memorable dispatch to the Speaker dictated late on the very day of the battle, he rightly praised Fairfax's conduct in it but said nothing about his own. He gave all the glory to God, but he did not forget the soldiery: 'Honest men served you faithfully in this action. Sir, they are trusty; I beseech you in the name of God, not to discourage them. . . . He that ventures his life for the liberty of his country, I wish he trust God for the liberty of his conscience, and you for the liberty he fights for.'[24] The Commons, in ordering his dispatch to be printed, deleted this whole passage. Fortunately the Lords sanctioned its publication intact, so both versions appeared on the bookstalls. The Lords also graciously assented to Cromwell's appointment as lieutenant-general, though only for three months, whereas the Commons voted to extend it indefinitely. Both reactions must have warned him, if he needed warning, that he would have political battles to fight when the military ones were won. But in the military sphere Naseby was the decisive one, and he was not mistaken about its bearing on the future liberty of his country. A modern government has honoured the dead of the most important battle on English soil since Hastings by driving a motorway through a part of the field over which Rupert's cavalry pursued Ireton's beaten men and later returned to the fight.

The king, after a brief stay in Hereford, spent the first half of July with the Marquis of Worcester at Raglan Castle. Within a week of the battle Digby was writing diplomatically that 'the consequences of this disaster will not have great extent',[25] and Charles was putting a good face on it. But on 23 June he wrote a letter to the 15-year-old Prince of Wales in terms which show that he was now, perhaps for the first time, contemplating the possibility of defeat.

---

[24] Abbott, *Writings and Speeches of Oliver Cromwell*, I, 360.
[25] Quoted in C. Carlton, *Charles I: The Personal Monarch* (1983), p. 288.

He solemnly commanded his son, should he, the king, ever be taken prisoner, not to yield to any conditions that were dishonourable, or 'derogatory to regal authority', even to save his father's life.[26] In more sanguine moments, however, he was still hoping to rebuild an army as good as ever he had commanded. For a nucleus he had the cavalry that had survived Naseby and about 3,000 infantry, mostly the Welsh levies that he had failed to collect before the battle. But Rupert, whom he had sent to defend Bristol, wrote to him in July, venturing his opinion that he should treat for peace, believing it to be 'a more prudent way to retain something than to lose it all'. Charles resented the advice and forbade Rupert to repeat it. 'Speaking as a mere soldier or statesman,' he wrote, 'I must say that there is no probability but of my ruin; yet as a Christian, I must tell you that God will not suffer rebels or traitors to prosper.'[27] That for Charles was an article of faith, and it would sustain him through all his misfortunes. For the present he was looking mainly to Ireland for help, and after Naseby he hastened the departure thither of the Earl of Glamorgan, whose mission will be described shortly.

Fairfax lost no time in ensuring that royalist hopes of a military recovery were dashed. His first priorities were to relieve Taunton and defeat Goring. He drove his men hard; between Marlborough and Dorchester, for instance, they marched an average of seventeen miles a day for five days on end. At Dorchester he was met on 3 July by the leaders of the Clubmen of Dorset and Wiltshire, who asked for passes to enable them to carry petitions to both king and parliament, calling for a cessation of hostilities and the handing over of all the places in Dorset that were garrisoned by either side to the Clubmen themselves. Fairfax naturally refused their request, though with courtesy and reasoned argument. Their numbers made them formidable, but their attitude thereafter softened as they came to appreciate his genuine consideration for local interests and the growing contrast between his army's respect for law and property and the habitual marauding of the western royalists.

Fairfax had no difficulty in making Goring give up the siege of Taunton, but experienced rather more in bringing him to battle on advantageous terms. His ranks were thinned by the casualties at Naseby, where many more had been wounded than killed, by the escort that he had had to provide for the 4,500 prisoners, and by the chronic drain of desertions. By way of reinforcement he called in Massey and his Western Association forces, which brought his strength up to about 14,000. Goring with about half that number was also counting on reinforcements, in his case from south Wales, and was avoiding battle until they arrived. He sent off a small force in a clever feint which deceived Fairfax into thinking that he was about to reinvest Taunton, and led

---

[26] Clarendon, *History of the Rebellion*, IV, 168–9; Carlton prints the letter in *Charles I*, p. 288.

[27] Quoted, along with Rupert's advice, in Carlton, *Charles I*, p. 290.

him to detach Massey with about 4,000 men to prevent it. This meant that when Goring at last had to face Fairfax on 10 July, after manoeuvres that showed his tactical sense to be undimmed, he had been able to select a strong defensive position at Langport, and was much less heavily outnumbered than he had been a few days earlier. But Fairfax attacked with boldness and skill, making good use of his artillery and precisely co-ordinating the deployment of his cavalry and infantry. Success hung upon a cavalry charge which had to negotiate a line wide enough for only four troopers to ride abreast before they engaged the waiting royalist horse, and it was executed with proud courage by units which had ridden under Cromwell before the New Model existed. By this time Goring's men could not match their spirit; they fled, and Cromwell reckoned that they lost 2,000 killed or captured. So many others, scenting defeat, just melted away that Goring's army ceased to exist as a fighting force, though he himself escaped westward.

Twelve days later Fairfax stormed the important garrison town of Bridgwater, and he took Bath soon afterwards. These successes made Charles and Rupert abandon their tentative plans for a new campaign in the West Country, with Bristol as their base. Their position in south Wales was endangered by a combined operation by Vice-Admiral Batten and Major-General Laugharne, who routed the local royalist forces at Colby Moor (near Haverfordwest) on 1 August. A few days later Fairfax laid siege to Sherborne Castle, which had a large garrison, and took it by assault on the 14th. By then Charles, who had been in Cardiff, was already on his way northward, for he had felt the trap closing upon him. Leaving Rupert with what he thought a sufficient force to defend Bristol, he set off with the idea of making a junction with Montrose. After his triumph at Auldearn Montrose had won another brilliant and bloody victory over Baillie and the Covenanters at Alford on 2 July, and was advancing upon Glasgow. Baillie was now longing to be relieved of his command, for he was let down by his troops, ill supported, and distrusted by his masters in Edinburgh, and shadowed by an interfering committee of estates. When he again faced Montrose, eleven miles from Glasgow at Kilsyth on 15 August, the committee of estates overruled his choice of ground and plan of battle, and his army of 6,000 was utterly routed; only a few hundred escaped with their lives. Montrose, with his own forces now grown to at least 4,400 foot and 500 horse, entered Glasgow soon afterwards, and for a brief while he was master of Scotland.

By then Charles had got as far as Doncaster on his way to meet him, but there he learnt that Leven and his army was on his tracks and only ten miles away. Leven had been besieging Hereford, but had broken off the operation to hunt larger prey. Poyntz's Northern Association forces were also threatening Charles's little army, if it can be so called, so in search of safety he took it on a long and exhausting march by way of Newark and Huntingdon before returning to Oxford, and thence to Worcester. By now his main concern was to save Bristol, though Rupert had assured him that it could hold out for at least four months. That proved to be a serious error of judgement.

Fairfax had had Bristol in his sights ever since Naseby. He overruled the cautious spirits in his council of war who advised him first to clear the far south-west, where Grenville, Goring, and Hopton among others were still under arms, but he did think it important to reduce the nearer royalist garrisons in Dorset and Somerset, as we have seen. One reason was that they were in league with some of the local Clubmen, who were numerous enough to hamper his operations. There were two distinct associations of Clubmen in the region. One, centred on the chalk downs of Dorset and neighbouring Wiltshire (predominantly arable country), had a markedly royalist bias. While Fairfax was besieging Sherborne its members had been in touch with the defenders and had agreed to try to force him to raise the siege. He frustrated their plan by surprising a meeting of their leaders at Shaftesbury and sending them up to London as prisoners, whereupon 2,000 or more of their associates assembled in arms on Hambledon Hill nearby, demanding their release. Three times Cromwell sent a party of horse to command them to disperse, and each time his men were fired on; some indeed were taken prisoner, and according to Cromwell 'used most barbarously'. Two of their most pugnacious leaders were Anglican clergymen. In the end it took a minor cavalry action to break them up, and though fewer than a dozen were killed, many more were wounded and about 300 captured. Cromwell kept them overnight in a church, took their names, warned them that they would be hanged if they were caught again opposing the parliament's forces, and then let them go.[28]

The other Clubmen association with which Fairfax dealt was drawn from the woodland and pastoral areas of Somerset and Gloucestershire, where a rural clothing industry flourished, and it was much more sympathetic to parliament. It quietly co-operated with Fairfax in his siege of Bridgwater, and when operations began against Bristol the Somerset Clubmen allowed him to recruit 2,000 auxiliaries from their ranks. Gloucestershire furnished a further 1,500, and both counties readily raised more volunteers as the siege progressed.[29]

Fairfax completed the investment of Bristol on 23 August, and despite its formidable fortifications he did not intend to conduct a long siege. Yet the alternative of storming the city was a daunting one, and Rupert's assurance to the king that he could hold out for four months shows that he anticipated no such exploit. Success depended on the new courage of the infantry, for

---

[28] Abbott, *Writings and Speeches of Oliver Cromwell*, I, 368–9.
[29] Underdown, *Somerset in the Civil War and Interregnum*, pp. 98–100, 105–8, 111–18; Gentles, *New Model Army*, pp. 61–6.

until a breach was made or a gate forced open cavalry could be of little help. For foot soldiers, a pitched battle at push of pike was a severe enough test of morale, but to scale high walls under fire from cannon and muskets, and with defenders waiting to club or run through the assailants as they came over the top, must have been quite terrifying. Yet Fairfax sent his men in at 1 a.m. on 10 September, even though six days of bombardment had failed to make a breach in the walls, and the New Model foot that had fallen back before inferior numbers at Naseby fought heroically. Their task was the harder because at most points of attack their scaling ladders were too short to reach the tops of the walls. Yet they forced their way in, and their sheer numbers told in the end. Fairfax had not far short of 10,000 men, including cavalry, backed by nearly 5,000 auxiliaries. There was plague in the city, and sickness and desertion had left Rupert with at most 2,000 regular troops and 1,000 trained bands and auxiliaries to man a perimeter three or four miles long.[30] The fighting raged for six hours, but when resistance became hopeless Rupert was offered honourable terms, and with the full support of his council of war he accepted them. His men were allowed to march out with their swords, though not their firearms, and were given safe conduct to Oxford. Fairfax and Cromwell personally escorted him on the first two miles of his journey.

Cromwell in his dispatch to the Speaker paid generous tribute to the gallantry of the soldiers which had secured this great victory. He testified (in a passage already quoted in part) that men of different religious professions had fought together as comrades, fired by the same spirit of faith and prayer, and he ended with an eloquent plea that they and 'the people of God all England over' should enjoy liberty of conscience. With obvious reference to the sterile pursuit of religious uniformity then in progress, he urged that the real unity was inward and spiritual, 'and from brethren, in things of the mind, we look for no compulsion but that of light and reason'.[31] The Commons deleted the whole paragraph when they published his letter, as they had done with the similar plea in his Naseby dispatch, but his Independent supporters had it printed separately and scattered in the streets. It probably received more public attention in the end because of the shabby attempt to suppress it.

No previous defeat so shocked and grieved the king as the surrender of Bristol. He saw it as a betrayal; he immediately dismissed his nephew from the command of his army, rebuking him in a curt letter for 'so mean an action'

---

[30] The mayor of Bristol told Cromwell that Rupert had about 1,000 horse and 2,500 foot, besides 1,200 or more trained bands and auxiliaries, but Rupert's own narrative states that though his garrison was nominally 2,300 strong, he could never man the line with more than 1,500 regular soldiers, and that the trained bands and auxiliaries were down to 800: Abbott, *Writings and Speeches of Oliver Cromwell*, I, 377; Warburton, *Memoirs of Prince Rupert*, III, 166–7.

[31] Abbott, *Writings and Speeches of Oliver Cromwell*, I, 377.

and directing him to seek his subsistence overseas. This was grossly unjust. Rupert could fairly be faulted for misleading Charles about his power to hold out, but not for seeking terms when an immensely superior enemy had forced its way into the city and had its defenders and inhabitants at mercy. If he had cared nothing for civilian casualties or for the lives of his own men he might conceivably have withdrawn into the fort for a do-or-die stand, but his own officers judged it untenable, and the only possible justification would have been that the king or Goring or both could have brought him swift and powerful relief. But Charles was in Raglan and in no position to help him, and Goring was still in Exeter; Fairfax intercepted a letter from him saying that he could not get to Bristol for three weeks.

Further disasters followed fast. Three days after Bristol fell, Montrose suffered a crushing defeat, and as it proved a decisive one, at Philiphaugh. David Leslie had a large superiority in cavalry and was reinforced by seasoned troops from Leven's army in England. Sheer hatred of the plundering Highlanders and Irishmen made the winners dishonour their victory. After about 250 Irish foot had been killed in action the remaining 50 or so laid down their arms on promise of quarter. Most of them were then shot, and about 300 soldiers' wives, with their children, were butchered on the field. The execution of some of Montrose's senior officers followed later; indeed two Irish officers were put to death without trial. The treatment of the Irish as sub-human was a vice common to English and Scots, and in this case it had the full blessing of the Scottish parliament. Montrose himself made his escape, but his hopes of doing the king further service were vitiated by the mutual enmity and jealousy between Huntly and the Gordons and himself.

Not knowing of his champion's defeat, Charles set out from Raglan on 18 September and made for Chester, hoping once more to join forces with him. The city was under siege but open from the south, and he still had Langdale's northern horse to screen him. But on 24 September, the day after he slipped into Chester, Langdale and some of the garrison forces were thoroughly defeated by Poyntz's northerners and some of the besieging army. Charles was forced on his travels again, with little more than a bodyguard by now, and he found refuge in Newark on 4 October. By then garrison after garrison had fallen to detachments of the New Model, Devizes, Laycock House, and Berkeley Castle all surrendering within four days.

Meanwhile Rupert was so desperate to clear himself that he and Maurice skirmished their way to Newark, defying the king's orders not to enter the city. Charles refused to see him, but Rupert obtained a hearing before members of the royal council of war, sitting as a court martial. They cleared him of any lack of courage or fidelity, but found him guilty of 'indiscretion' in surrendering Bristol prematurely. The order to leave the country was not enforced and eventually a sort of reconciliation was effected; Rupert ended the war in Oxford, though without a commission.[32] The contrast between Charles's severity towards his best commander and his indulgence towards Goring, whom he is not known to have reproached for persistently failing him in his need, makes sad reading.

During October Cromwell bombarded Winchester Castle into surrender on the 5th and then moved against Basing House, the strongly fortified mansion of the catholic Marquis of Winchester and a centre of heroic resistance. It had already withstood two sieges, the second lasting three months, but this one lasted only six days before Cromwell's siege guns blew two large breaches in its walls. The marquis, however, refused his summons to surrender, so he had to storm it. He did so with little loss, but the defenders fought almost to the last, and he let his men slaughter many of them, including six priests, before granting quarter to the majority. Since terms had been refused after essential defences had been breached they were not entitled to quarter, and a case could be made for punishing desperate resistance as an example, for the sake of saving soldiers' lives and shortening the war. Nevertheless it can hardly be doubted that Cromwell's uncharacteristic harshness sprang partly from Basing's notoriety as 'a nest of idolatrous papists'. The sack of the house was comprehensive, and its inmates, ladies included, were stripped of their clothes by the soldiers. One who got away, wrapped only in a blanket, was Inigo Jones.[33]

While Cromwell was mopping up the royalist strongholds in Hampshire and Wiltshire, Fairfax was embarking on the reconquest of the south-west. He took Tiverton after storming its castle on 19 October, but his campaign petered out because an increasingly wet autumn made the roads impassable for his guns and baggage train. There was much sickness in his cold and hungry army, and he was far from well himself. He suffered from kidney stones, rheumatism, and (so he wrote to his father) 'a benumbing coldness in my head and arms, especially on that side I had any hurts';[34] he had been wounded four times before he became Lord General. Cromwell and his part of the army rejoined him late in October, having taken the surrender of Langford House on the way. He gave its small garrison honourable terms, and when six of his soldiers tried to rob its officers they were court-martialled. Since they had done the same in Winchester their sentence was severe: they were made to draw lots for their lives, the loser was hanged, and the others were sent off to the governor of Oxford to deal with as he thought fit. He repaid the courtesy by setting them free. The contrast with the treatment of the Basing House

---

[32] Warburton, *Memoirs of Prince Rupert*, III, 162; Clarendon, *History of the Rebellion*, IV, 93.

[33] Abbott, *Writings and Speeches of Oliver Cromwell*, I, 385–7; Gardiner, *Great Civil War*, II, 344–7.

[34] Quoted in John Wilson, *Fairfax* (1985), pp. 86–7; cf. p. 55.

garrison needs no underlining; it paid to surrender. The reunited army spent the rest of the year in widely scattered winter quarters in Devon. It no longer had to reckon with Goring, who took ship for France late in November. Hopton, whom he had supplanted as commander-in-chief of the king's western forces by his intrigues, had the thankless task of taking over the demoralized remnants of his army.

At Newark Charles was having to bear not only bad news from all sides but troubles at his own court. They were partly of his own making, for he had dismissed Will Legge, the governor of Oxford, for no better reason than that he was Rupert's friend and Digby wanted him out of the way. Now he did the same to Sir Richard Willys, the governor of Newark and commander of its large garrison. This led to a disgraceful scene in which Rupert, Maurice, Willys, Lord Gerrard, and a dozen or more of their friends burst unbidden into the king's presence and demanded an explanation. Willys may have remembered his treatment when he betrayed the secrets of the Sealed Knot years later. Such quarrels did nothing to improve Charles's authority, but the passions simmered down, and on 5 November he returned to Oxford to face a cheerless winter.

After cashiering Rupert he had appointed his archenemy Digby as Lieutenant-General of all his forces north of Trent, and then in mid-October sent him with about 1,500 men, including what was left of Langdale's northern horse, to try and make a junction with Montrose on the Scottish border. In a rare and brief moment of co-operation in the king's cause, Huntly's son Aboyne had lately come in to Montrose with 1,500 foot and 300 horse. Two days out of Newark Digby surprised the infantry of Poyntz's northern army at Sherburne in Yorkshire and captured most of it, but in an ensuing cavalry action a lack of understanding between him and Langdale turned victory into defeat, and they and their disorganized horsemen fled all the way to Skipton Castle. Thence they resumed a circuitous journey northward, and though their cavalry took another beating from the Scottish forces based on Carlisle they pressed on as far as Dumfries. The news they were given there—largely false, as it turned out—about Montrose and the forces opposed to him was so discouraging that they hastened back to England. Their few remaining troops melted away in the Cumbrian fells, and with a small group of officers they were glad to find a little boat in Ravenglass to take them to the Isle of Man. Thence Digby sailed to Ireland, where he busied himself with a plan to bring over the Prince of Wales and make the country a base for a royalist resurgence.

Charles's own thoughts were turning more and more towards Ireland. There had been something of a stalemate there for a year or two on both the military and the political fronts, though since April 1644 Colonel Robert Monro, an experienced professional soldier, had been in command of both the Scottish and the parliamentarian forces in Ulster. Charles had received only limited benefit from the 1643 Cessation, and the longstanding negotiations between Ormond, his faithful Lord Lieutenant, and the Confederates for help from the Irish themselves were almost deadlocked. Ormond was bent on keeping Charles's powers as King of Ireland intact, whereas the Confederates were interested in assisting him only if he would grant them religious freedom and confirm at least some of the political gains that they had won by rebellion. Early in 1645 Charles commissioned his friend Edward Somerset, Earl of Glamorgan, Worcester's son and like him a devout catholic, to go to Ireland on his behalf. Glamorgan's official instructions were to assist Ormond, but unknown to the Lord Lieutenant he had a private mandate to negotiate with the Confederates for an Irish army. A shipwreck and other difficulties delayed his arrival in Ireland until late in June, by which time the king's almost desperate plight led him to interpret his brief very liberally. He did not, however, deal directly with the General Assembly in Kilkenny but with the Confederate delegates who were treating with Ormond in Dublin. On 25 August he concluded an agreement with them whereby in return for an army of 10,000 Irishmen he conceded on the king's behalf not only the repeal of the anti-catholic penal laws but public catholic worship in all the churches in Confederate-held territory. Furthermore Irish catholics were to be subject to no ecclesiastical jurisdiction but that of their own clergy. But the agreement was to be kept secret until this Irish army was on English soil, and Glamorgan insisted on signing a 'defeasance' which he hoped would give him a let-out if the king would not consent to the concessions he had made. It was a tortuous business, and Glamorgan probably went beyond his instructions, but having been briefed to negotiate behind the Lord Lieutenant's back he may well have been unsure how far his discretion stretched. The extent of Charles's double-dealing is further revealed by his readiness later in the summer to receive a special envoy from Mazarin named Jean de Montreuil, whose mission was to broker a rapprochement between the king and the Scottish Covenanters.

Glamorgan's treaty never stood much chance of being implemented, and it was doomed by the end of the year. In October the pope sent Giovanni Battista Rinuccini, Archbishop of Fermo, to Ireland as his nuncio. Rinuccini was a thoroughgoing ultramontane, and his overriding aims were to restore public catholic worship and the power of the catholic church in Ireland. He called Glamorgan to Kilkenny for discussions, and reached an agreement with him on 20 December which added further concessions to those of the August treaty. The church was to regain most of its lands, catholic bishops were to sit in the Irish House of Lords, and the next Lord Lieutenant was to be a catholic. Rinuccini's position was strengthened by two letters that Charles had written in his own hand on 20 October to the pope and the cardinal secretary of state, expressing his full confidence in Glamorgan and promising to ratify any agreement that he made. Unfortunately the Archbishop of Tuam had recently been killed in a skirmish near Sligo and a copy of Glamorgan's August treaty was found on him. It was sent to London and published on parliament's orders; consequently when Glamorgan returned to Dublin on 26 December Ormond had him arrested and charged with treason. A month later the king publicly disavowed Glamorgan's treaty, and denied that the earl had any commission to make concessions regarding religion, or to nego- tiate over anything but the raising of forces, without Ormond's 'privity and directions'. That almost put paid to the chances that any such forces would be raised. Ormond released Glamorgan when faced with a refusal by the Con- federates' Supreme Council to negotiate any further until he was freed, but Rinuccini had rather lost interest in him by then. The reason was that the queen had concluded a separate treaty with the pope on her husband's behalf, through her envoy Sir Kenelm Digby, and it granted the Irish catholics even more than Glamorgan had conceded.[35]

During January and February 1646 Charles was trying to keep open even more incompatible options than have been described so far. On 5 December, and several times subsequently, he proposed that parliament should send commissioners to discuss peace terms and asked for safe-conducts for com- missioners of his own. These overtures were rightly seen as a bid to buy time, and ignored. He met Montreuil on 2 January and encouraged a plan for the Scottish army to join with the English presbyterians in fighting for him, with armed assistance from France. The Scottish commissioners in London were interested, but he would not pay their price; he was prepared to tolerate Pres- byterianism, he told Montreuil, but not to make it the established religion of England. Henrietta Maria, who had persuaded Mazarin to send Montreuil, was impatient at such scruples, for she could see little to choose between one form of heresy and another. By January Charles was setting his hopes more on direct military aid from France, and was urging her to hasten the landing of 5,000 French troops at Hastings.

But there was no help to be had now from outside the realm, and nothing to stave off inevitable defeat within it. Early in January Fairfax set off on icy roads to clear the south-west, leaving enough troops to keep Exeter under siege. He took Dartmouth by assault on the 19th, then struck north- westward to engage Hopton. The crucial action was the storming of Tor- rington on the night of 16 February, for the ensuing pursuit left Hopton with only the tattered remnants of an army. Hopton went on resisting against

---

[35] This account of Charles's dealings with Ireland is based mainly on *A New History of Ireland*, III, 316–20; Ohlmeyer, *Civil War and Restoration in the Three Stuart Kingdoms*, pp. 160–5; M. Ó. Siochrú, *Confederate Ireland 1642–1649* (Dublin, 1999), chs. 2–3; and Gardiner, *Great Civil War*, ch. 39 (not included in the 3-volume edition cited elsewhere in this book, but printed near the end of the 4-volume edition).

hopeless odds for as long as the Prince of Wales and his council were still in the south-west, but the king was now writing to his son repeatedly, urging him to escape overseas. The prince was really in danger of capture now, and on 2 March, just as Fairfax's troops were occupying Bodmin, he sailed for the Scilly Isles. Soon afterwards Fairfax invited Hopton to treat on honourable terms, and he capitulated. The disbandment of the king's army of the west, such as it was, began on the 20th. Next day the 3,000 men who were left of his main field army, marching from Worcestershire towards Oxford under old Lord Astley, were utterly defeated at Stow-on-the-Wold. After that only a few garrisons remained under arms for him. Exeter was the most important after Oxford and Newark, and on 9 April Fairfax took its surrender on generous terms—generous not only in granting its defenders all the honours of war but in guaranteeing its cathedral and indeed all the city's churches against defacement. The chivalry with which Fairfax treated his enemies in their defeat and the discipline that he kept in his army helped to bring an end to resistance without pointless loss of life; so did the wide publicity given to the Glamorgan treaty and to the correspondence between king and queen over military intervention by France. Damaging letters from Henrietta Maria were intercepted when a French sea captain put into Dartmouth, believing the port to be still in royalist hands.

Once he was unopposed in the field, Fairfax set about preparing to besiege Oxford. Anxious at all costs to avoid capture, Charles slipped out of the city at 3 a.m. on 27 April, disguised as a servant, with only his friend Jack Ashburnham and his chaplain Michael Hudson for company. His intentions are something of a mystery, and he may not have been clear about them himself. He had told his council that he was going to London, and he first took a circuitous route towards the capital. Was this just a feint, or had he some kind of assurance that he would be well received at Westminster? He halted for three hours at Hillingdon, as if waiting for a message, and then rode on to Harrow, within sight of London's towers. After a night at Wheathampstead he turned north-eastward to Downham Market in Norfolk. He was heading now towards the Scottish army, which was besieging Newark and had its headquarters at Southwell. Montreuil was there, and Charles sent Hudson forward to seek his assurances that the Scots would support him. But since Montreuil had been negotiating with the Scots for over seven months, and Charles had been in personal touch with him since early January, it is strange that there was such uncertainty about his reception. The fact that Charles awaited Hudson's return so close to King's Lynn suggests that he was keeping open the option of fleeing overseas, if all else failed.

Hudson could not obtain the written assurance of Scottish armed support that Charles urged Montreuil to procure for him. The Scots commissioners did, however, assent verbally to four engagements that Montreuil set down on paper. The most important were that they would not press the king to do anything against his conscience, and that if parliament refused to restore him to his rights and prerogatives they would declare for him. With that he had to be content, and he rode into Southwell on 5 May. From the moment when he put himself into the Scots' hands he was treated as a prisoner, and he remained one for the rest of his life. They insisted for a start that he should order Newark to surrender, and he did so.

The inevitable surrender of Oxford followed, after a lengthy negotiation. A few other garrisons still held out, but there is no need to follow their capitulation in detail, for the first Civil War was to all intents and purposes over.

# PART II: FURTHER READING

On the events leading to civil war Conrad Russell, *The Fall of the British Monarchies 1637–1642* (Oxford, 1991) integrates developments in all three kingdoms as never before and is essential reading. Anthony Fletcher, *The Outbreak of the English Civil War* (1981) retains considerable value for England, while for Scotland David Stevenson, *The Scottish Revolution 1637–44* (Newton Abbot, 1973) is lucid and authoritative. Several essays in John Morrill (ed.), *The Scottish National Covenant in its British Context* (Edinburgh, 1990) bear on these years. For events in Ireland *A New History of Ireland*, vol. III, provides as ever an excellent survey (see Part I: Further Reading). It is supplemented by M. Percevall-Maxwell, *The Outbreak of the Irish Rebellion of 1641* (Dublin, 1994), the essays in Brian Mac Cuarta (ed.), *Ulster 1641: Aspects of the Rising* (Belfast, 1993; revised ed., 1997), Jane H. Ohlmeyer, *Civil War and Restoration in the Three Stuart Kingdoms* (Cambridge, 1993: focused on Antrim's career), Micheàl Ó Siochrú, *Confederate Ireland 1642–1649* (Dublin, 1999), and J. H. Ohlmeyer (ed.), *Ireland from Independence to Occupation* (Cambridge, 1995). New light on both Scotland and Ireland is cast by the essays in John R. Young (ed.), *Celtic Dimensions of the British Civil Wars* (Edinburgh, 1997).

On politics at Westminster, J. H. Hexter, *The Reign of King Pym* (Cambridge, Mass., 1941) has come under cogent criticism from John Morrill in S. Amussen and M. Kishlansky (eds.), *Political Culture and Cultural Politics in Early Modern England* (Manchester, 1997), but Hexter is still worth reading. Valerie Pearl gives masterly treatment to the vital topic of *London and the Outbreak of the Puritan Revolution* (Oxford, 1961). Since the late 1960s, however, there has been a most fruitful shift in the focus of historical research from the capital to the localities, which has shown how varied were the responses to the war and the patterns of allegiance. The best introduction to this field is by John Morrill in *Revolt in the Provinces* (1999), a revised and expanded version of his earlier *The Revolt of the Provinces* (1976). Morrill, besides writing one of the best county studies in *Cheshire 1630–1660* (Oxford, 1974), has explored the diversity of allegiance further in Part II of his collected essays, *The Nature of the English Revolution* (1993). On this topic see also David Underdown, *Revel, Riot and Rebellion* (Oxford, 1985) and Joyce L. Malcolm, *Caesar's Due: Loyalty and King Charles 1642–1646* (1983).

Studies of counties and other local communities have multiplied, and space forbids the mention of more than a selection. Mary Coate on *Cornwall in the Great Civil War* (Oxford, 1937; 2nd ed. Truro, 1963) and A. C. Wood, *Nottinghamshire in the Civil War* (Oxford, 1937) were honourable precursors, but the tide really began to flow with J. T. Cliffe on *The Yorkshire Gentry* (1969), A. M. Everitt, *The Local Community and the Great Rebellion* (1969), the same author's *The Community of Kent and the Great Rebellion* (Leicester, 1970), R. W. Ketton-Cremer, *Norfolk in the Civil War* (1969), Eugene A. Andriette, *Devon and Exeter in the Civil War* (Newton Abbot, 1971), David Underdown, *Somerset in the Civil War and Interregnum* (Newton Abbot,

1973), Clive Holmes, *The Eastern Association in the English Civil War* (Cambridge, 1974), B. G. Blackwood, *The Lancashire Gentry and the Great Rebellion* (Manchester, 1978), Anthony Fletcher, *A County Community in Peace and War: Sussex 1600–1660* (1975), Ann Hughes, *Politics, Society and Civil War in Warwickshire* (Cambridge, 1987), and Roy Sherwood, *The Civil War in the Midlands* (Stroud, 1992). See also note 17 to Chapter 8.

There are many narrative histories of the first Civil War as a whole, all of them indebted to S. R. Gardiner, *The History of the Great Civil War* (3 vols., 1886–91; 4 vol. ed. 1893), but for grace and readability none surpasses C. V. Wedgwood, *The King's War* (1958). Those who like their military history written by professional soldiers can best turn to Peter Young and Richard Holmes, *The English Civil War . . . 1642–1651* (1974), but particularly commendable for its integration of all three kingdoms is Martyn Bennett, *The Civil Wars in Britain & Ireland 1638–1651* (Oxford, 1997), the best one-volume history currently available. The authoritative work on the New Model is Ian Gentles, *The New Model Army in England, Scotland and Ireland 1645–1653* (Oxford, 1992). Mark A. Kishlansky, *The Rise of the New Model Army* (Cambridge, 1979) is illuminating but sometimes controversial on its formation; where he and Gentles differ, Gentles is generally to be preferred. C. H. Firth, *Cromwell's Army* (1902, repr. 1992) remains valuable on its composition, organization, and equipment. The experience of soldiering is vividly conveyed by Charles Carlton in *Going to the Wars* (1992), and the same author's *Charles I: The Personal Monarch* (1983) is the best biography for the war years. Two close studies of particular battles stand out: Peter Newman, *The Battle of Marston Moor* (Chichester, 1981), and Glenn Foard, *Naseby: The Decisive Campaign* (Guildford, 1995). Two books are particularly valuable for topography: Peter Gaunt, *The Cromwellian Gazetteer* (Gloucester, 1987) and Peter Newman, *Atlas of the English Civil War* (1985). Among recommendable biographies, John Wilson, *Fairfax* (1985) is a good popular life, though serious students will still turn to Sir Clement Markham's full and scholarly *Life of the Great Lord Fairfax* (1890). Similarly, Frank Kitson, *Prince Rupert* (1994) is sound and concise, but no modern work really supersedes Eliot Warburton, *Memoirs of Prince Rupert and the Cavaliers* (3 vols., 1849). John Buchan's exciting and well researched *Montrose* (1928) remains hard to beat. By comparison Vernon F. Snow, *Essex the Rebel* (Lincoln, Nebr., 1970) is pedestrian, though useful. For books on Cromwell see Further Reading for Part IV.

For religious disputes in England and the Westminster Assembly the standard work is still W. A. Shaw, *A History of the English Church during the Civil Wars and under the Commonwealth* (2 vols., 1900).

# PART III

## Towards a Kingless Britain
### 1646–1649

# ✝ ELEVEN ✝

# Between Two Wars

BETWEEN the last battle in the first Civil War and the first military action in the second, just over two years elapsed in which the British peoples licked their wounds and counted the cost of civil strife. Their experience naturally coloured their attitudes to the quest for a peace settlement and, when that quest failed, their animus against those whom they counted responsible for the renewal of war.

Enough has probably been said already about the unprecedented weight of taxation, the forcing of unwilling conscripts into a hard and dangerous service, the burden of free quarter, the commandeering of goods and horses, the unauthorized plunder by the soldiery of both sides, and the often oppressive demands made by the parliament's county committees and by royalist commanders. Here is perhaps the place to take stock briefly of the toll that civil war had so far taken in human lives, in the scars physical and mental that it had left on the survivors, and in the lasting material damage that it had inflicted. The main emphasis will be on England and Wales, because they were the main theatres of war and their peoples took the heaviest casualties. Ireland's agony still lay mainly in the future, and will be considered in its place.

It is very hard to assess the scale of fatal casualties, because contemporary estimates often varied wildly and tended to exaggerate. The tally of dead left on battlefields might be more or less accurately counted, but not the numbers of those who were cut down in a pursuit or who subsequently died of their wounds. Moreover major battles account for only about 15 per cent of fatalities; more than three times as many fell in skirmishes or other minor actions, and sieges were responsible for nearly a quarter. Most of the rest are attributable to exploding powder-barrels, bursting pistols, and fatal accidents with muskets. A careful recent estimate suggests that the total number who died by these various means in England and Wales between 1642 and 1651 came to over 84,000, and that over 62,000 of them perished in the first Civil War. In the seventeenth century, however, war-related diseases, especially typhus and dysentery and the ravages of plague in besieged cities which allowed no escape, regularly took a heavier toll than actual combat, and probably carried off at least 100,000. If these figures are anything like correct, they may mean that in proportion to the whole population the civil wars carried off more English and Welsh dead than the First World War, and certainly many more than the Second.[1]

Generally speaking, infantrymen suffered much higher casualties than cavalrymen, though it depended very much on whether they served in garrisons or in field armies. Those in the latter who survived the heavy slaughter in major battles, the gruelling marches with poor footwear and meagre rations, the epidemics of the camp and the nights in the open, often in wet clothes, were fortunate, though many lost limbs or bore other scars of war. Common soldiers who were wounded in the field were lucky if they received the services of a surgeon, and if they did so there was no anaesthetic to relieve the agony of an amputation and no effective antiseptics to stave off gangrene. Those who were made prisoners of war would expect to be plundered of any possessions and stripped of any clothes worth taking, and were likely to be crammed suffocatingly into churches or other buildings and half starved before further arrangements were made for them. Sometimes a triumphant enemy subjected them to collective public humiliation. The luckiest were exchanged, or set free under promise not to fight again; the unluckiest were sold as indentured servants to planters in Barbados and worked to death, though this happened mainly to those taken between 1648 and 1651. Many on both sides promptly enlisted in their captors' army, for war had become a way of life to them; they knew no other trade, and peace must have brought them problems.

The experience of garrison troops varied very greatly, from relative comfort and idleness if they never came under attack to sheer horror if they succumbed to a direct assault after a long siege. But with regard to sieges, one cannot draw a hard line between the experiences of soldiers and civilians, or indeed between those of men and women. All shared, if unequally, the blight of hunger and hardship and disease that a long siege imposed. Women often worked alongside men in building fortifications, putting out fires, taking their turn at guard duty, bringing food and drink to the soldiers under fire, reloading their muskets, and even sniping with them at the besiegers. There were famous defences in which women took full command, notably the Countess of Derby in Lathom House on the king's side and Lady Brilliana Harvey in Brampton Bryan Castle on the parliament's. But the worst civilian suffering occurred in populous towns which stood long sieges, for the attacking commanders seldom allowed women and children to leave since their departure would allow resistance to be prolonged. One can barely imagine the squalor and stench when water was too scarce for people to wash their clothes or

[1] Charles Carlton, 'The impact of the fighting', in John Morrill (ed.), *The Impact of the English Civil War* (1991), pp. 17–31, esp. 17–20. Charles Carlton writes vividly of the experience of the civil wars by both soldiers and civilians in *Going to the Wars* (1992).

bodies, when hunger made them too weak to bury their dead, and when sewage had no escape from a surrounding ditch or a sluggish mid-town river.

If the defending commander refused terms of surrender and the town was taken by storm, it was generally reckoned on both sides that the attacking troops were entitled to what they could get by sacking it. Soldiers who had been through the extreme danger of assaulting manned fortifications were apt to engage in indiscriminate slaughter and wanton destruction, wrecking what they could not take with them and sell. Yet in comparison with the continental wars there was generally some restraint, and there seems to have been very little rape. England experienced nothing remotely comparable to the sack of Magdeburg in 1631, in which a whole population of perhaps 24,000 perished, let alone the still ghastlier atrocities committed three centuries later in Japan's attempt to conquer China and in the war on Europe's eastern front. And things were on the whole getting better, not worse, by 1645. Before Fairfax stormed Bristol he promised his men two weeks' pay in lieu of a sack, and a grateful corporation was glad to help him find the money. The discipline of the New Model Army after Naseby, and Fairfax's readiness to grant honourable terms to garrisons, not only shortened a war that might have been prolonged by desperate resistances, but saved many lives and spared much property.

Scottish casualties in England were not very heavy in the first Civil War, because Leven's army did so little serious fighting after Marston Moor. They would be heavier when the Scots fought for the king in the Preston and Worcester campaigns of 1648 and 1651, which brought the number of those killed fighting in England to an estimated total of 6,120. In Scotland itself, Montrose's campaigns were small in scale but took a severe toll in men killed—an estimated 2,400 on his side and 12,300 on the Covenanters', though the figures are in the estimator's words 'inspired guesses'.[2]

Material damage in England was generally greater in the towns than in the countryside, though the destruction of crops and orchards and timber caused hardship enough at the time. At least 150 towns sustained significant destruction of property, though actual war damage was very unequally distributed, since in the first Civil War there was no serious military action east of a line drawn through King's Lynn, Cambridge, London, and Arundel. The Midlands and the Welsh borders were the worst affected areas, though parts of Wales itself and the West Country suffered considerably. Posterity has tended to focus on the ruination of churches and castles and mansions, but in terms of human suffering the destruction of ordinary dwelling-houses took a far heavier toll. It has been reckoned, necessarily very roughly, that 10,000 houses were demolished or burnt down in towns and at least 1,000 in villages,

[2] Carlton, *Going to the Wars*, pp. 211–12.

which would suggest that about one in ten inhabitants of provincial cities and towns were made homeless—and many more in the main theatres of war.[3] But it was not only in war-torn regions that people lost their homes, because many were deliberately demolished before an enemy came near. Few towns still had their medieval or Tudor defences intact, and some newer ones had never had any. Where defensible walls survived, many buildings had gone up outside them since the last serious fighting in the Wars of the Roses, and these gave cover to attacking troops and miners, or denied the defending gunners or musketeers the clear field of fire that they needed. Many suburban dwellings were pulled down when war broke out, sometimes by order of the corporation, more often on the insistence of the local military commander. And in most defended towns existing fortifications needed to be extended or new ones created; bastions were built out from old walls and sconces erected outside them. Usually this necessitated the demolition of dwelling-houses, though in the suburbs some were so flimsy that they could be taken down and reerected elsewhere.

Damage by direct military action took many forms. Bombardment was only one, and the slow rate of seventeenth-century cannon-fire and the limited effectiveness of solid shot fired at low velocity made it much less destructive than those who have been under modern aerial or artillery attack might imagine. Fires were a greater menace, especially where thatched roofs were the norm, and considerable use was made of red-hot shot to start them. Even more effective, and more damaging to civilian morale, were the hollow iron grenades filled with gunpowder or quick-burning material that were fired over the walls by large mortars with a high trajectory. But these were scarce and very expensive weapons; Essex had only one mortar in 1643, as did Fairfax when the New Model first took the field, though by the end of the war he could deploy six in an important siege. Fires were sometimes started by attacking troops, if they had the wind behind them, in order to blind or choke the defenders, and towns which refused terms of surrender were sometimes torched in the aftermath of an assault, if it had proved costly in casualties. Yet considering how combustible most houses were when timber, lath-and-plaster and thatch were the commonest building materials, serious firestorms were surprisingly rare and most fires were more or less successfully contained. Town corporations were well aware of the danger and made serious provision against it. The worst fire in England during the war years, which destroyed three hundred houses in Oxford in 1643, was started accidentally; the war had nothing to do with it.

In the most heavily war-damaged towns it might be thirty years or more before their stricken suburbs were fully rebuilt. Gloucester's population had

---

[3] Stephen Porter, *Destruction in the English Civil Wars* (Stroud, 1994), p. 66 and *passim*. This and the following paragraphs are heavily indebted to Dr Porter's excellent study.

not recovered its pre-war level by the end of the century, and York's was about the same in the 1760s as in 1640, but this was partly because the tide of economic expansion was passing these cities by. Elsewhere there was a great deal of reconstruction in the 1650s and 1660s, and most of the material ravages of war were repaired within a generation.

Some losses were of course irreparable, and the destruction wrought in some cathedrals, whether by military action as in Lichfield or bigoted iconoclasm as in Ely, was tragic. Churches in defended towns quite often suffered because their towers were manned by gunners and snipers, or because they became the last refuge for a desperate garrison. Not all were rebuilt, and one reason why some survive in ruins is that many towns had become over-provided with churches by the 1640s. It is always worth checking whether the smashing of medieval glass and statuary which the folk memory chalks up to 'Cromwell's soldiers' can be justly blamed on them. Often it turns out to have taken place in the first wave of the Reformation nearly a century earlier, under the aegis of Thomas Cromwell, and most of the deliberate wrecking that did occur during the Civil War had the authority of a parliamentary ordinance of August 1643 which *commanded* the general demolition of altars and defacement of paintings and images. One of the parliamentary visitors who executed this order, William Dowsing, destroyed more ecclesiastical treasures in the two counties of Cambridgeshire and Suffolk than all the soldiery of both sides in the whole course of the Civil Wars. This is not to excuse the vandalism committed by parliamentarian troops, who had been taught to regard cathedrals as centres of idolatry and did considerable damage to a dozen of them, as well as to Westminster Abbey. But parish churches suffered much less by them; of more than 9,000 in England and Wales they are known to have despoiled fewer than thirty.[4]

Castles and country houses suffered heavily during the wars, usually because they were garrisoned. Most castles underwent the greatest damage after the fighting ceased, when they were deliberately made indefensible. Some, like Banbury and Tickhill and Pontefract, were in large part demolished, but more often they were 'slighted', which generally meant having their outer walls destroyed while their living quarters were left relatively intact. That was the fate of Kenilworth, Sudeley, Dudley, Denbigh, Montgomery, Pembroke, and Raglan, among others. Many country houses too were garrisoned. The more important defended towns were commonly surrounded by a ring of satellite garrisons, often in suitably sited mansions strengthened by defensive works, and if the central stronghold had to be abandoned the satellites were sometimes demolished so as to deny the enemy the use of them.

---

[4] Gentles, *New Model Army*, pp. 109–10. St Paul's may be added to the eleven cathedrals named by Dr Gentles.

Between 150 and 200 country houses are reckoned to have been destroyed, including such a gem as Sir Baptist Hicks's mansion in Chipping Campden. In the later stages parliament made a conscious attempt to limit the damage. Countermanding a county committee's instructions to burn a great house in order to prevent it from being occupied and defended by the royalists, the Committee of Both Kingdoms stated in April 1646 that it did not 'think it fit that all houses whose situation or strength render them capable of being made garrisons should be pulled down. There would be then too many sad marks left of the calamity of this war.'[5] There were sad marks enough, but many country houses were rebuilt, and England was just entering upon her most glorious age of domestic architecture. The loss was not as great as in the case of medieval churches and castles, nor was the resultant distress to be compared with that of the poor whom the war rendered homeless.

The country was deeply war-weary when the fighting ended, but the prospects of its finding relief in a generally acceptable peace were heavily clouded. Superficially, a settlement might seem not to have been too difficult, since the war had not been a clash between irreconcilable ideologies. Both sides had professed to take up arms for much the same things: the rights and privileges of parliament, the just powers and prerogatives of the king, the true protestant religion, the fundamental laws of the land, and the liberties of the subject. That went for the Scots too, though their conception of the true protestant religion was different from that of most Englishmen. But the differences went deeper than the public rhetoric suggested, and they had deepened further with the years. In countries where government rested as much on consent as it did in England and Scotland, a durable peace demanded from the victors a certain magnanimity and a firm consensus about what they wanted, and from the losing side a realistic willingness to accept the minimal consequences of defeat. These desiderata were lacking in the Britain of 1646. The political divergences within the parliamentarian ranks, and the gap between the war aims of English and Scots, resulted in their jointly presenting the king with harsher terms than he could reasonably have been expected to submit to; while Charles was so dominated by his conviction that God would not let rebels proper, and that to give up any of his regal powers would be a sin, that his mind was closed to honourable terms even when (belatedly) they were offered to him. He never gave up the hope of somehow renewing the war and winning it.

 The main line of political division at Westminster continued to lie between the presbyterians and independents, but since the chief plank in the independents' platform had been to fight the war to a successful conclusion their

---

[5] Quoted in Porter, *Destruction in the English Civil Wars*, p. 63.

ascendancy was much less secure after it was won. The New Model Army, which was largely their creation, was still their ally, but it was the principal cause of the continuingly heavy taxes, and a large reduction in its establishment, and consequently in the excise and the assessment, became a popular policy. It was eagerly taken up by the presbyterians, who had always regarded the army, and Cromwell in particular, as their enemies. This, as we have seen, had forged a marriage of convenience between them and the Scots, which had tied the millstone of a Presbyterian religious settlement round their necks, though to be fair many of them embraced it with conviction. The popularity that they enjoyed, especially in the City, as the party which sought to cut military power and expenditure was, however, offset to some extent by their denial of liberty of conscience to Anglicans, Independents, and sectaries alike. The independents were also more interested in genuine constitutional reform, which would render the king's government permanently more accountable to the people's representatives, so long as 'the people' were not too democratically defined. The presbyterians were not entirely homogeneous, but Essex's party was still a power among them, and most were less concerned about reform than about ensuring that while the king remained under harness the reins should be in the hands of the presbyterian magnates and their clients. It was a paradox that while the presbyterians were the more anxious to see the king back on his throne and the war machine dismantled as soon as possible, they made demands regarding religion, the control of the armed forces, and the appointment of the essential officers of state that were more unacceptable to him than those which the independents were prepared to offer. For Charles, this was a chink in his enemies' armour that he would not be slow to probe.

He knew that the Scots distrusted the independents so intensely that they had been prepared to consider going over to his side, but it is remarkable that after all the months of Montreuil's mission he still did not know on what terms they would fight for him when he put himself in their hands. Can he have thought that his very presence would fire their loyalty and unsheathe their swords for him? If so he was soon disillusioned. They were amazed and delighted to acquire so strong a bargaining counter as his royal person, but having demanded and obtained his order for the surrender of Newark they took him back to Newcastle with them, where they treated him with little ceremony. He was very plainly a prisoner. He had not appreciated, though it should have been obvious, that their commitment to high Presbyterianism was as strong as his own to high Anglicanism, and that unless he would pledge himself to impose at least the Westminster Assembly's version of it on the whole English nation they would not be prepared to help him. He had to endure weeks of instruction in the true faith by Alexander Henderson, and much pressure from the commissioners to convert to it. He began to regret his surrender, and

sent a request to Westminster that he should be allowed to come and negotiate with parliament in person. But its members were steadily uncovering the
extent of his intrigues with the Scots, the French, and the Irish, and they went
on unhurriedly preparing their own peace terms. Argyll saw a danger that
England might come to a settlement with him that left the Scots out in the
cold, and he hastened to London to try and prevent it. Parliament's peace
propositions were ready when he got there and, though they fell short of the
Covenanters' full objectives regarding religious uniformity throughout
Britain, he and the Scottish commissioners accepted them without alteration.
Scottish fears of a separate English peace, and English suspicions of a deal
between Charles and the Scots, were thus allayed. There was no question of
inviting the king to Westminster, and the Propositions of Newcastle, as they
soon came to be called, were carried north to him by commissioners in
mid-July.

Although there was never a chance that he would accede to them, the
propositions deserve attention because for more than a year they were the
only peace terms to be formally put to him by either England or Scotland, and
they remained a basis for negotiation for longer than that. They were evidently drawn up on the assumption that as a prisoner, defeated in war, he had
no choice but to bow to the victors' demands. He was asked to swear and sign
the Solemn League and Covenant and to pass acts requiring all his subjects in
all three kingdoms to do the same. He must assent to further acts for the total
abolition of episcopacy, the reformation of religion according to the
Covenant, and the closest possible religious uniformity between England and
Scotland. An oath was to be imposed on all catholics, forcing them to for-
swear not only the pope's supremacy but their central doctrinal tenets, the
object being to leave no loophole for church papists. Those who declined
it were to be automatically subject to the penalties of recusancy, and to having their children compulsorily educated by protestants in the protestant
faith.

In secular matters, parliament was to have sole control of the armed forces
for twenty years, and the right to resume it at any later time when the two
Houses should declare the safety of the kingdom to be concerned. In twenty
years Charles would be 66, an age to which no King of England had lived
since Edward I. No peers made since 1642, nor any to be made in the future,
were to be admitted to parliament without the consent of both Houses.
All the major officers of state and all the judges were to be nominated in
perpetuity by both Houses, and were to continue in office *quam diu se bene
gesserint* (for so long as they conducted themselves satisfactorily). As for the
king's supporters, a long list of both English and Scots were to be excluded
from pardon altogether, more were to be banned from the court and public
employment, and all active royalists were to lose varying proportions

of their estates, from two-thirds downwards, according to the degree of their 'delinquency'.[6]

These were not all the humiliations that parliament proposed to inflict. A king who submitted to so much that offended his deepest beliefs and his sense of honour could have commanded no respect, and could have had none for himself. The radical limitations of the historic royal prerogative went far beyond what was necessary to prevent Charles from doing further mischief, and the savage penalties and prescriptions proposed for the beaten royalists might have been calculated to perpetuate divisions in the nation rather than to heal them. One wonders how many of the authors of these propositions had even considered what they would do if the king doggedly refused to accept them. The terms were not even offered as a basis for negotiation, for the delegates who brought them to him had to admit that they had no power to treat, but only to take his answers back to parliament. He was understandably angry; 'an honest trumpeter might have done as much', he told them. But Loudoun warned him that if he was intransigent he might end up by being deposed, so his formal reply was to request time to consider and for a safe conduct to London, so that he could negotiate in person.

That was not at the time a serious possibility, but it was the first move in a long stalling exercise from which he had much to gain. At Westminster, all the presbyterians and nearly all the independents wanted him back on his throne, and by playing them off against each other he stood a fair chance of securing easier terms. As for the Scots, the strict Covenanters were demanding a price that he was unwilling to pay, but Hamilton led a party of nobles and lairds who were prepared to fight for him without forcing his conscience, and their time would come. He had an iron in the fire too in Ireland, where after the fiasco of the Glamorgan treaty Ormond was still negotiating, on his instructions, with delegates of the Confederates in Dublin. Hostile as Rinuccini was towards Ormond and all he stood for, the nuncio was prepared to send 3,000 Irish troops to the relief of Chester, the last important town still holding out for the king. Ormond did sign a treaty with the Confederate delegates in March 1646, though nothing concrete was to come of it, since Chester surrendered in February. The negotiators agreed to keep it secret for the time being, but Ormond published it on 30 July. It was to divide the ranks of the Confederates even further than they were split already, for its concessions fell far short of what the clerical party wanted. It would have admitted catholics to office without taking the oath of supremacy, so long as they took the oath of allegiance, but it referred the repeal of the penal laws to the king's favour and left all other matters of religion to be dealt with elsewhere. Rinuccini was strongly opposed to the whole negotiation, and was furious when he heard

---

[6] Full text in Gardiner (ed.), *Constitutional Documents*, pp. 290–306.

that the treaty had been concluded, especially as he was not immediately informed of the fact. There was also much consternation at Westminster that Ormond had come so close to agreement with the catholic Irish, especially as the news of it came close on the heels of a severe defeat that Owen Roe O'Neill inflicted on Colonel Monro and his mainly Scottish forces at Benburb (near Armagh) on 5 June. Six weeks later the Confederates captured Bunratty and placed the important stronghold of Limerick under threat. These were sharp reminders that the reconquest of Ireland could not be put off indefinitely, and that England's own affairs needed to be put in order before an army could be released for the task. And before the problems of a peace settlement were tackled, the first Civil War was not quite over, for though the last royalist garrison in England surrendered in August 1646, the king's banner still flew over Holt, Chirk, and Harlech castles in Wales, and it was not hauled down at Harlech until 13 March 1647.

In Ireland, Ormond's treaty set the Supreme Council (which generally favoured it) at odds with the clerical party (which decidedly did not). There were three parties within the Confederation at this stage. Those who sought peace with the king in return for access to public office and de facto religious toleration were mostly laymen and included most of the Old English ascendancy, though they were by no means exclusively an Old English party, for no sharp lines could be drawn between the Old English and Old Irish nobles and gentry. They were intent on maintaining the king's rights to his Irish kingdom, even if he went down to defeat in England, though they expected reasonable concessions in return for their loyalty. Opposed to them were the clerical party which took its cue from Rinuccini, though not all the bishops were equally ready to follow his lead, and O'Neill was not the only prominent layman to support him; others of the Old Irish interest did likewise, not only in Ulster, and so did a few ultra-catholic Old English. This party sought the full restoration of the catholic church in Ireland and an independent Irish parliament. Rinuccini aimed at securing the enormous concessions which Henrietta Maria's representative Sir Kenelm Digby had agreed with Pope Innocent X, regardless of the fact that Charles would never confirm them. He was quite prepared to contemplate the defeat of the king; indeed he reported to Rome that it might actually help the cause, by uniting all Irish catholics against the English parliament. His preferred tactic was to pursue the complete military conquest of Ireland. Between these extremes there was for several years a middle group, whose leading figure was Nicholas Plunkett, a lawyer trained in Grays Inn, and the third son of Lord Killeen, an Old English Lord of the Pale. Plunkett was elected chairman of every General Assembly except the last, and he sat on every Supreme Council. He was a devout catholic (he counted the influential Bishop French of Ferns among his allies), but in the interests of unity, he and his group sought to moderate the positions assumed by the other two parties, and for considerable stretches of time they held the balance of power. At first Plunkett supported the Ormond treaty, but eventually he gave his full backing to Rinuccini, seeing the greatest threat to Ireland in a total victory for the English parliament.

Rinuccini did his best to wreck the Ormond treaty from the moment he learnt of it. He first got the majority of the bishops to sign a declaration, warning against the conclusion of any peace without his consent. He next summoned a national synod to Waterford, where the assembled Irish clergy pronounced an interdict on all places that accepted the treaty and excommunicated anyone who gave it any public support. In September the members of the Supreme Council who had promoted or encouraged it were imprisoned, and a new Supreme Council of sixteen, chosen by the synod, was set up with Rinuccini as its president. O'Neill fully accepted its authority, and supported the nuncio's plans to conquer the whole of Ireland, beginning with Dublin, by military force. Thomas Preston, the commander of the army of Leinster, was much less enthusiastic, partly because of his Old English lineage (his nephew Viscount Gormanston's title went back to 1478), and partly because he and O'Neill had been personal and professional rivals in the Spanish army of Flanders for a long time before their return to their native country. But for the present Preston obeyed the Supreme Council's commands, and the threat that his forces and O'Neill's posed to Dublin was immediate and formidable.

Faced with that threat, and with the likely rejection of the king's authority over Ireland that lay behind it, Ormond's position became intolerable. It would have been even more so if he had been aware that Charles had written to Glamorgan on 20 July, offering virtually to pawn his Irish kingdom in return for a large sum of money, and talking of coming over and putting himself in Glamorgan's and Rinuccini's hands. Nor did Ormond know that Rinuccini was manoeuvring to get him replaced as Lord Lieutenant by Glamorgan, who swore an oath of entire submission to the nuncio on 28 September. What he did know was that Charles had publicly repudiated the treaty that Glamorgan had concluded on his behalf in the previous year. Faced with an imminent attack on Dublin by the forces of Preston and O'Neill, it is entirely understandable that Ormond, as a protestant and as the senior Irish officer of the crown, could not contemplate surrendering the city to a body of rebels directed by an Italian servant of the pope, whose aims for Ireland clashed heavily with the real interests of his royal master, as well as with those of the Old English ascendancy that he represented. He therefore applied to the English parliament for help in defending Dublin, and it sent over commissioners to negotiate with him. Before they arrived, however, the city came under siege by the Confederate forces early in November.

It was not sustained. Rinuccini and O'Neill were afraid that Preston would strike a deal with Ormond (as he was ultimately to do), and O'Neill ordered him into winter quarters. Rinuccini backed the command with a threat of excommunication, and since it was so late in the year for campaigning O'Neill took his own troops into winter quarters. Their lawless and destructive behaviour outside their native Ulster made them widely unpopular, and was denounced not only by the moderate Plunkett but by Rinuccini himself. The immediate threat to Dublin collapsed, and the parliamentary commissioners began a negotiation there with Ormond on 14 November. But he had never contemplated unconditional surrender, and when he found them unwilling to allow the king to be any kind of a party to whatever treaty they might arrive at he broke it off, and they retired into Ulster. His conduct has recently been severely criticized, and Rinuccini's strategy of a total conquest of Ireland justified as constituting 'a pragmatic assessment of developments in the three Stuart kingdoms'.[7] But Ormond faced extraordinary difficulties in reconciling the opportunist tergiversations of his royal master (when he was kept informed of them) with the true long-term interests of the house of Stuart—not to mention his very sincere religious beliefs and his consciousness of his position as senior Old English magnate. On the whole he behaved with intelligence as well as with integrity. As for Rinuccini, his policy was not only bound to alienate a considerable part of the population of Ireland, but it was militarily unrealistic, for he grossly underestimated the power that England could bring to bear against his forces once her own civil war was over—as to all intents and purposes it was before he moved against Dublin.

The Scots were not as indifferent towards the king's fate as Rinuccini was, but for the time being they offered him little better prospect of armed assistance. Argyll's party continued to enjoy more support than Hamilton's among the nobles, lairds, and burgesses, and had the Kirk behind it. Since Charles persistently resisted its pressure to impose Presbyterianism on his English subjects, it came to regard him mainly as a bargaining counter for securing the payment of England's large debts for the maintenance of a Scottish army in England—debts which continued to mount for as long as it remained there. Charles came to see little prospect in his current situation beyond a possible change of gaolers, and from the early summer onward he began to plan an escape to France or Holland. To keep parliament interested in a possible negotiation, and to play upon its divisions, he found means from September onward of putting to it certain counter-proposals to those he had received at Newcastle. He would consider parting with control of the armed forces for ten years instead of twenty, and he would confirm the Presbyterian Church of England, now being established by ordinance, for three years, after which an assembly of twenty Presbyterian divines, twenty Independents, and twenty

<hr />

[7] Micheál Ó Siochrú, *Confederate Ireland 1642–1649* (Dublin, 1999), p. 107; see also pp. 77f., 106f., 248–9. Though I differ from Dr Ó Siochrú on some points of interpretation, I am much indebted to his work, especially concerning Plunkett and his middle group.

more of his own choosing should work out a final settlement. How seriously he intended these offers is doubtful, since he was simultaneously appealing to his wife and to his daughter Mary, William of Orange's wife, to provide the means for his escape. He was unhappily at odds with Henrietta Maria, who nagged him in her letters. She was impatient with his scruples about yielding to the Scottish demand that he should enforce Presbyterianism in England, which were making it harder for her to interest the French government in helping him, and she was shocked by his offer to cede control of the armed forces for ten years. Nevertheless a Dutch ship waited in New-castle harbour all through the late autumn, ostensibly to have its hull cleaned but really to carry him overseas. He hesitated, and when he did attempt a getaway on Christmas Day it was bungled. From then on his guards were doubled and his seaward escape route was patrolled by naval frigates.

He did not despair, because he had been receiving intelligence that large parts of England and Wales wanted so much to see him restored that they might be prepared to rise for him. It was not a vain hope, though it would be more than a year before the time was ripe for insurrections. The impetus behind this genuine popular discontent was not any great recrudescence of ideological royalism but rather a yearning to return to the old ways for which the monarchy stood in people's eyes. The peace had brought no substantial relief from crippling taxation, free quarter, the petty tyranny of county committees, and violence and plunder by ill-paid and mutinous soldiers. The New Model's discipline remained generally satisfactory, despite the fact that its pay was now far in arrears, but Fairfax's army accounted for less than half the men under arms in the country, not counting the Scots. Between May and September 1646 there were mutinies in no fewer than twenty-two English counties and in several Welsh ones, and the local population usually suffered through them.[8]

Hostility to the New Model itself remained strong in the City of London, which was always a centre of Presbyterianism, both religious and political, and became even more so with the autumn elections to the Common Council. The corporation petitioned parliament for the disbandment of the New Model Army, complaining of the widespread disaffection within it towards the new church government, and of the usurpation of pulpits by preaching soldiers in order to infect the people with 'strange and dangerous errors'. The Lords welcomed the petition with 'hearty thanks' and had it printed; the Commons received it coldly.[9] There had been an attempt by the party of Essex, Holles, and Stapleton to build up Massey's western brigade into a self-sufficient army, capable of counter-balancing Fairfax's, but in October

[8] John Morrill, 'Mutiny and discontent in English provincial armies', in *Nature of the English Revolution*, pp. 332–58; David Underdown, *Pride's Purge* (Oxford, 1971), pp. 39–40.

[9] Gentles, *New Model Army*, pp. 145–6.

parliament decided to disband Massey's force and to keep the New Model intact for a further six months. While the king was still in Scottish hands and known to be angling for armed assistance from abroad, it was the only sane decision.

It also showed that in such a crucial vote the independents could still command a majority. One reason was that from August 1645 onwards the Commons had been holding elections to the many seats made vacant in recent years by death or by the exclusion of active royalists. Nearly 270 new members were elected to the House between then and Pride's Purge, the great majority before the end of 1646. Most were chosen in the time-honoured way, in accordance with the candidates' standing in their county or other local communities, but a significant number of seats were contested on party lines. The net effect was to increase the strength of the independents and to add substantially to their radical wing. Among the recruiters, as they were called, were Cromwell's close associates Charles Fleetwood and Henry Ireton (who married his daughter Bridget in June 1646), the future republicans Edmund Ludlow and James and Thomas Chaloner, and the future Fifth Monarchists John Carew and Thomas Harrison. Henry Marten was readmitted to membership in January 1646, and though hardly anyone besides him was yet seriously contemplating the deposition of the king, the majority of the forty-three MPs who were to sign his death warrant were recruiters.

 The presbyterians were further weakened when Essex died in September 1646, following a stroke. He was genuinely mourned, and not only by his own party. Parliament voted £5,000 for the expenses of his funeral, which was the most magnificent since that of James I. He was buried in Westminster Abbey, whose chancel was draped in black from floor to roof for the occasion. Before the site of the then dismantled high altar, his funeral effigy, dressed in a military buff-coat and scarlet breeches beneath the parliamentary robes of an earl, was left standing after the ceremony, beneath a splendid catafalque designed by Inigo Jones. Five weeks later both effigy and catafalque were hacked to pieces in the night by a poor farmer from Dorset, who claimed that an angel had so commanded him, since Christ was dishonoured by the bringing of the image of a man into the house of God.[10]

With the passing of Essex, the baronial element in the parliamentary cause became more fragmented, and the thinly attended House of Lords had a diminished role in national politics. Saye, Northumberland, and Wharton still had a significant part to play, as leading independents. Manchester remained a presbyterian, though with a diminishing zest for public life; so too for the present did Warwick, though he was to side with the army in 1647. Warwick's vacillating brother Holland was entering his final royalist phase,

[10] Gardiner, *Great Civil War*, II, 533; Snow, *Essex the Rebel*, pp. 489–95.

which would cost him his life, whereas his one-time fellow-courtier Pembroke travelled the other way and was to finish up on the Council of State of the Commonwealth.

Despite some strengthening of the independents, parliament was so far committed to the religious settlement that the Westminster Assembly was working out that it continued to embody it in legislation, step by slow step. A Blasphemy Ordinance, imposing the death penalty for denying the Trinity, the Incarnation, and other central doctrines, and life imprisonment for rejecting infant baptism (among other disputed tenets), began its slow course through the two Houses in October. Presbyterians, Independents, and sectaries could at least agree in condemning episcopacy, whose formal abolition was effected when the Lords finally passed the necessary ordinance on 9 October. The main object now was to vest the hugely valuable episcopal lands in trustees so that they could be sold, for it was now becoming clear that a down payment of £200,000 would suffice to persuade the Scots to withdraw their army from England and hand over the king. The bishops' lands were immediately pledged for the raising of this sum. The Scots rather ambitiously reckoned England's total debt to them at £1,300,000, but they were prepared to accept £500,000, and further bargaining drove the sum down to £400,000. The Scottish commissioners obtained clearance from the committee of estates and the Scottish privy council in September to accept £200,000 on account as the price of withdrawing Leven's army. The decision was challenged, however, when the Scottish parliament met in November, and during December Hamilton, Lanark, and their party contended long and at first (it seemed) successfully that the army should be kept in England and the king granted his wish to go freely to London. But with busy support from the Kirk, Argyll and the majority finally carried it that unless Charles accepted the Propositions of Newcastle he should be delivered to the custody of the English parliament, and the army should come home. The Scottish parliament obtained face-saving assurances from Westminster that no peace would be concluded without the consent of both kingdoms, and that meanwhile the form of government in England would not be changed.[11] The Scots were predictably accused of selling their king, not least by Charles himself, and parallels with Judas were drawn from the day they handed him over. The strictures were unjust. The transaction may be unappealing, but the Scots had gone to war for the Covenant, and in face of his persistent rejection of it they were entitled to say 'no Covenant, no pikes and muskets'.

So he passed into the hands of the English parliament's commissioners, and the last of Leven's army left England on 3 February 1647. The place of his next imprisonment had been contested, and was a political decision. The

---

[11] Stevenson, *Revolution and Counter-Revolution in Scotland*, pp. 75–81.

Lords had voted to bring him to Newmarket, a favourite Stuart stamping-ground in country where political presbyterians and outright royalists were thick on the ground. But the Commons had their way and lodged him in Holmby (or Holdenby) House in puritan Northamptonshire, where he could be held more securely. It was the largest private house in England, built by Queen Elizabeth's Lord Chancellor Sir Christopher Hatton. Puritans or not, the gentry of the county turned out in force to greet him, and the regiments that guarded him were chosen for their presbyterian commanders. In overall command of them was Major-General Richard Browne, who had never fought in the New Model and would soon be openly defying it. Charles was given a large household and a lavish royal table, and the military presence was relaxed enough to allow him to ride over to neighbouring country houses, including Lord Spencer's Althorp, to play bowls. What he continued to miss most were the ministrations of his Anglican chaplains, and considering how much most of his captors wanted to come to terms with him the denial was as impolitic as it was ungenerous.

Once the Scots had gone home and the king was in English hands, the pressure for a massive reduction of the military forces was stepped up and the independents found themselves no longer strong enough to resist it. One of the New Model's most formidable assailants was Thomas Edwards, an intolerant and intemperate Presbyterian divine, who in the course of 1646 hammered the Independents and sectaries in the three massive parts of his *Gangræna*. The gangrene lay in the heresies with which they were infecting the body politic, and the third part, published late in December, particularly targeted the army. Bigoted though he was, Edwards did reckon that not more than a quarter of the New Model consisted of Independents and separatists, but he found this minority dangerous on secular as well as religious grounds. Besides the usual accusations that officers and soldiers preached in public, spread false doctrine, disturbed church services, and defied the parliament's ordinances regarding worship and church government, he charged them with harbouring subversively radical political beliefs, in particular that supreme authority rightly belonged only to the Commons, as the representatives of the people. He admitted, however, that he had found very little anti-monarchical feeling in the army.[12] There was indeed very little as yet, and no political activity as such, but many officers and men resented the overt hostility of the City and the Scots and cordially reciprocated it. They already feared that their enemies inside and outside parliament would combine together to impose a perfidious peace, probably after getting most of the army out of the way by sending it to Ireland.

[12] T. Edwards, *The Third Part of Gangræna* (1646); A. Woolrych, *Soldiers and Statesmen: The General Council of the Army and its Debates 1647–1648* (Oxford, 1987), pp. 21–3.

Their apprehensions were justified. As soon as the Scottish army departed, the Commons' chamber was resounding with complaints against preaching officers and soldiers, causing Bulstrode Whitelocke to remark that 'those who were so lately in their highest esteem and respect, as freers of their county from servitude and oppression, are now by the same people looked upon as sectaries and oppressors themselves'.[13] Cromwell was not present in the House to stand up for the army, since he fell seriously ill late in January and remained incapacitated until well into March. Just a fortnight after the last Scottish soldier left English soil, the Commons began to debate whether the axe should fall first on the New Model or on the various provincial forces, such as Poyntz's Northern Association army. It might have been supposed that on grounds of military effectiveness and natural justice the victorious regiments of Fairfax and Cromwell had an overwhelming claim to furnish the nucleus of whatever standing force was kept afoot, and so the independents urged, but they were narrowly defeated. Two days after that vote the Commons decided that the army in England should consist of just 5,400 cavalry and 1,000 dragoons, with no regular infantry beyond the complement of a few scattered garrisons. Even without our knowledge that a new civil war was little more than a year away, it should have been obvious that this provision was utterly inadequate, at least until the king and the Scots had been brought to binding peace terms.

Early in March the Commons voted that the army for Ireland should consist of 4,200 horse and dragoons, and that all of it was to be drawn from Fairfax's army. The aim to destroy the New Model as an entity was now blatantly obvious. Before deciding whether to incorporate any part of it in the home army of 6,400, the Commons voted to keep up the regiments of Poyntz and two other presbyterians in his northern forces. There was even an attempt to take the home command from Fairfax and give it to the presbyterian Richard Graves, who had been lieutenant-colonel of Essex's own regiment of horse and had fought at neither Naseby nor Bristol. This was defeated only by 159 votes to 147, but other motions equally hostile to the New Model, and to Cromwell in particular, were actually carried: for instance that no officer under Fairfax should rank higher than colonel, that none should be exempt from taking the Covenant and conforming to the Presbyterian ecclesiastical establishment, and that no MPs should hold military commands in England. That would have prevented Fairfax from standing again for parliament, as he had recently done, and would have forced Cromwell, Ireton, and several other old Ironsides to choose between resigning their seats or their commands.

[13] B. Whitelocke, *Memorials of the English Affairs* (1682), p. 240, and cf. p. 238; Gentles, *New Model Army*, p. 147.

It may well be wondered how so many provocative and ill-willed proposals were approved by a House in which a majority had supported the New Model from its inception to the end of the war. One answer is that not all who had accepted the need for the army loved it, especially when Cromwell and many of his fellow-officers had manifested opposition to the parliamentary religious settlement. The independents at Westminster were not so much a political party as a loose coalition of members, bound together mainly by a common dedication to outright military victory. Once victory was achieved, many of their more pragmatical adherents fell away. The concerted anti-military pressure of the City corporation, whose financial co-operation with parliament gave it a powerful lever, played its part. The presbyterians at this stage displayed rather more of the characteristics of a party, with a leadership that paid close attention to political management and pursued its ends with considerable short-term tactical skill. Holles and Stapleton, who had been Essex's closest friends and allies in the Commons, acted countless times as tellers in crucial votes, and they headed a tightly knit group of fellow-activists. They probably had no illusions about the possibility of forcing the Newcastle Propositions upon the king, but when the time should become ripe for compromise they wanted to set the terms and share out the spoils of office. They rightly saw the army as a potential obstacle to any such design, and they set about getting rid of it. But they could not rely solely on the uncertain votes of a now almost evenly balanced House of Commons; they needed an executive instrument, and they forged one.

With the end of the war, and still more with the departure of the Scottish army, the Committee of Both Kingdoms became less appropriate as a national executive, and in October 1646 parliament set up a new Committee for Irish Affairs, consisting of the older committee's still active members with the addition of Holles, his ally Sir John Clotworthy, and five others. From its place of meeting it came to be called the Derby House Committee. The newcomers gave it a heavily presbyterian bias, and since the recovery of Ireland and the necessary military and financial provision for it were matters of urgency, it gradually assumed most of the general executive role of its parent body, the Committee of Both Kingdoms. It was specifically entrusted with framing proposals for a general reorganization of the military establishment, as well as for an expeditionary force to Ireland. All the moves that drove the army into revolt were planned and managed from Derby House. Cromwell's illness kept him away during a crucial period, and the army's other friends on the older committee, outnumbered now and reluctant to be seen as parties to decisions they deplored, mostly stopped attending. The Lords showed some jealousy of the power that the Derby House Committee was assuming, but Holles and Stapleton squared them by securing a vote in April 1647 to add six more peers to it, along with five more MPs. Since the Lords' nominees were solidly conservative and the Commons' included Massey and others of like mind, the independents were left for a time with no answer to the presbyterians' political machine.[14]

'There want not in all places men who have so much malice against the army as besots them', wrote the convalescent Cromwell to Fairfax on 11 March; 'never were the spirits of men more embittered than now.'[15] That same day the Commons received a particularly venomous petition against it from Essex, where it had its headquarters at Saffron Walden, and within a week yet another from the corporation of London, calling again for its disbandment. But by then a very different petition was beginning to circulate within the army. It arose spontaneously among the troopers of the cavalry, who were reacting to the orchestrated public hostility to which the army was being subjected and to the treatment with which it was threatened. The men were chiefly concerned about three things: the threat of being disbanded without their full arrears of pay, which ran to forty-three weeks in the cavalry; their liability, when disbanded, to be prosecuted for acts committed in war; and the conditions of service that they faced if they were sent to Ireland. Including as they did many of the longest-serving soldiers in the parliament's service, and most of them having enlisted as volunteers, they did not see why they should be compelled to go to Ireland when shorter-serving conscripts were being paid off, and if they did go they wanted to fight alongside their old comrades, under the regimental officers and the general whom they knew.

Parliament first became aware of this petitioning movement after Waller, Clotworthy, and another MP visited Fairfax's headquarters on 21–2 March, as delegates from the Derby House Committee, to discuss with him the formation and dispatch of an army for Ireland. Apparently they were hoping to find enough officers ready to engage themselves and their men to constitute then and there the full force of 12,600 that had been voted, but Fairfax knew of his men's grievances and sympathized with them. To meet the commissioners he summoned an unusually large council of war—forty-three officers besides himself—and not one of them would undertake to serve in Ireland until they were satisfied on certain points. Severally, they raised four questions. What regiments were to be kept up in England? Who was to command those who went to Ireland? What assurances of regular pay and support could be given to those who enlisted? And how was parliament going to provide for the army's arrears of pay and its members' indemnity for acts committed in war? Somewhat taken aback, the commissioners probed the officers' solidarity by pressing each one individually on all four questions. All

---

[14] On the Derby House Committee and its treatment of the army see M. Kishlansky, *The Rise of the New Model Army* (Cambridge, 1979), *passim*. Kishlansky puts a kinder construction on the presbyterians' proceedings than I do.

[15] Abbott, *Writings and Speeches of Oliver Cromwell*, I, 430.

present held firm on the last two, but five dissociated themselves from the first and twelve from the second. It was the beginning of a rift between a minority of officers whose political sympathies were presbyterian, or who wanted to pursue their careers in Ireland, and the majority who sought to maintain the solidarity of all ranks in the army and distrusted the presbyterian politicians' intentions. The commissioners made what capital they could of this disagreement before leaving headquarters, and parliament was to play on it in the coming months.

More than one petition was circulating among the soldiery by this time, and it seems that sympathetic officers, of whom there were many, consolidated the men's grievances into a single document, persuaded them to address it to Fairfax, their general, rather than to parliament, and pruned away passages that strayed into political territory. It emerged as 'The petition of the officers and soldiers of the army', and it asked for just five things: a parliamentary ordinance to guarantee their indemnity, security for the payment of their arrears before they were disbanded, regular pay while still in service, no compulsion on those who had enlisted voluntarily to serve outside the kingdom and no conscription of cavalrymen into the infantry, and finally some provision for maimed ex-soldiers and for the widows and children of the fallen. These were all fair requests, respectfully expressed, and confined to the soldiers' interests as soldiers. The petition was not published until after parliament itself made it notorious by exploding in anger over it. The three commissioners somehow got hold of a copy while they were at headquarters, and Clotworthy produced it when he reported to the Commons on their mission on 27 March. The House immediately ordered Fairfax to suppress it, but though he tried to stop it going any further the petitioning movement had taken on a momentum of its own. When the Commons listened to letters of intelligence two days later, alleging (whether with any truth we do not know) that the campaign was being directed by a group of senior officers, Ireton among them, and that signatures to the petition were still being collected under threat of cashiering, they boiled over. They instructed the Derby House Committee to segregate all the officers and men who were willing to serve in Ireland and to disband the rest of the New Model Army at once. Not trusting Fairfax, who had given no cause for distrust, they summoned Skippon from Newcastle, where he was governor, to see to the recruitment for Ireland and the suppression of the petition. Holles, who with three other MPs had been entrusted with formulating a reply to the petition (which of course had not even been presented to parliament), left the House to draft it at about 9 p.m., when many independents had gone home. He brought his draft back shortly; the members still present approved it without a division, and the Lords passed it next day. It intemperately expressed parliament's 'high dislike' of the petition, and gave warning that all who went on promoting it would be 'looked upon and proceeded against as enemies of the state and disturbers of the public peace'.[16]

'Enemies of the state': those words were to be repeated in declaration after declaration from the army in the coming months, with justified indignation. To understand how otherwise sane (if mediocre) politicians could put forth a statement so wantonly provocative as this 'Declaration of Dislike', one must appreciate that their reaction to the army petition was coloured by the shock that they had received from another and altogether more revolutionary petition little more than a week earlier. This too had been intercepted before it was presented, and was treated as deeply subversive. It contained the fullest statement so far of the aims of a body of men who were soon to become known as the Levellers. They were at this time an essentially civilian movement, London-based, and consisting mainly of small traders, craftsmen, and apprentices, though of their leaders John Lilburne, William Walwyn, Maximilian Petty, and John Wildman came of minor gentry stock. Richard Overton, who was in some ways the most radical of them, had a humbler background; he had been in voluntary exile as a Baptist before the war and had since run an unlicensed printing-press. Lilburne, Overton, and Walwyn had long been prolific pamphleteers, and the first two had been in the Tower since the summer of 1646 for casting scandal upon the peerage. There were already a few links between the Levellers and the army; Lilburne, as we have seen, had been a lieutenant-colonel of dragoons in pre-New Model days, and Overton's brother Robert was a recently appointed colonel of foot. Edward Sexby, who was soon to be one of the most prominent army agitators, had visited Lilburne in the Tower, though his closeness to the Leveller leader at this time has been much exaggerated. A Major Tulidah, who had come to parliament to defend the Leveller petition, and had been personally assaulted by Stapleton for his pains and imprisoned without a hearing, was not at the time a member of the New Model.

There is no evidence that the Levellers instigated the petitioning movement in the army, and every indication that it arose spontaneously from the soldiers' sense of grievance. *Their* petition was wholly concerned with parliament's threatened treatment of them as soldiers, whereas the Levellers' March Petition was a highly political document. It was provocatively addressed to the Commons as 'the supreme authority of this nation', and its first demand was that neither the king nor the Lords should have any veto over what the people's representatives determined; nor should the peers have any jurisdiction over commoners. It called for the repeal of all oaths and covenants (the Solemn League and Covenant obviously included) that could lead to the persecution of law-abiding people for nonconformity in religion,

[16] *Commons Journal*, V, 129.

and demanded that no one should be punished for preaching or publishing his religious opinions in a peaceable way—a clear condemnation of the Blasphemy Ordinance then in course of enactment. It further called for the abolition of tithes, desiring that henceforth 'all ministers may be paid only by those who voluntarily choose them'. It pressed for a radical reform of the law and of legal proceedings, which (it demanded) should be conducted solely in English. It condemned the current prison system, run as it was for the private profit of prison-keepers, and with it the indefinite incarceration of insolvent debtors. Not least it looked to the Commons to 'provide some powerful means to keep men, women and children from begging'.[17] This was the most comprehensive formulation of the Levellers' programme so far, though some important parts of it, notably their proposals for parliamentary reform and indefeasible natural rights, were still to come. Even without them, however, the Leveller petition was sufficiently shocking to make conservative politicians overreact when they were faced with that of the army less than ten days later. The Levellers' petition itself they shuffled off to a committee until 20 May, when they responded to further popular pressure in support of it by ordering it to be burnt by the common hangman. The independents challenged the decision in a division, but mustered only eighty-six votes against ninety-four.

In the army, Fairfax obediently ordered that the soldiers' petition should circulate no further and that the Declaration of Dislike should be read at the head of each regiment. For two weeks there was scarcely a hint of the resistance to come, even in face of the Derby House Committee's final plans for the standing force to be maintained in England, which parliament approved on 8 April. From the New Model only Fairfax's and Cromwell's own regiments and three others were chosen, the latter for their supposedly 'safe' commanders, though Colonel Graves was to go over to the king within two years. That meant that six regiments of horse and all twelve of foot faced immediate disbandment unless their members took service in Ireland, and if they did that there was no undertaking that they would stay together as units, under their old commanders.

On 15 April another parliamentary delegation came to Fairfax's headquarters, still hoping to enlist the required number of officers and men for Ireland before disbanding the rest. It did not help that the Commons were represented by Waller, Massey, and Clotworthy, though Warwick was a more acceptable spokesman for the Lords. To meet them, Fairfax summoned not only the field officers of all the regiments within reach but the captains and lieutenants of every troop and company—nearly two hundred officers in all.

---

[17] Full text (with slight differences) in D. M. Wolfe (ed.), *Leveller Manifestoes of the Puritan Revolution* (New York and London, 1944), pp. 135–41, and G. E. Aylmer (ed.), *The Levellers in the English Revolution* (1975), pp. 76–81.

They all conferred about their responses before they heard the commissioners, and they chose five strongly independent officers to speak for them: Lieutenant-General Thomas Hammond, the commander of the artillery, and Colonels Lambert, Lilburne, Rich, and Hewson. Warwick pressed the urgency of recovering Ireland and Fairfax seconded him, but Lambert then asked on behalf of all present what parliament was doing about the four questions that had been put to the previous commissioners in March. In particular, who was to command those who went to Ireland? Skippon, they were told, with Massey in command of the cavalry. Skippon commanded everyone's respect, but he had never had independent charge of an army, and he was old for a service that would call for long marches and swift initiatives. Moreover he was still infirm after his serious wound at Naseby, and he had accepted the appointment only under pressure, after Waller had declined it. As for Massey as a substitute for Cromwell, the contempt can be imagined. The presbyterians had again overreached themselves, and the mood of the meeting became hostile; some shouted 'Fairfax and Cromwell, and we all go!'.[18] Afterwards, those present asked their five spokesmen to draw up a statement of their case to parliament, and 151 of them signed the resultant *Vindication of the Officers of the Army*. It powerfully affirmed that the officers stood four-square with their men, not only in respect of their grievances as soldiers but in a shared concern for their country's future, and it justified their right to petition their representatives in parliament. 'We hope, by being soldiers, we have not lost the capacity of subjects,' they said, 'nor . . . that in purchasing the freedoms of our brethren we have not lost our own.'[19]

The army's solidarity was not complete, however, since a minority of officers really did want to continue their military careers in Ireland. These the parliamentary commissioners segregated from the rest and encouraged with every kind of preferential treatment. They reported to parliament that 115 of them were willing to serve on the terms proposed, though they were nearly all infantrymen and mostly of junior rank. There was no certainty that their men would enlist with them, and some officers used dishonest or oppressive means to induce them to do so. At most 1,000 soldiers, almost all foot, engaged themselves for Ireland, and many of them returned to the New Model when its resistance to disbandment got under way. Holles and Stapleton's party had succeeded in creating a rift in the army, but had failed to raise a viable force for the recovery of Ireland. Moreover the split affected only some sections of the New Model, for in the greater part of it the politicians' machinations had positively strengthened the solidarity that knit all ranks together. This was firmest of all in the cavalry. The presbyterian-dominated Commons

---

[18] *Clarke Papers*, 7; Woolrych, *Soldiers and Statesmen*, pp. 44–7.
[19] Rushworth, *Historical Collections*, VI, 468–70.

proceeded to reinforce it with further provocations. They granted requests from the City corporation for the right (which it had lost in 1643) to nominate the members of its powerful Militia Committee, and for the trained bands of Southwark, Westminster, and the Tower Hamlets to be placed under its control. The result was that the committee became a solidly presbyterian body, which promptly carried out a purge of independent officers from the militias of the City and its principal suburbs. The threat to create a counter-force to a diminished New Model would soon become obvious, if it was not so already. Instead of giving a hearing to the officers' *Vindication* when it was presented on 27 April, the Commons summoned Colonel Robert Lilburne to the bar for discouraging his men from enlisting for Ireland and two other officers for distributing pro-army pamphlets; a fourth officer they imprisoned without a hearing. But their crowning folly was to carry a vote, also on the 27th, that the disbanded soldiers should receive only six weeks' pay.

Even before that, the men of the eight cavalry regiments in Essex and East Anglia had begun to take spontaneous action of their own. From about mid-April they met to elect agents or 'agitators'—both words then had the same neutral meaning—to formulate and represent their grievances. The movement seems to have started at grass-roots level, in individual troops, which were units of a hundred men, but the pattern of two agitators to represent each regiment soon became general throughout the cavalry, and during May the infantry regiments followed suit. The original agitators had no mutinous intentions, for they looked for and in many cases received the support of their officers, but they felt that they needed the means to act independently if circumstances should warrant it, and they had leaders of their own. Three of them, Edward Sexby, William Allen, and Thomas Shepherd, presented Fairfax on the 28th with a paper signed by the sixteen agitators of the eight cavalry regiments, and the same three took it to Westminster two days later. It was shortly to be published as *The Apology of the Common Soldiers of Sir Thomas Fairfax's Army*. It denounced the attempted recruitment for Ireland as 'but a design to ruin and break this army in pieces', and 'a mere cloak for some who having lately tasted of sovereignty, and being lifted beyond their ordinary sphere of servants, seek to become masters, and degenerate into tyrants'.[20] The Commons were belatedly considering the officers' *Vindication* when this fiery piece came before them, and they reacted with mingled anger and consternation. They immediately called in the agitators who had brought it, but the three gave nothing away about its authorship and stood up to a sharp interrogation with maddening aplomb. The House sat till ten that night and met again next morning, though it was a Saturday. It then ordered

---

[20] *The Apology of the Common Soldiers* (1647), quoted in Woolrych, *Soldiers and Statesmen*, p. 58.

Skippon, Cromwell, Ireton, and Fleetwood, all officer-MPs who (unlike its previous commissioners) would command the soldiery's respect, to repair to the army immediately, in order to investigate its 'distempers' and assure all officers and soldiers that an ordinance for their indemnity would be passed very shortly. The four were indeed respectfully received at headquarters, but the officers who had assembled in Saffron Walden church to hear them requested time to consult their men before they reported on what they preferred to call their grievances. A week's interval was therefore allowed before further meetings were held on 15 and 16 May.

All this time the agitators were developing and refining their organization. They had a kind of central council to concert policies and find printers for their pamphlets and petitions, and they acted in close liaison with a number of junior officers. They played a large part in preparing many regiments' statements of their grievances and desires for the next meetings with the parliamentary commissioners; indeed a central committee of agitators at Bury St Edmunds seems to have prepared a model version which a number of regiments adopted in whole or in part. Some of the agitators' pamphlets were already showing hints of radical political attitudes, and indeed the Levellers were not slow in trying to make use of their organization as a means of politicizing the army. But hostile allegations that the army was 'one Lilburne throughout' and that the soldiers took his tracts as statute law were wildly untrue at this stage. In all the regimental submissions that survive, only two or three show a distinctively Leveller cast, and they do so in only two or three articles. There was not a trace yet of the republicanism that was to emerge in parts of the army in the late autumn; indeed there was some concern about the amount of goodwill that some of its members were showing towards the king. There is evidence that some senior officers took soundings in mid-May about the possibility of sending propositions to him from the army, though nothing came of it. At a different level, soldiers in Norfolk and Suffolk were reported as saying that they had fought to bring the king to London, and to London they would bring him; nor was this the only testimony that most of the rank and file felt no personal animosity towards him.[21] There was no truth in a mischievous allegation which the Earl of Pembroke made in a speech to the Common Council early in May, when parliament sent him to request a City loan to help pay for the army's disbandment, to the effect that there were 4,000 (or by one report 7,000) cavaliers in its ranks, bent on restoring the king to his throne; indeed Pembroke's speech aroused great indignation in it. But since nobody was seriously contemplating a peace that would exclude the king, it was not unnatural for some in the army to speculate on whether the captive monarch might not prove a better line of approach to a settlement

---

[21] Ibid., pp. 69–71; Gentles, *New Model Army*, pp. 153–4.

than the presbyterian politicians. Soldiers have a way of thinking better of a brave former enemy than of present political masters whose honour they doubt. There was certainly a strong fear in the army, especially among the agitators, that the presbyterians were planning to make a quick peace with him that would secure their own interests and hasten the New Model Army's demise. This was strengthened when on 20 May the Lords invited the king to Oatlands, a mere sixteen miles from Westminster, though this was not supported by the Commons.

While the statements of the individual regiments' grievances were being digested at headquarters, the Commons made some conciliatory moves, passing an indemnity ordinance and increasing the pay to be given on disbandment from six weeks to eight. But this was nothing like enough. What they utterly failed to realize, or chose to ignore, was the affront that they had given to the army's sense of honour with their hostile votes and above all their Declaration of Dislike. If they had paid any attention to *A Second Apology*, which the agitators published on 3 May, they might have seen what a hornet's nest they were stirring on this account. Offended honour, and demands for a vindication of it, bulk large among the regimental statements drawn up between 7 and 15 May—even larger than the material grievances regarding pay, indemnity, and so on that we have met already. The political content in them was relatively slight, though two regiments urged that the army should resist disbandment and decline service in Ireland 'till the real freedom of the free people of England be established'. Surprisingly few statements touched on religious matters such as liberty of conscience or the imposition of the Covenant; taken together they show the soldiery to have been still overwhelmingly preoccupied with their specific concerns as soldiers, and as yet little subject to outside influences.[22]

After the regimental returns had been discussed in the adjourned meeting at Saffron Walden on 15 May, a committee of seven officers was entrusted with digesting them into a consolidated statement that could be presented to parliament in the name of the whole army. The presbyterian minority gave it a stormy passage when it came before the assembled officers, but it won the approval of much the greater number. It deserved to, for it conveyed in firm but respectful tones the substance and the spirit at the heart of the regimental submissions, only eliminating what did not concern them as soldiers and moderating their more extravagant and provocative expressions. It particularly praised the way in which officers had joined with the soldiers in most regiments, helping them to put their requests into acceptable words, and so

---

[22] The regimental statements, which are in the Clarke MSS in Worcester College, Oxford, and have as yet not been printed, are discussed in Kishlansky, *Rise of the New Model Army*, pp. 210–16; Woolrych, *Soldiers and Statesmen*, pp. 73–94; and Gentles, *New Model Army*, pp. 161–4.

counteracting their increasing tendency to act and organize on their own. Cromwell himself read it to the Commons on 21 May. He is said to have assured the House that the army would disband if so commanded by parliament, though this rests on the none too certain testimony of a royalist newswriter who was not personally present. But he also warned the members that the temper of the soldiers was passing beyond their officers' control, and that they were moving beyond their military grievances into broader political territory. Skippon and his fellow-commissioners had already reported that they had 'found the army under a deep sense of some sufferings, and the common soldiers much unsettled'.[23] The army was indeed on the very brink of a revolt that was to give the whole course of political events a new direction, yet it might yet have been persuaded to draw back from it. If the Declaration of Dislike had been revoked, if parliament had paid public tribute to the honour of the army that had won the war for it, if it had postponed disbandment until more of the soldiers's material grievances had been met and promised them much more of their overdue pay when in due course they were disbanded, and if it had agreed to reconsider the provision for an expeditionary force for Ireland, the situation could almost certainly have been saved.

Instead, the presbyterian politicians reckoned that they could dispose of enough force to take on the New Model Army if need be, and decided to disband it immediately. They had not far short of 20,000 trained bands in London and its environs, now under safe presbyterian commanders; they had Poyntz's northern army and the troops (admittedly few) already detached from the New Model for service in Ireland, and there were large numbers of disbanded men, called 'reformadoes', who were swarming in and around London in quest of their arrears of pay, and would readily re-enlist. On 23 May they talked with Lauderdale and the French ambassador about the possibilities of bringing a Scottish army back into England if it were needed, and of removing the king to Scotland if the English army threatened to seize him. Two days later the Commons approved orders for the disbandment of the entire New Model infantry between 1 and 15 June, directing the regiments to widely separate rendezvous so as to forestall any concerted resistance. Skippon, whose men they had been, was deeply troubled. He wrote to the Speaker:

I doubt [i.e. fear] the disobliging of so faithful an army will be repented of; provocation and exasperation makes men think of that they never intended. They are possessed as far as I can discern with this opinion, that if they can be thus scornfully dealt withal for their faithful services whilst the sword is in their hands, what shall their usage be when they are dissolved?[24]

[23] Abbott, *Writings and Speeches of Oliver Cromwell*, I, 446.
[24] *Clarke Papers*, I, 101–2. For the identification of writer and addressee see Woolrych, *Soldiers and Statesmen*, pp. 98–9.

Fairfax too was riven between a deep reluctance to disobey parliament and the strong corporate loyalty that he shared with his officers and men. Perhaps the strain contributed to the illness which kept him in London for a month from 21 April, and which despite the sneers of his enemies (including Holles) was genuine. He was still under treatment when at parliament's request he returned to headquarters, which he shortly moved to Bury St Edmunds. He wrote to every regiment on 24 May, ordering that soldiers should stop acting independently of their officers, and in particular that the agitators should hold no more central meetings. He was not obeyed; indeed the agitators were never more active than in late May and early June. They were well supplied with vital intelligence from London, notably by Lieutenant Edmund Chillenden of Whalley's regiment. Young Cornet Joyce, another of their close collaborators, was already organizing the cavalry force that was shortly to abduct the king. Rainborough's regiment set off without its colonel's knowledge to secure the army's train of artillery in Oxford, in case parliament should try to move it. Fairfax could not know all this, but he did receive a 'Humble petition of the soldiers of the army', signed by the agitators of ten regiments of horse and six of foot, calling upon him to summon a general rendezvous of the army, and more than hinting that the agitators would hold one anyway if he did not.

On 29 May he held an enlarged council of war of about a hundred officers at Bury St Edmunds, and there the crucial decisions about the future conduct of the army were taken. After the parliament's votes and the agitators' petition had been read and considered, he had two questions put to each officer individually. The first was whether enough had been done to satisfy the men's grievances for the proposed disbandment to be carried out without danger of disturbance, and an overwhelming eighty-six voted 'no'; there were only three ayes, though four officers reserved their position. Next they were asked whether in the light of the first vote they favoured a general rendezvous. Eighty-four were for it and only seven against, though nine left the meeting rather than commit themselves. He had now to decide between concurring with his army's decisively expressed wishes, or resigning his generalship because it would otherwise pass out of his control. He had probably made up his own mind, but he characteristically resorted to consultation, confident no doubt that it would bind his officers more closely to the course he wanted to pursue. He ordered the desired general rendezvous, which was to be held on Kentford Heath near Newmarket on 4 and 5 June, and his post-Restoration memoirs are not reliable evidence that he did so unwillingly.

Before the regiments marched to Newmarket, Cornet Joyce set off on his momentous exploit. He was the most junior officer of Fairfax's own life guard, but according to a plausible contemporary report the party of at least 500 horse that he commanded were drawn largely from the very three cavalry regiments that Derby House had chosen to guard the king—because their colonels were presbyterians. That choice backfired, for their men were by now far readier to obey the emissaries of the agitators than their own senior officers. Joyce and his force seem to have been acting under instructions from some central committee of the agitators' organization, and he and they were almost certainly engaged with the men of Rainborough's foot regiment, who were directed from the same source, in securing the artillery train in Oxford. While on that mission he received intelligence—we do not know whether or not it was true—that orders were being issued from Westminster to remove the king from Holmby. Fearing, as many in the army did, that Charles was to be brought nearer to London so that the presbyterians could strike a swift deal with him, he resolved to prevent it. But it was a heavy responsibility for a very junior officer to assume, and he might need more help, so on 31 May he left his men and rode up to London to talk to Cromwell. That evening he obtained Cromwell's approval for his plan to prevent the removal of the king, but it was probably not in the mind of either man that Joyce himself should abduct him. It was not long, however, before Cromwell's enemies were saying that Joyce and his party acted under his orders throughout the whole operation. But Cromwell consistently denied afterwards that he had authorized, let alone instigated, the removal of the king, and the charge is inherently implausible. It is surely inconceivable that Cromwell should on his own initiative have ordered an operation which involved the army so deeply, on the eve of its general rendezvous, without informing its commander-in-chief. His respect for Fairfax's authority as general had always been impeccable, and the relationship between the two men was reinforced by friendship and mutual trust. There can be no doubt about Fairfax's shock and consternation when he learnt that the king was on his way to Newmarket; his first reaction was to have Joyce court-martialled, though when he came to appreciate the cornet's motives he relented and promised him the captaincy of the first troop that became vacant.

After leaving Cromwell, Joyce sent orders to his troops to make their way to Holmby as fast as they could and set off on his own seventy-mile ride thither. He arrived a few hours ahead of them on 2 June, to find the king away playing bowls at Althorp. When his men caught up with him late that evening, the soldiers of Major-General Browne's garrison welcomed them as comrades; Browne found himself powerless. Joyce secured the house next morning, and after setting his guards dismissed the rest of his troops to their quarters. He still had no thought but to prevent the king from being moved, but he became worried when he learnt that Colonel Graves, who commanded one of the regiments that had been guarding him, had ridden away during the night, probably for London; some of his 'damming blades' were swearing that he would 'fetch a party', no doubt to conduct Charles there too. Joyce summoned his men for an urgent consultation—all their decisions were collective ones—and they unanimously advised that he and they should move the king, to prevent his removal by hostile forces. Joyce then had to talk his way past the parliamentary commissioners who were still in attendance at Holmby, but he entered the royal bedchamber at ten that night and warned Charles to be ready to depart early next morning. Charles was understandably alarmed and reluctant, but he was disarmed by Joyce's civility, and reassured when he willingly gave three promises: that no hurt would come to him, that he would be made to do nothing against his conscience, and that he would continue to be treated with the same respect as under parliament's custody, retaining his own servants. All these promises were kept.

Before they set out at six next morning, Charles pressed Joyce to tell him whose commission he had for what he was doing. 'The soldiery of the army', Joyce replied, quite truthfully. But had he no document, signed by his general? Finally under pressure Joyce said 'Here is my commission.' 'Where?', the king asked. 'Behind me', Joyce replied pointing to the ranks of his troopers drawn up for the march. 'It is as fair a commission,' Charles acknowledged, 'and as well written as I have seen a commission written in my life: a company of handsome proper gentlemen as I have seen a great while. But if I should refuse yet to go with you, I hope you will not force me.' Joyce replied that force was not their wish; they humbly entreated his majesty to go with them. But where, the king asked? By his own account Joyce suggested first Oxford, then Cambridge, but Charles himself proposed Newmarket, because its air agreed with him, and Joyce concurred.[25] There is no need to doubt his version, and it is further evidence that his abduction of the king was unpremeditated, since any pre-conceived plan would have specified his destination. Charles cannot have known that even as they set off most of the New Model Army was converging on Newmarket for a general rendezvous in defiance of parliament's orders.

Another rider on his way to Newmarket that day was Cromwell. Since the end of the war he had been putting his parliamentary duties first, and striving (except when prevented by illness) to counter the policies of the presbyterians on the floor of the House. But as soon as it became known that the army was resisting parliament's orders for disbandment there was talk of impeaching him, and if he had stayed until the seizure of the king became known he could not have been safe from arrest. The choice between his two commitments

---

[25] Joyce's narrative is in Rushworth, *Historical Collections*, VI, 513–19. For appraisals of the evidence see C. H. Firth in *Clarke Papers*, I, pp. xxiii–xxi, Woolrych, *Soldiers and Statesmen*, pp. 106–12, and Gentles, *New Model Army*, pp. 169–71. Gentles puts Joyce's force at 1,000 men, but 500 is Joyce's own figure, and I doubt whether as many as 1,000 could have been detached from their regiments without serious repercussions.

cannot have been an easy one, but he must have felt as a soldier that with the rendezvous in progress his place was at Fairfax's side, and as a politician that the army was a necessary safeguard against a partisan and unsafe peace. He had had nothing to do with the army's revolt, but his best service as he saw it now lay in helping to keep it on statesmanlike courses.

# ✝ TWELVE ✝

# Climacteric II:
# 'not a mere Mercenary Army'

THE general rendezvous on Kentford Heath opened not only a dramatically new chapter in the army's history but one of those phases of discontinuity and accelerated change that I have called climacterics. The next nineteen months witnessed repercussions that neither the soldiers nor most of the politicians had either foreseen or desired: an attempted conservative coup in London, a resultant military confrontation, the army's assumption (improvised step by step) of a dominant role in British politics, a second civil war in which the Scottish army fought against the English parliament, and finally the execution of the king and the abolition (in England) of the monarchy. In June 1647, however, the aims of the parties that precipitated the crisis were still largely negative. The presbyterian politicians wanted to eliminate the army as an obstacle to their own plans for reinstating the king, while the army sought only to avert its own destruction, secure its soldiers' rights, and prevent a partisan peace that would betray much that it thought it had fought for. Neither side was seeking drastic political change; they differed not as to *whether* the king should be restored to his regal authority but over the constitutional terms upon which he should be allowed to resume it.

This was in origin very much an English crisis, though its outcome would have profound implications for both Scotland and Ireland. The Scots watched it with acute concern, and its progress would determine whether Argyll and the strict Covenanters continued to dominate the political arena or whether the threat to their king would shift the initiative to the Hamiltons and their party, who were prepared to come to his rescue on less stringent terms. For the Irish, the new breach in England postponed the nemesis that awaited the Confederates, but they were powerless to affect its outcome—more powerless than they had appeared to be towards the end of 1646. If the situation in Ireland had remained as threatening as it looked then, the parliamentary presbyterians might have thought twice about provoking the army as they did in the spring of 1647, and the army leaders might not have felt free to defy them. The factions among the Irish themselves, however, largely neutralized

the threat posed by their rebellion until a radically changed English government was ready to deal with it.

The peace treaty which Ormond, as the kings's Lord Lieutenant, had concluded with delegates of the Confederates' Supreme Council in March 1646
had (as we have seen) been vehemently opposed by O'Neill, the clerical
party, and most of all Rinuccini, who had engineered the establishment of a
new Supreme Council dominated by his own faction. But Ormond was not
without his supporters, and the treaty had not yet come before a General
Assembly. Under pressure from the royalists within the Confederation,
Rinuccini agreed that one should be summoned to meet in January 1647,
expressly to consider it. It proved to be deeply divided over the treaty, but in
the end the majority rejected it on 2 February. By now the rifts in the Confederation were threatening it with dissolution, and Plunkett and his middle
group could not bridge them. On the one hand were those who maintained
their loyalty to the crown, even in its present defeat, provided they could practise their faith openly, have access to office and enjoy undisputed title to their
property. On the other hand were those who sought a total Roman Catholic
ascendancy, and if Charles was not willing to grant it were prepared to bid for
independence under the protection of a foreign power—perhaps also under a
king to be chosen by themselves. O'Neill was rumoured to have his eye on
the title.

Ormond, after the assembly's repudiation of his treaty, felt justified in
renewing his application to Westminster, since his opponents were now not
merely indifferent to his master's interests but ready to oppose them. He
offered to surrender his office of Lord Lieutenant to the parliament, which
now realized that it must take full responsibility for England's interests in Ireland and sent over a force of 2,000 men under Colonel Michael Jones. They
landed at Dublin in June; Ormond handed over his military command to
Jones, signed a treaty with the parliamentary commissioners and surrendered
his regalia. By the terms he agreed, all protestants were to be secured in their
estates, catholics who had remained loyal were to be favourably treated, and
all noblemen, gentlemen, and officers who wished to leave Ireland with him
were to have free passes. His action was not a betrayal, and Charles never
reproached him for it. He sought an interview with the king at Hampton
Court as soon as he arrived back in England, and received the full royal
approval of his conduct in Ireland. Not long after that, when the negotiations
that would lead to the second Civil War were taking shape, his royalism was
so unmistakable that he took ship for France to escape probable arrest by the
parliament. It would not be long before he was serving the house of Stuart
again in Ireland.

Nevertheless Ormond's capitulation divided his Old English adherents,
and some of them joined Preston, who with the army of Leinster set out again

to lay siege to Dublin. But Michael Jones stood in his way, holding a good position on Dungan's Hill near Trim. Many of Jones's men had been recruited from the provincial forces lately disbanded in England. Their conduct and discipline at first left much to be desired, but they knew how to fight. Preston was urged to give battle by civilian advisers who knew that the Confederates could not keep him supplied during a protracted campaign. He did so on 8 August, and was utterly routed. That left Leinster so vulnerable that O'Neill's dreaded Ulstermen had to be brought in to help protect the province, which led to a further worsening of relations between the predominantly Old English moderate party in the Confederation and the clericalist and Old Irish militants who followed Rinuccini and O'Neill.

Southward in Munster the English parliament still had the powerful support of Murrough O'Brien, Lord Inchiquin. He was that fairly rare bird, a strongly protestant Old Irish aristocrat. He had co-operated with Strafford, and in the early years of the Irish rebellion he had fought against its perpetrators as a royalist. But he was alienated by Charles's readiness to do business with Confederates and make large concessions to Irish catholics, and he was understandably dismayed when the king granted the presidency of Munster, whose functions he had been exercising and to which he had a strong claim, to the Earl of Portland. He declared for the English parliament in July 1644 and for the next four years he fought vigorously for it, not least when he repulsed a heavy incursion into southern Ireland by the catholic Earl of Castlehaven in 1645. His change of allegiance was not purely opportunist, for he genuinely had the protestant interest in Ireland at heart, and when he changed sides again in 1648 it would be because he could no longer bear to serve masters who threatened the very life of his king. All through 1647, however, he went on fighting hard against the Confederates. He took Dungarvan in May, so opening a threat to Waterford, and one castle after another fell to him after that. His storming of Cashel on 14 September was followed by a slaughter that prefigured the horrors of Drogheda and Wexford, and two months later he confronted the Confederate army of Munster under Viscount Taaffe in the battle of Knocknanuss, near Mallow. He virtually annihilated it, at a cost of only about 150 men killed, while Taaffe reputedly lost two-thirds of his 7,200 troops. By the end of the year Inchiquin was master of southern Ireland.

By then, too, there was nowhere in the whole country that could still pose a threat that need trouble the contending parties in England before they had resolved their own differences. Politically the Confederation was in as much disarray as its armed forces, for when the General Assembly met again in November its divisions threatened to destroy it. These arose chiefly over the election of a new Supreme Council, and over the choice of envoys to be sent to Spain, France, and the papacy in a quest for foreign aid. The clerical party carried a decision, if it came to a last resort, to ask the papacy to assume the protectorate of Ireland. Few of the Old English representatives relished this, and few cared to bow to O'Neill as military supremo in Ireland, which is what Rinuccini's plans entailed. The Assembly dissolved itself on Christmas Eve, and its less sanguine members must have faced the year 1648 with foreboding.

So it can be seen that when the English army confronted the parliament early in June 1647 neither party had much to fear in the short term from enemies outside England, and even less after Michael Jones's important victory at Dungan's Hill. The Commons, however, were so alarmed by the army's defiance and by its seizure of the king that they sat all through the night of 3–4 June, while the regiments were converging on Kentford Heath, and at two in the morning they voted to strike the Declaration of Dislike out of their Journal. Later in the day a lengthy 'Humble Representation of the Dissatisfactions of the Army' was read to each regiment at the rendezvous, signed by most of their officers and men (such as could write), and presented to Fairfax. Much of it was couched in the typical language of the agitators, and it voiced familiar grievances. It demonstrated the failure of the army's opponents to drive a wedge between officers and men, or between horse and foot. Fairfax, however, was anxious to keep defiance to a minimum and to maintain military discipline. In an exhausting day—indeed he did not even get to bed that night—he personally addressed each regiment in turn, urging it to show moderation and to respect the civil authority. Much the greater part of the army was present, though a few units were on duty too far afield to participate. The cheers that greeted Fairfax everywhere showed what a hero he still was to his men and how much they appreciated his sympathy and support, but he was not really a political animal, and now that the army was assuming such a political role it would need a different talent from his to guide it along constructive courses.

Much of the initiative in this field was assumed during the next two years by Cromwell's son-in-law Henry Ireton, the Commissary-General. He had the keenest and most original political mind in the army, though as a tactician and debater he had his limitations. He was almost certainly the main author of *The Solemn Engagement of the Army*, which was read to all the regiments on the second day of the rendezvous and assented to by them. It immediately assumed a much greater importance among the army's manifestoes than the agitators' Humble Representation, though it shows clear signs that agitators were conferred with in its preparation. It was indeed considerably more than a manifesto; it was, in that age of covenants, a covenant by the army. All its members engaged with each other, and with the parliament and kingdom, to disband cheerfully or to remain in service, as parliament should require, *when* they were given satisfaction for their stated grievances and *when* they received security that when disbanded neither they nor 'other the freeborn people of England' would remain subject to oppression and injury through the continuance in power of the men who had abused parliament in its past proceedings against the army. This was tantamount to a demand for a purge of the presbyterian leadership. Furthermore the redress and security thus requested must meet with the satisfaction of a startlingly new body which came to be called the General Council of the Army. It was to include not only the senior commanders who normally attended the general's council of war, but two officers and two soldiers elected by each regiment. This General Council was not to meet until mid-July, but until it was satisfied the *Solemn Engagement* declared that 'we shall not willingly disband nor divide, nor suffer ourselves to be disbanded or divided'.[1]

The solidarity of the army was not complete, because of those officers who had engaged with the parliamentary commissioners to serve in Ireland. They had been segregated, though a fair number of them changed their minds and came to Kentford Heath. There were others, however, who did not appear there because they were presbyterians by conviction and not prepared to defy the parliament, while yet others who had tried to oppose the rendezvous had been driven off by their men. The officers who left the army in May and June for one reason or another were a minority, but numerous enough for their departure to alter its political and social character significantly. Their total number cannot be accurately established, but among the 220-odd senior men who commanded regiments, companies, or troops—i.e. from colonels down to captain-lieutenants—57 left the service: almost exactly one in four.[2] They included eight colonels, two lieutenants-colonels, and eight majors, and since most of these were presbyterians their departure meant that the army no longer exhibited the broad political spectrum that had originally characterized it. Moreover since its formation 33 officers at or above company commander level had died or been killed and 25 had resigned earlier, so the turnover in senior officers amounted to 57 per cent by the end of June 1647. The great majority of those who died or departed were replaced by promoting men already within the army, and they were very often of humbler origin. The social level of the officer corps was thus lowered appreciably, though around half of those in the more senior ranks would probably still have styled themselves gentlemen. Nevertheless it was from this time that men of

---

[1] Full text in Rushworth, *Historical Collections*, VI, 501–2; greater part in A. S. P. Woodhouse (ed.), *Puritanism and Liberty* (1938), pp. 401–3.

[2] Gentles, *New Model Army*, p. 168, 487; I. Gentles, 'The New Model officer corps in 1647: a collective portrait', *Social History XXII* (1997), pp. 127–44. In this and the next paragraph I am deeply indebted to Professor Gentles's work. In respect of one detail, I would put the total of more senior officers slightly higher, since I see no reason not to count adjutant-generals, quartermaster-generals, and others attached to the general staff, whom Gentles excludes.

notoriously modest birth like Harrison, Pride, Okey, Goffe, and Tomlinson achieved a new prominence in the politics of the army.

About the junior ranks of officers—lieutenants, cornets, ensigns, and quartermasters—much less is known. They brought the total number of commissioned officers in the New Model to well over 700, while if noncommissioned officers were added the tally came to 2,320.[3] A pamphlet of June 1647 claimed to speak for 167 officers who had left the service, but it named none; its authors had a motive for pitching the number high, and some of those whom it counted may have returned to the army when it closed ranks. All that can be said with confidence is that proportionally fewer junior than senior officers left it; my estimate would be one in five at most. The number of soldiers who did so was only about 800 out of more than 19,000. The thinning of the officers' ranks in May and June left a virtually united army to confront the parliament, and the consequent promotions from the ranks narrowed further the social divide between subalterns, NCOs and troopers in the cavalry. When new divisions began to appear in the army during the autumn, they were of a quite different nature from those of the spring.

From Newmarket the army set off on a slow advance towards London, where it caused great consternation. The guards were doubled, the portcullises lowered, the City fathers obtained parliament's permission to raise their own cavalry, and Massey drove through the streets in his coach, urging the citizens to defend themselves. On 10 June Fairfax sent an assurance that the army sought 'no alteration of the civil government', but he allowed some of his officers to draw up articles of impeachment against Holles, Stapleton, Massey, Waller, Clotworthy, and six other MPs who were held to have been particularly responsible for the parliamentary campaign against the army, and he set up his headquarters at St Albans, little more than twenty miles from London. There on the 14th a summary of the charges against the eleven was delivered to the parliamentary commissioners with the army. It was of course quite unconstitutional for anybody but the House of Commons to institute impeachment proceedings, but that same day the army gave notice that it was advancing further into political territory. The general and his council of war approved a document that was shortly published as *A Declaration from Sir Thomas Fairfax and the Army*, which purported to be a vindication, as promised in the *Solemn Engagement*, clearing the New Model from all the scandals that had been cast upon it. But it went a good deal further than that, and again it was essentially the work of Ireton. Through it, the New Model staked a claim to speak and act for the whole kingdom, proudly asserting 'that we were not a mere mercenary army, hired to serve any arbitrary power of a state, but called forth and conjured by the several declarations of

---

[3] *Clarke Papers*, I, 19.

parliament to the defence of our own and the people's just rights and liberties'. It invoked the examples of the Scots, the Dutch, and the Portuguese in
associating by way of covenant to promote the principles of right and freedom against governments that denied them. Its first demand was that parliament should be purged of such members as had rendered themselves unfit to
sit by abusing their powers. Further, on the grounds that too long a continuance of the same men in power conduced to tyranny, it called for legislation
to set a maximum duration to each parliament's life, and in order to 'render
the parliament a more equal representation of the whole' it requested an
immediate and radical reapportionment of seats that would make the size of
constituencies proportional to what they contributed to national taxation.
These reforms were to be embodied in statutes, and when the king had assented to them and to whatever else was needed to secure the kingdom's future
peace, his own rights should be settled, 'so far as may consist with the right
and freedom of the subject'. Finally, the army had no design 'to overthrow
Presbytery' or to set up Independency as a national religion; it asked only that
those who dissented from the established forms should suffer no persecution
or civil disabilities.[4]

This advocacy of liberty of conscience and positive parliamentary reform
marked two vital differences between the army's proposals and any that the
parliament had yet put to the king. Another lay in their relative mildness
towards the beaten royalists, for after a few examples had been made they
desired a general act of oblivion and a burying of 'distinction of parties'. The
army's Declaration was a step towards the comprehensive alternative political programme that it would take into debate little more than a month later.

The situation remained very tense through most of June. The agitators continued to hold their own unauthorized meetings, and a number of officers
worked hand in glove with them. They kept pressing for a march on London
in order to enforce the arrest of the eleven impeached MPs, which the House
was resisting. Fairfax did indeed advance his headquarters to Uxbridge, only
fifteen miles from Westminister, and stationed some of his regiments even
nearer, in defiance of an order from the Commons not to bring the army within forty miles. The City went on organizing what defences it could and the
Lord Mayor called the trained bands to arms, but most of the citizenry
showed a sensible reluctance to engage in heroics against Fairfax's and
Cromwell's veterans. Both Houses voted on 15 June to bring the king to Westminster, but it was an empty gesture. Charles was firmly in the army's keeping, and happier with his new custodians than with his old. He appreciated
the courtesy with which the senior officers treated him, the ready access

---

[4] Printed with unimportant cuts in Woodhouse, *Puritanism and Liberty*, pp. 403–9 where it
is called (as it often is) 'A Representation of the Army'. I have used the title given to it on its first
publication, by the army's regular printer.

allowed to his friends, and most of all the ministrations of his favourite chaplains, Sheldon, Hammond, and Holdsworth. He spent the middle fortnight of June at his father's old hunting lodge at Newmarket, enjoying the chase as of old, and freely receiving the respects of large numbers of the East Anglian gentry. After that stay he was moved by comfortable stages to Hampton Court, and on the way he was reunited with his children James and Elizabeth, who were allowed to spend two nights with him.

Meanwhile, as June wore on, Fairfax took pains to establish better relations with London's Common Council, and when parliament made a number of conciliatory gestures he responded by drawing his headquarters back to Reading. But he could not tolerate the continued existence of potential rival armies, and on 16 July he wrote to the Speaker requesting that all the land forces in the kingdom should be put under one command. His pretext was that the Northern Association army had mutinied against Major-General Poyntz. There was irony here; Stapleton had ordered Poyntz to stand ready for action against the New Model, but emissaries from the latter's agitators had stirred up resistance among Poyntz's men, who arrested him early in July and took him to Fairfax's Reading headquarters as a prisoner. Fairfax released him on parole, and was promptly appointed by parliament as commander-in-chief of all the forces in England, including whatever part of them was to be sent to Ireland.

This was a most important gain, but it was going to take more than this to satisfy some of his agitators. On 16 July he convened at Reading the first meeting of the General Council of the Army, and a formidable new petition from the agitators kept it in debate until midnight. They called (among other things) for an immediate march on London, seeing that parliament and the City had gone back to their old ways since the army drew back; for the expulsion of the eleven impeached MPs within four days; for a prohibition by parliament on the raising or bringing in of any forces other than Fairfax's, on pain of treason; and for the release of John Lilburne and other Leveller prisoners, with reparation for their wrongful imprisonment. But Cromwell and Ireton urged strongly against resorting to force, and finally persuaded the agitators to drop their pressure for an immediate march. In return the General Council agreed to put their other main points before parliament, especially the restoration of the City's old militia officers and the liberation of the Leveller prisoners.

The army commanders had assembled the General Council for a larger purpose than the venting of old grievances, and they had good reason for wanting to allay dissension, both within the army's own ranks and between it and the parliament. On the second day of the debates at Reading Ireton read out the draft of a comprehensive scheme for the settlement of the kingdom which soon became known as the Heads of the Proposals. His hope and that of his fellow-generals was that they could, when perfected, be put to both king and parliament as the desires of the whole army, and provide a way out of the political impasse that had existed since the Propositions of Newcastle had been presented a year and more earlier. Until recently Ireton has always been regarded as their author, and there still seems to be no good reason for doubting that the conception and the formulation of the Heads of Proposals were essentially his work. But there is now evidence that they were put together in close consultation with a group of leading independents from both Houses, including Saye, Wharton, and Northumberland in the Lords and Vane, St John, William Pierrepont, and Saye's son Nathaniel Fiennes in the Commons. For about ten days before the Reading debates began messages passed frequently between this group and Cromwell and Ireton, and Wharton was a parliamentary commissioner at army headquarters from the end of June onwards.[5] What we are witnessing, therefore, is not an attempt by the army to promulgate peace terms over the heads of the parliament but a collaboration between the generals and the leaders in both Houses of the main party that had stood against the presbyterians all along. Nor were these the army chief's only important contacts, for the queen and her friends had lately sent over Sir John Berkeley, the one-time royalist commander in Devon, with specific directions to promote an agreement between the great officers and the king. Berkeley reached Reading on 12 July and soon established a remarkable rapport with Cromwell and Ireton, who made no secret of their hopes of finding a basis for peace that would be more acceptable to both king and kingdom than what had been offered so far. Berkeley gained the impression that the whole army, agitators included, would have been glad to come to terms with the king. The prospect looked promising; the main rub lay in Charles himself, who would not accept Berkeley's reading of the situation. He distrusted the chief officers, he said, because they had asked him for no personal favours or rewards.

It is a striking testimony to the openness of army politics that Ireton chose, obviously with Fairfax's and Cromwell's approval, to put his draft Proposals before the General Council, with over a hundred officers and the full complement of agitators present, before communicating them to either the parliament or the king, or even formally to the parliamentary commissioners at headquarters. The great difference between his scheme (concerted with the independents) and that of the presbyterians was that whereas the Propositions of Newcastle were mainly preoccupied with the disposal of power, the

---

[5] J. S. A. Adamson, 'The English nobility and the projected settlement of 1647', *Historical Journal* XXX (1987), pp. 571–9, 601. Dr Adamson throws new and valuable light on the role of Saye and Wharton in the formulation of the Proposals, but I think he goes too far in minimizing Ireton's. Cf. Gentles, *New Model Army*, p. 492n. 317, and Woolrych, *Soldiers and Statesmen*, pp. 151–2, 162–5.

Heads of the Proposals were much more concerned with genuine reform and with healing old enmities. Parliaments, they proposed, should be elected biennially, to sit for a minimum of 120 days (unless they agreed to dissolve earlier) and a maximum of 240. Following perhaps the Scottish example, each outgoing parliament was to appoint a committee to take care of parliamentary interests until the next one met. Rotten boroughs should be disfranchised and the number of county seats increased, with the aim of giving representation to counties in proportion to their contribution to taxation. Parliament was to appoint the great officers of state for the next ten years, after which, on a vacancy, the two Houses were to present three candidates and the king to make his choice from them. The privy council was to be replaced by a council of state consisting of 'persons now to be agreed upon', who were to hold office for a fixed term not exceeding seven years, and were to have the overall direction of the county trained bands, though the army and navy were to be controlled by parliament itself or its nominees for the next ten years. It is not clear whether the council of state was intended to be a permanent institution; perhaps it was envisaged as transitional, for nothing was said as to who should appoint its members in the future. Active royalists were to be debarred from the next two biennial parliaments, and for the next five years they were not to hold public office without the consent of parliament or the council of state. Not more than five were to be excepted from pardon; the rest were to compound for their estates according to the degree of their involvement, as in the Newcastle Propositions, but at much lower rates and only if worth £200 or more in land or goods. Those, however, who had shown a sincere disposition towards peace since the end of the war should be exempted, and terms granted to those who had surrendered were to be honoured. The king was to be restored with no other diminution of his rights than these proposals specified.

It was with regard to religion, however, that Ireton's proposed terms differed most refreshingly from the parliament's, and here he is said to have made some large concessions at a late stage, on the plea of Berkeley or even the king himself. The use of the Book of Common Prayer was to be permitted but not imposed, and there should be no penalties for not coming to the parish church or for attending other meetings for worship. Bishops were to be allowed to continue, though without coercive power or jurisdiction. No one was to be forced to take the covenant. The whole parliamentary settlement of church government and worship was passed over in silence.[6] Nothing so tolerant was to come before parliament again for more than forty years.

The immediate reaction of the General Council to the Proposals was favourable, if cautious. William Allen probably spoke for most of his

---

[6] Text in Gardiner (ed.), *Constitutional Documents*, pp. 316–26.

fellow-agitators when he said that there were 'things of great weight, having relation to the settling of a kingdom, which is a great work; truly the work we all expect to have a share in'. But he acknowledged 'that we are most of us but young statesmen', and would want some time for debate.[7] There was no opposition in principle to seeking a settlement on the lines proposed, but a wide range of grievances was evidently raised during the day's debate, for a miscellaneous list of matters for parliament's early attention, including tithes, the excise, the general inequality of taxation, and an assortment of legal abuses, were shortly added to the Heads of the Proposals. These were referred for further consideration to a committee of twelve officers and twelve agitators.

The prospects soon looked fair for a peace on terms that the king could in honour accept, and would have left Anglicans, Presbyterians, Independents, and even sectaries free to worship according to their consciences. The proposals were reported to parliament on 20 July and taken into debate immediately by the Lords, where the Saye–Northumberland group dominated the dozen or so peers who still attended. On the same day the eleven impeached members, sensing that the game was up, requested and obtained the Commons' leave to go overseas, and withdrew. Within the next two days parliament restored the control of the City's trained bands to the old Militia Committee, ordered the disbandment of the troops whom it had detached from the New Model Army and embodied in its own counter-force, and passed the desired declaration against the introduction of any forces from outside the kingdom.

This apparent surrender to the army, however, triggered a violent reaction from those in London who saw it as their prime enemy, especially the City presbyterians and the reformadoes. Many of the latter had lost their military employment when the New Model was created, and not a few had fought for the king. On the 21st large numbers of militiamen, reformadoes, apprentices, watermen, and others gathered in Skinners' Hall to sign a 'Solemn Engagement'—perhaps a conscious challenge to the army's recent one—pledging their utmost efforts to bring the king to Westminster, in order to restore him on the terms that he himself had offered. They addressed it not to parliament, which declared two days later that support for it constituted treason, but to the corporation of London. Next evening two or three thousand reformadoes demonstrated in St James's Field, clamouring for the City to join them in pressuring parliament to bring the king back to his capital. The Common Council was divided, but the Commons' vote to reinstate the old City Militia Committee temporarily reunited it. It welcomed two mass petitions urging it not to yield control over its trained bands, and on the 26th it processed in a body to Westminster to present them to parliament. An angry crowd of citi-

---

[7] *Clarke Papers*, I, 213.

zens followed the City fathers, with apprentices noisily prominent, and it was bent on no mere peaceful demonstration. It was actively encouraged, if not incited, by some prominent members of the City government, by a number of Presbyterian clergymen and militia officers, and almost certainly by some of the eleven impeached MPs. This mob first invaded the House of Lords, and bullied the peers into voting to restore the City's presbyterian militia Committee and rescinding parliament's condemnation of its Solemn Engagement. Then it forced its way into the Commons' chamber, abusing and insulting the members—some had excrement thrown in their faces—until they not only confirmed the Lords' votes but passed a resolution inviting the king to London forthwith. While under this intimidation they sent urgently to the Lord Mayor for some trained bands to protect them and restore order, but he ignored their request.

Once free of the mob the Speakers of both Houses, with eight peers and fifty-seven MPs, left Westminster and took refuge with the army. The futility of this attempt at counter-revolution was soon exposed, because it met with virtually no response outside London, and London itself quickly discovered that it had no means of defence. For a week the members remaining at Westminster made a show of carrying on business under illegitimate replacement speakers, and forbade the army to come within thirty miles. They tried to activate a counter-force against it, with Massey in overall command and Waller in charge of the horse. The City government had the drums beaten to muster not only the militia but all male citizens of military age; the response was humiliatingly feeble. Afterwards there were sneers at soft-living townsmen flinching from the rigours and dangers of the field, but they were quite misplaced. London's trained bands had fought bravely in pre-New Model days, when they had a cause they could believe in, but there was no good reason why they should take arms against the veterans who had won the Civil War for parliament, especially under orders of more than doubtful legality. And strong though the Presbyterians, both religious and political, were in the capital, their hold over it was by no means complete. London had large numbers of Independents and sectaries who took heart from the army's championship of freedom of conscience, and while many apprentices, fired with civic patriotism, had rioted happily on 26 July, many others were drawn to the Leveller movement and saw the army agitators as a means of promoting its aims. The army itself had friends in London, which was home to many of its officers, and where several of its regiments had been recruited. The populous suburbs of Southwark and the Tower Hamlets chafed under the City government's attempts to extend its authority over them, and welcomed the army as a liberator.

Fairfax had authority as well as power on his side when he announced on the 28th that at the request of both Speakers and the fugitive peers and members the army would shortly march into the capital to restore parliament to its freedom. The king, who was at Woburn when he heard of the tumults in London, reacted by sending to Fairfax and Cromwell and offering to treat on the basis of the Heads of the Proposals, which had been shown to him a few days earlier. Fairfax, before setting off, authorized Ireton, in company with Colonels Rainborough, Hammond, and Rich, to visit him and bring him to agreement if they could. The result was one of the crucial confrontations of the decade. The four spent three hours in discussion with the king, and in their eagerness to reach a quick and binding pact with him they made some substantial concessions. Berkeley's earnest advice had been that they represented the best terms that he could hope for, but Charles treated them as one more opportunity to play off one party of his quarrelling enemies against the other. The eagerness of many presbyterians to bring him to London made him confident that he could make the independents improve their offers further, and he was pretty clearly waiting to see whether the London counter-revolutionaries might do his business for him at an even lower rate. He took a very high tone with Ireton and his three companions, believing quite mistakenly that they needed him more than he needed the army. 'You cannot be without me', he kept saying; 'you will fall to ruin if I do not sustain you'.[8] He had been given much bad advice, counterbalancing Berkeley's good counsel: from Lauderdale, who gave him false hopes that the Scots and presbyterians were ready to fight for him; from Sir Lewis Dyve, his former major-general of Dorset, now a prisoner in the Tower, who grossly overestimated the fighting potential of the forces lately raised in the City; and by the presbyterian Colonel Joseph Bamfield, who poisoned his mind against Cromwell and Ireton.

Consequently he failed to appreciate that he was being offered a unique and fleeting opportunity. If he had grasped it, by pledging himself there and then to accept the proposals that Ireton and his colleagues offered in the name of the army, Fairfax would have escorted not only the Speakers and the independent peers and members back to London but the king himself. But what, it will be asked, if parliament declined to accept those terms as a basis of settlement? Berkeley sought a meeting with Ireton and his fellow-emissaries in order to put that very question. He was given to understand that the army would if necessary force parliament to endorse them, presumably by excluding enough presbyterians to secure a majority. The army did indeed purge a parliament sixteen months later, with unhappy and deeply unpopular results. But whereas the purpose of Pride's Purge was to *prevent* the conclusion of a treaty that would restore the king, that of a purge in August 1647 would have

---

[8] Quoted from Berkeley's *Memoirs* in Gardiner, *History of the Great Civil War*, III, 172; cf. Woolrych, *Soldiers and Statesmen*, pp. 175–8.

been to *effect* his restoration. It need not have been on nearly so large a scale as Colonel Pride's operation, and it would surely have been widely popular. Since the first Head of the Proposals was for an early dissolution, followed by a general election, the probable result would have been a landslide in favour of a settlement which already had the support of the army, the 'royal independents', and the king himself.

But of course Charles did not assent to the Proposals. Deeply disappointed, Cromwell, Ireton, and other officers asked him urgently to write ' a kind letter to the army', giving it his blessing in restoring order and disowning the actions of the mob. What he wrote was too little and too late; it was much less supportive than what they asked for, and he delayed it until it was quite clear that London's resistance was collapsing; indeed the City formally submitted before it appeared in print. In one crucial week he threw away not only his best chance of regaining his throne but the goodwill of a great part of the army.

The New Model's entry into London was a well staged demonstration of its strength and discipline. Fairfax did not hasten it, for he wanted no bloodshed. He drew up his 15,000 men on Hounslow Health on 3 August—their ranks stretched for a mile and a half—and escorted the two Speakers, fourteen peers, and about a hundred MPs in a review of them. Not a shot was fired nor a sword drawn when his regiments encircled the City next day, and when he escorted the returning members to the Palace of Westminster on the 5th his men wore laurel leaves in their hats and the church bells pealed. To complete the triumph, all his twenty regiments paraded in Hyde Park on the 7th, a Saturday, before marching to Cheapside with colours flying, trumpets playing, and drums beating. From that artery of the old City they spread out and moved through all its streets, to be greeted not sullenly but with enthusiastic plaudits. Their orderliness impressed everybody; they took not so much as an apple, it was said, and the contrast with the recent behaviour of the reformadoes was taken to heart. What would it have been like, one wonders, if they had been able to bring back the king!

But ceremonies do not resolve serious political crises, and the army still faced difficult relations with the parliament and (quite soon) growing dissensions in its own ranks. Saye and most of the other active peers were friendly, but although Holles, Stepleton, and three others of the impeached MPs went into exile during August the co-operation of the Commons was much less certain. It needed the concerted pressure of Cromwell, Ireton, and the other officer-MPs to goad them into annulling the proceedings of the members who had sat in the absence of Speaker Lenthall after the July tumults. This same pressure induced the House to impeach the Lord Mayor and three prominent aldermen for high treason, while others who were identified as leaders of the violence against the parliament, including City officials, militia officers, ministers, apprentices, and other citizens, were indicted for treason before King's Bench. Fairfax was made Constable of the Tower, and he appointed the radical independent Colonel Robert Tichborne as its new Lieutenant. London's new Lord Mayor was also the army's choice. In mid-August Fairfax set up his headquarters at Kingston, so the military presence remained close, though apart from one regiment temporarily guarding the Tower he quartered his troops well outside the capital. The City's Militia Committee was made to restore its independent members, and the militias of Southwark and Westminster were freed from their subjection to it. But the army's greatest triumph over the City was its success in securing that all London's Civil War fortifications, the so-called lines of communication, eleven miles in compass, were demolished. This of course was meant to prevent the presbyterian City fathers from ever again deploying their military resources as they had tried to do in June and July, but it is an interesting indication of how little either the army or the parliament foresaw that there would be a new civil war in less than a year's time. The one thing the army could not do was to make the City pay its taxes, which remained scandalously in arrears, to the detriment of the soldiers' pockets. The men did receive a month's pay on account in August, but nothing at all in September.

Despite Charles's treatment of them during the recent crisis, the army commanders still had a common interest with the parliamentary independents, who now dominated the Lords, in bringing him to accept the Heads of the Proposals as the basis of a settlement. The Commons, however, were anxious to keep on the right side of the Scottish Covenanters and merely rehashed the Propositions of Newcastle with a few amendments. These were sent to Charles early in September, but he in collusion with Cromwell and Ireton replied on the 9th that he preferred the Heads of the Proposals, which he asked parliament to take into consideration, as a prelude to admitting him to a personal treaty. But he bound himself to nothing, and Cromwell and Ireton lost credit with the more radical spirits in the army for persisting in seeking agreement with him.

Fairfax was having difficulty in holding its discordant elements together. At the only meeting of its General Council during August, at Kingston on the 18th, a carefully worded *Remonstrance* was approved, and was subsequently read at the head of each regiment. It declared that 'we shall rejoice as much as any to see the king brought back to his parliament . . . on such sound terms as may render the kingdom safe, quiet and happy'.[9] It asked parliament to take the Heads of the Proposals into speedy consideration, and to exclude all the members who had sat on during the recent absence of the Speakers, until

[9] Quoted in *Woolrych, Soldiers and Statesmen*, p. 186; full text in *The Parliamentary or Constitutional History of England* (1751–66), XVI, 251–73.

they had expressly disavowed the votes that had been passed under pressure from the mob. The Lords immediately approved the *Remonstrance* and returned their thanks to Fairfax, but the Commons took no action on its main requests. It did not satisfy a growing section of the agitators, who had been clamouring (and continued to clamour) for the total expulsion of the members who had sat on in Lenthall's absence. Since over a hundred MPs had done so on one day or another, that would probably have united the parliament and most of the public against the army and wrecked its leaders' plans for a settlement.

Fairfax moved his headquarters to Putney early in September, and there he instituted regular weekly meetings of the General Council, on Thursdays in the parish church. The Heads of the Proposals were further debated in three consecutive sessions; that on the 9th specifically considered the rights of the king and his heirs. Major Francis White, the senior officer-representative of Fairfax's own foot regiment and a committed Leveller, spoke against restoring him on any such terms as those proposed, declaring that there was now no visible authority in the kingdom but the power of the sword. He was promptly expelled from the General Council without a dissentient voice, and in publicly announcing the fact Fairfax reaffirmed that the army upheld the fundamental authority and government of the kingdom. Soon afterwards the army's printer put out a new edition of the Heads of the Proposals, with some modifications approved at the General Council's meeting on the 16th.

The Levellers were stepping up their efforts to indoctrinate the agitators and the soldiery generally, but they were making only limited progress in face of the respect in which the generals were held and the common desire to preserve the army's solidarity. They had the active support of a number of officers, including (despite White's expulsion) some on the General Council, such as Commissary Cowling, Lieutenant Chillenden, Captain Edmond Rolfe, and Major William Rainborough, whose brother Colonel Thomas Rainborough was also strongly sympathetic. The army being so close to London, it was from there that it recruited to vacancies in its ranks during the late summer and autumn, and a fair number of active Levellers enlisted with the purpose of spreading the word in it. The Leveller leaders were thoroughly disillusioned by now with the present parliament, and bent on an altogether more radical programme of reform than the Heads of the Poposals offered; Richard Overton had given a taste of it in July in a tract which he significantly called *An Appeal from the Degenerate Representative Body, the Commons at Westminster, to the Free People in General.* Lilburne nursed a grudge against Cromwell for not having secured his release from the Tower, though now that the sympathetic Tichborne was its Lieutenant he was allowed to go about London by day almost as he pleased. He rightly regarded the Lords, whom his attacks had deeply offended, as the main obstacle to his release, and he viewed Cromwell's and Ireton's close rapport with Saye and Wharton and their allies with strong suspicion and resentment. Early in September he asked to see Cromwell, who readily visited him and urged him in as cordial a way as he could to drop his attacks on the parliament. If he would just be patient, Cromwell promised, he would receive satisfaction for the wrongs that he had suffered and honourable employment in the army; but if he was released, would he promise to be quiet? Lilburne utterly rejected such a condition. He wanted not just his freedom but a public vindication, and reparations for his sufferings.

Very soon after seeing Cromwell, Lilburne wrote a widely publicized open letter to the soldiers of the army, advising them not to entrust the same men as agitators for too long, since their hopes of gaining promotion were making them too compliant. But he urged them above all 'not to trust your great officers at the general's quarters no further than you can throw an ox', for by their cunning they had 'most unjustly stolen the power both from your honest general, and your too flexible agitators'.[10] Ireton was Lilburne's and the Levellers' *bête noire*; they held him responsible for perverting Cromwell. They went on to develop a theory that the army, by means of its *Solemn Engagement* in June, had sealed a mutual compact which had turned it into a corporation independent of the state and vested ultimate power over it in its representative General Council. Consequently its officers, 'being only admitted by mutual consent . . . would have no power but what was betrusted to them by the soldiers'.[11]

These were notions that the army commanders would not possibly countenance. During September and most of October the General Council served to contain the discontent in the army's ranks and to provide a forum for its material grievances, though from the meagre news of its debates that leaked out it seems that the agitators were showing increasing opposition to the senior officers' dealings with the king. In the Commons on 22 September Marten and Colonel Rainborough moved that no further addresses should be made to him, but Cromwell, Ireton, Vane, St John, and Nathaniel Fiennes strongly opposed them, and the motion was defeated by 84 votes to 34. In practical terms the army had more to lose than to gain by quarrelling with the parliament, which in the course of September approved a new establishment for the home forces under Fairfax's command. They were to total 26,400, which was an advance of 20,000 on what parliament had proposed only six months earlier. In October the soldiers even got another month's pay. For all their professions the Levellers were doubtful friends to the army, for

---

[10] J. Lilburne, *The Jugglers Discovered* (1647), pp. 10, 12, quoted in Woolrych, *Soldiers and Statesmen*, p. 192.

[11] *England's Freedom, Soldiers's Rights* (1647), reprinted in D. M. Wolfe (ed.), *Leveller Manifestoes of the Puritan Revolution* (New York and London, 1944), pp. 243–7.

their demands regarding taxation were utterly inconsistent with its financial needs. When they came to publish their comprehensive plan for a democratic commonwealth it would (as we shall see) find no place for a standing army at all.

These considerations were not lost on the greater part of the army, and Lilburne and his associates were so disappointed with the performance of the existing agitators that towards the end of September they set about engineering the emergence of new ones. These appeared in five cavalry regiments, to which Fairfax's horse should probably be added since Edward Sexby was its senior agitator. For more than a month they spread no further, and it is not clear whether they were actually elected by the men they claimed to represent. In two or three regiments they probably received some form of assent,[12] but they did not displace their original agitators or gain a place on the General Council. They were commonly referred to as 'the agents of the five regiments' or 'the London agents', and it was in London that they regularly met—daily in the early stages. They were essentially proselytizers for the Leveller movement, and they seem to have been organized mainly by Lilburne's young friend John Wildman, a man of radical temperament and gentry background who had some knowledge of the law. They were probably acting already as a caucus before they sought any mandate from their fellow-soldiers.

From this source there came a challenge that shook the army to its roots and threatened to give a revolutionary turn to national politics. It was a paper called *The Case of the Army Truly Stated*, which was signed by the agents of the five regiments (and nobody else) and presented to Fairfax by two of them on 18 October. Its main author was almost certainly Wildman, though Sexby may well have had a hand in it, and the other agents probably added passages here and there. It alleged, with much rhetoric but little truth, that the army was in a worse situation than when it had gathered at Newmarket in June, and that its senior officers had been perverting the whole intention of its *Solemn Engagement* by their sinister manipulation of its General Council. They had, it claimed, frequently discouraged the agitators from consulting over the means of redressing the people's grievances and warned them not to meddle with matters that did not concern them. They had not pressed for the reforms and the redress of grievances that the army's declarations had called for, and they had failed to insist on the expulsion of the members who had sat on in early August; nor had they secured an early date for a dissolution and the abolition of monopolies, tithes, and the excise (there was no mention of the monthly assessment, on which the army's pay mainly depended). They were proposing to restore the king with his royal veto intact, and allowing his

---

[12] Gentles, in *New Model Army*, pp. 199–200, persuades me to modify the scepticism that I expressed in *Soldiers and Statesmen*, pp. 203–6.

evil councillors free access to him (though that in fact was put a stop to in mid-October).

The positive demands of *The Case of the Army* were based on the principle that all power rested originally in the whole body of the people, and that supreme authority, both legislative and executive, lay in their elected representatives. It called for an immediate and drastic purge of the present parliament, a dissolution within nine or ten months, and thereafter biennial elections at an appointed date in which 'all the freeborn' aged twenty-one or over should have the vote unless they had forfeited their freedom through delinquency, which in the context meant royalism. It did not need saying that the freeborn were exclusively male. Liberty of conscience and freedom from conscription were to be guaranteed, and a range of radical reforms was proposed, including the codification of the entire law of England in one compact volume, written in plain English. The lands of deans and chapters should be sold to meet the army's arrears (they would in fact have met only a third of them), and its current pay should be found from the allegedly vast sums that had gone to court parasites and the millions lying frozen in the 'dead stocks' of City companies. This was hogwash; as Ian Gentles has written, 'The notion of paying the army £45,000 a month out of sinecurists' salaries and the hidden capital of City companies is akin to the belief that the modern welfare state can be financed merely by soaking the rich'.[13] *The Case of the Army* is remembered chiefly for the memorable debate on manhood suffrage which it prompted, but its main purpose when it was written was to challenge the political direction that Cromwell and Ireton were giving to the army, particularly in their pursuit of a treaty with the king, and to renew the bid to control army politics from the bottom up. Leveller elements were already present among its demands, and its signatories, the new agents, would very soon be part of a Leveller campaign to weld the army into an instrument of revolutionary action.

Fairfax, sensing the danger of the document, put it before the next weekly meeting of the General Council, on 21 October. The day before, Cromwell made a very long speech in the Commons, totally dissociating himself and Fairfax from the proposals in *The Case of the Army*, which was already on the bookstalls, and reaffirming his commitment to the historic monarchy and to the reinstatement of the present king. The General Council gave the manifesto a cool reception, not relishing its allegations that it had been merely the generals' poodle and that the army was rent by faction. The regular agitators of the five regiments for which it claimed to speak repudiated it. It was referred to a committee with a view to disciplinary action against its authors or instigators, but probably because of the presence on it of Sexby, Lockyer,

---

[13] Gentles, *New Model Army*, p. 201.

and Allen the committee took a softer line and sent these three to the new agents' meeting with a cordial invitation to send representatives to explain their position to the next Thursday General Council.

It was not a time for the army to weaken itself by internal discussion. In Scotland the convention of estates had just voted to keep its army afoot until at least March 1648, and Hamilton's party was now in almost even balance with Argyll's. Hamilton's brother Lanark travelled south with Loudoun to see the king; they visited him at Hampton Court on 22 October and raised his hopes of getting armed support from Scotland without having to take the Covenant himself. A day or two later they reappeared with fifty armed horse-men and urged him to escape with them then and there. He was not quite ready for that yet, but the option made him less responsive to any propos-itions that either the parliament or the army might have to offer. In the Com-mons it was getting harder for Cromwell and the royal independents to keep their peace process afloat in face of the growing minority who already re-garded Charles as unfit to treat with.

Such was the background to the most famous non-parliamentary debates in British history, those held at Putney from late October into early Novem-ber. They took a very different course from what the senior officers expected. Fairfax, Cromwell, and Ireton had hoped that the General Council would reject the accusations in *The Case of the Army*, reaffirm the army's essential unity of purpose, and get on with the business of agreeing a set of terms that could be put to the king in its name. What Trooper Robert Everard, a new agent of Cromwell's own regiment, brought to headquarters on the day before the General Council's next meeting, however, was no mere reply to its committee's written objections to *The Case of the Army* but an entirely new document styled *An Agreement of the People*. It had been approved that very day by a meeting of the agents of the five regiments, together with other soldiers and some civilian Levellers, including Wildman, who was deputed to speak for it before the General Council. It seems to have been swiftly put together in order to grasp the opportunity to air the Levellers' larger aims before the army's representative body. Wildman almost certainly had a hand in drafting it, but its style, so concise and lapidary compared with the sprawl of *The Case of the Army*, suggests that its main another was William Walwyn.[14] When Cromwell read it he perceived at once that there were 'new designs a-driving' and that the General Council would have to thrash them out.

Whereas *The Case of the Army* set forth a programme for action in the spe-cific political circumstances of October 1647, the *Agreement of the People* dealt in first principles. That very fact widened the differences between its

---

[14] See Barbara Taft's introduction to *The Writings of William Walwyn*, edited by J. R. McMichael and herself (Athens, Ga., 1989), p. 31. Text of *An Agreement of the People* in Gardiner (ed.), *Constitutional Documents*, pp. 333–5.

authors and the army leaders. The latter were still seeking a settlement based on the ancient constitution and the fundamental laws of England, boldly though they proposed to modify them, and they still hoped to have it validated by the traditionally binding assent of King, Lords, and Commons. The Levellers by contrast had come to regard the present laws as largely a relic of 'the Norman Yoke', and now that the people had defeated the last of the Conqueror's successors they held the constitution to be a *tabula rasa*. Only the individual assents of the free people could legitimate a new and valid constitution, and to that end the *Agreement* was offered for their subscription— offered as something altogether higher than a statute, which future parliaments could repeal or modify, indeed as nothing less than an unalterable declaration of the principles upon which future parliaments must operate. The people's representatives in parliament, it affirmed, had full power, 'without the consent or concurrence of any other person or persons', to make laws, appoint officers of state and magistrates of every degree, declare war, make peace—indeed to do everything that the sovereign people did not reserve to themselves. Their power was 'inferior only to theirs who choose them', but some rights were so ineradicably planted in the people by nature that a paramount law must prevent even their chosen representatives from infringing them. Those affirmed in the *Agreement* included freedom of religion, immunity from conscription, and total equality before the law, regardless of birth, rank, or tenure. Parliament itself should be reformed by reapportioning constituencies according to the number of their inhabitants, not their contribution to taxation (as suggested in the Heads of the Proposals). That was consistent with manhood suffrage, but the *Agreement* said nothing about the franchise; nor did it specifically mention either the king or the Lords, or even suggest who was to govern in the eighteen-month intervals between parliaments, which were to sit no longer than six months. It is a document as remarkable for its silences, which were doubtless deliberate, as for its prescriptions.

The fact that Cromwell (who presided, Fairfax being unwell again) caused the debates engendered by the *Agreement* to be taken down almost verbatim shows that he and Ireton were aware of how much hung on their outcome. We owe their record to William Clarke, a Londoner of humble origin in his mid-twenties who had risen under John Rushworth in the army's secretariat and was now secretary to its General Council.[15] He was master of an early

---

[15] The text of the Putney debates is available in two editions: by C. H. Firth in *Clarke Papers*, I, 226–406, and by A. S. P. Woodhouse in *Puritanism and Liberty* (1938; 2nd ed. 1950) pp. 1–124. Firth provides an exact transcript of Clarke's text apart from an occasional transposition of phrases or sentences; Woodhouse judiciously edits it and modernizes the spelling, making it more accessible to the general reader. In quotations I have used Firth's text, but modernized the spelling; I have not thought it necessary to give page references for each one.

form of shorthand, which he later transcribed himself. His loyalty and intelligence won him new responsibilities under General Monck in the 1650s, and in 1661 he became Charles II's Secretary at War and a knight. Sadly, he was mortally wounded on Monck's flagship five years later, in a battle with the Dutch.

At the General Council on 28 October Sexby introduced the delegates from the new agents' organization: two soldiers, Everard being one, and the civilians John Wildman and Maximilian Petty. He then told Cromwell and Ireton to their faces that their 'credits and reputation hath been much blasted' by their striving to please the king and their support of a parliament of rotten members. Very soon the fundamental difference of purpose between the army commanders and the Leveller group stood revealed. The former held themselves bound by their pledges to respect the authority of parliament and to seek a settlement sealed by its authority, or (if not) by that of a new parliament following upon the self-dissolution of the present one. The Levellers on the other hand wanted the army to reoccupy London, break the parliament, and inaugurate a new and revolutionary constitution, which could only be done by force. The prospects of the *Agreement* gaining enough subscriptions to give it any kind of democratic validity, if it was imposed by a military dictatorship upon a nation yearning for peace and still devoted to its monarchy, were non-existent. No wonder the feelings of the General Council were divided. Many of those present, officers and soldiers alike, must have felt torn between on the one hand the powerful attraction of such ideals as equal political and legal rights and total liberty of conscience, and on the other a deep reluctance to divide the army and engage in political violence in defiance of its trusted general and lieutenant-general. Strong ties bound those who had marched and fought together, and who knew when they might have to do so again? We lack evidence, however, about the sentiments of the rank and file, for the only soldiers recorded as having spoken during the three days' debate at Putney (apart from one brief anonymous interjection) were Sexby, Allen, Lockyer, Everard, and the unnamed new agent who came with him, all committed Levellers or fellow-travellers, though Allen would not stay with them for long.

Although the *Agreement* was read to the General Council on the 28th, there was no debate that day of its specific contents. Cromwell and Ireton successfully insisted that the first thing to decide was whether the council was free to consider such radical changes at all. They argued that the army was bound by its public declarations from June onward, in which it had promised obedience to parliament if its legitimate demands were met, and that it remained morally committed to pursue the path of negotiation which it had opened up with the Heads of the Proposals, at least until they had been fully considered by king and parliament. The Leveller spokesmen, however, contended that parliament's rottenness was manifest, that the king had forfeited any right to be further treated with, and that no engagements were binding if they stood in the way of the rights of the people; if the matters propounded in the *Agreement* were the people's due, they stood self-justified. The outcome of the day's debate was the appointment of a committee to sift the army's declarations and itemize the commitments contained in them, so as to help the General Council, in a special meeting in a few days' time, to assess how far the *Agreement*'s proposals were compatible with them. This was not, as has sometimes been said, just an obstructive procedural stratagem, for the future political role of the army hung on the question. Nor was it a mere delaying tactic, for the committee was to convene next day, the new agents and their mentors were invited to come and put their case to it, and the General Council was to meet again next Monday to consider its findings. Cromwell's attitude was conciliatory, not confrontational; he assured the spokesmen for the *Agreement* that they would not find him and his fellow-officers 'wedded and glued to forms of government', and readily acknowledged for his part 'that the foundation and supremacy is in the people, radically in them'.

The famous debate on Friday the 29th, in which the Leveller spokesmen joined issue with Cromwell and Ireton over the very foundations of a free commonwealth, came about almost by accident. It took place neither in Putney church nor in a session of the General Council. In the Thursday meeting, before an hour was fixed for its committee to meet, Lieutenant-Colonel Goffe made an urgent and eloquent plea that they should gather first to seek the Lord's guidance in prayer. He probably spoke for many when he said that 'it hath been our trouble night and day that God hath not been with us as formerly'. This did not please Wildman, who spoke more than anybody else at Putney except Ireton, and was of all the Leveller leaders the one least touched by religion. But there was wide support for the proposal, and it was agreed that the next morning should be given to prayer, at an open meeting in the quartermaster-general's lodging in one Mr Chamberlain's house. The committee was to convene in the afternoon. There was a big attendance at the prayer meeting, and it was still hearing testimonies as to how God had worked on the hearts of its participants when representatives of the Leveller caucus arrived in the early afternoon to confer with the committee. Finding a large and potentially sympathetic audience before them, they wanted to launch a general debate on the Agreement there and then. Cromwell understandably opposed it, seeing that the General Council had sat until late last evening, its committee had not yet met, and he and the others present had already spent several hours together in seeking the Lord.

But several officer-representatives supported the plea for an immediate debate, the most insistent being Colonel Thomas Rainborough, whose contribution to it was to become immortal. His vehement stance may have taken his fellow-officers by surprise, since until the previous day he had not been seen in the General Council for over a month, and his right to attend it was highly questionable, though it was not in fact questioned. He had been a naval captain before he became colonel of a New Model infantry regiment, and he had lately been made vice-admiral. Cromwell had opposed his appointment, which had roused him to fury; not the first row between the two men. He was further incensed when Fairfax gave his regiment to another officer, but what did he expect, when he was returning to the navy? He was a brave, sincere, impetuous man and a genuine radical, but at Putney he did have a large chip on his shoulder.

Cromwell had to bow to pressure; the *Agreement* was read out in its entirety again, and then debated clause by clause. If he and Ireton had had time to think, and been fresher, they might have furthered their most immediate object, which was to preserve the army's unity and discipline, by focusing on those parts of the *Agreement* which commanded general consensus in it, such as liberty of conscience, equality before the law, and the superior authority of the people's representatives. Instead, Ireton seized on a point on which it was silent, and asked whether the proposal to equalize constituencies on the basis of population meant that every male inhabitant had a right to vote. This was what prompted Rainborough's memorable affirmation 'that the poorest he that is in England hath a life to live, as the greatest he; and therefore . . . that every man that is to live under a government ought first by his own consent to put himself under that government'. Against him, Ireton took his stand on the constitution of parliament from time immemorial and on the principle that only those should elect its members who had 'a permanent fixed interest in this kingdom, whether as freeholders or as freemen of corporations', the latter being mostly substantial traders. This led to a gladiatorial contest with Rainborough; for at least half an hour no one but these two got a word in, and both made long speeches after that. Sexby and Wildman also contributed substantially, and there is no doubt that the Leveller case commanded more sympathy than Ireton's. Sexby was passionately eloquent on behalf of his fellow-soldiers in challenging the claim that only those with a fixed estate should enjoy full political rights. Alluding to the famous declaration in June that this was no mere mercenary army, he declared that 'if we had not a right to the kingdom, we *were* mercenary soldiers'. He was echoing Rainborough, who had said he 'would fain know what the soldier hath fought for all this while'.

The irony is that Rainborough, who seems to have had little if any personal contact with the Levellers up to now, was going further than most of their leaders at this time in contending for unqualified manhood suffrage. The Levellers represented the interests of people of some modest economic independence, small traders and craftsmen and the like, rather than those of the great mass of the poor. When some of the officers present, in dismay at the heat being generated by Ireton's and Rainborough's long wrangle, tied to steer discussion towards a compromise, such as denying the vote only to foreigners and to those who were too dependent to make a free choice, Petty responded positively; he was quite ready to consider excluding servants and apprentices who lived in their masters' households, and men who subsisted by alms. Cromwell was prepared to enfranchise copyholders by inheritance. But just as the debate seemed set on a constructive course, Rainborough tried to move that the army should be called to a rendezvous, and its line of action settled there. He doubtless had in mind the precedent of the June rendezvous and the mass adoption of the *Solemn Engagement*, but whereas that occasion had served to unite the greater part of the army, what he proposed would have further divided it. The record of the day's debate breaks off before the end, but it seems that a straw vote was taken as to whether all but servants and beggars should have the vote, and (reportedly) only three voices were against it.[16] This did not of course betoken a general conversion to the Leveller programme as a whole; if the vote had been on whether to march on London and force the *Agreement* on parliament we can be sure that it would have gone very differently. Before the meeting broke up yet another committee was appointed, to prepare fresh proposals for the General Council's consideration in the light of the day's deliberations. As well as Cromwell and Ireton it included both the Rainboroughs, Chillenden, Sexby, and Allen, and it seriously set about seeking common ground, or compromises, between the Heads of the Proposals and the *Agreement*.

The Levellers, however, were rarely all of one mind, and Wildman was much less interested in compromise than in power. Unlike Lilburne, who as we shall see was not ill-disposed towards the king, Wildman was at this time a republican, and he had the kind of temperament that takes positive pleasure in conflict and conspiracy. He almost certainly wrote *A Call to All the Soldiers of the Army by the Free People of England*, which was in print and circulating among the regiments on 29 October, just as the great debate on the *Agreement* took off. It denounced Cromwell and Ireton in virulent terms, accusing them of leading the agitators by the nose in the General Council while they drove on the king's design in parliament, and of claiming as they did so that they spoke for the whole army. It called upon the soldiery to withdraw their obedience from all officers who would not go with them along the path blazed by the *Agreement*. 'Ye have men amongst you as fit to govern as others to be removed. *And with a word ye can create new officers.*' Let them form 'an exact council' and join hands in it with the 'truest lovers of the people ye can

---

[16] This vote has been variously dated; see *Soldiers and Statemen*, pp. 243–4 for my reasons for believing that it was taken at this meeting. It would not be binding, since this was not a session of the General Council.

find to help you ... Establish a free parliament by expulsion of the usurpers.'[17] Tens of thousands of supporters, they were assured, were standing ready to assist them. This of course was an open incitement to mutiny, and it was not the only one in circulation. New agents were now appearing in other regiments besides the original five, and the men of Colonel Robert Lilburne's foot regiment, which Fairfax had ordered to Newcastle, had already defied their officers and held an unauthorized rendezvous.

On Sunday the 31st Colonel Rainborough took advantage of a break in the intensive discussions to visit Lilburne in the Tower. It was probably their first meeting. Rainborough professed great friendship towards the Leveller leader, but deplored the 'foolish zeal' which was driving some spokesmen at Putney to express evil intentions towards the king, which 'he well knew the greatest part of the army abhorred to think of'.[18] This was probably not ill taken, for Lilburne (unlike Wildman) was not at this time a republican and had no special animus against the king. Our informant about Rainborough's visit is Lilburne's fellow-prisoner and friend Sir Lewis Dyve, who earlier in the month had transmitted his advice to Charles to send for his six or seven real enemies in the army, starting with Major White, Captain Reynolds, and Sexby. If Charles would reassure them about his intentions, Lilburne promised him that he would have the army at his devotion within six weeks!

If that is really what Lilburne believed he was greatly mistaken, for a tide of ill-feeling towards the king was rising in the army, and it made itself evident in the special session of the General Council on Monday 1 November. It probably owed something to Wildman's influence over the new agents and to his speeches at Putney, but it was partly religious in origin. Cromwell, who again presided, did not handle the meeting wisely. If he had directed attention to the common ground that the committee appointed on the Friday was exploring, it might have gone better. But he began by inviting those present to speak of any divine guidance they believed they had received in answer to their prayers, and this was an open invitation to the many, by no means all Leveller sympathizers, who felt that God had withdrawn his presence from them because they persisted in trafficking with the king. As Goffe put it, 'this hath been a voice from heaven to us, that we have sinned against the Lord in tampering with his enemies'. God's answer to Captain Bishop's prayers was that they were all distracted in counsel because of their 'compliance to preserve that man of blood, and those principles of tyranny, which God from heaven by his many successes [given] hath manifestly declared against'. The scriptural image of Charles as a man of blood was to gain even more potency when the second Civil War broke out. But such responses were not what

[17] Substantial excerpts in Woodhouse, *Puritanism and Liberty*, pp. 439–43; italics in original.
[18] 'The Tower of London Letter-Book of Sir Lewis Dyve', ed. H. G. Tebbutt, in *Bedfordshire Historical Record Society XXXVII* (1958), 95–6. See p. 92 for Lilburne's advice to the king.

Cromwell wanted to hear, and he let himself be drawn into a long altercation with Goffe as to how far they could expect God to pronounce on very particular political issues. For once he and Wildman were not far apart when the latter said 'we cannot find anything in the word of God what is fit to be done in civil matters'. He allowed a long and increasingly ill-tempered three-sided wrangle to develop between Ireton, Wildman, and Rainborough, who differed so far in principle that there was no reconciling their views. Yet despite this sterile session, the General Council agreed to go on meeting daily until all the proposals before it had been considered.

But further sittings only generated more division, and the army commanders became increasingly concerned about it. They had fresh cause to suspect the king's intentions. Charles had been free to see almost whom he pleased at Hampton Court because he had given his word that he would not try to escape, but on 30 October he withdrew his parole. The reason was obvious, as his actions would soon show. His guards were doubled, but in such a building it was very difficult to foil a determined escape plan without making him a close prisoner, which was politically unacceptable while he was still formally king and accorded royal honours. Still more worrying was the growing restlessness within the army. Leveller propaganda was making converts; the new agents were now claiming to have the support of sixteen regiments, including seven of foot. But not all the discontent was of their making, for 400 of Colonel Robert Lilburne's mutinous foot soldiers were reported early in November to have declared for the king, and his was not the only regiment in which royalist sympathies surfaced. More typical probably was a rising resentment against the agitators in perfectly loyal regiments, because of the divisions they were causing and because (it was said) they were acting as though they were the soldiers' masters. Whether such feelings were aroused by the original agitators or the new agents is not clear, but men who were not in direct touch with the proceedings at Putney may not have made the distinction. At any rate Fairfax is reliably reported to have received a petition from the majority of the regiments, asking him to send their agitators back to them until he felt a need to summon them again, and undertaking to submit to him and his council of war according to the old and accustomed discipline of the army.

Within the General Council the generals' hold on proceedings was precarious. On 5 November, when Fairfax was well enough to preside again and Cromwell was probably in the Commons, Rainborough secured the assent of the meeting to a damaging letter to the Speaker. Alleging that the House had been induced to make further propositions to the king because it was told that the army wished it, the General Council declared that any such representation of the army's desires was absolutely groundless. This was as good as to accuse Cromwell and Ireton of misrepresenting the army's sentiments to the House, and Ireton opposed the letter vehemently. When it was nevertheless approved he stormed out of the meeting, vowing not to return until it was recalled. The Leveller spokesmen also went on pushing for another general rendezvous, and on the 6th, a Saturday, they pressed hard for a free debate on whether the army and the people could safely allow any power at all to remain with the king. They later claimed that Cromwell promised they should have it at the General Council's next meeting.

They came to that meeting, on the 8th, seemingly bent on a crucial confrontation, and there was indeed another protracted clash over the franchise. But Fairfax and Cromwell had evidently decided over the weekend that the General Council was being made a platform for those who sought to divide the army and take control of it, and that the long debate must be wound up. They may also have had intelligence that the king was about to bolt, for it was during this weekend that Charles finally made up his mind to it. So when the talk seemed to have run its course, Cromwell moved that since Fairfax intended to call the army to a rendezvous shortly, and because 'many distempers are reported to be in the several regiments', the General Council should advise him to send the officer-representatives and the agitators back to their regiments until he should see cause to summon them again. There is no record of any dissent, and Fairfax reported to the Speaker that the regimental representatives had unanimously *offered* to return to their regiments and do all they could to restore discipline in them. To underline his support for his soldiers' real interests, he accompanied their letter with a request to the Commons for the immediate disbursement of six weeks' pay, the raising of the assessment from £60,000 to £100,000 a month, and the appropriation of dean and chapter lands as well as those of the bishops to the satisfaction of their arrears.

When the full General Council met next day—as it turned out for the last time—it approved a letter to the Speaker, explaining that its previous one on the 5th was not intended to mean (as it palpably did) that the army was opposed to parliament's sending any more propositions to the king. The generals were in control again. It was announced on the same day that the promised rendezvous of the army was to be spread over three separate dates and places between 15 and 18 November. The Leveller agents publicly denounced this as a base device to prevent the army from adopting their *Agreement* by general acclamation, and this was doubtless a consideration. But there were more compelling reasons for appointing three rendezvous, not least that Fairfax wanted to address each regiment in person, which could not be done in the course of one short November day. Moreover the regiments were dispersed over a wide area, and to have suddenly concentrated them in one place close to London would have not only set the political alarm bells ringing but caused much hardship to civilians. The Leveller agents, however, urged them in print to gather in a single rendezvous in defiance of orders.[19]

On 11 November Charles made his escape from Hampton Court. He had finally decided upon flight more than a week earlier, and he probably fixed the date on the 7th, before he had anything he knew of to fear from the army. Yet he told Sir John Berkeley on the night of the 9th that he was in fear for his life, for he had received a letter that day warning him that eight or nine agitators had met the previous night and resolved to kill him. The writer, who signed himself 'E.R.', was almost certainly Lieutenant-Colonel Henry Lilburne, brother and second-in-command to Colonel Robert, but of a very different temper from either him or his other brother, John the Leveller; Henry was quite shortly to declare for the king. How much he really knew, or believed, about a design on Charles's life is an unanswerable question, but there is some evidence of a shadowy plot among some of the Leveller agents to abduct the king, as Joyce had done in June, though not to kill him. Cromwell himself heard rumours of an attempt on his person, and wrote at once to his cousin Colonel Whalley, who commanded the guards at Hampton Court, to take special care against it, 'for it would be accounted a most horrid act'. [20] It suited Charles to declare publicly that he fled because he feared for his life, but he left a cordial personal note for Whalley, assuring him that this was not why he did so. His main reason, which he kept to himself, was doubtless that he wanted to be free to negotiate with the Scottish commissioners without members of either the army or the parliament looking over his shoulder.

It was not long before Cromwell's enemies were putting it about that he had deliberately frightened the king into fleeing, in order to get himself off the hook of a negotiation that was coming under increasing fire in the army, and even now the hypothesis gets an occasional airing.[21] It is altogether implausible. That Cromwell should have turned Charles loose when the army was as disturbed as it still was before Fairfax's three rendezvous is inconceivable. Nobody, not even Charles himself when he set out from Hampton Court, knew where he would head for. And Cromwell had not yet given up hopes of coming to terms with him, for only the day before his escape the Commons had put the finishing touches to a new set of peace propositions, based on the initiative of Cromwell's independent allies.

It was the second time in seventeen months that Charles had taken to the road before deciding where he was going. He had told the Scottish commissioners on the 9th that he was ready to make for Berwick, but he evidently changed his mind, and his companions Berkeley and Ashburnham gave him

---

[19]  *A Letter from Several Agitators to their Regiments* (1647), signed by Sexby, Everard, and thirteen others; mostly reprinted in Woodhouse, *Puritanism and Liberty*, pp. 452–4.

[20]  Abbott, *Writings and Speeches of Oliver Cromwell*, I, 551–2.

[21]  Cf. Antonia Fraser, *Cromwell Our Chief of Men* (1973), pp. 222–3.

conflicting advice. He decided in the end to place his hopes in the 26-year-old Colonel Robert Hammond, who had come to kiss his hand at Hampton Court. Though he was a cousin of Cromwell, Hammond had become increasingly unhappy about the army's political role during 1647, and with Fairfax's concurrence he had given up his regimental command in favour of what he hoped would be a quieter life as governor of the Isle of Wight. Charles knew that he had supporters in the island, and he reckoned that even if Hammond did not take his part he would be well placed to take ship for the continent. Hammond was utterly horrified when Berkeley and Ashburnham arrived at Carisbrooke Castle, his headquarters, and delivered the king into his hands, but he immediately informed Cromwell, and despite an agonizing conflict of loyalties his sense of honour compelled him to obey parliament's command to set a guard on his unwanted guest and prevent his escape. Once again Charles had exchanged one captivity for another, but for a while at least he was less subject to surveillance than he had been in the custody of either the parliament or the army. Two days after his arrival he sent a request to parliament for a personal negotiation in London, on the basis of a three-year trial period for Presbyterianism, liberty of worship thereafter for all but papists, and parliamentary control of the armed forces during his lifetime but not under his successors. That might have been a starting-point for a treaty eighteen months earlier, but his dwindling stock of credibility was now near to running out.

Meanwhile on the 15th Fairfax held the first of the three scheduled rendezvous at Corkbush Field near Ware. He brought with him a new *Remonstrance*, issued in the name of himself and his council of war, and prepared with the advice of a committee headed by Cromwell and Ireton but including several radical officers and agitators. It redefined the common objectives of the army, and it was hoped that by having it read to each regiment, personally commended by Fairfax, and then subscribed by officers and men, unity and discipline would be restored. But the Levellers had been very busy preparing to use the occasion for their own purposes, and the generals must have feared that they would try to turn it into a general rendezvous and get the *Agreement* acclaimed instead of Fairfax's *Remonstrance*. They did indeed find people distributing the *Agreement* among the troops, and two former officers, Colonel William Eyre and Major Thomas Scott, haranguing them in support of it. These were promptly arrested, but as soon as Fairfax appeared on the field he was confronted by a delegation headed by Rainborough, who presented him with the *Agreement* and a petition. Rainborough, being no longer of the army, had no right to be at any rendezvous, and he was moreover a member of the House of Commons, which six days earlier had condemned the *Agreement* as 'destructive to the being of Parliaments, and to the fundamental government of the kingdom'.

Seven regiments attended the rendezvous by Fairfax's command; all greeted him with enthusiasm and readily subscribed his *Remonstrance*. Two others, Harrison's and Lilburne's, appeared on the field without orders and without their officers, except for one Captain-Lieutenant Bray of Lilburne's. Many of the men wore copies of the *Agreement* stuck in their hats, overwritten with the Leveller slogan 'England's freedom and soldiers' rights'. This was mutiny, but it swiftly collapsed. The defiant soldiers found themselves isolated, and they were met with uncompromising firmness. Officers of Fairfax's staff rode in among them, snatching the papers from their hats. Lilburne's men, having marched twenty miles that day, arrived long after Harrison's had been dealt with, and when a major tried to remonstrate with them they stoned and wounded him. Fairfax left them until he had reviewed the seven regiments present by his orders, but they must have heard some of the cheers that greeted his speeches throughout the day. Encouraged by Bray, a vehement Leveller, they showed some truculence when he and his staff approached, but Cromwell and other officers charged at them with drawn swords, and they soon submitted.

The wisdom of holding separate rendezvous, where Fairfax's personal charisma could make its full effect, was now apparent. He had an equal success at the other two, on Ruislip Heath and at Kingston, and two other regiments which had been in a state of incipient mutiny read the signs and toed the line. The *Remonstrance* was well calculated to restore the army's solidarity. It accused the new agents of acting, without any mandate from their regiments, as a 'divided party' from the General Council, under the direction of non-members of the army. By printing false and scandalous propaganda, designed to discredit the chief officers and the General Council with the soldiery and the public, and by labouring to draw the army into engagements contrary to those by which it was already bound, they had jeopardized its very honour. Fairfax threatened to resign unless these abuses and disorders ceased. If he was to remain general, he required a promise from every officer and soldier to obey his superiors in accordance with military discipline, and to abide by what the General Council determined with respect to public engagements. In return he pledged himself to 'live and die with the army' in pursuit of its legitimate desires, which (as here set forth) went beyond the familiar matters of pay, arrears, indemnity, provision for the maimed and widows and orphans, and so forth. He would further join with it in pressing for an early dissolution, followed by a due succession of future parliaments at fixed intervals, 'and for the freedom and equality of elections thereunto, to render the House of Commons (as near as may be) an equal representative of the people that are to elect'.[22]

---

[22] Text in Abbott, *Writings and Speeches of Oliver Cromwell*, I, 557–60.

This was essentially a reaffirmation of what the army had stood for in its manifestos of the previous June, and all the regiments, including the lately mutinous ones, gave Fairfax the promises he demanded. Some sent him spontaneous loyal addresses, deploring the subversive activities of the new agents. This powerful reassertion of the army's unity and discipline did not spell an end to Leveller influences within it, but it did mark a widespread revulsion against recent Leveller tactics. With the king on the loose, the Scots' intentions highly uncertain, and the Irish rebels still undefeated, the army had need to close its ranks. Moreover, the Levellers articulated only one strain of popular idealism that sought expression in the later 1640s, whether in London or in the army. The radical Independent and sectarian congregations, which were currently swelling in numbers, nurtured quite another, and they had many adherents in the army. It was widely believed among them that the victory that God had granted in the recent war heralded a triumph of the saints and a major stage in the prophesied overthrow of Antichrist, so that to seek its fruits in such secular panaceas as those offered by the *Agreement* savoured of blasphemy. To such believers, Leveller democracy was a more than doubtful basis for a holy commonwealth. Just after Fairfax finished reviewing the army, the gathered churches of London published a declaration which bore the names of some of the best known Independent and Baptist ministers, including one who was probably Rainborough's pastor. A key passage in it obviously alluded to the Levellers' policies and their propagation in the army:

Since there is also so much darkness remaining in the minds of men, as to make them subject to call evil good, and good evil; and so much pride in their hearts as to make their own wills a law, not unto themselves only but unto others also; it cannot but be very prejudicial to human society, and the promotion of the good of commonwealths, cities, armies or families, to admit of a parity, or all to be equal in power.

They declared therefore 'that the ranging of men into several and subordinate ranks and degrees, is a thing necessary for the common good of men'.[23]

Considering how serious the threat of mutiny had been in the New Model, its perpetrators were dealt with remarkably leniently, especially by the standards of seventeenth-century armies. Only one of them paid the ultimate penalty. On Corkbush Field eight or nine ringleaders in Lilburne's regiment were court-martialled on the spot and sentenced to death, but Fairfax pardoned all but three, who were then allowed to draw lots for their lives. Only the unlucky loser was shot, and the Levellers made much of him as a martyr. Eleven others, including Bray, were taken into custody for future trial, and the London Levellers campaigned and demonstrated vociferously for their release, which led to further arrests. Their trials by court-martial were

---

[23] *A Declaration by Congregational Societies in and about London* (1647), p. 9 (misprinted as 7). See on this whole subject Murray Tolmie, *The Triumph of the Saints* (Cambridge, 1977).

strangely delayed—the last was on 23 December—and when held they proceeded uncertainly, revealing pockets of Leveller sympathy among the officers involved, and an unwillingness to judge harshly men who, however
mistaken, had acted out of conviction. Only two were condemned to death,
and both were reprieved. Rainborough, whose behaviour at the rendezvous
had been the most dangerous because of his seniority and popularity, was no
longer subject to military discipline. Being an MP it was for the Commons to
deal with him, and they did so on 10 December by annulling his appointment
as vice-admiral. By that time an attenuated General Council had resumed
occasional meetings, almost certainly without the soldier-agitators present.
Rainborough came before it to make a full acknowledgement of his misconduct on Corkbush Field, and in a spirit of reconciliation it asked Fairfax to
intercede for him, which he did. The Commons rescinded their vote, and
although the Lords still resisted his appointment Rainborough took up his
naval command on 1 January. Major White also made his apology for the
rash words that had caused his expulsion, and was readmitted to the General
Council. Even Bray was allowed to resume his regimental duties after making
due submission, though that was a decision that Fairfax would live to regret.

Consternation over the current wave of Leveller demonstrations and
anxiety as to what the king was up to were making parliament look more
kindly upon the army. Cromwell received the thanks of the Commons on
19 November for his part in restoring order in it, though Fairfax was ordered
to draw his headquarters back to Windsor. Getting the pay it needed took a
little longer, but the City began to open its purse-strings when Colonel Hewson
pointedly drew up his regiment in Hyde Park, and a firmly worded Representation from Fairfax and the General Council on 7 December, concerning the
army's financial and other material needs, got parliament moving towards
meeting them. Under the threat of having troops billeted on citizens who went
on defaulting on their assessment payments, measures were taken to put an
end to free quarter and enough money was found to pay off the men who had
been enlisted since 6 August. Most of those still in service were fully paid during the next six months; provision was made for maimed soldiers, widows,
and orphans, and apprentices were assured that their time in the army would
count as part of their term of service.

Parliament was not under the same pressure to attend to the king's latest
overtures, for it was plain to the clear-sighted that if he had been seriously
intent on negotiating he would have stayed at Hampton Court to hear parliaments's new proposals. The independent-dominated Lords responded first,
and they wanted some binding pledges from him before parliament would
treat further. They therefore framed four propositions, for the Commons to
convert into bills, intending that he should first give them statutory force by
his assent before being brought to London for a personal treaty. The first gave

parliament full control over all land and sea forces for the next twenty years, and made the king's disposal of them thereafter subject to parliamentary consent. The second annulled all oaths, declarations, proclamations, and judicial proceedings against parliament and its members and supporters since the start of the war. The third cancelled all peerages granted since May 1642, and ruled that no peers made from that time on should sit in parliament without the consent of both Houses. The fourth empowered the present parliament to adjourn to any place in England that it chose, for as long as it thought fit. Annexed to the Four Bills, as they came to be called, were a set of propositions, intended as parliament's further terms for a treaty, which included the abolition of episcopacy, the banning of the Book of Common Prayer, and the penalization of the king's supporters in the war on the lines of the Propositions of Newcastle.

The Commons approved the substance of the Lords' proposals by a mere nine votes, but stalled for some time before converting them into bills. The independents, who like the Lords were still prepared to restore the king on strict conditions, were almost balanced by a combination of presbyterians who would have had him back on easier terms and 'commonwealthsmen' who did not want him back on any. Charles tried his luck with the army commanders again and sent Berkeley to Windsor to ask them to intervene on his behalf, but they understandably gave his envoy a cool reception. Fairfax told him that they were the parliament's army, and would have to refer to parliament any proposals that he had to make. The Four Bills, when they were finally passed by both Houses, were presented to Charles on 24 December. He was given four days in which to reply.

More welcome to him than the parliament's commissioners were those from Scotland, Lauderdale, Loudoun, and Lanark, who came to Carisbrooke soon after. They were somewhat suspicious of him because he had not gone to Berwick, as he himself had suggested doing, but they were anxious that he should not make a peace with the English parliament in which Scotland had no say, and he almost certainly wrung easier terms from them by pretending that he was about to assent to the Four Bills. The political front in Scotland had been relatively quiet during 1647, when much of the country had been in the grip of a prolonged and deadly visitation of the plague. But the last of the Irish and the Macdonalds who had fought with Montrose had been savagely crushed, and there was no more resistance now from the royalist party under Huntly. No enemies of the Covenant remained under arms, so the political arena was dominated by the rival Covenanting factions headed by Argyll and Hamilton. Both wanted to see the king restored in all his kingdoms, but until at least the summer Argyll's and the Kirk's party had successfully maintained that he must take and impose the Covenant. From August onward, however, the prospect that he might come to terms with an independent-dominated

English parliament backed by the hated New Model Army swung the balance towards Hamilton's party, and so still more did the personal danger in which Charles was perceived to stand as the dissensions in the Army developed. He was Scotland's king as well as England's, and the view prevailed that it was better he should owe his restoration to Scottish arms, even if his commitment to Presbyterianism fell far short of what was to be wished, than that he should regain his throne on the ungodly basis of religious liberty, or not regain it at all. That is how Lauderdale and Lanark felt, though Argyll's kinsman Loudoun was full of misgivings.

The three signed the secret pact known as the Engagement with Charles on 26 December. Despite the distrust he inspired, their visits were not controlled. He was king still, and Scotland was still England's ally. His copy was wrapped in lead and buried in the castle garden, and two days later he formally rejected the Four Bills. He did not give much away in the Engagement. He would confirm the Solemn League and Covenant by act of parliament in both kingdoms, and would likewise confirm the Presbyterian ecclesiastical establishment in England for three years. But after that there should be a free debate in the Westminster Assembly, reinforced by twenty divines named by himself and any others whom the Kirk might send, and in the light of their deliberations the permanent form of the Church of England should be settled by king and parliament. Charles promised his assent to acts for the suppression of all Independents, Baptists, and separatists of every kind, and for the punishment of blasphemy, heresy, and schism. He condemned the actions of Fairfax's army since its refusal to disband, and all the propositions that had been sent to him thereafter without the Scots' assent. He promised to 'endeavour a complete union of the kingdoms'. In return the Scots engaged themselves to secure for him a personal treaty in London, upon propositions mutually agreed between England and Scotland. If this was refused, Scotland would declare his right to control the armed forces and the Great Seal, and to bestow offices and honours and to veto acts of parliament; and in order to restore him to his just rights would send an army into England.[24]

It was a foolish bargain on both sides. The Scots had no chance of raising an army that could engage that of Fairfax and Cromwell with any hope of success; they would have to count on powerful risings in their support, but they were hardly likely to win the hearts and minds of Englishmen by dictating in advance the answers to such delicate questions as the control of the armed forces, the appointment of ministers and the royal veto, and by closing the door to liberty of conscience. As for Charles, his calling in of a Scottish army before he had explored the possibilities of negotiating a peaceful restoration was the most disastrous decision of his life. If he had been in

[24] Text in Gardiner (ed.), *Constitutional Documents*, pp. 347–53.

Scotland, with a reasonable chance of escaping abroad if his champions were defeated (as his son was to do after Worcester), the gamble would have been less reckless, though he would still have faced heavy opprobrium for plunging two of his kingdoms in bloodshed again. He clearly misread the signs of a tide of popular feeling that really was running in his favour, and in favour of the old Anglican religion. Over Christmas there were riotous demonstrations for king and church, almost amounting to insurrections, in Canterbury, Ipswich, and other towns, while in London Christmas decorations appeared defiantly in churches and other public places. Ejected clergymen resumed their pulpits and used the Prayer Book services, and royalist newspapers and pamphlets appeared freely on the bookstalls. But these were mostly symptoms of a widespread nostalgia for the old days of peace rather than of any general willingness to go to war again, and Charles could have exploited this current of discontent much more profitably if he himself had shown a sincere and straightforward disposition towards peace.

Bad luck as well as bad planning frustrated his next move, which was an attempt to escape by sea; the wind was against him. As a result his guards were doubled and a squadron, commanded by Vice-Admiral Rainborough, was posted to guard the Solent. Charles lost his freedom to ride about the island and the company of his friends Berkeley, Ashburnham, and Legge; he was a closer prisoner now than at any time since the Scots had handed him over. In the Commons there was a proposal on 3 January to impeach him and settle the kingdom without him. That was going too far for most members, but the House did pass a Vote of No Addresses that day, declaring that it would send no more overtures to the king and receive none from him, and that for anyone else to treat with him without parliaments's leave would be high treason. The Lords at first would not concur in it; Saye was absent, conferring with his allies at army headquarters. He obtained a declaration from Fairfax and the General Council that the army would stand by the parliament and preserve the rights of the peerage, and on his return the Lords passed the Vote of No Addresses, though with some conspicuous absentees and some powerful dissenting voices, including Northumberland, Pembroke, Warwick, and Manchester. The party of royal independents was now seriously split, and the alliance between its leaders and the army commanders, which had produced the most statesmanlike proposals and the most hopeful strategy for giving the kingdom a lasting peace settlement, was fractured almost beyond repair.[25] The stage was now set for the second Civil War, but there were serious disagreements within the two Houses over what it was being fought for, and still wider differences between them and the army.

<hr>

[25] I am indebted in this paragraph to J. S. A. Adamson's unpublished Ph.D. thesis on 'The Peerage in Politics 1645–1649' (Cambridge, 1986), pp. 220–7.

# ✠ THIRTEEN ✠

# The Second Civil War

IT is hard to give a fully coherent account of the second Civil War, because the war itself was such an incoherent affair. What Charles and the Scots hoped was that his English and Welsh supporters would rise in arms just when a Scottish army invaded, for their only chance of success against Fairfax's and Cromwell's veterans lay in diverting and dividing the latter by simultaneous insurrections in several parts of the southern kingdom. But the king was a captive, and for all the freedom allowed to his visitors, he had no underground organization capable of marshalling his followers nationwide. The Scots did not have an army ready until July, and long before it crossed the border a series of uncoordinated royalist uprisings in southern and south-eastern England and in Wales had already spent their force. Most of them were spontaneous in origin, and motivated more by exasperation with the parliamentary regime than by positive enthusiasm for the king, and though some of his champions made heroic efforts to harness them to his cause they were suppressed or contained before Cromwell had to march against the Scots.

At the risk of repetition it is worth taking another glance at the grievances that sparked off rebellion in the spring of 1648. Most of them went back to the early years of civil war, but they had grown intolerable because nearly two years of nominal peace had brought so little relief. War taxation was the most obvious burden, and the excise was the most hated tax of all. Meat and salt were freed from it in 1647 (the government taxed producers instead), but it still fell on other articles of mass consumption, and violent attacks on excise collectors were an endemic problem for local authorities. The pay of the army rested on the monthly assessment, and Fairfax's pressure on parliament actually to increase its rate did not add to his troops' popularity. The shortfall in the soldiers' pay meant that free quarter continued to be a burden on many communities; it even caused Clubmen to reappear in some of them.

But fiscal oppression was not the only reason why parliamentary 'tyranny' had come to look worse in many people's eyes than that of Charles I's personal rule. Imprisonment by administrative fiat rather than due process of law had been a major issue in the Five Knights' Case and the Petition of Right, but it was widely resorted to in the 1640s, both by parliamentary committees and by county committees. Star Chamber and High Commission had been strongly attacked for causing people to incriminate themselves by forcing them to answer interrogatories, but the parliament's Committee of Examinations was at least as guilty of it, and the Levellers suffered particularly thereby. The Indemnity Ordinances of May and June 1647 protected ex-army men from prosecution for acts committed under the pressure of war, but many civilians who had had their goods or horses or crops or timber taken felt deprived of their legal rights. The county committees, being the agencies through which so many fiscal and administrative burdens fell upon the public, came in for special hatred. It was not fair to portray them as the willing and self-interested instruments of a tyrannous central government, for they quite often stood up for their communities against what they saw as unjust or excessive demands from Westminster, but that was how they were widely perceived. They did undoubtedly take much power out of the hands of the traditional local rulers, the JPs in their quarter sessions, and because so many of the old county elite tended in most regions to be royalist they generally shifted local authority downward in the social scale, towards lesser parochial gentry and townsmen.[1]

Unpopular though the military presence was because of its cost, neither the parliament nor the army could be justly accused of keeping up larger forces than the circumstances warranted. During the early months of 1648 no fewer than 20,000 soldiers were disbanded with two months' pay. The axe fell mainly on provincial forces, especially those in Wales and the adjacent border counties, many of whose officers had been in sympathy with the attempted presbyterian county-revolution of the previous summer. It looked as though they might join in a general mutiny against their disbandment, but some firm counter-measures by Fairfax stifled it. Some leaders of this movement remained dangerous, however, especially Major-General Rowland Laugharne, who had been commander-in-chief in Glamorgan, Cardigan, Carmarthen, and Pembrokeshire. Also disbanded were all but five regiments of the Northern Association army, whose commander Sydenham Poyntz had been deeply involved with Massey in 1647 in organizing a counter-force to the New Model Army. The garrisons of most of the defended towns and castles in England and Wales were discharged, a major operation in itself. Colonel Lambert was now in command of the remaining forces in northern England. The New Model itself was slimmed down to about 24,000 men, losing nearly 4,000 in the process. This was less than parliament had

---

[1] On civilian grievances underlying the second Civil War see Morrill, *Revolt in the Provinces*, ch. 3 and pp. 197–208; Robert Ashton, 'From cavalier to roundhead tyranny', in Morrill (ed.), *Reactions to the English Civil War*; and R. Ashton, *Counter-Revolution: The Second Civil War and its Origins* (1994), chs. 2 and 3.

recently legislated for, but Fairfax himself initiated the reorganization, with the Commons' consent. He got rid of his own lifeguard, whose political reliability he had strong reason to doubt. It proved him right by mutinying; so did half the men of Harrison's regiment, who had appeared on Corkbush Field against orders in November and were now discharged. The reorganized army had slightly more regiments, but fewer men in their troops and companies, a scheme which saved Fairfax from having to discharge officers of proven loyalty and efficiency.

Such a drastic overall reduction might look rash in view of the known possibility that a new war might be imminent, but it showed the public that parliament was serious about cutting the huge expense of the military establishment, even though the immediate cost of paying off the disbanded men imposed a heavy burden. It also ensured that virtually all the officers and men still under arms in England were wholly reliable. War was not a certainty, of course, at least until the Engagement became public knowledge late in February. The Commons showed their distrust of the Scots by voting to dissolve the Committee of Both Kingdoms when they passed the Vote of No Addresses, but it was not yet certain that the Scottish commissioners would be able to deliver what they had promised in the Engagement. Before they left London on 24 January, the commissioners held some secret talks with English royalists and presbyterians with a view to organizing risings in support of a Scottish invasion, but they were unable to set any date for the latter. When they reported the Engagement to the committee of estates in February it was favourably received, but no action could be taken on raising an army until the Scottish parliament met again on 2 March. Meanwhile the Engagement was hotly opposed by leading kirkmen, who found its commitment to Presbyterianism and the Covenant utterly inadequate. They were supported by Argyll, Balmerino, Lothian, and other powerful nobles, who were totally against going to war on its terms, while the free-spoken womenfolk of Edinburgh and Leith were heard to 'cry for peace, and say their husbands shall not fight'.[2]

When parliament met, however, the Engagers (as they were called) commanded a substantial majority, especially among the nobles, and Hamilton's hand was strengthened when his brother Loudoun was elected as its president. But division between his party and Argyll's was so bitter that it led to a notorious series of duels, and it deepened further when the powerful commission of ministers and elders that spoke for the Kirk in between general assemblies published an open denunciation of the Engagement. The Kirkmen organized a campaign of petitions against it, including one which split the Scottish army; Leven and David Leslie were among those who signed it.

---

[2] Quoted in Stevenson, *Revolution and Counter-Revolution in Scotland*, p. 99.

The Arch-Prelate of S^t Andrewes in Scotland reading the new Service-booke in his pontificalibus assaulted by men & women, with Cricketts stooles Stickes and Stones.

1 (*above*). Riot in St Giles's Cathedral, Edinburgh, on the reading of the New Prayer Book, 1637

2 (*left*). James Hamilton, Duke of Hamilton, after Van Dyck

3. The Short Parliament, 1640. The Long Parliament had the same setting and seating arrangements, until the exodus of royalist MPs depleted its numbers.

Groote Tiranev bedreuen aen Sʳ hy. syn vrau en kinderen
Groot Tiranny done agˢᵗ Sʳ his wife antchilderen.

4 (*above*). Atrocities in Ireland.
One of many propagandist
prints circulated in England.

5 (*left*). James Butler, Earl of
Ormond, by Van Egmont

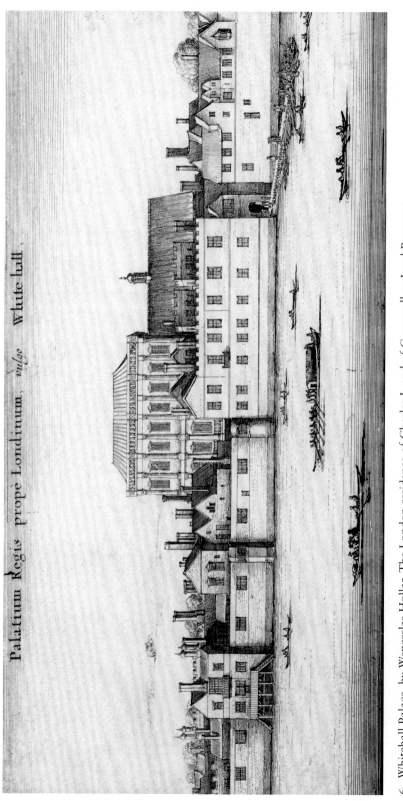

Palatium Regis propè Londinum, *vulgo* White hall,

6. Whitehall Palace, by Wenceslas Hollar. The London residence of Charles I, and of Cromwell as Lord Protector.

Sala Regalis cum Curia West-monasterij *vulgo* Westminster hall

7. Westminster Hall, by Wenceslas Hollar. The Hall, where the king was tried, is on the left; the Commons' chamber lies behind it.

8 (*left*). Charles as Prince of Wales, by Abraham van Blyenberch, 1620

9 (*above*). King Charles I, from a miniature probably painted by John Hoskins during his captivity at Hampton Court in 1647. Note the contrast between this care-worn face and that of the confident young prince above, as well as with the familiar (and somewhat idealized) pre-war portraits by Van Dyck.

11. Sir Thomas Fairfax, by John Hoskins

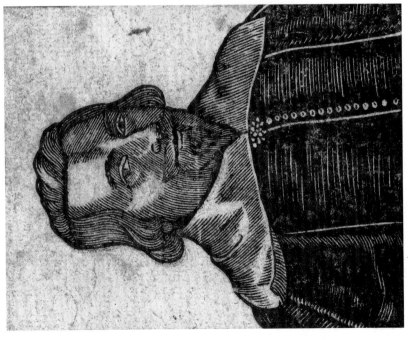

10. John Pym, after Edward Bower

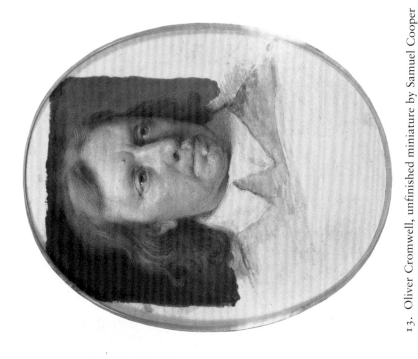

13. Oliver Cromwell, unfinished miniature by Samuel Cooper

VERA EFFIGIES ROBERTI DEVEREVX COMITIS ESSEX Aet.s.o Dom:1643

12. Earl of Essex, by Faithorne, 1643

15. Henrietta Maria, after Van Dyck

14. Prince Rupert, attributed to Gerrit van Honthorst

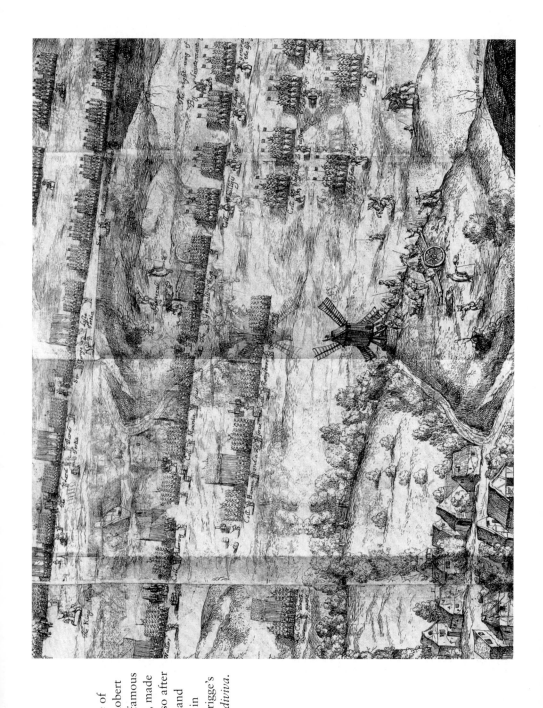

16. Battle of Naseby. Robert Streeter's famous engraving, made a year or so after the battle and published in Joshua Sprigge's *Anglia Rediviva*.

Though Englands Ark lime furies storms induru'd
By Plotts of foes and power of the sword
Yet to this day by gods almighty hand
The Arks preferud and almost safe at land

17. 'England's Miraculous Preservation'. Satirical print of 1646. The ark contains the two Houses of Parliament, and among those struggling in the flood are Henrietta Maria, Laud, Rupert, Strafford, Hamilton, and Newcastle.

18 (*inset*). Henry Ireton, attributed to Robert
Walker, after a miniature by Samuel Cooper

19 (*above*). The King's Trial, 1649

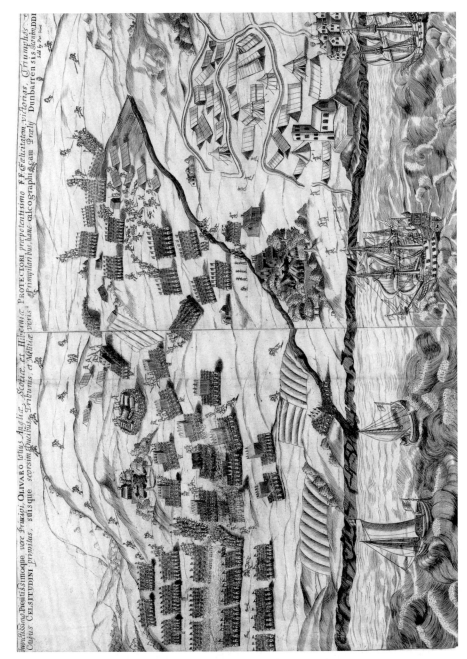

Triumphus Penitissimoque vere Principi, OLIVARO totius Angliæ, Scotiæ, et Hiberniæ PROTECTORI præpotentissimo F.F & Felicitatem, victorias, Triumphos Cujus CELSITUDINI primibus, suisque scorsim ducibus Tribunis, et Militiæ veris, primipilaribus, hanc calcographi Aeam Prælij Dunbarrensis Scenin DDD

20. Battle of Dunbar

22. Barebone's Parliament in session, 1653

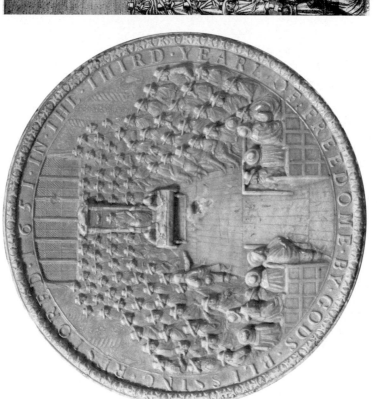

21. The Great Seal of the Commonwealth

24. Sir Arthur Haselrig, by Robert Walker

23. John Lambert, after Robert Walker

25. General Monck, miniature by Samuel Cooper

26. Edward Hyde, Earl of Clarendon, after Adriaen Hanneman

Hamilton, however, had qualified support from a party of royalist nobles led by the Earl of Callander.

For a while it seemed that Charles and his Scottish champions could hope for substantial support from Ireland. Ormond, although he had preferred to hand over Dublin to the parliament's commissioners rather than deliver the kingdom to the control of a Confederation dedicated to catholic supremacy and heavily influenced by Rinuccini and the catholic clergy, remained personally loyal to the king. The army's revolt drew Charles and his Lord Lieutenant closer together, until a suspicious parliament forbade Ormond access to his master. But during January 1648 Charles twice commissioned him by letter to seek a peace with the Confederates, if it could be had on honourable terms, and in February Ormond sailed to France. Before doing so he sent Colonel John Barry to Ireland to try to persuade Inchiquin, the commander of the parliament's forces in Munster, to declare for the king. Inchiquin did so early in April; he was furious at the way in which Lord Lisle, the parliament's Lord Lieutenant, had treated him, and he was alienated by the general course that English politics had taken in the past year. But he could not deliver over the whole army to the king's cause, for some of its protestant officers remained parliamentarian in sympathy—some even threatened mutiny. Moreover Rinuccini was opposed to a truce with Inchiquin, for it would strengthen the Ormond connection, and he did not want to see Ormond back as Lord Lieutenant. He would have preferred a truce with the Scots, but that did not appeal to O'Neill, who regarded the Scots already in Ireland as his enemies. The divisions that had bedevilled the Confederation through 1647 deepened further during 1648. Looking ahead for a moment, Inchiquin signed a truce with the Confederation on 20 May and most of the Old English came to support it, but Rinuccini was so hostile to it that he and three Irish bishops pronounced excommunication against all who gave it their support. Thereby he set himself at war not only with the Old English but with the majority of Irish bishops and with the Confederation's Supreme Council, which appealed to Rome against his action. Ironically, the only help that Charles was to receive from Ireland would come (as we shall see) from the Scottish Covenanting force under Colonel Monro, but it had absolutely no effect on the outcome of the second Civil War. Once that outcome was settled, the king's fate lay entirely in English hands.

Meanwhile, as the Engagement became more highly publicized during the spring, some hundreds of English royalists and reformadoes (disbanded officers and men) came to Scotland to offer their services. With their help, Berwick and Carlisle were occupied for the king on 28–9 April, by Sir Marmaduke Langdale and Sir Philip Musgrave respectively. But it was not until 4 May, when war had already begun in south Wales, that the Scottish parliament ordered the raising of an army of 27,750 foot and 2,760 horse. The existing

Covenanting army was to be absorbed into it, but its commander David Leslie refused to serve in the cause of an uncovenanted king. Hamilton himself was then named as general, with the Earl of Middleton commanding the cavalry and the luckless William Baillie the foot. The levying of the many men needed to bring it up to the specified strength (which was never achieved) went ahead in the face of curses from the pulpits, and its recruitment drew the Kirk into a broader conflict with parliament over the boundaries between spiritual and secular authority. It was not an auspicious launch to a perilous enterprise.

Meanwhile the king was having a tedious time waiting for the fates to decide his gamble on the renewal of war. He was being kept a closer prisoner after a hare-brained attempt to rescue him had failed late in December, and as suspicion of his pact with the Scots hardened into certainty his treatment hardened too. His servants were reduced to thirty, he was no longer allowed his own chaplains, and for exercise he had little more than a morning walk around the castle walls and a game of bowls within them. He and his friends hatched a series of escape plans during the spring, but because of Hammond's vigilance and the plotters' incompetence they all came to nothing. He was still, however, permitted a surprising number of visitors, many of whom came to be touched for the king's evil. This and the continuing news of a recrudescence of popular feeling in his favour kept his hopes alive.

This resurgent royalism was closely linked with dislike of the post-war religious settlement, which was currently being implemented through a series of parliamentary ordinances. The official Directory for Worship was a dead letter in many parishes. The authorities had a constant problem with parishioners withholding tithes from the intruded ministers who used the new services, and with parsons who were welcomed back to livings from which they had been ejected and there revived the Prayer Book ones. Many of these men were unrepentant royalists. The repression of Christmas celebrations in the second year of peace led to serious disturbances in London, Canterbury, and Ipswich. On 27 March, the anniversary of Charles's accession, bonfires blazed in the London streets and passengers in passing coaches were forced to drink the king's health. The oppressive sabbatarianism of the new Presbyterian order was another irritant, especially when an additional ordinance which threatened to intensify it came under debate in March and April. On 9 April crowds of young sabbath-breakers in London defied first the watch and then the trained bands, and the riot broadened further the next day, amid shouts of 'Now for King Charles!'.[3] The ban on stage plays lapsed on 1 January and the theatres enjoyed a brief though popular revival, but parliament clamped down on it with a new ordinance in February which not only renewed the prohibition but ordered that the playhouses should be demolished.

---

[3] Ashton, *Counter-Revolution*, p. 238.

Players who defied the ban were to be punished with a public flogging, and spectators with a five-shilling fine. But Presbyterian intolerance reached a new peak with the savage Blasphemy Ordinance of 2 May, which prescribed the death penalty for numerous deviations from 'orthodox' doctrine. This was some weeks before parliament published the Westminster Assembly's _Articles of the Christian Religion_, which at last enlightened the public as to just what that doctrine was. Milton could have been among its victims, but mercifully it was rarely enforced and was superseded in 1650.

Grumbling discontent first escalated into open insurrection in south Wales, where it was triggered by the attempt to disband the supernumerary forces. To speed the process, Fairfax sent Adjutant-General Fleming to relieve Colonel Poyer of the governorship of Pembroke Castle, but in February Poyer refused to hand it over. He was mainly concerned at this stage to secure his men's arrears and indemnity, but other troops of Major-General Laugharne's command joined with Poyer's in resisting disbandment, and the movement of defiance spread through the gentry of south Wales. Those of Glamorgan had risen twice before against the parliamentary regime. Hitherto Poyer and Laugharne had defended it, but Poyer now made common cause with the insurgents, and Laugharne threw in his lot with them early in May. But though Poyer talked with royalist agents he never accepted a commission from the king, and the declaration which he and his fellow-rebel Colonel Powel published on 10 April professed aims which moderate parliamentarians as well as royalists would have gladly endorsed—if only they had been realizable. It was their purpose, they declared, 'to bring the king to a personal treaty with his parliament, . . . that so the just prerogatives of the king, privileges of parliament, laws of the land, and liberties of the people, may be all established and preserved in their proper bounds.' They further pledged themselves to restore the Book of Common Prayer, 'with such regard to tender consciences as shall be allowed by act of parliament'.[4] Such a manifesto is a testimony of how unnecessary the second Civil War was. If the English parliament had been readier to present the king with terms that he could in honour accept, if he had been prepared to negotiate honestly and realistically, and if the Covenant had not tied the millstone of Presbyterianism round the English people's necks, how many lives might have been spared?

But armed insurrection demanded a military response. Fairfax sent Colonel Horton with a small mixed force to ensure that Laugharne's troops disbanded according to orders, but Horton found most of them defiant; many wore papers in their hats reading 'We long to see our king'. He engaged them at St Fagans near Llandaff on 8 May—it was the first clash of arms in the

---

[4] Quoted in J. Morrill, _The Revolt of the Provinces_ (1976), pp. 130, 203.

second Civil War—and beat them soundly; but it required larger forces than his to retake Pembroke Castle and subdue south Wales. Cromwell was already on the way to join him with three regiments of foot and two of horse.

By this time there were abundant signs that the Scots were preparing to raise an army, and the northern royalists' seizure of Berwick and Carlisle confirmed that an invasion was not far off. The reaction to the threat in many parts of England was a spate of petitions from counties and other communities, from late April to early June, calling upon parliament to admit the king to a personal treaty. This was understandable but unrealistic, since Charles had never been serious about negotiating when a chance remained of regaining what he had lost by force, and the momentum of war had already gathered too much strength to be checked. The Commons did however seek to reassure conservative spirits by voting on 28 April, by 165 to 99, that they would 'not alter the fundamental government of the kingdom, by King, Lords and Commons'. Vane voted with the majority, and Cromwell would probably have done so too, though perhaps with a mental reservation that Charles might have to be replaced by his youngest son the Duke of Gloucester. On the previous day Cromwell had moved, and Vane had seconded, that the House should grant the City's petition to restore the control of its trained bands to its own Militia Committee. The conciliatory gesture could safely be made, since the faithful Skippon had been chosen to command them. That was probably Cromwell's last appearance in the House until after Pride's Purge had changed the whole face of politics.

Just before he set off for south Wales, he joined a large body of officers who gathered in Windsor Castle to seek God's guidance in prayer before they took the field again. Their meetings lasted through 28 and 29 April and 1 May, and he was certainly present on the 29th, when he reportedly pressed them very urgently to search their hearts as to whether the army was guilty of any iniquity that could have caused God to withdraw his presence from it. On the third day came news that Fleming, who was a much liked officer, had been killed in south Wales. It hardened a feeling among the assembled officers that the army had drawn down God's rebukes by seeking to patch up a peace with the king and his party. Lieutenant-Colonel Goffe, who had harped on that theme in the Putney debates, had them all in tears with a homily on the text of Proverbs 1: 23: 'Turn you at my reproof : behold, I will pour my spirit unto you.' They were all fired with a resolve to go out and fight the enemies that threatened them: 'and if ever the Lord brought us back again in peace, to call Charles Stuart, that man of blood, to an account for that blood he had shed, and mischief he had done to his utmost, against the Lord's cause and people in these poor nations.'[5] 'That man of blood': the emotive scriptural image had

[5] William Allen, *A Faithful Memorial of that remarkable Meeting . . . at Windsor Castle*

been evoked before at Putney, and now that the king had clearly opted for a renewal of war its potency was all the greater.

One should be wary, however, of taking this episode, as some writers have done, as evidence that the army officers in general, Cromwell included, embarked on the second Civil War with a settled intention to put the king on trial for his life. The Windsor prayer meeting restored their solidarity and strengthened their will to fight, but we know that in the following November, long after the fighting was over, many officers including Cromwell needed a lot of persuading that to proceed against the king was the right course. Calling him to account, moreover, did not necessarily mean pursuing capital charges against him, and as for Cromwell there is no evidence that he was present on 1 May; he was more probably preparing for his imminent expedition into south Wales. We do not know when Cromwell made up his mind that Charles was unfit to be king, but it was almost certainly not yet. The republican soldier and MP Edmund Ludlow has an account of a conference that Cromwell called at his London lodging 'between those called the grandees of the House and army', probably not long before his Welsh campaign. Cromwell and his fellow-officers, according to Ludlow (if his often corrupt text can be trusted), 'kept themselves in the clouds, and would not declare their judgements either for a monarchical, aristocratical or democratical government; maintaining that any of them might be good in themselves, or for us, according as providence should direct us'.[6] It would have been unlike Cromwell to presume to judge the intentions of providence until after the outcome of the war that lay ahead. The only full account that we have of the Windsor prayer meetings was written eleven years after the event by the former agitator William Allen, who rose to become adjutant-general of horse and had his own republican axe to grind in 1659. He conveys the mood of a particular gathering of officers under the impact of what seemed a wanton renewal of war, and of the death of a popular comrade-in-arms, but just as he exaggerates in describing the army as hitherto 'in a low, weak, divided, perplexed condition', he overstates the unanimity that the religious exercises at Windsor restored to it.

One continuing difference was as to whether it was the army's business to promote a just secular settlement of the kingdom and leave matters of religion to the individual conscience, or whether its primary mission was to advance the interests of the people of God. The Levellers were of course among those who sought to prescribe a political role for it, and though Fairfax's triumph at the three rendezvous in November had checked their influence it had not erased it. During the winter and early spring they continued to direct

(1659), reprinted in *Somers Tracts* (1809–15), VI, 498–504, and discussed in Woolrych, *Soldiers and Statesmen*, pp. 332–5.

[6] *Memoirs of Edmund Ludlow*, ed. C. H. Firth, I, 184–5.

their propaganda at the soldiery, and they were striving to revive their organization among the soldiers right up to the outbreak of the new war. In this period they were approaching their peak of organization and activity, with a central committee meeting regularly and drawing funds from cells in each City ward and in the principal suburbs. Each cell had its chosen tavern where members met and planned. The Levellers' clandestine printing presses continued to be busy, and from June onward a weekly paper called *The Moderate* regularly supported their cause. John Lilburne had been freed on bail on 9 November, and at some meetings he provocatively wore the red coat of a lieutenant-colonel of dragoons, four years after he had left the service. He and his friends were trying to organize a petition to parliament with 100,000 signatures, but he was summoned to the bar of the Commons on 19 February, and despite one of his finest rhetorical performances he was recommitted to the Tower. Wildman was imprisoned in the Fleet; besides being active with Lilburne, he had hurled more bolts of invective against Cromwell and Ireton under the pseudonym John Lawmind in *Putney Projects*. He renewed his attack on them in March in *The Law's Subversion* under another *nom de guerre*.

In April the Levellers made a serious attempt to reinstitute the election of agitators in the army. The soldiery were urged to this in a tract entitled *The Army's Petition: or, a New Engagement of Many in the Army Who Are Yet Faithful to the People*, which vilified the grandees and lauded as heroes the 'honest soldiers' who had stood up to them in November. A meeting of agitators from several cavalry regiments, who were gathered to organize a petition to parliament in support of the *Agreement of the People*, was uncovered at St Albans on 24 April. Chief among them was Captain John Reynolds, a young lawyer of knightly family and a troop commander in Cromwell's own regiment who had been prominent in the agitator movement since its beginnings a year earlier. He and other ringleaders were court-martialled at Windsor while the prayer meetings were in progress; Reynolds was cashiered and imprisoned, and the rest were lucky to get off with a reprimand. Even Reynolds's disgrace was short-lived, for Cromwell had always thought highly of him, and in October he was made colonel of a new cavalry regiment that was to be raised for Ireland. At any rate, the combination of mutual exhortation and firm discipline sent the army into the field with its solidarity strengthened and with a firm resolve to defeat the common enemy. Its morale was to be more severely tested in the next four months than ever before, partly because the tide of popular feeling was running for the king in many areas where it fought, partly because it could never be quite sure of parliament's whole-hearted support, but most of all because it was to be physically divided as it had never previously been in time of war. Fairfax and Cromwell were never again to draw sword on the same field.

Kent, Surrey, and Essex were in an explosive condition as Cromwell

headed for south Wales. From Essex, 2,000 men marched to Westminster on
4 May with a petition bearing ten times their number of signatures, calling for
the king to be admitted to a personal treaty and the army disbanded. But the
spark which lit the powder barrel was struck in Kent by a special commission
which sat at Canterbury on 10 and 11 May to try the Christmas rioters. Legal
process required that they should be indicted by the county's grand jury, but
that body declined to find a case for them to answer and drew up a petition similar to the one just presented from Essex. The judges in the commission refused
to accept the grand jury's verdict and reimprisoned the accused, and the
county committee, anxious to suppress such a petition, supported them.
There was a furious popular reaction, which gathered further force when
3,000 armed men from Surrey brought up another such petition on the 16th and
invaded Westminster Hall. Fairfax still had two regiments in the capital to guard
the parliament, and they were called in. The result was a violent encounter
in which half a dozen petitioners were killed and many more wounded.

Popular risings followed in town after town in Kent, and the Derby House
committee ordered Fairfax into the county with all the force he could muster.
He had been intending to march north against the expected Scottish invasion,
but he promptly complied and many of the less determined insurgents went
home. Nevertheless, the bolder spirits held a large meeting at Rochester on the
22nd, to which they drew in many of the local gentry. Together they appointed
a general rendezvous of the king's supporters at Blackheath on the 30th,
hoping to be joined there by equal numbers from Essex. They were hugely
encouraged when most of the warships in the Downs joined them in declaring
for the king. Many of their crews were Kentishmen and shared the feelings of
their fellow-countrymen on land, but their defection was also inspired by a
general disgust, especially among the officers, at Rainborough's appointment
as vice-admiral. Cromwell was well vindicated for having opposed it.
Rainborough's earlier naval service was not remembered kindly, but it was his
association with the Levellers that made him most disliked. His predecessor
Vice-Admiral Batten had been popular, but he had been dismissed for assisting the escape overseas of five of the impeached presbyterian MPs, and he was
soon to go over to the king. The crew of Rainborough's flagship mutinied
while he was ashore, and when he tried to come aboard they sent him and his
family ignominiously packing on a small boat bound for London. Nine ships
were defying parliament within days of the outbreak of rebellion, and the
number grew thereafter. Their help enabled the Kentishmen to secure all the
maritime castles and their magazines with the exception of Dover.[7]

The insurgents lacked as yet an authorized military leader, and since the
king was a captive it fell to the exiled court of the queen and the Prince of

---

[7] Bernard Capp, *Cromwell's Navy* (Oxford, 1992), pp. 16–21.

Wales to commission one. Their unhappy choice, as commander of all the king's forces in England, was the Earl of Holland, a courtier who had changed sides twice but was still a favourite of Henrietta Maria. Holland appointed the veteran Earl of Norwich, Goring's father, to command the Kentish forces. He was hardly the ideal man to reconcile the divergent aspirations of the old cavaliers and of the majority who had risen primarily to reassert the rights and interests of their county community, but his leadership was accepted and he exercised it vigorously. By the end of May he had about 11,000 men under arms, and there was a great fear in London of a concerted attack from north and south of the Thames. But Norwich's forces were widely scattered, and Fairfax frustrated their planned rendezvous by occupying Blackheath himself. Thence he advanced with about 4,000 men against Maidstone, where Norwich found himself decidedly outnumbered. But he and the defenders were well posted and barricaded, and they had with them many determined seamen, watermen, and apprentices, as well as seasoned royalist officers. Fairfax's advance guard attacked them impetuously on the evening of 31 May, and he had a tough fight before he dislodged them, but by one in the morning his victory was complete. Many countrymen went home after that. Norwich tried to maintain his advance to Blackheath, but finding his further way to London firmly blocked, and with his total forces shrunk to about 3,000, he ferried all he could of them over the Thames into Essex and set about raising that county. Within the next week Fairfax's regiments reduced all of Kent except the castles of Deal, Walmer, and Sandown.

Essex was the main theatre of war during June, but rebellion threatened from so many quarters from mid-May onward that Fairfax's and Cromwell's forces were stretched, and it was well for parliament that their loyalty was unassailable. In Bury St Edmunds there was a riot when some revellers tried to set up a maypole, after which 600 armed men took over the town on 13 May, shouting 'For God and King Charles'. The trained bands dispersed them next day, but Colonel Whalley was sent down with a foot regiment to keep the country quiet. Meetings of old royalists at nearby Rusbrooke Hall, and at Newmarket, continued to arouse anxiety. There was another scare in May over a royalist design in western Norfolk, centred on King's Lynn, and reports in June of widespread disaffection in the Fens. These were old parliamentarian heartlands, but as in Essex most of the gentry had been dismayed by the rise of independency, and felt equivocal if not hostile towards the parliament.

Royalism of an older, simpler strain was raising its head in Devon and Cornwall; Fairfax had wisely sent Sir Hardress Waller there, and he had to suppress hostile tumults in both counties during June. The king's friends in Herefordshire were preparing to rise in support of the expected Scottish invasion, and some northern royalists under Langdale's orders seized Pontefract

Castle on 1 June. There was more disaffection in Shropshire, Cheshire, and north Wales, but Cromwell was able to send some small detachments to deal with it. He could spare them after he took the surrender of Chepstow Castle on 25 May and of Tenby Castle six days later, but because he lacked siege guns Pembroke Castle held out against him until 11 July. When it finally yielded Poyer, Laugharne, and Powel were sent up to London for trial.

So when Fairfax set about reducing Essex in June he had units of his army operating in six widely separated parts of England and Wales, and there was a serious danger of the conflagration spreading far into East Anglia if he did not scotch it. The Essex rising got under way when some of the county militia, led by a crypto-royalist colonel, seized all the members of the county committee as hostages, whereupon the grand jury publicly pledged its support for the king. Sir Charles Lucas was appointed to command the gathering royal forces, and Norwich joined him at Chelmsford with what were left of his Kentishmen. With them too were Lord Capel, Sir John Lisle, and the Tuscan Bernardo Guascone, better known as Sir Bernard Gascoigne, all seasoned soldiers. Together they made for Colchester, the county town, and set about organizing its defences. Fairfax appeared before it late on 12 June and summoned it to surrender the next day. The defenders refused, and he tried to storm it; but they withstood his assault through a fierce fight that lasted until midnight, with considerable losses on both sides. There was nothing for it but a long siege, for Fairfax's superiority in numbers was not overwhelming. He had about 9,000 against 4,000 or so defenders, but his troops included local forces from Essex and Suffolk. They had a miserable time of it, camping in the open through eleven weeks of an exceptionally wet and chilly summer, but it was nothing to the suffering of the inhabitants and the garrison as food and other necessities grew ever shorter. The siege was conducted with unusual harshness, and with a mutual bitterness between the two sides that was almost without precedent in the first Civil War. The whole experience of it heightened the feeling in the army that the king had wilfully renewed the shedding of blood, in the teeth of God's judgement. They saw him as what the modern world would call a war criminal.

Colchester was only fifty miles from London, and one reason for the hardening of the army's temper lay in its sense that its ostensible masters were not wholly behind it. Skippon could be counted on to hold the trained bands firm, but the City government was downright unfriendly, the Lords were equivocal and the Commons were wavering. Early in June the latter revoked their votes expelling the eleven impeached members, some of whom resumed their seats. The Tower and its garrison were now under presbyterian command, and on 19 June a train of wagons carrying munitions for the army through London was attacked and overturned by gangs of apprentices. Holland and the Duke of Buckingham were mustering the royalists of Surrey close to the capital, as part of an ambitious plan in which the warships which had gone over to the king were to sail up the Thames with the Prince of Wales and troops and munitions from France on board. But Sir Michael Livesey fell on them at Kingston on 5 July with a mixed force of Kentish levies and regulars and put them to rout, killing Buckingham's son and taking Holland prisoner. The Commons ordered Fairfax to hold Holland captive in Warwick Castle, pending trial, which he duly did; but it is typical of the Lords' attitude at this dangerous juncture that they ordered him, through their Speaker Manchester, to surrender Holland to their gentleman usher. Needless to say Fairfax did nothing of the kind, which so incensed the peers that they actually entertained a motion to revoke his commission, though they did not pass it.

Three key events in the war, the entry of the Scottish army into England, the surrender of the leaders of the insurrection in south Wales and the bottling up of the remaining royalists of the south-east in Colchester, all occurred within the span of six days. Hamilton's crossing of the border on 8 July was actually the first of them, but his army was in no condition to fight yet, and before it had spent a week on English soil every effective royalist movement south of Yorkshire and Lancashire had been crushed or contained. Hamilton had raised only about 9,000 of the projected 30,000 and more men, and most of them still needed basic training in handling their pikes and muskets. Even that many had been hard to muster, for the general levy which the Edinburgh parliament imposed on all Lowlands Scotland was resisted to the point of near-rebellion, not least because the Kirk continued to denounce the whole enterprise. In order to maintain the alliance between Engagers and royalists, Hamilton had had to accept the Earl of Callander as his second-in-command, and he could hardly have had a more difficult colleague. Callander, who had professionally commanded Scottish troops in the Dutch service, had much more military experience than Hamilton and thought he should have been made general. But he was not as good a soldier as he thought he was, and the arrogance with which he constantly disputed Hamilton's decisions weakened the latter's authority without contributing much to the army's efficiency. When it set out it had no guns, not nearly enough ammunition, and far too few horses for its wagons. The soldiers' morale was low and their discipline deplorable.

Lanark had advised delaying the invasion until the army was in a fitter condition to fight, but Lauderdale had helped to persuade Hamilton to answer the urgent calls of the royalists in northern England without delay. Yet Hamilton could not move fast, partly because of his transport problems and his need to train his men, but also because of the relentless rain and biting winds of that dreadful summer. Roads turned into quagmires, and streams that in a normal July were easily fordable became dangerous torrents. Hamilton dreaded the toll in sickness if he made his men sleep in the open. They had moreover large numbers of their womenfolk with them. On reaching Carlisle

he paused there for six days, during which he received the welcome reinforcement of about 3,000 foot and some hundreds of horse that Langdale had
raised in northern England. He was also expecting some 2,100 foot and 1,200
horse from the seasoned Scottish army in Ulster, under Colonel Robert
Monro's son Sir George, but these never caught up with him. Shadowed by
parliamentarian warships, they had to cross the rough Irish sea in little boats
by night, and after they landed in Galloway they found themselves cursed by
the ministers, cold-shouldered by the lairds, and refused quarters by the countrymen.

Since Fairfax was fully engaged in the south-east, it fell to Cromwell to
command the forces sent against Hamilton. He set out from Pembroke on
14 July with 3,000 foot and 1,200 horse, having sent much of his cavalry on
ahead of him. But there was already a small but efficient force in the north
which Major-General Lambert (as he now was) had built up out of the
remains of Poyntz's Northern Association army, and it was strengthened by
some very useful Lancashire levies under Colonel Ralph Ashton. Lambert,
however, had had to detach some troops to besiege Pontefract, whose royalist garrison had been harrying the surrounding country, and with only about
3,000 men in all he could not engage Hamilton in battle. But he could and did
watch his movements and harass his advance guards, and he gave time to
Cromwell to get his expedition into shape. After their long marches
Cromwell's infantrymen badly needed shoes from Northampton and stockings from Coventry, and these he collected as he passed through Leicester and
Nottingham early in August. If such an eastward route seems strange in a
campaign that reached its climax at Preston, neither Cromwell nor Lambert
expected Hamilton to take the western way south. They thought he would
want to relieve Pontefract and ultimately Colchester, so as to strengthen himself with their garrisons, and they expected him to try and make a junction
with the Prince of Wales and his ships, who were off Yarmouth by 22 July.

There was a danger that Hamilton would attack and destroy Lambert's
small force before Cromwell could join up with it, and a better general with a
better army might well have done so. But Lambert was adept at checking the
Scots' advance while avoiding a full engagement, and Hamilton was in no
hurry. He paused for a whole week in Kendal, from 2 to 9 August, and before
he moved further Cromwell had reached Doncaster. Hamilton rested for
another five days at Hornby, eight miles up the River Lune from Lancaster,
and while he was there Cromwell and Lambert joined forces at Ripon. It was
only at Hornby, in a typically bad-tempered council of war, that Hamilton
finally decided to continue southward through Lancashire rather than cross
the Pennines and strike for London by the faster eastern route. One reason was
that he hoped to recruit more royalists in Lancashire and Cheshire, but however the gentry may have viewed his approach the appalling conduct of his

troops was arousing a general loathing among the countryfolk. Having had a bad harvest in 1647, and now facing a ruinous one, they were already suffering from a serious dearth. Now the Scottish soldiers stripped the houses where they quartered of all they could carry, drove off the sheep and cattle, and sometimes seized the children and ransomed them at sword's point. Many poor Cumbrians were driven to flee their own homes.

Back in London, parliament and the City continued to give Cromwell's and Fairfax's officers and men cause to wonder what they were fighting for. On receiving the news that the Scots had invaded England, the Commons at least declared them to be enemies, but the Lords refused to concur. Ten days later the Commons consented to the king's persistent request for a negotiation without prior conditions, though they stipulated that it should take place on the Isle of Wight and not in the capital. Some City merchants suffered because the Prince of Wales, having no money to pay the crews of his warships, took to piracy; he seized merchant vessels passing through the Downs as prizes, and coolly wrote to the Common Council demanding ransommoney for their release. The City corporation's response was to petition parliament for an immediate armistice and for the freeing of the king. Meanwhile in the north-east the governor of Scarborough declared for King Charles late in July, and so on 9 August did the officer commanding Tynemouth Castle, who was none other than Henry Lilburne, brother of Freeborn John and Colonel Robert. Haselrig at once sent a detachment from Newcastle to recover the fortress, and in defending it Henry was killed. A few days earlier John Lilburne, who had just been unexpectedly released by parliament from the Tower, wrote to Cromwell to assure him of his support while the whole cause was under threat from the Scots and the king. He at least had the sense and magnanimity to recognize who were the real enemies of what they had once fought for together.

Cromwell of course had no doubts on the matter, and as soon as he and Lambert had joined forces they set off across the Pennines to give battle to the invaders, who were in the vicinity of Preston. The parliamentarians were outnumbered; Cromwell estimated their total strength at 8,600, of whom nearly a quarter were Ashton's Lancashiremen. Hamilton's army had been reinforced to about 10,000, not counting Langdale's 3,600, and Monro's Ulster brigade was not very far behind.[8] But Cromwell's confidence in the superior fighting quality and morale of his officers and men was not misplaced, and his intelligence, unlike Hamilton's, was excellent. He spent the last night before the crucial battle of the war in the mansion that is now Stonyhurst College,

---

[8] Contemporary estimates vary widely. I have modified one that I gave in my *Battles of the English Civil War*, p. 167, in the light of Gentles's discussion in *New Model Army*, pp. 261, 513, though I still think that the disparity between the two sides was probably greater than Gentles suggests.

and set off early on 17 August. He caught Hamilton with his infantry drawn up on Preston Moor, north of the River Ribble, and most of his cavalry (under Middleton) sixteen miles to the south at Wigan. Langdale, whose brigade was guarding Hamilton's eastward flank, had sent him a report of Cromwell's proximity the night before, but 'an eminent person' at his headquarters—surely Callander—had discounted it.

Cromwell had to decide whether to cross the Ribble and block the Scots' southward advance, or to strike at their infantry from north of the river. The latter was the riskier tactic, since if it failed the enemy horse and foot would recombine and resume their southward march unopposed. But if it succeeded he would have them at mercy, cut off from their homeward escape route and from the help of Monro's brigade. That was the course he chose, and his first task was to dislodge Langdale's men from the strong positions they had taken up on Ribbleton Moor, across his approach route. Hamilton's first plan was to draw up his infantry in battalia on Preston Moor, but Callander, probably wisely, talked him into getting them across the river so that they and Middleton's cavalry could rejoin before giving battle. The enclosures across Cromwell's line of approach helped Langdale's infantry to hold out heroically for four hours or more, and by the time most of them had been killed or captured the bulk of Hamilton's foot had got safely across the river. About 600 tried to defend the vital Ribble Bridge, but it fell before nightfall. By then the parliamentarians had captured the whole Scottish wagon train, along with 4,000 arms and almost as many prisoners, but Hamilton's troops probably still outnumbered Cromwell's, and most of them had not fought yet.

At a council of war that evening Hamilton decided to march them south, starting under cover of darkness, so as to bring his infantry and cavalry together again. But there were two roads between Preston and Wigan, and while the foot slogged southward through drenching rain down the westerly one through Standish, the horse came north by the easterly one through Chorley. Middleton's first contact therefore was not with his fellow-countrymen but with Cromwell's forward units within a mile or two of Preston, and they gave him a rough reception. He quickly retreated along the route taken by the foot, but Cromwell was soon in hot pursuit, his cavalry skirmishing with Middleton's all the way and doing heavy execution on Hamilton's infantry. The Scots tried to turn and fight on a height near Standish, but they could not stay and defend it because the powder in their flasks was soaked, and their supplies of it had been captured along with all their ammunition in Preston. Reaching Wigan that evening, Hamilton dared not let them rest but set them off on another long night march, this time for Warrington. There the Mersey might give him a line he could hold, and Byron, who had been raising some royalists in north Wales, might bring him relief. But Cromwell's pursuit was relentless. Just north of Winwick the Scots made a last stand and fought him off bravely for several hours, but they broke in the end, leaving (in Cromwell's estimate) a thousand dead and twice as many prisoners. From Warrington Hamilton and Callander rode off with what was left of the Scottish cavalry, leaving Baillie to make what terms he could for the infantry, of whom fewer than 2,600 were still under arms. Hamilton (unlike Callander, who got away to Holland), stuck with his fleeing horsemen to the last, but he and they had to surrender to Lambert at Stafford on the 25th. The army of the Engagers was not merely beaten, it was annihilated; Cromwell had nearly 10,000 prisoners on his hands, and had lost fewer than a hundred men killed, though many more were wounded. He had waged a brilliant campaign, though Lambert deserves his share of the credit for it.

The news of his victory hastened the surrender of Colchester, whose defenders were already preparing themselves for the inevitable. One may wonder perhaps why Fairfax had not tried again to storm the town, for its decaying walls offered no such challenge as Bristol's fortifications had done. One probable reason was that only three of his infantry regiments were old New Model units; the rest were locally raised in Essex and Suffolk. Moreover, he neither wanted nor needed to incur unnecessary casualties. Once all the other royalist movements south of Trent had been suppressed the Colchester garrison was isolated, and it posed no threat unless a Scottish army came to its relief. Fairfax's persistence with the siege shows that he had strong confidence in Cromwell's capacity to deal with Hamilton. The terms of surrender that he demanded were hard, and reflect the change in the army's attitude towards the royalist enemy between the first Civil War and the second. Soldiers and junior officers were granted quarter for their lives, but many of the men were sent to the West Indies as indentured servants. Captains and above, and gentlemen volunteers, had to surrender at mercy, and the stricken townsfolk had to pay a fine of £11,000 to save their city from being sacked. The fate of the commanders was decided by a council of war. Norwich, Capel, and Lord Hastings, being peers, were sent to London to be judged by parliament, but Lucas, Lisle, and Gascoigne were sentenced to military execution. Gascoigne was reprieved, probably because he was a foreigner, but Lucas and Lisle were shot by a firing squad that same evening. Fairfax has been much criticized for their deaths, and it was not long before the blame was being laid on Ireton, who was supposed to have talked him into a harsh decision. But Fairfax was his own man in military matters, and he acted entirely within the rules of war as they then stood. Not only had Colchester's commanders refused an earlier summons, but both Lucas and Lisle had been made prisoners in the first Civil War, and when exchanged for parliamentarian prisoners had given their parole not to fight again. Lucas, moreover, was reported to the council of war as having ordered between twenty and forty of a surrendered garrison to be slaughtered in cold blood. Fairfax may have reckoned, at a time when other royalist garrisons like Pontefract were contemplating desperate resistance, that a stern example would save bloodshed in the long run, but he does not need this kind of pleading. It should not be taken as a stain on his character, as it often has been, that he accepted his council of war's judgement in the circumstances, for much as we may regret the execution of men who had fought bravely for what they believed in, Fairfax's decision must be judged in accordance with the rules and conventions operative in his time. The fate of Lucas and Lisle does not seem notably harsher than that of Hamilton, Holland, and Capel, who after six months' captivity were tried by an unconstitutional High Court of Justice set up by the Rump and then publicly executed in front of Westminster Hall; or of Poyer, who was tried by court-martial on parliament's orders nine months after he surrendered and was publicly shot in the piazza of Covent Garden. Norwich was the lucky one; having been sentenced to death by a High Court of Justice, the Commons reprieved him, but only by the casting vote of the Speaker, who had allegedly received favours from him in the past.

The immediate reaction at Westminster to the news of Cromwell's victory was to repeal the Vote of No Addresses. Both Houses did this on 24 August, before Colchester had surrendered, while men were still in arms for the king in Carlisle, Berwick, Pontefract, and other fortresses, and while the Prince of Wales was still preparing to sail up the Thames. The repeal was avowedly in preparation for the negotiation to which parliament had committed itself while the outcome of the war still hung in the balance, but the army's reaction can be imagined. Cromwell may have wondered ironically why Charles was thought to be fitter to be treated with after all he had done to launch the second Civil War than he had been before it started, but for the time being he put his responsibilities as a soldier before his commitments as a politician. In spite of the fact that his cavalry were, as he wrote, 'so exceedingly battered as I never saw them in all my life', and that his infantry lacked clothing, shoes, and stockings ('these ways and weather have shattered them all to pieces'[9]), he sent Lambert off with 3,400 men in pursuit of Hamilton and led the rest of his forces in a vain attempt to cut off the retreat of Monro's brigade into Scotland. He also had to reduce Carlisle and Berwick, which were still held in the name of the Scottish committee of estates, and on arriving in the border country he judged the situation in Scotland to be so unsettled as to call for military intervention.

On hearing the news of Hamilton's defeat, those regions most hostile to the Engagement, namely Ayrshire and Clydesdale, rose in open revolt, and Galloway soon joined in. Loudoun and other noblemen of Argyll's party led the insurgents, in company with Leven and David Leslie, and Argyll himself

[9] Abbott, *Writings and Speeches of Oliver Cromwell*, I, 641.

was not long in joining them. Several thousand men were soon on the march toward Edinburgh, and what became known as the Whiggamore Raid threatened to develop into a Scottish civil war. But the Engagers had Monro's brigade and some other small forces with which to defend themselves, and on 12 September these fell on the westerners at Linlithgow and cut them up badly. They then established themselves in Stirling.

It might be thought that since Cromwell and these western insurgents had a common enemy in the Engagers they would make common cause, but the situation was not so simple. The westerners had risen for king and Covenant, and Cromwell and his heresy-ridden army were held in deep suspicion on two counts: their opposition to the true work of reformation and their disturbing attitude towards the king—Scotland's king too, of course. The insurgents and the Engagers preferred to negotiate with each other rather than have Cromwell and his forces on Scottish soil, and in mid-September Argyll on the westerners' behalf begged him not to cross the border until they invited him. Meanwhile, he promised, Berwick and Carlisle would be promptly surrendered. But in Cromwell's judgement there were too many Engagers still under arms for it to be safe to hold back, and he may have known that the royalist nobility in the north were arming to support them. The Scottish committee of estates was physically split now; the part dominated by Argyll sat in Edinburgh and on 4 October it renewed an act debarring all Engagers from public office. Cromwell entered Edinburgh that same day, and he evidently convinced Argyll's committee that it needed English support, for when he departed three days later it actually requested him to leave some troops behind for its protection. He entrusted the task to Lambert, with two cavalry regiments and two companies of dragoons, who all spent a miserable month, vilified and robbed by the people of Edinburgh, before they were given welcome leave to return home.

In England, meanwhile, the two major events of September were the opening of the promised negotiation between the king and fifteen commissioners of parliament in the town hall of Newport on the Isle of Wight, and the return of the Levellers to political activity after the truce that they had observed while the war lasted. The treaty of Newport, as it came to be called, began on the 18th and was scheduled to last no more than forty days, but in its anxiety to come to terms parliament let it run well beyond its appointed limit. Its pace was the slower because the commissioners differed much among themselves; the archpresbyterians Holles and Harbottle Grimston were relatively easy on the political terms but pressed Charles hard to accept the recently completed parliamentary religious settlement, while the independents Saye and Vane were stricter on the constitutional restraints but strove for the relative religious liberty envisaged in the Heads of the Proposals. Charles played his old game of exploiting their divisions, but he was weary of being a prisoner and aware of the danger he was under if he remained one much longer. As time went on he made larger concessions than he had ever made before—larger on his own admission than he hoped he would have to keep to. In a letter to a confidant on 9 October he wrote:

To deal freely with you, the great concession I made this day—the church, militia, and Ireland—was made merely in order to my escape, of which if I had not hope, I would not have done; . . . for my only hope is that now they believe I dare deny them nothing, as so be less careful of their guards.[10]

Among other things he surrendered to parliament his authority over the armed forces and over the government of Ireland for twenty years, and gave up his right to appoint the chief officers of government. By mid-November an agreement of a kind had been reached on everything except episcopacy, and if the army had not intervened he would have been restored to a diminished regal power—more reduced in fact than he could have had if he had closed with the army commanders and the royal independents and accepted the Heads of the Proposals more than a year earlier. But those offers were of course no longer open, and when he had to face the fact that there was to be no escape he suffered agonies of conscience, which he partly relieved by throwing the blame on his advisers.

The Levellers opened their new campaign just before the start of the Newport treaty (which they deplored) with a comprehensive petition *To The Commons of England in Parliament Assembled*. It was more moderate in tone than most of their previous manifestos—reproachful rather than denunciatory—and it dwelt on the many things that the people had hoped for from the parliament's victory but had yet to obtain. Most of the familiar objectives were reaffirmed: the removal of the king's and the Lords' power of veto, regular elections (this time annual, not biennial), freedom of religion, equality before the law, abolition of tithes, enclosures, and the excise, and a good deal more. But it was silent on the contentious question of the franchise, and in wishing that the Commons had 'declared what the duty or business of the kingly office is, and what not' it seemed to envisage the continuance of the monarchy in some attenuated form. It repudiated the common charge of levelling by advocating a paramount and irreversible law against 'abolishing propriety [i.e. property], levelling mens's estates, or making all things common'.[11]

In contrast with the extreme hostility with which they had received earlier Leveller addresses, the Commons thanked the petitioners for their care for the public good of the kingdom and promised to take their desires into early and

---

[10]  Quoted in Gardiner, *History of the Great Civil War*, III, 480.
[11]  Text in Wolfe, *Leveller Manifestoes*, pp. 283–90; excerpts in Woodhouse, *Puritanism and Liberty*, pp. 338–42.

serious consideration. Only a few members can really have meant it, but the House was aware of the interest that the Levellers were fostering in the army, for which the petition had a paean of praise. Fairfax soon received letters in support of the petition from several outlying regiments, and from early October a wave of petitioning swept over the army. Between then and the end of the year no fewer than thirty petitions came in, most of them from regular regiments but others from local forces and garrisons. Not all were prompted by the Levellers, but seventeen of them explicitly supported their programme. The great difference between this campaign and their agitation a year earlier was that the Leveller leaders were not trying now to divide the soldiery from their officers but to unite all ranks in making respectful and unexceptionable representations to their general. They were aware of the common interest that they now had with Ireton and most of the officers in preventing a deal between the parliament and the king which would have ended all prospects of the reforms that they sought, and would doubtless also have led to the early disbandment of most of the army itself. For his part Ireton (and many others) no longer felt obliged to seek a settlement through the consent of the present parliament, or within the bounds of the ancient constitution, and saw the value of an understanding with the Levellers, not least for the sake of preserving the army's unity.

A great deal of responsibility fell upon Ireton during the autumn, because Fairfax was often uncertain how to act in the circumstances and Cromwell was far away, in Scotland until 10 October and then in the north of England until the end of November. Edmund Ludlow, who had a footing in both army and parliament and saw what was going on from inside the House, tried hard to get the army to stop the Newport negotiations from proceeding. He rode down to headquarters early in September to warn Fairfax that the projected treaty was likely to betray the cause that they had fought for, indeed that those who pressed it were aiming to destroy the army altogether, and that the king would not feel himself bound by any promises that he made because he would regard them as given under duress. Fairfax acknowledged what Ludlow said to be true, but did not feel that he had a clear call to intervene. Ludlow took him to be irresolute, but it would surely be truer to say that he was torn between conflicting loyalties and duties. As always he felt obliged to uphold the interests of his men, who as usual when parliament was in a hostile mood were being starved of their pay; they got none all through September, October, and November. He kept up a steady pressure on the Commons to remedy this, and advanced his headquarters from Colchester to St Albans in order to make it felt. But he was unwilling to offer direct violence to parliament, and deeply unsympathetic to the rising demand in parts of the army that the king should be brought to trial and the kingdom settled without him. After failing to convince Fairfax, Ludlow talked with Ireton, who agreed that the army would have to intervene but differed about the timing. Ireton thought at the time that it would be better to wait until king and parliament had come to terms and revealed their intentions; that way, he thought, the army would get more popular support when it came to act.[12] He was soon to change his mind.

Before the end of September Ireton became so frustrated by Fairfax's refusal to intervene against the treaty that he tendered the resignation of his commission. But Fairfax would not accept it, and Ireton changed his mind about leaving the army, though he did withdraw from headquarters for a time to work out what he thought should be done. During October, if not earlier, he became fully convinced that the army must take action to terminate the negotiations at Newport, bring the king to trial, and secure the early election of an entirely new parliament. He prepared a manifesto of these intentions, soon to be famous as *The Remonstrance of the Army*, for signature by its officers. It was considered at a series of meetings of the General Council of Officers (which was still sometimes called the General Council of the Army, though it included no agitators) at St Albans between 9 and 15 November. At this stage there was no consensus in favour of forceful intervention, doubtless because Fairfax, who presided, remained so much opposed to it. The Council of Officers voted in fact to acquiesce in the treaty, but to submit to the king (and to parliament, if he accepted them) certain minimal conditions for his restoration. On the 15th, however, the Commons voted 'that the king shall be settled in a condition of honour, freedom and safety, agreeable to the laws of the land'.[13] This, it has been well observed, was just what those who had risen for him in the spring and summer had declared for.[14] It was too much for most of the officers at St Albans, who now approved the first draft of Ireton's *Remonstrance*.

This draft, however, contained expressions unfriendly to the Levellers, who were seriously seeking a broad alliance with the army, the civilian Independents of London, and the more radical MPs as a basis for action in the political crisis that was clearly looming. Leading Levellers and independents had been meeting in London at the Nag's Head tavern, and had agreed on 15 November to aim for a constituent assembly consisting of representatives of the army and well-wishers from every county. Its task would be to draft a new constitution in the form of a revised Agreement of the People, and they wanted to get it endorsed by the officers at St Albans, who had already received the outline of their proposals sympathetically. They were particularly anxious that the army should dissolve the parliament before any constitutional agreement had been reached, so some of them sought an urgent

[12] *Memoirs of Edmund Ludlow*, I, 203–4.
[13] *Commons' Journals*, VI, 76–7.    [14] Gentles, *New Model Army*, p. 272.

meeting with Ireton and a few fellow-officers at Windsor. There they had a tough negotiation, but they secured the amendment and expansion of the *Remonstrance* in some significant particulars. It now specifically commended the programme of reform in the Levellers' petition of September, and desired that 'matters of general settlement', including either annual or biennial parliaments, so reformed as 'to render the House of Commons, as near as may be, an equal representative of the whole people electing', should be legislated for by the present parliament, or by the Commons alone if need be, 'and to be further established by a general contract or agreement of the people, with their subscriptions thereunto.'[15] To frame such an agreement, Ireton and his visitors agreed that a committee should be set up consisting of four representatives apiece of the Levellers, the army, the London independents, and the 'honest party' in parliament.

This final version of the *Remonstrance* was approved by the Council of Officers on 18 November and laid before the Commons, to whom it was addressed, with a covering letter from Fairfax two days later. He must have winced at its central demand, which was for 'exemplary justice . . . in capital punishment upon the principal author and some prime instruments of our late wars'. It argued at length, and rather speciously, that the pledge in the Solemn League and Covenant to preserve the king's person and authority had ceased to be binding. It did not propose the abolition of monarchy, but stipulated that no king should henceforth be admitted except upon the election of the people's representatives in parliament, and after subscribing the proposed Agreement of the People. The same subscription was to be required of all other holders of public office. The House reacted by postponing any consideration of the *Remonstrance* for a whole week, and turned instead to debating the latest unsatisfactory answers from the king. Thereby it took a long step towards sealing its own fate.

It may seem strange that vital decisions were being taken about the army's most fateful intervention in politics without Cromwell being involved in them. His continued absence in the north is easily explained until early November, but thereafter the reason for it becomes more problematical. For at least two weeks after leaving Scotland he was busy stamping out the embers of resistance and arranging necessary garrisons in northern England, but by the end of October only Pontefract was holding out. Its siege had so far been conducted rather dilatorily by Sir Henry Cholmley, who commanded the local forces, and Fairfax had sent Colonel Rainborough (now back in the army, after the fleet had rejected him) with a foot regiment to take over the operation. Cholmley was deeply resentful and appealed to the Commons to uphold his authority as commander, but at Fairfax's request they directed

---

[15] Substantial extracts from the *Remonstrance* are in Woodhouse, *Puritanism and Liberty*, pp. 456–65; the quotation is from p. 457.

him to obey orders. Rainborough, partly because the Yorkshire county committee was showing reluctance to provide his men with their needs, spread them out widely in the surrounding countryside. The royalist garrison got wind of the fact that he had left himself vulnerable and sent out a party of horse to capture him in his lodgings in Doncaster. What ensued was more like a modern hostage-taking attempt that went wrong than a cold-blooded murder, as many have described it; the royalists wanted him alive, no doubt to exchange for their own prisoners. But they gained access to him by pretending to be carriers of a message from Cromwell, which angered him, and brave and intransigent as always he refused to come quietly. As he attempted to escape, his captors ran him through and killed him. The impunity with which they passed through the parliamentarian lines and the guards in Doncaster raised the suspicion that Cholmley was in league with them, and it still lingers. Rainborough's death roused a sense of outrage throughout the army, and most of the regimental petitions from then on called for vengeance on his 'murderers'. His body was brought to London, and the Levellers mounted a great funeral procession for him, followed by many hundreds of mounted men—one estimate said 3,000—and fifty or sixty coaches carrying their womenfolk.

In these emotive circumstances it was appropriate for Cromwell to take over the siege of Pontefract for a while, indeed Fairfax ordered him to do so. But he did not need to stay there for a whole month after Rainborough's death, especially as Lambert and his detachment rejoined him before mid-November; he could have left the operation in no more capable hands. He did not return south until Fairfax sent him a direct order to do so on the 28th, and even then he took a week over the journey. It is hard to escape the conclusion that he still had doubts about Ireton's efforts to commit the army to dissolving or purging the parliament and putting the king on trial for his life. It was to be typical of him to go through a prolonged period of heart-searching, or as he would put it waiting upon the Lord, before coming to a crucial decision; it would happen again before he dissolved the Rump, and perhaps in 1657 before he finally refused the crown. He would have been expected to take his seat in the Commons if he had returned earlier, and for that too he may not have felt ready. We get a glimpse into his mind through two precious letters that he wrote on 6 and 25 November to his friend and distant kinsman Colonel Robert Hammond, who was carrying such a heavy responsibility as governor of the Isle of Wight. The king had been enjoying greater liberty since the Newport treaty began, and Hammond was known to feel a personal sympathy for him. Could the young governor be trusted to take all necessary measures against his escape, or (if so ordered) to make him a close prisoner again? Cromwell's tortuous letters to his 'dear Robin' suggest that in trying to point where the path of conscience should lead Hammond he was wrestling with his own. He warned Hammond against letting his aversion to the Levellers lead him into 'meddling with an accursed thing'. The first letter reveals that Vane and other leading independents were concerned that his own agreement with Argyll amounted to 'a compliance with presbytery', and wished he had gone on to conquer Scotland. That, Cromwell wrote, 'was not very unfeasible, but I think not Christian', and he was commanded to the contrary by parliament. For himself, he had waited and prayed 'for the day to see union and right understanding between the godly people (Scots, English, Jews, Gentiles, Presbyterians, Independents, Anabaptists), and all'.[16]

The second letter, written after the Council of Officers' acceptance of *The Remonstrance of the Army*, shows Cromwell coming to terms with the necessity for the army to put a stop to the Newport treaty, 'this ruining hypocritical agreement', as he called it. Robin must not look for any good from it or from the king—'Good by this man, against whom the Lord hath witnessed'? Cromwell bade him 'seek to know the mind of God in all that chain of providence, . . . and then tell me, whether there be not some glorious and high meaning in all this? . . . I dare be bold to say, it is not that the wicked should be exalted, that God should so appear as indeed he hath done'. Invoking the principle of *salus populi suprema lex*, and seeing that by the present treaty 'the whole fruit of the war [was] like to be frustrated', he asked 'whether this army be not a lawful power, called by God to oppose and fight against the king upon some stated grounds', and whether as such it might not resist a corrupted parliament as well as a king. As for the *Remonstrance*, he wrote that he could perhaps have wished that it had been held back until after the treaty was concluded, but he hoped for God's blessing upon it.[17]

Before he received this letter Hammond was under arrest. He had refused to place the king under closer restraint, as Fairfax had commanded, without direct orders from parliament, so on 21 November Fairfax summoned him to headquarters (now at Windsor) and sent Colonel Ewer to escort him thither. Two radical officers, Lieutenant-Colonel Ralph Cobbett and Captain John Merriman, arrived in the Isle of Wight soon after and put the king under heavy guard. They were acting under the orders of Ireton and his close associates, and at daybreak on 1 December they roused Charles and removed him, breakfastless, to Hurst Castle on the mainland. Before they arrived there a sizeable part of the army was on the march for London. The Commons had made it clear that they were not going to give any time to its *Remonstrance* until they had fully considered the king's final answer to parliament's propositions, and that for Ireton was the last straw. A public declaration by Fairfax and the General Council of Officers[18] heralded the army's advance, claiming

---

[16] Abbott, *Writings and Speeches of Oliver Cromwell*, I, 677–9.     [17] Ibid., pp. 696–9.
[18] Greater part reprinted in Woodhouse, *Puritanism and Liberty*, pp. 465–7.

that it was 'necessitated to, and justified in, an appeal from this parliament, in the present constitution as it stands, unto the extraordinary judgement of God and good people'. It still aimed at a settlement based on a regular succession of parliaments, and its best wish was that the present House of Commons would expel its 'corrupt and apostatized members' and proceed to such a solution forthwith. If, however, that did not happen—and nobody expected it would—the army called upon the 'upright' members to withdraw, and undertook to recognize them as a provisional government until a new and reformed parliament was elected, which was to be arranged as soon as possible. Ireton's was the mastermind behind this declaration and the army's consequent moves, and clearly he envisaged a forcible dissolution and not a purge.

The Commons remained defiant. On 1 December they did not go as far as William Prynne, who urged them to cashier Fairfax and declare the army to be rebels, but they totally rejected its *Remonstrance* by 125 votes to 58 and ordered Fairfax not to bring his forces any closer to London. That was a futile gesture, for by the time he received the Speaker's letter Fairfax had 7,000 men drawn up for review in Hyde Park. Ireton and his fellow-officers did, however, listen to the pleas of members friendly to the army that they should purge the parliament rather than dissolve it. On that same crowded day parliament received the formal report by its recently returned commissioners on the king's final answer to the propositions put to him at Newport. A thin House of Lords voted without a division that it provided 'a ground . . . to proceed upon for the settlement of the peace of the kingdom'. The summer's alliance between Saye, the royal independents and the army leaders was in ruins. The Commons put off their response, being much occupied with even more urgent matters, the military threat above all. On the 2nd, a Saturday, the whole of Westminster from Whitehall to Ludgate was crammed with troops; the City itself was temporarily spared having to quarter them on condition that it immediately handed over £40,000 of its assessment arrears. When the Commons sat again on the Monday they argued their unhappy way through a record sitting of over twenty-four hours, unable to agree on how to respond to either the military presence or the king's answer. Their numbers shrank from over 340 to 214 before they finally voted, on the morning of the 5th, on the same motion as the Lords had passed, and concurred that the king's reply furnished a sufficient ground for proceeding to a peace settlement. Speaker Lenthall is reported to have warned them that they were voting for their own destruction.

He was right. Ireton and other officers met friendly MPs later in the day, and again tried to persuade them to agree to a dissolution rather than sit on as 'a mock parliament'. He failed, and a committee of three officers and three members was entrusted with deciding how a purge was to be conducted, who should be excluded and who arrested. Marked out for exclusion were those who in the previous August had refused to declare the Scottish invaders to be enemies and traitors, and those who had just voted in support of the king's latest answer. By 7 a.m. on 6 December several regiments were posted in the precincts of the parliament-house, and Colonel Pride stood in the lobby to execute the operation so widely known by his name. Lord Grey of Groby was at his side to help him identify who was to be excluded and who arrested. Fairfax seems to have given Ireton free rein and kept out of the business himself, but he must have known what was going on; his lodging was close by in Whitehall. When a committee of six MPs waited on him to explain the previous morning's vote he kept them waiting for three hours, and then would give them no straight answer to their questions about what his army was up to. Later in the day Cromwell arrived at last from the north. He declared then and later that he had not been acquainted with the purge beforehand, 'yet since it was done he was glad of it, and would endeavour to maintain it'.[19] It is scarcely conceivable that Ireton had kept his father-in-law and immediate superior in the dark about his intentions, but Cromwell probably took care not to know too much and timed his arrival so as not to be personally involved in the day's business.

But Pride's Purge was not the work of just one day. The military watch on the entrance to the House continued until the 12th, by which time forty-five members had been imprisoned (though all but twenty were released by the 20th). A rather larger number had been physically prevented from taking their seats. Just how many Pride actually excluded is not known, and estimates vary widely, but many members avoided his attentions by staying away, and many more expressed their outrage at the army's violation by voluntarily absenting themselves, either permanently or for a considerable period. The pre-Purge strength of the House was 471, since 18 seats were vacant and 18 more held by men who had already long been absent. Eventually just over 200 members would take their seats in the Rump, as the purged parliament came to be called, but at the time the army's action alienated most of the parliamentary independents as well as all the presbyterians. It was a thin company that carried on parliament's business during the dangerous weeks in which the king was tried and executed, and several times in December the House was short of a quorum. The number of members who attended at any time between 6 December and 5 February, or who signed the king's death warrant, totalled only just over seventy, and Vane, St John, and Haselrig were not among them. The attendance of the peers rarely reached double figures.[20]

---

[19]  *Memoirs of Edmund Ludlow*, I, 211–12.

[20]  The indispensable work on the Purge and the numbers of members affected by it is Underdown, *Pride's Purge*. Equally essential on the Rump and its membership is Blair Worden, *The Rump Parliament* (Cambridge, 1974), esp. Appendix A, pp. 387–91; on pp. 391–2 he convincingly revises Underdown's estimate of the number of members physically excluded by the army.

The army moved into the City on 8 December, since the corporation had failed to meet Fairfax's deadline for the demanded payment of £40,000. Fairfax had no compunction about helping his unpaid troops to £27,000 which his officers found in Weavers' Hall, banked there by the Committee for Advance of Money. The shrunken Commons spent the 8th as a day of fasting and humiliation, and then adjourned until the 12th, as the Lords had already done. Somehow during these hectic days of early December the committee which Ireton had conceded to the Levellers just before the army's *Remonstrance* was finalized managed to meet and thrash out a new *Agreement of the People*. We do not know how many of its sixteen members took part; though the chief negotiators were Lilburne, Ireton, Colonel Tichborne, and Henry Marten, the only MP who attended. By Lilburne's own account he and Ireton argued keenly over the contents of the document, which was much longer than the original *Agreement*, but it was drafted in time to be presented to the General Council of Officers on 11 December. Lilburne claimed to have understood that its text was final, to be accepted or rejected as it stood, but to the Levellers' disgust the Council of Officers examined it closely, debated it at intervals for five weeks, and modified it in significant respects. William Clarke recorded much of the proceedings, which took place in the Palace of Whitehall, and they are scarcely inferior in interest to the more famous Putney debates. At leat seventy-three officers participated at one time or another, attendances of over fifty being not uncommon. Some historians have supposed that Ireton conceded the drafting of a new *Agreement* only in order to neutralize the Levellers while the army went ahead with prosecuting the king, to which Lilburne for one was thoroughly opposed, but the length and intensity of the Whitehall debates surely prove that this blueprint for a settlement was being taken very seriously, not least by Ireton himself.[21]

First, however, the Council of Officers had to decide what to do about the king. It resolved on 15 December that he should be 'brought speedily to justice', and appointed a committee to consider how this should be done. Cromwell and Ireton were conspicuously missing from its membership, but this may be because they were too busy behind the scenes. The small number of MPs who still attended the House contained many who were more resentful of the Purge than keen to proceed against the king, and it was not until the 28th that they gave a first reading to an ordinance for the establishment of a High Court of Justice to try him. Nine days earlier they had driven out the few remaining seekers after accommodation by requiring members, as a condition of their continuing to sit, to make a formal declaration that they

---

[21] Two articles by Barbara Taft illumine the evolution of the second *Agreement*: 'The Council of Officers' *Agreement of the People*', *Historical Journal* 28 (1985), 169–85, and 'Voting lists of the Council of Officers, December 1648', *Bulletin of the Institute of Historical Research* LII (1978), 138–54.

dissented from the vote on 5 December which had accepted the king's answer as grounds for proceeding to a settlement.

Predictably, Pride's Purge was denounced by most of the Presbyterian clergy in London and acclaimed by most of the Independents—specially rapturously by the army's champion Hugh Peter. Before the end of the year parliament received a spate of petitions and declarations, by one account over a hundred, from radical puritans and commonwealthsmen in various counties and towns, praising the army, urging the members to complete the work of reformation, and in many cases calling for stern justice upon the king. They represented the views of a minority, but an articulate and organized minority. The majority who looked upon the proceedings against the king with horror were powerless to resist them, for they had spent what force they could command in the spring and summer. A presbyterian City corporation might just have attempted resistance, despite the military occupation, but no such body now existed. Just before the annual elections to the Common Council on 21 December, the Rump rushed through legislation disqualifying all who had sided with the king in the wars or signed the engagement of the previous June which had called for a personal treaty with him. As a result only a third of the old common-councilmen were re-elected, and the corporation's support for the revolution in progress was assured.

Since the motive force behind that revolution lay so much in the army, it is a strange thing that the attitude of both its senior commanders was equivocal. Fairfax seems to have been genuinely convinced that the treaty of Newport was a potential disaster and must be stopped, but he was deeply unhappy about the consequential moves to put the king on trial. Cromwell's standpoint during December is hard to penetrate, and historians continue to disagree about it. He had no qualms about terminating the Newport treaty and needed no convincing now that Charles was unfit to govern, but that did not necessarily justify pursuing him to his death or abolishing monarchy in Britain. If a way could have been found of sparing his life—if Charles could have been persuaded to abdicate in favour of his youngest son the Duke of Gloucester—Cromwell would probably have welcomed it. He may have found parts of the new *Agreement of the People* too radical for him, and he held three meetings with the old middle group men Bulstrode Whitelocke and Sir Thomas Widdrington, with Lenthall present at the third, to discuss proposals for a more conservative settlement. He was not at one with his son-in-law Ireton, at least until late in December. He was half drawn to a scheme advanced by the peers Denbigh, Pembroke, Salisbury, and North whereby Charles might even have remained king, with drastically reduced powers, and through Denbigh a final approach was made to him. But Charles was utterly unwilling to consider such terms, and rather than compromise his crown any further he was now resigned to what he saw as martyrdom. By 26 December the quest for a bloodless solution was over, and Cromwell was fully convinced that the king must pay the penalty for making war upon his people. He said in the House, probably during the debate on the first reading of the ordinance for a High Court of Justice, that if any *man* had pursued a design to put the king on trial and depose him he would be the greatest traitor in the world, but that since providence and necessity had cast it upon them he would pray God to bless their counsels, though he could as yet offer them no counsel himself.[22]

The Commons passed the ordinance for a High Court of Justice on 1 January, but next day the Lords unanimously threw it out and adjourned for a week. In an attempt to cover the legal and constitutional nakedness of their revolutionary tribunal, the Commons passed a vote on the 4th that was to provide the ideological basis for the Commonwealth to come. They resolved:

That the people are, under God, the original of all just power; that the Commons of England, in parliament assembled, being chosen by and representing the people, have the supreme power in this nation; that whatsoever is enacted or declared for law by the Commons . . . hath the force of law, and all the people of this nation are concluded thereby, although the consent and concurrence of king or House of Peers be not had thereunto.[23]

The ordinance, as first drafted, intended the court to consist of 150 commissioners, presided over by the Chief Justices of King's Bench and Common Pleas (St John now held the latter post) and the Chief Baron of Exchequer. But none of these three, nor any judge in the central courts, was willing to act, so they chose the best man they could find. He was John Bradshaw, the Chief Justice of Chester, a convinced republican and a friend of John Milton. Such was the unwillingness to serve that they had to reduce the number of commissioners to 135, but of these 55, including most of the lawyers named and all 6 of the peers, never attended the trial. Vane, Skippon, and Brereton were among those appointed who never appeared. Fairfax came to the initial meeting of the court for preliminary business on 8 January, when attendance was so poor that it adjourned until the 10th, but he never came again. The 26-year-old Colonel Algernon Sidney, later famous as a republican theorist and a Whig martyr, withdrew after the preliminary meetings, declaring that the king could not be tried by any court and that no one could be tried by this one. But at least one man of law had no doubts about its legality: John Cook, who was appointed solicitor to the Commonwealth on 10 January so that he could lead the prosecution. He was a thorough-paced republican and a puritan fanatic.

On the 20th General Council of Officers presented its amended *Agreement*

---

[22] Abbott, *Writings and Speeches of Oliver Cromwell*, I, 719. For differing opinions as to when Cromwell became fully convinced of the necessity of trying the king, see Underdown, *Pride's Purge*, ch. 6, and Gentles, *New Model Army*, pp. 284–5, 297 ff. I incline here towards Underdown, but both readings are possible.

[23] *Commons' Journals*, VI, 110–11, quoted in Gardiner, *Great Civil War*, III, 561.

*of the People*, in a fair parchment copy, to the Commons, but the eyes of the country were on the adjacent Westminster Hall, where the king's trial opened that day. The great building had been filled with tiered seats, so as to make as public a spectacle as possible of the hoped-for demonstration of his war-guilt. He had been at Windsor since 23 December, but he was brought on 19 January to St James's, where he spent the last eleven nights of his life. He appeared before the court dressed all in black, and he kept a high-crowned hat on his head throughout in token that he did not accept its authority. His hair was streaked with grey now, and his face betrayed the long-drawn strain he had been under, but when he spoke his voice was firm and quite free of its old stammer. His attempted objections could not prevent Cook from reading out the lengthy charge which he and others had (with some difficulty) prepared. Its main burden was that Charles Stuart, having been entrusted with a limited power to govern by the laws of the land, for the good of the people and the preservation of their rights, had pursued a wicked design to arrogate to himself an unlimited and tyrannical power, in order to rule as he pleased. To that end he had 'traitorously and maliciously levied war against the present parliament, and the people therein represented', and he had compounded his guilt by deliberately causing the war to be renewed during the past year.[24] Nothing was said, however, of the Engagement or the Scottish invasion; he was on trial solely as King of England, though the Scottish parliament had just been pressing that proceedings should be suspended until their country had been heard in the matter. But his traffic with Irish rebels and his encouragement of an Irish invasion of England formed part of the charge.

At the end of the reading he laughed in the face of his judges. Time and again, on this and subsequent days, he challenged Bradshaw to say by what authority the court sat, and when told that it was by the authority of the Commons of England he poured justified scorn on the idea that the Lower House of parliament was a court of judicature or that a small fraction of it, first elected more than eight years ago, had any claim to speak for the commons of England in the broader sense. If he had recognized the court's jurisdiction and been prepared to abdicate he could still have saved his life, but by refusing to plead guilty or not guilty he frustrated one purpose of his accusers, since until he did so the thirty-three witnesses who had been assembled to testify to his responsibility for the two wars could not be publicly heard. The further price he paid for refusing to plead was that he was not allowed to address the court himself; yet his regal dignity and self-possession on all three of his appearances before it won him many sympathizers. Finally the witnesses were heard by a committee on the 24th, and their depositions were read out in a public session in the Painted Chamber next day. Only forty-six commissioners

---

[24] Text in Gardiner (ed.), *Constitutional Documents*, pp. 371–4.

attended it, but they resolved that they could now proceed to a death sentence. In face of his brave defiance it was a foregone conclusion, and Charles was brought before the court to hear it on the 27th. He pleaded eloquently to be heard before the full body of the Lords and Commons, and in doing so he had the better of yet another exchange with Bradshaw, but all he won was a brief adjournment. In the course of it Cromwell used all his powers of angry rhetoric to bring round the waverers among the commissioners. The sentence was then read in open court, and all the sixty-seven commissioners present rose to signify their assent to Bradshaw's declaration that it was the judgment of the whole court. They must all be counted among the regicides, even though the king's death warrant was signed by only fifty-nine; indeed the regicides numbered sixty-nine, since two commissioners signed the warrant who were not present when the sentence was read.[25]

We are in the presence of tragedy in the final scene that was enacted three days later on a black-draped platform outside the upper windows of the Banqueting House of the Palace of Whitehall. Charles had passed up chance after chance of saving his life because he thought that by doing so he would compromise the sacred prerogatives of his kingly office. Those who had brought him to the scaffold were driven by a no less sincere conviction that they were doing justice upon a man against whom God had witnessed for shedding the blood of thousands of his subjects in an evil cause. His final ordeal was cruelly prolonged, largely because the Rump belatedly realized on that very morning that it was the custom, upon the death of a king, immediately to proclaim his successor, so they had to rush through an act to make such a proclamation illegal. The courage and dignity with which Charles bore his last hours surpassed even what he had shown during his trial, and probably did more for the future of the monarchy than all his acts of war. Not many of the thousands present on that wintry day can have heard his last words on the scaffold, but in them he recalled Strafford's fate, and accepted his own 'unjust sentence' as God's punishment for letting that earlier one take effect. He reaffirmed his central political beliefs, and rejected the charge that he was the enemy of the people; indeed he claimed to be 'the martyr of the people':

Truly I desire their liberty and freedom as much as anybody whomsoever; but I must tell you their liberty and freedom consists in having of government, those laws by which their life and their goods may be most their own. It is not for having a share in government, sir, that is nothing pertaining to them. A subject and a sovereign are clear different things.[26]

So most of his subjects still believed, and the groan that went up from the huge crowd as the axe severed his head has echoed down our history.

[25] A. W. McIntosh, 'The numbers of the English regicides', *History* 67 (1982), 195–216.
[26] Quoted in C. V. Wedgwood, *The Trial of Charles I* (1964), p. 191.

# ‡ FOURTEEN ‡

# Quest for a Settlement

NEITHER the people of England, nor those who watched aghast from Scotland, Ireland, and continental Europe, could tell what the outcome would be of that horrifying act at Whitehall on 30 January 1649. It seemed there might be no end to its revolutionary consequences. An anointed king had been brought to trial and execution by a fragment of one house of parliament, first elected more than eight years earlier, and now claiming to act by the supreme authority of the sovereign people's representatives. The Rump followed up the regicide with acts abolishing the office of king and the House of Lords. It called them acts, not ordinances, because they required no other assent now but that of the Commons. But behind the Rump stood the army, to whose force it owed its power, and the army might not sustain it for long, since its first intention had been to dissolve the parliament rather than purge it. The Rumpers themselves promised, in their act of 17 March that abolished the monarchy, 'that they will put a period to the sitting of the present parliament, and dissolve the same so soon as may possibly stand with the safety of the people that hath betrusted them'.[1] The army had seemingly committed itself to supporting a programme of radical reform, embodied in the revised Agreement of the People that it had presented to the Rump—a programme that would have transformed the constitution of parliament itself, regulated the frequency and duration of its sitting, brought large alterations to the law of the land, and changed the whole relationship between the church (or churches) and the state. The army and its supporters hoped and expected that this caretaker regime, as they saw it, would soon make way for a reformed and reforming parliament, elected on a far broader franchise than ever in the past. And what might the consequences of that be? The Levellers had reached the peak of their influence, through the share they had taken in drafting the new Agreement. From the early months of 1649 onward there was a burgeoning of various groups even more radical than the Levellers: the Fifth Monarchists, who felt a divine call to set up a regime ruled exclusively by their fellow 'saints' in preparation for Christ's prophesied kingdom on earth; the Diggers,

---

[1] Gardiner (ed.), *Constitutional Documents*, p. 380.

who called themselves True Levellers, and preached and practised the community of property; and people known as Ranters who believed that those who had discovered the godhead within them were liberated from all conventional morality. Of these groups only the Fifth Monarchists had any considerable following in the army, but there was an understandable fear in conservative hearts that with dissolution threatening the ancient constitution, the established church, and the known laws of the land, a dark and revolutionary future lay ahead.

Who could have foreseen that the Rump would go on wielding sovereign authority over England and Wales for four and a quarter years after the king's execution—longer than the whole duration of the first Civil War, and almost as long as Cromwell's whole rule as Lord Protector? The Rump, moreover, proved to be a far from revolutionary body, and its temper became more conservative with time. The majority of its members were deeply unsympathetic towards the aspirations of Levellers, Diggers, Fifth Monarchists, Ranters, and extremist sects of all kinds. Its concessions to religious liberty were to be limited and grudging, its record in social reform miserably meagre, and the professional interests of its influential lawyer-members made it deeply suspicious of any changes in the substance and operation of the law, where moderate reform was overdue. In the folk memory, the period in which the Commonwealth was ruled by the Rump is the least remembered and least known phase of the Great Rebellion, and the mistaken notion that Cromwell was the great shaper of national policy from the Civil Wars onward dies hard. He was of course immensely influential, but he was away on his campaigns in Ireland and Scotland for long periods, and when his military commitments did leave him free to attend the House he by no means always got his way in it.

The politics of the Rump defy simple analysis, because its lines of division were seldom clear-cut, and they changed considerably with time. The first distinction to be made is between the small core of members who led the House and bore the burden of responsibility during the critical, dangerous period between Pride's Purge and the execution of the king, and the much larger number who resumed their seats later. This committed nucleus totalled just over seventy, though the daily attendance was much smaller. The most prominent of them, apart from Cromwell, who had much military business to see to, were Thomas Scot, a Buckinghamshire attorney elected late in 1645, Henry Marten, and Thomas Chaloner, another 'recruiter'. All three were republicans and regicides. Two future leaders of the Rump were conspicuously absent, Haselrig because he was carrying out important military duties as governor of Newcastle, and Vane because he was opposed to putting the king on trial, as he had been to Pride's Purge. Forty-three MPs, less than one in ten of the unpurged House, sat in judgement on the king and subscribed his death warrant, though three of these seem to have been bullied into signing, for they withdrew from parliament soon afterwards. The forty unrepentant regicides can be regarded as committed revolutionaries, though not necessarily as allies of the army, for some of these hard-core Rumpers were as much concerned to assert parliament's rights against a military takeover as to condemn monarchical tyranny. Rather more members complied with the requirement, imposed from 20 December onward, that as a condition of sitting they must record their dissent from the unpurged House's vote to accept the king's answers to the Newport propositions as a basis for a settlement; thirty did so at once, and about twice as many more before the end of January. Not all of these, however, approved of the proceedings against the king. Most of them were more strongly committed to the new regime than the large number who resumed their seats even later, but some safeguarded their right to sit mainly out of a resolve to uphold parliament's authority against any threat of usurpation by the army.

By the end of January the House still had an active membership of only seventy or so and a much smaller average attendance. This worried it. So far it had excluded members who had voted on 5 December to keep the Newport treaty going, but on 1 February it resolved that during that month it would admit without further scrutiny any who would now register their dissent from that vote. Thirty at least took advantage at once, and at least forty more in the next three weeks. Most of these 'February dissenters' were cautious souls who had not cared to be politically involved while they might have been thought complicit in the act of regicide, but they were not all conservatives. They included those committed republicans Haslerig and Vane, who with Cromwell (or rather, usually, against him) were to be perhaps the most influential of all the actors on the political stage in the next four years. But most of them were opposed to radical change in religion, the law, and the social basis of political power, and most were strongly concerned to thwart any threat to parliamentary power by the army. Yet the Rump's historian has argued convincingly that the man most responsible for broadening its power-base and persuading so many members to return was Oliver Cromwell.[2] For all his record as a breaker of parliaments, he was a lifelong believer in parliamentary authority, and he could see no future for the Commonwealth under a narrow oligarchy upheld only by the sword.

Only about fifty more members were readmitted after February, and they were subjected to rather closer scrutiny. They tended to reinforce the Rump's unrevolutionary temper, though most of the latecomers, including the February intake, proved more dilatory in attendance than the original nucleus. Between the House's nominal membership and the actual presence in it there

---

[2] Worden, *Rump Parliament*, pp. 67–9. I am indebted to Worden's masterly study throughout this chapter.

was a huge gulf. Two hundred and eleven members took their seats at some time in the course of its existence, including nine added through by-elections after the Purge, but the average number present at divisions remained steadily in the fifties over the years, falling to forty-nine in 1653; the highest total ever recorded was seventy-one, including the four tellers. Only about thirty Rumpers treated their membership as a full-time occupation, though thirty or forty more sat reasonably often. These figures, however, do not convey a full picture of the active members' involvement, since the House delegated an increasing amount of business to committees, in whose demanding work they widely shared.

Much the most important delegation was that of general executive authority to a Council of State. The decision to establish it was taken on 7 February, immediately after the Rump had voted to abolish the monarchy, and the purpose was to fill the great gap in government left thereby. A powerful committee was set up to define the council's powers and propose the names of its initial members. The latter were to number forty-one, of whom thirty-one were MPs; the others included five peers, the three chief judges, an alderman to represent the City, and John Bradshaw, who had added to his stature by presiding over the king's trial with what dignity that difficult role permitted him. But only three of the peers, Denbigh, Pembroke, and Salisbury, proved willing to serve, and among the committee's nominees the House rejected Ireton and Harrison. This was a heavy slight to the army, whose only members on the council for the next two years were Fairfax, Cromwell, and Skippon. Since Fairfax was seldom seen and would eventually resign his command, and since Cromwell was to be absent most of the time in Ireland and Scotland, the army (to whom the Rump owed its being) was most unwisely underrepresented. That ill-considered vote can indeed be seen as an initial move in the quarrel that would one day lead to the Rump's expulsion.

The council was empowered to raise forces, conduct relations with foreign powers and their ambassadors, and imprison anyone who disobeyed its commands, but it was firmly subjected to whatever orders parliament gave it, and it was appointed for one year only. There was never a question of who was master, and the Rump elected a new council in every year of its existence. Barely half the original one was committed to the regime to the extent of having signed the king's death warrant or registered their dissents before February, and the political complexion of its successors did not change very much. Councillors were required, however, to formally engage themselves to pursue whatever instructions they received from parliament, and specifically to uphold whatever parliament settled with regard to 'the government of the nation for the future in way of a republic, without king or House of Lords'.[3]

---

[3] Gardiner, *Constitutional Documents*, p. 384; cf. pp. 381–3 for the act appointing a Council of State.

The price paid for selecting so many 'unrevolutionary' councillors was that many of them were little more inclined to give their time to the Commonwealth's business than the counterparts in the House itself. The council's attendance averaged barely fifteen in its first three months, and later in the year it sometimes had difficulty in assembling a quorum of nine. The average attendance in the four subsequent councils never rose to half their nominal strength.

The manner in which the composition of the Rump and its Council of State evolved goes a long way to explain why the early fears of radical change in political, legal, and social institutions—far beyond the abolition of the monarchy and the Lords—proved to be unfounded. Conservative spirits had been equally apprehensive about the influence of the army, and specifically about its leaders' collaboration with Lilburne and other Levellers in framing a new Agreement of the People as a basis for constitutional settlement. This Agreement was to sink into limbo, but this was not a foregone conclusion, and if its promoters had handled it more adroitly it might conceivably have given the Commonwealth quite a different political cast from the one it actually assumed. It will be remembered that the drafting committee of sixteen, which included Ireton, Lilburne, Marten, and Tichborne, completed its work on 10 December, but that to the outrage of the Leveller leaders the General Council of Officers proceeded to scrutinize and modify it extensively in the so-called Whitehall debates before presenting it to parliament on 10 January. Lilburne and his chief associates denounced their tampering with it on 28 December, but surely they were naive to expect the officers to adopt it without question or discussion, especially since the title-page of the printed edition, which was on sale before mid-December, described it as 'tendered *to the consideration of* the General Council of the Army'.[4] They too readily assumed, as many historians have done since, that Ireton was merely keeping them in play so that the army leaders could pursue their own quest for power without being troubled by Leveller unrest in the ranks. But it has been well asked why, if this was so, the Council of Officers debated the Agreement in such detail, and with such obvious seriousness.[5] Since it was presented to the Rump as the army's considered and agreed recommendations for the constitution of the Commonwealth, it deserves consideration as one of the most interesting might-have-beens of the Interregnum.

It was of course a compromise document from the start, since the Levellers were only one party to its composition. Nevertheless it began by repeating

---

[4] Wolfe, *Leveller Manifestoes*, p. 293; emphasis added. Most of the December text is also printed in Woodhouse, *Puritanism and Liberty*, pp. 356–67, with the alterations made by the Council of Officers in footnotes. The text in Gardiner (ed.), *Constitutional Documents*, pp. 359–71, is that presented to the Rump by the army.

[5] See above, pp. 423–4, 429, and the articles by Barbara Taft cited there. I have benefited much from discussing the Agreement with Dr Taft.

almost verbatim the preamble to the original Agreement of 1647, which had been debated at Putney. That had been a manifesto, dealing mainly with general principles; this was a more detailed prescription for the actual conduct of government, and was accordingly six times as long. Perhaps the most interesting questions are whether it was a practicable prescription, and whether the officers' modifications seriously compromised the proposals of the drafting committee, as the Levellers alleged. Both the committee's and the officers' versions agreed that the present parliament should be dissolved on or before 30 April next, and that parliaments should thereafter be elected by all male householders of twenty-one and over, provided they paid poor relief and were not servants or wage-earners dependent on any particular person. Parliamentary seats were to be radically redistributed, eliminating rotten boroughs and greatly enlarging the proportion of county constituencies. The committee proposed a total of 300 members, which would have been a severe drop from the existing 507; the officers raised it to 400, which like the reapportionment of constituencies would be followed both in the Rump's own bill governing future elections and in the Instrument of Government which defined the constitution of the Protectorate. By an obvious oversight the committee omitted to specify the frequency of elections or the maximum duration of parliaments. The officers followed both the Heads of the Proposals and the 1647 Agreement in appointing biennial parliaments, to sit no longer than six months (very much as in the first Agreement; the Proposals set a limit of 240 days). The officers cut out a requirement that all electors should subscribe the Agreement before being admitted to vote, which was a liberal amendment, since subscription would have been a stumbling-block to many, and insistence upon it would have made the Commonwealth a distant ancestor of the one-party state. Nevertheless the Agreement was to be publicly read at all elections, and the members elected were to pledge themselves to act according to its terms.

In the eighteen-month intervals between parliaments government was to be entrusted to a council of state, elected by the outgoing House and resigning when the next one met. It says something for the altruism of the officers that they accepted, without recorded protest, the disqualification of military (though not naval) officers from standing for parliament, along with treasurers and receivers of public money. Lawyers, if elected, were to be debarred from practising during their membership. More surprisingly—and to modern eyes this and the short duration of parliaments probably seem the biggest impediments to the workability of the whole scheme—serving councillors were also disqualified from being elected (or re-elected) to parliament. This looks like a recipe for friction between legislature and executive, and a denial of the value of political experience. But the whole document breathes a distrust of long-serving politicians, and a suspicion that new parliament-man could be old courtier writ large: in the business for what he could get out of it. On the constructive side it preserved one of the most forward-looking concepts in the original Agreement, the reservation of certain indefeasible natural rights from encroachment by even the people's representatives. These included liberty of conscience in religion, total equality before the law, the independence of the judiciary, and freedom from conscription (though the officers entered a sensible proviso to secure the continuance of county militias for purely local defence). Further, to reassure any who believed the propagandists who accused the Levellers of undermining property itself, no parliament was to abrogate 'any of the foundations of common right, liberty and safety contained in this Agreement, nor level men's estates, destroy property, or make all things common'. This was not a repudiation of the Diggers, whose experiment in communism still lay in the future, but a rebuttal of the unfair charge of aiming to undermine property that had haunted the Levellers since they first emerged.

The longest recorded debates at Whitehall were over religion, and the passionate intensity with which many officers, Ireton included, opposed the position taken by the sectaries and radical Independents is surely evidence that they thought the Agreement might really become the basis of England's government. The Agreement, as drafted by the committee, denied parliament any power to impose in matters of faith or worship through laws, oaths, or covenants, or to restrain people from worshipping and professing their faith according to their consciences; but it granted the people's representatives discretion to provide for 'the instruction or directing of the nation in a public way, for matters of faith, worship or discipline (so it be not compulsive, or express popery)'. That might seem moderate enough, and there was no disagreement over permitting a wide freedom of worship and belief. But the article concerning religion that emerged from the Whitehall debates, completely rewritten, envisaged that parliament would underwrite a public (though not compulsory) profession of the Christian faith, and that this should be taught by ministers maintained 'out of a public treasury', though not by tithes. The difference between the two schemes in actual operation might not have been large, but the officers wanted to maintain a more visible national church, more positively linked to the state, and with a publicly maintained parochial ministry. There can be no doubt that their version would have had wider public support, and indeed all their amendments to the Agreement were designed not to emasculate it but to make it more workable and acceptable.

What incensed the Levellers, however, was not just the officers' leisurely emendation of a text that they thought had been finalized, but the manner in which the army put the Agreement before parliament. It was presented on the very day the king's trial began, and Veronica Wedgwood has speculated that 'the lethal timing . . . could have been a final twist of Ireton's cold ingenuity'.[6] But that seems an unduly harsh reading of Ireton's character, and she grants that the coincidence may have been an accident. That is likelier, for the completed text had only received the officers' final approval earlier that week, on 15 January. A Machiavellian Ireton, supposing him to want to scupper the Agreement, might have postponed its presentation until after the king's head had fallen, and when the rapid influx of February dissenters was making the Rump's temper more anti-radical day by day. But it was not the timing that the Levellers resented so much as the tone in which the army's spokesmen tendered the Agreement to parliament. Instead of pressing it as a firmly agreed prescription for a settlement, to be endorsed intact by the mass subscriptions of the people, they humbly asked the parliament to take it into consideration and to commend as much of it as they thought fit to the public, with a request to the well-affected to signify their acceptance of it with their signatures. One can understand the Levellers' sense of betrayal, but Fairfax was still Lord General, and there was never a chance that he (or Cromwell) would present it in the manner they desired while the outcome of the king's trial was yet unknown. Still less likely was it that the army commanders would (as they had hoped) circulate it for mass signatures *before* putting it to parliament. It is no wonder, in the circumstances, that the Commons' only answer was that they would take it into consideration as soon as 'the necessity of the present weighty and urgent affairs would permit'.[7]

It may be argued that if Fairfax, Cromwell, and Ireton were lukewarm about the Agreement it was bound to be a lost cause. But the Levellers still had a considerable following among the junior officers and the politically conscious rank and file, especially in the cavalry, and Ireton tacitly acknowledged their influence when he entered into negotiation with them. If they, Lilburne especially, had not taken such umbrage at the officers' scrutiny of the Agreement, if they had joined in the debates at Whitehall, defended their position there, and had been prepared to accept a few compromises, they would have remained a force to be reckoned with. In face of their angry non-cooperation, the surprising thing is not that the officers made some modifications in the Agreement but that they accepted all its essentials (with the partial exception of the article on religion). If the Levellers had gone on behaving as allies, Ireton could not easily have abandoned a set of proposals which he had helped to draft, and to which by mid-January the General Council of Officers stood publicly committed. Unhappily it was the Levellers themselves who gave the army's commanders cause to wash their hands of the Agreement. They virtually gave up on it themselves, before the Council of Officers were half way through their debates on it. In an angry pamphlet

---

[6] Wedgwood, *Trial of Charles I*, p. 120.
[7] Gardiner, *Great Civil War* (1891), pp. 567–8.

published on 28 December, Lilburne and fifteen fellow-Levellers denounced them for contesting its contents, 'and that in things so essential unto our freedom, as without which we account the Agreement of no value!'[8] On top of this extravagant accusation, they demanded that strict rules should be fixed for the composition and procedure of the General Council of Officers, for instance that it should include at least the greater part of the officers within reach of headquarters, that its decisions should be subject to no veto or check by any senior officer, that there should be an agreed limit to how many times any member might speak to a question (clearly a hit at Ireton), that there should be no disbandments without its consent, and that it should in future regulate the enlistment of soldiers in the horse and foot. They further called for a wholesale revision of the present articles of martial law. The obvious intent was to take the formulation and control of army policy out of the senior commanders' hands, and it is no wonder that the latter, faced with such demands, presented the Agreement to parliament with something less than enthusiasm. If the army–Leveller *entente* that produced it had still held, they might have pressed it much more strongly, and the Rump might have found it less easy to shelve if the Leveller tail had not so obviously been trying to wag the army dog.

Before the Levellers fired their next salvo, Prince Rupert, now formally in command of the royal fleet, appeared off the Irish coast with ten warships and took station at Kinsale. Shortly after, on 5 February, the Scots proclaimed Charles II King of Great Britain. On the 22nd the new king appointed Montrose as his Lieutenant-Governor of Scotland and Captain-General of all the forces that could be assembled there. The only question was which springboard he would choose for his attempt to recover his English throne. The Rump could fairly claim that this was not the time for elections to a new parliament or debates on the long-term constitutional future. Still less was it a time for sowing strife between parliament and army. Yet on 26 February Lilburne and his associates presented the House with a bitter remonstrance under the guise of a petition, which they published under the title of *England's New Chains Discovered.*[9] These chains had been forged, they alleged, through an unholy alliance between the army grandees and the oligarchs at Westminster, who had joined in muzzling the press, discouraging petitioners, and seeking draconian powers to suppress the Levellers' current attempt to resuscitate the agitator organization in the army. The tract made a special grievance of the Council of State, which had existed for less than a fortnight when it was presented, and its main demand was that the Rump should dissolve it and transfer its functions to strictly accountable committees of short

---

[8] John Lilburne (and fifteen others named), *A Plea for Common-Right and Freedom* (1648); excerpts in Woodhouse, *Puritanism and Liberty*, pp. 472–4.

[9] Substantial excerpts in Aylmer, *Levellers in the English Revolution*, pp. 142–8.

duration. This of course was wildly unrealistic, and its further suggestion of a change in the highest commands in the army was equally irresponsible in face of the Commonwealth's urgent need to defend itself. Going back on the Agreement's demand for an early terminal date to the present parliament, this 'petition' urged the Rump to refuse to dissolve itself until a new representative of the people had been elected and could take its place the next day.

The Levellers stepped up their campaign against the generals and the Council of State during March. They were behind a petitioning movement among the rank and file to revive the full General Council of the Army of 1647, and to give its soldier-agitators an equal right with officers in determining army policy. When five troopers were cashiered for promoting a petition which supported *England's New Chains* and asserted the right of soldiers to address parliament directly, regardless of any possible objections by their officers, their Leveller friends drove them away in coaches and lavishly feasted them. On 21 March an angry pamphlet was published over their names, though it was probably written by Richard Overton, entitled *The Hunting of the Foxes from Newmarket and Triploe Heaths to Whitehall, By Five Small Beagles (Late of the Army).*[10] Its sub-title was 'The grandee-deceivers unmasked (that you may know them)', and much of it was a venomous attack on Cromwell and Ireton, charging them with ruthless self-advancement, tyranny, hypocrisy, and a systematic betrayal of the soldiers' interests. The clear implication was that the men were no longer bound to obey such commanders. Three days later Lilburne assailed the grandees in general and Cromwell in particular even more intemperately in *The Second Part of England's New Chains Discovered.* He appealed now to a new parliament, since the Rump had become a mere channel through which the decrees of a military junto were given effect. The accusation was absurd as well as offensive, and the House responded predictably. After three hours' debate it voted that the tract was 'false, scandalous, and . . . highly seditious, and tends to division and mutiny in the army, and the raising of a new war'. It ordered that its authors should be prosecuted as traitors, and as a consequence Lilburne, Overton, Thomas Prince, and (less justly) Walwyn were imprisoned in the Tower, where they were held until 8 November. After being interrogated by the Council of State, Lilburne claimed to have heard Cromwell thump the table and say 'I tell you, sir, you have no other way to deal with these men but to break them, or they will break you'.[11] We have only Lilburne's word for what he overheard from an adjoining room, but it has the ring of truth, and what Cromwell said was not unjustified.

---

[10] Full text in Wolfe, *Leveller Manifestoes*, pp. 358–83.

[11] Gardiner, *Great Civil War*, III, 37–40, quoting J. Lilburne *et al.*, *The Picture of the Council of State.*

Happily not all the Levellers were as confrontational as Lilburne and his main associates. Walwyn, who had not attended their meetings for months and seems to have had no part in inciting the army to disobedience, wrote a sober and moving vindication in *A Manifestation*, to which all four prisoners in the Tower put their names on 14 April. He pleaded that the Commonwealth should not let slip 'an opportunity which these 600 years has been desired, but could never be attained, of making this a truly happy and wholly free nation'. He and his fellows did not seek power for themselves, or look to force to attain their objectives, 'but solely upon that inbred and persuasive power that is in all good and just things, to make their own way in the hearts of men, and so to procure their own establishment'.[12] If only that had been true of all the Leveller leadership! The others were weakening their own movement, not only by engaging in sedition and alienating most of the army, including now such old supporters as Major Francis White and Colonel (formerly Captain) John Reynolds, but by antagonizing the gathered churches. Radical Independents and sectaries understandably saw a better future for themselves under the new Commonwealth, for all its imperfections, than under the unpurged Presbyterian-dominated Long Parliament. On 2 April William Kiffin headed a deputation of Baptist ministers which presented a petition to the Rump, disso-ciating themselves from *The Second Part of England's New Chains* and dis-avowing any intent to 'intermeddle with the ordering or altering civil government'. The Leveller organization had been so strongly linked to that of the General Baptists that the latter's withdrawal of support seriously weak-ened the movement. More unpleasantly, a group of separatist pastors pub-lished a pamphlet later in the month under the title of *Walwyn's Wiles*, which quite unjustly accused him of immorality, irreligion, and seeking to make all things common. It was mainly—perhaps wholly—written by a lay preacher of John Goodwin's church called John Price, but his co-signatories included Kiffin and Edmund Rosier, the pastor of the congregation to which Lilburne had belonged, and perhaps still did. Walwyn could and did answer their base-less slanders, but if he tried to check his fellow-Levellers' sowing of disaffec-tion in the army he did not succeed. The climax of their second attempt to wrest control over the soldiery from their officers—the first had been in the autumn of 1647—was imminent, and it was to prove fatal to the future of the movement. For clarity's sake its brief story will be told here before returning to the Rump's attempt to tackle the problems of settlement and defence.

Women played a conspicuous part in the Levellers' spring campaign. Ten thousand of them are said to have signed a petition for the release of the prisoners in the Tower, and for three days on and off, from 23 to 25 April,

---

[12] *A Manifestation* is printed in McMichael and Taft (eds.), *Writings of William Walwyn* (passages quoted at pp. 336, 341) and in Wolfe, *Leveller Manifestoes*, pp. 387–96.

several hundred demonstrated clamorously at the doors of the parliament-house. While they were doing so, there was a minor mutiny in Colonel Whalley's London-based regiment of horse, arising from a combination of Leveller agitation, lack of pay, and the soldiers' reluctance to serve in the forthcoming Irish expeditionary force. Fifteen troopers who publicly defied Whalley's personal orders to march were court-martialled, and six were sentenced to death. They made a humble submission, and Cromwell was for pardoning them, but Fairfax insisted that an example must be made of the one judged most culpable. Accordingly, Trooper Robert Lockyer was shot next day in St Paul's Churchyard. Fairfax, needless to say, was not deterred by the appearance in print of a menacing letter from Lilburne and Overton, accusing him and his court of treason and murder, and threatening a popular uprising if the sentence was carried out. Lockyer died bravely and defiantly, and the Levellers made of his funeral an even more spectacular demonstration than they had of Rainborough's. About 4,000 followed his coffin, including large numbers of women, and many of the mourners wore green ribbons, green having been Rainborough's colour. It was henceforth that of the Leveller movement. Worryingly for the army's commanders and for the government, hundreds of soldiers joined in the funeral procession.[13]

Leveller agents were active now not only in the regiments near London but in many far afield, and their aim was to get agitators elected in every one of them. They were given a fillip when the units destined for Ireland were chosen on 20 April, and in playing on the men's understandable reluctance to serve there they manifested a hitherto unsuspected sympathy with the misfortunes of the Irish people. Discontent verging on open disobedience was appearing by the end of April in the cavalry regiments under orders for Ireland (Scrope's, Ireton's, and Horton's), and also in Harrison's, which had been prominent in the Ware mutiny. By 1 May the Levellers felt ready to raise a far larger mutiny, indeed a general one, and that day the four prisoners in the Tower published a new Agreement of the People to serve as a manifesto for it. It is interesting as revealing (as they put it) 'the ultimate end and full scope of all our desires and intentions concerning the government of this nation', free now from any pressure to make compromises.[14] It opted for annual parliaments, sitting for at least four months, and it expressly forbade them to erect a Council of State. Servants and recipients of alms were excluded from the franchise—so much for 'the poorest he that is in England'. Not only

---

[13] On the Lockyer affair see Gentles, *New Model Army*, pp. 326–9; Woolrych, *Soldiers and Statesmen*, pp. 289, 342–3. It was claimed that Lockyer had championed the Agreement of the People on Corkbush Field in 1647, but it is most unlikely that he was there. His regiment (Whalley's) was not, and it was enthusiastically loyal to Fairfax at the rendezvous which it did attend. I am indebted to Phil Baker, who has made a close study of the agitators, for confirming my impression that Lockyer never figures in the strictly contemporary accounts of the Ware mutiny.
[14] Full text in Wolfe, *Leveller Manifestoes*, pp. 400–10.

excise but the customs were to be abolished; the sole tax was to consist of a pound rate on real or personal estate. As for defence, parliament was to appoint the commander-in-chief and other general officers, but the land forces were to consist solely of regiments and companies allocated to particular counties and towns. The same male electorate that chose MPs was to elect all civil magistrates and officials in counties, hundreds, and towns, all military officers below general rank, and all parish clergy, the latter on a contractual basis. By the criteria of practicability and acceptability, this Agreement was inferior in almost every way to the second one, whether in its original version or as modified by the officers. Curiously, it made no mention of monarchy. Can this omission have been intended to leave the way open for the dubious traffic with the exiled royal court in which some leading Levellers were to engage in the coming years?

It is impossible to put an exact date on the start of the mutiny, but its active phase and its suppression occupy the first half of May. It was more serious than the scale of the actual confrontations between mutineers and loyal forces might suggest, because some regiments which would almost certainly have joined it if they could were not given the chance. At one stage or another at least 2,500 men were in active mutiny or on the brink of it, and this does not include some outlying regiments whose temper was uncertain; they were awaiting the outcome before declaring themselves. Nearly all the mutineers were cavalrymen, and the loyalty of the great majority of the infantry was one factor that doomed the movement to defeat. The others were the wide scattering of the disaffected regiments, and above all the swiftness and determination with which Fairfax and Cromwell moved against them. Before they brought their forces to bear, however, one colourful character played a disproportionate part in stoking up subversion. William Thompson had been a corporal in Whalley's regiment, but on a drinking and gambling spree in September 1647 he committed such outrageous violence in a tavern brawl that he was cashiered. He still hung around army quarters, however, inciting his old comrades to defy their officers, and after the Ware mutiny he was one of the ringleaders condemned to death. He was reprieved, but he was in trouble for further crimes in the ensuing year, including stabbing a man to death. Lilburne, however, got him out of prison by paying his bail, so freeing him for his final adventure. Posing as a captain, he mustered a private army of about 300 men in the spring of 1649, and on 6 May published a full-throated attack on the Rump and the army commanders, demanding the release of the Leveller leaders and calling on all and sundry to join him 'for a new parliament by Agreement of the People'.[15] He drew in half the men whom Colonel

---

[15] For Thompson's exploits see Firth and Rait, *Regimental History of Cromwell's Army*, I, 221–3, and Gentles, *New Model Army*, pp. 229, 316–17, 331–3.

Reynolds had recruited for his new regiment, as well as a whole troop of Ireton's regiment, and he could have become really dangerous if he had succeeded in his aim of joining up with the units in the Bristol area which were at the main storm-centre of the mutiny. Ironically it was Reynolds, who had been so prominent in the original agitator movement two years earlier, who engaged Thompson's force with his three loyal troops and routed them near Banbury. Thompson himself got away, but died later in the month in a shoot-out with his pursuers.

What really broke the mutiny was the resolution with which Fairfax and Cromwell in person led a force of nearly 4,000 so far loyal troops against its focal area in Bristol. On 12 May, when they were marching through Hampshire, a shrewdly calculated declaration was published in Fairfax's name. It assured the whole army that no one would be compelled to serve in Ireland against his wishes and that the mutineers' grievances were being heeded. It claimed (with little justification) that the implementation of the Agreement was in hand, meaning of course the one presented to the Rump by the army, including provisions for the election of a new and equal parliament. It offered pardon to the mutinous regiments if they returned to obedience immediately, but if they did not they would be reduced by force. By this time the mutineers were becoming worried by their failure to mobilize more supporters, and their resistance began to crumble. The outcome was still uncertain, however, since a trickle of recruits was still coming in to them and the generals could not be wholly sure that their men would fight against their old comrades. Fairfax sent a delegation to parley with representatives of the mutineers, and trustingly appointed Major White, the former Leveller, to head it; but though White performed his mission bravely and faithfully the attempt at negotiation broke down. There followed a mini-campaign, at the end of which nine hundred or so mutineers who were still under arms were put to rout in a skirmish at Burford on the night of 14/15 May. There was little fighting; 340 were taken prisoner, and the rest made their escape in the darkness. With typical moderation only five ringleaders (three officers and two corporals) were court-martialled, and only three were shot. The other prisoners were not only released, but given debentures for their arrears of pay.[16]

Thereafter the Levellers rapidly lost coherence as a political movement, and their organization sank into terminal decline. The voices of some of them would be heard again at intervals in the 1650s, but they were never again serious contenders for power. A generation or two ago historians were apt to give them excessive prominence, but there is now perhaps a tendency to underestimate them. It will not do to ascribe their failure to their programme being 'ahead of its time', unless one particularizes as to what that glib phrase is

---

[16] Gentles gives an excellent account of the army mutinies in *New Model Army*, pp. 329–49.

supposed to mean in their case. Much of what they contended for was achieved at least in part in the 1650s: regular parliaments at minimal intervals, a radical and rational reapportionment of seats, a large liberty of worship and belief, freed from civil penalties, and the use of only the English language in legal proceedings. The Levellers were not the only champions of these objectives, but they took an early lead in asserting them. A household franchise, as defined in the second Agreement, would not have spelt the death of the English political system. What was perhaps the most fertile of all their concepts, the reservation of certain fundamental human rights from the power of even the people's representatives to infringe them, began its long road to fruition in the first Bill of Rights before the century was out. It has been argued here that they spoilt their best chances through errors in tactics, but that does not detract from the originality of their vision of a just and equal commonwealth. It may be true that they demanded a greater degree of political equality than was realizable in a society where social and economic inequality was so ingrained, but they set a goal that posterity has rightly honoured. It has been said that their programme, London-bred as it was and geared to the needs of the middling sort in the great city, had little appeal for the great mass of the rural population; but that is perhaps to underestimate the potential taste for liberty among our village Hampdens, who would certainly have benefited from the abolition of tithes and copyhold tenures—probably too from popular courts of law in every hundred.

Religion was probably the sphere in which the Levellers were most out of tune with the majority of their contemporaries. Their proposal to remove it altogether from parliament's and the state's authority proved the biggest bone of contention in the Whitehall debates, because Ireton and his fellow-officers were typical of the gentry in believing, in company with all beneficed clergy, that in a Christian commonwealth the civil magistrate had a God-imposed duty to ensure that the true faith was publicly professed and propagated. We should also remember that while we in the west today think of popular radicalism as aiming naturally towards democracy, and even communist dictatorships feel obliged to call themselves people's or democratic republics, this was by no means necessarily the way minds ran three and a half centuries ago. We have already noted the distrust felt by many of the sects and radical Independents, whose congregations sprang from much the same social soil as the Levellers, towards the latter's trust in purely secular panaceas, and towards their egalitarianism in particular. There was a fundamental incompatibility between the Levellers' tenets and those of the Fifth Monarchists, who were taking off as a political (as well as religious) force in 1649, just when the Levellers were entering upon their decline. Their reading of the books of Daniel and Revelation led them to believe that the thousand-year kingdom of the saints was imminent. This kind of millenarianism had been around in England for some time, but the Fifth Monarchists differed from its more sober exponents, who trusted to God to bring in Christ's kingdom in his own good time, in believing that they were called to do all they could to bring it in themselves, if necessary (many of them thought) by force. They differed as to whether they expected Christ to appear in person before the thousand years were up, but they agreed that until he came his kingdom was to be ruled by his saints, which of course meant people like themselves. In an address to Fairfax and the Council of Officers, shortly after they had presented the second Agreement to the Rump, the Fifth Monarchist churches of Norfolk asked: 'How can the kingdom be the saints' when the ungodly are electors, and elected to govern?'[17]

Between receiving this manifesto and confronting the main Leveller mutiny, Fairfax was directed by the Council of State to deal with a small incident in Surrey. He and the council would have been astounded if they could have learnt of the interest that posterity was to take in it three centuries and more later. The first Digger community, a company of thirty or so men who called themselves True Levellers, had gathered on common land on St George's Hill near Walton-on-Thames, and had dug it and sown it with parsnips, carrots, and beans, on which they proposed to live. They maintained that God had made the earth as a common treasury, and that the division of it into parcels of private property was the source of all bondage and bloodshed. But rights of common were an appurtenance belonging by law to the local landowners, and upon their complaint the Council of State instructed Fairfax to evict the intruders. Fairfax entrusted the task to Captain Gladman of his own regiment, but he listened courteously to two emissaries of the Diggers, even though they refused to remove their hats in his presence—a sign of the common intellectual ancestry that they shared with Quakers. Gladman judged their little community to be harmless, and it was left undisturbed through the summer. But after it moved on to nearby Cobham Heath in August it gave rise to further complaints, and this time the council gave the army firm orders to suppress it. The squatters' shacks were pulled down, their crops destroyed, and the men convicted of trespass and fined, but somehow the little colony survived into the spring of 1650. Other Digger communities sprang up in various parts of the country, but they were equally short-lived, and the movement was never large. By the summer of 1650 the ripple that it made on the Commonwealth's political history had all but died away.

Yet posterity's interest in the Diggers has not been misplaced, for in Gerrard Winstanley they had a leader and publicist of genius. He used to be celebrated as an ancestor of modern secular-inspired communism, but his

[17] *Certain Queries Humbly Presented in Way of Petition* (Feb. 1649); mostly printed in Woodhouse, *Puritanism and Liberty*, pp. 241–7.

ideas derived from Daniel and Revelation no less than those of the Fifth Monarchists, and his early writings read much like those of other radical millenarians. But by the spring of 1649, when he published his first Digger manifesto, *The True Levellers' Standard Advanced*, he had become convinced that the prophesied kingdom of the saints was to be brought into being through Christ, the second Adam, working in the breast of every man and woman, and inspiring them to redeem the first Adam's sin by renouncing lordship and property. Spiritual regeneration was to be attained through the sharing of the earth and its fruits. Further eloquent and often moving tracts followed, and they culminated in a full model of a propertyless commonwealth which he dedicated to Cromwell in February as *The Law of Freedom in a Platform*. The freedom that it offered was severely qualified, however, because Winstanley, like later devisers of communistic utopias, felt the need to hold his ideal community together through draconian laws and a strict regulation of education and ideas.[18]

At least the various programmes of Levellers, Diggers, and even Fifth Monarchists were borne up by a stronger conviction than the few dragging steps which the Commonwealth's actual government took towards shaping its constitutional future. It was past the middle of March before the Rump passed the two acts which formally abolished the office of king (as 'unnecessary, burdensome, and dangerous to the liberty, safety, and public interest of the people') and the House of Lords (as 'useless and dangerous to the people of England'). The latter act aroused far more controversy than the former, indeed Cromwell himself voted against it. The reason for it lay of course in the overwhelming opposition of the peerage as a class to the king's execution, but even after that event a substantial number of Rumpers wanted to retain the Lords in a purely consultative role. What tipped the balance was a printed royalist declaration, proclaiming Charles II as king and designating the House of Lords as the sole legitimate authority until he was able to exercise his regal powers in person. On its appearance the bill for abolition was rapidly passed, but by a majority of only fifteen in a House numbering seventy-three.

The Rump was being made aware almost daily of the deep unpopularity of its regime in the country at large. One evidence of it lay in the huge success enjoyed by a pious forgery entitled *Eikon Basilike*, which purported to record the late king's meditations and devotional exercises during his final captivity. It was compiled and probably mainly written by John Gauden, the future Bishop of Worcester, and published ten days after Charles's execution. Its tear-jerking portrayal of martyred innocence and piety had a very broad

---

[18] Christopher Hill (ed.), *The Law of Freedom and Other Writings* (which include *The True Levellers' Standard Advanced*) (Harmondsworth, 1973).

appeal; despite the government's attempts to suppress it it was reprinted thirty times within the year and translated into several European languages. One reader whom it exasperated, however, was John Milton. He had had no quarrel with monarchy as such when he took up his pen against the bishops in a series of tracts in 1641–2, but the course of events during the Civil Wars, especially the establishment of an exclusive Presbyterian national church, aligned him firmly on the side of the Independents and the New Model Army. His sonnet of 1646 'On the new forcers of conscience under the Long Parliament' ended with the famous line 'New Presbyter is but Old Priest writ large', and his sonnet to Fairfax two years later expressed his profound discontent with the whole ethos of the unpurged parliament's rule. He thoroughly approved of the proceedings against the king, and he was so incensed by the flood of outcries against them that he returned to prose polemics to defend them, directing his fire particularly against the Presbyterian clergy. *The Tenure of Kings and Magistrates* appeared two weeks after the king's execution, but most of it was written slightly before. The formality of its argument that kings are accountable to the whole body of their subjects, along with its splendidly orotund rhetoric and its piling up of biblical and classical authorities, seem to place it in an older world of controversy than the pamphlets of (say) Walwyn and Winstanley, but it was effective after its fashion, and Milton was already well enough known as a poet, scholar, and polemist for his support to be very welcome to the Rump, who had few enough defenders. Gratefully, the parliament appointed him Secretary for Foreign Tongues to the Council of State at £200 a year. His routine duties included rendering the council's letters to foreign states into elegant Latin, translating incoming diplomatic correspondence into English, acting as interpreter at audiences and conferences conducted in Latin (still the lingua franca of diplomacy), and examining papers and tracts suspected of being subversive. But he earned his quite handsome salary mainly by defending the Commonwealth in print against its literary assailants, and one of the council's first requests was for a reply to *England's New Chains Discovered*. He never wrote it, and some have taken this to imply that he felt some sympathy with the Leveller cause; but a much likelier explanation is that he gave priority to writing an answer to *Eikon Basilike*. This he did, to the extent of 242 pages, in *Eikonoklastes*, published in October 1649. No Miltonist loves this turgid piece much, but he devoted his failing eyesight to it, and to replying at length and in Latin to a piece of royalist apologetics by the French scholar Salmasius (Claude de Saumaise). By the autumn of 1651 he was almost totally blind, and his formal duties had thinned to a trickle.

Milton was right in sensing that the huge popularity of *Eikon Basilike* (and the uncritical acceptance of its genuineness) laid bare a great weakness in the young Commonwealth. This lay not so much in any direct threat from active royalists, raring to draw their swords again to avenge the regicide, for it would be six years before any significant number did so, as in a general lack of positive commitment or affection towards the new regime. It was to be an all but insoluble problem to win hearts and minds to a republic dedicated to the supreme authority of the sovereign people's representatives when so few of the people really wanted a republic at all. More than five months passed after Pride's Purge before the Rump defined what kind of a state it purported to govern. It did so in a one-sentence act declaring England 'to be a Commonwealth and Free State . . . governed by the representatives of the people in parliament . . . without any king or House of Lords'. Later still, in January 1650, it required all men aged eighteen and over to take an Engagement to be true and faithful to the Commonwealth, as now established without king or Lords, but it was subscribed with a good deal of casuistry by many ill-wishers, while it proved a stumbling-block to many honest men who had no intention of engaging in sedition.[19] But most did subscribe, and the widespread report that Fairfax refused it conceals the fact that he had already taken the Engagement in the earlier form prescribed for the council.

Long before it passed the Engagement, the Rump became aware that the state of public opinion made it impossible for it to keep its promise to hold early general elections. It was precluded from courting the popularity it so badly lacked by reducing taxation, because the threats from Ireland and Scotland forced it to keep up large land forces, which would grow even larger when conquered territory had to be garrisoned. The Commonwealth had a total of about 47,000 men under arms in March 1649, many with large arrears of pay and living at free quarter, and this would rise to about 70,000 in 1652.[20] Furthermore it had to go on building ships, not only to counter Rupert's small fleet and the much larger number of royalist privateers, but because it faced the hostility and rivalry of the greatest sea-power in the world. Charles II was currently the guest of his brother-in-law William II of Orange, who was much disposed to help him. The Rump hoped, vainly, to cut the monthly assessment at the end of 1649 from £90,000 to £60,000. Instead it was forced in the autumn of 1650 to raise it to an unprecedented £120,000.

It was as hesitant in grasping the nettle of religion as it was in putting the Commonwealth on firm constitutional foundations. The old line of division between Presbyterians and Independents was no longer so sharply drawn, since now many doctrinally orthodox Calvinists of both persuasions were prepared to put their differences aside in order to resist the rising tide of

---

[19] Sarah Barber, 'The Engagement for the Council of State and the establishment of the Commonwealth government', in *Historical Research* 63 (1990), 44–57, corrects previous accounts in important particulars. For text see Gardiner (ed.), *Constitutional Documents*, pp. 384, 391.

[20] The most authoritative estimates of the army's numbers are in the (unfortunately) unpublished Oxford D.Phil. thesis by H. M. Reece on 'The Military Presence in England, 1649–1660'.

radical sectarianism and popular heresy, of which the writings of the so-called Ranters were an extreme example. There was a small party of sectarian enthusiasts within the Rump, with the army men Harrison, Rich, Fleetwood, and John Jones prominent among them; they managed to secure the establishment of a Commission for the Propagation of the Gospel in Wales and a similar one for England's northern counties. But the majority of members were suspicious of religious enthusiasm and did not want to incur greater unpopularity by seeming to encourage it. They were aware of the strong preference in the country at large for retaining a national church with a publicly maintained parochial ministry, and many of them shared it. An established church was already in being when the Rump came to power, with its faith, worship, and government defined by the Westminster Assembly and given statutory authority by the unpurged parliament. In August 1649 there was a motion to confirm it; the division produced a tie and it was lost only by the Speaker's casting vote. That should not be taken as evidence that half the members present were committed Presbyterians (though a significant minority were), but that they preferred what they had got to any likely alternative. The positive task of establishing working classical presbyteries everywhere, based on ruling elders in every parish, was still very incomplete by the time of Pride's Purge, and it was not carried much further thereafter. But no new ecclesiastical regime to replace Presbyterianism was proposed until late in the Rump's existence, and in practice a wide variety of worship and church organization prevailed, including the continued (though illegal) use of the Anglican liturgy. But while the Rump shied off from the contentious business of providing for the propagation of the gospel on a national scale, it was happy to demonstrate that it was against sin. Between April and June 1650 it passed acts against non-observance of the sabbath and against swearing and cursing, as well as the notorious one which punished adultery, incest, and fornication with death, even on a first offence. Mercifully it was very little enforced. A Blasphemy Act followed in August, less savage than the Long Parliament's Blasphemy Ordinance of 1648 and aimed mainly against the Ranters, though George Fox and John Bunyan were among those whom it threatened. The House took longer to face the vexed question of toleration, but in September 1650 it repealed the recusancy laws to the extent of removing the penalties for not attending parish services on Sundays, provided that those who absented themselves took part in some other form of public worship.

When Fairfax, in the midst of the Leveller mutiny in May 1649, assured the army that elections to a new parliament were high on the Rump's agenda, he cannot have known how mistaken he was. But the current pressure in the army for an early dissolution did cause the House to debate the matter. It set up a committee, over which Vane was given special responsibility, to consider both the apportionment of seats in future parliaments and the date by which the present one should dissolve itself. But amid the genuine dangers to the Commonwealth from without, and the demoralizing symptoms of its unpopularity at home, the prospect of putting its future to the hazard of general elections became ever less attractive. Nothing was heard from Vane's committee, though the House did try in October to prod it into activity by ordering it to meet daily. When at last Vane reported from it in January 1650, its proposals were very different from what the army expected and what the Rump had promised less than a year earlier. It recommended that parliament should henceforth consist of 400 members, whom the present House should apportion between the counties and the towns within them, but that it should order elections only in as many constituencies as were necessary to bring its strength up to 400. The presently sitting members were to continue sitting, and be counted as part of the strength of the counties in which their seats lay. The Rump never formally adopted this recruitment scheme, as it came to be called, but it was clearly attracted by it. It was to be a potent source of friction with the army, which saw it as a device to keep its political opponents in power indefinitely. Its proposers could reply that its aim was to ensure not only that the next parliament was not more hostile to the army than the present one but that it could be trusted to preserve the very being of the republic.

Another area in which the Rump disappointed the army was that of law reform. The common law was a majestic edifice and the parliament-men were right to venerate it, but its procedures were riddled with archaisms, and the time was ripe for making it more rational, more accessible to the less well-to-do, and more humane. A very little was done, for instance for the relief of poor debtors, but the professional lawyers in the House formed a close-knit group and exerted an influence disproportionate to their numbers through their guidance of committees and their frequent employment in drafting legislation. They formed an almost solid bloc of opposition to any serious attempt to reform the law, and when the House at last took the matter in hand in 1652 they made sure that nothing came of it.

As time went on, the suspicion inevitably arose that the Rumpers were clinging to their seats for the sake of the material profit that power brought with it. Such a charge was indeed levelled against them by their opponents. In assessing how far it was justified we should judge by the standards of seventeenth-century Britain rather than by those we profess to uphold today, and under the Stuart monarchy holders of high office expected to enrich themselves very considerably, often more through patronage and perquisites than through their formal remuneration. There were limits to what was thought acceptable, and Buckingham and Strafford overstepped them, but the prewar view of where the bounds lay was a generous one. By the standards of the time the Rumpers as a body do not come out badly—certainly better than the ministers and courtiers of James I, viewed collectively. A fair number of them held lucrative offices, and profited from them in time-honoured ways. They were all subject to newer temptations. They were responsible for the sale of vast quantities of crown lands, royalists' lands, and the land of bishops, deans, and chapters, and it is not surprising that some of them secured choice bargains in real estate for themselves. Haselrig was sometimes referred to as the bishop because of the amount of diocesan land he bought in the see of Durham, and Colonel Philip Jones, who was born in Swansea's High Street of very minor gentry stock, rose by questionable means to become quite a magnate in south Wales. He was not the only army officer or ex-officer to do well for himself. Outright corruption in the form of taking bribes seems to have been rare, though one cannot be certain in an area where evidence is so elusive. Speaker Lenthall was alleged to be guilty of it, and so was his MP son, but the accusations were never substantiated. One Rumper, and only one, was actually convicted of taking bribes, and that was Lord Howard of Escrick. The fact that the House expelled him, disqualified him permanently from public office, fined him £10,000 (though this was soon remitted), and sent him to the Tower shows that it regarded corruption as a serious offence, from which rank gave no protection.

Some MPs took advantage of the immunity from prosecution for debt that membership conferred, including the Earls of Pembroke and Salisbury, who both won seats in by-elections after Pride's Purge; but no one would suggest that that was *why* they sought election. Some, mainly among the least active and committed members, took their chance to secure preferential repayment of debts owed to them by the state. Among over two hundred men who enjoyed opportunities for personal profit such as no previous parliament had afforded, it was inevitable that some abused their position. But they were creditably few, especially among the core of members who worked hardest, and the charge that the Rumpers as a body clung to power because they were doing so well out of it will not stand up.[21] The main reasons why they were so slow—and sometimes evasive—in providing for a successor to themselves were first the very real prospect that anything like free elections would return a majority of men hostile to the very principle of a republic, and secondly a desire to prevent the army from usurping political power. The two reasons were of course linked, since in the last resort only the army could ensure that a genuinely new parliament was not to be dominated by men disaffected towards the Commonwealth, and for many members this remedy would be worse than the disease. The Rump's contemporary critics went a lot too far in accusing it of corrupt self-interest, but they were more justified in complaining of its inertia, its dilatoriness in providing positive measures for

---

[21] The whole question is searchingly discussed in Worden, *Rump Parliament*, pp. 93–102, and Aylmer, *State's Servants*, pp. 139–55, 341–3.

constitutional and religious settlement, its aversion to reform in general, and the laxity of the majority of its members in attending to public business. Nevertheless, looking at the Commonwealth as a whole, it was managed by its councillors, officials, military and naval officers with more probity and a stronger sense of public service than the early Stuart monarchy had been, and that was to remain true right through the 1650s. One acid test was the administration of the navy, since the supply of timber and other material to the dockyards, and the provisioning of the fleet, involved very lucrative contracts and offered fertile fields for corruption. But this topic can best be considered in the context of the Commonwealth's defence of itself at sea; and since the most immediate threats to it were posed by land forces, its campaigns in Ireland and Scotland will be the main matter of the next chapter.

# PART III: FURTHER READING

For the effects of the Civil Wars on those who fought them, on the civil population, and on the material face of Britain, see particularly John Morrill, *The Impact of the English Civil War* (1991), Charles Carleton, *Going to the Wars* (1992), Stephen Porter, *Destruction in the English Civil Wars* (Stroud, 1994), and Martyn Bennett, *The Civil Wars Experienced: Britain and Ireland, 1638–1661* (2000). Ian Gentles remains authoritative on *The New Model Army* (Oxford, 1992). The army's role in politics between the wars is probed by the present writer in *Soldiers and Statesmen: The General Council of the Army and its Debates, 1647–1648* (Oxford, 1987) and by the essays edited by Michael Mendle in *The Putney Debates of 1647* (Cambridge, 2001), which also contains some of the best recent writing on the Levellers. A. S. P. Woodhouse presents the most accessible text of the Putney Debates, along with many other valuable documents and a good commentary, in *Puritanism and Liberty* (2nd ed. 1950, and later reprints). The debates were first published, with much else on the army and its political activities, in C. H. Firth's superb edition of *The Clarke Papers*, of which volumes I and II have been reprinted in a single volume by the Royal Historical Society (Woodbridge, 1992). Robert Ashton, *Counter-Revolution: The Second Civil War and its Origins* (New Haven, 1994) is illuminating on the inter-war years but stops short of the war itself. On this see Gentles (above) and S. R. Gardiner's magisterial *History of the Great Civil War* (various editions), and for the decisive Preston campaign A. Woolrych, *Battles of the English Civil War* (1961, 2000). On the navy's role see Bernard Capp, *Cromwell's Navy* (Oxford, 1989). Scotland is splendidly covered down to 1651 by David Stevenson, *Revolution and Counter-Revolution in Scotland* (1977). For Ireland, besides the ever-valuable *New History of Ireland*, vol. III and Micheál Ó Sliochrú, *Confederate Ireland 1642–1649*, already recommended, we have the essays edited by Jane Ohlmeyer in *Ireland, From Independence to Occupation, 1641–1660* (Cambridge, 1995).

The course of political events and the changes in political alignment that led to the execution of Charles I are wonderfully well traced by David Underdown in *Pride's Purge: Politics in the Puritan Revolution* (Oxford, 1971), whose scope is much wider than its title suggests. The story of the king's last weeks is incomparably told by C. V. Wedgwood in *The Trial of Charles I* (1964). On the political history of the Commonwealth down to 1653 Blair Worden, *The Rump Parliament* (Cambridge, 1974) is masterly. Worden also gives the best account of the early development of English republicanism in his contributions to David Wootton (ed.), *Republicanism, Liberty and Commercial Society, 1649–1776* (Stanford, Calif., 1994).

Frances D. Dow gives a fine brief survey of a big subject in *Radicalism in the English Revolution 1640–1660* (Historical Association, 1985), and Christopher Hill is at his memorable best in *The World Turned Upside Down: Radical Ideas during the English Revolution* (1972). He also writes affectionately about the Diggers in his edition of *Winstanley: The Law of Freedom and Other Writings* (1973). On the Levellers, the best short survey is G. E. Aylmer's introduction to the selection of documents that he prints in *The Levellers in the English Revolution* (1975); and see Mendle, *The Putney Debates of 1647* (above). Pauline Gregg is good on Lilburne in *Free-Born John* (1961). H. N. Brailsford's enthusiasm in *The Levellers and the English Revolution* (1976) is somewhat uncritical, but he is very readable. The spread of radical religious and especially millenarian ideas, and their influence within the army, are well covered in Murray Tolmie, *The Triumph of the Saints* (Cambridge, 1977), and Bernard S. Capp is definitive on *The Fifth Monarchy Men* (1972). The Ranters have been a controversial subject since J. C. Davis questioned whether they ever really existed in *Fear, Myth and History: The Ranters and the Historians* (Cambridge, 1926), but Gerald Aylmer has argued convincingly that they did in *Past & Present* no. 117 (1987), and Nigel Smith presents a selection of their tracts, with a perceptive introduction, in *A Collection of Ranter Writings from the Seventeenth Century* (1983). On one objective of all radicals, Donald Veall, *The Popular Movement for Law Reforms 1640–1660* (Oxford, 1970) is the primary recommendation, but Stuart E. Prall, *The Agitation for Law Reform in the Puritan Revolution* (The Hague, 1966) is also worth consulting. For the controversies over tithes, impropriations, and clerical maintenance, Christopher Hill, *Economic Problems of the Church from Archbishop Whitgift to the Long Parliament* (Oxford, 1956, and later paperback editions) is most helpful.

For books on Cromwell see Further Reading for Part V.

# PART IV

# *The Commonwealth*
# *1649–1653*

# FIFTEEN

# The Commonwealth at War

WHEN the nineteen-year-old Charles II heard the horrifying news of his father's death, he was at the court of his brother-in-law William II of Orange at Breda. William himself would have done all he could to help him, but the powerful regent class of Holland and Zealand, who dominated the States-General, were set against involving the United Provinces in any further warfare. It was only months since the Peace of Westphalia had formally brought to an end the exhausting struggle that we call the Thirty Years War; indeed their own war of independence had lasted with one break for eighty years. For Charles the great question was whether he should look first to the Irish or the Scots to help him back to his English throne. The Scots had been prompt to proclaim him King of Great Britain, but they made the actual exercise of his regal powers conditional on his giving satisfaction regarding religion and taking the Solemn League and Covenant. Ormond and his adherents in Ireland, needless to say, wanted to impose no such conditions.

Charles received conflicting advice from the three main groups of his supporters. His mother, and the so-called Louvre group of courtiers who attended her—the chief were Jermyn, Percy, and Berkeley—would have had him put himself in the hands of the Scots and rely on an alliance between them and the English Presbyterians, both religious and political. The constitutional royalists typified by Hyde and Hopton, however, were most unhappy about entrusting his cause and theirs to the Covenanters, who had first risen in arms against Charles I and had fought against him all through the first Civil War. As Anglicans, furthermore, they deplored the Scots' requirement that the king should take the Covenant himself and enforce it on others. They saw in the loyal protestant Ormond an ally after their own hearts, and they were ready not only to accept the concessions that he had made to Irish catholics but to extend at least some of them to English ones in return for their active support. They would rather the king did not rely on any foreign military aid if he could help it, but if it should prove necessary they would prefer that it came from Spain rather than France, for they thoroughly distrusted the Louvre party. The third royalist faction, who have been called the swordsmen, consisted mainly of Rupert and those who attached themselves to him. They were more opportunist, and tended to look to whatever quarter seemed to offer most in the way of military advantage and their own advancement.

Charles himself was eager to go to Ireland, and Montrose and several other Scottish royalists advised him to do so. He remained at Breda until June, despite his mother's urgent pleas that he should join her in St Germain. The Scottish parliament sent commissioners to treat with him there in March, hoping to negotiate terms to which he would commit himself in return for Scotland's armed support, but they received little satisfaction, and they went home empty-handed in June. His purpose was to keep the options open in case the Irish failed him, but the commissioners could not get him to dismiss Montrose, and he told them he was not prepared to impose the Solemn League and Covenant on England and Ireland without consulting their respective parliaments. So far he was playing his cards rather well, and for two or three months after he assumed the royal title his prospects looked quite promising. He had been proclaimed king in several places in England, as well as in Ireland and Scotland, and if he could launch an invasion from southern Ireland there seemed a good chance that the west country would rise for him; its residual loyalty had not been put under strain as that of northern England had been in the Preston campaign. There was considerable disaffection in London, where the Lord Mayor had been dismissed and sent to the Tower for refusing to proclaim the act abolishing the monarchy, and the Rump had had to resort to blatantly coercive methods to bring the City government to obedience. The relations between the parliament and the army were less than cordial, as we have seen, and in the army itself a new campaign of Leveller agitation was exploiting the soldiery's widespread reluctance to fight in Ireland. On the continent, all the powers that counted had given the new king assurances of their goodwill, and none had recognized the Commonwealth; Spain was to be the first to do so, towards the end of 1650. It is true that none was prepared to fight *for* Charles, but if he could recover his kingdoms without depending on foreign arms, so much the better.

Yet whatever the problems that the Rump faced at home, and however tentative its moves towards a long-term settlement, it showed a firm resolve in defending itself against its enemies. Soon after it was established the Council of State started to make serious plans for the reconquest of Ireland. It proposed to send 8,000 foot, 3,000 horse, and 1,200 dragoons to join the forces already there, and to maintain an army of 32,000 in England. It made a provisional choice of the regiments that should constitute the expeditionary force, but this caused great discontent among them, and fuelled the Levellers' agitation. It therefore directed Fairfax to consult his officers as to how they should be chosen, but he wisely replied that it should first be decided who should command them. Accordingly, on 15 March, Cromwell was named as commander-in-chief in Ireland; but he had misgivings about accepting the post, and asked for time to seek the Lord. Two whole weeks passed before he made his decision. On the 23rd he made a long speech to his fellow-officers in the General Council, who were urging him to accept. 'I had had no serious thoughts of the business', he said; but that is scarcely credible, since he was such an obvious choice. Yet he was probably wholly sincere when he said to them: 'I think there is more cause of danger from disunion amongst ourselves than by any thing from our enemies'. One can conjecture what the reasons for his hesitation were. The army really was in a state of some disunity, and with Fairfax somewhat out of his depth in the post-regicide political waters he probably felt his presence to be needed in England, at least for a time. He would not have been human if he had not felt some reluctance to remove himself from parliament and council for an indefinite period when so many critical decisions still had to be made about the Commonwealth's future. There were powerful men in the Rump, no friends to the army, who would be much happier to take those decisions with Cromwell and Ireton a long way away. On a tactical level, he probably reckoned that by delaying his acceptance he could exact firm assurances, as he did, that his forces would be constantly supplied, kept up to strength, and regularly paid. When finally he did make his decision, the aversion which many a soldier felt towards the Irish service must have been mitigated by the knowledge that Cromwell was going to lead them.

There was a long debate in the General Council of Officers as to how the regiments destined for Ireland should be selected. Eventually it was agreed that they should be chosen by lot, and on 20 April, after solemn prayers, a child drew papers out of a hat.[1] This did not eliminate the reluctance to serve, which played its part in the mutinies which soon broke out, but it did remove any suspicion of political bias in the composition of the force that Cromwell was to command.

Before the end of May the early signs of promise for the king's cause were fading. Those of his friends who had proclaimed him in some parts of England were not backing up their gesture with any serious plans to organize a rising for him if he should invade, and after Thomas Scot was put in charge of intelligence on 1 July the Commonwealth government was kept well informed of any stirrings of royalist conspiracy. There were few. The May mutinies failed; the combination of firmness with sympathy for the soldiers' grievances restored the discipline and unity of the army, but left the Levellers a spent force. Cromwell himself was preparing to lead a strong and reliable army to Ireland. There the situation was a little slower to deteriorate, but even before Cromwell landed in August it took a sharp turn for the worse. Here we must pick up the tangled threads of Irish politics where we left them, after the serious defeats of the king's supporters at Dungan's Hill and Knockanauss,

---

[1] Abbott, *Writings and Speeches of Oliver Cromwell*, II, 36–40.

and the opening of a fatal rift in the Confederation between the Old English who adhered to Inchiquin and the clerical party that took its cue from the papal nuncio Rinuccini.[2]

While the second Civil War was being fought in England, the only clash of arms in Ireland was not between the king's supporters and the parliament's but between the opposed factions of the Confederation. The royalists led by Inchiquin, now he was fighting for the king again, were allied to the moderate, pro-Ormond party in the Confederation and supported by what was left of the army of Leinster, which had been routed at Dungan's Hill. Ranged against them were the clericalist pro-Rinuccini Confederates, whose main military support lay in Owen Roe O'Neill's army of Ulster. So dominated was the Confederate Supreme Council by the moderate and royalist faction that O'Neill declared war on it in June 1648 and marched against Kilkenny, the Confederation's capital. He failed to take it, but during August he laid waste much of the surrounding countryside; so while Hamilton's Scots were marching to defeat at Preston, Inchiquin and most of the king's other supporters in Ireland were defending Leinster and Connaught against O'Neill.

Ormond received no reproaches from Charles I for surrendering his authority to the parliament's commissioners. Indeed Charles renewed his commission as Lord Lieutenant and sent him back to Ireland, where he landed late in September, with instructions to strengthen the bonds between Inchiquin, the Old English, and the loyal Confederates. Ormond brought with him arms for 4,000 foot and 1,000 horse, which were very welcome to Inchiquin, with whom he swiftly reached agreement. He then sought the support of the ninth and last General Assembly of the Confederation, which had been summoned to treat with him. Rinuccini's supporters boycotted it, declaring it to be unlawfully convened. That made it all the easier for Ormond to come to terms with it, and the resultant articles of peace were published just as the king's trial opened in Westminster. Rinuccini did his best to frustrate them; he no longer desired a royalist victory, because he believed that an English king would never give the catholics equal status in Ireland. Ormond's treaty, however, promised that the catholics would retain possession of their churches and church livings until all matters of religion had been considered by a free parliament. The government of the Confederation was formally dissolved, and the territory acknowledging Ormond's authority as Lord Lieutenant was placed under the management of twelve 'commissioners of trust'. Rinuccini found himself with no useful role in Ireland, for he lost O'Neill's support through his attitude to the king's cause. He sailed for Italy late in February, never to return.

A striking number of the main participants in the Irish wars changed their

[2] See above, pp. 366–9, 405.

allegiance at one time or another, and more often on grounds of principle than through self-interest. Colonel Michael Jones, commander of the parliament's forces based on Dublin and victor of Dungan's Hill, had left his studies at Lincoln's Inn at the outbreak of the first Civil War to join the king's army in Ireland. His father was the Welsh-born Bishop of Killaloe, his brother the Bishop of Clogher; but he himself was a strong protestant, with puritan leanings, and after the Cessation of 1643 he could not stomach the terms that Ormond agreed with the king, which to Jones seemed to be selling out to the Irish catholics. Rather than bring his men over to join the royal army in England, as the treaty envisaged, he went over to the parliament's side and took them with him. He fought with distinction with the parliamentary forces in Cheshire before being made governor of Dublin and commander in Leinster in 1647, and he was soon to fight one of the crucial actions of the whole war in Ireland. The two other chief officers on the parliamentary side were Sir Charles Coote, Lord President of Connaught, whose loyalty at this time was unswerving, though later he was to play an important part in the restoration of Charles II, and George Monck, commander of the English and Scottish forces in Ulster. Monck was a professional soldier who had learnt his trade in the Dutch service, and it was as a professional that he commanded the foot in the English army in Ireland in 1642–3, when the main objective was to suppress the Irish rebellion. The English Civil War had not started when he was first in action, and he was not under pressure to take sides between king and parliament until Ormond concluded the Cessation, which was designed to release his forces to fight for the king in England. Ormond required them all to swear their allegiance to the king and the Church of England and never to fight in the parliamentarian army. Monck refused the oath, so Ormond relieved him of his command and sent him to England as a prisoner—though with a commendation of his service, and a request to treat him with all possible civility. In refusing to swear allegiance, Monck's motive had probably been to keep his options open rather than to make a positive commitment to the parliament's cause. But George Digby, who had recently been appointed Secretary of State, persuaded the king to send for Monck, and Charles apparently gave him to hope that in time he might command all the forces now released from Ireland for service in England. Meanwhile he was to raise a regiment of his own. But before he could do so the regiments from Ireland, together with Byron's Cheshire forces, were engaged by Brereton and Fairfax in the battle of Nantwich. Monck fought as a volunteer in his old regiment, and in the total defeat of the royalists he was captured. He was brought to the bar of the Commons, accused of high treason and committed to the Tower of London during the House's pleasure. He remained there until Ormond, on coming to terms with parliament in 1646, secured his release. Viscount Lisle, Leicester's son and (briefly) successor as Lord Lieutenant, persuaded him to serve again in Ireland, and after a short spell of duty in Munster he was made major-general of all the English and Scottish forces in Ulster.

Before he assumed this command Monck took the 'negative oath' (not to assist the king) and the Solemn League and Covenant, and thenceforth he remained unswervingly loyal to his new masters until the Commonwealth itself was collapsing through its own internal dissensions. His claim to take over the Scottish forces in Ulster was naturally contested by Colonel Robert Monro, the commander appointed and recognized by the Scottish government. But in the second Civil War Monro sided with Hamilton and the Engagers and declared for the king, whereupon Monck had him seized in his bed and shipped him to England as a prisoner. For a time Monro seemed to have some hold on the Scottish regiments, but after the king's execution many Scottish officers would no longer serve under parliament's banners and had to be cashiered; indeed most of the Scottish forces that had been Monro's transferred their allegiance to Inchiquin.

A stranger test of loyalty came in the spring of 1649 when Owen Roe O'Neill approached Monck with a view to a treaty. O'Neill was in an isolated position, having been declared a traitor by the Confederation's last General Assembly for his abortive march on Kilkenny, yet remaining the enemy of Ormond and Inchiquin. His army of Ulster was so short of ammunition and provisions that it was threatening to disintegrate. He had already tried to enter into negotiation with Michael Jones, without success, and sent an envoy to London to propose a deal whereby the Ulster Irish would have their estates restored and their religious freedom assured, while he himself would be given a command in Fairfax's army. He was, however, simultaneously exploring the possibility of making his peace with Ormond. Monck himself was starved of money and supplies; he controlled only patches of territory in Ulster, and he could not defend Drogheda, which fell to Inchiquin late in June. In May Monck concluded a three months' cessation of arms with O'Neill, each man making undertakings which must have been at least in part insincere; Monck needed to buy time, and his armistice both neutralized his most immediate enemy and kept him from coming to terms with Ormond. O'Neill eventually did just that, but only after the cessation expired. Coote, who was besieged in Londonderry by the Scottish royalists, struck a rather similar deal with O'Neill, whose help saved the town from falling. Monck was not altogether happy about what he had done, for he did not inform the English government, and he waited two and a half weeks before reporting his action to Cromwell, now his commander-in-chief. His truce with O'Neill gave him no defence against Inchiquin, who advanced in strength from Drogheda to Dundalk. There Monck was forced to surrender to him, and most of his men promptly joined Inchiquin's army. But the terms allowed him and any other officers to return to England, and at Milford Haven on 4 August he had his first meeting with Cromwell, who was about to sail with his expeditionary force to Ireland. Cromwell ordered him to London, to explain his conduct to the Council of State. Both council and parliament had long known of his cessation, but they kept it secret while it could be of tactical value. Then, when its term had expired, Monck was reprimanded at the bar of the House for entering into it, though with a gracious assurance that since he had believed it necessary to preserve parliament's interest in Ireland he would not be taxed with it any further.[3] One outcome of this episode was to cement a mutual soldierly trust between Monck and Cromwell, in contrast with which Monck's well-grounded mistrust towards the Rump would resurface momentously after Cromwell was dead and buried.

A more unexpected convert to the Commonwealth's cause, whose importance to it was to grow through the next decade, was Roger Boyle, Lord Broghill, a son of Strafford's arch-opponent the Earl of Cork and elder brother to Robert Boyle, the great chemist. He was twenty when he took up arms against the Irish rebels in 1641, and he remained an active Irish royalist in the Ormond mould until the execution of the king. Some months after that he decided to offer his services to Charles II, and prepared to leave England for the exiled court. But Cromwell, who got wind of his intentions, sent for him and warned him that if he persisted in them he would be clapped in the Tower. Judging correctly that Broghill was a man of high ability and still moved by a strong desire to see the Irish rebellion crushed, Cromwell offered him a high command in his expeditionary force. All he asked was Broghill's word of honour that he would serve faithfully in the recovery of Ireland, and he assured him that he would not be called upon to fight any but the Irish. Broghill asked for time to consider, but Cromwell demanded an immediate answer. He got it, and made Broghill master of the ordinance in Ireland. It was an extraordinary chance for Cromwell to take on so slight a personal acquaintance, but Broghill kept his word, and mutual trust soon ripened into friendship. A remarkable partnership developed between Cromwell and the two ex-royalists Monck and Broghill, which was in time to bear even more fruit in Scotland than in Ireland.

To match the ex-royalists (including Jones) who were fighting for the Commonwealth, Ormond's chief lieutenant was the ex-parliamentarian Inchiquin, who (as we have seen) was much strengthened by the Covenanting Scots who had formerly fought as the parliament's allies under Monro. Late in May Inchiquin reckoned his total forces at nearly 13,000, though for want of money to pay them he was finding it hard to hold them together. Against him, Michael Jones in Dublin was greatly outnumbered, and he too

---

[3] The best account of these transactions is in Maurice Ashley, *General Monck* (1977), pp. 58–68. Ashley joins S. R. Gardiner in dismissing the story, still credited by some biographers, that Cromwell knew of Monck's treaty with O'Neill from the start, if he did not initiate it.

had dissatisfaction in his ranks. But in July the English government reinforced him with a little over 2,000 men, and seldom was so modest a force so timely, for Cromwell was not ready to sail until 13 August. Ormond played into Jones's hands. Misled by Cromwell's choice of Milford Haven as the port of embarkation for his army into believing that it would land in Munster, he sent Inchiquin south to counter it, and led his own forces in an attempt to capture Dublin. His intelligence was poor, and he may not have known that Jones could now engage him with not greatly inferior numbers. Jones took the initiative; he advanced against Ormond's quarters at Rathmines, just south of Dublin, and on 2 August he took him and his small army by surprise. It was a skilfully conceived and executed attack, under which Ormond's forces broke and fled. Ormond himself was nearly captured, and he lost all his guns and wagons and treasure, amounting to about £4,000 in gold. A fortnight later Cromwell disembarked his army close to Dublin, unopposed.

Jones's great victory at Rathmines made the expeditionary force's task immensely easier, as Cromwell gratefully acknowledged. There were still brave men in the field against him, and some hard campaigning lay ahead, but it was to consist of sieges rather than battles, and for these he had the heavy guns that his predecessors had lacked. His most troublesome enemies in the coming months were to be the Irish roads, the Irish weather, and the various maladies that afflicted armies in that damp and boggy country. Among the many who were carried off by sickness before the year was out were Michael Jones, who succumbed to a fever on 6 December, and Owen Roe O'Neill, who died exactly a month earlier. O'Neill had made his peace with Ormond after Rathmines and agreed to serve as his commander in Ulster, but he was too broken in health to bring him the swift military aid that he needed.

Cromwell's strategy was to reduce all the towns that mattered on the eastern and southern seaboards before he carried his campaign of conquest any distance into the interior. Whatever his personal feelings about the Irish nation, he tried to make it clear that he had no quarrel with unarmed civilians, for he published a declaration which strictly banned plunder and free quarter, and promised that countrymen who brought provisions to his forces would be paid in cash at the market rate. He was unable to go on paying his way for long after the end of the year, but his policy won him considerable support in Leinster and Munster. A fortnight after landing he set out against Drogheda, where Ormond had chosen to make a stand. Ormond had lately put the veteran English royalist Sir Arthur Aston in command there, while he himself remained with about 3,000 men at Tecroghan, more than thirty miles away. His own explanation was that the morale of these troops was too low for him to trust them in face of the enemy. Cromwell took six days in stationing his siege artillery before he summoned Drogheda on 10 September. Aston, outnumbered by nearly four to one, short of powder, and with Ormond ignoring his appeals for help, nevertheless refused the summons contemptuously. By late afternoon the next day Cromwell's guns had breached the walls in two places, and he sent in three foot regiments to storm the town. But they came up against well prepared and stoutly defended entrenchments within the walls, and they were beaten back with some loss. Accounts differ as to whether one assault or two were repulsed, but Cromwell himself and Colonel Hewson led a finally successful one on foot. It made enough ground to open a gate to the cavalry, but even then Aston and his men held out on a steep mound called Mill Mount. Infuriated, and as he wrote 'being in the heat of action', Cromwell ordered that all who were in arms in the town should be put to the sword. Out of about 3,100 soldiers there at least 2,800 were slain, most of them after they had stopped fighting. Friars and priests were killed too, but there was no general slaughter of civilians, except such as had taken up arms to assist the defenders. The total death toll probably exceeded 3,000, but not by much, compared with about 150 killed on the English side. By the rules of war that were then current, and still defended by Wellington two centuries later, a garrison that refused a summons after its fortifications were breached was not entitled to quarter, but Cromwell had not hitherto conducted his campaigns in such a spirit. He shared, alas, the prejudice of most of his fellow-countrymen which viewed the Irish as a savage and inferior people, and held them collectively responsible for the massacre of protestant settlers. Yet he can hardly have been unaware that many of Drogheda's defenders were English and protestant, even if he did not know that the town had actually been under siege by the catholic rebels at the time of the 1641 'massacre'. It is hard to stomach his pronouncement, in his report on the action to the Speaker, that 'this is a righteous judgement of God upon these barbarous wretches, who have imbrued their hands in so much innocent blood', though he showed a hint of compunction in trusting 'that it will tend to prevent the effusion of blood for the future, which are the satisfactory grounds to such actions, which otherwise cannot but work remorse and regret.'[4]

Ormond himself admitted that Drogheda's fate did indeed strike terror, and his forces suffered many desertions. When Cromwell moved against Wexford, his next major objective, its corporation and citizens were much divided as to whether to offer him any resistance. Wexford was the home and base of many privateers, and much of its wealth derived from their plunder of English shipping. It was also a strongly catholic town and had been very much on the side of Rinuccini's faction in the Confederacy. It had had no garrison when Drogheda fell, and it did not take kindly to the appointment of Colonel David Synnott as its governor on 28 September by the Earl of Castlehaven,

---

[4] Abbott, *Writings and Speeches of Oliver Cromwell*, II, 127. Tom Reilly, *Cromwell: An Honourable Enemy* (Dingle, 1999) and J. Scott Wheeler, *Cromwell in Ireland* (1999) offer contrasting interpretations of the campaign; see also Gentles, *New Model Army*, ch. 11.

whom Ormond had assigned to defend southern Ireland. Synnott with difficulty persuaded the citizens to resist Cromwell, on condition that Ormond furnished a competent garrison of exclusively catholic troops. Ormond agreed, so the city was by no means undefended when Cromwell summoned it on 2 October. Synnott made a show of negotiating terms, but Cromwell became exasperated when he discovered that his real purpose was to spin out time while Castlehaven brought in 1,500 reinforcements. Synnott's procrastinations, under cover of which he sent an appeal to Ormond for further relief, caused Cromwell to break off negotiations, and on the 11th his siege guns opened a heavy bombardment. Thereupon Synnott and the city magistrates proposed articles of surrender, but the terms they offered were so absurdly favourable to themselves that Cromwell justifiably described them as impudent. In return he offered quarter for their lives to the officers and soldiers, with leave to the latter to go home if they pledged themselves to fight no more against the English parliament. Civilian property would be respected, and the town spared from plunder. These were very reasonable terms in the circumstance, but they never reached Synnott, for just as they were being prepared Captain Stafford, who commanded Wexford Castle, surrendered it to the besiegers on his own initiative. It is unlikely that he was unaware of the renewal of negotiation, since he was one of the four men named by Synnott to conduct it. His motives have been variously guessed, but Cromwell's guns had heavily breached the castle walls. The troops who took over the castle promptly turned its guns on the defenders manning the adjacent city walls, who shortly abandoned them. The besieging forces then stormed them, and the garrison was soon in complete disarray. Some of them tried to get away across the estuary in boats, but in their scramble they so overloaded them that at least one sank, causing nearly 300 to drown. Others, together with some armed townsmen, tried to make a stand in the marketplace, where they were slaughtered indiscriminately. Priests and friars were again killed without mercy, but there was no general massacre of civilians, other than those who fought alongside the garrison troops. Among a total of nearly 2,000 who perished there may have been a few innocent civilians, but not many. The whole action was over in about an hour.

Cromwell's role in this tragic business is not easy to assess. His remarkable patience with the devious Synnott over nearly ten days, during which he held a commanding military advantage, bears out his assurances to parliament that he truly wished to avoid a repetition of the bloodbath of Drogheda. He gave no orders for the slaughter that occurred, and he was not on the spot when it began. The regimental officers who took immediate advantage of Stafford's surrender of the castle were very likely unaware that a new negotiation of articles of surrender was in process of being initiated. The big questions are whether Cromwell was physically in a position to countermand the killing of the defenders, and whether he made any attempt to do so. In his report to parliament there are again some intimations of compunction, yet it suggests that he saw Wexford's agony, unplanned by him, as a divine judgement, and forbore to interfere with it

And indeed it hath not without cause been deeply set upon our hearts, that we intending better to this place than so great a ruin, . . . yet God would not have it so; but, by an unexpected providence, in his righteous justice, brought a just judgement upon them, causing them to become a prey to the soldier, who in their piracies had made preys of so many families, and made with their blood to answer the cruelties which they had exercised upon the lives of divers poor protestants.[5]

The soldiers got very good booty, he wrote, but added: 'I could have wished for their own good, and the good of the garrison, they had been more moderate'.

Drogheda and Wexford are not such indelible stains on Cromwell's character as his detractors have often alleged, but they make painful reading, and not only because of compassion for the victims, for different though they are, both are out of key with the rest of his conduct as a soldier. At Drogheda he was strictly within the rules of war, but he did not apply their full rigour in any other of his campaigns, or during the rest of this one. Coote and Inchiquin and other commanders in Ireland sometimes acted with comparable severity, and brutality towards both armed enemies and hapless civilians was not confirmed to one side. But the fact that the carnage at Drogheda and Wexford was by no means unparalleled is not enough to condone it. Nor does it help much to invoke parallels from the German wars of the time, or the slaughter of civilians by Rupert's men in Leicester in 1645, for Cromwell would not have wished to be judged by such models. He was never guilty of the slaughter of women and children that legend has attributed to him, and he consistently tried to spare unarmed civilians from the ravages of war. But he gave hints that his conscience was not entirely at ease about either Drogheda or Wexford, and there was nothing remotely comparable with them in the subsequent actions that he fought in Ireland. His uncharacteristic conduct at Drogheda (Wexford being a less clear-cut case) is a reminder of the corrosive effect that assumptions about the inherent inferiority of race or creed, especially when stoked by persistent lying propaganda, can have even upon hearts and minds that are otherwise capable of nobility.

At least for a time the terror that he struck through these first two operations weakened resistance to him. He came before the walled town of New Ross on 17 October, and as soon as he opened his bombardment its governor Sir Lucas Taaffe sued for terms of surrender. Many of the defending troops were English, and at least five hundred of them promptly enlisted under Cromwell. The latter's own men were short of pay, however, and he felt obliged to issue

---

[5] Abbott, *Writings and Speeches of Oliver Cromwell*, II, 142.

a proclamation threatening severe punishment against any who were caught seizing the countrymen's plough horses and seed corn (presumably with a view to ransoming them). Good discipline and good politics went together here, because there were still many people in Leinster and Munster who would rather support the English parliament's forces than the remnants of the Confederates, and Broghill was of great help in bringing them in. He raised 1,500 foot and a troop of horse in his own family territory, and with the help of friendly forces in Cork, which had many inhabitants of English origin, he won control of that major port without bloodshed. He had many friends holding commands under Inchiquin, and with their collusion he persuaded a succession of Munster towns, including Youghal, Kinsale, Bandon, and Timoleague, to declare for the Commonwealth. Inchiquin's army was in a state of dissolution by the time the campaigning season ended, and Rupert's little fleet, which had been blockaded in Kinsale by Robert Blake, was lucky to get away and make for Lisbon when a storm forced Blake's ships out to sea.

By mid-November Waterford was the only port on the east or south coasts still in royalist hands, and it was a prize worth taking, vying as it did with Limerick as the second city in Ireland. Cromwell did not expect much resistance when he set out against it, for several inhabitants had let him know he would be welcome. But despite Waterford's strong English connections, most of its population and all its garrison were staunchly catholic, none more so than its mayor and its governor. Ormond sent them just the help they needed, and when Michael Jones in his last action tried to storm Duncannon, which covers the seaward approaches to Waterford, Colonel Edward Wogan (a former New Model officer who had changed sides) threw his men back in serious disorder. Sickness and the need to garrison captured towns had drained Cromwell's effective strength to only 3,000 men, who were all too anxious to get into winter quarters, and he was far from well himself. On 2 December he abandoned the only siege that he ever undertook unsuccessfully, and his woebegone troops marched away in teeming rain.

Yet he was soon heartened by the news that Dungarvan had surrendered to Broghill in the south and Carrickfergus to Coote in the north. Altogether the achievement of the four months since Rathmines had been impressive. Waterford and its estuary formed the only pocket of resistance along the whole coast from Derry round to Ireland's southern tip, though the territory firmly under English control did not stretch far inland. Most of Cromwell's sick soldiers would recover, and reinforcements were at last on the way. He continued to keep his troops in better discipline than Ormond's unruly and generally unpaid forces, who made themselves so unpopular that Waterford and Limerick refused them winter quarters.

The clericalist party that had followed Rinuccini became increasingly concerned over the tendency of the civil population to prefer co-operating with the Commonwealth's forces rather than support the remnants of the Confederates. They largely had themselves to thank, because Rinuccini had put the church's interests far above the king's, and his excommunication of all who supported Inchiquin's treaty with the Confederates had made him many enemies. His policies had caused rifts not only between the Old English and the Old Irish but among the bishops themselves. In an attempt to repair the damage, the majority of the Irish catholic bishops met at Clonmacnoise during the first half of December 1649. From there they published a declaration proclaiming themselves (not altogether truthfully) united in the defence of their faith and their king, calling for an end to dissension, and appealing to the people to support Ormond's and the king's cause loyally and generously. They warned them against putting any trust in Cromwell, who (they said) was planning to extirpate not only the catholic religion but the Irish people themselves, along with all their property.

Cromwell was greatly angered by this piece of propaganda, and by virtue of his office of Lord Lieutenant he published a very long counter-declaration. It has often been quoted to illustrate his bigotry against the Irish, and it does indeed display ignorance of their past and insensitivity towards their aspirations for the future. But though he gave his authority to the document it is extremely unlikely that he composed all 6,000 words of it himself, and large parts of it are quite unlike his authentic writings and utterances in style. Those, especially near the beginning, which focus on ecclesiastical matters and attack the authors of the Clonmacnoise declaration as popish prelates, are couched in a pulpit-rhetoric that suggests a clerical hand, perhaps that of Cromwell's trusted chaplain John Owen. But the most interesting pages, and the ones which seem most stamped with Cromwell's own tone and thought, are those which address the laity and challenge the bishops' misrepresentation of the Commonwealth's intentions towards them. Their gist is that England had no quarrel with the Irish people as such, but only with those in arms against her, and with the clergy who incited and supported them. The declaration hotly denied that the English government intended, along with extirpating the catholic religion, to 'massacre, banish and destroy the catholic inhabitants' of Ireland. That, it said, had been the historic method of the catholic church in dealing with those who rejected its authority, but a better might be found:

to wit, the Word of God, which is able to convert (a means that you as little know as practise, which indeed you deprive the people of), together with humanity, good life, equal and honest dealing with men of a different opinion, which we desire to exercise towards this poor people, if you, by your wicked counsel, make them not incapable to receive it, by putting them into blood.[6]

---

[6] Abbott, *Writings and Speeches of Oliver Cromwell*, II, 203.

To the accusation of intended massacre Cromwell replied: 'I shall not willingly take or suffer to be taken away the life of any man not in arms, but by
the trial to which the people of this nation are subject by law, for offences
against the same.' Banishment to the plantations would be incurred only by
prisoners taken in arms who would otherwise be liable to the death penalty.
He justified the confiscation of the estates of those who had engaged in rebellion, but to those who had not he promised that their lives, liberty, and property would have the protection of the law. To those who had once been in
arms but were so no longer, and to all who would now lay them down and
submit to the state of England, he promised that he would intercede with parliament for their merciful treatment. In summary, he declared:

We come to break the power of a company of lawless rebels, who having cast off the
authority of England, live as enemies to human society. . . . We come (by the assistance
of God) to hold forth and maintain the lustre and glory of English liberty in a nation
where we have an undoubted right to do it;—wherein the people of Ireland (if they
listen not to such seducers as you are) may equally participate in all benefits, to use
liberty and fortune equally with Englishmen, if they keep out of arms.[7]

One thing that Cromwell could not or would not understand was the depth
of the devotion that the majority of the Irish felt towards the catholic religion.
He frankly declared that he would not permit the celebration of mass where
he had power to prevent it, but he failed to recognize that this would deprive
most of the nation of the central rite of their faith; their devotion to it, he
thought, was a superstition inculcated by their priests. 'Alas,' his declaration
said, 'the generality of the inhabitants are poor laity (as you call them) and
ignorant of the grounds of the catholic religion', and like many Englishmen
he probably really believed that they were not so much catholic as unconverted. In all matters secular, however, he really does seem to have envisaged
a kinder treatment of the mass of the Irish people than the Commonwealth
was soon to mete out. One needs of course to be cautious of taking at face
value a public pronouncement by a conquering general whose main purpose
was to loosen the catholic clergy's hold on lay opinion, but there is other evidence that he really hoped that the bulk of the people might be won over by
decent treatment. Very shortly before issuing this declaration he wrote to his
friend John Sadler, a Master in Chancery, inviting him to come to Ireland as
Chief Justice of Munster at a handsome £1,000 a year. 'In divers places
where we are come,' he wrote, 'we find the people very greedy after the Word,
and flocking to Christian meetings.' They were so accustomed to tyranny and
oppression from their landlords, and so inured to getting nothing done without bribes, that a taste of cheap and impartial justice could win their loyalty,
and then 'the foregoing darkness and corruption would make it look so much

---

[7] Abbott, *Writings and Speeches of Oliver Cromwell*, II, 205.

the more glorious and beautiful, and draw more hearts after it'.[8] Sadler, however, declined the offer, whereupon Cromwell was instrumental in getting him made Master of Magdalene College, Cambridge. The Munster post went to John Cook, the late king's prosecutor, who filled it admirably.

Cromwell spent less than two months in winter quarters. It was a mild season, and the good recovery that most of his men made from their various sicknesses enabled him to take the field before the end of January. The only places of importance eastward of Connaught and the Shannon that still held out against him were Kilkenny, Clonmel, and Waterford, though a number of smaller strong points had to be reduced before he could tackle these major objectives. He quickly took the castles of Kilbeheny, Clogheen, and Rehill, and then appeared before the fortified town of Fethard on the wild, wet night of 2–3 February. The governor made a slight show of resistance, but a few cannon-shots persuaded him to treat, and he surrendered on honourable terms the next day. The defenders were allowed to march out with the honours of war, the priests in the town were specifically included in their safe-conduct, and protection was promised and given to the property of the townsmen. On 24 February Cromwell prepared to besiege Caher, a small town on the river Suir with a massive island fortress. His first summons was ignored, but as soon as he brought up his siege guns the governor surrendered on terms, which again were generous.

Kilkenny, the old capital of the Confederation, proved predictably a harder nut to crack, though plague was raging in the city. It was in the heartland of Irish resistance; it had a full circuit of medieval walls, an imposing castle, and a large garrison, commanded by Ormond's cousin Sir William Butler. Cromwell was in no hurry to attempt it, and he spent some weeks in reducing other minor strongholds in the vicinity, so as to isolate it. For all or most of this time he must have been aware that parliament had voted on 8 January to order him to prepare himself to return to England as soon as possible, but he received no official intimation, and he was most reluctant to leave Ireland until its reconquest was absolutely assured. For reasons still mysterious he did not receive the Speaker's letter formally summoning him home until 22 March, the very day on which he appeared before Kilkenny. He and Colonel Hewson, with forces from Dublin, threatened the city with a pincer movement, but Butler rejected his first summons. Two attempts to storm the walls were repulsed with considerable losses to the assailants, the second even after their capture of Irish Town, the suburb across the river Nore, had made Butler's position almost untenable. It was a gallant defence, and Butler finally agreed honourable terms of surrender on the 27th. The townsfolk had to pay £2,000 to be spared the pillage that the besiegers would normally have

[8] Ibid., pp. 186–7.

expected, but that did not save their churches from a good deal of vandalism by the angry protestant soldiers.

Meanwhile the royalists and Irish still in arms continued to weaken themselves by their own divisions. On 8 March Ormond and the commissioners of trust met the bishops and other Old Irish leaders at Limerick, the most important inland town still holding out, and the more so after Kilkenny fell. Ormond demanded that Limerick should admit a garrison under his command, and threatened to leave the country unless he received the obedience due to the king's Lord Lieutenant. But the bishops and their associates faced him with a catalogue of complaints of military and financial oppression, and refused to let in his garrison. He retired to Loughrea, the base of his commander in Connaught, the Marquis of Clanricard, and a long way from the scene of action in the coming months. He was wearying of his task; he had asked the king to recall him in the previous December, but Charles had told him to stay, hoping he might give support from Ireland to his own coming adventure in Scotland. Ulster was of course the province best placed to assist him, but there the royal cause was needlessly thrown away. The catholic nobles and gentry met there in March to appoint a commander to succeed Owen Roe O'Neill, and their choice fell on Heber MacMahon, Bishop of Clogher, the chief organizer of the recent Clonmacnoise meeting. He was an astute clerical politician, but he entirely lacked military skill and experience. Understandably, this thoroughly alienated Colonel Monro's Scottish forces in Ulster, who since the regicide had been supporting Charles II. Most of them, including Monro himself, went over now to the English parliament, while Viscount Montgomery threw in his lot with Ormond. To look ahead for a moment, the bishop, against his officers' advice, committed his army to battle against Sir Charles Coote's superior forces at Scarrifhollis on 21 June, and it was utterly routed, with about 3,000 men killed. This was quite as bloody a business as Drogheda and Wexford, and not a few officers were executed after quarter had been given. Bishop MacMahon escaped but was captured next day, and eventually hanged on Coote's orders.

All this was after Cromwell had returned to England. Before he did so he moved late in April against Clonmel, where he received perhaps the worst rebuff of his military career from its governor, Major-General Hugh O'Neill, Owen Roe's Spanish-born nephew. Hugh was a resourceful soldier with a nerve of steel, and he managed to increase his little garrison from about 1,300 to over 2,000 during the three weeks that Cromwell spent in forming his siege lines and planting his batteries. During that time his bold sallies inflicted considerable losses on the besiegers. When Cromwell's heavy guns eventually opened up, O'Neill got all hands to work at building makeshift defences where they were opening up a breach, so as to force the attacking troops to traverse a narrow lane, ending in a deep ditch. So when Cromwell sent his men in to storm the town on 16 May they marched into a cleverly set ambush, raked by guns firing chain-shot from behind the ditch and by musket-fire from the upper floors of the surrounding houses. He lost about 1,000 dead within an hour and perhap 500 more by the end of the day, by which time he found (as he had at one stage at Waterford) that he was pushing his soldiers further than they were prepared to go. Around midnight the mayor sent to him to ask for terms, and he quickly granted favourable ones. He was furious to discover, after signing them, that O'Neill and his men, who had run out of ammunition, had slipped away through the besiegers' lines in the darkness; nevertheless he honoured the terms that he had granted to the townspeople. O'Neill made for Waterford, twenty-eight miles away, but the city was plague-stricken and would not admit him, so his little remnant of the army of Ulster was forced to break up.

Cromwell sailed for England a week after taking Clonmel's surrender, leaving Ireton in command as Lord Deputy. Clonmel was a sour note on which to end his Irish campaign, but thanks to his efforts, combined with those of Jones, Broghill, and Coote, the completion of the subjugation of Ireland was only a mattter of time. The remaining garrisons in Leinster and Munster, including Waterford and Duncannon, capitulated during the summer, and only Limerick and the wilds of Connaught still offered resistance. If Cromwell had stayed, there can be little doubt that he would have taken Limerick before the year's campaigning season ended, for despite its strong fortifications the city had hardly any ammunition left and its magistrates were bitterly divided. Hugh O'Neill, by now probably Ireland's best soldier, had the greatest difficulty in persuading them to accept him as commander of its garrison. But Ireton was over-confident; he thought he could tackle Limerick and Athlone simultaneously, so he divided his forces. His conduct of his first independent campaign was indecisive, and by the time he concentrated his efforts on Limerick it was too late in the season for prolonged siege operations. When at last he set about besieging Limerick in June 1651 he counted on starving it out, and it was not until late October that he at last prepared to storm it. In addition to the suffering imposed on the inhabitants by hunger and plague, his troops were guilty of some unnecessary acts of cruelty. The terms of surrender that he insisted upon were harsh, especially towards the principal defenders, seven of whom were executed. He wanted O'Neill's blood too, and he twice virtually forced his council of war to vote for the death sentence. He finally gave way in face of the admiration most of his officers felt for their opponent's honour and courage as a soldier. But the strain of the five-month siege cut Ireton's own life short, for a neglected cold turned to high fever, and on 26 November he died.

By that time the king's cause in Ireland was in terminal disarray, not least through the action of the king himself. The simmering feud between the catholic prelates and Ormond came to the boil when the bishops met at Jamestown in August 1650 and published a declaration that the catholics of Ireland could no longer accept him as their leader. They released the people from their obedience to him as Lord Lieutenant, called upon him to resign his authority and leave for France, and proposed in effect to take over political authority themselves until a General Assembly could be called and the Confederation revived. They prepared a formal excommunication of all Ormond's supporters, but held it in suspension pending his reply. They appealed to the commissioners of trust to depose him. Predictably, he told their envoys that he had no intention of leaving and bade the bishops to stop wrangling and support the war. Thereupon they published their excommunication, not knowing that Charles himself had just totally repudiated them and simultaneously cut the ground from under Ormond's feet.

The king had been in Scotland since June, and more will be said shortly about the humiliating declaration that he was induced to publish on 16 August, as a condition of receiving Scottish armed support; but among other things he was made to revoke the peace that he himself had instructed Ormond to conclude with the Confederates in 1649, and to acknowledge the 'exceeding great sinfulness and unlawfulness' of treating with 'the bloody Irish rebels'.[9] There was no more for Ormond to do in Ireland; indeed Charles himself advised him to leave the country. With the grudging agreement of the catholic bishops he appointed Clanricard as Lord Deputy, and in December he sailed for France. With him went Inchiquin, Daniel O'Neill, and other pillars of Old English royalism. Most of the bishops, for their part, were no longer greatly interested in the king's cause, for they doubted whether he would ever give their church the rights and powers that they thought belonged to it. Their first loyalty was to international catholicism, and they were placing their hopes now in military aid from abroad. They were in negotiation with Charles, Duke of Lorraine, who had long ago been expelled from his duchy by the French, and had since been a mercenary commander in the imperial service. But it was most unlikely that either Spain or the papacy would back him with the necessary financial and logistical aid, and many of the old confederates, especially among the laity, remained loyal in their hearts to Ormond and the crown.

It is difficult to set a firm date to the end of the Irish rebellion and the completion of the reconquest. Both were assured by the time Cromwell sailed home, and after Coote took Galway in April 1651 virtually all the garrisons and forts in the country—over 350 of them—were subjected to the English Commonwealth. But there was little peace outside them, and though there was no further prospect of mounting an army that could challenge the

---

[9] R. Bagwell, *Ireland under the Stuarts* (3 vols., 1906–16), II, 239.

English in battle, royalist commanders could still muster considerable numbers of soldiers on a local basis, even though an estimated 34,000 Irishmen enlisted in continental armies during the early 1650s. The remnants of the Irish armies in Leinster, Munster, and Connaught made their formal surrenders between March and June 1652, but that did not spell an end to resistance. It took over 33,000 English troops to man the garrisons in Ulster, Leinster, and Munster, and mortality was so high among them that they needed to be constantly reinforced. Even so the peace that they maintained was precarious. Large numbers of dispossessed small landholders were living in the bogs and woods and mountains and subsisting by armed raids. These tories, as they were called, drove off so many cattle that few were left to their rightful owners, and they made cultivation so hazardous that four-fifths of the fertile land lay fallow and uninhabited. The process of depopulation and impoverishment was compounded when garrison commanders responded to tory raids and larger-scale military activity by laying waste the territory on which their tormenters subsisted. Dearth ensued; whereas even in 1650 food prices were lower in Ireland than in England, by the end of 1651 bread was much dearer. Actual starvation became common over large areas, and a serious visitation of plague followed in 1652. Accurate figures for population are not to be had, but Sir William Petty estimated that the total fell from 1,500,000 in 1641 to 850,000 in 1652, and the steepest decline came towards the end of that period.

The tragedy of so much suffering lies partly in the role that sheer misfortune played in bringing it about. It was a misfortune that the Irish rebellion was launched shortly before English military power was increased, for reasons scarcely connected with Ireland, to a degree that left the Irish with no chance of winning. It was rather more than misfortune that the rebellion was stained by atrocities which, when magnified by propaganda beyond all measure, encouraged those who suppressed it to reply in kind. It is interesting to speculate on what might have happened if the Irish rebellion had *preceded* the Scottish, and if those who launched it had controlled it more firmly. Might the Stuart monarchy, weak as it was in the late 1630s, have had to concede what both Old English and Old Irish leaders then most reasonably wanted, including an assured place in the constitution for an Irish parliament, firm titles for Irish landowners, and at least a de facto toleration of the religion of the great majority of the Irish people? Enough has been said of the ways in which the Irish weakened their cause by their quarrels among themselves, and of Ormond's shortcomings as a military commander, and of the difficulties that both Charles I and Charles II made for their loyal servant; once the rebels were up against the undistracted military and naval power of the English Commonwealth defeat was surely inevitable. Yet the real curse of Ireland was not Cromwell but a conjunction of attitudes, largely shared by both

English and Scots, which went back to before Cromwell's lifetime: attitudes which assumed Ireland to be a depedent kingdom, looked greedily upon her land as a field wide open for colonization, and equated popery with idolatry. England was already committed to a huge confiscation of Irish land before Cromwell set foot in the country, and the Act for Settling Ireland of 1652, which set that confiscation in motion and rendered around 80,000 Irishmen subject (on paper) to the death penalty, was the collective responsibility of the Rump Parliament, and passed at a time when Cromwell, far from dominating it, was seriously at odds with it. It will be described later in the context of the so-called Cromwellian settlement, taken as a whole.[10]

The reason why the Rump had been anxious from January 16 onward to call Cromwell home lay in their growing fear that the Scots were about to take up arms again for their king. Charles II had been in Jersey since the previous September, but in mid-February he sailed for France and spent three weeks conferring with his mother at Beauvais before going on to Breda to treat with commissioners from the Scottish parliament. That body was divided between representatives of the strict Kirk party, who were doubtful about negotiating with him at all, and the more flexible politicians like Argyll who saw the advantage of having him in Scotland, at least as a figurehead. The young king found that the price of Scotland's armed support was to be far higher than his father had paid in the Engagement. He was required to sign both the Scottish National Covenant and the Solemn League and Covenant, as well as to repudiate the treaty concluded on his behalf with the Irish. A still harder demand was that he should order Montrose to lay down his arms and leave Scotland, seeing that he had so recently commissioned his father's old champion to embark on his last and fatal enterprise. Montrose had raised about 1,200 men, mainly Danish, Swedish, and German mercenaries, and had landed with them in Orkney in the middle of March. There he found waiting for him a letter from the king, written in January, directing him to go ahead with his campaign, despite his (Charles's) negotiations with the Covenanters, in order to help him wring concessions from the Kirk party. Montrose accordingly landed his small force on the mainland in mid-April, hoping to recruit an army from the Highland clans that had fought with him before, but their morale had been so sapped by the years of defeat that very few came in. David Leslie marched against him, and on 27 April Montrose advanced into a trap skilfully set near Carbisdale by Archibald Strachan and the Covenanting cavalry. Nearly all his men were killed or captured or drowned in trying to escape, and though he himself got away he was caught a week later. He was treated ignominiously on his long journey south to Edinburgh, where the

---

[10] See below, pp. 573–9.

public hangman conducted him to the Tolbooth tied to a cart. On 21 May he was publicly hanged and quartered, dying with a bravery that moved the onlookers. Five of his leading officers were executed in the course of the next month.

Meanwhile Charles came to terms with the commissioners at Breda on 1 May, not knowing yet of Montrose's defeat, but without obtaining any guarantee of his safety. He wrote him a public letter on 3 May, ordering him to lay down arms and leave Scotland, and a private one two days later, promising to protect his interests and hoping to employ him again soon. He wrote to the Scottish parliament on the 8th, saying that Montrose had been ordered to disband and asking that he and his forces should be allowed to leave Scotland unharmed, but next day he sent privately to him (still not knowing of his defeat), telling him to remain in arms in case his treaty with the Scottish parliament should fall through. There are still some puzzles concerning his dealings with Montrose and the parliament, which were too complex to be recounted here in full, but it is clear that to some extent he publicly disowned responsibility for Montrose's efforts on his behalf, after so strongly encouraging them. There is no need to detail the other terms agreed in the so-called Treaty of Breda, because the Scottish parliament was not satisfied with them, but before he was admitted to Scotland Charles did sign both Covenants, recognized the supreme authority of the Kirk in spiritual matters and of the parliament in secular, and agreed to disown Ormond's Irish treaty if and when the parliament should so require. He set sail early in June before he knew of Montrose's execution in a warship provided by the Prince of Orange, and he only signed the final concessions just before his little flotilla, which had been hunted by the English fleet, arrived in the Moray Firth on Midsummer's Eve. Dismay at the terms he agreed to was not confined to the old royalists such as Hyde, Hopton, Nicholas, and Cottington, for his mother (who had been so keen on a Scottish alliance) and Rupert's circle felt it too. Whether, when he entered Edinburgh, he observed Montrose's severed head impaled on a spike on the Tolbooth is not recorded. He received a genuinely warm welcome from the common people of Scotland, but he was soon in bitter dispute with the parliament and the Kirk over the many old royalists he had brought with him as part of his household, and he was eventually forced to dismiss them. The crowning humiliation was the public declaration that he was forced to issue on 16 August, as a condition of Scottish support, in which he not only bound himself to a church he did not believe in and renounced the Irish who had fought for him, but humbled himself before God for his mother's idolatory and his father's sin in opposing the Covenant. Charles I may have been less than fastidious at times over the means of recovering his throne, but his son left him standing. To do the young king justice, his concessions left him very wretched, and he wrote to Secretary Nicholas on 3 September, asking through him that the Prince of Orange should have a boat lying ready off the nearest Scottish shore, in case he should decide to throw up the whole adventure.

By that time, however, the Scots were seriously at war for him. In England the Rump had long seen it coming; hence their increasingly urgent efforts to call Cromwell home. He landed at Bristol late in May, and parliament greeted his arrival with a grant of lands worth £2,500 a year, having already given him the use of St James's House, the Cockpit, and Spring Gardens. Many MPs, councillors, and officers came out to meet him at Windsor and many volleys were fired in his honour, but this company was nothing to the great crowds that gathered on Hounslow Heath to welcome him next day. Fairfax was among those who greeted him, and few of those present were probably gladder to see him home. The mutual warmth and regard born of long comradeship in arms were still undimmed, but Fairfax had still stronger reasons for welcoming him. Leading politicians were already persuaded that the safest way of countering the threat from Scotland was to strike first, and the obvious person to command an invading army was the Lord General. An army had to be sent north anyway, to meet a possible invasion from Scotland, and on 12 June Fairfax accepted the command of it, with Cromwell as his lieutenant-general. But in Fairfax's mind it was one thing to defend English territory and quite another to take the initiative in attacking an old ally, and when the Council of State formally voted on the 20th to invade Scotland he decided, after forty-eight hours' thought, to resign his commission. He took the view that England and Scotland were still mutually bound in alliance by the Solemn League and Covenant, and he met the objection that Scotland had cancelled the bond by invading England in 1648 by pointing out that a Scottish parliament had subsequently disowned and condemned Hamilton's enterprise. But his commitment to the Commonwealth was open to doubt on other counts, and his formidable wife's disaffection towards it was notorious. He had still not formally taken the Engagement, and though he attended the Council of State sporadically he seems never to have taken the seat in parliament to which he was elected early in 1649. The House appointed a powerful committee consisting of Cromwell, St John, Whitelocke, Lambert, and Harrison to try to overcome his scruples about carrying the war to Scotland, and Cromwell strove as sincerely as any of them to persuade him to accept the command. But though Fairfax treated the committee members as the old friends they were, and affirmed his continuing 'duty and affection' to the parliament, he resisted their arguments through almost a whole night. Pleading his 'debilities both in body and mind, occasioned by former actions and businesses',[11] he insisted on resigning. Charles II had tried, quite in vain, to tempt

---

[11] On Fairfax's resignation see Gardiner, *Commonwealth and Protectorate*, I, 287–96, and John Wilson, *Fairfax* (1985), pp. 158–62. Fairfax's own account in his autobiographical *Short Memoirs* reflects his political views after the Restoration rather than those he held at the time.

him with the earldom of Essex, £10,000 a year in land, and whatever office he might choose, but Fairfax was not to take up the king's cause until the Commonwealth was collapsing from within. Still only thirty-eight, he retired to Nun Appleton and cultivated his garden, whose beauties Andrew Marvell, his small daughter's tutor, celebrated in a memorable poem.

Inevitably, Cromwell succeeded to his office of Lord General, and so became commander-in-chief of all the parliament's land forces for the first time. He set out for Scotland on 28 June, the day on which he received his formal commission. It was less than a month since he had arrived back in London, and not many days since the king had set foot on Scottish soil. The Scottish parliament had only just passed an act of levy for the recruiting of its army by over 36,000 men, in addition to the few thousands that David Leslie already had under arms. It was a huge target for a small nation, and nothing like it was ever achieved. Cromwell's attacking force consisted of eight regiments apiece of cavalry and infantry, totalling over 16,000 men. By the time it crossed the Tweed on 22 July, Leslie had already raised his army to almost that number, and recruitment was still in full swing. Many of his levies were still raw and untrained, but their morale was much higher than that of the last Scottish army Cromwell had fought, and Leslie was a vastly better general than Hamilton—probably the best that Cromwell was ever up against. Though Leven, now about seventy, was still nominally commander-in-chief, Leslie was in actual control of operations. For all the English parliament's superior resources, they were severely stretched, since fighting was still continuing in Ireland, where garrisons were making mounting demands on manpower, and the danger of English royalists rising in response to the Scots' efforts necessitated the upkeep of considerable forces at home. A very testing time lay ahead for Cromwell. Faced with Leslie's rapidly increasing strength, he pressed to have his own army augmented to 25,000, but it was well into 1651 before it reached 20,000.

Leslie had fortified a line between Edinburgh and Leith, and his strategy was to leave Cromwell free to advance to it unopposed, having stripped the intervening territory of all provisions that his troops might need. This scorched earth policy, coming on top of the impressment of all men of military age, inflicted great hardship on the Lowlands countryfolk, and made them doubly hostile to the invaders; nor were they mollified by Cromwell's repeated proclamations forbidding his men to lay hands on their persons or property. He was forced to rely on seaborne supplies landed at Dunbar, but these brought him less than he needed, and their transport from the coast was impeded by persistently wet weather. Exposure to this caused much sickness in his army, reducing it to not much more than half the strength of Leslie's constantly reinforced opposing force. Nevertheless he tried hard to bring the Scots to battle. He advanced against Leslie's lines on 29 July, bombarded

Leith furiously, and even temporarily captured Arthur's Seat, but after his wet and weary men had stood in battle order all night he withdrew them to their camp at Musselburgh. Their first night's rest there was broken by a bold attack by fifteen troops of Scottish horse, which were beaten off with some difficulty.

Cromwell's attitude towards his Scottish opponents was markedly different from the one he had shown to the Irish. The Scots were fellow-protestants, if of a bigoted kind, and he and Leslie had fought side by side at Marston Moor. But in his mind the two peoples had one thing in common: both were being driven to fight for a bad cause by their clergy. In a war of words with the kirkmen which had begun with a long manifesto in the name of his army when it first crossed the border, he published a famous address to the General Assembly of the Kirk from Musselburgh on 3 August. He accused the ministers of claiming infallibility in interpreting the word of God, and teaching the people that the Covenant bound them to fight on their side in the present war. It was of course a highly partisan document, but it is expressive of his own convictions:

Your own guilt is too much for you to bear: bring not therefore upon yourselves the blood of innocent men, deceived with pretences of king and Covenant, from whose eyes you hide a better knowledge . . . Is it therefore infallibly agreeable to the Word of God, all that you say? I beseech you, in the bowels of Christ, think it possible you may be mistaken . . . There may be . . . a carnal confidence upon mistaken and misapplied concepts, which may be called spiritual drunkenness. There may be a Covenant made with death and hell.[12]

The suggestion that they might be mistaken hit the kirkmen on the raw. In a reply that smouldered with indignation they asked: 'Would you have us to be sceptics in our religion?' Their view, repeated again and again, was simply that Cromwell had signed the Covenant and was now breaking it.

It would be too much to say that they were fighting a war on two fronts, but Cromwell was not their only problem. His challenge to battle on 29 July coincided with an unofficial visit to the Scottish army by the king himself. Charles was joyously welcomed by both officers and men, so warmly indeed that Wariston and others of the Kirk party were thoroughly dismayed. They feared that a war for God and the Covenant would degenerate into a secular war for the king, with of course a consequent diminution in their own influence. They warned Charles that his continuing presence would discourage the godly and incur the wrath of God, who was jealous of any rivalry to his own glory. They put strong pressure on him to leave, which he reluctantly did on 2 August, and then, concluding that there were too many malignants (i.e. royalists) in Leslie's camp, they persuaded the Committee of Estates to

---

[12] Abbott, *Writings and Speeches of Oliver Cromwell*, II, 303, see p. 305 for the Scots' reply.

carry out a purge which rapidly removed about 80 officers and 4,000 men. This was folly on at least three counts: it damaged the morale of the Scottish army as well as reducing its strength, it roused the young king's deep resentment, and it widened the rift in the Covenanters' ranks between the fanatical clergy-dominated wing and the moderate and aristocratic one led by Argyll. Between Argyll and Cromwell a certain wary rapport persisted, despite the war.

Throughout August Cromwell tried intermittently to bring Leslie to a decisive engagement, but he always failed. Leslie was under frequent pressure to give battle, both from the politicians in Edinburgh and those precursors of modern political commissars, the ministers attendant on the army, but he steadily resisted them. He was justified, and in the complex tactical manoeuvres that he and Cromwell executed his generalship was arguably the better. He reckoned that the toll that dysentery and camp fever were taking of the English army, joined to the problems of supplying it by sea in continuingly atrocious weather, would force Cromwell to withdraw it across the border before winter set in, and it was not an unreasonable judgement. Although Cromwell had been reinforced, sickness and desertion had reduced his effective strength to about 11,000 by the end of August, and despite the continuing purge of malignants Leslie had at least twice as many in the field by then. During 31 August and 1 September, with the Scots harassing his rearguard, Cromwell fell back on Dunbar, whither his seaborne supplies and recruits were shipped from Berwick, and where his many sick soldiers could find some shelter. Leslie believed he had him cornered. He took up a strong position on Doon Hill, overlooking the town, and occupied a vital defile at Cockburnspath on the road to Berwick, so cutting off the English army's retreat by land. On the 2nd Cromwell wrote to Haselrig, who was still governor of Newcastle, plainly facing the possibility of defeat and warning him to muster all the forces he could against a possible Scottish invasion:

We are here upon an engagement very difficult. The enemy hath blocked up our way at the pass at Copperspath [Cockburnspath], through which we cannot get without almost a miracle. He lieth so upon the hills that we know not how to come that way without great difficulty; and our lying here daily consumeth our men who fall sick beyond imagination.[13]

But though defeat was a contingency against which it was his duty to provide, Cromwell's mind was all on battle, and he never despaired of victory. Leslie, with his two to one superiority (slightly more than that in infantry, slightly less in cavalry), did not conceive that the English would attempt any more than to make their escape with as few losses as possible, and he was confirmed in this expectation when Cromwell put 500 of his sickest men on shipboard; he thought the English were evacuating all their infantry. He came down from Doon Hill on 2 September and formed a battle-front about a mile long, mostly behind the shallow ravine of the Spott Burn (then called Brock's Burn), but stretching right across the Berwick road. Some sources state that he moved his army against his better judgement, under pressure from the Committee of Estates, who kept urging him to fall on his weakened enemy. But he needed no persuading to give battle now, and the decision may well have had his full concurrence, if it was not entirely his own. His move brought the English lines within range of his artillery, and gave his men some relief from the bitter winds and rain that swept Doon Hill.

Cromwell led the senior officers of his council of war on a mounted reconnaissance of the Scottish position late in the afternoon before formally consulting it, after sundown, as to what course to take. A number of colonels were for shipping the infantry to safety while the cavalry tried to cut through a path of escape, just as Leslie supposed would happen. But there were nothing like enough vessels for that, and Lambert, whose own reconnoitring had helped to discover a possibly fatal weakness in the Scottish position, gave Cromwell the support he wanted by pressing for battle. The decision was taken, not only to fight but to attack first.

Both armies spent a cold wet night in the field, ranged in battle order. But whereas most of the Scots were allowed to unsaddle their horses and extinguish their matches, and many of their officers went off to houses or tents behind the lines for a sleep, the English regiments stayed at the ready, and Cromwell rode round them all night, checking their positions and giving them encouragement. In his tense concentration he bit his lips until the blood ran unnoticed down his chin. Well before daybreak, Lambert and a brigade of horse opened the battle with an assault on the Scots holding the pass at Cockburnspath, and despite a strong cavalry counter-attack they cleared it after an hour's fighting. In the general engagement that followed, the infantry battle played at least as critical a part in the day's outcome as the initial cavalry action. Attacking against such heavy odds, the English foot were at first repulsed, but they rallied and drove the Scots back at push of pike over a distance of three quarters of a mile. When the Covenanters finally cracked and began to throw down their arms, Cromwell's cavalry inflicted a terrible slaughter upon them; they were, in his words, 'made by the Lord of Hosts as stubble to their swords'. As the sun rose over the sea, he shouted 'Now let God arise, and his enemies shall be scattered', and indeed they were soon in full flight. He never fought a finer battle, though Lambert deserves his share of the credit. Cromwell had faced possible destruction, but it was the Covenanting army that was all but destroyed. He may have underestimated his own casualties, which he variously put at twenty or thirty killed, but Leslie lost over 3,000 dead and nearly 10,000 prisoners; only about 4,000 men, mainly cavalry, subsequently rallied to him. For Cromwell, Dunbar was a very special providence of God, and he was anxious that his masters at Westminster should be worthy of it. In his dispatch to the Speaker next day he wrote:

We that serve you beg of you not to own us, but God alone; we pray you own his people more and more, for they are the chariots and horsemen of Israel. Disown your-selves, but own your authority, and improve it to curb the proud and the insolent . . . relieve the oppressed, hear the groans of poor prisoners in England, be pleased to reform the abuses of all professions; and if there be anyone that makes many poor to make a few rich, that suits not a Commonwealth.[14]

The officer entrusted with carrying this dispatch—one of those specially named in it for his service in the battle—was the same Major White of the General's own regiment of horse who had been expelled from the General Council for his Leveller opinions in 1647 and employed by Fairfax to negoti-ate with the Leveller mutineers in 1647. The House heard his account of the great victory with understandable enthusiasm and relief. It made some response to Cromwell's pleas, for it quickly passed an act repealing all laws that penalized non-attendance at Sunday services in the parish church, pro-viding that nonconformists engaged in some other form of worship on the Lord's Day. The Dunbar dispatch also probably prompted the setting up of a committee to look into excessive expenses and delays in the courts of justice, and a vote that henceforth all legal proceedings should be conducted solely in the English language.

Edinburgh learned of the disaster at Dunbar from the fleeing horsemen who sought shelter within its walls, and it reacted with panic. Leslie, after rallying what remnants of his army he could, withdrew with them to Stirling, and old Leven went with him. Stirling also became a refuge for the Commit-tee of Estates and the city fathers, besides very many burghers of Edinburgh and nearly all its hitherto bellicose ministers. No marriages took place in the capital for months, because there were no clergy to perform them. Cromwell sent Lambert to secure the city while he himself took Leith, which despite its strong walls and thirty-seven cannon offered no resistance. Leith was vital to him for the safe landing of supplies and reinforcements, and among the booty it yielded were three hundred tuns of French wine.

On arriving in Edinburgh Cromwell again sought to persuade the Scottish people that his quarrel was not with them. By proclamation and by personal assurances he promised them protection of their persons and property, and freedom to come and go from Edinburgh and Leith to sell their wares and hold markets. Edinburgh Castle still held out against him, but since its small

[14] Abbott, *Writings and Speeches of Oliver Cromwell*, II, p. 325; on the battle generally see also pp. 321–30 and Gentles, *New Model Army*, pp. 392–8.

garrison posed no threat while cut off from reinforcements he put no pressure on it, and he treated its governor, Sir Walter Dundas, with scrupulous courtesy. Some ministers from the surrounding country had taken refuge in the castle, and he sent Colonel Whalley to invite them to preach in the city churches if they wished, promising that they would not be molested. They were suspicious and refused. But the exemplary behaviour of the occupying troops under Colonel Robert Overton, and the steps he took to secure provisions for the hungry city, induced many of the fugitive burghers to return and restored its economic life to something like normal.

After a week in Edinburgh Cromwell set out to tackle Leslie and the remnants of his army in Stirling, which he summoned to surrender on 18 September. Leslie had no more than 5,000 men, including the garrison, but he refused, and Cromwell prepared to storm the town. But at the last moment he changed his mind, and by the 21st he was back in Edinburgh. Several considerations probably influenced his decision. An assault could have cost many lives, and with so much already gained he did not want to subject his brave army to unnecessary losses. It would have been a problem to garrison Stirling, since it could not be supplied by sea. But judging by his earnest public addresses and conciliatory gestures around this time Cromwell may well have decided to postpone any further use of force chiefly out of a genuine desire to win over most of the Scottish nation by persuasion. The internal divisions, which Dunbar had opened much wider, may have seemed to be doing his business for him, and they justified him in engaging in no further large-scale military action during the rest of the year.

For one thing Leslie's authority as general was seriously diminished. He was so much criticized for the defeat of his army that he tired to resign, but the Committee of Estates would not allow him to, chiefly because there was no other plausible candidate for his job. Some influential officers, however, notably Colonels Archibald Strachan and Gilbert Ker, blamed him so much for Dunbar that they refused to take orders from him. At this time the Committee of Estates was almost desperate to raise new levies, and early in September it accepted an offer from the counties between the Firth of Clyde and the Solway Firth, which had come together to form the Western Association, to raise more than their quota on condition that their men would constitute a virtually independent army. Glasgow and the south-west were the heartlands of militant, intolerant Presbyterianism, and many there looked to this force to prevent the strict Covenanting cause from being taken over by 'malignants', i.e. royalists. The Committee of Estates sent Strachan and Ker and Sir John Cheisly, a former Engager, to command the Western Association army, but by doing so they alienated the nobles and greater lairds of the region, who looked upon themselves as its natural commanders. The new army therefore was officered mainly by minor gentry and men of the middling sort, and took its colour from the large numbers of ministers who enthusiastically supported it. Many of the more strongly Presbyterian officers and men in Leslie's army left to join it without orders.

Both clergy and laity were split by the lessons they drew from the disaster of Dunbar. The more rational attributed part of the blame for it to the purges which had weakened Leslie's army, both in numbers and morale, and looking to the larger interests of the Scottish nation they were for bringing back into the army the Engagers, who had already proved their commitment to the royal and the national cause. The dogmatic party, who included laymen like Johnston of Wariston as well as the majority of ministers, believed that the Lord had withdrawn his presence from them because they had put too much trust in a prince who was not sincerely repentant of his parents' sins and was intent on worldly, not godly ends. In their view neither the purging of the army nor the conversion of the king had gone far enough.

Charles himself must have had mixed feelings when he heard of Leslie's defeat. On the one hand it gravely diminished the chances of his being restored to his English throne by a Scottish army, but on the other it gave him hope of loosening the shackles that the Kirk party had fastened on him. That result was slow in coming, however. He was in Perth, and so for most of the time was Argyll, striving to extend his influence over him. Charles disliked and distrusted the man, but at this stage the two needed each other, and on 24 September Charles agreed to make Argyll a duke and a knight of the garter at whatever time the foxy Campbell should choose. A few days later, the Committee of Estates banished twenty-four members from the king's household and replaced them with hard-line Covenanters. It was the last straw. Charles entered into a conspiracy with his northern royalist supporters to raise all their friends and clansmen north of the Tay, with the aim of seizing Perth and Dundee and making a platform for a general royalist rising. But the day before the coup was due to begin he told the Duke of Buckingham of it, who was so worried that he in turn told Wilmot. Together they persuaded Charles that the scheme was hopelessly rash, and he, too late, gave orders to cancel it. Next day, however, he changed his mind and tried to reactivate it. By then the Committee of Estates had wind of it, and the predictable fiasco ensued. Charles fled from Perth, perhaps (like his father on two previous getaways) without knowing quite where he was heading for. Colonel Montgomery and a body of Covenanting cavalry caught up with him, hiding cold and frightened in a squalid hovel in Glen Cova, and brought him back to Perth. He was humiliated, yet this foolish adventure, which became known as the Start, did him less harm than might have been expected. He had to make his submission to the Committee of Estates, but its members were rattled, and the saner Kirkmen realized that if they provoked their country's king too far they would raise questions about their claim to be the conscience of the Scottish people.

Some kind of deal was struck, and thenceforth Charles was allowed to attend all meetings of the Committee of Estates.

This was too much for the zealots of the Kirk, especially those who dominated the territory and the army of the Western Association. They increasingly questioned whether they should be fighting for a king whose commitment to the Covenant and indeed to the protestant religion in any form was highly doubtful (though they could not know that he was to die a catholic), and who seemed to prefer the support of malignants to their own. Some of them wondered whether Cromwell did not represent a better cause than Charles's; indeed Strachan and Ker were in touch with Cromwell during October, and would probably have entered into negotiation with him if Wariston and Cheisly had not vetoed it. Cromwell himself, with 9,000 men, paid a three-day visit to Glasgow in mid-October, probably in the hope of convincing its citizens and the westerners of his good intentions, as well as demonstrating his power, but he had limited success. Just after his return to Edinburgh, however, an important Remonstrance was published, addressed to the Committee of Estates, in the name of 'the gentlemen, commanders and ministers attending the forces in the west'. It was to widen the rifts in Scottish politics still further, and it gave its name to the party known as the Remonstrants. It castigated the government for not sufficiently purging malignants from its armies and from its own personnel, and for seeking to impose an unrepentant king on an unwilling England in order to grow rich on England's spoils. This was its central message, and the original spelling helps to convey its flavour:

But we are convinced that it is our sinne, and the sin of the kingdome, that quen the King had walked in the wayes of his fathers oppositione to the works of reformatione, and the soleme leauge and covenant, . . . that after all this, commissioners should have beine warrandit to assure him of his present admissione to the exercisse of his royall power, upone his profession to joyne in the causse and covenant, not onlie without aney furder evidence of his repentance, unto the renewing of the Lord's contraversie with his fathers housse, and without convincing evidences of the realitie of his profession and his forsaiking his former principalls and wayes; but quen ther was pregnant presumptions, if not clear evidences, of the contrarey.[15]

The main support for this sharply divisive document came from the clergy, especially those of the west and south-west (though many ministers in the north and east opposed it), and from the burghers of Glasgow. None of the nobility upheld it, though a few lairds came out strongly for it, especially in the south-west. Wariston defended it passionately in the Committee of Estates, but Argyll and other nobles, who wanted to bring the king to heel rather than to alienate him further, denounced it. After a delay, during which Leslie signed

[15] Croft, Dickinson, and Donaldson, *A Source Book of Scottish History*, III, 145.

an agreement with the northern royalists whereby they disbanded in return for an act of indemnity, the Committee of Estates condemned the Western Remonstrance. The Committee of the Kirk, which was entrusted with the voicing of ecclesiastical policy in the intervals between general assemblies, showed great reluctance in following suit, but finally did so in very mild and qualified terms, whereupon the Remonstrants withdrew from it.

But outside their home territory the Remonstrants spoke for only a minority of the Scottish people, most of whom deeply resented the presence of an English army on Scottish soil, and were ready to rally behind their king in affirming a united national interest. By late autumn Cromwell's forces were being harassed by a rising guerrilla movement in the whole territory between Edinburgh and Glasgow and the border, and he felt obliged to tackle the unreduced strongholds which were sheltering it. He himself moved against Borthwick Castle, one of the strongest and strategically most important. On the instructions of the Committee of Estates, Colonel Ker of the Western Association was ordered to relieve it. Ker refused, openly stating his unwillingness to fight for the king, and on 22 November Borthwick had to surrender. Cromwell and Lambert then launched a two-pronged attack into Western Association territory, perhaps as much to explore its army's willingness to resist as to force a battle. Ker came upon Lambert's cavalry force camped near Hamilton, and grossly underestimating its strength attempted a night attack, for which Lambert was thoroughly prepared. Next morning, 1 December, the rout of Ker's force was completed and he himself captured. Strachan tried and failed to rally his fleeing men, then gave himself up to Lambert. The Western Association army ceased to exist, for most of its soldiers who had not been killed or captured simply went home.

Faced with its liquidation and with Cromwell's steady consolidation of his military dominance over southern Scotland, the reassembled Scottish parliament, now dominated by Argyll and his party, recognized that it was no longer possible to raise an army with any chance of restoring the king unless it could draw on all who were prepared to fight for him, including royalists as well as Engagers. If the Kirk as a body opposed it, it would probably suffer the same fate as Hamilton's enterprise in 1648. So in mid-December parliament put intense pressure on the Commission of the Kirk, shorn now of the extremist Remonstrants, to pass a set of 'Public Resolutions' which countenanced the enlisting of repentant former enemies of the Covenant to help defend the Scottish kingdom against the invading English sectaries. Parliament then promptly ordered the raising of twenty-five new regiments, and to the consternation of strict Kirkmen their colonels not only included former Engagers but royalists who had taken part in the Start and were not repentant at all. This aroused a series of protests during late December and January, not only from hard-line Remonstrants but from a wider range of presbyteries, though still mainly in the south-west. The majority of more moderate ministers, however, were patriots enough to accept that the struggle had become primarily a national one, and that strict religious objectives must yield priority for a time to the prime necessity of driving out the English. They therefore supported the Resolutions, and the rift in the Kirk between Resolutioners and Protesters was to last right through the 1650s.

Cromwell and Owen scored some notable successes in their campaign of persuasion against the bigotry of Scottish Presbyterianism. Two influential members of the Committee of Estates, Alexander Jaffray and Alexander Brodie, became converts to Independency. Another who was shaken by doubts as to the worth of the king's cause, and perhaps also the authoritarian claims of the Kirk, was Walter Dundas, governor of Edinburgh Castle. Cromwell could not tolerate a hostile garrison in the capital indefinitely, but an attempt to mine the castle had run up against solid rock. Cromwell summoned it on 12 December, and it took only a brief bombardment to make Dundas sue for terms. He formally surrendered on the 24th.

Charles himself was now really benefiting from the recent changes in the Scottish political scene. The order banning the English royalists from his entourage was rescinded, and those of them who had been lying low in Scotland since the summer rejoined him. He attended every meeting of the parliament and the Committee of Estates, and he was not shy about making his wishes known to them. On New Year's Day 1651 he was at last crowned King of Scotland in the little church at Scone. The hereditary Earl Marischal, a royalist, escorted him; Loudoun, the Chancellor, proffered him the crown, and Loudoun's brother Argyll, the most powerful man in Scotland, placed it upon his head. He had to subscribe the Covenants once more and declare them sacred, and he did so with a convincing show of zeal, foreseeing no doubt that whether he won or lost the war ahead there was little chance that he would be forced to uphold them for long. Not long after, Argyll pressed a proposal that he should marry his daughter, but Charles adroitly parried it by insisting that he must obtain his mother's permission, and Henrietta Maria stymied it as neatly by stipulating that the match would have to have English approval. Argyll must have cursed his luck ten years later, for he would probably have kept his head on his shoulders if he had been the king's father-in-law.

The war marked time during the first half of 1651. The Scots had a whole new army to raise and train, but Cromwell found himself unable to take advantage of their weakness and force the pace. Defying a typically hard Scottish winter, he set out early in February to reduce Fife, but he was driven back by weather (in his own words) 'so tempestuous with wind, hail, snow and rain' that his troops could hardly find their way.[16] During the march back to

---

[16] Abbott, *Writings and Speeches of Oliver Cromwell*, II, 393.

Edinburgh he fell seriously ill, through a combination of ague, dysentery, and gallstones, brought on initially by exposure. He really thought he was close to death. His health fluctuated through March, and he attended to a certain amount of business, but his recovery was slow. He had confessed to his wife after Dunbar: 'I grow an old man, and feel infirmities of age marvellously stealing upon me'. On 12 April he began a tender letter to her with thankfulness for being 'increased in strength in my outward man', but ended it confessing: 'Truly I am not able as yet to write much. I am wearied'.[17] He had a relapse towards the end of the month, and around the middle of May his bouts of fever became so frequent that the Council of State, greatly concerned, directed him to return to England, and meanwhile sent hasting northward the two physicians who normally attended him in London. But he was too wrapped up now in the affairs of Scotland to leave his post, and on 9 June Doctors Wright and Bate felt able to report that his health was restored.

The main reason why the Scots failed to muster an army capable of taking advantage of Cromwell's temporary incapacitation lay in their continuing political divisions. Their parliament, which sat in Perth during Edinburgh's occupation, was in recess from 30 December. It should have reassembled on 5 February, but the Committee of Estates kept it prorogued until 13 March. The reason was that the full parliament reflected the strength of Argyll's party and the rising influence of the king and the royalists, whereas the Committee of Estates, which was elected by all four estates in the parliament, was dominated by the Kirk party. During its brief session in March parliament appointed a committee for managing the affairs of the army on which royalists were strongly represented, but when it adjourned, and as usual elected a new Committee of Estates to carry on the government until it met again, the votes of the clergy, lairds, and burgesses gave it the same Kirk-party complexion as the last. And like the last, this new Committee of Estates prevented parliament from reconvening on the appointed date, 17 April, and held it prorogued until 23 May. Again like the last, it strove to assert its authority over the raising of the army, with predictably adverse effects on recruitment. It tried in particular to reactivate the unrepealed Acts of Classes of 1646 and 1649, which had classified the royalists and (in 1649) the Engagers according to the degree of their 'delinquency', and disqualified them correspondingly from political and and military employment. It is doubtful whether Leslie had as many as 10,000 men at Stirling by the middle of May, and he was having great difficulty in feeding even them. Cromwell, reinforced, would soon outnumber him comfortably. On 4 June, however, parliament formally repealed the Acts of Classes, though it required those with a royalist past to sign a band (or bond), giving certain pledges demanded by the Kirk before they were appointed to offices or commands.

[17] Ibid., pp. 329, 404–5.

Cromwell took the field at the end of June, intent on bringing Leslie to battle. First, however, he resumed his attempt to gain control of Fife, 'the breadbasket of Scotland', which he had had to abandon in February. He now made use of fifty flat-bottomed boats, which he had then ordered to be built, in order to transport 4,000 men under Major-General Overton (as he now was) across the Firth of Forth, with orders to secure and fortify the peninsula between that water and the Firth of Tay. Leslie, whose immediate aim was to protect Stirling, had taken up a strong defensive position at Torwood, six miles down the Stirling–Edinburgh road. To distract attention from Overton's operation, Cromwell marched against Leslie and took up battle stations opposite his defences, challenging him to come out and fight. When that failed to draw him, Cromwell moved west to Glasgow and conducted forays into the territory in which the Scots were busy recruiting. This brought Leslie westward to Kilsyth on 13 July, and focused his whole attention on Cromwell during the next week, while the flatboats ferried the English forces over the Forth to North Queensferry. Cromwell entrusted the operation to Lambert, now promoted to Lieutenant-General. Leslie heard of it just too late, but sent Major-General Holborne with over 4,000 men to oppose it. Lambert immediately forced a battle at Inverkeithing, only a mile or so from where he had just landed. After some preliminary skirmishing the battle proper lasted just a quarter of an hour, and for the Scots it was an utter rout. Their cavalry were put to flight and their infantry, mostly Highland clansmen, were cut down where they stood. About 2,000 men were killed and 1,400 captured; perhaps 1,000 got back to Stirling.[18]

Cromwell thereupon brought his own forces back to Edinburgh and Leith, and then transported the greater part of them into Fife. He next marched not against Stirling, Leslie's headquarters, but against Perth, the current seat of Scottish government, far to the north-west. After Inverkeithing Leslie's demoralized men were deserting in droves, and Cromwell was deliberately leaving the way open for them to invade England. Confident now of complete military superiority, he was content to take the risk of fighting the decisive battle on English soil. Charles and Leslie realized that for them the risk was even greater. Argyll and Loudoun thought that invasion would be madness, and washed their hands of it. But Charles feared that if he stayed in Scotland and suffered military defeat there, as was now almost inevitable, he would become the prisoner of the Kirk party again. So he and his army set off southward from Stirling on 31 July, two days before Perth surrendered to Cromwell, as usual on generous terms. He and Leslie had little more than 12,000 men with them, and they were so short of firearms that fifty or sixty

---

[18] John D. Grainger, *Cromwell against the Scots: The Last Anglo-Scottish War, 1650–1652* (East Linton, 1997), p. 125.

archers had to make up the strength of each foot regiment. They would only have any chance of success against the military power of the Commonwealth if the English royalists rose in large numbers to support them; and the main reason why Charles invaded England was that once he had called them to arms, as he was bound to do, he could not in honour do anything else. But their response was all too disappointing, and the Commonwealth's local defences never showed any sign of cracking. Leslie led his army on long, rapid marches, in time to summon Carlisle on 6 August, but that well fortified city kept its gates shut against him. Scarcely any English came in to him during his progress through Cumberland and Westmorland.

One reason why the king found so little support lay in the northerners' detestation of Scotsmen, whose burdensome presence they had suffered twice in the last decade. To the countryfolk, they were alien, ill-disciplined plunderers. As for the gentry, most would want better expectations than Charles could offer before they exposed their estates for a third time to sequestration or confiscation. If the monarchy could have been magically restored on the basis of an all-round amnesty and constitutional guarantees against any repetition of the abuses of the 1630s, it would have received a wide welcome. But the reinstatement of an untried and obviously opportunist king on the back of a Scottish army, with the Covenant and rigid Presbyterianism as part of the package and no convincing assurance that the Long Parliament's constitutional gains would be confirmed—that was a prospect with little appeal.

A further reason why the royalist response was feeble was that good intelligence by the Commonwealth broke its back. There had been a premature attempt at insurrection in Norfolk in December 1650, small in scale and easily suppressed without a fight. Fiasco though it was, it alerted the Council of State to a flimsy network of royalist conspiracy over a much wider area of the country. The region of greatest danger lay in Lancashire and Cheshire, where the king's supporters were taking their directions from the Earl of Derby, then on the Isle of Man. But one of them, Isaac Berkenhead, was captured in March as he embarked for the island, and his disclosures under interrogation set the council on the track of Thomas Coke, the son of Charles I's Secretary of State, who had come over from Holland in the previous June to help organize royalist resistance. Berkenhead and Coke saved their lives by pouring out all they knew, and a string of arrests followed in Lancashire, Yorkshire, Worcestershire, Gloucestershire, Hampshire, Kent, and London. Derby did manage to raise about 1,500 men in Lancashire and Man to support the invasion, but before they could join it Colonel Robert Lilburne put them to rout at Wigan on 25 August, killing many and taking 400 prisoners. The contingents of royalists who succeeded in joining the king's army were numbered in scores rather than hundreds, and the largest, sixty horse under Shrewsbury's son Lord Talbot, did so only after it arrived in Worcester. This puny contribution makes it seriously misleading to describe the campaigns of 1650–1 as the Third Civil War, as has become the fashion in some quarters. This was essentially a war between the Scots, or at least such of them as obeyed the Scottish parliament, and the English Commonwealth.

Returning to the early days of the invasion, the counter-measures taken by both Cromwell and the Council of State were swift, effective, and cool-headed. Cromwell left Monck, recently promoted to lieutenant-general, with over 5,000 men to keep Scotland quiet and continue her military subjugation. He sent Harrison with not far short of 4,000 horse and dragoons to harass the royal army's eastern flank, and Lambert with a similar force to worry its rear. Both men moved swiftly; Harrison's brigade was in Newcastle by 5 August, the day the Scots crossed the border, and Lambert's in Penrith on the 9th. Cromwell had to move more slowly with his main body of about 10,000 men, since most of them were infantry, but he rode somewhat ahead of them and reached the Tyne by the 12th. He did not have to worry about Yorkshire, for Fairfax, who was to raise the county for Charles II in 1660, now emerged briefly from his retirement to secure it against the king, while the county committee set about raising 2,400 foot. When Cromwell reached Yorkshire Fairfax met him, and rode for three miles in his coach. What would one give to have overheard their conversation! But the Council of State was not relying only on local initiatives. It swiftly concentrated the regular troops outside Cromwell's immediate command, together with the trained bands and many newly raised additional militia, to cover the danger-spots in case the king's forces should break through into southern England. Four great musters were held late in August in Northampton, Gloucester, Reading, and Barnet, while on the 25th the trained bands of London, Westminster, and the inner suburbs paraded 14,000 men for the Speaker and members of parliament to review. The cost, coming on top of that of conquering and garrisoning Ireland, was very heavy. The monthly assessment rose to a record £157,096, which meant that without counting the excise or the income from sequestered estates the Rump was raising by direct taxation more than three times the crown's total revenue from all sources twenty years earlier. But the government was obeyed, and by the council's own account 'very cheerfully'. The picture presented in the summer of 1651 is not one of an oppressed nation groaning to restore its rightful king.

While Charles's Scottish army marched towards its doom, Monck was making the most of his opportunities in Scotland. He battered Stirling Castle into surrender on 14 August, by which time a force under Colonel Okey had put a stop to all resistance and recruiting in the west. The Committee of Estates, or rather those members of it who were still active, had taken refuge in Alyth, but Monck sent Colonel Matthew Alured there with a detachment of cavalry and they were all taken prisoner. St Andrews finally submitted at the end of August, and Monck stormed Dundee, the last significant Scottish stronghold, on 1 September. Before Charles's invading army was brought to battle and destruction, Monck and his lieutenants had secured all of Scotland south of a line drawn through Perth, except for the isolated strongholds of Bass Rock and Dumbarton Castle.

Harrison and Lambert shadowed the Scottish army all the way to Worcester, which it reached on 22 August. On the way the king summoned Shrewsbury, but its governor pointedly addressed his defiant reply to 'the commander-in-chief of the Scottish army'.[19] Charles had not wanted to stay in Worcester, but his weary soldiers needed rest, for since leaving Stirling they had marched 330 miles in three weeks and a day. He also probably reckoned that Worcester, with its Civil War fortifications and its rivers as additional defences, was the safest place in which to await reinforcements from the friendly territory of Wales, the Marches, and the West Country, which might yet show a better response than the north-west had done. But what he hoped would be a huge muster of his west Midlands supporters on Pitchcroft Meadow on the 26th brought in disappointingly few of the gentry and a derisory number of their tenants and followers—perhaps only two hundred.[20]

Meanwhile his opponents were closing in on him. Lambert and Harrison joined forces between Preston and Blackburn on 13 August, and two days later they collected an infantry contingent, in the shape of the Cheshire and Staffordshire militia, to balance their predominantly cavalry force. This was at Warrington Bridge, and they were very soon engaged in defending it against an assault by the royalist army, bravely led by the king himself. The Cheshire foot also fought bravely for over an hour and a half before Lambert wisely decided not to offer battle at a site where cavalry could not make their weight felt. His and Harrison's forces totalled slightly over 12,000 men, which was about the strength of the king's army at this stage, but the opportunity to engage the latter at overwhelming advantage was fast approaching. Lambert and Harrison made their rendezvous with Cromwell at Warwick on the 24th, and a few days later Cromwell was reinforced, at Evesham, by the trained bands of Essex and Suffolk. He now had an army of 31,000, not counting several thousand local levies. He could afford to take his time, and he did so. Some writers have surmised that he spun it out until 3 September because that was the anniversary of his triumph at Worcester, but this is profoundly unlikely. There is a world of difference between his deep belief in divine providence and the sort of superstition that sets its course by 'lucky

---

[19] John D. Grainger, *Cromwell against the Scots: The Last Anglo-Scottish War*, p. 104–7.

[20] Regarding the numbers of English royalists who joined the king's army there is a large discrepancy between Grainger in *Cromwell against the Scots* and Gentles in *New Model Army*. Grainger's much larger estimates derive mainly from royalist sources, with their natural tendency to overstate; I believe those of Gentles to be near the mark.

days'. He was strong enough to divide his army without either part of it being outnumbered if it had to fight on its own, but he had to take Worcester's defences seriously, for they were strenuously improved and extended during the twelve days between the royalists' arrival and the battle, and the rivers Severn and Teme complicated his problem. His plan was to attack the city from two sides simultaneously, and to draw the enemy into the open—a plan which involved two bridges of boats, one for each river. Their preparation took time, because they needed to be piloted into place and then spanned with planks just at the right moment for the cavalry to ride across them. Even with his great numerical superiority, an attack on an army protected as the king's was by man-made and natural defences ran the risk of heavy losses, and the most consistent characteristic of all Cromwell's campaigns is his care for his soldiers' lives and his pride in keeping casualties to a minimum.

He struck when he was ready, and he struck surely, though the day was not without its dangers. It was the longest and most complex of all his battles, fought in several stages and raging on several sites, and it lasted from early afternoon until after nightfall. In his own words, written that same night when he was 'so weary [as] scarce able to write', it was 'as stiff a contest, for four or five hours, as ever I have seen'.[21] He himself led his men across the bridge of boats over the Severn in the initial attack, timed to coincide with that of Fleetwood's brigade over the Teme, upon the Scots' position between the two rivers, and he was in the thick of the fighting at more than one later stage of the battle. The Scots and their English auxiliaries fought skilfully, as well as with the courage born of desperation, and Charles himself risked his life time and time again in encouraging them at the heart of the action. The course of the battle defies brief summary, but apart from one temporary setback its outcome was never in real doubt. Cromwell did not want it to be a bloodbath, and when the Scots were clearly facing defeat he rode round in front of their infantry lines at considerable personal risk, offering them quarter. They replied only with musket-fire. The battle was fully decided by 8 p.m., but the rounding up of prisoners and the slaughter of fugitives went on until after midnight. When they were counted the next day, the dead in and around the city numbered well over 2,000, and somewhere between 6,000 and 7,000 prisoners were taken. About 3,000 cavalry escaped from the field, but many did not get home, because they had to run the gauntlet of highly hostile countryfolk and townsmen all the way back to the border. Cromwell put the losses of all the Commonwealth's forces in the battle at under 200 killed, a crowning achievement in his record of low casualties.

The only royalist leaders who got clean away were the king himself, Buckingham, and Wilmot. The Scottish prisoners included the second Duke of

---

[21] Abbott, *Writings and Speeches of Oliver Cromwell*, II, 461.

Hamilton, who died of gangrene within a few days, Leslie, and Lauderdale, who languished in prison until the Restoration, and Middleton, who escaped from the Tower. The Earl of Derby was captured, though not until he had seen the king into the safe hands of the catholic Penderell family, tenant farmers in Wiltshire. Derby was court-martialled and executed for treason, even though Cromwell strongly supported his appeal to parliament against his sentence. As for Charles's own escape, the story of it became a legend, and as is the way with legends it accreted a wealth of dubious detail, some of it contributed by Charles himself, who never tired of recounting it. He was passed from household to household, generally disguised as a tenant farmer's son, and the catholic community played a crucial part in hiding and protecting him. Although he was frequently recognized and had the very large sum of £1,000 on his head, no one betrayed him in all the six weeks between the battle and his sailing from Shoreham to Fécamp in mid-October. And he really did spend a night amid the branches of that royal oak from which countless English pubs have taken their name.

Soon after he reached France the Duke of Orleans, the French king's uncle, asked him if the rumour was true that he intended to return to Scotland. 'I had rather have been hanged first', he replied, and he never in his life set foot in his northern kingdom again. His reaction was unkind to the thousands of Scots who had died for him, but it is understandable, and in any case there was soon nowhere in the country to which he could have returned. Monck's impressive progress in the absence of Leslie's army still left a vast area of northern Scotland unaccounted for, but the obstacles to tapping the reserves of royalist sentiment in the Highlands were formidable. The Earl of Crawford-Lindsay, whom Charles had designated as his commander-in-chief in Scotland, had been captured at Alyth, together with Leven and the Earl Marischal. Huntly, the greatest royalist magnate, had men under arms in his Gordon territory, but Aberdeen, the city at its heart, had no stomach for war now, and when Monck sent Okey with a body of cavalry to secure it, its council soon submitted. Its distinguished provost, Alexander Jaffray, was already one of Cromwell's and Owen's converts. The Highland nobility were never united. Huntly, always a firm royalist, never collaborated easily with Balcarres, who sat on the Committee of Estates and had been a Covenanter. Argyll continued to sulk at Inverary, and his brother Loudoun, who as Chancellor was the senior officer of state in the kingdom, remained a thorough Kirkman.

The difficulty after Worcester was to assemble any body or council that could speak as the government of Scotland, and to get it, if assembled, to speak with a single voice. Of the members of the Committee of Estates who had not been captured at Alyth, Loudoun managed to bring together seven nobles (including Argyll), three lairds, and three burgesses at Killin at the foot of Loch Tay on 10 September, but Balcarres refused to attend. Balcarres did agree, however, to bring his clansmen to a general gathering of the Highland forces, including Huntly's, at Dunkeld on the 24th, but in the event no such rendezvous took place. The Committee of Estates met again at Dumbarton on the 25th, but because the English forces in Glasgow were uncomfortably close it moved on first to Rosneath and then in mid-October to Rothesay on the island of Bute. By this time it lacked a quorum, but it nevertheless ordered that the parliament, which had been scheduled to reassemble at Stirling in November, should meet instead at Finlarig, near Killin. Argyll saw the hopelessness of it all and wrote to Monck on 15 October to propose peace negotiations. These did not materialize for some time, but when Loudoun went to Finlarig to preside over the parliament he found there just three nobles and no lairds or burgesses at all. The government of Covenanting Scotland had disintegrated, for even the remnant of the Committee of Estates faded away. Huntly signed articles of surrender later in the month, and Balcarres on 3 December. Meanwhile Monck and his subordinates encouraged the resumption of normal economic life in the Lowlands, including fishing, and most Scots welcomed the relief from the long rigours of war. The harvest had been poor, and the feeding of the forces and in places the scarcity of labour had created food shortages.

When the Rump first launched its pre-emptive strike in 1650 it had not intended to annexe the Scottish kingdom, but before the end of 1651 it had to deal with something like a political vacuum there. Amid the rejoicings after Worcester it gave a single reading to 'an Act asserting the title of England to Scotland', but the bill proceeded no further. Within a month the plan of annexation was quickly dropped, and the very different concept of a union substituted: Scotland was to be incorporated into one commonwealth with England. It is likely that Cromwell himself was mainly responsible for this change of policy. He was given a triumphal entry when he returned to London on 12 September, and the great cheering crowds that lined the streets testify to the very real popularity of his victory. Some republicans feared that it would give him notions about making himself head of state, perhaps even aiming at the crown, but there was (and is) no evidence of this. Describing his conduct amid all this celebration, Whitelocke wrote in his diary: 'He was affable and humble in his carriage, and in his discourses about the business of Scotland and of Worcester, he would seldom mention any thing of himself, but the gallantry of the officers and soldiers, and gave (as was due) all the glory of the action unto God.'[22] Modest though he was, however, there was little that the parliament could refuse him at this juncture, and we have the testimony of John Swinton, another Scottish convert of Cromwell's who had been with his army at Worcester, had travelled up to London with him and

---

[22] *The Diary of Bulstrode Whitelocke 1605–1675*, ed. Ruth Spalding (Oxford, 1990), p. 271.

returned home later in the month, that Cromwell opposed the many in England who favoured 'declaring this a conquest' and was 'for making it one nation'.[23] A declaration outlining the terms for a union of Scotland with England was prepared by the Council of State (on which Cromwell had of course resumed his place) during early October, laid before parliament on the 23rd, and agreed to with minor amendments after two days' debate. In it was enshrined the Cromwellian principle that England had no quarrel with the Scottish nation at large but only with those who had made war on her in the past four years. It promised in particular that the Scots should enjoy the same liberty of conscience in religion as the English. The precise terms of the union were to be defined after consultation between commissioners of the parliament and elected Scottish representatives; meanwhile, in January 1652, the Rump dispatched eight commissioners 'for the managing of the civil government'. The civilians among them included Vane and St John, the soldiers Lambert and Monck. They were given large powers and they were backed by the English army in Scotland, but they genuinely tried to persuade the Scottish people of the benefits of a union and to win their unforced assent to it. They naturally faced a considerable amount of opposition to it, not only from Scots who prized their national independence or were unwilling to renounce their king, but most of all from the clergy, who stridently denounced the very idea of religious toleration. They could not ignore the facts that a large part of the Scottish nation had recently been at war with England and that resistance was by no means over, but the process of consultation that they set in train was honestly aimed at winning agreement to benefits that they believed to be real, and was not a mere cover-up for a cynical process of subordinating Scottish interests to English.[24] How far they succeeded, and what shape the union eventually took, will be described in a later chapter. Meanwhile our account of the Commonwealth at war remains seriously incomplete, since it has so far considered only the campaigns fought on land.

[23]  F. D. Dow, *Cromwellian Scotland 1651–1660* (Edinburgh, 1979), pp. 30–1.
[24]  Dow writes that 'what was in theory to be a political merger . . . was in fact a take-over bid by the English', and that 'the period from January 1652 to April 1653 was one of unremitting and successful efforts by the English to subordinate the Scots to their will' (*Cromwellian Scotland*, p. 35). I think this is an overstatement, though I am greatly indebted to Dr Dow's scholarly study.

# SIXTEEN

# The Commonwealth in Crisis

THE navy had a vital role to play in the defence of the Commonwealth, but it was not in a healthy state when the republic was first established. The second Civil War and the execution of the king had, as has been seen, alienated many captains and crews. In addition to those who openly declared for Charles II and joined Prince Rupert, many others, while stopping short of changing sides, felt a strong dislike for the New Model Army and for sectaries and radicals in general. Warwick, the Lord Admiral, had been openly opposed to the king's trial and the abolition of the Lords; moreover he was 61, old for his age and in poor health. He had to be removed, but it was scarcely less necessary to get rid of the excessive personal authority and patronage that attached to his office. The navy needed to be brought more closely under the control of parliament and the council, so before discharging Warwick the Rump enlarged the powers of its Navy Committee. It dealt with Warwick simply by repealing, in February 1649, the act that had appointed him Lord Admiral, and then leaving that office in abeyance. The actual command of the fleet was entrusted jointly to three Generals at Sea, Robert Blake, Richard Deane, and Edward Popham, all former army colonels. Warwick had served the parliament well in his time and he suffered no disgrace, though he was unable to save his brother Holland, who had fought for the king in 1648, from execution. Warwick withdrew from public life for some years, but he was to support Cromwell as Lord Protector. He carried the sword at his second investiture in 1657, and a grandson of his was to marry Cromwell's youngest daughter.

The appointment of the Generals at Sea was part of a policy of bringing the navy into line with the army in its relations with the state, and of encouraging an interchange of personnel between the two services. Very soon after the Council of State was established it set up an Admiralty Committee, which assumed most of the administrative functions that had previously been under the Lord Admiral's authority. The dominant figure on it was Sir Henry Vane, who had been Treasurer of the Navy since 1642, but Cromwell's brother-in-law Valentine Walton was scarcely less influential. Since the council was elected annually there was a new Admiralty Committee each year, but Vane and Walton were regularly reappointed. Walton was a link with the parliament's Navy Committee, whose other most active members were his fellow-regicides Miles Corbet and Gregory Clement. The function of both committees was of course continuous, but to tackle the urgent immediate task of purging the disaffected elements from the officer corps, the ships' crews, the dockyards, and Trinity House, the Rump appointed sixteen 'Regulators', even before it established the Council of State, indeed even before the king was sentenced. They were sometimes known as the Committee of Merchants, for most of them were big men in the City, independents in their politics, and trading mainly with the colonies and other distant markets. That gave them a stronger interest in naval protection, and they formed a distinct interest from that of the Merchant Adventurers and other older chartered companies, whose political orientation tended to be presbyterian if not royalist. The Regulators tempered genuine zeal with discretion, and their recommendations were subject to parliamentary approval. Those whom they succeeded in removing included the Master of Trinity House, many ship's captains, and several of the Navy Commissioners, those very senior salaried officials who were responsible for the dockyards and the manning and fitting out of all warships. The Regulators were lenient towards those master-craftsmen in the dockyards and warrant officers, boatswains and gunners on board ship whose conduct had been suspect but who were now ready to serve the Commonwealth faithfully, but from officers and officials in higher positions they required unquestionable loyalty. They acted swiftly, and when they had done their work two-thirds of the captains of men-of-war were relatively new to their commands, having been appointed since 1647. A fair number of them were experienced masters of merchant ships rather than promoted naval officers. The Rump itself enacted a very rigorous disciplinary code for the punishment of crimes committed at sea, but this was generally held *in terrorem* rather strictly enforced. Those who reformed the navy in 1649 were not all above the suspicion of feathering their own nests, but on the whole they did an effective job. When Rupert issued a declaration in March, offering good employment to all ships and seamen who would join him, only one little sixth-rate responded, and she was soon recaptured.[1]

Even more impressive than the rapid transformation of a widely disaffected navy into an arm wholly loyal to the Commonwealth was the increase in its size. Within three years it was almost doubled. Twenty new warships were built between the spring of 1649 and the end of 1651, and twenty-five more were added to the strength either by capture or purchase. Of the latter, many were armed merchantmen suitable for conversion. The government's administrative structure, what with the overlapping and sometimes conflicting

[1] Capp, *Cromwell's Navy*, ch. 3; Aylmer, *State's Servants*, pp. 40–1 and *passim*.

authorities of the Navy Commissioners, the parliamentary Navy Committee, the conciliar Admiralty Committee and for a time the Regulators, may look like a recipe for confusion, and the placing of land warriors in command over ship's captains an invitation to disaster. But the navy was in fact on the brink of a heroic chapter in its history, and none of the Generals at Sea proved inadequate. Robert Blake, whose name is one of the greatest in British naval annals, was celebrated in 1649 only as the heroic defender of Lyme and Taunton, and he is not known ever to have gone to sea before that year, though as a member of a mercantile family in Bridgwater he may already have had some knowledge of shipping. His case is not unique; Monck, whose previous experience was wholly military, was soon to distinguish himself as a naval commander, and after the Restoration he fought the Dutch again at sea alongside his fellow-admiral Prince Rupert.

The role of the fleet was secondary to that of the armies during the first three years of the Commonwealth's existence, but it was nevertheless vital. It had to support, supply, and protect the land campaigns against the Irish and the Scots. The navy also had to combat the many royalist privateers that were preying on English merchant ships, mainly from French bases. Since Charles II's mother was a daughter of the royal house, France was ready at first to give him all possible support short of actual war, and did indeed wage an undeclared war against English shipping in the Channel and the Mediterranean. The losses became so heavy and the participation of the French navy so blatant that in 1650 the Rump authorized its Generals at Sea to attack French warships as well as merchantmen. English naval power commanded increasing respect, and before very long drove first Spain and then France to give formal recognition to the Commonwealth.

Long before that, however, the navy's first task was to deal with the flotilla of warships that Rupert commanded, and had brought to Kinsale to facilitate a possible landing by Charles II. Rupert was soon collaborating with a score or so of Irish privateers in preying upon English shipping, but he was not allowed to do so for long. Blake, Popham, and Deane joined forces in May 1649 with such ships as they had ready, and they soon had Rupert blockaded in Kinsale. The harbour, however, was too strongly fortified for a direct assault by sea, and for some months there was stalemate. But Cromwell's rapid progress laid Rupert's ships open to an attack from the land, and the threat became acute when Cork, only a dozen miles away, declared for the parliament on 16 October. Then in the next few days a heavy storm forced the blockading ships out to sea, and Rupert seized the chance to slip away with the seven men-of-war that he had manned and ready, along with four small frigates. He made first for northern Spain, but the authorities there had no desire to provoke the English Commonwealth and they gave him a cold reception. Spain still had the revolts of Catalonia and Portugal on her hands, as well as the long, exhausting war with France. King John of Portugal, however, was prepared to give the little squadron a welcome, and it wintered in the Tagus, taking toll of the English shipping that cruised along the Portuguese coast to and from the Straits of Gibraltar.

Blake was on Rupert's track by March 1650, and after sending a polite note to King John he sailed boldly into the Tagus to engage the royalist ships. But the forts on shore opened fire on him, and the king refused all his requests to hand Rupert's vessels over to him, or to let him attack them where they lay, or to order both fleets to leave. A period of stalemate ensued, with the two of them anchored a couple of miles apart, and their crews skirmishing at intervals ashore. But Portugal could not go on protecting Rupert indefinitely, because she depended on hiring English merchantmen to maintain her vital trade with Brazil, and Blake put the pressure on by capturing nine of them that were sailing under contract with the outward-bound Brazil fleet. Just after that Popham joined him with strong reinforcements, and it was increasingly clear that the Commonwealth was ready to risk war with Portugal in order to destroy Rupert's flotilla. In September Blake attacked the homeward-bound Brazil fleet as it entered the Tagus, sinking one ship and capturing seven. That was enough to make King John press Rupert to depart, and the prince shortly took his six remaining ships through the Straits into Spanish Mediterranean waters. There they took some prizes and forced their way into Spanish harbours to burn English merchantmen, but Blake caught up with them in November. One of them surrendered, five were driven ashore and wrecked or burnt; the offended Spanish authorities left them at Blake's mercy. Rupert himself and Maurice, his vice-admiral, had a lucky escape from Blake's attack because they had sailed off on their own to chase a prize, and they got away to Toulon. With French help Rupert managed to put together another tiny flotilla, which spent an adventurous two years in ranging down the west African coast and across to the Caribbean, where Barbados and other islands still remained loyal to the king. But he could inflict no serious damage on the Commonwealth's increasingly powerful navy or on the trade routes that it protected, and after he had lost all his ships save one he limped back to France in 1653.

The main task of the Generals at Sea during 1651 was to reduce the still resisting offshore islands, namely Jersey, the Scilly Isles, and Man, which the royalists were using as bases for privateering. The Scillies, where Sir John Grenville was governor, were the first to be tackled, and the task was initially entrusted to a small amphibious force under Sir George Ayscue, the Admiral of the Irish seas. But the situation became more serious when it was learnt that Admiral Tromp and his Dutch fleet were sailing against the islands. Grenville had had the folly to let his privateers take Dutch prizes and prisoners, despite the king's need to keep on the right side of the States-General—all the stronger now, since William II had died in 1650. There was a real danger that the Dutch might take possession of the Scillies and use them as a privateering base of their own, so Blake was sent to join Ayscue and make sure that the Commonwealth secured them first. It was not an easy operation, for Grenville had excellent defences, both natural and man-made, and he put up a stout resistance. But Blake took Tresco by assault with the loss of only four men, and after that Grenville was persuaded to surrender St Mary's Castle on honourable terms.

Blake's main responsibility during the summer of 1651 was to prevent any supplies or reinforcements from reaching the king and the Scots from overseas during their advance to Worcester, but after their defeat he could turn his attention to the Channel Islands. Late in the season though it was, he sailed from Weymouth with thirteen warships and numerous transports carrying about 2,000 soldiers. Sir George Carteret, the governor of Jessey, had slightly more men, but although he was stout of heart his foot soldiers were not. A major problem, however, was that Blake's transports drew too much water to put his troops directly ashore on those difficult coasts. He solved it by sending his smaller vessels—victuallers, probably—ahead, building bridges to them from his larger transports, and then getting his infantry swiftly on land under the protection of his well-armed seamen. Most of Carteret's foot fled before them, and though a few of his horse and dragoons fought bravely he was forced to take refuge in the island fortress of Elizabeth Castle. Colonel Heane completed the conquest of Jersey, and when Carteret surrendered on 12 December all resistance in the Channel Islands ceased.

The Isle of Man was the Earl of Derby's base, and after his capture in the Worcester campaign it was held by his French wife Charlotte de la Tremoille, who had already made a reputation as the gallant defender of Lathom House. Now, however, she tried to negotiate the surrender of the island in return for her husband's life, but in spite of Cromwell's pleas that he should be spared the Rump insisted that he should suffer death as a traitor. A force under Colonels Duckenfield and Birch, the governors of Chester and Liverpool, reduced the remaining strongholds in Man by the end of the year, an unnecessary little campaign if ever there was one.[2]

Meanwhile Ayscue was sent across the Atlantic with a small military force to prevent Rupert from setting up another nest of pirates in Barbados. Lord Willoughby, the royalist governor of the island, raised 6,000 men to defend it, but on receiving the news of Worcester he negotiated its surrender and was granted generous terms. The submission of the other West Indian islands soon followed. Another small amphibious force secured that of Virginia in March 1652 and of Maryland not long afterwards. There was now no patch

---

[2] For all these various operations see Capp, *Cromwell's Navy*, pp. 60–9.

of British soil in the world where a royalist could take refuge, and the naval strength of the Commonwealth was making all the European powers chary of offending it. By this time none of them could match its fleet, and none could boast a finer admiral than Blake. He was now in full command, for his friend Popham had died in 1651 and Deane had been made commander-in-chief of the army in Scotland.

If the surrender of Maryland marked the final tremor of the English Civil Wars, only weeks separated it from the Commonwealth's first war with a foreign power, which began with a clash between Blake and Tromp in the Downs. It may seem strange that the regicide state took up arms against its fellow-republicans and fellow-Calvinists in the United Provinces, rather than against either of the great catholic monarchies that had denounced the execution of Charles I so loudly. But Spain with Catalonia and Portugal still in revolt, risings in Sicily and Naples only recently suppressed, and the long war with France still on her hands, could not afford to add England to her open enemies. France had been more belligerent; her conflict with England at sea and her sympathy with the cause of Charles II as Henry IV's grandson had brought her to the brink of war in 1650. But from October of that year until 1653 she was locked in her own civil war, the second Fronde, as well as having Spain's Army of Flanders on her north-west frontier. Cardinal Mazarin was a realist, and he increasingly saw the advantages to be drawn from the English Commonwealth's friendship. It would not be long before France and Spain were competing for it.

There has been much argument as to whether the Dutch war came about mainly through long-term commercial and colonial rivalries or through more immediate political causes.[3] But the two explanations are not mutually incompatible, and both factors contributed. To take the economic ones first, Dutch maritime supremacy had rested since James I's time on two main foundations, their control over the trade in corn, timber, and other ship-building materials produced by the countries surrounding the Baltic Sea, and their ability to carry the goods traded between foreign nations at a cost that those countries' native merchants could not compete with. This carrying trade in north European waters was conducted in unarmed or lightly armed vessels called fluits (flutes or flyboats in English), which were far cheaper to build and man than England's typical armed merchantmen. By 1650 the total tonnage of Dutch shipping probably exceeded England's by at least five to one, and

---

[3] On the causes and issues of the Dutch war Charles Wilson, *Profit and Power: A Study of England and the Dutch Wars* (1957) retains great authority, especially on the economic factors, but Steven C. A. Pincus in *Protestantism and Patriotism: Ideologies and the Making of English Foreign Policy, 1650–1668* (Cambridge, 1996) has argued persuasively (if a little excessively) for greater importance to be given to political and religious motivation. See also Worden, *Rump Parliament*, ch. 14, and for source material *Letters and Papers Relating to the First Dutch War*, ed. S. R. Gardiner and C. T. Atkinson (5 vols., Navy Record Society, 1898–1912).

Dutch dominance of the Baltic trade was even more disproportionate. Dutch mastery of the carrying trade had steadily increased during the rapid colonial expansion of the last half-century; English merchantmen struggled against its competition not only in northern and Mediterranean waters but along the coasts of Africa and America, in the Caribbean and in all the seas plied by the East India Company. Dutch carriers depended for protection on the Dutch navy, which when Blake first put to sea was the largest in Europe, though the Commonwealth's great effort to enlarge and improve its own was altering the balance.

A source of grievance and controversy nearly as old as the century was the United Provinces' 'Great Fishery', which took most of its catches off the coasts of Britain, from the mouth of the Thames right up to the Shetlands. It is reckoned to have given employment to about a thousand fishing-boats and nearly half a million people on sea and shore. There had been more than one attempt to organize a government-supported Anglo-Scottish fishery, but each had foundered in face of Dutch superiority in organization, finance, and technical proficiency. England's greatest single concern, however, was to protect her cloth trade, which still heavily dominated her exports as well as her domestic industry. The old cross-Channel trade in traditional heavy broadcloths was still in the exclusive hands of the Merchant Adventurers Company, but these materials, whose market was increasingly under challenge from newer, lighter, more colourful fabrics, were sold 'in the white', to be dyed and finished by Dutch craftsmen, whose work contributed more than half to the value of the final product.

Commercial rivalries and resentments generated a strong current of anti-Dutch feeling in various quarters in England, but it was by no means inevitable that they would lead to war; nor was it obvious that war would be a good way of resolving them. When the Commonwealth was first established the Rump was so far from seeking a quarrel with the Dutch republic that in April 1649 it sent Dr Isaac Dorislaus, a Dutch-born lawyer in its service, on a mission to the States-General, with instructions to prepare the ground for an alliance between the two republics. But a deep rift ran through the politics of the United Provinces, so deep that it almost belied their name. On one side was the party of the Regents, the urban patriciate that governed the rich mercantile cities and was most dominant in Holland, the wealthiest of the provinces and the most powerful in the States-General. This, sometimes called the States party, was republican in sentiment, dedicated to promoting Dutch commercial interests, and generally disposed towards peace. Against it was ranged the quasi-monarchical Orangist party which supported the descendants of William of Orange, the original Stadholder and Captain-General. William II of Orange, who had succeeded to these offices in 1647, was Charles II's brother-in-law, and he nursed bellicose and expansionist aims. His strongest support came from the inland provinces, with their largely agrarian economies and their relatively strong nobilities, and from Zeeland. Unlike the Regents and the mercantile community, he had not welcomed the Peace of Westphalia in 1648, for he had hoped by continuing the war to enlarge his territory at the expense of the Spanish Netherlands. To this end he entered into secret negotiations with the French court, which remained at war with Spain, and at this stage shared his desire to see Charles II restored to his throne. He made English royalist exiles welcome, and when a group of them murdered Dorislaus in his lodgings there was suspiciously little effort to bring them to justice. Anglo-Dutch relations became very cool. But William died suddenly of smallpox in November 1650, and the political balance in the States-General shifted dramatically in the States party's favour.

The majority of the Rump was now keener than ever on a partnership with the Dutch republic as a basis for a wider protestant alliance, and in March 1651 it sent St John and Walter Strickland to the Hague with proposals aimed at averting war between the two commonwealths forever. These were for what the Council of State called a 'confederacy perpetual', but what this meant cannot be exactly known, because the envoys' secret instructions have not survived. It clearly involved, however, some permanent fusion of sovereignties and pooling of economic resources. It remains an astonishing conception, and it bespeaks a strange mixture of idealism, naivety, and arrogance in its authors. The proposals were never formally submitted, presumably because the envoys' general presentation of their drift was coldly received. To the Orangists they were obviously anathema, since they threatened the whole future of the stadholderate, and one can understand why they were quite unacceptable to the majority of the States-General. The Dutch were naturally jealous of their hard-won status as a sovereign power, which had finally won formal international recognition at Westphalia only three years earlier, and were little inclined to share their large commercial advantages, especially in the Baltic, with an up-and-coming maritime rival. Even while St John and Strickland were still at the Hague, the Dutch signed a treaty with Denmark which secured for the United Provinces, and for them alone, the privilege of paying a very favourable composition in lieu of the dues imposed on all other nations' ships when they passed through the Sound. This was seen in England as a bid to create a virtual Dutch monopoly in the indispensable naval stores produced around the Baltic shores. It has been interpreted as a deliberate death-blow to the Commonwealth's diplomatic initiative, but it more probably reflected a reluctant recognition by the States-General that there was little prospect of agreement on the terms that the English envoys sought. The States-General were certainly dismayed when St John obtained his and Strickland's recall to England, and they negotiated an extension of their stay so that they could consider a more conventional commercial and political treaty. But the two Englishmen were convinced that the Dutch were spinning out time until they saw the result of Charles II's campaign in Scotland, and it is true that the Scottish royalists were being supplied with ships and ammunition through Dutch ports.

St John and Strickland finally took their leave at the end of June, and on 9 October the Rump passed its famous Navigation Act. This has been attributed to the influence exerted upon the House by a particular group of London merchants, but though it was undoubtedly designed to serve mercantile interests the motivation behind it was at least as much political as economic. St John was plausibly reputed to be its prime mover, and he had returned home full of resentment at the way he and Strickland had been treated in Holland, where they had been the butt of many insults, as well as being (in their opinion) bamboozled by the Dutch commissioners. St John was as concerned to punish the Dutch as he was to promote English trading interests, and he had a strong tide of public opinion running on his side. The act passed smoothly. It reflected a widespread concern over the growing imbalance between imports and exports, which was causing a net outflow of bullion (or 'treasure'), and especially over the increasing extent to which England's imports, and those of her colonies too, were being carried in Dutch ships. Its chief provision was that no goods should be imported into England, Ireland, or the colonies except in English (or colonial) ships, or in ships of the countries where those goods had been grown or manufactured. As to the fisheries, no cod, herring, pilchards, or any other commonly salted fish were to be landed in England except what had been caught by English fishing-boats, and their catches must be cured in England.[4]

The act caused consternation in the Netherlands, not only because of its damage to Dutch commercial interests but because it potentially threatened a war which was bound to hit them even harder than it hit English shipping and taxpayers. They would not have let the act by itself cause a war, nor did the Rump intend that it should do so. The States-General sent a powerful embassy to England in December to try to mitigate its effects and put the two republics on course again towards a general agreement. But a growing number of clashes on the high seas were exacerbating the long-existing mutual animosity between Englishmen and Dutchmen at the popular level, and the presses in both countries were inflaming it. On the diplomatic front negotiations went well during the winter and spring, and by May the terms of an offensive and defensive alliance seemed almost to have been agreed.[5] But events at sea killed it.

The growth of friction was cumulative. In the course of the undeclared war at sea between England and France that developed from 1649 onwards,

[4] Text in Gardiner (ed.), *Constitutional Documents*, pp. 468–71.
[5] Pincus, *Protestantism and Patriotism*, ch. 4, esp. pp. 54 ff.

French warships had been sinking or capturing English merchantmen on the pretext that they were carrying contraband goods to the Spanish enemy, whether or not they were actually doing so. Consequently the Council of State in 1650 ordered its naval commanders to attack French vessels, whether men-of-war or merchantmen, and from early in 1651 English shipping in the Straits of Dover was furnished for the first time with naval convoys. English privateers were granted letters of reprisal, authorizing them to recoup the losses that England had suffered at French hands by seizing French ships and their cargoes. They increasingly executed this power against Dutch merchant ships whom they suspected of carrying French goods, and they seized not only the cargoes but the vessels and their crews. They were not always scrupulous in checking that the goods really were contraband or even French, and the Court of Admiralty found it necessary to threaten them with punishment if they went on torturing Dutch mercantile officers to make them declare cargoes to be French when they were not. The Dutch were naturally furious at such practices, and maintained that their neutral flag covered the cargoes that their merchantmen carried. That looked a plausible argument, but Dutch privateers were operating openly against English shipping from the French port of Dunkirk, some of them with commissions from Charles II.

Another irritant was the English claim to sovereignty over the 'British Seas', whereby they demanded that foreign vessels sailing them should salute English men-of-war by striking their topsails and dipping their flags. Moreover England claimed a right to stop and search any foreign ship in such seaways. The claim was not new, but the notional extent of the 'British seas' was now being extended from coastal waters into the whole Atlantic. Violent incidents arising from the claim to stop and search multiplied, in colonial seas as well as those nearer home, and public anger in both England and the Netherlands rose to match. Both governments dredged up grievances born of decades of commercial rivalry, England's being the more belligerent. The Commonwealth claimed the right to impose conditions and levy tribute on any foreigners who fished in the North Sea, and that was not the most preposterous of its demands.

What finally sparked the war was a clash off the Downs between Blake and the Dutch admiral Martin Tromp on 19 May 1652. Tromp was a fervent Orangist, and so were most of his captains; he had forty-two ships, against Blake's fifteen. These were English waters, so Blake demanded that Tromp should strike his topsail, and on his failing to do so fired several warning shots. Tromp replied by firing a broadside into Blake's flagship; he reportedly said he would strike sail if there were a king in England. A general engagement followed, which Tromp broke off at nightfall after losing two ships. The news of it left the Rump deeply divided; until then most members had been inclined to accept the treaty terms thrashed out with the Dutch commissioners, but now the majority demanded satisfaction. Public feeling in the Nether-lands was equally bellicose, and the States of Holland were almost isolated in continuing to seek a peace treaty. They sent their elderly Grand Pensionary, Adrian Pauw, to join the three Dutch envoys already in England, but his mission was hopeless. A public declaration by the Rump on 9 July explained that the war was the result of an Orangist-inspired design to subvert the Commonwealth and restore the house of Stuart, and alleged that the United Provinces had allowed their old protestant identity to become submerged by reason of state, worldly materialism, and the worship of Mammon.

Not all the Rump was in favour of war; Vane was one of the minority who opposed it to the last moment. Most prominent in the war party were the rad-icals Marten, Neville, Thomas Chaloner, and Herbert Morley, and the more moderate leaders Haselrig, Scot, and Whitelocke were in strong support. Curi-ously little is known of Cromwell's views at the time; his persistent absence from the Council of State during the crucial period of decision, despite a direct request for his attendance, suggests that he may have been going through one of his periods of heart-searching. But he seems to have been convinced that it was the Dutch who precipitated the war, and though he almost certainly regretted that the two leading protestant powers were in conflict there is no convincing evidence that he was opposed to it in principle when it was declared. Some of the most enthusiastic supporters of the war were the Fifth Monarchists and other extreme sectaries, including Harrison. They regarded the Dutch quest for world dominance in commerce as contrary to God's purpose for his people, and they saw the prevailingly moderate tone of Dutch Calvinism as akin to that of their opponents at home, the Presbyterians. They saw victory over these crea-tures of Mammon as an appropriate first stage in a career of universal conquest by the saints over the carnal kingdoms of this world.

In the country at large, reactions to the war were very mixed, and they were to fluctuate with its changing fortunes. Dislike of the Dutch was very wide-spread, and the combined impact of official propaganda, semi-official news-papers, and public preachers (especially in fast-day sermons) made its mark. But trade was hard hit by heavy losses of ships and crews sunk or captured, by the enforced conversion of merchantmen into warships, and by the press-ganging of seamen into the navy. The cost of maintaining a great fleet on a war footing, on top of garrisoning Ireland and Scotland, was huge. In Decem-ber the Rump restored the monthly assessment from £90,000 per month to the peak figure of £120,000 at which it had stood when the drain of the Scot-tish and Irish campaigns was heaviest, but that did not suffice. The war was mainly what made parliament step up the sale of the estates of selected 'delin-quents' to make up the shortfall in revenue. The process began when the lands of 73 royalists were put up for sale by an act passed in July 1651, when war first threatened, followed by another a year later when it actually broke out;

but this, which hit 29 victims, was nothing to the act of November 1652, which deprived no fewer than 678. These measures not only made the burying of old quarrels much harder, but deepened the growing animosity between parliament-men and army officers, since the confiscations in not a few cases infringed the articles of surrender that commanders had granted to royalists in the field. There had been similar clashes in the previous winter over a belated Act of Oblivion for the beaten cavaliers, which Cromwell and his fellow-officers in the House, allied for once with Marten, had sought to make as generous as possible. But Haselrig, 'that arch-enemy of delinquents',[6] managed with his various republican allies to clog it so heavily with exceptions and provisos as to frustrate its original intentions.

The first six months of the Dutch war were packed with incident, though no engagement was decisive. Late in June Blake sailed again to the Dutch herring fleet that was fishing south of the Orkneys and routed its naval escort, sinking three ships and capturing nine. That was not his only business in northern waters, for he next lay in wait off the Shetlands for the Dutch East India convoy, which was sailing round the north of Scotland because it no longer dared run the gauntlet of the Channel. While Tromp and most of his fleet were seeking Blake out, Ayscue showed how unsafe the Channel could be when on 2 July, with only nine ships, he attacked a large convoy of Dutch merchantmen. He captured six, burnt three, and drove twenty-six ashore on the Calais sands; only seven got away to safety. On the 26th Blake and Tromp came within sight of each other south of Shetland, but a fearsome north-westerly gale prevented what would have been a major sea-fight and forced both fleets to seek what safety they could. Blake found shelter in Bress Sound, and though all his ships were damaged, none sank. Tromp, however, lost at least ten wrecked on the Shetland coasts and six sunk at sea, though most of the East Indiamen eventually limped home. On his return an ungrateful States-General suspended him from his admiralship, though more because of his Orangist partisanship than because he was really to blame for his recent losses. They would soon find that they could not do without him. But in his absence the gallant Ayscue's luck did not hold. In mid-August he attacked about forty men-of-war under Admiral de Ruyter who were escorting the West India fleet of about sixty merchantmen, many of them heavily armed and very ready to join in the fight. Ayscue took something of a mauling, and he did well to lose no ships, but he was forced to retire to Plymouth for repairs, and only a sudden change of wind saved his battered vessels from being attacked by de Ruyter at their anchorage.

Blake fought two more major actions before the end of the year. On 28 September he engaged the combined fleets of Witte de With and de Ruyter off the

---

[6] Worden, *Rump Parliament*, p. 269, and for the act in general pp. 267–70.

Kentish Knock and worsted them in a hot fight, though his crews were short of victuals and showing signs of mutiny. De With too faced disaffection among his captains and seamen, and his setback was instrumental in deciding the States-General to restore Tromp to the overall command in November. Blake was further weakened by having to send twenty of his ships to the Mediterranean, leaving him with only forty-five, including some hired merchantmen. But when he heard that Tromp was escorting a huge merchant fleet through the Straits, he sailed to attack him on 10 December, even though Tromp had eighty-five men-of-war. The odds became hopeless when twenty of Blake's ships held off and declined to give battle, and after losing two more in action he was forced to fall back on Dover. It was a heavy defeat. Several of his captains, including his own brother, were subsequently sacked. Up to this action the honours in the war had been fairly even, but the year ended with the Dutch on top and in full command of the Channel. That situation was to change dramatically in 1653, but before the decisive actions of the spring and summer there were to be major political changes in England that were to be at least as important in setting the course towards peace.

One important side-effect of the Dutch war was upon the Commonwealth's so far heavily strained relation with France. Since September 1651 Spanish troops had been besieging Dunkirk, which had been part of the Spanish Netherlands until the French captured it in 1646. In September 1652 the Admiral of France sent a flotilla of six supply ships, with a guard of seven men-of-war, to help relieve it. Blake, under orders from the Council of State, fell on this convoy, capturing all but one of the warships and either destroying, capturing, or dispersing the store-ships. Loud protests came from the French government, but the Rump made it clear that if France wanted her warships back she must first formally recognize the Commonwealth. The outcome was the dispatch to Westminster of a French ambassador, Antoine de Bordeaux-Neufville, who after some shuffling fully acknowledged the present regime as the lawful government of England before the end of the year. This was not, however, the result of a single wartime incident, for Mazarin and his fellow-ministers had gradually been coming to a decision that France's interest lay in cultivating an alliance with England. The Commonwealth's reaction to Bordeaux's overtures was to be vitally affected, like its response to peace-seekers from the Hague, by the constitution of its own government, and that was to change radically, not once but twice in the course of the year 1653.

The most significant turning-point in the four-year history of the republic, as instituted in 1649, came with the revival of concerted political activity in the army after its campaigning years came more or less to an end after the battle of Worcester. Something has already been said about the impact that the return of Cromwell and other senior officers to Westminster made upon the political scene. This is not just a story of personalities, however, large though Cromwell's was. The army was not of one mind in matters either political or religious. It had maintained the conviction, asserted in 1647, that it was not a mere mercenary army, but had some claim to speak for the people's interests as well as its own. Since making that claim its years of fighting in Ireland and Scotland had strengthened a belief, shared by the articulate in all ranks, that its mission was to advance the interest of the people of God, and that God by conferring on it victory after victory had confirmed its right to a voice in speaking for their cause. It expected the regime that it served to show a similar commitment, by ensuring that the gospel was preached in every corner of the land, by remedying obvious social and legal injustices, and by establishing a constitution which would enable the people to elect representatives worthy of God's blessing at regular intervals. But members of the army, living as most did in a semi-closed community, and having in many cases been physically distanced through active service from contact with public feeling in England, failed to realize that many of the things they most desired were bound to increase the already disturbing unpopularity of the republic.

The Rump by contrast was well aware of how little it was loved, and this, combined with its internal divisions and innate inertia, largely explains why its record in reforming legislation was so barren. Its narrow basis in public support was not getting any broader. On the credit side the hated county committees had largely withered away, and in local government there had been some resumption of authority by the JPs and their quarter sessions. But the overall financial burden was as high as ever in the winter of 1652/3, and the commission of the peace was not what it had been. The widespread dislike of the Rump's regime among the established county families had led to a considerable piecemeal purge of the commissions, leaving the bench in most counties to be occupied by men of generally lower status than of old. The downward social trend had also characterized the setting up, by an act of 1650, of powerful militia commissioners in each county, who not only directed the trained bands but were empowered to search into conspiracies and disarm papists and other suspects. Some counties were to a great extent managed for the Rump by powerful local bosses, such as John Pyne in Somerset, Robert Bennett in Cornwall, and Wroth Rogers in Herefordshire—all styled colonel, though none was currently in the army. One way and another, the Rump's rule had alienated the traditional elite without earning any significant degree of genuinely popular support to compensate for it.

Whether a bolder reforming programme could have won such support for the Commonwealth is a question that does not admit an easy answer, for many of the areas in which the Rump's critics called for action were themselves beset with difficulties. Perhaps the most contentious issue before it was the settlement of religion, and here there was no way in which it could have pleased all parties. The even balance between Presbyterians and Independents in the House had the result that the Presbyterian settlement enacted by the unpurged parliament remained unrepealed, and nothing positive was erected to take its place. The system of church government decreed by it was only very patchily put in place by the time of Pride's Purge, and though it was not dismantled there was no longer any official drive to extend it. It did not retain much vitality outside London and the clothing towns of Lancashire. Presbyterians and orthodox Independents were closing ranks from 1649 onward against the rising threat from sectaries and other extremists who sought to abolish tithes, attacked the right of lay patrons to present incumbents to parish livings, and aimed at severing all links between church and state. But though there was much support in the army for these radical objectives, they would (if attained) have alienated many more people than they pleased, and there was never a chance that the Rump would espouse them. Tithes and advowsons were recognized as forms of property, and they never came under serious threat. Most MPs shared the strong public desire to retain a nationally maintained parochial ministry, and parliament showed its commitment to one by two measures in particular. One was a church survey, carried out during 1649–50, which established the yearly value of every benefice with cure of souls in the country; the other was the commitment of large powers to thirteen Trustees for Maintenance of Ministers, who had discretion to augment where necessary the stipends of preaching ministers. This partly offset the large depletion of the church's overall wealth through the sale of the lands belonging to bishoprics, deaneries, and chapters.

Where the Rump disappointed even moderate reformers was in its failure to do more to ensure that the word was preached in every parish, for there were still too many lazy, ignorant, or absentee parsons who left their flocks hungry in that sermon-loving age. As already mentioned, it did set up two local Commissions for the Propagation of the Gospel early in 1650, one for Wales and the other for the northern counties, but it made no progress at all with a bill intended to do the same for the country as a whole. The propagating venture got a bad name when the Welsh commission was powerfully infiltrated by Fifth Monarchist firebrands, notably Vavasor Powell and Morgan Llwyd, who had strong links with Harrison and his faction in the army. They were not only seen as perverting the organization in order to preach socially subversive stuff about the irrelevance of worldly rank and the imminent rule of the saints, but they were unjustly accused of misappropriating the tithes and other revenues of the church in Wales to their own sectarian ends. This was only one symptom of a growing polarization between moderate and extreme puritans. The year 1652 saw a spate of radical pamphlets and petitions, tending to the total removal of religion from the state's authority, as well as the rapid expansion of the Quakers and other highly unorthodox sects.

On the moderate side John Owen and a group of similarly inclined Independents pointed the way forward in February 1652 when they put a set of proposals before the Rump which prefigured the ecclesiastical regime of the Protectorate. They sought to preserve a broad established church, with a generous freedom of worship and association outside it, and with its own bounds set only by the acceptance of certain defined fundamentals of the Christian faith. For the clergy within the establishment who were to enjoy the public maintenance, they proposed two commissions, one to weed out the scandalous and ignorant, the other to adjudge the fitness of all those nominated to livings from then on, whether by traditional patrons or by anyone else. The Rump would have been wise to take this scheme into early consideration, not only on account of its considerable merits, but because Owen enjoyed Cromwell's special confidence. He had won it during the Irish and Scottish campaigns, and on Cromwell's recommendation he was made Dean of Christ Church in 1651 and Vice-Chancellor of Oxford University in the following year. But a whole year went by before the relevant parliamentary committee gave any attention to the proposals of Owen and his colleagues, and by then the Rump was under such heavy pressure from the army that all its intentions were suspect. If it had proceeded promptly and purposefully on the basis of these proposals, religion might have been a potent means of rallying the centre against the extremes. In the event, by contrast, it was to become a trigger for the parliament's expulsion.

There was considerable popular pressure for the reform of the law, and it was a consistent aim of the army. Lawyers tended to regard any proposal for change as an affront to the honour and prestige of their intensely conservative profession, but the radical minority in parliament strongly favoured it; indeed in November 1649 they proposed to exclude lawyers from the House, and next year they succeeded in getting a parliamentary committee appointed to consider just how (not whether) the law should be reformed. The drift back of conservative members, however, increased the number of lawyers in the Rump from fourteen when Charles I was executed to forty-four by the end of 1651, and the committee fell asleep. It was re-awoken briefly by Cromwell's victory dispatch from Dunbar, but no proposal got anywhere near the statute book until the army renewed its pressure after Worcester. Then a commission of non-members was set up, with the distinguished lawyer Matthew Hale as its chairman, and over the next eighteen months it did really valuable work. It prepared a whole range of moderate but beneficial measures for parliament's consideration, including the erection of accessible courts in every county and the total abolition of imprisonment for debt. But the resultant bills tended to get bogged down in committee through the lawyer-MPs' inveterate procrastination and their skill in spinning out the discussion of technicalities. The only one that actually passed—and that was just twelve days before Cromwell sent the Rump packing—was an act that established a court for probate of wills.[7]

Social reform fared no better. There was a clamour for the improvement of poor relief, but though the parliament-men spoke compassionate words they were collectively far more concerned with the interests of wealthy merchants than with those of the underprivileged. Apart from one minor act, which was confined to London, the Rump did nothing for the poor, and the only reason why the really needy did not suffer more in those depressed times was that the JPs in most counties cared more about relieving them than the national government did. Nothing was done, either, to remedy the arbitrary disadvantages suffered by copyholders; landlords' self-interest joined hands with lawyers' conservatism to frustrate any progress on that front.

The army's chief grievance against the Rump, however, came to centre on its failure to make satisfactory provision for the election of a new parliament, and here there is rather more to be said on its side. One can understand why the officers disliked Vane's scheme for 'recruiter' elections, which would have filled only the vacant seats while the sitting members went on sitting, but they did not appreciate as the Rumpers did that a genuinely free *general* election would in all likelihood return a parliament more conservative and anti-military than the present House—one indeed in which a majority might be opposed to a republic as such. Members would admittedly have had to take the Engagement before standing, but that pledge had already been taken already by so many who were no friends to the Commonwealth that as a shibboleth it was of little use. These were objections which very much deserved to be considered, but what rankled with the army was that the question of how to provide for future parliaments had so rarely been considered at all. Cromwell's dispatch from Dunbar had revived discussion of it, and the House had then opted for recruiter rather than general elections. But it had resolved to decide first how constituencies should be redistributed among counties and towns, and it was still at this task six months later. It took even longer in going through the names of all the members who had voluntarily absented themselves since Pride's Purge, in order to determine which should keep their seats, and it spared so many that recruiter elections would have wrought even less change in the personnel and temper of the House than might reasonably have been expected. In the summer of 1651 it laid even this unfinished business aside in face of the impending Scottish invasion.

    [7] Underdown, *Pride's Purge*, pp. 275–80; Worden, *Rump Parliament*, ch. 6; Mary Cotterell, 'Interregnum law reform: the Hale Commission of 1652', *English Historical Review* LXXXIII (1968); S. E. Prall, *The Agitation for Law Reform During the Puritan Revolution* (The Hague, 1966); D. Veall, *The Popular Movement for Law Reform 1640–1660* (Oxford, 1970).

Cromwell's victory at Worcester, however, had such an effect that on the very day he received the House's thanks it voted to take the provision of 'an equal representative in parliament' into consideration on the morrow. After three days's debate it resolved by thirty-three votes to twenty-six to bring in a bill which would set a date for its own dissolution and provide for the election of a new parliament. It was a narrow majority in a typically thin House, but the tellers for the ayes were Cromwell and his future opponent the republican Thomas Scot; the lines of division that were to bring the Rump to a violent end were not yet fully drawn, and that outcome was still quite unforeseen. The bill was introduced on 8 October and debated intensively in grand committee over the next five weeks. Many of the more dilatory members, alerted to the threat that they might really have to face their electors again, took to attending more often. Cromwell made a long speech on 14 November, urging that it was high time for the present parliament to fix a date beyond which it would not sit, and he secured a vote in favour, but only by forty-nine voices to forty-seven. When the House voted four days later on what the date should be, it plumped without a division for 3 November 1654, all but three years ahead.

By that time many members would have held their seats unchallenged for fourteen years, many constituencies would have had no opportunity to choose their representatives for as long, and many would have had no representative at all since Pride's Purge, all but five years ago. This went ill with the parliament's claim to wield supreme authority by virtue of the suffrages of the sovereign people. A case could be argued that early general elections would have been extremely hazardous, and that a space was needed for the Commonwealth to win new friends and reconcile old enemies before it went to the people. But during the next two years the Rump did practically nothing of the kind; indeed it gratuitously offended its radical critics without doing anything substantial to mollify its moderate ones. The impetus towards reform that the victory at Worcester generated soon lost momentum, as the earlier one after Dunbar had done. The bill to provide for the propagation of the gospel on a nationwide scale was revived on 1 October 1651, but was quietly dropped after a few weeks. It was not until February 1653 that the Rump took up the relatively conservative but nevertheless reforming scheme of Owen and his colleagues. As for healing old wounds, the successive acts for the sale of delinquents' estates often contravened the spirit and sometimes the letter of the terms of surrender that military commanders had negotiated with their royalist opponents, and the wretchedly imperfect Act of Oblivion increased the officers' suspicion of the Rumpers' motives.

The suspicion was reciprocated, and the Rump showed a particular animus against Harrison, whom hostile members too readily blamed for the malversations charged against the Commission for the Propagation of the Gospel in

Wales. He lost his place on the Council of State in the annual election in November 1651, and there was even a move to expel him from parliament. This was foolish as well as unjust, for although Cromwell did not share Harrison's Fifth Monarchist beliefs there were still strong ties of mutual trust and friendship between the two men. And while Harrison's treatment particularly incensed the religious enthusiasts in the army, another case involving John Lilburne roused the anger of those officers and men whose radicalism was of a more secular cast. Its details were complex, but it concerned a coalmine in County Durham, the property of a royalist delinquent, who had leased the greater part of it to one George Primate long before the Civil War. Primate had subleased it to Lilburne's uncle George and to another man, but after the war the whole estate had been sequestered, and in 1649 Haselrig, who was using his privileged position to amass royalists' as well as bishops' lands, acquired the lease of the colliery at an advantageous rate. Primate and George Lilburne tried to assert their continuing right to the lease, and George employed his nephew John as his counsel, but after long debate in the latter weeks of 1651 the Committee for Compounding found in favour of Haselrig. As the law then stood the decision may have been a sound one, whatever the equity of the case; but John Lilburne published a vitriolic attack on Haselrig and the Committee, accusing his old enemy of abusing his political position in order to obtain a corrupt judgment in his own favour. The Rump reacted furiously, and took the case into its own hands. The issue consequently was no longer who had the right to the coalmine but breach of privilege, so the members could pass what sentence they pleased, without worrying about any niceties of the law, or even hearing the accused. John Lilburne and Primate were punished with fines and damages totalling £7,000 each, a sum which would have taken Milton thirty-five years to earn from his salary as Secretary for Foreign Tongues. Haselrig had the decency not to enforce payment of his share of Lilburne's damages, but the Rump further passed an act of banishment against Lilburne, decreeing the death penalty if ever he set foot in England again. Granted that his attack on Haselrig had been extremely intemperate and perhaps ungrounded, his punishment was grossly disproportionate to his offence and smacked of vindictiveness. It was foolish too, for whereas there had been little Leveller activity in the army since the 1649 mutiny it reawakened the sympathy with Lilburne's sufferings that many soldiers and junior officers had shown in 1647–8. Cromwell did not share their feelings, but many caught the same whiff of parliamentary tyranny that had roused them to resistance in that earlier phase.[8]

---

[8] On the Lilburne–Primate affair see Pauline Gregg, *Free-Born John* (1961), pp. 309–11; Worden, *Rump Parliament*, pp. 282–4; Barry Denton, *Only in Heaven: The Life and Campaigns of Sir Arthur Hesilrige* (Sheffield, 1997), pp. 163–72.

For over a year after his return from Worcester, Cromwell strove continuously to avert a political polarization, whether between the army and the parliament or between the conservative and reforming factions within the House. About three weeks after the Rump had voted to give itself (if need be) until November 1654 before dissolving, Cromwell arranged a meeting of some leading MPs and officers at the Speaker's house, to consider whether they might put life into the almost deadlocked debate on the future government of the country by offering some jointly agreed proposals. They soon concurred that the central question was whether to aim at a pure republic or a mixed constitution with a monarchical element in it. The lawyers present, including Whitelocke, St John, Lenthall, and Widdrington, favoured the latter, and many were for crowning Charles I's youngest son, the twelve-year-old Duke of Gloucester, under firm constitutional restraints. Nearly all the officers present were firmly opposed to kingship in any form, but Cromwell himself took the view 'that a settlement with somewhat of monarchical power in it would be very effectual'.[9] There is no sign that at this stage he had any serious thought of setting up as king for himself, and his words may hint at a possibility that the monarchical role need not necessarily be assigned to an individual. If one can judge by certain strands that ran fairly consistently through his political thinking from at least 1647 onward, he probably hoped that a monarchical element, however embodied, would serve three main functions: to act as the guarantor of an accepted constitution while elected assemblies came and went, to check the evident tendency of an all-powerful single-chamber parliament towards electoral dictatorship, and to secure for the executive a degree of independence from the legislature. As Protector he was to be a strong believer in the separation of powers.

He did not find it easy to pursue a moderating course. It brought him under the suspicion of such influential millenarian preachers in London as Christopher Feake, Walter Cradock, Vavasor Powell, and the radical Independent John Goodwin, who all had a considerable following in the army. The open hostility of many Rumpers, especially the thorough-paced republicans, towards army officers did not help him. Skippon, a moderate if ever there was one, was dropped from the Council of State at the same time as Harrison, leaving the army almost insultingly under-represented. Then Lambert, who had deserved more from the Commonwealth than any soldier other than Cromwell for his service in the Dunbar and Worcester campaigns, was

---

[9] B. Whitelocke, *Memorials of the English Affairs* (1682), pp. 491–2. The account in *The Diary of Bulstrode Whitelocke*, p. 273, is much shorter and does not reproduce Cromwell's or any other participant's actual words, but it states that 'their debate . . . is more largely inserted in Wh[itelocke's] larger book', so I see no reason to doubt the authenticity of the record. I also find Whitelocke's date for the meeting (10 December) entirely plausible, but cf. Worden, *Rump Parliament*, p. 276.

gratuitously offended. After Ireton's death, parliament named Lambert to succeed him as Lord Deputy in Ireland, where he would have had almost vice-regal powers as well as the command of the armed forces, since Cromwell himself was the absentee Lord Lieutenant. There could have been no fitter appointment. Yet after Lambert had spent £5,000 on fitting out a suitable equipage for his post, he learnt in May 1652 that parliament had abolished it, along with the Lord Lieutenancy itself. Lambert, in deep offence, declined the far less prestigious post of commander-in-chief in Ireland, and became a lead-ing spirit among those in the army who were pressing for the dissolution of the Rump. The Irish command went to Fleetwood, who in June married Ire-ton's widow, and so became Cromwell's son-in-law.

Far more than personalities, however, were involved in the army's mount-ing hostility towards the parliament, which by the summer was rising beyond Cromwell's power to restrain it. There was pressure within the army for a comprehensive statement of its desires, and Cromwell and the Council of Officers held a nine-hour meeting on 2 August, the first of several, in order to frame it. A listing of the officers' demands was published on the 10th in the form of a declaration of the army addressed to Cromwell, but a revised version, probably bearing the marks of his restraining influence, was pre-sented to parliament by six senior officers, all but one of them staunch Cromwellians, as a petition from his Council of War. Much has been made of the fact that he did not expressly put his name to it, but that was probably because of the delicacy of his position as a member of parliament and coun-cillor of state. Since he presided over the Council of Officers there is no doubt that he countenanced it, and indeed he cited it as authoritative on two import-ant occasions in 1653.[10]

The petition was respectfully phrased and contained few requests that the army had not advanced before. The first, predictably, was for the removal of unworthy parish ministers and their replacement by godly preachers, main-tained by some more acceptable means than tithes. It called for the reform of the law and the speedy enactment of the Hale Commission's recommenda-tions. It wanted profane, scandalous, and disaffected officials removed, and public office entrusted solely to 'men of truth, fearing God and hating cov-etousness'. Reflecting the army's distrust of parliament-men, it called for a commission of non-members to investigate monopolies, pluralism, unneces-sary offices, and excessive salaries. It expected the rectification of abuses in the management of the public revenue, especially in the hated excise, and it pro-posed a total reorganization of the financial system under a single national

---

[10] Gardiner and Abbott are both somewhat misleading on this important document: For its provenance and progress see Worden, *Rump Parliament*, pp. 306–9; Woolrych, *Soldiers and Statesmen*, pp. 39–44; Gentles, *New Model Army*, pp. 419–20, 553. Strangely, the text of the petition, which is brief, has not been reprinted since 1652.

treasury. It demanded better provision for the poor, the old and infirm, for soldiers crippled by their war wounds, and for the widows and orphans of the fallen. It reiterated the old grievance of the men's arrears of pay, and it asked again that terms of surrender granted by commanders in the field should be honoured. But it left till last the matter that had come to preoccupy the officers most, namely the speedy provision for elections to a new parliament, under such qualifications that only 'such as are pious and faithful to the interest of the Commonwealth' should serve in it. According to a newswriter's report, this formulation was arrived at after Cromwell objected to a peremptory demand 'that a new representative be forthwith elected', but it poses some problems of interpretation. It suggests perhaps an attempt to accommodate both the moderate majority who believed (like Cromwell) that the 'representative of the people' should consist of members whom the people (however defined) freely chose, subject only to safeguards necessitated by the times, and the minority who held (like Harrison) that only those who could be counted among God's saints were qualified to bear rule in his dawning kingdom. This potential rift in the ranks was to open much wider in the year ahead.

Neither the politicians nor the officers foresaw what a crisis lay ahead when this petition came under debate, but in fact it heralded the third of those phases of accelerated and largely unplanned political change that I have called climacterics. As in the crises of 1641–2 and 1648–9, the consequences of the quarrel that developed in the winter of 1652–3 were neither desired nor foreseen by the participants. The great majority of them, however great their differences, expected them to be resolved eventually within the framework of the existing republic, ruled as it was by a sovereign single-chamber parliament. All now accepted that the Rump would have to make way for a successor before too long, however they might disagree over the time-table and how it was to be chosen. There seemed to be promising ways ahead on the nationwide provision of a preaching ministry in the parishes and on the reform of the law, if the Rump would only overcome its inertia. No one before the end of 1652 plotted or even desired what actually happened in 1653: the forcible expulsion of the Rump by the army, its replacement by a pseudo-parliament nominated by the Council of Officers, and after that failed the establishment of a quasi-monarchy with Cromwell as head of state under a written constitution. Yet all that was to ensue within a year, the climacteric year 1653.

There was nothing inevitable about such an outcome, and for a month or two the Rump made promising efforts to avert a breach. It set up a powerful and broad-based committee to report what progress had been made in the matters raised in the officers' petition and what more needed to be done to bring them under speedy consideration. The committee's chairman was the radical John Carew; it included his friend and fellow-millenarian Harrison, Cromwell,

Colonel Rich, and two other officer-MPs, along with several men who would be prominent in Barebone's Parliament and the Protectorate Council of State. Naturally they were balanced by members who were hostile to any pretension by the military to a voice in politics, but the army's arch-opponents Haselrig and Vane were conspicuously absent. (Cromwell and Vane, who had once been so close, had been moving apart, largely because of the army's challenges to the Rump.) Carew reported from this committee in mid-September that the bill for a new representative, which had gone to sleep in the committees of the whole House, would be better expedited by a select committee, whereupon his own committee was promptly entrusted with it. The committee sat daily at first, but before the end of the year it sank into inactivity. So did the committee entrusted with preparing measures for the national propagation of the gospel. As for improving the relief of the poor, the House debated a bill to that end on 12 October, but when it was due for further consideration on 11 November, Haselrig moved to put it off, and it never got any further. The little burst of reforming activity begotten by the army petition was sputtering out, just as in the aftermaths of Dunbar and Worcester. The Rumpers could not plead pressure of other business as an excuse for their dilatoriness, for they were currently sitting as a House on only four mornings a week. There was a motion on 11 November to restore Monday and Saturday sittings until the end of the year, but it was narrowly lost. Haselrig, who did not attend a single meeting of the Council of State between 27 July and 26 October, was a teller against it. When the House did sit it spent day after day in selecting one by one the 678 unlucky royalists whose estates were to be put up in their third Act of Sale. This in itself angered the army officers, for the victims included many who had surrendered on a promise that their estates would not be forfeit. An Act of Articles, intended to confirm surrender terms granted by military commanders, had long been under debate, but when it finally passed on 28 September it was so clogged with provisoes that neither officers nor royalists felt reassured. Worse still, a rider was added in November which excluded all those named in the Act of Sale from its benefits. The army's sense of honour was deeply offended, and after its coup in 1653 a number of the royalists concerned had their lands restored by a committee of officers.

Cromwell still went on striving to prevent an open breach. By his own account he arranged ten or twelve informal meetings between leading officers and MPs during the last six months of the Rump's rule. At some point, probably late in 1652, he complained to Quartermaster-General Vernon 'that he was pushed on by two parties to do that, the consideration of the issue whereof made his hair to stand on end'.[11] He named the two parties' leaders:

---

[11] *Memoirs of Edmund Ludlow*, I, 346. Ludlow, with hindsight, believed Cromwell's words to be hypocritical, but they were probably perfectly sincere.

Lambert, who headed those whose more secular outlook saw the Rump as clinging to power for selfish reasons while doing little to deserve it, and Harrison, whose faction lamented that its aversion to the work of reformation was obstructing the fulfilment of the promised kingdom of Christ. On one fine November afternoon Cromwell and Whitelocke happened to meet in St James's Park when both men were taking the air after their day's work. Cromwell dismissed his attendants so that he could seek Whitelocke's frank advice on what to do about the growing political impasse and the rifts which were splitting apart those to whom God had given victory over their enemies. He complained of the Rumpers' neglect of duty, their pursuit of power and profit, and the arrogance and corruption of many of them. But since they had constituted themselves the supreme authority, what other way was there to control them but by force? Whitelocke predictably argued that force could not safely or honourably be applied by the army. Cromwell then shocked him by suddenly asking 'What if a man should take upon him to be king?' He replied that if Cromwell took such a step it would do him more harm than good, since he already had as much honour and power as if he were king, and most of his officers and the dominant party in both the parliament and the City were for a commonwealth. If he took the crown he would change the question from whether England should be a republic or a monarchy to whether the king should be a Cromwell or a Stuart, and he would suffer a great loss of support thereby. Cromwell granted that Whitelocke spoke sense, and pressed him long and hard as to what line of action he would advise. With much hesitation, and under pledge of secrecy, Whitelocke suggested that Cromwell might consider 'bring[ing] in him that hath the legal right to be king, upon such conditions as you shall think fit, whereby you may secure the interest of yourself, and of your posterity and of your friends, and of the cause in which we are engaged'.[12] Whitelocke sensed a cooling in Cromwell towards him after this, but he continued to enjoy high public employment under the Protectorate, and less than five years after this conversation he was to play a prominent role in a parliamentary committee appointed to persuade Cromwell to accept the crown.

The interesting question, of course, is whether Cromwell was seriously thinking of assuming it towards the end of 1652. Whitelocke thought that he was, but his reading of Cromwell's motives, written up long after the event, was heavily coloured by hindsight, as in the case of that earlier meeting in the Speaker's house. It would be naive to suppose that the idea had not crossed Cromwell's mind, but he was to show a sincere aversion to the royal title in 1653 and 1657, and it is unsafe to conclude that he was actively seeking it while the Rump was still sitting. His whole conduct after the dissolution

---

[12] *Diary of Bulstrode Whitelocke*, pp. 281–2.

indicates the contrary, as we shall soon see. There were several other occasions on which he threw ideas into the air to see how his friends and associates would react to them, and he was probably drawing out Whitelocke because he knew him to be a shrewd and influential fellow-councillor with a special skill in public law. He cannot have relished the suggestion of a deal with Charles II, but he probably respected it as honest advice, honestly given.

By the turn of the year increasing numbers of officers were gathering in London, far beyond the membership of the Council of Officers, and meeting almost daily to seek the Lord in prayer and fasting. Radical ministers in the capital were preaching incendiary sermons against the Rump. Rumours, true or false, were feeding the discontent. Bordeaux heard in mid-December from a prominent MP's son-in-law that there was a plan afoot in the House to remove Cromwell from the generalship, and there were other reports of a design to recall Fairfax. On the last day of the year parliament voted to sell off Hampton Court, which it had fitted up as a residence for Cromwell after his return from Worcester. It had the crushing cost of the Dutch war as a pretext, but Ludlow thought it was because his fellow-members saw the palace as a temptation to 'some ambitious man to ascend the throne'.[13] Material grievances aggravated the army's discontent. Although the monthly assessment was raised in December to £120,000, a full third of it was earmarked for the navy, and each month the army's pay was falling a further £31,000 in arrears. There was disquiet too over disbandments. Since Worcester the land forces in England and Scotland had been brought down from 45,000 to 31,500—a wholly justified reduction, but it still hurt. Freedom of expression was also under threat, for *The Faithful Scout*, the newspaper which spoke for the army's interests and had recently become critical of the parliament, was suppressed after its issue for 18–25 December. The Rump could not look to popular support to shield it from the army's rising anger, since on top of the unprecedented weight of taxation the price of Newcastle coal, on which London absolutely depended to keep warm, was being driven up to unaffordable heights by the Dutch fleet's presence in the North Sea, and all through the winter naval press gangs were roaming the streets at night and dragging men from their beds.

It was therefore no single grievance that was heating the army's temper towards flash-point at the beginning of 1653, but the greatest one remained the Rump's apparent reluctance to proceed with its bill for a new representative. Presumably in the hope of mollifying the officers, it put Harrison in charge of the bill on 6 January, in place of Carew, and ordered that it should be brought in speedily. This is puzzling, because Carew and Harrison were soon to be close allies, if they were not so already. Both were Fifth Monarchists, and

---

[13] *Memoirs of Edmund Ludlow*, I, 347.

they were to be jointly in trouble in 1654 for opposing the Protectorate, chiefly on the grounds that 'it had a parliament in it, whereby power is derived from the people, whereas all power belongs to Christ'.[14] Harrison took no notice of the Rump's order, and seems to have done nothing at all about the bill. Probably he had already lost all faith in elected parliaments, for he was soon to believe that government should be vested in a Sanhedrin of godly men, chosen solely by the saints. When the House eventually heard a report on the bill on 23 February, including some amendments to it, the spokesman for the committee was the army's arch-enemy Haselrig. How he came to take charge of the committee is a mystery, for there is no record of his ever having been appointed to it; nor is it known what the proposed amendments were. They seem not to have been good news to the army, which far from moderating its agitation soon stepped it up. But at least Haselrig got the bill moving again, and thereafter the parliament spent every Wednesday except one in debating it in grand committee. Few members, however, troubled to attend: just forty-two on 23 March, for instance, and forty-four a week later.

By then Cromwell himself had almost certainly come to regard the Rump as incorrigible, though he went on resisting the army's growing pressure to put an end to it. On 11 March he and Desborough only just managed to dissuade an enlarged Council of Officers from voting to expel it forthwith. One reason he gave, surely a sincere one, was that it was working towards a peace with the Dutch. He was also troubled to know what to put in its place. Summon a new parliament, the officers said; but if they did that, he replied, 'then the parliament is not the supreme power, but this is the supreme power that calls it'.[15] Nevertheless there were signs that he was coming to the end of his patience with the Rump, for he never again attended the Council of State after 8 March and he stopped coming to the House soon after. It seems that he was going through a phase similar to that which had preceded Pride's Purge and the trial of the king, in which he was convinced that the way things were running was wrong and ought to be stopped—the treaty of Newport then, the Rump's clinging to power now—but was not yet certain that he had a clear call to perform the violently unconstitutional act that seemed requisite to set the ship of state on a better course. As before, it was a period of soul-searching and prayer, and this time he had to think hard how to provide for the Commonwealth's future government if he did dissolve the parliament by force. The puzzle is to explain why in the end he expelled it *before* he had decided what should take its place, and historians have differed quite widely in their attempt to solve it. Any such attempt is bound to involve a fair amount of hypothesis, since the evidence is inconclusive, if not contradictory.

[14] *Clarke Papers*, II, 244.
[15] Newsletter quoted by C. H. Firth in 'Cromwell and the expulsion of the Long Parliament in 1653', *EHR* VIII (1893), 527–8.

As April went on, however, it required only a small trigger to release the coiled spring of Cromwell's frustration, which was being wound tighter by the Rump's animus against the sects and religious unorthodoxy in general. In considering the proposals of its committee for the propagation of the gospel, it threatened to place restrictions on lay preaching, in which many members of the army had engaged. It gave a warm welcome to an orchestrated wave of county petitions, urging it to uphold a godly learned ministry against sectaries who were striking at the very roots of the established clergy, and calling for a new assembly of divines to help mend the present sad divisions in England—presumably by defining permitted doctrine more strictly. But for many the crux came when the Commission for the Propagation of the Gospel in Wales, which had been established for an initial three-year term, became due for renewal at the end of March. It had, as we have seen, become highly suspect because of the extent to which it had been colonized by the Fifth Monarchists, but the Committee for Plundered Ministers had cleared it of the charges of misappropriating ecclesiastical revenue. Many senior officers and garrison commanders in Wales, not for the most part extremists, were engaged in the commission's work, and it really had been promoting the preaching of the gospel in some rather dark corners of the land. On 1 April, the day appointed for considering the renewal of the act on which its authority rested, the House threw it out. Walter Cradock, the commission's most famous and distinguished pastor, was to have preached before parliament later in the month, but his engagement was cancelled. The anger of Harrison and his party can be imagined, and Cromwell shared it, though his religious convictions stood some way from theirs. When he explained his reasons for expelling the Rump to the Nominated Parliament which succeeded it, he said that its treatment of the Welsh Propagators 'was as plain a trial of their spirits as anything, it being known to many of us that God did kindle a seed there hardly to be parallelled since the primitive times'.[16] The Rump's historian has fairly commented that 'In its later stages the House seems at times to have been possessed of a death-wish',[17] but if its refusal to renew the commission at just this time looks like a piece of sheer folly, the blame for the impending crisis did not all lie on one side. Cromwell and Harrison could not convincingly complain about decisions that offended them when they had given up even trying to make their own case heard in the House, and registering their own votes. Their non-attendance may have led their opponents to believe that a violent end was imminent anyway, and that there was no longer any point in making conciliatory moves that went against their own convictions.

Debate on the bill for a new representative trickled on during March. On

---

[16] Abbott, *Writings and Speeches of Oliver Cromwell*, III, 57.
[17] Worden, *Rump Parliament*, p. 286.

the 30th the House voted to vest the franchise in all men possessing property, real or personal, worth £200. The annual value of land worth £200 was commonly reckoned at £20, which was roughly equivalent to the old 40s. when that rate was fixed before the great inflation, and the time-honoured restriction to freehold land was now removed. This cannot have been a bone of contention between parliament and army, for the same franchise, and the same redistribution of constituencies, were embodied in the written constitution that the chief officers presented to Cromwell eight months later. A week afterwards, however, the regular Wednesday debate on the bill was laid aside to make way for other business, and that may have been the last straw. The debate was resumed on 13 April, when the House voted unexceptionably that future members must be 'persons of known integrity, fearing God, and not scandalous in their conversation'. It may have meant this as a conciliatory move, but if so it came too late, because Cromwell had decided to cut the knot. Next day or the day after, he took his seat for the first time in over a month, and on the 18th and 19th he held crucial meetings of the Council of Officers, to which he put a drastic proposal for resolving what he saw now as a hopeless impasse. After the second session he put his plan again to about twenty officers and a select group of MPs whom he summoned to his apartments in Whitehall. What he proposed (if that is not too mild a word) was that the Rump should appoint a caretaker government consisting of about forty men, chosen from its own membership and from the army, commission them to exercise the supreme authority until the country was deemed to be in a fit temper to elect a new parliament, and then dissolve itself. This startling scheme had a mixed reception from the MPs present, but after it had been discussed far into the night Cromwell and his fellow-officers believed that those members had firmly agreed to get the next day's scheduled debate on the bill put off, and further proceedings on it suspended, until his proposals had been fully considered. He invited those present to another conference next afternoon or evening.

It seems strange that Cromwell counted on the score of members who came to this meeting to persuade the House to lay aside its bid in favour of his scheme, especially as they were by no means all won over to it; strange too that he had no thought of taking his seat next day and commending it to the rest of the members in person. He evidently counted on parliament to give it full consideration, and perhaps chose not to sway the debate by the pressure of his presence. At any rate he dressed simply and informally on the morning of the 20th, and resumed discussion of his plan for an interim government with a small group of members and officers at his Whitehall lodgings. He was taken totally by surprise when news was brought that the Rump was not only busy on its own bill but was bent on passing it into law that very day. He refused at first to believe it, but after a second messenger and then a third confirmed it he gave orders to assemble a body of soldiers and hastened to the House. There he found between eighty and a hundred members sitting, double or more the number that had turned up for the recent weekly debates on the bill. Obviously, those opposed to a dissolution had summoned all the supporters they could muster, knowing that if they could get an act for the election of a new parliament passed into law, a violent dissolution by the army would be a very hard action to justify. It was such a plausible tactic that it seems odd that Cromwell was so surprised at it, though he may have thought it incredible that a bill which had been on the stocks for nineteen months could be rushed through in two or three hours. He took his usual seat and listened in silence for a while. Only when the Speaker was about to put the final question, prior to the formal passing of the bill, did he rise and speak. He began by praising the parliament's care of the public good in the past, but with mounting fury he castigated its subsequent neglect thereof, its denial and delays of justice, its self-seeking, and its espousal of the corrupt, oppressive interests of Presbytery and the lawyers. Then, putting on his hat, he strode up and down the floor of the House, denouncing individual members as whore-masters, drunkards, and a scandal to the profession of the gospel. 'You are no parliament', he shouted at the climax of his wrath, 'I will put an end to your sitting', and turning to Harrison, bade him 'Call them in! Call them in!' The serjeant opened the doors, and in marched Lieutenant-Colonel Worsley with thirty or forty musketeers. Vane, in shock, protested: 'This is not honest, yea it is against morality and common honesty.' Cromwell turned on him, shouting 'Oh Sir Henry Vane! Sir Henry Vane! The Lord deliver me from Sir Henry Vane!' It seems likely that Cromwell thought he had a pledge from Vane to use his influence to get proceedings on the bill suspended, for he called him a juggler as he was leaving the House, and said he 'might have prevented this extraordinary course'.

Having ordered Worsley to clear the chamber, Cromwell laid hands on the mace, the sacrosanct symbol that the Commons were in session. 'What shall we do with this bauble?', he asked, then turning to a soldier said 'Here, take it away.' Not all the members left willingly; the Speaker refused to leave his chair until Harrison gave him an arm, as if to make him do so, and Algernon Sydney had to be similarly stirred out of his seat. But there was no crude physical violence, and as the members filed out Cromwell's mood seemed to be turning from anger to sadness. 'It's you that have forced me to do this,' he told them, 'for I have sought the Lord night and day, that he would rather slay me than put me upon the doing of this work.'[18] He may well have been unjust in his bitter attack on Vane, who for all he knew may have tried and failed to

---

[18] All the contemporary sources recording Cromwell's words and actions on this day are printed in Abbott, *Writings and Speeches*, II, 640–6. For valuable comments on them see Worden, *Rump Parliament*, pp. 334–9, and Firth's notes in *Memoirs of Edmund Ludlow*, I, 351–7.

persuade the House to give his proposals a hearing. At a distance of three and a half centuries those proposals look less plausible than they appeared to him. His caretaker government of forty men, however honest, could not have given the potential supporters of the Commonwealth the reforms that they had long craved, and who were they to judge when and how elections to a new parliament should take place? The decision was bound in practice to lie with the army. But if Cromwell was looking for the one man who did most to quash his scheme, rally his opponents, and try to force the Rump's bill through, that man was probably Haselrig. He had become the most implacable opponent of all challengers to the supreme power of parliament, whether royalist or military. He had somehow taken charge of the committee entrusted with the bill. He would lead the parliamentary attacks on the successive constitutions of the Cromwellian Protectorate, and when the Rump was restored in 1659–60 he would play a dominant role in it, pointing it on even more suicidal courses than in 1652–3. Ludlow, who knew him well, described him as 'a man of disobliging carriage, sour and morose of temper, liable to be transported with passion, to whom liberality seemed to be a vice'; but he had no doubts whatever 'concerning the rectitude and sincerity of his intentions'.[19]

Cromwell had not seen the last of Haselrig when he left the parliament-house that day. On returning to Whitehall he found some resolute members of the Council of State, including Haselrig, Scot, and Bradshaw, sitting in the Council Chamber as usual, evidently determined to carry on some semblance of constitutional government. Cromwell, accompanied by Lambert and Harrison, told them that if they met there as private persons they would not be disturbed, but that since the parliament had been dissolved the council's authority had terminated with it. 'Sir,' replied Bradshaw, 'we have heard what you did at the House in the morning, and before many hours all England will hear it: but, sir, you are mistaken to think that the parliament is dissolved, for no power under heaven can dissolve them but themselves; therefore take you notice of that.'[20]

It is much easier to recount *what* happened on 20 April 1653 than to explain *why* it happened; indeed historians still differ in their readings of Cromwell's motives, and acknowledge that an element of uncertainty remains. Two time-honoured interpretations have to be discarded. One, advanced by his opponents from an early stage, is that his coup was part of a premeditated design to take the supreme power into his own hands. His subsequent actions belie such a charge, no less than his words. If his breaking of the Rump had been a deliberate step on the path to a dictatorship, he would surely have planned the next step, but he clearly had not, and it is doubtful

---

[19] *Memoirs of Edmund Ludlow*, II, 133.    [20] Ibid., I, 367.

whether his fellow-officers would have stood for it if he had. He can be accused of naivety in supposing that his scheme for an interim ruling council of forty men would find acceptance with the Rump, but all the indications are that he saw it as a way forward to a resumption of government by a regular session of elected parliaments. When its summary rejection drove him to expel the Rump, it was an unpremeditated act, and he had so little idea of what to do next that he sent for his fellow-members Salwey and Carew and asked them to persuade St John, Selden, and other constitutional experts to draw up 'some instrument of government that might put the power out of his hands'. But Salwey boldly yet respectfully advised him that the way out of the temptations offered by the prospect of unrestrained authority was 'to rest persuaded that the power of the nation is in the good people of England, as formerly it was'.[21]

A much more enduring explanation of Cromwell's action, accepted by all historians until quite recently, was that the bill he was so desperate to prevent from passing was not really for a *new* representative, but for filling up the present one by means of elections only to the vacant seats. But though such a recruitment scheme had been considered on and off for years, Blair Worden has demonstrated beyond reasonable doubt that the bill that was before the House when Cromwell expelled it really did provide for general elections to a new parliament, which was to meet in November.[22] This leaves us with the problem of explaining why, when the Rump was apparently on the point of doing what the army had been pressing for ever since Worcester, Cromwell intervened so violently to prevent it. Worden's suggestion is that Cromwell had quite recently changed his mind about the desirability of a new parliament because he had become temporarily converted to Harrison's and the Fifth Monarchists' ideal of a kingdom ruled for Christ by his saints. But there are difficulties with the hypothesis that he had a rush of millenarian blood to the head. There is no positive evidence for it, his conduct of national affairs after the dissolution is inconsistent with it, and the Fifth Monarchists themselves had as yet no agreed model for an elitist rule of the saints. Harrison himself claimed to have warned Cromwell, just as he rose to dissolve the Rump, that 'the work is very great and dangerous', and that he should consider seriously before he acted.[23]

We are driven back to concluding that the main reason for his precipitate action lay in the bill itself, or in what he thought was in the bill. But the bill does not survive, for Cromwell seized it from the clerk's table before he

---

[21] *Memoirs of Edmund Ludlow*, I, 358. We cannot be sure that these were Salwey's precise words at the time, but he was a very close associate of Ludlow, who records them.

[22] Blair Worden, 'The Bill for a New Representative: the dissolution of the Long Parliament, April 1653', *EHR* LXXXVI (1971), 473–96; *Rump Parliament*, Part 5, *passim*.

[23] *Memoirs of Edmund Ludlow*, I, 352.

stormed out of the House, and it has never been seen again. He was to shift his ground suspiciously as to what he found most wrong with it, but he was consistent in some of his objections to it, and they were not groundless. One was that it contained no adequate safeguards against the next and future parliaments being dominated by members who were uncommitted to a Commonwealth, or even positively disaffected to it. He himself asked the conference that he convened on 19 April 'Whether the next parliament were not like to consist of all Presbyters? Whether those qualifications [in the bill] would hinder them? Or neuters?'[24] The bill by all accounts did disbar papists, Irish rebels, and all who had fought for Charles I, and it required members to take the Engagement to be faithful to the Commonwealth as it was established without a king or House of Lords. But so much casuistry had developed around the Engagement, and so many obvious non-republicans had taken it, that it was not a trustworthy political test. The problem was not to exclude royalists but to forestall the return of a majority of conservatives with irreproachable parliamentarian credentials who were opposed to religious liberty, social and legal reform, and all that the army and its friends understood by 'a godly reformation'.

Then there was the larger question of who was to ensure that the qualifications laid down for members, such as they were, were duly enforced. Normally the incoming House of Commons, and no one else, ruled whether its members had a right to take their seats and determined disputed elections. But it was evidently part of the Rump's bill that it should reconvene immediately before the new representative took its place, obviously with the purpose of determining whether the incoming members were duly qualified. The question that the Speaker was about to put on 20 April when Cromwell interrupted the proceedings was for appointing 3 November as the date of the present parliament's dissolution.[25] It seems to have been assumed that it would adjourn for part of the intervening period, but nobody could know for how long. Haselrig's close ally Thomas Scot said in the House in 1659 that they might have sat on for four or five months, to see the Dutch war to a conclusion.[26] But if the new House of Commons was unsympathetic to the qualifications laid down for its members, nothing could make it adhere to them once the Rump had gone—nothing, that is, but the intervention of the army. For its part, the army was all too conscious of recent rumours about an intention to remove Cromwell from the generalship and purge its senior ranks. By November, it feared, it might have been in no condition to act. A glance ahead to what was actually to happen in the spring of 1660 will show what it

[24] Woolrych, *Commonwealth to Protectorate*, p. 28.
[25] See the letter from Marten's unpublished papers quoted in Worden, *Rump Parliament*, p. 365, and the speech by Reynolds in ibid., p. 366.
[26] *Diary of Thomas Burton*, ed. J. T. Rutt (4 vols., 1828), III, 111–12.

genuinely had to fear. Before the restored Long Parliament finally dissolved itself in March 1660, the act that it passed to regulate the elections to its successor debarred not only all those who had fought against it in the 1640s but their sons too, as well as all papists and participants in the Irish rebellion. Yet the Convention Parliament ignored all such restrictions on its membership and proclaimed King Charles II within a fortnight of its first meeting. In 1653 there was of course no such tide of resurgent royalism running as in Restoration year, but there was no great enthusiasm for the Commonwealth either.

These considerations may be enough to explain why Cromwell thought it so urgent to prevent the Rump's bill from passing. A general election with parliament and army in partnership to see it through safely was a risk worth taking, but with the two at loggerheads, and with the Rump empowered to vet the returns in the interests of its own kind, it certainly was not. Yet there was probably something more to it than that. There are strong indications that when Cromwell hurried to the House on 20 April he really believed that the bill was somehow skewed to ensure that 'these present members were to sit and to be made up by others chosen, and by themselves approved of '.[27] These were the words of the first report of the dissolution, in the next days's issue of one of the two official newspapers, and they cannot have been published without authority. It was quite uncharacteristic of Cromwell to put out a direct falsehood, and it would have been damaging if its untruth could have been immediately exposed. But the paper printed what seems to have been generally believed at the time. On that same 21 April Bordeaux, the best informed of the foreign diplomats (he was in personal touch with several MPs), reported home that the Rumpers thought only about how to continue their own authority, and were legislating for a new representative with such conditions that they would be able to confirm their own places in it, and ensure that the army officers had none.[28] But as soon as Cromwell and his fellow-officers had had time to study the bill they began to backtrack. The declaration that they published on 22 April, to explain their action, said of the bill that the members 'resolved to make use of it to recruit the House with persons of the same spirit and temper, thereby to perpetuate their own sitting'[29]—an ambiguous allegation, but it marked the beginning of a retreat.

It may seem extraordinary to suggest that Cromwell was unfamiliar with the contents of the bill when he interrupted its passage, but it really does seem that he may have been surprised by what he read in it when he got it back to Whitehall. One can only conjecture what lay behind the inconsistencies in his

[27] *Severall Proceedings of State Affairs* no. 186, 14–21 April 1653, p. 2944; cf. Woolrych, *Commonwealth to Protectorate*, pp. 80–1.

[28] Woolrych, *Commonwealth to Protectorate*, p. 80.

[29] Gardiner (ed.), *Constitutional Documents*, p. 401.

utterances on the subject, but one hypothesis—and it is no more—seems to accord both with his own conduct and that of the bill's promoters. It is that when the bill was reintroduced by Haselrig in February 1653 it contained some provision which, without going as far as substituting a mere recruitment for a general election, nevertheless guaranteed a certain number of the present members a seat in the new parliament, conceivably as supernumerary county representatives. This would account for the army's manifest dissatisfaction with the bill from at least early March onward, especially if, as Bordeaux reported, serving officers were to be disqualified from standing. Bordeaux was not alone in reporting at the time that the leading Rumpers were bent on holding on to power. On our hypothesis Cromwell was aware of this provision in the bill, and disliked it so much that he was determined to prevent it from passing. His ultimatum on 19 April brought Haselrig hurrying to London, where he was seldom seen these days except for the Wednesday debates on the bill. He and his like-minded fellow-members may have then decided to rush the bill through without the offending clause, rather than lose it altogether, even though it meant giving up a guaranteed seat in the new parliament. This was perhaps preferable in their eyes to Cromwell's scheme, which threatened a large enhancement of the army's power, removed the Rump's intended control over the electoral process, and postponed elections indefinitely. Cromwell, it is suggested, did not know of this last-minute decision to drop the provision of assured places for favoured Rumpers when he went to the House on the 20th, and was surprised to find it missing from the bill when he read it back in Whitehall.

This would explain why Cromwell and the officers had to beat an awkward retreat from their first allegations that the bill would have perpetuated the Rumpers in power, and why he never published it. But the bill's authors were equally coy about publicizing its contents, either in 1653 or when they returned to power six years later. Only one member is known to have recorded an express denial that the bill contained anything like a recruitment clause, and he was describing it *as it was when Cromwell seized it.* His open letter survives among Marten's unpublished papers, and it may or may not have been written by him. It reads as though it was written for publication, but it was never printed. Professor Worden has fairly remarked that both sides may have had something to hide.[30]

Whatever the full explanation of the dissolution may be, it left Cromwell with the practical responsibility for providing the country immediately with some sort of government, and he seems to have had little idea in those first few days of how to go about it. The declaration which he and his officers put on

[30] Worden, 'The Bill for a New Representative', p. 495. The 'Marten' letter is discussed there and in *Rump Parliament*, pp. 364 ff.; also by myself in *Commonwealth to Protectorate*, pp. 81–3.

22 April announced a vague intention 'to call to the government persons of approved fidelity', and went on to say 'that as we have been led by necessity and providence to act as we have done, . . . so we shall . . . put ourselves wholly upon the Lord for a blessing'.[31] To profane ears that sounds very like 'Lord only knows where we go from here'.

---

[31] Gardiner (ed.), *Constitutional Documents*, p. 403.

# SEVENTEEN

# 'A Story of My Own Weakness and Folly'?

ADDRESSING members of another parliament four years later, Cromwell described his attempt to set up a new supreme authority in place of the Rump as 'a story of my own weakness and folly'.[1] Perhaps he took too much of the blame for what was really a collective decision, and perhaps he was rather hard on himself.

He started off with some advantages. The country and the capital took his coup very calmly, for the Rump had few mourners besides the Rumpers. He hardly exaggerated when he said later that 'there was not so much as the barking of a dog',[2] and a wag who pinned a notice on the door of the Commons' chamber reading 'This House is to be let, now unfurnished' caught the public mood. One small petition apart, there were no demonstrations of protest against the expulsion; the army was solidly behind Cromwell, and the gathered churches were positively jubilant. But he and his fellow-officers were so unprepared for the responsibility they had undertaken that they needed time to consider how to provide even temporarily for the government of the country. Their public declaration of 22 April promised vaguely enough to call to it 'persons of approved fidelity and honesty', and privately they consulted a number of the more sympathetic former MPs on how best to fill the constitutional vacuum. They took an early decision to set up a Council of State, to carry on day-to-day administration and conduct relations with foreign powers. It was much smaller than the Rump's council, numbering just thirteen members. Cromwell and three others, Lambert, Harrison, and Matthew Tomlinson, were officers in the field army. Colonels Philip Jones, Robert Bennett, and Anthony Stapley were primarily administrators with some authority over local garrisons, and the other six were civilians. Eight of the thirteen had sat in the Rump and one more in the pre-Purge Long Parliament. Only four were regicides, and Harrison and Carew were the only Fifth Monarchists. It was not an unbalanced body, or in temper a revolutionary

---

[1] Abbott, *Writings and Speeches of Oliver Cromwell*, IV, 489.    [2] Ibid., III, 453.

one, and its members mustered between them a reasonable amount of administrative experience.

Its functions, however, were strictly those of a caretaker executive. The Council of Officers kept in its own hands the decision of how to constitute the sovereign authority of the state over a longer term. The fact that they had to start by debating the most basic questions is further evidence that the expulsion of the Rump was no part of a premeditated scheme. The main division of opinion was between Lambert, who was for committing power to a compact council of not more than a dozen men, and those who wished to entrust a much larger body. The latter differed among themselves; Harrison, for instance, favoured a congregation of seventy godly men, after the model of the biblical Sanhedrin. Lambert, in view of his earlier share in framing the Heads of the Proposals and his authorship later in this year of the Instrument of Government, must have thought of his small council as the executive element in a constitution which would include an elected legislature when the temper of the country made it safe to go to the polls, but Cromwell and the majority carried a decision in favour of a larger assembly, sufficiently broad-based to set about the long-delayed work of reformation without waiting until a normal parliament could be summoned. Their opting for a larger body should not be seen, however, as a victory for the Fifth Monarchists, for Harrison told a friend soon afterwards that though his party had argued for having its members chosen solely by the saints they did not get their way. Not all Fifth Monarchists were of the same mind though, for one of their preachers, John Spittlehouse, published a bizarre proposal for a ruling assembly consisting of two officers elected by each regiment, together with some chosen by the navy. He soon changed his mind, for in mid-May he was urging that Cromwell should govern on his own, since he was as plainly called by God as Moses had been to rule Israel. John Rogers, another prominent Fifth Monarchist, did not go quite so far, though he too hailed Cromwell as a second Moses and advocated that he alone should select the members of the ruling assembly.

There was never any question of such advice being followed. Cromwell was acutely aware of his vulnerability to the charge of military dictatorship, and most of his senior officers shared his aversion to such a thing, whether personal or collective. They had long been pressing for a new elected parliament, but there were several cogent reasons why Cromwell could not summon one. He had no shred of legal right to do so, and the members of the Long Parliament would have claimed that their seats were still lawfully theirs, since they could be dissolved only by their own consent. Moreover, the Rump had been on the point of passing a bill for general elections to be held in November when he dissolved it; and even if these objections could have been overcome, a parliament elected in 1653 would have been even less likely to endorse a government inaugurated by the army than the first parliament of the Protectorate proved to be a year later.

So what Cromwell and the Council of Officers decided upon was a kind of surrogate parliament, to wield paramount authority for a strictly limited period of time, and so nominated that every county in England was represented, together with six members apiece for Ireland and Wales and five for Scotland. Seventy was clearly too small a number to accommodate a membership thus grounded, and Cromwell wanted an assembly weighty enough to enact laws that judges and magistrates would enforce. He later claimed that he himself proposed 140, the number agreed upon. But who was to select them? It was decided to entrust their choice to Cromwell and the Council of Officers collectively, and to debar serving officers from being nominated. This last was a remarkable self-denying ordinance, and it was credited to Cromwell himself; the one officer who is said to have been seriously disgruntled by it was Harrison. The two men, for long so close, were now clearly taking different directions.[3] But there is no sign of serious conflict within the Council of Officers, which had made considerable progress with the selection of representatives only two weeks after the Rump was expelled. Every officer present was free to propose whom he pleased, and the decision on each nomination was taken by a simple majority vote. Rank seems not to have counted; Cromwell said later that there was 'not an officer of the degree of a captain but named more than he himself did'.[4] The process of selection was complete early in June, when Cromwell signed the letters summoning the members in his capacity as commander-in-chief.

The character and purpose of the resultant assembly were until recently widely misunderstood, because generations of historians followed Gardiner in one of his rare errors (though Gardiner was not the first to fall into it). Because a few letters survive in which the gathered churches in certain counties and towns recommended particular candidates to represent them, he assumed that the Council of Officers sent out circular letters to the similar churches throughout England, *inviting* them to name men fit for the trust of government, and then chose the members from the lists submitted. But there is no evidence that any such circular letters were issued, and many indications to the contrary.[5] Those congregations or groups of congregations that sent in names did so without formal invitation, though it is likely enough that some individual officers consulted their pastors or fellow-churchmen about

---

[3] For the deliberations leading to the summoning of the Nominated Assembly, the fullest account is in Woolrych, *Commonwealth to Protectorate*, ch. IV; for Harrison's role see esp. pp. 108, 111, 115, 121–2, 142–3.

[4] Abbott, *Writings and Speeches of Oliver Cromwell*, IV, 418.

[5] A. Woolrych, 'The calling of Barebone's Parliament', *English Historical Review* LXXX (1965), 492–513, and more summarily in *Commonwealth to Protectorate*, pp. 114–21.

suitable candidates. Of the nominees in the surviving letters of recommendation from the churches, fifteen were actually chosen, and it is unlikely that many more members owed their seats to such sponsorship.

The supposition that the majority did so, and the association of the Independent and sectarian congregations mainly with the middling sort rather than with the county elites which traditionally dominated the House of Commons, also misled historians into accepting too readily the contempt with which royalists and other hostile commentators described the social standing of the membership at the time. 'A pack of weak, senseless fellows', Clarendon called them; 'much the major part of them consisted of inferior persons, of no quality or name, artificers of the meanest trades, known only by their gifts in praying and preaching.' Collectively they were certainly below the social level of a typical Stuart parliament, but Clarendon's description is a travesty. At least four-fifths and perhaps five-sixths of them could style themselves gentlemen in an age when that distinction was still crucial, however blurred it was round the edges. Lesser gentry outnumbered greater by about two to one, and a few had acquired their gentry status through success in trade or a profession, but the assembly included two peers, three future earls, four baronets, and four knights. At least a third of the members would not have been socially out of place in any seventeenth-century House of Commons; indeed nearly half of them were elected to subsequent parliaments, mostly under the Protectorate. Eighteen had sat in the Rump. Of the 128 who represented English or Welsh constituencies, 117 were justices of the peace, and though some of these were new to the bench 89 had been on it in 1650 or earlier. Twenty-eight members served as sheriffs of their counties at some stage in their careers. At least forty-four had been to a university, and the same number to one of the Inns of Court.

Allegations that the assembly consisted largely of religious fanatics and lay preachers were almost as exaggerated as the sneers at its social level. Most of the Council of Officers held strong religious convictions, and these were reflected in their choice, but their nominees included at most thirteen Fifth Monarchists and perhaps a dozen more who can be categorized as religious radicals. One of these was Praise (or Praise-God) Barebone, a warden of the Leathersellers Company and lay preacher to a congregation of his own. His published writings show him to have been no ranting fanatic (he was sceptical about the fifth monarchy, for instance), and he was a substantial enough citizen to serve more than once on London's Common Council. But his name chimed so well with the anti-puritans' stereotype of the assembly that some came in time to call it Barebone's Parliament (though not 'the Barebones Parliament'). It was a misleading label, for the membership spanned a wide religious spectrum, ranging from a very few like Viscount Lisle and Ashley Cooper who were not exactly burdened with spiritual convictions to the Fifth

Monarchist fringe. The prevailing confessional tone was that of a sober congregationalism, though as time went on the zealot minority were to wield an influence on proceedings out of proportion to their numbers.

Between the choosing and the meeting of the Nominated Assembly the Dutch war reached its climax. The Rump had taken so much care to remodel the navy with commanders and captains fully committed to the Commonwealth that Cromwell must have felt some anxiety about its reaction to his April coup. Blake was a member of the Rump and was reported to be strongly on its side in its quarrel with the army, but in February he had been severely wounded in the course of his hardest-won victory, in which he fought Tromp all the way from Portland to Beachy Head, and he was out of action until well after the change of government. It therefore fell to the other two Generals at Sea, Deane and Monck, to make sure that their ships' captains accepted the new regime, and they lost no time in getting them to subscribe a very neutrally worded declaration that was probably designed to paper over their varying reactions to it. But there was no reason to fear their disobedience. They were all in the thick of a gruelling war, and they had no doubt who the prime enemy was. Some were enthusiastic about the change, and those who had misgivings about it put their country's interest before their own political preferences. Captains and crews all fought magnificently in the decisive battle of the war, in which Deane and Monck confronted Tromp off the Gabbard on 2 June. More than a hundred ships on each side slogged it out, on and off, for four days, and the fight had already gone against the Dutch when Blake, still far from fully recovered, joined in it at a late stage. The English men-of-war were larger and better built, and by this time the skill and morale of their seamen and gunners were superior too. Tromp lost about twenty ships, the English not one, though Deane was killed on the first day.

The States-General sent commissioners to London in mid-June to explore the possibilities of a peace, but the Council of State was mostly inexperienced in foreign affairs, and some of its members insisted on excessively humiliating conditions. Even Cromwell, who really wanted peace now that the Dutch had been worsted and were ready to grant reasonable terms, clung to the dream of a closer union between the two commonwealths which had wrecked the earlier peace overtures while the Rump was still sitting. So one more battle had to be fought, and it proved the bloodiest of all. It was joined off the Texel on 31 July when Tromp attempted to break Monck's blockade of the Dutch ports, but Tromp himself was killed in it and about twenty-six of his ships were lost. Human casualties were high on both sides, but much heavier on the Dutch. Both countries were now groaning at the war's toll in lives, ships, and merchandise, not to mention its punishing financial burden, but the peace that both wanted had to wait until the government of England was in hands with a stronger grasp of political realities than the Nominated Assembly.

That body first met on 4 July. Cromwell, who had avoided the word 'parliament' in all references to it, significantly summoned it not to the Commons' Chamber in the Palace of Westminster but to the Council Chamber in the Palace of Whitehall. The day was hot and the room uncomfortably crowded, but he spoke to it for about two hours. For him it was a solemn occasion, for in his view he had taken the whole care of the Commonwealth on his shoulders when he dissolved the Rump, and he was now disburdening himself. He wept frequently as he spoke. He began by tracing the unbroken chain of providences that had brought him and his listeners through victory after victory to the establishment of the Commonwealth and beyond, and then traversed the frustrations and disappointed hopes that had ensued upon the 'crowning mercy' at Worcester. His purpose was to persuade the men before him that the juncture in which he and they now found themselves had not come about through human will or ambition but through the high destiny that God had in store for his people, and this led him into the second half of his speech, which was a solemn charge to them to be worthy of their calling. The authority that he was transmitting to them came 'by the way of necessity, by the way of the wise providence of God, though through weak hands . . . Truly you are called by God, to rule with him, and for him.' He struck an increasingly visionary note as he approached his final peroration. 'Jesus Christ is owned this day by you all,' he said, 'and you own him by your willingness in appearing here, and you manifest this (as far as poor creatures can) to be a day of the power of Christ by your willingness.' And a little later: 'Why should we be afraid to say, or think, that this may be the door to usher in things that God hath promised and prophesied of ? . . . Indeed, I do think something is at the door, we are at the threshold.'[6] These passages have been taken as evidence that Cromwell was temporarily converted to Fifth Monarchism and hoped that the kingdom of Christ was in process of being realized there and then. This is largely because in Abbott's standard edition of the speeches Cromwell is made to say 'you manifest this . . . to be *the* day of the power of Christ'. There is no authority whatever for this reading, and it distorts his whole sense. By '*a* day of the power of Christ' he was expressing a hope that his present entrustment of authority to men dedicated to the interest of the people of God would prove to be a milestone on the road to the promised kingdom, but he was not saying that they had already arrived at it. He had long been a millenarian, but he never shared the Fifth Monarchists' quest for a literal, physical rule of the saints. The kingdom he looked forward to was a spiritual kingdom, and it would be realized in God's good time. Meanwhile, the fact

---

[6] *The Lord General Cromwel's Speech delivered in the Council-Chamber* (1654), pp. 22, 24. The text of this speech in Abbott, *Writings and Speeches of Oliver Cromwell*, III, 52–66 is seriously unreliable. On the texts and their interpretation see Woolrych, *Commonwealth to Protectorate*, pp. 145–50, 399–402.

that those to whom he now spoke owned God, and were owned by him, put them on a footing 'with those that have been called by the suffrages of the people; who can tell how soon God may fit the people for such a thing, and who would desire any thing more in the world but that it might be so?'[7] Clearly he regarded elected parliaments as the norm, and longed for the time when it would be safe to return to them.

Before he finished he had a brief 'Instrument' read out, by which he committed the supreme authority and government of the Commonwealth to the present assembly, with just one restriction: they were to sit no longer than 3 November 1654, the terminal date that the Rump had appointed for its own dissolution. Three months before then, the present members were to choose others to succeed them. These were to sit for no more than a year, and during that time were 'to take care for a succession in government'.[8] The implication is that Cromwell hoped that before the end of 1655 the people would be sufficiently settled to return to regular elected parliaments. Finally he told the assembly that the Council of State's authority was subordinate to their own, and that its membership and duration were as they should order; but he hoped that for the sake of continuity they would respect the present council's authority until they saw fit to change it. He said nothing about his own authority, and he expressly handed over executive as well as legislative power. In so doing, and in entrusting his and his officers' nominees with selecting their own successors, he was taking large risks, but that is a measure of his reluctance to be seen as seeking power for himself.

Before they broke up that day the members voted to sit in future in the traditional Commons' Chamber. There they spent at least ten hours next day in prayer and humiliation, without the assistance of any ordained minister. Before they parted they elected Francis Rous as their chairman—an ecumenical choice, for although sometimes labelled a Presbyterian he is perhaps better described as just a broadly tolerant puritan. He was Provost of Eton and a learned and prolific author; he had been half-brother to Pym, and had sat in every parliament since 1626. They also invited Cromwell and the other four army officers on the interim Council of State to sit with them as co-opted members. They spent most of the first full day of secular business in debating whether or not to assume the title of parliament, and after much argument they voted to do so by sixty-five to forty-six. Most of the minority doubtless associated parliaments with mere 'carnal' government and felt their own calling to be from God, but the noes also included some relative conservatives, like Sir Gilbert Pickering, who felt that the title should be reserved for the elected body known to the law. But once the title was adopted the rest of the

[7] *Lord General Cromwel's Speech*, pp. 23–4.

[8] Abbott, *Writings and Speeches of Oliver Cromwell*, III, 67; printed from the official *Mercurius Politicus*, where the gist of the Instrument was immediately published.

trappings quickly followed; Rous was voted Speaker, the mace—Cromwell's 'bauble'—was daily carried before him, the Rump's Clerk of the Parliament and Sergeant-at-Arms were restored to their offices, and the Journal of the House was kept as of old.

A crucial test of the assembly's co-operativeness lay in its decisions regarding the Council of State, and here too the auspices looked good. It confirmed all Cromwell's interim councillors as members, starting with himself, and decided to make up their number to thirty-one—ten fewer than under the Rump, though the average attendance at this council was to be actually higher. Six of the eighteen new councillors were religious radicals, but they also included Charles Howard (the future Earl of Carlisle), Edward Montagu (the future Earl of Sandwich), Sir Anthony Ashley Cooper (the future Earl of Shaftesbury), Viscount Lisle, and Sir Charles Wolseley—not exactly 'artificers of the meanest trades'. All were members of the parliament (as we can now call it) except Charles Fleetwood, who was obviously chosen because of his almost vice-regal position as commander-in-chief in Ireland, but never attended because of his absence there. The council was a youngish body, with at least twelve members under forty and probably only seven (including Cromwell) over fifty. The average age of the parliament itself, as far as can be known, was only just over forty.

The parliament set about its business with enthusiasm. The divisions during its first month show an average of almost 105 members present out of 144 (including the co-opted ones), and the absentees included a few who declined their summons on principle. Cromwell was one of these; he seems never to have taken his seat, except on one day of prayer, but that was probably through a wish not to seem to sway an assembly that he himself had called. This attendance record contrasts sharply with that of the Rump, in which over the years the number present had averaged about 55 out of well over 200. And whereas the Rump had sat on only four days a week except in emergencies, and rarely for more than three hours, Barebone's Parliament met on every day except Sunday, and began its often lengthy sittings with prayers at 8 a.m. It very soon showed its commitment to initiating reform in areas where the Rump had stalled, by setting up committees to consider what should be done about tithes, financial administration (including the project of a single treasury), prisons and prisoners, trade and corporations, the relief of poverty, the advancement of learning, and most contentious of all 'the business of the law'. These were not all, and by 21 July every member so far present had been appointed to one of the House's ten committees, or to the Council of State, or to the Commission for the Admiralty and Navy. This early zeal and spirit of co-operation were not to be maintained, but in spite of the divisions which later afflicted it Barebone's Parliament managed to pass more than thirty statutes during its five months' existence. That was far more than the

Rump had ever achieved in such a term, and the first parliament of the Protectorate was to sit nearly as long and pass none. Barebone's has sometimes been written off as one in a series of 'constitutional experiments', but that is far from the mark—further indeed than the depiction of it as an attempt to establish a rule of the saints, since that really was the aim of a small minority of Fifth Monarchists in the Council of Officers and in the House itself. For Cromwell and the majority of his fellow-officers it was an expedient rather than an experiment. His expulsion of the Rump may have been a mistake, and in his several retrospective speeches he seems to have found it among all his actions the most uncomfortable to explain, but in the circumstance a nominated ruling assembly, to tide the nation over until it could safely return to elected parliaments, made a good deal of sense. With a little more goodwill and good fortune it might even have worked.

While it was getting down to business so purposefully, a figure from the recent past re-emerged to cause it some embarrassment. The banished John Lilburne had been intriguing with a number of fellow-exiles on the royalist side, and there were reports from several quarters that he had offered, for a consideration of £10,000, to bring about the destruction of Cromwell, the Rump, and the Council of State and to raise 40,000 men for the king. He and the Duke of Buckingham, the rakish son of James I's favourite, had formed a close attachment. He longed to return home, but he hated Cromwell as much as ever. Commenting in March 1653 on reports that the army was pressing to put an end to the Rump, he wrote that he was resolved 'never to see England, so long as Cromwell's most hateful and detestable beastly tyranny lasteth, unless it be in a way to pursue him, as the grandest tyrant and traitor that ever England bred'.[9] But when the Rump was expelled, Lilburne saw a chance of getting its act of banishment annulled and made his humble addresses to Cromwell, asking for a pass to let him back into England. He was told that he must wait for the new supreme authority to adjudge his case, but he decided to take a chance, and after a farewell dinner with Buckingham and other royalists he sailed for Dover on 14 June. On reaching London he tried and failed to get an audience with Cromwell, but he wrote him a letter full of false pathos, promising to serve the Commonwealth to his best ability, or if that was not acceptable to retire submissively 'to the most private life'.[10] His recent conduct and writings, however, made such a change of heart unbelievable. Cromwell referred him to the Council of State, which promptly committed him to Newgate. But he was not without sympathizers in the council, nor in the Nominated Parliament when it met. It was decided, to the credit of all concerned, that his case should be determined by due process of law, and

[9] L. Colonel John Lilburne Revived (1653), quoted in Pauline Gregg, Free-Born John (1961), p. 320.
[10] Gregg, Free-Born John, p. 322.

Cromwell promised him a fair trial. This was appointed for 13 July at the Old Bailey, and formally all that the court had to decide was whether the prisoner at the bar was the John Lilburne named in the act of banishment. If he was, it could proceed to the death sentence therein prescribed. This was unlikely to be carried out, partly because of his personal popularity and partly because of a reluctance to endorse one of the discredited Rump's more tyrannical acts; the new regime could have won credit for clemency by commuting his sentence to imprisonment.

But if this was Cromwell's preferred scenario—and the supposition is only a conjecture—Lilburne's was different. He hoped that the new supreme authority would repudiate the Rump's act, or failing that that a London jury would refuse to convict him. He and his friends mounted a campaign of pamphlets and petitions reminiscent of the heyday of the Leveller movement; two dozen of them appeared on the bookstalls during July and August. One, by Lilburne himself, appealed to parliament to suspend his trial, and this was refused only after considerable debate. When the trial did open, he and his friends made it into a great piece of public theatre. His supporters packed the courtroom and thronged the surrounding streets, women (as before in his career) being conspicuous among the demonstrators. The council had detailed three cavalry regiments to stand by, but found it needed considerably more of both horse and foot to keep some kind of order. Lilburne exercised all his oratorical skill and knowledge of the law to probe every chink in the prosecution's case, and in the course of four strenuous days he won several quite exceptional concessions from the court, which then adjourned until 10 August. When it resumed, the demonstrations grew in volume. He spun out the proceedings for ten more days, refusing to plead to the charge because he challenged its fundamental validity. He finally entered a plea of not guilty, but only when threatened with the ancient penalty of being crushed to death if he went on declining. The jury then went out, and after long deliberation returned its famous verdict that he was 'not guilty of any crime worthy of death'. This was of course utterly irregular, because juries are judges only of fact and not of law, but they were rewarded with a series of great shouts as the news of their boldness spread through the surrounding streets. The very soldiers who guarded them blew their trumpets and beat their drums. It is heartwarmingly typical of the times that twelve nameless London citizens, at real risk to themselves, refused to be party to what they saw as a piece of tyranny, and in effect passed judgement on the Rump's act of banishment and the penalty that it decreed. These jurors stood up subsequently to a severe grilling by the Council of State, but they were quite unrepentant and they went unpunished.[11]

---

[11] On Lilburne's trial and its contempary impact see Gregg, *Free-Born John*, ch. 28, and Woolrych, *Commonwealth to Protectorate*, pp. 250–62.

What to do with Lilburne himself was an embarrassing question. Few would have wanted to vindicate the Rump's treatment of him, but his relations with the exiled royalists and his reviving power to stir up the soldiery made him a real danger. His attitude to the present parliament was typically equivocal; just before his trial he had addressed it as 'the Supreme Authority for the Commonwealth of England', but since then some of the petitioners on his behalf had been questioning its claim to be a parliament at all. His fate was referred to the House itself, which resolved, though only after much contention, that he should remain imprisoned 'for the peace of this nation'. He was transferred to the Tower, where his devoted wife was given permission to join him. But he was allowed no visitors, and with his disappearance from sight the agitation for his release quite quickly died down.

By that time the parliament had sat for two months, and serious divisions had appeared within its ranks, chiefly over tithes and the reform of the law. Today it requires a stretch of the historical imagination to understand what strong feelings the issue of tithes aroused from the time of the Rump onward, but opposition to them ranged over several levels, both secular and religious, and touched on some deep convictions. On the material plane tithes fell very unequally on different sectors of the population. They were a severe burden on small landholders, who mostly had to part with literally a tenth part of the produce of their crops and livestock. Wealthy townsmen by contrast generally escaped or evaded them altogether, while many substantial landowners actually profited from them, since their forbears, in appropriating the estates of religious houses to their own use on long leases before and during the Reformation, had often acquired the rectorial tithes of the parish livings within the gift of the monasteries concerned. About a third of all the tithes paid in England went to these lay 'impropriators', and not to the parochial clergy for whom they were originally designated. They had become a marketable property, and those who owned or traded in them saw the movement to abolish them as part of a radical threat to property itself. Moreover such tithes as were still the clergy's by right rewarded them very unequally, leaving some lucky rectors very well off, while many a parish vicar got less than enough to live on.

At the spiritual level, many strong protestants condemned tithes as popish and superstitious, a relic of the age before the Gospel superseded the Law and an apostolic ministry replaced the Levitical priesthood. The most radical objection to them, however, came from strict separatists who rejected the whole conception of a national church with a publicly maintained clergy, and held that the state as such had no business with religion, except perhaps to punish gross blasphemy. In their view the only true church consisted of a body of believers voluntarily united by a covenant with God and with each other, and each such church should choose and maintain its own pastor.

Many members of Barebone's Parliament held this position, which was not confined to sectarian fanatics; John Milton was soon to write its classic defence. Few in the House took the wholly conservative view that had been defended in the Rump, namely that tithes had a scriptural authority that Christ had not abrogated, and that being also an ancient and integral part of the law of England they were the indefeasible property of those to whom they were legally due.

The main line of division in Barebone's Parliament lay between the outright abolitionists and the rather larger number who aimed to reform but not to remove the public provision for the parochial clergy, and so were against abrogating tithes until a superior system had been devised to replace them. The matter was referred to a large committee in which both parties were equally represented, and its brief was greatly extended a month later when the House instructed it to propose the best means of ejecting ignorant and scandalous ministers and encouraging godly preachers. This implied the continuance of a national ministry, but this and other evidence of a moderate reformist line in parliament was countered in the public mind by various extravagant excesses among the London sects, accompanied by a wave of millenarian petitions against not only tithes but any form of established church. These generated a counter-campaign of petitions in defence of a publicly maintained preaching ministry, and the effect of so much contention was to foster a widespread impression among the public that the church was in danger.[12]

The parliament's attempt to reform the law started out with just as good intentions as its efforts to promote the preaching of the gospel, and ended by becoming if anything even more divisive. All members agreed that the law needed to be reformed, but they differed radically over how it should be done. There were three broad schools of thought. The first, to which Cromwell and the moderate majority in the House adhered, wanted to preserve the historic common law of England in its essentials but to improve and expedite its procedures, clarify its obscurities and archaisms, abolish parasitic fees, make its benefits available to a wider public, and render it more humane, especially with regard to insolvent debtors and the excessive number of capital crimes. A more radical objective was pursued by the Levellers and their fellow-travellers, who regarded the current legal system as a product of the Norman Yoke imposed by the Conquest, and aimed to scrap it altogether. They wanted to replace it with a simple written code that would be easily comprehensible

---

[12] For a masterly account of tithes, impropriations, and the controversies over the provision for the clergy in mid-seventeenth-century England, see Christopher Hill, *Economic Problems of the Church from Archbishop Whitgift to the Long Parliament* (Oxford, 1956), esp. chs. 4–6. On the tithes debate in the Nominated Parliament see Woolrych, *Commonwealth to Protectorate*, pp. 235–50, 333, 336–8, 342–3.

by the laity and could be competently administered by popularly elected magistrates, holding court at frequent intervals in every county, without any need for professional advocates. The third school of reformers consisted of the Fifth Monarchist and other extreme sectaries, who believed that the kingdom of Christ was in process of being established and that the only laws fit to be observed in it were those contained in the Scriptures, whether in the Mosaic code or the teachings of Christ. Incredible as it may seem, they really were confident that these were 'perfect and sufficient, and so large as the wisdom of God judged needful for regulating judgement in all ages and nations. For no action or case ... possibly can fall out in this or other nations, by sea or land, but the like did or possibly might fall out in the land of Israel'.[13] This was of course the position of a minority, but it was a very vocal minority, both inside and outside the House.

The moderate reformist party had a programme ready-made in the work of the Hale Commission, which in the later days of the Rump had drafted fifteen bills for specific reforms and a comprehensive act for a more general restructuring of legal institutions and procedures.[14] The House chose its committee 'for the business of the law' on 20 July with particular care. Eight of its nineteen members had been called to the bar, two more had been attorneys, and another was a specialist in Scottish law. Seven MPs had actually served on the Hale Commission, and all were appointed to the committee. Six or seven of its members could be categorized as radicals of one hue or another, but none of these were extremists or Fifth Monarchy men. The committee took the Hale Commission's drafts as its starting-point, and two of them, including an act for civil marriage, were passed with amendments into law. But radical members were dissatisfied with the moderate tone and measured pace of the committee's work, and during August several developments coincided to make them press for more drastic action. One was Lilburne's challenge to the law's injustices, together with all the clamour and propaganda that accompanied his trial. Another was a debate on the Court of Chancery, which was notorious for its slow and arcane processes and for the fees exacted by its swollen body of officials and clerks; this ended in a vote in the House to abolish the court outright, before deciding who or what should take over its functions. A third was a set of charges that parliament heard on 17 August against the Keeper of the Marshalsea, Sir John Lenthall, brother of the Speaker of the Long Parliament. They were probably not all true, but they painted a

---

[13] William Aspinwall, *A Brief Description of the Fifth Monarchy* (1653), p. 11, quoted in Woolrych, *Commonwealth to Protectorate*, p. 264.

[14] The adverse view of the Hale Commission's work taken by older legal historians has been radically revised, notably by Mary Cotterell in 'Interregnum law reform', *English Historical Review* LXXXIII (1968), 689–704, and by Donald Veall, *The Popular Movement for Law Reform* (Oxford, 1970). On the Nominated Parliament's handling of law reform see Woolrych, *Commonwealth to Protectorate*, esp. pp. 262–73, 291–9.

shocking picture of venality and extortion, practised by the prison's whole staff upon the poor debtors within it. They occupied the House for most of two days, and they may have been the last straw in convincing its radical members that the legal system as it stood was rotten to the core. With many of the less zealous attenders absent, arranging for their families to join them for the winter, the hard-line reformers carried a vote by forty-six to thirty-eight to set up a new committee 'to consider of a new model of the law'—at least that is what they thought they voted for, but the Clerk of the Parliament misheard the motion and recorded it as for 'a new *body* of the law'. They tried twice to get the word corrected, but the moderates rallied and successfully insisted that 'body' should stand, thinking that this even more alarming prospect would discredit the whole enterprise.

The word in fact made little difference. The new committee had a predominantly radical membership, and it set out to codify all that it found good and just in the existing laws, harmonize them with the law of God, and prescribe proportionable punishments for specific offences. It invoked the example of Massachusetts, where such a written code had been promulgated ten years earlier, but England, with its age-old complexities of tenure and property rights, was not Massachusetts. The new committee did not supersede the original one 'for the business of the law', which continued to meet. The result was that the parliament was committed simultaneously to two fundamentally different programmes of law reform, which would almost certainly have proved incompatible, and would weaken the prospects of securing the very real benefits that the Hale Commission's projects held forth. The impact on conservative public opinion was deeply damaging.

Cromwell became increasingly disillusioned with the parliament as the summer wore on. Writing to Fleetwood on 22 August, he lamented the lack of mutual kindness among its members and their division into parties, each of which was turning upon himself. Shortly afterwards he was reported as saying that he was 'more troubled now with the fool than before with the knave'.[15] The millenarian enthusiasts who had so rejoiced when he expelled the Rump were coming to feel that he was no longer the chosen instrument of the work of the Lord, and no one preached that message with more histrionic ostentation than the Fifth Monarchist prophetess Anna Trapnel, whose performances had something of the pull of a raree-show. His old comrade-in-arms Harrison was drawing steadily further away from him. On the other hand the moderates were inclined to blame him, though much less publicly, for not supporting them more actively and for giving such a free rein to the zealots. Whether he was wise not to take the seat to which the parliament

[15] Abbott, *Writings and Speeches of Oliver Cromwell*, III, 89; Woolrych, *Commonwealth to Protectorate*, p. 274.

co-opted him may well be doubted, but he was ultra-sensitive to the charge that he had broken the Rump in order to secure power for himself, and he clung as long as he could to the belief, which he had expressed so passionately in his opening speech, that authority had come to the present assembly through divine providence. If that were so, providence must be trusted to guide it, and it would be wrong for him to usurp that role. The Council of State was not in a position to provide the management that he failed to offer, partly because of its lack of experience in such skills and partly because it was almost as divided as the House itself.

Cromwell's policy of non-intervention was eventually strained beyond breaking-point by the new government's ineptitude in foreign relations, when it could be brought to giving them any consideration at all. During the Interregnum between April and July, envoys from France, Spain, Portugal, and the United Provinces had attempted to open negotiations with him, as well as a minister representing the Prince of Condé and the rebel *frondeurs* besieged in Bordeaux—though any chance that England might support them, as Cromwell was inclined to do, ended when Bordeaux surrendered to Louis XIV on 20 July. France itself was seeking a closer accord with England, Spain wanted a commercial treaty, and the King of Portugal sought a treaty of peace that could help him in his struggle for independence from Spain. But the most urgent mission was that of four envoys whom the States-General sent in June, for the Anglo-Dutch war was having disastrous effects on Dutch commerce after the battle of the Gabbard, and even worse after the further defeat off the Texel. Cromwell referred all these diplomatic overtures to the interim Council of State, and implied that any long-term commitments would have to await the meeting of the new supreme authority.

The Dutch commissioners had their first meeting with the four Englishmen appointed to treat with them four days after Barebone's assembled. To Cromwell's dismay, the English commissioners demanded the same impossibly harsh preconditions that had wrecked negotiations under the Rump, including reparations for English losses in the war, the handing over to English occupation of several Dutch 'cautionary towns', to be chosen by England, and a humiliating public acknowledgement that Tromp had been the original aggressor. Several times Cromwell sent privately to one or other of the Dutchmen to suggest ways in which the terms might be modified, but he himself still clung to the idea of a partial fusion of sovereignties between the two republics, so as to form the united core of a triumphant 'protestant interest' in Europe. He would soon give this up when he came to realize how utterly unacceptable it was to the Dutch, but no such realism was to be expected from the parliament or its Council of State. The latter kept changing the composition of its committee for foreign affairs, and like the House itself was too engrossed in domestic issues for weeks at a time to give foreign policy any proper attention. The scales were tilted against a reasonable peace by a combination of ill-informed chauvinists who held inflated views about the terms that England's victories entitled them to demand, and the millenarian minority who were opposed to a peace altogether. It may seem strange that Harrison and his kind in the House and the Fifth Monarchist preachers outside it were so opposed to a treaty with a fellow-protestant power, but victory had gone to their heads—victory over the king (representing the fourth monarchy), over the Scots, over the Irish, and now over the Dutch. The latter's protestantism made little appeal to them, for its prevailing tone was an orthodox Calvinism akin to that of the English Presbyterians, who were their enemies. As they saw it, the Dutch obsession with trade and material wealth aligned the United Provinces with the carnal kingdoms that were soon to be overthrown, republican though they nominally were, and England's victory over them marked an early stage in a career of conquest which would culminate when the saints toppled the throne of the Roman Antichrist himself. Fundamentalist fanaticism tends to flourish when political institutions are in the melting-pot, and the firebrands took advantage of the loosening of traditional restraints, both secular and ecclesiastical.

The naivety and incompetence of the new government in diplomatic business became a matter of notoriety among the foreign envoys and ambassadors in London. The Dutch commissioners, hearing the Fifth Monarchist fulminations against their country and the projected peace, must have wondered what kind of land they had come to. But Cromwell kept in touch with them, often clandestinely, and he played an increasingly interventionist role as the autumn wore on. Understanding now how strongly disliked his conception of a 'coalition' was, he let them know that he would not pursue it. He worked closely with John Thurloe, the secretary to the Council of State, a born negotiator and intelligence-gatherer who had held the same post since the Rump's last year in power. Thurloe played an increasing role in conducting the council's diplomatic correspondence and contacts with ambassadors, and in so doing brought some sense to its handling of foreign affairs.

Although the main issues that were to split the parliament fatally can be seen emerging quite early, the House was not in a regular habit of polarizing until well into the autumn. It considered most other questions that came before it on their merits, without dividing along a predictable party line between moderates and radicals. Its legislative achievement was not negligible. Of its twenty-nine public acts (there were also a few private ones), many were of a purely administrative nature, or renewed existing statutes that were due to lapse. But its act for civil marriages was not the only one of more general interest. The act for the disposal of land in Ireland laid one of the bases of the Protectoral settlement of that country, and a bill to incorporate Scotland with England in a single commonwealth was ready by 23 November for its final passage when the outbreak of a royalist rising under the Earl of Glencairn caused it to be laid aside. An act for the relief of creditors and poor prisoners, though limited in scope and duration, was a step towards further reform under the Protectorate. Another act protected the persons and estates of lunatics, and several more ambitious reforms were in the pipeline when the end came. Two of them sought to provide for jurisdiction in equity after Chancery was abolished, but Chancery was an issue that split the House down the middle. A bill introduced in mid-October to suspend proceedings in the court for a month led to heated debates and a tied division; the Speaker gave his casting vote against it.

With the increase in dissension went a decline in attendance. After the counts of well over 100 in July, divisions in August show a presence ranging from 71 to 91, an average of 72 in September and of 70 in October—just under half the membership. One can guess that many moderates shared Cromwell's disillusion with the parliament, and found the zealots' constant pressing of their views repellent and tedious, but few of the absentees withdrew from it completely. They could still turn out in force for a vote on a matter of real concern to them, and they did so strikingly on 1 November, when the term of the Council of State chosen in July expired and a new one was elected. It had been decided that sixteen of the currently serving councillors, chosen by ballot, should be retained, and fifteen new ones elected. The polling left only four radicals in the whole council. Some of the busiest MPs in the House lost their places on it, and even Harrison only just scraped back—but then he had attended only seven council meetings since July, and he came to none at all after his re-election. By contrast every member present, no fewer than 113, voted to retain Cromwell. The voting also showed a strong preference for men of gentry rank.

If the moderate majority had maintained their presence and given their constant support to the council they had thus transformed, and to Cromwell's increasingly active role in it, they might just have enabled the parliament to run its appointed sixteen-month course. But it was not to be. On the very day after the council elections the attendance fell to sixty-five, and on 15 November to forty-nine. Yet two days later well over a hundred members turned up for a debate on the right of lay patrons to present to ecclesiastical benefices. This was an issue of great social and economic as well as religious significance. In four of the largest dioceses, York, Lincoln, Norwich, and Rochester, nearly two-thirds of parish livings were in the gift of lay patrons, and the proportion was high everywhere. Such patrons frequently bought and sold advowsons, which the law treated as freeholds. They often paid the vicars they appointed a mere fraction of the rectorial tithes which they themselves received, and bestowed benefices upon kinsmen dependants, and any clergymen willing to marry their dowerless daughters. Yet widespread though such abuses were, lay patronage was often employed to less selfish ends. Most of the puritan clergy who held parish livings owed them to like-minded peers and gentry who owned the advowson, and a few of these encouraged congregations to name the parson they wanted. The main opponent of lay patrons' rights before the Civil War had been Archbishop Laud.

The matter therefore was not a straight issue between conservatives and radicals, for the parliament included many sober Independents who while moderate enough on other questions believed deeply in the right of every congregation to choose its pastor. With their support, and after strenuous debate, the House voted by sixty to forty-three that a bill should be brought in to abolish 'the power of patrons to present to benefices'. This significantly added to the parliament's unpopularity among property-owners generally, and was cited by the first speaker on its last day as a prime reason for ending its existence. At about the same time the renewal of the excise and a new bill for the abolition of Chancery further alienated conservative opinion, and Lilburne hit the news-sheets again in a way that stirred populist feeling against the government. In mid-November he understandably tried to obtain his release through a writ of habeas corpus in the Upper Bench, as the former King's Bench was now called. A worried Council of State intervened and ordered the Lieutenant of the Tower not to deliver him, and on the 26th the House confirmed that he was to remain a prisoner 'until the parliament shall take further order'.[16] It was uncomfortable to be put in the position of overriding the due process of law, just when the pseudo-parliament's standing as a legitimate government was being questioned more strongly than ever before.

From mid-November onward the foreign diplomats in London were reporting that an early dissolution was widely expected, to be followed by a change in the whole form of government. They commonly named four reasons: the stresses and divisions within the parliament itself, the resultant frustration of the peace treaty that the majority of Englishmen and Dutchmen dearly wanted, the increasing seriousness of an incipient royalist insurrection in Scotland, and the stridency of the Fifth Monarchist preachers in London, whose jeremiads were rising to a pitch that no government could put up with. It was of course intolerable that peace with the Dutch should be denied by a combination of domestic distractions, ill-informed negotiators, and the Fifth Monarchists' crazy expectations of a career of universal conquest by the saints. Of the royalist movement in Scotland more will be said in the next chapter, but it was spreading from the Highlands where it originated and threatening to become a general national movement against the presence of English conquerors on Scottish soil. The Earl of Glencairn, whom the king commissioned to command his forces, was himself a Lowlander. Resolutioners were praying openly for the king, and even the Protesters, who had been so strict against an uncovenanted monarch, saw Glencairn's adherents as less of an enemy than the English. The latter were lucky that the powerful Earl of Argyll stuck to his alliance with them and resolutely opposed the insurgents, but there was a real danger that if the rising spread further it would encourage the English royalists to take to arms too. It was probably in November 1653 that the most active of them formed the highly secret committee which they called the Sealed Knot, with the aim of giving leadership and organization to royalist conspiracy throughout England.

The situation called for firm and competent hands at the helm, but a combination of factors was increasingly undermining the government's stability. Many of the moderate MPs, who commanded a majority when they were present in force and might have held the parliament on constructive courses, especially after the new council was chosen on 1 November, more or less gave up hope of it and stayed away, except when matters of special concern to them were voted on. This enabled the radical minority to promote projects like the codification of the law and the abolition of Chancery which deeply antagonized most of the political nation. But a major part in the downfall of Barebone's Parliament was played by the Fifth Monarchist preachers in London, particularly by those who led the great prayer meetings held each Monday at St Anne's, Blackfriars, where Christopher Feake was pastor. It may seem strange that incendiaries who thundered a message that sounds so absurd to modern ears could pose any serious threat, but what made them dangerous was that they received enthusiastic support from the Fifth Monarchist caucus and its fellow-travellers within the parliament, and from Harrison and his following in the army. Parallels may suggest themselves with movements of fundamentalist fanaticism today, but the fundamentalism of Feake and Harrison and their brethren was not based on the bible as a whole but on a few apocalyptic books, especially Daniel and Revelation, that fed their feverish visions and their hunger for power. Twice, in late October and early November, Cromwell sent for several of the Blackfriars preachers, and in the presence of such moderate divines as Owen, Nye, Marshall, and Jessey tried gently to persuade them that all those who professed to follow Christ should strive to agree in mutual love and refrain from reviling each other. It was to no avail. Two Mondays later the Blackfriars fulminators were blasting the parliament, the council, the army, and everyone in power in scurrilous terms, and by late November they were concentrating their shafts upon Cromwell himself, 'calling him the man of sin, the old dragon, and many other scripture ill names'.[17] Harrison was reportedly railing every day against him and the Anglo-Dutch peace negotiations, and there were allegations that

[17] *Thurloe State Papers*, I, 621.

he and his party were aiming to take over the command of the army. There was never any real danger of that, but Harrison was capable of seriously dividing it, and his favourite preachers were aspersing the loyal majority of its officers as janissaries and pensioners of Babylon, corrupted by wealth and power. Vavasor Powell 'told the sword-men in general, that the Spirit of God had departed from them; that heretofore they had been precious and excellent men, but that their parks, and new houses, and gallant wives had choked them up'.[18]

In the parliament's later stages its radical millenarian members were meeting frequently at the home of one Arthur Squibb, MP for Middlesex, to concert their policy. There were strong reports that they were plotting to secede from parliament and set up as an authority on their own, backed by their friends in the army. This sounds extravagant, but it may have been a contingency plan in the event of the great decisions still pending, concerning tithes, the ministry, and the law, going against them. It was indeed the question of a national clergy and the manner of maintaining it that triggered the end of the parliament. How to provide for the public ministry had been referred, it will be remembered, to the committee for tithes, whose recommendations were heard at last on 2 December. Six days of intense debate ensued, filling almost all of the parliament's remaining life.

What the committee proposed represented an honest attempt to secure the dedicated parochial clergy that most of the nation clearly wanted, and its scheme did not differ greatly in principle from that which Owen and his brethren had submitted to the Rump in 1652. The ultimate responsibility for ejecting unworthy incumbents and replacing them with godly and competent ones was to be vested in twenty-one commissioners, but England and Wales were to be divided into seven circuits, in each of which these national commissioners were to act in consultation with local ones, chosen on the basis of three or four per county. Tithes were to be retained, supplemented where necessary so as to give all parish clergy an adequate income, but people who had conscientious scruples about paying tithes were to be allowed to make an equivalent contribution in money or land, to be assessed by their nearest JP.

Few members can have been aware that the parliament's very existence would hang on the way they voted on these proposals. Major-General Lambert, however, had decided quite some time earlier that it was past saving, and that the country needed a new kind of government altogether. He had never thought that a nominated assembly was a good solution, and he had withdrawn from active political life from the day it met, ignoring its co-optation of him and ceasing to attend the Council of State. Years earlier he had

---

[18] *Strena Vavasoriensis* (1654), pp. 18–19, quoted in Woolrych, *Commonwealth to Protectorate*, p. 331.

assisted Ireton in framing the Heads of the Proposals, and now in his leisure at Wimbledon House, the former royal residence that a grateful Commonwealth had assigned to him for his outstanding military services, he worked from about mid-October on a written constitution. It bore a broad resemblance to Ireton's Proposals, and like them it was a prescription for a limited monarchy, though this time the monarch was to be Cromwell. It came to be called the Instrument of Government. At some time in the latter part of November, when Barebone's was visibly heading for the rocks, he took half-a-dozen fellow-officers into his confidence and discussed his draft closely with them. How far they contributed to its final form is unknown, but the general belief was and is that the Instrument was essentially Lambert's work. He and they brought it to Cromwell a few days before the committee for tithes reported, having assembled a large number of officers at Whitehall, without telling them why. He probably hoped to announce an imminent dissolution and to obtain their acclamation of King Oliver and the new constitution there and then. But in the course of long discussions with Cromwell, both on that day and the next, he and his coadjutors found him adamantly opposed to their proposals on two central points: he would not hear of the title of king, and he would not be a party to forcibly terminating an assembly whose authority he himself had given nearly a year more to run.

But if Cromwell would not dissolve the parliament, the parliament might be persuaded to dissolve itself. The pretext came when it took its first and only vote on the report from the committee for tithes, on Saturday 10 December. This was on its first clause, which prescribed the manner in which unworthy incumbents were to be removed and godly ones chosen to replace them. It was lost by just two votes in an exceptionally full House; 115 members were present, including the Speaker. There was no motion to recommit the clause, so the whole scheme was in effect rejected. It is evident that radicals who were opposed on principle to tithes and an established clergy were joined by conservatives who would rather have kept the traditional system of maintenance and patronage in place, but it is not impossible that some who voted with the majority were already in collusion with Lambert and his friends, and were deliberately helping them to bring the parliament to an end.

At its next sitting, on Monday the 12th, the moderate members took their seats earlier than most of them were wont to do, and in force. Clearly they were following a concerted plan, and there can be little doubt that Lambert and his group were parties to it. One member after another rose to denounce the radicals, for threatening not only the church and its clergy by throwing out the tithes committee's recommendations, but the army by opposing the assessment, the legal system by abolishing Chancery and projecting a 'new body of the law', and property itself by annulling the rights of patrons. Since the parliament had patently failed to answer the people's expectations, they proposed that it should abdicate. Speaker Rous was clearly in the plot, for he allowed no hearing to those who wished to speak against the motion, and when the resigners got up to leave the chamber he rose too and led them, without putting any question. Those who followed him numbered between forty and fifty, but they easily outnumbered the thirty or so members who sat on in the House in protest. It being a Monday, some of the zealots were away attending the weekly prayer meeting at Blackfriars. Two colonels and a file of musketeers soon arrived and cleared the protesters from the chamber, for it was as well not to let them reach a quorum. It looked as though Lambert had the situation in hand.

Rous and the majority processed to Whitehall Palace, where they considered and signed a one-sentence document whereby they resigned to Cromwell the powers that they had received from him. Late-comers soon swelled their number, and when they were ready Cromwell received them. He seemed surprised by their resignation, which he said placed a very heavy burden on him, but he accepted it. He solemnly told his next parliament that he had known nothing of it beforehand, and that was probably true, because once Lambert and his colleagues had come up against his blank refusal to dissolve the parliament by force it was only sensible for them and their friends in the House to keep their plans from him. But he had been in close consultation with Lambert and his collaborators over the terms of their proposed written constitution for several days before the resignation took place, so he was clearly envisaging at least a possibility of its being implemented. And if they found it politic not to tell him what they and their friends in the House were up to, perhaps he was wise enough not to ask questions. There was certainly no questioning the resignation itself, for within a couple of days nearly eighty members had signed it. They deserved better than to have their honest efforts for the Commonwealth wrecked by a wave of irrational fanaticism, inside and outside the parliament-house, but many had a future in the coming regime.

If the Rump had had few mourners but the Rumpers, Barebone's had fewer by far—not many indeed outside the ranks of the Fifth Monarchy men. There were predictably some angry sermons from Feake and his kind, but there were also bonfires in some of London's streets to attest a spirit of positive rejoicing. The question was how many of the gathered churches would align with the Fifth Monarchists in opposing the imminent change in government, and how the considerably larger number of Baptist congregations would react; 'Anabaptist' was a generic label for extremist sectaries in the hostile vocabulary of the time. But though some prominent Baptists such as Hanserd Knollys and Henry Jessey remained suspicious of the Protectorate, three others of high reputation, William Kiffin, John Spilsbery, and Joseph Fansom, published a circular letter to the Baptist churches in January 1654, urging them not to engage against it, because the Blackfriars prophets and their friends in Barebone's Parliament had been bringing magistracy itself, which was God's ordinance, into disrepute. In asserting that the civil magistrate must derive his power immediately from God, and be accountable to no one else, they were echoing the claims of Charles I.[19]

[19] Woolrych, *Commonwealth to Protectorate*, pp. 349–50. The letter by Kiffin, Spilsbery, and Fansom is in J. Nickolls (ed.), *Original Letters and Papers of State . . . among the Political Collections of Mr. John Milton* (1743), pp. 159–60.

# PART IV: FURTHER READING

On everything that concerns the government of the Commonwealth down to the expulsion of the Rump, Blair Worden, *The Rump Parliament* (Cambridge, 1974) is the prime authority. The fullest account of the next phase, through Barebone's Parliament to the establishment of the Protectorate, is in the present writer's *Commonwealth to Protectorate* (Oxford, 1982; repr., 2000). For Scotland, where David Stevenson, *Revolution and Counter-Revolution in Scotland* (1977) leaves off, the story is taken up by F. D. Dow's equally excellent *Cromwellian Scotland* (Edinburgh, 1979). On the military campaigns we have John D. Grainger, *Cromwell against the Scots: The Last Anglo-Scottish War, 1650–1652* (East Linton, 1997). For Ireland, the broad account in *A New History of Ireland*, III (Oxford, 1976) is filled out by Tom Reilly's spirited *Cromwell: An Honourable Enemy* (Dingle, 1999), J. Scott Wheeler's more critical *Cromwell in Ireland* (1999), and the essays edited by Jane Ohlmeyer in *Ireland, from Independence to Occupation, 1641–1660* (Cambridge, 1995). Ohlmeyer also gives the best concise account of 'The Civil Wars in Ireland', in *The Civil Wars: A Military History of England, Scotland and Ireland 1638–1660*, edited by John Kenyon and herself (Oxford, 1998).

On the challenge to successive Commonwealth governments by extreme millenarians, see Bernard Capp, *The Fifth Monarchy Men* (1972) and Murray Tolmie, *The Triumph of the Saints* (Cambridge, 1977). For the controversies over tithes, lay patronage, and clerical maintenance, Christopher Hill, *Economic Problems of the Church from Archbishop Whitgift to the Long Parliament* (Oxford, 1956 and later paperback editions) continues to be most helpful. Regarding the law, Donald Veall, *The Popular Movement for Law Reform 1640–1660* (Oxford, 1970) is the prime recommendation, but see also Stuart E. Prall, *The Agitation for Law Reform in the Puritan Revolution* (The Hague, 1966) and Mary Cotterell's seminal article in *English Historical Review* LXXXIII (1968).

On the first Dutch War, Charles Wilson's classic *Profit and Power* (1957) has been modified but not superseded by Steven C. A. Pincus, *Protestantism and Patriotism: Ideologies and the Making of English Foreign Policy, 1650–1668* (Cambridge, 1996). On the navy and naval operations, Bernard Capp, *Cromwell's Navy* (Oxford, 1989) continues to be the prime recommendation, but see also Michael Baumber, *General-at-Sea: Robert Blake and the Seventeenth-Century Revolution in Naval Warfare* (1989) and J. R. Powell, *Robert Blake, General-at-Sea* (1972).

For books on Cromwell see Further Reading for Part V.

# PART V

## Cromwell's Protectorate
### 1653–1658

# ✠ EIGHTEEN ✠

# A New Order in Three Nations

WITH Barebone's Parliament gone, nothing stood in the way of Lambert's Instrument of Government; indeed there was no other practicable way of filling the constitutional hiatus, short of bringing back the king. The day after the resignation, Lambert summoned a large concourse of army officers—considerably larger, it appears, than the regular General Council—to the Council Chamber in Whitehall, where he himself read the Instrument to them. He asked for their assent so that it could be formally presented to Cromwell in the name of them all. Some raised objections to it, as Harrisons's Fifth Monarchist faction was bound to do, but there may also have been a few uncompromising republicans among the unconvinced. Some may have remembered the many days spent in constitutional debate at Reading and Putney years earlier. But he persuaded the company that this was not a time for disputing over the document, for it had been under consideration for two months already, and it was important to keep the present Interregnum as brief as possible, with Feake and his brethren still ranting away and the cavaliers awaiting their chance. He secured the meeting's concurrence in general terms, promising that any suggested amendments would be considered. Cromwell's acceptance was already assured, for his title and other matters had been agreed in the course of close discussions with Lambert and his collaborators over recent days. A few details still probably remained to be settled, as did the important selection of the council, to which the constitution allotted a major role. But the new government was publicly inaugurated only three days after Lambert's meeting with the officers, and Cromwell was solemnly admitted to the office of Lord Protector on 16 December 1653.

The ceremony was staged in Westminster Hall, and its organizers took care to involve the Lord Mayor and aldermen of London in it as prominently as the new Council of State. Ranks of soldiers lined the route of the procession from Whitehall, but Cromwell himself wore a plain black suit and cloak. After the Instrument had been read out he took the oath prescribed in it, swearing to observe all its provisions, and in all else to govern England, Scotland, and Ireland according to their respective laws, statutes, and customs. He made a short speech, saying that his aim was that the gospel should shine in all its splendour and that the people should enjoy their just rights and property; then the company took coaches to the Banqueting Hall and heard a sermon. It is hard to gauge the public reaction to the day's show. There was some applause from those who turned out to watch it, but Bordeaux was not the only foreign diplomat to remark the general silence and indifference with which it was received. The ceremony was so little publicized in advance, however, that not many Londoners can have been fully aware of what was happening and what it signified. The Fifth Monarchists, of course, thought they knew perfectly. At Sunday service on 18 December Feake and Powell denounced Cromwell from the pulpit as 'the dissemblingest perjured villain in the world',[1] and at the next day's prayer meeting at Blackfriars preacher after preacher hurled Scripture-laden diatribes against him. Feake and Powell were imprisoned for a few days and the Blackfriars exercises banned, only for their brethren to shift their base to Christ Church in Newgate. But the Fifth Monarchists' excesses were losing them such public sympathy as they still commmanded, and they ceased to be a serious danger when they lost their places in the seats of power, both at Westminster and in the army. Harrison was asked for an assurance that he recognized and would obey the new government, and was quietly cashiered when he declined. Only two or three other officers of his persuasion resigned their commissions when faced with the same choice. Three or four colonels nursed more secular reservations about Cromwell's elevation which would surface later, but the army as a whole took it very quietly, and most of its senior officers welcomed it.

The constitution which defined Cromwell's powers, and which was to be the basis of Britain's government for the next three and a half years, was an honest and on the whole intelligent piece of work by Lambert and his collaborators, and not a mere cloak for a dictatorship. It did not establish a single sovereign power, but distinguished and partially separated the legislative authority and the executive.[2] The former was vested jointly in the Protector and parliament, the latter in the Protector 'assisted with a council', numbering not fewer than thirteen or more than twenty-one. The council was in fact accorded as important a constitutional role as the parliament, and limited the Protector's powers far more than the pre-war privy council had limited the monarch's. He was required to govern by its advice in all matters, and decisions of peace and war needed the consent of the majority of its members. Upon the death of a Protector, the election of his successor was entrusted to the council, and to the council alone. In exercising the all-important control and disposition of the armed forces by sea and land, the Protector had to act with the consent of the majority of the council when parliament was not

---

[1] *Thurloe State Papers*, I, 641.
[2] Text in Gardiner (ed.), *Constitutional Documents*, pp. 405–17.

sitting, and with parliament's own consent when it was. No limit was set to councillors' tenure of office, and neither the Protector nor parliament could dismiss them at pleasure, but an elaborate procedure was prescribed for removing and punishing any who were found guilty of corruption or other misconduct. When a councillor died or was dismissed, parliament was to nominate six candidates, the council was to select two of them, and the Protector was to appoint which of the pair he preferred. These provisions concerning the appointment and tenure of councillors were to prove highly controversial, and could have led to great friction if the Protector and parliament were ever at loggerheads, but they expressed Lambert's and his fellow-officers' embittered memories of the total subordination of the council to the Rump.

Parliaments were to be elected at three-year intervals, though the interval was to be measured from the dissolution of the preceding parliament, not from its election. This followed the precedent of the Long Parliament's Triennial Act, which set up procedures to ensure that not more than three years should elapse between one parliament's end and another's beginning. But whereas the 1641 act had fixed fifty days as a parliament's guaranteed minimum life, the Instrument protected it against dissolution (except by its own consent) for five months, and it set no explicit limit to its sitting. This may have been an oversight, because Cromwell certainly assumed that the constitution prevented parliaments from perpetuating themselves. But the authors of the Instrument were respectful towards the Long Parliament's decisions, including those of the Rump, whose abortive bill for a new representative they followed with regard to both the franchise (vested in adult males owning real or personal property worth £200) and the distribution of seats. There were to be four hundred members for England and Wales and thirty apiece for Scotland and Ireland. The English and Welsh constituencies were radically reapportioned, with only the larger towns retaining separate representation; county seats outnumbered those for cities and boroughs by more than two to one. Roman Catholics and Irish rebels were permanently disqualified from voting or standing; so for a limited period were former active royalists, unless they had since 'given signal testimony of their good affection'. The council was empowered to scrutinize the returns to the next three parliaments and to exclude members who fell outside the qualifications. The first parliament of the regime was to meet on 3 September next, the anniversary of Dunbar and Worcester, and until then the Protector and council were given a purely temporary power to make ordinances, whose continuance would be subject to parliament's assent.

The tricky question of a veto was resolved in a liberal spirit by providing that if the Protector did not consent to a bill within twenty days, and parliament then declared its wish to persist with it, the bill should become law, unless it contravened anything contained in the Instrument itself. The latter has been criticized for making no provision for its possible revision or amendment, but it left the way open for this to be effected by mutual consent. On the no less thorny matter of the revenue, it was written into the constitution that the state should have enough to support an army of 30,000 (which was little more than half the forces afoot late in 1653), 'a convenient number of ships for guarding of the seas' (thus left conveniently vague), along with £200,000 a year for civil government; but any further taxation, including what was needed to maintain 'the present extraordinary forces, both at sea and land', required parliamentary consent.

On the most sensitive of all issues the Instrument laid down 'That the Christian religion, as contained in the Scriptures, be held forth and recommended as the public profession of these nations', and its authors probably envisaged that a new confession of faith would be formulated, less rigid than that of the Westminster Assembly. This was not attempted until 1658, but it was intended to be binding only on the parochial clergy, whose funding from tithes was to be replaced 'as soon as may be' by a less objectionable provision (it never was). But though so much of an established church was to be retained, no one was to be compelled to attend its services or bow to its discipline. All who professed faith in God by Jesus Christ were to be free to practise their religion, so long as they did not abuse it to the civil injury of others, or disturb the peace, or invoke it to justify licentiousness. This liberty was not to extend to 'popery or prelacy', but there was a widespread de facto toleration of Anglican worship throughout the 1650s, and even towards catholics Cromwell's government was more indulgent than the letter of the law and the constitution prescribed. He was consistently more tolerant than his parliaments.

He certainly thought well of the constitution under which he ruled; he was to defend it passionately when it came under parliament's attack. But his immediate reason for assuming the office of Protector was that he saw it as a matter of necessity rather than choice, in order to prevent the country from heading further towards anarchy. 'I saw we were running headlong into confusion and disorder', he said in retrospect, 'and would necessarily run into blood, and I was passive to those that desired me to undertake the place that now I have.'[3] At a deeper level he believed that after the failure of each successive regime since the first Civil War to achieve settlement, and in view of the actual power and responsibility that he carried as commander-in-chief, divine providence was directing him to accept the headship of the state, on the terms that were so strongly pressed upon him. He felt the easier about it because those terms set strict limits upon a power which, after Barebone's resigned, he

---

[3] Abbott, *Writings and Speeches of Oliver Cromwell*, IV, 470.

had felt to be constitutionally unbounded. As he told his first parliament, 'In every government there must be somewhat fundamental, somewhat like a Magna Carta, that should be standing and be unalterable'. For him the Instrument filled that role. He endorsed the official apologia which Marchamont Nedham wrote in January 1654 and published as *A True State of the Case of the Commonwealth*; Cromwell expressly commended it to his first parliament. Nedham eulogized the Protectoral constitution for embodying elements of the three classic forms of government, monarchy, aristocracy, and democracy, in perfect balance, each contributing its particular virtues and restraining the possible abuses of the others.

In taking the council to represent aristocracy, Nedham was using the latter word in its classical rather than its modern sense, but the actual composition of Cromwell's council, no less than the powers given to it and to the parliament by the Instrument, should help us to judge whether the Protectorate deserves to be characterized as a military dictatorship, as it so often has been. Fifteen councillors were appointed by name in the Instrument, and three more were added during the next six months. Ten of the eighteen were civilians, and only Lambert, Fleetwood, Desborough, and the elderly, semi-retired Skippon were members of the field army. The remaining four were styled colonel, but three of them were administrators rather than soldiers, like Philip Jones, who commanded fifty men in Cardiff Castle but was really a sort of unofficial minister for Wales. The fourth, Edward Montagu, who was soon to be Pepys's patron and later Earl of Sandwich, had last commanded a regiment in 1645, though he was to become a General at Sea in 1656. Cromwell's council contained men of such diverse and independent views as Francis Rous, Viscount Lisle, Sir Charles Wolseley (still only twenty-three), Sir Gilbert Pickering, and Sir Anthony Ashley Cooper. Such a body of men was unlikely to act collectively as a rubber stamp to a dictatorship, nor did it. Cromwell wielded immense personal authority, and he would never have become Lord Protector if he had not been Lord General. But he had a genuine aversion to dictatorial power, and the constitution was genuinely designed to prevent such a thing. How far he observed its letter and spirit, and how far his rule can be characterized as military, can best be assessed when we have watched it in action over the next five years.

If 1653 was a climacteric year in the English political scene, it also marked a crucial phase in the resettlement of Scotland and Ireland, though in neither country did the process fit so neatly within a twelvemonth.

It will be remembered that after Worcester the Rump had first intended to annex Scotland to England, but had quite soon decided instead upon a union between the two commonwealths. While its terms were being considered at Westminster it sent eight commissioners north to lay the foundations of a peacetime administration, and they sat at Dalkeith from January to April 1652. Years of internal strife and occupation by an invading army had left both central and local government in serious disarray, and the commissioners did their honest best not merely to restore the *status quo ante bellum* but to set up something of a new and better order. They could not ignore the fact that large numbers of Scots had been at war with the English parliament on and off for years, and that resistance was still smouldering, especially in the Highlands. But since their main enemies, past and present, were among the nobles and lairds, and since the Rump had decreed that no jurisdiction should be exercised that did not draw its sanction from Westminster, they were able to make a clean sweep of some oppressive feudal survivals. The old baron (or barony) courts were abolished, to the considerable benefit of small tenants. Local justice now devolved upon the sheriff courts, and in each county the high sheriff's authority was shared between two men, one Scottish and one English. To head the judicial system at the national level, the parliamentary commissioners appointed seven Commissioners for the Administration of Justice, three Scottish and four English, and though the English judges were granted some superior powers (and double the salary), Scotsmen dominated the lower tiers of the judicial machine, which below the top level was left largely intact. The English judges were far more sceptical than their predecessors over accusations of witchcraft, and Scottish writers paid tribute to their even-handed and enlightened justice. Suits were not allowed to drag on as they had before, and smaller men pursued their rights at law against the rich and great to an extent they had not previously dared.

Restoring municipal government and jurisdiction was another major task, and the parliamentary commissioners linked it with a serious attempt to obtain the towns' acceptance of the forthcoming union. They organized the election of representatives of the shires and burghs, eighty-nine constituencies in all, to meet in Dalkeith during February 1652 in order to register their assent to a 'Tender of Incorporation' which was there presented to them. There was naturally considerable opposition to the union, and not just because Scotsmen valued their independent nationhood and were reluctant to renounce their king. The most hotly denounced of the English proposals was the one concerning religious toleration, and the clergy, both Resolutioners and Protesters, were vociferous in opposing the whole Tender on its account. But while the kirkmen could enjoy the luxury of protest, most of the laity saw sense in coming to terms, as a step towards ending the alien military presence, recovering a degree of self-government, and making sure of their lands and possessions. Seventy of the eighty-nine constituencies registered their assent to the Tender promptly, and a minority did so with positive enthusiasm. These were mainly in the west and south-west, where Cromwell and his army had been widely regarded as a lesser evil than Charles II and the 'malignants'.

Sixteen constituencies sent no delegates to Dalkeith, but in at least five it was on account of their poverty, and they were excused. That left only three— Glasgow, Morayshire, and Kirkcudbrightshire—which lodged positive dissents from the Tender, in each case on religious grounds.

In March the delegates who had met at Dalkeith sent in return a Tender to Parliament, which among other requests asked that fourteen representatives of the shires and seven of the burghs should be allowed to come to London and confer with the responsible members of the English parliament over the detailed terms of the Bill of Union, which was already on the stocks; it had its first and second readings on 13 April 1652. Their request was granted; the bill was put on one side until they got to London in October, after which they met the committee entrusted with its preparation twenty-two times before the expulsion of the Rump put an end to their consultations.

Long before this the eight parliamentary commissioners had returned from Dalkeith to Westminster, but before doing so they took measure with regard to two difficult issues. One was the treatment of the chief nobles and lairds who had been in arms against the parliament; their estates were naturally liable to sequestration, but the appointment of three commissioners to supervise the process inevitably aroused great fear among Scottish landowners and impelled many of them to join in Glencairn's rising. The other problem centred on the universities, and on the clergy generally. The latter's opposition to the union was so strident that their training-grounds, the universities, could not safely be left in ultra-Presbyterian hands. The new principals whom the commissioners appointed were all distinguished men in their way, and they covered a wide spectrum. Patrick Gillespie, their choice for Glasgow, was a leader of the Protesters, and became in time a close friend of Owen, Lambert, and Fleetwood. Robert Leighton, their nominee for Edinburgh, was by contrast a former Engager, and would eventually become Archbishop of Glasgow. John Row, whom the commissioners installed at Aberdeen, had already converted from Presbyterianism to Independency. They made no change at St Andrews.

Before leaving Scotland they appointed nine men—the four English judges, the three Sequestration Commissioners, the commander-in-chief (who was still Richard Deane until December 1652), and the governor of Edinburgh and Leith—as 'commissioners for visiting and regulating universities and other affairs relating to the ministry in Scotland'.[4] Their task of taming the Kirk's belligerence was made easier by the continued quarrelling between Resolutioners and Protesters, and they went about it with commendable tact. They allowed a General Assembly of the Kirk to meet in Edinburgh in

[4] Dow, *Cromwellian Scotland*, p. 58. This whole section is much indebted to Dr Dow's fine work.

July 1652, but it was a muted affair because the Protesters refused to recognize it. The Protesters were very much a minority, however, and the intransigence of such Presbyterian diehards was causing a small but significant stream of conversions to Independency, including some in high places. A few leading figures would in time go all the way to Quakerism, such as Alexander Jaffray, Keeper of the Great Seal of Scotland, and John Swinton, one of the three Scottish Commissioners for Justice. Both were to sit for Scotland in Barebone's Parliament. Such conversions were due to conviction and not to pressure from the Commissioners for the Universities and the Ministry. The latter were hated by strict kirkmen like Robert Baillie for their very existence, but they acted with moderation and impartiality. They attempted no wholesale removal of ministers who prayed publicly for the king, and in filling vacant benefices they generally respected the wishes of presbyteries and congregations.

The expulsion of the Rump naturally delayed the formal enactment of the union, though Cromwell and the Council of Officers assumed that it already existed by summoning representatives of Scotland to Barebone's Parliament. Five members was a meagre allocation, however, especially since one of them, Alexander Brodie of Brodie, a Lord of Session, decided after much heart-searching not to attend. Nevertheless Barebone's made good progress with a bill of union, which was ready for its final passage when worsening news form Scotland caused it to be suspended. The English military commanders there had somewhat overestimated the extent to which they had subjugated the Highlands, and in the course of 1653 they were still interpreting as endemic clan lawlessness what was becoming an organized royalist insurrection. As early as June 1652 a number of chieftains and noblemen sent a collective message to the king, signifying their willingness to rise for him, and he responded with a circular letter addressed to the nobles and gentry of Scotland, thanking them for their devotion and asking their fullest support for Lieutenant-General John Middleton, whom he appointed commander-in-chief of all his forces in the country. Middleton, once a zealous Covenanter but later an Engager, had been wounded and captured at Worcester, where he commanded the king's cavalry, but he had escaped from the Tower in his wife's clothes and joined his master in exile. In November 1652 Charles received word that a group of associated chieftains and clans had pledged themselves to raise some thousands of men for him, and were asking that Middleton should join them shortly with supplies of arms and ammunition. But Middleton did not judge the time ripe to take the field in person, nor was he willing that the Highland chiefs should choose an interim commander themselves, so Charles commissioned the Earl of Glencairn to command his Scottish supporters until Middleton himself took over. Glencairn, being a Lowlander and a former Engager, found his authority challenged by more than one of the most heavily involved Highland chiefs, whose enterprise was in the spirit of Montrose rather than of Hamilton. But his appointment was designed to appeal to the potential support of the many Lowland nobles and gentry who wanted to rid their country of the English invaders. There was never a chance that the Highlanders could do the king's business by themselves, and always a doubt that they could be brought to agree together wholeheartedly.

They never did, and Argyll, the greatest magnate and clansman in the country, chose to stick with the English. He had a low opinion of Charles II, and no illusions about his intentions towards Scotland. He made an equally shrewd appraisal of the Highlanders' chances of success, and reasonably concluded that a restoration of the monarchy by royalist arms was not only unlikely but would, if achieved, be against the interests of his clan, himself, and his country. He drove a hard bargain with Deane, securing financial advantages for his territory and himself, and then signed a full agreement in August 1652, promising to live at peace with the English government. Deane left Scotland in December to become a General at Sea, and Colonel Robert Lilburne, who took over the command of the English forces, was never quite sure of Argyll's loyalty. But Argyll gave tangible assistance to Lilburne's forces in the summer and early autumn of 1653, especially in their campaign to secure the islands of Lewis and Mull.

The royalists did indeed recruit significant numbers of Lowlanders, and from September 1653 onward they were raiding far into south-west Scotland. Lilburne, who at first lacked the political flair of Deane before him and Monck after, increased support for the insurgents' cause by overreacting somewhat; he dissolved a General Assembly of the Kirk in July 1653, and in the same month his troops broke up a convention of royal burghs at Cupar, though he did allow another one to meet in October. By January 1654 a royalist report claimed 9,000 or 10,000 men under arms for the king, but a contemporary English estimate put them at half that number. At any rate they were never a match for Lilburne, who disposed of 12,500 infantry and five regiments of horse. There were several reasons why they never realized their full potential. Too many Highland chiefs proved reluctant to honour their pledges when the call came to bring their clansmen to a rendezvous. The Lowland gentry, however much they wanted to see the English occupiers driven out, hesitated when it came to welcoming armed Highlanders into their territory, for the damage that they did to property was notorious. Smaller Lowland landholders felt the same way, but more strongly: they would much rather have disciplined English troops who paid their way in their midst than Highland raiders. Even in the Highlands, many clansmen preferred to pay their cess to the English rather than to their chiefs, because the reprisals they suffered for refusing it were so unpleasant. Furthermore, the royalist commanders and clan chiefs weakened their cause by constantly clashing among themselves.

To take just one example, Argyll's son and heir Lord Lorne defied his father and took the king's side, but did it more harm than good through his incorrigible quarrelsomeness towards his fellow-royalists. Finally, Lilburne deserves all credit for constantly striving to ensure that his troops did not oppress the common people or resort to free quarter, and to see that the assessment was levied equitably, which he did in full consultation with the gentry of each county. He also pressed continually for an Act of Oblivion which would identify the landowners who were liable to fines and forfeitures and leave the rest in untroubled enjoyment of their property. This was a measure that Barebone's took over from the Rump, but never got as far as enacting.

Middleton belatedly landed in Scotland in February 1654, bringing a modest supply of arms and powder. He was shocked by the state in which he found the king's supporters, for Glencairn's rising was already past its peak before it ever risked a battle. The Protectoral government took the situation in Scotland swiftly in hand, designating Monck as commander-in-chief. He took over from Lilburne, who was longing to be relieved, in April, and in the same month Cromwell approved an Ordinance of Union , based on the bill so nearly passed by Barebone's Parliament, which his council had been working on since January. Cromwell was taking advantage of the temporary power to legislate which the Instrument of Government gave to him and the council, pending the meeting of his first parliament. The ordinance formally abolished the royal office and the separate parliament of Scotland, and confirmed the country's representation in the parliament at Westminster. It promised free trade and proportionate rates of taxation between Scotland and England. It decreed that vassalage and feudal incidents were henceforth abolished, and that apart from the dues paid on death called heriots, tenants were to owe their landlords no other service than their rents. The private jurisdiction of the magnates was transferred to courts baron, which differed fundamentally from the old barony courts in being public tribunals, modelled on the English manorial courts. A separate ordinance defined their powers and prescribed their frequency, but it was Monck's aim to establish a system of justices of the peace in Scotland, and this (as will be seen) was to be put in hand when the country had been fully pacified and the transformation of its civil government completed. A third ordinance, promulgated on the same 12 April as the other two, was styled an 'Act of Pardon and Grace', and implemented the amnesty which the Rump and Barebone's Parliament had intended. It excepted twenty-four landowners whose estates were to be totally confiscated and seventy-three who were to suffer fines. It also excluded all who were actively engaged in the current rising, but Monck issued a proclamation on 4 May, promising pardon to all who submitted, except the ninety-seven named in the ordinance.

He lost no time in confronting Middleton and his dwindling forces. He marched into the Highlands in June, and in collaboration with Colonel

Thomas Morgan waged a vigorous campaign which broke the back of royalist resistance before the end of December. The decisive engagement was fought on 19/20 July at Dalnaspidal at the northern tip of Loch Garry, where Monck drove Middleton's men into the arms of Morgan's cavalry, who put them to utter rout. After that he pursued the royalist remnants relentlessly. Some of their leaders surrendered to him during August, and he granted them remarkably generous terms. By the late autumn Middleton commanded a mere 300 men, mostly infantry, and he was finding it impossible to recruit more. Those chiefs who were still loyal to him and the king were finding their clansmen refusing to fight. The winter of 1654/5 was an exceptionally harsh one in the Highlands, and Monck secured a fresh wave of surrenders from January onward. This was partly because chiefs and lairds had come to see the king's cause as hopeless, and partly because the terms that Monck was granting now allowed their men to keep their arms. Thereby he not only salved their pride, but recognized that in the endemically feuding Highlands the clans needed to defend themselves against each other. It was his realistic policy, once they submitted, to let them share in the enforcement of law and order within their own territory.

Early in 1655 Middleton was driven to take refuge in the isle of Skye, and in April he rejoined the king in exile. There was a brief stirring of activity while the English royalists attempted a rising during March, but by May Glencairn's rising was at an end. All its remaining leaders had surrendered, or were negotiating articles of surrender. Monck, who had no desire to place any more restraints on the ordinary people of Scotland than security demanded, felt able to relax the ban on the meetings of presbyteries and synods that Lilburne had imposed. The legislative foundations of the Cromwellian union had already been laid, and the way was now clear for placing the government of Scotland on a positive footing.

In the year or so following the expulsion of the Rump, Cromwell and his councillors were as keen to grasp the nettle of Ireland's future as they were to establish a new order in Scotland; but the problems posed by the two countries were utterly different, and so were the attitudes and assumptions with which the English government approached them. The Scots were overwhelmingly a protestant nation, the Irish a catholic one. Most of the Scots had been the Long Parliament's allies in the first Civil War, most of the Irish its bitter enemies. Gross exaggerations of the scale on which protestant settlers in Ireland had been massacred in 1641 were still being kept alive in 1653–4. Whereas the early Protectorate identified less than a hundred Scottish landowners as deserving fines or confiscation, it inherited assumptions about the collective guilt of the Irish that bound its hands. The so-called Cromwellian settlement of Ireland was to a large extent governed by decisions taken and measures passed by the Long Parliament over more than a decade before Cromwell became head of state, and a brief retrospect is necessary to show the position from which he started.

From a very early stage in the Irish rebellion the Long Parliament took the view that the cost of suppressing it should be met from the large quantities of land that it expected to confiscate from the rebels. Prompted by the need to secure a loan of £100,000 from the City of London, it passed an act in February 1642 for the confiscation of 2,500,000 acres, which was roughly 18 per cent of all the profitable land in Ireland, for the satisfaction of such 'adventurers' as would advance money for the war against the rebels. At this stage it was intended that the lands to be forfeited would be equally divided between Ulster, Munster, Leinster, and Connaught, and the adventurers were expected to settle in them personally. Parliament had as yet little knowledge of which provinces were most deeply engaged in rebellion and its attendant atrocities, and even less of the total acreage of Ireland. But the act assumed the almost universal guilt of Irish catholics, and by committing England to suppressing the rebels by force it killed any lingering possibility of negotiating with them. Charles I gave it the royal assent, partly because he dared not appear to condone the rebellion and partly because he was mortified by Phelim O'Neil's false claim to be acting under a royal commission.

Subscriptions were disappointingly slow in coming in, and one aim of the propaganda that so infamously exaggerated the horrors of the 'massacre' was to persuade more adventurers to put up their money. Two explanatory acts and an ordinance extended the scope and improved the terms of the original offer, and the response rose, though not as much as was hoped. Even a 'doubling ordinance' in 1643, which offered twice as much land to any investor who added only a quarter to his original subscription, found only 171 takers and brought in less than £12,000. Long before parliament could actually carry out the reconquest of Ireland, it was committed to a confiscation measured not by the rebels' supposed guilt but by its obligations to its own creditors. When it later decided to pay the arrears of its army in Ireland out of Irish land, the disproportion between 'crime' and punishment became even more blatant.

At the first launching of the adventure, it had been expected that the great majority of participators would be wealthy Londoners. But from an early stage it attracted people from all walks of life from yeomen upward, and during the unexpectedly long period between the launch and the final repossession of Ireland the investment changed in character. Irish land was seriously undervalued at the rates first offered, and many speculators bought and sold shares in it who had no intention of settling on it. By 1652, when the reconquest was complete, there were slightly over 1,500 adventurers to be satisfied, and they had raised a little over £300,000. Just over half were Londoners, and they contributed more than half the total. In parliament itself 119 MPs had put up nearly £70,000 between them. One disappointment, however, was the scheme's failure to attract many really large investors, for only fifty are known to have risked £1,000 or more, and only two more than £2,500. And though £300,000 was quite an impressive sum for the time, the total cost of suppressing the Irish rebellion came to almost ten times that figure.

There was a hope towards the end of the first Civil War that it might be suppressed very soon, but political conflict within the parliament killed it. Sir Hardress Waller, who had commanded the parliamentary forces in Munster during 1644, launched a proposal in December 1645 that Cromwell should be appointed Lord Lieutenant of Ireland, as a prelude to his undertaking the reconquest at an early date. Cromwell's political enemies responded, however, by putting forward Viscount Lisle, son of the Earl of Leicester, the last pre-war holder of the office. After hot debates Lisle was made Lord Lieutenant, though for one year only from 9 April 1646. This was a rebuff not only to Cromwell but to the New Model Army, the adventurers and the protestant interest in Ireland, for Lisle was justly seen as 'the do-nothing figurehead of a do-nothing Irish policy'.[5] He did not even go to Ireland until his commission was within six weeks of expiring, and once there he did the parliamentary cause positive harm by his bad relations with the Earl of Inchiquin. His presence was instrumental in impelling Inchiquin to make his peace with Ormond in 1648 and return to the king's service. The lack of clear purpose in English policy towards Ireland was largely due to the quarrels at Westminster between presbyterians and independents, and after the army had been goaded into revolt it was plain that the reconquest would not go ahead until the leading presbyterians had been driven from the political stage.

By the time the Irish campaigns had been fought and won, it had come to be assumed that the 35,000 officers and men engaged in them would be paid off with Irish land. There had been no firm parliamentary pronouncement, but the assumption took root because no one could think how else the huge cost of the operation could be met. It was going to call for far more land than would be needed to satisfy the adventurers, and was to alter the whole future pattern of English settlement in Ireland. But the adventurers were opening their mouths much wider by 1652, and one can partly understand why. They had been without the use of their money for far longer than they had anticipated. Ireland had become a war-torn, widely desolated country, and land values in it had severely declined. Much of it was unsafe, too, with bands of Irish 'tories' preying upon English invaders where they could, for reasons of survival as well as patriotism. The adventurers were no longer content to take

---

[5] Karl S. Bottigheimer, *English Money and Irish Land* (Oxford, 1971), p. 97. The treatment of Ireland in this chapter is deeply indebted to Bottigheimer's meticulous study.

land scattered among the four provinces; they wanted their settlement to be wholly within one undivided area, in Munster and adjacent parts of Leinster. They claimed not only over a million acres which they reckoned as their due under the original acts, but an extra half million to compensate for having had their capital tied up so long. They did not propose to settle any of their land until the fighting in Ireland had completely ceased.

They were opposed, however, from Dublin, by the four parliamentary commissioners who had constituted a provisional government since October 1650. The commissioners wanted the adventurers to begin planting immediately, on the terms originally agreed, in four 'allotments' spaced over sixteen counties. They favoured a total clearance of the native Irish from these settlement areas, but this did not appeal to the adventurers, who seem to have reckoned on exploiting cheap Irish labour. To provide ammunition for their case they turned to Henry Jones, who combined the offices of protestant Bishop of Clogher, Vice-Chancellor of Dublin University and Scoutmaster-General. He had been employed from early in 1642 in collecting reports of the atrocities attributed to the rebels; now he produced an enlarged and even more inflammatory compendium of them. It was read in the Rump on 19 May 1652, and published as *An Abstract of some cruel Massacres of the Protestants and English in Ireland*. It has been well compared to the Protocols of the Elders of Zion,[6] because its purpose had little to do with historical truth and everything with supplying justification for a wholesale confiscation and clearance. It had a pernicious influence on the Act for the Settling of Ireland passed in August 1652, for hitherto the Rump had been much divided as to how severely or leniently to treat the Irish people, and Jones's *Abstract* tilted the balance towards harshness.

The act did not tackle the really difficult problems of how much land should be confiscated and where, or how it should be distributed between the adventurers and the army in Ireland, but it did decree how the Irish people were to be dealt with. It granted pardon to all 'the inferior sort' who submitted, but with regard to men of substance it defined five categories who were to be excluded from pardon as to life or estate or both, according to their 'respective demerits'. A list of 105, headed by Ormond, were totally excepted by name; the other four excluded groups were all abettors of the rebellion in its early stages, all priests and Jesuits in any way involved in it, all who had murdered civilians, and all who failed to lay down their arms within twenty-eight days. Officers who had fought against the parliament were to be banished and their estates forfeited, though their wives and children were to be given land worth a third of what they had lost in a location to be decided by parliament. Non-belligerent catholics also faced forfeiture unless they

---

[6]    Bottigheimer, *English Money and Irish Land*, pp. 127–8.

had shown 'constant good affection' to the parliament, though they were to be compensated elsewhere with land valued at two-thirds of what they surrendered.

If the act had been rigorously implemented it might have initiated a huge bloodbath, for it has been reckoned that the one clause excluding abettors of the rebellion rendered up to 80,000 people liable to the death penalty. Fortunately the execution of the act was much less draconian than its letter. Its object, at least in the eyes of those who carried it out, was not to deal out wholesale retribution but to clear the way for confiscation on a scale not yet known (because the total quantity of disposable land and size of the army's claim on it had yet to be ascertained) by making nearly all land held by catholics subject to forfeiture. To try all those whom it rendered subject to the death penalty, the Rump set up a high court of justice in October 1652, and it sat in several provincial centres as well as in Dublin. Its records are very incomplete, but those who were executed under its sentence were to be counted in hundreds at most rather than in thousands. Sir Phelim O'Neill, who was captured in February 1653, was its only really prominent victim, and by the time Cromwell became Protector the court seems to have ceased to sit.[7]

Nearly all the Irish officers and soldiers who voluntarily surrendered in the course of the fighting and after its end were allowed to leave the country and take service in foreign armies, like so many Irishmen before them, and the great majority did so. Sir William Petty, the great political economist who was soon to know the country better than anyone, estimated that 34,000 left it to enlist abroad. A much smaller but still substantial number of prisoners of war were sent as indentured labourers to the West Indies and other plantations. Transportation had already been used to get rid of paupers and vagabonds and people who aided the tories, but what had been quite a stream thinned to a trickle from 1655 onward. Merchants came to fight shy of Irish bondsmen, for the planters regarded them as trouble-makers and found they got much more work out of African slaves. Figures are scarce, but by the late 1660s there were about 12,000 Irish in all the West Indies, compared with 50,000 black slaves.[8]

During June and July 1653, busy as they were with other matters, Cromwell and his interim Council of State took in hand the questions from which the Rump had shied away: which areas of Ireland were to be cleared for plantation and where the uprooted Irish should be settled. It was urgent to provide for the English forces in Ireland that were now in process of disbandment. The first need was for a national survey, since no one knew how much land there was in Ireland to dispose of. Three distinct surveys were instituted

---

[7] *A New History of Ireland*, III, 359–60. The excellent chapter on 'The Cromwellian regime, 1650–60' is by Patrick J. Corish.

[8] Ibid., p. 364.

in the course of 1653–4, the first two being of a necessarily rough and provisional nature; but at the end of 1654 Petty was entrusted with what came to be known as the 'down survey', which took him until 1659 but was unprecedented in its thoroughness. An immediate decision was needed, however, on where to begin settling the adventurers and members of the army. It was taken by Cromwell and the council and confirmed by much the longest act passed by Barebone's Parliament, which became law after seven days' close debate on 26 September. Irish catholic landlords who were to be transplanted, and that was to mean the great majority of them, were to be resettled in Connaught. The adventurers and members of the army of conquest were to have equal shares in an area of settlement covering ten contiguous counties, Antrim, Down, Armagh, Meath, Westmeath, King's, Queen's, Tipperary, Limerick, and Waterford. The adventurers drew lots for the lands made available to them; so many had sold their interests during the long wait that they were down now from 1,533 to 1,043. It was even more of a lottery than it looked, for the 'gross survey' which the authorities had to go by until Petty had done his work was often highly inaccurate. Many smaller investors sold their shares without leaving England, but at least half the adventurers actually settled on their estates, for about five hundred had their ownership confirmed at the Restoration.

The army's arrears presented greater problems which took years to settle, since there were so many claimants and not enough land to satisfy them—not even after Sligo, Leitrim, and part of County Mayo had been added to the territory available. Officers and men were given debentures for the sums owed to them, but these could not be exchanged for land immediately because the down survey took years to complete and there was clearly insufficient land to go round. Even those who held on to their debentures had to accept, under protest, a rate discounted to 12s. 6d. in the pound (i.e. 62.5 per cent). Most private soldiers received allocations so small that their parcels of land would not have provided a living, and most did not want to settle in war-torn Ireland anyway. They pined for the comforts of home, though in 1656 1,500 enlisted for service in newly conquered Jamaica. Very many sold their debentures to their officers or to other speculators, and according to Petty the going rate in 1653 was only 4s. or 5s. in the pound. A total of 33,419 debentures were issued, and about 12,000 ex-army men took their land and settled; about 7,500 had their titles confirmed at the Restoration. They did not establish the protestant yeomanry that the English government had envisaged, since the smaller landholders were thinly spread and were apt to go native, but ex-Cromwellian officers became a significant component in Ireland's new landlord class.

The lot of the transplanted Irish was seldom a happy one. There was just not enough land in Connaught to give them their due under the relevant acts, and many received very small allocations. Quite a few whose estates already lay in Connaught suffered transplantation. The land shortage in the province was exacerbated because quite a number of the 105 men whom the Rump's act totally excluded from pardon were not only spared but received land there. How far this was due to unrecorded compacts in the interests of clemency and future peace, and how far to bribery of the commissioners entrusted with the allocation of the land, are questions on which historians differ; the records are very incomplete, and of such as were taken many perished in the fire of 1922. But one decision did mitigate the general hardship. The 1653 act did not specify whether the counties earmarked for settlement by the adventurers and army members should be totally cleared or whether only their landlords should be transplanted. Most army officers took the hard line, but in a pamphlet controversy early in 1655 Vincent Gookin, a settler landlord who had sat for Ireland in Barebone's Parliament, pleaded the case of the Irish poor with a compassion untypical of his time. Probably through the influence of his fellow-member Henry Cromwell, Oliver's younger son, who came to Ireland in 1655 as commander-in-chief at the age of twenty-seven, it was decided that only landlords should be transplanted, though any of their dependants who chose to accompany them were to be free to do so. This was a practical as well as a humane decision, because the settlers needed Irish labour to work their land, and a total clearance would have exacerbated the land shortage in Connaught.

Politically, it was assumed by 1652 that Ireland was to be part of a union with England, since the Rump's bill for a new representative gave her, like Scotland, thirty seats in future Commonwealth parliaments. But it was to be a union on very different terms from Scotland's, since full political rights would be effectively restricted to the settler class and the military occupiers. Even so, three of the six members for Ireland nominated to Barebone's Parliament had genuine Irish roots, and they were not the only Irish sympathizers among them. Civil government in Ireland was still in an inchoate state when Cromwell assumed the Protectorship. The commissioners in Dublin to whom the Rump had delegated authority were divided; Ludlow as a strict republican resigned his place, and Cromwell's son-in-law Fleetwood, who had recently been appointed principal commissioner and acting commander-in-chief, was made Lord Deputy in July 1654. Next month a Council of State of six members was appointed from Westminster to assist him. Not one of them was Irish-born, but these were provisional arrangements. The direction of the Cromwellian government of Ireland was to change somewhat after Henry Cromwell's arrival in 1655, not least with regard to religious policy, and its course will be followed later.

# NINETEEN

# The First Phase of Cromwellian Rule

In England, during the dozen years prior to the Protectorate, each major political turning-point had alienated a significant section of the Long Parliament's original adherents, and so had narrowed the basis of support for the government of the day. When Civil War loomed, the constitutional royalists who had helped to pass the reforms of 1641 broke with Pym and his party and rallied to the king. In the crisis of 1648–9, most of the political presbyterians were driven into the wilderness by Pride's Purge and the regicide, and some of them became royalists. In 1653, Cromwell's expulsion of the Rump made enemies for life of such parliamentary republicans as Haselrig, Vane, Bradshaw, and Marten, while the Fifth Monarchists among others were never to forgive his elevation to the Protectorship at the end of the year.

Yet this latest turn was to bring some rallying of support. Pragmatic people who thought that almost any government was better than none, and had feared a drift towards anarchy while Barebone's Parliament was tearing itself apart, were ready to welcome a regime that combined firmness with moderation and pledged itself to respect the rule of law. Most were glad to see the strident prophets of a rule of the saints put in their place. The survival of a national church with a publicly maintained parochial ministry was assured. Many must have found it comforting that the constitutional balance between Protector, Council of State, and parliament bore a recognizable resemblance to the old trinity of king, privy council, and parliament, and many more were relieved that the ancient common law of England was no longer under threat, whatever reform it might face in particulars. Social conservatives were reassured by Cromwell's pride in having been born a gentleman and by his declared commitment to 'keep up the ranks and orders of men'.

But he had a long way to go before he could live down the fact the he had come to power as the head of an ambitious army, and win the positive support of the majority of the political nation. He would be on the way to doing so towards the end of his life, under a constitution devised by an elected parliament, but the result after his death was to make his disgruntled officers reassert themselves against his son, to their own ruin as well as Richard's. He nevertheless achieved a degree of acceptance which grew over the years. Not so long ago it was customary to account for this by portraying the Protectorate over-simply as a conservative reaction, but this was at best a half-truth. At least in its earlier years it showed a stronger impulse to reform than the Rump had done. Although Cromwell was at heart a constitutionalist, with a strong respect for parliament as an institution, he still believed that he had a higher duty to promote what he called 'the interest of the people of God' than to bow to the wishes of an unregenerate majority. And while he was conservative to the extent of preserving a national church and respecting the rights of tithes-holders, he upheld a broader religious liberty than any elected parliament did in his lifetime. He strove for what he called 'a reformation of manners', and he would not be afraid to employ his major-generals in promoting it.

One must be wary, however, of generalizing too far or too soon about the character of the Protectorate as a whole, for despite the continuity that ran through its five-and-a-half year term it fell into distinct phases. In the first, which ended with the dissolution of its first parliament, Cromwell and his council were concerned mainly with strengthening foundations and wrapping up unfinished business. The second was much affected by royalist conspiracy and by disappointment at the lack of parliamentary support, and its most notorious feature was the regime of the major-generals. The major change in the third phase came through the new constitution devised by the second Protectorate parliament, which revived the civilizing tendency of the regime and brought it closer to the monarchy, as modified in 1641. The brief rule of Richard Cromwell can be seen as a fourth phase, though it was essentially a continuation of the third.

During the early weeks of the Protectorate the first need was to secure it against those, mainly the Fifth Monarchists, who were publicly denying its legality, prophesying its early fall and inciting their flocks to disobey it. Feake and Powell were at it again immediately after their early release and were consequently rearrested, though Powell escaped to Wales. John Simpson and John Rogers were also disciplined, but Simpson was released in July on condition that he did not come within ten miles of London. Anna Trapnel threw a spectacular trance, lasting several days, in which she spouted doggerel prophesies of Cromwell's downfall, but then felt called by the Lord to Cornwall, where the local clergy reckoned her to be setting up as a second Holy Maid of Kent and got her arrested. But without friends at Westminster or active supporters in the army the Fifth Monarchists were ceasing to be a serious threat, especially as time passed and their prophesies went unfulfilled. Harrison could still have been a danger, but early in February 1654 he was ordered to retire to his father's home in Staffordshire. He took his time about obeying, but obey he did. There were still two regimental commanders with

Fifth Monarchist convictions, Nathaniel Rich and Robert Overton, but they were in Scotland and Hull respectively, and Cromwell took a chance on them. There will be more to tell about Overton in the next chapter. Three other colonels who were unhappy about the Protectorate because of their republican convictions nursed their misgivings until parliament met in September. There was a ripple of unrest among the officers in Ireland, on both millenarian and republican grounds. Edmund Ludlow, lieutenant-general of the cavalry, was a rigid republican; he obstructed the proclamation of the Protectorate in Ireland for weeks, and ceased to act as a commissioner for the government. A firmer superior than Fleetwood, his commander-in-chief and senior commissioner, would have made him either conform or get out, but Fleetwood was malleable in the hands of the many Baptist officers under his command who shared Ludlow's scruples, though not to the point of resignation. Cromwell was indulgent towards Fleetwood, who had married his daughter Bridget, Ireton's widow, and he did not have to fear serious opposition from the forces in Ireland. He let Ludlow retain his command until he was caught circulating seditious pamphlets early in 1655. The great majority of the army was so strongly supportive of the Protectoral regime, and he was so unwilling to make martyrs of old comrades in arms, that he could tolerate a few dissidents unless or until they engaged in open disobedience.

He was anxious at this stage, however, to play down the military origins of his authority and to clothe his government with as much legal respectability as possible. He had no difficulty with the judiciary, at least for the time being. There were twelve judges in the central courts of law, and ten of them were immediately reappointed. It is not known that the other two declined to serve; it is likelier that Cromwell and the council held objections to them. One was replaced by Mathew Hale, whose commission had served the cause of law reform so well under the Rump. Hale accepted appointment on condition that he would not have to take part in trying political prisoners, which was readily granted; but in fact there were to be remarkably few political prisoners under the Protectorate. Among such as there were, some were held without trial because the charges to which they were liable carried the death penalty, which the government was reluctant to inflict. Throughout the Protectorate, no one suffered death for a political offence unless he planned or engaged in armed rebellion or conspired to assassinate Cromwell. To try such offences, the regime only twice resorted to a high court of justice (the Rump had done so five times, in a shorter span of time), and only eight men suffered death by these courts' sentence. Torture was never employed by the Protectorate, and no civilian was ever tried by court-martial.

In Cromwell's England, as under the monarchy, most justice and most local administration lay in the hands of the county magistracy. The only period when their local supremacy was seriously encroached upon by the military was that of the major-generals, who will be considered in their place. Throughout England and Wales the commission of the peace was an over-whelmingly civilian body. Naturally some army officers were appointed to it, and some enjoyed a standing in the social hierarchy of their counties that would have made it anomalous not to appoint them. But there were at any one time at least 2,500 JPs in the country, and fewer than 90 of them were serving officers—roughly 1 justice in 30. Little more than half of these, most of the time, held commands in the national or field army; the rest were govern-ors of towns, castles, and other strong points, and many felt as least as strong a tie to their local communities as to the central government. There was an even smaller military presence among those other agents of central authority, the commissioners for collecting the monthly assessment. Out of about 3,000 in the whole country there were 72 serving officers, of whom 21 held only garrison commands.[1]

One civil authority whose goodwill mattered greatly to Cromwell was the corporation of the City of London, as he had acknowledged by giving it so strong a presence at his inauguration. They repaid the compliment by mount-ing a great reception and feast for him on 8 February 1654. Heading a large, richly-clad cortège, he was greeted at Temple Bar with an oration by the City Recorder, and from there all the way to Grocers Hall the streets were lined with benches, seating the members of the livery companies. Crowds turned out to watch the show, both in the morning and on the procession's return to Whitehall after dark, but they were depressingly silent.

The regime had to empower itself to punish its declared opponents, so one of the first of its ordinances proclaimed it to be treason to publish or preach that the supreme power did not lie in the Protector and parliament, and the administration in the Protector and Council of State. But no new political test was imposed to replace the 1649 Engagement to be faithful to the Common-wealth without a king or House of Lords, which was repealed. Hindsight might suggest that Cromwell was keeping the way open for later assuming the crown and creating a new second chamber, but all the indications are that such possibilities were far from his thoughts early in 1654, or for long after.

He and the council used their temporary power to legislate by ordinance more boldly to implement the Instrument's provisions with regard to religion and to speed the process of reform. Given that a broad established church was to be maintained, the problems were to ensure that its resources were effect-ively employed to maintain an able preaching ministry in the parishes, and to remove those clergy who were ignorant, idle, drunken, or immoral. The

---

[1] I examine the evidence more fully in 'The Cromwellian Protectorate: a military dictator-ship?', in *History* LXXV (1990), 207–3: see esp. 215–19. For the statistics I am deeply indebted to the unpublished Oxford D.Phil. thesis by H. M. Reece on 'The military presence in England, 1649–60', though my interpretation of the evidence differs somewhat from Dr Reece's.

solutions now provided were a refinement upon not dissimilar schemes that had been considered by the Rump and Barebone's Parliament, but never enacted. One ordinance, in March, set up a compact central body of Commissioners for Approbation of Ministers, who came to be known as the triers, whose function was to approve every candidate presented to a living in the church. A second ordinance, in August, nominated local commissioners in each county (or group of small counties), commonly called the ejectors, who were to identify the clergy in their areas who deserved to be removed. Lay patronage, which Barebone's had voted to abolish, was retained, but its abuses were checked because every presentee had to receive the triers' approval.

What happened when a parish living fell vacant was that the patron presented his candidate to the triers, with testimonials from three people who knew him personally, including at least one in holy orders. Where the advowson had belonged to the crown, or to a bishop or dean and chapter, or to a now-deprived royalist layman, the right to present had generally been taken over by one or other agency of the state, and in these cases the wishes of the parishioners were quite often consulted. The triers were an eclectic body, including laymen as well as clergy, with Presbyterians and Independents in roughly equal proportions and two or three Baptists as well. They were not empowered to impose any such doctrinal test as the Thirty-Nine Articles; Cromwell probably thought that the formulation of the 'public profession' envisaged in the Instrument required the sanction of parliament, as any change in the tithes system certainly did. The triers had to satisfy themselves of just three things: that the presentee was well grounded in the essentials of the Christian faith, that he was competent to preach, and that his moral life was above reproach.

As for the ejectors, they certainly made no clean sweep. Of all the parish clergy beneficed in 1640, only 27 per cent were actually removed during the next twenty years, though others retired voluntarily and many of course died. Many had already been put out as active royalists or unbending Anglicans, long before Cromwell became Protector. Where the ejectors took action, the commonest grounds were habitual drunkenness, notorious immorality, frequent or persistent non-residence, and unwillingness or inability to preach.[2] Some parsons were deprived for persisting in using the Prayer Book services, preaching against the government, or collaborating with royalist laymen to subvert it, but they were not very many. The fact is that the majority of the pre-war parish clergy accommodated themselves to the successive changes of

---

[2] The standard work on the fate of the clergy during the Interregnum is A. G. Matthews, *Walker Revised* (Oxford, 1948). For an admirable concise treatment see Claire Cross, 'The Church in England 1646–1660', in G. E. Aylmer (ed.), *The Interregnum* (Problems in Focus series, 1972).

the 1640s and 1650s, and before we sneer at vicars of Bray we should consider whether it was dishonourable of them if they thought it more important to go on ministering to the spiritual needs of their flocks as best they could than to observe the strict letter of the Anglican rite. In practice, many Prayer Book formularies were repeated from memory where parson and parishioners still treasured them, and in London and some larger centres of population elsewhere there were semi-private congregations that met regularly to enjoy the full Anglican services and sacraments. The authorities generally turned a blind eye to them except when the discovery of a royalist conspiracy caused a clamp-down.

Richard Baxter, who was no upholder of the Protectorate and regarded Cromwell as a usurper, paid a warm tribute to what the triers and ejectors achieved in the church. 'They saved many a congregation from ignorant, ungodly, drunken teachers', he wrote, and though the triers were 'somewhat partial' toward Independents, 'yet so great was the benefit above the hurt which they brought to the church, that many thousands of souls blessed God for the faithful ministers whom they let in'.[3] Baxter himself, who was minister of Kidderminster in Worcestershire, led the way in providing the sort of positive 'propagation of the gospel' by a collective effort of evangelization that had been so frequently urged, but was so hard to achieve by legislation alone. From 1653 onward he took the lead in uniting most of the clergy of Worcestershire in a voluntary association which overrode any distinctions between episcopalians, Presbyterians, and Independents in a common enterprise of spiritual dedication. All his associates were 'disengaged faithful men', and their first commitment was to instruct and inspire the laity. This they did not only by preaching but by reviving the practice of catechizing, and they also combined to regulate admission to holy communion. This did involve exercising a degree of moral discipline over the laity, though in a much less rigid manner than under a strict Presbyterian regime, and no one was forced to submit to it. The example of the Worcestershire Association was followed in at least thirteen other counties, not counting Cumberland and Westmorland, where a similar movement originated independently. A particular concern of the association was to identify, encourage, and support suitable candidates for ordination.

The ordinances which instituted the triers and ejectors were not the only ones that carried on the efforts of earlier regimes towards reform in the church, with rather more impetus. Another commissioned a new national survey of the value and source of revenue of all benefices, with a view to ironing out the grosser inequalities and ensuring that for the poorer clergy a living meant what it said. Another provided for the uniting of small parishes,

---

[3] Quoted by Claire Cross in 'The Church of England', p. 105.

especially in the older towns where they were obviously too thick on the ground, and the sub-division of very large ones where one minister could not possibly cope. These were widespread in the north; the parish of Whalley in Lancashire, to take an extreme case, covered 180 square miles and included nearly forty villages and hamlets with about 10,000 inhabitants between them.[4] Such measures as these might have initiated a comprehensive rationalization of the church's resources, but strong vested interests stood in the way of change, and fact-finding in itself took time in a pre-industrial age of communications. The Protectorate did not last long enough to see much progress.

Outside the broad Cromwellian national church, the separatist congregations which chose and supported their own pastors enjoyed considerable liberty, though it was not unlimited. It did not extend to those whose teachings or actions were accounted rank blasphemy, such as the anti-trinitarian John Biddle or the Quaker James Nayler, of whom more will be said later. Cromwell was reluctant, however, to see them punished as harshly as his parliaments would have liked, and he was more indulgent towards Quakers than most gentry magistrates. But he gave no countenance to those of them who tried to break up the services conducted by the parish clergy in what they called 'steeple-houses', and he was even firmer against so-called Ranters who preached and practised a belief that the spirit had liberated them from the moral code enjoined by Holy Scripture. He was not a tolerationist of the modern kind who regards an individual's religious convictions as entirely his or her business, so long as they do not impinge on the rights or liberty of others. His ideal was not a plurality of sects, tolerated out of indifference, but a community of all who 'had the root of the matter' in them, in a manner transcending differences over outward forms and rites. He expressed it memorably in a declaration that he issued on 20 March 1654, ordering a day of fasting and prayer for relief from a long and unseasonable drought. It urged the people to search their hearts as to why God seemed to be withdrawing his blessing from them, and among the questions that he urged them to ask themselves were these:

Is brotherly love, and a healing spirit of that force and value amongst us that it ought? . . . Do we first search for the kingdom of Christ within us, before we seek one without us? . . . Do we not more contend for saints having rule in the world, than over their own hearts? . . . Do not some of us affirm ourselves to be the only true ministry, and true churches of Christ, and only to have the ordinances in purity, excluding our brethren, though of equal gifts? . . . Do we remember old puritan, or rather primitive simplicity, self-denial, mercy to the poor, uprightness and justice?[5]

It may seem strange to modern readers, and it is certainly sad, that so

[4] Derek Hirst, *England in Conflict 1603–1660* (1999), p. 36.
[5] Abbott, *Writings and Speeches of Oliver Cromwell*, III, 226.

humane and ecumenical a concept of religious liberty excluded Roman Catholics. There were several reasons. The catholic church claimed for Rome a temporal authority that could and then did conflict with that of national sovereigns, and a spiritual authority that set the tradition of the church and the pronouncements of the pope on a level with Holy Scripture. Protestants were brought up to regard any challenge to the supremacy of God's word as impious, and much of catholic doctrine, especially concerning the mass, as idolatrous. This was an age in which seriously false beliefs were thought to be literally soul-destroying. At a more mundane level, most English and Scottish catholic peers and gentry had been royalist in the Civil War, or at best neutral, and the Irish rebellion had greatly heightened the national prejudice against the faith. Yet Cromwell was more reluctant than most puritan politicians to deal harshly with catholics, partly because of his desire to heal the divisions in the nation and partly because he sincerely disliked forcing consciences. He evidently wanted to free them from liability to the forfeiture of two-thirds of their estates if they defaulted on their fines for recusancy, which is what a harsh act of 1587 subjected them to. When the Protectorate was barely a month old the council gave two readings to an ordinance repeating this penalty, but it got no further, perhaps because other business crowded it out, perhaps because it was felt that the repeal of a statute should be left to parliament.[6] Cromwell contented himself with wielding executive authority leniently, and except when serious royalist conspiracies were under investigation his government turned a surprisingly blind eye to peaceable catholic activity. Late in 1656, when he was negotiating an alliance with France, Cardinal Mazarin wrote to him to urge a formal toleration of catholics. He replied that a public declaration granting them full religious freedom was politically impossible, but claimed that they had less cause for complaint under his government than under that of the Long Parliament. He himself, he said, had shown compassion to 'very many'; he had 'plucked many out of the fire—the raging fire of persecution, which did tyrannize over their consciences, and encroached by an arbitrariness of power over their estates'.[7] He hoped to do more for them as soon as he could remove certain impediments, but in the event his second parliament was to press him in the opposite direction. Nevertheless Bordeaux assured Mazarin that catholic priests were moving freely about London, and he and other foreign diplomats testified that the catholic laity thronged to worship in the chapels of foreign embassies, where they heard English priests preach in their own language. There were

---

[6] *Calendar of State Papers, Domestic 1653–4*, p. 360, cited (slightly inaccurately) in Abbott, *Writings and Speeches of Oliver Cromwell*, III, 164.

[7] Ibid., IV, 368. See Blair Worden's outstanding essay on 'Toleration and the Cromwellian Protectorate' in W. J. Sheils (ed.), *Persecution and Toleration: Studies in Church History* 21 (1984).

occasional crackdowns when complaints were raised in parliament or a royalist plot was uncovered, but it seems to have been rare for anyone to be punished.

In the secular sphere the Cromwellian ordinances mainly sought to tie up what the Rump or Barebone's Parliament had left unfinished, rather than to initiate new reforming policies. Many were of a routine or stopgap nature, such as those that renewed acts that were due to lapse. Cromwell was chary of using ordinances to break new legislative ground, partly because he had a true respect for parliament's paramount role in law-making and partly because he was anxious not to prejudice the endorsement of the Protectoral regime by the parliament due to meet in September. But the tally of ordinances—no fewer than eighty-two in little more than eight months, which were marked also by intense diplomatic activity—testifies to the prodigious amount of work that he and his councillors got through. Nor were they all of a politically 'safe' nature, by any means. Most contentious was one for the reform of Chancery. This was a problem that had occupied the Rump and Barebone's at intervals since 1649, and the new ordinance's provisions were as conservative as they well could be without failing altogether to ameliorate what was amiss. Almost everyone except the court's own personnel admitted that it badly needed reform, for the delays, costs, and general impenetrability of its procedures were notorious, but so far the professional conservatism of lawyer-MPs and the rich pickings for Chancery's underworked and overpaid officials, such as the Six Clerks, had ensured that nothing was done. The bid by Barebone's to abolish the court outright was unhelpful, since it would have left no jurisdiction in equity to fill the gaps where the common law's antique and formalized processes failed to provide remedies for palpable wrongs. But the new ordinance raised such objections from the judges in Chancery—Bulstrode Whitelocke, Sir Thomas Widdrington, and John Lisle, Commissioners for the Great Seal, and William Lenthall, Master of the Rolls and former Speaker—that Cromwell suspended its operation until they had been fully considered.

More than twenty of the 1654 ordinances dealt with finance; the two most ambitious brought all the revenues into one treasury and under the jurisdiction of the Court of Exchequer. Another group dealt with matters of public order and banned duels, cock-fighting, and horse races, the latter because they were notorious occasions for the meeting of royalist conspirators. (Bearbaiting had already been forbidden, not very effectually, by the Long Parliament in 1642.) Another ordinance took an important step towards providing a public postal service, and yet another towards maintaining the highways better. Another, in response to a petition from the Lord Mayor, regulated London's hackney-coaches, though not so much in the interests of their passengers as in an attempt to moderate their feuding with the Thames watermen. Taken as a body, the Cromwellian ordinances give little support to the stereotype of puritan repression, and convey an impression of sensible, unbiased effort to apply practical correctives to perceived ills.

One interesting phenomenon that links England and Scotland in the 1650s is the steep decline in prosecutions for witchcraft, though in England it began slightly earlier and is not to be attributed there to any one change of political regime. Before the Civil War, witchcraft trials in England had shown a very marked fall from the early 1620s onward, partly because James I grew out of the beliefs he had expressed in his *Daemonologie* of 1597, and partly because most of the circuit judges were meeting popular credulity regarding demonic possession with a wholesome scepticism. This trend was drastically reversed in the mid-1640s, largely through the efforts of one man, Matthew Hopkins, the self-appointed 'witchfinder-general' who operated in East Anglia for three years until his timely death in 1647. Belief in the public duty to punish witchcraft was part of the dark side of the orthodox puritanism that then prevailed, and Hopkins obtained a commission of oyer and terminer, empowering him to try witches. He caused about 250 to be prosecuted and about 100 to be executed, a sizeable proportion of all those who suffered death—probably not more than 500—during the two centuries (almost) in which witchcraft was a capital offence in England. For comparison, the total number of English catholic martyrs from Henry VIII's reign onward was 264. Hopkins owed his shocking success to the strength of popular beliefs in *maleficium* and the wartime suspension of the assizes; his death and the revival of the assizes restored something like normality, though there was a brief wave of witchcraft prosecutions in Kent in the early 1650s.[8]

North of the border the pattern was different. The Scots were much fiercer witch-hunters than the English; with about a quarter of England's population, they put between two and three times as many alleged witches to death, often after extracting 'confessions' by torture, before parliament finally put a stop to such savagery in both countries in 1736 (over half a century after the last known execution for witchcraft in England). There was a minor peak in prosecutions in 1643–4, but it was nothing to the witch craze of 1649–50, which was exceeded in ferocity only in the early 1660s. It was at its height between the Scots' proclamation of Charles II and the battle of Dunbar, when the Kirk party was straining every nerve to assert and enhance its authority. The kirkmen summoned the faithful to atone for the backslidings that had

---

[8] For excellent brief introductions to the subject, see Hirst, *England in Conflict 1603–1660*, pp. 49–51, and *The Oxford Companion to British History* (Oxford, 1999), under 'witchcraft'. The article in the latter is by J. A. Sharpe, whose *Instruments of Darkness: Witchcraft in England 1550–1750* (1996) is the best account on a much fuller scale; but for the broader picture see Keith Thomas's classic *Religion and the Decline of Magic* (1971) and Stuart Clark, *Thinking with Demons* (Oxford, 1997).

caused God to punish them with defeats in the field; they launched a drive against heinous sin of every kind, from fornication to fishing on the sabbath, and what could be more displeasing to the Lord than witchcraft? In contrast with England, where parliament and government showed little or no interest in witches after the Presbyterians lost their ascendancy, the Scottish parliament, the Committee of Estates, the privy council, and the Commission of the Kirk all played a part in harrying them. But the strain of fanaticism was strong at the grass roots too, for most prosecutions were initiated at parish level, in the kirk session. How many perished in 1649–50 is impossible to say; the best authority reckons 'certainly many dozens, perhaps hundreds'.[9] All that can be said in mitigation of these barbarities is that most of the wretched victims were strangled at the stake before being burnt.

The horrors all but ceased upon Cromwell's rout of the Covenanting army and the subsequent establishment of the English ascendancy in Scotland, for the Kirk party now had to bow to a degree of religious pluralism and could no longer sway the agencies of the state. The four English commissioners who went through Scotland on circuit in 1652 to administer criminal justice showed the same scepticism towards accusations of witchcraft as the assize judges in their own country, and they dismissed many cases for lack of evidence.

Further progress in settling Scotland had to wait until the terms of union had been defined and Glencairn's rising defeated. By May 1655, however, the last embers of royalist resistance in arms had been stamped out, and Middleton had rejoined the king in exile. In London, a strong committee of the Council of State had spent most of March considering the civil government of Scotland, which it proposed to vest in a Scottish Council. Cromwell formally approved its nine members, soon raised to ten, on 4 May, and they were all in place in Edinburgh by mid-September. Lord Broghill, the 34-year-old son of the Earl of Cork, was its all-important president, and Monck as commander-in-chief was his right-hand man. Of their fellow-councillors, two were distinguished Scotsmen, William Lockhart and John Swinton, and the rest were English; they included Charles Howard, the future Earl of Carlisle. Broghill was a bold choice, for he had been a staunch royalist until six years earlier, but Cromwell had been much impressed by the high ability that he had displayed in Ireland as diplomat and administrator, and his trust was not misplaced. The successful partnership that developed between the ex-royalists Monck and Broghill, differing as they did in age and social background, is a tribute to Cromwell's breadth of view and judgement of men.

Broghill for his part had become devoted to Cromwell, but he stipulated that he should not be required to hold the presidency for more than a year.

[9] Stevenson, *Revolution and Counter-Revolution in Scotland*, p. 144.

His success in Scotland is the more impressive for being achieved in so short a term. He never doubted that his prime obligation was to the Protectoral government, but he appreciated that a contented Scotland would be easier and cheaper to administer, and he genuinely aimed to better the lot of the middling and lower orders of the population. He shared Cromwell's desire to free them from feudal burdens and give them better justice than they had had under the hereditary jurisdictions of the magnates, and Robert Baillie and John Nicoll, Scottish patriots both, testify to his success in gaining the people's admiration, even their love. Monck's aim to establish a system of justices of the peace was realized during Broghill's presidency, and though some of the JPs were English officers the majority were Scottish lairds.

One of Broghill's thornier problems was to moderate the fierce differences within the Kirk, especially those between Resolutioners and Protestors, and to protect the religious liberty of protestants who wanted no part of either faction. As soon as Glencairn's rising was suppressed, Monck had lifted the ban on meetings of presbyteries and synods that Colonel Lilburne had imposed when many of them were acting as cells of conspiracy and agencies of recruitment against the Commonwealth, but the presbyteries could not be fully restored to their traditional role in admitting ministers to parish livings, because so many of them were dominated by Resolutioners, who were still praying openly for the king. Against such people, Lilburne had found a valuable collaborator from 1653 onward in Patrick Gillespie, the newly appointed Principal of Glasgow University, and in March 1654, on Lilburne's advice, Cromwell summoned Gillespie and two other ministers of his persuasion to London for consultation. In May Cromwell also invited two Resolutioners and a strict Presbyterian Protester, so that he could hear all sides, but none of the three accepted, so their case went by default. The outcome was an ordinance by Protector and council, erecting a commission of fifty-seven Scottish 'triers' with functions like those of their English counterparts. Not surprisingly, most of them were the more compliant sort of Protesters, laced with a few outright Independents, and the ordinance soon became known as 'Gillespie's charter'. For a long time it remained almost a dead letter, for the Resolutioners in general and the strict Presbyterians among the Protesters denounced it as an intolerable intrusion by the state on the indefeasible spiritual authority of the presbyteries.

While numerous Scotsmen were still in arms for the king it was natural that Lilburne, and Monck after him, had looked to the Protesters (or at least Gillespie's party among them) as friends and the Resolutioners as enemies. The trouble with such a policy was that the Resolutioners were in a huge majority; the Protesters included only a sixth of Scotland's parish clergy, and their adherents included rigid Presbyterians like Johnston of Wariston who were not friendly at all. Soon after Broghill arrived in Scotland he wrote to

Thurloe that the main difference between the parties was that the Resolutioners 'love Charles Stuart and hate us', while the Protesters 'neither love him nor us'.[10] He set about persuading the Resolutioners that the king was truly beaten and that their best interests lay in coming to terms with the Protectorate. He secured their leaders' agreement to stop their members from praying for the king by remitting the fines already imposed on those who had done so, whereupon the Protesters of the west, fearing a deal with their opponents that would leave them in the cold, sent a deputation to Edinburgh to find how best they could register *their* willingness to own the present civil power. Broghill wrung from them some kind of undertaking to put Gillespie's charter into execution, after which he and the Scottish Council announced that any of the triers who had not declared themselves willing to act by 1 December would be replaced.

The story of his negotiations with the various factions is too long and complicated to be told here, but his patience and diplomacy in dealing with men whose bigotry was so alien to his own nature were exemplary. By the spring of 1656 he had all the parties looking to the Scottish Council—and behind it the Protectorate—to umpire their quarrels and help them defeat their opponents. His aim was to create a new party, embracing the great majority of Resolutioners and the Gillespie wing of the Protesters, and in practical terms he largely succeeded. His final achievement, in August 1656, was to reach agreement with the Resolutioners on how parish ministers were to be selected, approved, and admitted to their benefices and stipends. The terms were that the presbyteries should nominate their candidate as of old, but must certify the Scottish Council as to his fitness, and that if approved the presentee must engage willingly to live peaceably under the established government. It was a triumph of common sense, for it preserved the essence of the Presbyterian system of appointment while ensuring, with the minimum of secular intervention, that the clergy were pledged to obey the civil authority. The system worked well, and went on functioning through the remaining years of the Protectorate.

Broghill came of a remarkable family. His elder brother, the second Earl of Cork, suffered through his staunch royalism throughout the Civil Wars and lived quietly on his ruined Irish estate, where through Broghill's intercession he obtained from Cromwell some relief from his acute financial problems. His youngest brother was Robert Boyle, one of the father-figures of modern science, and a leading spirit in the group of fellow experimentalists which he liked to call the 'invisible college', and which is famous as the nucleus of the Royal Society. Boyle chose to make his home in England in 1654, and his

[10] *Thurloe State Papers*, IV, 49, quoted in C. H. Firth, *Last Years of the Protectorate* (2 vols., 1909), II, 95, and in Dow, *Cromwellian Scotland*, p. 199.

Oxford lodgings were one of the regular meeting-places of this group, which also included Seth Ward, John Wallis, and Christopher Wren. The college had its origins in 1645, and its activities are to be linked far more with the longer-term developments in intellectual enquiry than with any particular changes in government; but it is not insignificant that it flourished in Cromwellian England, and in a university whose chancellor was Cromwell's appointee and former chaplain John Owen (though Owen and the scientists were not on friendly terms). It is not a simple matter to characterize a regime that is associated on the one hand with major-generals and the enforcement of moral regulation by the state, and on the other with scientific research, the enlargement of toleration, the encouragement of learning, and (as we shall see) the only attempt to establish a new university between the Middle Ages and the nineteenth century.

It is no easier to convey with a few broad strokes the style and spirit in which Cromwell actually wielded his power as Protector. He has been called a king in all but name,[11] but the description, while containing elements of truth, needs to be received with caution. He willingly accepted formal constitutional restraints on his authority that no previous English monarch would have dreamt of bowing to, and which had no parallels in contemporary European monarchies. He seems to have had a genuine aversion to the royal title and all the religious connotations that it carried, and he was anxious to avoid any outward appearances that would give ammunition to those who suspected that his rise to Protector was planned as a stage in his ascent to the throne. Yet he was much aware of the dignity due to the British state, which in the eyes of foreign monarchs and their diplomats he now personified, and in his dealings with them there was no other model than the monarchical one for him to adopt. Presidents, as heads of state, had not yet been invented. The stadholderate of Holland offered no pattern to follow, not only because its powers were quite different but because it had been closely linked with the house of Stuart and was currently in abeyance. The Doge of Venice provided even less of a model, being a byword for powerlessness and mere pomp.

The degree to which Cromwell assumed the outward trappings of monarchy changed considerably between the first and longer constitutional phase of the Protectorate, which was regulated by the Instrument of Government and lasted for more than three and a half years, and the final sixteen months that ensued upon his second investiture under the new parliamentary constitution of 1657. In the latter period he did assume a more regal persona, partly to mitigate the disappointment of those who had tried to make him king, but

---

[11] Roy Sherwood, *Oliver Cromwell: King in All but Name 1653–1658* (Stroud, 1997), and for what follows concerning Cromwell's court and entourage the same author's *The Court of Oliver Cromwell* (Cambridge, 1989). Sherwood is of course by no means the only historian to have delineated Cromwell's authority as essentially royal.

from the outset the only residences appropriate to his office were royal palaces, and their staffing and ceremony were bound to bear some resemblances to a royal court. The contrast between the early Protectorate and the preceding Commonwealth can, however, easily be exaggerated. The Rump had been well aware of the sensitivity of foreign ambassadors and other diplomats to the ceremonial, the accoutrements, and the whole physical ambience that they encountered when they did business with the regicide republic, and it had been much concerned to uphold the Commonwealth's dignity when transacting with them. Despite its chronic financial problems, it had reserved to the republic's use not only the palaces of Whitehall, St James's, and Hampton Court but also Somerset House, Greenwich House, Windsor Castle, and York Manor. When it sold Charles I's great art collection, it kept back many treasures to embellish the rooms in the royal residences that were still used for official purposes or to house senior officers of state.[12] After the battle of Worcester it had allocated Hampton Court to Cromwell's use, but in the dark days late in 1652, when the war at sea was going badly and its relations with the army were worsening, it decided to sell Hampton Court (among other assets) to help fill its empty coffers. Cromwell must have concurred, since he was on the committee for disposing of it, but on becoming Protector he had Hampton Court repurchased. Thereafter he spent most weekends there, from Friday to Monday. It gave him welcome relief after the hectic activity of Whitehall, where he lived and transacted affairs of state during the week. St James's and Somerset House were retained mainly for the entertainment of ambassadors and distinguished guests of the state, as they had been under the Rump, while Windsor Castle was used mainly as a prison.

There is a revealing contrast between the spontaneous, informal way in which Cromwell received and conversed with fellow-countrymen who came before him, from the republican Edmund Ludlow to the Quaker George Fox, and the protocol he observed on public and diplomatic occasions. He took over the Master of Ceremonies whom the Long Parliament had employed since late in 1643, Sir Oliver Fleming, who happened to be his distant cousin and had learnt his job under Charles I. Fleming was openly pleased at Cromwell's elevation and served him well; he must have enjoyed restoring the dignity and etiquette with which ambassadors had been received when he was younger. The scene for such occasions was the Banqueting House in Whitehall, beneath the ceiling on which Rubens had glorified the Stuart monarchy. Ambassadors had to come into the Protector's presence cap in hand and address him as Highness, and he insisted that in formal letters of state monarchs should call him 'brother', to the considerable embarrassment of

<hr/>

[12] Sean Kelsey, *Inventing a Republic: The Political Culture of the English Commonwealth, 1649–1653* (Manchester, 1997).

Mazarin and Bordeaux. Yet his concern was for his country's status rather than his own glorification, and whatever resemblances his household bore to the court of Charles I its cost to the taxpayer was a small fraction of what it had been under the monarchy. The sum allocated to its upkeep, and endorsed by parliament, was £64,000 a year, which was raised to £100,000 under the new parliamentary constitution of 1657, which deliberately approximated his office more closely to that of a king. This charge was formally separated from that of the civil government and its personnel in a manner that anticipated the modern civil list, a wholesome practice that would not be followed again until the reign of George III. Comparisons with early Stuart times cannot be precise, because no firm line had then been drawn between the functions and officers of what we would call the court and those of the civil government; all were the king's servants, and he remunerated them from what was still regarded as 'his own'—except that much of the income of many of them came from fees and gratuities paid by the public. But a very rough estimate of the cost of the royal court in the early 1630s, including that of the queen's and princes' households, would be of the order of £250,000, plus more than £131,000 paid from the king's coffers in annuities and pensions, though some of the recipients of these did render genuine political services. This was at a time when the total ordinary revenue of the crown had averaged less than £620,000 a year, whereas parliament in 1657 fixed the Protectorate's regular revenue at £1,900,000. Before Ship Money, the royal household had consumed at least half the king's regular income; under Cromwell the charge was more like a twentieth.[13] Again, we are not exactly comparing like with like, but we should be cautious about accepting the Protector as a king in all but name.

One pleasure on which he did not stint himself was music, which he greatly loved. He had the organ of Magdalen College moved from Oxford to Hampton Court, where it accompanied the musical entertainments he gave there, as well as solacing his leisure hours. He had an organ at Whitehall too, and music enlivened such occasions as ambassadorial banquets. The 'Gentlemen of His Highness's Music' actually outnumbered those of Charles I, though at least four had previously served the king, and in 1657 his council appointed a Committee for the Advancement of Music. Secular music was flourishing in England, and from 1652 the printer and publisher John Playford drove a fine trade in meeting the demand for songs and instrumental pieces for performance in the home. Nor was music-making exclusively domestic, for despite the ban on stage plays that the Long Parliament had imposed in 1642 the first full-length English opera, William Davenant's

---

[13] Aylmer, *King's Servants*, ch. 2 (iv), 4(v), pp. 436–7 and *passim*; Aylmer, *State's Servants*, pp. 322–3.

*The Siege of Rhodes*, was publicly performed in London in 1656. A certain relaxation of puritan austerity was in the air, though the trend was to be reversed during the brief regime of the major-generals. Gallants and their ladies were resorting again to such places of pleasure as Hyde Park and the more exclusive Mulberry Garden, while John Evelyn in 1654 'observed how the women began to paint themselves, formerly a most ignominious thing, and used only by prostitutes'.[14]

A very different sort of entertainment from that of Davenant's opera was the weekly dinner at Whitehall that Cromwell gave to the army officers in and around London. He probably enjoyed these relaxed and sometimes convivial occasions, for they kept him in touch with old comrades and helped him to keep his finger on the pulse of the army. They helped too by making the officers feel they were still valued, for their General Council had taken a sharp cut in the political influence that it had wielded on and off since 1647. In 1653 alone it (or most of it) had endorsed the dissolution of the Rump, selected the members of Barebone's Parliament, and given its vital approval to the Instrument of Government. Since then it had quite quickly sunk into obscurity, and no one knows how often it met. It resurfaced occasionally at moments of crisis, such as the challenge to the Protectorate by certain republican colonels during the sitting of the forthcoming parliament, but it never recovered any significant political initiative during Cromwell's lifetime. The role of the military in government was to increase significantly under the major-generals in 1655–7, but their regime derived its authority entirely from the Protector and his council, and bore no resemblance to the collective claims to a political role that the army had asserted between 1647 and 1649. When the General Council did resume regular and frequent meetings in the spring of 1659, it would be a sure sign that Richard Cromwell's grip on the reins was slipping and that the Commonwealth's days were numbered.

In examining the face that the Protectorate presented to the world, it is interesting to compare the vindications that were published by its two chief official apologists during the first half of 1654. It is hard to imagine two defenders of the same regime more different in their attitudes and arguments than Marchamont Nedham and John Milton, especially since both had quite recently been upholding the superior virtues of a republic. Part, but only part, of the differences lay in the audiences that they were addressing. Nedham's *A True State of the Case of the Commonwealth* was aimed at the educated British public, and it ran to fifty-two pages of good plain English. Milton in his *Second Defence of the English People* was writing for an international readership of scholars and political specialists, and he spread himself to three

[14] Diary of John Evelyn, under 11 Dec. 1654; p. 87 in the selection edited by Guy de la Bédoyère (Woodbridge, 1995).

times that length, in highly rhetorical Latin. Nedham, it will be remembered, saluted the Protectoral constitution as a perfect embodiment of mixed government, comprising the virtues of monarchy, aristocracy, and democracy while obviating the abuses to which each form was subject.[15] Milton by contrast scarcely concerned himself with constitutional matters, apart from praising Cromwell for spurning the title of king. Throwing consistency to the winds, he hailed Cromwell as the sole saviour of his cause and country. What, he asked, could be more just, more expedient, more pleasing to God and agreeable to reason, than the rule of the man most fit to rule? Fifteen pages of full-throated panegyric sustained the eulogy. Yet though Milton had nothing to say about formal limitations to the Protector's power, it is clear that his acceptance of it was not without reservations—clear from the names of the Commonwealth's heroes whom he celebrated alongside Cromwell, including the unbending republicans Bradshaw and Robert Overton, and clearer still in the advice he tendered on the self-restraints that Cromwell should observe in exercising his God-given authority. Chief among these was to refrain from employing it in anything that concerned religion and the church, since they by their nature lay outside the scope of the civil magistrate.[16] Milton must have known of Cromwell's commitment to a publicly maintained parochial clergy, to which he himself was totally opposed, and his failure to influence him on this, together with the monarchical direction of the constitutional changes in 1657, were gradually to alienate the poet from the regime he served.

Milton's views on church and state were diametrically opposed to those of Thomas Hobbes, who had published his *Leviathan* in 1651. Hobbes maintained that the civil sovereign, if he was a Christian, had the right and duty not only to regulate the temporalities of the national church but to appoint pastors and determine what doctrine might be taught and preached. It is interesting that the two greatest political philosophers of their time, Hobbes and James Harrington, both had strongly royalist connections and sympathies—Harrington was a groom of the bedchamber to Charles I throughout his captivity—but both lived and wrote untroubled in Cromwell's England. Hobbes, who had dwelt in Paris throughout the Civil Wars, chose to return home at the end of 1651, and engaged in vigorous controversy with members of the invisible college. Both men came more under threat after the Restoration than they ever had been under the Protectorate; Harrington indeed spent a spell in the Tower.

One aim on which Cromwell and Milton were agreed was a protestant foreign policy, with an alliance between Britain and the United Provinces as its cornerstone. The prospects had not been good while Barebone's Parliament

---

[15] Above, p. 567.
[16] *Complete Prose Works of John Milton* (8 vols., New Haven, 1953–82), IV, 666–8.

was sitting, and the sticking-points were not only the unacceptable English demands, which included a partial fusion of sovereignties and the permanent exclusion of the house of Orange from the stadholderate. There was a fear abroad in the Netherlands that England intended to swallow them up as she had swallowed Ireland and Scotland, and with this went a great surge of Orangist feeling. Town after town witnessed popular demonstrations in favour of the immediate revival of the stadholderate, even though William III was still an infant, and some even set up irregular Orangist municipal governments. Jan de Witt, the Grand Pensionary of Holland and chief proponent of peace with England, narrowly escaped being lynched in the Hague. It has been suggested that one reason why Cromwell and his colleagues stuck so long to their proposal for a 'coalition' between the republics was the need they felt to stem the pro-Orange, pro-Stuart tide that was running in the Netherlands.[17]

A sequence of events in the second half of 1653 opened the way to a peace acceptable to both sides. The violently Orangist Admiral Tromp was killed in action on 31 July, and his successor, the republican Jacob van Wassenaer, Lord of Opdam, quickly made enough changes among his ships' captains to ensure the full loyalty of the fleet to himself and the States-General. Soon after Tromp's death, Cromwell hinted to Beverning in an informal conversation that he personally would be content with a treaty that did not encroach upon Dutch sovereignty. The States party made a good political recovery, sweeping away the violent Orangist factions from most Dutch towns and restoring the dominant role of the States of Holland in the States-General. That body sent Jongestal and Nieupoort back to England in October, but hopes of a peace were dashed by the unrealistic terms presented to them by the Council of State responsible to Barebone's Parliament. These included not only such hardy perennials as the exclusion of the house of Orange and the striking of the flag by Dutch ships in the ill-defined British seas, but large reparations for English losses in the war, a mutual limitation of naval strength in England's favour (sixty ships to forty, it was rumoured), and payment by the Dutch for fishing rights off all British waters. Understandably, the two Dutch envoys asked for their passports, and they were only persuaded to delay their departure on receiving private messages from Cromwell and others close to him early in December, hinting that a change of government was imminent. As soon as Barebone's resigned, Cromwell sent to assure them that he truly desired a peace and was now in a position to treat for it.

There were, however, still some quite formidable difficulties in the way of it. The Dutch wanted their ally the King of Denmark included in it, but in

---

[17] Pincus, *Protestantism and Patriotism*, pp. 140–8. Pincus is illuminating on the whole peace process.

1652 he had detained twenty-two English ships in the Sound (the straits between Denmark and modern Sweden, whose shores were then both in Danish territory), and Cromwell at this stage refused. The two Dutchmen did return home early in January 1654, though they brought secret proposals for a compromise from Cromwell to de Witt, who sent Beverning back to London as his personal envoy before the month was out. Frederick III of Denmark eased the situation in February by sending an ambassador to England to congratulate Cromwell on his elevation. A negotiation followed, whereby eventually eighteen of the seized ships were freed and the fate of the other four referred to Anglo-Dutch arbitration. Long before that, Nieupoort and Jongestal returned with the States-General's formal authorization to conclude a treaty, and a London crowd cheered them as they made their formal entry. Both sides needed peace, but it took weeks of tough negotiation between the three Dutchmen and six commissioners chosen by Cromwell before the Treaty of Westminster was signed on 5 April. It proclaimed a 'nearer alliance, union and confederacy than heretofore', but made no encroachment on the actual sovereignty of either state. A compromise was reached on reparations, somewhat in England's favour, though the liability to pay them applied to both sides. No more was said about limiting navies, and as for saluting English men-of-war, Dutch ships were required to do so 'in the former manner', which was vague enough to leave the matter almost in the air. Neither country was to allow the other's rebels on its soil, which forced English royalists, including the Princess Mary, to depart from Dutch territory. The most contentious issue was over England's demand that the Prince of Orange should be permanently excluded from the offices of Stadholder and Captain-General. Cromwell gave way only to the extent of conceding that this should be a secret article, but he insisted that it should be ratified by the States-General. Perhaps he drove too hard, since it was as much in de Witt's interest as his to keep the Prince of Orange out of public office, but de Witt was new to his great office and his full stature as a statesman had yet to be revealed. The irony is of course that in the fullness of time the three-year-old prince was to become not only Stadholder but King of England, Scotland, and Ireland, and the champion of much that Cromwell believed in. Nevertheless, the facts that Cromwell got his way in this, and that the Navigation Act remained unrepealed, are measures of England's victory in the Dutch war.

Within a week of the conclusion of the Treaty of Westminster, Bulstrode Whitelocke completed a successful embassy to Queen Christina of Sweden. The Rump had decided on the mission at the end of 1652, when there was a real fear of a pact between the United Provinces and Denmark to close the Sound to foreign and especially to English shipping, but its chosen ambassador, Lord Lisle, procrastinated over his departure and finally resigned his appointment, pleading ill-health. Whitelocke was Cromwell's choice as his replacement, and Christina received (and hugely charmed) him just a week after the Protectorate was inaugurated. At that stage, with the Dutch war still on and Denmark the Dutch republic's close ally, Whitelocke was briefed to seek an armed alliance. But Christina and her shrewd old chanceller Oxenstjerna chose to see how the Anglo-Dutch negotiation prospered before committing themselves, and the Treaty of Westminster quickly eased the way to a satisfactory commercial treaty. Very shortly afterwards Christina abdicated in favour of her cousin, who ascended the Swedish throne as King Charles X. A similar treaty of commerce with Denmark followed in September, whereby British shipping was to pass through the Sound on paying the same dues as all other nations except the Swedes. This put them on equal terms with the Dutch, who did not gain their right to compound for their Sound dues. Britain's freedom to trade in the Baltic was assured, and the shadows of war in northern waters were lifted.

# TWENTY

# 'A Single Person and a Parliament'

ALTHOUGH Cromwell and his councillors and diplomats got through an impressive amount of work during his first nine months as Protector, they all knew that the regime would face a severe test when, as the Instrument of Government decreed, its first parliament met on 3 September 1654, the anniversary of Dunbar and Worcester. From July onward the first general elections for fourteen years were held in England, and the first ever to a parliament of all three kingdoms. The resultant assembly deeply disappointed Cromwell's hopes. It has been argued that he had largely himself to thank for this, since he failed to understand that parliaments in his revered Queen Elizabeth's days had been rendered co-operative only through skilful management by a core of privy councillors and other royal servants, who used their large electoral influence to secure the return of a nucleus of grateful clients, and with their support steered the House into voting the measures and the subsidies that the government needed.[1] But granted that his expectations were a shade naive and his mastery of the lower arts of politics limited, the kind of management that the Cecils (for example) had practised was quite beyond his reach. They and their kind had had power-bases in their counties such as Cromwell's councillors could not possibly match, partly through their personal territorial influence and partly through their ability to deploy royal patronage in bestowing local offices and dignities. Cromwell's men mostly lacked that kind of social and political standing, and he would have regarded the systematic manipulation of patronage for political purposes as an abuse. The large number of borough constituencies with very small electorates had made electoral influence relatively easy in pre-war parliaments, but the Instrument's multiplication of county seats and its restriction of direct borough representation to sizeable towns rendered it much harder. Above all, there had been a broad consensus about what the ancient constitution was and how it operated within a hierarchical society, and no stirring of doubt about its legitimacy until far into Charles I's reign.

---

[1] H. R. Trevor-Roper, 'Oliver Cromwell and his Parliaments', in *Religion, the Reformation and Social Change* (1956); reprinted in Ivan Roots (ed.), *Cromwell: A Profile* (1973).

Cromwell had none of these advantages. The legitimacy of his office and of the constitution under which he held it was highly questionable until an elected parliament confirmed both. Consensus in the constituencies had been destroyed by the Civil War and the successive political cataclysms that had followed it. Widely preferable though his regime was to that of Barebone's Parliament, and probably (though less widely) to that of the Rump, this was no guarantee that parliament would endorse it. He faced such a range of opposition: overt and covert royalists, successors to the political presbyterians, who had never aimed at abolishing the monarchy, republicans of the stamp of Haselrig, Scot, and Bradshaw, who had never forgiven his expulsion of the Rump, more populist 'commonwealthsmen' who included the remnants of the Leveller movement and particularly distrusted military power, and Fifth Monarchists who believed that he had usurped the authority that belonged by right to Christ and his saints. The first and last of these groups posed little threat in this parliament, though a few royalists got in. All who had fought or acted in any war against the parliament were debarred by the Instrument from either voting or sitting unless they had subsequently demonstrated their good affection, and the council was empowered to scrutinize the returns to this and the next two triennial parliaments and exclude any members who transgressed the prescribed qualifications. The council, however, exercised this power very sparingly. It refused letters of admission to fewer than a dozen members—probably no more than eight—and in nearly every case local electors had petitioned against the admission of the candidate concerned. At least half of the excluded had engaged in royalist activity since the Civil War, though they also included a minor and a man notorious for whoring, tippling, and swearing. Another to be debarred was the Leveller John Wildman, who was already engaged in conspiracy against the government. But the council gave the benefit of the doubt to a few other members who were petitioned against as royalist sympathizers.[2]

Crypto-royalists, however, were nothing like such a threat to the parliament's success (from Cromwell's point of view) as the vociferous ex-Rumpers led by Haselrig, who missed no chance to urge upon the many members who were new to the House that there was no power in the land as high as that of the people's representatives. More than half of the members were in fact sitting for the first time, though 125 had been in the Long Parliament (about two-thirds of them as recruiters), and 55 in Barebone's. Eighteen members were regicides.

That year 3 September fell on a Sunday, and the members spent much of the day at worship in Westminster Abbey, so Cromwell addressed them in the Painted Chamber only briefly and bade them return there next morning to

---

[2] Peter Gaunt, 'Cromwell's Purge?', in *Parliamentary History* VI (1987), 1–22.

hear him further. In that age when ceremonial bore such a weight of political significance, both English and foreign observers threw searching eyes on the pomp and symbols with which he chose to surround himself. He seems to have tried to strike a middle course, observing such formality as was proper to a head of state on a major public occasion, while minimizing the military origins of his authority and seeking to avoid any suggestion that he regarded it as a step towards the throne. The day started with another service in the Abbey, the preacher being the moderate Independent Thomas Goodwin, thus balancing the moderate Presbyterian Stephen Marshall, who had preached the day before. Cromwell rode the short distance from Whitehall Palace to the Abbey in a coach of state, escorted by the Yeomen of the Guard, attended also by his own life guard and other army officers, on foot and bare-headed, and followed in other coaches by his councillors and chief officers of state. Immediately before him Whitelocke carried the purse of state, containing the Great Seal of the Commonwealth, and Lambert bore the sword of state, but Cromwell himself wore unostentatious civilian clothes and conducted himself throughout the day with conspicuous modesty.[3] Hostile commentators made what they could of his summoning the members of Whitehall to hear him, rather than to the House of Lords as monarchs had done, but for him to have addressed them in the chamber of the abolished Upper House would have sent out quite the wrong signals.

The keynote of his speech, which Goodwin had already sounded in his sermon (a case of collusion, perhaps?), was the duty of 'healing and settling'.[4] He contrasted the state of the nation just before the Protectorate was established with what it was now. Then, the strife within it had grown so high as to threaten not only ordered government but the very fabric of society, 'the ranks and orders of men, whereby England hath been known for hundreds of years: a nobleman, a gentleman, a yeoman'. This of course was exaggeration, as even more was his allegation that 'men of Levelling principles' had been undermining property itself and bidding 'to make the tenant as liberal a fortune as the landlord'. He was to some extent playing upon his audience's prejudices, but he was quite sincere in presenting himself as a conservative with regard to some very central principles: a hierarchical society, founded in property, and a constitution geared to it, guaranteeing the rule of law, setting safeguards against arbitrary power, and giving a voice to all well-affected men of some small substance in choosing their legislators at regular intervals. Turning to religion (and again exaggerating), he said it had been in an even worse condition than the civil state, what with the unchecked preaching of 'prodigious blasphemies' and the invocation of so-called faith to justify the

---

[3] A much fuller description of the ceremonial is in Sherwood, *Oliver Cromwell: King in All but Name*, pp. 39–41.

[4] Abbott, *Writings and Speeches of Oliver Cromwell*, III, 435.

breaking of 'all rules of law and nature'. He referred to the Ranters, though he did not name them as such. Such horrors, he said, had brought to mind the iniquities prophesied for 'the last times', for Christ returned to earth in judgement. The power to check them had been undermined by a second sort of men, who while not justifying such evils denied the civil magistrate any authority to intervene, on the ground that matters of conscience and belief lay outside his sphere. Cromwell reaffirmed his own commitment to liberty of conscience, but defended the claim of the civil power to a role in promoting true religion and punishing manifest wickedness. He upheld the right of godly and gifted laymen to preach, but he repudiated the sectarian extremists who denounced the whole concept of an ordained ministry as antichristian. He adopted a gentler tone when he went on to condemn 'the mistaken notion of the Fifth Monarchy', acknowledging that many honest, God-fearing men adhered to it. It was one thing, however, to expect, as he hoped they all did, 'that Jesus Christ will have a time to set up his reign in our hearts', but quite another for men upon their own conviction of God's presence with them to claim a sole right 'to rule kingdoms, govern nations, and give laws to people'.

If these were but notions, they were to be let alone. Notions will hurt none but them that have them. But when they come to such *practices*, as to tell us that liberty and property are not the badges of the kingdom of Christ, and to tell us that instead of regulating laws, laws are to be abrogated, indeed subverted, and perhaps would bring in the Judaical law instead of our known laws settled amongst us,—this is worthy of every magistrate's consideration, especially where every stone is turned to bring confusion.[5]

Such people, he said, had not only threatened anarchy at home, but had obstructed the work of settlement in Scotland and Ireland and hindered the negotiation of peace with Holland, Portugal, and France.

To all these evils the present constitution and government had applied a remedy. He took pride in its achievements so far: its measures to raise the standards of the parish clergy, its conclusion of peace treaties with the Netherlands, Sweden, Denmark, and Portugal, and its reduction of the assessment by £30,000 a month, among other things. Yet, he said, 'these are but entrances and doors of hope, wherein through the blessing of God you may enter into rest and peace. But you are not yet entered.'[6] The completion of the work lay with the parliament now assembled, and what he most needed was its ratification of the Instrument as the legal and binding constitution of the three kingdoms. He was scarcely less anxious to obtain statutory authority for the ordinances of the last nine months. It was uncomfortable for him to have had to suspend the implementation of the reform of Chancery because

[5] Abbott, *Writings and Speeches of Oliver Cromwell*, III, 437–8; emphasis added.
[6] Ibid., pp. 439–42.

of the conscientious objections of such basically loyal men as Whitelocke, Widdington, and Lisle, the Commissioners of the Great Seal. And if the financial provisions were not confirmed, what was to stop ill-disposed people from refusing to pay taxes and customs duties? This was to happen soon enough.

The first few days' business did not bode well. Cromwell is said to have welcomed the House's election of Lenthall as Speaker, probably because he represented continuity with the constitutional past. But he must have been angry when Haselrig, on the first day of full business, proposed that parliament should give priority to religion, and urged that it should settle on one good form and suppress all the sects. This amounted to an outright rejection of the religious provisions of the Instrument, and must have been seen as a veiled attempt to restore the Presbyterian establishment formulated by the Westminster Assembly of Divines. It was a tactic designed to appeal to the religious conservatism of the majority of members and to encourage them to challenge the whole authority of the Instrument. It was somewhat cynical because Haselrig had in former times been accounted an Independent; he had married the sister of Lord Brooke, who had greatly influenced him when younger. Soon after this a member of the council, probably its president Henry Lawrence, proposed that parliament should take the Instrument into consideration as its first major business. There was general agreement, including that of the army officers and lawyers in the House and the Cromwellians generally, so the prospects looked hopeful. But soon after the great debate began, the House divided as to whether it should be conducted in its formal sittings or in grand committee (i.e. committee of the whole House). Cromwell's supporters preferred the former course, hoping to get the Instrument (or most of it) approved as it stood, but the vote went for a grand committee by 141 voices to 136, a narrow margin in a fuller than usual House. On the losing side were those who, while believing in parliament's paramount legislative power, accepted its place within a balanced polity, whereas the majority, without necessarily opposing the principle of a written constitution, upheld the superior right of the people's elected representatives to define its terms. The ensuing days' debates showed that many members regarded the constitution as a *tabula rasa*. Two proposals in particular were contrary to the whole spirit of the Instrument, one that the council should be elected afresh by each triennial parliament, and the other that the Protector's authority should be confined to civil affairs, while parliament appointed the commanders of the forces. Those who proposed such fundamental changes were contravening the indentures made at their election between the sheriffs, mayors, and other returning officers on the one part and the electors on the other, certifying (as the Instrument prescribed) 'that the persons elected shall not have power to alter the government as it is hereby settled in one single person and a parliament'; but that did not trouble them. They would have replied that the people's right to elect their legislators was fundamental, and that the authors of the Instrument had had no right to set terms to it.

Cromwell felt he could not let this go on, especially when he heard that Harrison was organizing a mass petition in the army and elsewhere, calling on parliament to extirpate the present tyranny, as being worse than that of Charles I. He had Harrison arrested, and on 12 September he summoned the members at very short notice to hear him again in the Painted Chamber. There he addressed them for an hour and a half, in one of his most self-revealing utterances. When last he spoke, he reminded them, he had told them they were a free parliament, but that had been on the assumption that they owned the government that summoned them. It implied some reciprocity, he said, and since that was evidently lacking, 'I see it will be necessary for me now a little to magnify my office, which I have not been apt to do'. He had not called himself to it, he insisted, and 'If my calling be from God, and my testimony from the people, God and the people shall take it from me, else I will not part with it.'[7] He said that after Worcester he had begged again and again to be relieved of his command and allowed to retire into private life, but his fellow MPs dissuaded him. He traced the steps which from then on had brought him to the point when he had felt it to be God's will that he should accept his present office. He had pressed the Rump repeatedly to make way for a more genuinely representative parliament, but he had found it bent on a self-perpetuating oligarchical dictatorship. Barebone's might have been a mistake, but he had known nothing beforehand of its resignation, and the framers of the Instrument had not taken him into their confidence until it was largely cut and dried. He had finally accepted it because it put an end to the brief military dictatorship created by the Nominated Assembly's resignation of its authority to him, and because it set firm constitutional limits upon his own authority. This was not of course the way in which his republican opponents viewed his ascent to the Protectorship, but it was genuinely his own sense of the matter.

His arguments that the people had already accepted his government were unlikely to convince the unconverted, but they were not wholly without substance. He cited the dignatories and officers of state who had witnessed his inauguration and oath of office, the judges and JPs who had acted under his commission, his feasting by a grateful City corporation, and the many addresses of loyalty he had received from counties, cities, boroughs, and not least from the army. The Instrument had been read out at all the recent elections, and the members themselves were committed to it by the indentures signed at their return.

Nevertheless he was not proposing to close the constitution to parliamentary debate. Many things in it were open to discussion, but he identified four

---

[7] Abbott, *Writings and Speeches of Oliver Cromwell*, III, 452.

principles which were fundamental and unalterable. One was the vesting of government in a single person and a parliament, neither of them absolute. Another was 'that parliaments should not make themselves perpetual'. Liberty of conscience was a third, and the fourth was joint control of the armed forces, by Protector and parliament when parliament was sitting, and by Protector and council in the intervals.[8] Interestingly he avoided the word Protector all through the speech, preferring 'single person' or 'chief officer', but that should be taken to suggest that he was deliberately leaving the way open to changing his title to king. He seems to have been uncomfortable about titles; 'Lord Governor' had been considered before he settled for 'Lord Protector'. He stressed the constitutional role of the council, who (he said) 'are the trustees of the Commonwealth in all intervals of parliaments, [and] who have as absolute a negative over the supreme officer in the said intervals, as the parliament hath whilst it is sitting'.[9] (But how absolute is that, members may have asked themselves.) He ended with an eloquent plea for their co-operation in giving the nation the peace and settlement that it desired and deserved. Before parliament met, he had considered requiring members to register their formal consent to the government which had called them before taking their seats, but had rejected the idea because he could not believe they 'came with contrary minds'. But now, to his deep regret, he found it necessary to require all members to sign the following 'recognition' before they resumed their seats:

I, AB, do hereby freely promise and engage myself to be true and faithful to the Lord Protector and the Commonwealth of England, Scotland and Ireland, and shall not (according to the tenor of the indenture, whereby I am returned to serve in this present parliament) propose, or give my consent, to alter the government, as it is settled in one single person and a parliament.[10]

About 140 members signed the recognition at once, and 50 more the next day. The number stood at 240 (a clear majority) within a month, and in the end only about 100 permanently absented themselves because they rejected it on principle.

Cromwell tried not to widen the rift. He released Harrison on the day of his speech and had him to dinner, but there was no mending the breach between them. Three days later he made an even longer speech to the Lord Mayor and corporation of London, enlarging on what his government had done to promote peace and free trade, and urging them to be on guard against three sorts of men, the violent cavalier, the rigid Presbyterian, and the militant Anabaptist. But his religious position was too liberal for the City fathers, who not long after petitioned parliament to make a firm settlement of church

---

[8] Ibid., pp. 458–9.
[9] Ibid., p. 460.    [10] Ibid., p. 463.

government. The House was very receptive to such advice, for if Cromwell had hoped that the recognition would render it compliant he was soon disappointed. At first it gave him hope. It endorsed the first of his fundamentals without demur; it renounced self-perpetuation by accepting triennial elections, and it confirmed Cromwell's power to dispose of the forces by sea and land during his lifetime, subject to parliament's consent when it was sitting. Thereafter things went less well, for although the recognition kept out Haselrig, Scot, Bradshaw, and other diehard republicans, there still remained a majority who were suspicious of military influence, unsympathetic towards toleration of the sects, and keen to tilt the constitutional balance in parliament's favour. It was soon clear that the parliament saw its main business to be not just to debate, approve, and if necessary amend the Instrument, but to redraw the whole map of government in a constitutional bill of its own, within the broad outlines of Cromwell's four fundamentals. It has been argued that he was naive to hope to get what he wanted from the House without putting a more specific programme before it and constantly keeping it on course through well-briefed managers within it. To this he might have offered two answers. First, he regarded the Instrument and the supplementary ordinances as sufficient agenda in themselves, and though they were open to amendment he hoped that in their essentials they would be self-justificatory to men of goodwill. Secondly, his unwillingness to intervene too closely in parliament's proceedings sprang from principle rather than from inexperience or negligence. One of his serious complaints against the Rump had been of 'how hard and difficult a thing it was to get anything to be carried without making parties, without things indeed unworthy of a parliament', and when he finally came to dissolve the present one he made a great virtue of never having interrupted or interfered in its business.[11] It is ironic that the man so often branded as a military dictator should come in for criticism as over-respectful of parliament's freedom of debate. Perhaps we should suspend both judgements.

One bone of contention was over the succession to the Protectorship, and an accident that Cromwell suffered on 29 September brought the question into prominence. He was enjoying a drive with Thurloe in Hyde Park, the more so because his coach was drawn by six grey Frieslands recently presented to him by the Count of Oldenburg. Always a lover of horseflesh, he took the driver's seat for a spell, but he used the whip too freely and the horses bolted. He was pulled to the ground with a foot caught in the reins, and dragged along for some short distance. He had a loaded pistol in his pocket, and the impact fired it. He was lucky not to be seriously hurt, but he was kept in bed for two or three weeks and was lame for several more. The succession

[11] Abbott, *Writings and Speeches of Oliver Cromwell*, III, 57, 580–1.

was not the burning issue that it might have been, for parliament had already agreed with the Instrument that it should be elective, despite a long speech from Lambert advocating that it should be hereditary. But whereas the Instrument firmly entrusted the election of a new Protector to the council, parliament claimed the power to determine the manner of his choice if the vacancy occurred while it was sitting.

More disturbing was the debate in November on the control of the armed forces after Cromwell's death, and the vote on the 20th, without a division, that they should be disposed of by parliament as it thought fit. It was becoming clear that a large number of members, perhaps the majority, were bent on reducing the standing army immediately to the minimum of 30,000 specified in the Instrument, and entrusting most of its defensive role to the militia. An irresponsible vote on the 21st to reduce the monthly assessment from £90,000 to £30,000 was seen as even more hostile to the army, though in the event it was not put into effect. These moves caused growing resentment among the senior officers, thirty or forty of whom met at St James's on the 25th to stand up for the Instrument unchanged, as Lambert and his colleagues had devised it. Four days later they passed a resolution to live and die with his Highness and 'the present government'.[12]

The army, however, was not unanimous in its support of the Protectorate. The Fifth Monarchist faction was a dwindling force within it since 1653, though Harrison, Rich, and Robert Overton were still capable of arousing disaffection. Rather more of a threat lay in a minority of rigid republicans or commonwealthsmen who clung to a belief in the unfettered sovereignty of the people's representatives. In October the council got wind of a petition to which three colonels, John Okey, Thomas Saunders, and Matthew Alured put their names, intending that it should be circulated throughout the army for signatures. But they did not write it. Its author was John Wildman, the former Leveller, and it stemmed from meetings which had begun in September (if not earlier) and included not only the three colonels but Vice-Admiral John Lawson, who was in effective command of the fleet in the English Channel. It would be interesting to know who sought out whom, for there was soon evidence of a wider web of conspiracy than the three colonels are likely to have spun on their own, and Wildman was never one to miss a chance to make trouble for Cromwell and his fellow-grandees. The three were arrested and their petition seized before it could be sent out for signatures, but it was nevertheless published as a broadsheet on the 18th, doubtless by Wildman, and packets of it were dispatched to army units in England, Scotland, and Ireland. Some batches were accompanied by copies of a pamphlet, probably also by Wildman, entitled *Some Mementos for the Officers and Soldiers of the Army,*

[12] Gardiner, *History of the Commonwealth and Protectorate*, III, 59–60.

which interspersed gobbets from the petition with inflammatory exhort-
ations to stand up for the people's rights and freedoms and not 'to settle the
powers of tyranny'.[13] The petition itself portrayed the Protectorate as at least
potentially a military tyranny, since for two and a half years in every three it
gave supreme power over the armed forces to a single person and a council
'whom he may control by a negative voice at his pleasure'. It urged that the
settlement of the Commonwealth should be entrusted to 'a full and free parliament', on the lines proposed to the Rump by the General Council of Officers in their version of the *Agreement of the People* nearly six years earlier. Its
specious rhetoric passed over the poor record of parliaments over the last five
years in caring for the people's freedoms and their frequent hostility towards
the army itself. It ignored the danger that a truly 'full and free parliament'
would bring back the king, as was to happen little more than five years later.
It was particularly disingenuous in looking to such a parliament as the guarantor of liberty of conscience, for although Cromwell was not a total tolerationist he strove for a broader religious freedom than any parliament of the
Interregnum would endorse—or indeed any parliament at all before 1689.
The colonels were lucky that Cromwell was reluctant to punish old comrades. Okey was court-martialled, found not guilty of treason, and set free
upon surrendering his commission. Saunders resigned his without demur,
and suffered no further penalty. Only Alured, who had been sent home from
Ireland for trying to stir up disaffection in the English forces there, was
imprisoned, and he was released after little more than a year.

There was a parallel movement of republican discontent in the forces in
Scotland, where it was headed by Colonel Robert Overton, who was a special
friend of Milton. He is also an example of the way in which the republican
and Fifth Monarchist strains of opposition could merge. He had been seconded in 1653 to serve (as he had done earlier) as governor of Hull, and he
had written to congratulate Cromwell in his expulsion of the Rump. But he
was known to be unhappy when Barebone's gave way to the Protectorate,
and of his own accord he went to London to see Cromwell personally. He
told him frankly of his misgivings, but promised to inform him if ever his conscience should forbid him to serve him further. Cromwell cordially took his
word and sent him back to Scotland, where he repeated his undertaking to
Monck. Before leaving London, however, he conferred with Wildman. During late October and November hostile pamphlets, including the three
colonels' petition and Wildman's *Some Mementos*, were found circulating
among the regiments in Scotland, and in December a group of disaffected

---

[13] Quoted by Barbara Taft in '*The Humble Petition of Several Colonels of the Army*: causes,
character and results of military opposition to Cromwell's Protectorate', in *Huntington Library
Quarterly* XLII (1978), 15–41. This is much the most thorough account of the whole episode,
though Dr Taft evaluates the petition itself more kindly than I do.

officers was meeting at Overton's headquarters. He did not inform Monck, and he countenanced the summoning of a more general meeting of officers, planned to be held in Edinburgh on 1 January in order 'to assert the freedoms of the people in the privileges of parliament'. Thurloe received intelligence that he intended to seize Monck and march the army in Scotland (or as much of it as would follow him) into England, there to join up with forces raised by Haselrig and Bradshaw. No evidence survives to substantiate this allegation and the extent of Overton's engagement in sedition must remain uncertain, but Cromwell had totally ceased to trust him and wrote to Monck on Christmas Day to order his arrest.[14]

Wildman is again the common denominator that links these ripples of unrest with that in the navy. Vice-Admiral Lawson had not only been meeting with him and the three colonels in September, but as a member of the corporation of his native Scarborough he had done much to get Wildman elected to parliament for that borough. He was a Baptist and a Leveller sympathizer, and he was currently in effective command of the Channel fleet because Blake was in Plymouth, preparing to sail to the Straits of Gibraltar, and Penn was ashore, planning the ill-fated 'Western Design' (of which more anon). At about the same time as the three colonels' petition was being hatched, Lawson encouraged (and very possibly drafted) a petition of the seamen in his squadron which besides expressing their more material grievances carried strong republican overtones. On 17 October he presided over a council of war on Penn's flagship off Spithead and persuaded the assembled captains to uphold the men's right to petition and to support their requests. Cromwell sensed the danger and sent Desborough to join with Penn in investigating its source. A prompt and generous distribution of pay allayed the seamen's discontents, and the crisis blew over. Remarkably, Lawson was allowed to retain his vice-admiralship, but he was an able and popular officer, and Cromwell decided to give him another chance. It was a gesture of confidence that Lawson did not repay.

During December Cromwell's relations with parliament remained under strain, partly through lack of communication, but they did not seem yet to be pointing inexorably towards a breach. He still had his supporters in the House, and the balance between them and his opponents fluctuated. It has often been said that the members spent nearly all their time on redrawing the map of government according to their own desires, to the neglect of all other public needs, but this is not true. This was a hard-working parliament, which sat morning and afternoon on six days a week, sometimes till late at night. Although the constitutional bill was by far its greatest business, it gave consideration to at least twenty-seven other public bills, thirteen of which

[14] Ibid., pp. 37–9; Abbott, *Writings and Speeches of Oliver Cromwell*, III, 557.

received one or more readings. None of them, however, not even an assessment bill, got as far as being passed.[15] As the year 1654 neared its end, hopes were still alive that Cromwell and the parliament might come to agreement. On 23 December Anthony Garland, a regicide member, moved that Cromwell should be offered the title of king. Henry Cromwell and Sir Anthony Ashley Cooper spoke in support, but the general feeling of the House was so clearly against the motion that it was withdrawn without being put to the vote. It is surprising, however, that at this stage it was made at all; surprising too that it made so little stir, and not least surprising that Cooper and Cromwell's son supported it. Oliver himself cannot have approved it, for he said in his speech at the dissolution that 'if . . . this government should have been placed in my family hereditary, I would have rejected it'.[16] As for Cooper, what was the future Earl of Shaftesbury and arch-Whig up to in proposing a Cromwellian dynasty? He had once been a royalist, certainly, but now, after serving for a year as a loyal and busy councillor, he was moving towards opposition. He may have thought that making Cromwell king under a constitution that limited his powers more strictly than the Instrument had done, as the bill under debate promised to do, would be the best guarantee against the regime turning into a military dictatorship. Whatever his motives, he attended the council for the last time on 28 December. It may well have been at that meeting (the next was not until 5 January) that Cromwell broached the idea of dissolving parliament after five lunar rather than calendar months, and that for Cooper may have been the last straw.

By that time Cromwell must have decided that some provisions in the constitutional bill were quite unacceptable unless he could get them modified. The established parochial clergy and the limits of religious toleration came much under debate during December, and parliament clearly intended to draw the lines more strictly than the Instrument had done. It proposed to allow the Protector no more than a twenty-day suspensive veto over any acts it might pass to restrain 'damnable heresies', as well as 'atheism, blasphemy, popery, prelacy, licentiousness and profaneness', and it intended to specify precisely what 'damnable heresies' came under its ban.[17] This could have been a persecutor's charter, and when, as a very late insertion on 12 January, the Protector was admitted to a share in enumerating the damnable heresies, the concession came too late. Parliament also busied itself over the case of John Biddle, the Socinian, and on 13 December committed him to prison. Cromwell's own tolerance did not extend to those who denied the divinity of Christ, as Socinians did—not at least until he readmitted the Jews—but as he

[15] Peter Gaunt, 'Law-making in the first Protectorate parliament', in C. Jones, M. Newitt, and S. Roberts (eds.), *Politics and People in Revolutionary England* (Oxford, 1986), pp. 163–86.

[16] Abbott, *Writings and Speeches of Oliver Cromwell*, III, 589.

[17] Gardiner (ed.), *Constitutional Documents*, p. 443. The whole bill is printed on pp. 427–47.

was to show in the case of the Quaker James Nayler two years later, he objected to parliament acting as a court of first instance in such matters, and assuming the roles of prosecutor, judge, and jury.

Probably the most seriously objectionable provision in the constitutional
bill, as it took all but final shape towards the end of 1654, concerned the
choice and tenure of the council. Under the Instrument, when a vacancy in the
council occurred parliament was to nominate six candidates, the council was
to select two of them, and the Protector was to choose the one he preferred;
but once chosen a councillor's appointment was to be permanent, unless he
was convicted of corruption or other serious misconduct. Under the bill,
however, new councillors were to be nominated by the Protector and
approved by parliament; but the whole council was to be subject to fresh
approval by each triennial parliament within forty days of its meeting. This
arrangement, taken together with parliament's claims to determine how a
new Protector should be chosen if the vacancy occurred while it was sitting,
and to dispose the control of the armed forces as it thought fit under
Cromwell's successors, made nonsense of the quest for a balance between the
legislative and executive powers, and for a measure of independence between
them. The bill would have subordinated the executive to the legislature. Its
financial provisions were less grossly inadequate than parliament had at times
threatened, but they fell far below the government's current needs, and by
implication confirmed the intention to reduce the standing army to the Instrument's minimum of 30,000 at an early date. Cromwell currently had about
57,000 men under arms, the majority of them garrisoning Ireland and
Scotland.

It became a crucial question whether parliament was prepared to negotiate
with him before finalizing the bill. Until a late stage he hoped, and his supporters urged, that the House would appoint a committee to treat, or at least
to hear him, on the points of controversy. This was refused; the bill was to be
presented to him for acceptance as it stood, and if he did not agree to every
article in it, it was to be void. Furthermore, parliament decided not to put any
other bill before him until he had passed its new constitution, so unless he did
so he could get none of his ordinances confirmed, or even the monthly assessment authorized.

Whether this uncompromising attitude would by itself have led to an early
dissolution cannot be known, but the situation was inflamed by the number
of plots which were threatening the government from more than one quarter.
Royalist conspiracy was now better organized and more widespread than
ever before, and by early January Thurloe and Cromwell knew for certain
that it would not be long before the king's friends attempted a general rising.
It was essential therefore that discipline and obedience in the armed forces
should be complete, but commonwealthsmen and Leveller sympathizers were

planning to raise unrest among the soldiery and link it to that of the seamen. Unauthorized rendezvous on Marston Moor, Salisbury Plain, and other sites were being planned for January, and Overton's activities in Scotland were plausibly seen as part of the same picture. Such subversive movements took encouragement from the fact that a parliament was not only sitting but striving to reduce Cromwell's powers, and when he dissolved it he more than hinted that some of its members had been working with the conspirators to pervert the army.

He wrote a self-revealing letter to his friend Lieutenant-Colonel Wilkes in mid-January, telling him how deeply saddened he was by the continuing opposition of men he had hoped to find on the same side as himself. His efforts to resolve the differences between 'the several interests of the people of God', had brought him 'reproaches and anger from some of all sorts'.[18] On the 22nd, the day on which five lunar months elapsed since the parliament first met, he dissolved it, though not without first subjecting it to two hours of reproaches. Thomas Carlyle, who first presented Cromwell's speeches to a wide readership, enthused about this one, but his hearers must have found most of it rather predictable, as well as very long. This passage conveys its main burden:

Instead of peace and settlement, instead of mercy and truth being brought together, righteousness and peace kissing each other, by reconciling the honest people of these nations, and settling the woeful distempers that are amongst us, . . . weeds and nettles, briers and thorns, have thriven under your shadow; dissettlement and division, discontent and dissatisfaction, together with real dangers to the whole, has [sic] been more multiplied within these five months of your sitting, than in some years before.[19]

He spoke of the royalists' preparations to rise in arms, and accused 'that party of men called Levellers, and who call themselves commonwealthsmen', of colluding with them. He defended the present constitution as in its essentials 'most agreeable to the general sense of the nation, having had experience enough by trial of other conclusions, judging this most likely to avoid the extremes of monarchy on the one hand, and democracy on the other, and yet not to found *dominium in gratia*' (as the Fifth Monarchists sought to do, by confining political participation to the 'saints'). He professed his continuing faith in the people of these nations as 'a people blessed by God . . . by reason of that immortal seed, which hath been and is among them, those regenerated ones in the land, who are all the flock of Christ, and lambs of Christ, though perhaps under many unruly passions and troubles of Spirit'.[20] Almost by way of conclusion he referred to the design to seize Monck and march the forces in Scotland into England as though it were a fact, which he believed it

---

[18] Abbott, *Writings and Speeches of Oliver Cromwell*, III, 572.
[19] Ibid., p. 582.     [20] Ibid., pp. 587, 590.

to be. With that and other conspiracies afoot, and all taking comfort from the differences between the parliament and himself, he did not believe the country to be safe.

Parties in opposition have a way of finding more in Common than when they have to bear the burden of government, especially when they have a common bugbear, which in this case was the political influence wielded by the army. Military dictatorship is a great evil, though how far the Protectorate deserved such an appellation is a question best considered after describing how it ran its whole course. Much of Cromwell's problem lay in the sheer range of opposition that he faced: royalists, Presbyterians, Rumper oligarchs, populist commonwealthsmen, proponents of a rule of the saints. None of these except the first was likely to command as much support or make a better fist of governing than he did, but they made it very hard for him to achieve what he really desired, 'a government by consent'.[21] As for the royalists, a plebiscite (if such an anachronism can be imagined) might have brought back the king, but the next five years would show how few were prepared to risk their lives for him. When a genuine tide of popular sentiment did urge in favour of returning to monarchy, it was in reaction not to the rule of a Cromwell but to that of the restored Rump.

[21] *Memoirs of Edmund Ludlow*, II, 11.

# TWENTY-ONE

# Cavaliers in Arms, Swordsmen in the Saddle

MUCH the most imminent threat that Cromwell faced when he dissolved parliament came from the royalists who were planning an early general rising, and it will soon be shown how he countered it. But he also had to protect his back against other sorts of opponents. He knew very well that if the royalists had not enlisted the old Levellers in their cause it was not for want of trying. John Wildman was arrested on 10 February in the act of dictating a declaration calling upon the people to take up arms against him. Sexby, even deeper in conspiracy, escaped to the continent from Portland, abetted by the mayor of the town and governor of the castle, who actually arrested the party of soldiers sent to apprehend him because they had no written warrant. Leveller renegades, however, posed no serious menace.

The Fifth Monarchists were less of a thorn in Cromwell's flesh than they had been a year earlier and he treated them as gently as he dared, but he could not ignore their persistent incitements to disown and disobey his government. John Rogers and Christopher Feake were still in confinement, Rogers at Lambeth. Early in February a dozen members of Rogers's church came to Whitehall to plead for the two pastors' release, and Cromwell accordingly summoned Rogers and a few of his friends to a conference with himself and a group of councillors and ministers. It did not help that Rogers came attended by an uninvited retinue of about 250. Cromwell nevertheless reasoned with him long and patiently, seeking an undertaking from him to live peaceably under his government; such a pledge could have released both preachers long ago. But Rogers would yield nothing; the issue, he said, was not between man and man but between Christ's government and Cromwell's. He demanded that he be brought before a regular court of law on a formal charge, well knowing Cromwell's reluctance to subject men to the rigour of the treason laws for their religious convictions. That same evening, Harrison, Rich, Carew, Hugh Courtney, Arthur Squibb, and Ireton's younger brother Clement came to Whitehall together and urged Cromwell to free 'the prisoners of the Lord'. He replied that if Rogers and Feake were truly the Lord's prisoners they would soon be at liberty, but that in fact they were in prison for railing, reviling, uttering falsehoods, and stirring up the people to arms. But this was at the end of a long day, and he said he would speak further with Harrison and his companions shortly. When he gave them an appointment two or three days later, however, they failed to keep it. He then summoned them by a written warrant to undergo interrogation by himself or the council on matters concerning the peace of the nation, but again they failed to appear. It was high time, he decided, to bring them to heel, so he had the five arrested and brought before him in custody. In this crucial confrontation he had with him, besides the council, the ministers Walter Cradock, Joseph Caryll, and Thomas Brooks, while the five prisoners were granted their request to have John Simpson and other Fifth Monarchist pastors present. Asked why they had refused the Protector's previous summons, they frankly said that by obeying it 'they should acknowledge the government, which they could not do, it being a government set up against the will of God, and in opposition to the kingdom of Christ, and was antichristian and Babylonish, and that they did expect God would pour out his wrath upon it'. Carew added that when Barebone's Parliament was dissolved Cromwell 'took the crown off from the head of Christ, and put it upon his own'. They flatly refused to pledge themselves not to disturb the peace, saying 'that the present authority is no authority, nor to be obeyed, and consequently arms may be taken up against it'. Their strongest objection to the Protectoral constitution was that 'it had a parliament in it, whereby power is derived from the people, whereas all power belongs to Christ'.[1] Cromwell conferred with the council, and then, despite their defiance, made them a generous offer: if they would retire to their native counties and promise not to leave them without permission, they would not be prosecuted further. They utterly rejected it, so they were committed to widely separated prisons, though not without hope of release. Harrison, for example, was freed after little more than a year and Rogers early in 1657, though both men were soon in trouble again.

Ten days after his clash of wills Cromwell gave a very different reception to a man who was widely regarded as quite as dangerously subversive as any Fifth Monarchy man. George Fox was in the midst of his strenuous evangelizing journeys round the Midlands and northern England, where he and his fellow Quakers were notorious for interrupting church services. This was reasonably resented as a breach of the law that could easily lead to a breach of the peace, but Quakers were perhaps even more widely abominated for challenging the very principles of social rank and deference by refusing 'hat-honour' and addressing all and sundry with the familiar 'thou' and

---

[1] The above quotations are from Thurloe's report of the interview to Monck, in *Clarke Papers*, II, 242–6, reprinted in Abbott, *Writings and Speeches of Oliver Cromwell*, III, 618–20.

'thee'. Such feelings were strongly shared by Colonel Francis Hacker, a Presbyterian officer who had commanded the guard at the king's execution and was now responsible for security in Leicestershire. He saw Fox's meetings in the county as a threat to the state, and sent him and others up to London in custody. Cromwell interviewed the Quaker leader while he was still dressing, and listened patiently to a long harangue. He treated Fox with true courtesy, but taxed him with his people's behaviour towards the clergy. A long exchange was broken off as more and more people came into the room, but before Fox left Cromwell caught him by the hand and said, with tears in his eyes, 'Come again to my house, for if thou and I were but an hour in a day together we should be nearer one to the other'.[2] He gave orders that Fox should be given dinner with his entourage in the Banqueting Hall, though the invitation was declined. He not only released him, but left him at liberty to address meetings in London or wherever he would. Fox returned more than once to Whitehall and preached to Cromwell's household and gentlemen of the guard, among whom he made several notable converts.

It is remarkable that Cromwell found time for these long interviews with the Fifth Monarchist leaders and Fox, considering how the evidence was pouring in of an imminent royalist rising. So many enemy agents were crossing the Channel both ways that he ordered the port authorities early in February to let no one leave the country without a license from himself or the council, and to examine any suspects who tried to enter it very strictly. But royalist leadership and organization in England were not in good shape. Since late in 1653 the king had committed the sole authority to raise his supporters in arms to a group of six men who called themselves the Sealed Knot. They had all held commands under his father, and were highly placed socially. The fathers of Lord Belasyse, Lord Loughborough, Sir William Compton, and John Russell were respectively Lord Fauconberg, the Earl of Huntingdon, the Earl of Northampton, and the Earl of Bedford. Edward Villiers was a nephew of the first Duke of Buckingham, and of the six only Sir Richard Wyllis, the former governor of Newark, had no close aristocratic connections. They got the king to agree that their activities should be known only to himself and Hyde and Ormond, and that he should countenance no other designs besides theirs without consulting them. They hardly deserved so exclusive a trust, for several reasons. They were cautious to excess; the time for them was never ripe. They were hostile to royalist groups outside the Hyde–Ormond ambit, especially to Rupert and the 'swordsmen' and to the Louvre circle attached to Henrietta Maria. There was bad blood between them and various other

---

[2] The account of the interview is of course Fox's own: *The Journal of George Fox*, ed. J. L. Nickalls (1975), pp. 198–202.

English-based royalists who might have done the king good service, and one of them was to prove a traitor.[3]

At least the Knot discountenanced wildcat plots, of which there had been more than one during 1654. The most serious of them, in May, centred around some kinsmen of Lord Gerard and had links with Rupert and the Louvre set, though most of its participants were more obscure. The design was to ambush Cromwell's coach and murder him as he drove from White-hall to Hampton Court for the weekend, but Thurloe had some inkling of it and Oliver changed his route, travelling as far as Chelsea by boat. The plan was changed to seizing him in his chapel a week later, but it was all uncovered within days and many were arrested, perhaps several hundred. These counter-measures were unpopular among the largely Presbyterian citizenry, so a High Court of Justice was set up to try the chief conspirators, the first of only two such tribunals under the Protectorate. It sentenced only two of them to death, John Gerard, a royalist colonel, and Peter Vowell, an Islington schoolmaster, and even they were spared the barbarities of hanging, drawing and quartering, the law's ancient penalties for treason. A few other plotters were transported to Barbados. Many royalists had held aloof from the whole conspiracy, some because of an honourable aversion to assassination, others because many of its promoters were dubious adventurers, and because the plans for following up the Protector's murder with a national uprising were so patently half-baked.

From the king's point of view the worst effect of this botched and some-what disreputable enterprise was to shrink the snail-like Knot further back into its shell. So far the Knot had formulated virtually no concrete plans for a general rising, and its continued inactivity caused such widespread dissatis-faction among committed royalists that a new leadership emerged, in rivalry with it. These activists, as they may be called (they had no special appellation at the time), were not as tightly organized as the Knot, nor so aristocratic. Most were country gentlemen of local rather than national social standing, though they did include Sir Hugh Pollard and Sir John Grenville in the West Country, the second Lord Byron in the Midlands and Sir Philip Musgrave in the north. The king, despite his ill-advised pledges to the Knot, was happy to listen to them, and though they would have done better with closer co-ordination at home and more regular contact with his ministers abroad, several brave agents passed increasingly frequently between England and the exiled court. Unlike the Knot, the activists were very ready to enlist the support of political presbyterians who had come over to the king since the first Civil War, and they were keener to engage former Levellers and other disaffected

---

[3] For a masterly account see David Underdown, *Royalist Conspiracy in England 1649–60* (New Haven, 1960), esp. chs. 5 and 6.

elements in the army and the fleet. The mutual jealousy between them and the Knot was predictably intense, but their plans and proposals were sufficiently advanced to be smuggled over to the king in two papers, in July and August 1654.

Thereafter they went ahead with preparations for a national rising, enlisting men, collecting arms, and allocating commands and areas of responsibility. They had very limited success with disaffected presbyterians; they won fairly positive undertakings from Major-General Richard Browne and Colonel John Booth, but Lord Willoughby of Parham blew hot and cold, and persistent attempts to engage Fairfax came to nothing. The king, despite his pledges to the Knot, in September 1654 commissioned Henry Wilmot, Earl of Rochester, his companion during his fugitive wanderings after Worcester, to command all such forces as should appear for him in England. But while the activists were urging Charles to order immediate action, the Knot sent him a deeply pessimistic report on 3 December, dismissing their rivals' sanguine assurances as illusions. Thurloe had his ear to the ground, and during the second half of the month the Knot's fears were confirmed as 3,000 troops were called home from Ireland, fresh regiments were brought into London, the Tower garrison was trebled, and artillery was positioned around Whitehall and St James's. The sharp action taken against Overton and his accomplices killed the activists' hopes of subverting any considerable elements in the army and the fleet. On New Year's Day Thurloe's officers made a major breakthrough when they uncovered and broke that part of their organization that was gathering and distributing arms in the Midlands.

Yet still Charles went on urging his supporters to action, and they duly fixed 6 February as the date for a general rising; it would have coincided with the dissolution of the parliament if Cromwell had let it run its five-month course. The hard-drinking Rochester was slow to take his leave of the taverns of Dunkirk, and did not sail for England until the 19th. Meanwhile the many adverse signs made the activists postpone the rising until the 13th, and they sent again to the king for his approval of their plans. Against the advice of Ormond, and despite a warning from all six of the Knot that an attempt at this time would destroy his friends, he readily gave it, though he failed to send positive orders to the Knot to give it all their support. He himself moved to Middelburgh on the Dutch coast at the end of February, hoping to put himself at the head of the insurgents as soon as they got under way, though he could bring them neither troops nor arms and supplies. Meanwhile the rising was again postponed, this time until 8 March, though the message failed to reach some of its intended leaders in Somerset and Wiltshire. They attempted to rendezvous in Salisbury on 12–13 February. Many arrests followed; one of the prisoners confessed all he knew of the design and its leadership, so in what was to have been one of its main centres it was already past saving.

What ensued on 8 March was predictable. Rochester had planned a great rally on Marston Moor, preparatory to an attack on York, but only about 150 men appeared, and on the approach of Colonel Lilburne's troops they rode off in such a hurry that they left four cartloads of arms behind them. Rochester made his escape disguised as a grazier, but other northern cavaliers were not so lucky. Even fewer men gathered for the intended attacks on Newcastle and Chester, and none at all for that on Hull, where recent reinforcements had killed any hopes of success. The largest turn-out—some 200 or 300—was in Nottinghamshire, but the expected commanders in the Midlands, Lord Byron and Sir George Savile (the future Earl of Halifax), stayed in London, so these men too ditched their arms and made for home. London itself stayed quiet, not only because of the powerful counter-measures already described, but because Cromwell had asked the Lord Mayor and corporation on 15 February to raise a special militia, and about 5,000 were swiftly embodied. Londoners had resented the number of arrests following the Vowell–Gerard plot, but a renewal of civil war by cavaliers in arms was the last thing that most of them wanted. Timely warnings from central government enabled local commanders to frustrate intended rendezvous in Shrewsbury and along the Welsh border, while Portsmouth and Plymouth slept undisturbed because the men who were to have attempted them were already prisoners.

Strangely enough it was in Salisbury, where the abortive rendezvous in mid-February might have seemed fatal to any further action, that one small body of royalists succeeded in getting under arms. The recent debacle did not deter Sir Joseph Wagstaff, a soldier of fortune who had fought for both sides in the first Civil War but had latterly shared the king's exile. He came over with Rochester and joined John Penruddock, the local royalist entrusted with the command in Wiltshire and adjacent parts. Their plan for 8 March was to enter Winchester and capture the assize judges who were there on circuit, but they were thwarted by the arrival of a troop of horse, so they postponed it for a few days and switched the venue to Salisbury, the next assize town. They entered the city with about 180 mounted men in the small hours of the 12th, seized the many horses belonging to visitors attending the assizes, broke open the jail, enlisted and mounted most of the prisoners, and dragged the two judges and the high sheriff from their beds. Wagstaff wanted to hang all three on the spot; Penruddock with difficulty dissuaded him. They rode westward out of Salisbury with somewhat less than four hundred men, including the jailbirds, counting on the promised support of the great Marquis of Hertford. But he never stirred, nor did the thousands that they had hoped to recruit in Dorset. Their numbers indeed shrank through desertion as their march into Devon became a flight, and they were finally routed in South Molton by a single troop of horse under Captain Unton Croke. They put up a fight, but

Croke took more prisoners than he had men. Wagstaff made his escape, but Penruddock to his honour would not abandon his men, and was taken.

Cromwell promptly sent Major-General Desborough to subdue the West Country, but he found when he got there that there were really no embers to stamp out. Many more prisoners were taken after Croke's original haul, and Desborough wrote that he could have brought in many more still of the meaner sort. But he sent in a list of 139, including 43 officers and gentlemen, hoping (he said) that these would suffice to be made an example of. Less than a third even of these were put on trial, and a fair trial is what they got—not by a high court of justice, but by judge and jury under a special commission of oyer and terminer. Of the thirty-nine who were sentenced to death for treason more than half were reprieved; Thurloe reported the number to be executed as fourteen or fifteen, including of course Penruddock, and even they were spared the butchery of hanging, drawing, and quartering. Nationwide there was a much larger number of prisoners, including those arrested before 8 March or taken when fleeing from abortive rendezvous in the north and Midlands. The majority of these were freed during the summer and autumn on giving bonds for their good behaviour, though a few were punished with fines. About seventy, including some taken with Penruddock, were transported to Barbados as indentured servants, with the prospect of regaining their freedom if they survived their term of servitude. When one compares this retribution with the hundreds who were summarily hanged after the rebellion of the northern earls in 1569, or the 250 hanged, drawn, and quartered after Monmouth's rebellion in 1685, Cromwell's lenience is striking. Penruddock's rising was of course a smaller affair, but it would not have been if all the men who conspired to take up arms and raise their tenantry had actually done so.[4]

Many factors contributed to the failure of the royalist effort in 1655: the penetrating skill of Thurloe and his network of intelligences, the strong nerve and vigorous counter-measures of Cromwell's government, the lack of co-ordination and mutual trust within the royalist leadership, the Knot's near-defeatism, the folly—encouraged by the king—of persisting with the rising in face of growing evidence that many of the plans for it had been unmasked, and the failure of nerve that made so many who had pledged their participation wait and see how the first few days went before risking their necks. The activists, especially some agents of the exiled court like Daniel O'Neill, had wildly overestimated both the popular appeal of the king's cause and the supposed unpopularity of the Protectoral regime. Even in the mainly royalist territory through which Penruddock marched, not only did he fail to raise the

---

[4] For the attempted risings and their suppression see Underdown, *Royalist Conspiracy*, ch. 7, Gardiner, *Commonwealth and Protectorate*, ch. 39, and for a briefer survey A. H. Woolrych, *Penruddock's Rising 1655* (Historical Association Pamphlet, 1955, repr. 1968).

countryfolk, but over 2,000 of them came into Taunton to help keep the peace against him, while 400 pro-government volunteers mustered in Gloucestershire, and a militia regiment was rapidly raised in Devon. Such responses, coupled with London's readiness in enlisting a special militia, might have encouraged Cromwell to make a virtue of clemency and pursue a steady policy of winning the positive support of former neutrals and moderate ex-royalists.

Instead, he threw the opportunity away within a few months by instituting the regime of the major-generals. It was almost certainly the biggest mistake of his political career, but it was not incomprehensible, and it should not be judged too hastily in the light of hindsight. The royalists' blunders in the early months of 1655 had been so crass that their potential for resistance had really not been measured. Cromwell was not to know that they would fail while he lived to heal the breaches in their own ranks, construct an effective underground organization, or fire something like the spirit of 1660 among the king's friends. Furthermore, however satisfying it was that Penruddock's followers had been dealt with by due process of law, there were other signs during the spring and summer that the Protectorate could not totally rely on the judiciary to support it. Parallel to the commission of oyer and terminer in the west, another such commission had been issued for the trial of the prisoners taken in the north and Midlands. But the three chief commissioners—two judges and a serjeant-at-law—proved reluctant to execute it. After taking refuge in legal technicalities, they admitted to doubts as to whether the offences charged against the prisoners constituted treason in law. That was to call in question the legality of the 1654 Treason Ordinance, and by implication that of the government itself. The two judges, Francis Thorpe and Richard Newdigate, were called before the council and dismissed from their posts. The prisoners were eventually tried before the assize judges, who imposed no heavier sentences on those found guilty than fines for riot or misdemeanour.

Three other challenges to the government's legality discomfited it in the course of the spring and summer. In April it felt that it could leave the reform of the Court of Chancery in abeyance no longer, so the three Commissioners of the Great Seal, Lisle, Whitelocke, and Widdrington, together with William Lenthall, Master of the Rolls, were summoned before the council and ordered in the Protector's name to implement the reforms prescribed in the ordinance of the previous year. Whitelocke and Widdrington resigned rather than comply, but Cromwell was so loath to lose such able and basically loyal servants that he appointed them both as Commissioners of the Treasury.

The other two cases were quite different, but they are interesting in showing further the genuine difficulties that senior lawyers experienced in executing the Protectorate's ordinances and commissions, and the genuine efforts that Cromwell and the council made to respect the law's processes. That of a London merchant called George Cony had begun in November when he refused to pay duty on some silk that he had imported, and then violently threw out the customs officers who came to distrain on his goods. Fined £500 by a committee of the council, he had refused to pay that either, and was duly imprisoned—whereupon he sued out a writ of habeas corpus. Being rich, he took three of the most distinguished lawyers in the country as his counsel, John Maynard, Thomas Twysden, and Wadham Wyndham. They were reluctant to engage in direct confrontation with the government and argued on points of procedure for as long as they could, but on 8 May they were driven to plead that the ordinance under which customs duty was levied and the fine imposed on Cony had no force in law. The case was heard before Chief Justice Rolle, who was one of the judges recently seized in Salisbury and one of those who subsequently tried Penruddock and his fellow insurgents. He made no demur at the argument of Cony's counsel, and was promptly summoned before the Council of State. The three counsels were separately brought before it, and on refusing to retract were briefly imprisoned, though they soon made their submission and were freed. Rolle agreed to adjourn the case until the following term, but he resigned his office before it came up. He may well have wanted no further part in this dubious quarrel; he was about 66, and he died a year later. Cony, seeing that the game was up, paid his fine and was released.

The third case was simpler but odder. In July 1655 Sir Peter Wentworth, a former Rumper and a friend of Milton, had the collectors of the assessment in Warwickshire arrested and prosecuted. He was brought before the council, and there told Cromwell to his face that 'by the law of England no money ought to be levied upon people without their consent in parliament'.[5] This was ironical, since twenty years earlier, as sheriff of Oxfordshire, he had been collecting Ship Money for Charles I. Cromwell asked him whether he would withdraw his action, to which he replied 'If you will command me, I must submit'. He had made his gesture, and submit he did; the assessors were set free to go about their business, and that was the end of the matter. These various cases did not seriously shake Cromwell's hold on power, but since his first parliament had fallen short of ratifying his authority it was uncomfortable to have his right to it questioned from so many quarters, and to have to rely on a judiciary that was reluctant to recognize that one cannot make revolutions without breaking a few constitutional eggs. It was probably his evident difficulty in putting the legal basis of his authority beyond doubt that led to a spate of rumours that he was about to assume the crown; indeed a large

---

[5] Abbott, *Writings and Speeches of Oliver Cromwell*, III, 862–3, quoting *Cal.S.P.Dom.* (1655), pp. 296–7, 300, and *Memoirs of Edmund Ludlow*, I, 413–14.

crowd gathered in Westminster on 1 June in the expectation that he would announce his royal title that day. There was probably nothing behind such stories but speculation and the tattle of foreign diplomats. In an affectionate letter to his son-in-law Fleetwood, in which he was clearly baring his heart, he wrote that 'The noise of my being crowned &c. are like malicious figments', though he lamented that 'The wretched jealousies that are amongst us, and the spirit of calumny, turns all into gall and wormwood'.[6]

From the spring to the autumn of 1655 Cromwell and the council were very much occupied by dramatic developments in Britain's foreign relations which called for major decisions of peace or war. These will be described shortly, but they help to explain why so many months elapsed between Penruddock's rising and the full establishment, between August and October, of the most controversial phase of Cromwell's rule, the regime of the major-generals. At any rate it was not a hasty decision, or a mere reaction to royalist insurrection. Cromwell was aware of three main problems on the home front, and he hoped that by a single expedient he could go a long way to tackling them all. His most obvious need was for security against further royalist conspiracy, for it would be tempting providence to expect the king's supporters to bungle their opportunities so feebly a second time round. He needed the protection of his army, but his second major problem was that he could not afford to maintain it at its current strength, because he had progressively reduced the monthly assessment from £120,000 to £60,000 and his government was falling steadily further into debt. His third great concern was over the lack of progress in 'the reformation of manners', that moral regeneration of the nation that he hoped would attend upon the better preaching of the gospel. He publicly asserted that 'the suppressing of vice and encouragement of virtue [were] the very end of magistracy',[7] and he knew all too well that most JPs rarely concerned themselves with lapses in personal morality unless they threatened a breach of the peace. 'Really,' he told his next parliament, 'a justice of peace shall from the most be wondered at as an owl, if he go but one step out of the way of his fellow justices in the reformation of these things.'[8] It was here, in his beliefs regarding government's duty in the sphere of private morality, that Cromwell's views stood furthest from those of the western world in the twenty-first century, but to puritans then it did not seem so wildly inappropriate to employ senior military officers as vice squad chiefs.

Cromwell was impressed by Desborough's efficiency in reducing the West Country to order and obedience, but months before he set up a similar

---

[6] Abbott, *Writings and Speeches of Oliver Cromwell*, III, 756. I find it surprising that Gardiner believed, on highly dubious evidence, that a proposal to make Cromwell king was seriously considered by both the Council of State and the Council of Officers: *Commonwealth and Protectorate*, III, 155–8.

[7] Abbott, *Writings and Speeches of Oliver Cromwell*, IV, 112.        [8] Ibid., p. 494.

organization nationwide he started raising a new mounted militia, quite separate from the old trained bands, who fought on foot. It was to be a step
towards reducing the regular army, whose cavalry was its most expensive
component. Its captains were appointed by the council in May, and they
enlisted their men, all volunteers and many of them old soldiers, during June.
They were organized in troops by counties, and they numbered 6,520 in all.
They were on call at forty-eight hours' notice, and on active service they were
to be paid as regular cavalry; otherwise they were due a retainer of £8 a year
(though whether they got it was another matter). It was primarily to co-
ordinate the operations of this militia and of the regular forces that England
was divided into ten (later eleven) districts, including Desborough's, each
under a major-general. The first ten were appointed in August, and their
instructions were finalized in October. Besides their obvious military duties,
they were to disarm all Roman Catholics, all who had fought for or assisted
the king, and 'all others who are dangerous to the peace of the nation'. They
were to take bonds of all heads of families in these categories for the good
behaviour of their whole households, and they did so in the case of over
14,000 former royalists, normally for £5,000 if they had borne arms for the
king. They returned full lists of these men to a central register in London,
where visiting royalists had to check in, after first reporting their intended
movements to the local major-general before leaving home. They were to
maintain a ban on horse races, cock-fights, bear-baitings, and stage plays, and
to seek out robbers and highwaymen in their respective areas.

But their instructions went far beyond the spheres of security and police.
They were directed that 'They shall in their constant carriage and conversation encourage and promote godliness and virtue, and discourage and dis-
countenance all profaneness and ungodliness';[9] and in company with the JPs
and other local officers they were to ensure that the laws against drunkenness,
swearing, blaspheming, sabbath-breaking, stage plays, and other such abom-
inations were more effectually enforced. They were to close down all out-of-
town alehouses, reduce their number everywhere, and suppress all gambling
dens and brothels in and around London. They were to put their weight
behind the enforcement of the ordinances for ejecting scandalous ministers
and schoolmasters, and to report regularly to the Protector and council on the
progress made therein.

In these various functions they were assisted by commissioners, appointed
by the council for each county, and to these some major-generals added
nominees of their own. In total about a thousand commissioners had been

---

[9] Abbott, *Writings and Speeches of Oliver Cromwell*, III, 845; the full instructions are on
pp. 844–8. I am greatly indebted to Dr Christopher Durston for enabling me to read his
authoritative study, *Godly Governors: The Rule of Cromwell's Major-Generals*, ahead of publication. The following pages owe much to his work.

named by the end of 1655, though not all were willing to act. They were never intended to supplant the existing magistracy, though there was a large overlap in function and in personnel between the new commissioners and the local bench. In Staffordshire, where they have been particularly closely studied,[10] fourteen of the twenty-two commissioners were already JPs. They also overlapped considerably with the officer corps of the local militia, both old and new. Most were to be identified with the 'godly interest', though few were fanatics; among Staffordshire's twenty-two, for instance, only two were separatists, and they were balanced by two of Anglican sympathies. Their social status varied from region to region and covered quite a wide spectrum. In Staffordshire, at least six ranked as middling gentry or above and four more as lesser gentry, while another nine claimed gentry status through success in trade or a profession. In neighbouring Cheshire the commissioners included a higher ratio of the county elite, but also a larger military presence. By contrast in Kent, Sussex, and Hampshire, where royalism had been predominant and the wounds of the second Civil War still throbbed, the proportion of lesser gentry and men of the middling sort was higher, and the same was generally the case in the West Country.

Although the commissioners were unpaid, the organization as a whole cost a lot of money, and the method of financing it was one of its most unpopular features. The main charges were the salaries of the major-generals themselves, the officers of the county troops and the civilian staffs of the commissioners; together these came to about £80,000 a year. Cromwell took the view that since royalist conspiracy had necessitated the regime, royalists should pay for it, and the result was the notorious decimation tax. All who had adhered to the king in any way, and who possessed land worth £100 a year or more or personal property worth at least £1,500, were made liable, though Cromwell's declaration which announced the scheme on 31 October held out the hope of exemption to those who testified to a genuine change of heart and fully accepted the present government. Otherwise they had to pay £10 a year for every £100 of landed income or £100 for every £1,500-worth of personal property. The obvious objections to the decimation were that it had no sanction from parliament and took no account of whether the decimated had actually engaged in plotting. The great majority who paid had been committed royalists in the wars, though a significant number had been only nominally attached to the king's side and a few had stayed neutral. How many had been active for him since 1648, or even 1646, was a large question. Some of the major-generals' commissioners who were otherwise loyal and willing subjects of the Protectorate were deeply unhappy about subjecting

[10] See John Sutton,'Cromwell's commissioners for preserving the peace of the Commonwealth: a Staffordshire case study', in I. Gentles, J. Morrill, and B. Worden (eds.), *Soldiers, Writers and Statesmen of the English Revolution* (Cambridge, 1998), pp. 151–82.

their neighbours to decimation and refused to take part. Many victims of the levy appealed against it to Cromwell and the council, who were quite generous in granting exemptions—to the dismay of the major-generals, at least seven of whom protested. They needed the money, for although four of them, in areas where royalists were thickest on the ground, collected a surplus, most found themselves short. Their own salaries and those of their militia officers fell heavily into arrears, and their troopers' retainers went unpaid.

It might be thought otiose to explain any further why their regime was very widely disliked, but in fact the major-generals were by no means universally unpopular. Several were struck by the enthusiasm with which they were greeted in their regions, especially by the more active commissioners. There really was a 'godly interest' in the country, and though it was in most parts a minority one Cromwell's eagerness to see the work of reformation go forward was more widely shared than is sometimes allowed. But among their so varied duties, this was the sphere in which their success was most limited. In some regions they did stir the local magistrates into greater activity, especially in administering poor relief and regulating alehouses. But though they closed some hundreds of the latter, tens of thousands survived them, and those they suppressed showed a strong tendency to spring up again. As for moral offences, in Middlesex under Major-General Barkstead there were three times more prosecutions in 1656 than in 1652, and he had some success in banning race-meetings and enforcing sabbath observance. But he was not typical; most major-generals seem to have found it as hard to keep the people chaste as to keep them sober. Some filled the local prisons with rogues and vagabonds, but most of the vagrant fraternity seem to have just moved on to where the heat was lower. In many areas the major-generals' efforts towards reformation were frustrated by the hostility of anti-puritan, anti-military JPs, but again there were wide differences in their relations with the established magistracy. It depended as much on their personalities as on the predisposition of their territories. Boteler in Northamptonshire, Bedfordshire, and Huntingdonshire, and Worsley in Lancashire, Cheshire, and Staffordshire both aroused animosity by the unyielding and abrasive manner in which they went about their business, whereas Whalley, sandwiched between them in Leicestershire and Warwickshire, achieved real progress through courtesy and considerateness. He gave much time to such practical matters as relieving poverty, checking enclosures that involved depopulation, regulating markets by standardizing weights and measures, and punishing cheating and overcharging. More controversial were the major-generals' efforts to purge the municipal corporations of obstructive or ungodly members, because their legal right to do so was very dubious. On the other hand their relations with the assize judges were generally good, and several rode the circuits with them. Few of them acted solely as enforcers of the interests of central government upon the reluctant localities; quite often they spoke up for their territories against its demands. They were not always well supported by Cromwell and the council, partly because the latter was so heavily stretched by other demands on its time. As Anthony Fletcher has said, 'Far too much was expected of men who were bound to be treated with the cynical mixture of wary deference and quiet obstructionism reserved for government inspectors'.[11] They inherited some of the opprobrium that had attached to the old county committees of the 1640s, and as with those bodies their unpopularity was exacerbated by snobbery. Of the sixteen men who acted as major-generals, or as their deputies where the titular major-generals were on duty elsewhere, only three were fully on the social level of the county elite, six were lesser gentry, and seven ranked still lower in the scale. Most were also considerably younger than most of the JPs whom they tried to spur into action, for only four of the sixteen were over forty.

In their primary role of stamping out conspiracy they succeeded triumphantly, for their control over royalists' movements and the bonds they took of them, distasteful though we may find such measures, were almost totally effective. There were one or two more assassination plots, but they were quickly discovered or betrayed; most royalists felt an honourable dislike for such methods. There were no further plans for a general rising until 1658, when they fell apart even more ineptly than in 1655. Long before then, Thurloe and his agents had such a grip on security that they no longer needed the major-generals' special militia. The Knot retreated into inactivity, and from November 1656 onward, if not before, one of its members, Sir Richard Wyllis, regularly divulged many of its secrets to Thurloe. If the major-generals failed to facilitate any considerable reduction in the regular army, that was not their fault. Cromwell was pursuing an adventurous foreign policy which necessitated a reserve of land forces, and anyhow the total of land forces afoot in England and Wales in October 1655—about 11,700 officers and men[12]—was modest enough by contemporary European standards.

The major-generals do not deserve the kind of anathema that they commonly received from historians steeped in the prevailing liberalism of late Victorian and Edwardian times, or from those writing under the shadow of the military dictatorships of the mid-twentieth century. Yet they have to be reckoned one of the mistakes of Cromwell's rule, not only because of the unpopularity that they brought upon it but because they were given an impossibly wide range of duties and responsibilities, too little support in carrying them out, and too little time—effectively less than a year—in which to fulfil them. Much of the bad press that they received stems ultimately from

---

[11] Anthony Fletcher, *Reform in the Provinces* (New Haven and London, 1986), p. 60.

[12] H. M. Reece, 'The military presence in England 1649–1660' (unpublished Oxford D.Phil. thesis, 1982), p. 287.

royalist sources, understandably enough, and from anti-Cromwellian republicans. Clarendon and Ludlow, who both branded them as 'bashaws',[13] the very type of oriental tyranny, exaggerated grossly, but it was never a good idea to commit to the same inexperienced soldierly hands the security of the government against conspiracy, the general invigoration of civil administration, and the promotion of a godly reformation. From Cromwell's point of view the worst damage that he did was to his own cherished aim of 'healing and settling'. He had set out as Protector with the laudable intentions of bridging over the rifts opened up by the wars, eliminating arbitrariness from civil government and putting the military origins of his power behind him. He let himself be deflected too far by the persistence of royalist plotting and by his disappointment with his first parliament, but it is curious that it took him so long to see how far he was compromising his own ideals.

It is not difficult to see why domestic business did not always get the attention it needed, because while the government was dealing with Penruddock's rising and its aftermath it was being faced with decisions of huge consequence in its relations with France and Spain. Both powers, it will be remembered, had been seeking England's friendship, and now that her civil wars were over and her great fleet free from its struggle with the Dutch, neither could afford to provoke her to war. Cromwell exploited this situation, sometimes coolly, sometimes rashly, but because English shipping had suffered so many losses at French hands during the years of undeclared war at sea, he at first displayed more hostility towards France than towards Spain. Back in February 1654, while still at war with the Dutch, he had sent Major Robert Sedgwick to organize an attack by the colonists of New England on what is now New York, but was then New Amsterdam. When his peace with the United Provinces ruled that out, Sedgwick, boldly stretching a clause in his commission that empowered him to seize French ships, attacked and captured three forts in the French colony of Acadia, which then included the coasts of modern New Brunswick and Maine as well as Nova Scotia. This was disputed territory between France and the New Englanders, who were delighted by Sedgwick's venture—the more so when Cromwell showed no signs of yielding to French pressure to restore the forts and the lands they protected.

Blake's fleet, which had sailed for the Mediterranean in October 1654, became an even greater source of friction. France was planning to invade Naples, the capital of the Spanish kingdom that embraced all southern Italy and Sicily, and the design involved the conjunction of two French fleets, one

---

[13] Clarendon, *History of the Rebellion*, VI, 17 (Book XV, § 25); *Memoirs of Edmund Ludlow*, I, 405–6. Blair Worden, however, has pointed out to me that this passage in Ludlow may be an editorial interpolation; see his introduction to E. Ludlow, *A Voyce from the Watch Tower 1660–1662* (Camden series, Royal Historical Society, 1978).

based in Brest, the other, under the Duke of Guise, in Toulon. Blake's orders have not survived, but they were probably to frustrate the invasion by all possible means. Cromwell requested and obtained the King of Spain's permission for Blake to have the use of Spanish ports in the Mediterranean, and his mere presence caused Guise to call the whole scheme off. It also secured the restoration of English merchant ships captured by the French. It caused widespread alarm all around the Mediterranean shores; the pope feared that Blake intended to attack the papal states, and some wealthy Roman citizens sought safety in rural retreats. But Blake's next mission was against the Barbary corsairs operating under the protection of the Dey of Tunis, and on 4 April he brought off an unprecedented feat by sailing into Porto Farino harbour and attacking nine warships that lay under the protection of a powerful fort and other shore batteries. His ship's guns silenced the shore-based artillery, and all the Dey's men-of-war were burnt. Consequently he met with a very different reaction from the Dey of Algiers when he anchored off the port later in the month. He was most courteously received, and he rapidly negotiated the release of the English captives who were toiling as slaves under Algerian masters.

Such was the provocation that Cromwell offered to France that Mazarin gave some passive support to the royalist conspirators in the early part of 1655. Yet it was with Spain that Cromwell went to war in the following October, and with France that he signed a treaty of peace and commerce in the same month. This was to ripen in time into a full offensive alliance. The story of his breach with Spain goes back to the spring of 1654, when he was in a rather bellicose and overconfident mood after concluding his successful peace with the Dutch. Both Cardenas and Bordeaux, ambassadors respectively of Spain and France, believed he was seriously seeking an alliance against the other's country, but for both the terms that he demanded were impossibly high. The price that he asked of Spain for going to war with France was free trade with the Spanish colonies, the right of protestant Englishmen in Spain to worship freely in private premises, the cession of Dunkirk as an earnest for the eventual handing over to England of Calais if the war went successfully, and a subsidy of £300,000 a year while it lasted. No wonder Cardenas sent to Brussels for authority before agreeing to such terms, but in May 1655 he thought he had Cromwell's assurance that he would declare war on France. Cromwell, however, was setting his mind, if he had not set it already, on acquiring by conquest one of Spain's most valuable colonies, Hispaniola. He seems to have thought that he could attack Spanish possessions on the other side of the world without engaging in war with Spain herself, but he was not afraid to face war if it should come. Such an unprovoked attack was by no means an unprecedented idea, for Warwick, Eliot, and Pym among others had urged it in the parliaments of the 1620s. Like them, Cromwell believed that if it succeeded it would quite soon pay for itself, and more. The project aroused keen debate in July in the Council of State, and thanks to jottings taken by Edward Montagu we have a rare glimpse of how it went. Fascinatingly, it shows how forcefully Cromwell's views could be opposed in council, in this case by Lambert in particular. Against the enterprise, he argued its cost and uncertainty, the heavy casualties to be expected, and the unlikelihood that it would advance the protestant cause. He gave higher priority to tasks and challenges nearer home, including the settlement of Ireland. He had a powerful case. But Cromwell was convinced that providence was leading them to the Western Design, as it came to be called. He contended that it would cost little more than laying up the ships engaged in it, and that it would give employment to a considerable part of the army.[14] Later, in justifying the consequent war to parliament, he invoked the example of 'Queen Elizabeth of famous memory', and maintained that the Spaniard was England's 'natural enemy', by reason of 'that antipathy that is in him providentially'.[15] So it was that prejudice, providentialism, and nostalgia for a half-mythical Elizabethan golden age impelled him towards the most ill-considered military decision of his career.

The leadership of the expedition was divided, with William Penn, General at Sea, in command of 38 ships, and Colonel Robert Venables at the head of a land force of nominally 3,000 infantry and 100 cavalry, to be reinforced by recruitment from Barbados. Relations between the two men were deplorable; Penn, who was suspicious and irascible by nature, not only treated Venables with contempt but allowed his subordinates to do so. But the responsibility for the Western Design's failure lay at least as much with the government that planned it as with the commanders who led it. The military force was too small for a start, and instead of being composed of entire regiments whose officers and men knew and trusted each other, it was made up of small drafts from many units scattered up and down the country. Their colonels, given *carte blanche* to name whom they chose, naturally rid themselves only of the men they were glad to lose, and their numbers had to be made up from the scourings of the streets. Venables pleaded and protested in vain. He had to sail with only 2,500 men, and his recruits in Barbados were nearly all untrained, poor-spirited, and ill-disciplined servants, since the colonists saw the expedition as a disruption of their trade and gave it a cold welcome. The soldiers' low morale was further depressed by nasty victuals and inadequate stores. Much the best of Venables' troops consisted of a regiment of about 1,200 seamen drawn from the fleet; they brought his total force to just over 9,000 men.

---

[14] *Clarke Papers*, III, 207–8; also in Abbott, *Writings and Speeches of Oliver Cromwell*, III, 377–8.

[15] Abbott, *Writings and Speeches of Oliver Cromwell*, IV, 261–2.

The attempt on Hispaniola began on 14 April 1655, and it was a predictable disaster. To reach their objective, San Domingo, most of the troops had a thirty-five mile march in torrid heat, on reduced rations, and dreadfully short of water. Dysentery struck down more and more of them, including Venables himself. When they finally came before the walls of the city they were in such wretched shape that he had to order a temporary retreat, and though he organized a second attempt on it his soldiers, the naval regiment excepted, were so demoralized by small-scale Spanish guerrilla attacks that he was forced to call it off. He re-embarked what was left of his men on 4 May, and Penn transported them to Jamaica, which had at most 500 troops to defend it. The island surrendered on the 17th, and its 1,500 or so Spanish settlers were all forced to leave. In English eyes Jamaica was no compensation for Hispaniola, which was nearly seven times as large and had far more colonists. Penn thought so little about a possible Spanish counter-attack that he sailed for home in June with all his larger warships. Venables, who was now very ill, followed soon after, leaving the very capable Colonel Richard Fortescue in command of the garrison. Fortescue was one of the few who had any idea of the prosperous future that lay ahead for Jamaica, which he considered a better site for British colonization than Hispaniola. Sadly, he died only three months after taking up his command.

Penn and Venables, on returning home, were summoned before the council, and after a lashing from Cromwell's tongue for deserting their posts both were committed to the Tower. Penn had the less to complain of, since by bringing most of his ships back without orders he had passed up a chance of capturing the Spanish silver fleet, though he had known it was in Havana, and vulnerable. Venables was harshly treated, for he sought his officers' consent before leaving his post, and he would probably have died if he had stayed at it. Neither commander was released until he abjectly acknowledged his guilt and surrendered his commission, which both did before the end of October. Penn deserved his disgrace more than Cromwell knew, for he had offered his services to the king in 1654, and on retiring to his estates in Munster after making his submission he resumed his correspondence with the exiled court. Venables was to be Monck's choice as governor of Chester shortly before the Restoration. It would be unjust to regard Penn and Venables simply as Cromwell's scapegoats, for both had failed to some extent to measure up to their responsibilities, and he did not place all the blame on them. He was deeply troubled by the expedition's failure to achieve its first objective, and he searched his own heart for reasons why the Lord had frowned upon his attempt at what he saw as 'promoting the glory of God, and enlarging the bounds of Christ's kingdom'. He wrote to Fortescue: 'We have cause to be humbled by the reproof God gave us at San Domingo, upon the account of our sins, as well as others''.[16] He might have beaten his breast less for his own and others' sins and more for inadequate planning, under-provision of troops, poor commissariat, and gross ignorance of the needs of soldiers campaigning in the tropics. Gardiner hit the nail on the head when he commented: 'Oliver, as ever, trusted in God. For once in his life he had forgotten to keep his powder dry'.[17]

Bordeaux naturally hoped that Cromwell's aggression in the Caribbean would propel him into the treaty with France that Mazarin had long been seeking. So it might have done, if the attack on Hispaniola had not coincided with an act of violence in some Alpine valleys in the duchy of Savoy that exercised Cromwell very powerfully. Savoy was then a virtual dependency of France, and its young duke's mother, the Duchess Christina, who had until lately been regent and still held the reins, was a sister of Henrietta Maria. The valleys of the Pellice and the Chisone were inhabited by a peasant community called the Vaudois or Waldenses, who had been unorthodox in their religion since the twelfth century and had converted to Calvinism in the sixteenth. In 1561 they had won toleration within strict geographical bounds, but they had subsequently expanded well beyond them; indeed by 1650 eleven of their 'temples' were in forbidden territory. In January 1655 an order from the duke, instigated by his mother, commanded them under pain of death to quit all areas outside the 1561 limits, unless they engaged themselves within three days to convert to catholicism or sell their property to catholics. The valleys to which they were required to withdraw were snowbound for much of the year and would have yielded their present numbers no adequate living, but when they petitioned against the decree Christina had the Marquis of Pianezza sent against them with a military force that included some French troops. Inevitably there was resistance, and the result (in April) was the so-called Vaudois massacre. Its scale cannot be precisely established, but the victims certainly ran into hundreds, and the slaughtered included women and children. Even more villagers were terrorized into renouncing their religion. A Huguenot captain, who resigned his commission rather than participate in such atrocities, testifies to the burning of houses and people, the killings in cold blood, and the extreme cruelty of the Piedmontese soldiery; he alleged that Pianezza, in his presence, ordered the killing of all prisoners, though it seems that some were taken.

On hearing of these events in May, Cromwell sent formal letters to the Duke of Savoy, expressing his outrage, to the King of France, urging his intervention, and to the rulers of Sweden, Denmark, the United Provinces, and Transylvania, inviting them to join him in securing redress for this dreadful

[16] Abbott, *Writings and Speeches of Oliver Cromwell*, III, 858, 891, quoted in Barry Coward, *Oliver Cromwell* (1991), pp. 133–5, in an admirable discussion.

[17] Gardiner, *Commonwealth and Protectorate*, III, 371.

wrong. Milton, as Secretary for Foreign Tongues, worked these missives into diplomatic Latin, and his own sonnet on the massacre, 'Avenge O Lord thy slaughtered saints', shows that his heart was in the job. Mazarin was angry at this ill-timed setback to the treaty he was seeking, for it was intimated to him that it would not proceed unless France at least disowned the Duke of Savoy's action. In the name of the seventeen-year-old Louis XIV Cromwell was assured that French troops had been used without his knowledge and for ends that he disapproved. The Duchess Christina, Louis's aunt, proved more recalcitrant, but under French pressure her son assured Cromwell that upon his intercession he would pardon his rebellious subjects. Cromwell duly interceded, and by the resultant treaty of Pignerol (or Pinerolo) in August the Vaudois had their freedom of worship confirmed within their territory, which was formally extended to include some but not all of the lower ground into which they had expanded since 1561. Neither they nor Cromwell were fully satisfied, but the treaty went ahead and was signed in October. It spelt out the terms of a firm peace and freedom of trade between England and France, and included a secret article whereby Charles II, his brother James, and seventeen other leading royalists were excluded from French territory. Since James Duke of York was then Lieutenant-General in the army of Marshal Turenne, this was a major concession.

The treaty did not provide for the offensive alliance that Mazarin hoped for, since England and Spain were not yet formally at war. But the government in Madrid was predictably unwilling to stomach the recent attacks on its colonies; it called Cardenas home, and in mid-September laid an embargo on all English goods and ships throughout Spanish territories and waters. In London the council was much divided as to whether to break openly with Spain, but Cromwell carried the majority in favour of war, which he justified in a very long and jingoistic manifesto.[18] This was published on 26 October, two days after he signed the treaty with France. It was only a matter of time before that matured into a full offensive alliance, and Cromwell's appointment of Sir William Lockhart as England's formal ambassador to the French court was a step towards it. The 35-year-old Lockhart was another former royalist to receive Cromwell's trust in a position of high responsibility; he had proved his worth in the council of his native Scotland. He did not leave for Paris until April 1656, probably because Mazarin was due to receive an envoy from Madrid, sent to explore possible terms of peace. But peace with Spain was not yet on Mazarin's agenda.

Sweden was another power that courted England's alliance, with a view to both military and naval aid. The young King Charles X was much more bellicose than Queen Christina and Oxenstjerna had been. He had overcome an

[18] Printed in Abbott, *Writings and Speeches of Oliver Cromwell*, III, 878–94.

initial inclination to give aid to the English king when he came to appreciate how useful a pact with Cromwell could be in pursuing his overriding ambition, which was to make the Baltic a Swedish lake by extending his hold over its southern and Norwegian shores. When he sent Peter Coyet to England as his envoy in March 1655, Cromwell gave him the warmest of welcomes. Oliver had hero-worshipped Charles X's uncle Gustavus Adolphus, and would have liked few things better than to make Sweden the cornerstone of his dreamed-of general protestant league, since the Dutch had proved so regrettably disposed to put commerce before religion. But Cromwell wanted the United Provinces included in any treaty that he negotiated, and Dutch and Swedish objectives were deeply opposed. The Dutch could not tolerate any stranglehold over the Baltic that threatened their vital source of timber and naval stores, as well as one of their major trading areas, and Britain's commercial interests required the maintenance of the hard-won Anglo-Dutch peace. The situation was further complicated when Charles X asserted a specious claim to the throne of Poland and declared war on that country in June 1655. All through the second half of the year he pursued an astonishing career of conquest; first Warsaw, then Cracow, next Thorn and Elbing fell to him, until by December Danzig was the one major Polish city still holding out against him. For Cromwell to have committed English warships to fighting Dutch ones in the Baltic, and English land forces to campaigns in Poland and northern Germany, which is what Charles X proposed, would have been madness. Nevertheless Charles's overtures, made through his ambassador Count Bonde, gave rise to keen and frequent debate in the council of state, where Whitelocke's pro-Swedish sympathies were balanced by the pro-Dutch stance of Lawrence, Pickering, and Strickland. So while Cromwell kept on cordial terms with Bonde, he parried his requests to raise troops in England, and kept up talks with the Dutchman Nieupoort. The negotiations continued, but no positive alliance resulted from them. Eventually, in July 1656, a satisfactory commercial treaty was concluded with Sweden, confirming English merchantmen's rights to trade in the Baltic on equal terms with those of other nations, and securing that the tolls levied in the Polish and Prussian ports now under Swedish control should remain no higher than they had been in 1650. This time the Swedish king did gain permission to raise 2,000 men in England, besides 1,000 in Scotland, who had been agreed upon earlier.

By now England was carrying more weight in European politics than she had done for half a century. Cromwell was learning his way through its tortuous paths. He had still been trailing clouds of Elizabethan glory when he launched the Western Design, but its ill success taught him greater realism—greater respect, too, for the interests of English merchants. It was natural that an East Anglian puritan whose adult life had coincided with the Thirty Years War should be intensely concerned for the protestant cause in Europe and the world at large, but by 1656 he had been forced to realize that his dream of a general league of protestant powers was likely to remain a dream. He was listening more to those of his councillors whose knowledge of European affairs was fuller than his own, and his conduct of foreign policy became more pragmatic over the years. This appraisal would have raised eyebrows two or three generations ago, when historians were still repeating the charge, first levelled quite soon after his death, that he acted against England's long-term interests by aligning her with the rising power of France, who was to be her national enemy through most of the long eighteenth century and beyond. But the Fronde was scarcely over when he first took up the reins, and no one could foresee during Mazarin's troubled years how far and how fast French power and aggression would advance under the mature Louis XIV, or how Spain's decline would accelerate during the miserable reign of Philip IV's successor. Cromwell had to care for his own security, and his slowly and cautiously negotiated alliance with France yielded substantial dividends. If he had cast his lot with Spain, France might seriously have supported the cause of Charles II, Louis XIV's first cousin. Admittedly his war with Spain enabled Charles to sign a treaty with Philip IV, but that king was too heavily stretched to give him any help, and Cromwell knew it. Charles in Bruges, where he took up residence, was less of a menace than he would have been on French or Dutch soil, from which Cromwell's diplomacy had excluded him. If Oliver had lived just a little longer, Britain would doubtless have been included in the Treaty of the Pyrenees.

## ✝ TWENTY-TWO ✝

# King or Constable?

WHATEVER one may think of the Western Design or the regime of the major-generals, neither fulfilled Cromwell's hope that it would be self-financing. Consequently the most important question that faced him and the council during the first half of 1656 was whether to summon a parliament before the appointed three-year interval had elapsed, and the main arguments for doing so were to remedy the government's growing indebtedness and to put its finances on a sounder legal footing. But another matter that they considered intermittently, and one that it would have been quite unprofitable to put before parliament, was the possible readmission of the Jews.

Since they had been expelled in 1290 there had been no recognized Jewish community anywhere in Britain. A small body of Jewish merchants did drive their trade in Elizabethan and early Stuart London, but their status was that of Spanish or Portuguese aliens, and their only synagogue was a private house, where they worshipped very circumspectly. In Holland, however, there was a tolerated and thriving Jewish community, and several factors inclined its leaders in the early 1650s to apply for the right of Jews to resettle in England. One was the Commonwealth's growing reputation for religious tolerance, even though it was never formally extended to those who denied the divinity of Christ. Another was the remarkable personality of the chief rabbi of Amsterdam, Manasseh ben Israel, whose *Spes Israeli*, published in 1650, was translated as *The Hope of Israel* and found a ready sale in England. The persecution of Jews had been intensifying in Russia, and ben Israel's hope was that England would offer a new refuge to his people. Thurloe met him in 1651 when he was in Amsterdam as Oliver St John's secretary, and he advised him to apply on their behalf to the Council of State. Thurloe was probably genuinely sympathetic, but he was also aware of the Jews' value, through their many commercial contacts, as expert purveyors of international intelligence. Ben Israel duly petitioned the council, which set up a committee (including Cromwell) to consider his appeal, but nothing came of it while the Rump remained in power. After the Protectorate was established, however, he decided to come to London and see Cromwell in person, and according to a plausible hint from John Sadler, who was known and trusted by both men,

Cromwell himself may have invited him. At any rate, when he arrived in September 1655 he did not stay with his fellow-Jews in the City but was officially lodged in the Strand, close to Whitehall. Cromwell received him personally, and ben Israel opened the interview with a glowing personal tribute to his host. Cromwell responded warmly, and invited his visitor to dine with him. But the eloquent petition that ben Israel presented required further consultation, for it asked for the right of Jews not only to reside and trade freely but to worship in public synagogues and have their own burial ground.

Cromwell referred it to the council, which appointed a sub-committee; but its four members had grave doubts about it and felt the need to consult more widely. So a conference was called that included a number of judges, ministers of religion, university dons, and representatives of the City, besides the four councillors. It met several times between 4 and 18 December, and Cromwell, who was always present, addressed it eloquently in favour of readmitting the Jews. He had more than one reason for doing so. He was not indifferent to the influx of capital that they would bring with them, and like Thurloe he appreciated their value as intelligencers, especially as many of them were of Spanish birth. But what probably weighed most powerfully with him were the scriptural prophecies that the coming of Christ's kingdom on earth would be preceded by the conversion of the Jews. That kingdom, he believed, would come in God's good time, but what a great work it would be for England to provide a setting for that essential precursor! And where likelier were the Jews to be converted than in what he told the conference was 'the only place in the world where religion was taught in its full purity'?[1] But the majority of the conference remained hostile. Many ministers, though not Cromwell's own chaplains, still regarded the Jews as a cursed people, from whom Christians should be spared contact. It seems, however, that the strongest opposition came from the mercantile community, who did not want to be exposed to open competition from some of the most skilled bankers and traders in the world.

For the conference's final debate, Cromwell threw the Council Chamber open to the public, but he had misjudged the strength of popular antisemitism. The room was thronged with opponents of the petition. The conference's role was only advisory, but he never took the logical next step of inviting the full council to pronounce on it, because he knew by now that its decision would be negative. But prerogative action remained open to him, for the two judges present at the conference had given their opinion that there was no law against readmitting the Jews, since they had been expelled by

[1] Abbott, *Writings and Speeches of Oliver Cromwell*, IV, 52; cf. pp. 18–19, 34–6, 45, 51–5. On the readmission generally, see C. Roth, *A History of the Jews in England* (Oxford, 1941) and David S. Katz, *Philo-Semitism and the Re-admission of the Jews to England 1603–1655* (Los Angeles and Oxford, 1982).

royal edict. So Cromwell assured their spokesmen, though only verbally, that the recusancy laws would not be enforced against them. They duly purchased a burial ground, and continued to worship without interference at their synagogue in Creechurch Lane. A test case arose when a rich Jewish merchant was denounced as a Spaniard and had his goods seized on the grounds that he was an enemy alien. The council had them restored to him, and its decision meant that Jews resident in England no longer had to assume the guise of Spaniards or Portuguese. Reassured by this de facto toleration, more Jews came to settle. There was no specific decree yet to legalize their readmission, but Jewish historians have rightly dated it from 1656, as English contemporaries did. It is pleasant to recall that Sigmund Freud named one of his sons Oliver, in acknowledgement of what Cromwell had done for English Jews.[2] At the Restoration there was a campaign in the City to get their rights withdrawn, but Charles II, who had himself received Jewish assistance, would have none of it. Formal legalization followed in 1664.

On the major question of whether to summon a parliament ahead of the prescribed three-year interval, Cromwell was obliged to act 'with the advice of the major part of the council'. But the decision should have been a formality, since the Instrument of Government also directed that 'in case of future war with any foreign state, a parliament shall be forthwith summoned for their advice concerning the same'.[3] He also needed parliamentary consent for the upkeep of military forces in excess of 30,000, and his army, including the garrisons in Ireland, Scotland, and Jamaica, far exceeded that number. At the end of 1655 it was costing more than half his government's total annual expenditure of very nearly £2m., and outgoings were exceeding revenue at the rate of over £230,000 a year. If these were not reasons enough, there was according to the Venetian resident a public clamour for a parliament during May 1656, and when the major-generals were called to London for a conference shortly after, they hammered home their difficulties in paying their militia and meeting their debts. Yet Cromwell was most reluctant to call a parliament, and when he finally gave way he was clearly bowing to the council's collective advice. He had reason to fear that a House chosen that summer, if elections were at all free, would endorse neither the constitution under which he ruled nor the policies he was currently pursuing, but he could not debar them from debate by the people's representatives indefinitely. And what were the alternatives, particularly with regard to finance? If he had extended the decimation to non-royalists, as he reportedly proposed, he could have wrecked his prospects of winning the broad support of the political nation irreparably. At any rate it was publicly announced on 26 June

---

[2] I owe this information to the sympathetic account of the readmission in Antonia Fraser, *Cromwell Our Chief of Men* (1973), p. 357 n.

[3] Gardiner (ed.), *Constitutional Documents*, p. 412.

that a new parliament would meet on 17 September, and the elections took place during August.

The opposition that he had most to fear in it was that of republicans of various shades, and the main danger was that the experienced tacticians who had never forgiven his expulsion of the Rump would go all out, as in the last parliament, to win over the many unattached but instinctively anti-military members who were sure to be returned. The prospect of elections did indeed generate a wave of republican activity, both in print and in behind-the-scenes intrigue. One of the first in the fray was Sir Henry Vane, who published *A Healing Question Propounded and Resolved* in May. It was a subtle piece, and it deserves attention both because it caused serious concern to Cromwell's government at the time and because it closely prefigured the kind of opposition that was to bring down that of his son. Its purpose was to provide a common platform for republican politicians of Vane's own type, commonwealthsmen of a more populist complexion, radical puritans who were uncomfortable about Cromwell's temporal power, and malcontents in the armed forces. Its clever rhetoric threw a smokescreen of evasion over the problems that faced and divided these interests. It centred on the concept of a 'good old cause' that had carried parliament to victory in the Civil Wars and was still in essence as good as ever, though it had become perverted by 'the private and selfish interest of a particular part' of its original adherents. The way to restore it was to declare sovereignty to lie in the whole body of those adherents, and to vest ultimate authority in a succession of supreme representative assemblies freely chosen by them. How 'the honest party' (or 'the good party'), as he called them, were to be identified at the polls was a problem that he did not address, and he simply ignored the extreme unlikelihood that any truly free elections would return a republican majority in the foreseeable future. Over matters of religion he asserted that the civil magistrate should exercise no coercive power, dodging the fact that most of the English and Scottish peoples desired the retention of a public preaching ministry, whose maintenance depended on the co-operation of the state. In asserting that a selfish interest was denying the honest party their due role in ordering their government, 'upon pretence they are not in a capacity as yet to use it', though really for that interest's own advancement and self-enrichment, Vane was careful not to identify the culprits with the army as such. The honest party needed, at least in part, to assume a military posture, but that part must serve the interests of the whole. For the day-to-day administration of the country and the conduct of foreign relations, Vane proposed 'a standing council of state settled for life', subject to overall direction by the representative assembly, 'but of the same fundamental constitution with themselves'. It would govern in the intervals between parliaments (a word Vane avoided), and fill any vacancies by the majority vote of its own members. So far, Vane had advocated what looks very like a one-party state with executive power in the hands of a self-perpetuating oligarchy, but he envisaged a third element in the constitution, subordinate to the supreme assembly but responsible for the execution of the laws. This function could be entrusted to a single person or to a greater number, as the supreme assembly should see fit. This was a sop to the many who admired Cromwell and recognized his indispensability, but were unhappy about his present powers. Once he was dead and his son over-thrown, the republicans, Vane included, would make the exclusion of any single person from any high constitutional role their first principle. In *A Heal-ing Question*, however, Vane proposed that Cromwell, as general of the army, should inaugurate the new order by summoning a constituent assem-bly, to be chosen by the well-affected throughout the country.[4]

Vane did not of course expect this to happen, but his tract was widely read and discussed. In July a number of leading commonwealthsmen and Fifth Monarchists, including Colonel Okey, Vice-Admiral Lawson, and Thomas Venner, met to consider a proposal that it should form a basis for a union of the two groups against the Protectorate, but they came to no conclusion, for Vane's model smacked too much of 'carnal' government for the extreme mil-lenarians. So far the council had taken no formal notice of Vane's pamphlet, but after this meeting it interrogated Okey, Lawson, Venner, and one other, though after examining them it let them go. It also sent for Vane, who at first ignored the order, as being contrary to the laws and liberties of England, but upon a second summons he appeared before it on 21 August. It found his tract subversive, and demanded a bond for £5,000 that he would 'do nothing to the prejudice of the present government, and the peace of the commonwealth'. He indignantly refused, accusing it of following the absolutist practices of Charles I. The council gave him two weeks in which to change his mind, and then imprisoned him in Carisbrooke Castle on the Isle of Wight, which like the other offshore islands was beyond the reach of the writ of habeas corpus. But Vane was released at the end of the year.

Bradshaw and Ludlow were two other former Rumpers whose persistent refusal to recognize the government's legitimacy brought them before the council, since they were still in places of authority. Bradshaw was dismissed from his office as Chief Justice of Chester and justice of three Welsh counties, but he suffered no other penalties. Ludlow, who was still lieutenant-general of the army in Ireland, had been circulating anti-Protectorate literature with-in it, and Fleetwood as commander-in-chief and Lord Deputy had demanded the resignation of his commission. Ludlow preferred to have it out with Cromwell in person, who granted his wish and tried earnestly to persuade

---

[4] *A Healing Question* is reprinted in *Somers Tracts*, ed. Sir W. Scott, 13 vols. (1809–15), VI, 303–15.

him of what he saw as the error of his ways. 'What is it that you would have?', he asked him; 'what can you desire more than you have?' 'That which we fought for,' Ludlow replied, 'that the nation might be governed by its own consent'; to which Cromwell retorted: 'I am as much for a government by consent as any man, but where shall we find that consent? Amongst the prelatical, Presbyterian, Independent, Anabaptist, or Levelling parties?'[5] Ludlow's own account of the long interview shows us two men of utterly sincere convictions at irreconcilable odds, though experience had given Cromwell a sharper sense of political realities than Ludlow ever had. As with Vane, the council demanded of Ludlow a bond of £5,000 for his peaceable behaviour, and like Vane he refused. The councillors differed as to what to do with him; Lambert was for peremptorily insisting that he give the bond or take the consequences, while Cromwell was prepared to send him back to Ireland. In the end he was allowed to retire to his brother-in-law's house in Essex without paying up. The reason for keeping him out of his native Wiltshire was that a substantial party there wanted to re-elect him to parliament.

At the radical end of the spectrum some remnants of the Leveller movement were still capable of giving a little trouble. Not all wished to, by any means; Walwyn for example had withdrawn from political activity and started practising as a physician. John Lilburne had become a devout Quaker. He was still formally a prisoner in Dover Castle, but he was often out on parole, free to enjoy the company of his devoted wife and his children, and to preach to his fellow-Quakers in various parts of Kent. He died on 29 August 1657. By contrast Edward Sexby, the former agitator, had been deep in intrigue with the royalists when the 1655 risings were brewing, and only escaped arrest by fleeing to Flanders. There he extended his royalist contacts and won the ear of the Count of Fuensaldaña, the commander of the Spanish Army of Flanders. That gullible officer was so taken with his proposal for a joint enterprise by Spain, the cavaliers, the commonwealthsmen, part of the fleet (so it was promised), and much of the army, to overthrow Cromwell and restore Charles II, that he sent Sexby to Madrid to lay his scheme before the king and his ministers. Needless to say, Sexby's notion that he could persuade a large part of Cromwell's army to support a Spanish-backed royalist rising was as chimerical as his supposition that Charles, in return, would implement a constitution modelled on the 1648 Agreement of the People. The Spanish government shrewdly promised no more than financial support, if and when a rising really got going in England, while Hyde and the wiser majority of exiled royalists were as suspicious of Sexby personally as of his design to compromise the monarchy. But in May 1656 Sexby got a letter through to John Wildman, who was still in the Tower after being caught dictating the seditious

---

[5] *Memoirs of Edmund Ludlow*, II, 10–14.

manifesto mentioned earlier. On 1st July Wildman was released on bail, and his quite considerable estates were freed from confiscation. He almost certainly obtained his liberty by betraying to Thurloe what he knew of the Leveller–royalist conspiracy and engaging to spy for him in the future. He had no intention, however, of transferring his allegiance to the Protectorate. Once out of prison he set about supplanting Sexby as the chief link between the Levellers and the royal court, and he would soon be deep in a plot to assassinate Cromwell.[6]

In the same year in which Vane published his pragmatic blueprint of a commonwealth and the seedier remnants of the Leveller movement were compromising their former republican principles, James Harrington put the finishing touches to the greatest work of republican political thought to be written by an Englishman in the early modern period. He had been working on *The Commonwealth of Oceana* for some years, and it appeared soon after the new parliament met. Oceana was a transparent synonym for England. Although it implied a deeply critical view of the Protectoral regime, it was not in intention a subversive work and it contained no incitement to resistance. The government kept a close eye on its printers and publishers while it was in the press, probably suspecting that it might run in the same channel of republican opposition as that exemplified by the three colonels of 1654 and by Lawson and others more recently, but Harrington himself was never troubled or interrogated over it while Cromwell lived. *Oceana*, for all its baroque extravagance of detail, was a serious attempt to prescribe for Britain's political needs in his own time. It was widely read and discussed, and when the fabric of government began to unravel after Oliver's death Harrington campaigned hard, and not without support, to get his solutions adopted.

Central to his argument was that the form of a country's government, if it is to be stable, must be matched to the distribution of property, especially landed property, within it. Ownership of all the land by one man, for example the Turkish sultan, results in absolute monarchy. Where most of the land belongs to a feudal nobility, as in medieval England, the appropriate form is a mixed monarchy, with the crown sharing power with the aristocracy. Where ownership is much more widely distributed, or as Harrington put it where the balance is popular, only a republic can provide durably stable government. He believed that this condition had been reached in England under the Tudors, through various measures but especially through the vast sales of monastic land. Queen Elizabeth, by 'converting her reign through the perpetual love tricks that passed between her and her people into a kind of romance', had concealed the mismatch between the 'superstructures' of government and its economic foundations, but the Stuarts, lacking her flair, had

[6] M. Ashley, *John Wildman, Plotter and Postmaster* (1947), pp. 95–103.

left it increasingly exposed: 'Wherefore the dissolution of this government caused the Civil War, not the war the dissolution of this government'.[7] To prevent the balance from ever swinging back to a dominant aristocracy, Harrington prescribed a fundamental 'agrarian law', whereby anyone who owned or acquired land worth more than £2,000 a year would be compelled to distribute the surplus among his younger children.

Another of his basic tenets was that the commonwealth should be defended by a citizen militia and not by a professional army, so he linked political rights with compulsory military obligation as well as with ownership of property. He therefore divided *Oceana*'s population into three classes: those worth upwards of £100 a year in land or goods, styled 'the horse' because they would perform their military service as cavalry; those worth less but with a modest competency, called 'the foot' because they would train and fight as infantrymen; and servants and the poor, who since they lacked economic independence would share neither the obligations nor the political participation allotted to the other two orders. At the heart of *Oceana*'s constitution was a legislature consisting of two elected chambers, a senate of 300 chosen wholly from and by the horse, and an assembly of 1,050 composed of horse and foot in the ratio of 3 to 4. The first was supposed to embody the wisdom, the second the interest of the commonwealth. That was a crude assumption, but Harrington was far ahead of his time in requiring that the elections to both chambers should be by secret ballot. Both were to remain continually in being, for in place of general elections he prescribed a system of rotation whereby a third of each body should retire each year. His most idiosyncratic proposal was that the senate should have the sole right to propose and debate measures; the more popular assembly was to ballot for or against them in silence, without the right to discuss or amend them. As for day-to-day administration, the highest offices of state were to be elected by and from the senate, but the 'magistracy' that executed the laws, from the national judges to the local JPs, was to be quite distinct from the legislature. All its members were to be publicly elected, and all subject to rotation. Some of the detail in *Oceana* invited and received ridicule, but in Harrington's lifetime it was more widely read, and on the whole more respectfully, than *Leviathan*, and its relevance was recognized anew during the American Revolution. Harrington believed that the legislator who successfully devised the institutions appropriate to his country's needs was creating a work of art, but his insights into the relationship between the structure of society and the structure of government place him among the pioneers of politics as a science.

---

[7] *The Commonwealth of Oceana* (1656), p. 25, reprinted in J. G. A. Pocock (ed.), *The Political Works of James Harrington* (Cambridge, 1977), p. 198. For distinguished commentaries, see Pocock's introduction, and chapters 2 and 3 by Blair Worden in *Republicanism, Liberty and Commercial Society, 1649–1776*, ed. David Wootton (Stanford, Calif., 1994).

However one may judge the relevance of *Oceana* to Britain's problems in 1656, the parliamentary elections that were held while it was in the press demonstrated that the country was still a considerable way from the degree of consensus needed to make 'a government by consent' possible. The major-generals, who devoted most of their energies to the elections during the summer, gave widely different predictions of their outcome. They all got themselves elected, and all the rest of the council of state got in except Lord Lisle and the Earl of Mulgrave, who probably did not stand. But such was the outcry against 'swordsmen and decimators' during the electioneering period and at the polls that the influence of the major-generals was on balance probably negative. They helped to get a disproportionate number of fellow army officers elected, but they were powerless to prevent the return of many republicans, with Haselrig and Scot in the van.

The council felt driven to make full use of the power conferred on it by the Instrument of Government to scrutinize the returns and exclude any persons who fell under the disqualifications therein laid down. These were primarily active royalists, Irish rebels, and Roman Catholics, but hardly any of those debarred by the council fell into these categories, so it was left to be inferred that they were not 'persons of known integrity, fearing God, and of good conversation'.[8] This was insulting, and in most cases untrue. But the worst blunder was to exclude so many—just over a hundred of those elected, which caused fifty or sixty more to decline to take their seats in protest. Contemporary allegations that many of the excluded were either not disaffected or of no political weight were almost certainly correct. At least a third of them had not sat in parliament before. Cromwell later declared that he had been against so many exclusions, but he could surely have put his foot down more firmly if he had felt that way at the time. All through its long first session, this was at best only two-thirds of a parliament.

The pageantry at its opening on 17 September was more military than in 1654. Only Lambert sat with Cromwell in his coach, and three hundred army officers marched in front of them from Whitehall to Westminster Abbey, where Owen preached an adulatory sermon. Cromwell addressed the members as before in the Painted Chamber, and despite its being very hot there he spoke for two or three hours. He may have been aware afterwards that it was not one of his best efforts, for it was not printed. Besides being too long for its content, much of it was rather truculently defensive or jingoistic. He would speak first, he said, of what had been done out of necessity to preserve the very being of the nation, and then of what was needed for its well-being—for the fulfilment, that is, of the great things that God had in store for it. Under the first head he justified the war with Spain, 'a natural enemy', made so 'by an

---

[8] Gardiner (ed.), *Constitutional Documents*, p. 411.

enmity put into him by God'. No honest or honourable peace was to be had with such a power, for it would be 'but to be kept so long as the pope said amen to it'. As for England's almost unprovoked aggression in the Caribbean, 'Being denied just things, we thought it our duty to get that by the sword which we could not otherwise do. And this hath been the spirit of Englishmen'.[9] He furiously denounced Spain's alliance with Charles II, not admitting of course that it was a consequence and not a cause of the war in which he had chosen to engage. It was a good thing that his actual conduct of foreign policy was becoming less crude than his public defence of it. He made all he could of the attempted risings eighteen months ago, portraying the royalists as hand in glove with papists, and both driven by the recently elected Pope Alexander VII, whose design it allegedly was to unite the catholic interest against the protestant throughout Christendom.

We need not follow his excoriation of the commonwealthsmen, whom he described as 'the Levelling party [going] under a finer name or notion'. He followed it with a lengthy justification of the major-generals and of the decimation tax that financed them. Their regime had not only preserved the peace, he said, but had 'been more effectual towards the discountenancing of vice and settling religion, than anything done these fifty years'. The tone of his speech took a turn for the better as he moved at last from the theme of 'being' to that of 'well-being'. He made one of his more eloquent vindications of liberty of conscience; he took pride in his government's efforts to promote a preaching ministry, regarding whose remuneration he said: 'I should think I were very treacherous if I should take away tithes, till I see the legislative power to settle maintenance to them another way'. He then warmed to his familiar theme of a reformation of manners, and linked it to his support for the established social order. 'We would keep up the nobility and gentry,' he said, 'and the way to keep them up is not to suffer them to be patronizers or countenancers of debauchery or disorders'. He appealed to the parliament to be fellow-labourers in the good work: 'Truly these things do respect the souls of men, and the spirits, which *are* the men. If that be kept pure, a man signifies somewhat; if not, I would very fain see what difference there is betwixt him and a beast.' He urged the need to reform the law, not in its essence but to ensure its more humane execution. It was abominable, he said, 'to hang a man for sixpence, threepence, I know not what; to hang for a trifle and pardon murder'.[10] After a belated and all too brief mention of the government's present financial plight, he ended with an exhortation based on the eighty-fifth Psalm to join with him in advancing the interest of the people of God.

It was only when the members went to take their seats in the House that some of them learnt that they were to be excluded from it. At the door, a

---

[9] Abbott, *Writings and Speeches of Oliver Cromwell*, IV, 261, 263.
[10] Ibid., pp. 267–74, for all the quotations in this paragraph.

guard headed by three colonels admitted only those who could produce a certificate of the council's approval. There was almost as much indignation among many of the approved members as among those thus debarred, and next day a letter of protest from seventy-nine of the latter was presented to the Speaker by Sir George Booth, MP for Cheshire, who was to make his own protest in arms in 1659. Nearly four days of tense and sometimes bitter debate ensued before a vote was passed to leave it to the excluded to put their case to the council and meanwhile to carry on with the nation's business. It was carried by just 125 votes to 29, a Pyrrhic victory in a House which should have numbered 460. Many members had walked out in disgust. Bordeaux reported home that the people were angrier at the exclusion of their representatives than over any previous infringement of their liberties, but how far he was aware of reactions outside London is hard to say. The government suppressed a printed remonstrance bearing the names of ninety-eight of the excluded (though how many of them were actually aware of it is not known), and from October the only weekly newspapers that it allowed to appear were the official *Mercurius Politicus* and *Publick Intelligencer*. There was a motion in the House on 31 December to admit the excluded members, but the Speaker left the chair before it was put to the vote.

The parliament, however, was by no means wholly uncooperative with the government, as one would expect when most known opponents were shut out of it. It quickly passed a bill to annul 'the pretended title of Charles Stuart', and also a treason act that put the penalty for any threat to the Protector's person beyond doubt. It declared its approval of the war with Spain as just and necessary, and showed some willingness to raise the money to finance it. It put off fixing the amount, however, on receiving the welcome news that on 8 September six smallish ships under Captain Stayner had engaged the Spanish Plate fleet off Cadiz, sinking two great galleons and capturing two more. Rumour valued the silver taken at £1m., but when it was brought home in October it was found to be worth only a quarter as much. How far the difference was due to natural exaggeration and how far to the no less natural tendency of pieces of eight to stick to seamen's hands is an unanswerable question.

Two developments, however, opened new rifts between Cromwell and the parliament before the end of the year. One was the *cause célèbre* of the Quaker James Nayler, who celebrated his release from a spell in prison by staging a triumphal entry into Bristol which was patently modelled on Christ's into Jerusalem. He rode a donkey, led by two of his many women disciples, while others spread their garments in his path or walked beside him singing 'Holy, holy, holy, Lord God of Israel'. He bore a natural resemblance to popular images of Jesus, and he emphasized it by the way he cut and combed his hair and beard. Parliament was outraged; it appointed a committee of no fewer than fifty-five members to examine him and his followers, and they took five weeks before they reported to the House on 5 December. Called to the bar next day, Nayler protested that as a mere creature he claimed no special glory, but shared the common Quaker conviction that Christ dwells in all believers. He was convinced that he had a revelation from God, commanding him to do what he did as a sign of Christ's coming. The House spent nine days in hot debate as to what to do with him, and it was much divided, as indeed were the members closest to Cromwell. To some extent the line of division exemplified a parting of the ways, by no means altogether new, between military and non-military Cromwellians. None denounced Nayler more fiercely than the soldiers Skippon, Boteler, and Goffe, while Lawrence, Pickering, Strickland, and Sydenham, all civilian members of the council of state, spoke in mitigation of his offence. Whitelocke and others took the wholly sensible line that he should be dealt with by the ordinary courts of law, but under the 1650 Blasphemy Act he could be given no more than six months' imprisonment for a first offence, and for the bloodthirsty majority that was nothing like enough. But had parliament the power to act as a court of first instance? It was highly questionable, but in the end the House was persuaded that it inherited the judicial powers of both the Lords and the Commons.

Nayler escaped the death penalty by only ninety-six votes to eighty-two, but parliament sentenced him to a series of savage corporal punishments in London and Bristol, to be followed by indefinite solitary confinement and hard labour. It is worth remarking that on the rare occasion when anything deserving the name of torture was inflicted in England under the Commonwealth and Protectorate, it was by order of parliament and not by the judiciary or executive. Flogged all the way from Westminster to the City on 18 December, 310 stripes (by the hangman's reckoning) left Nayler so weak that the next instalment had to be postponed. Before it was executed, many petitioners, by no means all Quakers, pleaded for the remission of the rest of the sentence, first (vainly) with parliament and then with Cromwell. He immediately wrote a note to the Speaker, expressing abhorrence of the 'crimes' imputed to Nayler, but asking the House to let him know 'the grounds and reasons whereupon they have proceeded'.[11] This plain challenge to the constitutionality of its actions caused much consternation and not a few pleas for mercy, but parliament nevertheless voted by nearly two to one to carry out the rest of the sentence. So before a crowd of thousands, nearly all sympathetic, Nayler was duly branded on the forehead and bored through the tongue with a red-hot iron. Parliament never replied to Cromwell's letter, but the episode helped to convince its wiser heads that the constitution needed further defining.

---

[11] Abbott, *Writings and Speeches of Oliver Cromwell*, IV, 366.

The second bone of contention appeared while controversy over Nayler was at its height. On Christmas Day, when the House was predictably thin, Desborough asked its leave to bring in a bill for the continuance of the decimation tax. He was supported by a succession of councillors and major-generals, but opposed by others in authority, including Whitelocke and Lenthall, on the strong grounds that the tax was contrary to the Act of Oblivion. Leave for the bill was nevertheless given, but when it was introduced on 7 January Cromwell's son-in-law John Claypole immediately moved its rejection, and one of its most eloquent opponents was Lord Broghill. With Lambert on the other hand strongly defending it, no one quite knew where Cromwell himself stood, and he was careful to hold aloof. It seems extraordinary that he was not consulted about the bill. A decision on it was delayed because the Speaker fell ill and other distractions intervened, but the several days' debate that it received were often angry to the point of disorder. The contest was less between friends and opponents of the Protectorate than between military and civilian Cromwellians, and the main issue for most members was whether the rule of the major-generals should continue. On 29 January the bill was defeated by 124 votes to 88, and the army party took it very badly. The majority by contrast were so pleased that on the very next day they voted a thumping grant of £400,000 for the prosecution of the war with Spain.

One of the interruptions that delayed the decision on the bill was the uncovering of the assassination plot that Sexby had been hatching for some time. His chosen hit-man was one Miles Sindercombe, an ex-quartermaster who had been a ringleader in the Leveller mutiny of 1649. Sindercombe and two fellow-assassins had first planned to shoot Cromwell as he drove to the opening of parliament, but finding him too well protected they changed their design more than once. They finally settled on burning down Whitehall Palace with him inside it, and it was only when the matches were already lit on their formidable fire-bomb of pitch, tar, and gunpowder that one of Sindercombe's two co-plotters informed on him. The other then revealed all he knew, and with the three safely under lock and key Thurloe told the whole story to the House on 19 January. The revelation that the Protector had been dogged by assassins for months had its effect, for his sudden death would have been a disaster for almost all the members. They all came to Whitehall four days later to congratulate him on his escape, and in the Banqueting House he made a modest and mercifully short speech in reply. He congratulated them in turn on representing 'the best people in the world', fortunate in enjoying civil rights and liberties 'very ancient and honourable'. Then warming to a favourite theme: 'And in the midst of this people, a people . . . that are to God as the apple of his eye; and he says so of them, be they many or be they few. But they are many, a people of the blessing of God, a people under his safety and protection.'[12] He exhorted them to make the laws of the land as conformable as possible to the law of God and the aspirations of God's people, and he closed with another invocation of the eighty-fifth psalm, commending to them the pairs of virtues that it linked: mercy and truth, righteousness and peace.

Such a deliberately irenical speech was well timed, not only because of the recent or current clashes over Nayler and the major-generals but because a major debate on the constitution was clearly imminent. On the very day that the House heard of the Sindercombe plot, the former Rumper John Ashe had moved that for his better security 'His Highness would be pleased to take upon him the government according to the ancient constitution'. This was of course by no means the first proposal that Cromwell should assume the crown, and in the present parliament Colonel Jephson had already suggested that the Protector's title should be made hereditary. Ashe's motion immediately aroused both opposition and support, and since the House was already deep in divisive business it was taken no further as it stood. But some of the leading civilian Cromwellians were soon at work, if they were not already, on a scheme to make Oliver king, not under the old constitution but as part of a new one. Lord Broghill was deeply engaged in drafting it and was perhaps its main author, but its promoters thought it best to have it set in motion by someone not too obviously connected with the government. Sir Christopher Packe, a recent Lord Mayor of London, readily agreed to do it, so on 23 February he duly rose in the House, presented a paper, and asked to have it read. Its purport must have been an open secret, for many members spoke vehemently against even giving it a hearing, and some would have had Packe called to the bar. Members of the council spoke on both sides, but Packe had the support of Broghill, Whitelocke, Wolseley, and Glyn among others, and his Remonstrance (as it was at first styled) won a reading by 144 votes to 54. On hearing it there was furious opposition to considering it any further, led by Lambert, but its supporters easily outnumbered its opponents.

The Humble Petition and Advice, as this draft of a new constitution came to be called,[13] began by asking Cromwell to assume the title of king, though not on the old hereditary basis. He was to name his own successor, and how the title should pass after that was left unstated, no doubt deliberately. Such was the strife over the royal title that it tended to divert attention from the other proposed changes, which represented an intelligent attempt to remedy the defects that experience had revealed in the Instrument of Government. The most striking was that parliament was to consist of two houses, with the new one approximating more to a senate than to the aristocratic and

---

[12] Abbott, *Writings and Speeches of Oliver Cromwell*, IV, 389.
[13] Text in Gardiner (ed.), *Constitutional Documents*, pp. 447–59.

hereditary House of Lords. It was to consist of between forty and seventy members, nominated by Protector and approved by the present House of Commons, though Cromwell got this modified to give the initial choice solely to himself. The filling of future vacancies was to be subject to the approval of 'the Other House' (as it came to be called) itself. This House was to have an appellate jurisdiction over cases referred to it by inferior courts, but parliament's criminal jurisdiction was to be confined to impeachments initiated by the Commons and adjudged by the Other House 'according to the known laws of the land'. This marked a reversion to traditional constitutional practice, and so did the renaming of the council of state as the privy council. In place of the complex method of filling vacancies in it that the Instrument had prescribed, new councillors were to be nominated by the Protector, subject to the consent of the council itself and the subsequent approval of both Houses of Parliament. The Protector was empowered to suspend councillors, given just cause, but only parliament could remove them. Appointments to the highest political and judicial offices in all three kingdoms were to be subject to the approval of both Houses. The Petition and Advice also fixed a regular annual revenue of £1m. for the armed forces and £300,000 for the civil government, and it required parliamentary consent for any taxation in excess of those figures. They were inadequate, and Cromwell subsequently negotiated an increase in the total of £600,000.

Regarding religion the new constitution was slightly more restrictive than the Instrument, but in practice it made little or no difference. There was to be a confession of faith, agreed by Protector and parliament, to which clergy who received the public maintenance must conform, but no such document was ever promulgated. For those who dissented from it, toleration was limited to those who accepted the basic doctrine of the trinity and acknowledged both Old and New Testaments to be the revealed word of God; it was explicitly denied to papists and prelatists and all who made religion a pretext for 'horrible blasphemies', or licentious practices, or disturbing the public peace. These last exceptions were aimed mainly at Ranters and Quakers, but the authors of the Petition and Advice had to steer a course between displeasing intolerant magistrates and offending Cromwell's notorious breadth of sympathy, since their whole enterprise was dependent on his acceptance.

Their proposals clearly pointed to a more civilian style of government, for they promised both to increase the overall power of parliament and to diminish that of the army. Among other things, they envisaged a separation of the office of commander-in-chief from that of Protector after Cromwell's death. The army reacted very promptly. The officers of the London-based regiments were in the habit of meeting weekly on Thursdays for prayer or discussion, and when they so gathered on 26 February, three days after Packe presented the Petition and Advice, they heard that the major-generals were meeting simultaneously at Desborough's lodgings. Contact was soon established, and as a result a delegation of a hundred officers waited on Cromwell next day to voice their dismay at the new proposals and their hope that he would refuse the crown. Lambert, who was especially piqued by the threatened supersession of his brain-child the Instrument of Government, took a prominent part in organizing the confrontation.

Cromwell received them with unconcealed anger, and in his temper he accused them of some things unjustly: for instance, of driving him to dissolve both the Rump and the last parliament against his better judgement. Both had been essentially his own decisions, and the officers must have bridled at being told 'that they had made him their drudge upon all occasions'. But he was right to remind them that seven of them had brought the Instrument to him with the title of king in it. He loved the royal title no more than they now did—'a feather in a man's hat', he called it—but it ill behoved them to startle at it as they were doing. The Instrument, he said, had been subject to too little debate and consultation before it was promulgated, and the last parliament's dissection of it had convinced him that it needed amendment. The major-generals' regime had been their idea, and he still thought it justifiable, but they themselves had undermined it. 'You major-generals did your part well', he said; 'you might have gone on. Who bid you go to the House with a bill and there receive a foil?' They had been impatient to call the present parliament; he had voted against it, but they were confident that they could 'get men chosen to [their] hearts' desire'. When they failed, they (meaning presumably the military party in the council of state) abused the Instrument to shut out whom they pleased:

And I am sworn to make good all you do, right or wrong, and because 120 are excluded I must think them malignants or scandalous whether they are so or not. Yet now you complain of those [who] are admitted. I have no design upon them or you. I never courted you, nor never will . . . Next time for aught I know you may exclude 400.[14]

It was time 'to come to a settlement and lay aside arbitrary proceedings, so unacceptable to the nation'. They objected to the proposed 'Other House', but the Commons stood in need of 'a check or balancing power', as Nayler's case demonstrated—the same could happen to them. He asked them to choose six or seven of them to come and speak with him at a later date, and then bade them good night without entering into further discussion. This was a turning point; the army's influence in politics would never be the same again while he lived.

---

[14] The full text of the speech has not come down to us; what survive are two synopses by officers present, both reprinted in Abbott, *Writings and Speeches of Oliver Cromwell*, IV, 417–19. The words I have quoted in this paragraph have the ring of Cromwell's own, but they may not reproduce exactly what he said.

The officers were abashed by such plain speaking, and also by the rapid progress of the Petition and Advice in the House. The members resolved to consider it clause by clause, but to reserve the first one, which asked Cromwell to take the title of king, to the end. The second, whereby he was to name his own successor, was passed unanimously on 3 March, despite an attempt by officer-MPs and others to get it similarly deferred. The temper of the army was already much quieter. When the small delegation that he had invited came to see him on the 5th the mood was conciliatory on both sides. They assured him that the officers were resolved to acquiesce in whatever he should judge to be for the good of the three nations, and he in response declared 'his constant regard to his army, and to the ancient cause of the honest people under his government'.[15] Two days later the article proposing the Other House, to which Thurloe and others had expected stiff resistance, was passed without a division. One suspects that some senior officers rather liked the prospect of getting a seat in the new chamber and being styled 'lords'. The only articles which occupied parliament for any considerable time were those regarding religion, the revenue and the royal title itself. Desborough, Lambert, and Fleetwood were the most vehement opponents of kingship; Whalley and Goffe spoke against it more moderately, but the 'kinglings', as they were soon called, carried it by 123 votes to 62. Probably anticipating that Cromwell would try to accept the rest of the new constitution without changing his title, parliament added a final clause, declaring that if he did not consent to all its provisions, none of them should be of force.

The great debate ended just five weeks after Packe first introduced his Remonstrance, when Speaker Widdrington, in a long and high-flown oration, presented the final document to Cromwell in the Banqueting House on 31 March. Cromwell spoke only briefly in reply. He acknowledged that parliament had been aiming sincerely 'at the glory of God, the good of his people, [and] the rights of the nation', but it had faced him with as weighty a decision as ever a man had had to take. He needed to give it 'the utmost deliberation and consideration', so for the present he asked only 'that . . . I may have some short time to ask counsel of God and of my own heart'.[16] Some writers have taken this response to signify indecision, but it was probably sound diplomacy. He must have been kept well informed of the contents of the Petition and Advice and the debates on it, and he had little reason to fear the army. Although most of the leading officers continued to oppose it, a small delegation had waited on him the evening before and told him that many of their more moderate colleagues would accept the new constitution, if he did, as a dispensation of providence, and Monck had assured him of the

[15] Firth, *Last Years of the Protectorate*, I, 138–9.
[16] Abbott, *Writings and Speeches of Oliver Cromwell*, IV, 443–4.

acquiescence of the forces in Scotland. But an immediate decision would have been bad tactics, robbing him of room for negotiation; for in spite of parliament's intention that he should accept or reject its whole package he was almost certainly hoping that he would not have to do either. He wanted the constitution without the royal title.

He did not keep the House waiting long. Three days later a committee attended him at his own request to hear his further answer. He warmly praised parliament's zeal for 'the two greatest concernments that God hath in the world', the one being the special interest of His own people, the other 'the civil liberty and interest of the nation'. He deeply appreciated the high honour that they had done him, but they had named him by another title than that which he bore, and all he could say was 'that seeing the way is hedged up so as it is for me (I cannot accept the things offered unless I accept all), I have not been able to find it my duty to God and you to undertake this charge under that title . . . Nothing must make a man's conscience his servant; and really and sincerely it is my conscience that guides me to this answer'.[17] There was nothing indecisive or equivocal about his position, and he held to it consistently. He made it clear that the proposed constitution appealed to him strongly in every respect but one, both because of its merits and because it emanated from a parliament, but his refusal of the crown was a matter of conscience.

His response caused jubilation among the opponents of kingship and consternation among the new constitution's promoters, many of whom had been over-optimistic. After debate the House voted to adhere to the Petition and Advice and press it further, but only by seventy-eight votes to sixty-five—a sadly thin attendance. Accordingly the Speaker and the negotiating committee went to Cromwell again on 8 April with an address inscribed on vellum. It stated respectfully that parliament had not yet received satisfaction regarding its Petition and Advice, which embodied what it judged most conducive to the people's good in both their spiritual and their civil concernments. It reminded his highness of his great obligation in respect of what parliament advised, and again desired his assent. He assured them of the very high value he placed on parliament's desires and advice, but advice was just that, and his scruples about the title were (he stressed once more) deep-rooted in his conscience. 'Give me leave therefore to ask counsel,' he said; 'I am ready to render a reason of my apprehensions, which haply may be overswayed by better apprehensions.'[18] There were also many other things in the Petition on Advice on which he would like further information and satisfaction from them. He was holding the door slightly ajar, and encouraging further negotiation over the constitution as a whole.

---

[17] Ibid., p. 446.     [18] Ibid., p. 454.

As a result he held four more lengthy meetings with the committee between 11 and 21 April, with a week's hiatus in the middle because he was unwell. In them he expounded his difficulties over the title, and the parliament's spokesmen, chiefly Wolseley, Glyn, Fiennes, Lenthall, and Broghill, strove to convince him that he should overcome them. Their chief argument was that the whole body of the law was geared to and guaranteed by the office of king, and that parliament as the voice of the people had voted to restore it. Wolseley, a prominent councillor, reminded Cromwell that he had, to his great honour, called himself a servant of the people. 'I hope then, sir [he said], you will give the people leave to name their own servant; that is a due you cannot, you will not certainly deny them.'[19] But while they were arguing on a legal and political plane, Cromwell continued to take his stand on a moral and religious one. He was not convinced that the laws of the land were so interwoven with the kingly office that they could not stand without it; they could be executed under another title, as they had been for the past eight years. 'I am ready to serve not as a king but as a constable', he said, 'for truly I have as before God thought it often, that I could not tell what my business was . . . in the place I stood, save by comparing it with a good constable to keep the peace of the parish'. He spoke affectionately of the men he had raised and led in the wars—'such men as had the fear of God before them, and made some conscience of what they did'—and begged 'that there may be no hard thing put upon me, things I mean hard of them, that they cannot swallow.' But what weighed most with him was a conviction that providence had pronounced against the royal title. 'God has seemed providentially not only to strike at the family but at the name . . . I would not seek to set up that providence hath destroyed and laid in the dust, and I would not build Jericho again.' Parliament's spokesmen had not convinced him; he summed up his position on the 13th by saying 'I do not think the thing necessary: I would not that you should lose a friend for it'.[20]

That speech expressed his objections to it so fully and unequivocally that it is surprising that his contemporaries, and some modern historians, could suppose that he was still undecided, and might yet accept the crown. But in between these formal conferences he would relax very informally with some of the champions of kingship, notably Broghill, Whitelocke, Wolseley, Pierrepont, and Thurloe, and would smoke pipes of tobacco and play rhyming games with them before settling down to serious discussion of the business in hand. He does not appear to have conferred with leading army officers about it; he knew their mind on the matter, and he was probably still angry with them for their recent attempt to put pressure on him. By contrast his affability towards the kinglings filled them with excessive optimism, which

[19] Abbott, *Writings and Speeches of Oliver Cromwell*, IV, 460.    [20] Ibid., pp. 470–4.

they communicated to the House, while his coolness towards the anti-kingship party, including its army element, made it fear that its cause was already lost.

When he next addressed the committee on 20 April, his speech was cloudier than before, but he made no concession over the title. 'I have no title to the government of these nations,' he said, 'but what was taken up in a case of necessity, and temporary, to supply the present emergency.' Not wishing to go over again the arguments that they had put to him at their last meeting, he would 'rather tell [them] what sense lies upon my heart out of the abundance of difficulty and trouble that lies upon me'. But there were other things in the Petition and Advice besides the title that he would like to discuss with them; he was drafting a paper on them, so he asked them to meet him again next day.

When they did so, he treated them to one of his longest speeches on record. Its theme was 'the providences of God, how they have led us hitherto', and he went over the events of the past six years at considerable length. Superficially, it can be read as an essay in self-justification, but his real purpose was to expose the shortcomings of every previous attempt at settlement and underline the responsibility that lay upon them all not to waste the opportunity that providence was now laying before them. The unspoken message was that since they were so close to settlement now, let them not let it slip because of disagreement over the title, a subject that he studiously avoided throughout this long oration. He was full of praise for the Petition and Advice as a whole:

I think you have provided for the liberty of the people of God and of the nation; and I say, he sings sweetly that sings a song of reconciliation betwixt these two interests, and it is a pitiful fancy, and wild and ignorant, to think they are inconsistent. They *may* consist, and . . . I think in this government you have made them to consist.[21]

But there were some points in the Petition and Advice that he would like to see modified or elucidated, and he spoke of these before handing over his 'paper of objections'. The most substantial of the latter concerned the revenue, which as proposed fell far short of his government's needs. He also expatiated on three of his constant objectives, about which the parliament's proposals had little or nothing to say: the regulation of the law, the reformation of manners, and the provision throughout the three nations of a godly preaching ministry.

There is no doubt of his strong and sincere desire to come to terms with the parliament over its new constitution. It seems likely that he temporarily diverted attention from the question of his title in the hope that by showing how close he and parliament were to agreement over the rest of the proposals

---

[21] Ibid., p. 490. The whole speech fills pp. 484–97; that of 20 April is on pp. 480–3.

he could persuade the House to stop pressing him over the crown, for the sake of securing virtually all its other desires. The actual effect, however, was to make the kinglings think that his keenness on the new constitution as a whole was causing him to waver over the royal title. The wish was father to the thought, for there is nothing in his recorded words, prolix and convoluted though they sometimes were, to warrant such a supposition.

Parliament spent a whole week in considering his 'objections', and it met his wishes on virtually all of them, including the vital matter of the revenue. It then attended to the acts passed by Barebone's Parliament and the ordinances made by the Protector and council during 1654, whose legality had been challenged by Cony, Wentworth, and others. It confirmed all of them that mattered, except that the act for civil marriages was extended for only six months. The triers, whose work Cromwell valued so highly, obtained parliament's blessing, though it asserted its right to approve future appointments to their commission. Parliament presented the results of its deliberations to him on 1st May, expressing a hope for his early decision on its whole offer. This he promised to give, but nearly a week went by without further word from him.

It is during these tense weeks of late April and early May that his thoughts and intentions are hardest to read. Until only a day or two before his final decision he kept them very much to himself. Thurloe wrote to Henry Cromwell on 21 April that his father was having 'very great difficulties in his own mind' about the choice that faced him, and on 5 May he still did not know which way it would go. It may be that Cromwell was having late doubts as to whether he really would be following the guiding hand of providence by refusing the crown, given the benefits that would flow from his reaching full agreement with parliament over the constitution, the succession, and the revenue. He may genuinely have wanted time for prayer and heart-searching before finally committing himself. But another possibility, and perhaps the likelier, is that he was taking time to gauge public reaction, and particularly that of the army, before choosing the moment to make his refusal public. The view most widely taken by modern historians from Firth onward is that he slowly made up his mind to accept the crown, but was deflected from doing so by opposition from the army, most particularly from Desborough, Lambert, and Fleetwood. This was what the foreign diplomats and many MPs believed, and the strongest evidence for it comes from Thurloe, who reported to Henry that on 6 and 7 May Oliver privately told several members that he was resolved to accept the Petition and Advice, royal title and all. He certainly arranged a meeting with the House on the 7th, and then countermanded it that same morning. But Thurloe's evidence should be treated with caution, for Cromwell made so many cloudy utterances during these long negotiations, in affirming his general goodwill towards the parliamentary constitution, that without knowing his actual words to those members on the 6th and 7th we should not attach too much weight to them.[22]

He did not have to fear the army, but he did need to keep an eye on its reactions, since its dissident elements were still capable of making mischief. It remained divided during the crucial stages of the negotiation. Whalley believed that the Petition and Advice held forth such prospects of settlement that he would acquiesce in the royal title if need be, and he said so in parliament. He was one of many senior officers on whose loyalty Cromwell could rely; 'great professions of fidelity have been made very lately', Thurloe reported on 29 April.[23] But Pride and Desborough, always more intransigent (and less intelligent), were so put out by what they, like others, assumed to be Cromwell's imminent acceptance of the crown that they went to John Owen on 6 May and persuaded him to draft a petition, which they then circulated among the officers in and around London for their signatures. It was not a direct challenge to Cromwell, for it was addressed to parliament and simply begged it not to press him to assume a title that he had already refused. But only about thirty officers signed it, and at least half of them ranked no higher than captain; only two were full colonels. On this same 6 May Desborough met Cromwell as he was walking in St James's Park and told him that if he took the crown he would not act against him, but he would serve him no further. Cromwell got the same message from Fleetwood and Lambert.

Naturally those officers liked to think that they had made him change his mind, and because of the widespread assumption that he was on the point of becoming King Oliver they have received more credence than they deserved. But they were most probably wrong. He had told the politicking officers what he thought of them in that memorable speech on 27 February, and when he heard of the new petition drafted by Owen he was filled with fury. It may well have been the reason why he cancelled his intended speech to parliament on 7 May. Supposing (as is supposed here) that he had been treading a diplomatic tightrope, waiting for his best chance of achieving his constant objective of closing with the parliament on the rest of the new constitution without having to change his title, the officers' intervention could have been gravely prejudicial, because it would make it appear to the world that in refusing the crown he was bowing to army pressure. That is what the world did assume, and it was probably quite untrue. The ease with which he sent Lambert into retirement shortly after this episode, and his devastating rebuke to Fleetwood for another crass political intervention nine months later, would show how little he felt he need defer to these officers. If he had wanted to be king, a few

---

[22] *Thurloe State Papers*, VI, 281, quoted in *Memoirs of Edmund Ludlow*, II, 25 n. 2. The whole negotiation is discussed at length and fully documented in Firth, *Last Years of the Protectorate*, I, ch. 6, though Firth's conclusions differ from mine.

[23] *Thurloe State Papers*, VI, 243, quoted in Firth, *Last Years*, I, 189.

dismissals would have been necessary to bring the army completely to heel, as in 1654 and again early in 1658, but that would have sufficed. Taken as a whole it was a less political army than it had been in the late 1640s. It was still capable of ideological arousal, as the events of 1659 would show, but for most of the middle-ranking and junior officers, and for nearly all the rank and file, soldiering had become a career.

Damaging though the officers' attempt at intervention was, Cromwell could not defer his answer to the parliament any longer. On 8 May he addressed the members in the Banqueting House in a short, plain, and patently sincere speech. He again praised their efforts to provide for 'the great fundamentals' of civil and religious liberty and declared 'that, *ceteris paribus*, no private judgement is to lie in the balance with the judgement of parliament'. But he had to ask of them the liberty to follow the dictates of his conscience, indeed he had an overriding duty to do so. That being the case, he said 'I cannot undertake this government with that title of king'.[24]

The House received his reply with shock and consternation; indeed the members were so nonplussed that they did not take it into debate until the 13th, and then they spent three whole days on it. They were divided between continuing to press the Petition as it stood or letting him retain the title of Protector, and again between leaving his office as it was or defining and restricting it further. Many were so frustrated that they ceased to come to the House; attendances grew thinner and thinner. Once his continuance as Protector was accepted, the question of his authority was referred to a committee. On the 22nd it recommended that he was 'to govern according to this Petition and Advice in all things therein contained; and in all other things, according to the laws of these nations and not otherwise'.[25] This report was adopted, but only by fifty-three votes to fifty, a paper-thin majority in a parliament shrunken to well under a quarter of its nominal strength. But it sufficed. Cromwell, who must have been in suspense as to whether his refusal had killed the Petition stone dead, gave it his formal assent in its revised form on 25 May, and was solemnly reinstalled as Lord Protector on 26 June.

This second investiture was a much more richly ceremonial occasion than the first, with the army much less in evidence; only the Yeomen of the Guard and the Protector's life guard attended the state coach to and from Westminster Hall. There he sat in the coronation chair—moved from Westminster Abbey for the only time in its history—in which English monarchs had been crowned since 1308. He rose from it to be invested by the Speaker with a robe of purple velvet lined with ermine, and was girded with a rich sword of justice. He bore a sceptre of solid gold weighing over ten pounds. Public reaction to the ceremony was muted; the crowd that came to watch the procession

---

[24] Abbott, *Writings and Speeches of Oliver Cromwell*, IV, 512–14.
[25] *Commons Journals*, VII, 537.

come and go from Whitehall was unusually silent, but how many in it, one wonders, knew just what was going on? To the average citizen the changes in the constitution made no great difference. The irrepressible Prynne had greeted the first appearance of the Petition and Advice with a piece entitled *King Richard the Third Revived*, but during the ensuing spring there had been no such pamphlet controversy as had attended earlier political changes since the first Civil War. How far this was due to lower public interest and how far to tighter control of the press is hard to say; probably something of both. Militant opposition to the new government came from the expected quarters, the Fifth Monarchists and their fellow-travellers, and the commonwealthsmen.

The government had released Feake and Rogers from prison in December 1656, and both promptly resumed their attack on it as fanatically as ever, in print and from the pulpit. They did not stop at words, for they were intent on overthrowing 'Babylon' by force. But they found their support much narrower than in the heady days of Barebone's Parliament, even among their fellow Fifth Monarchists. Harrison and Carew would have nothing to do with them, saying they 'were not of a Gospel spirit'; nor would John Simpson or the Baptists Jessey and Kiffin. In south Wales, once one of their heartlands, Morgan Llwyd had renounced militancy, and even Vavasor Powell held aloof from the current plans for a rising. Those plans centred on the congregation of Thomas Venner, a cooper, lay preacher, and former Massachusetts colonist, who had already been in trouble for plotting to blow up the Tower. The would-be insurrectionists prepared a manifesto, entitled *A Standard Set Up*, which comprehensively denounced Cromwell and his government and sketched the primitive theocracy that they aimed to put in its place. Supreme authority was to be vested in a Sanhedrin of saints, elected annually by 'the Lord's freemen', who were also to choose the judges and local magistrates. There were to be no tithes, no excise, indeed in peacetime no taxes whatever. This was offered as the constitution of the kingdom of Christ, but to the uninitiated it must have looked fitter for cloud cuckoo land. Venner's military plans were equally unrealistic, and Thurloe's intelligencers were on to them. When he and his comrades tried to rendezvous on 9 April, they were rounded up by a party of horse before they even laid hands on their modest store of arms. Thurloe's revelation of the whole affair to parliament two days later earned him the thanks of the House and gave an unintended boost to the kinglings. As another remarkable example of the government's leniency, Venner's life was spared, though he was imprisoned in the Tower until February 1659. Perhaps it wisely reckoned that the decline of the Fifth Monarchist movement would best continue if it refrained from making martyrs of men who no longer posed a very serious threat.[26]

---

[26] DNB; Firth, *Last Years*, I, 207–19; Capp, *Fifth Monarchy Men*, pp. 117–20.

The radical commonwealthsmen's designs against Cromwell's life had been thrown into disarray when Sindercombe's plot was uncovered, but Sexby was still at large in Holland, and as murderous in intent as ever. He was cogitating a printed piece that would justify the assassination of the Protector as a patriotic act and a blow for the people, but he knew he lacked literary skill and learning, so he enlisted one Captain Silius Titus as his co-author. Titus had originally fought for parliament, but had converted to royalism while attending upon Charles I in his captivity, and was now an active intermediary between the exiled court and the former Levellers. Together they concerted *Killing No Murder*, whose message was that to slay Cromwell, he being a tyrant both through his unlawful acquisition of power and his despotic exercise of it, would be no sin but an act of duty to God and man. It is a thoroughly unpleasant piece, but written with a wit and eloquence well calculated to appeal to all who shared its authors' hatred, and the more dangerous because it particularly incited members of the army to act the part of assassins. It was doubly disingenuous in that its title-page named as its author Sexby's old fellow-agitator William Allen, who had no part in it whatever. Sexby reckoned on exploiting the army's resentment at Cromwell's assumption of the crown, which he fully expected, but he did not get the printed copies over from Holland until after Oliver had refused it. About 1,700 were seized between 25 and 27 May, but a few probably escaped Thurloe's watchdogs. Sexby himself risked coming to England a month later, but an accomplice betrayed him just as he was re-embarking for Holland. He spent the short remainder of his life in the Tower, where he fell sick in mind and body and died in January 1658.

Immediately after his re-investiture, Cromwell adjourned parliament until January. It had been a long and strenuous session, and those who had sat it out deserved a rest. It would consist of two Houses when it met again, and since it had agreed to entrust the initial nomination of the Other House entirely to him he needed time to make his choice. Meanwhile the newly constituted privy council met for the first time on 3 July, though it was new only in name. Thurloe was formally admitted to it on the 13th, though he had been acting a councillor's part for a long time. No other new member was added until Cromwell's elder son Richard was appointed on 31 December. But all privy councillors were now required to take a lengthy oath, and since it was prescribed in the Additional Petition and Advice that had been formulated mainly in response to Cromwell's 'paper of objections', it is quite likely that he was its main instigator. Some councillors, mainly those of the military faction, jibbed at it, but only Lambert persisted in refusing to take it. One can only speculate as to what he found so objectionable in it, but he was plausibly rumoured to have his eye on the succession to the Protectorship. In a long interview with him on 11 July, Cromwell strove to persuade him to take the oath, but having failed, he ordered him two days later to surrender all his commissions—not just as councillor but as major-general, as colonel of two regiments, as Admiralty Commissioner, and as Lord Warden of the Cinque Ports. But he did not part with his old comrade-in-arms in anger, for he granted him a handsome pension. He also retained him as one of the leading commissioners of the new University of Durham, whose establishment he had formally inaugurated just two months earlier. But he could not tolerate Lambert's implied rejection of the constitution that he had so painfully negotiated with the parliament, and he had to show the army who was master. There was never any doubt. Of their own accord, the officers of both Lambert's regiments pledged their loyalty to Cromwell in writing, and so, unanimously, did a general meeting of the officers in and about London on 27 July.

# TWENTY-THREE

# The Protectorate in Scotland, Ireland, and Europe

IF Scotland and Ireland have remained in the background through the last three chapters, it is because their political role following the Cromwellian conquests was mainly passive. Both countries were to play a dramatic part in the restoration of Charles II, but throughout Cromwell's Protectorate they were subordinate to England, though in different degrees. Government in Scotland was far more considerate of Scottish interests, and more open to Scottish participation, than in Ireland.

Lord Broghill, it will be remembered, had stipulated when he accepted the presidency of the Scottish council that he would serve no longer than a year, and in August 1656 he duly departed. During his tenure the balance in Scottish government shifted from a military to a civilian predominance, and Monck, his right-hand man and commander-in-chief, who famously said on a later occasion that he had learnt his trade in a commonwealth (the Dutch republic) where soldiers obeyed orders but gave none, willingly concurred in the trend. This is not to deny that English army officers continued to be involved in Scottish government at all levels from the council downward, but they did not constitute a self-consciously military interest and they worked in harmony with their civilian colleagues. The army played a necessary role in countering conspiracy, maintaining law and order, and ensuring that decisions taken by the Scottish council and the government in London were implemented in the localities, but Scotsmen played a full part in the commission of the peace and the collection of the cess (the equivalent of England's monthly assessment) and the excise. Initially, the English council's instructions were to assimilate legal procedures in Scotland to those of English law 'as far as the rules of the court will permit', but Scottish law and its processes proved toughly resistant, and gradually won an impressive degree of acceptance from Westminster.

Broghill and Monck were of course always aware that the Scots had been in arms against the English government in more years than not between 1648 and 1654, and that some elements in the nation would never bow to English dominance or renounce the house of Stuart. But they made it as easy as they could for all those who were prepared to accept the new order to find a place in it. Cromwell and the English council passed an Ordinance of Pardon and Grace for Scotland in 1654, but it excluded from its benefits 24 leading royalists whose entire estates were declared forfeit, and 73 who were subject to punitive fines. Of the 24, however, eight won a total reprieve and others a partial one, while 55 of the 73 were let off with paying only a third or less of their nominal fines and none paid more than half. Resistance among the dwindling numbers of the irreconcilable was stifled by an effective military presence and an intelligence network that watched their movements and monitored their contacts with the exiled court.

The biggest single obstacle to Scottish acceptance of English overlordship lay in its cost, and the army was far and away the largest item of expenditure. The Scots were a poor nation compared with the English, and fifteen years of intermittent fighting from the Bishops' Wars to Glencairn's rising had further impoverished them. During that rising England had had over 20,000 officers and men in Scotland, and though they had been reduced to about 12,450 by October 1655, and fell by a further 3,000 or so by 1659, they were still costing over £270,000 a year to maintain when the Protectorate came to an end.[1] There was never a chance of meeting their cost from revenue raised in Scotland. That revenue came from four main sources, the estates of the Scottish crown, the customs, the excise, and the cess. The value of the crown lands was much diminished by what Charles I and his son had granted away to their loyal supporters, and the attempt to recover the income from these estates caused keen resentment among the nobility. The odium fell upon the radically reorganized Scottish Exchequer and its newly erected Exchequer Court, which were among Broghill's more impressive creations. Scottish nobles, like their counterparts elsewhere in that age, hated carrying their share of the fiscal burden, and by the spring of 1658 the crown estates were still bringing in only £5,300 a year. Duties on imported goods were yielding about £12,800 in 1656, another disappointing figure, but the new excise on beer, ale, and spirits which the Scottish council introduced and farmed out to the highest bidder, county by county, was producing a total of just over £35,000 in 1656-7, and more than £47,000 by 1659.

The cess was the largest source of revenue, and the most unpopular, partly because the Scots were not accustomed to regular direct taxation on such a scale and partly because it was earmarked for the upkeep of an occupying army. The government did constantly reassess the quotas imposed on the local communities in an effort to match its demands to their capacity to pay,

---

[1] H. M. Reece, 'The military presence in England, 1649-60' (Oxford, D.Phil. thesis), p. 287; Dow, *Cromwellian Scotland*, p. 219 and *passim*. I am much indebted to Dr Dow's work for all that concerns Scotland in this chapter.

and with the aim of involving the Scottish gentry in rating their neighbours and dependents it required all JPs to act ex officio as assessment commissioners. This, however, caused a mild setback to the laudable introduction of the commission of the peace to Scotland, because it made many lairds refuse to serve in either capacity. Broghill and Monck clung as long as they could to a target of £10,000 a month for the cess, for even if it had been attainable it would have covered nowhere near half the cost of the army in Scotland. But they came to accept that the ravages of war had put it beyond reach, and with Monck's full agreement parliament reduced it in 1657 to a more realistic £6,000. Scottish revenue never met half the costs of governing, defending, and policing the country. Just before the Protectorate was overturned in 1659, a parliamentary investigation showed a total annual expenditure on Scotland of £307,271, and a total Scottish revenue of £143,652; the balance fell on the English taxpayer. The Scots felt that they were heavily taxed, but the burden was not intolerable, and the government strove in association with local interests to ensure that it fell as equitably as possible on the various sectors of the community.

One way and another, Scotland was making steady progress from the status of a conquered country towards partnership in the Commonwealth of Great Britain. The process was very incomplete when Cromwell died, and the partnership was never likely to be an equal one. But the involvement of nobles and lairds in local administration and justice through the commission of the peace was a real blessing, and the regime's increasing respect for the distinctive principles and procedures of Scottish law was to its credit. Scotland's representation in the Westminster parliament, though limited to thirty members, became more of a reality in 1656–7 than it had been in 1654. In the first Protectorate parliament it had not been found possible to fill even thirty seats; we know the names of only twenty-two members, and nine of them were Englishmen. But in the second, all the Scottish seats were filled, fourteen of them by Scotsmen, and these were men of real political and social weight. The Englishmen holding Scottish seats included five councillors and several other high-ranking officials; only four were serving army officers. The Scottish council was indeed severely depleted during parliament's session, and the new Exchequer Court was rendered inquorate.

Civil jurisdiction at the highest level was committed to eight Commissioners for the Administration of Justice. Two of them were returned to parliament, and the death of two others reduced their number also below a quorum, just before the summer session of 1657. It was not very easy to replace them, because most learned English men of law were reluctant to wrestle with an alien and complex legal system in a far-away country, and many able Scots were unwilling to compromise the law of their fathers. Gradually, however, the government both in Edinburgh and Westminster eased up on trying to assimilate Scottish procedures to English and came to trust Scotsmen to administer Scottish law, at least in civil actions. The change of attitude was reciprocated. That fascinating diarist Alexander Brodie of Brodie had, as a Scottish patriot, refused Cromwell's invitation to advise him on the Ordinance of Union, declined his seat in Barebone's Parliament, and turned down a judgeship early in 1657. But he accepted one in January 1658, and thereby Scottish judges (in the civil sphere) came to outnumber English by five to four. They were a distinguished group. The number of cases that the commissioners adjudged rose steeply in 1657–8, which strongly suggests that people were engaging in litigation more willingly because they trusted the justice that the court was dispensing.

The government was understandably slower to entrust Scottish judges with the exercise of criminal jurisdiction, for in a country so lately subdued and pacified there were bound to be strict limits to the civilizing trend so far described. Most crimes above the petty level were tried by the circuit judges, and the cases that they dealt with were presented to them by the justices of the peace. The commission of the peace was one of the success stories of the Cromwellian regime. The main reason why it throve now, after James's attempt to establish it had failed, was that in his time the nobility had correctly seen the JPs as a threat to their hereditary jurisdictions, whereas it was a consistent policy of the Commonwealth and Protectorate to curb their excessive powers. The majority of JPs were local lairds and other men of substance, but there were a few army officers on the commission in every shire, and the army played an essential part not only in keeping track of the government's political enemies but in apprehending thieves, moss-troopers, and other common law-breakers. The only major exception was in the Highland regions, where Monck allowed the clan chiefs to deal with cattle-thieves and other malefactors, and let them keep arms for the purpose. He kept as strict an eye as he could on the passage of enemy agents from overseas and any stirrings of unrest among the Scots themselves, but he found himself with less and less to worry about. Royalism was a declining force in Cromwellian Scotland, partly because security was so effective, but partly because the maintenance of the longed-for peace and the dispensing of even-handed justice gave it little discontent to feed upon.

As to religion, Broghill had laid sound foundations by establishing a modus vivendi between the government and the warring factions of Protesters and Resolutioners. The presbyteries continued to enjoy their cherished right to appoint ministers to parishes, subject only to a check that their candidates were fit for their trust and not positively disaffected towards the government. The latter was attacked for its tolerance, not its intolerance, and posterity will hardly be shocked, as the stricter brethren were then, that distinguished Scotsmen felt free to convert to Independency and Quakerism. Indeed only

Roman Catholics were formally denied the right to practise their religion. They were commanded to surrender all arms and ammunition in their possession, and to pledge themselves not to correspond with the king or his agents. But the protestant clergy complained that so long as papists gave bonds for their good behaviour the government was not concerned to interpose further in suppressing their exercise of their religion, which suggests that a de facto tolerance of discreet catholic worship prevailed where it posed no political threat. From March 1656, however, catholic priests were declared subject to the death penalty if found on Scottish soil, though this may have been a reaction to Charles II's imminent treaty with Spain rather than the inauguration of a more rigorous policy.

The year of Broghill's presidency in Scotland witnessed something of a turning-point in the affairs of his native Ireland, though the problems of governing the two countries, and England's approach to them, were very different. The vast majority of Scots were fellow-protestants, and most of them had been the English parliament's allies in the first Civil War. Despite all that had happened between 1648 and 1654, the Protectorate's policy was to win back the friendship of the Scottish people and to involve them as far as was safe in the administration of their country. By contrast, not only were the overwhelming majority of the native Irish Roman Catholics, and tarred in English eyes (however unjustly) with the brush of the 1641 massacres, but a substantial proportion of protestants, whether Old English or more recent settlers, had been royalists. In their sympathies many still were. The situation was complicated by the large number of Presbyterian Scots settled in Ulster, who associated the Protectorate and its agents with Independency, sectarianism, and the toleration of heresy.

When Cromwell became Protector Irish government was still officially in the hands of four commissioners appointed by the Rump, though the republican Rumper John Weaver had already resigned, and Ludlow was so openly opposed to the new regime that he tried to prevent it from being proclaimed in Dublin. A heavy responsibility lay upon Fleetwood, who had been made commander-in-chief in 1652. That was just after he had married Ireton's widow, and so became Cromwell's son-in-law. Cromwell had a great affection for him, and for some time to come he let it get the better of his generally shrewd judgement of character. Fleetwood was a brave soldier and a devout and upright man, but he had neither the flair nor the intelligence for a major political role, and he was apt to be putty in the hands of men who spoke the canting language of the saints. He regarded the bulk of the Irish people as past saving, and he saw it as his function simply to keep a conquered country quiet, rather than to cultivate the co-operation of those inhabitants who might be prepared to give it. Consequently he had no compunction about exercising military rule, and few qualms about his army's unpopularity, even among the best disposed of Irishmen. His personal loyalty to Cromwell was beyond question, strained though it became when he thought that his father-in-law was about to become king, but that of some of his officers was more doubtful. There had been more disquiet among them over Cromwell's elevation as Protector than in the army in England, probably because Ireland had come to be seen as a suitable posting for officers whose republican or sectarian leanings made them look likely to rock the boat in the home forces. A significant proportion of them were Baptists, and radical Baptists made an extraordinary number of conversions in the army of Ireland during the 1650s. One can understand why. Among fairly simple men who felt isolated in an alien environment, amidst what they saw as a hostile, barbarous, and antichristian (i.e. papist) population, the thunderous certainties of a fundamentalist faith gave them comfort and knit them closer together. The gospel preached by Baptist firebrands in Cromwellian Ireland was very different from the gentle religion of the heart that we know in modern Britain, or from that of such moderate contemporary Baptist leaders as Jessey and Kiffin. Fleetwood remained an Independent, but he made no attempt to stem the militant Baptist tide; indeed conversion was said to open the path to promotion. William Allen, the former agitator and now Adjutant-General in Ireland, was one such convert; he and his fellow-Baptists Quartermaster-General Vernon and Colonel Axtell led the faction whose fidelity to the Protectorate was most in doubt. It was reported in 1655 that the military governors of five Irish towns were Baptists, and that some had used their resources to import Baptist preachers from England. This heavy Baptist bias, with its disturbing political overtones, made the army doubly unpopular with the older protestant interest that had adhered to the Church of Ireland, and with the Presbyterian Scots settled in Ulster.

Cromwell never doubted Fleetwood's personal loyalty, but he became sufficiently concerned about the temper of his subordinates to send his son Henry over in March 1654 to investigate. Henry was only just twenty-six, but he knew something of Ireland, having served there as a colonel of horse in 1649–51 and fought alongside Broghill. Reporting on his return home, he was reassuring about the reliability of the officers in general, but he recommended that Ludlow should be stripped of his commissions—something that Fleetwood should have done immediately when Ludlow refused orders to proclaim the Protectorate. Henry found Fleetwood himself over-partial towards his Baptist and other sectarian officers, and hinted that it might be better to call him home. Fleetwood was perturbed by Henry's mission, for it set rumours flying that the younger man was being lined up to supplant him. He communicated his fears to Cromwell, who replied in June that the idea of putting Henry in his place had never entered his heart. Indeed Fleetwood was raised in August to the office of Lord Deputy, and furnished with a council of six to assist him in the government of Ireland. Not long afterwards the Council of State recommended that Henry be made acting commander of the forces of Ireland with the rank of major-general. He was formally commissioned and added to the Irish council in December, but he did not return to Ireland until July 1655.

These were not good decisions. It made little sense to advance Fleetwood, whose only talents were military, to a virtually vice-regal post at the head of the civil government, and to saddle Henry, who had real political ability but little standing in the army, with the responsibilities of commander-in-chief, over the heads of colonels all older than himself. The result was to leave Irish government from the council downward riven by faction for as long as the Protectorate lasted. Furthermore there were just not enough councillors to carry out the work in hand, partly because three of them doubled as judges and could only attend to their heavy political duties when the courts were not sitting. It was a perennial problem to find really able Englishmen who were willing to serve in Ireland, whether as judges or administrators, and it was compounded because those who did so were most inadequately supported from Westminster—and not only in the matter of finance. Time and again, when they appealed for measures or orders to underpin their efforts, they were ignored or kept waiting for months. No parliament ever got around to passing an act of union, though a bill for that purpose did receive two readings in December 1656. The constitutional basis of much of Irish government was therefore always more uncertain than that of Scotland. This was partly because Cromwell and his council had too much on their hands, what with suppressing conspiracies, managing the major-generals (who had also felt under-supported), pursuing the long negotiation over the Petition and Advice, and conducting the war with Spain. But another reason was that parliament, when it was sitting, and to a lesser extent the council, evinced less concern and sympathy towards Ireland's problems than Scotland's. To most MPs Ireland was something of a bore, if it did not inspire positive hostility.

Cromwell himself might have given his son stronger support. He was commendably anxious not to incur the charge of advancing his own kin, and Henry, besides being very young to carry high responsibilities, was not without his faults: he was not strong on tact, his temper had a short fuse, and his correspondence with Thurloe suggests a streak of paranoia in his attitude towards his opponents. But he had a broader vision of Ireland's needs and England's interests in the country than anyone else in high authority there, and it would have been better if the home government had heeded him more and the army party less. His relations with the latter were made more difficult because his arrival coincided with the first considerable disbandments, to which Fleetwood was openly opposed. It also coincided with the revival of the four courts of justice in Dublin which parallelled those at Westminster,

Upper Bench, Common Pleas, Exchequer, and Chancery; but they were wretchedly understaffed, and they remained so. They also shared the deficiencies of their Westminster counterparts, especially in their profusion of archaic technicalities and their separation of common law from equity. The army party saw their revival as a betrayal of the cause of radical law reform, but for most property-owners in Ireland it was a step in the right direction; unreformed courts were a great deal better than none. At the same time there was a marked revival of the JPs' authority in the localities, and with it the termination of the summary judicial powers that army officers had been exercising since the reconquest. There were of course many officers in the commission of the peace, but the benches also included a proportion of older protestant settlers, and Henry used his authority to add to their number wherever possible. All in all his arrival in 1655 marked a turning-point in Irish administration, tilting the balance from a military to a civilian predominance, though the process was gradual and never fully achieved.

Henry's position, both as councillor and acting military commander, was almost impossible while Fleetwood remained in Ireland as Lord Deputy, and his father knew it. Oliver did not actually recall his son-in-law, but he wrote suggesting that he might return home 'if you have a mind',[2] and Fleetwood did so in September 1655. Many of his supporters remained in places of power and influence, however, and for a considerable period the council was split three a side between his faction and Henry's. Deplorably, Cromwell did not bestow the title and authority of Lord Deputy on his son until Fleetwood's commission expired in 1657, and even then he took nearly seven weeks to make up his mind to do so. This sent the wrong signals to the older-established protestant interest in Ireland, with whom Henry was trying so hard to establish a rapport. It also hampered his efforts to make ends meet financially.

One thing that the Irish situation had in common with the Scottish was that neither country could pay for the cost of governing and policing it, and that in both the occupying army was far and away the heaviest item of expenditure. It was estimated that in December 1654 England had 23,115 officers and men in Ireland, at a cost of nearly £500,000 a year. By July 1657 they had been reduced to slightly over 16,000, and by the end of the Protectorate to less than 12,000, but in 1658 their annual upkeep was still reckoned at £336,000, and their pay was nine months in arrears. Henry made himself further unpopular with the army by proposing that to reduce it further part of its duties should be taken over by an unpaid, locally based militia, but the scheme was not adopted. With the civil administration costing a modest £46,000 a year in

---

[2] Quoted in T. C. Barnard, *Cromwellian Ireland: English Government and Reform in Ireland, 1649–1660* (Oxford, 2nd ed. 2000), p. 20. In these pages I have drawn heavily on Dr Barnard's authoritative study.

1658, there was no chance of balancing overall expenditure with revenue, and in that year the deficit was reckoned to be running at £96,000. The resultant financial burden was keenly resented in England. The sources of revenue were similar to those in Scotland: land owned by the state or forfeited to it by the rebels, customs and excise, and the monthly assessment. The loss of records makes it impossible to calculate the yield from land, though it was felt to be very disappointing. But customs and excise, which had brought in around £35,000 a year in the early 1650s, had improved to nearly £50,000 by 1657, and were put out to farm in 1658 for £70,000. That target proved too high, but the rising yield suggests a considerable recovery in trade and living standards, as well as more efficient collection. Soon after Henry's arrival in Ireland, many heavy restraints on her trade were lifted. The bans on the export of cattle, beef, pork, hides, tallow, and butter were removed. Cattle and sheep farming flourished, clothmaking throve in a modest way (thanks partly to the needs of the English soldiery), linen manufacture was encouraged, and grain exports to England rose strikingly. Irish merchants, however, still had to pay customs duty on exports to England, including wool, and they were not allowed free trade with the American colonies, as the Scots were. Ireland's commercial interests remained firmly subordinated to those of England, as they had been under Strafford, and would be again, even more rigorously, after the Restoration. In this respect Cromwellian government was running to form. One obstacle to the revival of trade, especially foreign trade, that government should have addressed but did not was the wretchedly debased state of the Irish coinage.

As in Scotland, the monthly assessment was the most unpopular tax because it was appropriated to the upkeep of the occupying army, but it was hated even more in Ireland because it was fixed so high. The target was £12,000 in 1656, £13,000 in 1657, and would have been raised to £14,000 for 1658 if the Irish MPs at Westminster, with Henry's full support, had not got it reduced to £9,000. Some English members were so outraged that they moved that the representatives of Ireland should be sent to the Tower. But the latter, and Henry, were fully justified, because the assessment had been unfairly apportioned as well as set too high, and punitive taxation was deterring new settlers as well as retarding economic recovery.

The greatest economic injustice, and the heaviest blow to recovery, had been perpetrated by the Long Parliament long before Cromwell became Protector, when it decided not only to exclude Roman Catholics from municipal government and trading guilds but to expel them from all walled towns. Many of the less wealthy just moved out into the suburbs, and some simply evaded the ban, but most of the substantial catholic merchants left the country and settled abroad; St Malo was their favourite refuge. They took with them their ships, their stocks, and their expertise, causing a serious shortage of Irish-based shipping to carry Irish trade, and much urban decay, especially in Cork, Galway, Limerick, and Waterford. The Commonwealth's attempts to induce well-to-do protestants to settle in these and other towns met with a mediocre response, though Martin Noell, a rich revenue farmer who shared the office of Postmaster-General with Thurloe, did have some success in establishing an English merchant community in Wexford.[3] Henry Cromwell played a strong part in aiding the revival of borough corporations, to which Fleetwood and the army party had been thoroughly hostile. Only Dublin, Belfast, and two other towns had with difficulty hung on to their charters during the period of reconquest, but from 1656 onward charters were granted or restored to Cork, Waterford, Limerick, Kilkenny, Derry, Wexford, New Ross, Cashel, and other places. Since catholics were debarred, and members of the corporations were probably named in the charters (which do not survive), this was only a limited step towards urban self-government; the mayors of Galway and Limerick, for instance, were army officers or ex-officers. But it was another step in the right direction, and another success for Henry and his friends over the military faction.

The two parties were no less divided over religious policy. The army interest looked little further than providing for the religious needs of the occupying forces and such new settlers as came in under their auspices. Ideally, they would have liked to convert all protestants in Ireland to their own Independent or Baptist faiths, though they were welcoming towards Quakers, who made many converts in the army, especially in Munster. They were unsympathetic towards the Church of Ireland, with its episcopal structure and Anglican liturgy, and the antagonism between them and the Presbyterians of Ulster was mutual. Henry by contrast, as part of his policy of building bridges between the Protectorate and the older-established protestant interest, cultivated the clergy of the Church of Ireland. Thereby he laid himself open to criticism, because of that church's links with the proscribed Church of England and royalism, but given his assumption that the regime that he served had a long-term future in Ireland it was a risk worth taking. He also sought good relations with the Ulster Presbyterians, since they were obviously there to stay, though not to the extent of encouraging their ambition to impose their own brand of theocracy on the rest of the country.

The difficulty of revivifying some kind of ecumenical national protestant church, which was Henry's aim, lay not only in the existing Church of Ireland's commitment to episcopacy and its dubious political affiliations, but in its generally run-down state. This was evident even before the 1640s, but still more so after 1649. Very many of its livings were so poor that incumbents

---

[3] Barnard, *Cromwellian Ireland*, pp. 56–7; life of Noell by G. E. Aylmer in *The Dictionary of National Biography: Missing Persons* (Oxford, 1993), pp. 497–8.

could only keep alive by taking more than one, and many of its churches were already dilapidated before the fighting of the 1640s wrought further damage. The Rump abolished episcopacy and banned the Book of Common Prayer, but set up no other church polity or form of worship to replace them in Ireland; such matters were deferred to the act of union that was never passed. After the reconquest, however, the English government began appointing salaried preachers in Ireland, at first primarily for the benefit of its own garrisons and administrators, but increasingly from 1655 for that of the protestant community in Ireland as a whole. Between 1651 and 1659, 376 state-salaried ministers were appointed, most of them after Henry's arrival in the country. At least 67 of them had held benefices in the Church of Ireland; an equal number were Presbyterians, and nearly all the rest were Independents.[4] They included a few Baptists, but the stricter members of that sect refused the state's stipend on principle, and some who took it lost their appointments under Henry—not because of their religious beliefs but because of their political partisanship. Henry's checks on the Baptist ascendancy in parts of the army, and his promotion of a broad religious front that would embrace the old as well as the new settler interest, led four of the five leading Baptists in the army, Adjutant-General Allen, Quartermaster-General Vernon, and Colonels Axtell and Barrow, to resign their commissions in November 1656. The fifth, Colonel Hewson, a particular opponent of Henry, had recently left Ireland to take command of a new regiment in England and a seat in the Other House. His Irish regiment remained nominally his, but he did not return.[5] Henry at first regarded the Quakers as a seriously subversive influence in the army, where they made many converts, for Quakers were not yet committed as a body to pacifism. The Irish council ordered the arrest of all Quakers late in 1655, and some officers were cashiered. But Henry soon came to realize that most of the Friends in Ireland posed no threat, and the number of them held in prison fell rapidly from seventy-seven in 1655 to one in 1659.

On the positive side of religious policy, Henry worked to restore tithes as part at least of the clergy's maintenance, subject to the proviso that no incumbent should receive less than £80 a year. In April 1656 he instituted a committee of eleven members, including four ministers, who were to consult with two councillors and recommend the best method of adjudging fit candidates for livings and removing unworthy ministers. They seem to have taken over the job themselves, though Munster kept its own commission for the approbation of ministers, and in Ulster the presbyteries were allowed to retain their role therein. Lay patrons recovered their rights of presentation from 1655

[4] Barnard, *Cromwellian Ireland*, p. 166; Patrick J. Corish in *New History of Ireland*, III, 377–9.
[5] *DNB*, *sub* Hewson, Henry; Firth and Rait, *Regimental History of Cromwell's Army*, II, 409–11.

onward, subject to their nominees satisfying the committee for approbation. In 1657 a general inquisition was instituted into the value of all benefices, the names of incumbents, patrons, and impropriators, and the physical contribution of churches. The commissioners' main task was to recommend changes in parish boundaries that would bring livings up to the £80 minimum. The result of these various measures was to improve the income of the parish clergy substantially, reduce the charge of the state-salaried preachers upon the exchequer, and increase the overall number of active pastors. Even so, Henry admitted in 1658 that little more than a third of the country was adequately supplied with ministers; but there were large tracts of it in which protestant worshippers were very thin on the ground and his reckoning probably did not include the episcopalian chaplains who were kept at their own expense by some protestant magnates like the Earl of Cork, as well as by several town corporations and Dublin guilds. It can hardly be doubted that such chaplains practised the Anglican rites behind closed doors, and that Henry, like his father except in times of crisis, looked the other way. As in the economic and judicial spheres, he made large progress in his four years towards a state of affairs in which the whole protestant community could live together in harmony, and by the end of his time his standing was high throughout it, except among the dwindling and now harmless band of Baptist and other fanatics.

Where his regime failed, and was bound to fail, was in its avowed objective of evangelizing the catholic Irish. There were one or two tentatives in that direction, but the scarcity of able and willing Irish-speaking preachers, the inadequate financial resources, and the low priority of the enterprise combined to doom them. There were some conversions, but they were mostly of the kind that had produced church papists in Elizabethan England: outward only, and motivated by a desire to protect property and escape penalties. But at least the Protectorate was not a time of active religious persecution. It would have been if Cromwell's second parliament had had its way, for it passed an Act against Popish Recusants which it expressly extended to Ireland. It required all suspected catholics in both countries to take an oath whereby they not only abjured the pope's spiritual jurisdiction and power to depose, but denied the doctrine of transubstantiation and affirmed 'that the church of Rome is not a true church'.[6] Irishmen who took it were further required to bring up their children to speak only English and conform to the English catechism. Henry deplored this oath of abjuration, which naturally caused great consternation among Irish catholics, but having failed to prevent its extension to Ireland he seems to have made no attempt to impose it. Nor was there any drive to compel catholics to attend the services and receive the sacraments of a church that their consciences rejected, as there had been in

[6] Firth, *Last Years*, II, 147–8.

Elizabethan and early Stuart England. Priests were officially proscribed; from January 1653 the policy was to banish them on pain of the penalties for high treason if they returned, and perhaps a thousand or more went into exile. But a considerable number returned and led an underground existence among the catholic population, despite a price of £5 on their heads. Those that were caught were commonly transported to the West Indies, but they were not in Henry's time subjected to a traitor's death. The number of Irish martyrs subsequently recommended to Rome for beatification comes to 119, including 22 laymen, for the years 1649–53, and of these 84 suffered in 1651–2; but the toll fell to 2 in 1654 and 3 in 1655, the year of Henry's arrival. There were none thereafter. Tragic though it was that the great majority of the Irish people could not practise their religion openly, Henry was moving in the direction of de facto toleration of discreet catholic worship, and the penal laws throughout the Cromwellian Protectorate were less harsh than they were to be under William III and after.

The best testimony to the fairness and good intentions of Henry's treatment of the Irish, given the circumstances, came from the royalists Ormond and Clarendon after the Restoration. The great transplantation of catholic landlords to Connaught was none of his doing; it was largely implemented before he came over. He was a benign Chancellor of Trinity College Dublin, which had almost ceased to take in students before he presided over its revival. He resurrected a dormant proposal of the Rump to found a second college in Dublin, which was well on the way to establishment when the troubles of 1659–60 overtook it. Archbishop Ussher, whom he admired, died in 1656, leaving a magnificent library, which was threatened with sale and dispersal. Henry ensured that it was bought for the new college at the considerable cost of £22,000, a significant part of which was raised from contributions by officers of the army in Ireland.

As if the Petition and Advice and the problems of Scotland and Ireland were not enough to keep Cromwell and the council busy, they had on their hands a war with Spain, a threat of renewed war with the Dutch, a northern war in and around the Baltic which came close to involving Britain, and in 1658 a joint campaign with France by land and sea, resulting in the acquisition of Dunkirk.

The Spanish war was relatively uneventful in 1656. Spain lacked the resources for any serious attempt to recapture Jamaica, so although a squadron was kept in the Caribbean under young Captain Christopher Myngs (he was only thirty when first appointed), such action as there was took place in Spanish rather than colonial waters. Late in March 1656 a fleet of thirty-seven ships set sail for the Spanish coast under the joint command of Blake and Edward Montagu, who had recently been appointed General at

Sea. The command was shared at Blake's request, no doubt because of his failing health; it had never been robust since his wound. Montagu was Cromwell's choice, and a bold one, for he too was only thirty and he had never been to sea. But he had fought at Marston Moor as a colonel of foot before he was nineteen, and he had impressed Oliver in a number of employments since then. The main aim of the expedition was to capture the Plate fleet and generally prey on Spanish shipping, though the two commanders were authorized to attack Spanish territory if they saw a good opportunity. They reconnoitred Cadiz and Gibraltar, but wisely decided that to take and hold either was beyond their resources. The Spanish home fleet would not come out and challenge them, and they found few prizes because Spain had few merchant ships of her own at sea. But Portugal's Brazil fleet was then nearing home, and by threatening it they forced King John to ratify the treaty on which he had been stalling since 1654. They next made a foray into the Mediterranean, leaving Vice-Admiral Stayner with a squadron before Cadiz. Their aim was to extirpate the corsairs of Tripoli, but it was frustrated by a devastating storm which scattered Blake's contingent. Nevertheless five frigates made a spectacular raid on Malaga, burning nine ships and raking the town with fire. The success of the year, however, fell to Stayner, when he had been driven from Cadiz by a gale, and on 8 September caught the Plate fleet running for home without a convoy. The seven great galleons mistook his six small ships for fishing vessels, and were taken wholly by surprise when they opened fire. Stayner captured two and sank two more without loss to himself. The amount of captured treasure that reached England proved much less than expected, as mentioned earlier, but the loss to Spain was great, and the rather scrappy operations of 1656 certainly succeeded in crippling Spanish commerce.

Montagu sailed home with part of the fleet late in October, but Blake kept up the blockade of Cadiz all through the winter, which was an unprecedented feat. There was considerable alarm when the Dutch admiral de Ruyter appeared off Cadiz late in January 1657, for it was rumoured that he had been sent to join the Spaniards in fighting Blake. But though de Ruyter had secret orders to resist any attempt by English warships to search the merchantmen that he was convoying, his primary targets were the French privateers and Barbary corsairs that had been plundering Dutch merchant shipping. Neither the Dutch nor the English government wanted war, and Cromwell and de Witt between them made sure that the danger passed.

By February Blake's ships were mostly in poor shape through having been so long at sea, and his crews were on short rations in both food and drink. Blake himself was in wretched health. When news came that another Plate fleet had been sighted heading for the Canaries he felt bound to resist his captains' eagerness to take a squadron and cut it off, for he judged his fleet to be in too weak a state to be divided. But late in March the victualling ships from

England reached him at last, and during the next two weeks he received increasingly sure intelligence that sixteen vessels of the Plate fleet, seven of them great galleons, had landed their treasure on Tenerife and lay at anchor in the Bay of Santa Cruz. Despite a worrying report that de Ruyter was on his way with sixteen warships to convoy them to Flanders, Blake sailed for the Canaries with nearly all his own twenty-three ships. At Santa Cruz, however, the harbour was so strongly defended with six or seven stone forts, and the fire-power of the sixteen ships at anchor in it was so formidable, that the Spaniards felt quite safe from attack. But Stayner formulated, and with Blake's approval executed, a bold and brilliant plan. On 20 April he led twelve frigates straight into the harbour in line astern, trusting to the smoke from his guns to protect him from the worst of the enemy musketry and counter-fire. An extremely fierce fight ensued, but Stayner sank or burnt every Spanish ship and lost none of his own, though his flagship, the Speaker, barely managed to limp away. Only about 50 of his men were killed and 120 wounded. Most of the treasure remained ashore in Tenerife, but Spain lacked the available naval force to ship it to the mainland, and suffered very seriously through the lack of it. Her land campaign against Portugal had been going promisingly, and might have achieved outright victory within the year, but by July her armies were disintegrating for lack of pay.

Parliament heard the news of the victory three days after Cromwell accepted the Petition and Advice. It appointed a day of national thanksgiving and voted Blake a jewel worth £500, but it gave nothing to Stayner. Cromwell, however, knighted him as soon as he returned to England. Blake was called home too, but he never quite made it. He had been subsisting for a year past on 'broths, jellies and cordials', and he died within sight of Plymouth harbour. He was given a hero's burial in Westminster Abbey, but he was not allowed to rest there long. To the enduring shame of England's new masters in 1660, his remains were disinterred and cast into a common pit. He had played no part in the trial and execution of Charles I.

By 1657 the centre of diplomatic and operational activity was shifting nearer home. Mazarin had long been hoping to convert France's treaty of peace and commerce with England into an offensive alliance against Spain. The distractions of the Fronde had set France back in her long war with Spain, and territory that she had earlier won in the Spanish Netherlands had recently been lost again. Mazarin wanted both English naval support in the Channel and English land forces for a campaign in Flanders. Cromwell was the more disposed towards such an alliance after Charles II signed his treaty with Philip IV, and he was attracted by the prospect of acquiring a port and naval base across the Channel, but he baulked for some time at committing English troops to a continental campaign. Nevertheless he allowed his ambassador Sir William Lockhart to come to an outline agreement with Mazarin in

November 1656 (and knighted him soon afterwards), and this ripened into a formal treaty in March 1657. Cromwell had been angling for a league that would unite England, France, Sweden, Denmark and the United Provinces against both branches of the house of Hapsburg, but Denmark, and Sweden were on the brink of war with each other—Denmark was to declare it in May—and as Mazarin pointed out the Dutch were visibly more pro-Spanish than pro-British. The cardinal gently brought the Protector to a sense of diplomatic realities, and the treaty that they signed had the limited objectives of joint attacks by land and sea on Gravelines, Mardyke, and Dunkirk. England was to contribute a fleet and 6,000 infantry, France an army of 20,000 under Turenne. When captured, Dunkirk and Mardyke were to be awarded to England, and Gravelines to France. On the sensitive matter of religion, Cromwell agreed to guarantee both regular and secular clergy in possession of their revenues and churches, as well as to preserve full freedom of catholic worship, in such Flemish towns as fell under his authority.

Cromwell had no reason to fear the invasion proposed by Charles II's recent treaty, since Spain was no more able to find the 6,000 troops that it promised than the English royalists were to seize the stipulated port for their unopposed disembarkation. Spain concentrated her limited resources on reinforcing Dunkirk and Gravelines against the Anglo-French threat, and she did so to such effect that Turenne, with Mazarin's approval, put off attacking them for months in order to clear more of the territory inland of them. The 6,000 English foot joined him at St Quentin early in June. About a quarter were drawn from the regular army; the rest were volunteers, raised by beat of drum, and a mixture of old soldiers and raw recruits. Their commander was Sir John Reynolds, the same man who as a captain in Cromwell's own regiment of horse had played a leading part in the agitator movement of 1647. He had since earned a knighthood for distinguished service in Ireland, where he was Commissary-General and a pillar of strength to Henry Cromwell. He had married a sister of Henry's wife, and he left Ireland reluctantly. His second in command was Major-General Anthony Morgan, who had been Monck's right-hand man in the pacification of Scotland. Their soldiers all wore the red coats of the New Model Army.

They performed in action to the admiration of the French commanders, but their officers were bemused and then disgruntled at the type of warfare in which they were engaged, with its endless sieges of minor strong points and its studied avoidance of battle. 'Fighting is not the fashion of the country', wrote Reynolds to Henry on 1 September, and he made no secret of his wish to be recalled to his old employment. Sickness and desertion, he told him, had reduced his 6,000 men to less than 4,000.[7] They were discontented with their

[7] Firth, *Last Years*, I, 277, 279.

small and irregular pay, and their health suffered from their poor rations, mainly 'ammunition bread' of rye and bran. But Lockhart had already been remonstrating at their misemployment, and a letter from Cromwell was on the way, instructing him to threaten Mazarin with the withdrawal of the English forces if the French did not immediately strike against Dunkirk or Gravelines. Turenne in fact was already on the move. He set siege to Mardyke on 19 September, battered its main fortress into surrender within four days, and promptly handed it over to the English. It was less than Cromwell wanted, for he believed that Turenne could have taken Dunkirk if he had struck earlier. But Mardyke was so much a part of Dunkirk's outer defences that it had to be taken first, and Spain cared enough about it to send Don Juan with over 4,000 men to try to recapture it. There was a brisk fight, notable because both Charles II and his brother James Duke of York took part in it, but Mardyke held out. The fortress, however, had to be considerably extended to hold its English garrison, and the troops who had to dig entrenchments, raise palisades, and build lodgings had a wretched time of it. Reynolds reckoned that he had 1,000 men sick and only about 1,800 fit for service, and Cromwell's relations with Mazarin became very strained. He reproached France for failing to provide his troops with timber, fuel, shelter, and other necessaries; Turenne laid the blame on their own laziness and the neglect and absenteeism of their officers.

In mid-November a strange episode took place that was to have tragic consequences for Reynolds. The Duke of York, who was now serving in Spain's Army of Flanders, was one of the most senior officers in Dunkirk, which was only a stroll across the dunes away from Mardyke. Informal contacts between the officers of the two garrisons took place frequently, especially outside the campaigning season. One such meeting took place between Reynolds and James, whether at Reynolds's instance is not clear. Curiosity was probably the main motive, and it was probably mutual, since James had been lieutenant-general in Turenne's army until Cromwell's treaty with France drove him out of the country. Nothing significant seems to have passed beyond an exchange of civilities. But tongues began to wag, and some officers in Mardyke reported the meeting to Cromwell, expressing doubts about Reynolds's loyalty. According to James's own memoirs, Reynolds's chief accuser was Lieutenant-Colonel Frances White, who had very recently been sent from England to be temporary Governor of Mardyke. White too had been an officer-agitator, but he and Reynolds had taken very different lines during the Leveller mutiny in 1649; perhaps there were old scores to settle. At any rate, when White set out for England to inform against his commander, Reynolds sailed in the same ship. He had obtained leave to pay a short visit home, but whether his main reason was to plead the case of his forces, or see to his private affairs, or clear himself from White's charges, is uncertain; probably something of all three. But the ship was wrecked on the Goodwin Sands in a December storm, and all on board were drowned.[8] The command of the English forces in Flanders passed to the faithful Morgan.

Cromwell reinforced the Mardyke garrison during December to a strength of at least 2,500, which was more than the fortress could comfortably hold. He met opposition in the privy council to the resources that he was pouring into it, and it may well be asked why he was so keen to acquire continental territory that was almost sure to cost more to maintain and defend than it brought in. There were several reasons. Prestige was one; all the major European powers in his time shared the same acquisitive itch, and Cromwell felt a special urge to redeem Mary Tudor's loss of Calais. He also saw that a base across the Channel would strengthen his splendid fleet's position in the Narrow Seas. In the short term, he intended to recall parliament soon, and he hankered after a triumph to put before it, because the session promised to be a difficult one. But perhaps more importantly, he had evidence through Thurloe's intelligencers that the Spaniards were now planning to honour their pledges to Charles II, and that the royalists in England were plotting another rising early in 1658. Nothing could deter a Spanish invasion more effectively than the acquisition of Dunkirk, and the reinforcement of Mardyke was a preparation for just that.

Earlier in 1657 Dunkirk was not the only bait to attract Cromwell, for he had expressed a serious interest in acquiring Bremen. To explain the full circumstances would take us deep into the complexities of the northern war that Charles X of Sweden launched with his assault on Poland in 1655, and that is not necessary because despite prolonged pressure Cromwell kept England out of it. But his sympathies and those of most Englishmen were strongly on Charles's side, partly because of the golden aura that clung to the memory of his kinsman Gustavus Adolphus and partly because the Swedes were a protestant nation and the Poles a catholic one—though Cromwell would much rather Charles had turned his sword against the Habsburg emperor. He received a series of envoys from the Swedish king in the course of 1655–6, and he treated them with exceptional cordiality and favour. His dream of a grand protestant alliance against the catholic powers was still distorting his view of Baltic politics. He signed a trade treaty with Sweden in July 1656 which expanded the one negotiated by Whitelock two years earlier, and he allowed 2,000 English volunteers to be recruited for the Swedish army, but he steadily resisted the envoys' pleas to commit England to war by a full offensive alliance. It would, he rightly feared, have provoked a closer accord between

---

[8] On Reynolds and White, see (besides earlier references) Firth, *Last Years*, I, 294–8; Gentles, *New Model Army*, pp. 320–1, 332–3, 340–7.

Denmark and the United Provinces, thus etching deeper the line of division within the protestant interest; it might have pushed the Dutch further into friendship with Spain. It would have upset the balance in the Baltic, and so jeopardized a vital source of England's naval stores. He would have welcomed a treaty that also included the Dutch, but that was not on the diplomatic cards, and anti-Dutch feeling was strong in his own council.

From December 1656 Charles was pressing hard for a loan of £100,000, and in January Cromwell replied that he would consider it if Sweden would hand over the duchy of Bremen by way of security. This was a fairly preposterous proposal—for one thing it would have made an enemy of the Great Elector of Brandenburg—and it is hard to say how seriously Cromwell intended it. He certainly could not afford to lend Charles £100,000, and he may have thought that an impossible request was diplomatically preferable to an outright refusal. He repeated it in May, when Denmark declared war on Sweden and threw her for some time on the defensive. In the same month the Archduke Leopold, who was shortly to be elected Emperor in succession to Ferdinand III, signed a treaty with Poland, promising her 12,000 Austrian troops. Charles's grip on that country had already been seriously weakened since his early conquests, and now he was simultaneously threatened not only there but by three Danish armies, on two fronts in Sweden and in Bremen and western Germany. War on this scale in the Baltic was most unwelcome to Cromwell. His relations with the United Provinces were worsening, and he felt bound to resist Sweden's urgent and constant pleas to send an English naval squadron to the Sound lest it should spark off another Anglo-Dutch war.

When the feared attack by Denmark fell early in August, Charles sent Cromwell some quite extraordinary offers. In return for substantial military and naval aid, he proposed that Denmark, once beaten, should be partitioned, with England taking a large part of Jutland along with East Friesland and Münster, and Sweden annexing the rest. At one stage he was prepared to throw in Iceland and Greenland too, and to offer a four-year alliance for a joint war against Habsburg Austria as soon as Denmark had been disposed of. Cromwell received all these propositions with profuse expressions of goodwill, but his mind was really set on mediating between the warring kingdoms. For this purpose he sent the experienced diplomat Philip Meadowe to Copenhagen and the bluff soldier Major-General William Jephson to the Swedish king. Since Mazarin and de Witt were equally concerned to set limits to the northern war and to broker a peace if they could, his policy of reconciliation was in line with the best diplomatic minds in Europe, as well as with England's best interests.[9] He was well placed to help save Denmark from

---

[9]    Michael Roberts, 'Cromwell and the Baltic', in *Essays in Swedish History* (1953).

a humiliating peace when Charles X transformed the whole situation by his devastating march across the ice against Copenhagen early in 1658, but that sensational episode, and England's reactions to it, will find their place in the next chapter. Meanwhile the next chapter for Cromwell, and for Britain, was to be his last clash with parliament.

# ‡ TWENTY-FOUR ‡

# Unfinished Business

WHEN Cromwell reopened parliament for its second session on 20 January 1658, it wore a very different aspect from the one it had presented when he last addressed it. It now consisted, of course, of two Houses, but the Commons themselves were transformed by two changes that were bound to make them harder to manage. In the first place the Petition and Advice ruled that no member could be excluded except by authority of the House itself, so all those who had been excluded by the council in 1656 were free to take their seats, and most did so. Secondly, thirty MPs had been nominated to the Other House, and they included many of the Protectorate's staunchest and ablest supporters.

It had been given to Cromwell to name the members of the Other House, subject originally to the approval of his nominees by the Commons; but in subsequent negotiation he had obtained that the choice should lie solely with himself and his successors. This concession had been won in a thin House by ninety votes to forty-one. Three considerations probably swayed the majority: approval by the Commons would have implied the elected chamber's superiority; it would have deterred the peers who had been faithful to parliament in the wars from accepting membership (and there was a hope among conservatives that in time they might all have been incorporated); and on the analogy of the peerage, sole choice by the titular head of state accorded with ancient constitutional practice. There was probably also a fear that ambitious MPs might exercise a right of approval in pursuit of their own self-promotion. As Thurloe wrote to Henry Cromwell, the great difficulty was to sift 'those who are fit, and not willing to serve, and those who are willing, and expect it, and are not fit'.[1]

Cromwell did not seriously embark on the business of selection until November, and he completed it on 10 December. He gave it much thought, and his choice fell on sixty-three men (out of a permitted maximum of seventy). Seven were peers of the realm, but only two of them took their seats: Lord Fauconberg, who had recently married Cromwell's daughter Mary, and

---

[1] *Thurloe State Papers*, VI, 648, quoted in Firth, *Last Years*, II, 10.

the impoverished Lord Eure, who had sat in Barebone's Parliament and had been elected to the Commons in 1654 and 1656. Those who declined or ignored the summons included such close earlier associates of Cromwell as Manchester, Saye and Sele, Warwick (whose grandson and heir had lately married another Cromwell daughter), Wharton, and Mulgrave. They were not necessarily disaffected towards the government, but with Cromwell visibly ageing and the future uncertain they were probably reluctant to compromise their future as peers by endorsing this dubious surrogate for the 'real' House of Lords. Seventeen of Cromwell's nominees were serving army officers, but they included his sons Richard and Henry, as well as Monck and Howard, all opponents rather than supporters of the military party as it had evolved since 1654. That party was well represented by Fleetwood, Desborough, Hewson, Pride, Whalley, Berry, and Goffe (though not of course Lambert), but its presence was not so large as to distort the balance of the House. Among republicans, Haselrig received a summons (which he ignored), but not Vane or Scot or Ashley Cooper or Marten, still less anyone associated with the Leveller or Fifth Monarchy movements. Experienced middle-of-the-road stalwarts such at St John, Pierrepont, Nathaniel Fiennes, Lenthall, Whitelocke, Glyn, Wolseley, Montagu, Strickland, Sydenham, Lawrence, Philip Jones, Francis Rous, and Broghill formed the core of the membership. Exactly two-thirds of Cromwell's nominees took their seats and were sworn in, but the absentees included a few who were kept from attending by urgent duties, such as Monck, Lockhart, and Henry Cromwell.

The address with which Cromwell opened the new session was the utterance of a tired man in failing health, and he twice excused its brevity on account of his 'infirmities'. He spoke mainly on his old themes of 'our civil liberties as men, our spiritual liberties as Christians', and he blessed God for the Petition and Advice, which had done so much to secure both.[2] He left it to Fiennes as Commissioner of the Great Seal to speak further about public affairs. It had been the accepted practice for monarchs, at state openings, to delegate to the Lord Chancellor (to whose office Fiennes's corresponded) the task of opening up in more detail the state of the nation and the work for which parliament was called, but all that the members got from Fiennes was more rhetoric about the virtues of the new constitution. They were told not a word about the progress of the war with Spain, or the operations in Flanders, or Britain's position with regard to the northern war, or even the serious state of the nation's finances. And whereas Cromwell had informed the last parliament frankly about the imminence of a royalist rising, this one was told nothing as yet about the preparations in progress for another. In his current ill health he could not be blamed for not briefing it as a head of state should, but

---

[2] Abbott, *Writings and Speeches of Oliver Cromwell*, IV, 705.

it speaks badly of the collective competence of his councillors that they failed to see that this was done on his behalf. It was an unhappy omen for what would happen when he died.

An early brush occurred when the Other House sent a message to the Commons, asking their concurrence in calling the three nations to a day of prayer and humiliation. The Speaker described it as coming from the Lords, and it sparked off an immediate debate on how the new chamber was to be addressed: as the House of Lords, as it appeared to be styling itself, or as the Other House, as the Petition and Advice called it? Cromwell, perhaps because he saw a constitutional row brewing, or perhaps because he sensed how inadequate his opening speech had been and was feeling better by the weekend, summoned the whole parliament to the Banqueting House on Monday 25 January to hear a much longer and more specific address. Its theme, he announced, was to be the dangers that faced Britain abroad and at home. He claimed, with staggering over-simplification,

that the greatest design now on foot, in comparison with which all other designs are but low things, is whether the Christian world should be all Popery; or whether God hath a love to, and we ought to have a brotherly fellow-feeling of, the interest of all the protestant Christians in the world.

The house of Habsburg on both sides of Christendom was in league with the pope 'to destroy the whole protestant interest'. Against this monstrous design stood 'a poor prince! Indeed poor, but a man in his person as gallant, and truly I think I may say as good, as any these late ages have brought forth'— and he was 'now reduced into a corner'.[3] Cromwell knew enough by now about Charles X and the tangled issues of the northern war to be aware that he was presenting a distorted picture, but he was anxious to deflect the members from their constitutional bickering and rouse them to face the seriousness of the international situation. He did not paint it all in black and white, for he had kind things to say about France and harsh things about the Dutch, who he said were pledged to transport a Spanish invading force to England in support of Charles II. He appealed for money to defend the country. He was briefer about the dangers at home, but he lamented once more the nation's internal divisions, 'whether sects upon a religious account, or upon a civil account', each striving to get power into its own hands. Only two things kept the peace in the three nations: the army—'a poor unpaid army, the soldiers going barefoot at this time, in this city, this weather, and yet a peaceable people, seeking to serve you with their lives'—and the recent settlement of the constitution that had vested power in the two Houses of Parliament and himself. He had something to say about the progress made in Ireland and

---

[3] Abbott, *Writings and Speeches of Oliver Cromwell*, IV, pp. 713–14.

Scotland, and the blessings that six years of peace had brought to them and to England. 'We have peace and the gospel. Let us have one heart and soul, one mind to maintain the honest and just rights of this nation.'[4]

The latter part of the speech, pleading for unity and co-operation, was truly eloquent and deeply felt, but it fell on many deaf ears. Haselrig, scorning his summons to the Other House, led a concerted attack on it in company with Thomas Scot, who on one occasion spoke for a whole morning. The two had formed a partnership in the Rump and were to maintain an even stronger one in 1658 and 1659. With the support of other ex-Rumpers like Ashley Cooper and Weaver, they attacked the claim of any second chamber or any other body whatever to set a check upon the sovereign authority of the people's representatives. There were cogent arguments on the other side, notably from Serjeant Maynard, but defences of the Petition and Advice got nowhere because the slender majority that had carried it was gone. The republicans also borrowed from Harrington, who was widely read, the contention that power follows property, and maintained that the members of the Other House owned nothing like enough land between them to stand as a balance to the Commons. That was true as far as it went, but if the constitution had been given longer to take root there was every prospect of the membership being enlarged, with perhaps all the 'faithful' old peers incorporated in it. Moreover, as Major-General Boteler pointed out, there were other qualifications besides broad acres, indeed even better ones, such as 'religion, piety and faithfulness to this commonwealth'.[5]

Parliament was not the only platform from which the republicans promoted their cause. They got up a petition which was designed to appeal to commonwealthsmen and radical puritans in general and to members of the army in particular. It was circulated for signatures within the army and among the citizenry of London while the debates were in progress, and its authors planned to present it to the House of Commons on 4 February. It was addressed to 'the Parliament of the Commonwealth of England', as if the Other House did not exist. It commands attention, not only because it led directly to the dissolution of this parliament, but because it was revived and presented to the next one a year later. It defined the tyranny against which parliament had fought the Civil War as consisting in the king's and the Lords' power of veto, the king's claim to control the armed forces, the exercise of arbitrary powers over subjects' persons and estates, and the raising of money without parliamentary consent. It implied, of course, that the Protectorate was perpetrating all these evils. Its requests covered them all, but its chief

[4] Ibid., pp. 717, 720.
[5] *Diary of Richard Burton Esquire*, ed. J. T. Rutt (4 vols., 1828) II, 409, quoted in Firth, *Last Years*, II, 23–4.

demand was that the present Commons should provide for a succession of parliaments in which the representatives of the people ('the original of all just power') should have supreme authority to make laws, define the offices and institutions of government, and call judges and ministers of state to account. It coyly refrained from claiming for parliament similar power over the army; indeed it demanded that no officer or soldier should be dismissed from the service except by sentence of a court-martial. This would have deprived the state of the essential power to remove members of the services who engaged in political subversion. Religion was glossed over with a request that provision should be made for all sincere professors and that no tender conscience should be oppressed, thus evading the really divisive questions of the limits of toleration and the upkeep, if any, of a national parochial ministry. The petition was cunningly contrived to appeal to all the Protectorate's opponents except the royalists and the rigid Fifth Monarchy men, but it contained no practical solutions to the political problems of the present.[6] When the republican politicians did recover the power for which they lusted seventeen months later, their enjoyment of it was to be short indeed.

Cromwell decided that there was so much potential mischief in this petition that he must prevent if from coming before parliament. On the day it was to be presented he made his way hurriedly to the Lords' House without telling any of his councillors—not even Thurloe—what he intended. He had meant to go by water, but the Thames was partly ice-bound, so he took the nearest hackney coach. Once at the Palace of Westminster, he sent for the judges from their courts in Westminster Hall and dispatched Black Rod to summon the Commons. Fiennes and Fleetwood, hearing of his unheralded arrival, came to ask him what his purpose was, and were astonished to hear that it was to dissolve parliament. Fleetwood begged him to think hard about it first, for it was a decision of great consequence. 'You are a milksop,' Cromwell replied; 'by the living God I will dissolve the House.'[7] Haselrig tried to persuade the Commons to ignore Black Rod, but after keeping him waiting some time while they discussed his summons they obeyed it. Cromwell's speech that put an end to their sitting was fairly brief and powerfully reproachful. He had expected that when he framed his government to a constitution proposed by them, and agreed with them after long negotiation, the country might have enjoyed the peace and settlement that had so long been striven for. Instead, disaffected members had been working to overturn the settlement that parliament itself had authored, and 'designing a commonwealth that some tribune of the people might be the man that might rule all'. This was 'but the

---

[6] The petition was published by its anonymous author in March, as *A True Copy of a Petition ... intended to have been delivered to the late Parliament* (British Library, E 936(5)). Strangely, it has never been reprinted since 1659.

[7] Abbott, *Writings and Speeches of Oliver Cromwell*, IV, 728.

playing of the King of Scots's game'; and the worst of it had been their 'endeavours . . . to pervert the army whilst you have been sitting, yea and to draw the army to the state of a question, a commonwealth, a commonwealth.' His closing words were 'I do dissolve this parliament. Let God judge between you and me'; to which some of the members responded 'Amen'.[8]

The dissolution led to much premature rejoicing among both royalists and commonwealthsmen, who misread it as the act of a desperate man facing defeat. But Cromwell knew what he was doing, and actually strengthened his position by nipping the republican design in the bud. Much had changed since the outgoing parliament had been elected under the shadow of the major-generals, and there was good reason to hope that a new one, chosen under the terms of a parliamentary constitution, would endorse it and act co-operatively under it, as the next parliament indeed did. Cromwell's one real worry was about the temper of the army, or rather that of a small minority within it; he had inspected the night watch at Whitehall in person for some days before the dissolution. Two days after it he summoned all the officers in and about London, some two hundred or so, and addressed them for about two hours, explaining how providence had brought him to his present unsought place and why he had felt obliged to dissolve the parliament. The officers applauded him, and pledged themselves anew 'to stand and fall, live and die with my Lord Protector'. He toasted them; they drank to him, and the occasion became convivial as bottle after bottle was drained.[9] The only centre of real disaffection in the army in England was Cromwell's own regiment of horse. He cannot have had much personal contact with it in the past five years, and Monck had long regarded its effective commander, Major William Packer, as a dangerous trouble-maker and the source of its discontents. Packer was an extreme Baptist of the type that vexed Henry in Ireland, and he had brought many officers and men of his kind into the regiment; three of his troop commanders were new. Cromwell argued with him and his troop captains over several days, trying to satisfy their objections, but finding them unmovable in their rigid republicanism he cashiered all six of them.[10]

His firm action made a considerable stir, but it had the desired effect. At Monck's prompting, the regiments and garrisons in Scotland sent him addresses of loyalty. All the more senior officers around London met in Whitehall on 24 March to hear Fleetwood introduce a collective address, which was read twice and laid open to discussion. There was none; everyone present signed it on the spot, and four days later, after it had been circulated, Fleetwood presented it to Cromwell with a roll of 224 officers' signatures. It specifically affirmed their commitment to the Petition and Advice, as well as

[8] Ibid., pp. 731–2; Firth, *Last Years*, II, 41.
[9] Firth, *Last Years*, II, pp. 44–5.
[10] Firth & Rait, *Regimental History*, I, 70–4.

their fidelity to Cromwell. A very full declaration from the army in Ireland was not long in following. Predictably it met with more discussion, but only a dozen men, some of them private soldiers and only one ranking as high as major, dissented from it. As for popular reactions, London took the dissolution calmly, apart from some radical sectaries. The City corporation made no official response until Cromwell sent for the Lord Mayor and aldermen and informed them of the advanced state of royalist preparations. Ormond, he revealed, had been in their midst for three weeks and had only just returned to the continent. This produced not only a loyal address, warmly supporting the Petition and Advice, but a substantial reinforcement and reorganization of the City's militia.

Cromwell certainly had the measure of his opponents now, partly of course because of the force he could dispose of, but partly too because his regime commanded respect in quarters where it had earlier been opposed. The Fifth Monarchists had already been made aware in the spring of 1657 that they stood no chance of overthrowing him by force, and his refusal of the crown took some more wind out of their sails. After he dissolved parliament they published fresh incitements to resist him, aiming them particularly at the army, but they found little response and they were promptly dealt with. Venner was already in the Tower; Rogers, Courtney, Portman, and (soon after) Feake were sent to join him there, but Rogers and Feake were released in April, and only Portman was held for a whole year. When the Baptists of the West Country held a conference at Dorchester in May 1658, some senior Fifth Monarchists including Carew urged that their two groups should combine, but Kiffin and others vigorously opposed the proposal and it was rejected.[11] Moderate sectaries recognized how well off they were with the toleration that in practice they enjoyed.

The royalist threat was punctured even more comprehensively than in 1655. Vice-Admiral Lawson with twelve frigates blockaded Ostend from 27 February, arriving just in time to engage the Dutch transports that Spain had hired to carry the troops assembled in Flanders for the invasion of England. He captured three of them and drove two more ashore. Three weeks later the royalists called off the whole enterprise, at least for the current year, for they saw no chance of securing an English port, as the treaty had stipulated. But the government did not drop its vigilance, and it arrested a number of important suspects, including three members of the Sealed Knot, during late March and April. One Sussex royalist, Anthony Stapley, whom Cromwell examined in person, gave way under interrogation and confessed all he knew. Quite soon Thurloe uncovered most of what mattered about the whole conspiracy, and in May, on the council's advice, the second and last High Court

---

[11] Capp, *Fifth Monarchy Men*, pp. 120–1.

of Justice of the Protectorate was convened to try its chief actors. It is symptomatic of the strengthening constitutional spirit of the time that only about 50 of the 140-odd commissioners appointed to constitute the court consented to act, and that all the judges of the regular courts declined, holding that the prisoners should be tried by a jury. But Cromwell was evidently not prepared to risk the acquittal of proven conspirators, and this High Court was scrupulous in requiring proof of guilt.

Chief of the accused were a Yorkshire knight, Sir Henry Slingsby, who was rather unpleasantly ensnared into treasonable activity in order to uncover his fellow-plotters; Dr John Hewitt, an Anglican clergyman; and John Mordaunt, a son of the Earl of Peterborough, and fast becoming the most active and effective royalist agent in England. Slingsby and Hewitt were convicted and beheaded, but Mordaunt was spared by the casting vote of the president because the evidence against him was not found to be conclusive. Three other prisoners, engaged in the Sussex plot and betrayed by Stapley (who saved his neck thereby), were tried separately; one had his case dropped, another was acquitted, the third was convicted but reprieved. While these trials were pending, a break-away faction of plotters in London decided bravely but madly to go it alone and raise the City on 15 May. The government was well informed of their plan and pounced just as they were going into action, taking forty or fifty prisoners before a blow was struck. Seven ringleaders were tried by the High Court of Justice; six of them were found guilty but three were reprieved at the foot of the gallows, and only three were hanged, drawn, and quartered—a very rare example of the application of the traditional punishment of treason in Cromwellian England.[12]

The total failure of these designs put an end to serious royalist conspiracy for as long as the Protectorate lasted. Repeated frustration did at least make some of the activists overcome their reluctance to seek an alliance with the former political presbyterians, and among their chief targets were Manchester, Sir William Waller, Robert Harley, and Fairfax, whose daughter had married the second Duke of Buckingham in September 1657. But whatever guarded civilities were exchanged they made very little progress, and Manchester, Waller, and Fairfax held back from anything that can be called conspiracy. Most presbyterians remained unwilling to support a restoration except on terms similar to those of the Treaty of Newport, which true royalists found quite unacceptable. The situation would change radically when Richard Cromwell was overthrown, but the Protectorate, while it lasted, accorded better with presbyterian political values than a Stuart restoration effected by force of arms (especially Spanish arms), and hence likely to be unconditional.

[12] Firth, *Last Years*, II, 76–82; Underdown, *Royalist Conspiracy*, ch. 10, esp. pp. 226–9.

How well the constitutional settlement might have bedded down if Cromwell had had even a year or two more of full vigour is a matter for conjecture, but declining health took an increasing toll of him during 1658. It had been his practice through most of his rule to attend a majority of council meetings, but of the seventy-four held between January and his death he was present at only nineteen. Fatigue and worry sometimes told on him, especially since the dissolution had left his government with steadily mounting debt and his soldiers' and seamen's pay perilously in arrears. The fatal cancer of his favourite daughter Elizabeth Claypole—she died on 6 August—grieved him deeply. But to picture him (as some have done) as a broken man, or losing his grip on affairs, is seriously to overstate the case. He continued to take a keen interest in foreign policy, especially in the progress of the Flanders campaign, and he frequently dealt with foreign diplomats in person.

The French alliance needed to be renewed in March, having initially been given a year to run. Lockhart drove a hard bargain with Mazarin, not without seriously offending him, but he secured his commitment to a joint operation against Dunkirk by land and sea between 20 April and 10 May. After the port had been handed over to England, the English fleet engaged in its capture would be at France's disposal for the siege of Gravelines. Mazarin had good cause to complain, however, that England was extremely slow to bring her troops in Flanders up to strength, despite urgent pleas from Lockhart to Thurloe. Nevertheless Turenne did lay siege to Dunkirk on 15 May with a combined army of at least 25,000, supported by an English fleet of over twenty warships. The English troops, which had attracted some resentment, mainly through their quarrelsomeness, redeemed themselves by fighting like heroes in the siege operations, which cost them quite heavy casualties.

On the Spanish side Don Juan was slow to respond because he took the siege of Dunkirk to be a feint to cover an attack on cities and forts inland, but once convinced that it was the prime objective he concentrated the whole Army of Flanders, about 14,000 strong, on relieving it. Turenne had no intention of waiting passively for an attack on his siege lines, so leaving about 6,000 men to guard them he marched out the rest of the army and drew it up in battle order, facing the strong position that Don Juan had taken up among the sand-hills. British troops fought on both sides in the Battle of the Dunes, which was fought on 4 June. Don Juan had an English, a Scottish, and three Irish regiments, all fighting as professionals in his Army of Flanders, as well as the Duke of York and his life guard. Turenne's force included seven English regiments, numbering between 4,000 and 5,000 men, and they were ranged against Spanish veterans, the toughest opposition on the field. Their courage impressed both French and Spanish commanders, but they had a hard fight, scrambling up steep sand-hills on hands and knees under fire, and out of about 400 killed in Turenne's army they accounted for almost half. But few of the old Spanish infantry that they fought escaped death or capture, and the Anglo-French victory was total; Don Juan lost about 1,000 men killed and 4,000 taken prisoners.

Dunkirk capitulated ten days after the battle, and the nineteen-year-old Louis XIV, who had accompanied his army throughout the campaign, entered the town in state next day. He wrote a letter of congratulation to Cromwell in his own hand, and he himself handed the keys of Dunkirk to Lockhart, but he personally shared the widespread French resentment at the delivery of so valuable a place to the English. There was a considerable party in France that deplored her alliance with the heretical regicide republic, but Mazarin held firm to it, and the four English regiments which were not assigned to garrisoning Dunkirk and Mardyke did good service under Turenne during the rest of the campaigning season. Indeed Mazarin sounded Lockhart informally late in July about extending the league, and suggested that Ostend might be the reward for a larger-scale English participation. It was an unlikely possibility, however, given the Protectorate's financial problems, and Cromwell's death put an end to it.

Whether Dunkirk would ever have been worth the £70,000 or so a year that it cost to garrison, over and above what could be raised locally, is debatable, but its acquisition should not be glibly dismissed as the product of a Tudor hangover. It put paid to any possibility of using the Spanish Netherlands as a launching-pad for a royalist invasion, and Thurloe rightly described it as 'a bridle to the Dutch'. It was a blessing to English merchant shipping that Dunkirk was no longer a nest for privateers. Lockhart, now made its governor, had no doubts about it value: 'It is not only an excellent outwork for the defence of England, but a sally-port by which his Highness may advantageously sally forth upon his enemies, as often as he shall see occasion for it.'[13] Possession of Dunkirk set the seal upon the success of the English army on both land and sea, and very significantly raised the Protectorate's status among the European powers. No one appreciated this better than Clarendon, writing of Cromwell many years after the Restoration: 'But his greatness at home was but a shadow of the glory he had abroad. It was hard to discover which feared him most, France, Spain, or the Low Countries, where his friendship was current at the value he put upon it.'[14] Samuel Pepys, commenting in 1667 on the recent disaster in which a Dutch fleet had sailed right up the Thames estuary and the Medway and destroyed many of England's proudest men-of-war as they lay at anchor in Chatham, remarked. 'It is strange how ... everybody doth nowadays reflect upon him

---

[13] *Thurloe State Papers*, VI, 853, quoted in Firth, *Last Years*, II, 218.
[14] Clarendon, *History of the Rebellion*, VI, 94 (Book XV, § 152).

[Cromwell] and commend him, so brave things he did and made all the neighbour princes fear him.'[15]

Cromwell scrupulously honoured his treaty obligations to the catholic inhabitants of Dunkirk, and most of the burghers (priests and religious orders apart) seem to have been more content under English than under Spanish overlordship. But he himself hoped that his foothold on the continent would advance the protestant interest in western Europe, envisaging that converts and settlers in and around Dunkirk would spread their faith in the Low Countries, and give encouragement to the Huguenots in France.

Such hopes were over-optimistic, and passed into limbo when the restored Charles II promptly sold Dunkirk back to France. But Cromwell's enhanced prestige increased the diplomatic influence that he could wield in the northern war—never in a dominating role, of course, but still to an extent that the belligerents had to take notice of. Charles X transformed the situation by two sensational marches across the ice in January and early February of 1658, which brought Copenhagen under the immediate threat of his army and forced the Danish king to sue for peace. Frederick III sent urgently for help to Philip Meadowe, Cromwell's envoy to his court, and Meadowe in collaboration with the French ambassador did all he could to moderate Charles's demands, which at first included the whole of Norway and the island of Zeeland. That would have given Sweden both shores of the Sound, with power to dictate access to the vital sources of naval stores in the Baltic. By the Treaty of Roskilde Charles had to be content with acquiring the southern provinces of modern Sweden that had hitherto been Danish, but the opposite shore remained Denmark's. The part that Meadowe played in negotiating the terms earned him the respect of both kings and the sincere gratitude of Frederick.

Cromwell never altogether abandoned his dream of uniting the protestant interest in Europe, but he showed an increasingly sophisticated awareness of the realities of the diplomatic situation, and he used his influence on it responsibly, with the object of limiting rather than extending war in northern Europe. He chose his diplomats well. He sent George Downing to the Hague to try and repair England's relations with the United Provinces, which had recently gone to war with Portugal, mainly because both countries laid claim to Brazil. That war brought the Dutch closer to Spain, and the underhand aid that they were giving to the Spaniards, coupled with England's acquisition of Dunkirk and the frequent seizure of English prizes by Dutch captains, made Downing's task as a negotiator difficult. But after many months he did secure the restoration of some English ships that the Dutch East India Company had impounded in Bantam, and he gradually established a relationship with

---

[15] *Diary of Samuel Pepys*, VIII, 332 (*sub* 12 July, 1667).

Grand Pensionary de Witt. He managed to bring the latter into closer touch with the Swedish envoy at the Hague, and won his personal agreement to a proposal that Cromwell should arbitrate between the United Provinces and Sweden over the vexed question of the Sound dues. Cromwell also took up the cause of the protestants who were currently being persecuted in Poland and Silesia, much as he had in the case of the Vaudois. In March he launched an appeal for them in England which brought in £10,685.

He was steadily learning how little religious ideals had to do with the realities of northern European politics. In February 1658 Frederick William, Elector of Brandenburg, concluded an offensive league with Austria and Poland, aimed primarily against Sweden, and designed (in a secret article) to open the way to his own acquisition of Pomerania. There was no love lost between the Calvinist Frederick William and the Lutheran Charles X, who debarred Calvinists from holding office in his dominions. During the spring Charles tried to draw England further into an offensive league against Austria and Spain, but financial stringency would have ruled that out for Cromwell, even if he had not seen that Charles's main reason for threatening the Habsburgs was to deter Austria from ganging up with Poland, Brandenburg and Denmark against him. Cromwell did send Jephson to Berlin in April, primarily to promote if he could a better understanding between Brandenburg and Sweden, but also (too late) to try to secure the Great Elector's vote against the election of Leopold as Emperor. He also sent Meadowe to East Prussia to offer his mediation in the peace negotiations that then seemed imminent. It cannot be said that these missions effected anything very significant, but the very fact that they were received with respect testifies to England's enhanced standing in the counsels of Europe. Far more was achieved by the League of the Rhine, which was master-minded by Mazarin and signed three weeks before Cromwell died. It conjoined a powerful body of German princes with the Kings of France and Sweden in a joint undertaking to maintain the terms of the Peace of Westphalia and those under which Leopold had just been elected Emperor. Effectively, it prevented the Emperor from taking Austria into a war against France in alliance with Spain. Cromwell had no share in negotiating the League of the Rhine, but against the opposition of the Spanish ambassador and the papal nuncio Mazarin had a clause inserted in the treaty that extended its benefits to France's allies. That meant that none of its signatories could aid Spain against England, and if Cromwell had lived Mazarin would surely have insisted that the Protectorate was included in the Treaty of the Pyrenees.

It must have been a bitter disappointment to Cromwell to hear, as his life was running out, that Charles X had broken the Treaty of Roskilde and laid siege to Copenhagen. But Sir Charles Firth was for once mistaken in concluding that this spelt the ruin of the Protector's policy in the Baltic, for France, the United Provinces, and England together decided that the terms agreed at Roskilde should be upheld, and so they essentially were when the Treaty of Copenhagen was concluded in 1660; indeed its modifications actually improved the balance of power in the Baltic.[16] By then Cromwell of course was dead, and so, more recently, was Charles X, who left a successor less than five years old. Cromwell, however, did live long enough to hear cheering news from Jamaica, where the plantation was just beginning to prosper. Colonel Edward Doyley, who took over as governor when Major-General Brayne died in 1657, defeated an attempt by about 1,000 Spanish troops to recapture the island that year, killing about 120 and losing only 4 of his own men. In May and June 1658 his small but gallant garrison routed a considerably larger invading force, which lost about 300 in action, not counting those who perished after taking to the forest for refuge.

Cromwell's health was collapsing during August. On a good day he could still ride out and take the air in Hampton Court Park, and there around the middle of the month George Fox accosted him at the head of his life guard. Fox came to plead for his imprisoned fellow-Quakers, and Cromwell bade him come to the palace next day. But, Fox writes, 'I saw and felt a waft of death go forth against him, and he looked like a dead man'.[17] Cromwell was indeed too ill to see him the next day, and on 3 September, the anniversary of his victories at Dunbar and Worcester, he died peacefully. He was conscious on his deathbed of leaving much unfinished business, and it is tantalizing to speculate on what course public affairs might have taken if he had had just a little longer. There had been much debate in the council from February onward on whether to summon a new parliament soon, and though Desborough and a few others were for relying on the sword and collecting money by force, the consensus was that only a parliament could solve the government's mounting financial problems. It was proposed, though not yet formally agreed, that the Commons should be elected by the traditional constituencies, and that all the old peers who had been faithful to the parliamentary cause should be summoned to the Other House alongside Cromwell's nominees. In June a council committee consisting of five officers and four civilians was appointed to consider an agenda for the parliament, but by then it was too late to get it elected before the harvest, and Cromwell's fatal illness put it in limbo. There seems little reason to suppose, however, that a parliament assembled in the autumn of 1658 would have been less amenable and co-operative than the one summoned by Richard Cromwell early in 1659.

It would probably have repeated its predecessor's attempt to make Cromwell king; indeed it was the talk of the town even in the spring of 1658

---

[16] Compare Firth, *Last Years*, II, 290 with Michael Roberts, 'Cromwell and the Baltic', in *Essays in Swedish History* (1953).

[17] *Journal of George Fox*, ed. J. L. Nickalls (1975), p. 350.

that a coronation was imminent. Bordeaux was sure of it, and other foreign diplomats thought the same; Cromwell's son-in-law Fauconberg believed that only the timing was uncertain. Firth thought it probable that Cromwell would have accepted the crown if he had lived, but presumptuous though it is to differ from that great historian twice in one chapter it may be doubted. There is no evidence that Oliver had overcome the patently sincere scruples about the royal title that he had persistently expressed during 1657. Moreover he knew his army. Some but by no means all of the senior officers had become reconciled to the prospect of kingship, but the disquiet that it would have caused among those below field rank would probably have been serious; the rift that was to develop under Richard between the senior commanders on the one hand and the captains and subalterns on the other would have opened up earlier, and perhaps even more damagingly.

One major piece of unfinished business when Cromwell's life was ebbing was the nomination of his successor, and it caused much anxiety, both as to whom he would name (or had named?), and as to whether he would do it at all. The evidence regarding his nomination of his elder son is confused and in places contradictory, and controversy over its interpretation has been revived in our own time.[18] As late as 30 August he had not confided his wishes to anyone. Earlier in the month he told Thurloe that there was a sealed letter, addressed to him, on his study table in Whitehall, in which he had named his successor soon after the Petition and Advice empowered him to do so. The letter could not be found, however, and he never told Thurloe whose name it contained. After the Restoration, the story spread in varying guises that the lost letter had nominated Fleetwood, and some modern scholars have credited it. It is conceivable that in the early years of the Protectorate Cromwell did contemplate Fleetwood as his favoured successor, for he had a strong affection and regard for his son-in-law. But by 1657 Fleetwood had so fully exposed his defects of leadership and lack of political judgement in Ireland that it is simply not credible that Cromwell was still considering him as the next Protector. Whatever happened to that letter in his Whitehall study, it can surely have named no one but Richard, and the latter's subsequent appointment to the privy council and to the command of a cavalry regiment point the same way. What evidently happened during his last days was that on 30 August he discussed the succession with four or five of his council, declaring his choice of Richard, though as Thurloe reported to Henry 'his illness disenabled him to conclude it fully'. During the next two days he showed signs of recovering, and perhaps even now he felt that his hold on the helm would remain firmer

---

[18] I have discussed the evidence and conflicting interpretations of it in 'Milton and Cromwell', in M. Lieb and J. T. Shawcross (eds.), *Achievements of the Left Hand* (Amherst, Mass., 1974), pp. 200–8.

if he did not publish his intentions further. On 2 September, however, he was clearly dying, and when asked in the presence of several councillors whether he still wished Richard to succeed him he gave his assent—according to his physician by a nod of the head. There can be no reasonable doubt that Richard really was his choice, and the council accepted it unanimously. It was doubtless a difficult decision, but who else could he have chosen? Henry had far more political talent than Richard, but there were question marks over his temperament, and in those days it would have been very difficult to advance a younger brother above an elder. None of Cromwell's civilian councillors had the stature for the job, or could have managed the army, while in the army itself Lambert had put himself in the wilderness and Desborough was even more unthinkable than Fleetwood.

Here seems to be a good point at which to take stock of the regime that Oliver bequeathed to his son. It has often been called a military dictatorship, and it may be remembered that when the question arose earlier of whether it deserved the description an answer was deferred until an account had been given of its whole course. The reason for postponing it was that the Protectorate was in constant transition, and how far it constituted a dictatorship at any one time is partly a question of degree. At a superficial level it was always a military dictatorship in that Cromwell was an active commander-in-chief as well as head of state, but that is only a small part of the truth. In another sense he was never a dictator, because his powers were always limited by a written constitution, though the Instrument of Government was an imperfect one, and devised by a small group of army officers. With only slight over-simplification it can be said that Cromwell's aim was to shed the military origins of his government and to broaden its basis, both in its constitutional checks and balances and in its acceptance by as much as possible of the political nation. This process was temporarily interrupted during the regime of the major-generals, when it lurched back somewhat towards military rule, though not to the extent that its enemies claimed. From the autumn of 1656 the Protectorate resumed its progress towards civilian dominance and constitutional propriety, in which the promulgation of a new frame of government devised by a parliament marked a major step. When Cromwell died the Petition and Advice had yet to be put to the test of a truly free parliament, but there were strong indications that it would pass it.

Our present-day preoccupation with dictatorship is very much a product of twentieth-century experience, and some of the things we associate with it are of doubtful relevance to an age which knew nothing of mass media or concentration camps or professional state police, to mention only three phenomena. But perhaps we need not be too nervous of falling into anachronism, for Cromwell's contemporaries had very clear ideas about what constituted tyranny and how it differed from the rule of law, and their criteria were not so very different from ours. To apply some common touchstones, there were remarkably few political prisoners, and no one suffered death for his political convictions unless he was taken in arms or actively conspired to overthrow the state or assassinate the Protector. Unless they were active plotters, Britons did not have to fear the knock on the door in the early hours of the morning. Rebellion, when it was attempted, was punished more leniently than it had been under the Tudors and would be again in 1685. Judicial torture to extract confessions, which had last been authorized by Charles I's own warrant in 1640,[19] passed out of use and was never again officially authorized in England. Throughout the Protectorate both civil and criminal jurisdiction remained in the hands of the ancient common law, whose procedures were marginally—many would have said insufficiently—reformed. The central courts at Westminster were staffed by judges with a healthy sense of independence towards executive government, and their control of justice at the highest level was only twice breached during the Protectorate by the erection of High Courts of Justice to try very specific conspiracies against the state or the Protector's life.

Enough has probably been said already about liberty of conscience in the sphere of religion, whose breadth under the Protectorate contrasts starkly with the straitjacket imposed by the post-Restoration Act of Uniformity. The great limitation was the continuance of the Long Parliament's formal ban on the Book of Common Prayer, but the widespread de facto tolerance of Anglican forms of worship would doubtless have increased as their link with active political royalism diminished in the course of time—had the Protectorate lasted longer. On the debit side the press was somewhat more closely controlled than it had been before Penruddock's Rising, and only the two official weekly newspapers were allowed to appear. But censorship was not strict—far less so than it was to be under the Licensing Act of 1662. Pamphlets continued to pour fairly freely from the presses, many of them unlicensed. There was only one year (1658) in which the bookseller George Thomason, who tried to buy every tract and news-sheet that appeared, collected fewer than 300 new titles, and even then his count came to 282.

Chequered though Oliver's relations with his parliaments had been, Richard inherited a regime in which parliament had an assured place, and larger powers than any predecessor had enjoyed prior to 1641. Parliaments met more frequently in the 1650s than in the 1680s, and they were elected by more rationally apportioned constituencies, on the basis of a more uniform franchise, than at any time until far into the nineteenth century. Unfortunately, Richard's council was to jettison this very real achievement in parliamentary reform. The council itself was given powers by the Petition and

---

[19] Above, p. 140. On the use of judicial torture in England and its ending see John L. Langbein, *Torture and the Law of Proof* (Chicago, 1977), esp. pp. 134–5.

Advice that constituted a genuine check upon any tendency to dictatorship, the more so because on contentious issues it rarely spoke with one voice. On major decisions of policy Cromwell had his way, but recent research has shown how much work was necessarily delegated to the council, and the significant number of occasions on which its collective decision or advice ran counter to his own inclinations. Its real weakness lay not in subservience, nor in its internal divisions (though these could be serious), but in its lack of first-rate talent. The men of real ability tended to be rather young, like Howard and Wolseley, or very old, like Francis Rous, and they were greatly outnumbered by mediocrities. Collectively they were to prove unequal to the heavy responsibilities that Oliver's death and Richard's limitations were to lay upon them.

It is clear that the institutions and powers defined by the Petition and Advice were not those of a dictatorship, but it needs to be considered whether the permeation of both central and local government by army officers made it one. Constitutional checks and balances do not necessarily tell the whole story. At the highest level senior officers always played a powerful role in the council, though there was never a time when they were not outnumbered by civilians. A simple head count, however, can be misleading, since the civilians Walter Strickland and Sir Gilbert Pickering often supported the military faction, while Colonel Montagu, later General at Sea, tended to oppose it, and Colonel Philip Jones was essentially an administrator. The army party reached its peaks of influence when Cromwell accepted the Instrument of Government and during the rule of the major-generals, but he signalled his disillusion with it in the speech that he made to the hundred officers in February 1657. The notion that he refused the crown because he feared the army's reaction dies hard, but it is surely implausible. In the remodelling of the privy council under the Petition and Advice, the exclusion of Lambert and the admission of Thurloe and Richard Cromwell shifted the balance decisively against the military faction, but the process was already far advanced. Cromwell had to respect the susceptibilities of his officer corps, since there was still a vein of republican sentiment running through its middle and junior ranks, but he knew how to manage it. The trouble that the military grandees made for Richard in the spring of 1659 does not testify to a continuing ascendancy, but to the reaction of mediocre men smarting under a sense of defeat.

In the seventeenth century so much government was local government, and so much justice was locally administered by unpaid magistrates, that any appraisal of the quality of Cromwellian rule must take great account of the commission of the peace. How freely did it function, and how representative was it of local interests? Something has already been said of the military presence within it.[20] The county committees, which had encroached heavily on

----

[20] Above, pp. 582–3.

the JPs' authority during the war years, were a thing of the past in the 1650s, and the county magistracy suffered only a partial and quite brief eclipse under the major-generals. For most of the time thereafter, out of at least 2,500 JPs in England fewer than 90 were serving officers, and nearly half of these held purely local commands, as governors of towns, castles, and other strong points. A significant minority of officer-JPs were of the social status to warrant inclusion by any criteria, and they would have been shocked by the suggestion that the profession of arms should disbar them from the commission.

As for the extent to which the bench represented the traditional elite of the county communities, active royalists who had suffered sequestration or who still openly upheld the king's cause were of course excluded, and in most counties that caused a certain drop in the social level of the bench. But it was Cromwell's policy from the time he first became Protector to win the support of the moderate gentry and broaden the social basis on which his government rested. Not only did the JPs recover most of their old authority, but much of the old social life of the country houses revived, often crossing the divide that the Civil Wars had created. The crackdown on royalist suspects in 1655, together with the major-generals and the decimation tax, reversed this trend for a time, but from about the end of 1656 the process of reconciliation within the gentry class was resumed at a greater pace. The old families returned to the commission of the peace in larger numbers now, especially as active royalists died out and were succeeded by sons who had been too young to take part in the wars. Horse races, hunting, country-house parties, and intermarriages all helped to push the old divisions further into the past. The process was of course incomplete, and it did not occur everywhere. In some counties the government continued to rely on powerful local bosses, and Kent was ruled by a narrow clique of rigid puritans, mostly relative newcomers to gentry status. But Kent's social structure was atypical, and besides having been the seedbed of rebellion in 1648 it was the county through which royalist agents most frequently passed to and from the exiled court.[21]

The decimation is a rare example of an arbitrary tax under the Protectorate, for most of its revenue was derived from sources devised by parliament long before Cromwell became head of state. Taxation was fairly heavy, but it was not unduly inequitable in its incidence. Except for those who had suffered sequestration as royalists, people were secure in the enjoyment of their property, and had ready access to the courts if they had need to defend it. There were of course irksome aspects of Cromwellian rule, such as the notorious ban on the public celebration of Christmas, but this too predated his access to power, and the prohibition was widely ignored or defied. As for the folk memory of a civil populace groaning under the oppression of

---

[21] David Underdown, 'Settlement in the counties 1653–1658', in Aylmer (ed.), *Interregnum*.

red-coated soldiers, the presence of about 13,500 well-disciplined officers and men on English soil, amid a population of at least 5,000,000, was small by the contemporary standards of continental Europe, and well below what James II would have on foot in the year of Sedgemoor.

There was still a proportionately larger military presence in Scotland, but nothing approaching a dictatorship, and little to give Richard cause for concern. The Scots were enjoying a reasonable share in the government of their own country, and their much valued judicial system was now secure. There was a positive improvement in the quality and accessibility of the justice that the public courts had to offer and, although strict Presbyterians deplored the degree of religious toleration that prevailed, its benefit to the greater part of the nation seems incontestable. The indications are that the majority of Scots had come to value the union with England, and would be loath to see it go. The majority of the Irish were nothing like as fortunate, and no conceivable regime in England was likely to reverse the fate that had befallen them. But government in Ireland was stable, and much more representative of the older protestant community than it had been before Henry Cromwell came to the country. There was every prospect of his relative success continuing, so long as his brother was not overthrown in England.

It has often been too easily assumed that only Oliver's strong hand had held the union and the Protectorate together, and that the collapse of both was only a matter of time. His untimely death certainly bequeathed a precarious situation, but it was an extraordinarily open one. There was always a possibility, of course, that things would fall apart, but it was not a foregone conclusion, and the manner in which they did so is full of interest. The tendency of old textbooks to race through the twenty months between Cromwell's death and Charles II's return as a period of predictable anarchy with an inevitable outcome committed a serious distortion. Speculating again on what might have happened if Oliver had lived a few years longer, with his faculties undiminished and a competent successor, the net result might have been not unlike what the so-called Revolution Settlement of 1689 achieved: a constitution such as Europe came to envy, embodying as it did a guarantee of frequent parliaments and the rule of law, and a broad toleration for protestants of all denominations. Whether or not it would have been a constitutional *monarchy* is of secondary importance. Oliver's successor, or the successor of his successor, might well have been persuaded in time to take the crown, and who is to say whether a Cromwellian dynasty could not have been as acceptable as a Hanoverian one? As things were, Oliver's passing removed from English government something that it was to lack for the next thirty years: a touch of the heroic.

# PART V: FURTHER READING

S. R. Gardiner died when his great *History of the Commonwealth and Protectorate* had reached the year 1656, at which point the thread is taken up by his pupil C. H. Firth in *The Last Years of the Protectorate* (2 vols., 1909), which is perhaps even finer in its grasp and scholarship. There are valuable essays on the period in G. E. Aylmer (ed.), *The Interregnum* (Problems in Focus series, 1972), especially by Ivan Roots on Cromwell's ordinances, Claire Cross on the church, and David Underdown on settlement in the counties. Books on the central figure of Cromwell are legion; particularly recommendable are C. H. Firth, *Oliver Cromwell and the Rule of the Puritans in England* (1900), Christopher Hill, *God's Englishman* (1970: controversial but stimulating), Barry Coward, *Oliver Cromwell* (1991), Peter Gaunt, *Oliver Cromwell* (1997), J. C. Davis, *Oliver Cromwell* (2001), and the collections of essays edited by John Morrill in *Oliver Cromwell and the English Revolution* (1990) and by Peter Gaunt in *Cromwell 400* (Cromwell Association, 1999). The latter contains a good up-to-date select bibliography. Antonia Fraser, *Cromwell, Our Chief of Men* (1973) is not invariably reliable but is on the whole a good popular biography. Roy Sherwood is informative about the Protector's whole entourage in *The Court of Oliver Cromwell* (Cambridge, 1989), but is sometimes more controversial in *Oliver Cromwell: King in All but Name* (1997). Cromwell's own major utterances are probably more accessible to most readers in Ivan Roots (ed.), *Speeches of Oliver Cromwell* (1989) than in W. C. Abbott's massive edition, which is convenient for its completeness but mediocre in its commentary. Among other interesting essays in Ivan Roots (ed.), *Cromwell: A Profile* (1973) is H. R. Trevor-Roper's much discussed article on 'Oliver Cromwell and his parliaments'. Blair Worden's long promised study of Cromwell's life and work is still eagerly awaited at the time of writing; meanwhile, appetite is whetted by his *Roundhead Reputations: The English Civil Wars and the Passions of Posterity* (2001), which is specially illuminating on Cromwell's posthumous reputation. Parliamentary diaries for all three Protectorate parliaments are printed in J. T. Rutt (ed.), *The Diary of Thomas Burton* (4 vols., 1828). Roots has written good short accounts of the major-generals in his *The Great Rebellion* and in R. H. Parry (ed.), *The English Civil War and After* (1970), but the definitive work on them is now Christopher Durston, *Cromwell's Major-Generals: Godly Government during the English Revolution* (Manchester, 2001).

As in earlier periods, the versatile Bernard Capp remains the prime authority on *The Fifth Monarchy Men* (1972) and on *Cromwell's Navy* (1989). On foreign policy, Firth's full coverage in *Last Years* (above) may be supplemented by Steven C. A. Pincus, *Protestantism and Patriotism* (Cambridge, 1996), Timothy Venning, *Cromwellian Foreign Policy* (1995), and Michael Roberts's important article on 'Cromwell and the Baltic', reprinted in his *Essays in Swedish History* (1953). On the political thought of the period I have attempted a brief survey in Chapter 2 of *The Age of Milton*, ed. C. A. Patrides and R. B. Waddington (Manchester and Totowa, NJ,

1980), but for more searching treatments see Blair Worden's chapters in David Wootton (ed.), *Republicanism, Liberty and Commercial Society* (Stanford, Calif., 1994), and J. G. A. Pocock's introduction to his edition of *The Political Works of James Haprington* (Cambridge, 1977). There is quite a large literature on Cromwell's readmission of the Jews. Cecil Roth, *A History of the Jews in England* (Oxford, 1941) is a standard work; it is valuably supplemented by David S. Katz, *Philo-Semitism and the Readmission of the Jews to England* (Los Angeles and Oxford, 1982).

For Scotland, few readers will need to go beyond Frances D. Dow's excellent and comprehensive *Cromwellian Scotland 1651–1660* (Edinburgh, 1979), but three volumes published by the Scottish Historical Society furnish rich compendia of source material with authoritative commentaries, two edited by C. H. Firth, *Scotland and the Commonwealth* (1895) and *Scotland under the Protectorate* (1899), and the third by C. S. Terry, *The Cromwellian Union* (1902). Ireland is equally well served by T. C. Barnard, *Cromwellian Ireland: English Government and Reform in Ireland 1649–1660* (Oxford, 2nd ed. 2000: with a valuable survey of the literature on the subject published since 1975), while on a smaller scale Patrick J. Corish, 'The Cromwellian Regime, 1650–1660', in *A New History of Ireland*, III (Oxford, 1976) is highly recommended. On the land settlement see Karl S. Bottigheimer, *English Money and Irish Land* (Oxford, 1971).

# PART VI

## The Collapse of the
## Good Old Cause
## 1658–1660

# ✠ TWENTY-FIVE ✠

# The Overthrow of the Protectorate

RICHARD CROMWELL's brief tenure of the Protector's office began auspiciously. The privy council accepted without question that Oliver had nominated him to it, and Fleetwood and the senior army officers in and around London were as prompt to recognize his title. The Lord Mayor and aldermen of London were enthusiastically co-operative, and the proclamation of the new Protector, performed with due pomp, was greeted with warm applause at Whitehall, Westminster, Temple Bar, Cheapside, and the Royal Exchange. In most provincial towns too the proclamation was celebrated with bell-ringing, bonfires, parades, and cannon-fire. Only in royalist Oxford do we hear of students pelting the sheriff and his attendant troops with the tops of carrots and turnips, but that tells us more about the agelessness of student protest (probably directed there mainly against the military) than about the response of the public as a whole. Addresses of loyalty and congratulation poured in during the next three months from at least twenty-eight counties, twenty-four towns (besides London), and half-a-dozen groups of ministers covering a wide religious spectrum, as well as from the fleet and sundry garrisons and other outlying military units. There were the predictable hostile rumblings from a few Fifth Monarchists and other seekers after a rule of the saints, but they found no response outside their own diminished ranks. The exiled royalists, who had hoped that Oliver's death would herald a resurgence of the king's supporters in England, were deeply disappointed. Richard Baxter testifies that many who had regarded Oliver as a 'traitorous hypocrite' were prepared to give allegiance to his son, since he had had no hand in the war, had never pursued his own advancement, and was 'now seeking to own the sober party'.[1]

Richard himself was easy to like, for he was not at all the clownish 'Tumble-down Dick' of royalist lampoons. He lived on the friendliest terms with the Hampshire squirearchy, regardless of whether his neighbours' background was royalist or parliamentarian. His personal morality seems to have been above suspicion, yet he had none of the proselytizing zeal for a 'reformation of manners' that had grated so in recent years. His genuine affability struck

---

[1] *Reliquiae Baxterianae*, p. 100, quoted in Godfrey Davies, *The Restoration of Charles II* (San Marino, Calif., 1955), pp. 15–16.

everybody, and on public occasions he conducted himself with grace and dignity. He could deliver quite an effective speech, so long as someone told him what to say, and he instinctively found the right words with which to thank the presenters of loyal addresses and send them away glowing. But the wooden phrasing and confined expression of his surviving letters confirm that his was hardly a towering intellect, and there is no suggestion that he had minded being kept out of any position of political or military influence until he was thirty-two and his father's powers were obviously declining. He had no instinctive political flair, and he lacked the sheer zest for the exercise of authority that his office demanded.

With all his limitations, however, he might have managed if he had been guided by a competent and reasonably united council, and if the army's officer corps had been unequivocally loyal to the government that employed it. If more of his councillors had been of the calibre of Montagu, Thurloe, and Wolseley, and if the army had taken its cue from Monck rather than Fleetwood and Desborough, the story might conceivably have been different. But enough has probably been said of the mediocrity and factionalism of most of the council, and Richard suffered fatally from his lack of standing among the army officers, who were in the habit of referring to him as 'the young gentleman'. Not unreasonably, he looked for advice to friends and well-wishers outside the council, including Broghill, Fauconberg (his brother-in-law), St John, Pierrepont, and Whitelocke, but this aroused the resentment of Fleetwood, Desborough, and other councillors of their faction. He wanted to bring Broghill, Fauconberg, and his brother Henry into the council, but since (by the Petition and Advice) the appointment of new councillors required the collective assent of the existing ones there was never a chance. It is interesting to note how many of the men who could offer him the wisest counsel and the most loyal service either had a royalist background or had lost their seats in Pride's Purge. Monck in particular sent him an admirable letter of advice from Scotland soon after his accession, urging him to cultivate the men of power and interest in the localities, to admit more of them to the Other House, along with the more prudent of the old peers, to encourage moderate Presbyterian and Independent divines to form a common front against the blasphemies of the extremer sects, to amalgamate regiments in order to rid the army of 'insolent spirits' and reduce its cost, and in all this to consult Whitelocke, St John, Broghill, Pierrepont, and Sir Richard Onslow.[2] But sound though the advice was, there was little chance of Richard being able to follow it, even if he had the will.

Fleetwood, as Lieutenant-General and as his brother-in-law, bore a special responsibility for maintaining Richard's good relations with the army, and he

---

[2] *Thurloe State Papers*, VII, 387–8.

played an ambivalent role. On 21 September he appeared at the head of over two hundred officers to present Richard with an address of loyalty in the name of the armies in England, Scotland, and Ireland, but its profession of allegiance to the Petition and Advice was qualified by a reminder that Oliver had 'in his armies . . . reckoned the choicest saints his chiefest worthies', and by an exhortation to 'carry on that good old cause and interest of God and His people'. That catch-phrase, the Good Old Cause, would soon be carrying more and more subversive overtones. The army address also strayed into political territory by asking that vacancies in the privy council should be 'filled up with men of known godliness' and 'that a work of reformation, tending to good life and manners, may be vigorously carried on by the hands of good magistrates'.[3] A more serious political challenge appeared early in October in the form of a petition from a large gathering of more junior officers, asking that Fleetwood should be made commander-in-chief, with power to commission all officers below field rank, and that no officer should be dismissed or cashiered unless he was convicted by a court-martial. To give a generalissimo so much independence of the head of state, and worse still to make *all* officers potentially immune from dismissal if their activities should threaten the state, was intolerable. A commander with more sense and integrity than Fleetwood would have let the petition go no further, but all he did was to pass it on to Richard. 'The young gentleman' decided to address the assembled officers in person on 18 October, and armed with a draft prepared by Thurloe he temporarily quieted them with an effective speech. He had commissioned Fleetwood as Lieutenant-General of all the land forces, he said, so making him commander-in-chief under himself, and would always consult him when granting commissions, and he promised that no officer would be arbitrarily punished or dismissed.

Monck's diligence ensured that there would be no such stirrings in the forces in Scotland, where the change of Protector brought little alteration until the government in England was undermined. Richard was proclaimed with due ceremony in Edinburgh and elsewhere, and the only hitch in the smooth running of the civil administration arose through the English government's failure to fill two vacancies on the Scottish judges' bench. Monck had already weeded out the disaffected elements in his forces, but to make sure he placed a ban on all meetings of officers and soldiers that might tend 'to interpose in public affairs'.[4] In Ireland too the Dublin government took Richard's accession in its stride, and in October Henry was rewarded for his patient work with promotion to the office of Lord Lieutenant, which had long been his due. Without his father's support he was more vulnerable to the coolness,

[3] *Parliamentary or Constitutional History of England* (24 vols., 1751–66), XXI, 233–4; well discussed in Davies, *Restoration of Charles II*, pp. 8–10.
[4] Dow, *Cromwellian Scotland*, p. 234.

to say the least, of the military faction in the English council, headed by his old adversary Fleetwood, but the Irish situation, like the Scottish, was to remain stable until the stability of the Protectorate itself was seriously undermined by disruptions in England.

The major political event that was to involve all three countries early in 1659 was the calling of a parliament. Since the intention of Oliver and his council to summon one in the autumn of 1658 had been abandoned only because of his mortal illness, and since the financial plight that Richard inherited clearly needed a parliament to alleviate it, there is a hint of drifting government in the fact that three months passed after his accession before the decision to call one was formally taken, and nearly five before it actually met. Richard's position stood to be greatly strengthened by a freely elected parliament's recognition of his title and confirmation of the constitution under which it was elected, and the welcome with which most of the country had greeted his peaceful accession gave a fair prospect that both such votes could be secured. Thurloe feared a concerted attack on the Petition and Advice by the commonwealthsmen, but the main reason why the council was so divided on whether to hold an election, and postponed its decision so long, must surely have been that the military faction feared opposition to its current ascendancy and a check to the army's bid to recover the power that had been slipping from it since 1656. In the council the rift between the civilian and military parties was widening, and there were rumours early in November of an intention to purge it of all but the army men and their allies. At a council meeting in December, Desborough absurdly accused Montagu of conspiring with Fauconberg to have Fleetwood and himself seized and imprisoned in Windsor Castle. Amid these broils, Oliver's funeral was belatedly solemnized on 23 November, though he had been buried earlier. What the council had planned as a great public pageant ended in near-fiasco, because the funeral procession set off so late that Westminster Abbey was dark by the time it arrived there, and nobody had thought to provide candles. So Oliver's effigy was abandoned after a brief flourish of trumpets, without prayers or funeral oration or any further ceremony.

Meanwhile the effects of Richard's conciliatory speech to the army officers was proving short-lived. There were far too many officers in London who should have been with their regiments elsewhere, and during November a dangerous new demand was heard at their Friday meetings at St James's, namely that the officers cashiered by Oliver should be reinstated. These included not only republicans like Okey and Packer and Fifth Monarchists like Harrison and Overton but of course Lambert, and Fauconberg for one was positive that Lambert was covertly fanning the officers' discontents.[5]

[5] *Thurloe State Papers*, VII, 528, 612, discussed by Davies in *Restoration of Charles II*, p. 38 n. 35.

These rose higher when Richard rather tactlessly gave a regiment to Montagu, who was still General at Sea, and there was a new move to restrict the Protector's power to grant commissions. As soon as the summoning of parliament was announced the leading republican politicians stepped up their contacts with the disaffected officers, and it was the alliance between the two groups that gave Richard and his loyal councillors most to fear.

For the elections, the government went back to the traditional pre-war franchise and constituencies. Its opponents alleged that it did so in order to manipulate the returns more easily and pack the House, but since Oliver and his council had reportedly taken the same decision when they were contemplating holding elections in the autumn of 1658, this is unlikely to have been the motive. The Petition and Advice had laid down that in the calling of parliaments 'the laws and statutes be observed' in all particulars except for the disqualification of royalists and catholics, and since it said nothing specific about the franchise and the apportionment of seats, very possibly through sheer oversight, the council probably felt that to follow the provisions of the superseded Instrument of Government would have laid the forthcoming parliament's legality open to question. At any rate there was great eagerness to get elected, and the republicans in particular strove to secure as many seats as they could get. They concerted their electioneering tactics in frequent meetings at Sir Henry Vane's London house. At the formal opening of parliament on 27 January 1659 they made their hostile intentions clear. The ceremony was performed with a decent pomp, similar to that with which Oliver had inaugurated his last parliament, and Richard launched it with a speech that struck many of the notes that his father had sounded: faith in the two Houses' advice and appeals for the pay of his patient army, for the prosecution of the war with Spain, for the care of the people of God, for the reformation of manners at home, and for the protestant cause abroad. No doubt he was well coached by Thurloe. He left it to Lord Keeper Fiennes to give a fuller account of the state of foreign relations, but Fiennes roamed far beyond his brief and talked far too long.

Many MPs, however, heard neither him nor Richard, who in the traditional manner delivered their speeches in the Lords' chamber. About 150 members ignored Black Rod's summons and sat tight in the Commons, either because they did not recognize the Other House or because they challenged Richard's own title (in which case they rejected both). It is impossible to give a remotely accurate breakdown of parties in Richard's parliament, partly because the fundamental division between supporters and opponents of his Protectorate overlays some quite wide differences of outlook within both sides, and partly because so many members' views are unknown. More than half had never sat before, and many were unusually young. The republican veterans of the Rump strove hard and none too scrupulously to win these newcomers over to their own views about the paramount authority of the people's representatives, but though they had some success in obstructing measures that the government wanted and needed, they quite failed to command an overall majority.

The council played into their hands by bringing before parliament a bill to recognize Richard as Protector and the Petition and Advice as the constitution under which he and the two Houses governed. Thurloe introduced it on 1 February, but it must have emanated from a conciliar decision. It was an open invitation to question both Richard's authority and that of the Petition and Advice, and the anti-Protectorists managed to hold off a second reading for a full six days. When it was at last read again, Haselrig launched the debate with a speech that lasted two or three hours and surveyed the course of English history over the past thousand years, from the heptarchy onward. He and Scot were the main leaders in a campaign of blatant filibustering, which Richard's supporters failed signally to counter. Not until 19 February did the Commons finally vote to recognize Richard as Lord Protector, but only subject to additional clauses (yet to be formulated) that would further limit his powers and secure both parliament's authority and the people's liberties. Thereafter the republicans switched their main attack to the Other House, which they portrayed as so full of swordsmen and government officials as to constitute a mere extension of the Protector's authority, at the expense of that of the people's representatives. Haselrig's language became extravagant, even by his standards. 'If this should pass', he said, 'we shall next vote canvas breeches and wooden shoes for the free people of England.'[6] Eventually, but not until 28 March, the Commons did vote to transact with the Other House as a house of parliament, but with the proviso that it should not exclude the old peers who had been faithful to the parliamentary cause. Their admission had long been discussed, and this proviso was not a republican victory, but for Haselrig and his cohorts this spinning out of debate was part of an anti-Protectorate campaign that was now shaping mainly outside parliament. For however well versed they were in delaying tactics, they could make little headway against the majority of politically unattached and conservatively inclined members who appreciated the Protectorate's pursuit of peaceful settlement at home and endorsed its policies abroad. Their procedural wrangles and general obstructionism increasingly irritated the House.

They found more fertile ground outside it, in the middling and junior ranks of the army officers and among the millenarian and other radical sectaries. They were helped by the tactless hostility that the moderate majority in the Commons often displayed towards the army and the sects. William Prynne, writing in May 1659, correctly attributed Richard's downfall to 'the

---

[6] *Diary of Richard Burton*, IV, 79.

confederated triumvirate of republicans, sectaries and soldiers'.[7] Things
began to go seriously wrong when the republicans and their supporters in the
army revived the petition, first framed just over a year earlier, which had led
Oliver to dissolve his last parliament rather than let it come under debate
there. This time it was actually presented, with a roll of signatures variously
estimated between 15,000 and 40,000, by three prominent London Baptists,
Samuel Moyer, William Kiffin, and Josiah Berners. Moyer, who had been a
conspicuous firebrand in Barebone's Parliament, subjected the Commons for
nearly an hour to 'a great deal of cant language', but whereas he had been a
consistent oppositionist Kiffin and Berners had hitherto sided with the Protectorate against its extremist attackers. Their appearance on this occasion
was a sign that Richard's cultivation of conservative support was arousing
unrest at the radical end of the spectrum. The petition itself was addressed as
before 'To the Parliament of the Commonwealth of England', as though the
Other House had no part in it, and called upon it to restore to its elected members 'the supreme power and trust, which the people (the original of all just
power) commit unto them'. It also demanded that no tender consciences
should be oppressed, and that no officers or soldiers should be cashiered
except by sentence of a court-martial. The republican MPs were clearly
expecting it, and among others not only Haselrig, Scot, Vane, and Neville
but Lambert too urged that it should receive a vote of thanks. But that motion
was lost by 202 votes to 110, and the petitioners were given a coldly non-
committal answer.[8]

Despite their support of his petition, the republicans were not yet openly
campaigning for the outright abolition of the Protectorate, though they
would change their tune when they had sufficiently undermined it. For the
present they recognized that it was quite widely popular and that they were in
a minority, so one after another they declared their willingness to accept it in
a modified form, so long as it was based not on the Petition and Advice but on
the free grant of parliament, under such limitations as parliament should
impose. In particular, the Protector must have no veto over the Commons'
enactments and no absolute control over the armed forces. On the latter point
they had much support within the army, where a new remonstrance was
being agitated while the mass petition already described was being canvassed.
Lambert was reported to be fomenting it, and among other things it demanded again that the army should have a commander-in-chief distinct from the
Protector. Fleetwood, Desborough, and the other officers of general rank
should have put a stop to it, but they showed no disposition to do so. For one

---

[7] W. Prynne, *The Republicans and Others' Spurious Good Old Cause Briefly and Truly Ana-
tomized* (13 May, 1659: British Library E983(6), p. 1.

[8] For fuller accounts of the petition and its reception, see Firth, *Last Years*, II, 30–4; Davies,
*Restoration of Charles II*, pp. 57–9; and *Complete Prose Works of John Milton*, VII, 20–1.

thing they had no inclination to alienate the mass of middle-ranking and junior officers, because they needed their support for their efforts to secure their own political ascendancy, and for another they shared their subordinates' resentment over Richard's habit of taking counsel from the army's opponents. It was no doubt on the latter's advice that Richard went in person to Wallingford House, Fleetwood's palatial residence at Stoke Newington where the senior officers in and about London habitually met. He told them he would part with the generalship and his life together, and shamed Fleetwood and Desborough into publicly repudiating the proposed remonstrance. Neither officer was yet engaging in open disloyalty to Richard, or conniving actively with the republican opposition in parliament, but that would come quite soon.

Two incidents throw light on the rise of feeling against Richard within the army, especially among its radical puritans. One arose from a violent public quarrel in Westminster Hall between Colonel Ashfield, a leading army commonwealthsman (and a Baptist) whose regiment was in Scotland, and Major-General Whalley, a conspicuously loyal supporter of the Protectorate. Ashfield reportedly dared Whalley to strike him, whereupon Whalley, as his superior officer, reported him to the Protector as commander-in-chief. Richard ordered Ashfield to apologize to Whalley on pain of being court-martialled, but a deputation from the gathered churches came and pleaded with him not to put their brother on trial. Richard forbore, but it was a pity he did not at least follow Monck's excellent advice to send Ashfield back to Scotland. The man's impunity must have seemed a sign of weakness. The other episode began when a godly cornet in the cavalry regiment of Colonel Ingoldsby, another of Richard's most loyal officers, brought charges against his major of favouring moral delinquents and browbeating honest men in the regiment. The case came before Richard, who furiously accused the cornet of trying to arraign his major because the latter was one of his own supporters. 'You talk of preaching and praying men, they are the men that go about to undermine me', he reportedly said, and clapping his hand on Ingoldsby's shoulder, added 'Go thy way, Dick Ingoldsby, thou canst neither preach nor pray, but I will believe thee before I believe twenty of them'.[9]

There was something of a lull on the political front between mid-February and the end of March. The republicans, while ostensibly courting the army, went on obstructing the financial measures that were needed to meet the soldiers' arrears of pay, but they rarely won a vote. They were not the government's only opponents, for a small number of crypto-royalists had found seats—probably fewer than a score—and they were encouraged by the exiled

---

[9] *A Second Narrative of the Late Parliament* (1658), pp. 30–1, fully quoted in *Memoirs of Edmund Ludlow*, II, 62–3 n. 2. Ludlow gives his own account of the episode and of the Ashfield affair.

court to side with the republicans. They usually did so, though not invariably. The republicans' best chances still lay in stirring trouble outside parliament, and from February onward they made considerable use of the presses. In the course of 1659 the bookseller George Thomason collected 652 separate pamphlets, compared with 282 in 1658. The theme of tract after tract was 'the Good Old Cause'—the cause for which the Civil Wars had been fought and won, but whose purity had since been lost through the selfish ambitions of sectional interests. These pamphleteers were very coy about just what the good old cause consisted in, because they were courting quite a range of Richard's political opponents, whose particular interests were not identical. Until his regime was totally on the rocks they refrained from calling openly for its overthrow, and despite their strong republican overtones they were generally vague as to what specific form of government they favoured. They professed friendship towards the army as a whole, and they sought to engage the support of radical Independents and sectaries who leaned towards an ascendancy of the saints as well as that of commonwealthsmen whose republicanism was more secular. Their prevailing tone was emotional rather than rational; they invoked a generalized nostalgia for an imaginary time when all who fought against the king had been united in a selfless common cause, and lamented that self-regarding sectional interests had since dimmed its light. The same sort of appeal had been sounded by Sir Henry Vane in *A Healing Question* in 1656, coupled with the same evasiveness; the words 'the good old cause' appear in its postscript, and Vane was almost certainly one of the orchestrators of the 1659 campaign.

One of the first manifestations of that campaign came in *XXV Queries*, a tract that was widely circulated, and even distributed within the House of Commons, soon after Richard's parliament met. It asked:

Is there not an apparent necessity for those of the old parliament, the officers and soldiers of the army, and all others that pretend to be friends to the good old cause, to lay aside all personal animosities, . . . and to unite their forces together, to keep out the common enemy, and to promote those principles of public interest, and common right and freedom, which have been held forth from time to time in the declarations of the parliament and army?[10]

*The Good Old Cause Dressed in its Primitive Lustre*, published in mid-February, sighed that 'there was in those virgin days such a mutual, strict, and lovely harmony and agreement . . . between the parliament and the honest unbiassed people of the nation', and identified the 'first and virgin-cause' as having consisted in parliament's control over the armed forces and its freedom

---

[10] *XXV Queries* (1659), reprinted in *The Harleian Miscellany*, ed. T. Park (1808–13), IX, 424 f.

from a monarchical veto.[11] This sexual imagery was not uncommon; for instance *A Call to the Officers of the Army* urged them to 'do our first works, and remember the loves of our virginity', for the cause that had once shone with the freshness of a bride was now soiled and faded, 'misshapen with a strange dress, we had almost said with the attire of an harlot'.[12] Early in March a longer piece entitled *The Cause of God and of These Nations Sought Out and Lifted up into Sight* was more overtly republican. The cause had reached its zenith (it affirmed) in the year of Worcester, but since then public interest had yielded to private, 'the old spirit of the gentry brought in play again', and the profane pomp and vanity of the court revived. Triers were keeping the true spirit of God from the pulpits, and the army was purged to serve the usurpers. All was running back into the old channels of King, Lords, and Commons, and the root cause was the present powers' enmity to 'the growing light of the people of God'. The true good old cause, the cause of God, lay not only in restoring a commonwealth, or even in civil and religious liberty, but in a spiritual awakening that would deliver the whole creation from the bondage of corruption into the liberty of the people of God. It is significant that this anonymous author's heroes were Ludlow, Okey, and Overton, but above all Vane.

Robert Overton was very much in the news. He had been held a prisoner since 1654, but on a petition from his sister the Commons had sent for him from Jersey. He was warned to enter London quietly, but his fellow, commonwealthsmen and millenarians stage-managed a hero's welcome for him. At Brentford 1,500 supporters turned out to greet him, and 400 or 500 horsemen carrying laurel branches escorted to Westminster—not to Lambeth, whither he had been directed—the coach in which he sat crowned with laurels and bowing to the acclaim of the crowds. When the Commons heard his case a few days later, Thurloe and other government speakers tried in vain to justify his imprisonment, and he was triumphantly released.

The literature of the good old cause, as one would expect, had a lot to say about liberty for tender consciences, but it was a matter on which the parliamentary republicans did not all speak with one voice. Early in Richard's Protectorate a conference of about 200 representatives of 120 Independent (i.e. Congregational) churches had met at the Savoy and deputed six ministers including Owen, Nye, and Thomas Goodwin to draw up a confession of faith. It was an ecumenical document, minimizing the differences between Independents and Presbyterians at home and seeking the fullest concord with the churches' brethren in New England. Published in October 1658, it was followed by local initiatives towards an accommodation between Independents

[11]  The tract was by R. Fitz-Brian, and has never been reprinted; the press-mark of the British Library copy is E968(6).

[12]  By 'S.R. H.W. R.P.': British Library E968(8).

and Presbyterians, though without prejudice to peaceable sectaries. It urged the churches to give all their support to Richard and his government, and in its preface John Owen thanked God for a regime that 'vouchsafed a forbearance and mutual indulgence unto saints of all persuasions that . . . hold fast the necessary foundations of faith and holiness'.[13] Its definition of doctrine was considerably less restrictive than the Westminster Confession of a decade earlier, and in particular it declared that the civil magistrate had no authority to dictate what people believed, beyond punishing the publication of gross blasphemies and errors that could imperil their souls. Even this, however, was more than many would allow—and not only extreme sectaries but the poet Milton, who published *A Treatise of Civil Power in Ecclesiastical Causes* in February 1659. That power, in Milton's book, should be as near to nil as made no difference.

The prevailing attitude in Richard's parliament was less liberal than the Savoy Declaration, and one reason was that the gentry's animosity against the Quakers, as subverters of social order as well as religious truth, was at its height. The Commons held long debates early in April on a declaration ordering a day of national fasting and humiliation. It attributed the current dearth, the decay of trade and the high mortality among both men and cattle to God's wrath at the many blasphemies and damnable heresies that were abroad, and (most provocatively) at the failure of the civil magistrate to punish them. It specially deplored the 'crying up the light in the hearts of sinful men, as the rule and guide of all their actions'. This was a direct allusion to the Quakers' doctrine of the inner light, and an incitement to JPs to be more severe on them. In fact there were 140 Quakers in prison at the end of Richard's brief rule, not counting 21 who had died in gaol, compared with 115 at the beginning, no doubt because of the cessation of his father's frequent interventions to curb the gentry's intolerance. At much the same time the Commons were debating in grand committee the adoption of a 'public profession' of the nation's faith, and ordered that it should consist of the doctrinal articles of the Westminster Confession. According to a well-informed reporter no minister was to receive the public maintenance unless he subscribed it. As in Oliver's time, parliament wanted a more strictly defined national church and a narrower range of tolerance outside it, but whereas the old Protector had used his large powers to preserve a very wide liberty of conscience, the new one's notorious aversion to preaching and praying men strengthened the fear that toleration was under threat. When some London Quakers presented a petition early in April on behalf of their brethren in prison, member after member inveighed against them, and one moved that they should be whipped home as vagrants.

---

[13]  A. G. Matthews (ed.), *The Savoy Declaration of Faith and Order, 1658* (1959), p. 56.

Another source of concern in the middling ranks of the army and among the gathered churches lay in a crop of rumours from February onward that this parliament intended to revive the last one's attempt to make the Protector king. There was probably very little behind them, though a few conservative members spoke openly in the House of their preference for the old monarchical constitution. But such talk of kingship fostered a suspicion among the discontented army officers that 'this gentleman, who they would have made so much haste to dress and set on horseback, was but to warm the saddle for another whom they better loved and liked'.[14] The openly expressed hope of presbyterian and crypto-royalist MPs that the army would shortly be much reduced, if not disbanded, and give way to a territorial militia, encouraged a whisper to circulate among the junior officers 'That the Protector did intend to cast them out of their places, and put the army into the hands of the nobility and gentry of the nation, thereby to bring in the king, and destroy that liberty of the gospel they had so long contended for'.[15]

A little earlier, on 22 March, Thurloe had written to Henry Cromwell: 'It is a miracle of mercy that we are yet in peace, considering what the debates are, and what underhand working there is to disaffect the officers of the army: but for ought I can perceive, they remain pretty staunch, though they are in great want of pay.' A week later Fauconberg thought that the prospects were improving, but both men were over-optimistic. The senior officers who met at Wallingford House decided late in March to seek an *entente* with the parliamentary republicans, and through Colonel Kelsey they invited Ludlow, currently MP for Hindon and one of the inner ring of their policy-makers, to come and meet them there. Whether their primary motive was to take some of the sting out of the republicans' subversion of their own juniors, or to strengthen their own position vis-à-vis Richard's civilian advisers, it was certainly not loyalty to the Protector. They seem not to have realized that the republicans could hold a stronger hand than they did. Ludlow told them that an alliance must be based on their commitment to restoring a republic and going all the way with the commonwealthsmen in the army; to start with they should back Ashfield in his quarrel with Whalley. They jibbed at that, as well they might. Vane and Haselrig approved the line he had taken, but would not meet the officers themselves; all they would say was 'that when they saw it seasonable they would be ready to assist them in all things tending to the public service'.[16]

If, on a charitable appraisal, Fleetwood and his fellow-commanders acted more out of misjudgement than disloyalty in making overtures to Richard's

---

[14] *Clarke Papers*, III, 211.

[15] Sir Richard Baker (continued by E. Phillips), *Chronicle of the Kings of England* (1670), p. 659.

[16] *Memoirs of Edmund Ludlow*, II, 63–5.

republican enemies, it is harder to offer the same defence of their second injury to him within a week or so. They persuaded him to sanction the summoning of a General Council of Officers, including all of commissioned rank who were in and about London. These numbered about 500, and many if not most of them belonged to regiments stationed far from the capital. One might think that commanders worth their salt would have ordered a large part of them back to their units, but these ones persuaded Richard that they could not keep the army under control unless they gave them a hearing in a General Council. They would have been shocked if accused of deliberate treachery; they probably had in mind the precedent of 1647, when the army had united against the Long Parliament's threat to its very existence. But there was no Fairfax and no Cromwell now to keep the army's protest within bounds and its discipline intact, and no Ireton to help guide it towards responsible, constructive goals. Fleetwood and his fellow commanders had much lower aims, and they grossly overestimated their influence over their unruly juniors. They probably hoped to enlist republican support just far enough to make Richard give up his preferred counsellors and bring the army back to its political eminence of earlier years, but they soon found that they could not ride the tiger.

When the General Council met on 2 April, it agreed to submit a petition to parliament and appointed a committee to draft it. The commonwealthsmen were in the ascendant; the committee was dominated by their leaders, including Ashfield, Robert Lilburne, and Mason, and it omitted not only all Richard's personal supporters but even Fleetwood and Desborough. The resultant petition 'smelt of gunpowder and ball'[17] and deeply shocked the officers still loyal to the Protector, who managed to tone it down somewhat in the next General Council. It was naturally much concerned about the army's arrears of pay, but it lamented that 'the good old cause is very frequently and publicly derided' and that 'its implacable adversaries were showing themselves in the highest places'. Ominously, the officers collectively resolved 'to stand by and assist your highness and parliament, in the plucking the wicked out of their places, wheresoever they may be discovered, either amongst ourselves or any other places of trust'.[18]

When a delegation of officers presented the petition to Richard on the 6th he received them most cordially, greeting them as the old friends of his father and the faithful servants of the public interest. His words were well taken, and serious trouble might yet have been averted if the parliament had taken proper notice of the points that the petition legitimately raised, concerning the army's pay, the signs of resurgent royalism, the law suits brought against soldiers for acts committed under orders, and the apparent threats to freedom of

---

[17] [Arthur Annesley], *Englands Confusion* (1659), reprinted in *Somers Tracts*, VI, 518.
[18] Text in *Parliamentary or Constitutional History of England*, XXI, 340–5.

worship. But after the petition was read in the Commons on the 8th the House gave it no more consideration for the next ten days, and proceeded instead to give the army further provocation. It stalled on a move to make the farmers of the excise pay up their arrears, and showed no inclination to raise the monthly assessment above £50,000, its lowest level since the Civil Wars, despite the government's total debt having risen to about £2,000,000. It engaged in a sharp attack on Major-General Boteler for his activities when he had been major-general of four Midland counties in 1655–6—chiefly for his seizure of a certain delinquent's property. Boteler's plea that he had acted by the Protector's orders won him no sympathy; a very hostile House voted to strike him out of the commission of peace, and a motion to debar him from all employment might have passed if Thurloe had not firmly argued that he should at least be heard before being punished. If the Commons were intent on pursuing the case, Thurloe rightly said, their proper procedure was to hear witnesses, draw up articles of impeachment, and send them to the Other House. A committee was appointed to act accordingly, and the reaction at Wallingford House can be imagined. In the same interval the offensive declaration for a fast was approved and carried to the Other House on the 14th, and the Commons' bitter reaction to the Quaker petition followed two days later.

Events in both parliament and army were moving fast toward a crisis. Richard and his councillors, together with some senior officers, held tense consultations between 16 and 18 April. He still had some totally loyal friends in the army; indeed Howard, Goffe, Ingoldsby, and others, along with Fauconberg, even offered to seize the chief men at Wallingford House so that he could place himself at the head of his troops. Thurloe and others advised him against such a coup, and he wisely rejected it, but it seems that a dissolution of parliament was seriously discussed. It was indeed coming to be a question whether parliament's provocations or the General Council of the Army's febrile temper posed the greater threat to the Protectorate's survival.

The Commons precipitated the parliament's fate late in the afternoon of 18 April, when sitting behind locked doors they passed two resolutions that had no chance of being enforced. One was that there should be no further meetings of officers without the consent of the Protector and both Houses, the other that no officer should retain his command unless he pledged himself not to interrupt the free meetings of parliament. That same day Richard summoned all the officers about London to Whitehall, and before the Commons passed their fateful votes he ordered that the meetings of the General Council should cease and that all officers should return to their regiments. Not only Ashfield (whose regiment had not seen him for two years) but Desborough too defied him openly; yet when the General Council tried to convene for its next scheduled meeting on the 20th Fleetwood dismissed the officers and took his seat in the Other House, where the Commons' votes of the 18th were meeting strong opposition. Probably that same evening, Richard assured Fleetwood and Desborough of his goodwill to the army, and gave them to understand that he would not countenance any move by parliament to assert his own generalship at the expense of their authority.

He probably meant it, for on the 21st he consulted with his closest confidants, including Broghill, Fiennes, Thurloe, Wolseley, and Whitelocke, as to whether he should dissolve parliament as the officers wished. Most were in favour, but that same day the Lord Mayor and aldermen brought him the City's promise to stand by him and the parliament to the last. Much of the City militia, however, declared for the army and its petition. The Commons, having at last taken the soldiers' pay into consideration, spoilt the brief good impression on the 21st by debating the control of the national militia at length and showing a strong bias towards putting all the forces, army and militia alike, under the immediate joint authority of the Protector and parliament. The result was that the officers at Wallingford House took Richard's pledge to be worthless, and word soon spread among the lower ranks that he meant to disband them and trust instead to a militia commanded by the nobility, as a step toward restoring the house of Stuart.

Fleetwood was persuaded that it was time for a trial of strength, and late on the 21st he gave orders for a general rendezvous of all the regiments about London, to take place next day at St James's. Richard ordered a counter-rendezvous at Whitehall, but when the colonels loyal to him tried to comply, most of their own subordinate officers took their men to St James's instead. Only two troops of horse and three foot companies obeyed his call; the rest rallied to Fleetwood. That night Desborough came to him and demanded that he should dissolve parliament and entrust himself to the officers, who had promised to take care of him, which they signally failed to do. One wonders what Mrs Desborough, who was Oliver's sister, thought of the betrayal. Perhaps her thick-skinned, thick-skulled husband persuaded her not to see it that way. Richard at first refused, but seeing the hopelessness of resistance he bowed to pressure and signed a commission for the dissolution. Next day the Commons thrice refused to let Black Rod deliver his summons to attend the Other House for the final ceremony, but he broke his emblem of office at their door to signify that their sitting was at an end.

It was the second time that the army had broken a parliament without knowing what it was going to put in its place, and the parallels with 1653, as well as with the army's first defiance of parliament in 1647, were in many people's minds. Both those earlier actions had inaugurated one of those phases of accelerated political change, resulting in unforeseen consequences, that I have called climacterics. So did the current crisis. The officers at Wallingford House who precipitated it had no desire to bring the Protectorate to an end, but only to manipulate Richard and ensure that he exercised his authority through councillors of like mind to themselves. They wanted to consolidate their power over the army, but they found themselves having to share it with the men whom Oliver had wisely purged, and to bow to the pressure of subordinates whom they could no longer control. What those subordinates wanted cannot be stated with any clarity, so befuddled were they with the foggy rhetoric of the Good Old Cause. It was surely something better than a return to the unsolved problems of the early 1650s, and it was certainly not the almost unconditional restoration of the king, which their conduct brought so much nearer. The only group who achieved their aims in the short term were the parliamentary republicans, and they seem to have failed utterly to grasp how low their stock lay in the country at large, and hence how little able they were to impose any kind of acceptable settlement upon it. All those involved in the forced dissolution on 22 April 1659 would have been dismayed to learn that just over a year later, on the orders of a freely elected parliament, Charles II would be proclaimed king in London, with no conditions but such as he himself had offered.

As in April 1653, it was a restricted Council of Officers, not the all-inclusive General Council, which took up the reins after the dissolution of parliament. It immediately acclaimed Fleetwood as commander-in-chief, but restored the powerful figure of Lambert to his command. It removed Ingoldsby, Fauconberg, and other loyal supporters of Richard from their colonelcies, and reinstated Okey, Saunders, Rich, Overton, and other old commonwealthsmen whom Oliver had cashiered. Thus the whole political balance in the army's upper ranks was altered, and Fleetwood's and Desborough's promises to look after Richard's interests became mere empty words. Moreover, even this refashioned Council of Officers had nothing like the freedom of action that its predecessor in 1653 had enjoyed, for it was under vociferous pressure from a large mass of junior officers, who held their own packed meetings at St James's, where impassioned preachers exhorted them to be true to the Good Old Cause. A medley of emotions went into the potent brew that they imbibed there: an exaggerated sense of apostasy in high places, resentment at parliament's hostility towards them and undervaluation of their service, nostalgia for the heroic years when ideals had been brighter, a fear that the cause of the people of God was being betrayed, and a strong strain of the populist republicanism of which the Levellers had been the main exponents. There were indeed meetings in London of soldiers and NCOs who called themselves the Army's Agitators, but it was the captains and cornets at St James's who were making the running.

The masterpiece of republican propaganda was to persuade them to identify the Good Old Cause with the Good Old Parliament, and look to the restoration of the Rump as the one way of redeeming the nation's 'backsliding'. A barrage of pamphlets and petitions, directed to that end and aimed mainly at the army, appeared in late April and early May, and the weekly *Faithful Scout*, the army newspaper of 1650–5, now revived, reprinted many excerpts from them. *Some Reasons Humbly Proposed to the Officers of the Army, for the Speedy Readmission of the Long Parliament* denounced the Petition and Advice as 'a mere Chimera', and urged the army to renew its old partnership with the Rump, whose political skill and experience were now essential; only by restoring it could they avoid further faction and bloodshed, revive the Good Old Cause, restore trade, terrify the Commonwealth's enemies, and of course provide for the army's pay. 'Cleanse therefore and purge your councils and commands', urged the commonwealthsmen of Southwark; 'root out those Canaanites, those court-parasites and apostates . . . if once you touch or give any way to their politics, farewell, Good Old Cause'. Nearly four hundred men of Goffe's regiment, who had defied their colonel's call to rally to Richard on the night of 21 April, published a *Humble Remonstrance* demanding the recall of 'the Good Old Parliament'. 'Our camp-court creatures going about to bridle the army, have given them just occasion to take the bit into their own teeth', wrote *A Perambulatory Word to Court, Camp, City and Country*. All these pieces appeared on the bookstalls between 26 April and 4 May, and many more could be quoted.[19] They effectively prevented the Wallingford House party from maintaining the Protectorate in any form.

Although this well orchestrated burst of propaganda called overwhelmingly for the restoration of the Rump, it was not the only voice to be heard. The Fifth Monarchist Christopher Feake, who was at least consistent, fulminated that the Rump was still the accursed thing that it had been when it was expelled, in 1653 and urged the faithful remnant to proclaim 'the name and interest of the approaching King of Saints'.[20] Some millenarian congregations tried to persuade the junior officers at St James's to stand up for a Sanhedrin of seventy godly men, but they were cried down. No more heed was given to a couple of tracts that called for a new nominated assembly, after the pattern of Barebone's Parliament.

After the dissolution, two weeks passed before Britain again had a settled government. It was soon clear to informed observers that the question was not *whether* the Rump would form it, but on what terms. John Owen, whom Oliver had so trusted and whose career he had so greatly advanced, played an equivocal part in the negotiations that ensued; he obtained a list of the surviving Rumpers from Ludlow and took it to Wallingford House. Early in March he had formed a gathered church from the senior officers about

[19] British Library press-marks for all the tracts quoted above, together with further similar quotations, are in *Complete Prose Works of John Milton*, VII, 67–9.
[20] C. Feake, *A Beam of Light* (1659), preface and pp. 47–8.

London, including Fleetwood, Desborough, Berry, Goffe, Whalley, and also Sydenham and Lambert. He had probably intended to try and heal the breach that had opened between Richard's supporters and the Wallingford House faction, but he took part in the great meeting of officers on 13 April for fasting and prayer which did so much to fan the army's rising temper against the parliament, and during the subsequent crisis he joined in the devotions of the junior officers at St James's as well as those of the commanders at Wallingford House. There is no evidence that Owen did or said anything positive to Richard's prejudice, and indeed it is unlikely, but the fact that he preached before the Rump on the day after it returned to power made it appear that he at least condoned the change of government. He had in fact been literally sick with worry while the coup was imminent, but as his biographer has remarked he might have been better in Oxford, attending to his duties as Dean of Christ Church, where he was missed.[21]

Two crucial conferences took place at Vane's house on 2 and 5 May, at which Haselrig, Ludlow, Salwey, and Vane himself met representatives of the Council of Officers, including Lambert, Berry, Kelsey, and John Jones, but apparently neither Fleetwood nor Desborough. The officers tried to set three conditions to the re-instatement of the Rump: an act of indemnity to cover the army's past actions; some face-saving place of authority and a generous subsistence for Richard; whatever measures were necessary for the reform of the law and the clergy; and 'That the government of the nation should be by a representative of the people, and by a select senate'. The first and third were agreed without difficulty. The second was rejected outright; the Rump would honour Richard's public debts, but would not preserve any shred of his authority as Protector. The select senate was the most controversial proposal, and it would remain so all through the summer and autumn. After four or five hours' argument the former Rumpers declined to commit their fellow-members in advance, but promised the officers a sympathetic hearing for any proposals that the army put to the parliament after it had reconvened.[22]

That had to satisfy the officers, and when they returned to Vane's house on the 5th they not only agreed to restore the Rump but urged that it should meet as soon as possible. There was now no other way they could provide for the country's government, and their own subordinates would stand for nothing else. Next day the Council of Officers published a declaration lamenting the failure of all the army's attempts at settlement, and the daily decline of 'the good spirit which formerly appeared amongst us . . . so as the good old cause itself became a reproach'. Searching for the reason why the Lord had

---

[21] Peter Toon, *God's Statesman: The Life and Work of John Owen* (Exeter, 1971), pp. 109–14.

[22] *Memoirs of Edmund Ludlow*, II, 74–7. The marginal date on p. 74 should be 2 May, not 29 April.

withdrawn his presence from them, and 'calling to mind, that the Long Parliament, consisting of the members which continued there sitting until the 20th of April, 1653, were eminent asserters of that cause, and had a special presence of God with them', they judged it their duty to invite them to return to their trust.[23]

Richard did not go down without a fight. Helpless at Whitehall, he wrote to Monck in Scotland, Henry in Ireland, Montagu as General at Sea and the commander in Flanders, appealing for armed support. But he failed to contact the last two, and the first two could not help him; Monck's officers, as he privately explained to Richard, sided so strongly with the Council of Officers in London that he had to fall in with it himself, and the forces in Ireland were so divided that Henry could do nothing.

On 6 May just forty-two Rumpers—barely a quorum—took their seats again in the House of Commons. One of the hardest to persuade was old Speaker Lenthall, now in his late sixties, no friend to the Wallingford House party, and reluctant to relinquish his 'lordship' as a member of the Other House. But within days the chamber filled up a little more, and on 13 May it was given something to chew on in the Humble Petition and Address of the Officers of the Army. Significantly it was Lambert who presented it, not Fleetwood, though perhaps that was because Fleetwood was a member of the House. Most of its requests relate to the settlement of the restored Commonwealth, so the debate on it will be described in the next chapter. But it asked that generous financial provision should be made for Richard and his heirs, and though the Protectorate was virtually at an end it could not be totally written off until he accepted the fact. Accordingly the Rump appointed a committee to consider his financial circumstances, he being quite heavily in debt, and to receive his submission. From one or two royalist sources there are allegations that he came to the brink of offering to work for the restoration of the king but drew back from it, but in the absence of firmer evidence they are best discounted. The Rump accepted its committee's recommendations that Richard's debts should be paid and his future financial independence quite handsomely assured, and on 25 May he signed a dignified submission to the restored Rump's authority that came as close as need be to a resignation. The new government, however, being itself in severe financial straits, failed to honour its promises to him, and he hung on in Whitehall until far into July, not because he still entertained any political pretensions but in order to escape arrest by his creditors. In that month the Rump first gave him six months' immunity from them and then made his debts a charge upon the public purse. But again the promise was not kept, and in the spring of 1660 he was still flitting from one hiding-place to another to avoid arrest. In May Richard sailed for France, and for years he lived in Paris, helped by subventions from his friends, under the name of John Clarke, which he kept for the rest of his life. Later he moved to Geneva, but in or around 1680, having inherited an interest in his mother's estate, he returned to England and made his home in Cheshunt. There he died in 1712, not far short of his eighty-sixth birthday, having seen another revolution rescue and consolidate much that his father had fought for. His only son predeceased him, so Oliver's descent in the male line passed to the sons of his brother Henry, who died in 1674.

# ‡ TWENTY-SIX ‡

# The Commonwealth Restored

ONCE back in power, the Rump faced two obligations that would be difficult to reconcile: to content the army that had restored it, and to provide for the political needs of the nation (or nations) that it purported to represent. It failed to do either; but just whom did it represent? It recognized only seventy-eight members as entitled to sit, less than a seventh of the Long Parliament's original strength. Some even of these did not take their seats. It contained no representatives of Scotland or Ireland, and though it claimed authority over both countries it did not recognize the terms of the Cromwellian union with Scotland.

Yet for the present it seemed secure enough. There were some doubts as to how the fleet would react, in view of the strong attachment of its commander, Edward Montagu, to the house of Cromwell, but he called his officers to a council of war and they resolved to obey the parliament's commands. He was holding his fire, as would soon be seen. Monck sent the Speaker a rather fulsome assurance of the loyalty of the forces in Scotland, and Lockhart pledged that of those in Flanders. From Ireland, Henry Cromwell responded with honesty and dignity. He could not profess to welcome the change of government, he wrote, but since his brother had submitted to it he did so too. The army in Ireland would concur with their comrades in England and render obedience to the parliament, but he himself felt unable to continue serving, so he stood ready to hand over his charge.[1] The Rump accordingly vested the government of Ireland in five commissioners, and sent Ludlow over as commander-in-chief, to take over six regiments of horse, one of dragoons, and eleven of foot, besides sundry detachments—a formidable army.

At home it set up a new Council of State, consisting of twenty-one MPs and ten non-members. Haselrig, Vane, and Ludlow got the most votes in the former category, and the latter included Lambert, Desborough, and Berry to represent the army. Among the others nominated by the Rump were Bradshaw, who was mortally ill and died on 31 October, and Fairfax, who maintained his aloofness from current politics and never took his seat.

---

[1] A statement by Sir Edward Hyde on 25 October 1659 that Henry had been on the point of declaring for the king but lost his nerve is not to be believed; see Davies, *Restoration of Charles II*, p. 244.

The nomination of Johnston of Wariston gave Scotland a token presence in English government, and the late addition of Sir Anthony Ashley Cooper and the crypto-royalist Sir Horatio Townshend (who sought the king's permission to sit) introduced further elements of disharmony. The army officers made no secret of their dislike of the council's overall composition. The most conspicuous omission from it was Thurloe, whose skill and experience could ill be spared, but his exemplary loyalty to Richard had earned him the enmity of both the officers and the republicans. One of his last acts was to respond cordially to an offer from France to lend assistance in keeping the Protector in power, but there was nothing by then to be done. His office of Secretary of State was left unfilled, and this and the council's failure to set up a committee for foreign affairs were signs that Britain was withdrawing from the international stage on which Cromwell had played so conspicuous a part.

Fortunately that stage was becoming a quieter place, thanks partly to Thurloe's efforts to restore peace in the Baltic after Charles X's attack on Copenhagen, and partly to England's fortune in having a first-class resident at The Hague in the person of George Downing, who fully shared Thurloe's aims. At the same time France and Spain were moving towards an armistice, in the negotiation of which England played no part, thanks to her preoccupation with domestic strife in the spring of 1659. It was signed in the middle of the hiatus between the dissolution of Richard's parliament and the Rump's return to power.

The reaction of the nation to its recall is hard to gauge, but except among the strident minorities of commonwealthsmen and radical puritans it was muted at best. There were some addresses of loyalty—thirty-one at a generous count spread over three months—but they were far fewer than had greeted Richard's accession, and more narrowly based. Nearly all came from south-eastern England, and many emanated from sectional groups rather than whole communities. Others were mere covers for specific requests.[2] The effect of the change on local government was mixed, but there were large displacements of personnel in most counties. In a few the local bosses who had ruled them before 1653 returned to power: John Pyne in Somerset and Herbert Morley in Sussex, for example. But in most of the country the trend in the social standing of JPs and militia commissioners was downward. 'There is a strange contempt and hatred throughout the nation of this present parliament', wrote Wariston in his diary in July, and James Harrington, Bordeaux, and the Venetian resident all thought that the Rump was more widely unpopular than the Protectorate had been.[3]

[2] Ronald Hutton, *The Restoration: A Political and Religious History of England and Wales, 1658–1667* (Oxford, 1985), pp. 46–7, 51–2.

[3] A. Woolrych, 'Last quests for a settlement', in Aylmer (ed.), *Interregnum*, pp. 195–6.

The majority of its members faced the same problem that had confronted them in the early 1650s. They were dedicated to the republican principle that supreme power belonged of right to the chosen representatives of the sovereign people, yet most of the political nation did not want a republic at all. Since they soon voted that they would not sit beyond 7 May 1660, they had to find, rather urgently, a form of government that would guarantee the continuance of the Commonwealth's very being. They spent every Wednesday in grand committee debating how to do it, and they never came to a positive conclusion. The first proposals to come before them were contained in the Humble Petition and Address of the Officers of the Army, which Lambert presented a week after they resumed their sitting. These were in essence what the Council of Officers had put to them before readmitting them to power, and most were uncontroversial. But the most interesting was this:

That . . . the legislative power may be in a representative of the people, consisting of a House successively chosen by the people in such way and manner as this parliament shall judge meet, and of a select Senate, co-ordinate in power, of able and faithful persons, eminent for godliness, and such as continue adhering to this cause.[4]

The words 'co-ordinate in power' imply that the senate's assent would be necessary to acts of parliament, to decisions of peace and war, and to the ultimate control over the Commonwealth's armed forces, among other things. At a superficial level it could be seen, and was seen, as a bid to compensate the senior officers for their lost 'lordships' in the Other House and secure them a permanent voice in affairs of state, for it soon became clear that senators were intended to be appointed for life. This was beyond doubt part of the senate's appeal to the Council of Officers.

On a more altruistic plane, however, this was a serious attempt to protect the fundamental principles of the Commonwealth against the vagaries of future elected assemblies that might seek (as was all too possible) to bring back monarchy or set undue limits to liberty of conscience. Something very like this 'select senate' had been advocated by Vane three years earlier in *A Healing Question*, though then he had called it a 'standing council'. Vane may well have been the source of its revival now, for he was drawing closer to Lambert and further apart from Haselrig, Scot, and the majority of republican Rumpers, who would brook no check upon the supreme authority of the people's representatives. Since the Council of Officers kept up their advocacy of a senate through the summer, and reiterated it when their relations with the Rump were coming to another crisis in October, its intended role is a matter of some interest. But evidence is scarce as to its intended size, and how it was

---

[4] Text in Baker, *Chronicle of the Kings of England*, pp. 662–4, and *Parliamentary or Constitutional History of England*, XXI, 400–5.

to be chosen, and just what powers it was to wield. Scattered references in petitions and pamphlets suggest that it was to be instituted by some form of election, that membership was to be for life, and that it should be considerably larger than the Council of State, which the army petitions included in their proposals as a quite distinct institution; seventy was a number canvassed several times, no doubt for its biblical associations and consequent appeal to millenarians. The chances that the Rump would accept a senate were extremely small, for in late July Vane was reckoned to command only sixteen or seventeen votes in the House.[5]

The situation was complicated by the fact that James Harrington was taking advantage of the constitutional hiatus to run a serious campaign in favour of his own model of a commonwealth, as elaborated in *Oceana*. That model, it will be remembered, included a senate of 300, elected by men of property, and a popular assembly of 1,050, elected on a very broad franchise, with the former having the sole right to frame and propose measures and the latter restricted to balloting for or against them. Late in May (probably) Vane published anonymously *A Needful Corrective or Balance in Popular Government*, which set forth his own version of a senate in the form of an open letter to Harrington.[6] He agreed with Harrington in seeking a government of laws rather than men and in deriving it from the people's consent; but for him the central problem was not to strike a balance between property interests but to ensure that the corrupted and self-interested will of the people at large should be guided so as persuade them 'to espouse their true public interest'. The depraved will of man needed 'the balancing and ruling motion of God's Spirit to keep him steadfast'. In order that the 'Ruling Senate or Body of Elders' should provide this guidance, it should be elected only by 'such as are free born, in respect of their holy and righteous principles, flowing from the birth of the Spirit of God in them', or 'else who, by their tried good affection and faithfulness to common right and public freedom, have deserved to be trusted with the keeping or bearing their own arms in the public defence'.[7] In view of the difficulty of identifying the 'saints' in the first category, this meant in effect entrusting the choice of senators to members of the army and the militia, which may well have been what Lambert and his colleagues wanted.

As for Harrington, he himself published five pamphlets between May and August, and they spoke with a new directness, even passion. Pieces by his supporters brought the number up to a dozen, and a club was formed in Bow Street to debate his ideas. But not everyone shared his faith that perfectly devised institutions would make people better citizens and guarantee that

---

[5] *Thurloe State Papers*, VII, 704.

[6] I set out the evidence for Vane's authorship and the probable date in 'The Good Old Cause and the fall of the Protectorate', *Cambridge Historical Journal* XIII (1957), 154.

[7] Quoted more fully in *Complete Prose Works of John Milton*, VII, 104–6.

their political needs were met, while the Rumpers were never going to take seriously his principle of rotation, which would have sent them into the wilderness after three years, the maximum tenure both for representatives and for office-holders. The air was full of projects for reform in the summer of 1659, but at Westminster there was much talk but little action. There were mass petitions again for the abolition of tithes, but the Rump voted that they should continue *unless* it devised a fairer and more acceptable maintenance for the clergy. The word in the motion had been 'until'; its change, without a division, to 'unless' amounted to a rejection. As for the pressing problem of the soaring national debt and the army's lengthening arrears of pay, the Rump's failure to respond to the repeated promptings of its own revenue committee confirmed that in its six years in the wilderness it had not only forgotten nothing but had learnt nothing either.

It continued to give offence to the army, not merely by neglecting its financial needs and cold-shouldering its requests for a select senate, but by more positive means. It could hardly refuse its demand to confirm Fleetwood as commander-in-chief, but it did so only for the duration of its current session, and it denied him the powers of appointment that normally went with such a post. The selection and promotion of all officers was entrusted to a Committee of Nominations, in which he had only one voice alongside those of Haselrig, Vane, Ludlow, Lambert, Desborough, and Berry; moreover every one of its recommendations was subject to parliament's approval. As for officers already in post, the House ordered on 6 June that every one of them must come and receive a new commission from the hands of the Speaker. Thereafter it closely scrutinized the regimental lists, and a considerable purge of known Cromwellians resulted. Another of the army's requests, both before and after it restored the Rump, was for an act of indemnity to protect its members from prosecution for actions done in the course of their military duties. The House took seven weeks to pass it, and in the course of long debates in grand committee some outrageously hostile proposals were ventilated. The act that finally emerged struck the officers as insufficient; Lambert complained to Haselrig that it left them still at mercy. 'You are only at the mercy of the parliament, who are your good friends', Haselrig replied; to which Lambert retorted: 'I know not why they should not be at our mercy as well as we at theirs.'[8] A drastic remodelling of the militia in the counties and cities caused further friction, especially since the House insisted on approving every single officer by name and requiring that his commission be signed by the Speaker. The army suspected it of erecting a rival force of its own devotees, prior to a large-scale disbandment of regular regiments. Nor was this implausible, since the only means whereby Haselrig and the dominant faction in the

---

[8] *Memoirs of Edmund Ludlow*, II, 100; Davies, *Restoration of Charles II*, pp. 112–14.

Rump could hang on to power indefinitely was by disposing of effective military force.

Two considerations deterred the leading officers from allowing their dis-satisfaction with the Rump to swell to bursting-point: the sizeable number of commonwealthsmen within the army, and the knowledge that the king's sup-porters were far advanced with plans for another rising. This time the royal-ists posed a greater threat than in 1658 or even 1655, because the Rump's rule was much more widely unpopular than the Protectorate had been, especially in its later years, and many more political presbyterians were now willing to join them in arms. The man who gave his name to the rising in August, Sir George Booth, had raised troops for parliament in 1642–3 and been elected MP for Cheshire in 1646; and though secluded in Pride's Purge he was a trusted militia commissioner in the time of the major-generals. He was one of a number of participants with a similar past. Even a few Cromwellians, loyal to the Protectorate until the moment it fell, were ready to join the rising; Richard Ingoldsby and some of his officers did so, even though he himself was a regi-cide. These were not turncoats; in their eyes England's present masters had destroyed the regime that had given the country its best prospect of stable government, based on consent, and were incapable of providing it them-selves. They were arguably more principled, and certainly braver, than the majority of royalists, who stayed at home until they saw how things went. In committing themselves they took great risks, for there was little sign yet of the surge of popular royalism that would arise in the following winter and spring.

The risks were the greater because of the usual lack of unity and deficien-cies in organization on the royalist side. By far the most active and devoted of the king's friends in England was John Mordaunt, who had escaped execu-tion in 1658 only by the casting vote of the president of the High Court of Just-ice that sentenced Slingsby and Hewitt. He wrote to the king in November, offering to resume working for him, and Charles responded with a warrant for a viscountcy and a new empowerment entitled the Plenipotentiary or Great Trust and Commission—henceforth (for convenience) the Trust. This was addressed not only to Mordaunt but to five of the six members of the old Sealed Knot, but they as always proved broken reeds. They rejected the new commission because it infringed their original one and because Mordaunt and his friends were too ready to bring presbyterians into their designs, but underlying these objections was a strong reluctance to risk their own necks. So Mordaunt looked elsewhere, and the eight men whom he certainly re-cruited to the Trust by August 1659 included the presbyterian Lord Willoughby of Parham as well as such tried and trusted royalist activists as the Earl of Northampton, Sir John Grenville, Sir Thomas Peyton, and Will Legge. Close-ly associated with them were the former parliamentarian generals Waller and Massey, Silius Titus (who had written *Killing No Murder*), and of course

Sir George Booth. It was at least as much a presbyterian as a royalist enter-prise, and its greatest weakness was that the great royalist nobles who could have done most to make the rising a success held aloof from the Trust. This was partly because they resented the authority assumed by and accorded to Mordaunt, but as David Underdown has written, 'underneath can be detect-ed the continued preference of the peers for self-preservation rather than mar-tyrdom'.[9] Northampton proved to be only a partial exception.

Unheroic though so many of the old royalists were, they did have much to fear. Although the master-hand of Thurloe had been removed, Thomas Scot was back in the council and he was well versed in uncovering conspiracy. Thanks to assiduous intelligence and effective counter-measures, many parts of the design were already scotched or doomed before 1 August, the appointed date for the rising, came round. Secrets were certainly betrayed by men whom the king trusted, though how far Sir Richard Willys of the Sealed Knot kept up his role of informant after Thurloe left the stage is not clear. But the active discouragement that Willys and others of the Knot gave to their friends in the final stages of preparation did much to condemn the enterprise to failure.

As in 1655, the plans were for the rising to be launched simultaneously in a number of centres spanning a large part of the country, but only one of these got under arms with even temporary success. A major difference, however, was that the Trust was so anxious to enlist the support of presbyterians and other opponents of the Rump that its commission gave participants discre-tion as to whether or not they should declare outright for the king. In fact none of them did. Booth's own manifesto accused the present government of 'subjecting us under the meanest and fanatic spirits of the nation, under pre-tence of protection', and declared that its dependence on an army that had twice already violated parliament, in 1648 and 1653, would have the result that 'A mean and schismatical party must depress the nobility, and under-standing commons'.[10] What the Cheshire insurgents demanded was either a freely elected new parliament or the restoration of the old Lords and Com-mons, as they had sat before Pride's Purge. Hereby they anticipated the gen-eral call for 'a full and free parliament' which was to be a rallying cry in the coming winter for all who wanted the old monarchy restored; but when some of Booth's supporters openly proclaimed Charles II he complained that it would be their ruin. However, by contrast with Booth's own printed declar-ation, a broadsheet published a week later and claiming to emanate from the

[9] Underdown, *Royalist Conspiracy in England 1649–1660*, p. 238. Chapters 11 and 12 of Underdown's work give the fullest and best overall account of the Trust and of Booth's Rising, but J. S. Morrill, *Cheshire 1630–1660: County Government and Society, during the English Revolution* (Oxford, 1974), pp. 300–25, has considerable independent value.

[10] Quoted in *Complete Prose Works of John Milton*, VII, 108–9, and discussed there and in Morrill, *Cheshire 1630–1660*, pp. 318–22, and Davies, *Restoration of Charles II*, pp. 135–7.

knights and gentry engaged with him in Cheshire (though probably concocted in London), professed fellowship with the 'gathered separate churches', opposed all coercion in matters of religion, and called among other things for the annual election of all office-holders and magistrates, drastic reform of the law and the restitution of the enclosed common land to the poor. This was patently incompatible with the real aims of Booth and his followers, which were quintessentially conservative. One reason why they made a better showing than would-be insurgents elsewhere was that they were drawn from the main area of Presbyterian strength outside London, and the Presbyterian clergy urged them to arms with tales that a Quaker uprising was imminent— a scare that was also raised in Norfolk, Hampshire, Gloucestershire, and Devon, though with less effect.

The main reason why the rising was nipped in the bud lay in the vigorous counter-measures taken by the council, which set up a standing committee for intelligence with Scot as its guiding spirit. As the appointed day approached, the council itself sat all day and much of the night, sleeping at Whitehall and grabbing meals as chance afforded. Many activists were arrested, including three members of the Trust itself. Worst of all, the Knot sent out messengers to intending participants on 30 July to tell them that the council had uncovered the design and that it was therefore abandoned.

Some of the largest preparations had been made in Gloucestershire and its neighbouring counties, and no one could have been more active in organizing them than Edward Massey, the former major-general of the Long Parliament's Western Association, who had since become an open royalist. But the Rump's supporters in Gloucester sent out several troops of horse to scour the countryside on 31 July, and Massey and other leaders were arrested. Massey himself escaped overseas, but the failure of his enterprise had a domino effect on others in the West Country, and Devon and Cornwall did not even stir. Grenville and his colleagues had agreed to rise only if Bristol and Gloucester were first seized and if the king or the Duke of York came to lead them in person. All too many of the old royalists were prepared to join a rising only if and when it was clearly on the way to success. Lord Falkland, son of Hyde's friend who had perished on Chalgrove Field, tried rather harder in Oxford, but vigorous counter-measures made him call off the rendezvous at the last moment, and he was soon in the Tower. There were elaborate plans to draw the Commonwealth's forces out of London by risings in all the home counties, but Mordaunt's own design in Surrey and Sussex collapsed as feebly as Peyton's in Kent; the few who turned up at the appointed rendezvous at Redhill, Blackheath, and Tunbridge Wells were easily taken prisoner. In Berkshire, Buckinghamshire, and Bedfordshire very little happened at all. In East Anglia, where the Knot was most influential, its active discouragement killed the enterprise stone dead, and in Northamptonshire and the neighbouring Midlands the Earl of Northampton abandoned it just before it was due to begin. From Shropshire and Worcestershire fifty or sixty men gathered on the Wrekin in soaking rain, but they had fled by early morning on 1 August. In the northern counties other than Cheshire and Lancashire the Trust had done little to organize the king's friends, who were still in disarray after previous designs had failed, and little happened except the round-up of some of the usual suspects. Such was the degree of enthusiasm for the king's cause nationwide, only months before he actually returned.

Why then did Sir George Booth manage to hold together a force of about 4,000 men in Cheshire and south Lancashire for nearly three weeks, while everywhere else the attempted rising had collapsed within hours—if it was attempted at all? For a start, Booth was exceptionally able and resolute; he stood high among the elite of his county and was greatly respected. Equally importantly, the council seems not to have had any such intelligence of preparations in Cheshire as it had from the other centres where it acted so promptly, and in recent years the county had not given it grounds for suspicion. It made all the difference that Booth was able to hold his rendezvous at Warrington on 1 August and at Rowton Heath near Chester next day without interruption. Still unhindered on the 7th, he was recruiting in Manchester. He had the support of the Earl of Derby, but more significant was that of the Presbyterian clergy, who used their pulpits—31 July was a Sunday—to call their flocks to arms. He was dismayed when the Knot's discouraging letter reached him that day, but he was not deterred. His initial declaration for a free parliament was a popular one, though he was compromised when his ally Sir Thomas Middleton, another former parliamentary commander, proclaimed the king in Wrexham. For a fortnight or more Booth controlled all of Cheshire and much of Lancashire, but his force did not grow in numbers after the first week, and he gradually became aware that he was utterly isolated. Lambert was after him with a competent force, picking up reinforcements as he rode north, and Ludlow had dispatched a brigade of horse and foot from the forces in Ireland to Wales. Just in case the rising got off the ground, the council had also recalled three regiments from Flanders. Lambert caught up with Booth's men near Northwich on the 19th, and though they put up something of a fight at Winnington Bridge it was more of a skirmish than a battle. Lambert lost only one man killed, Booth about thirty, but most of his men just scattered. Booth made his escape southward, disguised as a woman, but an innkeeper in Newport Pagnell became suspicious after his three companions, having called in a barber to shave them, tried to buy his razor. It was soon discovered that 'the Lady Dorothy' was not what she seemed. Booth and his fellow leaders spent the next six months in the Tower, but the obvious imminence of the Restoration brought their release in February, and soon a grateful king rewarded Booth with the barony of Delamere, to which parliament added a grant of £10,000. The handsome additions that he made to his family seat at Dunham Massey testify to his prosperity, but he remained a firm Presbyterian and was later a prominent Exclusionist.[11]

We shall probably never know for certain how close his rising came to receiving the support of a major part of the fleet. When the news of Richard's overthrow reached Montagu and his squadron in the Sound, most of his captains shared his own dismay, though Vice-Admiral Goodson rejoiced in the Rump's return to power. But they all agreed to obey its orders, and they accepted their new commissions signed by the Speaker, as the army officers had done. Among Montagu's officers, however, was a young cousin, also called Edward Montagu, who was thought to be more positively inclined towards the king's cause. Hyde wrote to him in June, urging him to press his kinsman to come over, and promising that if he brought his ships to Flanders the king would embark for England at once. But Charles and Hyde spoilt whatever chances they had by employing another agent in the person of Thomas Whetstone, a nephew of Cromwell and former naval captain who had been disgraced some months earlier. Whetstone persuaded them that he could still wield great influence among the ships' crews, and he set off from Brussels for Copenhagen with letters from the king to Montagu and his flag-officers Goodson and Stayner. Meanwhile the Rump, uncertain of Montagu's loyalty, had sent new commissioners to the Sound to treat with the Dutch and keep an eye on him. They were headed by Colonel Algernon Sidney, a strongly republican MP and a member of the council, and they arrived off Cophenhagen on 20 July. They found Whetstone behaving with extraordinary indiscretion, and Sidney soon guessed what he was up to. Montagu dared not meet him, and sent him hastily back to Brussels with only a vague verbal message of goodwill towards the king. His young cousin wrote a frank letter to Hyde on the 27th, probably unaware that the rising in England was timed to start four days later, but perhaps knowing that plans for it were afoot. If the moment had been seized when Richard was first overthrown, he wrote, something might have been done; but now that the captains had received their new commission and were 'not only forgiven but courted by the present power', only half of them at the most could be expected to follow the General at Sea if he declared for the king, and if they did so the sailors might deliver up their own officers. Yet he hinted that if the army and the civil government fell out, and there was a party able and willing to stand for the king, Montagu's help could be hoped for.[12] In fact Montagu and his ships did set sail for home on 24 August, when he knew that the rising had began but not that it had failed. Shortage of victuals was the reason he gave to his

[11] For his post-Restoration career see Douglas R. Lacey, *Dissent and Parliamentary Politics in England 1661–1689* (New Brunswick, 1969), esp. pp. 464–6.

[12] Capp, *Cromwell's Navy*, pp. 333–41.

officers, and afterwards to the Rump. His motives cannot be read with certainty. He would certainly have preferred a monarchy restored upon suitable terms to an indefinite continuance of the rule of the Rump, but he was a patriot, and it is most unlikely that he would have turned his ships' guns against an English government still firmly in being, to the detriment of his country's standing in the world at large. If, however, he had found that that government had already fallen he would have been happy to serve those who, like Booth, put their trust in 'a full and free parliament', and he would probably have been as glad as they if it had brought back the king. The council sent three Admiralty Commissioners to interrogate him as soon as he dropped anchor in English waters, and he was closely examined by the council. But there was no solid evidence against him, and after some debate the Rump let him resign his command and retire to his estate at Hinchingbrooke.

The most unhappy consequence of Lambert's easy victory in Cheshire, for both the Rump and the army, was that it removed the main check upon the mounting quarrel between them. Both parties must be judged to have shared responsibility for its escalation, but on balance the Rump was to a larger extent the author of its own downfall. When the House heard the news of Winnington Bridge, Fleetwood moved that Lambert should be restored to his old rank of major-general. It would have been a politic recognition of his recent services and his actual standing in the army, but Haselrig opposed the motion strenuously and it was rejected. Lambert was voted £1,000 to buy a jewel, but he preferred to distribute the money among his troops in Cheshire.

There was more friction, especially between Haselrig and Vane, when the former's party introduced on 3 September a new Engagement, to be taken by all militia officers, requiring them to abjure the pretended title of Charles Stuart and swear to be faithful to 'this Commonwealth', without a king, single person, or House of Lords. Vane, who was now closely allied with Lambert, opposed it sharply, partly because the form of the Commonwealth had yet to be defined, so that the oath could be used to prolong the power of one party (Haselrig's), and partly because it suggested a suspicion within that party that Lambert was aiming at a role akin to that of Protector. Vane was also sensitive to the scruples that many radical puritans felt against the multiplying of public oaths, as a tempting of God.

Simultaneously a row had been developing between the parliament and the City of London, partly generated by the former's overriding of the corporation's authority when it reorganized the City militia in July. The Lord Mayor was Sir John Ireton, a brother of the late Henry Ireton, and he and most of the aldermen supported the Rump. But most of the common councilmen and very many citizens sympathized with Booth's call for a free parliament, and many Presbyterian ministers in London refused to read the government's proclamation of him as a traitor from their pulpits. Ireton was under heavy pressure during August to call a Court of Common Council, and he even had to get troops posted at the Guildhall to prevent it from meeting without his summons. The annual election of a new Lord Mayor was due in September, but the Rump voted on the 2nd to override the City's historic right and to keep Ireton in office for another year. This aroused such a storm of protest that the House gave way later in the month, and the City gratefully elected one Thomas Allin, who could be relied upon not to make waves.

Meanwhile the government's financial difficulties deepened. The special militia raised against the August risings was stood down, but it took many weeks to find the money to pay the men off; in Suffolk and Staffordshire they seized the militia commissioners as hostages for it. The forces called back from Ireland and Flanders and the men of Montagu's fleet were extra burdens on the Exchequer, and the old evil of free quarter bore heavily again on the civil population. Belatedly, on 18 August, the Rump decided to raise the monthly assessment, but a bill to double it was still just short of passing four weeks later when the parliament was again interrupted.

If finance was one intractable problem, the settlement of the constitution was another. Since the House had made so little progress in grand committee, it set up a select committee on 8 September, with instructions to sit every day and present a draft by 10 October at the latest. But with twenty-nine members of very diverse views—with Haselrig and Scot pitted against Vane and Salwey, with Fleetwood confronting the anti-militarist lawyers St John and Whitelocke, and with the Harringtonian Henry Neville differing from them all—the committee was unlikely to deliver the wisdom of either Solomon or Solon; nor did it. In parliament itself, there was debate early in October on how to fill the vacant seats in the House. This can only mean that Haselrig's faction was still pursuing the same design that had brought it into disrepute seven or eight years ago, namely of holding only 'recruiter' elections and trusting to a compliant army to keep out undesirable candidates. Since the army's current mood was far from compliant, quite a small provocation could set it and the parliament on collision course again.

This arose in the shape of a petition from the brigade that Lambert had led against Booth. It was signed on 16 September, addressed to parliament, but quite properly sent to Fleetwood for prior consideration by the General Council of Officers. It became known as the Derby Petition, since that was where the brigade—only one small part of the military forces in England—was stationed when it was composed. Lambert had left Derby for London before it was drafted, and there is evidence to support his strenuous subsequent denials that he had had any part in it. It asked for action on the officers' Humble Petition and Address of May 12, whose main unfulfilled request had been that for a select senate. Its only really new proposals were that Fleetwood's appointment as commander-in-chief should be made permanent and that general rank should be conferred on three other officers: on Lambert as second-in-command and on Desborough and Monck as chief officers of the horse and foot respectively. It was provocative of the officers at Derby to send their petition to Monck in Scotland and to the acting commanders in Ireland, asking them to invite their officers to subscribe it, but this did not warrant the explosive reaction that it aroused at Westminster. On receiving it, Fleetwood was inclined to suppress it, but indecisive as always he showed it to Haselrig, suggesting that they should meet with Vane and Salwey and discuss what to do about it. Instead, Haselrig took it straight to the House, had the doors locked, and denounced it with all the inflammatory rhetoric at his command. Assuming without any positive evidence that Lambert was responsible for it, he moved that he should be committed to the Tower for high treason. This was monstrous; Lambert was so shocked by the suspicion that had fallen on his subordinates that he asked Fleetwood for leave to resign his commission, but Fleetwood, who believed him innocent, would not hear of it. After a second day's heated debate the motion to commit Lambert was dropped, but Fleetwood was ordered to reprimand the officers of his brigade, who were now back in London. Furthermore the House voted 'that to have any more general officers than are already settled by the parliament, is needless, chargeable and dangerous to the Commonwealth'.[13] Those last four words were utterly gratuitous; did no one in the House remember what had happened when it had branded an earlier body of army petitioners as 'enemies of the state' in 1647?

The officers about London were now meeting daily again, as they had done in April when the last coup was brewing. They appointed a committee to draft an address that would clear the army's reputation by publicly reaffirming its loyalty to the Commonwealth, but what Fleetwood had hoped would pour oil on troubled waters had the opposite effect, as the document emerged from the officers' debates. Those debates were heated; Haselrig, having been made colonel of a regiment again in the summer's reshuffle, asserted in the Council of Officers that absolute power lay in the parliament, whereas most of the officers were equally positive in claiming that they were employed against arbitrary government in any form whatsoever. Fleetwood tried to persuade them all 'to sleep upon the whole business', and Lambert sat silent, wisely (at this stage) declining to engage himself. The address that emerged, and was presented to the House by Desborough on 5 October, was styled The Humble Representation and Petition of the Officers of the Army, but humble it was not. So far from disowning or even qualifying the Derby Petition, it vindicated it, and blamed the current tension on those who had misrepresented

---

[13] *Commons Journals*, VII, 785, where the repetition of 'dangerous' is surely a clerical error; 'needless' is supplied from Baker, *Chronicle of the King's of England*, p. 678.

its authors' intentions. It vehemently denied that the army intended to interrupt the parliament's sitting, or to 'set up a single person, or another General'. It urged the Rump to get on with settling the constitution and reminded it again of the officers' address in May, whose proposal of a select Senate had been allowed to sleep. It repeated the dangerous demand that no officer or soldier should be dismissed unless convicted by a court-martial, though it did make an exception of cases in which they lost their employment because their regiments were disbanded. And there were new requests, in particular that soldiers should have the same right as other citizens to petition parliament, and that those who wrongfully aspersed the army should be tried and punished. Yet it did pledge the army's fidelity to the parliament and the Commonwealth, and expressed hopes for 'a cordial and affectionate union of the parliament and army, and an uninterrupted good understanding of each other'.[14]

At first the Rump responded temperately to the army's petition, debating its requests one by one and framing conciliatory answers to the first five of them. But on 11 October Colonel Okey divulged to Haselrig a letter signed by Lambert and eight other senior officers, inviting himself and the officers of his regiment to sign the Humble Representation and Petition. It transpired soon afterwards that similar letters had been sent to other commanders of regiments and garrisons and to the armies in Scotland and Ireland. To canvass thus for signatures to an essentially political petition *after* it had been presented, and before parliament had responded to it, was inexcusable, but the Rump fully shared the responsibility for the breach that followed. Upon Okey's revelation, it rushed an act through all its stages in a single day, declaring all legislation passed since April 1653 to be null and void unless the present House confirmed it, and making it high treason to collect any taxes, including customs and excise, without parliament's consent. The obvious purpose was to make lawful government impossible if the army should again dissolve the Rump, but this was almost daring it to do so.

Worse was to follow, and on the very next day. Early that morning, Haselrig, Scot and Valentine Walton received a secret message from Monck that if the parliament was resolute in standing up to the army he would if necessary bring the army in Scotland to its support. At this stage there is nothing to connect Monck with any design to bring back the king, whose chief agents in Britain were quite in the dark as to his intentions. He was making a reasoned judgement that Lambert and the leading officers in England were posing a greater threat to ordered government than the Rumper politicians, and he cannot be blamed for the latter's self-destructive response to his pledge. As soon as the House met on the 12th, Haselrig, Scot, and Walton caused its

---

[14] Text in Baker, *Chronicle*, pp. 679–81.

doors to be locked and had the letter from Lambert and his colleagues to Okey read out. After a long debate the House voted to cashier Lambert and his eight co-signatories, who included not only Desborough, Berry, and Kelsey but such staunch commonwealthsmen as Ashfield, Packer, and Creed. No less rashly, it revoked Fleetwood's commission as commander-in-chief and vested the command of the army in seven commissioners. Although Fleetwood was one and Monck another, all the rest were republicans: Haselrig, Scot, Ludlow, Walton, Morley, and Overton. This cannot have been what Monck wanted. He had offered to defend the parliament against the army if need be, but not to launch it upon a suicidal frontal attack.

On the evening of this same 12 October, Haselrig, Walton, and Morley used their new military authority to order two regiments (one being Morley's own) to occupy Westminster Hall and the precincts of the House, where some members camped for the night. But the majority of the regiments about London chose to obey Lambert rather than the new commissioners, and he posted them so as completely to surround the parliament's defenders. Through that night and all next day the opposing forces faced each other with muskets loaded and matches lit, but more and more of the defenders went over to Lambert, including the parliament's life guard. His blockading forces prevented any members from entering the House, including Speaker Lenthall. 'I am your General', he told them, and demanded obedience, to which they replied that they would have known him as such if he had marched before them on Winnington Bridge. The members who had spent the night in the House sent for help to the City militia, but it declined to meddle in the quarrel; indeed the citizens generally took the whole confrontation very calmly and went about their business as if unconcerned.

They had seen violent changes of government enough in the past dozen years, and by now they had little to hope for from either warring party. It was the second time within five months that the army had forcibly interrupted a political regime that it had been largely responsible for establishing, and in October it had even less prospect of settling the civil government of the three nations than it had had in April. Then, it had confronted and destroyed the Cromwellian Protectorate, and pinned its faith on putting the clock back to 1653. Now, though provoked almost beyond endurance by the incorrigible leaders of the restored Rump, not even its own generals had any clear idea of what they could set up in its place. In earlier years, between 1647 and 1648 and again in 1653, the army's incursions into politics had been fired by positive ideals and accompanied by constructive proposals for what it truly hoped would be a better political order, but in 1659 it was sinking into political bankruptcy.

No one, not even the army leaders themselves, knew whether their latest coup was meant to signify the dissolution of the Rump or merely an interruption, designed to bring it to terms. The indications are that if Lambert and his colleagues had been given assurances that the House would rescind the hostile votes of 11 and 12 October, and give serious attention to the army's requests, they would have restored it. But there was no chance that Haselrig and his party would agree to such terms, now that they had the secret promise of Monck's support. Two whole weeks went by before the Council of Officers gave any clear indication of its intentions, and the delay was probably due more to a lingering hope of striking a deal with the Rumpers than to a total inability to decide what to do next. A remnant of the Council of State sat on until 25 October, and five of its members, including Vane and Whitelocke, engaged in negotiation with five army spokesmen—Fleetwood, Lambert, Desborough, Sydenham, and Berry—as to how best to carry on the civil government. Not surprisingly, the councillors insisted that the first move must be the readmission of the Rump, and the generals adamantly opposed it. Faced with deadlock, the Council of Officers set up a Committee of Safety as a provisional government. It consisted nominally of twenty-three members, including the ten who had been treating during the past two weeks, but the officers had difficulty in finding as many men of experience who were willing to serve; Ludlow, Vane, Salwey, and Whitelocke were among those who were persuaded only with difficulty. Not more than twelve are certainly known to have ever taken their seats, and those who did attend found agreement very difficult. They did, however, appoint a sub-committee 'to prepare a form of government'.

Nothing came of it, for its members were as divided as the Committee of Safety itself, and the centre of political gravity very soon shifted elsewhere. But the intermission of regular government, which lasted until almost the end of the year, witnessed a spate of pamphleteering, which offered remedies for the commonwealth's ills that ranged from the restoration of monarchy to our old friends an Agreement of the People and a rule of the saints. Harrington's proposals continued to be vigorously discussed; indeed the Rota Club was established in October for that very purpose. Its regulars included Harrington himself, his close friend the Rumper Henry Neville, the former Levellers John Wildman and Maximilian Petty, the Cromwellian councillor Sir Charles Wolseley, the Earl of Dorset, the diarist Samuel Pepys, John Aubrey of the *Brief Lives*, and such early lights of the soon-to-be-founded Royal Society as Dr William Petty and Sir John Hoskins. Miles's coffee-house in New Palace Yard, where it met, was crammed every evening, and according to Aubrey 'the arguments in the parliament house were but flat to it'.[15] A balloting-box was a central feature, and each proposal was subjected in true Harringtonian fashion to its verdict. But for Harrington himself the urgency seems to have

---

[15] *Aubrey's Brief Lives*, ed. Oliver Lawson Dick (1949), p. 125.

gone out of the passionate promotion that he had given to his model of an ideal commonwealth during the spring and summer, when he had thought it had a real chance of being adopted. What had then seemed serious proposals for an actual political settlement had been relegated by the follies of both soldiers and politicians to an intellectual entertainment for the wits and virtuosi of the town.

Although the Committee of Safety remained the nominal governing body in England until late in December, its authority was fatally compromised almost from the start by General Monck's reaction to the English army's latest coup. There has been much disagreement about Monck's political standpoint at this stage, and in the face of conflicting evidence it is impossible to be completely certain about it. What is beyond doubt is that his loyalty to the Protectorate had been impeccable throughout, and that he felt no sympathy or solidarity with the army leaders in England who overthrew it. But he had little reason to love the restored Rump either, not only on account of its dubious credentials and the intransigence of Haselrig's faction, but because it proceeded to remove and replace officers in the regiments under his command without consulting him. The king and his ministers were aware that with his disciplined army Monck was in a unique position to serve the royal cause, and early in August they employed his younger brother Nicholas, a Cornish rector with royalist affiliations, to carry a letter offering him the huge sum of £100,000 a year for life if he would do so. The general received his brother with extreme caution and declined to accept the letter, though Nicholas divulged its contents to him. According to his chaplains Thomas Gumble and John Price, he nevertheless decided at this point to work for the king's restoration, and was preparing to give his support to Booth's rising when he heard of its defeat. But Booth had declared for no more than a full and free parliament, and that is what Monck himself would have preferred to either a military dictatorship or the self-perpetuation of the Rump—or so his brother reported.

Gumble and Price wrote their accounts after the Restoration, when it was in their interest as well as Monck's to antedate his commitment to the king's cause. They are not to be trusted, and the narrative by Edward Phillips in his continuation of Sir Richard Baker's *Chronicle of the Kings of England*, published in 1670, should be received with equal caution. There are at least three strong indications that Monck was not yet committed to restoring the king when he reacted to the news of the army's interruption of the Rump by immediately demanding its reinstatement and preparing to use his forces to bring this about. One is his refusal to receive the letter that his brother brought him in August, or to be lured by the immense reward that it offered. Nicholas would have loved to give his royalist contacts some assurance of George's good intentions, but he could not. Another is his reaction to the Rump's tampering with his army: he wrote to the Speaker on 3 September, asking leave to resign his commission and retire into private life. His brother-in-law Dr Thomas Clarges, another clergyman, managed to intercept the letter and gained Lenthall's collusion in withholding it from the House for ten days, by which time Monck had changed his mind about resigning, but it is surely inconceivable that if he had had as yet a firm intention to serve the king he would have deprived himself of the means of doing so. The third testimony to his non-commitment is the total mystification of the king's most trusted agents as to what he was aiming at, even as late as January 1660.

Monck's own explanation of why he took the stand he did in October is probably the true one. He thought that the army's seizure of power was wrong in itself and would deliver the country over to anarchy. He had a low opinion of the Rump, but he saw it as still the most likely channel through which the three kingdoms could be brought back to constitutional rule. On 31 October, however, before he knew that it had been turned out again, he wrote to remind it of the need 'to hasten the settlement of the government of these nations in a commonwealth way, in successive parliaments, so to be regulated in elections as you shall think fit'.[16] He almost certainly had an open mind as to what form that government might take, so long as it could reasonably claim the sanctions of law and consent. He must have contemplated the possibility that the outcome of his intervention would ultimately be the restoration of the monarchy, but there is no strictly contemporary evidence that he intended to push it that way, and he seems genuinely to have wished to give the Rump at least one more chance. His preference was for a regime with a broad basis of support among sober, non-partisan, propertied people, and though he was not a strongly religious man he firmly supported a national church. He probably shared in an undogmatic way the beliefs of his Presbyterian wife. Fanatics were anathema to him, whether in church or state; indeed, it has been suggested that what chiefly moved him to stand up for the Rump against the English army in October was the 'Quaker terror' that swept through the ranks of the gentry in 1659.[17] This was no doubt one factor in his response, but his main concerns were surely to counter the drift towards anarchy and to set his country back on course towards ordered and acceptable government. He was widely misunderstood, and it suited his purpose to keep people guessing about his intentions, but behind his bull-like appearance, his blunt speech, his coarse humour and rough temper—behind his whole

---

[16]  A *True Narrative of the Proceedings in Parliament* (1659), pp. 22–3; his public declaration for the Rump, dated 20 Oct., is printed in ibid., pp. 24–5. The case that Monck was not yet committed to restoring the king is argued by Davies in *Restoration of Charles II*, by myself in *Complete Prose Works of John Milton*, VII, and by Hutton in *Restoration*. Maurice Ashley stands by the more traditional belief that he made his decision for the king in August 1659 in *General Monck* (1977), ch. 12.

[17]  Barry Reay, *The Quakers and the English Revolution* (1985), ch. 5, esp. pp. 97–8; Hutton, *Restoration*, pp. 71, 74–7.

cultivation of the persona of a plain, tobacco-chewing, aleswilling professional soldier—lay a shrewdness, a seriousness of purpose and a sense of honour that have often been underrated. A superficial reading of his career
between 1640 and 1660 could suggest a series of self-interested tergiversations, and that is what his enemies portrayed. But every choice of allegiance
that he made in those two decades can be justified on grounds of principle,
and he never betrayed a cause to which he committed himself unless the cause
itself disintegrated.

His first step, on hearing that the Rump was shut out again, was to institute
a purge of his own forces, removing all those officers who he thought might
side with those in England. But he made great efforts to cement the loyalty of
the rest, and not only that of the officers. He addressed many regiments in
person, and summoned a great council of all the officers within reach, patiently
explaining and debating the reasons for his stand, and countering their misgivings about his setting of one army against another. He made it clear that
those whose consciences forbade them to serve would be allowed to withdraw into England. One way and another he lost ninety-seven officers within
a month, but he filled their places by promoting men of junior rank from
within his forces and recruited as many as he could to plug the gaps left thereby. He had to conduct a large-scale reorganization of his army before he
marched into England, but he lost no time in sending considerable numbers
of his most loyal units towards the border.

In London the Committee of Safety soon decided to send all the forces it
could spare against him, keeping only two infantry regiments and eight
troops of horse in the capital. Robert Lilburne, who commanded in the north,
supported the committee and secured Carlisle and Newcastle, though Overton in Hull distrusted both parties and stayed neutral. Lambert set off on
3 November to take overall command of the forces ranged against Monck's,
and soon outnumbered them by at least three to two. But neither side was
keen to fight, and Monck willingly accepted a proposal from Fleetwood that
each should send commissioners to negotiate. Each appointed three, and on
the 15th they agreed on the terms of a treaty. But Monck's commissioners
breached their instructions, which (though secret) one of them betrayed to the
other party. They were directed to insist that the Rump should be readmitted
and that 'no form of government be established over these nations but by parliament, unless they shall refuse to sit'.[18] Instead, the draft treaty provided
that a new parliament should be speedily summoned, but that its constitution
and manner of calling, along with the whole form of future government,
should be determined by a specially constituted General Council of the Army
and Navy, consisting of two officers from each regiment in England, Scotland

---

[18] *Clarke Papers*, IV, 98.

and Ireland, the commanders of garrisons, and ten officers of the fleet. It was to meet on 6 December. The qualifications of MPs, however, were to be decided by a special committee of nineteen, chosen from the Committee of Safety and the three armies. These arrangements were calculated to ensure that even if this General Council succeeded in getting a new parliament elected, its composition and its powers would be heavily subject to the dominant military faction. Its chances of securing the confidence of the political nation would have been small, and its authority would have been strongly challenged by the surviving members of the Long Parliament, both the Rumpers and those secluded in 1648.

Whether or not Monck had ever hoped for a successful negotiation with the Committee of Safety, he certainly could not accept the treaty that his commissioners signed. He had already summoned commissioners from the Scottish shires and burghs to meet in Edinburgh on 15 November to consider how the peace of Scotland should be secured if he had to march his army into England. He was evidently expecting at the end of October that he would have to do so, for his letters of summons requested each shire to send a quota of baggage horses and packmen to Edinburgh by 20 November. On convening there, the nobles and lairds of the shires chose as their president the Earl of Glencairn, the leader of the royalist rising five years earlier, while the burgh commissioners elected a Remonstrant, Sir James Stewart; but all accepted Monck's authority. In his opening speech on the 15th, he charged them and all the JPs to preserve the peace, suppress all tumults, counter any signs of correspondency with Charles Stuart, and support the godly ministry in the land. Next day the commissioners agreed to comply with his desires, but they asked for some direction as to how they were to prevent disorder or worse in their territories, in the absence of his forces. Behind this lay the difficult question of whether the Scots should be allowed to bear arms for their own defence, against both raids from the Highlands and enemies of the Commonwealth. Monck must have known this, but he said he had not had time to consider specific provisions, and would welcome suggestions. These would be discussed at a further meeting at Berwick on 12 December, to which he asked each shire to elect one representative.

His purpose in deferring the hard decision about arming the Scots may have been to gain time and see how the situation developed, for in England it was becoming increasingly fluid and unpredictable. There was great dismay and resentment in the Committee of Safety and at Wallingford House when he repudiated the draft treaty that his commissioners had signed. He proposed that the negotiation should be resumed at York or Newcastle with two additional commissioners on each side, and this was agreed, on condition that the new treaty should contain nothing directly contrary to that signed on 15 November, and that the representative General Council of Officers scheduled for 6 December should go ahead. In mid-November, however, some members of the Rump's Council of State, including Haselrig, Scot, Walton, Morley, Neville, and Ashley Cooper, began to meet again in private, and on the 24th they sealed a commission to Monck as commander-in-chief of all the land forces of England and Scotland. It empowered him to march into any part of either country and to fight all who were in hostility to the parliament or opposed its sitting.

The Committee of Safety was facing a rapidly worsening situation. France and Spain had concluded the Treaty of the Pyrenees on 28 October, and there were fears—groundless, as it turned out—that they would combine to help Charles II to his throne. The temper of the citizens of London, and that of the regiments hitherto loyal to Fleetwood and Lambert, gave more genuine cause for concern. The period between Cromwell's death and the king's return has often been loosely labelled as one of anarchy, but the description just does not fit the first twelve of the twenty months concerned. There had been a breach of continuity when the Protectorate was overthrown, but the civil population had not taken much notice of it; JPs had continued to hold their sessions, the courts at Westminster went on dispensing justice, and though trade was depressed merchants and shopkeepers carried on their businesses much as usual. But a dramatic change came about after the second exclusion of the Rump. Some judges at Westminster ceased to sit immediately; the rest closed their courts on 20 November because their commissions from the parliament expired that day. An organized movement sprang up amongst the citizenry of London to call for a full and free parliament and to refuse to pay any taxes that lacked parliament's sanction. A series of associations were formed in the provinces to the same end. Troops had to be used to help levy the assessment and other dues, and they were made to fear for their lives. Their morale was all too plainly wilting; it was at this point that they were heard saying that 'they will not fight, but will make a ring for their officers to fight in'.[19]

The City apprentices were specially busy in canvassing for signatures to a petition of their own for a free parliament, with enough success for the Committee of Safety to issue a proclamation forbidding such agitation, and ordering the Lord Mayor to publish it. By this time the City fathers were very ambivalent; the Court of Aldermen, which typically regarded any government as better than none, so long as it enabled trade to be carried on, was supportive, but the Lord Mayor asked for time to consult the Common Council, which was more in tune with the movement for a free parliament. Encouraged by a letter from Monck, appealing for its support, it had just refused the Committee's request for a loan point-blank. Then came news that on 3 December Haselrig, Morley and Walton had gained control of Portsmouth

[19] *Clarke Papers*, IV, p. 300.

and its garrison, with the warm support of its governor, magistrates, and citizens. They had been sent by the still active members of the Council of State, and their success meant that the champions of the Rump now had a substantial power-base only seventy-five miles from London.

On the 5th, unable now to trust the City authorities, the Committee of Safety sent the parliament's serjeant-at-arms, backed by a squadron of horse, to read its proclamation against the apprentices' petition at the Royal Exchange. The young men were out in force against him. They beat the troopers into disorderly retreat, while others pelted them from the roof-tops with tiles and blocks of ice from the gutters. As the riot became general, all the shops were shut, and angry citizens closed the gates at Temple Bar. The Committee sent in stronger forces under Colonel Hewson to break them open and restore order, but as they advanced towards the Exchange they were met with a hail of stones and cries of 'a cobbler! a cobbler!', alluding to Hewson's pre-war occupation as a shoemaker. Cavalrymen of the old New Model Army were not used to such humiliation and they eventually opened fire, killing at least two young men and wounding more. While the riot raged, the Common Council met and received a delegation from the apprentices, bearing a mass petition calling for either a new parliament or the restoration of the present one as it had been constituted before Pride's Purge. Either course would have brought back the monarchy, and by now everyone knew it. The Common Council appointed a committee to consider the petition, but ordered all householders to keep their sons and apprentices from raising tumults. Late in the evening it sent a deputation to Fleetwood, requesting that he withdraw his troops from the City. He agreed to do so in return for an order from the Lord Mayor commanding all citizens back to their homes. Next day, however, when the Committee of Safety summoned the Court of Aldermen to Whitehall it flatly refused to attend, and on the 9th the Common Council entrusted the keeping of the peace in the capital to a committee of safety of its own. A coroner's court returned a verdict of wilful murder on the citizens killed in the riot, and Hewson was indicted. On the 12th Desborough was only just in time to take over the Tower of London, whose Lieutenant was in league with Scot, Ashley Cooper, Okey, and others in a plot to bring it out in support of the forces in Portsmouth.

These developments in Portsmouth and London had repercussions in the fleet, in Ireland, and in northern England that were to contribute much to the overthrow of the Committee of Safety, and they overshadowed the deliberations of the specially constituted General Council of Officers that convened on 6 December. Broadly representative though it was intended to be, only thirty-seven members were attending it after six days' sitting, and none came to it from Scotland, Ireland (apart from several already in England), or even from Lambert's forces in the north. It was deaf to Ludlow's and Rich's pleas for the recall of the Rump, and it took little notice of the 'model or form of civil government' drafted for it by the Committee of Safety's sub-committee on the constitution. It soon decided instead that a new parliament should be called, consisting of two assemblies, one of the nature of a senate, the other a version of the House of Commons. Both to be elected by those of the people who were 'duly qualified'. Besides these two chambers there were to be twenty-one Conservators of Liberty, who were to determine any disagreements that might arise between the army and the parliament, and whose consent was required to any disbandments or changes of command in the army as it stood. These conservators were immediately elected by the General Council, and since it rejected not only Haselrig, Walton, Morley, Neville, Wallop, and Rich but also Monck himself, their chances of acting as umpires between the now irreconcilable factions were nil. The sub-committee also approved a set of seven predictable 'Fundamentals', which among other things ruled out not only kingship, or any single chief magistrate, but a House of Lords. Next day, before it had been decided how either assembly should be constituted or who was to wield executive authority, the Committee of Safety drafted a proclamation announcing that writs would be issued for the election of a parliament, to meet on 24 January. Weeks before then both the Committee and its General Council were to vanish from the scene, but such were the depths of political incompetence that they plumbed before they finally disintegrated.

The republicans' securing of Portsmouth was doubly damaging to them because of its impact on the fleet. With Montagu in enforced retirement, Vice-Admiral Lawson was in effective command. Lawson's sympathies lay firmly with the Rump, as did those of his senior subordinates Goodson and Stayner, and his hostility towards the officers who had interrupted it was increased when money earmarked for his unpaid seamen was diverted by the Committee of Safety to sweeten the soldiery on whom it so much depended. But in mid-October there was little he could immediately do, because at that point nearly all his ships were disposed on convoys and other duties, and he was persuaded by Vane and Salwey, in their capacity as Admiralty Commissioners, to go on taking orders from the still active members of the Rump's Council of State. Most of Lawson's captains, little as they loved the Committee of Safety, regarded it as a lesser evil than a restoration of the king and were deeply distrustful of Monck's intentions; Goodson, Stayner, and twenty others of them signed a letter to him early in November, bluntly telling him so. When the naval officers around London were asked to elect representatives to the General Council of Officers due to meet on 6 December they chose both Lawson and Montagu, as well as (among others) Goodson, Stayner, and Bourne. Montagu, however, held aloof and stayed at Hinchingbrooke.

This election showed that there was quite a wide range of political feeling in the fleet, but Lawson had a strong hold on the loyalty of the seamen, and on most of the officers too. His choice of action was not easy. As a republican and a Baptist he was sincerely opposed to the restoration of the monarchy, and as a believer in the rule of law he was quite out of sympathy with the army chiefs who had usurped power. He might have seen the way forward, as his friend Vane did, in the election of a new parliament with a senate as a guarantor of agreed 'fundamentals', including the rejection of monarchy or any one-person rule, but the dependence of such a scheme on army dominance, and (by December) the crumbling of the Committee of Safety, put it out of the question. He consistently saw the reinstatement of the Rump as the essential first step to a settlement, but he feared that if he allied with Monck, who was outwardly its strongest champion, he would be aiding those whose secret agenda included the restoration of the king. What probably tilted him into a public decision were the persuasions of Okey and Scot and their companions, who sought refuge in the fleet after they had failed to seize the Tower. On 13 December Lawson and his captains addressed an open letter to the Lord Mayor and corporation of London, announcing that they would back the recall of the Rump by force if necessary and calling for the City's support. They also published a seven-point programme of reform which they hoped the parliament would take in hand. The City fathers, who were mostly no friends now either to republicans or to radical reform, ignored his appeal. A day or two later he set sail from the Downs with twenty-two ships and headed for the Thames, to play his vital part in bringing about the Restoration, but before describing it we must catch up with events in Scotland, northern England and Ireland.

Monck's main difficulties were that it would be hard for him to leave Scotland undefended without laying the country open to the common enemy, and that the forces that Lambert had mustered in northern England considerably outnumbered his own. If he could create a diversion in Lambert's rear it could enormously help his own march south, when he was ready to make it, and greatly encourage his supporters in England. Early in November, his trusted former second-in-command Major-General Morgan, who was laid up in York with the gout, visited Fairfax of his own accord at his Nun Appleton seat, showed him Monck's declaration for the Rump and sought his support for it. Fairfax, as we have seen, had hitherto resisted all overtures by the royalists, but the latest exclusion of the Rump was evidently the last straw for him, not only because it threatened his own ideals of representative government and the rule of law but because it dishonoured his once heroic army. Through Morgan he returned a friendly message to Monck, along with a letter from his influential Presbyterian chaplain Edward Bowles, saying that many like-minded gentry in Yorkshire were well-disposed towards Monck's stand, but troubled that he had pledged himself to support no government but a republic and to restore only the Rumpers, rather than all the surviving members of the Long Parliament. Monck at once sent Clarges to explain that in the current circumstances he could not publicly declare all that he had in mind, and from then on plans went cautiously ahead for a rising of the Yorkshire gentry, including all but the extremes of the political spectrum, in support of his intended march into England. By this time one can assume that he was well aware of what it would probably lead to, though he was prepared to lie stoutly about his objectives in public. He certainly kept the royalists in the dark about them; even in mid-January, when he was well on his way to London, Mordaunt wrote to the king: 'He is a black Monck, and I cannot see through him'.[20] He was probably intent on keeping his own options open for as long as possible, and the fact that the Restoration was bloodless owed much to his coolness and inscrutability.

In preparation for his march into England, he set up his headquarters on 8 December at Coldstream on the Tweed. Today's Coldstream Guards descend directly from his own regiment of foot, and they wear white facings in remembrance of the undyed woollen coats that kept his soldiers warm in the harsh border winter. His reorganized army numbered four cavalry and six infantry regiments, with a nominal total of 8,400 men, though they were probably under strength. Lambert, when he first moved north to face him, had had not far short of 12,000, including the troops already in the region and the brigade that had been brought over from Ireland to counter Booth's rising, but so few of Lambert's men were willing to fight Monck that numbers soon became meaningless. On 12 December Monck met representatives of the Scottish shires as arranged at Berwick, thirteen miles from Coldstream. They chose five delegates to present their proposals to him, and significantly four of the five were nobles, Glencairn again being the chief of them. Monck granted some but not all of their desires. He allowed each shire to appoint a committee to regulate its own affairs, subject to its engaging not to act against the Commonwealth's interests or in favour of Charles Stuart's. He agreed that the shires adjacent to the Highlands should raise armed guards for their own defence, and promised to reconsider the case of the others if and when he took his army out of Scotland. Noblemen and gentlemen who pledged themselves to live peaceably regained the right to wear swords and have armed attendants. But he stalled over the Scots' proposal to raise men in arms to assist him actively in his campaign, saying he would allow it only if Lambert defeated him in battle. This was a typically shrewd handling of the situation, and it testifies both to the trust that Monck had won from the leaders of the Scottish people, at least south of the Highland line, and to the trust that he in turn was prepared to repose in them. Such threats as there were to the peace of

[20] *Clarendon State Papers*, III, 651. 'All the world is at a loss to think what Monck will do', wrote Pepys in his diary on 18 January.

Scotland probably came more from robbers and other lawless men than from conspirators against the Commonwealth, while those who did hope strongly for the king's return probably guessed that Monck would be the likeliest means of bringing it about. [21]

In Ireland, the senior of the commissioners whom the Rump had placed in charge after Henry Cromwell's resignation and return home was Colonel John Jones. Under his guidance the officers of the army there responded to the coup in October with a very cool and non-committal acceptance of the change of regime, and dispersed to their commands to frustrate any possible attempt by the royalists. Ludlow had named Jones as acting commander-in-chief of the army in Ireland when he returned to England in October 1659, and he was disgusted that Jones submitted to the English army's usurpation and rejected Monck's appeal to support him in demanding the reinstatement of the Rump. But only fifteen officers had signed Jones's letter to Fleetwood, and it was soon clear that his basis of support was narrow. Monck had had assurances that Sir Charles Coote, Sir Theophilus Jones, and a considerable part of the army were resolved to assist him, and that they hoped to win over Sir Hardress Waller. On 20 October he wrote to Ludlow, as nominal commander-in-chief in Ireland (though he had just returned to England) and as his fellow-commissioner under the recent act for the command of all the land forces, calling on him and the Irish army to assist him in restoring the Rump. The letter was replied to by Jones and just four other officers in Dublin, who professed themselves 'very much troubled and startled' by Monck's stand, which they feared would open the way to the common enemy.[22]

Jones was unhappily aware, however, of serious divisions within the army in Ireland. Ludlow had submitted it to quite a drastic purge during his brief period as commander-in-chief under the restored Rump. Besides removing officers with strongly Cromwellian sympathies, he got rid of others on the grounds of loose morals, heavy drinking, or corruption; but many of those he put in their place were Baptists or other sectaries, so the lines of division that had troubled Henry Cromwell when he faced Fleetwood in the mid-1650s were opened afresh. When the call came to elect delegates to the representative General Council of the Army and Navy, there was no time to get officers serving in Ireland to it by 6 December, and the only members of the Irish army who sat on it were drawn from the Irish Brigade that had been sent over to help suppress Booth's rising. Elections were held, however, but only the more radical officers co-operated, and they were finding themselves increasingly threatened and isolated. The opposition to them came mainly from men with

---

[21]   Here I follow the excellent discussion by Dow in *Cromwellian Scotland*, pp. 254–7.
[22]   Quoted by Aidan Clarke in *Prelude to Restoration in Ireland* (Cambridge, 1999), p. 98. Clarke provides the fullest and best account of these transactions.

their roots in Ireland whose authority did not rest wholly on their military commissions, and in particular from Sir Charles Coote, Sir Hardress Waller, and Sir Theophilus Jones, though Jones had been displaced from the governorship of Dublin by Ludlow. By the autumn of 1659, if not before, they cordially wanted the king back, and they had an ally in Lord Broghill. In the current quarrel they sided with Monck against the Committee of Safety. There had been coolness and rivalry between Coote and Monck, but they were prepared to sink their differences now in a common cause. That cause was supported also by the Scots in Ulster, who were giving the commissioners in Dublin an increasingly difficult time.

This old Cromwellian party organized a clever coup against Dublin Castle on 13 December. While two former officers diverted a sentinel, a mere thirty or forty infantrymen jostled their way in, took the hundred-strong guard by surprise and disarmed them. Troops of horse then rode through the streets with drawn swords, shouting 'A parliament! A parliament!', while others arrested John Jones and his two fellow-commissioners. Those of the garrison who did not go over to the conspirators were disarmed, and the new masters of Dublin acclaimed Sir Hardress Waller as their commander-in-chief. The citizens lit bonfires to express their joy at the overthrow of the unpopular commissioners. Next day Waller and twenty-one other officers issued a declaration condemning the 'sinful interruption' of the parliament, which they sent out to all garrisons in Ireland, as well as to Speaker Lenthall and the parliamentary commissioners in Portsmouth. Waller wrote privately to Monck, pledging his support, and (with tongue in cheek) professing confidence that he would not 'betray this good old cause to the Cavalier party'.[23]

In the provinces, Leinster fell into line after Captain Lisle was sent to seize Drogheda from its governor, Lieutenant-Colonel John Desborough (presumably a kinsman of the major-general). Ulster took a little longer to secure, but there was no serious resistance to the new order. Sir Charles Coote and his three brothers made sure of Connaught, where Athlone was the only place to show any resistance. In Munster, Clonmel and Limerick were gained by strikes clearly linked with the one in Dublin, and Broghill played his part behind the scenes in helping to overcome other pockets of resistance. There as elsewhere, the military adherents to the Committee of Safety, especially the Baptist element among them, were cordially detested by the local magistrates and people. A new council of officers was constituted to represent the overwhelming majority of the forces in Ireland that now supported the parliament against the committee. It scathingly criticized Ludlow's exercise of authority as commander-in-chief, and formally resolved on 26 December, without a dissenting voice, not to allow him back into Ireland unless the Council of

---

[23] *Clarke Papers*, IV, 202–3, quoted in Clarke, *Prelude to Restoration*, pp. 113–14.

State or parliament should order his return. Two days later it addressed letters to all the counties and major towns, requiring their well-affected protestant inhabitants to elect representatives to an assembly in Dublin, to meet on 24 January, subject to parliament's approval. It was following the precedent set by Monck in his summoning of representatives of the Scottish shires and burghs on 15 November and 12 December. It was indeed reporting to Monck in Scotland as well as to the Council of State in London and the parliamentary commissioners in Portsmouth. What it did not yet know was that the Rump had just been restored to power.

As December advanced, the Committee of Safety's authority fell away week by week, and latterly day by day. The City corporation kept up its own committee of safety to maintain order in the capital, but the apprentices and younger citizens were furious at its failure to secure the expulsion of Fleetwood's troops and to entrust London's defence solely to its own militia. Some of them stoned the Lord Mayor's coach, and despite posting large guards at the City gates and other key points the army could barely keep order. Sentries were shot at after dark, soldiers took their lives in their hands if they wandered off the main thoroughfares, and officers off duty dared not wear their swords. As late as the 14th the Common Council was sufficiently mollified by the Committee of Safety's promise of a new parliament to order all householders to keep their sons and servants and apprentices off the streets, but on the 20th it utterly rejected the seven 'fundamentals' by which it was to be limited, and pledged the City to support the speedy summoning of a fully free parliament. Next day came the annual elections to the Common Council, and the result was a turnover in which more than a third lost their seats to newcomers, most of them hostile to republicans and sectaries and ready to welcome the king back to his throne. The new Common Council promptly set about reorganizing the militia and taking over the defence of the capital.

A few days earlier a force that the Committee of Safety had sent to recover Portsmouth went over to its republican defenders, and Haselrig got ready to march on London with 1,500 horse. On the 21st two regiments on guard near Whitehall defied their colonels and declared for the Rump, and over large parts of southern and Midlands England and in south Wales other military units and garrisons were doing the same. Lawson and his fleet, whom we last saw setting sail from the Downs in mid-December, dropped anchor at Gravesand on the 17th, cutting London off from the sea. Before he got there Lawson was met by Vane and Salwey and other delegates from the Committee of Safety, who tried to persuade him that the best hope for the future lay in the new parliament that it had decided to summon for 24 January. But Okey and Scot were still with him, and they helped to hold him and his captains firm to their resolve to support the Rump. He really needed no persuading, for the fleet was not prepared, he said, to allow a pseudo-parliament 'to be a mask to the army's tyranny'.[24]

Whether that parliament would ever materialize was now in doubt. Writs for elections were sent to the City on the 21st, but countermanded on the 22nd. That day Whitelocke went to see Fleetwood, on the personal advice of Lord Willoughby of Parham, Major-General Browne, and several other prominent presbyterians, who had called to confirm his suspicions that Monck intended to bring back the king, and to suggest that Fleetwood should immediately send Charles an offer of good terms and so get in first. After much thought, Whitelocke put it to Fleetwood that he should choose between two courses: either to draw all his forces together and put himself at the head of them, so as to gauge his strength, and then if it proved as small as he expected to join with the City corporation and declare for a free parliament; or to send to the king as his presbyterian friends suggested. Fleetwood asked Whitelocke if he would act as his emissary to the king, and on getting a favourable answer told him to prepare himself to begin his journey that evening or early next morning. But Vane, Desborough, and Berry came to see him just as Whitelocke was leaving, and after a quarter of an hour with them Fleetwood came out, and in much passion said to Whitelocke "I cannot do it! I cannot do it!"[25] The three had reminded him that he had promised Lambert not to do such a thing without his consent.

The active nucleus of the old Council of State now judged the Committee of Safety's authority to have collapsed, and seized their chance. They called at Speaker Lenthall's home in Chancery Lane on the 23rd and obtained his authority to order all the troops in London to parade in Lincoln's Inn Fields next day under their supporters, Colonels Okey and Allured. Fleetwood, summoned by the Speaker to surrender the keys of the Commons' House, confessed as he handed them over 'that the Lord has blasted them and spit in their faces, and witnessed against their perfidiousness'.[26] The troops who had refused to recognize Lenthall as their general in October now marched from Lincoln's Inn Fields to his house to acclaim him as such with happy shouts and volleys of shot. It was a problem, however, to find enough Rumpers about town to constitute a quorum, and what would soon be called Christmas Day again was spent in rounding them up. They had announced that they would sit on the 27th, but they heard that the members secluded in Pride's Purge were planning to take their seats too; so Lenthall led them quietly by back ways from Whitehall to their chamber on the evening of the 26th, to hold a brief pre-emptive session.

So began the third incarnation of the Rump. Only forty-two MPs were

[24] Quoted in Capp, *Cromwell's Navy*, p. 349.
[25] *Diary of Bulstrode Whitelocke*, pp. 552–3.   [26] *Clarke Papers*, IV, 220.

present on the 27th, but Haselrig, Morley, and Walton got back to London two days later and went straight to the House without changing their riding clothes. Haselrig, unused to being cheered by the citizenry, was in a state of almost manic euphoria, but he refused to enter the chamber until Vane left it. Vane was in deep trouble for having sat on the Committee of Safety, and there was an attempt to impeach him, but after debate the House was content merely to expel him. It was on the point of electing a new Council of State when Haselrig rejoined it, and he topped the poll. But its choice of members put paid to any lingering hopes that the Rump would, without further pressure, offer any kind of settlement that the country could accept. Among the members who lost their seats were Vane, Salwey, Ludlow, Whitelocke, and Algernon Sidney, as well as the army chiefs Fleetwood, Lambert, Desborough, and Berry. A phalanx of Haselrig's henchmen took their places, along with a few republican army officers and City aldermen. So narrowly based a body could scarcely keep London quiet from day to day, let alone govern three nations and provide for the future. The Common Council showed its quasi-independence by meeting nine times between 20 December and 4 January—more often in two weeks than in a typical peacetime year. It approved a petition to parliament for the readmission of the secluded members and for free elections to the vacant seats, and was only just persuaded by Haselrig, Morley and Walton, in a meeting with its own committee of safety, to suspend it. But throughout England and Wales, in most of Scotland and among those of the people of Ireland who had a political voice the pressure for a free parliament had become irresistible. The great question was whether the political nation could move towards its desired end peacefully, or whether a further descent towards anarchy would plunge it once more in civil war. One man more than any other held the answer in his hands: George Monck.

# TWENTY-SEVEN

# The Monarchy Restored

IT is not often that historical turning-points fall on neatly memorable dates, but in a real sense the story of the Restoration can be said to have begun on 1 January 1660, for that was the day on which Monck's army began its march on London. The return of the monarchy had been inevitable for the past two months or more, but how and when it would come about were wide open questions. Monck held the key to the answers. He alone now commanded a coherent and obedient army, partly because he had recently purged and re-organized it, partly because his officers and men—those he had not dis-placed—felt a personal loyalty to 'honest George Monck' (their own name for him), and partly because he had shrewdly obtained enough money to keep them in regular pay, while Lambert's and Fleetwood's soldiers went penniless. Yet his intervention was not a foregone conclusion, for he knew perfectly well before he set forth that the Rump had already been restored, and the letter it sent to thank him for his support said nothing about march-ing into England. Haselrig and his party, now they were back in the saddle, would surely have much rather he stayed quietly in Scotland. He had indeed written to the Council of State on 29 December, promising absolute obedience to parliament's orders, and saying that while he was ready to march 'I shall attend your farther commands'.[1]

So it is not idle to ask why he did march three days later, *without* any fur-ther commands. It is no use looking to his own utterances, for he gave no encouragement to the addresses in favour of a free parliament, whether through the election of a new one or by readmitting the secluded members to the present one. On 23 January, from Leicester, he wrote a reply to one such declaration, published by the gentry of his native Devon, which was printed and avidly read. 'Monarchy', he wrote, 'cannot possibly be admitted for the future in these nations, because its support is taken away', and because it was incompatible with the variety of new interests begotten by the Civil Wars: vast diversity in religion, and on the material plane the rights of the pur-chasers of crown lands, church lands, and delinquents' estates. The secluded

---

[1] *Parliamentary or Constitutional History of England*, XXII, 40–1.

members, he went on, were monarchists who wanted to annul all laws passed since 1648, and to recall them would outrage the army and lead to a new and bloody civil war.[2] Two days earlier he had written to congratulate St John on his 'noble resolution to endeavour the just settlement of these nations in a Commonwealth way'.[3]

There is always an element of speculation in gauging a person's unspoken motives, especially in one as secretive as Monck. The prospect of high rank and a princely income must have counted, but he was never purely mercenary. On a higher level he must have rightly judged that a government dominated by Haselrig's faction and propped by Fleetwood's remnant of an army would never have given the nation the settlement that it so badly wanted and needed, and he knew that he, almost uniquely, possessed the means of setting it on course towards that goal—moreover without bloodshed. He also had a perfect pretext for marching when he did. He had engaged Fairfax to raise the gentry of Yorkshire in support of his advance into England, and the same messenger who informed him of Fleetwood's submission to the Rump brought him news that Fairfax's friends were already on the move. It would have been too late to cancel the rendezvous, even if he had wanted to. In fact Fairfax's supporters moved a day or two earlier than they had at first intended, because Colonel Lilburne got wind of their intentions and set off from Newcastle with reinforcements for the garrison of York. Fairfax had undertaken to appear with his forces before that city on New Year's Day, but the various local rendezvous of the gentry mostly took place two days earlier. He himself was so crippled by gout and in such pain from the stone that he had to ride in his coach, but the charisma that clung to his name enabled him to create a powerful diversion in Monck's favour. It was all the stronger because he excluded committed royalists from his company; he sent his own son-in-law Buckingham home, much to the latter's disgust. Nevertheless when he finally mustered his forces on Marston Moor—what resonances that scene must have had for him!—for the march on York they numbered about 1,800. Among them was the Irish Brigade that had been brought over to fight Booth, and some of Lambert's and Lilburne's own units came in to him. So far he had made no public declaration of his intentions, and it seems that he rather deftly avoided doing so now, but the whole company on Marston Moor acclaimed him with loud shouts before they marched off together towards York.

On arriving before its walls at about midday, Fairfax summoned the city to surrender, threatening to assault it if Lilburne and its defenders did not open its gates. Lilburne's garrison was small, and the citizenry were becoming

---

[2] Text in *Parliamentary or Constitutional History of England*, XXII, 68–70, where Monck's letter is misdated 21 January.
[3] *Clarke Papers*, IV, 249.

more vociferous in support of Fairfax by the hour. But he still hoped that Lambert might send him reinforcements, and he resourcefully bought time and divided his opponents by agreeing to admit only those who engaged themselves to support the present parliament as it had sat on 10 October (i.e. without the secluded members) against a king or any other single person whatsoever. Fairfax indignantly tore up this engagement, so York was held that night for the Rump by the Irish Brigade and some of Lilburne's men, while Fairfax and the gentry and their men quartered in neighbouring villages as best they could. Lambert was indeed at Ripon, thirty-seven miles away, and some of his cavalry did appear before the walls of York during the night, but he was by now in no condition to help Lilburne, let alone to resist Monck. His forces, miserable in their northern quarters and without pay, had been disintegrating since late December, when they got news of the collapse of the Committee of Safety. Most obeyed the Rump's orders to return to their former quarters, but many just melted away and made for home, and some rallied to Fairfax.

When Monck followed his forward units across the Tweed on 2 January, he did not have to fear resistance by any part of the army in England. Lilburne made his submission to parliament that day, and admitted Fairfax and his levies into York. Overton held out obstinately in Hull, but he was totally isolated and quite unable to take the offensive. Monck was able to choose his own pace for his advance southward, and he did not hurry it. There was no point in exhausting his foot soldiers, who had to contend with short days and snow-covered roads. He gave them a rest after he made a triumphal entry into York on the 11th, for he stayed there for five days, on one of which Fairfax entertained him and his staff at Nun Appleton. Back in Westminster the Rump, faced with the fait accompli of his southward advance, put the best colour they could on it by writing on 7 January to request him to come to London with such forces as he thought fit, to confer about the organization of the Commonwealth's armies. He had other business in mind, and the church bells that rang for him as he made his steady progress through the Midlands showed that most of England guessed it.

Haselrig's party did their best to frustrate the purpose of which they suspected him, but despite the expulsion or withdrawal of all the members who had acted with the Committee of Safety their hold on the House was very uncertain. On 2 January they managed to add a clause to the oath to be taken by members of the Council of State, requiring them to renounce totally the pretended title of Charles Stuart and to abjure the setting up of any single person or House of Lords. Next day Haselrig introduced a bill requiring all MPs to take the same engagement. It gained a first reading by twenty-four votes to fifteen, but after long debate, in which the member's language became so bitter that the Speaker threatened to leave the chair, it was dropped. Only thirteen councillors ever took the oath. Narrow as the basis of government now was, some of its members were preparing themselves to abandon the sinking ship, in order to swim with the tide that was bearing Monck towards his impending triumph. But the intransigents clung on. The Rump sent two of its members, Thomas Scot and Luke Robinson, to attend him on his march, ostensibly to bring him its thanks but in reality to watch over him in the manner of latter-day political commissars. He seems not to have been embarrassed; indeed he may have been quite glad to leave it to them to respond to the addresses for a free parliament that he kept on receiving. How little the Rump was prepared to grant one was shown when it voted on 5 January that the members excluded by Pride's Purge were now expelled and that writs should be issued for elections to fill the vacancies so created, though it did not make public its plans for the future of parliament until after Monck's arrival in London.

When he reached St Albans, only twenty miles from Westminster, Monck wrote to the Speaker to propose that all the regiments currently quartered in and around the capital, except for those of Morley and Fagg, whom he trusted, should be moved out to make room for his own three regiments of horse and four of foot. He further proposed that the outgoing regiments, whose colonels included such friends of the Rump as Okey, Rich, Streater, and Haselrig himself, should have their constituent troops and companies scattered over widely separated quarters. His intention to ensure military dominance for himself if he and the Rump fell out was transparently obvious, and the House debated his letter furiously for four hours. Eventually a compromise proposed by Haselrig was defeated, and Monck's requests were granted to the letter. He had a valid pretext for wanting his own troops about him, for the discipline and morale of those already in London were cracking. One regiment, when paraded prior to going on guard on 1 February, refused to march without its pay; the men threatened to strip and hang their officers, and drove them out of St James's Fields. Next day the troops in Somerset House tore up their colours and fired their guns, demanding pay before they would move, and so many companies came in to join them that there were soon well over 2,000 in full mutiny. Some called for a free parliament, some for the king, some for Lambert and their old officers; others said they would serve anyone who paid them. The Council of State was so scared that it sent Scot posting to Monck's headquarters at Barnet, to rouse him out of bed (it was past midnight) and urge him to march into London immediately. But Monck soon went back to bed again, saying he would make his entry next day as planned. By the time he did so, most of the mutinous troops had accepted their officers' promise that they would be paid on reaching their next quarters.

He rode into the City at noon on 3 February at the head of his life guard, soberly clothed but finely mounted. About a hundred notables followed him in coaches, and behind them came his cavalry. There were few manifestations of the popular enthusiasm with which he had often been greeted earlier in his march, but many cries for a free parliament. Relations between the City and the Rump were very tense, and the citizenry must have been unsure which side Monck was on, especially if they saw him embracing the Speaker, who met him before Somerset House, and being greeted at Whitehall by most of the members. On the very day after his entry, the House voted that it should be 'filled up to 400 members', on the basis of the apportionment of seats that it had approved in 1653, and that a committee should decide which seats were vacant and how they should be elected to. Nothing seems to have been heard of its vote, when first restored, that it would not sit beyond 7 May 1660. This massive recruitment, which could not have been completed until far into April, suggested that it meant to go on sitting at its pleasure.

For all the compliments that passed between Monck and the Rump during his first few days in London, there were tensions in their relationship. When he was invited to take his place on the Council of State, he declined the new oath abjuring the king's title and the House of Lords. It had not escaped him that parliament had recently been styling him Commissioner-General Monck, as if he was still just one of the seven placed over the army by the act of 12 October, despite his having asked and obtained its confirmation of his commission from the former Council of State as commander-in-chief. Haselrig had angrily said in parliament that Monck 'was no more General than himself was'.[4] When he attended the House in state on the 6th to receive its formal thanks, the speech that he made in reply to the Speaker's rhetoric, though totally respectful, contained blunter advice than many members were prepared to take from him. With an obvious allusion to the oath he had just declined, he said 'That the less oaths and engagements are imposed, . . . your settlement will be the sooner attained to'. He urged them to cultivate 'all the sober gentry . . . as knowing it to be the common concern to amplify, and not to lessen our interest, and to be careful that neither the Cavalier nor fanatic party have yet a share in your civil or military power'. He gave them similar advice about Ireland ('there as here, it is the sober interest must establish your dominion') and Scotland, where he entreated them to provide for the civil government; indeed he submitted the names of the commissioners and judges whom he recommended. Scot and other members only just managed to refrain from interrupting him.[5]

They could not afford to antagonize him, because London seemed to be on the brink of a tax strike, and if that happened the domino effect upon the counties and cities of provincial England could be disastrous. If it came to

[4] Historical Manuscripts Commission, *Leyborne-Popham MSS*, p. 210.
[5] Text in Baker, *Chronicle of the Kings of England*, pp. 705–6.

open defiance, only Monck's forces could protect the government. In an excited meeting on 8 February the Common Council seriously debated whether London should continue to pay any taxes voted by the Rump, but though a majority seemed in favour of refusing them no such decision was taken. It seems likely that the Lord Mayor invoked the Court of Aldermen's right of veto. The Council of State, however, reacted as though the City *was* openly defying parliament's authority. It sent urgently to Monck and ordered him to occupy the City with his army, take down its gates, wedge its portcullises open, and arrest eleven leading members of the Common Council. Long after the Restoration, Ludlow alleged that Monck himself proposed these severe measures with the object of luring the Rump into its own ruin, but this is even less plausible than the earlier allegations that the parliament-men set him upon an odious task in order to deflate his dangerous popularity. The probability is that the council genuinely overreacted, and that Monck obeyed because he had not yet given the Rump quite enough rope to hang itself (if you can hang a Rump), and because he had not yet had a chance to meet the secluded members and agree terms with them.

At any rate he marched his regiments into the City at daybreak on the 9th. His officers protested against the tasks imposed on them, but carried them out nonetheless, while great crowds of citizens watched in silence. The House when it met not only confirmed the council's orders but added that the City's gates and portcullises should not just be put out of action but totally destroyed. Then it listened to an address presented by Praise-God Barebone on behalf of London's gathered churches, deploring the advancement of the king's interest under the guise of demands for a free parliament or the read-mission of the secluded members, and praying that no one should be admitted to parliament, civil office, military command, or church living unless he solemnly abjured the house of Stuart and the promotion of any single person, senate or House of Lords. It was to rankle greatly with Monck that the Rump thanked the petitioners for their constant good affections.

Haselrig was exultant when he heard that Monck was carrying out his orders, exclaiming 'All is our own, he will be honest'.[6] But his tune changed that afternoon when the Speaker read out a letter from Monck, asking for a respite from the House's orders. He had arrested nine of the eleven designated common councilmen and made the City's defences unusable; to totally destroy the gates and portcullises would merely exasperate it. He believed that the Common Council would prove compliant over the taxes when it met next morning, and he begged parliament to decide quickly about the qualifications of members so that elections to the vacant seats could go forward soon. Haselrig's faction was deeply incensed; led by it the House not only

---

[6] *Memoirs of Edmund Ludlow*, II, 219.

ordered Monck to destroy the gates and portcullises but declared the City's Common Council dissolved.

Next day Monck duly burnt some of the gates, even though some of his most loyal officers were begging to resign their commissions rather than carry out such odious orders. But he conferred long and earnestly, not only with his senior officers but with Clarges, his trusted chaplains, and other confidants. That morning the Rump gave a first reading to a bill to put the command of the army into commission, as it had done just before the army had interrupted it in October. He was not going to put himself in the wrong by expelling it himself, but if parliament was going to deprive him of the command of the forces that it had so recently entrusted to him he needed to defend himself. Further close conferences ensued that evening, at the end of which he ordered fourteen of his senior officers to meet him at six next morning. All this consultation may carry a suggestion of indecision, and perhaps he partly intended it to. After the Restoration quite a number of men claimed the credit for persuading him to work for the king, but one can be fairly certain that he remained his own man throughout. He had the sense to listen to advice, and his decisions were all the more effective for carrying the concurrence of a wide range of associates.

At that early morning meeting on 11 February he put to his chosen officers the gist of a letter he proposed to send to the Rump. They gladly agreed to its terms, and as soon as it was drafted they all signed it. It was in effect an ultimatum. It complained that the use of force against the City was grievous to the army, which had acted not only to restore the parliament but to uphold the people's liberties. It protested at the retention in military commands of men who had acted with the Committee of Safety, at parliament's tolerance of Lambert's and Vane's continuing presence in London, contrary to its orders, and at its friendly reception of Barebone's pernicious petition, which would have forced a new oath on the nation and thereby excluded 'the most conscientious and sober sort of men' from civil and military employment. All this, however, was merely prefatory to the letter's main demand, which was that the Rump should issue writs for the promised elections by 17 February—just six days ahead. On hearing it read, Haselrig stormed out of the House in a fury, but he was back in the afternoon to help push through the bill to entrust the command of the army to commissioners. There were to be five, including of course Haselrig, and a motion that Monck should always be one of a quorum of three was defeated.

But while this was under way Monck was attending a packed meeting of the full City corporation at the Guildhall and explaining what he had done. Word soon spread abroad that he had come out on the side of the City and a free parliament, and when he came out Pepys heard the crowd greet him with such a shout as he had never in his life heard before. Monck and his soldiers were suddenly heroes, and that evening all the church bells rang and bonfires blazed in every street. Rumps were sacrificed at dozens of impromptu barbecues; boys begged passers-by for pennies for 'the roasting of the Rump', or invited them to 'kiss my parliament', and some citizens dared to kneel in the street and drink the king's health. Monck and his army stayed within the City, and he himself was happy to be put up by an alderman of known royalist sympathies. On both the next two days the Council of State requested him to come to Whitehall and take his seat, but he respectfully declined. The councillors' oath still stuck with him, and though the Rump tried to lure him with a series of concessions he maintained that the presence of 'fanatic and disaffected persons' necessitated his stay in the City.

The parliament did make some attempts to meet his wishes during the week following the receipt of his letter. It modified the councillors' oath. It ordered Vane's expulsion from London, summoned Lambert before the council, and ordered other members of the Committee of Safety to appear before the House itself. It ordered a month's pay for all the forces about London, though it could only find £5,000 of the £16,500 needed. Above all it went steadily ahead with the bill for elections to the vacant seats, and had it ready for printing by the 18th. But it never was printed, and its text has not survived. The amendments recorded in the Commons' Journal, however, reveal that it would have debarred anyone whose father had been sequestered, or had ever advocated a single person as chief magistrate, or refused to take the councillors' oath or was married to a papist—not to mention drunkards and blasphemers. Monck was clearly preparing himself to be dissatisfied with the Rump's response. He made no secret of being in contact with the secluded members; indeed he arranged two meetings between representatives of them and of the Rump at his headquarters, the first on the 14th. Among the many addresses that he received calling for their readmission, one that was most widely remarked came from Fairfax and a select band of the leading Yorkshire gentry; four of them presented it to him personally on the 17th, though it had been agreed a week earlier and had already been printed in both York and London. The council of officers in Ireland declared for their readmission on the 16th, though Monck cannot have known this before he took his crucial decision.

When did he take it? Historians still do not agree, and only a rash one would set a precise date. He had several good reasons for moving slowly and keeping people guessing as to his intentions. He genuinely wanted to avert the kind of uncontrolled royalist reaction that would undo all that the Long Parliament had fought for in church and state; his professed preference for 'a commonwealth way' was not wholly insincere, even though the Commonwealth's professed champions seemed intent on political suicide. He had to make sure of carrying his own officers with him, for some of them must have been uncomfortable about assisting in any way at the restoration of the king. He needed to cement his newly established friendship with the City corporation. He had given the Rump an ultimatum, and honour required that he should allow it the stipulated time to meet his demands. It was only one day late in settling the conditions and qualifications for the promised elections, and we know enough about them to be confident that they were too restrictive to satisfy—as he doubtless expected them to be. According to Whitelocke's diary, Monck decided on the 19th, the day after the 'act of qualifications' was passed, to admit the secluded members on the 21st.[7] But while all these considerations must have counted with him, surely his overriding reason for giving himself time before he took the crucial step was to reach agreement with the secluded members themselves and make certain that they would do what he expected of them. He had to guard on the one hand against generating an unrestrained and possibly violent royalist reaction that would lead to a totally unconditional restoration, and on the other against the possibility that once the secluded members were restored the Long Parliament would avail itself of the 1641 'own consent' act to go on sitting indefinitely. What we can surely discount is the view that he spent his first eighteen days in London in a state of dithering uncertainty until his more politically sophisticated confidants, Sir Anthony Ashley Cooper being the loudest-mouthed claimant, persuaded him that readmitting the secluded members was the only way forward.[8]

On Monday 20 February the Rump ordered the Speaker to sign a warrant for the issue of writs for the promised elections, but he stubbornly refused to do so, saying that every secluded member whose seat was thereby filled might sue him at law. It is quite likely that Monck tipped him to do so; it is not the only sign of collusion between the two men. At any rate seventy-three secluded members met Monck at Whitehall early next morning and gave their assent to a declaration that his secretary read to them. In it he charged them to settle the command of the armies (implying his reinstatement as commander-in-chief), to provide for the pay of all the forces, to appoint a new Council of State, to cause writs to be issued for elections to a new parliament to meet on 20 April, and to enact the legal dissolution of the present one. They readily signed this paper, and Monck's Adjutant-General then escorted them straight to the House, where their arrival took most of the Rumpers (though not, we can be sure, the Speaker) completely by surprise. Their dismay can be imagined, but that evening the citizens of London celebrated as jubilantly as

---

[7] *Diary of Bulstrode Whitelocke*, p. 571.

[8] For this version see K. H. D. Haley, *The First Earl of Shaftesbury* (Oxford, 1968), pp. 129–32. Aidan Clarke in *Prelude to Restoration in Ireland*, pp. 153–4, sees Monck as changing course twice between 10 and 21 Feb. My disagreement on this particular point implies no lack of general admiration for Haley's and Clarke's fine books.

they had done ten days earlier. Pepys sat in a Thames-side café with the composer Matthew Locke and Henry Purcell of the Chapel Royal (father of the
composer), and marvelled 'to see the City from one end to the other with a
glory about it, so high was the light of the bonfires, and so thick round the
City, and the bells rang everywhere'.[9] Many a provincial town kept holiday
the same way, if on a smaller scale.

The political situation was indeed transformed, for the secluded members
far outnumbered the Rumpers. They lost no time in voting to hold general
elections at an early date and in choosing a new Council of State. This was
dominated by presbyterians whose attachment to monarchy was no secret; its
wisely chosen president was Arthur Annesley, whose moderation and lenity
matched Monck's own. Monck was not only confirmed as commander-
in-chief but was made General at Sea in partnership with Montagu. A potentially embarrassing bill to settle Hampton Court on him was laid aside, but he
was voted a grant of £20,000 in lieu. Parliament made sweeping changes in
the militia commissioners throughout the country, to make sure that the
trained bands complied with whatever political changes lay in store. One of
those appointed for Cheshire was Sir George Booth, who had so recently been
in arms against the Rump. The main danger that the now inevitable restoration might be resisted lay in the remaining regular forces. We shall shortly
see how Monck kept those in England in obedience, but a bigger question
mark lay over those in Ireland.

After the coup in Dublin in mid-December most of the army in Ireland had
declared for the Rump against the Committee of Safety, but though Monck
was in contact with Coote and Broghill there was no certainty as to how it
would react to the readmission of the secluded members. Ludlow muddied the
waters by returning to Ireland as soon as the Rump was restored, hoping to
resume his command there. He arrived before Dublin on 31 December, but
on learning that Waller and the officers there intended to arrest him if he landed he made for Duncannon, where adherents to the old army interest represented by Fleetwood were holding out. He did not stay there long, for Waller
and his Dublin colleagues framed articles of impeachment against him. These
were presented to the Rump on 19 January, and Ludlow hastened home to
defend himself. Meanwhile, on hearing of the Rump's reinstatement, the officers in Dublin had cancelled the meeting of representatives that it had called
for 24 January. The Rump for its part formally annulled its former commission for the government and issued a new one, whose five recipients
included Coote and Waller. The latter pair and their friends were already carrying out large changes in the command of the regiments in Ireland. Waller and
Coote were given two each, while Coote's three brothers got one apiece and

[9] *Diary of Samuel Pepys*, I, 61.

a cousin of his a third. Monck, when he addressed the Rump on 6 February, assured it that these and other alterations in the Irish army were necessary to correct recent abuses of the power to appoint officers; but when, five days later, the House turned on Monck and put the command of the army in England and Scotland into commission, Marten at Ludlow's prompting moved that that in Ireland should be included, and so it was carried. This put all the recent changes in command there into the melting-pot.

During the tense days between Monck's ultimatum to the Rump and his re-admission of the secluded members, the officers in Ireland were sharply divided. While Coote and his party were enthusiastically in favour of filling the House up and opening the gates to the king's return, possibly by way of Ireland, Waller was a regicide and a firm republican, deeply suspicious of Monck's intentions. At a meeting of the Council of Officers early in February he presented an 'engagement' opposing the readmission of the secluded, and on finding the majority against him he formed a plan to arrest their leaders and confine them in Dublin Castle. It was betrayed, and on the 15th Coote, Sir Theophilus Jones, and others rode through the city streets with a trumpeter and a party of horse, calling for a free parliament, and followed by a cheering crowd. Next day the council of officers formally approved a declaration for a full and free parliament through the readmission of the secluded members and the filling of the vacant seats by new elections. They sent it to Monck with fifty-five signatures, eighteen of them being those of colonels or lieutenant-colonels. Waller, now under siege in Dublin Castle, wrote to Monck to explain his opposition to readmitting the secluded, claiming quite rightly that he had been upholding the General's own publicly declared policy. But with the active help of the citizenry the Castle was swiftly brought to surrender, and Waller and his associates were packed off to Athlone as prisoners. On the 17th an extraordinary assembly of Dublin citizens gave its support to the council of officers' declaration.

These events meant that neither Monck nor the restored Long Parliament had anything to fear from the forces in Ireland, but on the political front the situation might not have been as simple as it looked. Whether still uncertain of Monck's intentions or simply hoping to steal a march on him, Coote had sent a messenger to the king earlier in February, assuring him of his service and inviting him to come to Ireland. But Hyde wisely foresaw the adverse effect that this would have on the rising tide of support for his master in England, as well as the practical difficulties of using Ireland as a springboard. One reason why Broghill held aloof from the Dublin officers' declaration of 16 February, but sponsored another on the same lines from Munster, was that much as he wished now for the king's restoration he did not want it to be on terms dictated by the old royalists, as might well have happened if Charles had been swept back to power by force. Coote and his fellow-officers took another step that had no authorization from either Monck or the government in Westminster: they revived the plan to hold a convention of representatives of the Irish counties and towns, and summoned it to meet on 27 February. Their object was partly to secure nationwide assent to the policies outlined in their declaration of the 16th, which had covered more than just a free parliament for England, and partly to secure financial provision for their forces in case they should fall out with the powers at Westminster, whoever they might turn out to be. By one account the mayor and aldermen of Dublin petitioned for such an assembly. Between the ordering of elections and its actual meeting, however—it did not get down to business until 3 March—Monck readmitted the secluded members and the whole situation changed. The Convention was to have some slight influence on the Restoration settlement in Ireland, but it had little or none on the train of events that was to bring the king back to England.

Scotland too watched that train of events in outward calm, but with intense anticipation. The attenuated forces in Scotland, mostly garrison troops and now under the command of Major-General Morgan, had some difficulty in preventing the nobles and gentry from exceeding their limited right to bear arms and mount guards, but the large part of the nation that now wanted to see their king restored had some confidence that Monck would do the business, and refrained from distracting him from it by making trouble north of the border.

He had most cause for concern in the reaction of the army in England after he readmitted the secluded members, for there was still a strong current of republican feeling within it, especially in those regiments that had been most loyal to the Rump. They had been widely dispersed, but in at least nine major provincial towns they clamped down on the popular celebrations. The most dangerous officers still in post were Okey, Rich, and Overton, though the regiments of the first two were divided into several quarters, and Overton was now isolated in Hull. Rich was forced into submission, made to resign his commission, and spent some weeks in confinement. Overton too was put under intense pressure, but after days of hesitation he obeyed Monck's summons to London, where he was cashiered. Yet even if he had wished to, which he did not, Monck could not have carried out a wholesale purge of all those officers who were disquieted by the Militia Bill and fearful that the forthcoming general election would fill parliament with supporters of the king. Considerable numbers of them held unauthorized meetings in London, from which emerged a declaration which they desired Monck to present to parliament in the name of the whole army. It would have demanded that parliament should pledge itself to maintain a commonwealth without a king or House of Lords, and threatened that if it refused the army would take its own measures to save the nation from destruction. Monck made his response known to a heavily attended General Council of Officers on 7 March, which Okey opened with a long and bellicose speech. Clarges delivered the gist of Monck's reply, which was that if the army put such pressure on parliament it would promptly dissolve itself and leave the country in a state of anarchy. His argument that the act for the forthcoming elections debarred all who had fought against the parliament since 1641 cut little ice, since it would be a dead letter if the incoming House declined to enforce it. There was evidently a party of officers, however, who wanted Monck to take the government upon himself, for he declared in winding the meeting up that he would rather lose his life than do so. 'Nothing', he told them, 'was more injurious to discipline than their meeting in military councils to interpose in civil things', and he forbade them to do so in future.[10] To help defuse the situation he arranged a meeting next day between ten officers and ten MPs, but immediately after that he ordered all officers back to their stations. Meanwhile Lambert, who had been lurking in London, had been removed from harm's way. The Council of State summoned him on 5 March and demanded £20,000 as surety for his good behaviour. Predictably, he could not find so huge a sum, and was committed to the Tower. There were slight stirrings in the army when parliament annulled the Engagement to be faithful to a commonwealth without a king or House of Lords, which the Rump had imposed on all adult males in 1650, but they were safely contained.

The parliament at last enacted that it should dissolve itself on 16 March. The past five weeks had been the trickiest phase in Monck's whole operation, and he had negotiated it with impressive skill. He had been abundantly justified in concealing his precise intentions, keeping his options open, and lying stoutly when necessary. He not only managed the army but played his part as joint General at Sea with Montagu in preventing any resistance by the navy. Until their appointment on 6 March Lawson had been in effective command of the fleet, and we have seen the vital part he played in restoring the Rump in December, for which he was elected to the Council of State and given lands worth £500 a year. But his well-known republican principles and his old association with Okey, Overton, and others of their kind made it very doubtful how he would respond to the readmission of the secluded members. It did indeed shake him, for he had trusted Monck as an old colleague, and by his own later admission he was strongly tempted to join his republican friends in open resistance. On Monck's insistence, however, parliament kept him in the service as vice-admiral, and royalist agents found him willing to listen to them. He immediately wrote to Monck and Montagu, submitting to their authority, and it seems that he went on hoping even now for a settlement without the king. Self-preservation obviously played a part in his decision,

---

[10]  Baker, *Chronicle of the Kings of England*, p. 716.

but he probably felt a genuine repugnance at the prospect of setting one part of the navy against the others, and by March an orderly and conditional restoration may well have struck him as a better solution than any other that was then feasible. At any rate he responded gratefully to a letter of goodwill from the king that he received early in April.

One man whom February's turn of the tide caught sadly adrift was John Milton. He had seen how dangerously the current was running as the quarrel mounted between the army and the Rump in the autumn of 1659, and between October and December he had twice taken up his pen to propose the outlines of a constitutional settlement that would heal their rifts and guarantee the future of the Good Old Cause. He was possessed by a heightened sense of urgency, however, amid the clamour for a free parliament that followed upon Monck's arrival in London and his ultimatum to the Rump. In haste he set about dictating a larger tract which he called *The Ready and Easy Way to Establish a Free Commonwealth*, though he knew the way would be far from easy. What he proposed was by no means his ideal model of a republic, supposing one could have been devised from scratch, but what in the straitened political circumstances of February 1660 he thought might yet avert the absolute evil of a return to monarchy. In his words, 'to fall back, or rather to creep back so poorly as it seems the multitude would, to their once abjured and detested thraldom of kingship, not only argues a strange degenerate corruption suddenly spread among us, fitted and prepared for new slavery, but will render us a scorn and derision to all our neighbours'. The Rump had voted to fill up the House, so if the people will elect 'able men, and according to the just and necessary qualifications decreed in parliament, men not addicted to a single person or House of Lords, the work is done: at least the foundation is firmly laid of a free Commonwealth'. Then comes the shock: once chosen, let the resultant assembly be renamed the Grand or General Council and empowered to sit in perpetuity, with full authority to dispose of the land and sea forces, raise revenue, make national laws, control relations with foreign powers, take decisions of peace or war, and appoint a Council of State for day-to-day administration. The only spheres that Milton would have withheld from its sway were those of religion and civil justice. Matters ecclesiastical, he held, should be outside the authority of the civil magistrate. In civil affairs, his one concession to anything remotely resembling democracy was a proposal that every county in the land should be made 'a little commonwealth' and its capital town a city, 'where the nobility and chief gentry may build houses or palaces, befitting their quality, may bear part in the government, make their own judicial laws, and execute them by their own elected judicatures, without appeal, in all things of civil government between man and man'. From their ranks would be filled the vacancies in the Grand or General Council when they occurred, though he did not say how. An inveterate townsman, his vision was probably based partly on the urban palazzi that he had seen on his Italian travels and partly on the example of the regent class in the cities of Holland. Not loving Oxford or Cambridge, he anticipated the civic universities of centuries later in his hope that the county elites would have in their local capitals 'schools and academies at their own choice, wherein their children may be bred up in their own sight to all learning and noble education, not in grammar only, but in all liberal arts and exercises'.[11] His central proposal for a perpetual Grand Council was of course quite impracticable, and even Miltonists seem to have stopped supposing that his scheme as a whole might conceivably have worked. But there is no inherent reason, *pace* Shelley and his 'unacknowledged legislators of the world', for expecting a composer of sublime poetry to be an infallible guide in practical politics, and Milton deserves respect for deciding that in what he saw as a near-desperate situation desperate remedies were better than none.

He deserves something rather more than respect for his courage, for besides putting up with a great deal of ridicule and vilification from pamphleteers who were swimming with the royalist tide he put out a second edition of *The Ready and Easy Way* early in April, when the elections to the Convention Parliament (of which more anon) were in full swing and the Restoration was all but inevitable. The first edition had been overtaken by the readmission of the secluded members, just after he finished dictating it but before it was printed. The second was much more than a mere update, and in bringing out so vehement an attack on monarchy at that moment he was putting not only his liberty and perhaps his life on the line but also his supreme masterpiece, for he had begun to dictate *Paradise Lost* in 1658 and it would be at least three more years before he finished it. Taking what hope he could from the fact that the writs for the current elections were issued not in the name of the king but of the Keepers of the Liberties, and that they debarred the old royalists and their sons from being returned, he proposed that the forthcoming parliament should be constituted a perpetual Grand Council. This time, however, the powers that he would have accorded it were somewhat less sweeping, and he was more prepared to consider that its membership should be renewed by means of the sort of rotation advocated by Harrington. He still disliked it, for, he said, 'I could wish that this wheel or partial wheel in state, if it be possible, might be avoided; as having too much affinity with the wheel of fortune'. He filled a gap in the first version by proposing the manner in which elections to vacant places should be held, and his elaborate method, in three or four stages, 'not committing all to the noise and shouting of a rude multitude', was clearly designed to keep out royalists rather than to give the people their choice. Indeed the most striking features of the second edition,

---

[11] Quotations from *Complete Prose Works of John Milton*, VII, 356–7, 362, 383–4.

and perhaps his major objects in composing it, are its arguments that an 'unfree' majority has no right to dictate to a 'free' minority, and its passionate denunciation of the moral degradation that the nation will inflict on itself if it brings back monarchy. As to the first he asked:

Is it just or reasonable, that most voices against the main end of government [i.e. freedom] should enslave the less number that would be free? More just is it doubtless, if it come to force, that a less number compel a greater number to retain, which can be no wrong to them, their liberty, than that a greater number, for the pleasure of their baseness, compel a less most injuriously to be their fellow slaves.

As for 'the new royalized presbyterians',

let them but hear the insolencies, the menaces, the insultings of our newly animated common enemies crept lately out of their holes, their hell I might say . . . Let our zealous backsliders forethink now with themselves, how their necks yoked with these tigers of Bacchus, these new fanatics not of the preaching but the sweating-tub, inspired with nothing holier than the venereal pox, can draw one way under monarchy to the establishing of church discipline with these new-disgorged atheisms.[12]

Milton had a reason for addressing Presbyterians in particular, because in its dying days in March the Long Parliament made an attempt to reinstate the Presbyterian religious settlement that it had enacted in 1645–6. A series of swiftly passed acts declared the Westminster Confession to be the public profession of faith of the Church of England, ordered that the Solemn League and Covenant should be republished and read in every church in the country, resumed the process of dividing the counties into classical presbyteries, and appointed a Presbyterian-dominated body of commissioners to approve all candidates presented to ecclesiastical benefices. These measures would very soon prove to be little more than gestures, since no parliament can bind its successor, and the chances that one elected in the spring of 1660 would endorse them were nil. But they were bad news to the likes of Milton, and still more to the much greater number of English men and women who trusted that the return of the king would bring back the Church of England that they or their parents had loved in pre-war times. Much more pleasing to such people was the outgoing parliament's vote that the House of Lords had a right to form part of all future ones.

Intense speculation filled the interval of nearly six weeks between the dissolution of the Long Parliament on 16 March and the meeting on 25 April of the Convention, as it came to be called, since strictly a parliament could be summoned only by writs issued by the king. The two great questions before the country were whether any conditions would be set to the now inevitable

---

[12] Quotations from *Complete Prose Works of John Milton*, VII, pp. 435, 452–3, 455; and for the dates of both editions pp. 177–8, 204–6.

Restoration, and whether diehard republicans inside and outside the army would make any attempt to resist it by force of arms. There was much talk of resuscitating the so-called Newport treaty of nearly a dozen years ago, which the presbyterian majority had been close to concluding with Charles I when Pride's Purge removed them. But though the Newport terms had their supporters, several factors dashed their hopes. The tide of public opinion was flowing too strongly now in the king's favour to be held by such a breakwater, and men in public life must have thought of the massive patronage that he would soon dispose of again, and felt reluctant to exclude themselves from it: call it the bandwagon syndrome. Furthermore if there were to be any conditions set, they would have had to be agreed by the incoming parliament, and the outgoing one's attempted disqualification of active royalists from sitting in it was widely breached. But perhaps the decisive factor, thanks probably in large part to Monck's advice to Hyde, was that Charles himself offered pledges which spiked the guns of those who might have tried to impose terms on him. For the king and Monck were at last in touch. As soon as the Long Parliament had dissolved itself, Monck allowed his kinsman Sir John Grenville to deliver a royal letter that he had been nursing for nearly eight months, and it was not until Grenville arrived in Brussels at least ten days later that Charles knew for certain that the General was ready to sacrifice life and fortune in his service. Monck also sent him the sound advice to get out of Spanish territory, since England and Spain were still formally at war, and Charles accordingly moved to Breda in the Dutch republic.

Monck, however, put nothing in writing, and announced no change of policy in public. He still had to be careful of the temper of his troops, and his caution was justified when Lambert escaped from the Tower on 10 April and tried to rally his former forces. His call now was to restore Richard Cromwell to his Protectorship, he having done so much a year earlier to eject him from it. But he found little response in London, and not much more when he switched his efforts to the regiments in the Midlands and the north. Monck's strategy of splitting up their component troops and companies was paying off, and the Council of State helped by promising their full arrears of pay to all soldiers who stayed with their colours and by making judicious arrests. Lambert eventually made his rendezvous at Edgehill, where he mustered the equivalent of only four troops of horse and no infantry at all. There on the 22nd, Easter Sunday, Colonel Richard Ingoldsby caught up with him; Monck may have chosen Ingoldsby for the task to help him redeem his past as a regicide. There was much parleying and a few shots were fired, but Lambert and his fellow-officers—they included Okey, Axtell, Cobbett, and Creed—had to surrender. Lambert was made to stand under the gallows at Tyburn before returning to an imprisonment that was to last until his death twenty-three years later.

Among the republican old guard, Ludlow had been girding himself and his friends to support Lambert if his rising got under way, but Haselrig had fallen into deep depression and given up hope—not that he had much in common with Lambert now except a detestation of Stuart monarchy. He had lately thrown himself on Monck's mercy, and Monck had genially offered to save his life and estate for twopence, so long as he retired to his country seat and lived quietly. Haselrig wrote to Monck again on 30 April, protesting his innocence of any part of Lambert's enterprise and enclosing two pennies. Honest George was to be as good as his word.

Meanwhile England was enjoying the first general elections in all but twenty years that were open to the whole body of traditional voters, for the electorate (unlike the future members) was subject to no political disqualifications. They were contested by an unprecedented number of candidates, and fought on great national issues to an extent never seen before the Civil Wars, not even in 1640. A barrage of pamphlets, many of them overtly royalist, offered advice to the electorate. The main issue at the hustings was between those who favoured and those who opposed the setting of conditions to the king's restoration, though the candidates' record over the past dozen or so years generally had a large bearing on their success. There were naturally some places where local rivalries of the traditional sort determined the result, but generally speaking the more unqualified a candidate's royalism was the likelier he was to get in. It went very hard with the republican old guard. Haselrig, as far as we know, did not even stand, while Ludlow and Scot were unseated after disputed elections. Of all the Rumpers who had sat since their return to power in May 1659 only sixteen were re-elected, and three of these were soon expelled from the House. Lenthall was among those defeated, despite two strong commendations from Monck. In defiance of the outgoing parliament's ban, at least 62 of those elected had been active royalists in the wars or were the sons of such, including more than a quarter of the knights of the shire; indeed Bordeaux wrote to Mazarin that the number of members who should have been thus disqualified was between 100 and 120. No action was taken against them, because the temper of the Convention House of Commons, from the moment it met on 25 April, was overwhelmingly royalist. Nearly half its members had never sat in parliament before.

There was much interest in the peers' response to the outgoing parliament's assertion of their right to a place in the new one. On the opening day just ten of them, all former parliamentarians, took their seats in the upper chamber, but the 'young lords' who had been minors or had not yet inherited when the Rump abolished their House quickly asserted their right to sit, and by the 27th the attendance was up to thirty-six. In the Commons some members wanted a debate on whether to acknowledge the House of Lords, but the majority welcomed its return as a step towards that of the king. The royalist peers soon came in and brought its numbers up to about 145.

Three days after the Convention Parliament met Sir John Grenville appeared before the council, bearing a declaration that the king had signed on 4 April. Its timing and content were perfectly judged. Hyde, who had been Lord Chancellor since 1658, probably deserves the credit that he has usually been given for it, though to a considerable extent it reflected the advice that Monck had sent to the king, who also consulted Secretary Nicholas and Ormond in the framing of it. The Declaration of Breda pulled the rug from under the feet of those who still sought to set conditions to the Restoration. In it, Charles promised a free and general pardon to all his subjects, however guilty, who pledged their loyalty and obedience as good subjects within forty days, with the exception only of those who should be excluded from it by parliament. He further declared 'a liberty to tender consciences', promising his assent to such an act of parliament as should ensure that none should be troubled for differences of opinion in matters of religion, so long as they did not disturb the peace of the kingdom. As for disputes over title to the vast quantities of land that had changed hands as a result of the Civil Wars and subsequent confiscations, he granted that they should be settled by parliament; and he finally promised his assent to whatever acts of parliament would fully satisfy the arrears due to the officers and men under Monck's command, whom he would take into his own service on as good pay and conditions as they currently enjoyed.

The beauty of the declaration was that for all its apparent magnanimity and respect for parliamentary authority, most of it was shifting on to parliament's shoulders the problems which were likeliest to raise animosities: the decisions about whom to punish for Charles I's fate and how to sort out the conflicting claims to confiscated estates, and the raising of yet more taxes to pay the army—or pay it off. As for the promise of religious liberty, it was parliament that would in due course have to take the responsibility for breaking it, not the king. But in face of such voluntary pledges, so cordially phrased, what hope was there of imposing further conditions on his return? The declaration was read in both Houses on 1 May, and rapturously received. The Lords passed a formal vote 'That according to the ancient and fundamental laws of this kingdom, the government is, and ought to be, by King, Lords and Commons'. The Commons concurred that same afternoon, and the Restoration can be dated from that moment.

That evening Monck summoned all the officers about London to hear the Declaration of Breda and a letter that the king had addressed specifically to the army. It was couched in the same gracious terms as those in which Charles had written to the two Speakers, and it swiftly produced an address professing the army's loyalty to the king and confirming its promise to conform to whatever parliament should enact. Montagu obtained an equally satisfactory response from the fleet, whose captains and crews showed a positive enthusiasm for the restoration of monarchy that could not have been predicted even a week or two earlier. Meanwhile London celebrated its happiest May Day in living memory with a night of bonfires, bell-ringing and heaven knows how many loyal toasts, and the rejoicing spread rapidly throughout the provinces. There was a similar outburst, in this season of hangovers, when Charles was formally proclaimed king, with all the old pageantry, on 8 May.

The Restoration was very much an English transaction. Scotland remained quiet under the precautionary arrangements that Monck had made for keeping the peace, and in March the Long Parliament, before it dissolved, named a new set of judges for Scotland (four English and six Scots) and a new body of five (subsequently four) commissioners for the government of the country. As for the forthcoming parliament, Monck had recommended to the outgoing one that its constituencies should follow the reforms devised by the Rump in 1653 and implemented in 1654 and 1656, but his advice was not taken, so no Scottish or Irish representatives sat in the Convention. Powerful men in Edinburgh pressed him to allow the Scots to elect commissioners to attend it, but he firmly refused. The country as a whole awaited the inevitable Restoration with more mixed feelings than the English did, largely because the king's intentions towards it, particularly regarding episcopacy, were so little known. No declaration came from Breda to Scotland. Nevertheless there were celebrations in Edinburgh on 7 May when the news arrived of the Convention's votes on May Day, and still more a week later when Charles II was ceremonially proclaimed.

Ireland had its own Convention, for that was the name given to the representative assembly summoned by the recently transformed council of officers in Dublin. It met in the Four Courts on 2 March, slightly later than first intended. It had little positive influence on the course of events, and it articulated the interests of the protestant minority rather than those of the Irish nation as a whole. But it is of considerable significance for the light it throws on the aspirations of protestant Ireland on the eve of the Restoration, and of the balance within that community, since a very large majority of the representatives had roots in, or strong links with, the counties or towns that they represented. There were supposed to be two each for every shire and for Dublin, and one each for every town normally represented in the Irish parliament. That gave a nominal total of 158 members, though only 138 are known to have attended. Of these at least 98 were 'Old Protestants', with roots in the country stretching back to before the rebellion, often long before. Of the forty newcomers, twenty-seven had come to Ireland with the English army and chosen to settle there, though only ten had been in Cromwell's expeditionary force of 1649; the rest had fought in earlier campaigns. A longstanding tradition, repeated in respectable textbooks until quite recently, that the Convention was dominated by Cromwellian settlers, even by Cromwellian officers, is quite untrue.[13] Even in the Ulster contingent, twenty-nine of the thirty-six representatives stemmed from the pre-1641 community, and only two in the whole assembly were Scots.

This makes it comprehensible that the great majority of members found common ground in opposing sectaries but were much divided as to whether they wanted to see episcopacy restored. They were divided too on the political front over whether or not the king's restoration should be subject to conditions, but understandably they were far more concerned about its implications for Ireland than about constitutional arrangements in England. They declared that Ireland had a lawful right to its own parliaments, and that the successive English regimes that had imposed taxes on the country had invaded the rights of the parliament of Ireland. Nevertheless they resolved 'for ever to adhere to England' and affirmed that the welfares of the two countries were inseparably interwoven.[14] Their declaration evaded the question of episcopacy, but came out in favour of an established parochial ministry, maintained by tithes, with no toleration of dissent. They also assumed executive authority, issuing instructions on 13 March that all those who had been transplanted to Connaught should remain there, and that those who had since left the province should be sent back. They ordered the suppression of unlawful assemblies, especially those of priests, friars, and Jesuits, and banned 'dangerous papists' from within two miles of any city, garrison town, or fort.

Yet in the eyes of the government at Westminster it was more than doubtful whether they had the authority to give such directions. Communications between London and Dublin were slow, and made slower at the time by adverse winds. The Convention did not know when it first met that the secluded members had been restored, and it did not hear until 17 March that on the 8th the Council of State had appointed new commissioners for 'the management of the affairs of Ireland' in the persons of Broghill, Coote, Clotworthy, and Sir William Bury. They took up authority in Dublin late in March, and they did not defer to the Convention, though Broghill continued to attend it, at least on occasion. The situation was complicated by the fact that Broghill and Coote were at odds with each other, and both were independently in correspondence with the exiled court. At any rate the Convention completed the representations that it wished to put before the government in England, and after some disagreement as to whom to address them sent them to the Council of State. Its emissaries passed through Chester on 3 April, but they were not welcome at Westminster, for the council had

---

[13] The personnel and transactions of the Convention are examined in fine scholarly detail by Clarke in *Prelude to Restoration in Ireland*, chs. 6–8.

[14] Ibid., pp. 249–50.

just ordered that the Convention should cease meeting. With the English Convention due to meet later in the month, it clearly wanted to keep the terms of the Restoration firmly in English hands. Annesley, who as Lord Mountjoy's Dublin-born son knew Ireland so well, was keeping a watchful eye on the country, and probably persuaded the council to appoint Sir William Waller as commander-in-chief of its army. Waller, the 'William the Conqueror' of early Civil War days, was a cousin of Sir Hardress Waller, but of very different political and religious views, for he had secretly pledged himself to the king's service in 1659.

By this time the complexities of Irish politics defy brief summary, but one way and another Broghill, and to a lesser extent Coote and Annesley, deserve credit for preserving Ireland from bloodshed and easing a tolerable path to the king's restoration—tolerable that is to the protestant minority. It was not an easy path, for the Irish Convention defied the English council's direction to bow itself out. It was still unwilling to do so even when the English Convention opened on 25 April, though on 1 May it published a declaration that the execution of Charles I had been 'the foulest murder' and adjourned for six weeks. Long before that period elapsed, Charles II had not only been proclaimed king in all his three kingdoms but was back on his English throne.

Indeed after the Convention's crucial vote on May Day it only remained to bring him home. He chose to meet its emissaries at the Hague, and he was feted there for a triumphal week while Montagu's fleet readied itself to carry him across the Channel. Fairfax was prominent among the twelve members whom the Convention sent over with its formal invitation to return to his own, and Charles spent some time with him alone. Monck waited to greet him at Dover, along with a huge crowd. Charles raised him from his knees and kissed him, calling him father. The king made his leisurely way to London, holding his first privy council at Canterbury and worshipping in its much delapidated cathedral. He was 'extremely nauseated' by the crowd of old cavaliers who beset him there, clamouring for places or other rewards. At Blackheath he reviewed five regiments of cavalry, many of whose faces belied the declaration of their joy at his presence that their commander presented to him. But his triumphal entry into his capital aroused enormous popular enthusiasm, and the Londoners' celebrations lasted three days and nights. In some provincial towns they went on even longer, and the drunkenness was sometimes accompanied by vengeful attacks on former enemies' property and by the harassment of sectarian congregations. Quakers were attacked in fifteen counties, and prosecutions for witchcraft, which had fallen off so markedly since the Civil Wars, climbed for a while sharply again.[15]

---

[15] On popular reactions to the king's return see Davies, *Restoration of Charles II*, pp. 350–4, Hutton, *Restoration*, pp. 125–6, and the sources cited in both works.

Nevertheless there is no mistaking the breadth and depth of the rejoicing that accompanied the Restoration. It represented a return to order and stability after a year and more in which the quality of government had deteriorated to the point of threatening the livelihood of ordinary folk, as well as undermining the prosperity of the more well-to-do. The reaction was partly against things that had been unpopular for a dozen years or more: the unprecedented weight of taxation; the unwanted presence of soldiers in large numbers; the repeated intervention of the military in civil affairs; the proscription (at least on paper) of the much loved Prayer Book services, the ban on Christmas, maypoles, stage plays, and other pleasures; the antics of the extremer sectaries, Quakers especially; and the efforts of the civil magistrate to promote a reformation of manners. But it has been argued here that during Cromwell's rule as Protector, especially after 1655, things had been getting broadly better, and that the efforts of the royalists to bring back their king, which (with honourable exceptions) were never very impressive, became feebler and feebler until 1659, partly because there was less discontent to exploit. If Charles II had been restored by force of arms in (say) 1657 or 1658, there would undoubtedly have been considerable rejoicing, but it would have been much less general than in 1660, and tempered by much wider regret for the Good Old Cause. The Commonwealth perished through its own ineptitude and internal strife before any tide of royalist enthusiasm swept its remnants away.

# Epilogue

WITH the return of the king to his capital the narrative part of this book comes to an end. Readers who are gluttons for punishment might have expected it to be rounded off, textbook-fashion, with a summary of the so-called Restoration settlement. But that is a complex and partly illusory subject, for the regulation of the return to monarchical government in the state and to an exclusive Church of England occupied a considerable period of time, and some matters that really needed to be determined were not settled at all in Charles II's lifetime. Even by the end of 1662, the constitutional and ecclesiastical scenes were taking markedly different turns from what had appeared to be their direction in the first months of the reign. So I shall take my leave by addressing, as briefly as I can, three tasks: to tell as a story-teller should what became of his chief characters; to assess how far the peoples of the three Stuart kingdoms attained and held on to the objectives for which they had taken up arms, and finally to answer the question I posed at the beginning, namely how far, or in what senses, the upheavals that they underwent constituted a revolution.

To start with the most obvious losers at the Restoration, the Declaration of Breda left it to parliament to determine who should be excepted from the promised royal pardon and how they should be punished. The most vulnerable were the regicides, and of the sixty-nine who had passed sentence of death on Charles I forty-four were still alive. The most fortunate of these was 'Dick Ingoldsby, who can neither pray nor preach',[1] for he not only escaped punishment but was made a Knight of the Bath at Charles II's coronation, thanks to his recent success in routing and capturing Lambert. That was not the act of a turncoat, for he had been conspicuously loyal to the Protectorate up to the moment when Lambert's faction overthrew it. He sat as MP for Aylesbury from 1660 until his death in 1685. For the rest, the Convention showed considerable lenity in singling out only seven of the regicides in custody to be tried for their lives, along with John Cook, the king's prosecutor, Colonels Axtell and Hacker, who had commanded the guard at his trial, and Hugh Peter, whose vehement support of the regicide from the pulpit put him in royalist eyes on a level with the king's judges. Among those executed with them were Thomas Scot and the Fifth Monarchists Thomas Harrison and

---

[1] See above, p. 714.

John Carew, who all bore the public butchery of hanging, drawing, and quartering with conspicuous courage. It has been well said by Ronald Hutton that 'The regicide itself had been a solemn and tragic ritual: these men died amidst the atmosphere of a bear-baiting'.[2] Some, perhaps most of them, stayed in England expressly so that they could bear witness to their cause from the scaffold, but others understandably fled abroad, whether like Whalley and Goffe to the American colonies or like Hewson and many more to the continent. Ludlow bravely waited until the Convention had unseated him before he left for a long exile in Switzerland, in company with other old commonwealthsmen. Okey, Barkstead, and Miles Corbet took refuge together in the Netherlands, but George Downing, who had swum with the tide at the Restoration and won his continuance in his old post as resident in The Hague, secured their arrest by means akin to entrapment in 1662 and sent them home to suffer the death of traitors. They were not the last to perish that year, for the Cavalier Parliament, which had succeeded the Convention, was baying for the blood of Lambert and Vane, though neither was a regicide and both had been reprieved in 1660. Both were put on trial. Lambert expressed contrition and obtained the king's mercy, if that is the right name for twenty-one more years of lonely imprisonment in island fortresses, in the course of which he lost his reason. But Charles had no mercy for Vane, whose death he sought with an animus that can only be called vindictive, simply because Vane had been such a persistent and principled opponent of monarchy.

But it would be wrong to dwell on the hardest cases. Most of the regicides who surrendered and appealed to the king's mercy were spared, and some including Fleetwood suffered nothing worse than being disqualified from public office for life. The same penalty was imposed on such non-regicide pillars of the Commonwealth as Lenthall, St John, Whitelocke, and Berry. Marten was in danger of being executed along with the other arch-regicides, but he defended himself at his trial with great spirit, and it was remembered that he had interceded for the lives of a number of royalists, so he was sentenced to life imprisonment. He lived for another twenty years, and the tower in Chepstow Castle where he spent the last twelve of them still bears his name. He was so poor that according to Anthony à Wood he was 'glad to take a pot of ale from any that would give it to him'.[3] There was no spirit left in Haselrig, even though he had not sat in judgement on Charles I. He had been named to the High Court, but prevented from attending it by his military duties in Newcastle at the time. Nevertheless his impassioned opposition to monarchy put his life in danger, and he needed Monck's promised intercession to secure his exemption from the ultimate penalty. A broken man, he died in the Tower

---

[2] Hutton, *Restoration*, p. 134, and see Christopher Hill, *The Experience of Defeat* (1984), pp. 69–75.

[3] Quoted in Ivor Waters, *Henry Marten and the Long Parliament* (Chepstow, 1973), p. 71.

in 1661. There were no proceedings against Richard or Henry Cromwell, whose retirement into obscurity has already been mentioned, but a posthumous vengeance was taken against Oliver. His rotting body and those of Ireton and Bradshaw were taken from their tombs in Westminster Abbey and publicly hanged in their shrouds, before their skulls were impaled in Westminster Hall.

Milton paid a less heavy price than he probably feared for his last-ditch literary stand against the Restoration. One MP did propose that he should be one of the twenty non-regicides excepted from pardon under the Act of Indemnity, and though this was not seconded the Commons did order on 16 June that Milton and John Goodwin should be immediately arrested. Curiously, the Commons' sergeant-at-arms did not execute the order until November, though before then two of Milton's earlier books in defence of the Commonwealth were burnt by the common hangman. He was persuaded to sue out his pardon, which he duly received after the Commons considered his case on 15 December. He was not troubled again, and Goodwin too obtained a pardon. As for the latter's namesake Thomas Goodwin, he and John Owen, who shared the leadership of the moderate Independents, both formed their own congregations in post-Restoration London and ministered to them through thick and thin, far into what was then old age. In 1674 Charles II gave Owen a private audience and a thousand guineas for the relief of those suffering under the current penal laws against dissenters. As usual, the king was more tolerant than his parliament-men and his prelates.

There were rewards for some of the old presbyterians who had never countenanced the abolition of monarchy. Cromwell's old general Manchester became a privy councillor and Lord Chamberlain; Denzil Holles also joined the council and was made a peer, and Booth became Baron Delamere. There were knighthoods for Edward Massey and Richard Browne, but rather strangely nothing for Sir William Waller, though he had been in the Tower as a royalist conspirator in 1659 and was useful to Monck early in 1660. The greatest rewards went naturally to those former Cromwellians who had done most—more indeed than any old royalists except perhaps Hyde and Ormond—to bring the Restoration about. Monck himself was made Duke of Albemarle and Captain-General, Montagu became Earl of Sandwich and Admiral of the Narrow Seas, and both received princely endowments of land. Both continued their careers as fighting men in the naval wars against the Dutch, and Montagu perished when his ship was blown up in 1672. Broghill, who was still under forty when the king came home, was created Earl of Orrery and a Lord Justice of Ireland, and made some additional reputation as an author of rhymed tragedies. Sir Charles Coote became Earl of Mountrath, but died in 1661. His fellow Anglo-Irishman Annesley was made Earl of Anglesey and rose through a succession of offices to Lord Privy Seal.

   The fate of the Scotsmen who have figured prominently in these pages can be told most conveniently in the context of the plight of their country as a whole at the Restoration. Of Charles I's three kingdoms, Scotland had been the first to take up arms and England the last, so in considering how far each one achieved and held on to what it had fought for it seems appropriate to take them in the order Scotland, Ireland, England. In the first two the settlement had more to do with muscle than with justice, for Charles II was under far less pressure to make concessions to his father's former opponents than he had been when he was still winning his way back to England. He was slow to take any positive steps at all regarding the government of Scotland, but on a petition from some prominent Scots who had come to London to attend him he restored it in August 1660 to the Committee of Estates, pending the election of a Scottish parliament, which met on 1 January 1661. The Cromwellian union with England was of course assumed to be invalid. Meanwhile he chose men of contrasting political backgrounds as his chief ministers and officials. The Earl of Lauderdale, who as John Maitland had sat on the Committee of Both Kingdoms in 1644 but had sided with the king in the second Civil War, became the all-powerful Secretary of State for Scottish Affairs and eventually achieved a dukedom. Glencairn was made Lord Chancellor, and John Middleton, the former Engager and Lieutenant-General, became the king's commissioner for parliament, with an earldom. But the men whom Charles chose as Treasurer and Justice-General, Crawford-Lindsay and Cassilis respectively, did not last long because they fell out with him over his religious policy and lost their offices. Early hopes that Presbyterianism would be retained were gradually confounded. When eleven Protesters framed a petition to the king in August, congratulating him on his restoration but deploring the use of the Prayer Book in his household and reminding him that he was under obligation to observe the Covenant throughout his dominions, the Committee of Estates had them arrested (bar one who escaped) and imprisoned in Edinburgh Castle. One, James Guthrie, who obstinately rejected the king's ecclesiastical authority, was tried for treason by parliament in 1661, as was the Marquis of Argyll. Both were executed. Johnston of Wariston was marked down for the same fate, but he had fled abroad. He was captured, brought home, and put to death in 1663.

   The elections to the parliament were so managed that it represented royalist Scotland rather than the nation as a whole, but at least it did not revert to the early Stuart procedure which had made it a mere rubber stamp for the Lords of the Articles. Its first session lasted over six months, and it really did debate the highest matters of state. The voice of opposition, never silent, was increasingly heard in its successors. Its main measure in 1661 was a comprehensive Act Rescissory which cancelled the proceedings and enactments of every parliament since 1633 except that of 1650–1, which had been called by the young king when he was in Scotland. It thus swept away all the statutory authority that had supported the National Covenant, the Solemn League and Covenant, and the whole system of Presbyterian church government as it had evolved during and since the troubles of Charles I's reign. Another act virtually exempted the nobility and the more substantial lairds from the jurisdiction of the JPs, whom it reduced to mere agents of the Scottish privy council's authority.

This privy council was established immediately after the parliament's first session ended on 12 July 1661, and its members were named on the king's authority alone. It met at Holyroodhouse, but its role was mainly confined to routine administration. Major decisions of policy were taken in London, where Lauderdale, the hub round which Scottish affairs revolved, lived permanently on the king's orders, and conferred with Hyde (now Earl of Clarendon), Monck, Ormond and Manchester, who were tacked on to the Scottish council as special advisers. It was hence that the council in Edinburgh heard in September 1651 of the king's decision to restore episcopacy in Scotland, and obediently gave effect to it by an act of council. A proclamation followed, forbidding presbyteries, synods, or kirk sessions to meet without the authorization of the bishop, and an act passed on 27 May 1662, soon after parliament began its second session, completed the restoration of episcopal church government. Ministers who were not presented by a lawful patron and collated by a bishop, or who declined the oath of allegiance and supremacy, were to be deprived of their livings, and as a result of these and other decrees between a quarter and a third of all the parish clergy in Scotland lost their benefices, mainly in the Presbyterian west and south-west. Laymen too were subjected to religious tests, for all in public employment were forced to swear an oath abjuring the Covenants, as well as affirming the unlawfulness of taking up arms against the king.

So it was that for all those Scots who had fought in the Bishops' Wars, or as England's allies in the first Civil War—indeed for the larger number who sincerely adhered to the Covenants—the Restoration spelt almost total defeat. Even the Engagers of 1648, and those who fought for Charles II in 1650–1, would have got more generous terms if they had won, and even the royalists who had fought with Montrose or Glencairn would have expected a larger say in the government of their own country than their king and his crony Lauderdale allowed them. The only mitigations were that the nobility, despite being jurisdictionally over-privileged, did not retain such an oppressive power over their inferiors and tenantry as they had formerly enjoyed, and that the restored bishops did not recover much of the political role that had made them doubly unpopular in the 1620s and 1630s.

Of all who took to arms in the three kingdoms between 1637 and 1642, the Irish rebels of 1641 were the most comprehensive losers. They had fought for the free exercise of their catholic faith, for the eligibility of catholics to public office, for the right of a truly representative Irish parliament to legislate for their country unfettered by Westminster, and for secure titles to their estates. Although they had always professed their loyalty, they obtained none of these things. An Irish parliament did meet in 1661 and sat intermittently until 1666, but apart from a handful of catholic peers in the Lords it was a wholly protestant body, and its initiative remained shackled by Poynings' Law. After its dissolution Ireland did not get another parliament for twenty-three years, by which time the Glorious Revolution had changed the political scenery in all three kingdoms. While the Restoration parliament sat it was in no mood to honour Ormond's agreement in the peace of 1649 that it should free catholics from all penalties that hindered the practice of their faith; indeed it called for a bill to suppress the catholic hierarchy entirely. This was blocked by the government, and Ormond warmly encouraged a remonstrance, framed by his ally the Franciscan Peter Walsh, that would have secured religious freedom for catholics provided that they disclaimed the pope's power to absolve subjects from their king's authority, and affirmed kings to be God's lieutenants on earth, whatever their religion. This promising scheme failed mainly because the majority of the Irish clergy, taking their cue from the Vatican, opposed its concessions and partly because Walsh himself would brook no compromise.

The degree of de facto toleration of unobtrusive catholic worship varied from province to province, and also from period to period, as the ascendency of the various parties in England changed. There was seldom any shortage of priests; in the early 1670s there were said to be 1,000 seculars and 600 regulars in Ireland, but many had little education and they had to minister in masshouses rather than in the parish churches that they reasonably thought should be theirs. They made little progress during Ormond's first term as Lord Lieutenant from 1662 to 1669 (he had a second from 1677 to 1685), partly because the Vatican appointed no Irish bishops until it was over. The lieutenancy from 1670 to 1672 of Lord Berkeley, the former Colonel Berkeley with whom Cromwell and Ireton had negotiated in 1647, brought considerable relaxation, including a general synod of Irish catholic bishops in Dublin, but this brought a protest in 1671 from the Westminster parliament and a request that the king should expel all priests from Ireland. He did not do so, but upon a second address in 1673 he issued a proclamation expelling all bishops and regulars. This caused considerable hardship, but it was only partially enforced, and matters had returned to normal when the Popish Plot of 1678 brought further trouble to Irish catholics, culminating in the outrageous trial and execution of Archbishop Plunkett of Armagh for high treason. The situation eased during Charles II's last years, but most of his reign was a tense and unsettled time for the Irish catholics and their clergy, a time made no easier by the latter's quarrels among themselves.

It was little better for a high proportion of Irish protestants, perhaps as many as half. Most protestant ministers in 1660 were Presbyterians or Independents, but the Restoration brought with it the immediate re-establishment of the episcopal Church of Ireland, and the bishops, who were soon made up to their full number, ejected all incumbents who would not conform to the Book of Common Prayer. They were reinforced in 1666 by an Act of Uniformity which prescribed a revised version of it, and required all clergy to be episcopally ordained and all school-masters to be licensed by a bishop. In 1672 Sir William Petty reckoned that there were 300,000 protestants in the whole of Ireland, of whom 100,000 were Scots Presbyterians. He thought that rather more than half the rest conformed willingly to the established church, which suggests that the number who did not, the Scots included, totalled more than half. The discrepancy between the wealth of the prelates, a number of whom had four-figure incomes (the Archbishop of Armagh's was over £3,500 a year in 1668), and the poverty of very many parish clergy, who were forced into pluralism to survive, was matter for scandal. No wonder that under such a sick ecclesiastical establishment the Quakers spread and throve in Restoration Ireland.

In civil affairs, the land question posed the most heated conflict and the most intractable problems, and the attempts to solve them generated a rancour that rumbled all through Charles II's reign and beyond. It is a story too complex to be told here in more than the barest outline. The problems were indeed insoluble in any way compatible with justice, for the claims of the adventurers and soldiers who had settled in Ireland since the 1640s were irreconcilable with those of the catholics who had fought loyally for the king and claimed the benefit of Ormond's peace of 1649. There was nothing like enough disposable land in Ireland to satisfy both. Taken as a body, the greatest permanent losers were the catholic landowners, and they lost on a huge scale. According to the best evidence we have (and it is imperfect), catholics owned 59 per cent of the land of Ireland on the eve of the rebellion in 1641, and they predominated in all but two counties outside Ulster. By 1688 the proportion had shrunk to 22 per cent, and Galway was the only shire in which more than half the land was owned by catholics. Dr Simms's valuable map (opposite) shows the distribution at both dates.

The two chief measures which attempted to tackle the land problem, both passed by the Cavalier Parliament in Westminster, were the Act of Settlement of 1662 and the Act of Explanation of 1665. Their broad intention was to make restitution to Irishmen who had lost their estates through loyalty to the crown, and where these were currently occupied by Cromwellian settlers to compensate the latter with land elsewhere. But since there was far too little land to go round, the Act of Explanation cut the knot by requiring the great majority of post-1641 adventurers and soldier-settlers to surrender one-third

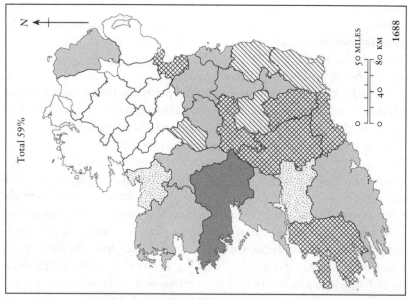

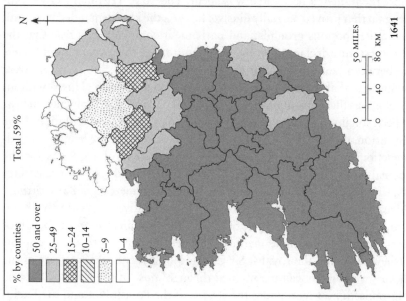

MAP 3. Land owned by Catholics in 1641 and 1688.

of their holdings. The natural result was that both catholics and protestant claimants were left with strong grievances, which were exacerbated by the greed and opportunism of Charles II's ministers and courtiers, who wheedled from him excessive grants of Irish land for themselves.

Turning finally to England, it would narrow the question unduly to ask merely how far the parliamentarians secured permanently the objectives for which they first took up arms. We should take account of what they had already gained in 1641 before it came to war, and of the broadening of their aims in the course of the fighting. The battle against arbitrary taxation was already largely won; there would be no revival of anything like Ship Money, and the financial settlement at the Restoration, imperfect though it was, was based on the basic principle of the abortive Great Contract of 1610: namely that the crown should renounce its objectionable fiscal rights, such as the exploitation of wardship, and that in return parliament should supply it with a regular annual revenue, supposedly sufficient in peacetime. The snags were that the Convention got its sums badly wrong, and that even if it had got them right, parliament was bound to suffer if it retained no right whatever to a say in how the money it had voted was spent. The 1641 Triennial Act was another gain that proved partially illusive. In 1664 the king demanded its repeal, citing quite specious grounds, and parliament complied. It is true that the repealing statute declared that by law no more than three years should intervene between parliaments, but the means for enforcing the principle were now gone, and at the end of the reign more than four years elapsed without one. Nor was there any limitation to the life of particular parliaments, such as had been sought by successive regimes since 1647. After the dissolution of the Convention, the so-called Cavalier Parliament, elected at the height of royalist reaction in 1661, was kept in being until the end of 1678. As for the Triennial Act's guarantee that each parliament should sit for at least fifty days, Charles dissolved his last one, in 1681, after a mere eight days' sitting.

At least there was no attempt to revive the prerogative courts of Star Chamber and High Commission and, thanks to the prominence on the bench of judges of such honourable men as the one-time adviser to the Rump Sir Matthew Hale and the royalist Sir Orlando Bridgeman, the integrity of the judiciary was pretty well maintained through most of the reign. It became compromised, however, under the strains of the Popish Plot and the Exclusion Crisis.

The most immediate issue at the outbreak of the Civil War in 1642 was the control of the armed forces, and in the 1646 Propositions of Newcastle parliament had demanded sole authority over them for the next twenty years, after which the king should dispose of them only after obtaining the consent of both Houses. At the Restoration the command of the armed forces returned unequivocally to the crown, as the Militia Act of 1661 expressly confirmed, but a dislike and suspicion of standing armies was one of the most lasting legacies of the Interregnum, so Charles II was never in a position to rely on military power. The plots and rumours of plots in the early 1660s, however, followed by the second and third Dutch wars and other continental entanglements, compelled him to keep up a modest standing force, though it was much hated and occasionally subject to parliamentary challenge. Ruling without a parliament in his last four years, he could barely keep up six regiments and a few garrison companies. It would take the ineptitude of James II to ring the alarm bells by building the army up to a really formidable size, and the result, after his overthrow, was a clause in the Bill of Rights that made it illegal for the monarch to maintain a standing army in peacetime without the consent of parliament.

With regard to religion, it is impossible to say with any precision what the parliamentarians had fought for because their personal convictions had ranged all the way from moderate Anglicanism to extreme sectarianism. They were committed to the Solemn League and Covenant because they needed Scotland's military assistance, though only a smallish minority really wanted the mandatory Presbyterian establishment that it prescribed. Their aim to abolish episcopacy was coloured by the peculiar slant and the exorbitant pretensions that Laud and his fellow Arminians had conferred upon 'prelacy', and by the fact that most of the bishops were committed royalists. Attitudes had greatly changed during the eighteen years since the outbreak of war. The familiar Prayer Book services and rites of passage had been badly missed, where they did not clandestinely survive. Deprived Anglican clergymen won many hearts and minds as chaplains or tutors in the households of nobles and gentlemen, and not only in those of active royalists. The rapid spread of radical religion in the 1650s, and especially the Quaker scare late in the decade, had caused the main line of division to run no longer between Anglicans and puritans, or between Presbyterians and Independents, but between on the one hand the growing number of people who like Richard Baxter and his Worcestershire association had sunk their differences for the sake of Christian community in a sober, orthodox protestantism, and on the other the passionate radicals who threatened social subversion as well as soul-destroying heresy. The prospects for toleration were further damaged in January 1661 when the Fifth Monarchist Thomas Venner led a wildcat attempt at rebellion in London.

For a brief period there was a genuine attempt, encouraged by the king, to make the established church more comprehensive by building bridges between Anglican episcopalians and moderate Presbyterians. Charles set in motion the talks between representatives of both that led to the Worcester House Declaration, which he issued in October 1660. It proposed that when bishops ordained ministers or exercised their ecclesiastical jurisdiction, they should act with the concurrence of elected lay 'presbyters'. It allowed some elasticity in the enforcement of the Book of Common Prayer, especially with regard to the disputed ceremonies. It promised a synod representing Anglican and puritan divines, that would be summoned shortly to define the final settlement. Historians have disagreed about the Worcester House Declaration. Some have seen it as a smokescreen, put up by Clarendon and the senior High Church prelates to distract attention from the real operation of filling the bishoprics—two-thirds were vacant in 1660—and other commanding positions in the church with staunch, uncompromising Anglicans.[4] But it is very doubtful whether Clarendon and Bishops Sheldon and Morley were insincere in their intentions, and virtually certain that the king was not. The religious situation was in rapid flux between 1660 and 1662, and it had changed even by the time the promised synod met at the Savoy in April 1661. The vacant sees had been filled; the Presbyterians (to use the term loosely) Baxter and Calamy had been offered bishoprics but had refused them, and most of the new prelates were High Churchmen. Those of their party at the Savoy took heart from the reaction against puritanism in the country generally, and still more from the rout of Presbyterian candidates in the elections to the Cavalier Parliament. The representatives of the puritan interest were weakened by their own disagreements, and by Baxter's rather poor tactical skill as their chief negotiator. The Savoy Conference was a sad failure, for the Cavalier Parliament took the religious settlement into its own hands, and the result was the Act of Uniformity of 1662: a brutal nullification of the promises held forth in the Declaration of Breda and of the concessions proposed at Worcester House. It authorized a new Book of Common Prayer, revised in minor particulars but in essentials the same as that of 1559. It was to be strictly adhered to, and no other form of public worship was allowed. All beneficed clergy were required to declare publicly their 'unfeigned assent and consent' to everything contained in it, or forfeit their livings. Under the same penalty, they had to obtain episcopal ordination if they had not already received it. All schoolmasters must be licensed by a bishop and conform to the Prayer Book; all clergy and teachers whatsoever must abjure the Solemn League and Covenant as an unlawful oath and declare their abhorrence of taking arms against the king or his commissioned officers.

Charles considered suspending the whole act; then with Clarendon's full support and advice, he tried to limit the damage and save his honour as the author of the promises made from Breda by issuing a public declaration, proposing that parliament should pass an act to recognize what he regarded as his inherent power to grant dispensations from the strict letter of statute

---

[4] This is the view of R. S. Bosher, *The Making of the Restoration Settlement* (New York, 1951); it is challenged by Anne Whiteman, 'The Restoration of the Church of England', in Geoffrey F. Nuttall and Owen Chadwick (eds.), *From Uniformity to Unity 1662–1962* (1962).

law, in this case in favour of loyal nonconformists and catholics who worshipped in private. The Commons responded with a polite but total refusal. The number of clergy ejected as a result of the Act of Uniformity came to 936, but over 800 had already lost their livings since 1660, either because a previously ejected Anglican had reclaimed his own or because the local squire or noble patron had jumped the gun in getting rid of a puritan 'intruder'. The total number of those ejected between 1660 and 1662 was about 1,760, and they included many of the most gifted and dedicated pastors in the land.

The responsibility for the dreadful intolerance of the 1660s and 1670s lies squarely with the Cavalier Parliament, in which the bishops were only a small element numerically. It derived partly from fear, for in the 'sixties the air was alive with rumours of threatened Presbyterian plots, but a spirit of vengeance played a large part in it. The screw was tightened after the so-called Yorkshire Plot of October 1663. The Conventicle Acts of 1664 and 1670 made it an offence, subject to progressive fines, for five or more persons who were not of the same household to meet for worship, even in private houses. The Five Mile Act of 1665 forbade nonconformist preachers to come within five miles of the place of the previous ministrations or any corporate town, unless they took an oath declaring it unlawful to take arms against the king. In 1672 Charles made a brave bid to suspend all the penal laws against nonconformists and recusants by issuing his Declaration of Indulgence, but when parliament met again in the following February it forced him not only to cancel it but to pass the Test Act, which required all holders of public office, civil or military, to receive Holy Communion in a parish church and sign a declaration 'that there is not any transubstantiation in the sacrament of the Lord's Supper'.

These measures were enforced with very varying rigour, both in time and place. Their authors recognized that while they might discourage nonconformity by penalizing it, they could not hope to stamp it out. Here was a major difference between the pre-Civil War and the post-Restoration religious scene in England. From the Reformation to the Long Parliament there had been a genuine quest for unity among English protestants, and a hope that it could be achieved. The rapid spread of religious diversity during the 1640s and 1650s, and the irreconcilable positions taken up by Presbyterians, Independents, Baptists and Quakers, to name only the principal denominations outside the Anglican fold, made this impossible. The line of division between church and chapel, which was to have so deep an effect on the lives of men and women—at least for so long as England remained a church-going nation—had come to stay. It was not yet the social division that it soon became, for moderate puritanism still had highly placed defenders such as Annesley, as well as plenty of adherents in the county elites. But the imposition of political tests on holders of public office thinned them out, and the typically close association between squire and parson subjected them to some degree of social discrimination, at least in rural society.

The best of the nonconformist ministers and the most faithful of their flocks held together, despite sporadic persecution, with a tenacity that commands respect. Their sufferings were often considerable; we owe *Pilgrim's Progress*, for example, to the fact that John Bunyan spent twelve years in prison for unlicensed preaching. No work better exemplifies the kind of faith that carried them through. It might be thought that Cromwell's quest for a reformation of manners was the most total casualty of the Restoration, but mercifully not all of England took its moral tone from the court. The nonconformist conscience had a long history, and the Cromwellian years were surely a formative stage in it.

So we come back at last to the question posed at the very beginning of this book: in what senses if any is the word 'revolution' applicable to the events that it describes? It may be remembered that I identified three main ways in which it has been used with reference to historical events.[5] The first and oldest, still current in the seventeenth century, signified circular motion, comparable to that of a planet orbiting the earth or simply a wheel turning full circle; it implied that the country in question went through a process of upheaval but returned to something very like the *status quo ante*. From Macchiavelli's time, however, 'revolutions' could be used to describe any major cataclysms that violently interrupted the history of the body politic, whether they permanently changed its institutions or not. Since the French Revolution, and more widely in the political thought of the twentieth century, the word has generally been used less loosely by serious writers. It has come to signify a complex of interlinked events, commonly including the collapse or overthrow of the existing institutions of the state, the violent competition for power between deeply opposed interests or classes, and the consequent restructuring of the body politic and even of society itself. To declare my hand, I am sceptical about the quest for a morphology of revolution that will accommodate the upheavals that began in France in 1789, in Russia in 1917, in China under Chairman Mao, and other later convulsions elsewhere. Their differences strike me as at least as significant as their common features. I am particularly sceptical of any attempt to fit the English Civil War and Interregnum into such a model, and I welcome signs that the designation of them as 'the English Revolution', so widespread a generation ago, is fading out of use. But revolution in the second sense identified above, as signifying a breach of continuity deeper in its causes and effects than just a rebellion, remains a useful concept, and its applicability varies between the different parts of the

[5] See above, p. 1.

Stuarts' multiple kingdoms. The most revolutionary thing that happened to them collectively was their union with England in a single Commonwealth. That was silently swept away at the Restoration, along with all the other measures that had not received the royal assent, but like so many of them it was to have a future undreamt of in 1660.

The concept of revolution is clearly less apposite to Ireland or Scotland than to England. The Irish rebellion was indeed in its origins and early stages a rebellion and nothing more, an attempt to attain limited ends by force of arms, but not to change the structures of the state or society. The rebels were seeking to secure what they saw as their rights within those structures. They reached out towards revolution in the heyday of the Confederation of Kilkenny, at least among those of its adherents who glimpsed the possibility of an Ireland independent of England, but they were defeated. Post-Restoration Ireland was again a dependent kingdom, its institutions not so very different from those over which Strafford had presided. The huge changes in landownership altered the ascendant class's character on such a scale that it would be absurd to talk of a return to the status quo, but in other respects Ireland reverted to a relationship of subordination, not least in the restoration of the Church of Ireland, not so very different from that of early Stuart times. The Presbyterian Scots settled in Ulster were among the losers, as well as the catholic Irish.

The Scots themselves, in the wake of the Bishops' Wars, the Civil Wars, and the English conquest, had experienced changes in church and state profound enough to be called revolutionary, but for the most part they were not lasting. Of the three kingdoms, Scotland came nearest to conforming to the original meaning of revolution as a rotation through years of commotions, ending in a return to the position from which she had started. Superficially, her political, judicial, and ecclesiastical institutions look much the same under Charles II as they had been before 1637, and such changes in landownership as had occurred were not large enough to alter the essential social structure of the country. But the experiences of the intervening decades had left their mark. In religion, Presbyterianism was weakened by the deep and lasting rift between Protestors and Resolutioners, and there were to be no more General Assemblies until after the Revolution of 1688. But at the Restoration parish ministers were not required, as in England, to undergo reordination by a bishop or to conform to the Prayer Book, though many did so. There was no attempt to re-introduce altars or surplices or kneeling at communion. Just over a quarter of all ministers holding livings in 1660 were deprived, 270 in all, many because of the restoration of patronage. That compares with more than half in 1690, when Presbyterianism was restored. Episcopacy was not as widely unpopular as might have been expected, partly because the new bishops kept their noses out of politics.

In the secular sphere it has already been noted that Scottish parliaments recovered a voice of their own, and became platforms for a quite vocal opposition. There was much to oppose, for the ministers through whom Charles II
governed Scotland, Lauderdale especially, were thoroughly corrupt and
enriched themselves shamelessly at their country's expense. One thing that he
and they had learnt from the Commonwealth period was how to tax his Scottish subjects more efficiently, but that did not exactly endear him to them.
When William of Orange landed at Torbay in 1688, he soon became aware
that he faced a deeply divided nation north of the border.

And so back to England. It should not need saying by now that rebellion is
a totally inadequate term with which to describe what happened in the 1640s
and 1650s. Even the original war aims of the Long Parliament went well
beyond remedying the specific grievances of the Personal Rule, and between
the first and second Civil Wars the Levellers and the New Model Army were
bent in their different ways on leading the country deep into revolutionary
waters. Despite the collapse of the Commonwealth and all that the Restoration purported to restore, it has (I hope) been shown that the England to
which Charles II returned would never be the same as the one his father had
governed, and that even the institutions that bore the same names had suffered an irreversible sea change. What Thomas Hobbes called 'a circular
motion of the sovereign power, through two usurpers, from the late king to
this his son', was in fact very much more than that, and we can be sure that at
heart he knew it.

So what is wrong with 'the English Revolution' as a handy label for these
two decades? It is nothing to go to the stake over, and to demur mildly at it
certainly does not imply condemnation of those historians, many of them
highly distinguished, who have used it. The objections, such as they are, are
threefold. In the first place it may imply that the commotions in England can
be understood in isolation from those in Ireland and Scotland, whereas historians like Conrad Russell and John Pocock have been demonstrating afresh
how closely they were interlinked—as Gardiner and Firth had been well
aware. Secondly, the term was always used (though not exclusively) by writers who were convinced that England underwent a social as well as a political
revolution in the period; so much landed property changed hands, they
thought, that a crucial shift took place in the composition of the governing
class. Marxists saw it as the decisive phase in the bourgeois revolution in English history; others identified a large-scale change in the balance between the
court and the country, with the 'ins' giving place to the 'outs'. But pains-
taking research in county after county, in local record offices and family
archives, has revealed that the changes in the ownership of real estate, and
hence in the composition of the governing class, were nothing like as great as
used to be thought. Crown lands and church lands that the Rump had put on

the market reverted to the crown and the church respectively. Virtually all the 780 nobles and gentry whose estates had been confiscated by act of parliament recovered them, or their heirs did. A much greater number, however—well over 3,000—had had their estates sequestered and had had to redeem them by paying composition fines, and many had had to sell land in order to raise the money. But a high proportion of these sold to kinsmen or agents or friends who held the property unofficially in trust until the original owner could buy it back, as most did, more often before the Restoration than after. Some royalist landowners did go under, especially if they were heavily in debt, and some Civil War careerists did invest in real estate and hang on to it; for instance Colonel Philip Jones, who had started with a yeoman's income and became Cromwell's Comptroller of the Household, remained in possession of Fonmon Castle and a four-figure landed income. But many, perhaps most, of the permanent acquirers of royalists' estates came from a gentry background, and the social complexion of the county elites probably did not change much more between 1640 and 1660 than in any other two decades of the early modern period. As a force in English politics, aristocracy had a long future before it, all through the eighteenth century and beyond.

The third reason for quibbling at the 'English Revolution' as an appellation is its suggestion that this was a self-contained episode in our history, which reached a kind of terminus in 1660. There lies a particular danger in books like this one that end there, and I would not wish to leave the reader with any such notion. The revolutionary years can be more fruitfully and accurately seen as part of a process: a process that reached some kind of a period (there are no full stops in history, at least while the human race survives) in the Revolution settlement of 1689 and after—for Scotland in 1707. The failings of Cromwell's immediate successors led to a partial reaction at the Restoration, in which some of the political gains since 1640 were consolidated and others were lost. But they were not forgotten for long, and they were not lost permanently. Large parts of the reigns of Charles II and James II were filled with bitter political and religious strife, and this was partly because the problems with which the Commonwealth and Protectorate had wrestled were real problems, and they had not been solved. The mercy was that they would not be solved, then or thereafter, by war; 'Forty-one is come again' was a common cry when the going threatened to get really rough in the 1670s, and it was an effective deterrent. The Toleration Act of 1689 was a grudging measure, excluding catholics from its benefits as it did, but at least it ensured freedom of worship for protestant dissenters and Quakers. Parliament's control over the very existence of a standing army in peacetime has been mentioned, and from 1689 the king required an annual act of parliament to legalize the punishment by court-martial of mutiny and other military offenses in such forces as he was permitted to maintain; he could not have maintained them without it. The Bill of Rights declared the crown's claim to suspend laws or dispense from them to be illegal, in the course of determining the succession to the throne. The succession was further regulated by the 1701 Act of Settlement, which took the opportunity to secure decisively the independence of the judiciary and to debar the king from pardoning anyone impeached by parliament. After the Triennial Act of 1694 there could be no more parliaments of indeterminate length and no long intervals between parliaments. Not everything that the reformers of the Interregnum had striven for was secured, for parliamentary reform had to wait for the nineteenth century, and democracy as the Levellers understood it was won even later; but enough has been said to show that they had not striven in vain.

# PART VI: FURTHER READING

Sir Charles Firth died before he had carried *The Last Years of the Protectorate* beyond Oliver's death, but his mantle fell on Godfrey Davies, who covered the ensuing period on the same scale in *The Restoration of Charles II 1658–1660* (San Marino, Calif., 1955). The book is essential for specialists, but Davies lacked Firth's narrative gift and power of organization, and most readers will be happier with Ronald Hutton's lively, more up-to-date and never unscholarly *The Restoration: A Political and Religious History of England and Wales 1658–1667* (Oxford, 1985), which is admirable too on the post-1660 phases of the settlements. On the latter see also the collection edited by J. R. Jones, *The Restored Monarchy 1660–1688* (Problems in Focus, 1979). I have described the events and ideas of the years 1658–60 in my Historical Introduction to *The Complete Prose Works of John Milton*, VII (revised ed., New Haven, 1980). On Ireland the key work is Aidan Clark, *Prelude to Restoration in Ireland* (Cambridge, 1999), while J. G. Simms's chapter 17, on 'The Restoration, 1660–85', in *A New History of Ireland* III is a good concise account of the settlement. Frances Dow remains as good as ever in *Cromwellian Scotland*, and has an epilogue on the settlement. Maurice Ashley, *General Monck* (1977) is a good popular biography, and so is Richard Ollard's *Cromwell's Earl* (1994), i.e. Edward Montagu, Monck's ally in 1659–60. Of the restored king we now have two excellent biographies of complementary qualities: Ronald Hutton, *Charles II: King of England, Scotland, and Ireland* (Oxford, 1989), and John Miller, *Charles II* (1991). John A. Butler was a brave man to tackle so unpromising a subject as *A Biography of Richard Cromwell, The Second Protector* (New York, 1994).

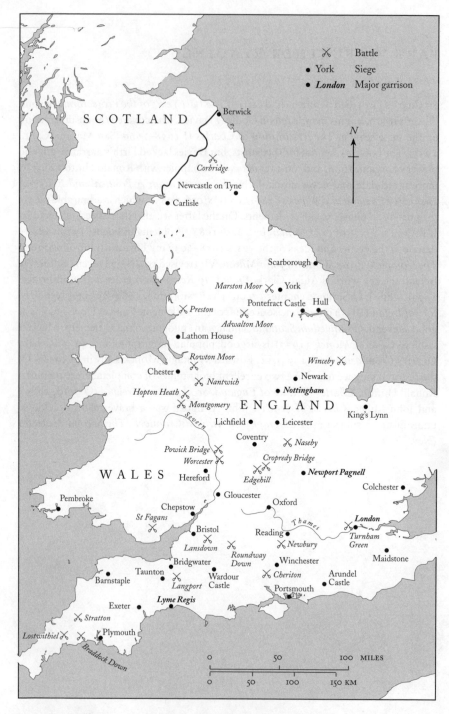

✕    Battle
● York    Siege
● *London*    Major garrison

SCOTLAND

N

● Berwick

✕ *Corbridge*

Newcastle on Tyne ●
● Carlisle

Scarborough ●

*Marston Moor* ✕ ● York
Pontefract Castle ✕   ● Hull
✕ *Preston*
*Adwalton Moor*
● Lathom House
*Rowton Moor*   *Winceby* ✕
Chester ●   ✕
✕ *Nantwich* ● Newark
*Hopton Heath* ✕   ● ***Nottingham***
✕ *Montgomery*   ENGLAND
Lichfield ●   ● Leicester   ● King's Lynn
*Severn*
Coventry ●
✕ *Naseby*
*Powick Bridge* ✕   *Cropredy Bridge*
*Worcester* ✕   ✕
WALES   Hereford ●   *Edgehill* ✕   ● ***Newport Pagnell***
  Colchester ● ●
Pembroke ●   ● Gloucester
Chepstow ●   Oxford ●
*St Fagans*   *Thames*
✕   ● Bristol   ● ***London***
*Lansdown*   Reading ●   *Turnham*
✕   *Newbury* ✕   *Green*
*Roundway*   ● Maidstone
Bridgwater ●   *Down*   Winchester ●
Taunton ●   Wardour   ✕ *Cheriton*   Arundel ●
Barnstaple ●   *Langport* ✕   Castle   Portsmouth ●   Castle ●
***Lyme Regis*** ●
Exeter ●
✕ *Stratton*
*Lostwithiel* ✕   ✕ ● Plymouth
*Braddock Down*

0    50    100   MILES
0    50    100    150 KM

MAP 4. Civil Wars in the three kingdoms (England).

Field of Battle

Dunbar

LAMBERT
CROMWELL
PRIDE
MONCK

Broxmouth
House

Pass over road

Spott Burn

LESLIE

Doon Hill

0        1 MILE
0    1    2 KM

Lewis

Harris

Caithness

Carbisdale ✕

Skye

Spynie 🏰          Banff ●        Turriff ●
Inverness ●   Auldearn   Strathbogie   Towie-Barclay 🏰
                    Balvenie 🏰    Fyvie 🏰
                Strathdon ✕    Don   Alford ✕
                         Dee   Aberdeen ●
Lochaber                           Megra Hill ✕
Ardnamurchan  Inverlochy ✕        Dunottar 🏰
          Mingary 🏰
       Morvern                Blair Atholl ✕   Careston   Montrose 🏰
                                            Alyth ✕
Mull   Lagganmore   S C O T L A N D   Tay   Dundee ●
              Inveraray 🏰      Tippermuir ✕   Perth ●
         Craignish ✕                          St Andrews ●
Jura                   Forth   Stirling ●
              Dumbarton 🏰   Kilsyth ✕   Inverkeithing ✕   Burntisland ●
         Dunoon ●                    Leith ●   Dunbar ●
Loch Gorm ✕   Islay 🏰        Edinburgh ●   Dunglass ●
              Skipness 🏰   Greenock ●   Glasgow ●   Musselburgh   Berwick ●
         Rhunahaorine ✕            Hamilton ✕      Duns ●
Dunyveg 🏰                    Irvine ●         Kelso ●
                              Ayr ●          Tweed   Coldstream ●
         Dunaverty 🏰
                              Mauchline ✕
                                          Philiphaugh ✕

                         Dumfries ●   Annan
                    Caerlaverock 🏰  Moor ✕
                         Threave 🏰

                                          E N G L A N D

                         N ↑

✕          Battle
Perth    Town/Garrison
🏰          Castle

Dates of all battles can be found
in the index under 'battles'.

0    10   20   30 MILES
0      20      40 KM

MAP 5. Civil Wars in the three kingdoms (Scotland).

×     Battle
● Derry    Siege
● *Dublin*   Major garrison

Coleraine

Derry

Carrickfergus

ULSTER     *Belfast*

Benburb ×
Charlemont

Enniskillen

Newry

Carlingford

Sligo           Dundalk

Boyle    Carrick on Shannon

Jamestown

Drogheda

CONNAUGHT

Roscommon

Dungan's ×
Hill   *Dublin*

Athlon       LEINSTER     × *Rathmines*

*Galway*

Galway Fort          Ballyshannon

Carlow

Bunratty         Kilkenny

Limerick

New
Ross   Wexford

Clonmel         Duncannon

MUNSTER     Waterford
Passage

Dungarvan         N

Cork

Youghal

Kinsale

0           50           100 MILES

0         50       100     150 KM

MAP 6. Civil Wars in the three kingdoms (Ireland).

# Index

Abbott, George, Archbishop of Canterbury 39–40, 73, 76–8
Aberdeen 95, 102, 115–16, 123, 142, 294, 499
  the Aberdeen Doctors 106
Accommodation Order 300
Adwalton Moor 263
agitators (or adjutators) 358–63, 369–76, 381–3, 392–3, 410, 443
  new agitators or agents (1647) 383, 393–4
*Agreement of the People* (1647) 385–90, 395–6, 410
  second *Agreement* (1648–9) 423–4, 429–32, 434, 438–42, 643
  'third' *Agreement* (1649) 445–6
Alford 321
Allen, William 358, 375–6, 385, 387, 390, 409, 662, 674
Almond, Lord (James Livingstone) 190
Alured, Col. Matthew 496, 609–10, 755
Andrewes, Lancelot, Bishop of Ely, later Winchester 39, 76–7
Annesley, Arthur 766, 778, 782
Antrim, Earl of (Randal MacDonnell) 107–8, 115–16, 128, 199, 296, 273, 279, 293
Archer, John 140
Argyll, Earl, later Marquis of; Lord Lorne until 1638 (Archibald Campbell) 25, 94, 97, 104–8, 112–14, 124, 142, 144, 189–91, 270, 294, 342, 346, 349, 383, 399, 404, 419–20, 480, 489–90, 492–4, 499–500, 555, 783
Arminians and Arminianism 37–40, 49–50, 60, 75–83, 132, 200
army, parliamentary 229, 234
  *see also* Eastern Association, Essex, Earl of, and New Model Army
army of the Commonwealth 434, 454, 515–35, 563
  in 1659–60 729, 738–42, 757, 768
  *see also* army in Ireland, army in Scotland
army of the Protectorate 563–4, 566, 596, 609–10, 640, 652–3, 659–60, 686–7, 689–90, 700, 707, 709–25
  *see also* major-generals
army in Ireland (1649–60) 462–79, 582, 668–72, 690, 727, 752–4
army in Scotland (1651–60) 572–3, 664–5, 689, 745

army, royal, in first Civil War 236–7, 308–30 *passim*
  *see also* Array, Commissions of
army, Scottish, in England (1644–7) 272, 279, 281, 285–9, 294, 311, 324, 326, 329, 337, 349
army plots (1641) 178–83
Army (Spanish) of Flanders 207, 231, 345, 692–3
Array, Commissions of 225–6 274
Articles of Perth 46, 85, 90, 93, 104, 109, 113, 124
Arundel, Earl of (Thomas Howard) 73–4, 117–8, 120, 126–7, 175–6
Ashburnham, Jack 248, 314–15, 329, 394–5, 401
Ashfield, Col. Richard 714, 718–20, 741
Astley, Sir Jacob, later Lord 114, 318, 329
Aston, Sir Arthur 468–9
Aubrey, John 742
Auldearn, 311
Aylmer, Gerald 251

Bacon, Francis, Viscount St Albans 54
Baillie, Robert 118, 169–70, 272, 294, 570, 591
Baillie, William, Lieut.-Gen. 294, 406, 418
Balfour, Sir William 179, 240
Balmerino, Lord (John Elphinstone) 93, 95, 98–9, 404
Bancroft, Richard, Archbishop of Canterbury 45, 46, 76
Baptists 45, 444, 558–9, 582, 584, 689–90, 713
  in Ireland 669–70, 752
Barbados 506
Barebone, Praise-God 540, 762
  Barebone's Parliament *see* Nominated Assembly
Barkstead, Maj.-Gen. John 628, 781
Baro, Peter 36–7
Barrington, Sir Thomas 132, 230
Basing House 325
Bastwick, John 81, 168–9
Batten, Vice-Admiral William 411
Baxter, Richard 249–50, 585, 707, 789
Beale, Thomas 199–200
Bedell, William, Bishop of Kilmore 162
Bedford, fourth Earl of (Francis Russell) 126, 132, 144–5, 165–7, 172–3, 178, 185